TODAY'S HOTTEST
COLLECTIBLES

2nd Edition

From the publishers of *Warman's Today's Collector* and *Toy Shop*

© 2000 by Krause Publications, Inc.

Items on cover courtesy of:
Bill and Mai Larson, Mark Rich, and Downtown Antique Shops Stevens Point, Wisconsin.

Published by

krause
publications

700 E. State Street • Iola, WI 54990-0001
Telephone: 715/445-2214

www.krause.com

Please, call or write us for our free catalog of antiques and collectibles publications.
To place an order or receive our free catalog, call 800-258-0929.
For editorial comment and further information, use our regular business telephone at (715) 445-2214.

Library of Congress Catalog Number: 98-84625
ISBN: 0-87341-907-3

Printed in the United States of America

TABLE OF CONTENTS

INTRODUCTION

Welcome to the second edition of *Today's Hottest Collectibles*, a guide to nearly one hundred of the most popular categories of antiques and collectibles. Like the first edition, published two years ago, this volume puts its emphasis on what things are worth—and how to separate the trash from the treasure. It's intended for the collector, the rummage-sale scavenger, the flea-market fanatic, or the guy who finds a bunch of old junk in his attic or basement.

But this book provides more than just pricing information. To really understand an antique or collectible, you need to know a little about its history and background. Each chapter provides enough background to make you an informed buyer or seller, but not so much history that you think you're back in high school. You'll find general guidelines, collecting tips and lots of other interesting and valuable tidbits—whether you're a long-time enthusiast or just a beginner.

Action Figures to Yo-Yos

Included in this volume are more than ninety-five collecting categories—presented in alphabetical order -- that represent the hottest collecting areas in America today. Some of these categories were included in the first edition of *Today's Hottest Collectibles*—after all, much of what was "hot" two years ago is still hot today. Those chapters, of course, have been updated and revised to reflect new trends and values. Many of the categories covered in the first edition have a different emphasis this time around. For example, the chapter on collectible magazines in the first edition dealt mainly with *Life* magazines and *TV Guide*. This edition highlights *Playboy* magazines and *Sports Illustrated*. The chapter on kitchen collectibles in this edition concentrates on vintage appliances, and so on. More than half of the chapters are entirely new to this edition.

In all, you'll find a wide range of categories—everything from action figures and American stoneware to World's Fair collectibles and yo-yos. The list includes lots of traditional antiques and collectibles (like stamps, coins and Depression glass) as well as many relatively new collecting categories (like space memorabilia and transistor radios) and some categories that some may consider a bit wacky (California Raisins and PEZ dispensers).

RECOMMENDED READING

Most of the chapters in this volume include a list of resources where collectors can go for more detailed information. In addition to those books and publications, we also recommend the following general references, which could be included in virtually every category.

BOOKS

Warman's Antiques and Collectibles Price Guide, 34th Edition, Ellen Schroy
Antique Trader's Antiques & Collectibles Price Guide 2000, Kyle Husfloen
Maloney's Antiques & Collectibles Resource Directory, 5th Edition, David Maloney, Jr.
Warman's Flea Market Price Guide, Ellen Schroy and Don Johnson
Warman's Americana & Collectibles, Ellen Schroy

PERIODICALS

Warman's Today's Collector
Antique Trader Weekly

The primary goal is to help you find the value of your antiques and collectibles, assist you in appraising items, and give you an edge in spotting bargains at the local flea market and neighborhood garage sales. But we also hope that, in the process, we'll pique your interest a bit. Spend some time with this volume and you'll be exposed to some new categories you may find fascinating but never seriously considered. We'll give the information you need to get started.

Included for most categories are clubs you can join and recommended reading for more information. The club listings are not intended to be all-inclusive, but just a sampling to get you started. We apologize in advance for clubs not listed and for address changes that may have occurred after this book went to press. The books and periodicals listed in each chapter are all from Krause Publications. Yes, it's a bit self-serving, but these are the books and publications we can recommend with the most confidence. As the world's largest publisher of books and magazines for collectors, Krause has dependable books, price guides, catalogs and publications in nearly every collecting category.

Welcome to the 21st Century

This book, of course, is not designed to be read in strict order, from front to back; but we strongly suggest that you do read the short introductory chapter "Collecting on the Net" before you dive into the rest of the book. It seems like something of a contradiction to use the words "antiques" and "Internet" in the same sentence, but no doubt about it, computers and the Internet have invaded the world of antiques and collectibles just as thoroughly as anything else—perhaps more. The Internet offers a tremendous resource for collectors—much of the background for this book, in fact, was researched on the Internet. We highly suggest you read "Collecting on the Net" (page 6) and try the recommended web sites, especially the sites that get you in touch with the thousands of collecting clubs available on the web.

About Krause Publications

This volume is a product of Krause Publications, the world's largest publisher of books and periodicals about antiques and collectibles. The Krause Publications lineup includes more than forty magazines and periodicals about antiques and collectibles—everything from stamps and coins to comics and sports memorabilia—as well as hundreds of books, standard catalogs and price guides. You can visit Krause Publications on the Internet at *www.krause.com* or access individual Krause publications using the domain names listed in this section.

Dozens of people and resources contributed to this book—all of them experts in their particular fields. Much of the pricing was compiled by the editors and staff of the various Krause Publications, using their own expertise, as well as information from other sources, such as auctions, shows, dealer lists, etc. Steve Ellingboe, founding editor of *Warman's Today's Collector*, compiled this Second Edition of *Today's Hottest Collectibles*.

COLLECTING ON THE WEB:

BUYING AND SELLING COLLECTIBLES ON THE INTERNET

When you think about it, it almost seems wrong to use the Internet to buy and sell antiques. Most collectors, after all, are attracted to antiques and collectibles for their nostalgic value—reminders of the days when life was easy and people did their chatting in the parlor. But suddenly here we are in the 21st century, and if you're not on the Internet, you might as well be living in a cave. The Internet, sooner than anyone thought, has invaded nearly every aspect of our lives—including our collecting.

According to one estimate, more than $3.3 billion was spent on Internet auction sites in 1999. The figure could double by 2001. And although online auctions are an exhilarating part of the Internet collecting experience, they are certainly not the only thing this new "dot.com" technology has to offer. Collectors online can find collecting clubs, chat with other collectors, research the history of their favorite collectibles, check price guides, view photos, explore new collecting categories, peruse dealers' for-sale lists and more.

Getting Started: The key to navigating around the Internet—whether you're after collectibles or recipes—is to get to the Internet site you're looking for as quickly as possible. If you know the web site address (that's the string of letters that starts with www. and usually ends with .com) there's no problem; simply type it in. But, even if you don't know the address (or if a web site even exists), there's still no problem—thanks to the magic of search engines. Search engines allow you to type in a key word or phrase (such as "Depression glass" or "cereal boxes") and uncover a list of all web sites dealing with the subject.

There are more than a dozen search engines available to Internet users (see the Web Site Directory at the end of this chapter for a list of the major ones). Their basic operation is similar, although each operates in its own distinct way that might make some search engines more attractive than others for your particular needs. There are even at least two Internet sites designed to help take the confusion out of selecting a search engine. You'll find them at: www.notess.com and at www.searchenginewatch.com.

Whatever search engine you use, there are some general guidelines to follow:

Refine your search. If you begin your search too broadly (for example, typing in the word "radios"), your search may yield too many sites that are not really what you want. Adding a modifier (such as "transistor radios") targets your search more directly.

Double-check your spelling. This may seem elementary, but a too-hasty keystroke may turn "pottery" into "potteru," which would yield no results and merely be a waste of time.

Use "bookmarks" once you find a site you like. Adding certain sites to your "favorites" list saves time when you want to return to these sites at a later date.

Become familiar with your regular search engine. Each search engine has its own design, layout and search techniques. Get to know the search engine you use and see how well it works for the tasks you generally perform. If one search engine is not satisfactory, try another one. If you get lost or have a problem, most search engines offer a "Help" or an "Advanced Search" section to guide you along and give you tips for more effective searching.

Take advantage of "links." Most web sites have "links" to related sites that might also be of interest. Clicking on these "links" often provides more information than the original site.

The Top Sites: The number of antiques and collectibles web sites is seemingly endless—and continually growing. There are sites for auctions, dealers, clubs, publications, individual collectors, manufacturers, museums, shows, and more. The staff of *Warman's Today's Collector* magazine recently selected its Top Ten web sites for collectors. They include:

Antique Resources *(www.antiqueresources.com)*—This may be the ultimate site for true antiques and collectibles junkies, offering a wide variety of information ranging from articles on how to date your antiques based on patent dates or origin marks to tips for cleaning and caring for your collectibles. There are also book reviews, an events calendar, an online antiques mall, bulletin board, glossary of collectible terms and lots more.

Maloney's Online (*www.maloneysonline.com*)— This site, an extension of the popular *Maloney's Antiques & Collectibles Resource Directory*, is a great place to go for more information in hundreds of collecting categories. Simply type in a keyword or browse the many categories to find experts, appraisers, collector clubs, auction services, etc.

eBay (*www.ebay.com*)—eBay is the king when it comes to Internet auction sites, easily dwarfing its competition in terms of quantity of items offered and number of items sold. It is the ultimate marketplace for buying and selling antiques and collectibles. A ratings system lets you know the past history of the buyers and sellers you're dealing with, so you can buy with safety and confidence. You can also chat with fellow collectors or search past (and present) auctions to learn the going rates of virtually any type of collectible.

Collecting Channel (*www.collectingchannel.com*)—Tune in here for a plethora of collecting information. Visit one of the many "channels" to explore specific categories, such as antiques, collectibles, glass, pottery, toys and more. The site also offers feature stories on a wide range of collectibles, collecting news and shopping. It also provides plenty of links to other collecting sites.

Antiques Roadshow (*www.antiquesroadshow.com*)—Fans of the phenomenally popular PBS show *The Antiques Roadshow* will love this site, where you can check out what's happening on each episode and get a closer look at the show's highlights. You can also try your own hand at appraising. A monthly contest tests your knowledge. The site also includes the *Roadshow's* upcoming schedule of cities, memorable stories, collecting tips and a glossary of terms.

Butterfield & Butterfield (*www.butterfields.com*)—This is the top site when it comes to auction houses. It allows collectors to view Butterfields' past and present auction catalogs and participate in online auctions. Butterfields' "Online Collector Magazine" includes features stories, auction news, and the opportunity to ask experts questions about your antiques and collectibles. You can even submit a photo for a free appraisal. (Incidentally, Butterfield & Butterfield, one of the nation's largest auction houses, is owned by eBay.)

Web Swap (*www.webswap.com*)—With its slogan of "Swap what you've got for what you really want," this site offers a different twist than the usual buy-and-sell web sites. The site allows collectors to list what they have and what they want, and then matches up people so that they can make trades.

Collector Online's Club Directory (*www.collectoronline.com/club-directory.shtml*)—This is the place to go to find a club for your particular collecting interest. At press time, the directory listed nearly one thousand collecting clubs related to antiques and collectibles. Most listings include contact names, addresses, phone numbers, links to e-mail and related web sites.

Kovels Online Price Guide (*www.kovels.com*)— If you're looking for the value of an item, you're likely to find it on the Kovels' web site. After free registration, users can access over 250,000 prices, along with other collecting information. There are also articles on antiques and collectibles and collecting news.

The Internet Antique Shop (*www.tias.com*)— TIAS has been dubbed "the Internet's largest catalog on antiques and collectibles." The catalog's 220,000 items can be searched by any of 600 categories or by typing in a key word. Although the catalog is this site's strength, TIAS is more than a buy-and-sell site. You can connect with other collectors on the bulletin board or read the "What's Hot" list or feature stories.

Don't forget the Krause Publications web site (*www.krause.com*) to learn more about the world's largest publisher of books and periodicals for collectors.

Online Auctions: Reading about collectibles, chatting with fellow collectors, and checking the activities of various collectors' clubs is certainly rewarding, but eventually, most collectors will want to use the Internet to participate in online auctions.

When it comes to online auctions, the three biggest names are eBay (*www.ebay.com*), Amazon (*www.auctions.amazon.com*) and Yahoo (*www.auctions.yahoo.com*), but there are dozens—actually hundreds—of other Internet auction sites for collectors. Some are general, like the big three listed above, while others are very narrow, perhaps offering auctions exclusively for coin collectors or for beer can collectors, etc. There is even a web site that helps you keep track of them all—*auctionwatch.com.*

But no matter which online auction site you use, there are some general guidelines to keep in mind. Most of them aren't much different from the common-sense safeguards you should use for any buy-sell transaction. They include:

Do your homework. Check what the item is selling for at shows, in magazine ads, and elsewhere on the

Internet. With items that are bought and sold frequently online, a bit of research can pay off quickly.

Do check the ratings and comments made about the seller. Most online sites provide a place where bidders can review a seller's past performance. If a seller has negative feedback on his record, think twice about bidding.

Don't succumb to "auction fever." It's easy to get caught up in the excitement and exhilaration of an auction, especially online. Don't pay more than you should.

Do keep price guides and catalogs handy. Use them to confirm that what you're bidding on is what the seller says it is. Is there more than one variety? What is the current price guide value?

Don't be intimidated. The online auction is just another tool to get buyer and seller together. The actual transaction isn't much different than ordering from a dealer ad in a collecting magazine.

Do feel free to ask questions. Most online auction sites allow the bidder to e-mail questions to the seller. If you need more information (about condition, variety, shipping costs, etc.) take advantage of this opportunity.

Don't believe everything you read. Descriptions of items, especially condition, are subjective, and buyers and sellers don't always agree. Ask questions before you bid.

Do remember that a bid in an online auction is a legal obligation. Don't bid unless you actually plan to buy.

Don't be afraid to return material if it fails to live up to what was advertised and promised. Reputable sellers should be glad to accept returns as part of the cost of business. (But don't return something because you decided you really don't want it or you found it cheaper somewhere else.)

Do figure out what a special item is worth to you and bid with confidence at that level. If you are outbid at your maximum price, you won't feel bad about losing the item. If you win, you'll be happy—and you may get it well under your top bid.

Don't rely on "sniping"—the practice of putting in a last-second bid at a level slightly above the current high bid—to get an item you really want. Sniping works sometimes, but usually not against intelligent and determined competition.

Do keep complete and accurate records of all your online transactions.

Don't forget to contact the seller when the auction is over (if you are the high bidder) to arrange payment and shipping. Pay promptly, and if the transaction is a good one, leave a positive rating for the seller.

More Resources from Krause Publications
Collecting in Cyberspace, Shawn Brecka

Web Site Directory

The following list of collecting web sites was compiled by *Warman's Today's Collector* magazine and represent some of the major Internet sites in each of several categories. This list is just a small sampling of the thousands of web sites available to collectors. Use your search engine to find others.

Online Auction Sites

AcuBid.com (*www.acubid.com*)

Amazon (*www.amazon.com*)

Auction Addict.com (*www.auctionaddict.com*)

Auction Interactive 2000 (*www.auction2000.net*)

Auction Page (*www.auctionpage.com*)

Auction Port Online Auction House (*www.auction-port.com*)

AuctionRover.com (*www.auctionrover.com*)

Auction Watch.com (*www.auctionwatch.com*)

AuctionWeekly.com (*www.auctionweekly.com*)

The Bargain Hut (*www.thebargainhut.com*)

Bidder's Edge (*www.biddersedge.com*)

Boxlot (*www.boxlot.com*)

Books By Bid (*www.booksbybid.com*)

buynsellit.com (*www.buynsellit.com*)

City Auction (*www.cityauction.com*)

Collector Auctions (*www.collectorauctions.com*)

Collectors Universe (*www.collectorsuniverse.com*)

cyrbid.com (*www.cyrbid.com*)

eBay (*www.ebay.com*)

eHammer (*www.ehammer.com*)

icollector (*www.icollector.com*)

L.H. Selman Ltd. Auctions (*www.pwAuction.com*)

Manion's (*www.manions.com*)

NiceBid.com (*www.nicebid.com*)

Out of theAttic.com (*www.outoftheattic.com*)

Pottery Auction (*www.potteryauction.com*)

SoldUSA.com (*www.soldusa.com*)

Sotheby's Amazon. com (*www.sotheby's.amazon.com*)

Yahoo! Auctions (www.auctions.yahoo.com)

Auction Houses

Antiquorum (*www.antiquorum.com*)

Block's Box (*www.blocksite.com*)

Butterfield & Butterfield (*www.butterfields.com*)

Christie's (*www.christies.com*)

Cincinnati Art Galleries (*www.cincinnatiartgalleries.com*)

Copake's (*www.copakeauction.com*)

Early American History Auctions (*www.earlyamerican.com*)

Eldred's (*www.eldreds.com*)

Frank Boos Gallery (*www.boos.com*)

Garth's (*www.garths.com*)

Greg Manning Auctions (*www.gregmanning.com*)

Gene Harris Antique Auction Center (*www.geneharrisauctions.com*)

Guyette and Schmidt (*www.guyetteandschmidt.com*)

Hake's Americana & Collectibles (*www.hakes.com*)

Historic Collectibles Auctions (*www.hcaauctions.com*)

Jackson's Auctioneers and Appraisers (*www.jacksonsauctions.com*)

James D. Julia (*www.juliaauctions.com*)

Norman C. Heckler & Co. (*www.hecklerauctions.com*)

Phillips (*www.phillips-auctions.com*)

Randy Inman Auctions (*www.inmanauctions.com*)

Skinner (*www.skinnerinc.com*)

Swann Galleries (*www.swanngalleries.com*)

William Doyle Galleries (*www.doylegalleries.com*)

General Antiques and Collectibles Sites

Antique Info Center & Cyber Mall (*www.antiqueinfo.com*)

Antique Resources (*www.antiqueresources.com*)

Antiques & Collectibles Associations (*www.antiqueandcollectible.com*)

AntiquesOnly.com (*antiquesonly.com*)

Antiques Roadshow (*antiquesroadshow.com*)

Antiques World (*www.antiquesworld.com*)

Collect.com (*www.collect.com*)

Collecting Channel (*www.collectingchannel.com*)

Collectit.net (*www.collectit.net*)

Collector Online (*www.collectoronline.com*)

Collectors.org (*www.collectors.org*)

CollectorsWeb.com (*www.collectorsweb.com*)

Curioscape (*www.curioscape.com*)

Harry Rinker (*www.rinker.com*)

Kovels (*www.kovels.com*)

Krause Publications (*www.krause.com*)

Maloneys Online (*www.maloneysonline.com*)

SeriousCollector.com (*www.seriouscollector.com*)

The Internet Antique Shop (*www.tias.com*)

ACTION FIGURES

Adventure heroes and superstars are everywhere—on comic pages, television and movie screens and, of course, in toy store aisles. The action figure likenesses produced by numerous toy companies are among today's hottest collectibles.

The action figure hobby is one of the fastest growing and potentially largest areas of collecting. For proof, walk through the toy section of any store and look at the vast number of figures—Star Wars, Star Trek, Spawn and many others, as well as the numerous sizes, ranging from 3-3/4 inches to 12 inches. It's been speculated that action figures bring more collectors into toy collecting than G.I. Joe, Hot Wheels and model kits combined.

Even new figures, originally priced at $5 to $10 have jumped 50 percent or more in value in just a few years as buyers become more aware of the figures' future potential.

Background: Action figures date back to the 1960s. Prior to that time, boys often played with toy soldiers made of iron, lead or plastic, with no movable parts.

The 1960s saw American culture and technologies change in countless aspects of everyday life, including how toys would be made and sold. Mattel's Barbie doll, marketed on television commercials, was taking the toy world by storm. No one dreamed boys would play with dolls, but toy executives believed boys would play with dolls if they were called "action figures." Hasbro's 12-inch G.I. Joe action figure was unveiled at Toy Fair in 1964. (See "G.I. Joe" for more details.) G.I. Joe was the first true fully articulated action figure for boys, but he wouldn't be alone for long. A.C. Gilbert introduced James Bond figures in 1965, but for the first time in his career, Ian Fleming's super spy failed in his mission. Marx also entered the ring with the Best of the West series, but G.I. Joe had a seemingly limitless arsenal of battle-geared apparel.

The first reasonably successful challenge to G.I. Joe came from Ideal's Captain Action. While Joe's identity was well established, Captain Action was a man of many faces. Ideal designed Captain Action to establish not only his own identity, but also to capitalize on those of many popular superheroes. Joe was just Joe, but Captain Action could become Spider-Man, Batman, the Phantom, the Green Hornet and others. Today, Captain Action figures and sets command the second highest prices in the action figure market, second only to classic G.I. Joes.

Mego joined Hasbro and Ideal as a major player in the action figure market when it released its first superhero series in 1972, 8-inch cloth and plastic figures called the Official World's Greatest Super Heroes. It later added figures based on TV characters from shows such as *Planet of the Apes, Star Trek* and *The Dukes of Hazzard.*

Five years later, another action figure milestone unfolded when Kenner released the first toys based on the smash film *Star Wars.* As well as being the first to capitalize on the film's success, the company also introduced a new, smaller size for its figures. Unlike G.I. Joe (12 inches) and Mego figures (8 inches), Kenner's Star Wars figures stood only 3-3/4 inches tall, a smaller size that's remained as a standard industry size today. Out of nowhere, George Lucas' *Star Wars* had become a worldwide smash, but nobody except Kenner had bothered to secure rights to merchandise toys. When Kenner realized the magnitude of *Star Wars'* potential, it rushed toys through production, but it didn't have time to get action figures on the shelves by Christmas. Instead, Kenner essentially presold the figures as the mail order Early Bird set. By Christmas 1978, the line had grown to 17 figures and became the first wave of a deluge of accessories and related toys. (See "Star Wars" for more.)

In 1981, Mattel offered the next highly successful and lucrative series when it issued 6-inch figures from its *Masters of the Universe* series. Mattel, which first made the toys, then sold the licensing rights to television and film, added new innovations too, such as punching and grabbing movements. This enhanced their play value and set another action figure standard.

General Guidelines: Action figures in original packages (boxes or on blister cards) command the highest prices.

THE TOP 10 ACTION FIGURES

(IN MINT IN BOX CONDITION)

1. Batgirl, Comic Heroine Posin' Dolls, Ideal, 1967 .... $4,500
2. Wonder Woman, Comic Heroine Posin' Dolls, Ideal, 1967 .... $3,000
3. Supergirl, Comic Heroine Posin' Dolls, Ideal, 1967 .... $3,000
4. Mera, Comic Heroine Posin' Dolls, Ideal, 1967 .... $3,000
5. Scorpio, Major Matt Mason, Mattel, 1967-70 .... $2,250
6. Batman's Wayne Foundation Penthouse, 1977, fiberboard, Mego, 1972-78 .... $1,200
7. Mission Team Four-Pack, Major Matt Mason, Mattel, 1967-70 .... $625
8. Romulan, Star Trek, 1976 .... $600
9. Callisto, Major Matt Mason, 1967-79 .... $600
10. Mad Monster Castle, vinyl, Mad Monster Series, Mego $600

Don't pass up unpackaged figures, though—look for examples in the best possible condition and those with a recognizable character. But be aware that action figures without boxes can be difficult to identify.

Remember, the fewer figures that were made, the more the figure will likely be worth. Fewer figures are usually made of females or those of minor characters like aliens (as opposed to major characters), so they're often harder to find and generally worth more to collectors.

In addition to action figures, related accessories such as vehicles, play sets and weapons can be worth just as much if not more than original boxes.

Trends: Today's generation of microchip-powered voice simulation and sound effects-laden toys are now the industry standard, but even these will undoubtedly be made obsolete by future evolutions of controllability and interaction.

Action figures are big business, and hot series such as Star Trek and Spawn are now regularly ranked in the top 20 best selling lines by industry trade magazines. An enduring character identity is a key to continued demand and future appreciation. *Star Trek* has proven itself a worthy long-term franchise and is joining the ranks of *Star Wars* as the blue chip stocks of the action figure market.

The action figure aisles are now attracting more adults, and they are not always buying for their kids. More adults today are buying action figures as collectibles and investments. And those investments will in years hence feed the needs of tomorrow's collectors—the ones who are now sitting on the floor playing with Captain Picard, Batman and Spawn.

Contributor to this section: Anthony Balasco Figures, P.O. Box 19482, Johnston, RI 02919

Clubs

• Action Figure Mania
  515 Ashbury St., San Francisco, CA 94114

• Classic Action Figure Collectors Club
  P.O. Box 2095, Halesite, NY 11743

Recommended Reading

Books

2000 Toys & Prices, Sharon Korbeck and Elizabeth Stephan
The Encyclopedia of Marx Action Figures, Tom Heaton

Periodical

Toy Shop

VALUE LINE

Values shown are for figures Mint-in-Package condition, the condition that serious collectors demand.

American West, Mego, 1973

Buffalo Bill Cody, boxed	$75
Buffalo Bill Cody, carded	$100
Davy Crockett, boxed	$110
Davy Crockett, carded	$140
Sitting Bull, boxed	$90
Sitting Bull, carded	$125
Wild Bill Hickok, boxed	$75
Wild Bill Hickok, carded	$125
Wyatt Earp, boxed	$75
Wyatt Earp, carded	$125

Batman, The Animated Series, Kenner, 1993-95

Bruce Wayne	$20
Catwoman	$25
Combat Belt Batman	$40
Infrared Batman	$10
Joker	$20
Killer Croc	$30
Manbat	$25
Mr. Freeze	$20
Penguin	$85
Poison Ivy	$30
Riddler	$50
Two Face	$20

Best of the West, Marx, 1960s

Bill Buck, 1967	$200
Brave Eagle, 1967	$90
Daniel Boone, 1965	$200
Davy Crockett	$200
General Custer, 1965	$80
Geronimo, 1967	$90
Jane West, 1967	$80
Johnny West, 1965	$80
Sam Cobra, 1972	$90
Thunderbolt Horse	$75

Captain Action, Ideal, 1966-68, 12-inch

Captain Action, box photo, 1966 .... $900
Captain Action, parachute offer on box, 1967 .... $1,150
Captain Action, photo box, 1967 .... $1,250
Captain Action, with blue-shirted Lone Ranger
    on box, 1966 .... $900
Captain Action, with red-shirted Lone Ranger
    on box, 1966 .... $900
Dr. Evil, 1967 .... $1,200

Dukes of Hazzard, Mego, 1981-82

Bo Duke $15
Boss Hogg $20
Cletus $30
Cooter $30
Coy Duke $30
Daisy Duke $25
Luke Duke $20
Rosco P. Coltrane $30
Uncle Jesse $30
Vance Duke $30

Ghostbusters, Kenner, 1986-91

Bad to the Bone Ghost, 1986 .... $15
Dracula, 1989 .... $15

Most serious collectors look for action figures that are Mint-in-Package, like this Brainiac figure from the 1980s Kenner "Super Powers" Collection.

Ecto-1, 1986 .... $40
Ecto-Glow Peter, 1991 .... $30
Ecto-Glow Ray, 1991 .... $30
Ghost Pooper, 1986 .... $10
Ghost Zapper, 1986 .... $15
Gobblin' Goblin Terrible Teeth, 1990 .... $15
Gooper Ghost Slimer, 1988 .... $25
Highway Haunter, 1988 .... $20
Mummy, 1989 .... $15
Slimed Hero Winston, 1990 .... $15
Slimer with Pizza, 1986 .... $40
Slimer with Proton Pack, red or blue, 1989 .... $35
Zombie, 1989 .... $15

Legends of Batman, Kenner, 1994

Catwoman $25
Crusader Batman $10
Crusader Robin $10
Dark Rider Batman $15
Future Batman $10
Joker $25
Riddler $25
Viking Batman $10

Legend of the Lone Ranger, Gabriel, 1982

Buffalo Bill Cody $25
Butch Cavendish $20
General Custer $20
Lone Ranger $40
Lone Ranger with Silver $90
Scout $20
Silver $30
Smoke $25
Tonto $15
Tonto with Scout $50

M*A*S*H*, Tristar, 1982

B.J. $15
Colonel Potter $15
Father Mulcahy $15
Hawkeye $15
Hawkeye with ambulance $35
Hawkeye with helicopter $20
Hawkeye with jeep $25
Hot Lips $20
Klinger $15
Klinger in drag $35
M*A*S*H* Figures Collectors Set $65
Winchester $15

Major Matt Mason, Mattel, 1967-70

Callisto, 6" $600
Captain Lazer, 12" $520
Doug Davis, 6" $300
Jeff Long, 6" $500
Major Matt Mason, 6" $225
Mission Team Four-Pack $625
Scorpio, 7" $2,250
Sergeant Storm, 6" $400

Masters of the Universe, Mattel, 1981-90

Battle Armor Skeletor $20
Blade $25
Buzz-Off $15
Clamp Champ $15
Dragstor..$15
Evil-Lyn $30
Faker $40
Fisto $15
Grizzlor $15
Jitsu $20
King Randor $25
Mer-Man $25
Mosquitor $15
Moss Man $15
Prince Adam $25
Ram Man $35
Roboto..$15
Scare Glow $35
Snake Face $20
Snout Spout $20
Sorceress $25
Stinkor $15
Teela $25
Trap Jaw $25
Tri-Klops $100
Two-Bad $15
Whiplash $15
Zodac..$20

Movie Maniacs, McFarlane, 1998

Chucky and Bride $15
The Crow $15
Eve $8
Freddy Krueger $15
Ghost Face $15
Jason...$8
Leatherface...$15
Michael Myers $15
Norman Bates...$15
Patrick $8
Pumpkin Head..$15

Planet of the Apes, Mego, 1973-75

Astronaut Burke, boxed $130
Astronaut Burke, carded $100
Astronaut Verdon, boxed $140
Astronaut Verdon, carded.............................$125
Astronaut, boxed $150
Astronaut, carded $100
Cornelius, boxed $140
Cornelius, carded $100
Dr. Zaius, boxed $150
Dr. Zaius, carded $100
Galen, boxed $140
Galen, carded $100
General Urko, boxed $130

General Urko, carded $100
General Ursus, boxed $120
General Ursus, carded $100
Soldier Ape, boxed..$140
Soldier Ape, carded.......................................$100
Zira, boxed $150
Zira, carded $100

Pocket Super Heroes, Mego, 1976-79

Aquaman, white card $100
Batman, red or white card..............................$40
Captain America, white card..........................$100
Captain Marvel, red card $40
Green Goblin, white card $100
Hulk, white card $40
Joker, red card $40
Penguin, red card $40
Robin, red or white card................................$40
Spider-Man, red card $30
Superman, red or white card $30
Wonder Woman, white card............................$45

Shogun Warriors, Mattel, 1979

Daimos $150
Dragun..$175
Dragun, second figure $150
Gaiking..$150
Godzilla...$200
Godzilla, second figure $250
Mazinga...$175
Mazinga, second figure $150
Raydeen...$150

Spider-Man: The Animated Series, Toy Biz, 1994

Alien Spider Slayer..$8
Carnage $15
Dr. Octopus $12
Green Goblin $15
Hobgoblin $12
Kingpin $15
Kraven...$12
Lizard $15
Peter Parker $15

Rhino..$25
Scorpion $15
Shocker $15
Smythe $12
Spider-Man (multi-jointed)......................$15
Spider-Man, with Spider Armor, Web Parachute, Web
  Racer, or Web Shooter.............................$15
Venom $15
Vulture $15

Star Trek, Mego, 1974-80, 3-3/4 inch

Acturian...$150
Betelgeusian...$150
Captain Kirk...$35
Decker $35
Dr. McCoy...$35
Ilia $20
Klingon $150
Megarite $150
Mr. Spock $35
Rigellian..$150
Scotty $35
Zatanite $150

Super Powers (Kenner, 1984-86)

Aquaman $35
Batman $55
Cyborg...$200
Darkseid $15
Flash..$25
Green Arrow $55
Green Lantern $60
Lex Luthor $15
Mantis $30
Mr. Freeze $35
Mr. Miracle $200
Penguin $40
Plastic Man...$80
Robin...$50
Superman $35
Wonder Woman..$20

World's Greatest Super Heroes, Mego, 1972-78

Aquaman, boxed or carded $150
Batgirl, boxed...$300
Batgirl, carded...$250
Batman, fist fighting, boxed $350
Batman, removable mask, boxed $350
Captain America, boxed...........................$200
Captain America, carded..........................$150
Catwoman, boxed or carded.....................$225
Conan, boxed or carded $300
Falcon, boxed...$150
Falcon, carded $200
Green Arrow, boxed $250
Green Arrow, carded $400
Green Goblin, boxed.................................$225
Green Goblin, carded................................$300

Future Treasure? Action figures from today's popular TV shows and movies, like this "X-Files" figure of Agent Fox Mulder, have tremendous investment potential. Make sure you keep them Mint-in-Package.

Incredible Hulk, boxed..............................$100
Incredible Hulk, carded.............................$50
Iron Man, boxed...$125
Iron Man, carded.......................................$250
Isis, boxed $250
Isis, carded $125
Joker, boxed or carded $150
Lizard, boxed $200
Lizard, carded $250
Penguin, boxed..$150
Penguin, carded...$125
Riddler, boxed $250
Riddler, carded $400
Robin, fist fighting, boxed.........................$350
Robin, removable mask, boxed..................$400
Shazam, boxed $200
Shazam, carded $150
Spider-Man, boxed....................................$100

The majority of action figures, like this Boss Hogg figure from Mego, are based on characters from popular movies or TV shows.

Spider-Man, carded	$50
Supergirl, boxed or carded	$450
Superman, boxed	$125
Superman, carded	$100
Wonder Woman, boxed	$250
Wondergirl	$240

X-Men/X-Force, Toy Biz, 1991-95

Beast	$20
Cannonball, pink	$35
Cannonball, purple	$20
Colossus, 1991	$20
Cyclops #1, blue	$20
Deadpool	$35
Deadpool, 1992	$35
Forearm	$20
Forge	$25
Gambit, 1992	$20
Ice Man, 1992	$45
Ice Man, 1993	$25
Juggernaut, 1991	$25
Morph	$20
Nightcrawler	$25
Phoenix	$25
Rogue	$25
Storm, 1991	$40
Storm, 1993	$20
Stryfe	$25
Warpath	$25
Wolverine #1, 1991	$20
Wolverine #3	$25

ADVERTISING COLLECTIBLES

The fact that millions of non-football fans tune in the Super Bowl each year just to watch the new commercials is a testament to the power—and popularity—of advertising. It is, in fact, among the most popular of all collecting categories. Much of today's advertising is found on TV and the Internet, but advertising actually began with the first crude symbols and signs that hung over shop doors centuries ago. It wasn't until the invention of printing in Germany in the mid-1400s that advertising really got going. Newspapers followed in the 1600s, and modern advertising began in earnest in the 1800s and especially in the early 1900s. Magazines, tins, paper items, bottles and ceramic objects all carried advertising, often in highly colorful and beautiful artwork. The nostalgia bug is probably most responsible for the popularity of advertising items.

Background: Advertisements were put on almost every household object imaginable and were constant reminders to use the product or visit a certain establishment.

The earliest advertising in America is found in colonial newspapers and printed broadsides. By the mid-19th century, manufacturers began to examine how a product was packaged. The box could convey a message, help identify and sell more of the product. Before the days of mass media, advertisers relied on colorful product labels and advertising giveaways to promote their products. Stylish lithographs and bright colors were used on containers to appeal to the buyer. Many of the illustrations used the product in the advertisement so that even an illiterate buyer could identify a product.

The advent of the high-speed lithograph printing press led to regional and national magazines, resulting in new advertising markets. The lithograph press also introduced vivid colors. Simultaneously, the general store branched out into specialized departments or individualized specialty shops.

By 1880, advertising premiums such as mirrors, paperweights and trade cards arrived on the scene. Through the early 1960s, premiums remained popular, especially with children.

The advertising character developed in the early 1900s. By the 1950s, endorsements by popular stars of the day became a firmly established advertising method. Advertising became a lucrative business as firms, many headquartered in New York City, developed specialties to meet manufacturers' needs. Advertising continues to respond to changing opportunities and times.

General Guidelines: The field of collectible advertising is broad and among the most popular of all collecting categories. The better and brighter the artwork on a particular piece of advertising memorabilia, the more valuable it usually is.

Collectors tend to collect by theme (for example, beer, coffee or tobacco), company (Coca-Cola, Campbell's or Kellogg's) or type of material (tins, bottles or signs). One of the reasons advertising pieces can get so pricey is that they appeal to so many different collecting groups. For example, a DeLaval match holder in the shape of a cream separator is collected by people looking for DeLaval items, match holders and farm-related collectibles.

Condition, of course, is a major factor, along with the company that produced the item. When considering condition, keep in mind that items that are 50 or 100 years old aren't normally found in Mint, pristine condition.

Collectors should be aware of reproductions and fantasy items. Many are obvious reproductions as they are marked as such, but other items are not marked and can often fool the uninitiated.

Don't overlook current advertising items being offered as premiums. For instance, a few years ago, Ragu offered a disposable 35-mm camera with Ragu advertising on it just for buying a few jars of spaghetti sauce. There probably weren't many of these items produced, and few people probably had enough interest to send for one. Add to this equation that, of the people who ordered them, many likely used the camera, leaving those still in Mint-in-the-Package even harder find. Someday, this nice-looking advertising piece will be a true prize for someone who collects disposable cameras with advertising (a very HOT trend these days).

Also, don't overlook current store displays. The large standees are interesting items, as are some of the smaller cardboard signs. Store managers often toss these items, so you might be able to get them free for the asking. Especially look for advertising with celebrities, such as Michael Jordan or Hollywood stars.

THE TOP 10 ADVERTISING TOYS
(IN MINT CONDITION)

1. Quisp bank, Quaker Oats, 1960s $850
2. Reddy Kilowatt bobbin' head, Reddy Communications, 1960s $450
3. Mr. Peanut figure, Planters Peanuts, 1930s $375
4. Esky store display, Esquire Magazine, 1940s $375
5. Elsie the Cow cookie jar, Borden's, 1950s $350
6. Speedy figure, Alka-Seltzer, 1963 .... $350
7. Vegetable Man display, Kraft, 1980 .... $275
8. Barnum's Animal Crackers cookie jar, Nabisco, 1972 .... $275
9. Vegetable Man bank, Kraft, 1970s $275
10. Clark Bar figure, Beatrice Foods, 1960s $275

Among vintage advertising items, there are several categories that are especially popular with collectors. They include the following:

Advertising characters—A colorful part of everyday life, advertising figures have promoted everything from tires and shoes, to fast food and dairy products, in a variety of means, such as vinyl figures, bendy figures, wind-up toys, radios, telephones and beanbag toys. Advertising characters were used in the early 1900s to help sell products; customers who could not read could recognize specific products by the colorful characters. Soon, trade laws were established to protect companies by allowing them to register their characters as part of a trademark. These trademarks and characters can be found on product labels, in magazines, on other types of advertising, and as premiums. Popular cartoon characters have even been used to advertise products.

Some advertising characters, such as the Campbell Kids, who first appeared on streetcar advertising in the early 1900s, and Mr. Peanut, were created to pitch specific products. Other advertising characters, such as Kayo and the Yellow Kid, are no longer used in contemporary advertising. But many, such as Aunt Jemima, have enjoyed a long advertising run and are still popular today. Cereal characters seem to be among the most popular among collectors. Quisp is extremely popular, but hard to find. General Mills monsters (Frankenberry, Boo Berry, Fruit Brute and Count Chocula), Tony the Tiger, and Snap, Crackle and Pop are also favorites. (See "Cereal Boxes" for more.)

Also popular are vintage advertising characters that presented stereotypical (often negative) ethnic characters. In addition to Aunt Jemima, there was Uncle Mose (pancake mix), the Mohawk Carpet Indian and Rastus, the black character used to advertise Cream of Wheat cereal.

Because of their wonderful display potential, advertising collectibles are among the most popular of all collecting categories.

Tobacco—The first tobacco advertisement appeared around 1790. Since then, there have been innumerable advertising items created for cigarettes, cigars and pipes. Collectors can look for tins, cigar boxes, tobacco tags, signs, postcards, ashtrays and lighters, along with flat paper items of all kinds. Most collectors focus on one area of items or a particular brand of tobacco. Collecting everything isn't realistic because these items can be extremely pricey. Many reproductions exist in this area. (See the chapter on tobacco-related collectibles for more.)

Kitchen—The kitchen is a good place to begin collecting advertising items. There are innumerable spice, coffee, peanut butter, tea, candy and oyster tins available. As is the rule in collecting anything, focus in on one area. Oyster and peanut butter tins have increased greatly in value over the past five years. Small spice tins, even recent ones from the 1960s and 1970s, are usually marked at a minimum of $3 to $5.

Other tins—Typewriter ribbon tins and phonograph needle tins are very neat and becoming very expensive. Fuse box tins are another up-and-coming area.

Toiletries—People are collecting all the "unmentionable" tins and bottles that spent their lives in bathrooms. Cough syrup, cough drop, deodorant, salve and hair tonic containers of all sorts are now highly collectible. Most are also reasonably priced, from $10 to $35. Talcum powder tins, along with prophylactic tins, are likely the two hottest powder room items going today. Talcum powder tins depicting babies are extremely popular. Many collectors treasure these items for their nostalgia and, often, their humorous claims and/or phrases.

Toys—You simply can't beat the combination toys and advertising. Dolls and banks are two of the more common types of advertising toys. Some of the more popular advertising characters that have had toys made in their likenesses are found on cereal boxes (Quisp and Cap 'n Crunch are two good examples). Many companies today still offer toy premiums (see "Cereal Boxes" for more).

Signs—Perhaps the most desirable form of advertising is signs, especially the metal signs with enamel. Because of their purpose (to be hung on the wall), they look great on collectors' walls. Signs can run from $50 into the thousands. Any original sign, no matter what the subject, is worth buying; however, be aware of the many reproductions on the market. Reproductions sell for $10 and up.

Advertising Trade Cards—Advertising trade cards are small, thin cardboard cards made to advertise the merits of a product. They usually bear the name and address of a merchant. With the invention of lithography, colorful trade cards became a popular way to advertise in the late 19th and early 20th centuries. They were made to appeal especially to children. Young and old alike collected and treasured them in albums and scrapbooks. Very few are dated; the prime years for trade card production were 1880 to 1893; cards made between 1810 and 1850 can be found, but rarely. By 1900 trade cards were rapidly losing their popularity, and by 1910 they had all but vanished.

Clubs

- Antique Advertising Association of America, P.O. Box 1121, Morton Grove, IL 60053

- Trade Card Collector's Association, 3706 S. Acoma St., Englewood, CO 80110

- Campbell's Soup Collector Club, 414 Country Lane Court, Wauconda, IL 60084

- Porcelain Advertising Collectors Club, P.O. Box 381, Marshfield Hills, MA 02051

- Tin Container Collectors Association, P.O. Box 440101, Aurora, CO 80044

Recommended Reading

Books

Hake's Guide to Advertising Collectibles, Ted Hake
Campbell's Soup Collectibles from A to Z, David and
 Micki Young

Periodicals

Warman's Today's Collector (magazine)
Antique Trader Weekly (newspaper)

VALUE LINE

Prices shown are for items in Exellent condition. For more pricing on similar items, also see the chapter on Country Store collectibles.

Bottles

Ballard's Horehound Syrup, 4 oz., cork, label, with box and directions	$25
Cuticura Resolvent for Affections of the Skin, two labels, embossed	$40
DeWitt's D&C Expectorant, label, screw cap, with box	$30
Dr. Guns Cough Remedy, embossed, labeled bottle, box	$20
Dr. Koenig's Hamberg Drops, clear bottle, label	$25
Dr. W.H. Bull's Chill Syrup Cure, cork, label, box and instructions	$155
Eucaline Malaria Chill Tonic, label, screw cap, sealed	$45
Gardner-Barada Urinary Urisepetin, label, wrapped	$50
Golden State Liniment, B.F. Hewlett, clear	$17.50
Hobson's Sarsaparilla, Pfeiffer, cork, label with box	$40
Karl's Clover Root, for constipation, full, with box	$75
Mrs. Winslow's Syrup, screw-top bottle	$20
Powers & Weightman Benzoali Ammonium, label	$40

Victorian-era advertising trade cards are extremely popular. Most sell in the $10-$20 range, but some especially rare and desirable examples can sell for $100 or more. This example, which would also appeal to Santa collectors, is probably worth $10-$15.

St. Joseph's Lax-Ana Tonic, label, cork	$25
Swanson's 5 Drops, label, cork with box	$35
Triena Laxative for Infants, with box	$10
W.S. Merrell Genitone, two labels, amber	$70

Phonograph needle tins

Edison Bell, Chromic Needles, England	$350
Embassy Radiogram, England	$30
Golden Pyramid, Medium, England	$175
Golden Pyramid, Radiogram, England	$155
Marschall, five-pack, Germany	$130
Natural Voice	$30
Songster Needles, five-pack of needle tins	$125
Taj Mahal, Extra Loud Tone	$30
Verona Needles, five-pack of needle tins	$125

Soup's On!
Collecting the Campbell's Kids

The Campbell's Soup Kids are a good example of the different kinds of advertising items collectors can pursue. Printed ads, generally $3 to $10, are a good place to start; they have appeared monthly in national magazines since September 1905, when Ladies Home Journal first ran an ad featuring the Kids. Four different colorful postcard sets were issued as free giveaways from 1910-1913; these series are still quite affordable today. Other paper items to look for include place mats from the 1950s (set of six for $30) and place cards from the 1930s (set of four for $50).

Dolls are also popular with collectors. "Can't Break 'Em" dolls, created by the E.I. Horsman Co. from 1910-1914, wear various costumes. They have molded, painted hair and corked, jointed bodies. Another jointed composition doll, the Petite Campbell Kid, was created by the American Character Doll Co. in 1929, in various costumes featured in Campbell's ads.

Many dolls were offered as premiums to those who turned in soup can and product labels. These free, or nearly free items (sometimes a small fee and postage had to be included), can now command higher values. For example, a pair of cloth dolls in Near Mint condition can bring $100, while a plastic pair may bring $75 to $100. In 1976, Campbell's issued dolls in colonial costumes to celebrate the bicentennial; these dolls can bring $150 to $200 for a pair.

Other toys have also been made, including squeak toys, kitchen and food-related items, candles, bed linens, books, dishes, and other items. Salt and pepper shakers from the 1950s can bring $25 to $35 a pair, while a Campbell Kid Chef rubber squeeze toy from the 1950s can sell for $65 to $75.

This rare tin advertising sign has a value of at least $1,000.

Verona Needles, unopened tin...$30
Vintage advertising signs
  Borax Dry Soap, red and white, metal.........................$45
  Butternut Bread, tin...$30
  Bull Frog Shoe Polish, double-sided tin litho..........$4,400
  Crest Flour, cardboard, 5" x 8", 1920 ....$10
  Dixon's Stove Polish, paper, 6" x 8"..........................$65
  Fisk Tire, porcelain, 36" x 28".................................$45
  Grape-Nuts, self-framed tin, 20" x 30" $5,500
  Kibber's Candies, brass, 9" x 8" $50
  Mikado Pencils, paper, 1930.....................................$85
  Munsing Wear, woman with two cherubs.................$3,300
  New York Daily News, paper, 1890............................$35
  Oh Boy Gum, tin, 17" x 10", 1930 ....$90
  Parker's Cold Cream, stand-up, 1905 ....$100
  Rexall, porcelain, 70" x 46"....................................$225
  Salada Tea, figural tea box, porcelain, 1940s.............$125
  Sherman-Williams, Covers the Earth, 36" $395

Sunbeam Bread, tin...$65
Vintage tins
  Acme Coffee $135
  Allspice, red and gold $5
  Bee Brand Insect Powder..$15
  Bliss Coffee, key wind...$25
  Butternut Coffee, key wind.....................................$30
  Campfire Marshmallows...$25
  Central Union..$35
  Cloverine Salve $5
  Dairy Maid Crackers..$25
  Dream Girl Talc $35
  Johnson & Johnson Baby Powder.............................$20
  Jolly Time Popcorn...$40
  Molasses Crunch..$30
  Old Judge Coffee, key wind....................................$35
  Ovaltine, 1921..$25
  Paste Shoe Polish $15
  Peter Pan Peanut Butter $20

Planters Blanched Almonds $70
Sanka Coffee, key wind $30
Wizard Carpet Clean, 1901 ....$45
Yum Yum $250

Vintage trays

Beamer Shoes, Victorian woman, 1900 ....$65
Buffalo Brewing, Sacramento, Calif., 1910 ....$295
Croft Ale, round $45
Diamond Wedding Rye, 1900 ....$215
Evervess Sparkling Water, parrot $50
Fairy Soap, 13" $125
Lomax's Celery Tonic, 10" x 13" $85
Resinal Soap for Skin Diseases $45
Staley's Flour, 1905 ....$45
Teaberry gum, glass $110
Wolverine Toy Co., 1920 ....$95

Advertising Toys

7-Up, Spot wind-up, 1990 ....$12
Alpo, Dan the Dog cookie jar, 7" ceramic, 1980s $50
Aunt Jemima Syrup, doll, cloth, red checkered dress,
    1950s $70
Bazooka, Bazooka Joe doll, plush pirate, 1973 ....$25
Borden's, Elsie the Cow doll, moos when shaken,
    1950s $75
Borden's, Elsie the Cow lamp, electric,
    ceramic, 1947 ....$175
Chiquita, Chiquita Banana doll, plush,
    fruit on head, 1974 ....$20
Crest Toothpaste, Sparkle telephone,
    snowman-type character, 1980s $35
Dow Brands, Scrubbing Bubble Brush,
    light blue brush, 1980s $10
Eveready Batteries, Energizer plush bunny $40
Funny Face Drink, Funny Face mugs, 1969, each $10
Funny Face Drink, Goofy Grape pitcher, 1973 ....$95
General Mills, Boo Berry figure, 1975 ....$95
General Mills, Count Chocula figure, 1975 ....$85
General Mills, Frankenberry figure, 1975 ....$95
General Mills, Fruit Brute figure, 1975 ....$90
General Mills, Lucky Charms Leprechaun doll,
    17" plush, 1978 ....$25
General Mills, Trix Rabbit figure, 1977 ....$40
Heinz, Aristocrat Tomato, 1939 ....$200
Kellogg's, Dig 'Em doll, 16", 1973 ....$20
Kellogg's, Rice Krispies towel, 1972 ....$20
Kellogg's, Snap, Crackle, Pop figures, arms at side,
    1975, each $25
Kellogg's, Tony the Tiger figure, vinyl, 1974 ....$60
Kellogg's, Toucan Sam backpack, 1983 ....$20
Kentucky Fried Chicken, Colonel Sanders bobber,
    1960s $85
Mohawk Carpet Co., Mohawk Tommy doll,
    16" stuffed, 1970 ....$15
Nabisco, Fig Newton girl figure, 4-1/2", 1983 ....$18
Nestle's Quik, Bunny doll, 24" plush, 1976 ....$35

COLLECTOR'S ALERT!

As original advertising items have gained popularity and value and sources have dried up for collectors who are looking for them, reproductions and fantasy items have surfaced, aimed at inexperienced collectors. Reproductions, often created to be sold at the cost of an authentic item, copy the exact likeness of the authentic item. Fantasy items, however, are designed and made to represent an advertising collectible never actually authorized or distributed by the advertiser named or depicted.

Both reproductions and fantasy items generally have telltale distinctions that are obvious to a trained eye. Sometimes, however, the counterfeit is more skillfully done and more difficult to detect, as is the case with metal watch fobs, for example.

There are several items—sometimes unknowingly being sold as originals—which have been subject to reproductions: small pins, pin-backs, pocket mirrors, larger trays, signs, Coca-Cola items, brewery serving trays and advertising signs. Collectors can learn more about reproductions and fantasy items by using reference guides on the specific items, by joining collector's clubs and reading their newsletters, and by buying from reputable dealers.

Oscar Mayer Foods, die-cast Wienermobile $4
Oscar Mayer Foods, Wienermobile,
    11" car, 1950s $95
Pillsbury, Jolly Green Giant figure, vinyl, 1970s $100
Pillsbury, Little Sprout figure, vinyl, 1970s $10
Pillsbury, Little Sprout inflatable figure, 24", 1976 .$30
Pillsbury, Poppin' Fresh doll, white velour, 1972 .....$25
Planters Peanuts, Mr. Peanut doll,
    21" pillow, 1967 ....$20
Proctor & Gamble, Hawaiian Punch radio, 1970s $35
Proctor & Gamble, Mr. Clean figure, 8", 1961 ....$100
Quaker Oats, Cap'n Crunch bank, 1969 ....$65
Quaker Oats, Quisp cereal doll, 10", 1965 ....$85
Raid, Raid Bug radio, 1980s $200
Sony, Sony Boy figure, 1960s, 4" vinyl $200
Squirt Beverage, Squirt doll, 17" vinyl, 1961 ....$150
Starkist, Charlie the Tuna radio, 1970 ....$60
Starkist, Charlie the Tuna scale, 1972 ....$65
U.S. Forestry Department, Woodsy Owl bank,
    ceramic, 1970s $125
Wonder Bread, Fresh Guy figure,
    4" loaf of bread, 1975 ....$150

Trade cards

A&P Tea Co. $17.50
Alden's Vinegars $10
American Breakfast Cereals, 1883 ....$15
Ayer's Hair Vigor $15
Ball's Health Preserving Corsets $10
Bazin & Sargent's Face Powder $4

Brown's Dentifrice	$15
Buster Brown Shoes, 1909	$12
Campbell's Hair Cutting & Shaving Saloon	$45
Carter's Little Nerve Pills	$7.50
Coderre's Infant's Syrup	$7.50
Davis Sewing Machine	$5
Deep Sea Mess Mackerel	$7.50
Deering Implements	$15
Dixon's Stove Polish	$7.50
Emerson Piano Co.	$4
Eureka Health Corset	$4
Eureka Silk	$10
Fairbanks Gold Dust Twins	$50
Globe Cocktail Bitters	$6
Hire's Root Beer	$20
Howard's Lotus Flower Cologne	$5
Jap Rose Toilet Talcum Powder	$12
Jayne's Expectorant, 1890	$7.50
Jewel Stoves	$17.50
Kenton Baking Powder	$10
Mack's Milk Chocolate	$4

Metropolitan Life	$30
Packer's Tar Soap	$4
Pear's Soap, baby	$12
Pillsbury's Best	$10
Red Rose Tea, Rockwell, 1958	$7.50
Remington Sewing Machine	$7.50
Shaker Oven Baked Beans	$35
Soapine	$7.50
Solar Tip Shoes	$155
Standard Sewing Machine	$15
Tarrants Seltzer Aperient	$15
Thorne's Hair Bazaar, 1881	$12
Victor Coffee	$7.50
Wheellock Piano	$10
Wilcox & White Organ Co.	$7
Williamatic Thread	$17.50
Wilsons Cooked Meats	$15

Miscellaneous Items

Almanac, Doan's Pills Birthday Directory, 1906	$8

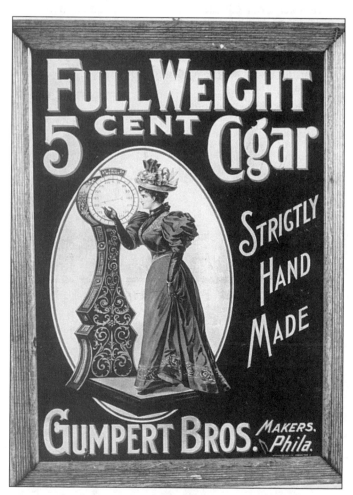

This extremely rare tin sign for Gumpert Bros. Cigars sold for nearly $15,000 at an auction conducted by James Julia.

Advertising tins are very popular with collectors for their display potential. Especially desirable are coffee tins, tobacco tins and peanut butter pails.

Ashtray, Firestone, copper tire $20
Ashtray, Universal Studios, cameras and crew $20
Bank, Pittsburgh Paints, glass $45
Banner, Kellogg's Corn Flakes, 48x23, 1920 ....$265
Blotter, Morton's Salt, 3-1/2" x 6-1/8"..........................$5
Book, Tip-Top Bread Horoscope Book, 1940s.............$10
Booklet, 60th Anniversary of Woolworth's,
    merchandise photos, 1939......................................$22
Box, Daylight Soap, wood $25
Box, Honor Bright Soap, cardboard $8.50
Box, Jessop's Cough Drops $5
Box, Quaker Puffed Rice, 1919 ....$20
Box, Royal Baking Powder, wood, 1880s $150
Box, White Swan oatmeal, 4 ounce $30
Brochure, Arm & Hammer,
    Cleansing Help for the Housewife, 1922 ....$3
Brochure, Bon Ami,
    "The Chick That Never Grew Up"..........................$12
Brochure, Magic Yeast, 3" x 5" $7
Brochure, Westinghouse, Today's Ben Franklin,
    1943..$3
Chair, Red Goose Shoes, folding $75
Coloring Book, Ben Franklin Stores Bicentennial,
    1974..$8
Cook Book, Gold Medal Flour, 1917 ....$25
Display, Pearson's Snuff, easel with containers............$50
Map, Dial Soap, Map of the Moon, 18" x 24",
    1958..$5

Mending kit, Real Silk Hosiery $4
Mirror, Haines Shoe Wizard $30
Mirror, Morton's Salt, 1930...$125
Mirror, Schaeffer Piano, yellow....................................$50
Mirror, Whirlpool Washer..$25
Paperweight, Bell System, bell, glass, blue $95
Paperweight, Golden Pheasant Gunpowder..................$35
Paperweight, Smith Bros. Cough Drops, cast iron $40
Pail, Uncle Wiggily Peanut Butter, 1923 ....$550
Pencil clip, Ritz Crackers, litho tin, 1930 ....$7.50
Pinback button, Aunt Jemima Pancake Flour,
    1896...$90
Pinback button, Hostess Cake, 1940s $20
Pinback button, Maypo, 1960s......................................$25
Poster, Arm & Hammer, birds $35
Poster, Bull Durham, includes cow figure $375
Pot scraper, Sharples Cream, 1909 ....$295
Ruler, Clark Bars, wood...$7.50
Tape Measure, Fab $35
Thermometer, Kerns Bread..$55
Thermometer, RC Cola $35
Tumbler, Coon Chicken Inn...$15
Wallet, Rock Island Plow, cloth $20
Whistle, Atwater Kent Radios $15
Whistle, Buster Brown Shoes, 1930s............................$65
Whistle, Oscar Mayer Wiener, hot dog shape,
    1950..$10
Yardstick, Kaiser Automobile..$15

AMERICAN STONEWARE

Antique stoneware—the old 19th and early 20th-century crocks and other items that were used to store food and drink in the days before refrigerators and glass jars—is a wonderful reminder of country life in rural America. It has always been popular with collectors but has become much more so in the past decade.

Background: Utilitarian stoneware (as opposed to more decorative forms of pottery) was used throughout the 1800s and into the early 1900s to store water or spirits or to preserve or pickle a variety of foodstuffs. It was made, primarily in the Northeast, by hundreds of American potteries and was inexpensive enough to be available to most American families, who used it on a daily basis. Stoneware took the form of crocks, jugs, jars, pails, pitchers, bottles and churns—all in various sizes. Stoneware was ideal for its purpose; it was safe and did not taint the food it held with any unwanted tastes or odors.

Collectible American stoneware can be divided into two broad categories. The first includes the early hand-thrown pieces that were individually made on a potter's wheel. Some were plain, while others were decorated, all by hand, of course. The second category consists of the newer pieces (dating from the late 1800s and early 1900s) that were molded or machine-made. These newer pieces are sometimes referred to as "blue-and-white" stoneware because of the blue designs or lettering that was typically stenciled or printed on the grayish-white background.

Both categories are avidly collected; but the older, hand-thrown and hand-decorated pieces are, by far, the more valuable. These are the pieces that serious collectors look for and the pieces that bring the highest prices.

General Guidelines: The value of 19th-century stoneware depends on several factors, including decoration, condition, age, the type of piece and the maker—pretty much in that order. The type of decoration displayed on a piece plays a huge role in determining its value. Pieces with elaborate or intricate decoration—such as birds, animals, people, battleships, etc.— commands much higher prices than similar pieces displaying simple swirl designs or uncomplicated flowers. Plain pieces, without any decoration, will, of course, be worth even less.

The method used to apply the decoration will also help date a piece and affect its value. The earliest pieces, dating from the early 1800s, were decorated by "incising," where the artist used a metal tool to actually scratch the design into the pottery. Incised stoneware is scarce today and almost always very expensive. A second method of applying the decoration was known as "slip-cupping," where the artist poured a thin stream of cobalt slip from a cup to form the design. Authors and experts Don and Carol Raycraft, who have written extensively about American stoneware, accurately compare this process to "decorating a cake," and say it was popular from the 1830s to the 1880s, with the best examples produced in the 1850s and 1860s.

The most common method of decorating stoneware between 1850 and the 1880s, according to the Raycrafts, was brushing, which, in effect, meant painting the surface of the stoneware with a brush dipped in the cobalt slip. The designs could range from something as simple as a quick swirl or a capacity mark to something as complicated as a group of birds, a country scene, or even people (a true rarity). Of course, the more complex the design, the more valuable the piece will be.

The least desirable type of design, as far as collectors are concerned, is the stencil design, which, because of cost-saving measures, saw increasing use beginning in the 1880s and extended into the 1900s, when the stoneware industry was taken over by mass-produced molded stoneware that was machine-made.

Collectors of 19th-century stoneware are, of course, concerned about condition but, unlike some other collecting categories, they don't insist on absolute perfection. Stoneware was rather crudely and quickly made. It was not art pottery but was intended to be inexpensive and utilitarian. Much of it was far from perfect when it left the factory, and once it got in the home, it was subjected to heavy daily use. Few pieces survived in pristine condition.

These three one-gallon preservative jars are signed "Lyons," "Cortland," and "Penn Yan." All have brush floral designs and are valued at between $300 and $600.

COLLECTOR'S ADVISORY!

Modern stoneware that has the look of vintage stoneware—complete with decorations of birds, flowers, etc.—is still being made today. Experienced collectors can identify the contemporary pieces because they are thinner and lighter in weight. Perhaps more of a danger to collectors are plain pieces of 19th-century stoneware that are painted with a cobalt decoration that is made to look original.

This three-gallon churn with a bird design is signed "E. and L.P. Norton, Bennington, Vt." It is worth a minimum of $750.

Collectors are especially forgiving about imperfections during the firing process—flaws described by the Raycrafts as minor surface cracks, "fried cobalt," flaking glaze, chips, burns or brown spots, or "salt tears."

Larger chips, cracks and other damage caused by mishandling and abuse, however, are another matter, and will subtract from the value of the piece, depending on the severity of the damage, the scarcity of the piece, etc. Most serious collectors would have little interest in a chipped or cracked common piece of stoneware displaying a simple decoration. They might be more forgiving, though, when it comes to a rare, early piece of stoneware with a complex, intricate design. (The Raycrafts suggest that any decorated stoneware pieces of great value should have chipped areas professionally restored.)

Also, unlike many other types of collectibles, most collectors of decorated stoneware generally do not place tremendous importance on the manufacturer of the piece. Over the course of the 19th century, there were hundreds of potteries that produced stoneware. Some marked their pieces, others did not.

This one-gallon unmarked butter pail, dating from the 1870s, is worth $500 or more.

As prices continue to rise for the original hand-thrown and hand-decorated stoneware of the 19th century, more and more collectors are turning to molded stoneware, which was produced mostly in the late 1800s and early 1900s. The mass-produced, machine-made pieces were either plain, or decorated with stencils, often indicating the capacity of the crock or piece. Small and simple molded stoneware pieces, without decoration, are the least expensive, typically available for $20 to $50. Pieces with decorations, designs or advertising are generally available for $35 and up, with prices going into the hundreds.

Clubs

• American Stoneware Collectors Society, P.O. Box 281, Gaithersburg, MD 20879

Recommended Reading

American Stoneware, Don & Carol Raycraft
Country Antiques & Collectibles, Dana Morykan and Harry L. Rinker
Antique Trader's Country Americana Price Guide, Kyle Husfloen
Country Americana Price Guide, Kyle Husfloen
Wallace-Homestead Price Guide to American Country Antiques, Don & Carol Raycraft

VALUE LINE

Decorated Stoneware

Batter Jug, long-tailed bird design, 9" high,
bottom chips, surface flakes $600

Batter Pail, 1-1/2 gallon, all-around flower design,
Sipe, Nicholas & Co., rim chips $1,100

Butter Churn, four-gallon, handles, stenciled eagle
with "E. Pluribus Unum" 16" high $225

Butter Churn, four gallon, handles, floral design,
W.H. Farrar & Co., 16" high, minor chips $350

Butter Churn, five-gallon, handles, floral design,
18" high, minor chips $575

Canning Jar, 2-quart, simple design $550

Churn, 6-gallon, "starface" decoration,
T. Harrington $5,000

Crock, apple butter, 1 gallon, floral design,
D Ack $400

Crock, butter, covered, side handles,
11-1/2" diameter, flower design $500

Crock, J. & E. Norton, intricate scene of house
and lion, handles $9,000

Crock, J. & E. Norton, 5-gallon, elaborate scene of
deer in woods $7,000

Crock, traveler viewing sign
"11 miles to Hartford" $700

Crock, 9" high, handles, flower design $400

Crock, 5-gallon, flower design, 18" high $450

Crock, 4-gallon, ovoid-shape, Mead,
simple decoration $200

Crock, 2-gallon, floral design, handles,
E. & L. P. Norton $150

Crock, 2-gallon, floral design,
New York Stoneware Co. $175

Crock, 2-gallon, Union Stoneware $55

Jar, 3-gallon, merchant ship and floral design $525

Jar, ovoid-shape, Bennett & Choliar,
shoulder handle, star design $425

Jar, 12" high, bird on flowering branch,
shoulder handles $550

Jar, eagle on cannon and "Charlestown" $600

Jar, ovoid-shape, girl looking between her legs,
17" high $10,000

Jar, 14" high, simple floral design,
W.E. Welding, strap handle $125

Pitcher, 1-gallon, handles, floral design $775

Molded Stoneware

"As You Like It Horseradish" pail, with handle $75

Bean Pot, covered, 7-1/2" high, relief of two
children and "Boston Baked Beans" $325

Butter Crock, covered, molded cherries and lid,
wire bale and wooden handle $250

Crock, Red Wing, 10-gallon $50

Crock, Red Wing 6-gallon $40

Crock, Western Stoneware, 6-gallon,
leaf decoration $60

Jug, "National Pickle & Canning Company,"
drop handle $75

Pitcher, 7" high, cattails design $200

Pitcher, 8", tree bark and flower design $165

Pitcher, 8", tree-lined roadway $200

Pitcher, 8", cattle in oval $200

Pitcher, 8", eagles and shields $375

Pitcher, 8", deer in one oval, swan in another $550

Salt Cellar, butterflies design $100

Salt Cellar, peacock design $85

Sugar Crock, 9" diameter, 4-1/2" high, stripes,
crow's foot in bottom $200

"Wesson Oil" jar, stenciled label $185

This set of one-to-three-gallon brown-and-cream covered crocks is worth about $300-$350 for the set.

This rare three-gallon crock decorated with a deer scene, is signed J.E. Norton, Bennington, Vt." Dating from the early 1850s, it is valued at over $7,500.

ANIMATION ART

As animation art becomes more and more popular, the market becomes ever more diluted with modern pieces that are wonderful for decorating children's rooms, but should be distinguished from original animation art production cels. The difference between "sericels" (short for serigraph cel) and "cels" (short for celluloid) adds up to thousands of dollars.

Witness the five-figure prices paid for distinguished animation art cels from some of Disney's most popular films—*Lady and the Tramp*, $57,500; *Peter Pan and Tinkerbell*, $21,850; *Snow White and the Seven Dwarfs*, $85,000.

Although animation art is not cheap, with the addition of sericels, limited editions and a vast number of television cels, there are also many items that retail in the hundreds, rather than the thousands, of dollars.

Background: Animation cels are the hand-painted sheets that are placed over a background and photographed to make animation films and cartoons. These are the original pieces used to make animated films, cartoons and television shows. One second of film requires more than 20 cels.

Through the years animation studios destroyed a majority of their animation cels, making those that survived extremely valuable. Winsor McCay's 1909 *Gertie the Dinosaur* is frequently referred to as the first animated cartoon. But the celluloid process—an animation drawing on celluloid—is attributed to Earl Hurd. These early pioneers paved the way for animation giant Walt Disney. To this day, Disney Studios remains the leader in animation. As the animation process changes—1995's *Toy Story* made history as the first full-length animation film to be completely computer-generated—many believe vintage animation art will become even more cherished as an art that no longer exists in its purest form.

Even newer animation cels can bring tremendous prices. This cel from the 1995 Disney film "The Lion King" brought a price of $37,000 at a Sotheby's auction in New York.

General Guidelines: In general, cels depicting the main characters from a film will garner the highest prices. There are exceptions to this rule, however. Two examples are cels featuring *Sleeping Beauty's* evil character Maleficent, and the Queen from *Snow White*. Values for both of these secondary characters exceed those of the films' stars.

If a film is recognized with an award or in any other high-profile way, the cels will likely bring higher prices.

Many original Disney animation cels are truly expensive. At a recent auction, an original production cel of Mickey Mouse garnered a bid of more than $400,000.

Cels from today's animation films are recognized immediately for their value and are auctioned by the most high-end auction houses. A sale of cels from *The Lion King* in 1995 grossed over $2 million.

In recent times Disney and other animation houses have begun producing limited editions—hand-painted cels created specifically for collectors in limited quantities (usually 250 to 2,500). The scenes shown may not even be from the film, but they can still retail in the thousands of dollars. They offer animation houses the chance to put popular characters in a scene together, even if such a meeting never occurred in a film.

A sericel is a non-production silk-screened cel. These are similar to limited editions, but no work is done by hand and they're usually produced in editions of 5,000. These are not actually "cels," but they are the most affordable items in animation art, usually selling for less than $300.

Warner Brothers is another animation industry giant, whose characters are second only to Disney's in collectibility. Bugs Bunny is king of the Warner line, with the Road Runner, Wile E. Coyote, Daffy Duck, Taz and Marvin the Martian not far behind.

Animation art from Japan is currently underappreciated and undervalued, making it some of the more affordable on the marketplace. Some original Japanese productions cels are still available in the $100 to $200 range.

Collectors should also consider cels from Saturday-morning cartoons and animated commercials as a less expensive way to collect animation art. The cels are much more plentiful and often sell in the $100 to $300 range. Cels from today's animated prime-time television shows are also very popular, and available for affordable prices.

Clubs

• Animation Art Collectors of Washington, 2972 Yarling Court, Falls Church, VA 22042

• Animation Art Guild Ltd., 330 West 45th Street, Suite 9D, New York, NY 10036

VALUE LINE

Disney

101 Dalmatians, Cruella, original animation
   art production cel $3,000

101 Dalmatians, Cruella, limited edition,
   framed size 18" x 21"............................... $2,000

101 Dalmatians, Pongo with puppy on his head,
   original animation art production cel,
   Disneyland mat and gold seal $3,800

101 Dalmatians, Pongo carrying one puppy,
   original animation art production cel $2,000

101 Dalmatians, Puppy Disguise, sericel,
   framed size 19" x 22"................................ $275

Aladdin, Aladdin with master background,
   unframed $2,500

Aladdin, Aladdin plucks a tasty treat for
   Princess Jasmine, limited edition,
   framed size 16" x 34"............................... $2,500

Aladdin, Aladdin and lamp, sericel,
   framed size 19" x 22"............................... $275

Alice in Wonderland, Down the Rabbit Hole,
   limited edition, framed size 18" x 38" $2,000

Anastasia, original production master
   background... $1,000

Anastasia, original production drawing of
   Anastasia $300

Bambi, Bambi, original production cel.................... $5,000

Bambi, Bambi and Faline, sericel,
   framed size 18" x 21"............................... $275

Bambi, Thumper and his mom,
   original production cel $4,000

Bambi, Faline, original production cel $1,000

Bambi, owl, original production cel $1,000

Beauty and the Beast, Belle and the Beast,
   limited edition, framed size 20" x 24-1/2............ $2,500

Beauty and the Beast, Belle and the Beast
   by the fire, Sericel, framed size 19" x 22".......... $275

Cinderella, Bruno, original production cel $1,000

Cinderella, Bruno, color model animation cel,
   3" x 5" $800

Cinderella, Lady Tremaine, original animation
   production drawing, signed by Frank Thomas,
   7-1/2" x 4"... $500

Cinderella, The Duke, original production cel........ $1,000

Cinderella, The King, original production cel $1,000

Donald Duck, character shown from back,
   original animation production cel $100

Donal Duck, Donald's Better Self (1938 short),
   original animation production cel $1,500

Donald Duck, Hockey Champ, Huey,
   Dewey and Louie original production cel $850

Donald Duck, Lonesome Ghosts, Donald emerging

LEARN THE LINGO!

Collectors of animation art have a language all their own. Here are some of the terms you should be familiar with:

12-Field and 16-Field—These are terms used to indicate the two most popular sizes in which original animation art was produced. A "12-field" cel measures 10-by-12 inches, while a "16-field" cel is a larger 12-by-16 inches.

Courvoisier—This refers to a cel set-up created and sold by the Courvoisier Galleries in the late 1930s and early 1940s. Characters were often trimmed to image and covered with a protective top cel. They were also glued to one of several backgrounds—wood veneer, hand-painted watercolors, dots or stars. Most Disney pieces from this era are Courvoisiers.

Master background—One of the most sought-after types of background, this can increase the price of a piece of animation art up to tenfold. This is a background from the same film as the cel, but the two did not appear together in the film. A "key master set-up" is a cel that appears with its original background as seen in the film.

Pan (Cinemascope)—This refers to a cel or drawing up to 12-by-30 inches.

Production—Any cel or drawing created for the production of an animated film, which may or may not appear in the film.

from box, original animation production drawing,
   4" x 4" $450

Donald Duck, Mickey's Circus, Donald with fish
   in bill, original animation production drawing,
   4" x 4" $495

Donald Duck, from 1961 short Mathmagic Land,
   original animation production cel, 5" x 4" $650

Donald Duck, 1950s/1960s original animation
   production cel, Disneyland set-up with
   gold seal, 6" x 8" $600

Donald Duck, 1985 television commercial,
   original animation production cel,
   9-1/2" x 5-1/2"....................................... $450

Dumbo, Dumbo and his mother inside the
   circus tent, limited edition, framed size
   18" x 21" $1,850

Dumbo, Dumbo and Baby Mickey, original
   production cel, framed size 16" x 18".................. $700

Dumbo, original animation art story drawing of
   Dumbo, matted and framed, 8" x 11" $1,900

Fantasia, animation drawing of Sorcerer Mickey,
   in color $4,200

Fantasia, centaur, original animation art
   production cel, 8" x 6" $3,900

Goofy, 1985 television commercial,
   original animation production cel, 10" x 6" $350

Goofy, Batter Up, sericel, framed size 16" x 26"........ $375

A piece of animation art from the classic 1937 Disney film, "Snow White and the Seven Dwarfs" sold for over $35,000 at a Sotheby's auction.

Goofy, Goofy Golf, sericel,
    framed size 34" x 20"... $450
Goofy, The Art of Skiing, original cel $2,000
Jungle Book, Baloo, original production cel
    with laser background $950
Jungle Book, Mowgli and Flunkey Monkey,
    original production cel $1,100
Jungle Book, Shere Khan, full figure
    original production cel $2,400
Lady and the Tramp, Lady and Tramp over a
    color laser background, original animation
    production cel, framed, 7" x 4-3/4" $4,900
Little Mermaid, Ariel, original animation
    production cel.. $1,500
Little Mermaid, Scuttle, original animation
    production cel.. $750
Little Mermaid, Triton, with trident original
    animation production cel..................................... $1,300
Little Mermaid, Ursula, original animation
    production cel, full figure................................. $1,800
Little Mermaid, Ursula, original cel,
    tentacles not showing $1,300
Lion King, pan-sized sericel, framed size
    17" x 38" $650
Lion King, Rafiki teaches Simba, sericel,
    framed size 17" x 20".. $275
Lion King, Simba introduces Pumbaa and
    Timon to Nala, limited edition,
    framed size 20" x 25".. $2,650
Mickey and Minnie, serigraph $250
Mickey, Camping Out, Mickey and Minnie,
    original animation art production drawing,
    3" x 4" $450

Mickey, Canine Caddy, Mickey swinging golf club,
    original animation art production drawing,
    matted and framed, 6" x 7-1/2" $950
Mickey, Mickey's Elephant, Mickey holding a saw,
    original animation art production drawing,
    4" x 2-1/2" $525
Mickey, Puppy Love, Mickey holding flowers
    and candy, original animation art production
    drawing, matted and framed, 3-1/2" x 3-1/2"......... $850
Mickey, Society Dog Show, Mickey dragging Pluto,
    original animation art production drawing,
    5-1/4" x 6" $575
Mickey, Steamboat Willie, original animation
    art production drawing, 3-1/2" x 6-1/2" $2,400
Peter Pan, Lost Boy and Indians,
    original production cel $500
Peter Pan, Peter Pan and Tiger Lily,
    original production cel $3,000
Peter Pan, Hook, original animation production
    drawing, 10" x 4-1/2" $975
Peter Pan, Michael yanked up pirate sail, original
    animation production drawing, 3" x 10-1/2" $425
Peter Pan, Peter Pan in headdress, original animation
    production drawing, 5-1/4" x 5-1/2" $595
Pinocchio, Coachman, original animation production
    drawing, green highlights, 5" x 8-1/2" $850
Pinocchio, Figaro, original production cel.............. $1,000
Pinocchio, Jiminy Cricket and Gideon, original
    animation art production cel $3,000
Pinocchio, Pinocchio, Figaro and Cleo, original
    animation art production cel, original paint,
    Courvoisier set-up with original label $13,500
Pinocchio, Pinocchio and Jiminy, original animation
    art production cel, Courvoisier set-up $11,000
Pinocchio, Stromboli, original animation production
    drawing, red accents in ax, 7-1/2" x 7-1/2" $700
Pluto, Donald's Garden, Pluto fighting with
    gopher for bone, 2-3/4" x 10" $475
Pluto, Just Dogs, original animation art production
    model drawing of Pluto and different poses of
    the same dog, framed $950
Pluto, Mickey's Elephant, Pluto as devil.................... $350
Pluto, Society Dog Show, Pluto and judge,
    6-3/4" x 8-1/4".. $400
Rescuers, original production cel of Orville.............. $400
Sleeping Beauty, Briar Rose, original animation
    art production cel over a color laser background,
    4-1/2" x 3-1/4".. $1,950
Sleeping Beauty, Briar Rose close-up of face
    with cape, original animation art production
    drawing, 7-1/2" x 4-1/2"... $450
Sleeping Beauty, Briar Rose full-figure pose,
    original animation art production drawing,
    5-1/2" x 2-1/2".. $495
Sleeping Beauty, Fauna original animation
    art production cel $650

Sleeping Beauty, Goon, original animation art production drawing, 4-1/2" x 3" $250

Sleeping Beauty, The Jester, original animation art production cel $650

Sleeping Beauty, Maleficent and Diablo, original animation art production cel over a color laser background, 7-1/2" x 6" $4,900

Sleeping Beauty, Merryweather original animation art production cel $950

Snow White, Bashful, original production cel......... $3,500

Snow White, blue bird on Snow White's fingers, original animation art production cel, Courvoisier set-up with labels........................ $14,500

Snow White, original animation drawing $950

Snow White, raccoon and his reflection, original animation art production cel, Courvoisier set-up with labels, original Courvoisier framing, 3-1/2" x 2-1/2" $950

Sword in the Stone, Wart as squirrel and lady squirrel, 5" x 10" $550

Winnie the Pooh, Blustery Day, Pooh and Owl original production cel $1,500

Winnie the Pooh, Christopher Robin and Owl, original animation production cel $450

Winnie the Pooh, Pooh, Eeyore, and Piglet, 1980s, sericel with Disney seal.......................... $195

Winnie the Pooh, Tigger Bouncing, 1980s, original animation art production cel $195

Winnie the Pooh, New Adventures of Winnie the Pooh, Rabbit, 1970s, original animation production drawing $125

Other Characters

Beavis and Butthead, two characters, original production cel $500

Bugs Bunny, Bugs and Daffy Duck, Hunting Season, limited edition, signed by Chuck Jones, framed size 18" x 21"............................. $850

Bugs Bunny, limited edition cel of Bugs and Chuck Jones, signed by Jones, one of 350 .... $950

Bugs Bunny, A Hare Grows in Manhattan, limited edition, framed size 16" x 34", signed by Virgil Ross $845

Bugs Bunny, Show Biz Bugs, 4-panel scene, limited edition, framed size 18" x 39", signed by Virgil Ross $995

Bugs Bunny, A Wild Hare, Bugs and Elmer Fudd, limited edition, framed size 16" x 18", signed by Virgil Ross $650

Daffy Duck, original production drawing.................. $195

Daffy Duck, Daffy Duck's Fantastic Island, 1983, Daffy and Yosemite Sam, signed by Friz Freleng, framed $600

Daffy Duck, 1960s, original animation production drawing, matted and framed................................ $500

Dilbert, Wally, Dilbert and Alice, original production cel $400

Dilbert, Dogbert, original production cel.................. $175

Dilbert, original production drawing $175

Fat Albert and the Cosby Kids, Filmation Studios, 1970s, tempera background sheet, framed............. $900

Felix the Cat, Biker Felix, limited edition, signed by Don Oriolo, framed size 18" x 21" $600

Felix the Cat, Felix and his magic bag, limited edition, signed by Don Oriolo, framed size 18" x 21" $600

Felix the Cat, Felix time line, limited edition, signed by Don Oriolo, framed size 18" x 36".................... $700

Felix the Cat, Felix Dentist, limited edition, signed by Don Oriolo, framed size 16" x 18"........................ $400

Foghorn Leghorn, 1960s, original animation art production $325

King of the Hill, Hank, original production animation cel, color laser background $375

King of the Hill, Hank and Peggy, original production animation cel, color laser background $375

King of the Hill, Hank, Bill and Dale, original production animation cel, color laser background $375

King of the Hill, Hank, Peggy and Bobby, original production animation cel, color laser background $450

King of the Hill, Hank and three neighbors, original production animation cel, color laser background $400

Marvin the Martian, limited edition, signed by Chuck Jones, framed size 16" x 18" $675

Marvin the Martian, Marvin and Hugo, 1980s $1,400

Peanuts, Charlie Brown, original production cel........ $175

Peanuts, entire gang, circa 1970s original animation production cel....................................... $500

Peanuts, Linus with blanket, original production drawing... $200

Peanuts, Marcie, original production drawing............ $100

Peanuts, Snoopy, original production drawing $150

Pink Panther, Anteater, original production cel, 4-1/2" x 4" $125

Pink Panther, Inspector, early cel in grease pencil...... $150

Popeye, limited edition cel, edition size of 250 .... $450

Ren & Stimpy, original production cel $500

Road Runner and Wile E. Coyote, late 1950s animation production background by Maurice Noble $2,800

Road Runner, 1980s original animation production drawing.. $295

Roger Rabbit, original production cel showing both
    Disney and Warner Bros. characters $7,000
Roger Rabbit, original production cel,
    Roger Rabbit $1,400
Simpsons, opening sequence, family on couch,
    original animation production cel $2,000
Simpsons, Homer, original animation
    production cel $400
Simpsons, Bart, original animation production cel..... $500
Simpsons, Bart and Homer, original animation
    production cel $600
Simpsons, Marge, original animation
    production cel $400
Simpsons, Bart and Millhouse, original animation
    production cel $600
Simpsons, Lisa and Marge, original animation
    production cel $500
Simpsons, Lisa, Bart and Homer, original animation
    production cel $600
Sylvester, 1990s, original animation cel, promo......... $395
Tasmanian Devil, original animation art $95
Tom and Jerry, That's My Pup, 1953, Tom, Jerry,
    Spike, original production cel on master
    background $3,000
Tom and Jerry, Tom's Photo Finish, 1957, original
    production cel on master background $2,200
Tom and Jerry, Jerry and Tuffy, original animation
    production drawing $450
Tom and Jerry, 1990, original animation art production
    cel from a commercial... $295

Some animation art can bring staggering prices. This scene from "Pinocchio" went for $120,000 at a Sotheby's auction.

Tom and Jerry, Royal Cat Nap, 1958,
    Tom Jerry and Tuffy, original production cel on
    master background $2,900
Wile E. Coyote, 1980s, original animation
    production drawing $300
Yellow Submarine, John Lennon and Ringo Starr,
    Heinz Edelman, King Features, 1968, 7-1/2" x 9"
    gouache on celluloid $2,500

ART DECO

Although the style now known as Art Deco dates from roughly 1920 to 1940, the term itself was not coined until the Art Deco revival of the 1960s. At the time, the sleek, clean style known as Art Deco was referred to as modernism, although some purists will claim clear differentiation between the two. Whatever one chooses to call it, the style was a clear departure from the swirling excesses of Art Nouveau. Most art historians agree true Art Deco began slowly in the early 1900s and attained the height of its glory in the *Exposition Internationale des Arts Decoratifs et Industriels Modernes*, held in Paris in 1925.

After the abundantly embellished motifs of Art Nouveau, the clean geometric lines and form-that-follows-function philosophy of Art Deco was a welcome breath of fresh air.

Although the lines are strong and simple, Art Deco is actually very sumptuous and luxurious. The use of exotic woods, precious metals, exquisite fabrics, ivory, mother-of-pearl, snakeskin and animal hides implies understated refinement. The devotion of Art Deco designers to fine craftsmanship, the clean geometric lines and avoidance of prettiness in embellishment is a fine combination.

As with any design style, some Art Deco pieces were designed and produced with the elite in mind, while others were produced for the average consumer. For the most part, those differences are reflected, now and in the 1920s, in price differences. In a few instances, simple functional pieces made of modest materials are disproportionately expensive, due to the name of the designer.

Clarice Cliff pottery is a perfect example. Cliff, a self-taught decorative British painter, worked her way up to designer, from line painter, in a famous pottery factory. Her

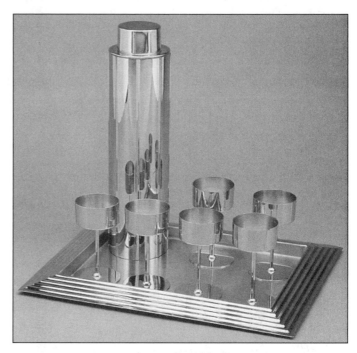

One of the classic Art Deco designs is this "Sky-scraper" cocktail shaker set with a "Manhattan" serving tray, designed by Norman Bel Geddes. Nice examples have sold for over $3,000. This example, from the Stephan Visakay Collection, was part of a display at the Seagram Museum.

challenge was to decorate styles of blank pottery whose sales had slumped in recent years, and to generate enough interest to sell off the remaining stock of blanks. The success of her designs is the stuff of which legends are made. Today, a teapot featuring one of her signature designs can sell for thousands.

Art Deco examples can be found in paintings, furniture, pottery, fashion, clocks, glassware, inkwells, frames, radios, lamps, ceramics and pottery, perfume bottles, figurines, vases, clothing, and almost any other works. A variety of materials, including chrome, colored glass, metals (nickel-, silver- and chrome-plated) and Bakelite were used. Works often feature sharply angular and geometric lines, vivid and contrasting colors. Often they depict speed and movement.

Clubs

• National Coalition of Art Deco Societies, One Murdock Terrace, Brighton, MA 02135-2817, Newsletter: NCADS Bulletin

• Art Deco Society of California, Suite 511, 100 Bush St., San Francisco, CA 94104

IT'S TIME TO LOOK FOR ART DECO CLOCKS!

Although a clock's primary function is for keeping time, those used in the 1920s were not only functional, but decorative, too. And, because by that time they were quite affordable, people could have a clock in each room—perhaps a mantel clock in the living room, a grandfather clock in the hall. Clocks were made of everything from celluloid to bronze, with animals and female figures commonly found on the clocks.

Some Art Deco timepieces also came with matching side panels, which were not attached to the clock. They were purely decorative and gave the appearance of being like bookends on either side of the clock. An Art Deco clock complete with its side panels would be a great find.

LOOKING FOR A BARGAIN!

Barware in general is a favorite category for many Art Deco collectors. During the carefree 1920s, despite Prohibition, alcohol was consumed, making barware a necessity for those who drank at home. Numerous items were needed to stock a personal bar, everything from ice buckets to soda dispensers. "Portable bars" are quite popular finds. Because of the range of collectibles, collectors can easily specialize in this area. Plus, most of the barware that can be found is still very usable.

- Art Deco Society of Chicago, 5801 N. Lincoln, Chicago, IL 60659

- Art Deco Society of Cleveland, 3439 West Brainard RD #260, Woodmere, OH 44122

- Art Deco Society of Detroit Area, PO Box 1393, Royal Oak, MI 48068-1893

- Art Deco Society of Los Angeles, PO Box 972, Hollywood, CA 90078

- Art Deco Society of New York, 385 Fifth Ave., Suite 501, New York, NY 10016, Newsletter: Modernist

- Art Deco Society of Northern Ohio, 3439 West Brainard Rd. #260, Woodmere, OH 44122

- Art Deco Society of the Palm Beaches, 820 Lavers Circle #G203, Del Ray Beach, FL 33444

- Sacramento Art Deco Society, PO Box 162836, Sacramento, CA 95816-2836

- Art Deco Society of San Diego, PO Box 33762, San Diego, CA 92163

- Art Deco Society of South Carolina, 856-A Liriope Lane, Mount Pleasant, SC , 29464

VALUE LINE

Magazines and Ephemera
American Home, 1930s ....$10-$12
Child Life, July 1938 ....$10-$12
Colliers, 1922 ....$25-$30
Judge, May 1924 ....$20-$25
Needlecraft Magazine, July 1928 ....$15-$20
Picture Play, April 1922 ....$20-$25

Decorative Pottery and Glass
Bottle, cut glass, European, black geometric designs,
    a la Josef Hoffman style ....$350-$400
Candy dish for piano ....$125-$150
Chandelier, molded glass and brass,

Deco foliate designs ....$1,300-$1,400
Dish, free-form, colorless, oval, white and purple
    stripes, Almeric Walter ....$550-$650
Dish, with painted floral design, Japan ....$25-$30
Goblet, snifter, peacocks and nude women design,
    European ....$300-$500
Jar, Gouda pottery, glazed, several colors ....$600-$800
Planter vase, bulbous rectangular, turquoise blue glass
    with cobalt blue, etched, LeVerre..................$700-$800
Urn, glass, raspberry pink goblet form, two handles,
    Degue, 8" ....$400-$450
Vase, Amphora, Austria, enameled stylized
    flowers ....$600-$700
Vase, Cameo etched, bulbous colorless vessel, three
    repeating design elements ....$150-$200
Vase, Muller, etched, colorless jardiniere-form,
    four blue glass-faceted ornaments.................$200-$400
Vase, Nelson McCoy, pink, in shape of hands.......$50-$60
Vase, Roseville, blue glaze, flared neck
    and base ....$75-$100
Vase, Schneider LeVerre, white body, swirled orange and
    brown-green glass etched with blossoms......$800-$900
Vase, Silvercrest, bronze, with elaborate overlay of
    abstract organic forms ....$175-$225

Fiestaware
Cobalt pitcher with chip.......................................$30-$35
Lamp of nude female figure ....$400-$450
Pair green cornucopia wall vases, Hall ....$50-$75
Small green tray ....$35-$45
Small plate ....$10-$15

Kitchen Items
Bowl, Hesques, colorless oval body,
    stylized floral border ....$150-$175
Bread basket, Manning-Bowman, 1941.............$150-$200
Centerbowl, transparent green, etched
    geometric motif, Daum, French ....$1,000-$1,500
Cream and sugar set, Chase Breakfast set, bowl,
    tray and creamer..$100-$150
Napkin holder, chrome, Chase ....$75-$85

This black chrome mirror-brush-and-powder-box set is valued at about $100-$125.

Pitcher, yellow, Hall China Co. ....$40-$50
Pitcher, colorless, spaced bubbles throughout,
    orange handle, Daum ....$500-$700
Refrigerator containers, covered, Hall China Co.,
    blue...$30-$35
Serving dish, tulip shaped, Chase, copper ....$25-$35
Salt and pepper shakers, Kensington, chrome,
    Raleigh model, 1950, set...................................$40-$60
Salt and pepper shakers, ceramic ....$40-$55
Syrup jug, Chase, chrome and clear glass,
    ribbed ....$40-$50
Table glass, 18-piece set, crystal, Steuben,
    "Cut Star and Punty" pattern, 1934,
    moon and star motif ....$600-$650
Teapot, chrome, electric, with cord........................$40-$45
Tea set, silver and rosewood, four-piece, plus tray,
    French..$3,000-$4,000
Toaster, General Electric #179T77 ....$50-$75
Toaster, Sunbeam, Model T-9, 1930s...................$75-$100
Waffle iron, Westinghouse, chrome and
    walnut..$45-$75
Waffle set, Chase, includes pitcher, sugar shaker,
    syrup pitcher and tray...................................$200-$300

Jewelry

Belt buckle, blue enamel, two pieces ....$60-$75
Bracelet, copper and oxidized silver with molded
    glass and simulated carnelian,
    Chinese influence ....$100-$125
Bracelet, elaborate rhinestone..............................$45-$60
Bracelet, Bakelite ....$30-$40
Dress clip, blue rhinestones and turquoise
    beads...$30-$40
Dress clip, rhinestone...$75-$85
Necklace, molded glass, French, Rene Lalique style,
    colorless ovals, bird and leaf design.............$200-$250
Necklace, Mayan and Egyptian influence, green enamel
    and faux jade in German silver mounts..........$75-$100
Necklace, rhinestone, with matching earrings .....$75-$100
Shoe slips, pair, rhinestone ....$30-$40

Desk Items

Bookends, dogs, Rockwood, 1937.....................$475-$500
Boudoir lamp, pot metal, green, nude dancing
    figure, American......................................$300-$350
Clock, wooden, with female figure ....$175-$200
Desktop clock/pen holder, Bakelite ....$75-$125
Digital clock, bronze, Silvercrest, California,
    19" long, 1930...$250-$300
Floor lamp, General Electric Sunlamp................$75-$100
Foyer lamp, iron...$225-$275
Lamp, chrome, trilevel shade, green and red
    interior lights ....$400-$600
Lamp, dancer figural, bronze and ivory, cast from
    model, cast after model, 1930 ....$2,000-$3,000
Letter stand, cast-iron..$75-$100
Light, sculptural figure of woman dancer on

    drum platform, Italian ....$400-$425
Pen holder, with inkwell, chrome ....$50-$75
Table lamp, reverse painted, domed heavy wall
    glass shade, painted with repeating Deco
    foliate elements, 20-1/2" tall ....$900-$1,200
Vase, mounted as a lamp, Scandinavian,
    silver-plated, 1925....................................$700-$1,000

Perfume Bottles

Black-glass perfume atomizer...............................$50-$60
California Perfume Co. ....$75-$85
Chypre Moiret Paris ....$55-$75
Danse Galante eau toilette ....$35-$45
Nuit de Gala (Francois Gerard)...........................$45-$55
Pink glass, with glass stopper ....$40-$50
Tiny Shalimar, with blue top................................$20-$25

Compacts

14K gold (no mark)..$600-$650
All-in-one (Richard Hudnut)...............................$75-$85
Coty "envelope"...$50-$60
Illinois Case Co (square, with watch, powder and
    rouge...$100-$125
Pentagon-shaped compact with lipstick............$150-$175

Garments
Beaded white silk dress (early 1930s) ....$150-$175
Barware
Bottle opener, chrome parrot, with corkscrew,
    Negbaur ....$250-$300
Cocktail cups, copper and glass, Gilley Inc.,
    each ....$5-$10
Cocktail set, silver, shaker, 12 goblets,
    Tiffany Co. ....$1,200-$1,300
Cocktail shaker, glass, "Sweet Ad-aline" and
    two drunks..$30-$40
Cocktail shaker, chrome, Manning-Bowman,
    the "Good Fellowship"..................................$75-$125
Cocktail shaker, Zeppelin-shaped, chrome,
    12" high ....$50-$75
Drink mixers, chrome, golf clubs, set of 4,
    Chase ....$75-$100
Ice bucket, Claridge, chrome and brass, 1937,
    with tongs..$50-$75
Manhattan Cocktail Ensemble, chrome,
    complete set with tray, shaker and four cups,
    Norman Bel Geddes ....$1,000-$1,500
Seltzer dispenser, chrome ....$45-$55
Soda dispenser, chrome, "Soda King" ....$35-$50
Smoking Accessories
Ashtray, "Globe," chrome, Chase ....$75-$100
Ashtray, "Commodore," Chase, 1935 ....$75-$100

Ashtray, marble, with figurine ....$125-$150
Cigarette box, "Rollaround," Chase...................$125-$150
Cigarette box, Heisey, glass ....$150-$175
Cigarette case, chrome, with attached lighter ....$25-$30
Cigarette container, Chase, polished nickel ....$50-$75
Lighter, "Triumph," Ronson...............................$50-$75
Match holder/ash tray, Chase, chrome,
    Bakelite holder ....$50-$75
Standing ash tray, Howell Manufacturing Co.
    ....$100-$150

Furniture
Armchairs, pair, fruitwood, rectangular back,
    curved armrests, French, 1930s...............$3,000-$3,500
Cabinet, walnut, two sections, fall front desk
    and liqueur cabinet, Austrian, 1930s.......$4,000-$6,000

This bronze and ivory figure, "The Archer," was cast and carved after a model by Ferdinand Preiss, circa 1930, and shows classic Art Deco design. It sold for a whopping $23,000 at a Butterfield & Butterfield auction.

WHO'S WHO IN ART DECO?

Several giftware manufacturers created Art Deco products, including:

American Thermos Bottle Co.: "Thermos" bottles, coffee-pots, decanters, desk sets, barware

Chase Brass & Copper Co.: lamps and lighting fixtures, housewares and consumer products

Everedy Co.: serving pieces, smoking accessories, skillets, trays, cocktail sets, vases, cooking utensils

Farber Brothers: cocktail memorabilia

S.W. Farber Co.: brass and copper kitchenware, barware

W.H. Howell Co: smoking stands, plant stands, flatirons, tables, piano benches, furniture

Kensington: cooking utensils

Manning-Bowman & Co.: coffee sets, cocktail sets, toasters, blenders, irons, waffle irons, appliances, clocks

Napier: ladies jewelry, matchboxes, watch chains, cocktail shakers

National Silver Co.: electric shavers, cameras, tableware, wallets, dinnerware, vases, compacts, hairbrushes, percolators, glassware

Park Sherman: lamps and smoking accessories

Revere Copper and Brass Inc.: plant holders, serving trays, candy containers

Shanklin Manufacturing Co.: smoking accessories

Chess table and chairs, coral-black lacquered board, with pieces, 1937..$2,500-$3,500

Console and mirror, wrought-iron, 1930s..$1,000-$1,750

Desk, rosewood, French, one cupboard with shelves, the other has drawers, 1930.......$5,000-$6,000

Extension dining table, rosewood, 1930s..$2,500-$3,000

Low table, rosewood, circular top, four legs, 1930s..$1,500-$2,000

Stained oak tables, Chinese-styled, circular top, three legs, 1930 ....$1,200-$1,750

Vanity and stool, maple and walnut, English, 1934..$1,000-$1,500

Miscellaneous

Book ends, "Crescent," Chase ....$100-$125

Books, red painted metal of two leaping greyhounds on marble base ....$125-$150

Candlesticks, polished copper, chrome base..........$30-$40

Clock set, three-pieces, rhombic-form clock, two candlesticks ....$1,000-$1,500

Figure, alabaster, Pan and reclining nude nymph, cast from model, 1925..................................$700-$900

Figure, Balinese dancer, patinated bronze, 1925, cast from model, Gorham Foundry ....$750-$1,200

Figure, female archer, patinated bronze, 1925, French, Susses Freres Foundry ....$2,000-$3,000

Figure, female snake charmer, patinated bronze and ivory, German, 1930, cast from model..............$2,500-$3,000

Figure, tiger, crouching, patinated bronze on marble, 1930, cast from model............................$1,500-$2,500

Glass ball slide fastener, black woven cord with pierced silver slide, suspending two clear glass balls, 1920s...$100-$150

Hand mirror, silver, bird and foliate design ....$175-$200

Mirror, brass and enamel, foliate design 22-1/2" tall ....$175-$200

Panel, oak, carved, depicts animal figures ....$475-$500

Panel, depicts Ida Reubenstein and Nijinksy, 1913 by G. Barber...................................$1,000-$1,200

Rug, wool, patterned after Jules Leleu design, fringed, beige, maroon border, 1930....................$2,000-$2,500

Traveling alarm clock, chromed brass, Jaegar, Switzerland...$75-$100

Watering pot, copper with brass handle................$75-$85

AMERICAN ART POTTERY

American art pottery is an immensely popular and a huge collecting category, far too large for the space allowed here, but the following should serve as a good introduction to this vast collecting area and provide some general guidelines to help separate the treasures from the trash. (The majority of American art pottery probably falls somewhere in between.)

Although hundreds of various potteries existed in America during the 19th and 20th centuries, only the major ones—in terms of collecting interest—will be covered here. The emphasis also is on decorative *art* pottery, rather than on ceramic dinnerware or the more general lines of utilitarian pottery (which, of course, are also collectible, but generally considered a separate category).

Fortunately for collectors, pottery is one category where there are plenty of references and resources available for further study. Collectors can choose from numerous books and price guides to learn more about American pottery in general or about a specific pottery and its wares.

Background: In the early 1870s, the art of ceramic and china painting caught the attention of the public as a form of self-expression and a potential field of employment—primarily for women. Within ten years, the popularity of ceramics was sweeping the country, and potteries were springing up literally from coast to coast.

Pockets of successful potteries, however, were centered in areas known for their indigenous clay. One such well-known pocket was centered around Zanesville, Ohio. In these pockets, the business of pottery-making flourished, with each company working feverishly to develop new shapes, glazes and painting techniques; guard their precious trade secrets; and market lines of decorative ware to a waiting and adoring public.

The popularity and demand for decorative ware peaked and then dimmed with the economic crisis of the late 1920s and '30s. By the late 1940s, many once-prolific potteries had closed their doors forever.

Because these potteries are no longer producing their wares, collectors find the American art pottery pieces produced between 1880 and 1950 particularly desirable. A beginning collector would profit from reading a few library books and attending a museum exhibition or two before jumping into this highly competitive market.

Although the demand for well-known collectibles is keen, pieces by lesser-known potteries are still available at very reasonable prices, making this a good collecting category for beginners.

General Guidelines: Each type of pottery often has its own specific guidelines, but the following applies in nearly every case. Condition is absolutely critical. An undamaged, perfect piece commands a higher price than one with even minor blemishes. Any chips, cracks, flakes, crazing, or hair-

COLLECTING TERMS!

Here are some general terms collectors of art pottery should know:

Earthenware—Pottery made of clay fired at temperatures lower than porcelain. It is considered good for everyday use because it is cheaper to produce than porcelain.

Flint enamel glaze—A finish usually applied to yellow ware consisting of powdered metallic glazes sprinkled on a coat of wet, clear glaze. When fired, the melting metal produced streaks of brilliant blue, green, white, and orange.

Gadroon—Dinnerware with molded-rope decoration.

Lug—Small tab handles on a bowl or jardiniere.

Paste—A mixture of clay and chemicals from which pottery pieces are made.

Red ware—Represents the widest category of American pottery, due to the availability of the raw material-red clay. The pieces are relatively fragile.

Rockingham—Clay glazed with dark brown, sometimes mottled glaze.

Scroddled or agate ware—Ceramic pieces made of mottled or swirled colors created by incompletely mixing several different clays. When fired, they would create a variegated effect. This is felt to be the least-known American ceramic product.

Toby jug—A mug or pitcher with the face or entire figure of a person.

Vitreous or vitrified—Non-porous pottery, which resists stains.

Yellow ware—Common, inexpensive American pottery, which takes its name from the color of the clay. Often associated with pie plates and mixing bowls, plain or decorated with a simple colored band or sponged glaze.

lines substantially decrease a piece's value. With a few exceptions, a well-known pattern, preferably one advertised in a catalog, is more desirable than an unknown pattern. A marked piece is more desirable than an unmarked piece. To sum it all up, a marked piece of a well-known design (or a rare-but-known design) in pristine condition, signed by the artist, will command the highest price. Also, with some exceptions, larger pieces will generally be more valuable than a corresponding smaller piece. A 12-inch vase, for instance, will usually be worth more than a similar 6-inch example.

Collectors should also be aware that regional differences in pricing are more dramatic than with most other collecting categories. Demand by competing collectors in a specific area can also cause artificially high prices.

This group of Rookwood vases, sold at a Don Tread-way Gallery auction in Cincinnati, includes (from left to right) a scenic vellum that sold for $4,125, a floral vellum that brought $3,850, and a scenic vellum that went for $2,420.

Grueby Pottery

Background: The Grueby Faience Company, based in Boston, Mass., was formed in 1890s and remained in business until 1921. In addition to art pottery, the company made architectural tiles, garden statues and other items, including lamp bases for other companies. Its hand-molded art pottery was decorated with handpainted flower and leaf designs. It employed various colored glazes, but cucumber green was its most popular and most successful, often copied by competitors.

General Guidelines: Grueby art pottery was usually marked, but often the marks were rendered unreadable by the firm's heavy glaze. Pieces after 1905 were marked "Grueby Pottery." Paper labels were also used.

Hull Pottery Company

Background: The Hull Pottery Company, located in Crooksville, Ohio, was founded in 1905 and produced various forms of art pottery and dinnerware until the company closed in 1986. Popular designs include Blossom Flite (mid 1950s), Bow Knot (late 1940s), Butterfly (mid 1950s), Calla Lily/Jack In The Pulpit (late 1930s), Capri (early 1960s), Crab Apple (mid 1930s), Dogwood/Wild Rose (mid 1940s), Ebb Tide (mid 1950s), Iris/Narcissus (mid 1940s), Magnolia (matte finish, mid-1940s; gloss finish, mid-1950s), and Morning Glory.

General Guidelines: Distinctive markings on the bottom of Hull vases help with identification. Early stoneware pottery has an "H." The famous matte pieces, a favorite of most collectors, contain pattern numbers. Camellia pieces, for example, are marked with numbers in the 100s, Iris pieces have 400 numbers and Wildflower pieces have a "W" preceding the number. Most Hull vases are also marked with their height in inches, making it easy to determine their value. Items made after 1950 are usually glossy and are marked "hull" or "Hull" in large script letters. Hull collectors are just now beginning to seriously collect the glossy ware and kitchen items.

McCoy Pottery

Background: McCoy Pottery was founded in 1848 by W. Nelson McCoy and W.F. McCoy near what is now Zanesville, Ohio. The firm was passed down through four generations of McCoys, until it was eventually sold to Designer Accents in 1985 and ceased production by 1990. Popular lines include: Hobnail, Lily Bud, Stretch Animals, Butterfly, Blossomtime, Wild Rose, Cascade, Brocade, Rustic, Harmony, Floraline, Antique, Starburst, and Golden Brocade.

General Guidelines: Several marks were used by the McCoy Pottery Co. Collectors should take the time to learn the marks and the variations. Pieces can often be dated based upon the mark. Most pottery marked "McCoy" was made by the Nelson McCoy Co.

Newcomb Pottery

Background: Founded at the Sophie Newcomb College for Women in New Orleans, La., in the 1895, the Newcomb Pottery continued to sell art wares until about 1940. Each piece was hand thrown and individually decorated, so no two pieces are the same. Most Newcomb pieces have a matte glaze.

General Guidelines: Most Newcomb Pottery is marked with the printed letters "NC," although various marks were impressed, incised or painted on the individual pieces. Starting in 1910, each shape was assigned a different number.

Niloak Pottery

Background: Often called Mission ware, Niloak pottery is recognized by its marble-like swirling layers of browns, blues, reds and tans. The firm was founded in 1911 in Benton, Arkansas by Charles Dean Hyten. He named the unique pottery after kaolin, the type of local clay used to make it ("Niloak" is simply "kaolin" spelled backward).

Overbeck Pottery

Background: Overbeck Pottery was started by the four Overbeck sisters in their family home in Cambridge City, Indiana, in 1911 and continued until 1955, when the last sister died. Overbeck made various sizes of vases, tumblers, and small figurines of animals and people, which are especially popular with today's collectors.

General Guidelines: Most Overbeck pieces are marked with a highly stylized "OBK" mark. Prior to around 1937, the pieces also included the initial of the sister who decorated the piece.

Red Wing Pottery

Background: The Red Wing Stoneware Company (established 1878) and the Minnesota Stoneware Company (1883) merged in the early 1900s to form the Red Wing Union Stoneware Company. The well-known art ware was developed in the early 1930s and the name officially changed to Red Wing Potteries Inc. in 1936. The lines included vases, flower arrangers, figurines, etc. The company shut down production in 1967.

General Guidelines: Red Wing Pottery can be found with various marks and paper labels. Some of the marks include a stamped red wing, a raised "Red Wing U.S.A. #____," or an impressed "Red Wing U.S.A. #____." Paper labels were used as early as 1930. Some pieces were identified only by an easily-lost paper label. Many manufacturers used the same mold patterns. Collectors should study the available references to become familiar with the Red Wing forms.

Rookwood Pottery

Background: Rookwood Pottery was founded in 1880 by Maria Longworth Nichols (in an old schoolhouse purchased by her father at a sheriff's auction) in Cincinnati, Ohio. It ceased production in 1967. Rookwood was known for its quality vases, jardinieres, lamps, tea pots, chocolate pots, sugar bowls, creamers, mugs, steins, candlesticks and ginger jars. Rookwood had more than 500 glazes, but eight glaze lines comprised the company's identity: Cameo, Dull Finish, Standard, Aerial Blue, Sea Green, Iris, Mat and Vellum.

General Guidelines: With very few exceptions, all pieces of Rookwood Pottery were marked and dated. The vast majority of pieces—all but the very earliest—display the famous "R" and "P" with the "R" reversed and the letters conjoined, surrounded by flames. In the very early years, you could determine the year of issue by counting the flames. By 1901, the date was indicated with a Roman numeral.

Production pieces (cast, undecorated) of Rookwood Pottery are usually available for about $50 and up. Most in demand, however, are the artist-signed pieces. Values depend

The Weller Dickensware vase (left), standing just under 9 inches, sold for $1,210 at a Don Treadway Gallery auction in Cincinnati, while the Owens standard glaze vase (right) went for $3,080.

largely on the particular artist. Expect to pay at least $500 and often more depending on artists, quality, scarcity and condition of the piece. Very high-quality pieces can bring thousands.

Roseville Pottery Company

Background: Started in Roseville, Ohio, in 1890, the firm also had a plant in Zanesville, Ohio. Rozane, Roseville's first art line, was renamed Rozane Royal in 1904. Roseville made more than 150 different lines or patterns.

General Guidelines: The prices for Roseville's later commercial ware are stable and unlikely to rise rapidly because it is readily available. The prices are strong for the popular middle-period patterns, which were made during the Depression and produced in limited numbers. Among the most popular patterns from this middle period are Blackberry, Cherry Blossom, Falline, Ferella, Jonquil, Morning Glory, Sunflower and Windsor. Desirable Roseville shapes include baskets, bookends, cookie jars, ewers, tea sets and wall pockets. Most pieces are marked, however during the middle period paper stickers were used. These often were removed, leaving the piece unmarked.

Shawnee Pottery Company

Background: The Shawnee Pottery Co. operated out of a complex of buildings in Zanesville, Ohio, starting in 1937. Shawnee pottery was an inexpensive, mass-produced pottery that was sold by large retailers. Shawnee began production in the midst of the Great Depression and continued into the new decade of the 1940s. It survived during the World War II years with a greatly curtailed, though highly profitable, operation. The late 1940s and early 1950s were the booming years for Shawnee; this was when it produced most of the figural lines and corn dinnerware that is so highly collected today. Production during the late 1950s and into the 1960s consisted mainly of corn dinnerware, ashtrays, kitchenware and non-figural floral items such as planters and vases.

General Guidelines: Shawnee pottery was made with a variety of marks, each indicative of a certain time period of production. Wares produced in the 1930s and into the early 1940s were generally marked with an incised "U.S.A." on the glazed bottom. Later, the "U.S.A." mark was combined with a three or four-digit number. Post-war items often had the embossed word "Shawnee" on the bottom, along with "U.S.A." and a number. In 1953, Shawnee began producing lines under the name Kenwood, and this name appears on many of those pieces along with "U.S.A." and a number.

Prices of Shawnee pottery increased dramatically during the 1990s, dictated in large part by supply and demand. Figural items such as cookie jars, pitchers and creamers have always been preferred to non-figural items such as planters and vases. Miniatures are some of the least expensive yet most highly sought-after Shawnee items. These miniatures are mostly non-figural pre-World War II items averaging three inches high and made as small vases, baskets, etc. in solid colors. Finding what is considered a "Mint" condition piece is difficult, and any defects decrease the value considerably.

One of Shawnee's policies was to sell all of its "seconds" to outside decorators, who would then add gold trim, decals or hand-painted features such as hair, bugs, patches, etc., to cover flaws on the pottery and sell these decorated items to higher-priced gift shops and stores. Items that have been decorated in this way are highly sought and often command from 50 to 100 percent more than the same item without the additional decoration.

Weller Pottery

Background: Weller Pottery was founded by Samuel A. Weller in 1872 near Zanesville, Ohio. The first pieces were sold door-to-door until the business grew large enough to open a factory operation in 1882, in Zanesville. Eventually, the business became one of the largest potteries in America; at one point, three Weller plants were operating. The firm ceased production in 1948. There are well over 100 Weller patterns.

General Guidelines: Because pieces of Weller's commercial ware are readily available, prices are stable and unlikely to rise rapidly. Forest, Glendale and Woodcraft are the most popular patterns in the middle price range. The Novelty Line is most popular among the lower-priced items.

Clubs

• American Art Pottery Association, PO Box 525, Cedar Hill, MO 63016

• Collectors of Illinois Pottery & Stoneware, 1527 East Converse St., Springfield, IL 62702

• Dedham Pottery Collector's Society, 248 Highland St., Dedham, MA 02026-5833

• Pottery Lovers Reunion, 4969 Hudson Dr., Stow, OH 44224

• Red Wing Collectors Society Inc., PO Box 184, Galesburg, IL 61402-0184

• Rosevilles of the Past Pottery Club, PO Box 656, Clarcona, FL 32710-0656

• Shawnee Pottery Collectors Club, PO Box 713, New Smyrna Beach, FL 32170-0713

Recommended Reading

Warman's American Pottery and Porcelain, Susan and Al Bagdade
20th Century American Ceramics Price Guide, Susan N. Cox
American & European Art Pottery Price Guide, Kyle Husfloen
Pottery and Porcelain Ceramics Price Guide, Kyle Husfloen and Susan N. Cox

VALUE LINE

Values shown are for pieces in Excellent condition with no flaws.

Grueby Pottery

Bowl, 11" diameter, cucumber green glaze, inscribed "RE" and "4/4"...$1,450
Bust, laughing boy, 11" high, unglazed terra-cotta.....$265
Tile, Spanish Galleon, ivory, brown, green and amber, "AS/GM" on back, 6" square $1,500
Tile, Knight, brown figure on blue background, 6" square...$265
Tile, Tree, green tree, blue sky, white clouds on light green ground, approx. 6" square $425
Vase, 9" high, 6" diameter, bulbous shape, cylindrical neck, gently flared rim, green matte glaze $725
Vase, 2" high, 3" wide, green matte glaze...................$295
Vase, 7" high, 4-1/2" diameter, bulbous shape, cylindrical neck, tooled and applied leaves and buds, cucumber green matte finish $2,500
Vase, 6" high, compressed spherical body, seven broad molded leaves, cucumber green glaze....................$875

Hull Pottery

Pre-1950 Patterns

Bow knot, B 7, 8-1/2" vase $300
Bow knot, B 13, double cornucopia............................$300
Dogwood (Wildflower), 504, 8-1/2" vase $165
Dogwood (Wildflower), 507, 5-1/2" teapot $375
Dogwood (Wildflower), 514, 4" jardiniere $115
Iris, 405, 4-3/4" vase $75
Iris, 406, 7" vase...$135
Iris, 412, 7" hanging planter.......................................$175
Jack-in-the-Pulpit/Calla Lily, 505, 6" vase $135
Jack-in-the-Pulpit/Calla Lily, 550, 7" vase $150
Magnolia, 4, 6-1/4" vase $60
Magnolia, 8, 10-1/2" vase $150
Magnolia, 22, 12-1/2" vase $250

REPRODUCTION ALERT!

Unfortunately, Nelson McCoy never registered his McCoy trademark, a fact discovered by Roger Jensen of Tennessee. As a result, Jensen began using the McCoy mark on a series of ceramic reproductions made in the early 1990s. While the marks on these recently-made pieces copy the original, Jensen made objects that were never produced by the Nelson McCoy Co. The best known example is the Red Riding Hood cookie jar, which was originally designed by Hull and also made by Regal China.

A mark alone is not proof that a piece is period or old! Knowing the proper marks and what was and was not made in respect to forms, shapes and decorative motifs is critical in authenticating patterns.

Magnolia (Pink Gloss), H 5, 6-1/2" vase $35
Magnolia (Pink Gloss), H 17, 12-1/2" vase $200
Open Rose (Camelia), 114, 8-1/2" jardiniere $395
Open Rose (Camelia), 120, 6-1/2" vase $115
Open Rose (Camelia), 140, 10-1/2" basket............. $1,400
Orchid, 301, 10" vase.. $325
Pinecone, 55, 6" vase $150
Poppy, 606, 6-1/2" vase $200
Poppy, 607, 8-1/2" vase $250
Poppy, 609, 9" wall planter $450
Rosella, R 1, 5" vase $40
Rosella, R 8, 6-1/2" vase $80
Stoneware, 536 H, 9" jardiniere $115
Tulip, 101-33, 9" vase $250

This 10-1/2-inch Weller Eocean vase sold for $3,300 at a Don Treadway Gallery in Cincinnati.

Waterlily, L-8, 8-1/4" vase $150
Wildflower, 54, 6-1/2" vase... $150
Wildflower, 66, 10-1/2" basket $2,000
Wildflower, 76, 8-1/2" vase $325
Wildflower, W-3, 5-1/2" vase $65
Woodland (matte), W1, 5-1/2" vase........................... $100
Woodland (matte), W25, 12-1/2" vase $425

Post-1950 Patterns (Glossy)

Blossom Flite, T8, basket.. $130
Blossom Flite, T11, candleholders, pair $85
Butterfly, B13, 8" basket $150
Ebbtide, E7, 11" fish vase $175
Figural planter, 27, Madonna, standing $35
Figural planter, 82, clown $50
Figural planter, 95, twin geese $50
Parchment & Pine, S-5, 10-1/2" scroll planter............. $85
Serenade (Birds), S7, 8-1/2" vase $65
Sunglow, 95, 8-1/4" vase.. $50
Tokay (Grapes), 4, 8-1/4" vase................................... $100
Tokay (Grapes), 12, 12" vase $135
Tropicana, T53, 8-1/2" vase $500
Woodland, W-9, 8-3/4" basket $125
Woodland, W-13, 7-1/2" shell wall pocket $75

McCoy Pottery

Bank, sailor, large duffle bag over shoulder................. $22
Basket, black and white, weave, double handle............ $25
Birdbath.. $32
Hanging basket, stoneware, marked "Nelson McCoy,"
   1926... $22
Jardiniere, 6" diameter, glossy black,
   marked "McCoy 6" $75
Jardiniere, 6" diameter, yellow, 1940s $60
Jardiniere, 7" diameter, Spring Woodline, 1960 .... $50
Jardiniere, 7" diameter, Swirl, black matte $40
Planter, Arcature, green and yellow $32
Planter, Wishing Well $20
Vase, Blossomtime... $45
Vase, Bud, green $20
Vase, Double Handles, green, 8", 1948......................... $50
Vase, Maroon Gloss, 6", 1940s $35
Vase, Swan, pink $25
Vase, Triple Lily, 8-1/2", 1950 .... $95

Newcomb Pottery

Candlesticks, corset shape, carved green, yellow and
   blue blossoms and leaves on blue ground, marked
   "NC/HB/232/HZ52" and "HZ53," pair $2,500
Vase, 4-1/4" high, bulbous shape, carved blue trees,
   pink and blue sky, marked
   "NC/JM/HW89/240/77" $2,500
Vase, 5-1/2" high, highly glazed, white clover,
   green leaves, blue ground, marked
   "NC/AFS/JM/M/Q/DB91"................................. $3,700
Vase, 6-1/2" high, three-color floral design on blue ground,
   marked "GK31AM" and "NC/JM,"
   mold mark 252 .... $1,850

Vase, 10" high, 6-1/2" diameter, bayou scene, large yellow moon, oak trees, marked "NC/JM/JA45/150, paper label, 1917 .... $5,000

Vase, 11" high, 5" deep, bottle shape, white and yellow flowers, on blue ground, 1904, marked "NC/JM/SE Wells/UU47/Q" $8,750

Niloak Pottery (Mission Ware)

Hatpin Holder, swirled clay $725

Vase, 4", swirled light and dark brown $95

Vase, 5-3/4", swirled blue, tan, light and dark brown $115

Vase, 7", swirled blue, tan, brown and cream $200

Vase, 16" high, 7" diameter, bulbous shape, swirled brown, blue and red $825

Wall pocket, 6", swirled blue, light and dark brown $350

Overbeck Pottery

Figure, bluebird, on flower, 2" high $275

Figure, dachshund, 4" long $225

Figure, Southern man, blue pants, pink coat.............. $235

Vase, 5", bulbous shape, matte blue fir trees, brown underglaze, marked "OBK/EH...................................... $1,350

Vase, 6", matte white excised birds on light blue ground, marked "OBK/EH" $2,900

Vase, 8", white carved birds, matte raspberry ground, marked "OBK/E" $6,500

Red Wing Pottery

Basket, white, semi-gloss... $35

Bookends, fan and scroll, green, pair........................... $25

Candleholders, Medieval, pair $50

Candy dish, 3-part, hexagon, gray, semi-gloss $15

Flower block, Dolphin $35

Planter, Birch $25

Planter, Loop shape, green and silver $50

Vase, calla, blue and yellow $85

Vase, classic shape, 9", swan handles, cream, high glaze, "Rumrill" $85

Vase, fan shape, 7-1/2", #892, blue, pink $50

Wall pocket, Gardenia, matte ivory.............................. $35

Rookwood Pottery

Ashtray, harp, light green high glaze, 5-1/2" diameter... $225

Ashtray, rook, butterscotch high glaze, 6-1/2"............ $265

Ashtray, rook, green mat glaze, 6-1/2" $295

Ashtray, rook, white mat glaze, 6-1/2" wide............... $275

Bowl, flower, wax primrose glaze, 12-1/2" diameter.. $695

Bowl, squat with banded dentil work, brown mat glaze, 6" diameter $250

Jar, lidded, art deco, pink matte glaze, 6" $275

Urn, two-handled, white matte glaze, 12-1/2" high, 10-1/2" diameter.. $535

Vase, art deco, pink matte glaze, 8-1/2"...................... $375

Vase, beet red high glaze, 5" $250

Vase, blue high glaze with dark accents, 7" $295

Vase, butterfly design, yellow-green high glaze, 4-1/2" high.. $150

Vase, charcoal with turquoise high glaze, 7" $360

Vase, cobalt blue high glaze, 10-1/2"........................... $425

Vase, crab apple motif, green glaze, 4-1/4" $175

Vase, deco motif, green matte glaze, 5-1/2" $195

Vase, deco motif, pink matte glaze, 5-1/2" $325

This pair of matte glaze Newcomb vases were offered at a Don Treadway Gallery auction in Cincinnati. The example on the left went for $2,750, while the one on the right brought $935.

These examples of quality Roseville pottery were offered in an auction conducted by Cincinnati Art Galleries.

Vase, diamond pattern, turquoise matte glaze, 5" $300
Vase, floral motif, brown high glaze, 6" $195
Vase, fluted, two-handled, cream high glaze, 8" $225
Vase, footed, blue highlights on maroon porcelain glaze, 4-1/2" $295
Vase, incised decoration around base, light blue matte glaze, 5-1/2" $160
Vase, incised leaf design, mat green glaze, 5" $185
Vase, lidded with decorative border, rose matte glaze, 5-1/2" $215
Vase, Mexican motif, yellow-green high glaze, 5-1/2" $175
Vase, narrow neck, dark blue matte glaze, 7" $150
Vase, raised pattern, light blue matte glaze, 7" $365
Vase, tulip, pink and green mat glaze, 5" $140

Roseville Pottery

Ashtray, Silhouette, brown $35
Basket, 10" diameter, clematis, brown $65
Basket, 10", Magnolia, green, marked "385-10" $100
Basket, 10", Peony, yellow flowers $115
Basket, 10", Pine Cone, marked "308-10" $225
Basket, 10", Rozana, ivory, marked "1-66-2-2" $100
Bookends, Foxglove, blue, pair $135
Bookends, Snowberry, pink, pair $135
Bookends, Zephyr, brown, pair $115
Bowl, Apple Blossom, 8", green $50
Bowl, Carnelian II, blue and purple $100
Bowl, Corinthian, 6-1/2" $55
Bowl, Magnolia, 10", blue $65
Candlesticks, pair, Baneda, pink, 4-1/2" $625
Candlesticks, pair, Bleeding Heart, blue $100
Candlesticks, pair, Clematis, blue, marked "1158-2" $95

Ewer, Bushberry, 6", blue $75
Ewer, Columbine, 7", blue $85
Ewer, Freesia, 6", green $70
Ewer, Gardenia, 6", brown $55
Ewer, Silhouette, 10", ... $75
Ewer, Snowberry, 10", blue.. $110
Floor vase, Velmoss, green, 14" high........................ $425
Flower frog, Fuchsia, green $200
Hanging basket, Mock Orange $275
Jardiniere, Florentine, 8" diameter, brown................. $100
Planter, Artwood, yellow, '1056-10" $135
Planter, Earlam, green, 89-8.. $200
Vase, Apple Blossom, pink, 7", #382 .... $125
Vase, Apple Blossom, pink, 8", #385 .... $175
Vase, Apple Blossom, pink, 10", #388 .... $265
Vase, Carnelian II, blue, 8" $185
Vase, Clematis, dark green, 6", #103 .... $95
Vase, Foxglove, 6", blue, double open handles, "44-6" $100
Vase, Thorn Apple, blue... $85
Vase, Wisteria, brown, 630-6 .... $395
Wall pocket, Corinthian, 12".. $235
Wall pocket, Donatello, 11-1/2".................................. $185
Wall pocket, Florentine, 9-1/2", brown...................... $135
Wall pocket, Imperial II, #1264, orange and green $450
Wall pocket, Mostique, 9-1/2" $200
Wall pocket, Tuscany, pink $125

Shawnee Pottery

Ashtray, arrowhead 4-1/2" wide $150
Ashtray, flair #408.. $12
Ashtray, flying geese #403 .... $25
Aster vase, 5" $8
Bank, tumbling bear.. $175
Birds on driftwood #502 .... $45
Blackie the cat #642... $15
Bookends, setter (dog) heads, pair $45
Boy at gate, 4" tall... $10
Boy and wheelbarrow, #750... $22
Calla lily planter #181 .... $14
Canopy bed #734 .... $100
Chihuahua and dog house #738 .... $25
Chinese girl with book #574 .... $12
Clock, trellis $50
Donkey and basket #671 .... $22
Duckling and egg #753 .... $15
Dutch windmill #715 .... $25
Elephant #759 .... $15
Fawn and log #766 .... $30
Figurine, Mumpy Kitty 5" $35
Figurine, crane 5-1/4" $12
Figurine, dolphin 1-3/4" $15
Figurine, flying bird 2-1/2" $15
Figurine, spaniel 3-1/2".. $15
Figurine, standing lamb 2-1/4" $15

Figurine, terrier 6"..$22
Figurine, turtle 3-1/2" $15
Floral planters and vases, 1950s, each $15
Flying mallard #707 ....$20
Frog on lily pad #726 ....$35
Giraffe and baby vase #841 ....$50
Globe #635 ....$25
Lamb, black w/gold trim #724.......................$25
Piano #528 ....$25
Rabbit and stump 3".......................................$12
Rooster #503 ....$25
Southern girl 7-1/4" $20
Wall pocket, bird on cornucopia $18
Wall pocket, girl with rag doll #810 ....$30
Wall pocket, Scottie dog $55

Weller Pottery
Ashtray, Coppertone, frog seated at end $100
Ashtray, Roma, 2-1/2" diameter $35
Ashtray, Woodcraft, 3".................................$75
Basket, Melrose, 10"....................................$165
Basket, Sabrinian $175
Basket, Silvertone, 8"..................................$365
Bowl, 5-1/2" tall Ivory ware $85
Bowl, 4-1/2" tall Ivory ware $60
Flower frog, figural, Muskota $135
Flower frog, figural, Silvertone, 1928...........$125
Flower frog, figural, Woodcraft, figural lobster,
    1917...$135
Jardiniere, Claywood, 8", cherries and trees..............$100
Jardiniere, Marvo, rust, 7-1/2" $95
Planter, blue drapery $65
Planter, Klyro, small $45
Planter, Woodrose, 9"...................................$65
Vase, Bonito, blue flowers, two small handles, 5" $75
Vase, Claremont, 5", two handles $65
Vase, Coppertone, 8-1/2" $275
Vase, fan, 7", small flake $65
Vase, floretta, 7-1/2", grapes decoration,
    high-gloss glaze.....................................$185
Vase, forest, 6" $175
Vase, Glendale Thrush $250
Vase, Hudson, floral dec., 7" high, signed "D
    England"..$215
Vase, Hudson, floral dec., 7", signed
    "Timberlake" $395
Vase, Louwelsa, 10"....................................$210
Vase, marbleized, 6"....................................$85
Vase, Muskota, boy fishing, 1915, 7-1/2" $200

Vase, oak leaf, 7-inch, double bud type, green and
    brown accents, blue ground.....................$90
Vase, Roma, grape dec., 6", scenic $75
Vase, Tutone, 4", three-legged ball shape $85
Wall pocket, Roma.......................................$200
Wall pocket, Sabrinian $500
Wall pocket, Suevo.......................................$200

A nice Cambridge vase, standing 24 inches tall, sold for $1,540 at a Don Treadway Gallery auction.

AUTOGRAPHS

Autograph collecting is a centuries-old hobby that has enjoyed a tremendous increase in popularity in recent years. This resurgence is due in large part to a big boom in "celebrity" signatures—primarily sports and entertainment autographs—but the residual benefits have spilled over into the more traditional fields of autograph collecting, such as literary and historical signatures. Today, more than five million people in the United States collect autographs, making it one of the nation's most popular pastimes.

General Guidelines: Autograph collecting is a hobby that offers something for every budget. In fact, the most satisfying autographs may be those obtained for free—either by mail or, even better, in person. The old-fashioned method of getting a free autograph at the ballpark or in a hotel lobby is probably tougher than it used to be, but it is still the most fun

and the most rewarding. And there is never any doubt about the authenticity of a signature that you obtain in person. Plus, if you're able to have someone take a picture of you getting a celebrity's autograph, you not only have another great reminder of the experience, but also pretty good documentation of the signature's authenticity for the future.

Also fun and almost free is the age-old practice of requesting an autograph through the mail. This unfortunately isn't as easy as it used to be, with many celebrities becoming more guarded about their personal lives and their personal time, and with many stars being turned off by the recent commercialization of the autograph hobby. Still, there are many,

---

LEARN THE LINGO!

Autograph collectors have their own terms and abbreviations. Here are some of the more common ones you may run across:

SP: Signed photo

ISP: Inscribed signed photo (a photo inscribed to an individual, such as "To my best friend Steve." These generally have less value, because most collectors don't want someone else's name on their photo.)

ALS: Autographed letter signed (the letter is both hand-written and signed by the person. This form is generally the most valuable.)

TLS: Typed letter signed (a typed letter that is hand-signed by the person)

LS: Letter signed (usually refers to a letter hand-written by someone else but signed by the person)

Sig: A simple signature of the person, either on a small card or paper, or cut from a letter or document (then usually called a "cut signature"). This form is always the least desirable.

DS: Document signed (any type of document that was hand-signed)

AQS: Autographed quote signed (usually associated with literary figures, this very desirable piece would be a short hand-written excerpt from a literary work signed by the author)

AMQS: Autographed musical quote signed (same as above but for music)

ND: No date (the autographed letter or document contains no date)

NP: No place (the items makes no reference to location or address)

This rare carte-de-visite photograph signed by Abraham Lincoln sold for $39,100 at a Christie's auction in New York.

many celebrities who will still graciously respond to a nicely worded autograph request through the mail. (See "Collecting Tips" for some specific advice.)

Signatures obtained through the mail, of course, do not have the same absolute guarantee of authenticity that an in-person autograph does. The vast majority of celebrities will sign their own autographs, but a few (and the list is growing) will send out facsimile signatures or autographs signed by secretaries, relatives or even a sophisticated device known as an "autopen." Sometimes it takes a trained expert to tell the difference.

As rewarding as free autographs are, sooner or later, even the most casual collector will start buying autographs, and this is when the hobby can start getting expensive—and, often times, tricky.

For living celebrities, the safest method is still an in-person autograph—one obtained from an autograph guest at a baseball card show, record show, comics show, book-signing, etc. Prices vary, of course, from a few dollars to a hundred dollars or more, depending on the celebrity and, sometimes, on the item being signed (it has become commonplace in the baseball hobby, for instance, that it costs more, for some reason, to get a bat signed that a ball or a photo).

Paying $25 and standing in line to get an autograph of Eddie Mathews or Johnny Unitas isn't the same as getting a signature at the ballpark, but at least you know it's genuine, and you get to actually see the celebrity, and, in some cases, even shake his hand or take a picture. The popularity of this assembly-line style of autograph collecting coincided with the rise of the sports memorabilia hobby over the past two decades and has now spilled over into other areas of autograph collecting as well.

Everything stated above, of course, applies only to autographs of living persons. Collecting historical autographs or the signatures of deceased personalities almost always requires purchasing autographs from a dealer, through an auction, etc. When you reach this level of the hobby, it is critical to buy only from reputable dealers and collectors. Generally, members of the Professional Autograph Dealers Assocation (PADA) or the Universal Autograph Collectors Club (UACC) are trustworthy and dependable, Both groups do a good job of self-policing.

To further safeguard yourself, when buying expensive autographs, make sure they are backed up by a written guarantee of authenticity with no time limit, and, if there is any question about an autograph, send it to an expert to be authenticated.

Values: The value of an autograph depends largely on subject (who signed it), demand, scarcity, condition, form (what was signed) and content.

Subject, demand and scarcity are all tied together. As Mark Alan Baker points out in his *Standard Guide to Autograph Collecting*, Babe Ruth, for example, was a very cordial and prolific signer; he signed thousands of autographs during his lifetime. Ruth's signature is not considered rare, comparatively speaking, but, as the greatest ballplayer in history, it is in tremendous demand, making it relatively expensive.

COLLECTING TIPS!

It's still possible to request autographs through the mail. Here are some tips to increase your chances of getting a response:

Always include a self-addressed, stamped envelope with sufficient postage to mail the autographed item back to you.

Write a polite, courteous letter requesting the autograph. Make the letter sincere and personal. Mention you enjoyed their latest movie, CD, etc., or were thrilled by their performance at a game or whatever.

Keep the letter brief; no more than one page. Celebrities are busy people.

You may either type or hand-write the letter, but keep it neat and make sure you sign it by hand.

Be patient. Some celebrities get hundreds or thousands of requests a week.

Include an item you want signed (an index card, photograph, etc.), but don't send a piece of memorabilia you don't want to lose. There's no guarantee you'll get it back. (A strategy that some sports collectors use is to send two trading cards to a player; one for him to keep and the other for him to sign and return. Many players appreciate getting the extra cards of themselves.)

For your own records, and to help other collectors, keep a list of who responds and who doesn't.

The most expensive autograph in the sports hobby is that of Shoeless Joe Jackson, the great player who was banned from baseball after the 1919 "Black Sox" scandal. Basically illiterate, Shoeless Joe signed his name only a few times during his whole life. His autograph is both rare and in demand, and when offered for sale, can command over $25,000.

Certain events can also affect demand. For living persons, certain achievements cause a sudden increase in demand—such as an actor's winning an Oscar, a politician's being elected president, an athlete's breaking a record or entering the Hall of Fame, etc. All of these increase the value of an autograph. Obviously, the biggest impact on the value of a living person's autograph is death, especially an unpredictable one, such as in the case of Princess Diana, etc., which may cause the value to double or triple overnight.

Form (what was signed) and content are also closely related and can also have a great impact on value. Joe Namath's signature on a football is certainly more desirable than on a napkin or the back of an envelope. And, as Baker points out in his book, a simple signed photo of Clark Gable might typically sell for about $700, but an autographed photo of Gable as Rhett Butler may bring twice that.

Generally speaking, a "cut" signature or a simple signature on a card or piece of paper is the least desirable form. An autograph on a letter, document, or photo will almost always bring two to three times the price of a simple signature.

Legal documents, such as signed contracts, deeds and canceled checks, are interesting autographed items and generally tend to have fewer problems with authenticity than some other pieces.

Content comes into play primarily with signed documents and letters. The better the content, the more valuable the piece. For example, a letter written by Jimmy Stewart discussing his role in *It's a Wonderful Life* would be more desirable than a note from Stewart to his plumber about a broken water pipe.

Content is especially important when it comes to historical autographs. A letter from President Truman discussing his decision to drop the atomic bomb, for example, or a document from President Lincoln promoting a Civil War general, would be tremendously desirable and command a huge premium over more mundane correspondence.

Trends: Most autograph collectors specialize in a certain area. According to Baker, the most popular current areas of autograph collecting include: sports figures, movie and TV stars, astronauts, famous women, rock-and-roll stars and other music-related personalities, artists, writers, business leaders, politicians, government leaders and foreign heads of state, scientists and inventors, famous Black Americans, social reformers, religious leaders, educators, and famous criminals.

There are three more traditional categories of autograph collecting that have been strong for decades among serious collectors. They are Presidential autographs, Civil War autographs and signers of the Declaration of Independence. The last category is especially significant. Owning the autographs of all 56 men who signed the Declaration of Independence is considered the Holy Grail of autograph collecting. According to Baker, only 40 or so complete sets may exist. (The key to a complete set is the signature of Button Gwinett, who only signed an estimated 54 items during his lifetime.) At a Superior Galleries auction in 1991, a complete set of signers sold for just under $400,000. If offered today, a set could bring a million dollars or more.

A nice set of Presidential autographs, by comparison, could probably still be assembled for less than $50,000. Also attracting more interest in recent years are autographs of American First Ladies and U.S. Vice presidents.

The category of Civil War-era autographs has typically been dominated by generals, but now there is demand for virtually any autographed material relating to the war. Soldiers' letters describing battles and conditions during the war are especially desirable.

Clubs

• The Universal Autograph Collectors Club (UACC), P.O. Box 6181, Washington, DC 20044-6181

• The Professional Autograph Dealers Association (PADA), P.O. Box 1729, Murray Hill Station, NY 10156

Recommended Reading

Standard Guide to Collecting Autographs, Mark Allen Baker
Advanced Autograph Collecting, Mark Allen Baker
Signatures of the Stars, Kevin Martin
Celebrity Autographs, Mark Allen Baker

VALUE LINE

The following values are taken from The Standard Guide to Collecting Autographs by Mark Allen Baker (Krause Publications, Iola, WI).

Entertainment/Celebrities

Bud Abbott (SP)	$450
Aerosmith (SP, entire band)	$225
Louisa May Alcott (LS)	$300
Alan Alda (SP)	$35
Gracie Allen (SP)	$150
June Allyson (SP)	$15
Julie Andrews (SP)	$50
Maya Angelou (LS)	$35
Paul Anka (SP)	$15

A signed photo of Frank Sinatra is about a $300 item.

This first-day postal cover is signed by President Gerald R. Ford.

Fatty Arbuckle (SP)	$800
Louis Armstrong (SP)	$500
Desi Arnaz (SP)	$160
Fred Astaire (SP)	$185
Gene Autry (SP)	$65
Frankie Avalon (SP)	$30
Johann Sebastain Bach (LS)	$24,500
Joan Baez (SP)	$20
Lucille Ball (SP)	$500
Drew Barrymore (SP)	$50
John Barrymore (LS)	$275
Frank Baum (Sig)	$1,265
The Beach Boys (SP)	$450
The Beatles (SP)	$3,000
The Bee Gees (SP)	$70
John Belushi (SP)	$550
Peter Benchly (LS)	$55
Jack Benny (Sig)	$100
Ingrid Bergman (SP)	$400
Milton Berle (SP)	$35
Irving Berlin (Sig)	$200
Chuck Berry (SP)	$100
Big Bopper (J.P. Richardson) (SP)	$350
Mel Blanc (SP)	$200
Humphrey Bogart (SP)	$2,725
David Bowie (SP)	$125
Elizabeth Barrett Browning (LS)	$1,250
Ted Bundy (LS)	$75
Edgar Rice Burroughs (LS)	$500
James Cagney (SP)	$250
Karen Carpenter (SP)	$300
Jim Carrey (SP)	$65
Johnny Cash (SP)	$40
David Cassidy (SP)	$30
Lon Chaney (SP)	$2,000
Charlie Chaplin (SP)	$850
Cher (SP)	$60
Eric Clapton (SP)	$60
John Coltrane (SP)	$1,250

Sean Connery (SP)	$130
Gary Cooper (SP)	$595
Lou Costello (SP)	$500
Jim Croce (SP)	$395
James Dean (LS)	$7,000
Leonardo DiCaprio (SP)	$125
Charles Dickens (LS)	$1,250
Emily Dickinson (LS)	$2,400
The Doors (with Jim Morrison) (SP)	$2,500
Arthur Conan Doyle (LS)	$700
Bob Dylan (LS)	$750
Duke Ellington (SP)	$500
The Everly Brothers (SP)	$75
Douglas Fairbanks (SP)	$365
William Faulkner (LS)	$1,250
W.C. Fields (SP)	$1,500
F. Scott Fitzgerald (SP)	$2,600
Fleetwood Mac (SP)	$250
Robert Frost (LS)	$650
Annette Funicello (SP)	$40
Clark Gable (SP)	$900
Greta Garbo (SP)	$9,350
Judy Garland (SP)	$925
Marvin Gaye (SP)	$300
The Grateful Dead (SP) (with Jerry Garcia)	$550
Alex Haley (LS)	$150
Tom Hanks (SP)	$100
George Harrison (SP)	$350
Rita Hayworth (SP)	$440
Ernest Hemmingway (LS)	$2,750
Jimi Hendrix (SP)	$2,000
Alfred Hitchcock (LS)	$550
Billie Holiday (LS)	$1,000
Buddy Holly (SP)	$1,250
Harry Houdini (SP)	$2,000
Rock Hudson (SP)	$125
Michael Jackson (SP)	$275
Janis Joplin (SP)	$2,000
Boris Karloff (SP)	$575
Grace Kelly (SP)	$525
Jack Kerouac (SL)	$2,000
KISS (SP)	$150
Led Zeppelin (SP) (with J. Bonham)	$1,200
Bruce Lee (SP)	$1,100
John Lennon (LS)	$2,500
Sinclair Lewis (LS)	$275
Rush Limbaugh (SP)	$25
Jack London (LS)	$750
Madonna (SP)	$300
The Mamas and the Papas (SP) (with Cass Elliott)	$450
Jayne Mansfield (SP)	$480
Charles Manson (LS)	$250
Bob Marley (SP)	$2,250
Groucho Marx (SP)	$300
Paul McCartney (SP)	$350

Steve McQueen (SP)	$400
Herman Melville (LS)	$2,500
Margaret Mitchell (LS)	$3,000
Marilyn Monroe (SP)	$5,500
Edward R. Murrow (LS)	$300
Ricky Nelson (SP)	$225
Nirvana (SP) (with Kurt Cobain)	$500
Roy Orbison (SP)	$250
Lee Harvey Oswald (sig)	$2,000
Pearl Jam (SP)	$275
Anthony Perkins (SP)	$85
River Phoenix (SP)	$360
Pink Floyd (SP)	$300
Edgar Allan Poe (LS)	$5,000
Elvis Presley (SP)	$950
Queen (SP) (with Freddie Mercury)	$600

Handwritten letters are always more valuable than simple signatures and get very expensive, depending on the content of the letter and the person who wrote it. This page is part of an historic six-page handwritten letter written by John Lennon about the breakup of the Beatles. It sold for a stunning $90,500 at a Butterfield & Butterfield auction.

Gilda Radner (SP)	$175
Otis Redding (SP)	$750
Donna Reed (SP)	$185
George Reeves (SP) (Superman)	$1,250
Will Rogers (LS)	$1,000
The Rolling Stones (SP) (original lineup)	$1,250
J. D. Salinger (LS)	$3,250
Carl Sandburg (LS)	$250
Rod Serling (LS)	$300
Frank Sinatra (SP)	$300
Simon and Garfunkel (SP)	$150
Ringo Starr (SP)	$225
Steven Spielberg (LS)	$230
Bruce Springsteen (SP)	$200
John Steinbeck (LS)	$1,825
James Stewart (SP)	$160
Barbra Streisand (SP)	$300
The Supremes (SP) (original trio)	$500
Dylan Thomas (LS)	$1,250
Leo Tolstoy (LS)	$2,350
Mark Twain (LS)	$1,575
John Updike (LS)	$100
Rudolph Valentino (SP)	$2,100
Van Halen (SP)	$175
Jules Verne (LS)	$700
Fats Waller (SP)	$450
John Wayne (SP)	$725
Orson Welles (SP)	$300
H.G. Wells (LS)	$350
Mae West (SP)	$250
Walt Whitman (LS)	$2,750
The Who (SP) (original lineup)	$1,000
Hank Williams (SP)	$1,500
Oprah Winfrey (SP)	$50
Natalie Wood (SP)	$560
Frank Zappa (SP)	$225

Sports Autographs

Hank Aaron (SP)	$25
Muhammad Ali (signed glove)	$155
Arthur Ashe (SP)	$75
Cool Papa Bell (sig)	$25
Johnny Bench (SP)	$25
Larry Bird (SP)	$50
Bill Bradley (SP)	$40
Jim Brown (SP)	$30
Roy Campanella (signed ball)	$3,500
Roberto Clemente (SP)	$700
Ty Cobb (SP)	$2,150
Bob Cousy (SP)	$30
Jack Dempsey (SP)	$200
Joe DiMaggio (SP)	$200
Dale Earnhardt (SP)	$40
Bret Favre (football)	$200
Lou Gehrig (SP)	$5,750
Red Grange (SP)	$200

Wayne Gretzky (SP)......................................$75
Ben Hogan (SP) $200
Paul Hornung (SP) $25
Gordie Howe (SP) $25
Michael Jordan (SP)....................................$175
Sandy Koufax (SP) $50
Carl Lewis (SP) $25
Vince Lombardi (SP) $400
Joe Lewis (SP) $400
Mickey Mantle (SP)...................................$150
Rocky Marciano (SP)..................................$650
Willie Mays (SP) $40
Mark McGwire (SP)....................................$150
Joe Montana (SP) $40
Stan Musial (SP) $30
Jack Nicklaus (SP) $50
Mel Ott (SP)..$750
Arnold Palmer (SP) $50
Richard Petty (SP).......................................$25
Pee Wee Reese (SP) $35
Oscar Robertson (SP)....................................$40
Jackie Robinson (SP)..................................$700
Pete Rose (SP) $30
Babe Ruth (baseball)................................$8,000
Pete Sampras (SP) $35
Tom Seaver (SP) $20
Casey Stengel (SP) $200
Fran Tarkenton (SP) $25
Jim Thorpe (SP) $1,325
Johnny Unitas (SP) $30
Honus Wagner (sig) $400
Ted Williams (SP) $150
Cy Young (SP) $1,500

Historical, Political and General
John Adams (sig) $1,850
John Quincy Adams (sig)..............................$375
Buzz Aldrin (SP)..$150
Susan B. Anthony (ALS) $1,750
Neil Armstrong (ALS) $1,500
John James Audubon (ALS) $1,500
Alexander Graham Bell (ALS) $3,000
Daniel Boone (sig) $7,500
Omar Bradley (DS) $200
John Brown (ALS) $4,500
James Buchanan (DS) $800
George H.W. Bush (SP) $200
Andrew Carnegie (DS) $675
Jimmy Carter (SP)......................................$225
Winston Churchill (ALS) $3,425
Grover Cleveland (DS) $650
Bill Clinton (SP) $400
Calvin Coolidge (DS) $600
Jacques Cousteau (ALS) $250
George Custer (ALS) $12,750
Charles Darwin (DS)................................$2,000

TV cast photos are a favorite category for collectors of celebrity autographs. This photo signed by the cast of "The Munsters" sold for over $200.

Jefferson Davis (ALS) $2,500
Charles DeGaulle (ALS).............................$2,500
Princess Diana (ALS) $6,750
Walt Disney (SP).....................................$4,000
Amelia Earhart (ALS) $2,000
Thomas Edison (ALS) $1,750
Albert Einstein (ALS) $3,125
Dwight Eisenhower (DS) $800
Mamie Eisenhower (DS) $125
Gerald Ford (DS) $400
Betty Ford (DS)...$130
Benjamin Franklin (ALS) $16,625
Sigmund Freud (sig) $1,725
Yuri Gagarin (DS) $700
James Garfield (ALS) $1,500
Herman Goering (DS)................................$2,000
U.S. Grant (ALS) $1,725
Virgil "Gus" Grissom (SP)..........................$1,200
John Hancock (sig) $2,125
Warren Harding (ALS)..................................$850
Benjamin Harrison (ALS) $950
Rutherford B. Hayes (ALS) $800
Adolf Hitler (DS) $2,500
Oliver Wendell Holmes (DS) $325
Herbert Hoover (DS)....................................$325
Sam Houston (ALS)..................................$3,000
Howard Hughes (sig) $1,500
Andrew Jackson (ALS) $3,650
"Stonewall" Jackson (ALS) $22,500
Thomas Jefferson (ALS) $11,500
Andrew Johnson (ALS) $7,000
Lyndon Johnson (SP)................................... $500
Helen Keller (sig)......................................$225
John F. Kennedy (DS)...............................$2,150

A Harry Houdini autographed photo is generally valued at about $2,000. This one was sold at a Swann Galleries auction.

Jacqueline Kennedy (DS)	$1,200
Robert Kennedy (DS)	$700
Edward Kennedy (SP)	$20
Martin Luther King(DS)	$3,250
Robert E. Lee (DS)	$6,750

Abraham Lincoln (DS)	$5,000
Charles Lindbergh (SP)	$2,100
Douglas MacArthur (DS)	$500
James Madison (DS)	$2,250
Dolly Madison (DS)	$1,850
Malcom X (DS)	$4,000
Nelson Mandela (DS)	$400
Thurgood Marshall (DS)	$200
Karl Marx (DS)	$2,000
James Monroe (DS)	$1,500
Elijah Muhammad (SP)	$250
Benito Mussolini (DS)	$500
Napoleon I (sig)	$800
Issac Newton (sig)	$3,500
Richard Nixon (DS)	$650
Maxfield Parish (sig)	$250
Louis Pasteur (ALS)	$2,000
George Patton (DS)	$2,600
James Polk (DS)	$1,650
Ronald Reagan (DS)	$600
Paul Revere (sig)	$3,500
John D. Rockefeller (DS)	$1,500
Norman Rockwell (DS)	$300
Franklin D. Roosevelt (DS)	$1,000
Theodore Roosevelt (DS)	$1,120
Joseph Stalin (DS)	$5,000
William H. Taft (DS)	$525
Mother Teresa (DS)	$350
Harry S. Truman (DS)	$400
Martin Van Buren (DS)	$925
Andy Warhol (SP)	$260
George Washington (DS)	$12,500
Eli Whitney (DS)	$2,250
Woodrow Wilson (DS)	$600
Frank Lloyd Wright (DS)	$1,850
Andrew Wyeth (DS)	$500

AUTOMOBILIA

Americans have had a love affair with the automobile since Stanley invented the Steamer. No wonder anything related to vintage and classic automobiles is collectible—everything from vintage advertising to the automobile itself.

Background: Karl Benz and Gottlieb Daimler introduced the first successful gasoline-powered motor vehicles in 1886. The American automobile industry began ten years later, in 1896, when the Duryea Motor Wagon Co. mass-produced thirteen cars of standard design. From that point, the auto industry introduced countless new developments and it didn't take long for the first cars to become outmoded and historically interesting.

By the mid-1920s, automotive trade magazines were publishing silver jubilee editions that celebrated the 25th anniversary of the industry. This focused attention on the history of the automobile and soon led to the formation of the first antique car clubs in the early 1930s.

General Guidelines: In addition to vehicles, hobbyists collect automotive memorabilia, better known as automobilia—things that are related to vehicles, but are not actually a part of that vehicle. In the early days of the hobby, two types of collectibles—clothing and literature—got the automobilia ball rolling.

Clothing—When the hobby first began, most of the cars collected were built before 1916. These cars were from an era when motorists, driving in open-bodied cars, wore special clothing—such as dusters, cloth helmets, goggles and fur coats—to protect against the elements. Naturally, old-car collectors want to look the part when driving their cars, and dressing up in vintage motoring garb has become part of the hobby.

When cars of the classic era (1920s-1940s) became popular, Gatsby-style clothing was the rage among car collectors. In the 1950s, the Model A Ford became a hot collectible, so it was barbershop quartet-style duds that antique-auto lovers sought in thrift shops. Today, the rock-and-roll style clothing of the 1950s—like poodle skirts and saddle shoes—is popular with postwar car fanciers. Don't look now, but bell bottoms and double-knit leisure suits should be coming on strong as interest in 1970s cars develops.

To be collectible, clothing must be in good or better condition. Items with the look of a specific era are especially desirable, as are articles of clothing made of fur or leather, like hats or jackets.

Literature—Antique auto restorers have always sought automotive literature. There has been a lot of material published about cars, from service manuals to magazines to travel guides.

Various companies published guides to help motorists buy the best cars at the right price. Other firms printed books that estimated values for second-hand cars. As early as 1902, Studebaker produced a press kit with photos to help publicize its electric cars. Hobbyists also fall head-over-heels for sales brochures that illustrate their favorite car and all its features.

The first car magazine was published around 1900. Thousands of other titles have launched and folded since, but hundreds are still in circulation. All of these are collectible, as are books written about the romance or the history of the automobile. Books of this nature began appearing in good numbers after World War II.

Other collectible automotive literature includes old advertisements, posters, corporate reports, stock certificates,

---

IT'S NOTHING NEW!

A past issue of The Horseless Carriage Club Gazette predicted that "automobiliana is going to be the scarcest and most valuable of all collector items in a few years." The quote comes from a newsletter printed in 1938!

Collectors of automobilia have a huge variety of items to choose from.

technical literature, publicity photos, promotional giveaways and showroom decorations.

Collectors often seek automobile literature more for the subject than the condition of the book or manual, so items in lesser condition are collectible. However, paper items free of rips and stains are most desirable.

Badges, Mascots and Parts—In the early days of the hobby, there was a tremendous fascination with the many brands of automobiles that had been produced. In America alone, over 5,500 companies had built cars. Each of these marques had its own nameplate, badge or logo, distinctive radiator shape and hood or radiator mascot.

The nameplate was usually a brass name or initials affixed to the front of the radiator. The badge or logo decorated the top face of the radiator and sometimes the hubcaps. Radiator shapes ranged from barrel-like, as on the Franklin, to coffin-like, as on the Stanley Steamer. Mascots or ornaments sat atop the radiator caps of early cars. Later, when the radiator was moved under the hood, they decorated hoods. Mascot designs ranged from birds to elephants, nude women to Indian heads. Some were made by famous artists and sculptors.

Hubcaps, steering wheels, headlights, taillights and anything else that can be removed from an automobile also became common collectibles.

Collecting badges and mascots is not as common as it was years ago, when such items could be found in salvage yards. Most newer collector cars don't have hood ornaments, and even the use of badges has slowed down in recent years. Complete collections put together years ago often find their way to high-end collectors. Muscle cars of the 1960s and 1970s usually have trim badges to set them apart from look-alike family cars; some of these decorative items are very rare and extremely valuable. Parts are more valuable as usable parts than they are as collectibles.

Dealer and Corporate Memorabilia—Car makers turned out all kinds of items bearing the name or logo of their products. Matchbooks used as sales premiums carried the same name and logo as the giant neon sign hanging outside the dealership. Today both the matchbook and the dealer sign have collector appeal, along with anything else the dealer owned, stocked or gave away.

Collectors have also been known to buy items such as factory security badges, corporate employment anniversary

Early dealer license plates, like this 1915 example from Pennsylvania, are scarce and worth $200 or more, depending on condition.

pins, sales contest prizes and myriad other items related to their favorite brand of car.

Corporate and dealer memorabilia is a very hot field. Old-car fans tend to be loyalists and go to great financial extremes to obtain factory merchandise missing from their collection. Rarity is everything to serious buffs, and there are many rare trinkets. Promotional items with limited, or regional distribution, are most valuable.

License Plates—In the early days of the automobile, motorists made their own license plates, sometimes by decorating leather tags with house numbers. Porcelain plates were also used for a time. However, the metal plates used today have a long history.

States and territories use distinctive colors and designs on their plates. Special plates are made for trucks, taxis, official vehicles and school buses. In addition, unique designs have been created for presidential inaugurations, Vietnam veterans and United Nations ambassadors. The designs have changed many times over the years, as have the colors, though less frequently.

All of these factors make license plates attractive and appealing to collectors. The plates or "tags" are miniature artworks—produced in a more or less standard format—that reflect both history and creativity.

In addition to license plates, auto enthusiasts also collect old vehicle titles and registrations, tag toppers (small advertisements bolted onto the plates) and special license plate frames, such as those sold in Florida with palm trees in the frame design.

License plates are often collected in series, such as collecting all the years and variations of plates issued by one state. Others collect specialty issues. Antique auto hobbyists collect plates from the year their favorite car was built. Plates should be in the best condition possible; however, most plates can be restored with minimal time, effort and cost. Therefore, a rare plate in poor shape can still be worth more than a near-perfect common plate, as long as it can be restored.

Traffic Devices—After the invention of the automobile, it didn't take long for two horseless carriages to collide. After the first crash, it became obvious that traffic controls were essential. This led to stationary traffic signs, which evolved into semaphore-style signals. These evolved into the common red/yellow/green traffic lights.

Early examples of stoplights, with only green and red lights, were perched atop ornate fluted cast-iron poles. Later, yellow caution lights were added.

Parking meters and reproductions of traffic signs are other popular collectibles.

General Guidelines: Stoplights are bulky and heavy and not usually available for sale, so they bring relatively high prices. Functional lights are most desirable.

Motorsports Memorabilia—Stock car racing has become the recent hot spectator sport. Most of the hot collectibles now have links to the National Association of Stock Car Auto Racing (NASCAR). Die-cast toy vehicles and apparel

IT'S A COLLECTOR-FRIENDLY HOBBY!

Sizewise, automobilia runs the gamut, from small factory workers' badges to an old-fashioned gas pump. The prices range too, from inexpensive road maps to gas pumps, but it's generally easier for someone to collect automotive memorabilia than old cars. In fact, the cost of purchasing, restoring and maintaining a vintage vehicle may have stimulated the growth of the automobilia hobby. As old car prices soared, car lovers turned to collecting automobilia instead of the cars themselves. For one thing, a collection of old advertising, for example, does not demand the constant care that a vintage vehicle does. Such a collection just sits there, inviting all who pass to stop and admire it. You don't have to change its oil or rebuild its transmission. Oh, you may have to dust those "Oilzum" tins or occasionally wind that Packard pocket watch, but by and large, automobilia is collector-friendly.

are especially collectible. Among the most popular items to collect are those associated with drivers Dale Jarrett, Dale Earnhardt, Kyle Petty, Rusty Wallace and Jeff Gordon.

Historic memorabilia from the glory years of racing is becoming quite valuable. For newer racing collectibles, buy as much of the cheap stuff - lemonade boxes and coffee cans - as you can, since anything that depicts the driver can send its value skyrocketing. On the other hand, save some of your money to invest in high-end, limited-edition merchandise. This can be pricey, but worth it in the long run.

Trends: Trucks have been overlooked too long by collectors. Pickups and sport utility vehicles are the hottest sellers in today's new car market; this interest has spilled over into the collectibles market. Truck salesman's awards, promotional models and toys are less common than automobile memorabilia of the same year. The traditional "Big Three" trucks (Ford, Dodge, Chevy) offer plenty of collectibles, but memorabilia from International's dependable trucks and 4x4s is more difficult to find and also very popular. There are also a number of hardcore Jeep lovers out there looking for Jeep stuff.

Motorcycle memorabilia also continues to accelerate, especially early items from before World War I. This includes AMA (American Motorcycle Association) Gypsy Tour awards, motorcycle club membership pins and Harley-Davidson memorabilia. Look for the more unusual motorcycle advertising memorabilia, from names like Henderson, Flying Menkel and Excelsior to come on strong.

Racing memorabilia is always hot, but lately it has been even more popular with collectors. Even people who don't love old cars or don't collect or restore them enjoy auto racing. The vintage racing market is driven by nostalgia for the "good old days," when any number of shade-tree mechanics could jump in their daily driver and run out to the race track

on a warm summer night to participate.

For racing collectors, programs, pit passes and felt pennants are hot items right now. Pennants are really in demand, especially if they designate a specific race, and are dated. Modern die-cast is especially popular with today's NASCAR and drag racing fans, as are autographs.

Print advertising is among the most plentiful and easiest to collect. Automobile manufacturers have always had big promotional budgets to work with, so print advertising materials are abundant on the market. Print ads offer one of the least expensive means for someone who is beginning a collection. Many ads from the 1920s to 1960s are quite attractive and colorful, offering snapshots of that time; some feature illustrated scenes which capitalize on themes such as recreation and the family. These ads can generally be found at flea markets and antique shows for $5-$10. But, if you're willing to do some reading, you can peruse old magazines for their ads, too, and remove the ad yourself.

Clubs

- Automobile License Plate Collectors Association, Inc., Gary Brent Kincade, P.O. Box 77, Horner, WV 26372, 304-842-3773 / 304-269-7623

- Automobile Objets D'Art Club, David K. Bausch, 252 N. 7th St., Allentown, PA 18102-4024, 610-820-3001 / 610-432-3355

- Spark Plug Collectors of America, Jeff Bartheld, 14018 NE 85th St., Elk River, MN 55330-6818, 612-441-7059

- Hubcap Collectors' Club, Dennis Kuhn, P.O. Box 54, Buckley, MI 49620, 616-269-3555

- Antiques Motorcycle Club, P.O. Box 333, Sweetser, IN 46987

Recommended Reading

As the leading publisher of books for collector-car enthusiasts, The Krause Publications' catalog currently has over seventy-five books for collectors of automobilia—too many to list them all here. For the complete list, visit the Krause Publications Books web site at *www.krause.com/Books*. Here are a few of the more general titles:

Books

Car Memorabilia Price Guide, Ron Kowalke and Ken Buttolph
Standard Catalog of American Cars 1805-1942, Beverly Rae Kimes & Henry Austin Clark, Jr.
Standard Catalog of American Cars 1946-1975, Ron Kowalke
Standard Catalog of American Cars 1976-1999, James M. Flammang & Ron Kowalke
2000 Standard Guide to Cars and Prices, James T. Lenzke and Ken Buttolph

Publications

Old Cars Weekly
Old Cars Price Guide Monthly
Toy Cars & Vehicles

VALUE LINE

Values shown are for items in Excellent condition. (Note: For more pricing on related items, also see the chapter on Petroliana.)

Accessory catalogs, 1939 Nash accessories booklet, 16 pages, 6" x 9" $35

Accessory catalogs, 1970 Ford Maverick accessories brochure, 2 pages, 11" x 9" $22

Advertisement, 1937 Lincoln-Zephyr, from 10/12/36 *Time* $8

Advertisement, 1958 Edsel, from 9/2/57 *Life* $3

Ashtray, Brockway, chrome, with 6-1/4" gold Husky $150

Bank, Pro Street drag race car, glazed ceramic, limited edition, Willy $50

Battery charger, 6-volt, pre-1950s $75

Bell, hand held, "I'm ringing the bell with the Pontiac" $35

Belt buckle, GMC Astro 95, 1970s.............................$21

Bumper sticker, Chrysler, "Rapid Transit System," 1970s $5

Business card, Edsel dealer, late 1950s.........................$7

Candy jar, Volkswagen, with cork stopper, amber........$50

Cigarette box, Firestone battery, shaped like a battery...$185

Cigarette lighter, Ford logo, 1950s $30

Coasters, 4" square, Cadillac, blue plastic, 1960s, set of 4 ....$7

Cooler, Pinto/Coca-Cola, the California Compacts $15

Cuff links, Michelin Man, blue and white, 1960s.........$45

Dealership sign, Chrysler, neon, blue, 1940s...........$1,000

Decal, STP 1967 Parnelli Jones Turbine, vinyl sticker, 7" x 2" $15

Decal, United States Auto Club, 1959 shield, 3" x 3" $4

All vintage advertising brochures, owner's manuals, parts catalogs, and magazines dealing with cars are collectible. This issue of "Motor World" dates from 1923.

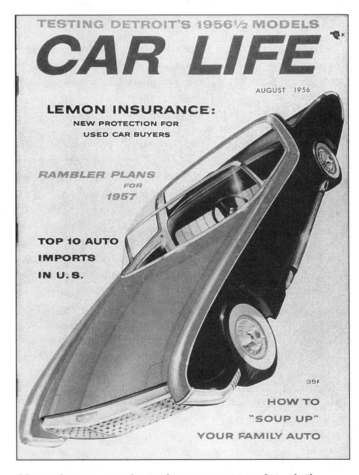

Magazine covers featuring concept or futuristic cars, like this 1956 issue of *Car Life*, are especially desirable.

This advertising button promotes the "New Chevrolet Six." It would probably sell for about $10.

Decal, Wynn's Joie Chitwood Thrill Show,
 with '58 Chevys, 4".....................................$10
Factory photograph, 1932 Packard, with actress
 Jean Harlow..$10
Factory photograph, 1937 Nash Ambassador,
 with Babe Ruth..$10
Factory photograph, 1957 Pontiac Bonneville.............$12
Flyswatter, wire with wood handle, Chevrolet dealer,
 1940s...$17
Fuzzy dice, large, 4" white with black dots...................$7
Hood mascot, 1933 Buick goddess............................$200
Hood mascot, 1934 Ford, greyhound.........................$275
Hood ornament, 1931-34 Studebakers, goose...........$150
Hood ornament, 1938-40 Packard, pelican.................$175
Hood ornament, 1951 Dodge,
 Ram mascot refined....................................$100
Hubcap, Cadillac, screw-on..$40
Hubcap, Ford, screw-on...$10
Jacket patch, Indianapolis 500, May 25, 1986.............$15
Key chain, AAA Golden Wheel Driving Award..........$12
Letter opener, Oldsmobile, 1950s.............................$30
License plate, 1940 Arizona, "Grand Canyon State,"
 white with dark numbers...$35
License plate, 1971 New Hampshire, "Live Free or Die,"
 white with dark numbers...$20
License plate tag topper, American Automobile

Advertising license plate attachments are popular with many collectors. This 1930s Farmers Insurance attachment is worth about $50.

 Association...$15
Literature, 1905 ALAM Hand Book of Gasoline
 Automobiles (original)...$150
Literature, 1915 Official Automobile Blue Book.......$100
Literature, 1923 NACC Hand Book (original).............$50
Literature, 1973 Kenworth 50th Anniversary booklet,
 8 pages...$15
Lunch box, Adam-12, tin, Aladdin Industries,
 1973...$90
Matchbook, Brockway..$4
Magazine, Motor Trend, September 1949,
 first issue...$125
Magazine, Rod & Custom, May 1953, first issue.........$45
Magazine, Speed Age, September 1958.....................$15
Model kit, Richard Petty's NASCAR Road Runner,
 MPC...$225
Model kit, 1957 Chevrolet "Pepper Shaker," ATM......$40
Model kit, Red Barron Show Rod, 1985.....................$20
Model kit, Mercedes-Benz, #H1285............................$75
Money clip, Prestone antifreeze...................................$15
Owner's manual, 1946 Buick owner's manual,
 100 pages...$32
Owner's manual, 1966 Chevelle owner's manual,
 228 pages...$34
Parking meter, Duncan, two-hour limit......................$25
Pedal car, Plymouth Speedway Pace Car,
 1958 convertible..$850
Pin, Ford, "Have a Good Ford Summer," 1970s.............$7
Publicity photo, movie cast from "The Three Stooges
 Go Around the World in a Daze," with 1933
 Ford taxi..$12
Racing program, Daytona 500 Official Program,
 1959, first event...$250

Racing program, Indianapolis 500 Official Program, 1911, first event $1,500

Radiator script, Cadillac.. $40

Ruler, 1938 Pontiac ad, 15" wooden............................. $35

Sales literature, 1912 Ford sales literature $75

Sales literature, 1914 Rolls-Royce sales catalog $225

Sales literature, 1934 Plymouth sales catalog.............. $50

Sales literature, 1955 Chevrolet sales catalog.............. $30

Sales literature, 1964 Cadillac sales brochure, 24 pages.. $20

Sales literature, 1974 Chevrolet Corvette sales catalog $20

Shaving mug, 1917 Chevrolet illustration $25

Spark plugs, AC, in tin box.. $65

Spark plug, Spitfire, lightning bolt logo $15

Steering wheel knob, Rod and Custom logo, white plastic $35

Sticker, AAA, 1950s, decal.. $5

Sunglasses, Chevrolet, 1962 .... $15

Technical literature, 1923 Ford reference book $25

Technical literature, 1932 Chevrolet reference book.. $35

Technical literature, 1956 Ford Truck, shop manual $37

Technical literature, 1963 Ford color selection chart.. $14

Technical literature, 1964 Mercury paint chart............. $10

Tire pressure gauge, Ford, crest on dial, 1950s............. $65

Trading card sets, Bowman, antique autos, 48 cards, 1953.. $400

Trading card sets, Tip Top Bread, sports cars, 28 cards, 1950s.. $600

Transmission grease, Acme, from Purity Oil Co. $20

Turn signal, 1920s Outlook combination stop/taillight $125

Uniform, mechanic's Ford overalls, logo, 1950s $45

Vanity mirror, Hudson, 1951... $45

Whiskey decanter, 1978 Jim Beam, 1978 Corvette $175

Yo-Yo, Chevrolet advertising, wooden, 1955 .... $20

BANKS

Antique cast-iron banks are generally considered to be the royalty of vintage American toys. Wonderfully intricate in their design, these old banks are prized by today's collectors as if they were rare examples of fine art, and many of them are priced accordingly.

Background: Banks have been around as long as there have been coins to put in them. Made of cast-iron, die-cast metal, plastic and other materials, they take all shapes and sizes—from cartoon characters like Popeye, to historical figures like Uncle Sam, and monuments like the Statue of Liberty. Often depicting scenes and situations both whimsical and well-known, some banks serve a dual purpose—holding change and advertising products.

The most collectible banks, and certainly the most valuable, are cast-iron banks. Made primarily between the 1870s and the 1920s (the 1880s were truly the golden age), cast-iron banks can be divided into two main categories: mechanical banks and still banks.

Mechanical banks are banks with moving parts. When a coin is deposited, it sets in motion a mechanism that makes the bank perform. The action can be as simple as the opening of a mouth or a door, or the nodding of a head; or as complex as making a figure dance, juggle, or skip rope. (See the descriptions in "Value Line" for some specific examples.)

Still banks are banks that don't have any moving parts; they stand "still." Many of the same companies that made the innovative mechanical banks—Arcade, Ives, and Stevens, among them—also made still banks as a less expensive alternative. Some banks, in fact, can be found in both mechanical and still versions. Buildings were probably the most common designs for still banks. They were made in the shape of churches, banks, skyscrapers, log cabins, Victorian mansions and other common buildings; as well as in the form of famous buildings, such as the Washington Monument, U.S. Capitol, Eiffel Tower, etc. Other still banks depicted animals, safes, clocks, mail boxes, globes and even people.

One category of vintage cast-iron bank—the registering bank—seems to straddle the line between still and mechanical. Often in the shape of either a safe or a cash register, these banks typically accept only one type of coin—nickels or dimes, for instance—and keep a running total as the coins are deposited. Once the deposits reach a certain total, usually five or ten dollars, the bank automatically pops open. While this limited action has earned registering banks a place in some mechanical bank collections, most collectors classify them as still banks.

Advertising banks are of interest to bank collectors and advertising collectors. Die-cast banks have been manufactured in the form of vehicles since 1981, when Ertl introduced its 1913 Model T Parcel Post Mail Service. Producing limited-edition runs that usually advertise prominent companies (ranging from Amoco to Winchester), die-cast bank manufacturers include First Gear, Racing Champions, Scale Models and Spec-Cast. These banks are of interest to bank collectors, die-cast collectors and brand-specific collectors.

General Guidelines: Antique mechanical banks are the true treasures of the bank-collecting hobby. Due to their limited supply and huge demand, they have a tremendous following with serious collectors, and a history of unequaled investment potential. A few rare examples have sold at specialty auctions for over $100,000, and while prices that high are not common, it is quite ordinary for nice examples to sell for prices in the thousands.

Rarity, condition, and the complexity of a bank's design and mechanism are all key elements in determining the value of a mechanical bank. Banks in good operating condition with their original paint are the most valuable. Condition is so important with mechanical banks that a single example—like the popular Calamity Bank—could have a price range from $5,000 to over $50,000, depending on condition. Because of their novel mechanisms, mechanical banks saw heavy use, and many were broken. As a result, today's collectors pay a huge premium for condition as well as scarcity. Popular themes, like Black Americana or sports, can also make a bank more desirable.

Prominent cast-iron bank manufacturers include Arcade, Ives, Kenton and Stevens. Building-shaped banks are regarded as the single largest type of still banks, followed by animals, busts, people, clocks, globes, mailboxes and safes. Featuring monuments such as the Eiffel Tower, commemorative banks are particularly popular among collectors.

Early cast-iron examples can be expensive. Due to rising values, many cast-iron mechanical banks have escalated into a price range reasonable only to the wealthiest and most major collectors. While still banks mirror this trend somewhat, their values are generally a fraction of mechanicals. Closer to the range of casual collectors, still banks have become attractive investment vehicles for those with modest means. Die-cast and plastic banks are the latest examples both available and affordable to average and beginning bank enthusiasts.

COLLECTORS' ALERT!

Reproductions run rampant in the collectibles cast-iron bank market. Poor paint jobs, different gloss and lighter weight due to inferior grades of iron are just three ways to spot an imitation. Reproduction labels and imprints can easily be filed away and removed, and metals can be artificially aged.

Trends: While cast-iron still and mechanical banks remain the most desirable collectible banks, die-cast examples continue to hold their popularity and are often more affordable.

The importance of condition to a bank's value cannot be underestimated. Cast-iron banks in Near Mint condition, featuring all original parts and little paint wear, are rarely found. Such examples will likely bring two to five times as much as one in Average or Very Good original condition with no repairs or restoration. As with many other collectibles of this type, restoration of banks is strongly discouraged in the marketplace. Unless done by an experienced professional, the restoration or re-painting of a vintage bank can seriously damage its potential value. The use of replacement parts and the dreaded refinishing or overpainting significantly depreciates a bank's worth.

Clubs

•Mechanical Bank Collectors Club of America, P.O. Box 128, Allegan, MI 49010,616-673-4509

•Still Bank Collectors Club of America, 1456 Carson CT., Homewood, IL 60430, 708-799-1732

Recommended Reading

Books

2000 Toys & Prices, Sharon Korbeck and Elizabeth Stephan
O'Brien's Collecting Toys, Elizabeth Stephan

Periodical

Toy Shop

VALUE LINE

Mechanical Banks

Values are for cast-iron banks in Very Good condition. Banks in Excellent condition are worth apeypproximately twice the value shown, while banks in Good condition are worth half the value shown.

Acrobat, 1883, J&E Stevens, gymnast kicks clown who stands on his head $4,000
Bad Accident Mule, 1890s, J&E Stevens, boy jumps into road, frightening mule pulling cart $1,500
Bear and Tree Stump, 1880s, Judd, 5" tall, coin on bear's tongue is dropped into bank $700
Billy Goat Bank, 1910, J&E Stevens, goat jumps forward when wire loop is pulled and coin falls in slot.... $1,000
Boy Scout Camp, 1912, J&E Stevens, scout raises flag as coin is dropped into tent $4,500
Boy Stealing Watermelon, 1880s, Kyser & Rex, dog comes out of dog house and boy moves toward watermelon when coin is dropped $1,500
Bulldog Bank, 1880s, J&E Stevens, put coin on dog's nose, pull his tail, dog opens mouth and swallows coin $1,200

Butting Ram, 1895, Ole Storle, ram butts coin on tree into bank while boy thumbs his nose $6,000
Circus Bank, 1888, Shepard Hardware, pony runs around ring as clown deposits coin $12,000
Clown Bank, 1939, Chein, place coin on clown's tongue, release lever and clown swallows coin................... $100
Coin Registering Bank, 1890s, Kyser & Rex, when the last nickel or dime is deposited to total $5, the door pops off $2,500
Dapper Dan, 1910, Marx, wind the key and Dan dances.. $500
Dentist Bank, 1880s, J&E Stevens, dentist pulls patient's tooth, patient falls backwards, dropping coin in gas bag $6,000
Dog Tray Bank, 1880, Kyser & Rex, dog takes coin from plate and deposits it in vault............................... $3,000
Fortune Teller Savings Bank, 1901, Nickel, Baumgartner and Co., drop nickel in slot, wheel spins, pull lever to read fortune $800

One of the true classics among vintage mechanical banks is "The Mikado," valued at $25,000 or more, depending on condition. This example was offered at a Christie's auction in New York.

Both of these mechanical banks date from the late 1800s. The "Speaking Dog Bank" (left), by Shepard Hardware, is valued at about $1,500 in Very Good condition and about twice that in Excellent condition. Depositing a coin on the girl's plate causes the dog's tail to wag and his mouth to open. The "Clown on Globe Bank" (right), by J&E Stevens, is worth about $1,500 in Very Good condition and about $4,000 in Excellent. When you deposit a coin, the clown stands on his head.

Girl Skipping Rope, 1890, J&E Stevens, ornately housed mechanism causes girl to jump rope, a classic.. $20,000

Hall's Lilliput, 1877, J&E Stevens, coin on plate is carried by cashier and placed in bank $700

Hoop-la Bank, 1895, J. Harper & Co., dog with coin in mouth jumps through hoop and deposits coin in barrel $1,500

Humpty Dumpty Bank, 1882, Shepard Hardware, Humpty's hand drops coin into bank $2,200

Jonah and the Whale, 1890s, Shepard Hardware, Jonah drops coin into whale's mouth (do not confuse with J&E Stevens Jonah and the Whale Bank worth as much as $50,000) $2,500

Lion Hunter, 1911, J&E Stevens, hunter shoots coin into lion's mouth.. $5,000

Little Moe, 1931, Chamberlain and Hill, place coin in Moe's hand, press lever on left shoulder, right arm raises, tongue flips in and Moe swallows coin while lowering his arm and tipping his hat $400

Mammy and Child, 1884, Kyser & Rex, put coin on apron, Mammy lower spoon to baby, baby's leg lifts as coin drops $4,500

Mikado, 1886, Kyser & Rex, coin mysteriously moves from under right hat to under left hat when crank is turned, a classic $25,000

Monkey Bank, 1920s, Hubley, monkey drops coin from mouth to organ $900

National Bank, 1873, J&E Stevens, place coin on door ledge, push doorbell, door revolves, slinging coin into bank as man moves quickly to get out of the way $3,500

Paddy and the Pig, 1882, J&E Stevens, pig kicks coin from its nose into Paddy's mouth................................ $2,500

Popeye Knockout Bank, 1929, Straits Mfg., when coin is deposited, Popeye knocks out opponent $600

Red Riding Hood, 1880s, W.S. Reed, moving lever makes grandma's mask move to reveal wolf; Red turns her head and coin drops.. $12,000

Santa at the Chimney, 1889, Shepard Hardware (and by Marx in 1910), Santa drops coins from hand into chimney $2,200

Sportsman Fowler, 1892, J&E Stevens, sportsman shoots flying bird, bank can use paper caps for sound effects $10,000

Uncle Sam with Carpet Bag, 1886, Shepard Hardware, Sam puts coin into carpet bag $3,500

Still Banks

Values listed are for cast-iron banks in Excellent condition.

Air Mail on base, Dent, 1920....................................$1,400
Alamo, Alamo Iron Works, 1930s $450
Amish Boy, John Wright, 1970.................................... $65
Amish Girl, John Wright, 1970.................................... $65
Andy Gump, Arcade, 1928 ....$1100
Arabian Safe, Kyser & Rex, 1882.............................. $300
Aunt Jemima, AC Williams, 1900s.............................$335
Barrel, Judd, 1873 .... $225
Baseball Player, AC Williams, 1909...........................$450
Battleship Maine, Grey Iron Casting, 1800s............$4,500
Beehive, Kyser & Rex, 1882.......................................$500
Billiken, AC Williams, 1909....................................... $125
Billy Possum, JM Harper, 1909 ....$5,500
Boss Tweed, 1870s...$3,750
Buster Brown & Tige, AC Williams, 1900s...............$375
Campbell Kids, AC Williams, 1900s $350
Captain Kidd, 1900s...$450
Cat on Tub, AC Williams, 1920s $200
Circus Elephant, Hubley, 1930s................................. $350
City Bank with Teller, HL Judd $750
Covered Wagon, Wilton Products $25
Daisy, Shimer Toy, 1899 .... $175
Dog Smoking Cigar, Hubley....................................... $850
Doughboy, Grey Iron Casting, 1919 .... $850
Dutch Boy, Grey Iron Casting.................................... $850
Dutch Girl, Grey Iron Casting $850
Egyptian Tomb, Kyser & Rex, 1882........................... $750
Electric Railroad, Shimer Toy, 1893 ....$6,000
Fido, Hubley, 1914.. $225
GE Refrigerator, Hubley, 1930s..................................$225
Gunboat, Kenton $1,800
Holstein Cow, Arcade, 1910 .... $650
Humpty Dumpty, 1930s.. $850

Ice Box, Arcade	$650
Laughing Pig, Hubley	$295
Lighthouse, Lane Art, 1950s	$250
Limousine, Arcade, 1921	$2,850
Lion on Wheels, AC Williams, 1920s	$225
Little Red Riding Hood, JM Harper, 1907	$4,500
Main Street Trolley, AC Williams, 1920s	$400-475
Mammy with Hands on Hips, Hubley, 1900s	$425
Mermaid Boat, Grey Iron Casting, 1900s	$850
Mulligan Policeman, AC Williams, 1900s	$450
Nest Egg, Smith & Egge, 1873	$850
Newfoundland Dog, Arcade, 1930s	$225
Organ Grinder, Hubley	$350
Palace, Ives, 1885	$3,750
Pavillion, Kyser & Rex, 1880	$575
Pay Phone, J&E Stevens, 1926	$2,000
Puppo on Pillow, Hubley, 1920s	$275
Rooster, Arcade, 1910	$400
Sailor, Hubley, 1910	$525
Santa Claus, Hubley, 1900s	$1,000
Seal on Rock, Arcade, 1900s	$500
Statue of Liberty, Kenton, 1900s, approx. 6"	$125-$175
Statue of Liberty, Kenton, 1900s, approx. 10"	$1,200
Thoroughbred, Hubley, 1946	$150
Three Wise Monkeys, AC Williams, 1900s	$550
US Navy Akron Zeppelin, AC Williams, 1930	$575
Villa, Kyser & Rex, 1880s-90s	$700-$850

Yellow Cab, Arcade, 1921	$2,500

Advertising Banks

Values shown are for banks in Excellent condition.

Alka-Seltzer, Speedy Figure, 1960s, vinyl	$260
Ballard Biscuits	$20
Big Boy, 1970s, vinyl	$45
Bosco, 1960s	$50
Bubble Yum	$20
Buddy L, Easy Saver, 1970s	$40
Buster Brown, 1980s	$45
Cap'n Crunch, 1975, molded vinyl	$25
Chrysler Mr. Fleet figure, 1973	$375
Chuck E. Cheese, vinyl	$20
Coca-Cola, 1950s	$75
Coca-Cola, Linemar	$470
Cocoa Puffs	$30
Curad Taped Crusader figure, 1975, vinyl	$35
Esso Oil, 1992, plastic	$65
Esso Oil Tiger, vinyl	$30
Eveready Batteries, 1981, vinyl	$12
Farmer Jack Supermarkets, 1986, vinyl	$30
Greyhound Bus, Jimson, 1960s, plastic	$45
Howard Johnson's, 1950s, plastic	$50
Husky Dog Food	$5
Icee Bear, 1974, plastic	$25
Ivory Soap	$30
Keebler Ernie the Elf, ceramic	$50
Kentucky Fried Chicken, 1960s-70s, plastic	$30
Kraft Cheeseasaurus Rex, 1992	$25
Magic Chef, 1960s, vinyl	$20
Marky Maypo, 1960s, vinyl	$50
Nestle Quik, 1980s	$12
Oscar Mayer Wienermobile	$25
Pepto Bismol, soft plastic	$65

Here are four examples of vintage cast-iron still banks. Sold at a Gene Harris auction, they include (from left to right) an Indian Scout bank that sold for $275, a Statue of Liberty bank that went for $350, a smaller Statue of Liberty bank that brought $93, and a Santa Claus bank that sold for $412.

The 1912 "Boy Scout Bank," by J&E Stevens, is a classic mechanical bank, valued at about $3,500 in Very Good condition and over $10,000 in Excellent. When a coin is deposited, the scout raises the flag.

Pillsbury, tin $25
Planters Mr. Peanut, 1950s, molded plastic $17
Royal Gelatin King Royal, 1970s, vinyl $250
Spam $10

Ertl Die-Cast Banks

Values are for banks in Mint-in-Box condition.

4-H Clubs of America, 1913 Model T $40
4-H Clubs of America, 1917 Model T $35
4-H Clubs of America, 1905 Ford Delivery $40
AJ Seibert Co, 1913 Model T $125
AC Rochester #1 UAW, 1950 Chevy Panel $125
ACE Hardware, 1918 Runabout $75
Agway #1, 1913 Model T $315
Agway #2, 1918 Runabout $45
Alka-Seltzer #1, 1918 Runabout $140
Allied Van Lines #1, 1913 Model T $85
American Red Cross #1, 1913 Model T $75
Amoco, 1913 Model T $165
Anheuser-Busch #2, 1926 Mack $65
Arm & Hammer, 1913 Model T $100

Atlas Van Lines #1, 1926 Mack Truck 1 .... $100
Barq's Root Beer #1, 1913 Model T $65
Bell Telephone #1, 1950 Chevy Panel $65
Breyer's Ice Cream, 1905 Ford Delivery $85
Canada Dry Ginger Ale, 1918 Barrel Runabout $45
Comet Cleanser, 1905 Ford Delivery $35
Dairy Queen, 1913 Model T $135
Dolly Madison, Step Van $65
Frito-Lay, 1950 Chevy Panel $40
Hamm's Beer, 1926 Mack Truck $75
Heineken Beer #1, 1918 Barrel Runabout $185
Henny Penny, 1932 Ford Panel $45
Hershey's Chocolate Milk, 1926 Mack Tanker $50
Hershey's Kisses, 1950 Chevy Panel $145
NASA, Step Van $45
Pepsi-Cola, 1917 Model T $135
Stroh's Beer, 1918 Ford Runabout $55
Titleist Golf Balls, 1913 Model T $70
Wonder Bread #1, 1913 Model T $80
York Peppermint Patties #1, 1932 Ford Panel $115

BARBIE DOLLS

Barbie is without doubt America's favorite doll and has been for over four decades. And why not? Who else has passed her 40th birthday and hasn't aged a day since 1959? Hasn't gained any weight, either. Plus she's got all those glamorous outfits and all that jewelry. You have to love her. And collectors certainly do.

Background: The inspiration for the Barbie doll came in the mid-1950s, as Ruth Handler, co-founder of Mattel Toys, watched her young daughter, Barbara, and her friends playing make-believe with paper dolls. She immediately recognized the potential for a three-dimensional teenage fashion doll—a doll that young girls could imagine in the role of cheerleader, teacher, nurse or college student. Handler and her staff designed the doll, named it after Handler's daughter, and introduced it at the 1959 annual Toy Fair in New York, where it became an instant hit. At the time, the children's doll market was limited to baby and toddler dolls, so the teenage Barbie doll was a huge sensation.

Over the years, Barbie has maintained her immense popularity by changing with the times. In the 1960s she reflected Paris high fashion and the elegance of Jackie Kennedy. In the 1970s she was a disco queen and a California girl. By the 1980s, Barbie was a business executive and a rock star; and in the 1990s she was a country girl, an international traveler and even a presidential candidate. For over forty years, Barbie has been a playmate and a role model for millions of girls—and a hot collectible.

General Guidelines: For serious collectors of Barbie dolls, age and condition are everything. Because the dolls were favorite playthings, finding examples in Near Mint condition

LOOKING OUT FOR NUMBER ONE!

The ultimate find for a Barbie collector is a nice example of the 1959 Ponytail Barbie, the first one made. Mint examples are very rare, but typically sell in the $5,000-$10,000 range when offered. (They must be in the original box to command the highest prices.) One Mint-in-the-Box example of a #1 Barbie sold for a record $13,000 at a 1999 auction. The first Ponytail Barbies all look somewhat similar to the non-collector, but there are subtle ways to identify a rare #1 1959 Ponytail Barbie. Here's what to look for:

- Holes in the bottom of the feet with copper tubes
- Zebra-stripe swimsuit
- Blonde or brunette hair with soft, curly bangs
- Red fingernails, toenails, and lips
- Gold hoop earrings
- White irises of the eyes and severely pointed black eyebrows
- Pale, almost white, ivory skin tone

(or better yet, still in the box) is difficult. But having that original box can add 50 percent or more to a doll's value. While some 1959 and 1960s Barbies have sold for thousands of dollars, those in poorer condition are worth much less. Most "played-with" vintage Barbies—especially those with missing fingers, neck splits, cut hair, or other similar flaws—are worth much less, often only about 10 percent of the Mint price.

Still, it is Barbie dolls from the 1960s that have the most value. Identifying the year of a Barbie doll is tricky and requires a good identification guide, plus lots of experience. Don't be fooled by the year listed on the back of the doll. This is not an issue date, but rather a copyright date. (For many, many years, Barbie dolls displayed a 1966 date mark.) If a doll has a mark saying it was made in China, Malaysia or the Philippines, it is not from the 1960s. No Barbies were made in those countries until later. Also, clothes may make the doll, but don't try to date a Barbie doll by her clothing. Fashions are

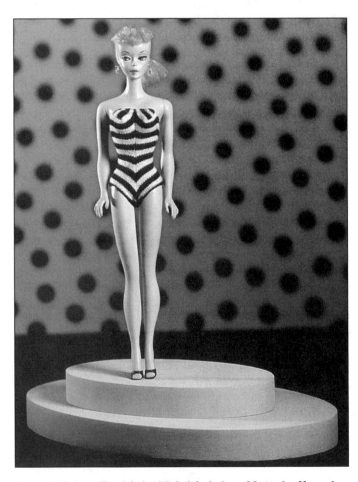

To celebrate Barbie's 35th birthday, Mattel offered a 35th Anniversary Barbie in 1994, looking just like the original 1959 #1 ponytail model.

often switched from doll to doll. Ken, Midge, Skipper and other Barbie friends are collectible, but Barbie herself remains the most popular with collectors. Don't overlook vintage accessories. Barbie houses, vehicles, cases and other toys bearing the Barbie logo are also collectible—the older the better. Vehicles still in the box remain the most valuable accessories.

Barbie fashions, of course, are also collectible and many are rising in value faster than the dolls themselves. Barbie's attire throughout the years has changed with the times. Some of her fashions alone have sold at specialty auctions for hundreds of dollars still in the original package. One interesting thing about Barbie clothing is that the large pieces of an outfit usually have the smallest value. For example, an outfit may be valued at $60 complete, but separately the dress may be worth $10, the shoes $20 and the necklace $30. This is because the smaller pieces were much more easily lost and fewer have survived.

With a few exceptions, regular-issue Barbie dolls from the 1970s and newer have not yet appreciated much in value. This could change as prices for the 1960s dolls escalate beyond reach and as more children from the 1970s begin to collect. Regular-issue Barbie dolls from the 1980s and '90s, however, are generally considered too new and too plentiful to ever have much investment potential.

The special limited-edition Barbies introduced by Mattel in recent years are showing mixed results, depending mostly on the size of the production run and the popularity of the doll. For example, the 1988 Holiday Barbie—the first doll in that popular series—which originally retailed for under $30, is now valued at as much as $800 still in the original box. Other limited-edition dolls have not increased in value at all since their day of issue. A few have even dropped in price. Still, if you decide to buy or collect the limited-edition Barbies as an investment, make sure you do not remove them from their original box. This is the condition that serious collectors demand, especially for newer Barbies.

Also popular with many collectors (and sometimes a good bet to increase in value) are limited-edition "exclusives," Barbies that were made exclusively for one retail outlet, like FAO Schwarz, Target, Toys R Us, etc.

Clubs

• Barbie Collectors Club International, P.O. Box 586, North White Plains, NY 10603

• Barbie Doll Lover's Club, 399 Winfield Road, Rochester. NY 14622

Recommended Reading

Books

The Ultimate Barbie Doll Book, Marcie Melillo
Contemporary Barbie Dolls—1980 & Beyond, Jane Sarasohn-Kahn
Barbie's Closet—Price Guide to Fashions and Accessories 1959-1970, Patricia Long

Periodical

Toy Shop

COLLECTING TIP!

Blondes may have more fun, but when it comes to Barbie dolls, brunettes are worth more. Because fewer were made, brunette versions of vintage Barbie dolls are worth more than their corresponding blonde counterparts.

VALUE LINE

Regular-Issue Barbie & Friends

Prices listed are for dolls in Mint condition without the box. Add 50 percent or more for Mint dolls in Mint original boxes.

Most regular issue Barbies, 1970s-present	$5-$25
Allan, bendable leg, 1966	$150
Allan, straight leg, 1964	$60
American Girl Barbie, "Color magic Face," 1966	$1,200
Astronaut Barbie, 1985	$25
Barbie with Growin' Pretty Hair, 1971	$100
Beautiful Bride Barbie, 1978	$75
Bubblecut Barbie, 1962	$325
Color Magic Barbie, midnight hair, 1966	$1,200
Fashion Queen Barbie, 1963	$150
Feelin' Groovy Barbie, 1985	$100
Francie, 1966, straight leg	$200
Francie, 1966, bendable leg, white doll	$150
Francie, 1966, bendable leg, black doll	$900
Hawaiian Fun Barbie and Friends, 1991	$3
International Barbies, 1980s-1990s, most examples	$15-$50

Some of the most valuable include:

International Barbie Eskimo, 1982	$50
International Barbie Italian, 1980	$65
International Barbie Oriental, 1981	$55
International Barbie Royal, 1980	$65
Ken, original flocked hair, 1961	$100
Ken, painted hair, 1962	$50
Ken, bendable legs, 1965	$150
Malibu Barbie, 1970s	$15
My First Barbie, 1980s, many variations	$3-$10
Ponytail Barbie #1, 1959	
Blonde	$4,000
Brunette	$4,500
Ponytail Barbie #3, 1960	
Blonde	$600
Brunette	$800
Quick Curl Miss America, 1974	$50
Rocker Series Barbie and Friends, 1985-86	$7
Skipper, straight leg, 1964	$50
Skipper, bendable leg, 1965	$125
Tropical Barbie or Ken, 1985	$3-$5

Twist and Turn Barbie, 1967......................................$150
Walk Lively Barbie, 1972 ....$75
Walk Lively Ken, 1972 ....$45

Collectors' Editions and Store Exclusives

Prices listed are for dolls in Mint condition in the original box. Subtract 50 percent or more for Mint dolls without the original box.

After the Walk, Coca-Cola, 1997..............................$200
Avon Barbies, 1996...$25
Barbie Loves Elvis Gift Set, 1997 ....$50
Bloomingdale's Barbies, 1990s ....$90-$125
Bob Mackie Designer Gold, 1990 ....$800
Bob Mackie Empress Bride Barbie, 1992................$1,200
Bob Mackie Fantasy Goddess of Africa/Asia,
    1998-99 ....$250
Bob Mackie Goddess of the Sun, 1995......................$175
Bob Mackie Jewel Essence Series, 1997 ....$85

The 1962 Bubblecut Barbie is worth over $400 Mint-in-Box.

CONTROVERSIAL BARBIE!

One of the most controversial Barbies ever issued was the 1993 "Teen Talk" Barbie, which was equipped with a computer chip that allowed the doll to talk. It was a popular model, until some feminist groups objected to one of the programmed phrases. The phrase, "Math class is tough," they argued, promoted the dangerous stereotype that girls aren't good in math and science.

Bowing to pressure, Mattel deleted the controversial phrase from all future "Teen Talk" models, but made no attempt to recall the dolls already on store shelves. At the time, it was estimated that only about 3,500 dolls were programmed with the objectionable phrase. (Each doll could say four phrases, picked at random from some 270 that were recorded.) Today, "Teen Talk" Barbies with the controversial phrase are valued at $200-$300 (in the original box), while versions of the doll without the objectionable phrase are worth about $45.

Bob Mackie Starlight Splendor, 1991 ....$700
FAO Schwarz Barbies, 1990s (most examples)
    ....$90-$225
40th Anniversary Barbie, 1999 ....$50
Gap Barbies, 1997...$35-$50
Happy Holidays, 1988 ....$800
Happy Holidays, 1989 ....$300
Happy Holidays, 1990 ....$200
Happy Holidays, 1991-94 ....$75-$100
Happy Holidays, 1995-96 ....$40-$60
Happy Holidays, 1997-98 ....$15-$30
Hollywood Legends, 1990s (most examples)........$40-$75
JC Penney Barbies, 1990s.....................................$50-$75
K-B Toys, 1990s $25
K-mart, 1990s $25
Pink Jubilee (1,200 made), 1989...........................$2,250
Sears Dream Princess, 1992...$50
Spiegel Regal Reflections Barbie, 1992......................$325
Spiegel Winners Circle, 1997 ....$70
Target Barbies, 1990s (most examples) ....$20-$40
Toys R Us Harley Davidson Barbie, 1997 ....$200-$400
Toys R Us 35th Anniversary Midge, 1998....................$50
Toys R Us Barbie for President, 1992...........................$65
Toys R Us Barbies (most examples), 1990s ....$30-$65
Wal-Mart Ballroom Beauty, 1991 ....$40
Wal-Mart Frills and Fantasy, 1988...............................$50
Wal-Mart Barbies, 1990s (most examples)............$15-$35
Woolworth's Barbies, 1990s (most examples).......$10-$20

Porcelain Barbies

Prices listed are for dolls in Mint condition in their original box. Subtract 50 percent or more for Mint dolls without the original box.

Blue Rhapsody Barbie, 1986 ....$600
Blushing Orchid Bride, 1997 ....$175

Gay Parisienne blond, Disney, 1991 ....$400
Gay Parisienne redhead, Disney, 1991........................$650
Holiday Ball, 1997..$175
Mattel's 50th Anniversary Barbie, 1995 ....$600
Solo in the Spotlight, 1990 ....$225
Wedding Day Barbie, 1989...$600

Barbie Accessories

Prices are for items in Excellent condition.

Double Barbie Case, 1960s..$15
Fashion Queen Case, 1963..$75
Skipper Case, 1964 ....$15

Barbie Goes Travelin' Case, 1965 ....$100
Barbie's Austin Healy Convertible, 1962 ....$125
Ken's Hot Rod, 1963...$125
Barbie Fashion Shop, 1962 ....$100
Barbie's Dream House, 1962 ....$35
Malibu Barbie Colorforms Set, 1972...........................$10

Barbie Vintage Fashions, 1959-1966

Prices listed are for fashions in Mint condition without original box.

American Airlines Stewardess, #984 ....$75
Barbie Skin Diver, #1608...$40
Beautiful Bride, #1698..$650
Candy Striper Volunteer, #0889 ....$125
Easter Parade, #971 ....$1,500
Enchanted Evening, #983 ....$125
Fashion Editor, #1635...$350
Fraternity Dance, #1638...$195
Little Red Riding Hood/Wolf, #0880..........................$220
Nightly Negligee, #965 ....$55
Pajama Party, #1601 ....$25
Pan American Stewardess, #1678 ....$1,000
Roman Holiday, #968 ....$1,500
Skater's Waltz, #1629 ....$150
Solo in the Spotlight, #982 ....$125
Wedding Day Set, #972 ....$140
Winter Holiday, #975 ....$50

Don't try to date Barbie dolls by their outfits. This is a 1960 #3 Barbie dressed in the 1970 Lemon Kick ensemble.

This Barbie and Midge vinyl lunch bag from King Seeley dates from 1965. You could add it to your collection for about $110.

BATTERY-OPERATED TOYS

The invention of the little dry-cell battery brought toys to life for kids the world over—and created one of the hottest categories of collectibles for the generations that followed. Battery-operated toys are, of course, still made today, but it's the charming tin character toys and robots of the 1940s-1960s that are most in demand by collectors.

Background: The heyday of battery-operated toys began in the 1940s with Japanese companies leading the charge. "Made in Japan" are the words toy collectors look for in their pursuit of high-quality vintage mechanical tin toys. Popular wind-up and friction toys, often of vehicles or human and animal characters, were being replaced by longer-lasting battery-operated versions.

Thousands of designs were made with toys featuring a variety of creative characters—from bubble-blowing monkeys to robots to cigar-smoking clowns. Disney and other cartoon characters like Popeye were also popular. The ingenuity of the Japanese created some truly unique novelty toys, valued today for their animation, design and humorous appeal.

Toys were often complex and could replicate several motions, such as walking, lifting or drumming. The tin lithography was usually quite interesting and detailed.

It is often difficult to identify the manufacturer of a battery-operated toy. Many companies used only initials to mark toys; some didn't mark them at all. Major manufacturers of battery-operated toys from the 1940s-1960s include Marx, Linemar (Marx's Japanese subsidiary), Alps, Marusan, Yonezawa, Bandai and Modern Toy (MT). The manufacture of tin toys dropped off in the 1960s in favor of cheaper methods and materials.

General Guidelines: While American-made Marx toys were popular, those made by Linemar and other Far East firms, were common.

To command top value, battery-operated toys should be operational and free of rust. But it is difficult to find most battery-operated toys in Mint condition in original boxes since the toys are highly susceptible to rust, corrosion and yellowing of fabric/plush.

Toys with character ties generally command more money. Space-related battery-operated toys, especially robots, are also popular.

Having the original box greatly increases the toy's desirability. Instructions were often printed on the box, and the name of the toy on the box often didn't match the toy exactly.

The complexity of the toy also determines value. A toy with three or more actions will generally be worth more than a toy that performs only one action. Even though they may be nice display pieces, toys that don't work command much less.

Made in Japan: Japan produced a lot of inexpensive, poor-quality toys until after the second World War, when the third-rate toy manufacturing nation's surrender resulted in economic chaos for this industrial nation.

In their quest for economic recovery and to compete in a toy market already dominated by Germany and America, the Japanese knew they had to come up with a new, different and exciting type of toy that would be more desirable than those produced by their competitors.

The Japanese toy designers concentrated their technology on a different type of toy operation. Not satisfied with the limited action and short duration of spring-driven or flywheel-propelled toys, the toy engineers developed a small electric motor powered by flashlight batteries. This mini-motor took up less room than other mechanisms, had a longer-running duration and enabled the toy to perform more functions. This development opened up an entirely new dimension in toy design—it introduced the concept of the battery-operated toy.

The toy designers integrated this new concept into hundreds of automation-like toys, capable of as many as eight different types of action in one cycle. These unique toys were an instant hit with the foreign market, especially in the United States. These clever, unusual and high-quality toys were made Japan the dominant toy producer and exporter for the next twenty to thirty years.

It should be noted that Japan flooded the market with these ingenious, well-made toys while quality control remained a high priority. These merits were not only apparent in their figural toys, but also in their vehicle line. The Japanese toy makers concentrated on very fine detail and quality, especially in their scale-model passenger cars. Their ultimate goal was to produce toys that looked like the real thing. They

---

THE TOP 10 BATTERY OPERATED TOYS
(MINT CONDITION)

1. Mickey the Magician, Linemar, 1960s................$2,500
2. Bubble Blowing Popeye, Linemar, 1950s............$2,500
3. Gypsy Fortune Teller, Ichida, 1950s....................$2,200
4. Smoking Spaceman, Linemar, 1950s...................$1,600
5. Kooky-Spooky Whistling Tree, Marx, 1950s......$1,600
6. Drumming Mickey Mouse, Linemar, 1950s........$1,600
7. Nutty Nibs, Linemar, 1950s...............................$1,400
8. Main Street, Linemar, 1950s..............................$1,200
9. Tarzan, Marusan, 1960s.....................................$1,000
10. Super Susie, Linemar, 1950s............................$1,000

Indian Joe," a politically incorrect though popular 1960s battery-operated toy, is valued at about $150 in Mint condition.

succeeded. Their workmanship carried over into their other vehicle lines—motorcycles, emergency and construction vehicles, novelty (silly) and comic character cars, trucks and space toys.

No other nation was able to equal (much less surpass) the impetus and determination of the Japanese toy makers until Japan relinquished its domination by redirecting its economy.

Now that they are approaching middle age, it is no wonder that these fine toys remain in great demand today and often command a very high price.

Recommended Reading

Books

Vintage Toys, Volume I: Robots & Space Toys, Jim Bunte, Dave Hallman and Heinz Mueller
2000 Toys & Prices, Sharon Korbeck and Elizabeth Stephan

Periodicals

Toy Shop
Toy Cars & Vehicles

VALUE LINE

Prices listed are for toys in Good to Excellent condition without original box.

ABC Fairy Train, MT, 1950s, 14-1/2" long	$80-$95
Air Control Tower, Bandai, 1960s, 11" tall	$210-$315
Aircraft Carrier, Marx, 1950s, 20" tall	$275-$450

DO YOUR TOYS MAKE THE GRADE?

Condition is critical to value. Here are some general guidelines regarding the grading of battery-operated toys.

Mint—A Mint toy is in the condition in which it was originally issued (perfect), regardless of age. It is also in perfect mechanical condition, complete with all accessory parts when applicable, and looks brand new. The cloth or fur (plush) covering on some battery toys may reveal some discoloration (yellowing) due to age, but this should not affect its value as a Mint toy as long as it is clean. All toys in this category must be in perfect working condition. The original box in Mint condition significantly enhances the value.

Very Good—A battery toy that has seen some use and is starting to show its age is described as Very Good. It must still be in perfect working order and have all its accessory parts when applicable. It may have some age soiling, but it has no rust or corrosion. Overall, it has an appearance of freshness and is still highly desirable to the fussy collector.

Good—This term applies to a toy that has seen considerable use, wear and tear, and some age-soiling, but is still in perfect working condition with no missing parts or accessories. The "wet" toys may show some slight surface rust that can be easily removed. A toy in Good condition is still a welcome addition to any toy collection, but would be targeted for upgrading by a piece in better condition.

Fair to Poor—Any battery toy below the condition of Good reflects a drastic reduction in value. Toys in good shape, but missing accessory parts, do not lose as much value as those that are severely rusted, corroded, painted over, have parts broken off, or are totally inoperable. These toys in Poor condition are usually collected for their scrap value by the toy repairer. Seldom are they worth more than $10.

Army Radio Jeep – J1490, Linemar, 1950s, 7-1/4"	$75-$125
Barber Bear, Linemar, 1950s, 9-1/2" tall	$175-$300
Barnyard Rooster, Marx, 1950s, 10" tall	$100-$150
Big Max Robot, Remco, 1958, 7" tall	$80-$125
Blushing Gunfighter, Y Co., 1960s, 11" tall	$120-$200
Bongo Player, Alps, 1960s, 10" tall	$75-$110
Brewster the Rooster, Marx, 1950s, 9-1/2" tall	$150-$200
Bubble Blowing Monkey, Alps, 1950s, 10" tall	$125-$150
Busy Housekeeper, Alps, 1950s, 8-1/2" tall	$175-$300
Calypso Joe, Linemar, 1950s, 11" tall	$190-$310

Caterpillar, Alps, 1950s, 16" long.........................$80-$125
Central Choo Choo, MT, 1960s, 15" long ....$30-$40
Charlie the Drumming Clown, Alps, 1950s,
    9-1/2" tall...$135-$200
Chippy the Chipmunk, Alps, 1950s, 12" long .....$75-$120
Circus Fire Engine, MT, 1960s, 11" long ....$110-$175
Clown on Unicycle, MT, 1960s, 10-1/2" tall .....$180-$280
Coney Island Rocket Ride, Alps, 1950s,
    13-1/2" tall..$300-$450
Crawling Baby, Linemar, 1940s, 11" long.............$45-$75
Doxie the Dog, Linemar, 1950s, 9" long ....$20-$25
Drummer Bear, Alps, 1950s, 10" tall.................$130-$200
Ducky Duckling, Alps, 1960s, 8" ....$35-$55
Fred Flintstone Bedrock Band, Alps, 1962,
    9-1/2" tall...$400-$500
Fred Flintstone Flivver, Marx, 1960s, 7 long.....$400-$600
Godzilla Monster, Marusan, 1970s,
    11-1/2" tall..$125-$160
Great Garloo, Marx, 1960s, 23" tall...................$300-$450
Gypsy Fortune Teller, Ichida, 1950s,
    12" tall ....$1,100-$1,700
Happy Fiddler Clown, Alps, 1950s,
    9-1/2" tall...$200-$300
Hobo Clown with Accordion, Alps, 1950s,
    10-1/2" tall..$275-$425
Hooty the Happy Owl, Alps, 1960s, 9" tall ....$65-$100
Indian Joe, Alps, 1960s, 12" tall ....$75-$110
Jolly Bambino, Alps, 1950s, 9" tall ....$200-$300
Josie the Walking Cow, Daiya, 1950s,
    14" long..$125-$175

Kissing Couple, Ichida, 1950s, 10-3/4" long .....$145-$200
Kooky-Spooky Whistling Tree, Marx, 1950s,
    14-1/4"..$450-$760
Mac the Turtle, Y Co., 1960s, 8" tall ....$85-$135
Main Street, Linemar, 1950s, 19-1/2" tall.......$600-$1,000
Marching Bear, Alps, 1960s, 10" tall.................$150-$225
Mickey the Magician, Linemar, 1960s,
    10" tall..$785-$1,200
Musical Bear, Linemar, 1950s, 10" tall.............$200-$300
Odd Ogg, Ideal, 1962, turtle-frog creature ....$75-$200
Peppermint Twist Doll, Haji, 1950s, 12" tall .....$150-$225
Peppy Puppy, Y Co., 1950s, 8" long......................$45-$70
Picnic Bear, Alps, 1950s, 10" tall ....$100-$150
Pierrot Monkey Cycle, MT, 1950s, 8" tall ....$325-$460
Pistol Pete, Marusan, 1950s, 10-1/4" tall..........$250-$270

KEEPING THEM IN TOP SHAPE!

Battery toys should be operated periodically to keep them loosened up. A lightweight spray lubrication now and then helps considerably if the mechanism is accessible. However, do not over lubricate, as the excess may stain any cloth or fur covering on the toy.

A quality car wax or polish keeps the lithographed and bare metal parts looking like new, especially on "wet" toys. Always test an obscure lithographed area to make sure the polish doesn't soften or dissolve the paint. Care should be exercised when polishing metal parts adjoined to cloth or plush covering, as the cleaning substance may stain the coverings. Light surface rust usually disappears with a careful polishing. Nothing can be done for deep rust or corrosion without further ruining the value of the toy. Repainting will only further reduce the value and is not recommended.

Check the battery compartment for leaking batteries or corrosion that can damage toys. Should your battery toy fail to operate, the following steps might be helpful:

Be sure it is not gunked-up and that no moving parts are binding.

Make sure the battery contacts are not dirty or corroded. If they are, clean them with crocus cloth. Always use fresh batteries!

Lightly tap the toy with your finger or lightly nudge one of the moving parts while the switch is in the on position.

If none of the above works, then your toy may need major surgery, which is best left to an expert in toy repair. Expert repairs do not affect the value of a battery toy as long as the repair is undetectable and the toy looks and functions exactly as it did before the repair. Such repairs are acceptable in toy collecting circles. Expert repairs are expensive but well worth the investment if it means the difference between a highly-prized Mint toy and one below the grade of Good. An inoperable toy is practically worthless, regardless of condition.

Charlie Weaver, the battery-operated bartender, is valued at about $125-$150 in Mint condition.

Playful Puppy, MT, 1950s, 5" tall ....$100-$150
Roarin' Jungle Lion, Marx, 1950s, 16" long .....$175-$250
Roller Skater, Alps, 1950s, 12" tall....................$100-$125
Sam the Shaving Man, Plaything Toy, 1960s,
    11-1/2" tall...$125-$180
Saxophone Playing Monkey, Alps, 1950s,
    9-1/2" tall...$200-$300
Serpent Charmer, Linemar, 1950s, 7" tall..........$175-$300
Shoe Shine Bear, TN, 1950s, 9" tall ....$150-$225
Skipping Monkey, TN, 1960s, 9-1/2" tall ....$45-$60
Sleeping Baby Bear, Linemar, 1950s,
    9" long ....$195-$285
Sleeping Pup, Alps, 1960s, 9" long ....$45-$75
Slurpy Pup, TN, 1960s, 6-1/2" long.......................$45-$60
Sneezing Bear, Linemar, 1950s, 9" tall..............$200-$300
Sunday Driver, MT, 1950s, 10" long ....$55-$90
Tarzan, Marusan, 1960s, 13" tall ....$480-$765
Telephone Bear, Linemar, 1950s, 7-1/2" tall .....$200-$300
Television Spaceman, Alps, 1960s,
    14-1/2" tall...$400-$600
Trumpet Playing Monkey, Alps, 1950s,
    9" tall..$150-$225
Tumbles the Bear, Yanoman, 1960s,
    8-1/2" tall..$100-$150
Twirly Whirly, Alps, 1950s, 13-1/2" tall............$290-$450
Walking Elephant, Linemar, 1950s,
    8-1/2" tall..$80-$120
Walking Esso Tiger, Marx, 1950s,
    11-1/2" tall..$250-$350
Walking Itchy Dog, Alps, 1950s, 9" long ....$45-$75
Western Locomotive, MT, 1950s,
    10-1/2" long...$45-$65
Yo-Yo Clown, Alps, 1960s, 9" tall ....$150-$190
Yo-Yo Monkey, Alps, 1960s, 9" tall ....$100-$185
Yummy Yum Kitty, Alps, 1950s, 9-1/2" tall......$170-$270
Zero Fighter Plane, Bandai, 1950s,
    15" wingspan...$150-$230

**Good Time Charlie," a 1960s battery-operated toy
from Japan, is valued at $175 in Mint condition. It
stands about 12 inches tall.**

BEANIE BABIES

The Beanie Babies world was shocked to learn plans were to stop producing those cuddly, understuffed beanbag animals in 2000—they would all be retired. But fans flooded the company's web site, voting to stay the demise of these popular collectibles.

On Jan. 8, 2000, Ty announced a reincarnation of plush for 2000—Beanie Kids! The line debuted at gift shows in Philadelphia, Dallas and Atlanta. The new line, based on early information and photos gleaned from collector web sites, are plush versions of kids, not animals

Ty's official web site, *www.ty.com* , has previously divulged several of its year 2000 releases, including: Beanie Buddies, now available in three sizes—large (32 inches), extra large (38 inches) and jumbo (48 inches); twelve items in its Attic Treasures line; Ty Classic—a combination of Ty plush (stuffed animals) and new bears; and Baby Ty, a line of plush toys catering to infants.

Background: Beanie Babies became all the rage in 1997, but were actually introduced by Ty Inc. three years earlier, in 1994. When the company began "retiring" (ceasing production of) specific animals, the collecting fever hit, with people scrambling to find scarce Beanie Babies and paying top dollar for them.

A secondary market quickly grew. Soon, collectors were paying $50 or more for the tiny toys, which originally retailed for about $5.

Over 250 Beanie Babies exist, from Twigs the Giraffe and Tabasco the Bull, to Ziggy the Zebra and Hoppity the Rabbit. A 1997 McDonald's promotion offered 10 Teenie Beanie Babies, smaller versions of the beanbags, which were offered with Happy Meals. A 1998 McDonald's promotion offered a dozen more.

General Guidelines: Retired Beanies and those with older hang tags sell for the highest prices. Variations in tags, colors and styles increase the collectibility of certain Beanies. Each of the newer Beanie Babies is labeled with its name, a poem and its birth date on a heart-shaped tag. Old tags are paper "To/From" style tags or a tag sewn into the animal.

Beanies with hang tags intact are more desirable than those without tags. Teenie Beanie Babies have a higher value in original plastic bag packaging.

Regional variations (like the Canadian Maple bear) and special editions (like Princess, a Diana commemorative bear) are highly desirable. Special, very-limited-edition Beanies, typically given only to Ty employees, etc., can bring some staggering prices. Recently the #1 Sales Rep. Bear, one of only 253 special Beanies that were presented to Ty sales representatives, sold for an incredible $12,000.

Hang tags were used on every Beanie Baby and are designated as "generations," based on the style of the tag and the release date of the baby. First-generation tags were used until late 1994; second-generations were used from late 1994 to mid-1995; third-generation tags were used from mid-1995 to early 1996; fourth-generation tags appeared from early 1996 to fall 1997; fifth-generation tags were used in the fall of 1997 and used until summer 1998; sixth-generation tags were released in the summer of 1998.

There are many different ways to store Beanies—seamless boxes, stackable cylinders, seamless cribs. These items can generally be purchased for less than $1 each in large quantities. Buddy boxes are usually less than $10. UV-coated plastic "time capsules," in three sizes (12", 8" and 5-1/4"), are all generally between 50 cents and $2.50. Tag protectors come in various shapes and sizes—soft shell, heart shell, hard shell, slip-ons, square Bamm Beano's lockets, Bamm Beano's football lockets and Disney lockets. These can be purchased for less than $10 each in quantities.

Recommended Reading

Books
The Bean Family Pocket Guide, Shawn Brecka
The Bean Family Album and Collector's Guide, Shawn Brecka
Big Little Book of Bears

Periodicals
Toy Shop

VALUE LINE

The following list includes all Beanie Babies valued at $10 or more. Listings are for examples in Mint condition and include birth date, generation (where applicable) and value.

Ally the Alligator, March 14, 1994, 1st	$450
2nd	$250
3rd	$150
4th	$42
Baldy the Eagle, Feb. 17, 1996, 4th, 5th	$10
Bessie the Cow, June 27, 1995, 3rd	$140
4th	$45
Blackie the Bear, July 15, 1994, 1st	$300
2nd	$175
3rd	$100
4th, 5th	$10
Blizzard the White Tiger, Dec. 12, 1996	$10
Bones the Dog, Jan. 18, 1994, 1st	$200
2nd	$150
3rd	$100
4th	$15

Bongo the Monkey (brown tail), Aug.17, 1995,
    3rd...$120
    4th...$45
Britania the Bear (Europe), Dec. 15, 1997................$125
Bronty the Brontosaurus $600
Brownie the Bear, Nov. 14, 1993, 1st $2,500
Bubbles the Fish, July 2, 1995, 3rd.........................$225
    4th...$90
Bucky the Beaver, June 8, 1995, 3rd.......................$100
    4th...$25
Bumble the Bee, 3rd $350
    4th..$325
Caw the Crow, n/a, 3rd...$500
Cheeks the Baboon, May 18, 1999 ....$10
Chilly the Polar Bear, 1st, 2nd $1,500
    3rd...$1,300
Chipper the Chipmunk, April 21, 1999, ...$20
Chocolate the Moose, April 27, 1993, 1st $1,000
    2nd...$400
    3rd $150
    4th, 5th, 6th $8
Chops the Lamb, May 3, 1996, 3rd $225
    4th..$100
Claude the Crab, Sept. 3, 1996, 4th $12
    5th, 6th...$8
Clubby the Bear, July 7, 1998..................................$15
Clubby II the Bear, March 9, 1999 ....$20
Coral the Fish, March 2, 1995, 3rd...........................$225
    4th..$100
Cubbie the Bear, Nov. 4, 1993, 1st $700
    2nd...$400
    3rd $200
    4th...$35
    5th...$18

COLLECTOR CARDS

In 1998, Cyrk Inc. issued the first series of officially licensed Ty Beanie Babies collector's cards. Cards from the original nine Beanies can range from $40 to $1,300, depending on the creature and the color. Retired cards from this series range from $1 to $250; commons are generally less than $1, as are those in series two. The success of these led to a second series in 1999, including a limited number of autographed cards by Beanie Baby creator and Ty Inc. president H. Ty Warner.

While the autographed cards have helped fuel the hobby, the limited variations of the Rare Bear cards has kept the frenzy strong. These cards can bring anywhere from $15 to $1,200, depending on the bear and the color combination. Series 3 cards were released at the end of the summer in 1999, and included five subsets, with cards being available in turquoise, magenta, silver or gold variations. Retired cards bring $25-$500 depending on the Beanie and color combination, while common cards and artists proofs are generally worth 25 to 50 cents.

Curly the Bear, April 12, 1996 4th.............................$20
    5th, 6th..$12
Daisy the Cow, May 10, 1994, 1st $300
    2nd...$275
    3rd..$125
    4th, 5th...$9
Derby the Horse, Sept. 16, 1995, fine mane $2,500
Derby the Horse, coarse mane, no star, 3rd $200
    4th...$12
Derby the Horse, coarse mane, with star $8
Derby the Horse, furry mane, with star.........................$8
Digger the Crab, Aug. 23, 1995, orange, 1st $900
    2nd, 3rd..$400
Digger the Crab, red, 3rd $225
    4th...$60
Doodle the Rooster, March 8, 1996 ....$20
Ears the Bunny, April 18, 1995, 3rd $100
    4th, 5th..$8
Eggbert the Baby Chick, April 10, 1998.....................$10
Erin the Bear, March 17, 1997, 5th............................$12
Flash the Dolphin, May 13, 1993, 1st.......................$425
    2nd...$300
    3rd $200
    4th...$80
Flip the Cat, Feb. 28, 1995, 3rd $125
    4th...$25
Flitter the Butterfly, June 2, 1999............................$16
Flutter the Butterfly, n/a...$600
Garcia the Teddy, Aug. 1, 1995, 3rd $250
    4th..$100
Germania (Europe), Oct. 3, 1998..............................$175
Glory the Bear, July 4, 1997 ....$20
Goldie the Goldfish, Nov. 14, 1994, 1st....................$400
    2nd...$250
    3rd $125
    4th, 5th...$25
Groovy the Ty-Dye Bear, Jan. 10, 1999......................$25
Grunt the Razorback, July 19, 1995, 3rd $240
    4th..$100
Halo the Angel Bear, Aug. 31, 1998..........................$10
Happy the Hippo, Feb. 25, 1994, gray, 1st.................$750
    2nd...$500
    3rd $400
Happy the Hippo, lavender, 3rd $175
    4th, 5th...$15
Hippity the Bunny, June 1, 1996................................$10
Honks the Goose, March 11, 1999..............................$20
Hoot the Owl, Aug. 9, 1995, 3rd................................$90
    4th...$20
Humphrey the Camel, n/a, 1st................................$2,400
    2nd, 3rd $1,500
Inch the Inchworm, Sept. 3, 1995, felt antenna,
    3rd $200
    4th...$150
Inch the Inchworm, yarn antenna, 4th $20
    5th...$10

The patriotic "Glory" is worth about $20.

Inky the Octopus, Nov. 29, 1994, tan, without mouth,
  1st $900
  2nd $700
Inky the Octopus, tan, 2nd $800
  3rd $600
Inky the Octopus, pink, 3rd.. $200
  4th $20
Kicks the Soccer Bear, Aug. 16, 1998 .... $10
Knuckles the Pig, March 25, 1999.............................. $12
Lefty the Donkey, July 4, 1996.................................. $150
Legs the Frog, April 25, 1993, 1st $450
  2nd $350
  3rd $110
  4th $15
Libearty the Bear, Summer 1996 .... $250
Lipps the Fish, March 15, 1999 .... $16
Lizzy the Lizard, May 11, 1995, tie-dyed................. $750
Lizzy the Lizard, blue, 3rd.. $200
  4th... $28
  5th... $20
Lucky the Ladybug, 7 spots, May 1, 1995, 1st $500
  2nd $400
  3rd $200
Lucky the Ladybug, 11 spots $12
Lucky the Ladybug, 21 spots $400

Magic the Dragon, Sept. 5, 1994, 3rd....................... $175
  4th.. $45
Manny the Manatee, June 8, 1995, 3rd..................... $225
  4th.. $75
Maple the Teddy, July 1, 1996, 4th $225
  5th.. $160
  6th.. $125
Millennium the Bear, Jan. 1, 1999, 6th..................... $12
Mooch the Spider Monkey, Aug. 1, 1998 .... $10
Mystic the Unicorn, coarse mane, gold horn, May 21,
  1994, 3rd $75
  4th, 5th.. $20
Mystic the Unicorn, fine mane, gold horn, 1st........... $500
  2nd... $425
  3rd $300
Mystic the Unicorn, white mane, iridescent horn........ $10
Nana the Monkey, Aug. 17, 1995, 3rd..................... $3,500
Neon the Seahorse, April, 1, 1999, 6th...................... $12
Nip the Cat, white face and belly, March 6, 1994,
  2nd... $700
  3rd $600
Nip the Cat, all gold.. $800
Nip the Cat, gold face, white paws, 3rd..................... $260
  4th, 5th.. $15
Osito the Mexican Bear, Feb. 5, 1999......................... $15
Patti the Platypus, Jan. 6, 1993, maroon, 1st $1,000
  2nd... $875
  3rd $650
Patti the Platypus, magenta, 3rd............................... $175
  4th, 5th.. $12
Peace the Bear, Feb. 1, 1996, 4th $20
  5th.. $12
  6th... $8
Peanut the Elephant, Jan. 25, 1995, royal blue $5,000
Peanut the Elephant, light blue, 3rd.......................... $750
  4th.. $20
  5th.. $14
Pecan the Gold Bear, April 15, 1999 .... $10
Peking the Panda, n/a, 1st $1,700
  2nd... $1,500
  3rd $1,400
Pinchers the Lobster, June 19, 1993, 1st................... $700
  2nd... $600
  3rd $110
  4th, 5th.. $12
Pouch the Kangaroo, Nov. 6, 1996, 4th $10
Princess the Bear, n/a, 5th.. $12
Pumkin the Pumpkin, Oct. 31, 1998 .... $15
Punchers the Lobster, June 19, 1993, 1st................. $3,600
Quackers the Duck, April 19, 1994, with wings,
  2nd... $500
  3rd $100
  4th, 5th.. $10
Quackers the Duck, no wings, 1st.............................. $1,800
  2nd... $1,600

Radar the Bat, Oct. 30, 1995, 3rd $200
    4th $190
Rex the Tyrannosaurus, n/a, 3rd $650
Righty the Elephant, July 4, 1996 .... $150
Ringo the Raccoon, July 14, 1995, 3rd $75
    4th, 5th $8
Rover the Dog, May 30, 1996 .... $15
Santa, Dec. 6, 1998 .... $20
Scaly the Lizard, Feb. 9, 1999, 6th $20
Scoop the Pelican, July 1, 1996, 4th $10
Scottie the Terrier, June 15, 1996, 4th, 5th $17
Seamore the Seal, Dec. 14, 1996, 1st $600
    2nd $400
    3rd $175
    4th $80
Seaweed the Otter, March 19, 1996, 3rd $75
    3rd, 4th $12
Sheets the Ghost, Oct. 31, 1999, 6th $25
Silver the Grey Tabby, Feb. 11, 1999 .... $10
Slither the Snake, n/a, 1st $1,500
    2nd, 3rd $1,200
Sly the Fox, brown belly, Sept. 12, 1996 .... $150
Sly the Fox, white belly $8
Slowpoke the Sloth, May 20, 1999, 6th $16
Snowball the Snowman, Dec. 22, 1996 .... $25
Spangle the American Bear, June 14, 1999 .... $20
Sparky the Dalmatian, Feb. 27, 1996, 4th $80
Speedy the Turtle, Aug. 14, 1994, 1st $650
    2nd $175
    3rd $100
    4th $20
Splash the Orca Whale, July 8, 1993, 1st $700
    2nd $400
    3rd, 4th $70
Spooky the Ghost, Oct. 31, 1995, 3rd $125
    4th $20
Spot the Dog, without spot, Jan. 3, 1993 .... $1,800
Spot the Dod, with spot, 2nd $400
    3rd $125
    4th $30
Squealer the Pig, April 23, 1993, 1st $750
    2nd $300
    4th, 5th $15

Steg the Stegosaurus, n/a $600
Sting the Stingray, Aug. 27, 1995, 3rd $275
    4th $100
Stinky the Skunk, Feb. 13, 1995, 3rd $75
    4th, 5th $8
Stripes the Tiger, orange, June 11, 1995 .... $400
Stripes the Tiger, tan $8
Tabasco the Bull, May 13, 1996, 3rd $275
    4th $90
Tank the Armadillo, Feb. 22, 1995, 9 lines, no shell,
    4th $275
Tank the Armadillo, 7 lines, no shell $200
Tank the Armadillo, with shell $40
1997 Holiday Teddy, 4th $50
    5th $30
1998 Holiday Teddy $45
1999 Holiday Teddy $30
1999 Signature Bear $10
Teddy the Bear, Nov. 28, 1995, brown, new face,
    2nd $1,000
    3rd $500
    4th $75
Teddy the Bear, brown, old face $2,100
Teddy the Bear, cranberry $1,800
Teddy the Bear, jade $1,900

"Garcia" is a popular Beanie Baby, selling for $50-$100.

Teddy the Bear, magenta..$1,700
Teddy the Bear, violet,..$1,900
Teddy the Bear, teal...$1,800
The End, the Black Bear $45
Trap the Mouse $1700
Tusk the Walrus, Sept. 18, 1995, 3rd $225
  4th..$80
Twigs the Giraffe, May 19, 1995, 3rd.........................$90
  4th, 5th..$15
Ty 2K the Confetti Bear, Jan. 1, 2000...........................$25
Valentina the Bear, Feb. 14, 1998 ....$12
Valentino the Bear, Feb. 14, 1994, 2nd $225
  3rd $150
  4th..$28
  5th, 6th..$10
Velvet the Panther, Dec. 16, 1995, 3rd.....................$100
  4th..$20
Waddle the Penguin, Dec. 19, 1995, 3rd....................$100
  4th, 5th..$10
Wallace the Scottish Bear, Jan. 25, 1999 ....$40
Web the Spider $1,200
Weenie the Dachshund, July 20, 1995, 3rd.................$100
  4th, 5th..$15
Zero the Penguin, Jan. 2, 1998, 6th............................$12
Ziggy the Zebra, Dec. 24, 1995, 3rd............................$85
  4th, 5th..$10

The majority of later-edition Beanie Babies remain priced in the $5-$7 range.

Zip the Cat, March 28, 1994, white face and belly,
  2nd..$550
  3rd $475
Zip the Cat, all black...$1,200
Zip the Cat, white paws, 3rd $300
  4th..$38
  5th..$15

THE BEATLES

No musical group, before or since, has had the impact of the Beatles. The Fab Four from Liverpool shaped a generation of young people—changing not just music, but also hair styles, fashion, attitudes and society in general. Now, nearly four decades later, they are influencing another generation. The Beatles impact is truly incredible, and interest in their music and memorabilia continues to grow.

Background: The earliest Beatles memorabilia dates back to 1962 when the band first became prominent in England, but the majority of vintage Beatles memorabilia dates from 1964 to 1967, when the group enjoyed its greatest fame in the U.S. and beyond. Virtually every baby boomer remembers where they were the night the Fab Four made their first triumphant appearance on the Ed Sullivan Show. The date was Feb. 9, 1964, and the historic event was watched by over seventy million people—a record that stood until Super Bowl mania came along in the 1970s.

As you might expect, most Beatles collectors today are from the baby-boom generation, but there are also a huge number of younger collectors who did not experience the frenzy of Beatlemania firsthand. Along with all of the original Beatles records and albums—an area so big it is really a collecting category all its own—there was a staggering amount of Beatles merchandise produced and sold worldwide. Most Beatles memorabilia being sought today was produced 1964 and 1966, the years when the group absolutely dominated the American and European record charts.

General Guidelines: Original Beatles merchandise included magazines, books, trading cards, sheet music, jewelry, pinback buttons, puzzles, paint-by-number sets, toys, games, lunch boxes, fan club souvenirs, posters, pennants, school supplies, dishes, glassware, figurines, dolls, clothing, wallets, combs and hundreds of other items. In fact, no other musical group in history inspired more collectibles.

There was a second wave of Beatles memorabilia issued in conjunction with the 1968 movie *Yellow Submarine*, and these items are among the most popular of all vintage Beatles collectibles. Most were marked "KFS-Suba Films Ltd.," with the "KFS" standing for King Features Syndicate. Vintage *Yellow Submarine* collectibles include party coasters, alarm clocks, costumes, masks, posters, model kits, key chains, puzzles, banks and dozens more—all picturing the Beatles as they appeared in the animated film or other characters, such as "The Boob," the "Blue Meanies," the "Apple Bonkers," and others.

Much of the paper memorabilia from the Beatles, especially books and magazines featuring the group, are fairly common. Most collectors, therefore, demand these items in top condition. Items in lesser condition, with rips, tears, or missing pages, have little value for a serious collector.

As with all collectibles, condition for all Beatles memorabilia is critical. A Near Mint condition item is typically worth two or more times the value of the same piece in Good condition or worse. Plus, all the pieces, parts and accessories must be intact. This is especially true for items like the popular Beatles "Flip Your Wig Game" or the set of four Remco dolls, which originally came with instruments wrapped around their necks. Today, a complete set of these five-inch plastic dolls sells for $250-$400, but only about half that amount without the original instruments.

Most in demand by serious collectors are examples of officially licensed merchandise still in its original package or box. The Remco dolls mentioned above, for example, would sell for as much as $1,000 a set if found still in their original boxes. Generally, having the original box or package at least doubles the value of a vintage item.

Many items of clothing displaying the Beatles' likenesses were merchandised in the mid-1960s, including hats, sunglasses, sweatshirts, dresses, tennis shoes, etc. There were also items designed to be used and consumed, like Beatles bubble bath, shampoo and so on. Today, these items are among the most difficult of all Beatles memorabilia to find, and among the most valuable. A can of Beatles Hair Spray, for instance, might bring $500 or more, depending on condition.

Beatles records: Beatles records, of course, are very collectible, but determining their value may be a little trickier than what you might expect, especially for the earlier discs.

COLLECTOR'S ADVISORY!

Officially licensed Beatles merchandise from the 1960s was marked either "NEMS" or "SELTAEB." "NEMS" was the acronym for Beatles manager Brian Epstein's company, North End Music Stores; while "SELTAEB" was simply "Beatles" spelled backwards. Look for either of these marks on legitimate vintage Beatles memorabilia.

Some companies at the time tried to cash in on the Beatles' popularity without paying any royalties, either by producing unauthorized Beatles merchandise or by marketing "generic" items that looked similar to the Beatles without actually using their name. One company, for instance, designed items featuring guitar-playing insects (beetles!). Because of their immense popularity, even these unauthorized vintage Beatles items are collected today, but they don't command the respect, or the prices, that the legitimate, licensed collectible do.

Today's collectors should also be aware that counterfeits and fakes exist in the marketplace. Since the late 1970s, there have been attempts to market new memorabilia designed to look like it had been produced in the 1960s. Some of these unauthorized items even fraudulently display a 1964 date and the "NEMS" or "SEALTAB" mark. These items have little collector value, and most serious collectors try to avoid them altogether.

The Beatles were the most-merchandised band in history. Everything depicting the Fab Four is collectible and rising in value.

FUTURE TREASURES?

Collectors should be aware of a trend that is emerging now that compact discs are dominating the music scene. Virtually everything ever recorded by the Beatles is now available on CD, making the old vinyl records unnecessary for all but the most serious hardcore vinyl junkies. Typical fans now listen to their favorite Beatles tunes on CD; but they still might want to decorate their offices or playrooms with framed album covers or 45 rpm picture sleeves.

If this trend continues, there will be an increasing demand for nice-condition vintage album covers and picture sleeves as objects of art, with little or no regard to the condition of the actual vinyl record inside—or even whether there is a record inside. If you find an attractive Beatles album cover in nice condition at a rummage sale or flea market, it might be worth buying, even if the record inside is in poor condition or even missing—assuming, of course, the cover is priced cheap enough.

Because of their tremendous popularity, most Beatles singles and albums have had several pressings over the years, resulting in many different versions of what appears to be the same record. And every version is valued differently, depending on scarcity. There are, for example, more than a dozen different versions of *Introducing the Beatles*, one of their early albums originally released on the Vee Jay label. To a novice, the various versions may appear almost identical, yet they all have subtle differences that cause their value to range

from under $75 for the common examples to over $3,000 for the scarcer versions. There are similar examples for many Beatles records, making a good record price guide an absolute necessity. (We recommend the *Goldmine Standard Catalog of American Records*.)

No doubt, the Beatles' most interesting album, as far as collectors are concerned, is the so-called "butcher" cover for the original *Yesterday and Today* album. Reportedly to protest the way Capitol Records was chopping up the Beatles' British releases to make additional albums in the U.S., the Beatles originally issued their 1966 *Yesterday and Today* LP with a gory picture of the group dressed in bloody smocks surrounded by dismembered dolls and slabs of raw meat. For the Beatles, especially in the mid-1960s, the gruesome scene was horrifying and so embarrassing to Capitol Records executives that they ordered an immediate recall of the album cover—creating an instant collectible. Capitol solved the problem by pasting a new photo—the one picturing the Beatles standing around a steamer trunk—on top of the offensive photo.

Several versions of the "butcher" cover exist. Albums with the original "butcher" cover that have never been pasted over are known as "first-state" butcher covers and are rare, with stereo versions generally selling in the $5,000-$10,000 range (a pristine, never-opened example recently sold for a record $38,500) and mono versions bringing about half that. Albums with the new "trunk" cover pasted over the "butcher" cover (under a good light you can see it peeking through) are known as "second-state" butcher covers and typically sell in the $500-$2,000 range, depending on condition. A "second-state" butcher cover that has been peeled off (don't try this yourself) to reveal the original cover is sometimes called a "third-state" butcher cover, and, depending on how good the "peel-job" is, may be valued anywhere from $250 to $2,000. Regular "trunk" covers, meanwhile—those released later that never had the "butcher" cover underneath—are generally worth less than $20.

Not every Beatles record is that complicated, of course, but enough variations exist for most of the group's releases that a good record price guide is absolutely essential for evaluating a collection of Beatles records.

Clubs

• Beatles Connection, P.O. Box 1066, Miami, FL 33780

• Beatles Fan Club, 397 Edgewood Ave., New Haven, CT 06511

• Working Class Hero Beatles Club, 3311 Niagara St., Pittsburgh, PA 15213

• Beatlefan, P.O. Box 33515, Decatur, GA 30033

• Good Day Sunshine, P.O. Box 661008, Los Angeles, CA 90066

• Strawberry Fields Forever, P.O. Box 880981, San Diego, CA 92168

Recommended Reading

Books

The Beatles Memorabilia Price Guide, Third Edition, Jeff Augsburger, Marty Eck and Rick Rann

Goldmine Price Guide to Rock 'n' Roll Memorabilia, Mark Allen Baker

Standard Catalog of American Records, Tim Neely

Goldmine Record Album Price Guide, Tim Neely

Goldmine Price Guide to 45 RPM Records, Tim Neely

Goldmine 45 RPM Picture Sleeve Price Guide, Charles Szabla

Goldmine British Invasion Record Price Guide, Tim Neely and Dave Thompson

Periodicals

Goldmine
Discoveries

VALUE LINE

Most of the following values were compiled from the Goldmine Price Guide to Rock 'n' Roll Memorabilia by Mark Allen Baker, published by Krause Publications.

Airbed, Li-Lo, 3' x 6'...........................$325-$750

Alarm Clock, *Yellow Submarine*, 1968, Shefield Watch, $1,500-$3,000

Apron, white paper, shows pictures, names and song titles ....$125-$275

Ashtray, white plastic, with photo......................$175-$325

Assignment book, vinyl, Select-O-Pack ....$125-$250

Autographed photo, all four Beatles ....$2,500-$4,000

Balloon, "Blow up!...a FAB," United Industries, unopened ....$40-$75

Bandage, from movie *Help!* 3-1/2" long, unused, Curad bandage, sealed, 1965, rare, ...$50-$75

Banjo, Mastro, 22", four strings......................$500-$1,000

Bank, "The Beatles Bank," 10", white plastic ...$250-$500

Banks, *Yellow Submarine*, set of four bust figures of each Beatle, 7-1/2", plastic, 1968 ....$1,000-$2,000

Beach hat, red, white and blue ....$50-$75

Beach towel, 35" x 65", Towel Decorations for Cannon ....$125-$225

Beat seat, Unitrend Ldt. ....$200-$400

Bicycle seat, *Yellow Submarine*, Huffy, yellow..$200-$400

Binder, white cover with Beatles images, N.Y. Looseleaf Corp...$60-$125

Bingo Game, Toy Works....................................$40-$75

Birth certificates, set of four facsimile, Davidson's ....$35-$75

Birthday cards, American Greetings, six different, each ....$20-$40

Blanket, 62" x 80", Witney ....$125-$250

Board game, "Beatles Flip Your Wig Game," Milton Bradley, complete................................$95-$150

Bongos, Mastro, two sizes ....$300-$650

Book cover, 1967 Capitol Records promo "Back to Cool" ....$15-$25

Booty Bag, 10" x 15" ....$25-$40

Box, ice cream bar, four-count, Hood Co., 1960s ....$250-$500

Box, ice cream bar, four-count, Townhouse, 1960s ....$400-$800

Box, licorice, held 24 pieces of Record Candy, 1960s ....$300-$600

Bracelets, various styles and designs ....$15-$75

Bread bag, Ringo Roll (custom bag for loaf of bread), 1960s ....$400-$750

Brunch Bag, with Thermos, Aladdin ....$200-$500

Bubble Bath, Colgate, 1965, Paul and Ringo available, each ....$75-$200

Buttons, pinback, many available ....$5-$25

Cake decorations, several variations ....$10-$45

Candy, "Beatle Bar" wrapper, 1960s ....$35-$50

Candy, Lollipop wrapper, 1960s ....$20-$40

Candy, Ringo Candy Rolls, Argentina...................$40-$60

Candy, "Yeah Yeah Candy Sticks" packs, World Candies, set of six ....$800-$1,200

Candy, "Yeah Yeah Candy Sticks" box, held 25 two-stick boxes................................$500-$750

Candy, "Yellow Submarine Sweet Cigarettes" box, Primrose Confectionery ....$200-$300

Candy dishes, set of four, Washington Pottery ....$200-$400

Christmas cards, various available ....$10-$40

The Beatles Phonograph, worth as much as $3,000 in top condition, is considered a treasure among serious collectors.

Christmas Ornament, 1994, Hallmark, complete
with box, stage and microphones ....$100-$125

Christmas seals, Hallmark, 100 color stamps ....$20-$40

Clothes hangers, set of four, Saunders Enterprises,
U.K. ....$200-$400

Coasters, set of four, Canada, soft-drink premium
....$35-$65

Colorforms, Saalfield ....$30-$65

Comb, plastic, Lido Toys, various colors.............$50-$150

Comic Book, *The Beatles Story*, Marvel, 1978......$10-$17

Costumes, Ben Cooper, set of four ....$500-$1,000

Cuff links, PRESS Initial Corp. ....$50-$100

Diary, vinyl, 1965, H.B. Langamm Co.,
Scotland...$25-$40

Dolls, bendy, 10", Newfeld Ldt. ....$90-$175

Dolls, Bobb'n Head, Carmascot, each ....$50-$100

Dolls, inflatable, 13", purple, 1966 ....$60-$120

Doll, mascot, 29", Remco, with guitar and
tag...$400-$700

Dolls, set of four Remco dolls, with instruments,
no boxes ....$250-$400

Dolls, set of four Remco dolls, Mint-in-Box
....$800-$1,000

Dresses, various available ....$300-$650

Drinking glasses, various, each...........................$50-$150

Flasher Button, VariVue, George ....$15-$25

Guitar, Mastro, 21", Four Pops, red and pink plastic,
four-string, Beatles faces and facsimile
autographs on front, U.S. .... $350-$750

The famous, and controversial, "butcher cover" can sell for thousands.

Guitar, Mastro, 5-1/2", miniature pink plastic,
Beatles faces on front, two rubber bands
for strings, U.S. ....$75-$125

Guitar, Mastro, 14-3/4", Junior, pink and burgundy
plastic, four-string, Beatles on body and crown,
U.S...$700-$1,500

Guitar, Mastro, 21", Yeah Yeah, red and burgundy
plastic, six-string, Beatles faces and facsimile
autographs on body, U.S ....$1,000-$2,500

Guitar, Mastro, 30", pink and burgundy plastic,
six-string, Beatles faces and facsimile autographs
on body, U.S... $750-$1,500

Guitar, Selcor, 21" Big Beat, red and orange plastic,
four-string, color photo sticker, facsimile
autographs on front, U.K........................$1,000-$1,750

Guitar, Selcor, 32-1/2", Big Six, orange, red and
burgundy, 6-string plastic, issued in coffin-shaped
cardboard box, U.K....................................$500-$1,000

Guitar, Selcor, 14" Junior, orange body with color
paper photo, sealed with backing board, U.K.
....$1,200-$2,000

Guitar, Selcor, 32-1/2" New Beat, red and burgundy,
four-string, Beatles pictures and facsimile
autographs on front, U.K.............................$400-$750

Guitar, Selcor, 23", New Sound, red or orange and
cream, four-string, Beatles faces and facsimile
autographs on front, U.K............................$750-$1,500

Guitar, Selcor, 31" Red Jet Electric, red and white,
six-string electric, Beatles sticker and facsimile
autographs on front, coffin-shaped cardboard box,
U.K. ....$650-$1,200

Gumball charms, set of four, 3/4" diameter with
loop, reverse has song ....$15-$30

Gumball rings, set of four with mini-records
attached
....$40-$55

The popular Beatles "Flip Your Wig Game" is fairly common but still worth $100 or more.

Gumball wallets, set of four, 1" wide, set ....$35-$50
Hairbrush, Belliston Production, various colors ....$15-$30
Hair clip, "Yeh, Yeh, Yeh," brass ....$40-$75
Hair Pomade, H.H. Cosmetic Labs, unused packet,
    1964 .... $100-$150
Hand puppet, Ringo, World Candies ....$150-$300
Headphones, Koss, with box, earphone stickers
    ....$1,200-$2,000
Kaboodle Kit, Standard Plastic ....$400-$750
Lamp, various table and wall ....$225-$425
Lockets, various, brass ....$45-$80
Lunch Box, Aladdin...$150-$400
Lunch Box, *Yellow Submarine*, steel,
    with Thermos bottle, King Seeley, 1968 ....$200-$500
Magic Slate Game, Merit...................................$250-$500
Magazine, Rolling Stone, Jan. 22, 1981,
    John and Yoko on cover ....$10-$20
Megaphone, "Beatle Bugle," Yell-A-Phone.......$200-$400
Mobile, *Yellow Submarine*, Sunshine Art Studio,
    unassembled ....$50-$125
Model Kits, various, Revell ....$150-$350
Movie Poster, Concert for Bangladesh, 1971,
    one-sheet ....$60-$90
Movie Poster, *A Hard Day's Night,* 1964,
    one-sheet ....$200-$400
Movie Poster, *A Hard Day's Night/Help!*
    combo, 1965, one-sheet ....$400-$650
Movie Poster, *Help!* 1965, one-sheet.................$300-$450
Movie Poster, *Magical Mystery Tour*, 1967,
    one-sheet ....$250-$400
Movie Poster, *Magic Christian* (Ringo, John Cleese
    and Peter Sellers), 1969, one-sheet ....$35-$70
Movie Poster, *Yellow Submarine*, 1968,
    one-sheet ....$600-$900
Napkin, Rolex Paper Co.....................................$15-$20
Oil paintings, for Beatles Buddies Fan Club ....$20-$45
Paperback books, various, mid-1960s...................$10-$20
Perfume, Olive Adair Ldt., "With the Beatles"
    ....$250-$500
Pencil By Number set, Kitfix ....$300-$500

Pennants, many available ....$25-$75
Picture sleeve, from 45 rpm record, 1960s,
    typical example ....$25-$60
Pillows, three varieties, Nordic House, each ....$50-$200
Plate, bamboo, 12" diameter, Beatles photo in center,
    colorful, 1966 ....$125-$200
Playing cards, two decks in same box ....$200-$350
Pom-Pom, 3", black with eyes ....$25-$50
Pom-Pom poster, "We Have Official Beatles
    Pom-Poms" ....$250-$400
Purses, various available ....$90-$200
Program, July 8, 1963, show at Winter Gardens in Mar-
    gate, U.K. ....$300-$400
Puzzle, Fan Club, black and white, marked
    "The Official Beatles Fan Club" ....$30-$50
Puzzle, U.K., Beatles Jigsaw, four available,
    340 pieces, each ....$125-$225
Record carriers, various ....$100-$250
Record case, round, plastic, Charter Industries,
    1966..$50-$150
Record Player, Beatles model #1000 ....$1,500-$3,000
Record rack, Selcol, U.K., holds 40 singles.......$175-$300

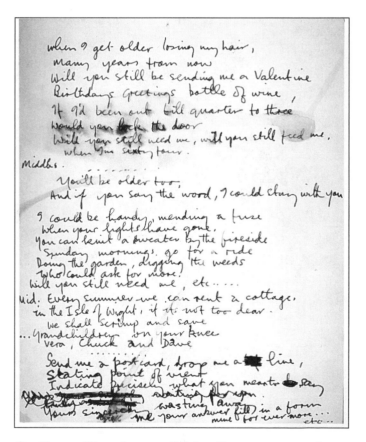

For the really serious collector, there are one-of-a-kind items, like Paul McCartney's handwritten lyrics to "When I'm Sixty-Four." Offered in a Butterfield & Butterfield auction, it sold for a stunning $40,250.

Rug, made in Belgium, 22" x 34" ....$150-$300

Scrapbooks, Whitman, various ....$25-$65

Shampoo box, Bronson Products,
    holds 12 bottles ....$150-$325

Shirts, various, vintage...$50-$150

Souvenir Book, *Hard Day's Night*, Whitman, ...$12-$20

Sunglasses, Solarex...$40-$80

Talcum Powder, Margo of Mayfair, U.K. ....$250-$525

Thermos bottle, blue, 1965 ....$90-$175

Thermos, Yellow Submarine, 1968....................$100-$225

Tennis Shoes, Wing Dings, pair.........................$100-$400

Tennis Shoes, Wing Dings, in original box ....$600-$900

Ticket, unused, pink and black print with photo, Candle-
    stick Park, last concert, Aug. 29, 1966..........$200-$425

Ticket, unused, white with black print, Suffolk Downs,
    Mass., Aug. 18, 1966 ....$75-$125

Ticket, unused, yellow with photo, Shea Stadium, Aug. 23,
    1966...$150-$300

Towel, made in Holland, 20" x 40"....................$100-$225

Tour Program, 1964, U.S ....$40-$75

Trading cards, 165 cards with original wrapper,
    1964 Topps ....$300-$600

Trading cards, *A Hard Day's Night*,
    unopened box of 24 packs, 1964...................$400-$500

Trading cards, *A Hard Day's Night*, set of 55,
    1964...$150-$225

Trading cards, *A Hard Day's Night*,
    one unopened pack, 1964..................................$50-$60

Wall hanging, Germany, linen...........................$150-$300

Wallet, vinyl, various ....$60-$130

Wallpaper, various, rolls or sheets ....$15-$40

Watch, Smiths, U.K. ....$125-$275

Water Color Set, Yellow Submarine ....$100-$150

Wig, two varieties, Bell Toys and Lowell Toys
    ....$300-$400

Wrapper, ice cream bar, Hood Co., 1960s ....$10-$15

Wrapper, ice cream bar, foil, Townhouse, 1960s
    ....$50-$100

Yellow Submarine submarine, Corgi,
    die-cast ....$145-$250

BICYCLES

If you're 35 or older, do you still have that status symbol of your childhood tucked away in your garage?

You know, the top-of-the-line Schwinn Black Phantom, with lots of chrome, a leather padded seat, a spring front fork, and huge balloon tires with wide whitewalls—the expensive model of the 1940s and 1950s, the '57 Chevy of the hobby. Or the "Sting Ray" or "Orange Krate" muscle bikes of the 1960s, with their sissy bars, banana seats, top-bar mounted stick shifts, slick small tires and high-rise handlebars, both which had you riding in style and said you were the coolest kid in the neighborhood…

Background: As far back as 1899, more than one million bikes a year were being produced in the United States. But numbers dropped as styles waned and automobiles became more affordable, until 1933, when Schwinn revived the market by introducing its balloon-tire bike during the "Century of Progress Exposition." But there were other manufacturers, too, who were soon building durable, solid, single-speed bikes tough enough to take the abuse kids could dish out. Although these bikes are still around, but may be lacking some original accessories, often all it takes to get these bikes rolling after years of neglect is a lube job and some air in the tires.

General Guidelines: There are collectors of bicycles from all eras, beginning with the old high-wheel models popular at the turn of the century; but the most active area of this hobby is probably bikes dating from the 1940s through the 1970s.

The beloved Schwinn Black Phantoms—made from 1949-1959, in thick enamel paints of red, green, blue or black—are not exceedingly rare (perhaps a million of them were made) but every collector wants one, especially in an original state. A poor condition Phantom, with original parts and an accessory or two, can be worth $500, while one in better condition, and fairly complete, might fetch $1,200-$2,000. But a nicely restored model will make you king of the neighborhood again—$3,500-$4,500's worth of coolness…

Mid-level models from the 1950s, such as the "Hornet" and "DeLuxe Hornet," were also produced during this time when bikes were gaining new heights of popularity. They are also hard to find in a complete, original state.

Many of these bikes were geared toward the youth market, for this was a time when adults were enamored with their new automobiles. But the styles, influenced by the automobile, had deluxe features, such as front brakes, taillights and spring forks. But even a Hornet in poor condition can bring $100, if it still has its tank and spring fork.

In the 1960s, Schwinn began producing its line of middleweight bicycles—gone were the heavy balloon tires (2.125 inches), replaced by those with a narrower rim and tire (1.75 inches). These bikes, which precede today's lightweight era,

can be found fairly regularly for reasonable prices ($50-$250) if you look at flea markets and garage sales. But remember that condition and completeness are keys to a bicycle's value. Are the paint, rubber and chrome still nice?

Popular Schwinn models from the 1960s include the one-, two- or three-speed model "Jaguar" (1955-60, in green, red, black or blue); the less equipped but similar "Corvette" (1956-63, in green, gold, black or red); and "Panther III," with its half-size tank and front carrier. Even less equipped was the "Tiger," with chrome rims, a chain guard and front rack (1958-67?), and the "Starlet," "Hollywood" and "Typhoon."

However, the core collectors set their sights on the streamlined, classic balloon-tire bicycles from the mid-'30s until the late '50s, when more than 38 million were made with comfort in mind. These fat-tired, shiny chromed bikes, especially prewar models from 1933-41, are among the most valuable and in greatest demand among collectors today.

If the bike from this era is in excellent condition and is an original boys model, it can sell for $3,000-$6,000, in part

The so-called "muscle bikes" of the late 1960s and early 1970s are very hot right now. This 1970 Schwinn Sting Ray "Cotton Picker" was offered at a recent Leslie Hindman auction in Chicago with an estimate of $400-$600.

CHARACTER AND NOVELTY BIKES!

Character-styled bikes were a trend during the late 1940s through the 1950s. (If a bike plays on fantasy or has a character theme, and if the price is right, buy it). Some of the more popular character and novelty bikes include:

The Donald Duck bike, which featured Donald's head mounted on the front, flashing eyes and a battery-operated horn that quacked, was made in 1949 by the Shelby Bicycle Co. in Ohio (in conjunction with Walt Disney).

The Gene Autry bicycle, with a fringed two-tone saddle blanket draped over the top tube and a pony's head in the front, plus a horn with a pistol grip handle, real leather holsters and jewel-studded fenders, was made by Monark Silver King Co.

The Hopalong Cassidy black-and-white "Hoppy" bike, with its six-shooters, horsehair grained saddle and frontier-fringed carrier, was a popular 1950 bike made by Rollfast of New York.

The Huffy Radiobike, introduced in 1955, was a nifty novelty bike that had a radio built into the horn tank and a speaker in the side.

The Bowden Spacelander, which, although designed in 1946, was not introduced to America until 1960, was a funky futuristic-looking model, with fiberglass fenders and frame. It was so far ahead of its time that most kids didn't like it. A failure then, it's considered a real treasure today. With only 300 or so known to exist, original examples in nice condition can sell for $5,000 or more. Although most Spacelanders are now primarily in museums and private collections, several original models have changed hands for prices near $15,000. In 1993, a Kansas firm began producing 150 limited-edition reproductions of the original Bowden Spacelander; each individually-numbered bike, handcrafted to be just like the original, had a $4,100 price tag.

The Schwinn "Phantom" from the late 1950s is considered a classic by collectors. This 1959 example was offered in a Leslie Hindman auction in Chicago with a pre-sale estimate of $1,500.

You can find these classics in antique shops or bike shops, or from a local bicycle repairman. Or you can pedal the pavement by attending flea markets and garage sales. It's also wise to contact your neighbors and friends, read hobby and trade publications, and search/advertise in the want ads of these magazines or local shoppers and newspapers.

Among the other major bike manufacturers is the Columbia Co., one of America's first, which created its showy, souped-up Five-Star Deluxe model in 1948, with a front fender light and rear taillight.

In the 1940s-50s, Dayton-Huffman, of Dayton, Ohio, was popular. The company, which, in 1953, became the more-commonly known Huffy Co., celebrated its 100th anniversary in 1992, making it one of the U.S.'s oldest surviving manufacturers. Models include its "Twin-Flex" (1939); from 1951 on, bikes featuring "Dial-A-Ride" suspension, which could be adjusted to the bike rider's weight.

Collecting Tips: Whether you're starting a collection of vintage bikes, or you're thinking about selling, here are some trends and tips to keep in mind.

Go for quality over quantity. Investing in one or two really nice bicycles is better than gathering a dozen junkers.

While the really old "high-wheelers" from the 1800s can often sell for tens of thousands—and most prewar bikes have more value than postwar bikes—bikes are not necessarily worth more because of age. Design, popularity, scarcity and condition are four key factors in determining a bicycle's value. Design, popularity, scarcity and condition are all more critical.

A hot area today is the "muscle era" bikes from the late '60s and '70s. These include the Schwinn Sting Rays; the "Krate" series, featuring the colors "Orange Krate," "Apple Krate," "Cotton Picker," "Pea Picker," "Lemon Peeler," and "Gray Ghost," the scarcest. Demand for these bikes is growing stronger.

Other leading manufacturers include Sears' Elgin, J.C. Higgins, and Murray.

because those boys, who were usually tougher on their bikes than girls were, often stripped their bikes of its custom-made fenders and chain guards. Today, these boys comprise the majority of those who are collecting bikes today.

Popular models from this time include the sporty "Aerocycle" (1934-35), the "Motorbike" (1935-39), the "Autocycle" (1936-41) and the "DX" models (1937-41). Many are bringing values that are more than 10 times their original retail price.

Unlike other manufacturers during this time, Schwinn, the name people think of most often for quality bikes, had control over every phase of the manufacturing process; in addition to the frames, it made almost all of its own parts and components. Those parts which weren't made by Schwinn were marked with a "Schwinn Approved" stamp.

Deluxe versions of bikes—those with lights, speedometers, horns and other original built-in accessories—are more popular with collectors than a stripped-down version of the same model. Many collectors also like flashy bikes with lots of chrome.

Generally speaking, boys' bikes in nice condition are worth more than the corresponding girls' models, in part because boys were tougher on bikes. Also, more men collect bikes today than women do.

Novelty and character bikes are also popular. Some of the most popular specialty bikes include the Hopalong Cassidy model from Rollfast, the Donald Duck model made by Shelby, Monark's Gene Autry model and Huffy's Radiobike.

Most collectors specialize, restricting their collections to one manufacturer, a certain era, or even a specific model. Once you have the bike in the condition you want, you can then concentrate on finding the corresponding memorabilia to go with it, including the original owner's manual, advertising and promotional material.

Caution: If a bike has been improperly or poorly restored, it might be worth less than as if it had been left alone. If done properly and expertly, however, a restored bike can be as valuable as a very good original. But in general, look for complete bikes; restoring and finding original parts can be costly, maybe more than would it would have cost to buy a nice-condition bike in the first place.

Today's 10-speed bikes and mountain bikes probably will not be considered collectibles. The end of the muscle bikes era marks the end of the bikes sought by collectors. Exceptions might include limited-edition versions of classics, however.

Clubs

• The Wheelmen, 63 Stonebridge Road, Allen Park, NJ 07042

• League of American Bicyclists, 1612 K Street NW, Washington, DC 20006

• Vintage Bicycle Club of America, 325 W. Hornbeam Drive, Longwood, FL 32779

• International Veteran Cycle Association, 248 Highland Drive, Findlay, OH 45840

COLLECTOR'S ALERT!

As bicycle collecting grows in popularity, more and more reproduction parts are becoming available. While purists want their bikes to be all original, some less serious collectors will often accept bikes with repro parts. Be sure you know what you're buying!

VALUE LINE

Ranges shown are for bicycles in Excellent to Mint condition.

Schwinn Classics

Aerocycle Model 34	$7,000-$10,000
Model 35 DeLuxe	$3,500-$4,000
B-107 Autocycle	$1,200-$2,000
B-607 DeLuxe Autocycle	$1,200-$2,500
Phantom Model B-17	$1,000-$3,500
Panther Model D-27	$750-$2,200
Panther Girl's Model D-77	$700-$1,400
Starlet Model D-67	$350-$700
Mark II Jaguar	$500-$1,200
Manta-Ray, 1971	$100-$150
Corvette	$250-$450
Tiger	$150-$300
Flying Star	$150-$300
Sting Ray Cotton Picker (white)	$400-$600
Sting Ray Lemon Peeler (yellow)	$300-$500
Wasp	$100-$300
Spitfire	$100-$300
Hornet	$200-$600
Traveler	$100-$300
Racer	$100-$300
Paramount	$500-$1,000

Columbia

Twinbar	$2,500-$4,000
3-Star	$300-$600
5-Star	$750-$2,000
Fire Arrow	$250-$450
Firebolt	$150-$400
Hartford Special, Ladies, 1938	$500-$800

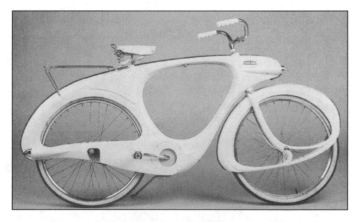

The Bowden "Spacelander" was so advanced in its design that kids didn't even want it. But today's collectors consider it a treasure, often paying as much as $5,000 or more when they come up for sale. This one was sold in a Leslie Hindman auction in Chicago.

Novelty and specialty bikes, like this 1949 Donald Duck model by Shelby, are very desirable. This example was offered in a Leslie Hindman auction in Chicago with a $2,000 estimate.

Elgin
Bluebird...$5,000-$10,000
Blackhawk...$2,750-$4,000
Skylark...$1,500-$2,500
Robin...$3,000-$4,000
Twin 30 ....$650-$800
Twin 40 ....$1,750-$2,500

Twin 50 ....$4,000-$5,000
Twin 60 ....$6,000-$8,000
Miscellaneous
JC Higgins Color-Flow ....$750-$2,000
JC Higgins Flightliner....................................$150-$400
Sears Spaceliner...$150-$350
Monark Silver King Hex Tube........................$850-$1,500
Monark Silver King Flo-Cycle ....$2,750-$3,500
Monark Super DeLuxe.................................$750-$2,200
Monark Holiday..$650-$1,750
Shelby Airflow...$7,500-$10,000
Hawthorne Standard Duralium ....$500-$700
Hawthorne Airflow ....$2,750-$3,500
Huffman Champion Model 10SF...................$750-$1,100
Rollfast Custom Built Model V-200 ....$2,500-$3,000
Evinrude Streamflow ....$6,000-$8,000
Roadmaster Jet Pilot ....$100-$300
Roadmaster Luxury Liner.............................$650-$1,000
Raleigh English Three-Speed ....$100-$300
Rudge tandem bicycle, three-wheeler, 1889
....$15,000-$18,000

Novelty, Character, Specialty
Rollfast Hopalong Cassidy model ....$2,000-$4,000
Monark Gene Autry model ....$1,500-$2,750
Shelby Donald Duck model........................$1,750-$3,500
Huffy Radiobike..$1,200-$2,500
Bowden 300 Spacelander............................$5,000-$9,000

Big Little Books &
Little Golden Books

As collectibles, Big Little Books and Little Golden books both have a lot going for them. They are wonderfully colorful, great to display, a manageable size, and, depending on your age, extremely nostalgic. There is hardly a person alive who doesn't have fond memories of these classic children's books.

Another advantage: For the most part, Big Little Books and Little Golden Books are still very affordable; and, unlike, many other collectibles, it is still possible to occasionally stumble across a real bargain at a garage sale or flea market.

Background: Whitman Publishing of Racine, Wisconsin, was the pioneer in this field. The company's line of Big Little Books was launched in 1932, and they lived up to their oxymoron name. The books were "big" in content, often topping 400 pages and an inch-and-a-half thick; but they were "little" in overall size, measuring just 3-3/4 by 4-1/2 inches— the perfect size for kids to carry.

The concept was right for the time. Priced at just ten or fifteen cents, even Depression-era families could afford them, and kids loved the easy-to-read format, which featured text on the left-hand pages and simple black-and-white illustrations on the right-hand pages.

The first title in the Big Little Books series was *The Adventures of Dick Tracy.* An instant success, it was soon followed by more books based on other characters from the popular comic-strips, radio shows and movies of the day, including Tarzan, Mickey Mouse, Little Orphan Annie, Moon Mullins, Roy Rogers, Captain Midnight, Flash Gordon and dozens of others. The Big Little Books were popular throughout the 1930s and '40s, and by 1950, there were more than 700 different titles in the series.

(Inspired by Whitman's success, a competing publisher, Saalfield, published a copycat line of books called "Little Big Books" in the mid- to late-1930s, which are often collected alongside the Big Little Books and bring similar prices.)

 Ten years after the introduction of Big Little Books, Western Publishing, the parent company of Whitman, introduced another line of inexpensive children's books called Little Golden Books.

The look was different—Little Golden Books were thinner volumes, usually about 42 pages, and they featured some pages with full color—but the concept was the same: Small, affordable books that kids could read and carry around with them.

When first introduced, Little Golden Books retailed for 25 cents. They measured approximately 6-1/2 inches wide by 8 inches high—an unusual size for the book industry at the time, but a size that was distinctive and proved to be very popular with both kids and their parents.

The first twelve Little Golden Books were released in October of 1942. The original titles in the series were: *Three Little Kittens, Bedtime Stories, The Alphabet From A to Z, Mother Goose, Prayers for Children, The Little Red Hen, Nursery Songs, The Poky Little Puppy, The Golden Book of Fairy Tales, Baby's Book, The Animals of Farmer Jones*, and *This Little Piggy.* Today, in nice condition, these original twelve can sell for $50 each or more.

The books were wildly popular, selling more than one-and-a-half-million copies within the first few months of their release, and the line quickly expanded to eventually include hundreds of titles over the next half-century. Some of the titles were based on things and events that kids experienced in their everyday lives (getting a pet, going to the circus, playing baseball, shopping with Mom, going to the doctor, etc.);

COLLECTOR'S TIP!

CHECK THE EDITION!

First editions are always the most valuable. With Little Golden Books, you can determine the edition by looking at the lower right-hand corner of the last page. The letter printed there will identify the printing. An "A" indicates a first printing, a "B" indicates a second-printing, and so on. First editions are most desirable and bring the highest prices. Subsequent printings may be valued at 25 to 75 percent the value of a first printing.

Little Golden Books were numbered (from 1 to 600), but they were not necessarily numbered in chronological order, and the numbering can be confusing. Many of the more popular titles were re-issued over the years with different numbers (Poky Little Puppy, for example, can be found with six different numbers, and each has a different value). So, when using the price list below (or when consulting a price guide) it is essential to know both the book title and its number.

Also, some Little Golden Books contained "extras." Doctor Dan the Bandage Man, for example, came with a half-dozen Band-Aids inside; and a book called Little Lulu and Her Magic Tricks had a small package of Kleenex attached to the cover. These books are extremely desirable with collectors today, but they must include the extras to command top dollar.

while other titles were based on licensed characters, like Snow White, Bugs Bunny, or Huckleberry Hound. To its credit, Western Publishing secured licensing agreements with almost every hot property to come along, so over the next several decades there were Little Golden Books featuring characters from Disney, Hanna-Barbera, Warner Brothers, Howdy Doody, Sesame Street, Barbie and others. All, of course, are extremely popular with today's collectors.

General Guidelines: For both Big Little Books and Little Golden Books, value depends on the title of the book, the edition of the book, and its condition. In general, the majority of Big Little Books (in average collectible condition) sell in the $20-$50 range; while vintage Little Golden Books (generally from the 1940s through the early 1960s) are often found in the $10-$35 range. Most Little Golden Books from the 1970s and newer are worth less than $5. (The Little Golden Books included in the listings below date mostly from the 1940s and 1950s.)

Condition is critical, however. Big Little Books, especially, are tough to find in nice condition. They were not designed for permanence. They were made with cheap, pulp paper and inexpensive bindings, and were intended for kids to carry around and read with dirty fingers. Few survived in Mint condition. Little Golden Books were of a slightly better quality, but they, too, saw lots of handling and rough treatment. Today, Mint examples from either series command substantial premiums—generally valued at a minimum of twice the value of an example in Very Good or Good condition. Most collectors today are happy with a nice, clean copy that displays well, so the condition of the cover is especially important. Examples with torn or missing pages are generally passed over by most collectors, and have very little value.

The majority of Big Little Books, like this example, sell for prices in the $25-$50 range.

Regarding titles, the books featuring licensed characters are far more desirable than the "generic" titles. This holds true for both Big Little Books and Little Golden Books. As you might expect, books featuring Disney characters are the most desirable. Also popular are other animated figures (Warner Brothers, Hanna-Barbera, etc.), Western heroes (Roy Rogers, Gene Autry, Red Ryder, etc.), space adventurers (Buck Rogers, Flash Gordon, etc.), other comic strip and radio and TV personalities (Blondie, Tarzan, The Shadow, Leave It to Beaver, etc.) and real-life celebrities, like Shirley Temple.

Clubs
•Golden Book Club, 19626 Ricardo Ave., Hayward, CA 94541

•Big Little Book Collector Club of America, P.O. Box 1242 , Danville, CA 94526

Recommended Reading
Collecting Little Golden Books, Third Edition, Steve Santi

VALUE LINE

Big Little Books
Values shown are for books in Fine condition. Books in Mint condition will be worth two to three times the value indicated; books in Good condition will be worth approximately half the value shown.

Ace Drummond	$22
The Adventures of Huckleberry Finn	$40
Alley Oop and Dinky	$25
Andy Panda and the Pirate Ghosts	$25
The Arizona Kid	$15
Bambi's Children	$40
Believe or Not by Ripley	$28
Betty Boop in "Miss Gulliver's Travels"	$90
Big Chief Wahoo	$22
Big Little Mother Goose (scarce)	$750
"Blondie" titles	$22-$27
Brenda Starr and the Masked Impostor	$25
Bringing Up Father	$40
"Buck Jones" titles	$25
Buck Rogers 25th Century AD	$100
Buck Rogers on the Moons of Saturn (softcover, scarce)	$250
"Buck Rogers" other titles	$50-$75
"Bugs Bunny" titles	$35-$40
Captain Easy Behind Enemy Lines	$15
Captain Midnight and the Moon Woman	$50
Charlie Chan Solves a New Mystery	$35
Chester Gump in the City of Gold	$25
Cowboy Lingo	$15
"Dan Dunn" titles	$25

David Copperfield..$18

The Adventures of Dick Tracy Detective (first title in BLB series) $600

"Dick Tracy" most other titles ....$30-$50

"Donald Duck" titles...$45-$50

Don Winslow Navy Intelligence Ace $25

Dumbo..$45

Eddie Cantor in "An Hour With You"...........................$75

"Felix the Cat" titles ....$50-$60

Flash Gordon and the Monsters of Mongo (softcover) $300

"Flash Gordon" most other titles ....$50-$75

Frank Merriwell at Yale $15

Gang Busters in Action $30

"Gene Autry" most titles..$30-$45

"G-Man" most titles...$20-$25

"Green Hornet" most titles.....................................$60-$80

Hall of Fame of the Air $18

Jack Armstrong and the Ivory Treasure $25

Jane Withers in Keep Smiling $40

Joe Louis the Brown Bomber $65

John Carter of Mars..$75

Kazan King of the Pack $20

Ken Maynard in Western Justice $25

Li'l Abner in New York..$40

Little Miss Muffet $22

Little Orphan Annie and the Ghost Gang (softcover) $160

Little Orphan Annie (#708)......................................$75

"Little Orphan Annie" most other titles.................$45-$60

Little Women $25

"The Lone Ranger" most titles ....$30-$35

Mac of the Marines in China $28

"Maximo" titles..$25-$32

Mickey Mouse (#717), first version with "Walt Disney" facsimile signature on cover, Mickey looking right), scarce..$750

Mickey Mouse (#717), second version, no signature, re-drawn Mickey looking left, scarce $500

Mickey Mouse and the Bat Bandit, scarce $375

"Mickey Mouse" most other titles ....$50-$75

Mickey Rooney Himself $35

Moon Mullins and the Plushbottom Twins (softcover) $200

Moon Mullins and the Plushbottom Twins (regular).....$32

Mutt and Jeff $65

Nancy and Sluggo $50

Og Son of Fire $20

"Peggy Brown" titles ....$20-$25

"The Phantom" most titles $50

Pinocchio and Jiminy Cricket $50

"Popeye" most titles...$35-$45

"Radio Patrol" most titles $20

"Red Ryder" most titles ....$30-$35

"Roy Rogers" most titles ....$35-$40

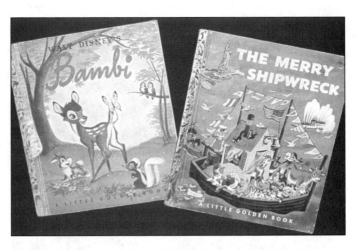

The majority of vintage Little Golden Books, those dating from the 1940s to the 1960s, sell in the $10-$30 range. Most examples from the 1970s and newer are worth $5 or less.

"The Shadow" most titles ....$90-$120

Skippy..$32

"Smilin' Jack" most titles $30

Snow White and the Seven Dwarfs.............................$50

The Spy..$25

Tailspin Tommy The Dirigible to the North Pole $140

"Tailspin Tommy" most other titles ....$30-$40

Tarzan Twins (softcover)..$275

"Tarzan" most other titles.......................................$35-$45

The Texas Kid $18

"Tim McCoy" most titles $35

"Tiny Tim" titles $50

Tom Mix the Fighting Cowboy (softcover)...................$175

"Tom Mix" most other titles $35

Union Pacific...$28

Wimpy the Hamburger Eater $35

"Zane Grey" most titles ....$25-$30

Little Golden Books

Values shown are for books in Fine-to-Excellent condition. Add approximately 25 percent for books in Mint condition. Examples in Good condition are worth about 25 percent less than values shown.

ABC is for Christmas (#108), 1974 ....$6-$8

Alphabet From A to Z (#3) ....$40-$50

Animal Babies (#39), 1947 ....$15-$20

The Animals of Farmer Jones (#11), 1942............$40-$50

The Animals of Farmer Jones (#211)......................$7-$10

Annie Oakley and the Rustlers (#221), 1955 ....$22-$27

Baby Dear (#466), 1962 ....$15-$20

Baby Listens (#383), 1960 ....$12-$16

Baby's Book (#10), 1942, original title ....$75-$85

Bambi (#D7), 1948..$20-$25

Barbie (#125), 1974 ....$10-$12

Bedtime Stories (#2) ....$40-$50

Bugs Bunny (#72), 1949.......................................$20-$25

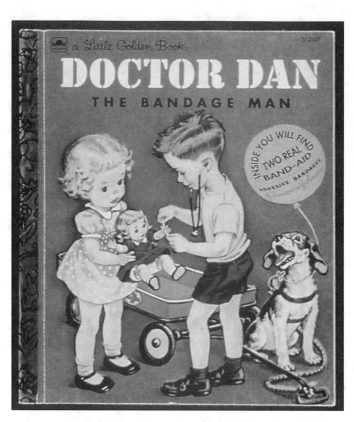

The "Doctor Dan" Little Golden Book, if found with the original Band-Aids inside the front cover, is worth about $125.

Bugs Bunny Gets a Job (#136), 1952.....................$12-$15
Bugs Bunny Pioneer (#161), 1977 ....$6-$8
Busy Timmy (#50), 1948 ....$30-$35
The Christmas Story (#158), 1952 ....$10-$14
Captain Kangaroo (#261), 1956 ....$14-$18
Counting Rhymes (#12), 1947..............................$15-$20
Dale Evans and the Lost Gold Mine (#213),
    1954..$22-$26
Davy Crockett's Keelboat Race (#D47), 1955 ....$20-$25
Dennis the Menace A Quiet Afternoon (#412),
    1960..$10-$15
Dinosaurs (#355), 1959 ....$7-$10
Disneyland on the Air (D43), 1958 ....$15-$20
Doctor Dan the Bandage Man (#111), 1950,
    with Band-Aids inside..................................$110-$125
Donald Duck Instant Millionaire (#D140),
    1978..$5-$10
Donald Duck Private Eye (#D94), 1961 ....$15-$20
Donny and Marie (#160), 1977 ....$6-$9
Exploring Space (#342), 1958 ....$7-$10
The First Little Golden Book of Fairy Tales (#9),
    1942, second cover..$20-$25
Five Little Firemen (#64), 1948 ....$20-$25
Fix It Please (#32), 1947.......................................$30-$35
Frosty the Snowman (#142), 1951 ....$12-$15

Fun With Decals (#139), 1952, uncut ....$135-$150
Fury (#286), 1957 ....$15-$20
Gene Autry (#230), 1955......................................$24-$28
Goofy Movie Star (#D52), 1956.............................$18-$22
The Golden Book of Birds (#13), 1943 ....$25-$30
The Golden Book of Fairy Tales (#9), 1942...........$40-$50
The Golden Book of Flowers (#16), 1943..............$30-$35
Gunsmoke (#320), 1958 ....$20-$25
Hansel and Gretel (#17) 1943, original cover
    (kids standing)..$25-$30
Hansel and Gretel (#17), 1943, second cover
    (kids sitting) ....$12-$16
Hansel and Gretel (#217), 1954 ....$7-$10
Heidi (#192), 1954..$10-$12
Hopalong Cassidy and the Bar 20 Cowboy (#147),
    1952..$30-$35
Howdy Doody and Clarabell (#121), 1951............$28-$32
Howdy Doody's Circus (#99), 1950......................$30-$35
How Big? (#83), 1949..$15-$20
J. Fred Muggs (#234), 1955 ....$18-$22
The Jetsons (#500), 1962 ....$28-$32
Lassie Shows the Way (#255), 1956......................$15-$20
Leave It to Beaver (#347), 1959 ....$28-$32
Let's Go Shopping (#33), 1948 ....$15-$20
The Life and Legend of Wyatt Earp (#315),
    1958..$17-$22
Linda and Her Little Sister (#214), 1954...............$75-$85
Little Black Sambo (#57), 1948, 42-page edition
    ....$160-$175
Little Black Sambo (#57), 1948, 28-page edition
    ....$100-$115
Little Black Sambo (#57), 1948,
    24-page edition..$60-$70
The Little Fat Policeman (#91), 1950 ....$15-$20
Little Golden Book of Hymns (#34), 1947 ....$15-$20
The Little Golden Paper Dolls (#113), 1951,
    uncut..$135-$150
Little Pee Wee (#52), 1948 ....$20-$25
Little Lulu and Her Magic Tricks (#203), 1954, with
    Kleenex $75
The Little Red Hen (#6), 1942, original cover showing hen
    on ground ....$40-$50
The Little Red Hen (#6), 1942, second cover showing hen
    at table ....$20-$25
Little Red Riding Hood (#42), 1948......................$15-$20
Little Red Riding Hood (#42), 1948 Puzzle Edition
    ....$100-$125
The Lone Ranger (#284), 1956 ....$24-$28
Mickey Mouse and His Space Ship (#D29),
    1952..$18-$22
Mister Ed the Talking Horse (#483), 1962 ....$20-$25
Mother Goose (#4), 1942.......................................$40-$50
My Baby Brother (#279), 1956 ....$24-$28
My First Book (#10), 1942, cover shows baby with teddy
    bear...$40-$50

My First Book (#10), 1942, new cover shows little girl
with book...$20-$25

My Teddy Bear (#168), 1953................................$25-$30

The New Kittens (#302), 1957 ....$8-$12

National Velvet (#431), 1961 ....$12-$16

The Night Before Christmas (#20), 1946, original cover
(Santa in sleigh) ....$30-$35

The Night Before Christmas (#20), 1949, second cover
(Santa on roof) ....$15-$20

The Night Before Christmas (#20), 1949, third cover (large
Santa) ....$8-$12

Noah's Ark (#109), 1969...................................$6-$8

Nursery Songs (#7), 1942, original cover showing boy and
girl on ground.......................................$40-$50

Nursery Songs (#7), 1942, second cover showing boy and
girl dancing ....$20-$25

Nursery Tales (#14), 1943.................................$25-$30

Old Yeller (#D65), 1957..................................$12-$16

Pets for Peter (#82), 1950 ....$15-$20

Peter Pan and Wendy (#D25), 1952.........................$20-$25

Pets for Peter (#82), 1950, Puzzle Edition.........$100-$115

Play Ball! (#325), 1958..................................$9-$12

Pollyanna (#D91), 1960...................................$20-$25

The Poky Little Puppy (#8), 1942.........................$40-$50

The Poky Little Puppy (#271)..............................$7-$10

Prayers for Children (#5), 1942..........................$40-$50

Rin Tin Tin (#276), 1956.................................$15-$20

Rootie Kazootie Baseball Star (#190), 1954.........$30-$35

Roy Rogers and the New Cowboy (#177), 1953 ....$25-$30

Rudolph the Red-Nosed Reindeer (#331), 1958 ......$7-$10

Ruff and Reddy (#378), 1959 ....$8-$12

The Saggy Baggy Elephant (#36), 1947.................$20-$25

Scuffy the Tugboat (#244), 1955 ....$7-$10

Sesame Street The Together Book (#315), 1971 ....$4-$7

Snow White and the Seven Dwarfs (#D4), 1948 ....$20-$25

This Little Piggy (#12), 1942 ....$50-$60

Three Little Kittens (#1), 1942..........................$40-$50

Tom and Jerry (#117), 1951 ....$15-$18

Topsy Turvy Circus (#161), 1953 ....$15-$20

Touche Turtle (#474), 1962 ....$20-$25

Toys (#22), 1945...$25-$30

Two Little Gardeners (#108), 1951 ....$15-$20

Winnie-the-Pooh Meets Gopher (#D117), 1972 ......$5-$10

Wizard of Oz (#119), 1975 ....$8-$10

Yogi Bear (#395), 1960 ....$20-$25

BLACK AMERICANA

As with Native American memorabilia, which was even slower to blossom, Black Americana hit the collecting scene late but quickly grew into a profitable and varied field. The category encompasses kitchen items, advertising, dolls and toys, photographs and paper items, political items, figurals and more. Items in this category either depict African-Americans or can be directly attributed to black artisans.

While controversy abounds as to the appropriateness of collecting black memorabilia—much of the vintage material features derogatory phrases and caricatured illustrations, made to reinforce ethnic stereotypes—black collectibles have been widely accepted as important reminders of a critical part of our nation's history. The field has been especially embraced by much of the black community. Many collectors, however, still avoid the extremely degrading works and focus on folk art, literature, photographs and everyday items.

Background: Often the early black collectibles portray slaves, exaggerate and distort facial features or—on the other extreme—depict Blacks of great beauty. Beginning in 1850 items were mass-produced and marked with the manufacturer's name. Products from earlier times are most likely handmade.

Throughout the first half of the 20th century, the production of black memorabilia greatly increased. Rag dolls, cookie jars, decorative items and other household items became common. Also on the rise were items created by

This Mammy cookie jar is one of many cookie jars with a Black Americana theme.

black artists—mainly furniture and decorative pieces—which were often unsigned or unmarked. It was not until the 1960s that many companies stopped using negative portrayals of African-Americans in their advertisements.

Much of the material produced since that time commemorates famous African-Americans and their accomplishments, and shows the strength and loving nature of the black family. Two of the most popular collections of limited edition items currently being produced are Thomas Blackshear's Ebony Visions line of elegant figurines, and the numbered and dated Daddy's Long Legs dolls by Karen Germany.

General guidelines: As this field develops and stabilizes, prices will also stabilize. In general, the early items—consisting largely of paintings, toys and dolls—can be quite expensive if found in good condition. Manufactured pieces of great quality and rarity can fetch prices as high as those paid for the handmade pieces. Vintage pieces that do not exaggerate peoples' features are considered very rare.

Pieces with specific historic ties—first-person accounts of slavery, photographs of influential figures—command some of the highest prices in this field. For example, a typed manuscript of a 1963 interview between Alex Haley and Malcolm X, done for Playboy magazine, sold in 1996 for more than $12,000.

Here are a few of the more popular categories among collectors of Black Americana.

Kitchen—Kitchen items are popular for their display potential. Salt-and-pepper shakers, creamer sets, glasses, teapots and cookie jars with a black theme are all plentiful. A common salt-and-pepper pair can be found for less than $20, while others can command prices upwards of $500, and scarce kitchen items can go for thousands of dollars. The immensely popular mammy cookie jar is most often found with quite a bit of paint wear and chips or dings. Prices reflect this, however pieces without such flaws are scarce.

Advertising—Advertising pieces depicting products and scenes of Black Americana are also appealing when displayed. They have been made for a wide variety of products, ranging from tobacco and whiskey to soap and pancake flour. The most derogatory ads are also often the most rare. Trade cards are a form of advertising that is highly collectible and increasing in value. These ads were given away with the purchase of any of a great number of household products. Many trade cards depicting Black themes are extremely degrading; but because of their historical significance, values are rising for these pieces as well. Average prices range from $5 to $25.

Condition dictates value with all ads, so look for pieces with the least number of tears and holes, and with the sharpest corners.

Paper collectibles and Photographs—Within the arena of vintage postcards, photos and pictorials, images of black children and babies are less common than those of men and women. Vintage pictures of famous personalities and black military men are very rare. The most rare pictorial images can cost more than $100. The postcard is the most common form of these pictorials, typically available for less than $10.

With books and magazines, vintage items published by black authors are rare, garnering the highest prices. Black-themed magazines, such as *Opportunity* and *Jet*, usually retail for $5 to $20 each. Vintage *Time* and *Life* magazines with blacks on the cover often sell for $20 to $75. Original-edition books by authors such as Sojourner Truth, Booker T. Washington and W.E.B. DuBois can command top dollar.

Toys and Dolls—Toys and dolls with black themes are highly collectible, especially when found in nice condition. The number of aggressive collectors looking for intact, working toys is great and growing, and prices reflect that demand.

Since most toys were played with, top-condition old toys are very expensive, due to their scarcity. Vintage toys with black themes vary greatly, ranging from as low as $40 on up into the thousands.

Black dolls, especially "golliwogs" (black rag dolls with exaggerated features), are especially collectible. Some of the more common dolls cost as little as $20; rarer dolls may sell for $400 or more. Look for rare blackface baseball and football bobbing-head dolls that were made in the 1960s; they are worth from $400 to $1,200 today.

Miscellaneous—Prominent Blacks were pictured on coins, paper money and tokens. Booker T. Washington and George Washington Carver appeared on commemorative silver half dollars (worth $30 to $50 each today). Confederate paper money may be found depicting blacks at work (valued at $10 to $30). Tokens known as "slave tokens" date back to the 18th and 19th centuries. Considered scarce, they are generally only found in museums and major private collections today.

Stamps that feature blacks are unusual, but can be found from most dealers for under $10, although some scarcer ones can go as high as $40.

Figurals and containers depicting Black Americans are typically ceramic, but are also found made of wood or metal. The figurals are mostly of men, and the best examples date back to the late 1800s and early 1900s. The value of figurals is considerable, usually $100 and up, with the scarcest running into the thousands of dollars. Containers can hold many types of things, from cookies to tobacco to salt and pepper. These items can run into the hundreds of dollars, but beware of reproductions.

Political memorabilia, posters and buttons that denounce racism and promote black rights are also very col-lectible. Vintage posters range in value from $50 to $125, with the rarest fetching up to $500. Buttons can be found in the $15 to $50 range.

Clubs
• Black Memorabilia Collectors Association, 2482 Devoe Terrace, Bronx, NY 10468

Recommended Reading
The Encyclopedia of Black Collectibles, Dawn E. Reno
Black Americana Price Guide, Kyle Husfloen

VALUE LINE

Values shown are items in Excellent or better condition.

Kitchen Items
Aunt Jemima's Restaurant paper plate, 1940s image of Aunt Jemima, 9" diameter $60
Aunt Jemima placemat, paper, 10-1/2" x 13-1/2", full color, "Story of Aunt Jemima and her Pancake Days," 1950s $35

Black figures were often depicted on boxes on food, soaps and other products, often in a stereotypical fashion. This vintage box of "Fun-to-Wash Washing Powder" is valued in the $20-$30 range.

Bottle opener, cast iron, figural black man and alligator $35

Coffee tin, paper label, mammy, Luzianne, 13" diameter $50

Condiment set, nude natives and straw hut, comical, Japan, 5" long $195

Cookie jar, "Someone's Kitchen," mammy, 1989, Department 56, 11" high, Mint $150

Covered sugar and creamer set, "Someone's Kitchen," Department 56, 1989, Mint $125

Salt and pepper, Aunt Jemima and Uncle Mose, F&F Mold & Die Co., 5" $65

Salt and pepper, Black babies in basket, three-piece ceramic set, 1950s, Japan $125

Salt and pepper, Black Jonah and the Whale, interlocking, brown-skinned boy wears only red shorts, exaggerated ethnic features, rides atop black whale, 1950s $95

Salt and pepper, native girl and alligator, girl is 4" high, vintage Japan $125

Salt and pepper, figural mammy and pappy $75

Salt and pepper, "naughty" female nude, three-piece set, red clay, body forms holder for two "large" shakers, Japan, 1940s $95

Salt and pepper, Sambo on alligator, ceramic, vintage Japan $125

Spice shakers, set of five, Mammy and Chef, 3", fully embossed figures, 1930s $250

Spoon, sterling silver, engraved "New Orleans," man eating watermelon, floral border $200

Spoon rest, pottery, mammy wall hanging, 8" x 6", dark brown pottery skin tone, bandanna features large embossed yellow polka dots, large rose lips and white teeth protrude $165

Sugar shaker, mammy, no stopper $30

Syrup holder, Aunt Jemima, plastic, 1930s $50

Swizzle sticks, glass, set of six, Black figures on top $130

Syrup pail, paper label, "Southern Plantation Pure Georgia Cane Syrup" $95

Victorian-era trade cards often had stereotypical depictions of Black Americans. This example sold at auction for $210.

Tablecloth, 48" x 52", mammy in each corner, dad and kids, red checks in center $125

Tablecloth, 48" x 52", man eating watermelon, woman carrying pie, children $125

Paper Items, Advertising and Photographs

Advertising packing label, Small Black Brand, Delta Packing Co., shows black baby $20

Book, *A Treasury of Stephen Foster*, hardcover, first edition, 1946, Random House, with dust jacket $75

Book, *All About Amos n' Andy and Their Creators*, hardcover, Correll & Gosden, 1929 .... $55

Book, *Little Brown Koko*, children's hardcover, dust jacket, first edition, illustrated, 1940 .... $95

Book, *Noddy Goes To Toyland*, Enid Blyton, no date, dust jacket, hardcover, 60 pp., color illustrations by Beek $50

Book, *Rowena Teena Tot and the Blackberries*, 1934, Albert Whitman & Co., school copy $50

Book, *Swanee River*, Stephen C. Foster $75

Book, *The Three Golliwogs* by Enid Blyton, 1968, Dean & Son, b&w illustrations $75

Book, *Where's Monkey?* by Enid Blyton, first story in 1930s *Collins Little Folks Annual*, England $90

Booklet, "The Gold Dust Twins at Work and Play," 1904, N.K. Fairbank Co., Chicago, sketched by E.W. Kemble $90

Cigar box label, Lime Kiln Club, 7-1/2" x 6-1/4", color litho, busy scene depicting a multitude of ethnic stereotypes including an alligator hanging from the ceiling, 1880s $195

Envelope cover, Deluth Imperial Flour, black chef with bag of flour and loaf of bread, picture of factory on back $50

Handbill, play, *Tourists in a Pullman Palace Car*, color, 3" x 5", features porters toting feather dusters, late 1800s $40

Matchbooks, case, "Golden West Hotel, San Diego, Calif.," colorful graphic on each matchbook, porter carrying bags $125

Paper doll book, *Betty and Billy*, Whitman, 1955 .... $125

Photo, framed b/w photo of black couple in Art Deco setting $20

Portrait, young lady in an old frame, 14" x 20" $135

Sheet music, "Dat's De Way To Spell Chicken," stereotype caricature of fellow at blackboard, 1903 .... $45

Sheet music, "Down in Alabam" by J. Warner, 1936 .... $18

Sheet music, "Sam the Accordion Man," six pages, 1926, Walter Donaldson $25

Pamphlet, "Aunt Jemima's Kitchen," shows picture of restaurant, 4" x 6" $65

Playing cards, double deck in box, Tamko Roof advertising, 1930s $165

Pop-up book, *Little Black Sambo*, 1934, Blue Ribbon Press $135

Postcard, advertising, "Jocular Jinks of Kornelia Kinks,"
No. 5 Series "A," 1907 The H-O Company $35

Postcard, embossed with silk insets, "Four of a Kind," car-
icatures of four young men wearing fancy silk
enhanced clothing, "Germany," postmarked
1908 .... $40

Print, "Lil' Moses Dog—Pore Lil' Dog," 1901,
15" x 11" $85

Print, "Little Black Sambo," in original mailing envelope,
1940s, color, artist-signed $95

Show program, "Rollicking Rotary Minstrels Fund
Raiser," 1918, brown-skinned minstrels with
banjo $65

Trade card, Aunt Jemima, die cut $50

Trade card, "Let Dinah Black Tell you the Story," mammy,
mechanical with moving eyes and mouth,
1920s $20

Trade card, Dixon's Stove Polish, mammy and
cherub $27

Trade card, Finnegan & Co., set of four, minstrels, pre-
1900, color litho $125

Trade card, Domestic Sewing Machine Company, pre-
1900, color litho $27

Trade card, Edwin C. Burn Fine Shoes, color litho $25

Trade card, Jackson Wagon, pre-1900, color litho $30

Toys and Dolls

Banjo, plastic carnival toy, 16" long, images of men playing banjo $40

Board game, "Rise 'N Fly," 1984, black heritage trivia
game $80

Bobbing-head doll, Chicago White Sox, 1960s $400

Dancin Dan, 1920s, wood dancer on wooden
paddle $75

Dancing Minstrel, wood jointed "dancer" on a wood pad-
dle $30

Doll, "Elis Joel" Cabbage Patch Kid by Xavier Roberts,
original design $120

Doll, Kewpie, 1913, Rose O'Neill, 2-1/4" $240

Doll, Merrythought, artist-signed limited-edition Golliwog, #118 of 500, tag signed Oliver Holmes, with tags
and labels $125

Doll, stuffed oilcloth, Aunt Jemima, 11", 1949 .... $95

Doll, plush Golliwog, 34" $185

Doll, wood and fabric, 1940s mammy, Wilson Ramp
Walker $65

Game, "Smoky Holler," 1916, target game, instructions
and box cover are intact, color graphics $250

Sambo, figural, hand-held, hard plastic dexterity puzzle,
1950s, Mint $38

Tin figure, dancer on a box, "Alabama" $200

Wood pull toy, Black child playing xylophone,
Japan $90

Miscellaneous Items

Amos n' Andy cloth patch, "Check-Double Check,"
1930s, fuzzy texture, embroidered features $60

**Postcards depicting Black Americana are very col-
lectible and can range in price from a few dollars to
over a hundred. This real photo postcard of a Black
baseball team is one of the better examples. It was
sold at an auction by Postcards International.**

Amos n' Andy Pepsodent radio premium, map and letter
in original mailing envelope, full-color, "Eagle's Eye
View of Weber City, Inc.," 1935 .... $95

Coal tag, "Little Joe," new, unused condition, 1930s $5

Fairbanks Gold Dust Washing Powder, giant size,
1920s $75

Figure, "Angel of Africa," ceramic, 1958, Artgift Corpora-
tion $55

Figures, "Barefoot Boys," cast-metal miniatures, 5" high,
1930s $150

Glass, Jazz Band, Art Deco style, 1930s, stylized black
musicians playing yellow instruments $45

Minstrel decanter, 8" high, hat is cork, outfit with red, yellow, white detailing, four shot glasses are suspended,
late 1940s $95

Noisemaker, tin, man playing harmonica, U.S. Metal Toy
Co. $45

Pin, decorative Art Deco-style, woman, goldtone metal
with green stones which dangle from the back to form
her eyes, turban has rhinestones, 2" $75

Record, 78 RPM, "Tales of Uncle Remus For Children
From Walt Disney's Song of the South," 1947, Capitol
Records, set of three, illustrated cover $90

Record, "Talking Book," 1919, "Watermelon Coon," Talking Book Corp., colorful graphic, boy eating water-
melon $500

Smoking box, wood-hinged box with decal of black butler
pointing to sign, Lake George, N.Y. $95

Stereo view, "Dis am de pick of dat roost," Underwood &
Underwood, 1901 .... $20

Stereo view, "Uncle Tom after Scraps," 1900 .... $20

Tin, round, Licorice Mint Candies "Black Beau," shows
black child on top of tin $75

Tin sign, "O' Baby Ain't That Sumptin," 10" x 16" $75

Tobacco jar, ceramic, figural of young man with hat as lid,
3" x 6", late 1800s to early 1900s $400

Wooden box, boy spring-loaded to "deliver" a cigarette,
4-1/2" x 3" $100

BOARD GAMES

Shake the dice, take a card, or spin the spinner. And don't forget to bring your price guide. The market for vintage board games is moving faster than a ride on the Reading. Board games—once considered mere playthings, used to pass the time and then discarded—are now being scooped up by collectors who want them for their nostalgic value and display potential.

The market for board games exploded in the mid-1990s, when a copy of the rare 1883 "Bulls and Bears" game sold at auction for a stunning $30,000. A few months later, a second example of the game (in a slightly lesser condition) went for $14,000. But it's not just the rare 19th-century games that have a monopoly on the action; board games from recent years are on the move too.

Background: The very first board game in America was "Travelers Tour Through the United States," a geography-based game released in 1822 when there were only 24 U.S. states to travel through. Board games entered their heyday in the later 1800s, when new printing techniques enabled games to be mass-produced with elegant and colorful lithography, the trademark of the Victorian-era games. Most in demand from this era are games made by McLoughlin Brothers. Other significant early game makers that collectors look for include Chaffee & Selchow, Clark & Sowdown, J.H. Singer, and R. Bliss.

Milton Bradley and Parker Brothers, the two perennial game-making giants, both got their start in the late 1800s, as well (Milton Bradley in the 1860s; Parker Brothers in 1883), and both have remained the industry leaders for decades. Modern game manufacturers have included Hasbro, Transogram, Ideal, Lowell, Cadaco and others.

General Guidelines: Factors that contribute to the value of a board game include box graphics, theme of the game or character depicted, age, manufacturer, and overall condition. For many collectors, who purchase games for their display potential, the keys are graphics and condition. Boxes with tears, faded colors, or crushed edges are worth less than boxes in nice, clean condition. Also, to command top value, games should be complete with all original pieces, board and instruction sheet intact. Age is often a factor, but older does not always mean better. A game from the 1950s or 1960s based on a popular TV show, for example, may be worth considerably more than a generic board game that is fifty years older. Likewise, games from the 1920s or 1930s featuring nice Art Deco designs or other interesting box illustrations may have a higher value than a less-interesting game from the turn-of-the-century.

Collecting is also generational, which affects pricing. In recent years, for example, TV-related games from the 1960s have been very much in demand; but, as the next gen-

eration starts to collect their own childhood memories, games from the 1970s and 1980s will increase in value. Those are the games to look for now at yard sales and flea markets. Most are still bargain-priced.

For serious game collectors, the three main collecting areas are Victorian games, sports games, and character-related (TV, Disney, comic, etc.) games.

Victorian-era games are primarily the domain of advanced collectors, who value the games for their historical significance and their elegant and colorful lithography. While five-figure prices are very rare, it is not uncommon for pristine examples from this period to sell for $1,000 or more.

Collectors of sports-related games generally prefer games associated with specific players (like Babe Ruth, Johnny Unitas or Mickey Mantle) rather than a generic-type sports game. TV and movie-related games are tremendously popular, especially from the 1950s and 1960s. Especially desirable are games based on TV Westerns, mystery and spy shows, popular sit-coms, and science-fiction shows. Less popular are board games based on TV game shows like Concentration, Password, etc., which have relatively little value.

Other games that are very popular with collectors include cartoon and comic related games (Disney, Hanna-Barbera, Warner Brothers, etc.); transportation games (featuring automobiles, trains, airplanes, boats, bicycles, etc.); space and science fiction games (everything from Flash Gordon and Frankenstein to Godzilla and Star Trek); and games with war or military themes (especially World War II-era games). Other popular specialty areas include games depicting Black Americana, Christmas and other holidays, and politics and social issues. In all categories: The more interesting and colorful the box graphics, the more desirable the game.

Among the more valuable post-war games is Johnny Quest, a 1964 Transogram game. It is worth $500 or more in Excellent condition.

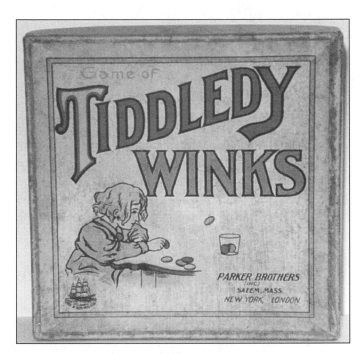

Age is not a major criterion in determining the value of board games. This early 1900s Tiddledy Winks game is valued at just $50 in Excellent condition. Most generic-type games have little interest to collectors.

This 1979 Parker Brothers game is a nice buy at $12-$15 in Excellent condition.

Clubs

• American Game Collectors Association, P.O. Box 44, Dresher, PA 19025

Recommended Reading

Books

2000 Toys & Prices, Sharon Korbeck and Elizabeth Stephan

Antique Trader Books Guide to Games and Puzzles, Harry L. Rinker

American Games Comprehensive Collector's Guide, Alex G. Malloy

Periodical

Toy Shop

VALUE LINE

Prewar Games (1945 or earlier)

Values shown are for games in Very Good condition.

Across the Channel, 1920s, Wolverine $75
Air Mail, The Game of, 1927, Milton Bradley $100

Alpha Football Game, 1940s, Replica $100
America's Yacht Race, 1904, McLoughlin Bros. $600
Astronomy, 1905, Cincinnati Game $50
Babe Ruth's Baseball Game, 1926, Milton Bradley ... $500
Bally Hoo, 1931, Gabriel $50
Barney Google and Spark Plug Game, 1923, Milton Bradley $150
Bell Boy Game, 1898, Chaffee & Selchow $550
Bible Quotto, 1932, Goodenough and Woglom.............. $8
Big Six Christy Mathewson Indoor Baseball Game, 1922, Piroxloid $600
Black Sambo, Game of, 1939, Gabriel $150
Buck Rogers in the 25th Century, 1936, All-Fair $250
Carl Hubbell Mechanical Baseball, Gotham $350
Dick Tracy Detective Game, 1937, Whitman $65
Famous Authors, 1943, Parker Brothers $12
Fire Alarm Game, 1899, Parker Brothers $1,500
Fox and Hounds, 1900, Parker Brothers $100
G-Men, 1936, Milton Bradley $45
Jack and the Bean Stalk, The Game of, 1898, McLoughlin Bros. $750
Knute Rockne Football Game, Official, 1930, Radio Sports $325
London Bridge, 1899, Singer..................................... $125
Lou Gehrig's Official Play Ball, 1930s, Christy Walsh $700
Lotto, 1932, Milton Bradley $6

Mickey Mouse Shooting Game, 1930s, Marks Brothers
.... $165
Monopoly, 1935 ed. only, Parker Brothers $20
Mother Goose, Game of, 1921, Stoll & Edwards $30
Motor Cycle Game, 1905, Milton Bradley $450
Ouija, 1920, William Fuld $25
Peter Coddle's Trip to New York, 1888, Parker Brothers
.... $40
Pla-Golf Board Game, 1938, Pla-Golf $900
Rival Policemen, 1890s, McLoughlin Bros. $3,000
Rough Riders, The Game of, 1898,
    Clark & Sowdon $500
Shopping, Game of, 1891, Bliss $1,500
Teddy's Ride from Oyster Bay to Albany, 1899,
    Jesse Crandall $4,000
Three Little Kittens, 1910s, Milton Bradley $75
Treasure Hunt, 1940, All-Fair $35
Uncle Wiggily's New Airplane Game, 1920s,
    Milton Bradley $95
Walt Disney's Uncle Remus Game, 1930s,
    Parker Brothers $75
Watermelon Patch Game, 1896,
    McLoughlin Bros. $1,500
World's Fair Game, 1892, Parker Brothers $1,000
Zippy Zepps, 1930s, All-Fair $450
Zoom, 1941, Whitman $45

Postwar Games (1946 to present)

Values shown are for games in Excellent condition. Examples in Good condition are worth approximately half the value shown. Examples in Mint condition are typically worth about 25 percent more than the value shown.

A-Team, 1984, Parker Brothers $10
Addams Family, 1965, Ideal $100
Alien, 1979, Kenner $50
Arnold Palmer's Inside Golf, 1961, D.B. Remson $95
Art Linkletter's House Party, 1968, Whitman $20

Games based on TV Westerns are a popular collecting category. This 1959 "Rawhide" Game by Lowell is worth $175-$200 in Excellent condition.

Barbie, Queen of the Prom, 1960, Mattel $65
Bart Starr Quarterback Game, 1960s $300
Baretta, 1976, Milton Bradley $25
Batman, 1978, Hasbro $30
Batman Batarang Toss, 1966, Pressman $250
Beatles Flip Your Wig Game, 1964,
    Milton Bradley $125
Beverly Hillbillies Game, 1963, Standard Toycraft $55
Bewitched Game, 1965, T. Cohn $85
Bible Baseball, 1950s, Standard $75
Big League Baseball, 1959, Saalfield $100
Boris Karloff's Monster Game, 1965, Gems $125
Branded, 1966, Milton Bradley $60
Calling All Cars, 1930s-40s, Parker Brothers $60
Calling Superman, 1955, Transogram $100
Casper the Friendly Ghost Game, 1959,
    Milton Bradley $12
Charlie's Angels, 1977, Milton Bradley $12
Cheyenne, 1958, Milton Bradley $65
Chutes & Ladders, 1956 ed. only, Milton Bradley $15
Cracker Jack Game, 1976, Milton Bradley $15
Creature from the Black Lagoon, 1963, Hasbro $425
Davy Crockett Adventure Game, 1956, Gardner $75
Denny McLain Magnetik Baseball, 1968, Gotham $200
Dick Van Dyke Board Game, 1964,
    Standard Toykraft $100
Dragnet, 1955, Parker Brothers $125
Dr. Kildare's Perilous Night, 1962, Ideal $40
Dukes of Hazzard, 1981, Ideal $10
E.T. The Extra-Terrestrial, 1982, Parker Brothers $12
Elvis Presley Game, 1957, TeenAge Games $700
Family Affair, 1967, Whitman $40
Family Feud, 1977, Milton Bradley $12
Felix the Cat Game, 1968, Milton Bradley $25
Flintstones Game, 1980, Milton Bradley $20
Flintstones Mechanical Shooting Gallery, 1962,
    Marx $125
Flying Nun Game, 1968, Milton Bradley $35
Frankenstein Game, Hasbro, 1962 .... $175
Garrison's Gorillas, 1967, Ideal $75
Gene Autry's Dude Ranch Game, 1950s,
    Warren Built-Rite $75

WHAT'S HOT!

For a recent Today's Collector article, game expert and author Bruce Whitehill was asked to name ten games that were especially in demand by collectors. His list (with approximate values in Excellent condition) included: "Red Barber's Big League Baseball" ($600); "Star Reporter" ($80); "Boom or Bust" ($100); "Mystery Date" ($100); "Dark Tower" ($75); "Jonny Quest" ($525); "Nancy Drew Mystery Game" ($75); "Park and Shop" ($60); "Green Ghost Game" ($100); and "Outer Limits" ($185).

Gentle Ben Animal Hunt Game, 1967, Mattel $75
Get Smart Game, 1966, Ideal $100
Gidget, 1966, Milton Bradley $35
Gilligan's Island, 1965, Game Gems $350
Globetrotter Basketball, Official, 1950s, Meljak $100
Godzilla, 1960s, Ideal $250
Green Hornet Quick Switch Game, 1966,
    Milton Bradley $300
Hank Aaron Baseball Game, 1970s, Ideal $85
Happy Days, 1976, Parker Brothers $25
Hawaii Five-O, 1960s, Remco $95
Hogan's Heroes Game, 1966, Transogram $85
Howdy Doody's Own Game, 1949, Parker Brothers .. $135
I Dream of Jeannie Game, 1965, Milton Bradley $75
Johnny Ringo, 1959, Transogram $125
Justice League of America, 1967, Hasbro $150
KISS on Tour Game, 1978, Aucoin $35
Land of the Giants, 1968, Ideal $100
Land of the Lost, 1975, Milton Bradley $50
Life, The Game of, 1960, Milton Bradley $15
MAD Magazine Game, 1979, Parker Brothers $12
Magilla Gorilla Game, 1964, Ideal $75
Mickey Mantle's Big League Baseball, 1958,
    Gardner $275
Mille Bornes, 1962, Parker Brothers $6
Monkees Game, 1968, Transogram $75
Monster Lab, 1964, Ideal $275
Mork and Mindy, 1978, Milton Bradley $20
Munsters Picnic Game, 1965, Hasbro $500
Mystery Date, 1965 ed., Milton Bradley $135
Partridge Family Game, 1974, Milton Bradley $30
Pee Wee Reese Marble Game, 1956,
    Pee Wee Enterprises $325
Petticoat Junction, 1963, Standard Toycraft $50
Phil Silvers You'll Never Get Rich, 1955, Gardner $75
Popeye, Adventures of, 1957, Transogram $75
Route 66 Game, 1960, Transogram $125

Simpsons Mystery of Life, 1990, Cardinal $9
Six Million Dollar Man, 1975, Parker Brothers $12
Star Trek: The Next Generation, 1993, Classic $25
Strike Three, 1948, Tone Products $500
Tarzan to the Rescue, 1976, Milton Bradley $15
Tennessee Tuxedo, 1963, Transogram $125
Three Stooges Fun House Game, 1950s, Lowell $295
Untouchables, 1950s, Marx $165
Waltons Game, 1974, Milton Bradley $20
Wanted: Dead or Alive, 1959, Lowell $75
Weird-Ohs Game, 1964, Ideal $150
Welcome Back, Kotter, 1977, Ideal $15
Wizard of Oz Game, 1974, Cadaco $15
Woody Woodpecker Game, 1959, Milton Bradley $100
Wolfman Mystery Game, 1963, Hasbro $175
Yogi Bear Break a Plate Game, 1960s, Transogram $80
Zorro, Walt Disney's, 1966, Parker Brothers $65

BOBBING HEAD DOLLS

Bobbing head dolls—along with PEZ dispensers and maybe Soaky bottles—fall into that category of wacky collectible that most people never thought would be collectible. Well, don't look now, but bobbing heads—those goofy figures from the 1960s with the big spring-loaded bouncing heads—are certainly worth a lot of money. Bobbing head collectors, it's time to come out of the closet and be vindicated.

Background: The heyday of vintage bobbing head dolls was from the early 1960s to the early 1970s. But bobbing head doll collecting really began in the mid-1980s, as kids from the 1960s decided to recapture their childhood. The fragile dolls, made of papier-mâché, were susceptible to cracks, chips and other misfortunes. Many of the original dolls were damaged or destroyed, so there wasn't a huge supply of collectible dolls available. Since the values of the dolls were being set by supply and demand, prices soared, as more and more collectors entered the hobby in the 1990s. The trend appears to be continuing into and beyond the year 2000.

General Guidelines: When trying to identify and evaluate your doll, the key factors to consider are the shape and color of the doll's base; the decals on its base or chest; and its features, such as the head, face and body design. Among sports bobbers, these characteristics have been used to create eight different categories for baseball dolls, 14 for football, five for hockey and one for basketball. Only by recognizing these subtle differences, will you will be able to identify and evaluate your doll.

The Beatles bobbing heads are worth about $75-$100 each.

It's difficult to find bobbers in nice condition; few survived in collectible condition. Therefore, top-condition dolls are truly valuable. Here are a few collecting tips:

Have a collecting goal, but collect for enjoyment. Most collectors specialize, collecting a certain series, sport, team, or different characters.

To find dolls, try the various Internet auctions or scan the ads in collectibles magazines such as *Toy Shop* and *Sports Collectors Digest*. This also allows you to develop contacts and reliable sources from whom you can purchase additional dolls.

If you're buying bobbers for their investment potential, buy dolls in Near Mint or better condition; these dolls are easier to sell and yield a greater return. Be patient, however; it takes time to find these quality items. If you are just looking for display pieces, you can often save up to 50 percent (or more) by buying dolls in Excellent, rather than Mint, condition.

It's best to display dolls in glass cases to keep dust and grime off. Keep your dolls out of heat or cold, out of the sunlight and away from smoky rooms. Handle the dolls with care; they can crack easily. Also, because the paint and decals are fragile, it is not a good idea to use strong cleaners on your dolls. You can also create a tissue "collar" around the doll's neck to prevent the head from hitting the shoulders.

Most of the bobbing head dolls produced after 1972 were not made in Japan, nor with papier-mâché, and, so far, are not considered collectible by "serious" collectors. Most of these post-1972 bobbers have not increased in value beyond their original issue price.

Club
• Bobbing Head Collectors Club, P.O. Box 9297, Daytona Beach, FL 32120

Recommended Reading

Book
Bobbing Head Dolls 1960-2000, Tim Hunter

Periodicals
Sports Collectors Digest
Tuff Stuff
Sports Cards
Toy Shop

VALUE LINE

Values shown are for dolls in Excellent condition, which may show average wear (such as thin hairline cracks or tiny paint chips) but cannot be missing any pieces. Any doll that is missing a piece or has been repaired is generally worth no

more than 15 percent of the value shown. Also, a doll's value drops by thirty percent or more if its decals are missing or damaged.

Non-Sports Bobbing Head Dolls

Value Notes: Non-sport dolls can be grouped into any of several categories, including advertising, cartoon characters, political (including JFK and Castro), celebrities, Disney, and miscellaneous. Some non-sport bobbers have not attracted much interest so far and have little value. They include the Oriental kissing pair and singles, generic animals, bums, clowns, lovable losers, etc.

Advertising

Big Boy	$600
Big Tex (Texas State Fair mascot)	$60
Brylcreem (kissing pair)	$150
Campbell's Kids (pair)	$200
Colonel Sanders (papier-mâché)	$100
Colonel Sanders (plastic)	$35
Happy Homer	$150
Icey	$50
American Indian with state or city stickers	$35
Knott's Berry Farm	$175
L.A. County Fair pig	$80
Mr. Peanut (with cane)	$100
New York World's Fair kissing pair	$75
Nugget Casino	$100
Phillips 66	$200
Ranier Brewing (papier-mâché)	$150
Ranier Brewing (Styrofoam)	$45
Reddy Kilowatt	$300
Smokey the Bear, three versions, each	$150
United Airlines	$300

Cartoon Characters

Batman or Robin	$500
Beetle Bailey	$75
Charlie Brown	$75
Pig Pen	$100
Schroeder	$70
Snoopy	$60
Woodstock (1970s mini)	$40
Bugs Bunny	$150
Elmer Fudd	$175
Porky Pig	$150
Speedy Gonzales	$200
Tweety	$175
Wile E. Coyote or Yosemite Sam	$150
Alvin (Dennis the Menace knock-off)	$80
Dick Tracy	$350
Li'l Abner Characters, 1975	$60
Popeye	$300

TV & Movie Characters

Ben Casey	$60
Bozo, "Capitol Records" stamped on bottom, rare	$300
Danny Kaye (kissing pair)	$140
Dobie Gillis	$140
Frankenstein, rare	$500
Phantom, rare	$500
Roy Rogers	$100
Universal Studios Werewolf, rare	$400

Political Figures

Castro	$100
Castro/Kruschev (kissing pair)	$150
Democrat Donkey	$25
John F. Kennedy (football player)	$250
Jack/Jackie Kennedy (kissing pair), rare	$500
Kruschev, "Banging Shoe"	$225
Mao	$250
"Nixon For President" (elephant)	$125

Other Celebrities

Beatles (16" promos), for set	$4,000
Beatles (regular size), with box, for set	$350
Davy Crockett	$75
NASA Astronaut	$100
Donnie Osmond	$80
Santa Claus (many different)	$50

Disneyland/Disney World

Donald Duck (early porcelain)	$65
Goofy	$60
Mickey Mouse, various	$50-$75
Pluto	$60
Winnie the Pooh	$125
Goofy, Donald, Mickey in car	$100

Kissing Pairs

Alaska	$80
Hawaii	$100
India, Russia, or Spain	$60
Japan, Mexico, or USA	$50
"Let's Kiss" on base	$20-$40

Even Fidel Castro was featured on a bobbing head. It's valued at about $100.

Colonel Sanders can be found in both a papier-mâché variety (worth about $100) and a plastic version (worth about $35).

Miscellaneous

Aloha Girls (originals, beware of repros) $20
Cleopatra $40
Confederate Soldier $40

Sports Bobbing Head Dolls

Value Notes: Unless noted differently, sports dolls are generally 6 to 7 inches tall; decals show the city name on the base and the nickname on the chest; a "Made in Japan" stamp or sticker appears on the bottom of the base. There is no price difference for such factors as holding a bat or ball, different hairstyle or color, etc.; Cardinals and Orioles are always on diamond-shaped bases. Although most teams were available each year of issue, only a few representative values are shown for each year to demonstrate the range of prices. Teams not listed fall between the lowest and highest values shown.

Baseball 1960-61 Square Color Base

There is no city designation on the base. The Orioles and Pirates dolls have mascot heads. All heads are connected to the neck by an older model "hook spring."

Baltimore Orioles (green diamond) $115
Chicago Cubs (blue) $100
Cincinnati Reds (red) $130
Los Angeles Angels (dark blue) $40
Minnesota Twins (dark blue) $40
New York Mets (blue) $100
New York Yankees (orange) $80
Pittsburgh Pirates $100
Washington Senators (dark blue), scarce $500

Baseball 1961-62 White Base Miniatures

Dolls stand 4-1/2 inches tall, on round white bases, with most still having magnets in the bottom.

Anaheim Angels $200
Chicago Cubs $250
Chicago White Sox $120
Detroit Tigers $250
Houston Astros $125
Milwaukee Braves $200
New York Mets $250
New York Yankees $100
St. Louis Cardinals $275
Mickey Mantle $750
Roger Maris $350

Baseball 1961-63 Square White Base

Anaheim Angels $85
Baltimore Orioles $150
Chicago Cubs $250
Chicago White Sox $150
Houston Colt .45s (blue uniform) $300
Los Angeles Dodgers $60
Kansas City A's $150
New York Mets $175
New York Yankees $125
Philadelphia Phillies $75
San Francisco Giants $135
Roberto Clemente $650
Willie Mays $250
Willie Mays, gold base $400

Baseball 1963-65 Black Players

African-American players on round green bases; bottom of the base is stamped "1962."

Baltimore Orioles $400
Chicago Cubs $500
Cleveland Indians $700
Houston Colt .45s $2,500
Los Angeles Dodgers $300

Baseball 1963-65 Green Round Base

"Made in Japan" or "1962" should be visible on the bottom of the base.

Baltimore Orioles $115
Chicago Cubs $200
Chicago White Sox $50
Los Angeles Angels $75

Milwaukee Braves $150
New York Mets $60
Washington Senators $125

Baseball 1966-71 Gold Round Base

Atlanta Braves $75
Baltimore Orioles... $100
Cincinnati Reds... $80
Cleveland Indians.. $125
Detroit Tigers (5/5) ....$100-$175
Los Angeles Dodgers $50
Kansas City A's $150
Milwaukee Brewers $30
Seattle Pilots $150
Washington Senators $150

Baseball 1970-72 Wedge Base

Faces have a "sad" look that is unique to this set.

Boston Red Sox $125
California Angels $60
Chicago Cubs $100
San Francisco Giants................................... $150

Miscellaneous Baseball Dolls

1960 rubber doll on wood base (Dodgers, Giants or
  Braves), each $50
Hawaii Islander, gold base $250
Little Leaguers $25
Little Leaguer on Globe $75
Minnesota Twins, green base with compass
  between feet $350
Umpires, various $100
Weirdo Los Angeles Dodgers, brown base,
  (player) $500

Football 1960-61 NFL Square Wood Base

*These do not have a city decal on the base, nor a wire
facemask. There are no decals on the dolls' helmets. Each team
has an embossed team nickname on the doll's chest. Some say
"Go Go Go For Falstaff" on the base, which adds a 20% premium to the value.*

Baltimore Colts $50
Chicago Bears $60
Cleveland Browns $100
Green Bay Packers $150
Pittsburgh Steelers....................................... $90

Football 1961-63 NFL Square Regular Base

*These dolls display the regular one-mold design where
the body and base are formed together in papier-mâché. Most
helmets display team decals.*

Chicago Bears $50
Cleveland Browns $100
Dallas Cowboys $150
Green Bay Packers $80
Los Angeles Rams $40
Philadelphia Eagles $60
Washington Redskins.................................. $100

**If your Bozo bob-
bing head says
"Capitol Records"
on the bottom, it's
worth $300.**

Football 1962-64 NFL Kissing Pairs

*Each pair includes a 4-1/2-inch football player and
majorette on a gold base. The city decal is on the player's
base; the chest has a team decal. Magnets in lip and cheek
make the couple "kiss."*

Baltimore Colts $150
Detroit Lions $200
Green Bay Packers $100
Los Angeles Rams (2/3).....................$80-$180
Washington Redskins.................................. $400

Football 1961-66 NFL "Toes-Up"

*Dolls stand on round bases of various colors with foot
and toes pointing up.*

Baltimore Colts $250
Chicago Bears $150
Cleveland Browns $350
Dallas Cowboys $400
Green Bay Packers $200
Los Angeles Rams $125

Football 1962-64 Black Players "Toes-Up"

*African-American players stand on round gold bases,
with toes-up.*

Baltimore Colts $400
Chicago Bears $200
Los Angeles Rams $125
Philadelphia Eagles $150
St. Louis Cardinals..................................... $350
Washington Redskins, scarce..................... $650

Football 1963-64 NFL Square Gold Base

City name or "NFL" is on the base, with an embossed team nickname on the chest. Helmets have wire facemasks.

Chicago Bears $75
Detroit Lions $200
Minnesota Vikings $250
St. Louis Cardinals $130

Football 1965-67 NFL Gold Round Base

Bottom of base should have a football-shaped sticker (contrasted to those from 1968, which have a circular decal).

Atlanta Falcons $50
Cleveland Browns $100
Dallas Cowboys $90
New Orleans Saints $40
Philadelphia Eagles $75
Pittsburgh Steelers $100

Football 1965-67 NFL Gold Round Base "Realistic Faces"

Dolls display "realistic" faces. Molded ear pads are on the helmet.

Atlanta Falcons $75
Baltimore Colts $200
Detroit Lions $150
New Orleans Saints $35
Washington Redskins $300

Football 1968-70 NFL/AFL Gold Round Base

The bottom of the base has a circular decal on it. NFL stickers are between the feet.

Atlanta Falcons $50
Boston Patriots $70

Big Boy is among the most valuable of all bobbing heads, worth about $600.

Buffalo Bills $100
Cincinnati Bengals $30
Dallas Cowboys $90
Detroit Lions $30
Green Bay Packers (5/5) .... $90-$190
Los Angeles Rams $40
Miami Dolphins $100
San Diego Chargers $50
San Francisco 49ers $100

Football 1961-62 AFL Round Base "Toes-Up"

Dolls display the "Toes-Up" pose, with wire facemasks.

Boston Patriots $200
Dallas Texans $300
Houston Oilers $250
New York Titans $400

Football 1965-66 AFL Round Gold Base/Ear Pads, AFL

Dolls are on round gold bases and have ear pads on the helmets.

Buffalo Bills $150
Denver Broncos $500
Houston Oilers $200
New York Jets $250

Football 1965 AFL Toes-Up

Miami Dolphins $175
Boston Patriots $100
Cleveland Browns $150
Denver Broncos .... $150-$250
Houston Oilers $75

1961-68 College Football, Round Green Base

Air Force $125
Air Force mini $75
Alabama $175
Army $100
Boston College $175
Clemson $200
Colorado $200
Duke $225
Florida (gold base) $100
Georgia Tech $150
Harvard $175
Illinois $150
Kansas $150
Michigan $250
Michigan State $175
Minnesota $90
Ole Miss $200
North Carolina $225
Notre Dame $100
Ohio State $225
Oklahoma $250
Southern Cal $100
Texas $200
Wake Forest $175
Wisconsin $200
Yale $175

Basketball Bobbing Head Dolls

Harlem Globetrotters (holding suitcase, 1962)........... $200
Los Angeles Lakers (1962, green square base) $175
Los Angeles Lakers (1967-68, gold round base).......... $35
Los Angeles Lakers (black player, gold round
    base) $150
New York Knicks (1962, orange square base)........... $180
San Diego Rockets (1967-68, gold round base) $150

Post 1972 Bobbing Head Dolls

1970s Plastic Dolls

Baseball dolls in box.. $20
Football dolls in box $10
Football dolls "Running Back"....................................... $15

1970s Ceramic Dolls

Cleveland Indians...$50-$60
Pirates... $50
Portland Blazers.. $15

1980s & 1990s Dolls

Golden Era Babe Ruth $25
Golden Era Lou Gehrig.. $25
Golden Era Joe Jackson $25
Golden Era Ty Cobb $25
Golden Era Honus Wagner $60
Golden Era Bronko Nagurski....................................... $50
Imus... $200
Negro League $25
Pete's Wicked Ale $25
Hayden Fry and Herkie Hawk $20

BREWERY COLLECTIBLES

Antique advertising is among the most popular and most enduring of all collectibles; and among the many types of vintage advertising being collected, one of the favorite categories is beer and brewery memorabilia—a category collectors call "breweriana."

Background: The rise of the brewing industry in the United States closely parallels the rise and success of our country as a whole. From the time Pilgrims were forced to land at Plymouth, Mass., beer has been an integral part of our culture. Brewing was a very localized industry until after the Civil War. Almost every town big enough to have a general store and a bank, also had a local brewer. In fact, many households brewed their own beer.

Two technological advances—efficient railroad transportation and mechanical refrigeration—changed the face of the industry. Once larger, more successful brewers were able to break out of localized markets, advertising became important.

From about 1870 until 1915, when prohibitionists began to hold sway, the brewing industry rode the crest of immigration, westward expansion and the industrial revolution. There were thousands of competing commercial breweries in the country and in those days—before radio and television advertising—signs, trays, posters and giveaways were the most effective ways to promote a product.

In 1919, Prohibition nearly wiped out an entire industry for 14 years. Upon repeal in 1933, some 750 breweries in

America reopened and began brewing again. Competition became intense, as the larger brewers poured millions and millions of dollars into advertising, and smaller brewers could no longer compete. The number of brewers gradually dwindled from the 1940s to the 1970s, until, by 1980, there were fewer than fifty major breweries left in the United States. Partly because of this disappearance of most local and regional brands, interest in collecting breweriana grew. Also, brand loyalty is famous among beer drinkers, and that is another element that makes beer collectibles so popular today.

Two of the oldest clubs for breweriana collectors were founded in 1970—the Eastern Coast Breweriana Association (ECBA) and the Beer Can Collectors of America (BCCA). In 1983, a new brewing industry trend developed with the opening of the first two new breweries in many years. These tiny companies were the first of what have come to be known as "micro" or "craft" brewers. By the end of 1999, there were more than a thousand of these micro or pub breweries nationwide, reversing the trend of the past 60 years and creating a new supply of brewery collectibles. Because of their small size and limited budget, most microbreweries do not produce many items of memorabilia. Items such as glasses and coasters from these microbreweries may prove to be wise investments.

General Guidelines: Prohibition, which lasted from 1919 to 1933, conveniently divides the breweriana hobby into two distinct periods—pre-Prohibition and post-Prohibition. All pre-Prohibition beer advertising is valuable and highly collectible. With the possible exception of embossed bottles, breweriana before 1870 should be considered extremely rare, from 1870 to 1890 very rare, and from 1890 to 1919 rare—with very few exceptions.

Advertising items from before 1919 generally include etched drinking glasses, cardboard coasters, lithographed metal signs and serving trays, lithographed posters and calendars, reverse painted glass signs, bottle labels, mugs and steins, pin-back buttons and cardboard, paper or metal signs. Workmanship and material was of high quality and highly detailed.

During Prohibition, many brewers attempted to stay in business through the manufacture of near-beer, malt syrup or soft drinks, so frequently the word "brewing" was dropped from the company name. Most brewery-related advertising from the Prohibition era (1919-1933) is considered rare and highly collectible.

Upon the repeal of Prohibition in 1933, brewing and beer advertising went wild in an apparent attempt to make up for lost time. Breweriana items introduced after 1933 include beer cans (first sold in January 1935), electric lights and signs, tap knobs for draft beer, statues, plastic signs and novelties.

Values for beer collectibles depend largely on condition, age and scarcity, although an exception to this rule would be the market for new "collectible" beer steins. Often a false mar-

Beer cans probably peaked in the 1970s but have always been popular with true collectors. Cone-tops, used from the 1930s to the early 1950s are desirable, with many valued in the $20-$30 range. Most beer cans produced since 1975 are worth less than $5 but still make a nice colorful display.

ket is created by manufacturers and dealers selling limited-edition steins that number in the thousands. The values in this market have more to do with hype than age or scarcity.

Materials are also important in some categories, with metal or glass signs commanding more interest than plastic or cardboard signs. Even damaged or worn beer advertising items can still be quite valuable if rare or old.

The most popular types of breweriana include the following:

Beer cans—Beer-can collecting became extremely popular in the late 1960s and early 1970s, when just about every kid on the block—and most of their dads—had a beer-can collection. The beer-can craze grew swiftly to an almost impossible crescendo, and then the air started coming out. The gusto was suddenly gone, and the beer can market fizzled like a keg gone flat. But out of all this emerged a core of dedicated beer-can collectors, who remained in the hobby long after the fad collectors were gone. These serious collectors are still very active and often pay substantial prices for the scarce cans they're looking for. There are even signs that the beer-can collecting hobby may be on the verge of a resurgence.

Beer in cans was first introduced in 1935 by G. Krueger Brewing of Newark, New Jersey, but it did not catch on with the American public until after World War II. The first cans of Krueger beer or ale may bring $300 to $350 today.

Serious collectors seek pre-1960 "flat-top" or "spout-top" cans, with pre-World War II cans commanding the top prices. Some 1964-1972 "pop-top" cans can be quite valuable, with the rarest labels bringing as much as $500. Most 1970s and 1980s beer cans are readily available and not valuable today.

The statement "Internal Revenue Tax Paid" was required to appear on all packaged beer from mid 1935 until 1950. Only the earliest cans (rare and valuable) or those made after 1950 will not have these words somewhere on the label. The appearance of the "IRTP" statement usually makes a can more valuable.

Spout-top cans—also called cone-tops or crown-tops because they had a conical top, which closed with a bottle cap—were made to be filled like a bottle. Nearly all spout-top cans are collectible; many are extremely rare. Prices range from $20-$30 for the most common to over $2,500 for the rarest brands. Spout-top cans were made from 1935 until the late 1950s.

WHAT IS IT?

The uneducated browser at an antique market probably wouldn't even know a beer foam scraper if he was holding one. They look like an oversized tongue depressor with a beer name printed on both sides. They were used in taverns in the days before health departments to scrape the foam from the top of an overfilled glass. Foam scrapers fell out of favor by the 1950s, and are highly collectible today. Common brands, such as Schaefer or Rheingold, may bring only $5-$10, but rare or pre-Prohibition scrapers sell for $50-$100.

Beer trays are extremely collectible. Common trays are still available in the $5-$20 range. Older and scarcer examples can sell for hundreds.

Among the rarest and most desirable beer cans are those pre-World War II flat-top cans with opening instructions on the side of the label. Pre-war flat-top cans range in price from $25 for a common brand like Pabst or Budweiser to over $2,500 for the rarest cans.

Because of the numbers of cans produced and the number saved by collectors, few cans made after 1975 are worth more than $5; most are worth much less. (And no matter what you might see in an advertisement or at the local flea market, a can of 1970s Billy Beer is never worth more than one dollar.) Also, misprinted cans are generally not worth more than perfect cans.

Beer-can collectors prefer to display near-perfect-condition, bottom-opened cans whenever possible. Full cans are not more valuable than empty ones.

Beer bottles—Beer bottles are less collectible than beer cans and many other forms of breweriana. The most sought-after bottles are those from the 1930s or earlier, especially unusual brands from small breweries. Early embossed beer bottles are important to breweriana collectors as often the sole link to early and short-lived breweries. Early embossed bottles are more collectible than the uniform brown bottles used after Prohibition. While the embossing makes each bottle unique, prices of early bottles do not approach the prices of other early breweriana. A typical 1880 to 1919 embossed beer bottle without a paper label will typically sell for $3-$20. The same bottle with a paper label in Good condition will sell for $15-$50.

Beer labels—Beer labels, the paper labels intended to be attached to bottles, are growing in popularity among col-

This selection of beer tab knobs sold for prices ranging from $35 to $85 at a recent auction conducted by Glasses, Mugs & Steins, a Sun Prairie, Wis., auction house that specializes in breweriana.

lectors because they are colorful and much easier to store and display than either cans or bottles. You can frame them like a small piece of art, or display them in albums, similar to photos or baseball cards. Another advantage is that they are, for the most part, quite reasonable. Extremely rare examples have sold for over $200, but many nice colorful labels are available for prices ranging from ten cents to ten dollars.

Bottle Caps—A favorite collectible of children in a much simpler time, bottle caps have achieved some recognition as a category of beer advertising memorabilia. Collecting beer caps (or crowns) offers the advantage of compact size and low cost. Many caps can be had for free or as little as five cents. Advanced collectors or specialists might pay as much as $5-$10 for a rare brand or a pre-Prohibition crown.

Trays—Often decorated with colorful scenes, trays were first used for beer advertising in the late 1880s. Pre-Prohibition trays are the most sought after and the most valuable. Early trays are normally characterized by low, flat rims and highly detailed lithography. Themes include women, brewery or drinking scenes and detailed and ornate depictions of products or logos.

Trays produced after Prohibition are generally less detailed and often pictured only the brewery name or logo. Contemporary trays are cheaper, lighter, smaller and often less desirable.

The most valuable trays are those that depict women or factory scenes. Common trays start at around $5; old and scarce examples can command thousands. Nearly all post-World War II trays sell for less than $60. Pre-war trays, made of heavier gauge metal with higher-quality paint and design, generally range from $50 to $250. Pre-Prohibition trays start around $100 and can range upwards of $2,500 for scarce examples in nice condition.

Signs and Lights—Neon signs are the most popular and most fragile of the lighted signs. Collectors pay as little as $25 for some less popular brands, although the typical price for a recent vintage neon sign in working order is $75-$150. Older, rarer neons can sell for $500 or more. Signs, lights or displays that incorporate movement into the advertisement are especially hot. These include motorized displays, lights with changing colors, and bubble lights. Bubble lights (when the sign is lighted, liquid bubbles in the lights), in working order, that feature the brand name spelled out in

bubble tubes start at $1,000. Other bubble lights range from $100 to $1,500. These lights are frequently pre-World War II and very rare. Other mechanical or motorized signs will vary in price based on age, size and condition. Small and recent signs start at $25, while displays from the 1950s and earlier, or large displays, bring from $100 to several thousand dollars.

Tin-on-cardboard signs consist of a piece of printed or painted metal folded over a heavy cardboard backing. What makes these signs collectible is their size (they are usually small enough to easily display), composition and variety. Those most in demand are 9-inch round "button" signs and signs that are scenic or show the product.

These signs were first used before Prohibition, and any of that age are rare and in high demand. Pre-World War II signs range from $100 and up, while postwar signs generally start at about $25 and can go as high as $125. Production of these signs faded by the mid-1960s, as cheaper materials replaced them.

Lithographs—Considered by many to be the ultimate beer collectible, lithographed posters and calendars are the crowning achievement of the printer's art. Stone lithography as executed around the turn of the century captured ornate art and minute detail not possible in any other advertising medium. Very scarce, by breweriana standards, lithographed posters from 1870 until 1919 are a solid investment. Low-end prices for a framed print that may be unique or one of a few known start at about $500. Beautifully executed prints of women with subtle advertisement or ornately detailed factory scenes may bring as much as $2,500.

Glasses and Mugs—One of the oldest forms of brewery advertising, a beer mug or a glass from an obscure local brewer, is an antique treasure worthy of preserving. Many pre-Prohibition glasses and mugs bore painted or etched designs and were created as gifts, or simply as drinking vessels.

Considering their age and scarcity, pre-Prohibition beer glasses and mugs are frequently underpriced today. Many scarce examples sell for less than $50. Post-Prohibition glasses, with painted or decal designs, were most frequently given to taverns to serve their customers. Prices today range from $1 for common types and brands (such as Budweiser) up to $100 for an older glass from a small brewer. The microbrewery movement that has swept the country, beginning on the West Coast in 1983, has supplied collectors with a seemingly endless variety of new glasses. Many can be found for less than $5.

Coasters—Beer coasters were meant to be used a few times and then discarded. Many beer coasters bear much more than a simple advertising message; some include puzzles and poems, songs and slogans, ladies and limericks, facts and fantasies. The rarest beer coasters can command $50 to $100, but the vast majority sells for less than $2 or $3. Ballantine Beer of Newark, New Jersey, was one of the most prolific coaster producers with nearly 300 to its credit.

Can and Bottle Openers—The small, hand-held can or bottle opener was a necessary accessory to the invention of the bottle crown and the beer can. Breweries gave away millions of small metal openers bearing advertising of the brewery. Prices range from 25 cents to several dollars for most openers. Pre-Prohibition openers, which frequently resemble a key (known as "church keys"), may bring $10-$20. Prior to bottle openers, some brewers issued advertising corkscrews, which are rare and highly valued.

Tap Knobs—Beer tapper handles from the 1930s through the 1950s were small round knobs with a porcelain insert. All tap handles are collectible, but the primary interest is in the early ball knobs and other types of early draft beer dispensers. Tap knobs from the 1950s and earlier generally start at $25 and can reach several hundred dollars for rare or unusual brands. Modern plastic, wood or composition tap handles typically bring $5 to $25. Designs from the 1960s are smaller and less showy and bring comparable prices.

Glass and China—Even delicate and decorative household items have borne the mark of brewery advertising. At least one brewer, Horlacher, of Allentown, Penn., offered carnival glass dishes and other decorative plates and bowls as premiums. These turn-of-the-century giveaways all bear the brewery name on the back. Some larger breweries, such as Pabst of Milwaukee, used brewery china bearing the company insignia in its brewery dining room or tap room.

Postcards and Ephemera—Perhaps more than any other industry, brewers used and issued scenic and advertising postcards to promote their products and special events. Before Prohibition in 1919, many brewers owned parks and gardens that were frequently featured on postcards. Letterhead, trade cards, bottle labels and booklets are all items used by brewers which appeal to breweriana collectors as well as more general collectors of these items.

Toys—Toy scale-model trucks and scale model railroad cars displaying beer logos and advertising are currently popular collectibles. Some brewers issued toy trucks bearing their logo as early as the 1940s, long before toy collecting became a fad. Playing cards and games have also been the target of brewery advertising.

Sports Collectibles—Sports figures have often served as beer spokesmen, and beer advertising and sporting events have been closely linked for nearly 100 years. Colonel Jacob Ruppert, the colorful owner of the New York Yankees during their earlier heyday, made his fortune on the success of Ruppert Knickerbocker Beer.

Contributor to this section: Lawrence Handy, 535 N. 8th St., Allentown, PA 18102.

Clubs

• Eastern Coast Breweriana Association (ECBA), P.O. Box 349, West Point, PA 19486, 610-439-8245

• Beer Can Collectors of America (BCCA), 747 Merus Ct., Fenton, MO 63026-2092, 314-343-6486

• National Association of Breweriana Advertising (NABA), 2343 Met-To-Wee Lane, Wauwatosa, WI 53226

• American Breweriana Association (ABA), P.O. Box 11157, Pueblo, CO 81001-0157, 719-544-9267

• The Microbes Micro Breweriana Collectors, P.O. Box 826, South Windsor, CT 06074

VALUE LINE

Ashtray, O'Keefe's Old Vienna Beer..............................$5
Ashtray, Tuborg Beer, white milk glass $15
Bottle, Andrew Liptak, Perth Amboy, N.J., 1890s $30
Bottle, Schmidt's, Hanover, Pa., 1890s........................$22
Bottle, Hoster, 1890s...$12
Badge, American Brewers Association Convention, 1899, "ABA" inscription, enamel and brass plated...........$20
Bell, Sterling Beer, girl $80
Blotter, 3" x 7-1/2", Bergdoll Brewing Co., 60th Anniversary, black and yellow Louis Bergdoll portrait, Christmas holly design, 1909, unused $50
Bottle opener, Fritz's Corner, Coeur D'Alene, Idaho $8
Bottle opener, Miller Beer, 1955....................................$35
Calendar, 1907, Yuengling & Son Brewers & Bottlers, Pottsville, PA, four puppies at the bar, 34" x 26" frame $1,850
Clicker, Gunther's Beer, white litho tin, red letters, "The Beer That Clicks," Kirchof Co., 1930s $30
Clock, Busch, electric, horse-and-rider scene...............$35
Clock, Piels Beer, 15" x 11"...$85
Clock, Schlitz, lights, 1959 ....$65
Coasters, Acme Beer, Cereal & Fruit Ltd., Honolulu, red and black letters $7
Coasters, Brugh Brau Beer, McDermott, Chicago, black and gold letters $15
Coasters, Champagne Velvet Beer, Terre Haute Brewing, Ind., man holding up glass of beer, red, blue and black $14
Coasters, Golden Age Beer, Fernwood Brewing, PA, center glass of beer, red, blue and yellow $50
Coasters, Gunther's Beer, Gunther Brewing, Baltimore, bear holding beer bottle, red, black and yellow $15
Cribbage board, Drink Rhinelander Beer $30
Doorstop, Hanley's Ale, cast iron, bulldog.................$595
Fishing lure, Schlitz, bottle shape $8
Foam scraper, celluloid, Goetz Brewery $18
Foam scraper, Meister Brau $20
Glass, Philip Best, Milwaukee, etched.........................$425

Regional beer glasses make nice display items. These, sold at auction by Glasses, Mugs & Steins of Sun Prairie, Wis., sold for prices ranging from $35 to $60.

Glass, Colorado Three Star Beer, Trinidad, Colo., enameled $325

Glass, Fox Head 400, Waukesha, Wis., barrel shape .. $725

Glass, F.W. Cook Brewing Co., Evansville, Ind., pre-Prohibition $200

Glass, Northwestern Beer, Superior, Wis., enameled $295

Glass, Silver Bar Beer, Tampa, enameled $160

Ice pick, Empire Lager, Black Horse Ale $30

Keychain fob, Schlitz Beer, brass charm, beer-keg shape, Schlitz trademark script name, early 1900s $25

Lapel stud, 3/4" x 7/8", Bert and Harry Fan Club, die-cut brass, blue paint, cartoon figures, National Bohemian Brewery Co., Baltimore, early 1950s $25

Medallion, bronze, Stroh's Run for Liberty $20

Memo Book, Pearl Beer, 1960-61 calendars $3

Menu, Old German Beer, Cafe Bischoff, York, PA, 1940 .... $10

Mugs, pre-Prohibition, Genesee Brewing Co., Rochester, NY $250

Mugs, pre-Prohibition, Hafemeister Brewing Co., Green Bay, Wis. $115

Mugs, pre-Prohibition, Schlitz, Milwaukee, salt-glaze $50

Patch, Lucky Lager, 7-1/4" x 6-1/2", large red X, white ground, yellow and red letters $20

Peanut dispenser, Miller Beer $15

Pinback button, American Beverage Co., "Hop Ale," red, white and blue $20

Pinback button, Bohemian Export, multicolored............ $3

Pinback button, Gluek's Beer, blue and white, 1911-20 .... $10

Pinback button, Budweiser Month, red letters, white ground, Anheuser-Busch logo, early 1950s $30

Pinback button, Rupperts Beer/Ale, dark blue and yellow, 1930s $25

Radio, Bud can, Mint-in-Box... $55

Sign, Adam Scheidt, Norristown, Pa., Valley Forge Special, die-cut, woman holding bottle standing behind case of beer, cardboard, 11" x 20"........................... $100

These Budweiser steins brought prices ranging from $170 to $715 at a recent auction conducted by Glasses, Mugs & Steins of Sun Prairie, Wis. The most valuable of the four is the lidded 1981 Chicago variation on the far right. The two steins on the left are worth about $350-$360 each.

Sign, Ballantine, Newark, N.J., Ballantine Beer, die-cut, 1960s pro-football schedule, cardboard, 12" x 20" $25

Sign, Falstaff Beer, Blacks in bar setting, lights, 11-1/2" x 18" $95

Sign, Old Dutch Bock Beer, Eagle, Catasaqua, Pa., referee holds up hand of standing ram prize fighter, cardboard, 13" x 19" $95

Sign, Schlitz, lighted, 1950s $95

Sign, Wunder Beer, Oakland, CA, cardboard, hanging type $65

Sign, Budweiser, 20" x 17", red and white $90

Sign, Coors, 22" x 23", red, white and gold $90

Sign, Old Topper Ale, 12" x 12", glass, illuminated..... $50

Sign, Schlitz, 10-1/2" x 33-1/2", white $60

Statue, Ballantine, wood, white, red and gold $18

Statue, Budweiser, wood, black, white and red $20

Statue, Hamm's, ceramic, black, white and red........... $18

Statue, Pabst, ceramic, white, black, red..................... $18

Statue, Piels, plastic, brown, gold, white and red $8

Tap handle, Schmidt City Club Beer, multicolored enamel design $85

Thermometer, Tannhauser Beer, brass case, paper dial, eagle logo, 1896 .... $100

Tip tray, Ballantine & Sons, back hanger $25

Token, Hamm's Beer... $20

Tray, Yosemite Lager $750

Tray, Ballantine's Ale, 12", 1940s $45

Tray, Bartels, 12", Bakelite $50

Tray, Berghoff Beer.. $75

Tray, Chester Pilsner, Ale and Porter, 12", blue and gold... $75

Tray, Columbia, Preferred Beer, 12", red, white and gold.. $65

Tray, Eagle Brewery, Catasauqua Beer, 12", eagle illustration $150

Tray, Falstaff, round, metal, maiden pouring beer $115

Tray, Genesee Cream Ale, 12" black, green and white $5

Tray, Hohenadel Beer-Ale, 13" $45

Tray, Kaier's Beer, 12", green and white $25

Tray, Old Reading Beer, Reading, Pa., 12" $40

Tray, Muehlebach Beer $20

Tray, Neuweiler's Ale, Allentown, Pa., 13", 1940s $40

Tray, Pabst Blue Ribbon, embossed plastic, blue $10

Tray, Schaefer Beer.. $10

Tray, Silver Bar Ale, Tampa, round $75

Tray, Stegmaier's Beer, 13-1/4", red, black and gold.. $14

Tray, Tru-Blu Beer, Northampton Brewing Co., 12", horse and dog illustration.. $50

T-shirt, Bud Man, dated 1988, Jostens.......................... $10

Watch fob, 1-1/2" diameter, die-cut silvered brass, Anheuser-Busch, enameled red, white and blue trademark $65

CALENDARS

Calendars are most commonly collected by year, subject or era. From Victorian children to popular advertising campaigns and Hollywood's pinup girls, the art that illustrates calendars is their most noteworthy feature. Each piece shows much more about the passing of time than just the ordering of the days and months, also revealing society's evolution.

Background: The earliest calendars were based on the moon's phases, called lunar calendars. In 46 BC, Julius Caesar dictated that the calendar should have 365 days, with a leap year every fourth year. Influential religious leaders were responsible for the inclusion of celebrations and church holidays into the calendar system. Called Gregorian, this calendar system was adopted first by Roman Catholic countries, and later by the rest of the world.

In more modern times companies embraced the calendar as a means to promote their goods and services. Advertising calendars were given away as premiums, and Hollywood also put its most famous faces on the pages of calendars. The most well-known artists and illustrators put their works on calendars.

Also included in this collecting category are calendar plates. Porcelain and pottery plates were first made in England in the late 1880s. They were popular in the U.S. from 1909-1915, and are also collected for their decorative scenes. They range in value from $10-$90.

Numerous subjects and designs are available to calendar collectors. Prices range from a few dollars to hundreds, but most are very affordable.

COLLECTING TIP

Calendars were made to be used and thrown away. As a result, many vintage examples are found in severely deteriorated condition and with pages missing. Consider altering and framing such pieces to preserve the pages that are still in good condition. If a calendar page is damaged around the edge, trim it, frame it using acid-free paper, and enjoy it as an inexpensive and highly displayable piece of art.

General Guidelines: Prices for calendars range from a few dollars to hundreds of dollars. Value is dictated by the condition of the paper, the popularity of the artist or product advertised, and age. Pinups and advertising calendars are extremely popular.

Although the price drops considerably, vintage calendars in fair or even poor condition are still considered collectible, as so few survived in top condition. Many older calendars are commonly reproduced, however, and then adhered to new pads. To spot such reproductions look for shiny staples on an old calendar, or more than one set of staple holes in the calendar's pad. Such a calendar is worth much less than an original, and should never be bought or sold as such.

Clubs

- Calendar Collectors Society, 18222 Flower Hill Way, #229, Gaithersburg, MD 20879

- Calendar Plate Collectors Club, 710 N. Lake Shore Dr., Tower Lakes, IL 60010

- Calendar Art Collectors' Newsletter, 45 Brown's Lane, Old Lyme, CT 06371

VALUE LINE

1890, Ivory Soap	$65
1890, Aetna Insurance Co., framed	$300
1893, Hood's Sarsaparilla, The Young Discoverers, some paper loss	$75
1894, Hoyt's, lady's perfume	$15
1898, Betsy Ross sewing American flag	$25
1898, John Hancock insurance	$25
1901, Colgate, miniature flower	$20
1909, Bank of Waupon	$35
1914, Youth's Companion, marching scene, easel back	$12
1919, Woodrow Wilson	$10

This 1918 Christmas calendar from Germany is made of pressed cardboard.

This unusual 1905 advertising calendar promotes Welch's Grape Juice. It is from a 1999 exhibit at the Concord Museum.

1922, Warren National Bank, Norman Rockwell
    illus. $300
1928, Hartney Machine & Motor Works,
    Discovered, full pad $55
1930, Scoony Products, celluloid calendar $20
1930, Winchester Arms Co. $300
1935, Lone Ranger and Silver $75
1942, Tydol-Veedol, wall type $40
1944, Dick and Jane school calendar $150

1944, Farmers Oil Co., full pad $7
1952, Mobil Oil, red Pegasus logo................................. $8
1952, Pinup, one page, Withers Hollywood,
    poor condition $10
1953, Standard Oil service station calendar.................... $8
1954, Shell Marine Lubricants, thin plastic $25
1955, Marilyn Monroe, full pad.................................... $25
1961, TWA, six sheets $15
1973, Playboy desk calendar, unused $20
1986, Charles Wysocki, excellent condition................ $30
1990, Traci Lords... $41

CALIFORNIA RAISINS

Are your hopes raisin' that that box of singing and dancing purple collectible creatures, wearing sneakers, white gloves and sunglasses, might be worth more than the dust that covers them?

Well, if those creatures are the California Raisins, you've got a sweet find. These cute, popular sun-wrinkled characters, introduced in 1986 by the California Raisin Advisory Board (CALRAB), have generated quite a stir since their debut as promoters of the goodness of raisins as a high-energy, natural snack. And most of the collectibles are still quite affordable.

They remain very popular among collectors today. But most collectors pursue only those items licensed by CALRAB depicting the Claymation characters created by Will Vinton Productions, the ones which sang and danced to the delight of television commercial viewers. The main licensee is Applause, which produced the original, 3-inch plastic PVC raisin toys— conga dancers with blue sneakers or orange sunglasses, a saxophone player and a lead singer, holding a microphone.

General Mills, hearing through the grapevine that these lovable raisins were hot commodities, promoted the California Raisins through its Post Raisin Bran cereal. Specially marked boxes offered a free figure; the complete set of four was available for two proofs of purchase and $4.95.

The original grapes, named through CALRAB's national "Name the Raisins" contest in 1987, are Justin X. Grape, Tiny Goodbite, and Ben Indasun. More than 300,000 fans participated. Soon a cast of backup raisins was on its way, triggering a national fan club, complete with a newsletter for keeping tabs on the characters' newly found fame and fortune, and special figures available to members.

There were even costumed dancers and singers, the California Raisins, who pitched the Raisins across the country from the comforts of their motor home. Fans were delighted by their appearances at the annual Macy's Thanksgiving Day parade in New York City, President Bush's inaugural parade and the Christmas tree lighting at the White House.

Hardee's restaurants jumped on the Raisins' bandwagon, too. Its first of four promotions began in 1987, when smaller 2-1/2-inch plastic versions of the three original Applause characters, plus a sax player, were produced. These Hardee's figures, which have different facial expressions and hand positions, generally sell for about $5 each. In addition to the original Applause story display, a Hardee's display board, featuring the Raisins and cardboard palm trees, is a highly sought collectible, worth about $200.

Hardee's sold millions of its six additional characters introduced during its second promotion—Waves Weaver (surfer), S.B. Stuntz (skateboarder), Rollin' Rollo (roller skater), F.F. Strings (guitar player), Captain Toonz (sun-

glasses and boom box) and Trumpy TruNote (trumpet player). Today they sell for $12-$15 Mint in Package with the trading card, or $5-$7 loose.

The third promotion pitched plush versions of the Raisins, featuring bendable legs and arms, followed by the final pitch in the 1980s—new PVC figures, which are more desirable than the previous Hardee's figures. These figures, individually wrapped with a trading card, depicted Anita Break (stylish, toting lots of bags); Benny (carrying a bowling ball); Buster (leaning on a yellow and orange skateboard); and Alotta Stile (with pink boots and a purple boom box).

By late 1989, in addition to now being overseas in Japan, the California Raisins were being sold nationally in American chain stores (Zayre's and K-mart), and at grocery, toy and card stores. Applause's plastic white display stage (with pink base and dark blue curtains for its PVC figures) is as popular as the Hardee's piece and sells for about $150.

Soon, more characters followed, such as a gloved Michael Jackson Raisin, a Valentine couple, and female figures in high heels. In addition to this cast, collectible figures (depicting several fruit and vegetable friends and foes) were made for the raisins' first TV movie, *Meet The Raisins*. This movie introduced fans to "those plump grapes from Fresno, California, who grew up to be hot Hollywood stars." These stars, featuring Leonard Limabean and Cecil Thyme (worth about $75 each), and Banana White, Rudy Bagaman and Lick Broccoli (about $20 each), are highly collectible.

More than one million copies of the group's first album, named, of course, *I Heard It Through the Grapevine*, were sold, making it platinum. This effort was a successful campaign, as were the 1987 and 1988 California Raisins' eight TV commercials. These commercials were ranked among the best each year.

In addition to the lovable figures, the Raisins were featured on a variety of items, such as radios, lunch boxes, coloring and play sets, wind-up walkers and game boards. General categories include figures; books (worth $5-$15 each); music/video (videos $20-$25, records $8-$10); time pieces (wall clocks $50-$75 each; wrist watches, $20-$25); drinking utensils (plastics are generally less than $10); pins and buttons (generally $5-$10); clothing/costumes; display and promotional pieces; trinkets; paper products; school supplies (erasers and notebooks $7-$10, folders $2-$5); toys, such as games and puzzles; and other miscellaneous items. Sun-Maid's AM-FM radio can sell for $150 Mint in Box. Produced by Nasta, it uses the raisin company's box motif and features a smiling raisin, with poseable arms and legs, leaning on a box of Sun-Maid Raisins. Nasta's wind-up walkers can bring $30 Mint in Box, or $15 loose.

Finding most of these items shouldn't be difficult. And

because the Raisins are still relatively affordable, it's an area ripe for younger, beginning collectors who are looking for a new hobby that may pay off in the long run as interest increases. Values are determined by factors such as scarcity, demand, condition and geographical location.

Hardee's second series of figures are plentiful on the East Coast and in Southern states, where most of this chain's restaurants are located. Look for Raisin collectibles at bargain values at garage sales and toy shows. Beware, however, that there are several unlicensed (those not licensed by CALRAB) lookalikes on the market. Generally, officially licensed products display the names CALRAB and/or Applause.

Two Claymation movies were produced—*The California Raisins Meet the Raisins* and *The California Raisins II, Raisins: Sold Out!* Several new characters appeared in these movies, which were later made into videos.

PVC key chains of the "Graduates," made in 1988, are usually about $50-$75 each.

Recommended Reading
Toy Shop magazine

VALUE LINE

Values shown are for items in Excellent or better condition (unless otherwise noted; "MIP" indicates Mint-in-Package).

Applause Figures
Banana White	$15-$20
Beach girl or boy	$15-$25
Cecil Thyme	$50-$75
Leonard Limabean	$50-$75
Lick Broccoli	$15-$20
Michael Jackson Raisin	$20-$25
Piano player, 3"	$35-$50
Rudy Bagaman	$15-$20
Surfer, 3", vertical board	$35-$45
Surfer, 3", horizontal board	$50-$60

This group of California Raisins is from the popular promotion at Hardee's restaurants in the late 1980s.

"Meet the Raisins" Movie
Banana White	$20-$25
Lick Broccoli	$20-$25
Red the Piano Player	$30-$35
Rudy Bagaman	$20-$25

"Meet the Raisins II" Movie
A.C.	$100-$125
Cecil Thyme	$100-$125
Leonard Limabean	$100-$125
Mom (Lulu Arborman)	$100-$125

Miscellaneous
Air freshener, MIP	$4-$5
AM-FM radio, Nasta, MIB	$125-$150
Board game, Decipher, 1987	$20-$25
Back packs, original, three types, each	$40-$50
Bookmarks, several varieties, each	$3-$5
Boxer shorts	$8-$12
Bulletin board, cork, several styles, used	$7-$10
Clay Factory, 11" x 8" box, MIB	$40-$50
Coffee mugs, ceramic	$15-$20
Colorforms Play Set, Colorforms	$18-$20
Crayon-By-Number, Rose Art	$18-$20
Display stage, for stores for Applause figures	$125-$150
Doorknob hangers, different styles, each	$5-$7
Elastic belts, different styles	$10-$15
Figural erasers, Imaginings	$8-$10
Finger puppet, Bendy Toys, MIB, 1987	$20
The Graduates, figures of four originals, 1988, each	$45-$55
Halloween costume, male, female or child, Collegeville, each	$30-$35
Hardee's paper bag, unused	$2-$4
Inflatable Raisin, 42", Imperial, MIP	$30-$35
Jigsaw puzzles, by American, 75 or 125 pieces, MIB	$25-$30
Just CrossStitch patterns, each leaflet	$12-$15
Key chain, PVC figure, Mint on card	$10-$12
Key chain, PVC figure, loose, each	$5-$7
Key chain, plastic, each	$4-$6
Key chain, metal	$8-$10
Magnets, PVC, each	$20-$25
Magnets, metal, round, each	$3-$5
Lunch box, plastic, with bottle, Thermos	$40-$50
Plush Raisin, 3-4 feet	$30-$40
Plush Raisin, 17-1/2"	$7-$10
Postcards, never mailed, Mint	$2-$5
Puffy Stick-Ons, MIP	$8-$10
Puppets, Fingertronic, Puppet Theatre, MIB, each	$30-$40
Purse	$20-$25
Raincoat, child's or girl's, depicts conga dancers	$20-$25
School kit, MIP	$20-$30
Store display stand	$125-$150

Sunglasses, child's, various colors, loose ....$5-$7
T-shirts, different designs.....................................$12-$20
Tractor-trailer, 18-wheeler, by Winross, diecast,
    MIB ....$200-$250
Valentines, boxed, Cleo...$10-$12
Wallet, MIP ....$20-$25
Wastebasket, plastic ....$40-$50
Wind-up walkers, Nasta ....$10-$15
Wind-up walkers, Nasta, MIP...............................$25-$30
Wristwatch, Nelsonic, 1988, 7-1/2", white band,
    conga dancer...$45-$50

PVC figures
Bass player ....$18-$20
Candy Cane Raisin..$10-$12
Drummer..$20-$25
Santa Raisin ....$10-$12
Valentine girl or boy...$10-$12

Original 2-1/2" figures, made in China, 1987
Ben Indasun, dancer with orange sunglasses.............$5-$7
Justin X. Grape, conga dancer with blue shoes ....$5-$7
Sax player...$5-$7

Tiny Goodbite, microphone singer ....$8-$10

Hardee's First Series
Ben Indasun ....$3-$5
Justin X. Grape...$3-$5
Sax player..$3-$5
Tiny Goodbite ....$3-$5

Hardee's Second Series
Captain Toonz ....$5-$7
F.F. Strings ....$5-$7
Rollin' Rollo ....$5-$7
S.B. Stuntz ....$5-$7
Trumpy TruNote ....$5-$7
Waves Weaver ....$5-$7

Hardee's Final Series (Mint-in-Package)
Alotta Stile ....$10-$15
Anita Break ....$10-$15
Benny ....$10-$15
Buster ....$10-$15
Loose figures (not in package).................................$5-$7
Hardee's display stage...$200

CARNIVAL GLASS

Carnival glass has a lot to offer collectors. Even the name makes it sound like fun -- especially compared to…oh, say…Depression glass. Both names, as it turns out, are a bit misleading. But, no matter, when it comes to collectible glassware, Carnival glass outshines them all.

Background: Simply stated, Carnival glass is merely colored pressed glass with a fired-on iridescent finish. It was made by various glass companies in the United States starting around 1905 as an affordable alternative to the more expensive art glass that was popular at the time but generally available only to America's wealthy. Although some form of Carnival glass has been produced ever since, the "classic" age of Carnival glass is generally considered to be from 1905 to the late 1920s. When collectors talk about Carnival glass, this is the era they're referring to.

Carnival glass was produced in numerous patterns— more than a thousand have been identified and cataloged. Knowing the pattern is essential to evaluating a piece, and fortunately for collectors, there are many books, price guides and collector clubs dedicated exclusively to Carnival glass. It is one of the most thoroughly researched and documented categories in all of collecting.

Carnival glass was produced by more than a dozen companies—both in the United States and abroad—and all of it is collectible. Five U.S. companies, however, were the acknowledged leaders in the field and produced the majority of the most popular patterns. They are Fenton, Dugan, Imperial, Northwood and Millersburg. Fenton probably produced the most Carnival glass, offering over 150 different patterns. Other U.S. firms identified with Carnival glass production, at least to a limited extent, include Fostoria, Heisey, Cambridge, Westmoreland, Indiana and a few others. Some patterns were offered by more than one company.

Together, these firms offered Carnival glass in the form of decorative vases, dresser sets, baskets, paperweights and perfume bottles, as well as more utilitarian pieces, such as bowls, ice cream sets, candy dishes, tumblers and all kinds of tableware. Carnival glass was inexpensive, especially compared to other glassware of the day, and Americans eagerly bought the glittery and colorful pieces. By the 1920s, tastes were changing, and America's love affair with Carnival glass began to dull. Companies holding excess inventory sold off huge quantities of their glassware at bargain prices. Much of it was sold cheaply or used for prizes at carnivals—resulting in the name that the glassware later came to be known by.

General Guidelines: Pattern and color are the two main factors in determining the value of Carnival glass— especially color. Collectors typically divide Carnival glass colors into "bright" or "pastel." The former group generally includes blue, green, amber, amethyst, marigold, purple and red. Marigold is, by far, the most common Carnival glass color and is generally the least valuable. On the other end of the scale is red. The most expensive color to produce, bright red pieces are relatively scarce today and typically bring the highest prices, often commanding five to ten times (or more) as much as a corresponding piece in a more common color.

The pastel colors, which include smoke, lavender, aqua opalescent, clambroth, blue, white and clear, are also generally more valuable than most of the "bright" colors.

As with all types of glassware, condition is critical, and pieces must be free of any chips, cracks or other flaws to be considered collectible.

Clubs

• American Carnival Glass Association, 9621 Spring-water Lane, Miamisburg, OH 45342

• International Carnival Glass Association, P.O. Box 306, Mentone, IN 46539

Note: There are also numerous regional Carnival glass clubs around the country. Many have Internet sites.

Recommended Reading

Warman's Glass, Third Edition, Ellen T. Schroy
Fifty Years of Collectible Glass 1920-1970, Tom and Neila Bredehoft
American Pressed Glass & Bottles Price Guide, Kyle Husfloen
Heisey Glass—The Early Years: 1896-1924, Shirley Dunbar

Carnival glass is among the most plentiful of all glass collecting categories. You can find it at virtually every antique shop and show in America.

VALUE LINE

Included are representative pieces from some of the more popular patterns. Values shown are for examples in Excellent condition in the colors indicated.

Acorn Burrs (Northwood)
Bowl, berry, 5", marigold...$25
Bowl, berry, 5", pastel...$75
Butter dish, covered, marigold..................................$275
Butter dish, covered, pastel......................................$700
Creamer, marigold $200
Creamer, pastel...$400
Punch cup, pastel $85
Punch bowl, with base, marigold $500
Punch bowl, with base, green $800
Punch bowl, with base, pastel $4,000
Tumbler, marigold...$85
Tumbler, pastel...$300
Water set, pastel $535

Blackberry Wreath (Millersburg)
Bowl, 5", marigold...$50
Bowl, 7", six ruffles, amethyst $90
Bowl, 8", ice cream shape, green $75
Bowl, 8-3/8", round flared, amethyst...........................$90
Bowl, 10", six ruffles, amethyst $180

Butterfly and Berry (Fenton)
Bowl, berry, 5", marigold...$45
Bowl, berry, 5", red...$1,000
Bowl, berry, 10", footed, marigold $75
Bowl, berry, 10", footed, blue $185

Captive Rose (Fenton)
Bowl, 10", blue or green $85
Bowl, 10", white $250
Plate, 7", blue or amethyst $165
Plate, 7", white $450
Plate, 9", marigold $150
Plate, 9", green $275
Plate, 9", white $550

Cherry (Dugan)
Bowl, 5", ruffled, marigold $35
Bowl, 5", ruffled, purple or amethyst...........................$55
Bowl, 8", ruffled, blue or green..................................$150
Bowl, 8", ruffled, marigold $65
Cruet, with stopper, purple..$225
Cruet, with stopper, pastel..$575
Sugar dish, with cover, amethyst or purple................$250
Sugar dish with cover, marigold $165
Water pitcher, marigold...$850
Water pitcher, green or purple................................$1,250

Coin Dot (Fenton)
Bowl, 6", marigold...$40
Bowl, 6", blue, green or purple $50
Bowl, 6", red $1,000

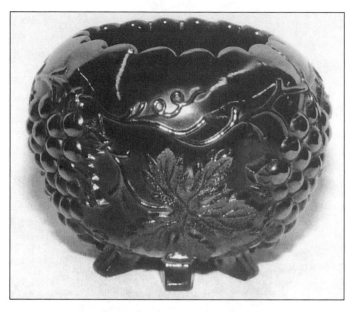

Many Carnival Glass patterns are difficult to distinguish. This rose bowl, in the Grape Delight pattern by Dugan, is worth about $100.

Bowl, 10", blue or green $60
Bowl, 10" pastel $295
Bowl, 10", red $1,200
Water pitcher, marigold...$300
Water pitcher, purple, green or amethyst $450

Corn
Bottle, smoke $250
Bottle, marigold $200
Vase, flower base, green...$475
Vase, marigold..$850
Vase, plain base, marigold $1,550
Vase, purple..$500
Vase, white...$175

Crackle
Bowl, berry, 6"-10", typical example.....................$20-$30
Creamer, green or purple $30
Punch bowl, with base, marigold...............................$135
Punch bowl, with base, green $250
Tumbler, typical example.......................................$20-$30
Wall vase, typical example....................................$35-$50
Water pitcher, typical example...................................$125

Fentonia (Fenton)
Bowl, 5"-7", footed, typical example.....................$40-$60
Butter dish, with cover, marigold................................$150
Water pitcher, marigold...$500
Water pitcher, blue or green $700
Vase, typical example..$200

Flute & Cane (Imperial)
Milk pitcher, marigold $130
Milk pitcher, small, marigold..$65
Water goblet, marigold...$40
Water pitcher, marigold..$145

This 5-inch bowl in Fenton's Peacock Tail pattern is worth about $40-$50. The pattern is very similar to Northwood's Nippon pattern.

Good Luck
Bowl, pie-crust edge, blue	$400
Bowl, pie-crust edge, basketweave exterior, green	$375
Bowl, ruffled, ribbed exterior, blue	$185
Bowl, ruffled, ribbed exterior, marigold	$230
Bowl, ruffled, ribbed exterior, purple	$225
Plate, 9"	$800

Grape & Cable (Fenton, Northwood)
Banana boat, ice green	$375
Banana boat, ice blue	$400
Banana boat, marigold	$175
Banana boat, purple	$220
Banana boat, white	$425
Bon Bon, amethyst	$75
Bon Bon, green	$90
Bon Bon, electric blue	$170
Bowl, 8-3/4", smooth exterior, green	$170
Bowl, master berry, amethyst	$85
Bowl, pie-crust edge, basketweave exterior, marigold	$110
Bowls, master and five small bowls, thumbprint, purple	$325
Butter dish with lid, tiny base nick, amethyst	$105
Candlesticks, pair, amethyst	$400
Compote, covered, marigold	$1,350
Cup and saucer, purple	$165
Orange bowl, 11", amethyst	$145
Perfume bottle, purple	$350
Plate, 6-1/4", basketweave exterior, amethyst	$125
Plate, 7", basketweave exterior, amethyst	$165
Plate, 8", hand grip, basketweave exterior, amethyst	$145
Plate, 9", basketweave exterior, amethyst	$175
Punch bowl and base, ruffled, purple	$350
Punch cup, purple	$27
Ruffled fruit bowl, amethyst	$325
Ruffled sauces, amethyst	$55
Sherbet, amethyst	$30
Tankard tumbler, amethyst	$55
Tumbler, amethyst	$42
Water pitcher, purple	$350
Water set, green	$575
Whiskey shot glass, amethyst	$210

Heavy Grape (Imperial)
Bowl, 10", ruffled, purple	$85
Chop plate, amber	$75
Chop plate, green	$85
Chop plate, purple	$125

Heisey
Creamer, marigold	$135
Creamer, pastel	$375
Sugar, marigold	$125
Sugar, pastel	$400
Toothpick holder, marigold	$185

Holly (Fenton)
Bowl, 8", blue or amethyst	$100
Bowl, 8", marigold	$70
Bowl, 8", pastel	$165
Bowl, 8", red	$1,850
Plate, blue or amethyst	$300
Plate, pastel	$500
Plate, red	$2,500

Lustre Rose (Imperial)
Bowl, 7", marigold	$40
Bowl, 7", pastel	$75
Spooner, purple	$125
Sugar, with cover, marigold	$50
Tumbler, purple	$65
Water pitcher, purple	$145
Water set, seven pieces, marigold	$130

Memphis (Northwood)
Berry set, seven pieces, marigold	$200
Fruit bowl, two pieces with four cups, marigold	$350

Orange Tree (Fenton)
Bowl, fruit, marigold	$85
Cream/sugar set, breakfast, blue	$100
Hatpin holder, blue	$400
Hatpin holder, marigold	$350
Loving cup, blue	$200
Loving cup, marigold	$185
Mug, shaving size, blue	$35
Mug, shaving size, marigold	$25
Mug, small, blue	$70
Plate, 9", blue	$500
Plate, 9", clambroth	$300

Plate, 9", marigold $325
Plate, 9", white... $200
Powder jar, marigold... $75
Tumbler, blue $55

Pansy (Imperial)
Bowl, 9-1/4", lavender $125
Bowl, 9", ruffled, purple...................................... $210
Pickle dish, oval, amber $50
Pickle dish, ruffled, amber $45
Pickle dish, ruffled, purple $70
Nappy, handled, purple $55

Persian Medallion (Fenton)
Bowl, 7", ruffled, green....................................... $55
Bowl, 8", candy ribbon edge, marigold $100
Bowl, 10", footed, ruffled, marigold $170
Bowl, 10", ruffled, blue....................................... $300
Bowl, ice cream shape with plain back, green........... $140
Chop plate, 10" small flake on back, blue.................. $400
Chop plate, 10-1/4", blue $500
Compote, crimped edge, large, blue $195
Compote, crimped edge, ruffled, large, marigold $175
Compote, ruffled, small, marigold $105

Hair receiver, marigold $115
Plate, 9", blue... $1,300
Sauce, round, red... $600

Ripple
Vase, 7", purple $105
Vase, 12", 4-1/4" top, purple.................................. $90
Vase, 12", 5-1/4" top, purple.................................. $95

Rooster
Hat pin, teal.. $100
Hat pin, electric blue... $50
Hat pin, lavender $175
Hat pin, white.. $80

Strawberry
Banana boat, typical example $2,500
Bowl, 5", marigold.. $55
Bowl, 5", vaseline $725
Bowl, 10", blue or green $375
Bowl, 10", marigold.. $200
Gravy boat, typical example $675
Gravy boat, vaseline.. $2,000
Plate, 7", marigold $300
Plate, 7", blue or green.. $450

CEREAL BOXES AND PREMIUMS

Collecting old cereal boxes is not as flaky as it sounds. These vintage boxes, in fact, offer everything a collectible should be. They're colorful, wonderfully nostalgic, challenging to find and great to display—plus, they're increasing in value. No wonder they're one of today's hottest collectibles.

Background: Although commercial breakfast cereals date back to the 1800s, the modern era of "cereal-box art" began with the birth of the television age in the early 1950s, when dozens of new cereals—most of them "pre-sweetened"—sponsored the Saturday-morning TV fare that shaped the lives of every baby boomer in America. The competition in the breakfast aisle was fierce, as cereal makers tried to lure youngsters (and their parents) with the cleverest names, the most colorful graphics and the best prizes. Nothing, it seems, was as enticing to a youngster as the image of their favorite cartoon character along with the magic words, "Free Inside!" As marketing became a bit more sophisticated, cereal boxes started appealing to more than just kids. In recent years, many boxes—especially Wheaties—have featured sports stars, NASCAR themes, movie themes, etc. All, of course, are collectible.

General Guidelines: In general terms, when it comes to cereal boxes, older is typically better. That's because of the supply factor. How many cereal boxes from the 1950s or 1960s have survived, especially in good condition. When you think about it, it's amazing that any survived. What would possess someone in the 1950s or '60s to save a cereal box? Still, for whatever reason, there are more vintage cereal boxes around then you might think. Even more exist from the 1970s and '80s, and boxes from the 1990s are plentiful.

But no matter what era you collect, the key to value is the character or personality depicted. In almost every case, a cereal box depicting The Lone Ranger, Superman, Tony the Tiger, Michael Jordan or the Beatles will be much more desirable than a "generic" box. Also valuable—and a specialty item among advanced collectors—are boxes from obscure cereals that were losers in the "cereal wars." Scarce, because they were not around for very long, they include names such as "Punch Crunch," "Fruit Brute," "Top 3," and "Crazy Cow." Some brands have attracted almost a cult-like following among cereal-box enthusiasts. Remember "Quake" and "Quisp?" They are both favorites among today's collectors. So are dozens of others.

Collector and author Scott Bruce, who publishes the respected fanzine *Flake* and owns one of the biggest collections of cereal boxes in the world, listed some of the hottest boxes in a recent *Today's Collector* article. Approaching the list by decade, Bruce came up with the following. From the 1950s, he chose: Mary Hartline Sugar Smacks, the Puffed Rice box featuring the Gabby Hayes cannon ring, Spoonmen Shredded Wheat Juniors, Superman Corn Flakes, Superman Frosted Flakes, Space Cadet Pep, Paul Jung Sugar Smacks, Wild Bill Hickok Sugar Pops, and Wheaties Lone Ranger.

The 1960s list includes Nabisco Wheat or Rice Honeys picturing the Beatles "Yellow Submarine" rub-ons, Yogi Bear birthday party Corn Flakes, Quisp, Quake, Twinkles, Linus the Lionhearted Crispy Critters, Mr. Spock Sugar Smacks (British), Quick Draw McGraw Sugar Smacks, Snagglepuss Cocoa Krispies, and Huck Hound All Stars.

From the 1970s, Bruce selected Moonstones, Freakies, Quangaroos, Dudley Doright Frosty-O's, Jean LaFoote's Cinnamon Crunch, Punch Crunch, Vanilly Crunch, Fruit Brute and Pete Max's Love Cereal. The 1980s list includes C-3POs, ETs, the Corn Flakes box picturing Miss America Vanessa Williams (it was quickly recalled), Mr. T, PB & Js, Gremlins, Donkey Kong, Donkey Kong Junior, Kellogg Ojs, and Mr. Cheapskates.

Cereal Premiums: Also collectible are cereal-box premiums—all of those little toys and trinkets that came free, either inside the boxes or by mail in exchange for a box-top or two. Sometimes, the premiums were on the back of the box, like baseball cards, phonograph records, or cut-out play sets, like the Lone Ranger "Frontiertown."

FUTURE TREASURES!

Using past experience as a guide, it's fairly easy to predict which of today's many cereal boxes might be collectible in the future. Most important, skip the generic boxes, and look for boxes featuring celebrities, characters and sports heroes. Also worth saving are boxes tied to movies, TV shows, and special events (like the special "Millennios" boxes issued by Cheerios last year to celebrate the new millennium). Cereal boxes are collected primarily for display, so look for boxes that have the best and most colorful graphics.

Any and all of the Wheaties boxes picturing sports stars or teams are worth saving. (If you're smart, you'll buy more than one.) And be aware that most of them are issued on a regional basis. This has made trading among Wheaties collectors in different parts of the country a common, and fun, practice.

Once you've found that box you want to save, open it carefully from the bottom and remove the bag of cereal. (Saving full boxes only attracts mice and insects.) If space is a problem, you can flatten a box by carefully opening both ends and folding it on the factory creases. In this way, you can safely store dozens, or even hundreds of cereal boxes, in a relatively small space. They are best displayed, however.

Every generation has its favorites when it comes to cereal premiums. The old-timers remember the classic Tom Mix and Jack Armstrong items, while baby boomers might recall Lone Ranger, Roy Rogers or Superman freebies, and the younger crowd might be turned on by Ghostbusters or Star Wars premiums. Today, the premiums are generally more plentiful than the boxes. There was a reason, after all, to save the premiums; the boxes were usually thrown out with the trash.

Some representative examples of cereal box premiums (mostly from the 1950s and '60s, along with some classic earlier examples) are included in the "Value Line" below.

Club/Fanzine

• *Flake,* Scott Bruce, P.O. Box 481, Cambridge, MA 02140

VALUE LINE

Values shown are for complete boxes in Excellent condition. Pay particular attention to description. Value shown is only for specific box described.

BooBerry, Star Wars Scene Stick-On Offer, 1977 ...... $125

Cap'n Crunch, Free Comic Book offer, 1963 .... $150

Cheerios, Lone Ranger "Frontiertown" offer, 1948 .... $750

Cheerios, Mickey Mouse on front, Free Walt Disney Pocket-Size Comic Offer, 1946 .... $600

Cheerios, Annette Doll offer on front and back, 1958 .... $350

Cheerios, King Leonardo mask on back, 1961 .... $85

Cheerios, Lone Ranger Frontier Hotel on front and back, 1957 .... $175

Cheerios, Lone Ranger Pocket-Size Comic Book offer, 1954 .... $350

Cheerios, Wyatt Earp Pistol and Target Game offer, 1955 .... $165

Frosty O's, One Million Dollar Offer, 1960 .... $125

Hunny Munch (Winnie the Pooh), Free 3-D Viewer offer, 1968 .... $200

Kellogg's Apple Jacks, Bowl & Mug Set offer, 1967 .... $225

Kellogg's All-Stars, Free Walking Finger Puppet offer, 1960 .... $100

Kellogg's Cocoa Krispies, Jose the Monkey on front, 1958 .... $125

Kellogg's Corn Flakes, Woody Woodpecker Contest/Win $2,000 on front, 1957 .... $100

Kellogg's Corn Flakes, Vote Eisenhower or Stevenson on front, 1952 .... $100

Kellogg's Corn Flakes, Flying Superman offer on front and back, 1955 .... $400

Kellogg's Corn Flakes, Yogi Bear Birthday Dell Comic offer, 1962 .... $375

Many collectors of cereal boxes and premiums also collect magazine ads promoting their favorite cereals, especially those featuring characters or celebrities pitching their favorite breakfast cereal. Clipped from magazines like Saturday Evening Post, Life, Look, Good Housekeeping, etc., a nice vintage full-page ad typically sells in the $5-$10 range. Matted and framed, they make a nice addition to a collection of cereal boxes or premiums.

Kellogg's Corn Flakes, Yogi Bear Head Mask offer, 1962 .... $125

Kellogg's Corn Flakes, Gary Lewis and the Playboys "Doin' the Flake" record offer on back, 1965 .... $135

Kellogg's Froot Loops, Toucan Sam Stuffed Toy offer, 1964 .... $275

Kellogg's Froot Loops, Batman Periscope offer, 1966 .... $300

Kellogg's Honey Smacks, Free Pop-Up Paint Set offer, 1984 .... $40

Kellogg's Hoots, "NEW," Newton the Owl on front, Safety Stickers Offer, 1972 .... $110

Kellogg's OKs, Big Otis Capault Game offer, 1959 ..... $90

Kellogg's Puffa Puffa Rice, Monkees Flicker Ring offer, 1967 .... $250

Kellogg's Raisin Bran, Monkees Picture Coins offer, 1967 .... $225

Kellogg's Raisin Bran, Free Bird Sticker Trading Card Offer, 1976 .... $45

Kellogg's Rice Krispies, Atom Sub offer on front and back, 1954 .... $150

Kellogg's Rice Krispies, "Free Inside Batman Ring," 1967 .... $350

Kellogg's Rice Krispies, Howdy Doody Cut-Out Mask offer $375

Kellogg's Rice Krispies, Annie Oakley Doll offer on back, 1955 $100

Kellogg's Sugar Corn Pops, Free True West Card Offer, 1976 .... $50

Kellogg's Sugar Frosted Flakes, Mary Hartline Magic Doll Offer on front and back, 1955 .... $275

Kellogg's Sugar Pops, Fort Tomahawk offer on back, 1963 .... $95

Kellogg's Sugar Smacks, clown Paul Jung on front, 1953 .... $350

Kellogg's Sugar Smacks, "Free Jig-Jag Puzzle," 1966 .... $100

Kellogg's Sugar Corn Pops, Wild Bill Hickok on front, 1953 .... $150

Kix, Family Size, Ding Dong School on back, 1953 .... $50

Kix, Lone Ranger Branding Iron offer on front and back, 1955 .... $275

Among the more valuable cereal boxes from the 1960s is this Nabisco Rice Honeys box that features an offer for the Beatles "Yellow Submarine" rub-ons. Because of the Beatles tie-in, the box is extremely desirable and worth about $700. A Wheat Honeys box had an identical offer.

Lucky Charms, Alphabet Cards offer, 1967 .... $100

Nabisco Wheat Honeys, Rin Tin Tin TV Mask offer, 1956 .... $100

Nabisco Wheat Honeys, "Yellow Submarine" Beatles Rub-Ons offer, 1969 .... $700

Nabisco Spoon Size Shredded Wheat Juniors, Tobor Mystery-Action Robot offer, 1959 .... $100

Nabisco Rice Honeys, Action Howdy Doody Ring offer, 1960 .... $185

Nabisco Wheat Honeys, Bert the Chimney Sweep (from Mary Poppins) offer, 1964 .... $175

Post Alpha-Bits, Fury Adventure Kit offer on back, 1960 .... $150

Post Cocoa Pebbles, Fred Flintstone on front, Trick Camera offer, 1976 .... $100

Post Corn Flakes & Peaches, 1966 .... $35

Post Crispy Critters, Linus the Lion Stuffed Toy offer, 1963 .... $225

Post Crispy Critters, Zillyzoo Animals offer on back, 1964 .... $135

Post Grape Nuts Flakes, full-panel photo of Mickey Mantle on back, 1960 .... $1,250

Post Mister Muscle, 1966 .... $125

Post Raisin Bran, Bugs Bunny Post Cards on back, 1961 .... $100

Post Sugar Crisp, Blackstone Magic Trick offer, 1955 .... $115

Post Sugar Crisp, Bugs Bunny mask on back, 1961 .... $135

Post Sugar Crisp, Roy Rogers Jigsaw Puzzle offer, 1957 .... $175

Post Sugar Crisp, Mighty Mouse Magic mystery Picture offer on front and back, 1957 .... $95

Post Sugar Sparkled Flakes, Action Football Players offer, 1963 .... $95

Post Super Sugar Crisp, Win Arcade Games Offer, 1984 .... $35

Post Top 3, "NEW! Three Top Favorites Mixed Into One!," 1960 .... $135

Post's Grape-Nuts Flakes, Hopalong Cassidy on front, "Mark a Trail" on back, 1950 .... $235

Post's Krinkles, elf-like character on front and back, 1951 .... $75

Post's Raisin Bran, Hopalong Cassidy Western Badge offer on front and back, 1951 .... $450

Post's Raisin Bran, Roy Rogers Western Ring on front and back, 1953 .... $400

Post's Sugar Crisp, Roy Rogers Paint Set on back, 1954 .... $235

Post's Toasties, Buck Rogers Ring offer, 1946 .... $750

Quake, "Free Comic Book Inside," 1966 .... $600

Quake, Cavern Helmet offer, 1967 .... $500

Quaker Puffed Rice, Sgt. Preston on front, Yukon Trail on back, 1950 .... $150

Quaker Puffed Rice, Gabby Hayes Shooting Cannon Ring offer, 1951 .... $425

Quaker Puffed Wheat, Western Wagons offer, 1952 .... $185

Quisp, "Free Quisp Ring," 1966 .... $600

Trix, Tonto Belt offer on front and back, 1955 .... $350

Trix, Walky Squawky Talkies offer and Trix Rabbit Pillow Case offer, 1965 .... $195

Wackies, "NEW" on front, 1965 .... $150

Wheat Chex, Magic Space Picture offer, 1953 .... $350

Wheat Chex, Checkerboard Squarecrow Doll offer, 1966 .... $75

Wheaties, Mousketeer Record on front, 1956 .... $135

Wheaties, Miniature License Plates offer, 1953 .... $45

Wheaties, Lone Ranger Hike-O-Meter offer on front and back, 1957 .... $350

Wheaties, Mary Lou Retton (18 oz.), 1984 .... $90

Wheaties, Pete Rose, 1986 .... $45

Wheaties, Walter Payton, 1986 .... $60

Wheaties, Minnesota Twins, 1987 ....$30
Wheaties, Detroit Pistons, 1989 (regional) $50
Wheaties, Jim Palmer, 1990..$45
Wheaties, Cincinnati Reds, 1990 (regional) $40
Wheaties, Joe Montana, 1991 ....$50
Wheaties, Rod Carew, 1991 (regional) $250
Wheaties, Minnesota Twins, 1991 (regional) $40
Wheaties, Pittsburgh Penguins, 1991 (regional)...........$45
Wheaties, Steve Largent, 1991 (regional)....................$70
Wheaties, Dallas Cowboys, 1992 (regional)................$40
Wheaties, Pittsburgh Steelers, 1992 (regional) $40
Wheaties, Washington Redskins, (regional) $40
Wheaties, Jagr and Lemieux, 1992 ....$45
Wheaties, Dallas Cowboys, 1993 (regional)................$30
Wheaties, Buffalo Bills, 1993 (regional) $40
Wheaties, John Elway, 1993 (regional) $40
Wheaties, Larry Bird, 1993 (regional) $35
Wheaties, Clyde Drexler, 1993 (regional) $40
Wheaties, Babe Ruth or Lou Gehrig or Willie Mays,
    1993...$25
Wheaties, Jerry Rice, 1994 (regional)..........................$35
Wheaties, World Cup Soccer, 1994 (regional).............$75
Wheaties, Atlanta Braves, 1995 (regional) $25
Wheaties, Cleveland Indians, 1995 (regional) $30
Wheaties, 30th Anniversary Super Bowl, 1995,
    18-oz...$25
Wheaties, 30th Anniversary Super Bowl, 1995,
    34-oz...$50
Wheaties, Jacksonville Jaguars, 1995 (regional) $40
Wheaties, Cal Ripken Jr., 1995 (regional) $35
Wheaties, Boston Garden, 1995 (regional)...................$25
Wheaties, Nebraska Cornhuskers, 1995 (regional).......$35
Wheaties, Dan Marino, 1995 ....$20
Wheaties, Atlanta Braves, 1996 (regional) $15
Wheaties, New York Yankess, 1996 (regional).............$15
Wheaties, San Francisco 49ers, 1996 (regional)...........$25
Wheaties, Kirby Puckett, 1996 (regional)....................$35
Wheaties, Negro Leagues, 1996 ....$25
Wheaties, Boston Marathon, 1996 (regional) $30
Wheaties, Peter Jacobsen (PGA), 1996 (regional)........$35
Wheaties, Michael Johnson, 1996 ....$20
Wheaties, Nebraska Cornhuskers "Back to Back,"
    1996 (regional) $35
Wheaties, QB's (Marino, Aikman, Elway), 1996.........$25
Wheaties, WR's (Brown, Rice, Reed), 1996.................$25
Wheaties, RB's (Thomas, Sanders, Allen), 1996..........$25
Wheaties, Women Gymnastics Team, 1996..................$25
Wheaties, Arthur Ashe, 1997 (regional) $25
Wheaties, Lambeau Field, "40 Years,"
    1997 (regional) $25
Wheaties, Marcus Allen, 1997.....................................$25
Wheaties, Tom Osborne (regional) $25
Wheaties, Walter Payton, 1997....................................$35
Wheaties, Jackie Robinson, 1997 ....$35
Wheaties, All-Star Outfielders (Bonds, Griffey,

Gwynn), 1997...$30
Wheaties, New England Patriots, 1997 (regional)........$25
Wheaties, Green Bay Packers, 1997 (regional) $30
Wheaties, Seattle Mariners, 1997 (regional).................$25
Wheaties, Michael Jordan, various,
    typical box..$30-$50
Wheaties, Chicago Bulls, various Championships,
    typical example ....$20-$25

Cereal Premiums

Values shown are for premiums in Excellent condition.

Apple Jacks Mug & Bowl Set, 1967 sendaway,
    Kellogg's Apple Jacks...$100
Atom Sub, plastic, 2" long, 1955,
    Kellogg's Rice Krispies...$20
Batman Ring, 1967, Kellogg's Rice Krispies $15
Beatles "Yellow Submarine" Rub-Ons, 1969
    Nabisco Rice (and Wheat) Honeys $50
Buck Rogers Badge, various, Cream of Wheat,
    typical example, 1930s...$100-$300
Buffalo Bee "Breakfast Buddy," plastic (hangs on
    rim of cereal bowl), 1961, Nabisco
    Wheat Honeys $5
Dick Tracy Badge, various, Quaker Oats,
    typical example, 1930s...$100-$200

The Batman offer on this box of Kellogg's OK's raise its value to $300 or more.

Dick Tracy Manual and Code Book, 1930s,
    Quaker Oats $225
Dick Tracy Secret Compartment Ring, 1938,
    Quaker Oats $400
Dick Tracy Pocket Flashlight, 1939, Quaker Oats $100
Don Winslow of the Navy, Squadron of Peace
    Membership Card, Creed and Manual, 1939,
    Kellogg's Wheat Krispies $125
Flash Gordon Ring, 1949, Post Toasties $85
Fury Adventure Kit, 1960 sendaway,
    Post Alpha-Bits $150
Cap'n Crunch mini-comic books, 1965,
    Cap'n Crunch $20
Captain Jolly Comic Book, 1954, Post's Corn-fetti $35
Gabby Hayes Cannon Ring, 1951, Quaker Oats $175
Gabby Hayes Movie Viewer, 1952, Quaker Oats $200
Hopalong Cassidy Trading Cards, 1950, Post, each $10
Howdy Doody Mask, cardboard cutout, 1954,
    Kellogg's Rice Krispies $25
Howdy Doody Ring, various characters, 1960,
    Nabisco Rice Honeys $25
Huckleberry Hound Stampets Printing Set, 1961,
    Kellogg's Corn Flakes $35

**The "Stampets Printing Set" advertised on this Corn
Flakes box has a value of about $25-$35.**

Jack Armstrong, Champion Belt, 1940s, Wheaties $300
Jack Armstrong, Six Man Football Book, 1938,
    Wheaties $25
Jack Armstrong, baseball cap, 1934, Wheaties............ $50
Jack Armstrong, Fingerprint Kit, 1939, Wheaties $65
Lone Ranger Hike-O-Meter, metal, 1957, Wheaties $60
Lone Ranger Bandanna, 1949, Kix............................. $50
Lone Ranger Billfold, 1942, Kix $90
Lone Ranger "Ranch Fun" Book, 1955, Cheerios........ $40
Mickey Mouse (and his pals) ring, plastic,
    various colors, 1956, Sugar Jets $40
Monkees Flicker Ring, 1967, Kellogg's Puffa
    Puffa Rice $35
Mouseketeers record, cardboard cutouts, 1956,
    Wheaties $15
Navy Frogman, plastic, various colors, 3", 1955,
    Kellogg's Corn Flakes $20
Rin Tin Tin Ring, plastic, 1955, Nabisco Ranger
    Joe Rice Honeys, 12 different $15
Roy Rogers Autographed Souvenir Cup,
    Quaker Oats, 1950.. $35
Roy Rogers Pop Out Card, early 1950s, Post $20
Shari Lewis finger puppet, 1962, Quaker Life.............. $12
Sgt. Preston Color Photo, 22" tall, contest prize,
    early 1950s, Quaker Oats $200
Sgt. Preston "10-in-1 Electric Trail Kit," plastic,
    1956, Quaker Shredded Wheat $135
Space Patrol Binoculars, plastic, 1953,
    Chex Cereals $135
Superman Belt, vinyl belt, metal buckle, 1955,
    Kellogg's Corn Flakes $225
Superman Satellite Launcher, plastic, 1956,
    Kellogg's Corn Flakes $45
Tobor Robot, plastic, 2", 1959, Nabisco Spoon Size
    Shredded Wheat Juniors...................................... $60
Tom Mix Badge, "Straight Shooter," silver or gold,
    1937, Ralston $65
Tom Mix Badge, "Ranch Boss," 1938, Ralston.......... $500
Tom Mix Belt and Buckle with Secret Compartment,
    1951, Ralston $225
Tom Mix Bandanna, 1933, Ralston $200
Tom Mix Cowboy Hat, 1933, Ralston $950
Tom Mix Ring, various, 1930s-1940s,
    Ralston .... $75-$150
Tom Mix Compass and Magnifying Glass,
    1940, Ralston $125
Tony the Tiger Doll, inflatable vinyl, 45", 1954,
    Kellogg's $300
Tony the Tiger stuffed toy, 25", 1963 sendaway,
    Kellogg's Sugar Frosted Flakes............................ $65
Walking Cornelius Toy, plastic, walking ear of corn,
    6", 1959, Post Sugar Coated Corn Flakes $175
Wild Bill Hickok Colt Six-Shooter, plastic, 10" long,
    1958 sendaway, Kellogg's Sugar Pops................... $165
Yogi Bear Cereal Spoon, silver, Canada, 1960,
    Kellogg's Rice Krispies....................................... $15

CHRISTMAS AND SANTA CLAUS COLLECTIBLES

Are you making your wish list and checking it twice? Are you sure you've covered everything?

If you collect Christmas collectibles, the possibilities are endless. You could fill Santa's sleigh with an assortment of items, including postcards, lights, ornaments and jolly old St. Knickknacks. Perhaps your home is decorated during the holiday season with other items being eyed up by the Grinch: Christmas seals, books, snow domes, candy containers, cookie cutters, angels, greeting cards, shopping catalogs, candles, artificial trees, figurines, nutcrackers, lead tinsel, cardboard Christmas village scenes, cake tins, tree stands, candleholders, dinnerware, records, wreaths, angel hair and icicles, stockings, trade cards, Christmas prints, Nativity sets, jewelry, dinnerware, and advertising items—especially those great Coca-Cola magazine ads showing Santa enjoying an ice-cold Coke!

Background: During the winter solstice—a time of the sun's rebirth, as the days grow longer—Christians celebrate Christmas to honor Christ's birth. Today, it is the most popular of the annual holidays. But even before Christ's birth, many cultures celebrated the winter solstice as the anniversary of several ancient gods' births. Although it is impossible to pinpoint Christ's exact birthdate, by the year 356, December 25 was accepted by Christians around the world.

As Christianity and birthday celebrations increased in popularity, pagan practices declined. However, some practices merged with Christian traditions. These included the Roman traditions of gift giving and decorating with flowers and candles, plus the Celtics' draping the home with holly, mistletoe and evergreens.

During the 14th century, religious celebrations marking Christ's birth involved the use of Christmas carols. Italians had live re-enactments of the Nativity. This tradition eventually evolved into the creation of Nativity sets and figures made from various materials to model Christ's birth.

During the 18th century, Germany used a Christmas pyramid to display scenes of Christ's birth. The pyramid was a forerunner to the Christmas tree; it was a set of shelves decorated with evergreen branches. As displays grew bigger and bigger, outgrowing the pyramids, they were moved to corners and altars in churches, where elaborate Nativity scenes were displayed.

The Moravian sect carried this tradition to America. Soon, people were recreating Nativity scenes in their homes. The Moravians' putz, meaning "to decorate," filled entire rooms. This practice was widely accepted, and by the turn of the century, homes commonly had crèche or putz scenes in them.

As the Christmas tree's popularity increased, the putz displays became the perfect way to fill the space beneath the tree.

In Europe by the 1500s, the evergreen tree had become an important part of the Christmas tradition, one which, with assistance from Martin Luther and Queen Victoria, spread around the world. Early trees were decorated with homemade fancies, cookies, fruit and small gifts. By the early 1900s, ornaments were being created specifically to decorate Christmas trees, which, by the way, were not always natural. In the late 1800s, artificial trees were made from materials such as goose feathers and aluminum.

And soon, Santa Claus was on his way to every town in the United States. The Christian St. Nicholas combined with traits from the Scandinavian Thor, the Anglo-Saxon Father Christmas, and the Russian Kolwada and Baboushka evolved into the Dutch Sinterklaas. Sinterklaas emigrated to America with the Dutch settlement of New York. With the help of Washington Irving, Thomas Nast and Haddon Sundblum of the Coca-Cola Co., Sinterklaas became our Santa Claus.

This slender papier-mâché Santa with a cotton beard was made in Japan in the 1940s. It is worth about $75 (Photo courtesy Susan Eberman).

This painted milk glass light bulb, about 3 inches tall and made in Japan, is valued at $15-$30.

COLLECTORS' TIPS!

In part driven by sentiment, Santa Claus is among the most popular subjects to ever appear on postcards. Postcard Santas were used for advertising, as well as to send annual Christmas greetings. Novelty Santas abound, including hold-to-light, mechanical, silks, transparencies, and installment styles. The demand for Santa postcards is also quite high, driving prices higher each year, and the supply is dwindling. But an average Santa postcard can still be had for anywhere from $5-$15 each.

Glittered cards can range from $2-$10; pop-ups, from $30-$40; mechanicals, from $35-$50; and silks, from $25-$50. Highly decorated costumes or backgrounds, styles such as those previously mentioned, and physical condition all influence the value. Full-length Santas (not just head and shoulders), long robes (not short jackets like the modern outfit), and nontraditionally colored suits (any color other than red) are all unusual, and therefore more desirable. Also desirable are postcards by noted publishers such as Raphael Tuck, John Winsch and Paul Finkenrath, which typically sell for about $30-$45.

As with all collectibles, condition is critical in determining value. When considering a purchase, or evaluating your own collection, look for the following defects, any of which would lower the value of a postcard: water damage; writing on the image; creases; tears; dirt on the surface (be extra careful when making purchases at outdoor flea markets); postal cancellation marks bleeding through from the back; paper gouges; added pencil, crayon or felt-tip marker repairs to the color; heavy eraser marks; bleaching of the card that leaves a chalky surface; off-register printing; and rounded corners.

Watch out for "sandwich cards," where an old back has been applied to a newer card. This is detected by the thickness of the card. You might also find trimmed cards, where a card has been cut smaller than its original size so that it has the appearance of having sharp corners and clean edges. The exception here is any card that was designed for a child to cut from the paper or box. These can be unevenly cut. Even in a set, not all cards are identical in size. However, avoid cards that look as though they were cut by a trained rat. Vintage cards were often trimmed at the turn of the century to fit into albums for display. This still detracts from the value.

Here are a few terms that even novice postcard collectors should be aware of as they pursue a collection of Christmas postcards:

Deltiology—the study and collecting of postcards.

Golden Age—1898 to 1918, when postcard use was at its peak.

Advertising postcards—issued as part of an ad campaign to promote a business or product.

Installment set—a series of postcards (usually four), intended to be sent one at a time, that form a completed

General Guidelines: Christmas memorabilia and Santa collectibles can be divided into several broad categories. They include:

Postcards—There are thousands of Christmas postcards available to collectors, most of them bearing good tidings at very affordable prices (starting at just $1-$5 each). They depict an array of Yuletide subjects and themes—Nativity, angels, winter scenes and landscapes, snowmen, holly, joyful kids, angels, Madonna, churches, Christmas trees, plants and more. But Santa Claus leads the way—be it on roller skates or guiding his sleigh. Some of the more elaborate Santa postcards even have real silk attached to his suit; these postcards can range in value from $50 to $100. Postcards also use a variety of colors and surfaces (flat; embossed; and "hold-to-light," which can sell for up to $100). Design, quality ad rarity are all factors which influence a postcard's value.

image when assembled side-by-side (similar to a puzzle). Among the most desirable installment sets is one picturing Santa Claus that was issued by Huld of Germany in 1907.

Hold-to-light postcards—die-cut cards, with small areas cut away so that certain graphic elements are highlighted when held to the light (for example, lights on a Christmas tree that "glow"). Hold-to-lights are considered very desirable and are usually among the most expensive.

Silks—novelty cards that use actual silk in their construction. For example, Santa's suit could be made of real silk, or the image may be printed on silk.

Transparency—a novelty card, similar to a hold-to-light, but not die-cut. A transparency card employs a thin layer of paper that reveals a hidden image when held to the light.

Mechanical card—another type of novelty card, it includes a moving part (a tab to pull, wheel to turn, etc.) to either enhance or change the image.

Christmas ornaments—German-made "kugels," a traditional collector favorite are heavy and can be quite large; some measure six to seven inches across. Most kugels were round, but some were oval. The first shapes produced (after the round kugels) were pinecones, grape clusters, nuts and apples. Popular shapes that followed included angels, snowmen, Santas, babies, animals, birds, butterflies, etc. Glass ornaments can have hangers or metal clips at the base. Butterfly ornaments had blown glass bodies and spun glass wings. "Wire-wrapped" glass ornaments, produced in the last half of the 1800s, were surrounded by a thin spiral-like wire.

As ornaments from the early 1900s are becoming scarce, and more expensive, collectors are looking for alternatives to these vintage collectibles. Some are turning to ornaments created primarily in America and Japan from the 1940s through the 1960s. Hand-painted balls from Japan from the late 1940s to early 1950s, often miniature and with solid colors, typically sell in the $3-$6 range. Their American counterparts, often produced by Shiny Brite, can bring up to $12 each. Shiny Brite was the leader in its field, producing ornaments in many different shapes, sizes, and colors. They were often sold in fancy boxed sets which, compared to individual ornaments, now command higher values if the set is complete. Postwar glass ornaments can readily be found in antique shops, secondhand stores and at flea markets, especially as the holiday draws near. Age, condition, size and design are key factors in determining the value.

Tissue paper is commonly used to wrap ornaments, but it can be abrasive and may damage the surface of a glass ornament or painted object. One alternative is to wrap ornaments in soft cloth, such as old sheets or pillowcases. Nesting fragile items in divided boxes padded with cotton also works well. It is also important to remove old hooks or wires from glass ornaments before storing them; they often poke holes in the glass or mar paint surfaces.

Christmas tree lights—The first person to illuminate a Christmas tree with electric lights was Edward Johnson, an employee in Thomas Edison's company. Johnson, in 1882,

Early depictions of Santa Claus do not show the jolly, roly-poly figure we know today. This postcard shows an almost sinister-looking Santa, dressed in white, rather than red. You'll find plenty of vintage Santa postcards in the $10-$20 range. Examples that show Santa dressed in colors other than the traditional red tend to be a bit more desirable. This particular white-robed Santa, because it is a colorized "real photo" postcard, is worth $50 to $60.

strung a set of 80 small electric lights on his Christmas tree. Ten years later, lights were being produced for commercial use and a new tradition was born. The first official White House Christmas tree to have electric lights was in 1895, displayed by President Grover Cleveland. Soon after, in 1901, General Electric began offering miniature lights, with Ever-Ready following in its wake. In 1925, American-based manufacturers united to form the National Outfit Manufacturers Association; its initials, NOMA, became a brand name to distinguish American lights from those produced by foreign companies, including Germany, Japan and Austria. As the lights have evolved, adaptations have been made in design, shape, colors and wiring, ranging from bubble lights (produced until the 1970s) and screw-in bulbs, to Santa Claus, Disney characters, Betty Boop and snowman glass figurals, to the tiny midget lights common today.

The variety and abundance of vintage Christmas lights makes it easy to find them at garage sales, antique shops and flea markets. But, although the lights' strings might still be in working order, use caution if you plan to actually use them. Check first for shorts in the wiring and potential overheating in the older strings. About half of the figurals you find will be in working order when you plug them in. If it's an $800 figural, you might want to keep it in a display case, rather than put it on your tree.

Christmas seals—Christmas seals are stamps sent out annually by the American Lung Association as part of its annual fund raising campaign. Quite often sentimental and colorful, they are an extremely affordable Christmas alternative. Sheets of Christmas seals from the 1930s can still be purchased today for a few dollars, while single seals can set you back but a quarter. But there are rare and early issues that command hundreds of dollars, too. (For more information, you can contact two clubs: The Christmas Seal and Charity Stamp Society, P.O. Box 39696, Minneapolis, MN 55439-0696; or The Christmas Philatelic Society, 5630 N. Greenwood Blvd., Spokane, WA 99205-7535. Both organizations charge annual dues, but offer newsletters.)

Club
•Golden Glow of Christmas Past, 6401 Winsdale Street, Minneapolis, MN 55427

Recommended Reading
Holiday Collectibles, Lissa Bryan-Smith and Richard Smith
Santa's Price Guide to Contemporary Christmas Collectibles, Beth Dees
Silver Christmas Collectibles, Clara Johnson Scroggins

Issued at a price of about $22, this "Favorite Santa" Hallmark Keepsake Ornament is now valued at about $50.

VALUE LINE

Values shown are for items in Excellent condition.

Vintage Christmas Postcards

Children, trimming tree	$7-$10
Christmas tree, decorated, real photo	$40-$50
Father Christmas, blue suit, "Christmas Greetings"	$15-$20
Father Christmas in bright purple, "Hearty Christmas Greeting"	$20-$25
Plum pudding, "Best Wishes For A Merry Christmas," Ellen H. Clapsaddle, International Art Pub.	$7-$8
Santa, adult erotic theme, with pretty young girl on his lap, Victorian Era	$50-$75
Santa, advertising for Lemp Beer, mechanical	$250-$350
Santa, advertising for Bloomingdale's, by R.F. Outcault, 21 Santas on trolley going to Bloomingdale's	$150-$250
Santa Cat postcards, Louis Wain artwork, each	$200-$400

CHRISTMAS AT WOOLWORTH'S!

In 1880 or so, F. W. Woolworth introduced German-made glass ornaments, kugels, in his Lancaster, Pa., dime store. He purchased a modest $25 worth from an importer; they were gone in two days. They were quite popular; the ornaments were his top-selling holiday decoration. At five and 10 cents each, he sold quite a few; his chain of stores brought in $25 million over the next 50 years from these!

Santa Claus, Wiener Werkstaette, Vienna..........$400-$650
Santa Claus, Raphael Kirchner, Art Nouveau....$350-$500
Santa, hold-to-light ....$450-$500
Santa, hold-to-light, "A Merry Christmas to You,"
    Malick ....$350-$450
Santas, mechanical, moving parts......................$150-$350
Santa, silk, "A Merry Christmas" ....$25-$50
Santa, sinister looking, in fur-trimmed blue
    robe...$15-$20
Santa, white-robed, colorized real photo ....$50-$75
Santa, red suited, driving sleigh............................$10-$15
Santa, with a gift-filled automobile........................$10-$15
Santa, "A Merry Christmas to You," Santa writing,
    toys at feet, sitting in woods, talking to angel,
    Germany, 1909 ....$8-$10
Uncle Sam Santa, hold-to-light, Ainbach, rare,
    four different, each ....$2,500-$3,000
Uncle Sam Santa, flat design, five different,
    each ....$200-$350

Christmas Ornaments
Angel, glass, Dresden trim, 5" ....$75-$100
Angel, red, glass, Germany, 3-1/2" ....$75-$85
Angel, chromolithograph, surrounded by spun glass,
    2-1/2", Germany.................................$12-$15
Angel, wax, 4" ....$100-$150
Angel, wax, tree top, 7" ....$650-$700
Baby Jesus, wax, in wooden oval, 3" ....$250-$300
Bell, glass, with clapper, 4" German,
    pre-1940s....................................$10-$40
Bird, glass, clip on, German, 1950s......................$25-$50
Candle, glass, with clip, 4" ....$75-$80
Candy cane, glass, silver with blue stripes,
    6-1/2"..$40-$50
Church, glass, 3" ....$20-$25
Church, pointed steeple, white, mica covered,
    cardboard, 3", Czechoslovakia........................$12-$15
Church, glass, red with frosted stencil picture of
    church, "Silent Night," 3", Shiny Brite ....$2-$4
Cross, with angel head, paper ....$35-$30
Father Christmas, glass, with clip, 4" ....$150-$175
Hand-painted glass balls, Japan, 1940s-50s, each .....$4-$5
Hand-painted glass, balls, Poland, 1960s....................$3-$4
Horns, blue and red, glass, Czechoslovakia,
    1980s, each.......................................$10-$15
Icicle, glass, silver with white mica snow, 6" ....$30-$35
Kugel, ball, German, late 1800s, 2-1/2" ....$25-$50
Painted and glitter glass balls, West Germany,
    1960s ....$3-$4
Peacock, glass, 5" $50-$75
Reindeer, Dresden, flat, gold, red and green foil,
    7" ....$65-$75
Reindeer, Dresden, 3-D, brown, 3"....................$150-$175
Rudolph, hard plastic, brown and white, USA ....$5-$6
Santa head, paper, with tinsel holder, 4"................$15-$20
Santa, in chimney, glass, 3" ....$50-$65

Santa Claus, red suit, foot in chimney, tinsel trim,
    6-1/2", Germany................................$30-$35
Shiny Brite mica-covered glass indents, reflector,
    1950s ....$4-$7
Shiny Brite bumpy glass indents, reflector,
    late 1940s-1950s ....$6-$12
Shiny Brite striped glass balls, 1950s ....$2-$4
Skier, cotton, bisque face, 3"....................$150-$200
Star, cotton batting stitched to cardboard, America,
    1880s ....$35-$50
Star, tinsel garland and die-cut foil, Germany,
    1890s ....$25-$30
Star, Dresden, flat, embossed gold, tinsel trim,
    3" ....$30-$35
St. Nicholas, with bag, glass, with clip, 5" ....$300-$325
Strawberry, large, glass Czechoslovakia, tin cap,
    1980s ....$25-$30
Snowman, unsilvered, white mica coating, Germany,
    3-1/2"..$30-$35

Christmas tree lights
Aurora Christmas Lights, boxed set, 1950s...........$15-$20
Candy cane, glass figural ....$5-$10

Dating from the 1950s, this plastic candy container is valued at about $30. (Photo courtesy Susan Eberman)

Many postcard collectors look for images of Santa driving an auto, rather than a sleigh. Typical examples sell in the $15-$20 range.

Clarabelle, glass figural, 1950s ....$250-$325

Christmas candle, glass figural, Avon....................$10-$15

Dick Tracy, glass figural ....$150-$200

Dealites, eight lights wired in series,
    1910s-1920s ....$75-$100

Ear of corn, glass figural, 1930s...........................$10-$15

Festive Lites, 1950s..$10-$20

General Electric Mazda Lamps, boxed.................$25-$30

Howdy Doody, glass figural, 1950s ....$125-$150

Jiminy Cricket, glass figural, hand painted............$35-$45

Kristal Star Lamps, glass lamps, star-like,
    Japan, each ....$5-$6

Mother Goose characters, glass figurals, 1930s.....$50-$75

NOMA Bubble-Lites, Watch Them Bubble,
    1940s ....$50-$75

NOMA, Christmas lights with Mazda lamps,
    seven lights, 1930s ....$35-$50

NOMA, Mickey Mouse Lights, 1939 ....$100-$150

Paramount Bubbling Lights, for use with
    candelabra base sockets, Raylight...................$50-$100

Paramount, Walt Disney Character Lites, boxed
    set of eight characters, 1960s ....$100-$150

Reliance Spark-L-Lite set, boxed, 1940s ....$15-$20

Santa Claus, glass figural, Japan ....$25-$30

Santa, Dresden, 6"..$175-$200

Santa, glass, double-sided ....$15-$20

Santa, in chimney, glass ....$15-$20

Snowman, glass...$10-$15

Snow White or Seven Dwarfs, glass figurals,
    1940s ....$100-$125

Sterling Bubble Light Outfit ....$50-$100

Timco Lighting Outfit, with General Electric
    lamps, 1940s-50s..$10-$20

Miscellaneous Christmas Collectibles

Angel hair, spun glass, fireproof, National
    Tinsel Mfg. Co., in box ....$15-$25

Artificial tree, green, with candleholders,
    red-white base, 36"...$300-$400

Bank, Santa, rubber, "A Christmas Club A Corp.,
    NY, 1972, 6"..$20-$25

Bank, Santa, hard plastic, Fanny Farmer, 7".........$30-$35

Book, The Night Before Christmas,
    Wm. B. Conkey Co., 10" x 7-1/2", 1905 ....$75-$100

Book, The Night Before Christmas, Bush and
    Bull Co. Dept. Store, Williamsport, Pa. ....$25-$35

Book, The Night Before Christmas, A Golden
    Book, Golden Press, Western Publishing Co.
    Racine, Wis., 1975 ....$10-$15

Book, Rudolph The Red-Nosed Reindeer,
    by Robert L. May, Maxton Publishers Inc.,
    New York, 1939 ....$15-$20

Book, Santa Claus in StoryLand, pop-up,
    Doehla Greeting Cards Inc.,
    Fitchburg, Mass., 1950....................................$25-$30

Book, Watching for Santa Claus, Hurst & Co. Pub.,
    New York, 1912 ....$15-$20

Book, The World With Santa Claus,
    McLoughlin Bros., New York, 1900 ....$30-$35

Booklet, Christmas Carol, by Charles Dickens,
    L.L. Stearn's and Sons, 100 pages, 5"................$7-$10

Candle, three in one base, hard plastic, white, 9" ......$6-$8

Candle, metal base, green, enameled, embossed,
    green and red cardboard tube, USA,
    3-1/2" x 9" ....$10-$12

Candy cane, chenille, 6", 1930s.............................$4-$5

Candy container, snowman, papier-mâché,
    German...$75-$100

Candy container, Santa in basket, celluloid head,
    string basket, Japan ....$100-$150

Candy container, Dresden ....$225-$275

Candy tin, Santa Claus on cover, Mrs. Steven's Co.,
    2-pound ....$10-$15

Christmas cake cutters, boxed set, made in Germany,
    1930s ....$50-$75

Cookie cutter, Christmas tree...............................$10-$12

Cookie cutter, Santa, vintage ....$50-$75

Feather tree, green, red wood tub,
    Germany, 1"...$12-$15

Feather tree, green, white wooden base with stenciled
    holiday design, Germany, 3" ....$300-$325

Feather tree, green with red composition berries and
    candleholders on branches, white round wooden
    base, Germany, 6" ....$575-$600

Feather tree, white with red composition berries,
    red wood round base, West Germany, 12" ....$50-$75

Figure, choir boy, hard plastic, red and white,
    3-1/2"..$3-$4

Figure, elf, bisque, different colors and positions,
    up to 3", Japan..$10-$15

Figurine, dancing snow babies, porcelain,
    Germany, pre-WWI, 2" ....$175-$225

Figurine, Santa snow baby, riding polar bear,
   German ....$250-$300
Greeting card, "Christmas Joys," silk tassel,
   Germany, 1910s...$15-$20
Greeting card, "Best Christmas Wishes," winter scene,
   held together with ribbon, Germany, 1932............$6-$7
Greeting card, "Christmas Greetings in My House,"
   pop-up, house with cat on fence, 1925.................$6-$7
Icicles, Double-Glo, fireproof, 1940s-1950s,
   in box..$10-$15
Jack-in-Box, Santa, 1930s..................................$175-$200
Mask, Santa, gauze, 1930s, Japan.......................$40-$50
Matches, Santa Claus, "Seasons Greetings,"
   Lion Match Co., 4"...$10-$12
Nativity scene, cardboard fold-out, Sweden,
   1950s, 7"...$8-$10
Nativity set, boxed set, 1950s, USA ....$20-$30
Nativity set, paper, fold-out, 4", Germany ....$20-$30
Nativity set, hand-carved and hand-painted,
   eight figures, box says "Made by the Peasants
   of the Tyrolean Alps," ....$30-$40
Nativity set, "Christmas Manger Set,"
   Concordia Product, USA....................................$20-$30
Package tags, 80 seals, 10 tags, Happee-Merree,
   1940s ....$5-$10
Tree stand, cast iron, with seven light sockets,
   American ....$50-$6

Plate, Santa and sleigh with holly, white with
   gold trim, "Souvenir of Sunbury, PA"...............$20-$25
Program, Christmas service, St. John's Rectory,
   South Williamsport, PA, 1925............................$3-$5
Record, O Little Town of Bethlehem, 78 rpm,
   Record Guild of America Inc................................$5-$7
Santa figure, Belsnickel, blue, 14"..............$1,000-$1,250
Santa figure, celluloid, in sleigh with two reindeer,
   8", Japan ....$75-$100
Santa figure, on paper skis, Japan, 4" ....$50-$60
Santa, battery operated, with bell, Japan............$175-$200
Santa, wind-up, on skis, Japan............................$75-$100
Santa, wind-up, on reindeer, Japan ....$150-$200
Sheet music, Santa Claus is Comin' To Town,
   Leo Feist Inc., New York ....$12-$15
Snow dome, Santa, reindeer on shoulders,
   Santa riding one inside globe ....$20-$25
Snowman, hard plastic, 9-3/4" ....$15-$20
Stocking, Santa, lithographed, 22"....................$200-$250
Stocking, filled with toys, Japan ....$30-$40
Telegram, "Holiday Greeting" by Western Union,
   1946...$10-$12
Toy, Santa and deer pulling green metal sled, wind-up,
   celluloid, Japan, 1930s ....$65-$75
Toy house, cardboard, Built-Rite, 1930s...............$10-$25

CIRCUS MEMORABILIA

Years ago, little boys (and girls, too) used to dream about running away to join the circus. Before movies and TV, the circus was as glamorous as things got in rural America. There are still people fascinated by the old-time circus, and, for them, collecting circus memorabilia is a national pastime. Circus collectibles abound—with more than two hundred years of circus history behind us, there is much to choose from, including circus posters, clown collectibles, animal acts, route books and cards, vintage photographs and circus wagons.

For those with enormous budgets—and room to spare—there is no better choice than an honest-to-goodness, authentic circus wagon. These beautifully carved wagons are reminders of the colorful and elaborate circus parades announcing that, yes, indeed, the circus was coming to town.

This 1913 poster for a Barnum & Bailey circus parade sold for $300 at an auction conducted by Collectors Auction Services of Oil City, Pa. The poster was one of many circus posters that were reproduced in the 1960s and 1970s.

But, in addition to being too expensive for the average collector, wagons require a large space to store them. For this reason, not too many collectors pursue these collectibles, instead opting to see them on display at museums such as the Circus Hall of Fame in Peru, Indiana, or the Circus World Museum in Baraboo, Wisconsin.

Background: The earliest "circus" was developed in England in the 1700s. America's first show opened in an amphitheater in Philadelphia in 1793, a one-ring horse and clown show. One hundred years later there were circuses touring the country, each billing itself as the biggest and the best, each trying to one-up the other with new daring acts and more exotic animals. In much of America, the circus was the biggest event of the year. When the circus came to town, all life revolved around it. By 1826, circus tents were being used, and the big top was born.

The years from 1870 to 1930 are considered the golden years of the circus. This period includes 1884, when the five Ringling Brothers started their own circus and performed for a hometown crowd in Baraboo, Wisconsin. Soon, they took their show on the road (228 performances in the first year) too, but for the next 34 winters, they returned to tiny Baraboo, Wisconsin, now the home of the Circus World Museum, the finest exhibit of its kind in the world.

The Ringling Brothers first traveled by wagons, but by 1890 they were traveling across the country by train. Phineas Taylor Barnum, P.T., was also making his mark during this time too, capitalizing on the "suckers" who were "born every minute." In 1907, The Ringlings bought out their biggest rival, Barnum & Bailey Circus, and by 1918 had combined the two performances into one—The Greatest Show on Earth!

General Guidelines: Circus posters are the best known of all circus collectibles. These timeless souvenirs offer some of the most colorful and thrilling publicity ever created. Posters from the late 19th and early 20th centuries can run into the thousands of dollars, but later ones are less expensive, often in the $75-$125 range, and are just as great to display.

COLLECTOR'S ADVISORY!

Posters used during Barnum's day cost only a few cents to produce at the time, so they were made by the hundreds of thousands. Not appreciated for their beauty at the time, they were considered throwaway items. Now, however, they are considered treasures. One rare poster, featuring "Mooney's Giants" (a bunch of elephants playing baseball) sold for just over $8,000!

A word of warning, however: Circus posters are being reproduced, and it is easy to wind up with a replica instead of the real thing.

SCHOENHUT'S CIRCUS TOY!

Schoenhut made a whole circus in the early 1900s. The "Humtpy Dumpty Circus" proved to be a very popular toy and was sold for many years. It included clowns, a ringmaster, lion tamer, lady circus rider, many animals and other accessories. When issued, the circus could be purchased in sets of various sizes for prices ranging from $1 to $35. Today, the Schoenhut "Humpty Dumpty Circus" is considered a rare treasure. Each of the figures sells for prices in the hundreds, while the larger pieces (like the tent and the circus wagon) can bring over a thousand dollars. An entire set-up would be worth many thousands of dollars.

Clown collectibles are probably the most plentiful—and affordable—line of collectibles. As P.T. Barnum used to say, "Clowns are the pegs used to hang circuses on." Collectors might want to paraphrase this and add, "Clown dolls and toys are the pegs used to hang a collection on."

There are many choices, most often very affordable, made in almost every medium. In addition to clown-related art, lamps and china, and figurines, clowns have been included in toy makers' lines of children's playthings.

Animals have also been created as tiny replicas, which are often inexpensive. Vintage advertisements, highly sought after, are collectibles too, depicting these animals' acts, such as trained seals balancing balls on their noses, tigers jumping through blazing hoops, horses prancing with their riders, and dancing poodles, bears and monkeys.

Often overlooked is printed material, such as route books, which told where the circus was going, provided information about the place, and listed the performers. These were made for the show people, not the general public, and were considered diaries, filled with hand-written entries such as: "Today we played Waycross, Georgia. It rained. One of the horses died and one of the clowns quit." The San Antonio, Texas, Public Library has what is considered one of the hobby's greatest treasures—an 1835 route book of a show called the Zoological Institute, the only copy known to exist.

Route cards, which were postcard-sized lists of the circus itinerary for the next two weeks, were often sent by performers to the folks back home, letting them know where they would be.

Photographs of these famous personalities are highly prized and can bring top dollar. From long ago, photos or Charles Sherwood Stratton, better known as General Tom Thumb, are some of the most popular. In 1995, a 19th-century quarterplate daguerreotype portrait of Mr. Thumb sold at an auction for $13,800. More in line with the budgets of average collectors would be photos of Emmet Kelly and Lou Jacobs, probably the two most famous circus clowns.

Most collectors also cherish the things they could carry away with them from circuses, such as colorful programs, ticket stubs, handbills, coloring books and songsters' booklets containing lyrics of songs sung by clowns during their acts.

This poster, showing both Mr. Barnum and Mr. Bailey, dates from the late 1800s. It sold for $210 at a Collectors Auction Services auction in Oil City, Pa. A popular example, the poster was reproduced in the 1960s and 1970s.

Clubs

• Circus Fans of America, P.O. Box 59710, Potomac, MD 20859

• The Circus Historical Society, 4102 Idaho Ave., Nashville, TN 37209

• The Circus Model Builders International, 347 Lonsdale Avenue, Dayton, OH 45419

• Society for the Preservation of Circus Art, P.O. Box 311192, Enterprise, AL 36331

VALUE LINE

Prices are for items in Excellent condition.

Miscellaneous Circus Memorabilia
Circus pass, Hunt Bros. Circus, child's pass,
Southington Kiwanis Club $5

Circus pass, King Bros. 3 Ring Circus, child's pass
for the "World's Newest Big Show, the World's
Finest," sponsored by Erlton Fire Co. $5
Circus pass, Von Bros. Three Ring Circus, 75 cents,
reserved chair coupon for "The Brightest New
Stars of the Circus World" $5
Circus tour routes, Ringling Bros. and Barnum &
Bailey, Tour Route #12 (1952, Mississippi,
Alabama, Tennessee, Virginia), has prancing
horse, clown and two elephants on front.................... $5
Circus tour routes, Ringling Bros. and Barnum &
Bailey, Tour Route #9 (1953, Utah, Idaho,
Montana, Washington, Oregon, California), has
prancing horse, clown and two elephants on front..... $5
Circus tour routes, Ringling Bros. and Barnum &
Bailey, Tour Route #10 (1954, Wisconsin,
Minnesota, Iowa, Missouri, Kansas), has prancing
horse, clown and two elephants on front.................... $5
Coffee cups, two different from the Emmet Kelly
Circus Collection, 1986...................................... $15
Coloring book, Saalfield, monkey on horse
jumping through hoop held by two clowns,
circa 1940s .... $5-$8
Figurine, Schoenhut Humpty Dumpty circus tiger,
1920s .... $50-$100
Figurines, Wade Red Rose Tea, complete
circus set of 15 .... $35
Glasses, tall frosted Big Top Circus glasses, set of six,
Libbey, includes ringmaster, giraffe, monkey and
lion, kangaroo, seal, elephant, and tightrope
walker, 1950s, mint in box .... $25-$35
Inflatables, two Ringling Bros. and Barnum &
Bailey Circus blow-ups, 1985 30" clown with
weighted feet and 1981 blue elephant............... $10-$15
Jigsaw puzzles, three, scenes from the big show,
Saalfield Publishing, 1952, beautiful color
illustrations $20
Magazine, Barnum & Bailey, 1932 season,
72 pages.. $50
Media Kit, Ringling Bros. and Barnum &
Bailey Circus, Gunther Gebel-Williams
Farewell Tour $10
Patch, Circus Fans Association of America
Membership patch, with elephant logo $5
Photograph, circus clowns leaving the Big Top,
vintage, stamped on back P.M. McClintock,
7" x 2-1/8" .... $15-$20
Photographs, six different black-and-white
photos of circus clowns, four show a car
called the "Black Dot Taxi" .... $15-$20
Plate, Ringling Bros. and Barnum & Bailey's lion
tamer Gunther Gebel-Williams, mint in box,
8-1/2" Hamilton.................................... $20-$25
Playing cards, 1959 Old Maid cards, circus edition,
35 cards, box, Ed-U-Cards .... $5-$10

Popcorn bags, 10 Ringling Bros. and Barnum &
Bailey popcorn bags, each shows clown holding
popcorn bag, 8-1/2" x 4-3/4"...................... $10-$20
Postcard, "Winter quarters of P.T. Barnum,"
Bridgeport, Connecticut $8.50
Program, 1948 Ringling Bros. Barnum & Bailey
Circus magazine and program, colorful clown on
the front cover, with articles, ads, comics and
photos, 76 pages................................. $10-$15
Program, 1949 Ringling Bros. and Barnum & Bailey
Circus program, cover has polar bear wearing
marching boots and hat while playing a drum,
80 pages.. $10-$15
Program, 1972 Ringling Bros. and Barnum & Bailey
Circus Souvenir Program and Magazine,

STEP RIGHT UP AND CHECK IT OUT!

The spectacle of the old-time circus is still very much alive at the Circus World Museum in Baraboo, Wisconsin, a picturesque riverside community that was the original winter home of the famed Ringling Brothers Circus. The museum, open to the public since 1959, is the world's foremost circus history institution, a fabulous 50-acre extravaganza of unique and colorful circus experiences and memorabilia. In addition to its historical displays and exhibits, the museum features various interactive programs and, during the summer season, live big-top circus performances with elephants, horses, clowns, acrobats, trapeze artists and other acts. During the peak tourist season, there are three shows a day.

Other popular demonstrations include juggling demonstrations and classes, clown make-up demonstrations, circus music concerts, circus wagon parades, a petting zoo, and an actual "elephant encounter," where you can touch and feed giant African elephants.

Of special interest to serious collectors is the Robert L. Parkinson Library and Research Center, the world's largest circus archives with unparalleled collections of vintage circus posters, photographs, books, business records and other documents. It is open year-round to researchers. Appointments are encouraged. For more information about the museum and archives, call 608-356-0800.

The Barnum Museum, which evolved from the Barnum Institute of Science and History, is also open to fans of the Greatest Show on Earth. The museum, which pays tribute to P. T. Barnum and his show, includes permanent exhibits focusing on the showman and his work, plus a 1,000-square foot scale model of his three-ring circus, featuring more than 3,000 miniatures. Temporary and traveling exhibits are also displayed at the museum, located in Bridgeport, Connecticut. For more information, call 203-331-1104.

Various circus-related toys have been produced over the years. This rare paper-on-wood circus wagon pulled by a pair of horses dates from the 1890s and measures over two feet long. It sold for $7,475 at a Christie's auction in New York.

Among the new limited-edition circus collectibles is this 1:43 scale model of a Ringling Bros. and Barnum and Bailey Circus truck. It was issued by the Franklin Mint in 1999 with a retail price of $135.

101st edition, 82 pages, 10" x 13"............................$10
Records, Bozo's Circus Band, 3 record set in sleeve,
 real circus music, Capitol Records, 1950.................$50
Record, Circus Time, A Little Golden Record & Book,
 No. 221, 24 pages, 33-1/3 rpm record......................$20
Signed letter, by P.T. Barnum, one page, Dec. 9,
 1878, personal embossed mourning stationery,
 Bridgeport, Conn., to Mr. E. E. Johnson, regarding
 giving a lecture, 4-1/2" x 7" ....$350-$400
Tin wind-up, Lionel Mickey Mouse five-piece circus
 train, Walt Disney Enterprises, 1930s, includes engine,
 and coal, circus, band and dining cars $1,250
Tin wind-up, wagon pulled by an elephant, plus four
 animals and a clown, "Barnum Bailey" on the
 side of the wagon sign (doesn't include Ringling
 Bros., so it may be from before 1919) $750
Toy, Big Performing Circus, Fisher-Price, complete
 set of 31, including circus wagon......................$1,000+
Toy, circus train, #991, 1973, Fisher-Price $35
Toy, circus wagon, #156, Fisher-Price ....$650-$800
Toy, Juggling Jumbo, Fisher-Price, #735, 1958..........$250
Toy, push toy clown, Fisher-Price, 1970s $15
Truck, Franklin Mint 1:43 scale circus truck,
 Ringling Bros. and Barnum & Bailey, 1999 ....$135
View-Master reels, "A Day at the Circus," set of
 three, 1952, scenes from the Ringling Bros. and
 Barnum & Bailey Circus................................$7.50-$10

Circus Posters and Window Cards
Barnum & Bailey poster, depicts various lion acts
 with women lion tamers, 1915 ....$300
Barnum & Bailey Circus Parade poster, depicts
 parade with elephants carrying performers, 1913,
 watch for reproductions......................................$300
Barnum & Bailey poster, depicts head of tiger
 with teeth exposed, 1916, reproductions exist $75

Bentley Bros. Circus poster, Springfield Ozark
 Empire Fairground, head of tiger with
 mouth open..$60-$120
Circus Varga poster, circus people and animals
 touting "a return to the rich tradition of the
 circus as it once was in America" ....$60-$120
Kelly Miller Three Ring Circus window card,
 large picture depicting clown face ....$50-$150
King-Royal Circus window card, depicts a clown,
 fairgrounds Summit...$60-$120
Ringling Bros. and Barnun & Bailey poster,
 Gargantua, the great ape, "the world's most
 terrifying living creature".. $60
Ringling Bros. and Barnum & Bailey poster, Terrell
 Jacobs, the lion king, "presenting the world's most sen-
 sational group of jungle-bred performers"............. $175
Ringling Bros. and Barnum & Bailey poster,
 depicts the backs of six clowns which spell out
 CIRCUS, watch for reproductions $500
Ringling Bros. and Barnum & Bailey poster,
 "Greatest Show On Earth," depicts four giraffes,
 1917, reproductions exist $100
Ringling Bros. and Barnum & Bailey poster,
 clown's face with big red nose, 1975 ....$50-$150
Ringling Bros. and Barnum & Bailey poster,
 horse with rider, clowns, motorcycle-riding
 monkeys, trapeze act, tigers, 1978 ....$50-$150
Ringling Bros. and Barnum & Bailey poster,
 huge white bear, surrounded by clowns, horse,
 tiger, rocket and girl, 1980 ....$50-$150
Rudy Bros. Circus poster, graphic of high wire
 act with three girls, Santa Ana Elks ....$60-$120
Rudy Bros. Circus window card, Santa Ana Elks,
 depicts clown, woman, elephant $25
Twin Lakes Shrine Club Circus window card,
 three-ring picture of lion, tiger and clown ......$60-$120

COCA-COLA COLLECTIBLES

When it comes to advertising collectibles, Coca-Cola is definitely the "Real Thing." For nearly a hundred years Coca-Cola has been the international model of mass marketing. Never mind that unfortunate "New Coke" disaster that would have doomed lesser companies; when it comes to soft drinks—and advertising collectibles—Coke is still the king.

Background: Coca-Cola has been around since before the turn of the century, so there are many items available to collectors. In 1886, Dr. John Pemberton, an Atlanta pharmacist, formulated Coca-Cola. From its humble beginnings—as a beverage that purportedly cured headaches and other ailments—it eventually grew into a worldwide phenomenon.

Coca-Cola has become such a huge collecting category today that virtually every Coca-Cola item now being produced is recognized as a potential collectible—not like the old days, when original advertising items were used and discarded. Items that survived are highly desirable today.

New items available to today's Coke enthusiasts include everything from die-cast cars and trucks to magnets and trading cards. These collectibles are, with some exceptions, not likely to be of any great value in the future.

The most desirable Coca-Cola collectibles are those made originally to advertise the beverage; most preferably, those items created prior to 1960. There are plenty of reproductions on the market, however, so new collectors should learn how to spot fakes and reproductions.

General Guidelines: Coca-Cola collectibles fall into the following general categories:

Tin Items—From the early 1900s to the 1920s, small pocket mirrors were produced featuring full-color artwork of

Coca-Cola tip trays are among the most popular of all Coca-Cola collectibles.

FAMOUS COKE SLOGANS!

Proper marketing went a long way to establish Coke's success. Here are some of the advertising slogans used by Coca-Cola over the years. They might help pinpoint the age of an item.

1900: Delicious and Refreshing
1905: Coca-Cola Revives and Sustains
1917: Three Million a Day (number of servings of Coca-Cola consumed per day)
1922: Thirst Knows No Season
1925: Six Million a Day
1929: The Pause that Refreshes
1932: Ice-Cold Sunshine
1938: The Best Friend Thirst Ever Had
1942: The Only Thing Like Coca-Cola is Coca-Cola Itself—It's the Real Thing
1948: Where There's Coke There's Hospitality
1952: What You Want is a Coke
1956: Making Good Things Taste Better
1963: Things Go Better with Coke
1970: It's the Real Thing
1971: I'd Like to Buy the World a Coke
1976: Coke Adds Life
1979: Have a Coke and a Smile
1982: Coke is It
1986: Catch the Wave
1989: Can't Beat the Feeling
1990: Can't Beat the Real Thing
1992: Always Coca-Cola

---

a woman, along with the Coke logo. Most of these sell in the $200-$350 range. Reproductions exist, most with a 1973 date; these are valued at $5 or less.

Some of the best-known Coca-Cola items are the change and serving trays that featured beautiful woman enjoying Coca-Cola. The company stuck with this mode of marketing for many years, from about 1900 to the mid-1950s. Coca-Cola trays are interesting items for many reasons. They established in the minds of marketers that beautiful women can help sell products. They also document changes in fashions and hairstyles from 1900 through the 1950s; and these colorful trays are great display items when found in top condition. The 1909, 1912, 1914 and 1917 trays were reproduced in the early 1970s; repros sell for from $8-$15, while originals are valued at several hundred dollars each.

Bottles—The classic curved Coca-Cola bottle shape that everyone is familiar with was first designed in 1915.

COKE VENDING MACHINES

The most serious Coca-Cola collectors, in addition to glasses and magazine ads and everything else, will often pursue a bigger bounty—vintage Coke vending machines, from the 1930s-1960s.

There are many different styles and designs (over one hundred models were made from the 1930s to the 1950s), but hardcore collectors look for older machines, with rounded corners and raised letters spelling out the slogan "Drink Coca-Cola in Bottles."

Some look for machines in their original state, in working condition. But most collectors look for restored machines to be display showpieces for rec rooms or kitchens. Professionally restored examples command the highest prices; the better the quality of the restoration, the higher the value goes.

For example, machines from the 1960s can range from $200 for a common machine in rough shape, to $1,000-$3,000 for nicely restored classics. These vending machines should have a complete work-over, including a disassembly of the entire unit, parts renewals, rewiring, rust and dent removal, a professional paint job, and a new enamel finish that matches that machine's particular Coca-Cola red color. It's important that the decals are authentic, too.

Three factors to consider when you are appraising an original condition machine include: general condition, mechanical condition and style and desirability. How many dents are there? Is there a lot of rust? Are all the parts there, and intact? Does the machine cool and dispense its beverages properly? Is the machine a classic rounded-corner version, or a square top one?

Models that have been nicely restored include a 1948 Jacobs Model 26, at $2,700; a 1931 Glascock "Counter Ice Cooler," at $1,500 or more; a 1955 Vendo Model 80, at $2,000 or more; 1949 Vendo Model 23, at $1,500 or more (lesser conditions are $350-$750); a 1959 Cavalier Model 72, at $2,500 or more (unrestored at $400 or less); a 1948 Vendorlator Model 27, with stand, at $2,500 or more; a Cavalier six-case air-cooled chest from the late '40s to mid '50s, at $1,000 or more; late '50s to early '60s Glasco Model GBV-50, known as the "Slider," at $1,750 or more; and a late '40s Cavalier Model 27, at $3,000 or more (lesser-conditioned versions are $500-$1,500).

The first Coca-Cola machine, dating from 1927, was known as the Icy-O. It was not a traditional vending machine because it did not take money. After taking a bottle, the customer was required to pay the clerk. For more information on Coca-Cola vending machines, we recommend Steve Ebner's book Vintage Coca-Cola Machines, Vol. II, which pictures nearly every Coke machine from 1959 to 1968. The 140-page book has sections on "Oddities and Rarities," fountain dispensers and accessories, too. It includes a price guide, which lists values for three conditions. You can contact the author at Fun-Tronics, P.O. Box 448, Middletown, MD 21769.

This Coca-Cola clock sold for $400 at an auction conducted by Collectors Auction Services of Oil City, Pa.

Prior to that, bottles were made in many different forms. Coke bottles can be dated by numbers on the bottom of the bottles. If there is one set of four digits, the last two digits indicate the year the bottle was made. Some pre-1920 bottles can be valued at $100-$300.

Some newer six-ounce bottles, from the 1980s and 1990s, were made to commemorate events, such as the Green Bay Packers' 1997 Super Bowl win. These new bottles are finding collectors; however, many were saved and there will likely be a better-than-average supply of Mint condition bottles well into the future. Some bottles do, however, sell for $4 to $20 or more apiece. The higher end prices can be partially attributed to the regional nature of many of these special promotions. For example, the Packers bottles were widely distributed in Wisconsin but not in other parts of the country.

Miscellaneous—Like serving trays, Coca-Cola calendars enjoyed their heyday from just before the turn of the century through the 1950s. Similar artwork was used on the signs and the calendars—in fact, sometimes the same artwork was used. Locating a calendar in top condition, with its pad still intact, is a rare find. The earliest calendars, those from about 1890 to 1905, can fetch prices in the low- to mid- four-figure range. Even calendars from the 1920s and 1930s sell for several hundred dollars.

Coca-Cola collectors have to fight radio collectors for several radios that carry the Coca-Cola logo. A 1930 bottle radio can have a value of more than $1,000, while a 1949 cooler radio can realize $400-$500. On a more contemporary note, look for 1960s-70s Coca-Cola transistor radios, in the shape of Coke machines, that are valued from $75-$150.

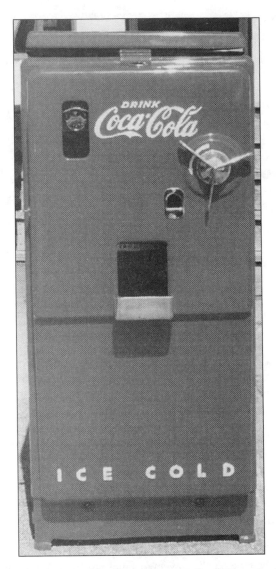

Serious Coca-Cola collectors may be interested in owning a vintage vending machine. This one, known as a Cavalier Model 27 dates from the late 1940s. In nice restored condition, it can sell for as much as $3,000. Lesser-condition examples can run from $500 to $1,500. (Photo courtesy Terry Kimble, Remember When Collectibles, Stone Mountain, Ga.)

Signs are another important area of Coca-Cola collecting. Made of wood, tin, porcelain, cardboard, chrome and plastic, these signs are popular as decorating items, as well as being collectibles in their own right. Many of the early signs breach the four-figure mark.

Coca-Cola sponsored drinking glass giveaways at fast-food restaurants, mostly in the 1970s and 1980s. These glasses, featuring the likes of King Kong, Star Trek, Popeye, Mickey Mouse and even Holly Hobbie, are generally inexpensive. These common items can be found for a few dollars, but some are valued at more than $10.

WHERE TO GO TO ENJOY A COKE!

Coca-Cola, headquartered in Atlanta, Ga., has its "World of Coca-Cola" fantasyland there too, featuring the largest collection of Coca-Cola memorabilia in the world. Located next to the famous Underground Atlanta, it features more than 1,000 artifacts, displayed in chronological order. Collectors can learn about the company's history, equipment and the changes made as the company evolved; ad campaigns; and packaging displays, including vending machines. A high-tech, futuristic soda-fountain offers thirsty viewers samples of Coke products; a retail store, "Everything Coca-Cola," offers just what it says. For more information, contact "The World of Coca-Cola" at 404-676-5151. A second museum has opened in Las Vegas.

The largest private collection of Coca-Cola memorabilia can be seen at Schmidt's Coca-Cola Museum, in Elizabethtown, Kentucky. It's located at Coke's bottling plant in the city and is operated by the Schmidt family, which has been producing Coca-Cola in Kentucky since 1901. Tours are offered.

Vintage advertising, old Coke trays, bottles, glasses, calendars, dishes, playing cards, ashtrays, sheet music, signs, posters and other items are among the hundreds of items on display.

Because Coca-Cola mania is a worldwide phenomenon, there is a wealth of foreign Coke advertising items available, as well. Unfortunately for collectors in the U.S., much of it is still in the foreign countries where it was made. There are a few ways you can get your hands on these items. First, if you or someone you know travels, look for the items yourself. If not, connect with other collectors in those countries and try a little horse-trading.

Club
•Coca-Cola Collectors Club International, P.O. Box 49166, Atlanta, GA 30359-1166

Recommended Reading
Petretti's Coca-Cola Collectibles Price Guide, Tenth Edition, Allan Petretti
Price Guide to Vintage Coca-Cola Collectibles 1896-1965, Deborah Goldstein-Hill
Classic Coca-Cola Serving Trays, Allan Petretti and Chris Beyer
Classic Coca-Cola Calendars, Allan Petretti

VALUE LINE

Values shown are for items in Excellent condition, unless otherwise indicated.

Airline cooler, mid-1950s, holds 18 bottles $400

Animation cel, Polar Bear, 1995, Mint $225

Bicycle, Huffy, 1986, 100th Anniversary, 25,000 made, Mint $750

Bottle, Albertville Olympics, 1992 .... $4

Bottle, Denver Broncos, 1993 .... $4

Bottle, Florida Marlins, 1993 .... $5

Bottle, NBA All-Star Weekend, Salt Lake City, 1993 .... $10

Bottle, World of Coca-Cola, 1993 .... $20

Bottle holder, metal, "Enjoy Coca-Cola while you shop. Place bottle here," 1950, Mint $75

Calendar, 1919 .... $1,750

Calendar, 1924 .... $900

Calendar, 1925 .... $750-$1,000

Calendar, 1933 .... $550

Calendar, 1936 .... $650

Calendar, 1944 .... $275

Calendar, 1958 .... $200

Camera, 35mm, shape of Coke can, made in Singapore, ... $30

Clock, 1951, metal, maroon with red logo, "Drink Coca-Cola" $125

Clock, 1960s, plastic, 15" square, "Things Go Better With Coke" $85

Cooler, 1950s, average condition $50

Drinking glass, Holly Hobbie Merry Christmas, each $3

Drinking glass, Mickey's Christmas Carol, 1982 .... $5

Drinking glass, Popeye, 1975 .... $15

Drinking glass, National Flag $10

Drinking glass, Star Trek: The Motion Picture $15

Lithograph, "Luge" commercial, polar bear holding bottle of Coke, 8" x 10", matted $45

Magazine ads, full page, 1910s .... $10-$15

Napkin holder, metal $40

COCA-COLA, THE IDEAL BRAIN TONIC—OR NOT!

Coca-Cola, one of America's true success stories, came about partly by way of a fortunate accident.

It had its start in 1886—in the days of "tonics" and "elixirs"—when pharmacist and businessman John Pemberton stumbled onto a secret mix of ingredients that formed the basis of the Coca-Cola syrup. Pemberton persuaded soda-fountain owner Willis Venable to mix the syrup with water and serve the tasty new concoction at his Atlanta business.

Later, quite by accident, Venable mixed the syrup with carbonated water, rather than plain tap water, and the real Coca-Cola was born.

Initially, Coca-Cola—so named because both words named two of the ingredients in the secret mix—was promoted as "The Ideal Brain Tonic," able to cure headaches and relieve mental and physical exhaustion.

Coca-Cola could easily have gone the way of many other elixirs and soda fountain drinks of the time, had it not been for Griggs Candler, a businessman who bought the company in 1888. Candler dedicated his life to making and merchandising Coca-Cola, and by 1914 he had acquired a staggering fortune of some $50 million.

Also making a fortune from the popular soft drink was Joseph A. Biedenharn of Vicksburg, Miss., who became the first bottler of Coca-Cola in 1894. Prior to that, Coke was available only at the soda fountain.

Interestingly, another early investor in the Coca-Cola Co. was baseball Hall of Famer Ty Cobb, who made millions—over and above his baseball success.

Some Coca-Cola collectibles can bring astounding prices. This rare Lillian Nordica Coca-Cola sign sold for a staggering $21,000 at a James Julia auction.

This self-framing tin sign, measuring 17-by-54 inches, sold for $750 at an auction conducted by Collectors Auction Services of Oil City, Pa.

A rather obscure Coca-Cola collectible is this deck of 1943 playing cards, valued at about $50-$60.

Pins, 1996 Olympics, various, each $5
Playing cards, Gibson girl images, 1909 ..... $2,000-$2,500
Playing cards, pink parasol, 1915 .... $1,200
Playing cards, sipping girl, 1928 .... $350
Playing cards, nurse, 1943 .... $75-$100
Playing cards, cowgirl, 1951 .... $75
Playing cards, ice skates, 1956 .... $85
Pushbar, porcelain enamel, 1950s,
    average condition $150
Radio, shape of Coke machine, 1980s, works $50
Serving tray, metal, woman under tree with flowers,
    1916 .... $350
Serving tray, metal, woman in blue hat, 1921 .... $1,000
Serving tray, metal, woman in white hat, 1922 .... $500
Serving tray, metal, woman in blue hat and fur,
    1925 .... $350
Serving tray, metal, boy with dog, 1931 .... $900
Serving tray, metal, woman on couch, 1936, ... $200
Serving tray, metal, woman in yellow bathing suit,
    1937 .... $350
Serving tray, metal, woman in white bathing suit,
    1939 .... $300
Serving tray, metal, woman in sailor hat on dock,
    1940 .... $425
Serving tray, metal, woman with ice skates, 1941 ...... $425
Serving tray, metal, two women by car, 1942 .... $425
Sign, cardboard, die-cut, shows boy fishing with dog,
    die cut, 36" tall, 1935 .... $2,500
Sign, cardboard, 36" x 20", shows cheerleader with
    megaphone, "Have a Coke," 1940s $275

Sign, cardboard, female clown, "Party Pause,"
    36" x 20", 1940s $500
Sign, cardboard, woman tennis player at cooler,
    "Welcome Pause," 1940s $325
Sign, metal, "Drink Coca-Cola," 48" diameter,
    1950s $250
Sign, tin, 30", white letters on red and green,
    "Ice Cold Coca-Cola Sold Here," $400
Sign, tin, couple with Coke, "Drink Coca-Cola
    Delicious & Refreshing," 1940s, 28" x 20" $625
Sign, tin "Drink Coca-Cola Ice Cold," 28" x 20",
    1930s $425
Sign, tin, shows girl, "Drink Coca-Cola," 28" x 20",
    1940s $500
Sign, cardboard, "Good With Food," 1951, 36" x 20",
    Niagara Litho Co. $250
Sign, glass, 1950s, "Drink Coca-Cola," $100
Sign, metal, "Drink Coca-Cola Ice Cold," 20" x 28",
    1950 .... $175
Sign, metal, "Coca-Cola A Sign of Good Taste,"
    1960 .... $160
Sign, neon, "Coca-Cola Classic: The Official Softdrink
    of Summer," 1989, Mint $2,400
Sign, plastic light-up, 12" diameter $55
Sign, porcelain, double-sided, 1939, 3" x 5",
    EX-NM $750
Sign, porcelain, "Drink Coca-Cola," 1950s,
    4' diameter, EX $500
Six-pack holder, metal, 1930s, NM $150
Six-pack holder, metal, 1950s, NM $125
Syrup glass, 1916, Mint $200
Syrup glass, 1970s, Mint $45
Syrup jug, 1940s, EX $45
Syrup jug, 1960s, EX $30
Tin tray, metal, 1907, "Relieves Fatigue,"
    woman in green dress $900

COINS

Coin collecting is among the world's oldest hobbies. It probably began shortly after the first coins were produced in Asia Minor some 700 years before the birth of Christ. Popular interest in coin collecting as we think of it today, however, didn't develop until the beginning of the 20th century.

Interest in collecting U.S. coins has grown significantly since World War II. Several valuable minting varieties, such as the 1955 and 1972 "doubled-die" cents (on which the dates appear to be out of focus) drew many new collectors into the hobby. They joined the ranks of true coin collectors while checking their pocket change for these rare error coins, of which only a relative handful were produced.

General Guidelines: If a coin is Uncirculated, has very little wear, or is dated before the 1960s, it is probably more valuable than newer or heavily worn coins.

The value of most coins depends largely on scarcity and condition. The first keys to determining the value of a particular coin are the date and the mint mark. The mint mark on a coin can make a significant difference in its value. Each mint that strikes coins uses a letter to identify its coins—"P" for Philadelphia (except on the cents, which are unmarked or "plain"), "S for San Francisco, "D" for Denver, "W" for West Point. Older United States mints included Carson City ("CC"), New Orleans ("O"), Dahlonega ("D") and Charlotte ("C"), the latter two used only on gold coins in the 1800s.

Besides the date and mint mark, the key element that determines the value of a coin is its condition, often called "grade" within the hobby. U.S. coins have come to be graded on a 70-point scale to indicate the amount of wear. At the top of the scale are uncirculated Mint-condition coins, which are identified with a number ranging from MS-60 to MS-70. (The "MS" stands for "Mint State.") All coins with an "MS" grade are uncirculated, never having been actually used in circulation. But some uncirculated coins are better than others, depending on the strength of the strike and other minting factors, allowing for the various grades even among "Mint-State" coins. An MS-67 coin, for instance, will have a better strike and be more desirable than an MS-62 coin, even though both are uncirculated. The difference in value between the two coins can be very large, but uncirculated coins will always be worth more than their circulated counterparts, which are known by numerical grades that range from G-4 (Good-4) to AU-50, which is used to describe a coin that is "almost" or "about" uncirculated. In between, are grades such as VG-8, F-12, VF-20, XF-40, to describe coins that range from Very Good to Extremely Fine. Of course, the better the grade, the higher the price.

In the MS-60 to MS-70 range, values may jump by hundreds, even thousands, of dollars for each grade point. Many higher-value coins are graded by a professional grading

The 1909-S VDB is the key to the Lincoln cent series. In Good condition is worth $360; in Very Fine or better condition, about $500.

service and then encased in a hard-plastic case for security. The grade shown is only valid if the sealed case is intact, 47so don't break it unless you want to pay to have the coin regraded.

Mintage figures are used to determine the relative scarcity of a coin. In this area, coin collectors have a distinct advantage over many other hobbies, in that they know exactly how many of each particular coin was made. The U.S. Mint keeps very complete and public records of mintages, which can be found in any coin price guide. In general, the lower the mintage, the more likely a coin is to be valuable.

Gold coins: All gold coins are worth at least the value of the bullion (raw metal) they contain. A U.S. $20 gold piece (made from 1849-1933) contains almost an ounce of gold, currently worth about $380.

Silver coins: From 1890-1964 U.S. dimes, quarters, half-dollars and silver dollars were made of 90 percent silver. If they've been circulated, these silver coins are worth about three times their face value for their silver bullion content alone. Many are worth more for their numismatic value to collectors.

Average circulated silver dollars with "common" dates minted between 1878 and 1935 are typically worth between $5 and $10 each; Eisenhower and Susan B. Anthony dollars are worth a dollar.

Kennedy halves were made from 1964 to 1970. Like the older silver coins, 1964 Kennedy halves are 90 percent silver. Kennedy halves dated from 1965 to 1970 are 40 percent silver; average circulated examples are worth about 60 to 75 cents each.

Average circulated half dollars and quarters dating from 1940 to 1964 are worth only their bullion value. Some Franklin halves (1949-S, 1953, 1955) are worth more, but unless the coins are in exceptional condition, the silver content rules the value.

Mercury dimes, minted from 1916 to 1945, have a winged liberty on the back. Average circulated examples are worth about 30 cents each, as are Roosevelt dimes with silver content (1946-1964).

Buffalo nickels were produced from 1913 to 1938. Buffalo nickels are often badly worn. A Buffalo nickel with the full date still showing is worth between 30 and 40 cents. If the date is completely worn away or has only one or two digits showing, the nickel is worth face value or can be sold for 20

FUTURE TREASURES IN YOUR POCKET CHANGE?

The coin collecting hobby has been energized in the past two years, buoyed by the release of the new "fifty states quarters" series, as well as the new one-dollar coin. The new quarters are creating the most interest, surprising even numismatic insiders.

The quarter series, which will eventually result in a 25-cent piece being issued for each of the fifty states, began in 1999. Five states quarters will be issued each year for ten years (ending in 2008), following the order that the states were admitted to the Union. None of the quarters will be scarce, but following the release of the first five in 1999, prices for uncirculated examples began to climb to as much as four times over face value -- an astounding amount for a new coin that is minted in the millions. In fact, of the first five quarters introduced, the lowest total minted (for the New Jersey quarter) was 290 million—certainly more than enough for every coin collector in America to have all he wants. Still, there is tremendous interest in the new quarters.

With such high mintages, it's not likely that any of the new states quarters will realize any long-term gain, but the numismatic hobby is enjoying the action while it lasts. If you do decide to collect the new states quarters—and they would make a nice collection, whether they increase in value or not—make sure you collect only uncirculated examples. With mintages this high, circulated pieces will never be desirable by serious collectors in the future.

Also, be on the lookout for mint errors. Almost every time a new coin is minted, some error coins sneak into circulation—and these are the coins that have the potential for real value. And with some forty quarters still on the way, there's plenty of opportunity for mistakes.

cents to be used in jewelry making.

Liberty nickels, or "V" nickels (for the Roman numeral five) were produced from 1883 to 1913. "V" nickels are usually worn flat and bring one dollar each. Common examples with full readable dates may be worth $2-$4.

Indian head cents were minted from 1859 to 1909. They are a common "starting place" for beginning coin collectors. Prices for average circulated examples typically run in the $1-$2 range.

"Wheat-back" Lincoln cents date from 1909 to 1958. There are a few key dates of wheat-back cents worth saving, but the majority of them are worth only about two cents in average-circulated condition. The 1909-S, 1914-D and 1931-S are valued at $30 and up. In all conditions, the scarce 1909-S VDB and 1922 wheat cents are worth from $300 to $600.

In 1943 Lincoln cents were made of zinc-coated steel, giving them a silver color, similar to a nickel. Often mistakenly thought to be valuable, they are very plentiful and often corroded; most are only worth two cents. Newer Lincoln cents with the memorial reverse (1959 to present) have only a few "keepers," which require specialized knowledge to spot.

Most coins found in circulation today are post-1964 and have no silver content.

Bicentennial: Bicentennial coins (quarters, half dollars and dollars) are worth only face value.

The above guidelines reflect values for average circulated coins with common dates. Higher-condition coins and those with scarcer dates and mint marks will be worth more. In every series of coins there are "key" coins that, primarily because of lower mintages, will have higher values. Some of those key coins are noted in the "Value Guide" below.

Proof Sets and Mint Sets: Both proof sets and mint sets are special sets of coins produced by the U.S. Mint on an annual basis specifically for collectors. They were not intended to be used in normal circulation.

A proof set consists of one coin of each denomination minted for a specific year, specially struck to have a sharper (sometimes "frosted") image on a clearer background (which is often "mirrored"). Proof sets are generally found in sealed cellophane packages or in hard plastic cases. They range in value from under $10 to over a thousand, so a coin price guide that includes proof sets is essential for the serious collector. Generally, proof sets dating from the 1930s and 1940s are worth between $500 and $4,000, depending on the specific date. Proof sets from 1950-1953 fall in the $125-$400 range. Proof sets dating from 1954-1960 are generally priced in the $15-$60 range. The majority of proof sets from the 1970s and 1980s are worth $5 to $10.

Mint sets consist of one uncirculated coin of each denomination from each mint for a specific year. Unlike proof coins, the coins in mint sets were struck to regular standards (just like coins intended for circulation) and were then packaged by the mint specifically for collectors. Mint sets from 1947 through 1958 contain two examples of each coin mounted in cardboard holders that caused the coins to tarnish.

Beginning in 1959, the sets were packaged in sealed Pliofilm packets and include only one specimen of each coin authorized for that year. The 1965 sets were packaged in Pliofilm, the 1966 and 1967 sets in plastic cases. Mint sets dating from 1947 to 1953 are valued in the $250-$600 range. Mint sets from 1954 to 1958 sell for prices ranging from $75 to $120. Mint sets from 1959-1999 range from as little as $4 to as much as $35, with the majority in the $5-$10 range.

Various Commemorative coins were produced in the United States from 1892 to 1954. These coins were intended for use as U.S. currency and most are relatively common. Average circulated commemorative coins are generally valued at several times their face value. Uncirculated commemorative coins should be checked in a guide to determine their value. Some commemorative coins are shown in the Value Guide below.

Clubs

• American Numismatic Association, 818 N. Cascade Ave., Colorado Springs, CO 80903-3279, 719-632-2646

• American Numismatic Society, Broadway at 155th St., New York, NY 10052, 212-234-3130

• Canadian Numismatic Association, P.O. Box 226, Barrie, Ontario, Canada L4M 4T2, 705-737-0845

Recommended Reading

As the leading publisher of books for coin collectors, the Krause Publications' catalog currently has over fifty books for collectors of coins and paper money—too many to list them all here. For the complete list, visit the Krause Publications Books web site at www.krause.com/Books. Here are a few of the more general titles:

Many Buffalo nickels found today have the date worn off. This example, dating from 1913 (the first year of the Buffalo nickel) has a nice strong date and is valued at about $8-$10 in Fine to Very Fine condition.

Books

Coins & Prices, Ninth Edition, David C. Harper
Warman's Coins & Paper Money, Allen G. Berman
Standard Catalog of World Coins, 28th Edition, Chester L. Krause, Clifford Mishler and Colin R. Bruce
2000 Auction Prices Realized, Bob Wilhite

Periodicals

Numismatic News
World Coin News
Coin Prices
Coins magazine
Banknote Reporter

VALUE LINE

Values shown are for grades indicated and are compiled from "Coin Prices" magazine, published by Krause Publications, Iola, Wis.

Cents

1864, 1865 Indian Head, Good	$5
1864, 1865 Indian Head, Fine	$18
1877 Indian Head, Good	$425
1877 Indian Head, Fine	$700
1866-1876, typical date, Good	$15-$45
1879-1909, typical date, Good	$1-$3
1879-1909, typical date, Fine	$2-$5
1909-S Indian, Good	$250
1909-S VDB Lincoln, Good	$350
1909-S Lincoln, Good	$37
1910-S, Good	$6
1911-S, Good	$16
1912-S, Good	$11
1914-D, Good	$85
1914-S, Good	$10
1915-S, Good	$7
Most Lincoln "wheat cents"	2-10 cents
1955, "doubled-die," XF	$550
1972, "doubled-die, XF	$150

Nickels

Shield Nickel, typical example, 1866-1876, Good	$10-$15
Shield Nickel, typical example, 1879-1881, Good	$175-$300
Liberty "V" Nickel, 1885, Good	$250
1886, Good	$100
1912-S, Good	$45
Liberty Nickel, most other typical examples, Good	$1-$4
Buffalo Nickel, 1914-D, Good	$45
1921-S, Good	$28
Buffalo Nickel, typical example, 1927-1937, Good	$1
Jefferson Nickel, 1939-D, XF	$10
1942-D, XF	$2

Commemorative half dollars are a popular collecting category. This Battle of Gettysburg commemorative half dollar dates from 1936 and is valued at $275-$325 in Uncirculated condition.

Dimes

Barber Dime, 1892-S, Good	$45
1893-O, Good	$12
1894-O, Good	$40
1895, Good	$55
1895-O, Good	$225
1895-S, Good	$28
1896-O, 1896-S, Good	$50-$60
1897-O, Good	$40
1901-S, Good	$50
1903-S, Good	$45
1904-S, Good	$25
1913-S, Good	$8
Barber Dimes, most other examples, Good	$2-$5
Mercury Dime, 1916-D, Good	$475
1921, Good	$20
1921-D, Good	$38
1926-S, Good	$6
1931-D, Good	$6
1942 (error coin 1942/41), Good	$275
Mercury Dimes, most other examples, Good	$1-$2
Roosevelt Dime, 1949-S, XF	$3

Quarters

Barber Quarter, typical example, 1892-1916, Good	$3-$6
Barber Quarter, 1901-S, Good	$1,750
Barber Quarter, 1914-S, Good	$50
Standing Liberty Quarter, typical example 1917-1924, Good	$15-$30
Standing Liberty Quarter, 1916, Good	$1,500
1919-D, 1919-S, Good	$75-$85
1921, Good	$100
1923-S, Good	$225
Standing Liberty Quarter, most other dates, Good	$3-$6
Washington Quarter, 1932-D, 1932-S, Good	$38-$45
1934-1940, typical example, Good	$2-$3
1941-1964, typical example, XF	$1-$3

Half Dollars

Barber Half, typical example, 1892-1915, Good	$6-$15
1892-O, Good	$165
1893-S, Good	$75
1896-S, Good	$60
1897-O, Good	$60
1897-S, Good	$110
Walking Liberty Quarter, typical example, 1917-1929, Good	$4-$10
1916, 1916-D, Good	$20-$25
1916-S, Good	$65
1921, Good	$75
1921-D, Good	$115
1921-S, Good	$20
Walking Liberty, typical example, 1930-1947, Good	$2-$4
Franklin Half, typical example, VF	$2-$5

Silver Dollars

Morgan Dollar, typical example, 1878-1921, VG	$12-$20
Morgan Dollar, typical "CC" mint mark, VG	$35-$100
Peace Dollar, typical example, 1922-1935, VG	$10-$15
Peace Dollar, 1921. VG	$30
1928, VG	$110

Commemorative Half Dollars

Values shown are for coins in Uncirculated MS-63 condition.

1921, Alabama	$425
1936, Albany	$210
1937, Antietam	$440
1935-37 Arkansas PDS set	$225-$275
1938, Arkansas PDS set	$450
1939, Arkansas PDS set	$825
1936, Bay Bridge	$110
1934, Boone	$80
1935, Boone PDS set with 1934	$750
1935-36 Boone PDS set	$275
1936, Boone PDS set	$255
1937, Boone PDS set	$650
1938, Boone PDS set	$950
1936, Bridgeport	$115
1925S, California Jubilee	$155
1936, Cincinnati PDS set	$750
1936, Cleveland, Great Lakes	$65
1936, Columbia PDS set	$575
1892-93 Columbian Expo	$75-$80
1935, Connecticut	$190
1936, Delaware	$210
1936, Elgin	$170
1936, Gettysburg	$285
1922, Grant with star	$1,450
1922, Grant	$160
1928, Hawaiian	$1,750

1935, Hudson	$500
1924, Huguenot-Walloon	$120
1918, Lincoln-Illinois	$110
1946, Iowa	$70
1925, Lexington-Concord	$95
1936, Long Island	$70
1936, Lynchburg	$165
1920, Maine	$145
1934, Maryland	$150
1921, Missouri two-star	$850
1921, Missouri	$700
1923S, Monroe	$120
1938, New Rochelle	$275
1936, Norfolk	$375
1926, 1926-S Oregon	$100-$110
1928, Oregon	$170
1933D, Oregon	$250
1934D, Oregon	$155
1936, 1936-S Oregon	$115-$150
1937D, Oregon	$140
1938, Oregon PDS set	$575
1939, Oregon PDS set	$1,200
1915S, Panama-Pacific	$600
1920, Pilgrim	$80
1921, Pilgrim	$145
1936, Rhode Island PDS set	$240
1937, Roanoke	$170
1936, Robinson-Arkansas	$110
1935S, 1936-D San Diego	$60-$65
1926, Sesquicentennial	$160
1935, Spanish Trail	$800
1925, Stone Mountain	$60
1934, Texas	$90
1935-37 Texas PDS set	$290-$300
1938, Texas PDS set	$730
1925, Fort Vancouver	$345
1927, Vermont	$155
1946, B.T. Washington PDS set	$50
1947, B.T. Washington PDS set	$73
1948, B.T. Washington PDS set	$105
1949, B.T. Washington PDS set	$195
1950, B.T. Washington PDS set	$105
1951, B.T. Washington PDS set	$130
1951-1954 Washington-Carver PDS set	$85-$95
1936, Wisconsin	$170
1936, York County	$155

Proof Sets

1936	$3,700
1937	$2,000
1938-1939	$850-$900
1940	$680
1941-1942	$590-$640
1950	$400
1951	$330
1952	$170

1953	$120
1954-1955	$65-$85
1956	$31
1957	$13
1958	$26
1959	$16
1960 large date	$11
1960 small date	$23
1961-64	$8
1968S-1989S, most regular sets	$5-$9
1968 S no-mint-mark dime	(scarce)$7,500
1970 S large date	$10
1970 S small date	$55
1970 S no-mint-mark dime	$365
1971 S no-mint-mark nickel	$630
1979 S Type II	$80
1981 S Type II	$210
1983 S Prestige set	$90
1983 S no-mint-mark dime	$340
1984 S – 1990 S Prestige sets	$21-$31
1986 S	$12
1990 S	$10
1991 S	$14
1991 S -1994 Prestige sets	$40-$50
1992 S	$12
1993 S -1998 Silver premier sets	$32-$40
1993 S	$26
1994 S	$13
1995 S	$40
1995 S Prestige set	$100
1996 S	$9
1996 S Prestige set	$140
1997 S	$32
1997 S Prestige set	$225
1998 S	$23
1999 S	$40

Peace dollars, minted from 1921 to 1935, sometimes turn up in old desk drawers or jewelry boxes. In average circulated condition, most are worth in the $8-$15 range. In Uncirculated condition they can be worth hundreds. This 1925-S example is valued at $9 in Good condition. In Uncirculated condition, its value ranges from about $60 to over $500, depending on the strength of the strike.

Mint Sets

Values listed are only for Mint Sets packaged and marketed by the U.S. Mint only.

1947	$595
1948	$225
1949	$365
1951	$370
1952	$295
1953	$230
1954	$115
1955	$95
1956	$75
1957	$105
1958	$88
1959-1960	$20-$22
1961	$28
1962-1964	$11-$13
1965-1967	$4-$6
1968	$4
1969	$6
1970 large date	$10
1970 small date	$37
1971-1972	$4
1973	$12
1974-1980	$6-$10
1981	$13
1984-1985	$5-$6
1986	$10
1887-1989	$6-$8
1990	$5
1991-1994	$9-$11
1995	$22
1996-1997	$14
1998	$10
1999	$26

COMIC BOOKS

We call them comic books, but some of the prices they bring are nothing to laugh at. The comic books we know today haven't been around long, compared to many other collectibles. But in a few cases, a single copy can bring tens of thousands of dollars to the lucky owner. In many more cases, comics can bring the delights of a well-told story in an American art form.

Some collectors are only interested in a specific era of comics publishing; some only care about a favorite character, whether he's Uncle Scrooge or Superman. Some collect issues with particular themes.

Background: Comic strips actually began to appear in American newspapers in the late 1800s, but modern collectors look on Richard Outcault's "Yellow Kid" as the first major modern comic strip character. He first appeared in 1896.

The evolution from comic strips to comic books took a bit longer. *Famous Funnies #1* went on sale in May of 1934 for ten cents and became the first regular monthly comic book. It eventually ran for 218 issues over the next 21 years. A Near Mint copy of that first issue can be worth $15,000.

Ten cents was the standard cover price for comics for more than 25 years after that and millions of children—and adults—bought them regularly. Today, any comic book with a 10-cent cover price is worth a second look, since it was distributed, at the least, more than 35 years ago. Though superhero characters had appeared in popular fiction—and even comic strips—before, *Action Comics #1* is considered to be the starting point for superhero comics. It was in that issue that Superman made his first appearance.

While many other types of comic books are collected today—and a few of them command prices of more than $1,000—the most collected comic books are those devoted to superheroes.

General Guidelines: Some collectibles challenge the collector because you have to be a detective to figure out what

you've found. But with comic books, it's easy, because they tell you about themselves, and excellent guides are available to fill in the rest. Just look for the little print that carries the copyright information; it's usually in the first few pages of the issue. That gives you the title and issue number and/or date. Then, it's easy to look it up in reference books.

Whether you're buying or selling comic books, one of the critical factors in determining value is condition. A scuffed, torn "reading copy" will bring only a fraction of the price of a copy of the same issue in like-new condition.

On the other hand, lesser-condition copies can be real bargains for collectors whose primary focus is reading the story. The same goes for reprints of comics which would otherwise be hard to find. Signs of repeated use (and abuse) include chunks (or even pages) missing; food stains; water damage; multiple folds and wrinkles; a rolled spine (permanently bent

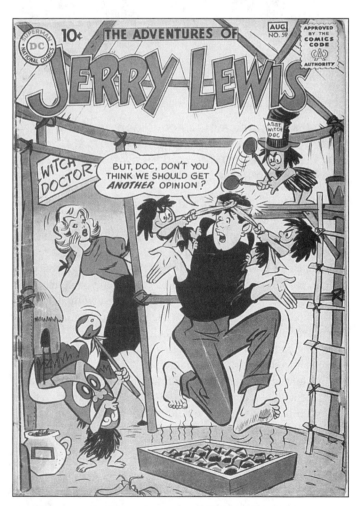

This issue of "The Adventures of Jerry Lewis" is worth about $12-$15 in Fine condition.

The classic comics in top condition can bring incredible prices. This example of "Marvel Comics" No. 1, dating from 1939, sold for a whopping $21,850 at a recent Sotheby's auction.

Is it Always Better to Be First?

Traditionally, the priciest issue of a comic book series is the first issue. This is because the first issue customarily marks the start of a series and is, therefore, a turning point. So it is that the reigning champion of comics in terms of price is also one of the most important: Action #1, which contained the first appearance of Superman. Another reason it's high in price is that very few copies survive, since it was created when comics were routinely tossed out. (Fewer than 100 copies may exist today.)

But it's the start of a popular feature that governs the importance of an item. So Detective Comics #1 (March 1937) brings only about a third of the price of a later issue in its series, Detective Comics #27 (May 1939)—because it was in #27 that Batman made his first appearance.

by folding back the pages); and tape repairs. These all reduce the market value of comic books. Comic buffs love to read what they buy. But comics get damaged easily. Folding back a corner of a cover, getting food on an issue or mending a tear with tape can lower its value. If you want to preserve your comic, put it in a plastic bag to protect it when you store it. That way, you can quickly find what you've got without tearing a cover off accidentally. You can even label the bag for fast identification without damaging the comic book.

Eras: Comic book collectors divide the early history of comics into the Golden Age and the Silver Age.

Golden Age indicates the first era of comic book production, which occurred in the 1930s and 1940s. It was a time of incredible creation in the field, when characters such as Superman and Batman first appeared.

Silver Age indicates a period of comic book production of slightly less nostalgic luster than that of the Golden Age. It is usually considered to have begun with the publication of the first revival of a 1940s superhero—the appearance of The Flash in *Showcase #4* (Sept.-Oct. 1956). However, that was a lone appearance at the time, so many collectors focus on

when Marvel entered the field, with the publication of *Fantastic Four #1* (1961). Both of these issues starred characters known today as superheroes.

Comic book collectors often look for comics from the Silver Age (1956-1969) because several superheroes from the Golden Age of Comics (1938-1945), such as Flash, Captain America and Green Lantern, were reintroduced to a whole new bunch of collectors.

But the Silver Age marked the debut of many other favorites, too, such as Spider-Man (first appeared in *Amazing Fantasy #15*, August 1962, $25,000) the Incredible Hulk (#1, May 1962 is $10,000) and the superheroes from the Justice League of America, including Wonder Woman, the Green Lantern and The Flash.

In 1956, when DC Comics used *Showcase #4* to reintroduce readers to Flash, wearing a new costume and having a new personality, the Silver Age began. This comic, in Near Mint condition, carries a $25,000 price tag, while a 1960 copy of *Brave and Bold #28*, featuring the first appearance of the Justice League of America heroes, can sell for $5,000. *Fantastic Four #1*, which appeared in November of 1961, has a value of $18,000 in Near Mint condition. Captain America appeared on the scene again, too; his revival issue from 1968, issue #100, is worth $250. Superheroes Batman and Superman also remained popular during this time.

Television shows from the 1960s were also turned into comic book subjects. Among those featured were (with first-issue values): *The Wild, Wild West* ($125), *Andy Griffith* ($300), *Green Hornet* ($150), *Dark Shadows* ($250), *Star Trek* ($450), *Space Ghost* ($325), *The Jetsons* ($225), and *The Man From U.N.C.L.E.* ($150).

Superhero comics are probably the foremost genre of collectible comic book today and as a rule bring the highest prices—especially for "key issues" (in which characters are introduced, a new plot element occurs, new costuming appears and the like). But other comics are also collectible, including "funny animal" comics, "noir" crime comics and comics based on movies and TV shows, just to name three types.

Recommended Reading

Books

2000 Comic Book Checklist and Price Guide, Sixth Edition, Maggie Thompson and Brent Frankenhoff
Comics Values Annual 2000, Alex Malloy
Comics Collectibles and Their Values, Stuart W. Wells III and Alex G. Malloy
The Comic-Book Book, Don Thompson and Dick Lupoff
All in Color for a Dime, Dick Lupoff & Don Thompson

Periodicals

Comics Buyers Guide

VALUE LINE

Values shown are for comic books in Near Mint condition.

First Appearances

Archie first appeared in *Pep #22*
(December 1941)....................................$8,500
Daredevil first appeared in *Daredevil #1* (April 1964)
from Marvel $1,750
The original Flash first appeared in *Flash Comics #1*
(January 1940)......................................$55,000
TV character Flash first appeared in comic books in
Showcase #4 and started the so-called Silver
Age of Comics (September-October 1956).......$25,000
Howard the Duck first appeared in *Fear #19* from
Marvel (December 1973) $20
The Hulk first appeared in *Incredible Hulk #1*
(May 1962)...$10,000
The Mask first appeared in *The Mask #1* from
Dark Horse (August 1991) $7
The Maxx first appeared in *Darker Image*
(March 1993) from Image.........................$2.50
The Rocketeer first appeared in *Starslayer #2* from
Pacific (April 1982) $7.50
The Silver Surfer first appeared in *Fantastic
Four #48* (March 1966) $800
Spawn first appeared in *Spawn #1* (May 1992) $20
Spider-Man first appeared in *Amazing
Fantasy #15* (August 1962)...........................$25,000+
Superman first appeared in *Action Comics #1*
(1938) $180,000
A version of Swamp Thing first appeared in
The House of Mystery #195 (October 1971)...........$15
Teenage Mutant Ninja Turtles #1 was their first
(Spring 1984, black-and-white from Mirage;
counterfeits exist, so beware!)...............$125

Uncle Scrooge first appeared in Dell Four-Color
#178, Donald Duck (December 1947)
"Christmas on Bear Mountain" story ....$1,000+
Wonder Woman first appeared in *All-Star #8*
(December-January 1941-1942).....................$24,000
The X-Men first appeared in *The X-Men #1*
(September 1963)..$5,000

TV-Related Comic Books

The Adventures of Bob Hope #1
(February 1950)...$1,000
The Adventures of Dean Martin and Jerry Lewis #1
(July 1952) $675
Beverly Hillbillies #1 (April 1963) $150
Captain Video #1 (February 1951) $750
Car 54, Where Are You #1? (1962) $75
Hogan's Heroes #1 (June 1966)................................$75
I Love Lucy #1 (1990) $2.50
I Love Lucy Comics #1 (1954) $500

"Cosmo the Merry Martian," was a little-known comic from the Archie Series. This example from 1958 is worth about $40-$50 in Fine condition.

This September 1961 issue of "The Flash" is very desirable because it features "The Flash of Two Worlds." In Fine condition, it sells for $275 or more.

Little Rascals #1 (1956) $75
The Monkees #1 (March 1967) $100
My Little Margie #1 (July 1954) $200
Our Gang #1 (1942)... $850
Roy Rogers Comics #1 (1948) $750
Roy Rogers Western Classics #1 (1989) $2.50
Star Trek #1 (1968) $450
Tarzan #1 (1948).. $1,000
Tekworld #1 (1992) $2.50
The Terminator #1 (September 1988)............................ $6
The X-Files #1 (1995) $10
The Young Indiana Jones Chronicles #1 (1992) $4.50
Zorro #1 (1966)... $75

Miscellaneous Comic Books

Abbott and Costello #1 (February 1948) $375
Adventures of the Fly #1 (August 1959) $525
All-American Comics #16, first appearance of the
    Green Lantern (1940)....................................... $60,000
All True Romance #1 (March 1951)............................ $100

GETTING STARTED!
COLLECTING TIPS

If you're buying and collecting comic books as an investment, you'll benefit from the following tips:

Learn as much about the field as you can before you invest large sums of money. Some titles do depreciate.

If you don't enjoy reading comics—if you have no feel for this art form—chances are you'll lose money.

If you decide to maintain a collection, it's well worth the added investment to preserve it. Buy plastic bags designed to protect comic books.

Handle comics gently. Don't snap them open sharply; the cover may split at the spine.

Don't fold the cover and early pages back on themselves so that you can conveniently hold the issue for reading; such handling can permanently damage the spine. Don't eat while you read. Don't write your name and address on the issue.

Don't file copies loosely in comics boxes designed to hold dozens of comics upright because the edges will bend under the weight of the comics.

Don't lend your comics to anyone.

The Amazing Spider-Man #1
    (March 1963)....................................... $18,000-$20,000
Archie Comics #1 (1942) $10,000
The Avengers #1 (September 1963) $2,250
Batman #1 (1940) $60,000
Beavis and Butthead #1 (March 1994) $3
Blondie Comics #1 (1947) $150
The Brave and the Bold #1 (1955).......................... $2,500
Captain America #100 (1968) $250
Casper the Friendly Ghost #1 (1949) $1,250
Conan the Barbarian #1 (October 1970).................... $200
Cracked #1 (1958) $125
Excalibur #1 (April 1988)... $5
Famous Funnies #1 (1933) $15,000
Fantastic Four #1 (November 1961)...................... $18,000
Green Hornet #1 (December 1940) .... $3,500-$4,000
Iron Man #1 (May 1968) $300
The Jetsons #1 (January 1963)................................... $225
Justice League of America #1 (1960) $3,000
Little Dot #1 (September 1953) $800
The Lone Ranger #1 (1948) $600
Mad #1 (1952)... $5,000
March of Comics #41 (Donald Duck)...................... $3,500
The Pink Panther #1 (April 1971) $40
Police Comics #1 (August 1941) $6,000
Richie Rich #1 (November 1960)............................. $1,500
Sad Sack #1 (September 1949) $350
Smash Comics #1 (August 1939)............................. $1,750
The Spirit #1 (June 2, 1940)....................................... $550

Strange Tales #1 (June 1951).......................$2,300-$2,500
Super-Book of Comics #1 (Dick Tracy, 1944) $150
Superboy #1 (March 1949) $6,500
The Swamp Thing #1 (May 1982)...................................$2
The Thing! #1 (February 1952)................................$500
Three Stooges #1 (1949) $750
Vampirella #1 (September 1969) $400
Wendy Witch #1 (October 1961) $100
Wolverine #1 (November 1988)...................................$20
Wonder Woman #1 (Summer 1942) ....$15,000-$17,000

Classic Comics (issues 1941-February 1947) and Classic Illustrated (March 1947-1969)

The Three Musketeers (October 1941)....................$4,000
Ivanhoe (December 1941).......................................$1,750
Moby Dick (September 1942) $1,200
Robin Hood (December 1942)....................................$700
Robinson Crusoe (April 1943)..................................$550
Dr. Jekyll and Mr. Hyde (August 1943) ....$800-$900
Huckleberry Finn (April 1944) $400
Frankenstein (December 1945)..................................$700
The Adventures of Sherlock Holmes
    (January 1947)...$900
Swiss Family Robinson (October 1947).....................$125
Twenty Thousand Leagues Under the Sea
    (May 1948)...$75
The Adventures of Tom Sawyer (August 1948)...........$100
Black Beauty (June 1949) $75
Treasure Island (October 1949) $75
The Jungle Book (May 1951)...............................$25-$35
Daniel Boone (August 1952) $20
The War of the Worlds (January 1955).........................$30
The Invisible Man (November 1959) $35

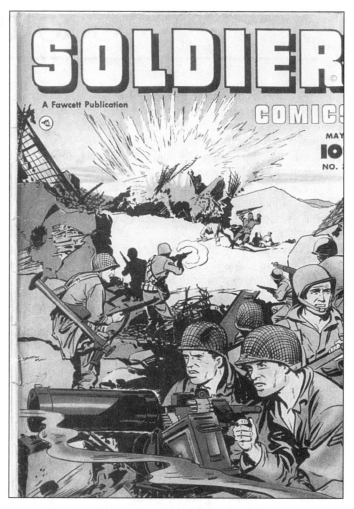

War comics were popular in the early 1950s. This 1952 issue of "Soldier Comics" is worth about $15-$20.

COOKIE JARS

Cookie jars came into common use in America during the early 1930s, and since then they've been made in hundreds of shapes and styles—at first mostly utilitarian but soon decorative as well. Today, memories of sneaking a cookie or two from those jars, when Grandma or Mom wasn't looking, is fueling one of the hottest collecting trends.

Background: The need for cookie jars in the family kitchen started during the Great Depression, when many Americans, unable to afford packaged cookies, began making cookies at home.

Although a few glass examples are available, the most popular cookie jars are ceramic, especially those made by McCoy Pottery. In addition to McCoy, Roseville Pottery in Ohio produced cookie jars in six patterns during the 1940s; five were floral designs (clematis, freesia, magnolia, water lily and zephyr lily). All floral jars are marked with the Roseville script signature, mold identification number followed by a hyphen and a number indicating size, and "U.S.A." Blue freesia and blue zephyr lily jars are the most sought after Roseville jars; clematis and magnolia are the most common. The sixth pattern, Raymor, is a glossy piece.

American Bisque in West Virginia began making airbrushed jars in the late 1930s, although it did not use fruit and vegetable motifs. These jars are difficult to identify, in part because most were only marked "U.S.A." and because the company was not the only one to use the unglazed heavy lugs called wedges. Wedges were used in these jars so they would not slip during firing or later when children reached for a cookie. American Pottery Co., Ludowici Celadon and Terrace Ceramics, all affiliated with American Bisque in some way before it closed in 1983, all used wedges.

This Little Red Riding Hood cookie jar by Regal China is valued at $350-$700, depending on condition.

Pre-World War II ceramic jars that are highly prized today were made by Brush Pottery. The company's first jars, dating back to the 1930s, were mostly glazed stoneware in cylindrical or beanpot shapes with only a few hand-painted leaves or flowers for decoration. It wasn't until the mid-1940s that figural cookie jars became the rage, jars depicting colorful animals and whimsical fantasy characters.

Twins Ross and Don Winton, who designed from the mid-1940s until 1971, created some of the most desirable Brush jars. The two also formed their own company, Twin Winton Co., which started in 1935 and closed in 1977, when it sold its molds to Treasure Craft.

A company that gained popularity in the 1980s was Brayton Laguna, founded in 1927. Today, this company's most sought after and most expensive jars are its African-American mammy jars. Other notables include the company's Walt Disney jars from 1938-40, when it was the only company with a license to do Walt Disney jars.

Shawnee Pottery (1937-61) produced identical molds with variations in the color and style of decorations; many collectors want to include variations of the same jar in their collections. Smiley pig, Winnie pig, and Dutch boys and girls are among this company's most popular jars.

The Regal China Co. is best known for one style in particular—Its Little Red Riding Hood jars. During the 1940s, the company purchased Little Red Riding Hood blanks from the Hull Pottery Co. in Ohio. Regal China then put the finishing pieces on the undecorated pieces. Collectors eagerly collect examples of jars with even small variations in detail, such as a different floral pattern on her skirt border. These well-made jars have lasted surprisingly well and are readily available, but demand for them keeps their prices up.

General Guidelines: Cookie jars made by particular manufacturers are especially desirable. Top names to look for (markings are often found on the bottom of the jar) include Abingdon, Brush Pottery, American Bisque, McCoy, Hull, Shawnee, Red Wing and Metlox.

Condition is essential, but remember that cookie jars were meant to be used on a daily basis, and that normal wear is a part of a jar's overall charm.

Much of the decoration found on jars was painted on top of the glaze or on the bisque itself, making this paint susceptible to flaking, chipping and marring after years of regular use. Chips and cracks, however, will greatly reduce the value of a jar, as will a poor attempt at restoration or paint job. Among the hottest cookie jars to look for include those with the following themes: Black Americana, advertising and character (Disney, Hanna-Barbera, etc.).

Trends: Most of the fluctuation in the market has been artificial, based on an event, and not reflective of the true market. The cookie jar market has remained active and strong. Many cookie jars are available for under $35, but jars in the $50, $100 and $150 range are not uncommon.

Cookie jars from the past are not the only ones being sought by collectors. Advertising jars and new designs are hot items, too.

Advertising cookie jars are a favorite cross-collectible. This popular idea began when companies used a colorful cookie jar as an eye-catching way to package their products, much the way tins are used today.

In other instances, figural jars were available to consumers who saved the required number of boxtops and labels and mailed them to a company, along with a nominal amount of money, in exchange for a cookie jar advertising one of that company's products.

Collectors also appreciate the fine new jars on the market. Shirley Corl of Caro, Michigan, began manufacturing jars in 1990. She now produces more cookie jars than any other American artist. Her works have been very successful in both their original limited edition sales and on the secondary market. Companies such as Treasure Craft and Fitz and Floyd are also hot companies.

Clubs

- Cookie Chat, Darcie Currier, 2978 W. Deckerville Road, Caro, MI 48723

- Cookie Jarrin', Joyce Roerig, RR2 Box 504, Walterboro, SC 29488-9278, 803-538-2487

- Exclusively Shawnee, P.O. Box 713, New Smyrna Beach, FL 32170-0703

- Our McCoy Matters, c/o Carol Seaman, 216-526-2094

- Cookie Jar Collectors Express, P.O. Box 221, Mayview, MO 64071-0221, 816-584-6309

- National Cookie Jar Show/Tennessee State Fairground, Walter F. Sill, Jr., 557 Forest Retreat Road, Hendersonville, TN 37075-2247, 615-824-4646

- The Cookie Jar Museum, Lucille Brombereck, 111 Stephen St., Lemont, IL 60439, 708-257-5012

There are dozens of mammy cookie jars available to collectors of Black Americana. This example was made by McCoy.

VALUE LINE

The following are representative values for collectible cookie jars. Prices reflect items that are in Excellent to Mint condition.

Abingdon

Cookie Time Clock	$150-$225
Jack In The Box	$575-$675
Pineapple	$150-$200
Train	$335-$430

Advertising Cookie Jars

Case Tractor	$165-$200
Coca-Cola Bottle, Doranne	$140-$180
Green Giant Sprout, Benjamin & Medwin	$85-$115
Mr. Peanut, Benjamin & Medwin	$100-$135
Pillsbury Doughboy, Benjamin & Medwin	$30-$60
Quaker Oats, Regal China	$150-$175
Spuds McKenzie	$300-$325

American Bisque

Davy Crockett, coming from the forest	$775-$825
Dino, with golf clubs	$1,000-$1,300
Dog, with toothache	$725-$800
Little Lulu	$3,750-$4,000
Pig	$115-$165
Rudolph the Red Nosed Reindeer	$650-$750
Tugboat	$250-$300
Yogi Bear	$700-$850

This nice Snow White cookie jar, featuring the seven dwarfs dancing around her skirt, sold at an ESAU's Antiques and Collectibles Extravaganza for $1,000.

CAN YOU HAVE TOO MANY?

It's a common problem—finding storage space when your collection grows from one jar to five, to a dozen, to two dozen, to five dozen jars. You may have to create custom-made shelves, because most bookshelves and cabinets do not have enough height for cookie jars.

The tops of shelves or kitchen cabinets are another possibility, because these spots often are not used for much, anyway. Plus, they will keep your collection safely out of reach. Other nooks and crannies may suffice, too, so look for these places.

Any jars that are not being displayed should be carefully packed away; you can rotate the ones you show. It's better to not see one for a while, than to have it broken.

Brush

Bear, smiling with cap	$500-$550
Cinderella's Coach	$335-$385
Fish	$445-$510
House, gray, marked W31	$165-$200
Humpty Dumpty, with cowboy hat	$340-$360
Puppy Police	$625-$655
Tulips	$110-$145

Character

Alf, made in USA, with tie	$275-$400
Bambi, Tree Stump, antique finish	$650-$850
Bambi, Tree Stump, color	$1,600-$1,850
Bugs Bunny, Warner Brothers	$35-$45
Cookie Monster, California Originals	$85-$115
The Count, Sesame Street, California Originals	$950-$1,150
Garfield, Enesco	$85-$105

Howdy Doody, Purinton	$700-$800
R2-D2, Cumberland Ware	$125-$175
Raggedy Ann, Bobbs Merrill Co.	$325-$375
Sylvester & Tweety Bird, Warner Brothers	$35-$45
Wizard of Oz, Clay Art	$80-$120
Wonder Woman, California Originals	$1,000-$1,250
Woody Woodpecker, California Originals	$1,100-$1,250
Yosemite Sam, Warner Brothers	$35-$45

McCoy

Apollo, space capsule, #260	$1,000-$1,250
Clown	$75-$100
Dog, with tail in the air	$20-$30
Freddy the Gleep, green	$600-$700
Grandma, #159	$125-$150
Green Pepper	$50-$70
Hamm's Bear	$300-$350
Harley-Davidson Hog	$650-$850
Keebler Tree House	$120-$140
Raggedy Ann, marked "USA 741"	$100-$165
Smiley Face	$50-$75
Traffic Light	$65-$80
Woodsy Owl	$310-$330
Yellow Pepper	$90-$120

Metlox

Apple Barrel	$70-$90
Ballerina Bear	$100-$150
Bluebird on Pinecone	$210-$235
Drummer Boy	$525-$625
Grapes	$300-$345
Hen	$300-$375
Little Red Riding Hood	$1,400-$1,600
Mammy, in polka dress	$450-$600
Santa head	$850-$950
Standing Santa	$650-$850
Uncle Sam Bear	$1,500-$1,600
Watermelon	$800-$900

Regal

Dutch Girl ....$800-$900
Humpty Dumpty ....$300-$350
Little Red Riding Hood, many variations ....$300-$700
Quaker Oats ....$140-$180

Shawnee

Corn Queen ....$230-$285
Sailor Boy, with blue scarf...............................$140-$180
Smiley pig, many variations..............................$350-$1,400

Sigma

Circus Lady ....$375-$425
Circus Man...$150-$200
Fireman Beaver..$260-$335
Hortense ....$200-$250
Kermit, on television...$700-$800
Mrs. Tiggy-Winkle..$400-$500

Treasure Craft

Bart Simpson, holding cookie...........................$60-$80
Baseball...$65-$85
Bull Dog Cafe ....$125-$200
Famous Amos Cookies ....$50-$60

Indian Tee Pee..$55-$65
Honey Bear ....$85-$115
Mickey Mouse ....$60-$80
Slot Machine ....$120-$140
Wurlitzer Jukebox ....$125-$175

Twin Winton

Castle...$875-$1,000
Friar Tuck...$80-$90
Hillbilly Outhouse...$350-$400
Howard Johnson's ....$2,000-$2,500
Mother Goose, color ....$315-$360
Mother Goose, gray ....$150-$200
Noah's Ark, blue ....$200-$225

Miscellaneous

Baseball Boy, California Originals ....$50-$65
Calico Dog, Brayton Laguna ....$375-$450
Clown, Fitz and Floyd..$135-$165
Elf, California Originals......................................$110-$160
Felix the Cat, Benjamin & Medwin......................$35-$50
Graduation Owl, Doranne ....$45-$60
Gumball Machine, California Originals ....$135-$145
Lunch Box, Doranne ....$50-$65
Mailbox, Doranne ....$90-$100
Monk, DeForest of California............................$135-$180
Moo Juice, Omnibus ....$45-$60
Police Paddy Wagon, Henry Cavanagh..............$300-$400
School Bus, California Originals ....$240-$290
School Bus, Doranne ....$125-$150
Seated Turtle, California Originals ....$30-$55
Shopping Rabbit, Maddux of California............$450-$525
Taxi Cab, Glenn Appleman................................$775-$895
Toaster, Clay Art ....$45-$65
Tuggle, Sierra Vista...$160-$235
Wind-up Car, California Originals.....................$225-$260
Wise Owl, Robinson Ransbottom.....................$160-$185

Collectors will have no trouble finding vintage cookie jars in a variety of designs and price ranges at collector shows, flea markets and antique shops across the country. They range in price from $25 to over a thousand.

COSTUME JEWELRY

Originally created as a cheap substitute for "real" jewelry, costume jewelry has come to be recognized as a legitimate art form. Pieces were made by substituting rhinestones or glass for gemstones, and silver or white "pot" metal for platinum. Many of the pieces were remarkably well-made, and designers experimented more because the components were not precious. This has resulted in a greater variety of pieces than exists in the category of fine jewelry.

Background: Costume jewelry was not immediately accepted upon its introduction. It would take renowned couturiers like Coco Chanel and Elsa Schiaparelli to bring costume jewelry to the attention of affluent, fashionable women. The two were foremost among Parisian couturiers in designing and promoting the wearing of faux jewelry as an accessory to clothing, and as a means of self-expression.

In the world of fashions for the average woman of the 1920s and '30s, the Eisenbergs of Chicago positioned themselves at the forefront of a new movement. In what would prove to be a marketing coup, they added sparkling baubles to their clothing. The brooches and clips soon disappeared while many of the clothes remained unsold, and so the Eisenbergs concentrated their efforts on costume jewelry, giving it further respectability and bringing it into the mainstream of fashion.

These rhinestone pin and earrings are part of a suite that also includes a bracelet and necklace.

During the 1930s, costume jewelry appeared on famous stars of the silver screen, and women could afford to buy similar items at their local emporiums.

Because they were made from non-precious materials, costume jewels gave manufacturers and designers a greater freedom to experiment with designs, and the opportunity to cater to fashion's whims and trends.

By the 1940s, the industry had a difficult time meeting the demands of an eager public. However, World War II forced many factories to take up the production of metal parts for the defense industry instead of costume pieces. When the war ended, the interest in costume jewelry escalated, continuing the frantic pace for over three decades.

Hundreds of manufacturers and designers flooded the market with costume jewelry, yet most were barely able to keep up with the demand. As a consequence, many pieces by the higher-end participants went unsigned, or sometimes only one piece of a pair bore identification, leading to still more unsigned items when pieces were separated or lost.

The boom would last through the late 1970s, when modestly priced delicate gold pieces and tiny chains would become the rage. Always eager for something new, the "gold rush" was on, leading to the unfortunate demise of many stalwarts in the costume jewelry industry. For those able to weather the bad times, a turnaround was inevitable, and by the mid-1980s the lure of quality costume jewelry once again found a place in the hearts, and jewelry boxes, of women around the world.

General Guidelines: Most costume jewelry made in the 1920s is unsigned.

Many collectors search for pieces produced during specific time periods—like Art Deco or Victorian—while others devote their efforts to finding examples from specific manufacturers or designers. Some collectors focus on both, covering periods from the past, as well as collectibles of the future being made today.

Designer names to look for in costume jewelry include Eisenberg, Chanel, Schiaparelli, Boucher, Hobe, the Mazer and Jomaz lines of the Mazer family, Schreiner, DeLillo, Polcini, Panetta, Hollycraft and Mimi d'N.

Beware of reproductions. Fake Eisenberg, Weiss and Trifari pieces have appeared in abundance.

Be particularly wary of "jelly bellies." Primarily featuring animals, insects, etc., the originals most often bore the names of Trifari and Coro. They can be distinguished by a clear, domed "belly" that dominates whimsical figurals of fish, turtles, frogs, etc. Usually in sterling silver, the bogus pieces also bear what is purported to be the authentic manufacturer's mark. Pay attention to the bellies, which were originally made of a clear synthetic material; fraudulent ones are

CARING FOR YOUR COSTUME JEWELRY!

Repairs to costume jewelry are costly and difficult, so it's best to fix any problems before they surface, and to store the pieces properly. Sometimes thought of as "throw away" jewelry, it was not made to withstand the tests of time and can come undone with little or no warning due to temperature changes, jostling, etc. Costume jewelry should not come in contact with perfume oil or even the natural oils in skin, as they can affect any glue or other adhesives. Gloves should be worn when handling the pieces. To store them, first wrap the pieces in soft cloth and then store them in a sealed plastic bag, to avoid moisture.

most often of glass. Potential buyers need only tap their teeth against them to tell the difference.

Of special appeal are the works of designers who used wired-on faux pearls and gems, beads, and mirrorbacks—most notably Miriam Haskell, Robert, and DeMario—as well as those bearing the names of couturiers Hattie Carnegie and Nettie Rosenstein, and the varied designs of Kenneth Jay Lane are also in demand.

Particularly popular with collectors are the distinctive designs of Eugene Joseff, known as Joseff of Hollywood.

Most of the aforementioned designers and manufacturers had distinctive styles. Just as many signed pieces are by manufacturers whose offerings were generally of poor quality or of no significance in today's collectibles market. Also, not every piece of jewelry by even the higher-end and sought-after names was particularly noteworthy. Consequently, it's wise to give attractive unsigned pieces careful attention.

Still, many of the finest and most treasured pieces in the collections of astute buyers do not bear identifying marks.

Pieces are most valuable in their original condition, with no changes or restorations made to any part of the piece. Learn the marks and identification signatures of the major manufacturers.

The age of a piece can be determined by the style and manufacture of the pinbacks, clips and other closures on the jewelry. Still, if the parts were replaced this can be unreliable. A fun way to learn what jewelry was produced when is to track down and browse through old catalogs, advertisements and other literature that originally showcased the jewelry.

Contributor to this section: Joanne Ball

Clubs

•Costume Jewelry Collectors Showcase, P.O. Box 656675, Fresh Meadow, NY 11365

•Vintage Fashion and Costume Jewelry, P.O. Box 265, Glen Oaks, NY 11004

Recommended Reading

Warman's Jewelry, Second Edition, Christie Romero
Collectible Costume Jewelry ID and Value Guide, Third Edition, S. Sylvia Henzel
Answers to Questions About Old Jewelry, Fifth Edition, C. Jeanenne Bell, G.G.
Antique Jewelry With Prices, Second Edition, Doris J. Snell
Collecting Rhinestone and Colored Jewelry, Fourth Edition, Maryanne Dolan
Bakelite Bangles Price & Identification Guide, Karima Parry

VALUE LINE

Signed items

Boucher reversible "night and day" brooch; one side as gold flower with pearl center, the other paved rhinestones; rare style and design; 2-1/2" diameter; 1940s-1950s $375

Coro Duette (one brooch that separates into two clips); rose-colored enameled love birds, pave and floral accents; 2-1/2"; 1940s .... $200-$350

CoroCraft Duette, sterling (vermeil) bees; multi-enamel and pave rhinestones; 2-3/4"; 1940s .... $350-$450

Eisenberg sterling floral spray fur clip featuring large clear stones; scrolled "E"; 3-1/4"; 1930s .... $800-$1,200

Eisenberg lead-backed spray brooch; red/clear stones; Marked Eisenberg (in script) Original; 4-1/2"; 1930s .... $400-$650

Florenza multi-colored enamel clown, head and torso; white finish; 2-3/4"; 1950s .... $50-$75

Georg Jensen sterling silver brooch; Nouveau design featuring large Chrysoprase cabochon .... $850-$950

Hobe faux ivory Chinese figural brooch, pink robe, large headdress of pink and green stones set in scrolled wire; 3-1/2", 1940s $1,000

Hobe sterling floral brooch; large aqua stones, engraved leaves and bow design; 4-1/4"; 1940s-1950s $500

Hollycraft necklace; coppery marcasite and amber stones, matching copper-colored snake chain; 1940s-1950s .... $250-$350

Hollycraft Christmas tree; rare; openwork antique finish; multi stones featuring clear candles, red stone "flames;" 1950s $200

Jeanne Peral jet beaded collar, French lattice work jet pendant, large black jet drop .... $600-$800

"Joseff of Hollywood," double section, silver leaf brooch, center flower featuring giant faux sapphire stones, 1940s.. $1,000

Joseff 3" diameter burnished gold brooch; angelic figural of children surrounded by openwork design of flowers and rhinestones; five 3" dangles capped with faceted crystals; 1940-1950s..... $500-$800

KJL (Kenneth Jay Lane) 1-1/4" center opening, heavy gold cuff bracelet; two 1" square-cut faceted crystals; 1960s ....$225-$300

KJL 18-3/4" triple-strand, faux pearls necklace; large center section in 3D floral design encrusted with crystals; 1960s-70s........................... $1,500

Maison Gripoux for Maggy Rouff double-strand necklace of red glass and crystal ovals, accented by large pearl drops ....$800-$1,000

McClelland Barclay rectangular gold brooch; Deco-style with overlapping raised section of pave rhinestones featuring three large red stones; 2-3/4"; 1930, early 1940s ....$250-$350

Mimi d'N domed brooch, pavé rhinestone design with faux amethysts and emeralds, emerald center; 2-3/4" diameter....................................... $450

Miriam Haskell 1/2" cuff bracelet; florentine finish, center section encasing mobe pearl encircled with seed pearls; 1950s-1960s ....$225-$275

Napier sterling bow brooch; 3-1/4" wide; large dangling marbleized amethyst stone; 1940s-50s ....$225-$325

Nettie Rosenstein vermeil enameled fur clip; aqua and red beads encased in open-topped flower; 3-1/4"; early 1940s $700

Pennino five-strand, four-sectioned faux pearl bracelet; pave rhinestone clasp and section dividers; 1950s ....$175-$250

Robert necklace, bracelet and earrings; pink beads and stones, rhinestone spacers; elaborate layered center designs featuring large pink stones, wired on beaded flowers and rhinestones; 1960s $1,000

Schiaparelli bracelet, confetti and rough hewn stones in shades of green and yellow; 1950s ....$350-$500

Schreiner maltese cross brooch, giant clear stones; elaborate center section with jeweled sceptres at each corner; decorative prongs......................$600-$900

Schreiner bib necklace; 38 strands of multi-colored and shaped stones, edged in scalloped design; earrings of large emerald-cut stones $1,800

Trifari necklace of large, high-quality double-strand faux pearls; gold beaded clasp; 28-1/2"; 1950s-60s ....$275-$375

Trifari three-dimensional green enameled frog brooch, silvertone accents, red eyes; 3"; 1950s................... $350

This rhinestone tiara with adjustable band would cost you $200 or more.

Trifari sterling (vermeil) crown brooch; large blue cabochons, red, green, pave clear accent stones; 2"; 1950s ....$300-$400

Vendome paper-tagged, long-stemmed flower; 2-1/2" diameter yellow/green enamel flower; raised center stones of faux amber and citrines; long-stemmed, 4-1/2" overall length; 1950s ....$175-$250

Weiss "apple" brooch, closely-spaced red stones set in japanned (black) backing, green enamel leaves; 2-1/2"; 1960s ....$125-$175

Unsigned Items

Bracelet, cuff, faux ivory, center designs of raised gold; unsigned Accessocraft; 1940s-1950s.......$30-$45

Brooch, silver gilt, Egyptian revival, 1925, postage stamps; enameled in red, green and blue $125

Brooch, sterling, three-dimensional featuring matador with cape and sword; signed Mexico; 1940s-1960s ....$135-$175

Brooch, circular, openwork design, layered stones in intricate design, clear and faux emerald stones; 3-1/4" diameter; 1950s........................... $275

Brooch, necktie-style; multi-colored stones; sectional design with eleven strands capped with turquoise beads; 9"; 1950s-1960s ....$300-$500

Brooch/pendant, four layer; bottom layer of six-pointed openwork "star" rimmed with rhinestones, six four-sectioned "rays" in blue/clear rhinestones above, overlaid with blue/white enamel star rimmed with silver and centered with high-set blue crystal; all prong-set stones; 4-1/2" diameter............................ $450

Brooch, heavy gold florentine-finish floral; faux pearl center; 2" diameter; 1960s........................$45-$60

Brooch, gold eagle in heavy design; raised feathers; unsigned Accessocraft; 2-1/2"; 1950s ....$55-$75

Brooch, layered; intricate design of multi-shaped, blue-hued stones; prong set; heavy silver backing; 1-3/4" sq.; 1960s-70s........................$75-$95

Earrings, similar to Eisenberg and Weiss style of the period; clear paves over green/blue multi-shaped, prong-set stones; 1950s ....$45-$65

Necklace, gold, elliptical sectioned; pave rhinestone spacers; three teardrop faux pearl dangles; 1950s-'60s ....$50-$65

Pendant, silver, Art Nouveau with moonstone "spacers" on chain; elaborate pendant featuring large center moonstone; probably German ....$850-$950

Pendant, black onyx drop overlaid with sterling filigree; silver chain; 1920s ....$65-$95

Pin, shield, gold crown top; blue/green enamel centered with 3 raised Napoleonic bees; 2-1/4"; marked Italy; 1950s-'60s................................$55-$75

Pin, sterling jelly belly frog, large red eyes; 1940s ....$350-$450

COUNTRY STORE COLLECTIBLES

There aren't many people alive who can remember the old turn-of-the-century country store, but any baby boomer (or Gen-Xer with cable) who's ever watched TV is probably familiar with the concept—the small-town general merchandise store that sold everything from dry goods and groceries to hardware and hosiery. Few things offer as much nostalgia and charm as the old-time country store, and today, virtually everything associated with it is a hot collectible.

Background: The general merchandise store became common in small-town America in the mid-1800s and continued in some rural locations into the 1950s, but its heyday was probably from the 1870s to the 1930s. Today, we can see the old country store fairly accurately depicted in many TV Westerns and movies. Viewers of period shows like *Gunsmoke* or *Little House on the Prairie* get an occasional glimpse of the old country store, and regular fans of *The Waltons* will recall that Ike Godsey's little mercantile was featured on nearly every episode (although this period really represented the very end of the general store's golden age).

For many rural Americans, the country store was the center of activity—a place not only to shop, but also to meet friends, hear the latest news, and pick up the mail, for in many towns, the owner of the general store was also the postmaster. He also sometimes served as the town's undertaker, barber and veterinarian. He not only dispensed the latest rumors and gossip, but also the latest medical advice and elixirs. And more often than not, he served as the town's welfare and social services department, extending both credit and counsel to his regular customers. And once the automobile age was ushered in, the general store also became the town's gas station and the auto repair shop. The proprietor of the old country store certainly wore many hats.

General Guidelines: As a collectible, country store memorabilia is a very broad—and rather vague—category, including everything from vegetable bins and tobacco tins to cash registers, coffee grinders, and everything in between. Many "country store" items—like advertising and tobacco (both, of which have their own chapters)—overlap into other popular collecting categories. In general "country store" collectors seek anything and everything associated with the old general store. Here are a few of the more popular areas that together make up the broad category of country store collectibles.

Tins and other containers—Tins, no doubt, are the most popular of all the "country store" categories. Much of the food sold in the old general stores was sold in bulk, out of large barrels or floor bins, and much what wasn't sold in bulk, came in a tin. Most popular with collectors today are coffee, tea, spice, and tobacco tins. Peanut butter tins are also popular, but because of their size and shape, vintage peanut butter containers are more appropriately called "pails." Tins came in

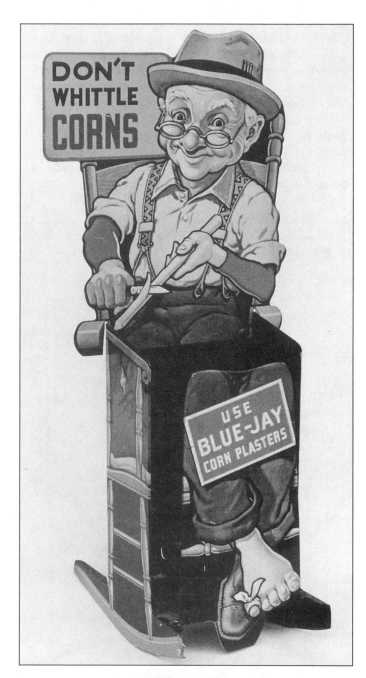

Vintage advertising signs, displays and store dispensers are very desirable and be quite valuable. This handsome tin lithographed dispenser for Blue Jay Corn Plasters sold for over $400.

lots of different shapes and sizes, but most collectors look for nice, clean examples that have lots of bright color and nice graphics. With their colorful lithographs, vintage tins from the early 1900s look great displayed in today's country kitchens. Serious collectors look for near-perfect examples, which can sell for hundreds. The average collector who just wants to add some nostalgic charm to his old-fashioned kitchen can find some nice examples (with at least one good side for display) for as little as $10 or $20. The majority of collectible tins probably fall in the $25-$100 range, but more desirable and scarce examples can sell for prices in the hundreds.

Often collected alongside tins are early vegetable cans (mostly from the 1920s and '30s), and paper and cardboard containers, like those typically used for rolled oats, powdered soaps, etc. Again, prices typically range from $10 to $75, with some especially desirable examples selling in the hundreds.

Patent Medicines—The apothecary section of the old country store was probably the most fascinating—and the

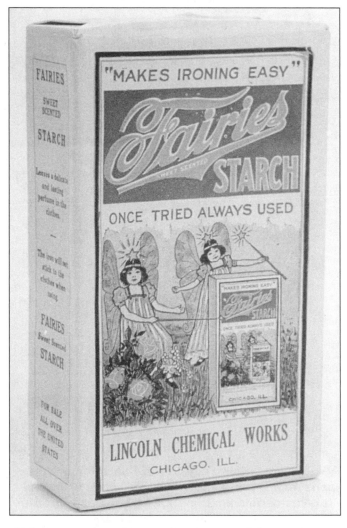

Old tins, cans and boxes in nice condition make nice display items. This box of Fairies Ironing Starch is valued at about $50-$60.

most frightening. In the days before the Federal Food and Drug Administration, sellers of drugs and health products could make pretty much any outrageous claim they wanted—and sell just about anything they cared to. In a time and a place where physicians were scarce and most people did their own doctoring, the general store was the place to go for most medical needs. The apothecary shelves were lined with a huge assortment of patent medicines, powders, syrups, oils, elixirs, tonics, pills, liniments, bitters, ointments and other miracle remedies that promised to cure everything from snake bites and toothaches to "liver complaints and "female weakness." The "secret" to most of these amazing cure-alls was that they were loaded with alcohol; some were laced with morphine or cocaine, while others even added arsenic or strychnine. When you think about it, it's amazing anyone survived this period in American history.

But not only did the patients survive, so did many of the bottles, boxes, cartons, tins, advertisements and other reminders of this bizarre period of do-it-yourself quackery—and all of it, of course, is very collectible, often, in fact, considered a separate collecting category. Prices for old medicine bottles, tins and other containers vary greatly, depending on age, condition and the product itself, but the majority of these items typically sell in the $10-$75 range.

Less controversial, but just as collectable, are vintage items related to beauty and grooming. Especially popular are talcum powder tins, shaving items, tooth powders, hand soap, hair dressings, and other common toiletries. Emerging as an extremely hot collectible in recent years are vintage condom tins, which are suddenly soaring in demand—and value.

Advertising—There are lots of advertising items associated with the old country store—signs, posters, calendars, counter displays, floor displays, and various premium items, like pocket mirrors, bottle openers, pen knives, serving trays, paperweights, drinking glasses, etc.—all displaying the name, trademark or slogan of a product. Especially popular during the time of the country store were advertising trade cards, which are prized by today's collectors for their wonderfully colorful graphics. (For more information, see the "Advertising Memorabilia" chapter of this book.)

Equipment and Fixtures: Serious collectors (with lots of spare room) who are not satisfied with a nice display of vintage tins or old medicine bottles might be interested in collecting the fixtures and original equipment from the old country stores. Included here are heavy wooden counters, wood-framed glass display cases, string holders, wooden or tin storage bins, cabinets, cash registers, large coffee grinders, meat cutters, cheese cutters, store-sized scales, clocks, lighting fixtures and more.

Because many food items were sold in bulk, the typical country store had an abundance of bins, barrels, crocks, crates, kegs, boxes, and cabinets that held everything from pickles and potatoes to sewing thread and chewing gum. Some of the cabinets, cases and containers were strictly utilitarian; others were like finely constructed pieces of furniture, with polished oak, cherry or walnut. Some of the glass displayed beautiful etching. These better pieces, of course, are the ones most in demand by today's collectors.

Especially popular are "Diamond Dyes" display cases and cabinets featuring beautiful color illustrations. In nice condition, they typically sell for $500 to $1,000 or more. Spool cabinets, which once held dozens of spools of thread are another popular collecting specialty.

Vintage cash registers—those dating from the late 1800s and early 1900s—make a country store display look authentic. Most in demand are nice, fancy ornate models made by National Cash Register that are in good shape and working condition. Most were of brass, nickel or bronze and featured fancy decoration and extras, like marble coin shelves. Nicely restored examples typically start at $750 and go up from there. Large, store-size coffee grinders stand three feet tall or higher. The most famous manufacturers included Star Mill, Enterprise and Elgin. Today, they typically sell for anywhere from $200 to $1,000 or more, depending on condition. Expect to pay at least $500 for a really nice example. Store-size scales sell in the $100-$400 range in nice condition.

Miscellaneous—Other items of interest to country store collectors include original old photographs of country stores (values range from $10 to over $100), as well as any stationery, envelopes, bills of sale, receipts, etc. containing the letterhead or logo of a country store. These types of items have, so far, been overlooked by many collectors, and prices have remained cheap, typically under $10 for nice examples. Matted and framed, they make a nice display piece. Also generally inexpensive, but a nice addition to a country store collection, are vintage burlap sacks, cloth bags, and similar items that have a country store connection.

Recommended Reading

American Country Store, Don and Carol Raycraft
Antique Trader's Country Americana Price Guide, Kyle Husfloen
Warman's Country Antiques and Collectibles, Third Edition, Dana Morykan and Harry L. Rinker
Wallace-Homestead Price Guide to American Country Antiques, 16th Edition, Don and Carol Raycraft

VALUE LINE

The following list includes some of the more interesting and desirable pieces. More common items will be worth less than the values shown. Values indicated are for items in Very Good to Excellent condition. (For more pricing on similar items, see chapters on advertising and tobacco collectibles.)

Boxes
Adam's Gum, 6-1/2" long, paper lithographed label of a New York street, 1880 .... $475
Barnum's Animal Crackers, 1920s $225

Old store display cases, like this one for Hickory Elastic, are relatively scarce and generally sell for prices in the hundreds. This example is probably worth about $250-$350.

Hershey's Mint Flavor Chewing Gum, cardboard, 6" long $700
Mickey Mouse Cookies, 1940, Mickey and Donald Duck $185
Purity Ice Cream, Canada, half-gallon, shows children at the beach $200

Coffee Tins
Aunt Nellie's Coffee, 1 lb. $300
Blue Bird Coffee, 1 lb. $200
Blue Bonnet Coffee, 1 lb. $350
Bridal Coffee, 1 lb., paper label with portrait of bride $525
Camp Fire Coffee, 2-1/2 lb. $225
Cupid Coffee, 1 lb., paper label $200
Devotion Coffee, 1 lb., early pry lid $115
Federal Club Coffee, 1 lb., paper label shows early automobiles $400
Pride of Arabia Coffee, 1 lb., Canada $115
Splendora Coffee, 1 lb., image of woman in Grecian style gown on both sides $1,600
Tartan Coffee, half-pound, red plaid label showing Scotsman $200
Wampum Coffee, 3 lb., Indian maiden image on both sides $650
White Swan Coffee, 3 lb., keywind can $175

Condom Tins
Altex, Western Rubber Co., Canada $325
Aristocrat, three-pack $500
Caravan, camel with riders in desert $200
Double Tip, depicts woman seated at water's edge $500
Hy-Pure $600
Silver Bell, Tiger Skin Rubber Co. $400

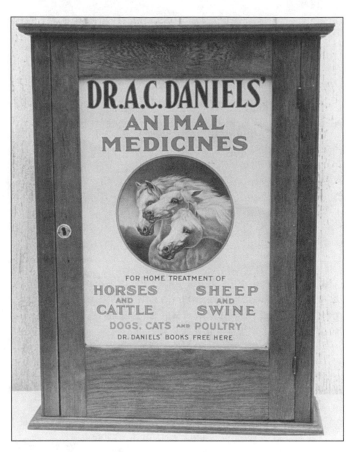

Vintage store cabinets often have nice advertising graphics on the front. Nice examples generally sell for prices in the hundreds.

Counter Displays

Baker Chocolate, tin, 22", serving-tray top $1,500
Beech Nut Gum rack, tin lithographed,
    14" high $1,100
Bull Frog Shoe Polish, tin lithographed...................... $375
Diamond Dyes, embossed tin front, 30" high,
    shows children playing.. $650
Green River Whiskey, elderly black man with horse
    .... $525
Harris Flavoring Extract, die-cut cardboard $125
Primley Chewing Gum, die-cut, figural bear $225
Sanfords Ink, oak and glass, 16" high........................ $500
Squirrel Peanut Butter, tin lithographed, die-cut,
    24" high.. $750
Waterman's Ink, tin lithographed, 21" high $775

Medicine Bottles

Black Swamp Syrup.. $50
Dr. Davis' Compound Syrup of Wild Cherry and
    Tar $40
Hayman's Balsam of Horehound $20
Dr. Henley's Celery, Beef and Iron, 9" high $120
Dr. McMunn's Elixir of Opium $140
Hick's Capudine Cure... $325

Kimball's Anodyne Toothache Drops...................... $425
Sanderson's Blood Renovator, 1840s, 8" high............ $650
Shaker Anodyne.. $250
Smith's Anodyne Cough Drops, 1850s.................... $140

Peanut Butter Pails

Armour's Veribest, 1 lb. $100
Capitol Peanut Butter, 14-oz., depicts children
    with toys... $475
Eat More Brand Peanut Butter, 1 lb. tin shows
    animal figures... $225
Hoody's Peanut Butter, 1 lb., graphic of two
    girls seesawing over large peanut...................... $175
Jack and Jill Peanut Butter, Canada, 13-oz. $245
King's Peanut Butter, 1 lb. $850
Peter Pan, 11-oz., snap top lid...................................... $60
School Boy Peanut Butter, 1 lb. $170
School Days, 14-oz., scenes of children playing $325
Squirrel Peanut Butter, 5 lbs., image of squirrel
    on both sides.. $400
Teddie Peanut Butter, 1 lb. $85
Van Dyks Peanut Butter, 1 lb., scene of
    Mother Hubbard and children $875

Tobacco Tins

Cardinal Cut Plug, vertical pocket-type..................... $200
Century, Lotilard & Co., flat pocket type, dial under
    lid rotates to show 1880 presidential candidates.... $650
Checkers, black-and-red checkered design................. $400
Colonial Cubes, pocket-type, image of
    George Washington $650
Dixie Queen, canister-shaped $175
Edgeworth Juniors... $125
Eve, vertical pocket-type, shows Eve covered by
    fig leaf $100
Fast Mail Tobacco, flat pocket-type........................... $275
Forest & Stream, shows fishermen in canoe $400
Fountain Tobacco, canister, 6-1/4" high $225
Greek Slave Tobacco, image of statue on red can $300
Honey Moon Tobacco, vertical pocket-type,
    image of couple in moon...................................... $900
Lucky Curve Plug Cut Tobacco, shows baseball
    player on red background.................................. $1,850
Maryland Club, vertical pocket-type $550
North Pole Tobacco, shows two polar bears killing
    walrus $140
Old Rip, shows Rip Van Winkle in Catskills $350
Pedro Cut Plug, image of straight flush poker
    hand $250
Real Thing, canister $250
Squadron Leader, shows 1920 airplane $75
Three Feathers, vertical pocket-type........................... $250
Times Square Smoking Mixture, vertical pocket-type,
    view of New York skyline at night........................ $425
Tuxedo, canister-type... $100
Yankee Boy, vertical pocket type, image of
    boy playing baseball... $625

Trade Cards

Typical example ....$5-$15
Agate Iron Ware, cat in coffee pot $25
Alaska Down Bustles, shows woman wearing
    bustle $18
American Breakfast Cereals, 1880s $15
Arbuckle Coffee $5
Automatic Shoe Heel Co., diecut................................$45
Ayer's Hair Vigor $15
Ball's Health Preserving Corsets $10
Bickford & Huffman, farm tools....................................$25
Bon-Ton Polish, girls playing with dog $5
Broadhead Dress Goods..$12
Buster Brown Shoes..$15
California Wine...$25
Capadura Cigar $10
Carter's Little Nerve Pills $18
Claredon Pianos, girl holding tennis racket $35
Deep Sea Mess Mackerel...$8
Dixon's Stove Polish...$8
Domestic Sewing Machine $15
Dutch Boy Paints, mechanical diecut $25
Eureka Mower..$18
Eureka Silk, girl at tea party $10
Fairbanks Gold Dust Twins...$50
German Corn Remover $35
Glenwood Rangers & Heaters, girl in hat......................$8
Hires Root Bear...$20
Horsehead Tobacco $10
Horsford's Acid Phosphate $25
Kenton Baking Powder, owl and moon........................$10
Libby & Spier, clothing $15
Marshall & Ball Clothiers..$5

Vintage cash registers are often very ornate.

Merrick's Thread, hot-air balloon $10
Niagara Starch...$5
Old Judge Cigarettes $12
Packer's Tar Soap, mother washing baby $5
Peckham's Croup Remedy $5
Princess Plow Co., four pages.......................................$18
Standard Sewing Machine, woman playing
    croquette $15
Syrup of Figs..$12
Standard Java $15
Target Plug Tobacco..$35
Taylor & Rogers Clothing..$25
Walter Baker & Co., cocoa $10
Williams' Yankee Soap, flag...$100

COWBOY HEROES

Astronauts, presidents and sports stars all have their place, but for millions of Americans (and thousands of collectors), no figure is more of a national hero than the good old American cowboy—the brave buckaroo who tamed the Wild West with his riding and roping and shooting and singing. From the time of the pioneers' first push westward, generations of Americans have been reared on cowboy tales and steeped in Western lore. In print, on radio, in big-screen films, and on television, dozens of cowboys have galloped their way into America's hearts and homes.

Of all the countless cowboys who rode through weekly radio shows and movie serials, four truly epitomized the American cowboy spirit—Roy Rogers, Gene Autry, Hopalong Cassidy, and The Lone Ranger. Within the category of cowboy collectibles, items bearing the names, images and likenesses of these "Big Four" are, by far, the most sought-after. Which of the four is the most popular depends on whom you ask. For many years, Hopalong Cassidy items probably attracted the most interest, but the recent deaths of both Roy Rogers and Gene Autry brought increased attention to their collectibles as well. Lone Rangers items, meanwhile, have always been hot.

Background: Two of the "Big Four"—Roy Rogers and Gene Autry—were real-life singing cowboys. The other two—Hopalong Cassidy and the Lone Ranger—were fictional characters (although William Boyd, the actor who played Hopalong Cassidy was so closely identified with the role that he actually became the character).

Hopalong Cassidy was based on a character created by novelist Clarence Mulford in the early 1900s. He first rode onto America's movie screens in 1935. William Boyd starred as Hoppy in over five dozen adventured-packed films, and then brought the character to television in an NBC program that premiered in 1949. On the popular TV show, Hoppy,

riding his horse "Topper," was foreman of the Bar-20 Ranch. During the 1940s and '50s, Hoppy was such an American superstar that he was featured on hundreds of toys, books, games and other items, becoming one of the earliest fictional characters to be so commercially marketed.

Gene Autry was really the first of the singing cowboys. He recorded his first record, "No One to Call Me Darling, in 1927, the first of over 400 songs he released during a sensational five-decade recording career that earned him a spot in the Country Music Hall of Fame. Autry's Christmas classics, "Here Comes Santa Claus" and "Rudolph the Red-Nosed Reindeer," remain seasonal favorites and are among the best-selling records of all time. Autry started his radio career as Oklahoma's "Yodeling Cowboy" in the early 1930s, and then moved up to Chicago's powerful WLS, where he had his own show, and also was featured on the "National Barn Dance." By the end of the 1930s, he was hosting "Gene Autry's Melody Ranch," one of the most popular shows on radio.

Autry also began his film career in the mid-1930s and was one of the cinema's biggest matinee idols, eventually appearing in some 89 feature-length films, before moving on to television in 1950. His half-hour "The Gene Autry Show," which co-starred his perennial sidekick Pat Buttram, ran for most of the 1950s and featured Autry singing the show's familiar theme, "Back in the Saddle Again."

Between radio, TV, movies and records, Gene Autry was one of the biggest stars of his generation and one of the shrewdest businessmen and toughest negotiators. He was featured on countless items—all of which are collectible today—and he invested his earnings and endorsement money wisely, eventually becoming "the richest cowboy in the world." Autry loved sports and for years was the owner of the California Angels baseball team.

Roy Rogers (born Leonard Frank Sly in 1911) also started his career as a singer, originally performing with his cousin as "The Slye Brothers" in California in the early 1930s. He eventually joined the "Sons of the Pioneers," the best known of all the early Western groups. The Pioneers enjoyed regular radio appearances and were featured in various Western movies during the mid-1930s. Sly was a natural.

Roy Rogers collectors have hundreds of items to look for.

COLLECTOR'S TIP!

For the really serious Hopalong Cassidy collector the ultimate treasure might be a Hopalong Cassidy bicycle. Made by Rollfast in 1950, a nice example can sell for $3,000 or more. Even a store display sheet advertising the bike is a desirable item. One sold at a recent auction for over $300.

He was soon given bigger roles and quickly established himself as a singing cowboy. Republic Pictures, looking for another Gene Autry, saw Sly's potential and gave him his own movie to star in, *Under Western Stars*, in 1938. They also gave Sly a new name—Roy Rogers.

One of the biggest names in Hollywood, Rogers went on to star in some 80 feature films, many with Dale Evans, whom he first appeared with in the 1944 film, *The Cowboy and the Senorita*. Roy and Dale married in 1947, a year after his first wife died. Rogers was also among the biggest radio stars of his day, hosting the radio "Roy Rogers Show" for nearly a dozen years, ending each episode with his trademark song, "Happy Trails to You."

In 1951, Roy and Dale moved to television, hosting their weekly show that also featured sidekick Pat Brady, Roy's horse, "Trigger," his dog, "Bullet," Dale's horse, "Buttercup," and a temperamental jeep called "Nellybelle." The show was one of the most popular Saturday morning offerings and continued on in syndication, long after the original episodes were done. By the mid-1950s, Rogers was endorsing over 400 products carrying his name, second only to Walt Disney in terms of licensing at the time.

The Lone Ranger first rode into living rooms via radio airwaves in 1933, accompanied, of course, by his white stallion Silver and his faithful Indian companion Tonto. One of the longest-running shows of radio's golden age, The Lone Ranger remained on the air until 1955. For most of those years the character was played by radio actor Brace Beemer. By then, The Lone Ranger had already been on television for six years, where Clayton Moore and Jay Silverheels had the starring roles. The Lone Ranger remained a TV favorite until 1961, filming some 221 episodes in all.

In 1956 Warner Brothers released *The Lone Ranger*, the first of two movies starring the TV characters. The second film, *The Lone Ranger and the Lost City of Gold*, came in 1957. One of the most revered characters in all of American pop culture, the Lone Ranger was also featured on hundreds of toys, guns, books and games.

General Guidelines: For years, Hopalong Cassidy items were greatest in demand, leaving Roy Rogers and Gene Autry riding in close second; but the deaths of Rogers and Autry, both in 1998, resulted in renewed interest in their items. Always a standout for his legendary status, Lone Ranger collectibles come next.

Movie memorabilia (especially posters and lobby cards) and toys are two biggest areas of interest for cowboy collectors. For Roy Rogers, Gene Autry and Hopalong Cassidy collectors there are dozens of movie posters to look for (although they are becoming quite pricey). However, as stated above, there were only two vintage Roy Rogers films (along with a rather poorly received *The Legend of the Lone Ranger* movie released by Wrather Productions in 1981) for which to search for memorabilia.

For all four cowboys, there are countless games, books, comics, capguns, holsters, clothing, lunch boxes, puzzles and

Here's a smiling Hoppy on the cover of the Aug. 29, 1950 "Look" magazine. It would probably cost about $25 to add it your collection.

other toys. Perhaps most popular among cowboy collectibles are cap pistols, either in holsters or by themselves. As always, condition is critical; items still in their original boxes command top dollar.

Clubs

•Friends of Hopalong Cassidy, 4613 Araby Church Road, Frederick, MD 21705

•Roy Rogers & Dale Evans Collectors, P.O. Box 1166, Portsmouth, OH 45662

•Gene Autry Fan Club, 4322 Heidelberg Ave., St. Louis, MO 63123

•Lone Ranger Fan Club, 19205 Seneca Ridge Court, Gaithersburg, MD 20879

•Western & Serials Fan Club, 527 S. Front Street, Mankato, MN 56001

•Cowboy Collector Newsletter, P.O. Box 7486, Long Beach, CA 90807

Having the original box can double the value of a vintage cowboy gun and holster set.

Recommended Reading

Books

2000 Toys & Prices, Sharon Korbeck and Elizabeth Stephan
Hake's Guide to Cowboy Character Collectibles, Ted Hake
Collecting Western Toy Guns, Jim Schleyer

Periodicals

Toy Shop

VALUE LINE

Ranges listed are for items in Excellent to Mint condition.

Gene Autry

Adventure Comics Book, Pillsbury, 1947	$85-$200
Boston Garden Rodeo litho button, 1940	$50-$75
Bread labels with photos, 1950s	$12-$15
Cello button, 1940s	25-$45
Columbia Records publicity photo, 1950s	$15-$18
Composition statue, 1930s	$300-$450
Dixie Ice Cream picture, 1948	$25-$50
Dell Comics U.S. flag plastic ring, 1948	$150-$200
Dell Picture Strip, 1950s	$60-$75
Flying A brass wings badge, 1950s	$50-$75
Flying A cardboard wrist cuffs, 1950s	$125-$200
Gene Autry & Champion cello button, 1950s	$25-$35
Gene Autry ring, 1940s	$125-$150
Litho tin club tab, 1950s	$40-$60
March of Comics #25, 1940s	$75-$150
March of Comics #120, 1954	$25-$50

Medal of Honor, 1950s	$200-$300
Movie poster, typical one-sheet	$100-$300
Movie lobby card, typical example	$35-$50
Official club badge cello button, 1940s	$30-$40
Paper doll book, Whitman, 1950	$60-$100
Penguin Melody Ranch cigarette lighter, 1950s	$55-$80
Plastic ring, 1950	$15-$20
Puffed Wheat/Rice Comics, Quaker, 1950	$40-$75
Republic's Singing Western Star Cello Button, 1940s	$50-$75
Republic Studio fan photo, 1940	$20-$35
Rodeo souvenir photo, 1957	$15-$20
School tablet, 1950s	$35-$50
Stroehmann's Bread trail map, 1950s	$75-$100
Sunbeam Bread cardboard gun, 1950	$50-$65
Sunbeam Bread color photo, 1950	$18-$30
Sunbeam Bread litho button, 1950	$15-$25
"The Big Show" Wheaties box back, 1937	$25-$35
Thunder Riders Club button, 1935	$450-$700
World Championship Rodeo handbill, 1940	$50-$85
Wrigley Doublemint Gum store sign, 1940s	$75-$125

Hopalong Cassidy

Adult hat, 1950	$225-$450
Aladdin steel lunch box, 1950	$125-$300
Aladdin steel Thermos bottle, 1950	$75-$150
Bar 20 bracelet, 1950s	$85-$175
Bar 20 chow set boxed glassware, 1950	$60-$85
Barclay Knitwear photo, 1949	$25-$40
Big Top Peanut Butter Bar 20 TV chair, 1949	$500-$1,000
Big Top Peanut Butter ID bracelet, 1950	$100-$150
Big Top Peanut Butter Junior Chow ad, 1950	$25-$50
Big Top Peanut Butter premium catalog, 1950	$100-$200
Bill Boyd/For Democracy cello button, 1942	$225-$350
Binoculars, 1950	$70-$100
Bond Bread book cover, 1950	$25-$35
Bond Bread hang-up album, 1950	$60-$850
Bond Bread label flyer, 1950	$75-$125
Bond Bread loaf end labels, 1950	$8-$12
Bond Bread store sign, 1950	$175-$250
Bond Bread postcard, 1950	$18-$25
Boxed camera, 1950	$150-$225
Burry's Cookies cut-out panel, 1950	$45-$65
Butter-Nut Bread Troopers News Vol #1, 1949	$175-$250
Cap gun, Wyandotte, 1950s	$125-$175
Capitol Records cardboard noisemaker gun, 1950	$65-$100
Child's hat, 1950	$85-$150
Chinese Checkers, Milton Bradley, 1950	$150-$200
Cole Brothers circus pennant, 1948	$50-$80
Compass hat ring, 1950s	$250-$350

Dairylea Ice Cream carton, 1950 ....$75-$150
Dairylea Milk class, 1950 ....$150-$300
Dairylea Milk paper poster, 1950 ....$100-$150
Dixie Ice Cream picture, 1938 ....$40-$75
Drinking straws, box, 1950 ....$85-$140
Fan club letter, 1946 ....$60-$100
Film and viewer set, Acme Plastics, with four films
....$225-$350
Glass mugs, 1950, each ....$22-$30
Grape-Nuts Flakes comic book, 1950 ....$40-$85
Grape-Nuts Flakes radio show handbill, 1950 .... $75-$125
Guitar ....$200-$350
Hammer Brand pocketknife, 1950 ....$75-$125
Honey Roll Sugar Cones box, 1950 ....$300-$450
Hoppy's Favorite Bond Bread cards, 1950 ....$8-$15
Hoppy's Favorite litho button, 1950 ....$25-$50
Ideal hard plastic figures, 1950 ....$65-$100
Marionette, National Mask & Puppet ....$400-$750
Melville Milk cardboard sign, 1950s ....$165-$250
Movie poster, typical one-sheet ....$100-$225
Movie lobby card, typical example ....$35-$50
NY Daily News cardboard clicker gun, 1950 ......$65-$125
NY Daily News cardboard poster, 1950 ....$175-$250
NY Daily News cello button, 1950 ....$35-$50
Picture gun and theater, Stephens, 1950s ....$150-$200
Pillsbury Farina punch-out gun and targets set,
1940 ....$85-$175
Pillsbury promotional sign, 1940, ...$400-$600
Plastic bank, 1950 ....$75-$125
Plastic wrist compass, 1950 ....$50-$75
Portrait ring, 1950 ....$45-$60
Post Cereals trading cards, 1951, each ....$8-$15
Post Raisin Bran badge, 1950 ....$30-$50
Post Raisin Bran box, 1950s ....$500-$650
Puzzle set, Milton Bradley, 1950s ....$65-$80
Radio, Arvin, 1950s ....$450-$600
Rollfast Bikes and Skates ad card, 1950 ....$85-$125
Round-Up Club Special Agent pass card, 1948 .....$35-$50
Saving Rodeo Bulldogger Litho Button, 1950 ......$25-$35
Saving Rodeo Tenderfoot Litho Button, 1950 ....$45-$60
Saving Rodeo Wrangler Litho Button, 1950 ....$20-$25
Savings Club Thrift Kit, 1950 ....$175-$300
Silvered Tin Badge, 1950 ....$40-$75
Stationery, Whitman, 1950s ....$50-$100
Stroehmann's Sunbeam Bread Ranch House Race
Game ....$70-$125
Table utensils, 1950 ....$25-$35
Timex painted latex store display, 1950 ....$1,500-$2,500
Tin potato chips can, Kuehmann Foods,
1950 .... $125-$200
Topper bracelet, 1950s ....$65-$120
Topps candy bag, 1950 ....$50-$75
Topps chewing gum wrapper, 1950 ....$50-$90
Troopers Club application card, 1949 ....$25-$40
US Time watch, 1950 ....$450-$600

US Time watch paper sign, 1950 ....$225-$400
Wonder Bread TV show special guest sign,
1950 ....$125-$200

Roy Rogers
Alarm clock, Ingraham, 1950s ....$325-$425
Book, typical child's hardcover with dust jacket,
1950s ....$35-$50
Book, typical child's with laminated color cover,
1950s-60s ....$25-$35
Bubble gum album, 1951 ....$150-$250
Bullet tin ring, 1953 ....$35-$60
Camera, Herbert George Co. ....$75-$125
Chuck Wagon and Jeep set, Ideal ....$175-$250
Child's ring, 1940s ....$225-$300
Coloring book, Whitman, 1975 ....$30-$35
Crayon set, Standard Toykraft, 1950s ....$50-$75
Dale Evans Fan Club cello button, 1940s ....$70-$100
Dale Evans statue, Hartland, 1950s ....$100-$200
Dale Evans tin ring, 1953 ....$40-$60
Dale Evans wristwatch, Ingraham, 1951 ....$125-$195
Dixie Ice Cream picture, 1938 ....$45-$75
Exhibit card, Exhibit Supply Co. ....$10-$20
Fix-It Chuck Wagon & Jeep, Ideal, 1950s ....$200-$300
Harmonica, "Cowboy Band," 1940s ....$40-$75
Hartland figure, Roy on Trigger, 1950s ....$100-$200
Horseshoe Game, Ohio Art ....$60-$85
Jigsaw puzzle, Whitman ....$35-$50
Little Golden Record, with picture sleeve ....$15-$25
"Lore of the West" storybook record album,
RCA ....$75-$135
March of Comics #47, 1949 ....$65-$150
March of Comics #77, 1951 ....$45-$110
Marx Play Set ....$250-$400
Microscope ring, 1949 ....$85-$125
Microscope ring ad, 1949 ....$35-$50
Movie poster, one-sheet, 1950s ....$125-$250
Movie lobby card, 1950s ....$25-$50

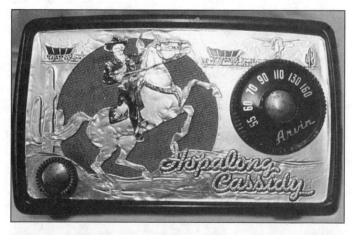

**The Arvin Hopalong Cassidy radio from the early
1950s is a collector favorite, fast approaching $500
in value.**

Movie or TV magazine with Roy on cover,
1950s ....$25-$50
Neckerchief, cotton or silk, 1950s ....$$75-$125
Nelleybelle pedal car.....................................$500-$1,000
Nodder, Japanese ....$185-$260
Paper dolls, Whitman, complete, uncut,
1954..$100-$125
Paper pop gun, 1951 ....$35-$50
Phonograph, RCA Victor ....$250-$325
Post Cereals RR Bar Ranch Set, 1953 ....$235-$325
Quaker brass badge, 1950..................................$65-$100
Quaker Cereals branding iron/initial brass ring,
1948 ....$175-$225
Quaker Oats contest card, 1948 ....$25-$40
Quaker Oats plastic mug, 1950 ....$22-$30
Raisin Bran rings sign, 1953 ....$425-$625
RCA Victor store sign, 1940s ....$375-$550
Republic Studios "My Pal Trigger" poster,
1946..$165-$250
Republic Studios publicity photo, 1940s ....$20-$30
Rodeo board game, Rogden, 1949......................$140-$200
Rodeo souvenir cello button, 1940s.......................$35-$65
Rodeo sticker fun book, Whitman, 1953 ....$60-$110
Roy Rogers and Trigger figures, Hartland,
1950s ....$125-$225
Roy Rogers club membership card, 1948 ....$30-$50
Roy Rogers cookie box, 1951 ....$425-$600
Roy Rogers Riders Club member pack,
1950..$500-$800
Sheet music, typical example...............................$10-$25
Sons of Pioneers photo card, 1935.....................$125-$200
Spurs, Classy Products or George Schmidt ....$75-$150
Stagecoach, Ideal, 1950s...................................$75-$100
Sterling silver saddle ring, 1948 ....$400-$550
Tattoo transfers kit, 1948 ....$75-$125
Toothbrush, Owens ....$35-$60
Three-gun double holster set, Classy, 1958 ....$600-$800
Thrill Circus pennant, 1950 ....$40-$75
Toy chest, 1950s...$325-$550
Toy football, 1950s ....$40-$66
Trick Lasso, 1947..$45-$65
Trigger tin litho ring, 1953..................................$30-$45
Trigger trotter, 1950s ....$250-$350
Truck, Marx, 1950s..$150-$250

**The "Roy Rogers Fix-It Chuck Wagon and Jeep" set
from Ideal is worth over $300 complete in the box.**

The Lone Ranger

Banjo figure, Gabriel, 1979....................................$40-$65
Bat-O-Ball, 1939..$100-$150
Bestyett Bread brass star badge, 1938 ....$85-$125
Betty Crocker Soups bandanna, 1950.................$65-$100
Bond Bread cardboard sign, 1940......................$200-$300
Bond Bread color cellophane picture sheet,
1939..$75-$125
Bond Bread color photo, 1940 ....$30-$50
Bond Bread Safety Club application postcard,
1939.. $20-$35
Bond Bread Safety Club badge, 1938...................$30-$45
Bond Bread Safety Club roundup newspaper,
1939..$100-$150
Bond Bread poster, 1938....................................$115-$175
Bond Bread World's Fair penny premium,
1939..$45-$65
Bond Bread wrapper, 1940 ....$45-$75
Buffalo Bill Cody figure, Gabriel, 1980 ....$20-$35
Butch Cavendish figure, Gabriel, 1980.................$20-$35
Cheerios Comic Story of Silver, 1954 ....$50-$110
Cheerios frontier town box, 1948 ....$400-$600
Cheerios Lone Ranger deputy kit, 1980 ....$25-$40
Cheerios paper mask, 1951 ....$65-$100
Cheerios Wild West Town figure set, 1957........$350-$450
Cobakco Bread calendar, 1939 ....$150-$200
Cobakco Bread picture card, 1938 ....$30-$50
Cobakco Bread Safety Club badge, 1938 ....$65-$100
Coloring book, Whitman, 1975 ....$10-$15
Dr. West's Toothpaste cello button, 1938.............$65-$110
General Mills Lone Ranger standee,
1957 $2,000-$3,000
General Mills movie film ring, 1950s ....$150-$300
Hand puppet, 1940s ....$95-$160
Horlick's Malted Milk picture, 1939 ....$30-$50
Kix Atomic Bomb Ring, 1947......................$100-$150
Kix blackout kit, 1942....................................$200-$300
Kix Cereal "Name Silver's Son" contest poster,
1941...$2,000-$3,000
Kix decal sheet, 1944......................................$40-$60
Kix luminous blackout belt, 1941 ....$75-$150
Lone Ranger and Silver figure set, Gabriel,
1979...$85-$150
Lone Ranger and Tonto target set, Multiple Toymakers,
1970s ....$35-$50
Lone Ranger cello button, 1938...........................$50-$75
Lone Ranger figure, Gabriel, 1979 ....$28-$55
Lone Ranger figure, Hartland, 1950s...................$90-$150
Lone Ranger lucky ring, 1938, ...$2,000-$3,500
Magic lasso, 1950s...$325-$400
Merita Bread brass star badge, 1938.....................$55-$75
Merita Bread coloring book, 1955.......................$25-$40
Merita Bread photo, 1938 ....$50-$75
Merita Bread Safety Club branding booklet,
1956...$50-$85

Meteorite ring, 1942......................................$2,750-$5,000
Movie serial ticket with Sears offer, 1938 ....$60-$100
National Defenders look-around ring, 1941 ......$115-$165
National Defenders secret portfolio manual,
    1941...$150-$250
New Haven Time Co. lapel watch, 1939 ....$250-$500
Oke Tonto photo card, 1934...............................$25-$50
Orange Pops cardboard sign, 1940 ....$300-$500
Record player, Dekka, 1940s ....$250-$450
Sheriff jail keys, Esquire Novelty, 1945 ....$65-$125
Silver Bullet Defender leaflet with .45 silver bullet,
    1941...$75-$150
Silver figure, Gabriel, 1979.................................$40-$75
Silver's lucky horseshoe brass badge, 1938..........$50-$75
Silvercup Bread Lone Ranger hunt map,
    1938..$125-$200
Silvercup Bread photo, 1938................................$40-$75

Silvercup Bread radio sponsorship brochure,
    1934..$100-$150
Silvercup Bread Safety Club folder, 1934 ....$65-$100
Silvercup Chief Scout brass badge, 1934 ....$225-$335
Silvercup Bread Safety Scout badge, 1934............$25-$50
Six-gun ring, 1947 ....$95-$125
Smoking click pistol, Marx Toys, 1950s.............$85-$150
Supplee Milk newsletter, 1940..............................$50-$75
Tonto and Scout figure set, Gabriel, 1979...........$75-$135
Tonto figure, Gabriel, 1979...................................$25-$45
Tonto bracelets, 1948 ....$100-$200
Tonto lucky ring, 1938 ....$1,750-$3,000
Victory Corps brass tab, 1942...............................$35-$60
Victory Corps cello button, 1942 ....$65-$100
Victory Corps club promo, 1942........................$100-$200
Weber's White Bread victory wrapper, 1942..........$45-$6

It uses a perfect blend of ingredients, but Cracker Jack's recipe for success has always been that coveted prize inside each box.

Though the combination of popcorn, molasses and peanuts had been around for nearly 20 years, it wasn't until 1912 that F. W. Rueckheim's snack packs included prizes, designed for pure fun and instant gratification.

And, since then, there have been more than 17 billion toys distributed in Cracker Jack boxes. Cracker Jack collecting is perhaps one of the easiest fields to enter today; the product is readily available and inexpensive, too.

Background: Although he didn't have a name for it yet, F. W. Rueckenheim introduced his popcorn confection to the world during the 1893 Chicago World's Fair. Only years later did a salesman, who was enjoying the snack, exclaim what would become the product name—"That's a cracker jack!" Soon after, the company slogan was adopted: "The more you eat, the more you want."

Cracker Jack toys, be it ecological cards of the 1980s, "groovy" tattoo sentiments of the 1970s, or political pieces from the 1940s, often reflected the changing times.

Cracker Jack bought out its competitor from its early years, Checkers, which also included prizes along with its popcorn product. But consumers liked Cracker Jack's idea of issuing prizes in series.

General Guidelines: Anything associated with Cracker Jack is collectible. In addition to the toy prizes, collectors can pursue boxes, advertisements, dolls, display pieces, posters, postcards baseball cards and other memora-

Cracker Jack has been putting prizes in their boxes for nearly a hundred years.

THE CRACKER JACK MYSTERY CLUB!

During the Depression years, the Cracker Jack Mystery Club offered members the chance to collect various prizes. Via a mail-in promotion, more than 200,000 members joined the club. Prizes offered included tin and paper items, presidential books and movie star cards. Some toys from this period are considerably scarce and command prices from $25-$100.

bilia bearing the company's famous mascots, Sailor Jack and dog Bingo, introduced on red, white, and blue boxes during World War I.

Vintage boxes and other memorabilia from the earliest period in Cracker Jack history are among the favorites, especially early 1900s boxes. If you can still find one, it might be worth $100-$200, while early boxes featuring the two mascots can bring $200-$250 in top condition. On the more affordable end are Saturday Evening Post ads from 1918-20, each worth $20 or more.

But the headliners among all Cracker Jack collectibles are two sets of 2 -1/4-by-3-inch baseball cards issued in 1914 (144 cards) and 1915 (176 cards). There's a crossover effect here; these sets, which combined, are worth more than $105,000 in Near Mint condition, are pursued by baseball card and Cracker Jack collectors.

The 1914 set ($65,000) is more difficult to find because the cards were only included in boxes, one per box. The set features cards for Walter Johnson ($2,400), Ty Cobb ($6,000), Honus Wagner ($3,000), Christy Mathewson ($2,250) and Frank Chance ($1,600). But Shoeless Joe Jackson sets the pace; his card can bring $15,000 from either set.

The 1915 set was available by mail for one Cracker Jack coupon and 25 cents. Cobb is the big-ticket card in this set, at $7,000, with Mathewson, Johnson, Tris Speaker, Nap Lajoie and Eddie Plank all commanding $1,000 or more.

Also desirable is a 1912 116-page catalog which featured sporting goods and other premium items, available via mail-in coupons on the back of the Cracker Jack boxes. The catalog today is worth $200.

Prior to 1912, boxes had these redeemable coupons. In 1907, for just 10 cents and one box side, or for 10 box sides, you could get what today is another popular collectible—a set of 16 Cracker Jack bear postcards. The colorful mail-in premiums bring up to $30-$40 each today.

Some early boxes also included prizes inside, but these unmarked items were not produced exclusively for Cracker

Jack. In the coming years, "Cracker Jack" or CJ was marked on prizes, although many prizes remained unmarked.

Although many of the early prizes were unwrapped, some were wrapped in unmarked brown paper envelopes or cellophane. But by the late 1940s, the toys were being wrapped in the familiar red, white and blue envelopes similar to those still being used today.

During this time, Cracker Jack supplied rations to the U.S. government during World War II. C-ration boxes from this effort are now valued at $50-$75. While the country was at war, Cracker Jack offered propaganda and war toys, such as Allies and Axis military aircraft cards, and toys featuring the American flag.

The company, to aid the war efforts, also switched its efforts to paper prizes instead of the metal toys issued in the early 1940s. Today, metal and paper toys from the 1940s-50s, such as tin clickers ($25-$40), paper whistles ($35) and an Indian headdress ($250), are highly sought-after, due in part to their uniqueness.

In the late 1940s, Cracker Jack launched its plastic collectibles, which were prominent during the next decade. These toys included animals, spinners, rings, cowboy characters and spinners; they have not appreciated significantly in value because they were so plentiful. Riddle books and coloring books were also common, too, but are more valuable than the plastic toys.

When Borden Inc. purchased the company in 1964, packaging and production changes were made. But the main change was the introduction of multi-part plastic toys, an unpopular idea among collectors, who wanted an "instantly satisfying" toy, not one that required assembly. Popular slogans during this era were also featured on the company's most common prizes—notepads, transfers and books.

By the time the 1970s-80s rolled around, Cracker Jack was following consumer protection laws that curtailed production of toys that were small enough to be swallowed accidentally by children. In general, Cracker Jack prizes from 1960–present are relatively worthless ($1-$5 each, depending on style and scarcity), but still fun to collect. The earliest toys are the most expensive and hardest to find.

Trends: The current prizes, such as the company's re-issue of its 1915 baseball cards, have been successful, in part to Borden's strong marketing and promotions. New collectors are doing it the old fashioned way—buying a box, eating the snack and keeping the prize.

Cracker Jack issued mini (1-1/4-by-1-3/4 inches) 72-card baseball-card sets in 1991 (Topps) and 1992 (Donruss), featuring modern players. These cards can usually be purchased for less than 25-50 cents each. A 20-card All-Star set was issued 1997, featuring players from that era; these cards bring at least $1 each. But Cracker Jack, in 1993, as part of its 100th anniversary celebration, did issue a 24-card set of mini replicas of its 1915 cards. With the exception of Shoeless Joe Jackson ($2) and Ty Cobb ($1), these cards will cost you less than a buck each.

The early tin and metal toys are the most valuable, often selling in the $20-$75 range. Plastic toys from the 1950s and 1960s typically sell in the $1-$5 range, sometimes a bit more.

Prizes from just after World War II, primarily made of paper, are fairly easy to find, usually at inexpensive prices. Common prizes included stickers and books, but plastic toys were on the way.

Toys from 1930-46 are more expensive and were made from a variety of materials—glass, ceramic, tin and paper. Display and promotional pieces, and dealer incentives, are also quite popular today.

The most expensive toys are the very early pieces, most of which are unmarked. Since they are so expensive and difficult to find, these items are not sought by many collectors.

Club
•Cracker Jack Collectors Association, P.O. Box 16033, Philadelphia, PA 19114

VALUE LINE

Miscellaneous Items
Model T Ford, tin, standup, unmarked,
    1916..$700-$750
Horse-drawn wagon, pot metal, unmarked,
    early 1930s ....$400-$450
Nodding head elephant, four animals to the set, tin,
    1930s ....$400-$500

The Cracker Jack Bears postcards are also popular with postcard collectors and are among the more desirable of all Cracker Jack collectibles. The 16 different cards in the series were originally a mail-in promotion available for just 10 cents for the entire set. Today, they are worth $25-$35 each.

Harmonica, full-sized, coupon item, marked "CJ", 1910-12 ....$300-$350

Cash register bank, tin, 1920s ....$250-$300

School house tin, unmarked, 1930s ....$225-$250

Cracker Jack baseball cards, 1914-15, common players each ....$150-$200

Radio, marked "Tune in with Cracker Jack," tin, 1930s ....$150-$175

Book-shaped bank, tin, marked, 1930s.............$100-$125

Coupe, tin, unmarked, 1930s ....$100-$125

Boat on wheels, unmarked, 1930s ....$100-$125

Train engine, #512, marked, 1930s...................$100-$125

Baseball score counter, paper, early 1900s ....$100-$150

Circus wagons, tin, five different, marked Cracker Jack Shows, 1947 ....$85-$100

Cracker Jack Air Corps. Wings, pot metal, 1930s ....$85-$100

Garage tin, unmarked, 1930s ....$75-$100

Yellow taxi, unmarked, 1920s...........................$75-$100

Miniature grandfather clock, metal, 1947..............$50-$75

Sled, tin, unmarked, 1930s....................................$35-$40

Boat, motor, with man driving, tin, unmarked, 1930s ....$35-$40

Bear postcards, mail-in premium, 1907, each........$30-$40

American flag, tin, standup, 1936-46.....................$30-$35

Globe, two sizes, tin, unmarked, 1930s ....$25-$30

Soldiers, tin, unmarked, 1930s...............................$20-$30

Halloween masks, paper, four different, 1950s......$15-$20

Clicker beetle, tin, unmarked, 1930s-50s.................$5-$15

Assorted plastic toys, 1950s-60s...............................$1-$5

Plastic Toys

Assorted animals, standup, 1950s.............................$3-$5

Cagey Animals, with paper pictures, unassembled, 1970s...$2-$4

Circus figures, standup, 1950s ....$2-$4

Comic character disks, 1950s ....$10-$12

Magic drawing pads...$3-$6

Magnifying glass, 1960s, various ....$2-$3

Martians, various colors and shapes, 1960s.............$2-$4

Other plastic toys, 1950s-60s...................................$1-$5

Pinball games, 1960s-70s....................................$2.50-$4

Plastic animals, curve bottom, 1950s.......................$2-$4

Plastic animals, flat bottom, 1950s ....$1-$3

Plastic snap-together toys, unassembled, 1960s ....$3-$5

Road signs, 1950s ....$3-$5

Whistle, with animals on top, 1950s.......................$7-$10

Whistles, 1950s..$2-$5

Tin and Metal Toys

American flag, oval standup, 1936-46 ....$35-$45

Bank, 3-D book form, 2" ....$100-$125

Boy and dog, standup, early 1900s ....$100-$150

Clicker, aluminum, pear-shaped, 1949 ....$30-$40

Horse and wagon, 2 1/8"...$60-$75
Horse and wagon, 3 1/8", gray/red ....$375-$425
Miniature grandfather clock, 1-3/4", 1947............$50-$75
Miniature tray, early...$100-$125
Train car, red coach, 1941 ....$20-$25
Wheelbarrow, 1931, 2-1/2" ....$40-$50

Paper Items

Baseball score counter, 3-3/8" ....$150-$175
Bear postcards, mail-in offer, each ....$30-$40
Book, "Bess & Bill," 1937 ....$75-$100
Booklets, riddles, jokes, etc., 1965 and on................$1-$2
Disguise, glasses, hinged with eyeballs, 1933 ....$7-$10
Disguise, glasses, hinged, cellophane lenses,
    1933..$150-$175
Disguise, mustache, 1949 ....$50-$75
Fortune wheel, 1-3/4" ....$65-$80
Indian headdress, 2-1/2", 1930s........................$100-$125
Indian headdress, 5-3/8", 1950s........................$275-$300
Little Books, with Japanese writing...........................$1-$3
Magic game book, erasable slate, 1946 ....$25-$30
Midget auto race game, 1949...................................$50-$75
Movie, pull tab for second picture, 1943 ....$75-$100
Paper whistles, 1940s...$35-$40
Sand picture, 1967 ....$7-$10
Slide cards, 1970s, questions and answers................$1-$3
Strange Facts sheets, animal trivia............................$1-$3
United States states cards, with trivia ....$2-$4

The famous Cracker Jack mascots, Sailor Jack and his dog Bingo, first appeared on boxes in 1919. Early Cracker Jack boxes are scarce, worth as much as $100 or more.

DEPRESSION GLASS

Depression glass is a generic term used to describe the inexpensive, machine-made glassware that was very popular in America from the 1920s to the 1940s. It was produced in various colors and was made by more than a dozen companies in over a hundred different patterns, resulting in thousands and thousands of different pieces for today's collectors to choose from. So many, in fact, that most collectors of Depression glass decide to specialize—usually by pattern, sometimes by company or color.

Background: Depression glass, as the name implies, came along at a time when America was struggling through hard economic times, and was born out of necessity. American families could no longer afford the hand-cut crystal and other forms of handmade glass that had been popular in better times, so America's glass factories responded with a very inexpensive form of glassware that was made and etched by machine using very inexpensive materials and production methods.

The result was tremendously successful. Dozens of companies mass-produced pieces by the millions, offering everything from colorful glass tumblers for a few cents each to complete table-settings for not much more than a dollar. Families could buy not only tumblers, plates, cups, saucers and soup bowls, but also a huge variety of accessory pieces including salt-and-pepper shakers, butter dishes, sugar-and-creamer sets, serving dishes, water pitchers, platters and more. Some patterns offered more than seventy-five different pieces.

Major manufacturers of Depression glass included Hocking, Federal, Cambridge, Imperial, Indiana, Hazel Atlas, Jeannette, MacBeth-Evans, Paden City, U.S. Glass and others. These companies produced and sold this new inexpensive glass in such huge quantities that for many Americans it took the place of traditional china dinnerware. So inexpensive was the manufacturing process that many pieces of glassware were given away free as premiums at movie houses and grocery stores or were packaged inside boxes of oatmeal or detergents. Today, all of this inexpensive glassware—made by various companies in lots of colors and patterns—is known collectively as Depression glass.

General Guidelines: Depression glass first became popular with collectors in the 1960s and has since become the most commonly collected glassware in America—and probably the most researched and documented. There is no shortage of information about Depression glass. In addition to dozens of collecting clubs across the country, there are several wonderful identification and price guides that list and illustrate thousands of different pieces with their current values. Anyone trying to appraise a large collection or considering becoming a serious collector should first invest in a good price guide. *Warman's Depression Glass* by Ellen T. Schroy, for instance, lists nearly 10,000 different pieces from 140 of the most popular patterns.

Although a separate price guide is recommended, there are some general guidelines that can help novice collectors and flea market scavengers separate the trash from the treasures.

Prices vary widely depending on pattern and color. Pink and green are the most common colors, along with yellow. Blue, black, amethyst, red and other colors were also produced. Crystal (or clear) Depression glass is generally the least desirable and almost always the least valuable (often about half the value of a corresponding piece in a more desirable color), but it may be a good starting point for beginning collectors. The scarcer colors are always worth more.

The type of piece can also determine value. Common, mass-produced pieces, like plates and bowls, are more plentiful and less valuable than corresponding accessory pieces that sold in smaller quantities.

Likewise, accessory pieces that saw everyday use, such as cookie jars and butter dishes, may also be more valuable because fewer survived without being damaged. In many patterns, salt-and-pepper shakers, and pitchers command higher prices. Unusual pieces, such as lamp shades, dresser sets, punch bowls, cake trays, ice tubs, etc. are almost always among the most valuable pieces in any pattern.

As with every collectible, condition is critical. But, because Depression glass was produced as a cheap everyday tableware—not expensive art glass or hand-cut crystal—collectors are generally more forgiving about minor manufacturing flaws, such as tiny airfs bubbles, slight color variations or small lines of excess glass. On the other hand, however, because Depression Glass is still relatively plentiful and for the most part quite affordable (compared to more exotic types of collectible glass), most collectors have no interest in pieces that are chipped, deeply scratched, or missing handles, etc. Pieces displaying this type of damage have virtually no value.

The key to collecting or appraising Depression glass is to know the various patterns. As stated above, there are dozens of patterns to chose from, so once again, an identification and price guide is essential. The "Value Line" below includes representative pieces from some of the more popular Depression glass patterns, along with some general value guidelines.

This Depression Glass berry set in the Moonstone pattern consists of a master bowl and four dishes. In white opalescent, the set would probably sell in the $28-$40 range.

Club

•National Depression Glass Association, P.O. Box 8264, Wichita, KS 67209

Note: There are numerous regional Depression glass clubs around the country, many of which have web sites.

Recommended Reading

Warman's Depression Glass, Ellen Schroy
Depression Era Glassware, Carl F. Luckey
Warman's Glass, Third Edition, Ellen T. Schroy

VALUE LINE

All values shown are for pieces in Mint condition with no chips, scratches, etc.

Adam

Jeannette Glass Co., 1932-1934 (Known for the square design of its plates; pink and green are most common colors; blue, topaz and yellow pieces are considerably more valuable; crystal pieces are about half the value of corresponding pink or green. Note: the butter dish has been reproduced in both pink and green.)

Ashtray, 4-1/2", pink or green ....$25-$32
Bowl, 9", covered, pink or green ....$75-$85
Bowl, 9", open, green $45
Bowl, 9", open, pink $30
Butter dish, covered, green $325
Butter dish, covered, pink $95
Candlesticks, pair, 4", pink or green ....$100-$125
Casserole, covered, green or pink ....$75-$90
Cereal Bowl, 5-3/4", pink or green $46
Creamer, pink or green..$20-$22
Pitcher, 32-ounces, 8" high, pink or green............$45-$50
Plate, salad, 7-3/4" square, pink or green $17
Plate, diner, 9" square, pink or green ....$30-$32
Salt and pepper, pair, 4", pink or green...............$80-$100
Sugar, covered, pink or green ....$42-$48
Tumbler, 4-1/2", pink or green...............................$28-$30
Vegetable bowl, 7-3/4", pink or green $30

American Pioneer

Liberty Works, 1931-1934 (Made in amber, crystal, green and pink.)

Bowl, 5", with handle, amber.......................................$44
Bowl, 5", with handle, pink or green ....$22-$25
Bowl, 5", with handle, crystal......................................$22
Candy jar, covered, 1-pound, crystal $100
Candy jar, covered, 1-pound, pink or green.......$110-$115
Creamer, 3-1/2" high, amber..$60
Creamer, 3-1/2" high, pink or green ....$30-$32
Creamer, 3-1/2" high, crystal $30
Dresser set, two cologne bottles, powder jar, tray,
     crystal $300
Dresser set, two cologne bottles, powder jar, tray, pink or
     green...$350-$375

Pitcher, covered, 7" high, amber $300
Pitcher, covered, 7" high, crystal $175
Plate, 8", amber..$28
Plate, 8", pink or green...$14
Plate, 8", crystal $10
Tumbler, 12-ounce, 5" high, pink or green ....$40-$55
Tumbler, 12-ounce, 5" high, crystal.............................$40

American Sweetheart

MacBeth-Evans Glass Co., 1930-1936 (Made in blue, cremax, monax, pink, red, and color-trimmed monax; blue pieces are most valuable, followed by red; most common are monax and pink.)

Cereal bowl, 6", pink $16
Cereal bowl, 6", cremax or monax........................$11-$14
Cereal bowl, 6", monax with color trim......................$38
Console bowl, large, 18" diameter, blue $1,000
Console bowl, large, 18" diameter, red $850
Console bowl, large, 18" diameter, monax $375
Cup, red or blue...$75-$100
Cup, monax or pink..$8-$15
Lamp shade, monax or cremax ....$400-$450
Plate, salad, 8", blue or red $75
Plate, salad, 8", cremax $25
Plate, salad 8", monax or pink ....$8-$11
Tumbler, 5-ounce, 3-1/2" high, pink $100

Aunt Polly

U.S. Glass Co., late 1920s (Made in blue, green and iridescent; blue is most valuable, often worth up to twice as much as a similar piece in green or iridescent, except for rare pieces such as the butter dish, which is high-priced in any color.)

Berry bowl, individual, 4-3/4" diameter, blue...............$18
Berry bowl, individual, 4-3/4" diameter, green or
     iridescent $9
Butter dish, covered, blue, green or iridescent
     ....$200-$225
Pitcher, 48-ounce, 8" high, blue $175
Plate, luncheon, 8", blue $20
Salt and pepper, pair, blue $225
Sugar, blue $48
Sugar, green or iridescent..$32

Bubble

Hocking, Anchor Hocking, 1937-1965 (Also called "Bullseye" or "Provincial"; was made in crystal, pink, green, ruby and blue; crystal is least valuable, often worth less than half of identical pieces in other colors; pink saw very limited production.)

Berry bowl, individual, 4" diameter, blue $18
Berry bowl, individual, 4" diameter, crystal $5
Candlesticks, pair, green $40
Candlesticks, pair, crystal $24
Creamer, blue $40
Creamer, green or ruby ....$14-$17
Creamer, crystal $4
Cup, green, ruby or blue ....$9-$14
Cup, crystal $4
Goblet, green or ruby $15

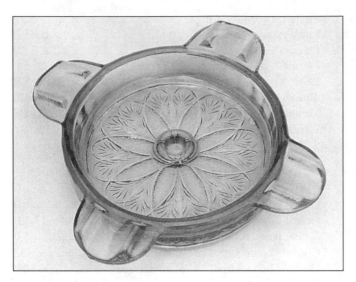

This ashtray in the Sunflower pattern is valued at about $10-$15 in pink.

Goblet, crystal $8
Plate, dinner, 9-3/8", green or ruby .... $22-$25
Plate, dinner, 9-3/8", crystal $8
Sugar, blue $20
Sugar, crystal $6
Tumbler, water, 9-ounce, ruby $10
Tumbler, water, 9-ounce, crystal $5

Cherry Blossom

Jeannette Glass Co., 1930-1939 (made in crystal, delphite, green, jadite, pink and red; delphite is the least valuable of the colors; production was very limited in crystal, jadite and red. Note: reproductions exist of the small berry bowl, butter dish, cake plate, cereal bowl, pitcher, divided platter, 6- and 9-inch plates, salt shaker, sandwich tray, saucer and footed tumbler; reproductions are in blue, delphite, green, pink and red.)

Berry bowl, individual, 4-3/4" diameter, delphite, green or
    pink .... $15-$19
Bowl, 9" diameter, two handles, pink $46
Bowl, 9" diameter, two handles, green $65
Bowl, 9" diameter, two handles, delphite $25
Cup, delphite, green or pink .... $20-$25
Pitcher, 8" high, green or pink $55
Plate, dinner, 9", green or pink .... $22-$26
Plate, dinner, 9", delphite $18
Salt and pepper, pair, pink (very scarce) $1,200
Salt and pepper, pair, green $975
Sherbet, delphite, green or pink .... $15-$18
Tumbler, 5" high, green or pink .... $70-$72
Tumbler, 5" high, delphite $20

Cloverleaf

Hazel Atlas Glass Co., 1930-1936 (Made in crystal, green, pink, yellow and black; there is little collector interest in crystal pieces; yellow and black are by far the most valuable; black pieces have become very popular with many collectors in recent years and should increase even further in value.)

Cup, pink or green .... $7-$8

Cup, yellow $10
Cup, black $16
Plate, sherbet, 6", green $5
Plate, sherbet, 6", yellow $7
Plate, sherbet, 6", black $38
Salt and pepper, pair, green $15
Salt and pepper, pair, black or yellow .... $75-$100

Cube or Cubist

Jeannette Glass Co., 1929-1933 (Made primarily in pink, green and crystal, with very limited production in amber, white and ultramarine; crystal is by far the least valuable, often only one-third the value of a similar piece in either green or pink, which are valued almost identically.)

Butter dish, covered, green or pink .... $60-$65
Creamer, 2-5/8" high, ultramarine $70
Creamer, 2-5/8" high, green or pink .... $9-$10
Creamer, 2-5/8" high, crystal $5
Pitcher, 45-ounce, 8-3/4" high, green or pink
    .... $215-$230
Plate, luncheon, 8", green or pink .... $8-$9
Salt and pepper, pair, green or pink $36
Tumbler, 9-ounce, 4" high, green or pink .... $65-$70

English Hobnail

Westmoreland Glass Co., 1920s-1983 (Among the most diverse and extensive of all Depression glass patterns, it was made in crystal, amber, cobalt blue, ice blue, pink, red, green, and turquoise. In this particular pattern, amber and crystal are priced nearly identically. The most valuable colors are ice blue, cobalt blue, red and turquoise, which may bring as much as two times the values listed for other colors.)

Ashtray, 3" diameter, amber, crystal, green, or pink
    .... $20-$22
Bowl, 8" diameter, footed, green $48
Bowl, 8" diameter, footed, amber or crystal $28
Bowl, 11" diameter, rolled edge, ice blue $85
Bowl, 11" diameter, rolled edge, amber, crystal,
    green or pink .... $35-$40
Cigarette box, with cover, pink $55
Cigarette box, with cover, amber or crystal $25
Cup, pink $25
Cup, green $18
Cup, amber or crystal $7
Demitasse cup, green or pink $55
Demitasse cup, amber or crystal $18
Egg cup, amber or crystal $10
Goblet, water, round, 6-1/4" high, pink $35
Goblet, water, round, 6-1/4" high, amber or crystal $12
Ice tub, 5-1/2" high, pink $100
Ice tub, 5-1/2" high, green $65
Ice tub, 5-1/2" high, amber or crystal $36
Lamp shade, 17" diameter, amber or crystal ...... $165-$175
Oil bottle, 2-ounce or 6-ounce, with handle,
    amber or crystal $25
Pitcher, 64-ounce, straight side, pink or green $310
Pitcher, 64-ounce, straight side, amber or crystal $75
Plate, 6" square, amber or crystal $5
Plate, 8" round, pink $15

Plate, 8" round, amber or crystal......................................$9
Plate, 10" round, pink..$65
Plate, 10" round, green..$45
Plate, 10" round, amber or crystal..................................$14
Punch bowl, with stand, amber or crystal..................$215
Punch cup, amber or crystal..$7
Salt and pepper, pair, round foot, green or
    pink...$150-$165
Salt and pepper, pair, round foot, amber or crystal.......$25
Saucer, round, green or pink..$6
Saucer, round, amber or crystal $2
Sugar bowl, square foot, green or pink.................$48-$55
Sugar bowl, square foot, amber or crystal $9
Tumbler, water, 8- or 9-ounce, amber or crystal...........$10
Vase, flared top, 8-1/2" high, pink $235
Vase, flared top, 8-1/2" high, green..............................$120
Vase, flared top, 8-1/2" high, amber or crystal.............$40

Florentine No 1

Hazel Atlas Glass Co., 1932-1935 (Sometimes called 'Old Florentine" or "Poppy No. 1," this pattern was made in crystal, green, pink and yellow with very limited production in cobalt blue, which is by far the most valuable. The other colors are valued nearly the same, with pink and yellow slightly higher on some pieces. Note: Salt and pepper shakers have been reproduced in cobalt blue, pink and red.)

Ashtray, 5-1/2" diameter, green, pink or yellow
    ....$24-$28
Ashtray, 5-1/2" diameter, crystal...................................$22
Berry bowl, 5" diameter, cobalt blue $18
Berry bowl, 5" diameter, crystal, green, pink or
    yellow ....$11-$15
Butter dish, with cover, pink or yellow..............$160-$170
Butter dish, with cover, crystal or green ....$110-$115
Cereal bowl, 6" diameter, crystal, green, pink or
    yellow ....$20-$24
Creamer, pink or yellow.......................................$18-$25
Creamer, crystal or green..$8
Cup, cobalt blue...$85
Cup, crystal, green, pink or yellow ....$8-$10
Pitcher, 36-ounce, footed, 6-1/2" high,
    cobalt blue $850
Pitcher, 36-ounce, footed, 6-1/2" high, crystal,
    green, pink or yellow......................................$40-$50
Plate, 10" dinner, pink or yellow.........................$22-$24
Plate, 10" dinner, crystal or green $16
Tumbler, 10-ounce, 4-3/4" high, footed, crystal,
    green, pink or yellow......................................$20-$23
Vegetable bowl, with cover, oval, 9-1/2" long, pink or
    yellow $60
Vegetable bowl, with cover, oval, 9-1/2" long,
    crystal or green...$40

Forest Green

Anchor Hocking Glass Co., 1950-1957 (Although not manufactured during the Golden Age of Depression glass, this pattern is, nonetheless, popular with collectors of the more traditional Depression glass. It was made in forest green only.)

Ashtray ....$4-$8
Bowl, 6" square...$18

Bowl, 4-1/2" square $6
Goblet, 9-ounce..$10
Pitcher, 22- or 36-ounce...$22-$25
Pitcher, 86-ounce, round $45
Plate, 7" square...$7
Plate, dinner, 9-1/4" $30
Punch bowl with stand $45
Tumbler, small..$4-$7
Tumbler, larger..$7-$10
Vegetable Bowl $24

Indiana Custard

Indiana Glass Co. 1930s and 1950s (This pattern was made in a custard color known as French Ivory in the 1930s; and then brought back in a white color in the 1950s.)

Berry bowl, individual, French Ivory...........................$14
Berry bowl, individual, white $6
Cereal bowl, French Ivory $4
Plate, bread and butter, 5-3/4", French Ivory $7
Plate, dinner, 9-3/4", French Ivory...............................$28
Sugar bowl, with cover, French Ivory...........................$30

Jubilee

Lancaster Glass Co., early 1930s (Made in pink and yellow; in most pieces, the pink version is slightly more valuable than the yellow.)

Bowl, 8" diameter, 5-1/8" high, 3 legs, pink...............$265
Bowl, 8" diameter, 5-1/8" high, 3 legs, yellow $215
Cake tray, 11" diameter, 2 handles, pink or yellow
    ....$75-$85
Cup, pink..$40
Cup, yellow $15
Plate, salad, 7" diameter, pink......................................$25
Plate, salad, 7" diameter, yellow $15
Sandwich tray, 11" diameter, with center handle, pink or
    yellow ....$200-$250
Sugar bowl, pink or yellow ....$40-$50
Tumbler, 10-ounce, 6" high, footed, pink $75
Tumbler, 10-ounce, 6" high, footed, yellow $50
Vase, 12" high, yellow $375

This covered butter dish in the Royal Lace pattern is worth several hundred dollars in blue.

Madrid

Federal Glass Co., 1932-1939 (Made in amber, blue crystal, green, iridescent and pink. Amber and crystal are the most common. Note: Reproductions include candlesticks, cups, saucers and vegetable bowl and are found in amber, blue, crystal and pink. Federal Glass reissued this pattern under the name "Recollection" in the 1970s; some were dated 1976. Indiana Glass later purchased the bankrupt Federal Glass Co. and reproduced the original line in crystal. Several pieces were added in recent years that were not part of the original line, including a footed cake stand, goblet, two-section grill plate, preserves stand, squatty salt and peppers, 11-ounce tumbler and vase. Values listed below are for the original 1930s Madrid.)

Ashtray, 6" square, amber or crystal ....$250-$265
Berry bowl, small amber or crystal $5
Butter dish, with cover, green $95
Butter dish, with cover, amber or crystal ....$65-$75
Cake plate, 11-1/4" diameter, amber, crystal or
    pink...$20-$28
Cookie jar, amber or crystal.....................................$40-$50
Gravy boat and platter, amber or crystal.....................$500
Pitcher, square, 60-ounce, 8" high, blue, crystal or
    green...$135-$150
Pitcher, square, 60-ounce, 8" high, amber or
    pink...$36-$45
Plate, salad, 7-1/2", amber, crystal, green or
    pink...$9-$12
Plate, dinner, 10-1/2", amber or green ....$40-$45
Plate, dinner, 10-1/2", blue $60
Plate, dinner, 10-1/2", crystal.....................................$22
Salt and pepper, pair, 3-1/2", green..............................$70
Salt and pepper, pair, 3-1/2", crystal $100
Salt and pepper, pair, 3-1/2", amber or blue ......$125-$135
Tumbler, 9-ounce, 4-1/2" high, green or pink..............$24
Tumbler, 9-ounce, 4-1/2" high, blue $38
Tumbler, 9-ounce, 4-1/2" high, amber or
    crystal ....$15-$18

Manhattan

Anchor Hocking, 1938-1943 (Made primarily in crystal and pink, with a very pieces in ruby, green and iridescent. Long overlooked, this pattern is growing increasingly popular, especially with the Art Deco crowd. Because of its distinctive pattern, it is sometimes known as "Horizontal Ribbed.")

Ashtray, round, 4" diameter, crystal or pink ....$9-$12
Bowl, 8" diameter, handle, crystal or pink.............$25-$30
Cookie jar, with cover, crystal or pink ....$32-$37
Cup, crystal $20
Cup, pink..$160
Pitcher, 80-ounce, crystal...$55
Plate, dinner, 10-1/4", crystal.......................................$25
Plate, dinner, 10-1/4", pink $120
Salad bowl, 9" diameter, crystal....................................$20
Salt and pepper, pair, crystal or pink...........................$50
Saucer, pink...$50
Saucer, crystal $7

Mayfair Open Rose

Hocking Glass Co., 1931-1937 (Made primarily in green, ice blue, pink, pink satin, and yellow. A 37-ounce juice

pitcher was the only piece produced in crystal; it is valued at $18-$20. This pattern includes some of the most valuable pieces in all of Depression glass collecting, especially for some of the accessory pieces. In general, for pieces that were made in all colors, green and yellow pieces are valued nearly identically and are the most valuable, followed by ice blue. Pink and pink satin are usually the least valuable, with the pink satin versions slighter higher than the plain pink. Note: Reproductions have existed since the late 1970s and include cookie jars, salt and peppers, juice pitchers and whiskey glasses. The reproductions are found in amethyst, blue, cobalt blue, green, pink and red.)

Butter dish, with cover, green or yellow $1,300
Butter dish, with cover, ice blue.................................$300
Butter dish, with cover, pink or pink satin ....$70-$80
Cake plate, 10" diameter, footed, pink or pink satin
    ....$35-$45
Cake plate, 10" diameter, footed, ice blue $75
Cake plate, 10" diameter, footed, green $115
Celery dish, divided, 9" long, green or yellow
    ....$150-$160
Celery dish, divided, 9" long, ice blue.........................$60
Claret, 4-1/2-ounce, 5-1/4" high, green or pink..........$900
Console bowl, 9" diameter, 3-1/8" high, 3 legs, green or
    pink (rare)..$5,000
Cookie jar, with cover, yellow $875
Cookie jar, with cover, green $575
Cookie jar, with cover, ice blue...................................$300
Cookie jar, with cover, pink or pink satin ....$40-$50
Cordial, 1-ounce, 3-3/4" high, green or pink
    ....$925-$1,000
Cup, pink or pink satin...$20-$25
Cup, ice blue $55
Cup, green or yellow..$150
Goblet, 9-ounce, 7-1/4" high, thin, ice blue or
    pink...$190-$225
Pitcher, 80-ounce, 8-1/2" high, green or yellow $550
Pitcher, 80-ounce, 8-1/2" high, pink or pink satin
    ....$125-$135
Pitcher, 80-ounce, 8-1/2" ice blue...............................$300
Plate, 5-3/4" diameter, green or yellow........................$90
Plate, 5-3/4" diameter, pink or pink satin ....$13-$15
Plate, 5-3/4" diameter, ice blue $25
Plate, dinner, 9-1/2" diameter, green or yellow..........$150
Plate, dinner, 9-1/2" diameter, ice blue $90
Plate, dinner, 9-1/2" diameter, pink or pink satin
    ....$55-$60
Salt and pepper, pair, flat, green...............................$1,000
Salt and pepper, pair, flat, yellow $800
Salt and pepper, pair, flat, ice blue $300
Salt and pepper, pair, flat, pink or pink or pink satin
    ....$65-$70
Tumbler, 9-ounce 4-1/4" high, ice blue $100
Tumbler, 9-ounce 4-1/4" high, pink.............................$30
Vegetable bowl, 10" diameter, with cover, yellow $900
Vegetable bowl, 10" diameter, with cover, ice blue,
    pink or pink satin...$120

Miss America

Hocking Glass Co., 1935-1938 (With its distinctive diamonds, this is a very popular pattern among collectors. It was made in crystal, green, ice blue, jadite, pink and royal ruby. Any piece found in royal ruby is valuable, as are most pieces in ice blue. Crystal pieces are by far the least valuable. Reproductions exist for the butter dish, creamer, 8-inch pitcher, salt and peppers, sugar and tumbler. Reproductions are found in amberina, blue, cobalt blue, crystal, green, pink and red.)

Berry bowl, 4-1/2" diameter, green..............................$15
Bowl, 11" diameter, shallow, royal ruby....................$800
Butter dish, with cover, pink......................................$550
Butter dish, with cover, crystal $200
Cake plate, 12" diameter, footed, pink......................$45
Celery dish, 10-1/2" long, ice blue $160
Celery dish, 10-1/2" long, crystal $17
Cup, crystal, green or ice blue ....$10-$12
Cup, pink..$23
Cup, royal ruby $235
Pitcher, 65-ounce, 8" high, pink...............................$175
Pitcher, 65-ounce, 8" high, crystal $45
Plate, 6-3/4" diameter, green....................................$12
Plate, dinner, 10-1/4", ice blue................................$150
Plate, dinner, 10-1/4", pink $40
Plate, dinner, 10-1/4", crystal...................................$17
Salt and pepper, pair, green.....................................$300
Salt and pepper, pair, pink...$65
Salt and pepper, pair, crystal $35
Saucer, crystal $4
Sugar bowl, royal ruby..$175
Sugar bowl, crystal or pink ....$10-$20
Wine glass, 3-ounce, 3-3/4" high, red......................$250
Wine glass, 3-ounce, 3-3/4" high, pink.......................$85
Wine glass, 3-ounce, 3-3/4" high, crystal $25

Moonstone

Anchor Hocking Glass Co., 1941-1946 (This World War II-era glass was very popular at the time because it was an affordable version of the earlier and more expensive hobnail glass. It was produced in crystal and ocean green, both with opalescent hobnails. Both colors are nearly identical in value today. Comparatively inexpensive, the majority of Moonstone pieces are still available in the $10-$20 range.)

Berry bowl, 5-1/2" diameter $18
Bowl, 6-1/2" diameter, crimped, handle $20
Candleholder, pair..$25
Cigarette box, with cover $25
Cup...$8
Goblet, 10-ounce..$24
Plate, luncheon, 8-3/8" diameter................................$15
Saucer...$6
Sugar bowl, footed $10
Vase, several sizes...$8-$10

Old Cafe

Hocking Glass Co., 1936-1940 (Made in crystal, pink and royal ruby, there is little price difference among the colors. Royal ruby pieces are generally worth the most and crystal the least, but the range is not as wide as in most other patterns.)

Berry bowl, 3-3/4" diameter, crystal or pink $4
Berry bowl, 3-3/4" diameter, royal ruby $6

This Depression Glass tumbler is in the New Century pattern.

Cup, crystal or pink...$6
Cup, royal ruby $10
Olive dish, oblong, 6" long, crystal or pink ....$6-$8
Pitcher, 80-ounce, crystal or pink $90
Plate, 10" dinner, crystal or pink.................................$35
Vase, 7-1/4" high, royal ruby $22
Vase, 7-1/4" high, crystal or pink..........................$15-$18

Princess

Hocking Glass Co., 1931-1935 (Made in apricot yellow, blue, green, pink, and topaz yellow. There are very few pieces in blue, and all are expensive. The two yellows are priced nearly identically and are also more valuable than similar pieces in green or pink.)

Ashtray, 4-1/2" diameter, green or pink.................$70-$80
Ashtray, 4-1/2" diameter, apricot or topaz $90
Butter dish, with cover, green or pink.................$95-$100
Butter dish, with cover, apricot or topaz $650
Cookie jar, with cover, green or pink.....................$55-$75
Cookie jar with cover, blue $875
Cup, green or pink...$12-$14
Cup, blue..$115
Pitcher, 37-ounce, 6" high, green or pink ....$55-$65
Pitcher, 37-ounce, 6" high, apricot or topaz...............$575
Plate, 8" diameter salad, apricot, topaz, green, or pink
....$10-$15
Salad bowl, octagonal, 9" diameter, green or pink
....$40-$45
Salad bowl, octagonal, 9" diameter, apricot or topaz
....$125
Salt and pepper, pair, 4-1/2" high, apricot, topaz, green or
pink..$60-$75
Saucer, apricot or topaz..$3
Saucer, blue...$65
Tumbler, 9-ounce, 4" high, apricot, topaz, green or
pink..$25-$28

Vegetable bowl, oval, 10" long, green or pink ....$28-$30
Vegetable bowl, oval, 10" long apricot or
    topaz ....$60-$65

Royal Lace

Hazel Atlas Glass Co., 1934-1941 (Made in cobalt blue, crystal, green, pink, and some amethyst.) Cobalt blue is by far the most valuable, bringing several times the value of other colors for many pieces. Crystal is usually the least valuable.)

Berry bowl, individual, 5" diameter, blue, green or
    pink..$27-$30
Berry bowl, individual, 5" diameter, crystal $15
Bowl, 10" diameter, 3 legs, straight edge, green or
    pink..$40-$45
Bowl, 10" diameter, 3 legs, straight edge, crystal.........$24
Butter dish, with cover, green $250
Butter dish, with cover, pink......................................$150
Butter dish, with cover, crystal $65
Cookie jar, with cover, blue $500
Cookie jar, with cover, crystal, pink or green ....$50-$75
Nut bowl, blue..$1,000
Nut bowl, green or pink $375
Nut bowl, crystal..$190
Plate, 8-1/2" diameter, luncheon, blue $30
Plate, 8-1/2" diameter, luncheon, pink or green.....$15-$20
Plate, 8-1/2" diameter, luncheon, crystal $8
Salt and pepper, pair, blue..$250
Salt and pepper, pair, green...$130
Salt and pepper, pair, pink..$65
Salt and pepper, pair, crystal $45
Tumbler, 10-ounce, 4-7/8" high, blue $100
Tumbler, 10-ounce, 4-7/8" high, green or pink.............$60
Tumbler, 10-ounce, 4-7/8" high, crystal $25

This cup-and-saucer set is in the Circle pattern. In a common color it is worth about $10.

Sunflower

Jeannette Glass Co., 1930s (Made primarily in green, and pink with some delphite).

Ashtray, 5" diameter, pink or green ....$10-$14
Cake plate, 10" diameter, 3 legs, pink or green $16
Cup, pink or green...$12-$15
Saucer, pink or green ....$10-$13
Trivet, 7" diameter, 3 legs, turned-up edge, pink or
    green..$300-$315
Tumbler, 8-ounce, 4-3/8" high, footed, pink or
    green..$30-$35

Tea Room

Indiana Glass Co., 1926-1931 (Made mostly in green and pink, with a few pieces in crystal and amber. Any piece in amber is valuable, and because of their scarcity, crystal pieces have a higher value in this pattern than is usually the case. Tea Room was originally sold for use in restaurants and soda fountains, so it is heavier than most other types of Depression glass.)

Banana split bowl, 7-1/2" long, pink $150
Banana split bowl, 7-1/2" long, green.........................$100
Creamer, 4-1/2" high, footed, pink or green ....$18-$20
Creamer, 4-1/2" high, footed, amber $80
Ice bucket, pink or green....................................$80-$85
Goblet, 9-ounce, pink or green ....$65-$75
Pitcher, 64-ounce, amber or crystal ....$400-$425
Pitcher, 64-ounce, pink or green ....$135-$150
Plate, 8-1/4" luncheon, pink or green ....$35-$38
Saucer, pink or green ....$25-$30
Sugar bowl, with cover, 3" high, pink or
    green..$100-$115
Tumbler, 6-ounce footed, pink or green...............$32-$35
Tumbler, 8-ounce, 5-1/4" high, footed, amber..............$75
Tumbler, 8-ounce, 5-1/4" high, footed, pink or
    green..$32-$35

Waterford

Hocking Glass Co., 1938-1944 (Made mostly in crystal and pink; A few pieces were produced in white, yellow and forest green.)

Ashtray, 4" diameter, crystal or pink.............................$5
Berry bowl, individual, 4-3/4" diameter, crystal............$8
Berry bowl, individual, 4-3/4" diameter, pink $16
Butter dish, with cover, crystal $28
Butter dish, with cover, pink.......................................$225
Cereal bowl, 5-1/2" diameter, crystal...........................$18
Cereal bowl, 5-1/2" diameter, pink $30
Cup, crystal $7
Cup, pink $15
Goblet, 5-1/4" high, crystal...$12
Pitcher, 80-ounce, tilted, ice lip, crystal.......................$32
Pitcher, 80-ounce, tilted, ice lip, pink $150
Plate, 7-1/8" salad, crystal or pink ....$7-$8
Salt and pepper, pair, crystal $7
Sugar bowl, crystal...$5
Sugar bowl, pink $12
Tumbler, 10-ounce, 4-7/8" high, footed, crystal $16
Tumbler, 10-ounce, 4-7/8" high, footed, pink..............$24

DISNEY COLLECTIBLES

Disney memorabilia may be the most beloved category in all of collecting. Walt Disney is considered one of the greatest contributors to American pop culture—and with good reason. Cheerfully led by Mickey and Minnie Mouse, the artist's endearing characters have propelled Disney's collectibles through over seven decades of pioneering prosperity, in the process creating one of the broadest and most active toy collecting genres. From *Steamboat Mickey* to *Hercules*, Disneyana thrives.

Disneyana refers to merchandise licensed by the Walt Disney Co. Disney collecting may be divided into three major categories—dimensional ware (dolls, figurines, jewelry, toys); ephemera (printed matter including books, catalogues, periodicals and sheet music) and animation art (cels, drawings, backgrounds and such).

From Mickey Mouse's 1928 debut until today, the Walt Disney Co. has produced literally millions of items and issued licensing rights to thousands of other companies. However, Disneyana was not widely collected prior to the 1970s.

General Guidelines: Due to the enormity of the Disneyana field, beginning collectors should become acquainted with the field. Knowing the availability, vintage and value of desired pieces will save effort, time and money.

Disneyana collectors may choose to generalize and collect everything from Disney or specialize by character, group of characters (heroes, princesses, villains), by film, date or vintage, by event (anniversaries, character birthdays, movie premieres), by type of merchandise, by artist (Carl Banks, Bill Justice and Ward Kimball are popular), by manufacturer, by limited editions or by country (German and Japanese pieces are favorites).

Tin toys, especially those made by the Louis Marx Co., are among some of the most highly-prized Disney collectibles. Puzzles, games and books—especially those made prior to World War II—are eagerly sought.

Markings: There are three types of copyright markings for Disney collectibles. The earliest pieces, from the late 1920s to early 1930s, bear the marking "Walt E Disney" or "Walter E Disney." The majority of vintage Disney items produced during the 1930s bear the marking "Walt Disney Enterprises," which is sometimes reduced to the three initials "WDE." Items from 1940 on carry the "Walt Disney Productions" mark. Items from 1984 and later are marked "Disney/Walt Disney Company."

Dating Disney: Often the look of a particular character can help date the item. Mickey Mouse first appeared in the animated sound cartoon *Steamboat Willie* in 1928. At that time, he had rat-like features with triangular pie-slice-shaped eyes, a longer snout and toothy grin. Donald Duck, introduced in 1934, originally had a long orange bill and feet with feathery hands. Later his bill was shortened, and his hands looked more human. Beware of reproductions, however.

Trends: Disneyana continues to be desirable and grow in popularity because the characters and products are merchandised almost continually, with new characters being added to the old favorites. Their perennial appeal alone suggests that people will always collect Disney.

The Walt Disney Co. continually produces numerous items associated with its characters; many are limited editions. Demand for Disney items such as videotapes usually increases every time a release is withdrawn from the marketplace, only to be re-released at a later date.

Over the years, the particular type of Disneyana in greatest demand will likely shift to reflect the changing eras, as collectors usually tend to seek out items associated with their childhood. Every Disney era has been represented on the collectible scale so far, from Mickey Mouse's pot-bellied beginnings to Annette Funicello's memorable television turn as a charter Mouseketeer on *The Mickey Mouse Club*.

Vintage Disney remains a strong force, as the merchandise manufactured prior to 1950 was produced strictly for user enjoyment and not intended as collectibles. As toys were abandoned by children after use, so too were early animation cels thrown out by the Disney company itself. For this reason, items in Excellent or Mint condition show the greatest demand.

Contemporary limited-edition pieces may or may not increase in value over time. It's important to understand the item's price in relation to edition size. Higher-quality pieces will most likely see values rise. But the nature of limited-edition pieces means most will be kept, which ensures a future supply (as opposed to a toy that may be discarded).

First editions of any Disney collectible are often highly valued.

Auction prices vary considerably from one auction to another based upon the items, their condition, and, most significantly, the competition.

Know the prices and values of the Disney items you want. Subscribe to collector magazines, read price guides, consult other collectors, join clubs and attend auctions, antique shows and flea markets.

While specifics about those future collectibles are hard to predict, demand is not. The trend is clear—the market for classic toys featuring Mickey Mouse, Donald Duck, Pinocchio and other early Disney characters is secure and will likely stay that way. We can only imagine what those first few vintage 1930s Disney toys will be worth when they become a century old, or how much today's *Toy Story* gems will escalate in value by 2099.

Finally, be aware that many Disney products (perhaps most) qualify as "cross-collectibles," which means they appeal to more than one kind of collector. Cross-collectibility always makes an item more desirable and, due to this increased demand, often makes it more valuable. For example, a Mickey Mouse cookie jar would appeal to cookie jar collectors as well as Disneyana collectors.

Contributor to this section: Joel Cohen, Cohen Books and Collectibles, P.O. Box 810310, Boca Raton, FL 33481 (text only, not values).

Clubs

• National Fantasy Fan Club for Disneyana Collectors, P.O. Box 19212, Irvine, CA 92713

• Disneyana Dreamers of San Diego County, P.O. Box 106, Escondido, CA 92033

• National Fantasy Fan Club for Disneyana (NFFC), P.O. Box 19212, Irvine, CA 92713

• The Mouse Club, 2056 Cirone Way, San Jose, CA 95124

Recomended Reading

Books

2000 Toys & Prices, Sharon Korbeck and Elizabeth Stephen
O'Brien's Collecting Toys, Ninth Edition, Elizabeth Stephan
Hake's Guide to Comic Character Collectibles, Ted Hake
The Golden Age of Walt Disney Records, R. Michael Murray

Periodical

Toy Shop

VALUE LINE

Ranges listed are for items in Near Mint to Mint condition.

Miscellaneous Disney

Disney ferris wheel, Chein	$625-$1,000
Disney rattle, Noma, 1930s	$125-$275
Disney shooting gallery, Weslo Toys, 1950s	$125-$225
Disney Treasure Chest set, Craftman's Guild, 1940s	$125-$200
Disney World globe, Rand McNally, 1950s	$50-$175
Disney bunnies, Fisher-Price, 1936	$125-$175
Disneyland puzzle, Whitman, 1956	$25-$40
Disneyland View-Master set, View-Master, 1960s	$25-$75
Disneyland wind-up roller coaster, Chein	$650-$750
Fantasia bowl, Vernonn Kilns, 1940	$225-$325
Fantasyland puzzle, Whitman, 1957	$25-$35
Horace Horsecollar hand puppet, Gund, 1950s	$50-$125
Pecos Bill wind-up toy, Marx, 1950s	$150-$225
Robin Hood Colorforms, Colorforms, 1973	$25-$40

Alice in Wonderland

Adventures in Costumeland Game, Walt Disney World, 1980s	$125-$200
Alice bank, Leeds, 1950s	$80-$125
Alice cookie jar, Regal	$1,600-$2,500
Alice cookie jar, Leeds, 1950s	$125-$175

Alice costume, Ben Cooper, 1950s-70s	$35-$50
Alice Disneykin, Marx, 1950s, unpainted	$15-$25
Alice doll, Duchess, 1951	$75-$100
Alice doll, Gund, 1950	$35-$50
Alice figure, Sears, 1980s	$15-$25
Alice figure, Haken-Renaker, 1956	$250-$400
Alice figure, Sydney Pottery, 1950s	$325-$500
Alice Little Golden Book, #D-20, Whitman, 1951	$25-$50
Alice coloring book, Whitman, 1974	$7-$10
Alice punch out book, Whitman, 1951	$80-$125
Alice marionette, Peter Puppet, 1950s	$75-$150
Alice mug, Disney, 1970s	$25-$35
Alice wristwatch, US Time, 1950s	$175-$250
Fan card, Walt Disney, 1951	$65-$75
Looking Glass cookie jar, Fred Roberts Co.	$260-$500
Mad Hatter costume, Ben Cooper, 1950s-70s	$35-$50
Mad Hatter Disneykin, Marx, 1950	$50-$75
Mad Hatter doll, Gund, 1950s	$35-$50
Mad Hatter plush doll, Gund, 1950s	$225-$350
Mad Hatter figure, Hagen-Renaker, 1956	$225-$350
Mad Hatter figure, Shaw, 1951	$150-$300
Mad Hatter figure, Marx, 1950s	$20-$25
Mad Hatter marionette, Peter Puppet, 1950s	$75-$150
Mad Hatter nodder, Marx, 1950s	$35-$50
Mad Hatter teapot, Regal, 1950s	$975-$1,500
March Hare costume, Ben Cooper, 1950s-70s	$30-$50
March Hare Disneykin, Marx, 1950s	$20-$25
March Hare plush doll, Gund, 1950s	$325-$500
March Hare figure, Hagen-Renaker, 1956	$225-$400
March Hare figure, Shaw, 1951	$325-$400
March Hare figure, Marx, 1950s	$20-$25
March Hare marionette, Peter Puppet, 1950s	$75-$100
Queen of Hearts Disneykin, Marx, 1950s	$50-$75

Some vintage Disney collectibles can be very valuable. This rare tin Mickey and Minnie toy from Tipp & Company has sold for more than $10,000.

Queen of Hearts doll, Gund, 1950s.........................$40-$50
Queen of Hearts figure, Sears, 1980s.....................$15-$25
Queen of Hearts figure, Disney Store, 1992 ....$13-$20
Queen of Hearts figure, Marx, 1950s.....................$20-$25
Tea set, Banner Plastics, 1956............................$325-$500
Tea set, Disneyland, 1990s.....................................$10-$15
TweedleDee and TweedleDum dolls, Gund,
    1950s, each..$35-$50
TweedleDee and TweedleDum figures, Shaw,
    1951, each ....$150-$200
TweedleDee and TweedleDum salt/pepper shakers,
    Regal, 1950s..$325-$500
Walrus doll, Lars/Italy, 1950s ....$325-$500
Walrus figure, Shaw, 1951 ....$225-$350
White Rabbit Disneykin, Marx, 1950s ....$50-$75
White Rabbit doll, Gund, 1950s ....$35-$50
White Rabbit plush doll, Gund, 1950s...............$225-$350
White Rabbit doll, Buena Vista/Disney,
    1974..$100-$150
White Rabbit figure, Sears, 1980s.......................$15-$25
White Rabbit figure, Shaw, 1951 ....$130-$200
White Rabbit figure, Marx, 1950s.......................$16-$25
White rabbit sugar bowl, Regal, 1950s ....$325-$500

Bambi
Bambi book, Grosset & Dunlap, 1942...................$25-$45
Bambi Soaky..$20-$40
Thumper bank, Leeds, 1950s...............................$80-$150
Thumper pull toy, Fisher-Price, 1942 ....$75-$150
Thumper Soaky, Colgate-Palmolive, 1960s...........$30-$60

Cinderella
Cinderella & Prince wind-up, Irwin.....................$65-$175
Cinderella paper dolls, Whitman, 1965 ....$45-$65
Cinderella puzzle, Jaymar, 1960s ....$25-$35
Cinderella Soaky, 1960s..$20-$30
Cinderella wind-up toy, Irwin, 1950 ....$100-$175
Cinderella wristwatch, US Time, 1950................$75-$125
Gus doll, Gund..$125-$175
Prince Charming hand puppet, Gund, 1959...........$50-$75

Donald Duck
Donald Duck & Pluto car, Sun Rubber................$60-$150
Donald Duck alarm clock, Bayard, 1960s ....$150-$350
Donald Duck bank, Crown Toy, 1938................$100-$425
Donald Duck camera, Herbert-George, 1950s.....$50-$125
Donald Duck car, Sun Rubber, 1950s..................$75-$125
Donald Duck Choo Choo pull toy, Fisher-Price,
    1940..$175-$275
Donald Duck Disney Dipsy car, Marx, 1953.....$650-$900
Donald Duck doll, Knickerbocker, 1938 ....$325-$850
Donald Duck doll, Mattel, 1976 ....$50-$75
Donald Duck dump truck, Linemar, 1950s........$150-$375
Donald Duck figure, Seiberling ....$80-$125
Donald Duck figure, Dell, 1950s ....$75-$125
Donald Duck figure, Fun-E-Flex, 1930s..............$80-$275
Donald Duck Funee movie set, Transogram,
    1940..$150-$250

Featuring the stars of "Mary Poppins," Julie Andrews and Dick Van Dyke, this paper doll book was issued originally in 1964 and then re-issued in the early 1970s. It is valued at $35 to $40.

Donald Duck marionette, Peter Puppet,
    1950s ....$75-$125
Donald Duck nodder, 1960s................................$50-$125
Donald Duck paint box, Transogram, 1938.........$30-$125
Donald Duck pocket watch, Ingersoll, 1939......$125-$375
Donald Duck scooter, Marx, 1960s ....$150-$225
Donald Duck telephone bank, NN Hill Brass,
    1938..$150-$275
Donald Duck tricycle toy, Linemar, 1950s ....$450-$675
Donald Duck wristwatch, US Time, 1940s........$225-$350

Dumbo
Dumbo figure, Dakin ....$25-$50
Dumbo roll over wind-up toy, Marx, 1941 ....$250-$500
Dumbo squeak toy, Dakin ....$20-$45
Dumbo squeeze toy, Dell, 1950s...........................$20-$45

Ferdinand the Bull
Ferdinand doll, Knickerbocker, 1938.................$200-$275
Ferdinand figure, Delco, 1938 ....$75-$125
Ferdinand figure, Seiberling,1930s.....................$50-$125
Ferdinand figure, Disney, 1940s ....$150-$275
Ferdinand hand puppet, Crown Toy, 1938 ....$80-$125

Ferdinand savings bank, Crown Toy....................$50-$175
Ferdinand the Bull book, Whitman, 2938............$35-$125
Ferdinand/Matador wind-up, Marx, 1938..........$425-$750
Ferdinand wind-up, Marx, 1938 ....$350-$450

Goofy
Backwards Goofy wristwatch, Helbros,
  1972..$500-$750
Goofy car, Madem/Spain ....$30-$45
Goofy figure, Arco..$20-$25
Goofy figure, Marx ....$35-$50
Goofy night light, Horsman, 1973 ....$30-$45
Goofy Rolykin, Marx...$50-$75
Goofy safety scissors, Monogram, 1973.................$7-$15
Goofy Twist 'n Bend figure, Marx, 1963..............$20-$30

Jungle Book
Baloo doll, plush ....$20-$25
Jungle Book carrying case, Ideal, 1966 ....$50-$85
Jungle Book Magic Slate, Watkins-Strathmore,
  1967...$16-$30
Mowgli figure, Holland Hill, 1967 ....$35-$65
Shere Kahn figure, Enesco, 1965 ....$25-$35

Lady and the Tranp
Lady and Tramp figures, Marx, 1955 ....$50-$80
Lady doll, Woolikin, 1955 ....$80-$150
Perri doll, Steiff, 1950s ....$40-$80
Tramp doll, Schuco, 1955 ....$100-$200

Little Mermaid
Ariel doll ....$16-$25
Eric doll..$16-$25
Flounder doll...$16-$25
Little Mermaid figures, Applause ....$4-$5
Scuttle doll ....$20-$30
Sebastian doll..$16-$25

Mary Poppins
Mary Poppins doll, Gund, 1964...........................$50-$175
Mary Poppins paper dolls, Whitman, 1973 ....$30-$65
Mary Poppins tea set, Chein, 1964 ....$75-$100

Mickey and Minnie Mouse
Mickey and Donald Duck alarm clock, Jerger,
  1960s...$100-$150
Mickey and Donald Jack-in-the-Box, Lakeside,
  1966...$50-$150
Mickey and Minnie dolls, Gund, 1940s............$225-$550
Mickey and Minnie flashlight, Usalite Co.,
  1930s...$75-$100
Mickey and Minnie sled, SL Allen, 1935 ....$275-$400
Mickey and Minnie tea set, Ohio Art, 1930s ....$80-$125
Mickey and Three Pigs spinning top,
  Lackawanna..$75-$135
Mickey Mouse bank, Crown Toy, 1938 ....$100-$350
Mickey Mouse bank, Transogram, 1970s..............$25-$35
Mickey Mouse Bean Bag game, Marks Bros.,
  1930s...$125-$200
Mickey Mouse Bump-N-Go Spaceship, Matsudaya,
  1980s ....$75-$100

DISNEY ON THE RECORD!

An interesting specialty category for Disney collectors are Disney phonograph records. Between 1933 and 1988, Walt Disney issued more than 3,300 records, under several different labels. Most of these 78 rpm, 45 rpm and LP records featured original Disney artwork on their paper or cardboard covers.

Today, you might find these records at flea markets, garage sales, resale shops and collector/toy shows. But you might have to fight for them with those who collect Mickey Mouse Club material, toy collectors, Davey Crockett fans, those who pursue rock music recordings by Hayley Mills and Annette Funicello, and those who want animation art.

Serious collectors look for all of the record's original components, such as the paper or cardboard cover, inserts and cutout figures, in the best condition possible (never opened, never played).

In general, Disney records fall between $20-$50, depending on age, condition, subject matter and if the original cover is included. As a general rule, the older the better. Also, pursue the stereo versions instead of their mono counterparts. Albums that did not sell well at the time of release are now among the hardest to find today. These include early Buena Vista pressings by such artists as Stan Jones, The Yachtsmen, Clara Ward and the Elliott Brothers.

In the 1970s, Disney produced records in Spanish; these records, under a Disneylandia label, are quite desirable today, in part because they are difficult to find and often have different artwork than their English counterparts.

The book The Golden Age of Walt Disney Records 1933-1988 offers pricing and comprehensive information and about these records. The book, written by R. Michael Murray, was published in 1997 by Antique Trader Books, The 248-page book lists more than 3,300 recordings and includes 200 color pictures.

Mickey Mouse camera, Ettelson, 1960s ....$35-$50
Mickey Mouse Choo Choo pull toy, Fisher-Price,
  1938..$225-$325
Mickey Mouse Club Fun Box, Whitman,
  1957..$75-$125
Mickey Mouse Club Magic Kit, Mars Candy,
  1950s..$50-$75
Mickey Mouse Club marionette, 1950s.............$100-$225
Mickey Mouse Club Mouseketeer doll, Horsman,
  1960s ....$50-$100
Mickey Mouse Club Mouseketeer ears,
  Kohner...$20-$30
Mickey Mouse Club toothbrush, Pepsodent,
  1970s ....$7-$10
Mickey Mouse Colorforms set, Colorforms,
  1976..$20-$50

TOP TEN MOST VALUABLE DISNEY RECORDS

From "The Golden Age of Walt Disney Records" by R. Michael Murray

"Who's Afraid of the Big Bad Wolf?" Parts I and II, RCA 224, Frank Luther & Orchestra, 1934 (Churchill), 7-inch, 78-rpm picture disc (add $100 for original sleeve)..$500

"In a Silly Symphony"/"Mickey Mouse and Minnie's In Town" RCA 225, Frank Luther & Orchestra, 1934, 7-inch, 78-rpm picture disc (add $100 for original sleeve)..$500

"Lullaby Land of Nowhere"/"Dance of the Bogey Men" RCA 226, Frank Luther & Orchestra (Churchill/Harline), 1934, 7", 78-rpm picture disc (add $100 for original sleeve)..$500

"Silly Symphony" Bluebird BC-2, 1937, three-record set, 78 rpm, with paper picture sleeve, Bluebird label, records numbered BK-5, BK-6, BK-7 ....$500

"Mickey Mouse Presents Walt Disney's Silly Symphony Songs" Bluebird BC-3, 1937, three-record set, 78-rpm, with paper picture sleeve, Bluebird label, records numbered BK-8, BK-9, BK-10 ....$500

"Annette and Hayley Mills (Singing 10 of Their Greatest All Time Hits)" DL-3508, Disneyland label LP, 1964, with jacket $450

"Alice In Wonderland" WDL-4015, 1957 (Fain/Livingston), Camarata, Disneyland LP...........................$350

"Songs from Walt Disney's Snow White and the Seven Dwarfs" Victor J-8, 1937, three-record set, 78 rpm, with cover $300

"Snow White and the Seven Dwarfs" RCA Victor PMS-09898, technically not an album, but more than a single, this is a promotional 16" radio transcription $300

"Teenage Wedding" / "Walkin and Talkin" Buena Vista 414, 45 rpm single with picture sleeve (sleeve is rare) $300

Mickey Mouse Dart Gun Target, Marks Bros., 1930s ....$75-$225
Mickey Mouse dinner set, Empresa Electro ......$250-$375
Mickey Mouse doll, 1930s................................$575-$875
Mickey Mouse doll, Schuco, 1950s..................$225-$350
Mickey Mouse doll, Knickerbocker....................$350-$525
Mickey Mouse doll, Knickerbocker, 1935.........$225-$325
Mickey Mouse fireman doll, Gund, 1960s.............$50-$75
Mickey Mouse talking doll, Hasbro, 1970s ....$35-$50
Mickey Mouse drum, Ohio Art, 1930s ....$75-$175
Mickey Mouse electric table radio, General Electric, 1960s ....$50-$125
Mickey Mouse figure, Marx, 1970 ....$20-$35
Mickey Mouse figure, Seiberling, 1930s ....$100-$150

Mickey Mouse figure, Goebel, 1930s ....$75-$100
Mickey Mouse fire engine, Sun Rubber ....$80-$135
Mickey Mouse fire truck w/figure, Sun Rubber..$80-$125
Mickey Mouse figure, Fun-E-Flex, 1930s ....$475-$700
Mickey Mouse gumball bank, Hasbro, 1968 ....$30-$45
Mickey Mouse Jack-in-the-Box, 1970s ....$45-$65
Mickey Mouse circus train, Lionel, 1935..$1,100-$1,600
Mickey Mouse circus train handcar, Lionel.......$450-$675
Mickey Mouse Magic Slate, Watkins-Strathmore, 1950s ....$30-$45
Mickey Mouse marbles, Monarch ....$7-$10
Mickey Mouse mechanical robot, Gabriel.........$125-$135
Mickey Mouse movie projector, Keystone, 1934..$275-$400
Mickey Mouse music stand, Schmid ....$125-$175
Mickey Mouse night light, Disney, 1938 ....$175-$250
Mickey Mouse ornament, Hallmark, 1978 ....$20-$50
Mickey Mouse pocket watch, Ingersoll, 1930s ....$350-$700
Mickey Mouse print shop set, Fulton Specialty, 1930s ....$150-$200
Mickey Mouse pull toy, Fisher-Price, 1936 ....$175-$250
Mickey Mouse pull toy, Toy Kraft.....................$550-$850
Mickey Mouse pull toy, NN Hill Brass, 1935....$250-$375
Mickey Mouse puppet forms, Colorforms, 1960s ....$20-$40
Mickey Mouse radio, Emerson, 1934 ....$700-$3,000
Mickey Mouse record player, GE, 1970s...........$100-$150
Mickey Mouse riding toy, Mengel, 1930s ......$725-$1,200
Mickey Mouse Rolykin, Marx ....$16-$25
Mickey Mouse sand pail, Ohio Art.....................$80-$225
Mickey Mouse sand shovel, Ohio Art.................$50-$125
Mickey Mouse sled, Flexible Flyer, 1930s ....$225-$600
Mickey Mouse squeeze toy, Dell, 1950s.............$60-$95
Mickey Mouse squeeze toy, Sun Rubber, 1950s ....$40-$60
Mickey Mouse steamboat, Matsudaya, 1988.......$55-$125
Mickey Mouse telephone bank, NN Hill Brass, 1938..$150-$275
Mickey Mouse toy tractor, Sun Rubber ....$55-$85
Mickey Mouse tricycle toy, Steiff, 1932.........$800-$2,000
Mickey Mouse wind-up toy, Gabriel, 1978 ....$15-$35
Mickey Mouse wooden bell pull toy, NN Hill Brass..$225-$350
Mickey Mouse wristwatch, Timex, 1958..........$225-$325
Mickey Mouse wristwatch, Bradley, 1978.........$125-$175
Mickey Mouse wristwatch, Ingersoll, 1939.......$375-$575
Mickey's Air Mail plane, Sun Rubber, 1940s......$75-$125
Minnie Mouse car, Matchbox, 1979 ....$10-$20
Minnie Mouse Choo-Choo train pull toy, Linemar, 1940s ....$125-$250
Minnie Mouse doll, Petz, 1940s ....$225-$325
Minnie Mouse doll, Knickerbocker, 1930s........$200-$475

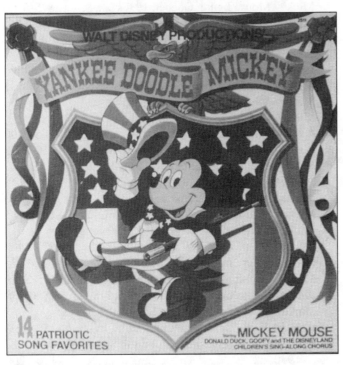

Disney records with colorful sleeves are becoming especially popular with collectors. For the most part, they are still very affordable. This patriotic "Yankee Doodle Mickey," a 1980 LP is worth about $25, according to R. Michael Murray, author of "The Golden Age of Walt Disney Records 1933-1988."

Minnie Mouse figure, Ingersoll, 1958.....................$55-$85
Minnie Mouse figure, Fun-E-Flex, 1930s..........$225-$350
Minnie Mouse hand puppet, 1940s.....................$100-$150
Minnie Mouse music box, Schmid, 1970s.............$25-$50
Minnie Mouse wristwatch, Timex, 1958 ....$100-$150
Mouseketeer cut-outs, Whitman, 1957 ....$50-$75
Spinning top, Chein, 1950s...............................$100-$225

Peter Pan

Captain Hook figure...$15-$25
Captain Hook hand puppet, Gund, 1950s ....$75-$100
Peter Pan baby figure, Sun Rubber, 1950s...........$80-$125
Peter Pan doll, Duchess Doll, 1953 ....$275-$425
Peter Pan doll, Ideal, 1953 ....$200-$275
Peter Pan hand puppet, Oak Rubber, 1953 ....$80-$95
Peter Pan nodder, 1950s....................................$150-$250
Peter Pan paper dolls, Whitman, 1952.................$75-$100
Peter Pan push puppet, Kohner, 1950 ....$50-$80
Tinkerbell doll, Duchess Doll, 1953 ....$225-$325
Tinkerbell figure, A. D. Sutton and Sons,
      1960s ....$50-$75
Wendy doll, Duchess Doll, 1953 ....$225-$325

Pinocchio and Jiminy Cricket

Figaro figure, Multi-Wood Products, 1940 ....$75-$150
Figaro figure, Knickerbocker, 1940s..................$150-$250
Figaro friction toy, Linemar, 1960s....................$125-$250

Figaro wind-up toy, Marx, 1940 ....$225-$400
Gepetto figure, Multi-Wood Products, 1940......$100-$150
Jiminy Cricket doll, Ideal, 1940........................$250-$450
Jiminy Cricket doll, Knickerbocker, 1962 ....$45-$80
Jiminy Cricket figure, Marx ....$50-$75
Jiminy Cricket figure, Ideal, 1940s ....$200-$350
Jiminy Cricket hand puppet, Gund, 1950s.............$50-$75
Jiminy Cricket marionette, Pelham Puppets,
      1950s ....$150-$275
Jiminy Cricket ramp walker, Marx, 1960s.........$125-$250
Jiminy Cricket Soaky ....$20-$35
Jiminy Cricket wristwatch, US Time, 1948 ....$125-$225
Pin the Nose on Pinocchio Game, Parker Bros.,
      1939...$75-$125
Pinocchio doll, Knickerbocker, 1962.....................$45-$80
Pinocchio and Jiminy hand puppet, Marx,
      1960s ....$50-$100
Pinocchio bank, Crown Toy, 1939 ....$125-$250
Pinocchio book set, Whitman, 1940 ....$175-$300
Pinocchio color box, Transogram ....$30-$60
Pinocchio cut-out book, Whitman, 1940 ....$75-$125
Pinocchio doll, Knickerbocker, 1940.................$350-$650
Pinocchio doll, Ideal, 1939 ....$200-$400
Pinocchio figure, Crown Toy ....$100-$200
Pinocchio figure, Multi-Wood Products,
      1940...$100-$200
Pinocchio hand puppet, Knickerbocker, 1962 ....$45-$75
Pinocchio hand puppet, Gund, 1950s ....$50-$100
Pinocchio paint book, Disney, 1939 ....$35-$85
Pinocchio plastic cup, Plastic Novelties, 1940 ....$50-$100
Pinocchio pull toy, Fisher-Price, 1939 ....$150-$300
Pinocchio push puppet, Kohner, 1960s.................$25-$65
Pinocchio Soaky..$25-$45
Pinocchio tea set, Ohio Art, 1939 ....$100-$200
Pinocchio the Acrobat wind-up toy, Marx,
      1939...$550-$900
Pinocchio walker, Marx, 1939 ....$400-$750
Pinocchio wind-up toy, Linemar........................$175-$350

Pluto

Pluto alarm clock, Allied, 1955 ....$125-$250
Pluto bank, Disney, 1940s..................................$75-$125
Pluto figure, Seiberling, 1930s...........................$75-$125
Pluto figure, Fun-E-Flex, 1930s........................$50-$100
Pluto hand puppet, Gund, 1950s ....$35-$75
Pluto Pop-A-Part toy, Multiple Toymakers,
      1965..$30-$45
Pluto pop-up critter figure, Fisher-Price,
      1936..$150-$175
Pluto purse, Gund, 1940s.....................................$50-$85
Pluto push toy, Fisher-Price, 1936 ....$150-$250
Pluto Rolykin, Marx ....$30-$60
Pluto sports car, Empire.......................................$16-$25
Pluto the Acrobat trapeze toy, Linemar ....$200-$250
Pluto the Drum Major, Linemar, 1950s ....$325-$700
Pluto toy, Linemar...$75-$200

MICKEY MOUSE TO THE RESCUE!

When the great Lionel Train Co. was teetering on the brink of bankruptcy in the 1930s, Mickey Mouse saved the day in his usually colorful way. Lionel's Mickey Mouse Circus Train and Mickey Mouse Hand Cart were two toys that essentially brought the legendary trainmaker back on the profitable track towards prosperity. In 1933, Disney's famous mouse rescued the Ingersoll watchmakers from a similarly perilous fate.

Pluto tricycle toy, Linemar, 1950s ....$325-$650
Pluto Watch Me Roll Over, Marx, 1939 ....$275-$425

Sleeping Beauty

Fairy Godmother hand puppets, 1958.................$75-$200
King Huber/King Stefan hand puppets, Gund,
    1956...$50-$125
Sleeping Beauty alarm clock, Phinney-Walker,
    1950s ....$75-$125
Sleeping Beauty Jack-in-the-Box, Enesco...........$60-$135
Sleeping Beauty Magic Paint set, Whitman ....$45-$65
Sleeping Beauty squeeze toy, Dell, 1959..............$45-$65
Sleeping Beauty sticker fun book, Whitman,
    1959..$25-$35

Snow White and the Seven Dwarfs

Bashful doll, Ideal, 1930s ....$100-$200
Doc and Dopey pull toy, Fisher-Price, 1937......$150-$350
Doc doll, Ideal, 1930s ....$100-$200
Dopey bank, Crown Toy, 1938...........................$100-$175
Dopey doll, Ideal, 1930s ....$100-$125
Dopey doll, Chad Valley, 1938 ....$100-$200
Dopey doll, Krueger..$175-$250
Dopey doll, Knickerbocker, 1938 ....$175-$375
Dopey Rolykin, Marx ....$50-$100
Dopey Soaky, 1960s..$20-$30
Dopey ventriloquist doll, Ideal, 1938.................$225-$500
Dopey walker, Marx, 1938...................................$175-$350
Grumpy doll, Knickerbocker, 1938 ....$175-$350
Happy doll, 1930s ....$75-$175
Seven Dwarfs figures, Seiberling, 1938.............$225-$450
Seven Dwarfs target game, Chad Valley,
    1930s ....$225-$325
Sneezy doll, Krueger...$225-$325
Snow White doll, Knickerbocker, 1940.............$150-$350
Snow White doll, Horsman...................................$25-$75
Snow White doll, Ideal, 1938 ....$450-$700
Snow White marionette, Tony Sarg/Alexander,
    1930s ....$125-$225
Snow White paper dolls, Whitman, 1938 ....$150-$225
Snow White Soaky..$25-$35
Snow White tea set, Ohio Art, 1937 ....$125-$250
Snow White tea set, Marx, 1960s ....$75-$150

Three Little Pigs

Big Bad Wolf pocket watch, Ingersoll, 1934 .....$350-$525
Three Little Pigs sand pail, Ohio Art, 1930s ....$80-$125
Three Little Pigs Soaky set, Drew Chemical,
    1960s ....$125-$175
Three Little Pigs wind-up toy, Schuco, 1930s ...$450-$700
Who's Afraid of the Big Bad Wolf game, Parker Bros.,
    1930s ....$125-$175

Toy Story

Flying Buzz Lightyear figure, Thinkway, 1996 ....$4-$8
Hamm figure, Thinkway ....$4-$8
Karate Buzz figure, Thinkway, 1996 ....$4-$8
Kicking Woody figure, Thinkway, 1996 ....$4-$8
Quick-Draw Woody figure, Thinkway, 1996 ....$4-$8
Rex figure, Thinkway, 1996 ....$4-$8
Talking Buzz Lightyear figure, Thinkway,
    1996...$15-$40
Talking Woody figure, Thinkway, 1996.................$15-$40

101 Dalmatians

101 Dalmatians snow dome, Marx, 1961 ....$75-$100
101 Dalmatians wind-up, Linemar, 1959.........$125-$375
Dalmatian pups figures, Enesco, 1960s ....$25-$125
Lucky figure, Enesco, 1960s................................$75-$100
Lucky squeeze toy, Dell ....$15-$35

This vintage Pinocchio tin wind-up toy by Marx is valued at about $300.

ELVIS COLLECTIBLES

Rock and roll memorabilia is among the hottest areas in all of collecting, and clearly topping the charts in this category are Elvis Presley and The Beatles, undoubtedly the two most popular—and most collected—musical acts in history. Both acts inspired generations of young people to rock and roll; and both put fear into the hearts of parents—especially Elvis, with his dangerously gyrating pelvis. The mania that surrounded Elvis during his career resulted in thousands of collectibles' being produced; and the enduring popularity of his music has caused many of these collectibles to keep rising in value. (See "The Beatles" for tips on collecting the Fab Four.)

Background: It's almost something of an enigma that Elvis Presley, a shy, religious, Southern boy who was extremely close to his mother, would grow up to become the "King of Rock and Roll." His natural modesty and genuine politeness seemed to contradict his image as a rock-and-roll rebel. Still, his lofty place in rock-and-roll history is no mistake. Since recording his first songs in the mid-1950s, Elvis has sold more than a billion records worldwide, recorded nearly a hundred gold singles and more than three dozen gold albums. He placed a record 149 singles on the pop charts; with 37 of them hitting the top ten; and 18 shooting to number one. He had numerous other entries on the gospel and rhythm-and-blues and country charts. Elvis was also a huge Hollywood screen idol, starring in some 33 feature films—more than even most Elvis fans remember. For most of the Sixties, Elvis was making at least three films a year—along with all of the requisite soundtrack albums. His TV appearances were legendary—especially his first appearance on the Ed Sullivan Show, where he was only shown from the waist up so his jiggling hips wouldn't offend an American audience not quite ready for his smoldering sensuality. After his death, Elvis was in the first class of artists inducted into the Rock and Roll Hall of Fame.

The list of accomplishments is impressive enough, but Elvis Presley's real appeal was something less tangible. It was his raw sexuality, his ability to combine rhythm and blues with country music and gospel to literally create what the world would know as rock and roll. Now, more than two decades after his death, Elvis's star is shining brighter than ever.

General Guidelines: As perhaps the most popular personality of his generation, Elvis Presley was featured on hundreds of items that are now collectible. The merchandise starting coming almost as soon as the young singer became a national star in 1956. The initial offerings, aimed mostly at the young female audience, included earrings, necklaces and other jewelry, Elvis perfume, lipstick, trading cards, handkerchiefs, shoes, scarves, poodle skirts and other clothing items. There were also Elvis scrapbooks, photo albums, pencils, school supplies and other trinkets and novelty items. In 1958, when Elvis was drafted into the army, merchandise included a series of "dog-tag" bracelets and other jewelry, all displaying Elvis's service number (55310761). Originally selling for about a dollar, this Elvis "dog-tag" jewelry is now valued at $50 to $200 or more, depending on the piece. Examples still attached to their original cardboard display cards always bring the highest prices.

Much of this Elvis memorabilia from this 1956-1958 period now sells in the $200-$700 range, depending on condition and scarcity. Two especially desirable items from this period include the "Elvis Presley Game," a scarce board game manufactured by Teen-Age Games that now sells for $1,000 or more in nice condition; and a 16-inch Elvis doll—the only doll issued during the King's lifetime—that commands $1,500 or more.

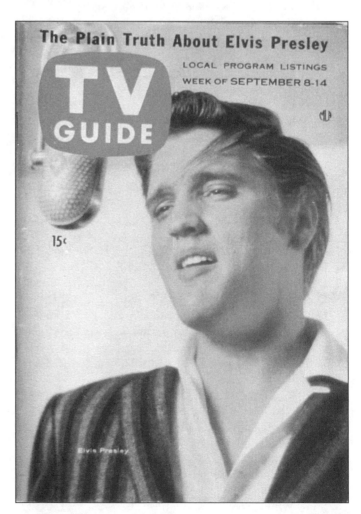

Relatively scarce, "TV Guides" from the 1950s with Elvis on the cover are worth $200 or more in nice condition.

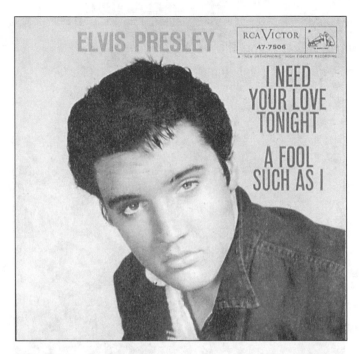

Nice Elvis 45 rpm picture sleeves from the 1950s and early 1960s (even without the record) are generally worth about $35-$50, depending on condition.

Magazines—Elvis appeared on hundreds of magazines during his lifetime and after his death, and all are collectible. Prices generally range from $5 or so for a recent magazine with Elvis on the cover to $75 or more for a nice magazine from the Fifties picturing Elvis. Especially in demand are the 1950s-era TV Guides with Elvis on the cover, which can sell for $200 in nice condition. The typical Elvis fan magazines from the 1950s and 1960s sell in the $25-$60 range.

Records—Elvis Presley records, of course, are a huge collecting area—but also a confusing one. Because of Elvis's tremendous and enduring popularity, many of his records—both singles and albums—have been issued and reissued countless times over the years, resulting in many different versions of essentially the same record. And every version has a different value. To a beginning collector, the various versions may not be easy to differentiate, but sometimes they can affect values dramatically. To fully understand the market for Elvis records, a good record price guide is a necessity (*the Goldmine Standard Catalog of American Records* is highly recommended), but here are a few general guidelines:

More than a thousand different Elvis Presley records have been released over the years. His material has been packaged and repackaged perhaps more than any other artist in history. While any Elvis record can be considered collectible, not all are necessarily valuable.

The more unusual the record is, the more valuable it is. The most sought-after Elvis records are his first five singles—all released on the historic Sun label in both the 45rpm and 78 rpm formats. In nice condition, any Elvis record on the Sun label is probably worth $1,000 or more.

Promo and radio station copies of Elvis records are almost always worth more than their corresponding regular-issue counterparts.

Over the years, millions and millions of Elvis records were sold, and many survived. But most of these records were played to death. The real treasures are the top-condition Elvis records, the earlier the better. Near Mint examples, especially those from the '50s, are nearly impossible to find. When they do turn up, they often sell in the $40-$60 range (sometimes more) for singles and over $100 for albums. Some Near Mint examples of Elvis's very first albums can sell for $500 or more.

Picture sleeves (the little paper jackets that many 45 rpm records came in during the '50s and '60s) picturing Elvis are very collectible and are often worth more than the record itself. Nice examples from the 1950s typically sell for $40-$60, while examples from the 1960s bring $20-$35, and examples from the 1970s sell for $5-$15. (These prices are the picture sleeves only, without the record.)

Common Elvis 45s and albums—the stuff you're likely to find at the neighborhood garage sale, or on your own record shelf—are plentiful and generally not valuable, unless they are in pristine condition.

Movie memorabilia: Memorabilia from Elvis Presley's movie career is another popular specialty area for Elvis collectors. The King appeared in some 33 feature films, and there are posters, lobby cards, still photos, press kits and other collectibles available from each one.

Prices vary, but in general, memorabilia from Elvis's first four films (*Love Me Tender, Loving You, Jailhouse Rock,* and *King Creole*) are most in demand. A one-sheet poster from any of these films typically sells in the $200-$600 range, while a lobby card might bring $45-$100. One-sheet posters from later Elvis films typically sell in the $50-$150 range, with lobby cards going for $15-$35 each.

The real treasures: Recent years have seen a new trend developing among advanced collectors of Elvis memorabilia. Not satisfied with the commercially mass-produced merchandise, they seek out the one-of-a-kind items that were actually used by Elvis—things like stage outfits, guitars, jewelry, even the King's driver's license and automobiles. Needless to say, prices for these rarities reach into the thousands. Major Elvis auctions in recent years have included such treasures as the glitzy stage capes worn by Elvis during his numerous Las Vegas shows (they sell for $50,000 or more) and the King's personal American Express card (worth about $10,000).

Modern collectibles: In the years since Elvis's death in 1977, more and more Elvis collectibles continue to be released, including collector plates, decanters, pillows, paintings, dolls, figurines, books, etc. These items are all wonderful to display and look good in an Elvis collection, but few of these items see any appreciable increase in value over their initial issue price, a fact that is probably not even a concern to the true Elvis fans, who collect with their hearts rather than their pocketbooks.

Clubs

- Elvis Forever, P.O. Box 1066, Miami, FL 33780

- Graceland News Fan Club, P.O. Box 452, Rutherford, NJ 07070

- Graceland, P.O. Box 16508, Memphis, TN 38186-0508

Recommended Reading

Books

Goldmine Price Guide to Rock 'n' Roll Memorabilia, Mark Allen Baker
Standard Catalog of American Records, Tim Neely
Goldmine Record Album Price Guide, Tim Neely
Goldmine Price Guide to 45 RPM Records, Tim Neely
Goldmine 45 RPM Picture Sleeve Price Guide, Charles Szabla
Goldmine British Invasion Record Price Guide, Tim Neely and Dave Thompson

Periodicals

Goldmine
Discoveries

VALUE LINE

The following are estimated values for some vintage Elvis collectibles. Most items shown are from the late 1950s, the period of greatest interest to serious collectors. Values shown are for items in Excellent or better condition. The "EPE" notation on many of the items indicates that it was licensed by "Elvis Presley Enterprises." Note that in some cases, prices are given for items still in their original packaging, a condition that increases the value substantially.

Anklets, 1956, EPE, two pairs attached to card	$1,200
Anklets, card only from above	$350
Ashtray, 1956, EPE, facsimile autographed photo in glass	$425
Elvis Presley autograph, "cut signature" on piece of paper	$450-$600
Elvis Presley autographed photo	$500-$1,000
Elvis Presley autographed picture sleeve or album cover	$700-$1,200
Autograph Book, 1956, EPE, line drawing of Elvis on front	$450
Belt, 1956, EPE, leather	$700
Belt, 1956, EPE, plastic	$650
Belt Buckle, 1956, EPE	$260
Billfold, 1956, EPE	$500
Binder, 1956, EPE, "Love Me Tender" zipper model	$1,100
Bolo Tie, 1956, EPE	$200
Bookends, 1956, EPE, pair	$600
Elvis books (dozens available), with dust cover	$15-$50

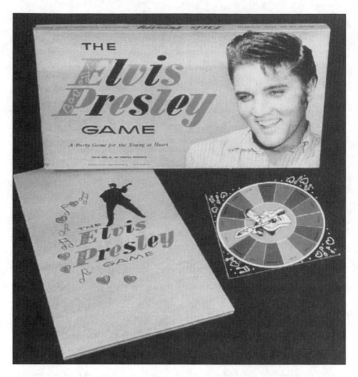

The 1956 "Elvis Presley Game" is a seldom-seen treasure that can sell for $1,000 or more in top condition.

Bracelet, 1962, EPE, various styles	$35-$65
Carrying Case, 1956, EPE, with insert	$675
Ceramic Tile, 1956, EPE, "Best Wishes, Elvis Presley," 6" square	$860
Charm Bracelet, 1956, EPE, with original card	$175
Charm Bracelet only (no card)	$125
Coaster, 1956, EPE, facsimile autographed photo in glass	$150
Coin Purse, Key Chain, Elvis pictured in striped shirt	$165
Cuff Links, 1958, EPE, in original box	$425
Cuff Links only, (no box)	$260
Diary, 1956, EPE (with lock)	$525
Dog Tag Bracelet, Key Chain, Anklet, 1958, EPE, (many styles)	$25-$50
Dog Tag Necklace, 1958, EPE, on original card	$95
Dog Tag Necklace only (no card)	$40
Dog Tag Sweater Holder, 1958, EPE, on original card	$200
Sweater Holder only (no card)	$135
Doll, 1957, EPE, in original box with all clothing	$2,250
Doll, original clothing, no box	$1,500
Earrings, 1956, EPE, picture of Elvis, on original card	$250
Earrings alone (no card)	$165
Elvis Fan Club Membership Package, 1956, complete	$300-$550

Fan Club Membership Card....................................$40-$50
"I Like Elvis and His RCA Records"
    Pin-On Button $75
"Personal Note to You From Elvis" $115
Framed Portrait, 1956, EPE "Love Me Tender,
    Sincerely, Elvis Presley" $525
The Elvis Presley Game, 1956, EPE,
    board game in box $1,000
Drinking Glass, 1956, EPE $210
Toy Guitar, 1956-57, EPE, Emenee,
    with carrying case ....$1,500-$2,500
Guitar only (no case)..........................$1,000-$1,500
Song Book For Emenee Guitar Including
    Elvis Presley Song Hits $50
Handbag, 1956, EPE, clutch style............................$550
Handkerchief, 1956, EPE......................................$325
Hats, EPE, Magnet, 1956, with manufacturer's
    tag...$100
Hat, paper army to promote "G.I. Blues," 1960............$40
Hat, Styrofoam straw, "Elvis Summer Festival"..........$25
Hound Dog, 1956, EPE, 10" dog with "Hound Dog"
    hat...$275
Hound Dog, 1972, 12-15", "Elvis Summer
    Festival" $50
Jeans, 1956, EPE, Blue Ridge, with "Elvis Presley Jeans"
    tag...$200
Keychain, EPE, Pictorial Products, 1956, flasher $20
Hawaiian Lei, promoting "Blue Hawaii" album.........$100

Lipstick, EPE, Teen-Ager Lipstick Corp., 1956,
    on original card $1,200
Lipstick only (no card).....................................$325
Locket, 1957, EPE, heart shaped Elvis $50
Elvis magazines, 1956-1960 (hundreds exist) ....$25-$75
Elvis TV Guides (several different) ....$50-$200
Medallion, 1956, EPE, "I Want You, I Need You,
    I Love You;" "Don't Be Cruel;" "Hound Dog;"
    "Heartbreak Hotel" $175
Mittens, 1956, EPE, pair $350
Necklace, 1956, EPE, heart-shaped, engraving
    of Elvis, original card...........................$235
Necklace only (no card) $165
Opening Night Invitations, Las Vegas, Lake Tahoe,
    printed paper $20
Paint-by-Number set, 1956, EPE, complete $500
Pajamas, EPE, pictures a singing Elvis, lists
    "Hound Dog," "Don't Be Cruel," others $450
Paperweight, "Sincerely Yours, Elvis" $16
Patches, 1956, EPE, heart-shaped, "My Heart
    Belongs to Elvis Presley," "I Love Elvis Presley,"
    and "Elvis Presley is a Doll" on display card $100
Single Patch (no card)......................................$35
Tour Patches, Ribbons (1970-77)...........................$30-$40

This group of original Elvis merchandise from the 1950s sold at a Butterfield & Butterfield auction. Included are a plastic Elvis guitar that sold for $860, an Elvis souvenir pillow that went for $488, a pair of Elvis drinking glasses that brought $430, an Elvis doll with rubber head and cloth body that sold for $1,600, an RCA Elvis phonograph in its case that went for $1,150, and an Elvis poodle skirt that brought $1,955.

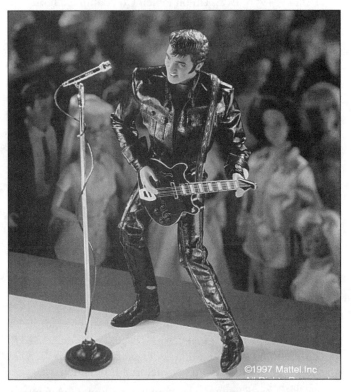

©1997 Mattel Inc

Among the dozens of newer limited-edition Elvis collectibles is this Mattel Elvis doll commemorating Elvis's 1968 Hawaii TV special.

Elvis records on the Sun label are considered genuine treasures by serious record collectors. In Near Mint condition, any Elvis single on the Sun label is worth at least $1,000.

Pencils, 1956, EPE, Union Pencil Co., complete box,
    one dozen packs of Elvis Presley Pencils $2,100
Single Pencil ....$15-$20
Pencil Sharpener, 1956, EPE $125
Perfume, 1957, EPE, "Elvis Presley's Teddy Bear
    Eau de Parfum," 1957 picture of Elvis on label $300
1965 version of above (1965 photo) $50
Phonograph, 1956, EPE, portable, facsimile
    autograph model.. $1,000
Printed Instructions, "How to Use and Enjoy
    Your RCA Victor Portable Phonograph" $85
Photo Album, 1956, EPE.. $360
Elvis Presley Photo Albums (souvenir and concert)
    1956 "In Person Elvis Presley—Country Music's
      Mr. Rhythm $425
    1956, "Elvis Presley Mr. Dynamite"........................ $335
    1956, "Souvenir Photo Album Elvis Presley"........... $310
    1957, "Elvis Presley Photo Folio"............................ $225
    1970-1977 Examples...$25-$50
Pillow, 1956, EPE $525
Pin, 1956, EPE, framed picture of Elvis attached to
    a guitar, with original card $375
Pin only (no card)... $225
Pin, 1956, EPE Vari-Vue or Pictorial Productions,
    flasher $35
Pocket Watch, 1964, pictures Elvis wearing jacket and
    playing guitar, polished finish $215
Pocket Watch, above, but with knurled finish.............. $45

For the true fanatic, there are one-of-a-kind Elvis items—guitars, articles of clothing, automobiles and other things actually used by the King. Sold at a Butterfield & Butterfield auction, this Elvis jumpsuit from one of his stage shows sold for a whopping $101,000.

Purse, 1956, EPE, clutch style, three pictures of Elvis, lists "Hound Dog," "Heartbreak Hotel," "I Want You I Need You I Love You" $365

Record Case, 1956, EPE $425

Ring, 1956, EPE, adjustable $110

Flasher Ring, 1957 .... $65

Scarves, 1956 EPE, three drawings of Elvis, lists "I Want You I Need You, I Love You," "Love Me Tender," "Don't Be Cruel," "You Ain't Nothing But A Hound Dog," reads "Best Wishes, Elvis Presley" $195

Scrap Book, 1956, EPE $310

Elvis Presley Sheet Music, (various picturing Elvis) 1956-1959 .... $25-$50

Sheet Music, 1960-1977 .... $15-$30

Shirt, 1956, EPE, Blue Ridge, green-and-white striped $150

Shoes, 1956, EPE Faith Shoe Co., pumps, pair in box $600

Pair of shoes without box $435

Skirt, 1956, EPE, Little Jeans Togs $675

Socks, 1956, EPE, Two pairs of bobby socks on original card $200

Socks, card only from above $45

Statuette, 1956, EPE, 8" bronze figure $575

Teddy Bear, 1957 EPE, 24" with "Teddy Bear" and "Elvis Presley" ribbons $295

International Hotel Bear, 1971, pink and white with pin on badge $45

Trading Cards, 1956, Topps, any one card .... $8-$12

Trading Cards, 1956 Topps complete set (66 cards) $600

Unopened Pack of 1956 Topps cards .... $60-$125

Wrapper from 1956 Topps cards .... $35-$75

Trading Cards, 1978, Donruss, any one card .... 50-75 cents

Trading Cards, 1978 Donruss complete Set .... $40-$50

Trading Cards, 1992-93, The River Group, any one card .... 20 cents

Trading Cards, River Group, one complete series $40

Wallet, 1956, EPE (several styles) $325

Elvis Records and Picture Sleeves

Values shown are for examples in Excellent condition. Values for picture sleeves are for picture sleeves only, without the record. All values are taken from the Goldmine Standard Catalog of American Records.

Typical 45 rpm single on Collectables label, 1970s-1990s $2

Any 78 rpm or 45 rpm on Sun label .... $1,500-$2,500

Typical RCA Victor 45 rpm single, 1950s .... $15-$40

Typical RCA Victor 45 rpm single, early 1960s ...... $8-$20

Typical RCA Victor 45 rpm single, later 1960s-1970s .... $4-$10

Typical 45 rpm picture sleeve, 1950s .... $40-$60

Typical 45 rpm picture sleeve, 1960s .... $20-$35

Typical 45 rpm picture sleeve, 1970s .... $5-$15

Album, typical 1970s Pickwick label .... $4-$6

Album, typical 1970s RCA Camden .... $6-$10

Album, typical 1970s-1980s RCA Special Products .... $8-$15

Album, RCA Victor, typical example, original 1950s .... $40-$200

Album, RCA Victor, typical example, original early 1960s .... $25-$75

Album, RCA Victor, typical example 1970s-1980s .... $5-$15

FAST FOOD TOYS

Although kids' meal toys and boxes were formerly discarded as fast as the food was eaten, these items have come into their own as collectibles.

More than two dozen national restaurant chains currently issue toys for young and old to collect. This simple marketing inducement has given collectors an inexpensive way to acquire high quality toys representing characters from comic books, movies, sports and television. The hobby is an investment in fun, where affordability is the key driving force.

Background: Burger Chef, one of the early fast-food chains became the first restaurant to regularly promote the concept of the kid's meal in 1972. Their initial effort was called a "Funmeal," a forerunner of the now-common box in which these meals are served. The Funmeal box featured the restaurant's own cast of characters, including Burger Chef and Jeff. Like the modern fast food toy meal boxes to follow, the box itself was designed to be played with, complete with games and pictures.

Burger Chef's Funmeal concept quietly continued until their first truly recognizable promotion took the fast food industry by surprise. In 1977, the Triple-Play Funmeal baseball team box set featured one box of each of the 24 different Major League Baseball teams. The use of a nationally known subject matter—in this case, baseball teams—was a major breakthrough. Today, a mere two decades later, this set of 24 Funmeal boxes is worth over $1,000.

The Triple-Play Funmeal success was soon followed by the introduction of the seven-box Star Wars Funmeal set in 1978. Burger Chef continued to issue boxes and related items until 1983, finishing with Indy 500 race cars with stickers and boxes.

Most restaurants issued toys or promotions for kids in the 1960s on an irregular and limited basis. McDonald's was primarily responsible for taking the industry to the next level with regular kids' meal toys and related box promotions. In 1978, they began tests of what are now known as Happy Meal toys. After mixed results, they hit upon a Star Trek promotional tie-in which gave them the same kind of success Burger Chef had enjoyed with their Triple-Play Funmeal baseball box program. By 1988, one thing seemed clear to both McDonald's and fast food toy collectors alike—recognizable characters were fun to collect.

General Guidelines: Since the typical kids' meal consumer is under age 12—an age range known for rough play habits—this makes condition of fast food toys a critical factor. Only the rarest toys hold any value if found in less than perfect condition. Fast food toys and restaurant premiums are generally valued using only two grade classifications, Mint in Package (MIP) and Mint No Package (MNP), also known as "loose."

As these designations suggest, MIP toys have never been removed from their original packaging or played with.

GOING DAFFY AT THE LOCAL ARBY'S!

Arby's has done several spectacular premiums. The two that have the highest collector value are the successive Looney Tunes sets from 1987-1989. Bugs Bunny, Daffy Duck, Taz, Elmer Fudd, Road Runner and Wile E. Coyote were the six freestanding figures that made up the initial set. Some collectors consider the second set as one of the best fast food promotions ever done. This time Bugs and the gang were on oval bases. One seldom seen character, Pepe Le Pew, was included. Pepe is rarely, if ever, included in Looney Tunes sets; his inclusion here seems to have been done on a regional basis. Pepe alone is valued at $75 in Mint condition.

On average, MIP toys are valued at 200 percent of MNP toys. Loose toys in "played-with" condition are generally of little or no value to collectors. If relatively new, most loose toys sell for 25 cents each or less. Toys fsthat are missing parts, scratched or worn are worthless to collectors.

More recent MIP toys, meanwhile, generally sell for around $1. Older toys in MIP condition—including scarcer regionals and "under three" toys—may sell for $3 to $10 or more. In general, while some scarce and especially desirable fast food toys and boxes may sell for $25 or more, ninety percent of all fast food toys and boxes are still available for under two dollars.

You may find fast food toys at neighborhood garage sales for pennies, but they usually aren't in Mint condition. It is the search for the Mint toy that keeps the hobby healthy and active. A spotty collection can be temporarily filled in with flea-market finds, but a collector may have to search toy shows, scan the ads in *Toy Shop* magazine or search the Internet to find that Mint-in-Package toy. Collector clubs and conventions allow people to swap toys, exchange information and create friendships that can last a lifetime.

Fast food toys are so new as a collectible that any pre-1986 McDonald's toys and any pre-1992 non-McDonald's toys are considered the "early" stuff. Although less than ten or fifteen years old, some of it is scarce.

Rarity does have an impact on value, as do a toy's age, cross-collectibility and overall popularity. Modern movie tie-in toys, such as Disney's *Toy Story*, are frequently worth more than older toys, due to the strong Disneyana collector market. The same holds true for well-known cartoon and comic character items.

Distribution also affects rarity. Some fast food toys and premiums, called "regionals," are offered only in designated geographic areas. Due to their limited distribution, regionals command higher than average prices.

Toys designed for children under age three ("under three" toys) are valued 20 percent higher than the standard toys in a promotion. Special "under-three" toys, which are manufactured in smaller quantities, are desirable—even out of the package. Loose, these toys typically sell for between $2 and $5 apiece.

Crossover categories such as Disney characters, professional sports teams, cartoon, comic book and TV characters are often most popular. They are easily recognizable by collectors in other fields, which adds to their appeal and fuels the demand for these collectibles.

DID YOU WANT BEANIES WITH THOSE FRIES?

McDonald's has dominated the fast food industry in general; it is only natural that they dominate the world of fast food premiums. McDonald's outsells every other restaurant chain when it comes to kids' meals. In the two decades since the Happy Meal was launched, they've reaped sales of more than 3.6 billion meal-and-toy combos worldwide.

McDonald's is generally able to secure the most lucrative licensing agreements and distribute the most toys. Their marketing clout made their toys the most collectible, most desirable and the most abundant ones made.

McDonald's most successful promotion to date was the Teenie Beanie Baby Happy Meal of 1997. A second Teenie Beanie Baby promotion followed in 1998. While these promotions were the most popular, they were flawed. Caught off guard by the craziness caused by the first Teenie Beanie Happy Meal, McDonald's tried to meet the demands of collectors by setting up specific rules and regulations regarding the purchase of Happy Meals and toys during the 1998 promotion.

The Beanie Baby craze was at its zenith. Any attempt made by McDonald's to control the distribution of the Teenie Beanies, while well intentioned, was futile. In order to meet the demands of Teenie Beanie Baby collectors, fast food toy collectors, and the kids who just wanted a Happy Meal, McDonald's increased the production of the 1999 series (reportedly 350 million were made), laid out very specific rules and made sure the buying public was aware of these rules before the promotion began.

It seemed the public had tired of the Teenies, or maybe the rumors of increased production numbers were true. Either way, the third promotion did not meet with the same success as the previous two.

Trends: Toys aren't the only thing collectors want. Displays, boxes, bags and inserts are seen by many as the sleeper of this young hobby. While the ephemera associated with fast food hasn't increased in value so far, it will. Paper disintegrates, especially when mixed with fries, hamburgers, condiments and children. Older boxes from kids' meals are emerging as some of the most valuable of the hobby's collectibles because of their great artwork and relative scarcity. Nobody kept them!

Along with the boxes and the fast food toy premiums themselves, various store displays used to advertise the special promotions are also becoming hot collectibles—if you can acquire them. Displays aren't readily available to the public; to get one, you need an "in" at the restaurant. Your best bet? Ask a restaurant manager about store policies.

Contributor to this section: Jeff Escue, Fundamental Research Inc., 164 Larchmont Lane, Bloomington, IL 60108-1412.

Club

• McDonald's Collectors Club, 1153 S. Lee Street, Suite 200, Des Plaines, IL 60016

Recommended Reading

Books

Ultimate Price Guide to Fast Food Collectibles, Elizabeth Stephan

2000 Toys & Prices, Sharon Korbeck and Elizabeth Stephan

Periodical

Toy Shop

VALUE LINE

Prices are listed for toys in Near Mint to Mint-in-Package condition. Prices are for each toy in a set, not the entire set.

Arby's, 1981-present

Barbar's World Tour finger puppets, 1990, set of four .... $3-$5

Barbar's World Tour license plates, 1990, set of four .... $1-$2

Barbar's World Tour puzzles, 1990, set of four .... $2-$4

Barbar's World Tour squirters, 1990, set of three ...... $1-$3

Barbar's World Tour vehicles, 1990, set of three .... $2-$4

Little Miss figures, 1981, set of eight .... $4-$10

Little Miss stencil, 1985 .... $15-$25

Looney Tunes figure, Pepe Le Pew, 1987, on base .... $25-$75

Looney Tunes Car-Tunes, 1989, set of six .... $3-$6

Looney Tunes figures, 1987, set of seven, on bases .... $4-$10

Looney Tunes figures, 1988, set of six, freestanding .... $3-$6

Looney Tunes flicker rings, 1987, set of three .... $20-$40

Looney Tunes pencil toppers, 1988, set of six.........$5-$10
Yogi & Friends fun squirters, 1994, set of three........$2-$4
Yogi & Friends Winter Wonderland Crazy Cruisers, 1995,
    set of three..$2-$4

Big Boy, 1960s-present

Action figures, 1990, set of four ....$2-$5
Big Boy bank, 1960s, large, 18" tall ....$125-$300
Big Boy bank, 1960s, medium, 9" tall................$50-$165
Big Boy bank, 1960s, small, 7" tall ....$40-$100
Big Boy board game, 1960s................................$50-$120
Big Boy kite, 1960s...$10-$25
Big Boy nodder, 1960s, papier-mâché...........$900-$1,500
Big Boy playing cards, 1960s, four designs ....$15-$45
Big Boy stuffed dolls, 1960s, set of three ....$40-$80
Helicopters, 1991, set of three ....$1-$3
Monster in my Pocket, 1991, various packs ....$2-$4
Sport poses, 1990, set of four.....................................$3-$5

Burger Chef, 1970s

Burger Chef and Jeff glass, 1975 ....$5-$10
Burgerilla hand puppet, 1970s ....$5-$10
Burgerilla window clinger, 1970s ....$5-$10
Crankenburger iron-on, 1978 ....$5-$10
Friendly Monsters glasses, 1977, set of 6 ....$5-$10
Halloween bag, 1978 ....$5-$10
Hand puppet, 1960s, Burger Chef character..........$10-$15
Klickety Klips, 1971, bag of straw bits for
    bike spokes..$5-$10
NFL Collectors glasses, 24 different NFL teams,
    each ....$5-$10
Playing cards, pre-1970s, Burger Chef pictured......$5-$10
Star Wars posters, 1977, set of four ....$10-$15
Yo-Yo, 1972, set of three, with Burger
    Chef & Jeff..$10-$20

Burger King, 1984-present

Aladdin figures, 1992, set of five ....$1-$3
Alf puppets, 1987, set of four ....$3-$8
Alvin and the Chipmunks, 1987, Super Ball,
    stickers and pencil topper....................................$1-$2
Archie cars, 1991, set of four.....................................$1-$3
Beauty and the Beast figures, 1991, set of four ....$2-$5
Beetlejuice figures, 1990, set of six ....$1-$2
BK Kids Club Bug Riders, 1998, set of five..............$1-$3
BK Kids Club Glo-Force figures, 1996, set of five,
    glow-in-the-dark..$1-$2
Bone Age Skeleton Kit, 1989, set of four dinos ....$3-$6
Burger King Clubhouse, full-size ....$15-$35
Capitol Critters Cartons masks, 1992,
    set of seven...$2-$4
Chicago Bulls bendies, 1994, set of four ....$3-$6
Dino Crawlers, 1994, set of five................................$1-2
Disney Afternoon, 1994, shovel, treasure chest,
    sun shoes, beach balls ....$2-$5
Freaky Fellas, 1992, set of four ....$1-$2
Goofy Movie, 1995, set of five ....$2-$5

McDonald's Happy Meal toys often feature licensed characters, like Disney or Barbie characters.

Hunchback of Notre Dame figures, 1996,
    set of eight..$1-$2
Hunchback of Notre Dame finger puppets, 1996,
    set of four ....$2-$4
Lion King Collectible Kingdom figures, 1994,
    set of seven...$2-$3
Lion King finger puppets, 1995, set of six................$1-$2
M&Ms, 1997, set of five ....$2-$5
Mr. Potato Head, 1998, set of five.............................$1-$3
Nerfuls, 1989, set of four ....$5-$10
Nickel-O-Zone, 1998, set of five ....$1-$3
Nightmare Before Christmas wristwatches,
    set of four ....$15-$30
Pinocchio Inflatables, 1992, set of four ....$3-$5
Pocahontas figures, 1995, set of eight.......................$1-$3
Pocahontas tumblers, 1995, set of four......................$3-$5
Scooby Doo, 1996, set of five ....$2-$4
Simpsons cups, 1991, set of four ....$1-$2
Simpsons dolls, 1990, set of five, plastic ....$2-$4
Simpson figures, 1991, set of five ....$4-$8
Teenage Mutant Ninja Turtles poster, 1991 ....$2-$4
Teletubbies, 1999, set of six......................................$1-$3
Toy Story, 1995, set of six...$4-$8
Toy Story puppets, 1995, set of four.......................$4-$10
Trolls Dolls, 1993, set of four ....$1-$2
Universal Monsters, 1997, set of four........................$4-$8

Chuck E. Cheese, 1980s

Chuck E. Cheese PVC figures ....$4-$7

Dairy Queen

Circus Train, 1994..$4-$5
Dennis the Menace, 1993, set of four ....$4-$6
Funbunch Flyer ....$3-$5
Rock-A-Doodles, 1992, set of six............................$6-$10
Supersaurus puzzles, 1993, set of three ....$2-$3
Tom and Jerry figures, 1993, set of six ....$4-$6

Denny's, 1990-present

Dino-Makers, 1991, set of six.....................................$1-$2

Flintstones Dino Racers, 1991, set of six...................$3-$6

Flintstones Fun Squirters, 1991, set of six................$2-$4

Flintstones mini plush, 1989, set of four ....$2-$4

Flintstones vehicles, 1990, set of six ....$2-$4

Jetsons Go Back to School tools, 1992, set of six .....$2-$4

Jetsons Space Balls planets, 1992, set of six ....$2-$4

Domino's Pizza, 1987-present

Noids figures, 1987, set of seven ....$2-$4

Quarterback Challenge cards, 1992,

pack of four cards..$1-$2

Hardee's, 1987-present

Apollo 13, 1995 ....$2-$5

California Raisins, 1987, set of four ....$2-$4

Days of Thunder Racers, 1990, set of four cars........$2-$4

Flintstones First 30 Years, 1991, set of five ....$3-$7

Ghostbuster Beepers, 1989, set of four.................$10-$15

Gremlins Adventures, 1989, set of five

record/book sets ....$2-$4

Home Alone 2 cups, 1992, set of four ....$1-$2

Marvel Super Heroes, 1990, set of three....................$3-$6

Pound Puppies, 1986, set of four ....$5-$10

Ren & Stimpy, 1994...$1-$3

Smurfs figures, 1987, more than 100 different ....$2-$4

Smurfin' Smurfs, 1990, set of four ....$5-$9

Super Bowl cloisonné pins, 1991, set of 25...............$2-$6

Waldo and Friends holiday ornaments, 1991,

three sets of three ....$2-$4

X-Men, 1995, four sets of two ....$3-$6

International House of Pancakes (IHOP), 1992

Pancake Kid cloth dolls, 1992, set of three..............$7-$10

Pancake Kids, 1991, set of 10.....................................$4-$6

Pancake Kids Cruisers, 1993, set of eight..................$4-$6

Kentucky Fried Chicken, 1960s-present

Animorphs, 1998, set of five.......................................$2-$3

Beakman's World, 1998, set of six ....$2-$3

Carmen Sandiego, 1997, set of six..............................$2-$3

Colonel Sanders nodder, 1960s,

papier-mache ....$50-$150

Cool Summer Stuff featuring Chester Cheetah,

1996, set of five ....$1-$2

Pizza Hut offered "Land Before Time" toys in a 1988 promotion.

Extreme Ghostbusters, 1997, set of six.....................$2-$3

Garfield Catmobiles, 1996, set of six.........................$2-$3

Ghostly Glowing Squirters, 1996, set of six ....$2-$3

Giga Pets, 1997, set of four..$2-$3

Koosh, 1995, set of three ....$1-$2

Marvel Super Heroes, 1997, set of six.......................$1-$2

Pokémon, 1998, set of six...$2-$3

Pokémon beanbags, 1998, set of four ....$2-$5

SI for Kids, 1998, set of four......................................$1-$2

Slimamander, 1998, set of six.....................................$1-$2

Wallace & Gromit, 1998, set of six............................$2-$3

Long John Silver's, 1989-present

Berenstain Bear books, 1995 ....$2-$5

Dinoworld, 1997, set of six...$1-$3

Fish cars, 1986 ....$8-$12

Garfield in Space, 1998...$2-$4

Lost in Space, 1998...$2-$4

Magic School Bus, 1997, set of four...........................$1-$3

Peanuts Easter, 1997 ....$2-$4

Pound Puppies, 1996, set of eight...............................$2-$4

School House Rocks, 1998 ....$2-$4

Sea goggles, 1996 ....$1-$3

Sea walkers, 1990, set of four.....................................$3-$8

Space Goofs, 1999, set of five.....................................$1-$3

Superstar Baseball Cards, 1990,

eight players/five cards each ....$10-$15

Treasure Trolls, 1992, set of six.................................$1-$3

Water Blasters, 1990, set of four................................$3-$5

Winter Muppetland, 1998, set of four.........................$2-$4

McDonald's, 1977-present

101 Dalmatians, 1991, set of four..............................$1-$3

101 Dalmatians snow globes, 1996 ....$2-$5

A Bug's Life wind-ups, 1998, set of eight..................$1-$2

A Bug's Life watches, 1998, set of three....................$2-$3

Adventures of Ronald McDonald figures, 1981,

set of seven ....$6-$12

Alvin and the Chipmunks figures, 1991,

set of four ....$4-$8

Animal Pals plush toys, 1997, set of six ....$1-$2

Animaniacs, 1994, set of eight....................................$2-$3

Babe plush toys, 1996, set of seven ....$1-$2

Back to the Future, 1992, set of four ....$2-$4

Bambi, 1988, set of four ....$2-$4

Barbie/Hot Wheels, 1990, set of four with

dioramas ....$25-$125

Batman, 1992, set of four..$1-$2

Beach ball, 1986, set of three...............................$10-$15

Beach toys, 1989, set of four ....$10-$15

Berenstain Bears figures, 1986, set of four ....$30-$75

Bicycle reflector stickers, 1978, set of four ....$6-$12

Black History coloring books, two, 1988 ....$200-$500

Cabbage Patch Kids/Tonka, 1992, set of five ....$2-$3

Captain Crook Hat, 1976 ....$15-$20

Changeables figures, 1987, set of six.........................$4-$8

Chip 'N Dales Rescue Rangers figures, 1989,
 set of four ....$2-$4
Circus Wagon, 1979, set of four ....$2-$3
Combs, 1988, set of four..$1-$2
Crazy Creatures with Popoids, 1985, set of four .....$6-$12
Crazy Vehicles, 1991, set of four................................$3-$5
Dexterity Games, 1965, set of two......................$75-$100
Dink the Little Dinosaur figures, 1990,
 set of six ....$4-$12
Dino-Motion Dinosaurs, 1993, set of six....................$1-$2
Disney Favorites activity books, 1987,
 set of four ....$3-$4
Double Bell alarm clock, wind-up ....$20-$40
Duck Tales, 1988, set of four ....$2-$4
Dukes of Hazzard vac-u-form container vehicles,
 1982, set of five ....$20-$50
E.T. posters, 1985, set of four ....$8-$12
Feeling Good grooming toys, 1985, set of six ....$1-$3
Flintstones Kids, 1988, set of four ....$4-$8
Flintstones, 1994, set of five ....$1-$2
Florida beach ball, 1985, set of three.....................$20-$25
Fraggle Rock, 1987, set of four ....$20-$40
French Fry radio, 1977, large red
 container/fries...$12-$25
Fun ruler, 1983, white, plastic....................................$3-$5
Funny Fry Guys, 1989, set of four.........................$15-$25
Furby, 1999, 80 different designs............................$5-$10
Garfield, 1988, set of four.......................................$20-$50
Glow-in-the-dark Yo-Yo, 1978 ....$2-$5
Golf ball, with McDonald's logo ....$1-$3
Grimace bank, 1985, purple, ceramic ....$10-$20
Grimace pin, enamel ....$6-$12
Grimace ring, 1970 ....$8-$15
Halloween figures, 1995, McDonald's figures...........$2-$3
Halloween buckets, 1986, pumpkin shaped................$2-$4
Halloween pumpkin ring, orange pumpkin face........$1-$3
Hamburglar doll, 1976, stuffed, Remco..................$12-$25
Happy Teeth, 1983, Reach toothbrush,
 toothpaste ....$15-$20
Hook, 1991, set of four ....$1-$2
Hunchback of Notre Dame, 1997, set of eight...........$1-$2
Jungle Book wind-ups, 1990, set of four ....$1-$3
Lego building sets, 1983, set of four.......................$25-$40
Little Mermaid, 1989, set of four................................$1-$3
Looney Tunes Quack Up Cars, 1993, set of five ....$3-$5
Lunch boxes, 1987, set of four.................................$5-$10
Mac Tonight puppet, 1988, foam ....$6-$15
Matchbox Mini-Flexies cars, 1979, set of eight ....$2-$4
McDino Changeables, 1991, set of eight...................$2-$3
McDonald's sunglasses, 1989, set of four ....$5-$7
McDonaldland Carnival floaty toy, 1990,
 Grimace...$10-$15
McDonaldland Express train cars, 1982,
 set of four ....$15-$40

McDonaldland Play-Doh, 1986,
 set of eight colors ....$2-$4
McNugget Buddies figures, 1989, set of 10...............$1-$2
Michael Jordan Fitness Fun Challenge, 1992,
 set of eight..$2-$4
Mighty Morphin Power Rangers, 1995,
 set of four ....$1-$2
Minnesota Twins baseball glove, 1984 ....$40-$75
Moveables bendies, 1988, set of six ....$5-$15
Mulan, 1998, set of eight ....$1-$2
Muppet Babies, 1986, set of four............................$25-$50
Muppet Kids, 1989, set of four ....$25-$50
Mystery of the Lost Arches, 1992, set of five.............$1-$2
Nature's watch, 1992, set of four ....$1-$2
Nickelodeon, 1993, set of four....................................$1-$2
Norman Rockwell ornament, 1978 ....$3-$7
Old McDonald's Farm, 1986, set of six...................$3-$12
Oliver & Company finger puppets, 1988,
 set of four ....$3-$5
Olympic beach ball, 1984, set of three ....$15-$20
Olympic Sports puzzles, 1984, set of five..............$15-$30
Paint with Water, 1978, coloring board ....$5-$10
Peanuts, 1990, set of four..$2-$4
Peter Rabbit books, 1988, four books....................$10-$25
Play-Doh, 1983, set of four containers ....$15-$20
Playmobile, 1982, set of five...................................$10-$20
Raggedy Ann and Andy, 1989, set of four...............$5-$10
Real Ghostbusters school tools, 1987, set of five.......$3-$5
Rescuers Down Under camera toys, 1990 ....$2-$4
Ronald McDonald doll, 14", Dakin ....$15-$35
Ronald McDonald doll, 7", Remco........................$18-$25
Sailors floating toys, 1988, set of four ....$5-$10
School Days, 1984, set of pencils and erasers ....$5-$10
Sindy Doll, 1970, old uniform ....$4-$8
Smart Duck figures, 1979 ....$2-$3

Snow White and the Seven Dwarfs, 1993,
  set of nine ....$2-$4
Sonic 3 The Hedgehog, 1994, set of four ....$2-$4
Space Aliens, 1979, set of eight................................$2-$4
Space Jam plush, 1996, set of six ....$3-$5
Spider-Man, 1995, set of eight.................................$1-$3
Spinner Baseball game, 1983....................................$2-$4

CHECK IT OUT!

Chicago's Museum of Science and Industry houses the largest and most comprehensive collection of fast food toys ever assembled. These items of our pop culture, animated works of art, have become cultural icons that decorate our desks, windowsills and collector's shelves. The museum, however, focuses on their connections to manufacturing, from plastic and polyvinyl chloride to injection molds, from engineering to the tiny power sources that allow the toys to roll, walk or hop across the table. Boxes, bags and counter displays are also featured on permanent display at the museum, located near downtown Chicago.

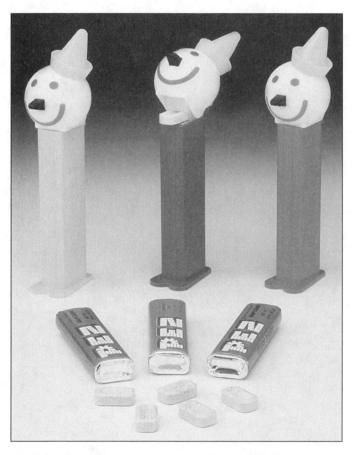

Jack in the Box restaurants had a promotion that included PEZ dispensers featuring a likeness of "Jack" himself.

Star Trek iron-ons, 1979, glittery..........................$10-$20
Star Trek rings, 1979, set of four ....$15-$20
Star Trek video viewers, 1979, five different........$15-$30
Storybook Muppet Babies books, 1988,
  set of three ....$2-$5
Super Mario Brothers figures, 1990......................$2-$4
Tamagotchi key chains, 1998, set of nine ....$2-$4
Teenie Beanie Babies, 1997, set of 10 ....$5-$10
Teenie Beanie Babies, 1998, set of 12 ....$2-$4
Teenie Beanie Babies, 1999, set of 12 ....$2-$4
Tinosaurs figures, 1986, set of eight ....$5-$10
Tom and Jerry Band, 1990, set of four......................$4-$8
Turbo Macs, 1990, set of four.................................$2-$4
Water Games, 1992, set of four................................$3-$5
Wild Friends, 1992, soft rubber panda....................$5-$10
Wrist wallets, 1977, set of four ....$5-$10
Yo Yogi, 1992, set of four ....$3-$5
Yo-Yo, 1979, red and yellow....................................$2-$5
Young Astronauts models, 1986, set of four............$5-$20
Zoo Face masks, 1987, set of four ....$20-$30

Pizza Hut, 1988-present
Air Garfield, 1993, attached to parachute or
  suspended in spaceball ....$2-$4
Air Garfield cups, 1993, set of two ....$1-$4
Beauty and the Beast puppets, 1992, set of four........$4-$8
Dinosaurs! cups, 1993, set of four ....$4-$8
Eureeka's Castle puppets, 1991, set of three.............$3-$6
Fievel Goes West cups, 1991, set of three ....$4-$6
Land Before Time puppets, 1988, set of six ....$4-$8
Universal Monster cups, set of three.....................$10-$20
Young Indiana Jones Chronicles, 1993,
  set of three ....$4-$6

Subway, 1993-present
Blue's Clues, 1998, set of four................................$2-$4
Cat's Don't Dance, 1997, set of four ....$1-$2
Conehead pencil toppers, 1993, set of three ....$2-$3
DC Super Heroes backpack hangers, 1998,
  set of four ....$3-$5
DinoStompers wind-ups, 1997, set of four ....$1-$2
Kool-Aid, 1998, set of three toys............................$1-$3
Marvin the Martian, 1998, set of four
  back-to-school toys ....$3-$5
Sea Splashers inflatable fish, 1997, set of four ....$1-$2
Space puzzles, 1997, set of four...............................$1-$2
Stunt Racers die-cast cars, 1998, set of four.............$1-$2
The King and I, 1999, set of four..............................$1-$2
The Simpsons figurines, 1997, set of four ....$3-$5
Tom and Jerry, 1994, set of four ....$2-$3

Taco Bell
Chihuahua plush talking dogs, 1999, set of four ....$3-$7
Happy Talk Sprites, set of two ....$2-$4
Hugga Bunch plush dolls..$2-$4
Star Wars, 1997, set of seven ....$3-$5
Star Wars Episode I—The Phantom Menace
  cup toppers, 1999, set of four...............................$2-$3

Wendy's, 1984-present

Alf Tales, 1990, set of six ....$2-$4
Alien Mix-Ups, 1990, set of six.................................$1-$2
Animalinks, 1995, set of five ....$1-$3
Bruno the Kid, 1997, set of six ....$1-$3
Carmen Sandiego, 1994, set of five ....$2-$4
Definitely Dinosaurs, 1988, set of four.....................$2-$4
Dino Games, 1992, set of five....................................$2-$4
Drinking tubes, 1994, set of five straws.....................$1-$3
Endangered Animal Games, 1993, set of five............$2-$4
Felix the Cat, 1996, set of five ....$2-$4
Gear Up! bike accessories, 1992...............................$2-$3
Glo Friends, 1988, set of 12......................................$2-$4
Jetsons figures, 1989, set of six.................................$2-$4
Laser Knights, 1996, set of four.................................$1-$3
Mighty Mouse, 1989, set of six ....$3-$5
Muppets from Space, 1999, set of five.......................$2-$4
NHL Kids, 1998, set of five ....$1-$3
Potato Head Kids, 1987, set of six.............................$4-$8
Sarus Sports Balls, 1991, set of four..........................$2-$3
Sharks, 1996, set of five ....$1-$3
Silly Sippers masks with straws, 1991, set of five .....$2-$3
Snoopy, 1998, set of five...$2-$4

Teddy Ruxpin, 1987, set of five ....$3-$10
Tricky Tints, 1992, set of five ....$2-$3
Wacky wind-ups, 1991, set of five ....$2-$3
Where's the Beef stickers, 1984, set of six ....$1-$3
Wishbone, 1996, set of five..$1-$3
Write and Sniff, 1994, set of five ....$1-$3
Yogi Bear and Friends, 1990, set of six ....$2-$4

White Castle, 1991-present

Bendy Pens, 1992, set of five......................................$2-$4
Camp White Castle orange bowls...............................$3-$6
Castle Friends bubble makers, 1992, set of four........$3-$5
Castleburger Dudes wind-up toys, 1991,
    set of four ....$3-$6
Fat Albert and the Cosby Kids, 1990,
    set of four ....$10-$20
Food squirters, 1994, set of three...............................$2-$4
Glow-in-the-dark Monsters, 1992, set of three........$4-$10
Godzilla squirter..$3-$6
Nestle's Quik Rabbit, 1990, set of four......................$2-$4
Silly Putty, 1994, set of three.....................................$2-$4
Stunt Grip Geckos figures, 1992, set of four ....$2-$4
Tootsie Roll Express train set, 1994, set of four........$3-$5
Water balls, 1993, set of four......................................$2-$3

FIESTAWARE

Fiestaware has been called the most popular dinnerware in American history—and the most collectible. Introduced by the Homer Laughlin China Company at the 1936 Pottery and Glass Show in Pittsburgh, Fiesta was an instant success and became a huge seller for the next four decades and beyond. Bright, colorful and affordable, it was just what Americans needed as they emerged from the Great Depression. It was not an expensive formal dinnerware, but it was a step above the cheap dime-store china.

Fiesta was designed by Fredrick Rhead in the Art Deco style that was so popular at the time. Beautifully simple, Fiestaware is recognized by its bands of concentric rings and its solid, bold tones that allowed American families to mix and match in a dizzying display of customized color. Adding to its popularity then—and its collectibility now—were all the accessory pieces that enabled families to constantly complement and expand their table service. In addition to several sizes of plates, bowls, cups and saucers, the Fiestaware line included pitchers, salt and pepper shakers, casseroles, coffee mugs, tumblers, platters, gravy boats, eggcups, teapots and more. You could even get Fiestaware ashtrays and candlesticks.

General Guidelines: The original Fiesta came in five rich, vivid colors: light green, yellow, cobalt blue, ivory and "Fiesta Red," a color that may actually be closer to orange. Turquoise was added in mid-1937. Over the years, other colors came and went; there were eventually eleven colors in all.

(Interestingly, Fiesta Red was temporarily dropped from the line starting in 1943, when the U.S. war effort took control of the nation's uranium oxide, the ingredient needed to produce the vibrant color. Fiesta Red did not return to the line until 1959, prompting fears among some consumers that the red glaze might be dangerously "radioactive." Follow-up studies proved the fears unfounded, and Homer Laughlin assured the buying public that the uranium oxide content in its red Fistaware was well within the limits considered to be safe.)

COLLECTOR'S ADVISORY!

Thankfully for today's collectors, authentic, original Fiestaware is relatively easy to identify. With only a few exceptions, the distinctive "Fiesta" trademark appears on every piece.

The exceptions include juice jumblers, demitasse cups, and salt and pepper shakers, which are not marked. Also, most teacups were not marked, although some are found with a "Fiesta" ink stamp. Sweet comports, onion soups and ashtrays are found both marked and unmarked. Most experienced collectors can easily identify authentic Fiesta pieces.

In the 1950s, four colors—forest green, rose, chartreuse and gray—were added. Today, collectors refer to these four colors as the "Fifties colors," a term that is frequently encountered in Fiestaware price guides and sales lists.

1959 saw not only the return of Fiesta Red, but also the introduction of another new color—medium green, which, for some reason, was produced in far fewer numbers than other colors. As a result, any piece found in medium green today is considered a real treasure by serious Fiesta collectors and always commands a premium price.

Several factors contribute to the value of Fiestaware, including color, scarcity, type of piece and condition. Pieces should be in Mint to command top prices. Pieces with minor scratches are typically valued at about 30 percent below Mint prices, while pieces with heavy scratches may be valued at half the Mint price or less.

While color plays a primary role in determining value, the popularity of colors has shifted through the years. Ivory, for instance, was for years largely ignored by collectors but is now as popular as the other original colors, perhaps more so. But, while certain colors may grow and fade in collector popularity, there is one constant when it comes to Fiestaware values: Pieces in medium green, because of their scarcity, are always more valuable than other colors. In fact, you can assume that nearly any piece in medium green is worth at least twice as much as the corresponding piece in a more common color.

As with every other kind of collectible, some pieces of Fiestaware are scarcer than others. In general, accessory pieces have more value than ordinary plates and bowls. Two accessory pieces, because of limited production, are especially tough to find. Fiesta carafes, only made until 1946, are one treasure, generally valued at $200 or more. Even scarcer are onion soup bowls, made only in 1936 and in very limited quantities (perhaps as few as 200 total). Today, any onion soup (with cover) is valued at a minimum of $500.

Collectors should also be aware that from 1939 to 1943, the Homer Laughlin company stimulated the sale of Fiestaware with a promoitional campaign that included the release of several specialty items that were offered for just a dollar. These one-dollar promotional specials are tough to find today and are highly prized by collectors. They include a four-piece refrigerator set; a salad bowl with fork and spoon; a casserole with pie plate; a chop plate with a detachable metal holder; and jumbo coffee cups and saucers.

Club
• The Fiesta Club of America, P.O. Box 15383, Love Park, IL 61132

TRUE TREASURES!

Because of limited production, the following pieces are considered true treasures by serious Fiesta collectors:

- Any piece in medium green
- Flower vases in the 10-inch and 12-inch size, which were only produced from 1936 to 1942
- Syrup pitchers
- Marmalades
- Onion soup bowls (with cover)
- Mixing bowls

VALUE LINE

Values shown are for items in Mint condition.

Ashtray, red, cobalt, or ivory	$50
Ashtray, yellow, turquoise or light green	$42
Ashtray, Fifties colors	$85
Ashtray, medium green	$150
Bowl, covered onion soup, cobalt and ivory	$550
Bowl, covered onion soup, red	$600
Bowl, covered onion soup, turquoise	$2,400
Bowl, covered onion soup, yellow and light green	$465
Bowl, cream soup, red	$55
Bowl, cream soup, cobalt or ivory	$55
Bowl, cream soup, yellow, turquoise or light green	$40
Bowl, cream soup, Fifties colors	$75
Bowl, cream soup, medium green	$3,200
Bowl, 6" dessert, red, cobalt or ivory	$48
Bowl, 6" dessert, yellow, turquoise or light green	$35
Bowl, 6" dessert, Fifties colors	$55
Bowl, 6" dessert, medium green	$340
Bowl, footed salad, red, cobalt or ivory	$295
Bowl, footed salad, yellow, turquoise or light green	$235
Bowl, 11-3/4" fruit, red, cobalt or ivory	$250
Bowl, 11-3/4" fruit, yellow, turquoise or light green	$195
Bowl, 4-3/4" fruit, red, cobalt or ivory	$32
Bowl, 4-3/4" fruit, yellow, turquoise or light green	$25
Bowl, 4-3/4" fruit, Fifties colors	$35
Bowl, 4-3/4" fruit, medium green	$395
Bowl, 5-1/2" fruit, red, cobalt or ivory	$35
Bowl, 5-1/2" fruit, yellow, turquoise or light green	$27
Bowl, 5-1/2" fruit, Fifties colors	$38
Bowl, 5-1/2" fruit, medium green	$70
Bowl, 7-1/2" individual salad, red, turquoise or yellow	$85
Bowl, 7-1/2" individual salad, medium green	$105
Bowl, #1 mixing, red, cobalt or ivory	$160
Bowl, #1 mixing, yellow, turquoise or light green	$135
Bowl, #2 mixing, red, cobalt or ivory	$100
Bowl, #2 mixing, yellow, turquoise or light green	$85
Bowl, #3 mixing, red, cobalt or ivory	$110
Bowl, #3 mixing, yellow, turquoise or light green	$95
Bowl, #4 mixing, red, cobalt or ivory	$125
Bowl, #4 mixing, yellow, turquoise or light green	$110
Bowl, #5 mixing, red, cobalt or ivory	$150
Bowl, #5 mixing, yellow, turquoise or light green	$135
Bowl, #6 mixing, red, cobalt or ivory	$195
Bowl, #6 mixing, yellow, turquoise or light green	$175
Bowl, #7 mixing, red, cobalt or ivory	$275
Bowl, #7 mixing, yellow, turquoise or light green	$225
Bowl, 8-1/2" nappy, red, cobalt or ivory	$50
Bowl, 8-1/2" nappy, yellow, turquoise or light green	$38
Bowl, 8-1/2" nappy, Fifties colors	$55
Bowl, 8-1/2" nappy, medium green	$115
Bowl, 9-1/2" nappy, red, cobalt or ivory	$65
Bowl, 9-1/2" nappy, yellow, turquoise or light green	$50
Bowl, 9-1/2" nappy, red, cobalt or ivory	$65
Bowl, unlisted salad, red, cobalt or ivory	$315

The value of Fiestaware depends partly on the color. The carafe, shown here, is worth $175-$185 in yellow, turquoise or light green; but about $225 in red, cobalt or ivory.

Bowl, unlisted salad, yellow $95
Candleholders, bulb, red, cobalt or ivory $115
Candleholders, bulb, yellow, turquoise or
    light green $90
Candleholders, tripod, red, cobalt or ivory $500
Candleholders, tripod, yellow, turquoise or
    light green $395
Carafe, red, cobalt or ivory $235
Carafe, yellow, turquoise or light green $195
Casserole, red, cobalt or ivory $195
Casserole, yellow, turquoise or light green $135
Casserole, Fifties colors $285
Casserole, medium green $525
Casserole, French, red, cobalt or ivory $495
Casserole, French, turquoise or light green $495
Casserole, French, yellow $265
Casserole, promotional, any color complete $150
Coffee pot, red, cobalt or ivory $215
Coffee pot, yellow, turquoise or light green................ $175
Coffee pot, Fifties colors... $270
Coffee pot, gray $365
Coffee pot, demitasse, red, cobalt or ivory $325
Coffee pot, demitasse, yellow, turquoise or
    light green $250
Comport, 12" red, cobalt or ivory $175

Comport, 12" yellow, turquoise or light green............ $130
Comport, sweets, red, cobalt or ivory $80
Comport, sweets, yellow, turquoise or light green........ $70
Creamer, red, cobalt or ivory $30
Creamer, yellow, turquoise or light green $25
Creamer, Fifties colors.. $40
Creamer, medium green.. $70
Creamer, individual, red.. $215
Creamer, individual, turquoise $310
Creamer, individual, yellow $65
Creamer, stick-handled, red, cobalt or ivory $50
Creamer, stick-handled, yellow, turquoise or
    light green $40
Cup, demitasse, red, cobalt or ivory............................. $65
Cup, demitasse, yellow, turquoise or light green $60

NEW FIESTA!

The Homer Laughlin company made Fiestaware from 1936 until about 1969, when it was discontinued from the product line. But in 1986, to celebrate Fiesta's 50th anniversary, the company revived the name with a brand new line of Fiestaware. Since then, more than three dozen different pieces have been produced in any of fourteen different colors.

The colors (along with the years they were produced) include: white (1986-present), black (1986-1998), rose (1986-present), apricot (1986-1998), cobalt blue (1986-present), yellow (1988-present), turquoise (1988-present), periwinkle blue (1989-present), seamist green (1991-present), lilac (1993-1995), persimmon (1995-present), sapphire (1997), chartreuse (1997-1999), and gray (1999-present).

This new generation of Fiestaware is known as "new Fiesta" by collectors. At first glance, some of the new Fiesta might fool a beginner, but serious collectors can easily differentiate the new pieces from vintage Fiesta. Although some of the new colors have the same names as the originals, none of the new colors is an exact duplication. Most collectors seem to think the new colors are not as bright or brilliant as the originals. Also, an experienced eye will detect that the new pieces are slightly restyled, although the differences may not always be immediately apparent (especially on pieces made in the late 1980s). And, most of the new Fiesta is slightly heavier than the vintage.

Even the new Fiestaware is collectible, and some of it already has considerable value. Among the new Fiesta offerings, lilac and sapphire pieces were limited and currently have the most value. A medium-size (9-1/2") vase in sapphire, for example, may bring as much as $200, while a lilac example may command twice that. Chartreuse, another limited color, is also in demand and rising in value, typically bringing about 50 percent more than a corresponding piece in a more common color.

The Fiesta syrup is a $260-$275 item in yellow, turquoise or light green. In red, cobalt or ivory, it is worth $310-$330.

Cup, demitasse, Fifties colors $285
Eggcup, red, cobalt or ivory $65
Eggcup, yellow, turquoise or light green $55
Eggcup, Fifties colors $150
Lid for mixing bowl #1-3, any color $625
Lid for mixing bowl #4, any color $685
Marmalade, red, cobalt or ivory $235
Marmalade, yellow, turquoise or light green $195
Mug, Tom and Jerry, red, cobalt or ivory $80
Mug, Tom and Jerry, yellow, turquoise or
    light green $55
Mug, Tom and Jerry, Fifties colors $95
Mug, Tom and Jerry, medium green $105
Mustard, red, cobalt or ivory $225
Mustard, yellow, turquoise or light green $185
Pitcher, disk juice, gray $2,300
Pitcher, disk juice, red $350
Pitcher, disk juice, yellow $45
Pitcher, disk water, red, cobalt or ivory $155
Pitcher, disk water, yellow, turquoise or
    light green $105
Pitcher, disk water, Fifties colors $225
Pitcher, disk water, medium green $1,000
Pitcher, ice, red, cobalt or ivory $145
Pitcher, ice, yellow, turquoise or light green $110
Pitcher, 2-pt jug, red, cobalt or ivory $100
Pitcher, 2-pt jug, yellow, turquoise or light green $70
Pitcher, 2-pt jug, Fifties colors $135
Plate, cake, red, cobalt or ivory $750
Plate, cake, yellow, turquoise or light green $635
Plate, 13" chop, red, cobalt or ivory $45
Plate, 13" chop, yellow, turquoise or light green $35
Plate, 13" chop, Fifties colors $85
Plate, 13" chop, medium green $175
Plate, 15" chop, red, cobalt or ivory $65
Plate, 15" chop, yellow, turquoise or light green $45
Plate, 15" chop, Fifties colors $100
Plate, 10-1/2" compartment, red, cobalt or ivory $40
Plate, 10-1/2" compartment, yellow, turquoise or
    light green $35
Plate, 10-1/2" compartment, Fifties colors $75
Plate, 12" compartment, red, cobalt or ivory $55
Plate, 12" compartment, yellow, turquoise or
    light green $55
Plate, deep, red, cobalt or ivory $52
Plate, deep, yellow, turquoise or light green $40
Plate, deep, Fifties colors $50
Plate, deep, medium green $110
Plate, 6", red, cobalt or ivory $8
Plate, 6", yellow, turquoise or light green $6
Plate, 6", Fifties colors $10
Plate, 6", medium green $18
Plate, 7", red, cobalt or ivory $12
Plate, 7", yellow, turquoise or light green $10
Plate, 7", Fifties colors $15

Plate, 7", medium green $30
Plate, 9", red, cobalt or ivory $18
Plate, 9", yellow, turquoise or light green $12
Plate, 9", Fifties colors $25
Plate, 9", medium green $42
Plate, 10", red, cobalt or ivory $40
Plate, 10", yellow, turquoise or light green $30
Plate, 10", Fifties colors $55
Plate, 10", medium green $115
Platter, red, cobalt or ivory $45
Platter, yellow, turquoise or light green $32
Platter, Fifties colors $60
Platter, medium green $125
Salt and pepper shakers, red, cobalt or ivory $30
Salt and pepper shakers, yellow, turquoise or
    light green $20
Salt and pepper shakers, Fifties colors $40
Salt and pepper shakers, medium green $115
Sauce boat, red, cobalt or ivory $60
Sauce boat, yellow, turquoise or light green $40
Sauce boat, Fifties colors $75
Sauce boat, medium green $135
Saucer, red, cobalt or ivory $6
Saucer, yellow, turquoise or light green $5
Saucer, Fifties colors $6
Saucer, medium green $10
Saucer, demitasse, red, cobalt or ivory $20
Saucer, demitasse, yellow, turquoise or light green $16
Saucer, demitasse, Fifties colors $95
Sugar bowl with lid, red, cobalt or ivory $55

**Among the more colorful pieces is the lazy susan;
the base and each section are a different color.**

Sugar bowl with lid, yellow, turquoise or
   light green $45
Sugar bowl with lid, Fifties colors $70
Sugar bowl with lid, medium green $135
Sugar bowl, individual, turquoise $325
Sugar bowl, individual, yellow $100
Syrup, red, cobalt or ivory $320
Syrup, yellow, turquoise or light green $275
Teacup, red, cobalt or ivory $32
Teacup, yellow, turquoise or light green $25
Teacup, Fifties colors $38
Teacup, medium green $55
Teapot, large, red, cobalt or ivory $195
Teapot, large, yellow, turquoise or light green $165
Teapot, med, red, cobalt or ivory $175

Teapot, med, yellow, turquoise or light green $150
Teapot, med, Fifties colors $275
Teapot, med, medium green $650
Tumbler, juice, red, cobalt or ivory $40
Tumbler, juice, yellow, turquoise or light green $35
Tumbler, water, red, cobalt or ivory $65
Tumbler, water, yellow, turquoise or light green $55
Vase, bud, red, cobalt or ivory $85
Vase, bud, yellow, turquoise or light green $65
Vase, 8", red, cobalt or ivory $550
Vase, 8", yellow, turquoise or light green $465
Vase, 10", red, cobalt or ivory $695
Vase, 10", yellow, turquoise or light green $635
Vase, 12", red, cobalt or ivory $1,000
Vase, 12", yellow, turquoise or light green $825

FIRE KING

This stuff's so hot you're going to need oven mitts. In fact, the term "hot" collectible seems entirely appropriate when used to describe Fire King, the popular "oven-proof" glassware made by Anchor Hocking in the 1940s and '50s. During its heyday, Fire King was an amazingly successful commercial product, found in kitchens throughout America. In just the past few years, Fire King dinnerware and kitchenware has emerged as a hot collectible.

Background: The Hocking Glass Company was founded in 1905 near Lancaster, Ohio, by Issac J. Collins. He named the firm after the Hocking River, on whose banks the company was located. Hocking was one of dozens of glass companies in America at the time that produced mainly pressed glass dinnerware. By the 1930s, Hocking was firmly established. Many of the companies glassware patterns from that era fall into the category that collectors now call "Depression" glass.

In 1937, Hocking Glass merged with the Anchor Cap Company to become the Anchor Hocking Glass Corporation. Within a few years of the merger, the company began manufacturing a new type of glass ovenware that could safely withstand the high temperatures of a kitchen oven. Production of the "oven-proof" glassware began in 1942. Marked "FIRE-KING," it was very popular with housewives across America, who eagerly purchased matching sets of dinnerware and ovenware in various patterns and colors. The company offered pre-packaged starter sets, along with luncheon sets, baking sets, snack sets and casseroles. There were enough accessory pieces to stock the entire kitchen. Anchor Hocking continued to produce Fire King until the mid-1970s.

General Guidelines: Fire King was available in a variety of patterns that included Alice, Charm, Fieurette, Game Bird, Honeysuckle, Jane Ray, Laurel, Primrose, Swirl and Wheat. Fire King colors included azurite, forest green, gray, ivory, jadeite, peach luster, pink, white, ruby red, sapphire blue, and turquoise. Some pieces were also made in white with various colored rims, and other pieces were dressed up with applied decals.

Fire King is a fairly new collectible, growing in popularity over just the past eight to ten years, and firm prices have not been established. But, for the most part, it is still very inexpensive; many Fire King pieces sell in the $5-$10 range, and prices over $20 or $25 are uncommon. It is still entirely possible to find Fire King at bargain-basement prices at neighborhood rummage sales or flea markets. This is truly a collectible where it is still possible to get in on the ground floor before prices take off.

COLLECTOR'S TIP!

Fire King pieces were marked and should be easy to identify. Look for either a mold mark directly on the piece or an oval foil paper label.

Collectors generally focus on a favorite pattern or two, or perhaps on specific colors. The older patterns and colors attract the most collector interest. In the 1940s, some Fire King dinnerware pieces were used as premiums. Cups and saucers in the Alice pattern were given away free inside packages of Quaker Oats. Anchor Hocking was hoping that once housewives had the free cups and saucers, they would go out and buy the more expensive plates to complete the set. Today, there are still many more cups and saucers in the Alice pattern than dinner plates.

Because the older patterns are generally more valuable, it is helpful to know the years each pattern was produced. Among the more popular are the following:

Bubble—1940s-1960s
Jane Ray—1945-1963
Alice—1945
Charm—1950s
Jadeite Restaurant Ware—1950-1956
Peach Lustre—1951-1965
Turquoise Blue—1957-1958
Golden Shell Swirl—1963-1976
Anniversary Rose—1964-1965
Blue Mosaic—1966-1968

Club

•Fire King Collectors Club, 1406 E. 14th Street, Des Moines, IA 50316

VALUE LINE

Values shown are for pieces in Excellent condition without any damage or flaws. Fire King was sold in sets. Add 30 to 35 percent to the values of the individual pieces for a set still in its original box.

Fire King Ovenware

Baker, individual, 6-oz., sapphire blue $4
Casserole, covered, ivory, 1-1/2-quart, knob lid $15
Casserole, covered, peach lustre, copper tint,
    French style $5
Casserole, covered, sapphire blue, one-pint $15
Custard cup, 6-oz., crystal $2
Custard cup, 6-oz., sapphire blue $3
Loaf pan, sapphire blue $16
Pie plate, crystal, 10-oz., deep $4
Pie plate, ivory, 15-oz. $16
Pie plate, sapphire blue, 9-1/2" diameter $7
Pie plate cover, sapphire blue, 9" $15
Roaster, sapphire blue, two-piece $90
Set, peach lustre set including 1-1/2-quart casserole,
    loaf pan, 9" pie plate, utility pan, 8" round cake pan,
    6-oz. custard cup, with original box $50

Table server, sapphire blue................................$20
Utility bowl, sapphire blue, 7" diameter.......................$12

Fire King Kitchenware

Batter bowl, 7-1/2" diameter, jadeite, one handle........$25
Coffee maker, Silex, two-cup, two-piece.....................$20
Hot plate, sapphire blue $15
Measuring cup, sapphire blue, one spout......................$18
Mixing bowl, 4-7/8" diameter, white, beaded rim $6
Mixing bowl, sapphire blue, turned rim.......................$24
Mixing bowl, Swirl, 6" diameter, jadeite $12
Mixing bowl, Swirl, 9" diameter, white $10
Mug, jadeite $8
Mug, sapphire blue, thick....................................$25
Refrigerator dish, 4-1/2" x 5-1/2", open, jadeite...........$16
Refrigerator dish, 5" x 9", covered, jadeite.................$40
Utility bowl, sapphire blue, 6-7/8" diameter.................$15
Utility bowl, sapphire blue, 8-1/4" diameter.................$18

Fire King Dinnerware

Bowl, 4-1/2" diameter, Meadow Green $4
Bowl, 4-5/8", Wheat $3
Bowl, 4-3/4", Charm, azurite $5
Bowl, 4-7/8", Jane Ray, jadeite $6
Bowl, 4-7/8", Swirl, Sunrise $8
Bowl, 9", Turquoise Blue.....................................$15
Bowl, 8-3/8", Bubble, Peach Lustre...........................$8
Cake plate, 9" diameter, Country Kitchens....................$5
Cereal bowl, Charm, Azurite $18
Cereal bowl, Sapphire Blue $22
Cereal bowl, Turquoise Blue..................................$12
Children's Ware, alphabet mug................................$14
Chili bowl, Peach Lustre $5
Creamer, Game Bird with pheasant decal.......................$10
Creamer, Laurel, Peach Lustre $3
Creamer, Swirl, azurite $6
Creamer, Vienna lace $3
Creamer and Sugar, Jane Ray, jadeite.........................$10
Custard Cup, Candleglow $2
Custard Cup, Peach Lustre, ruffled $1
Cup and saucer, Alice, blue and white........................$15
Cup and saucer, Alice, jadeite...............................$6
Cup and saucer, Charm, azurite $4
Cup and saucer, Charm, jadeite $12
Cup and saucer, Honeysuckle $6
Cup and saucer, Turquoise Blue $5

Demitasse cup and saucer, Fishscale Lustre $35
Demitasse cup and saucer, Lustre Shell.......................$6
Dessert bowl, Game Bird with duck or
    pheasant decal $6
Dessert bowl, Royal Ruby $6
Dessert bowl, Vienna Lace....................................$2
Mug, Bubble, Peach Lustre....................................$3
Mug, Game Bird with decal....................................$11
Mug, Red Rose..$3
Mug, Sapphire Blue $25
Mug, Turquoise Blue $10
Pitcher, Milano, aqua, ice lip $35
Plate, salad, Blue Mosaic $5
Plate, salad, Charm, azurite $15
Plate, salad, Meadow Green $4
Plate, salad, Swirl, Sunrise $8
Plate, luncheon, Charm, azurite $5
Plate, 10" dinner, Blue Mosaic $8
Plate, 10" dinner, Game Bird with decal......................$10
Plate, 10" dinner, Leaf and Blossom..........................$8
Plate, 10" dinner, Swirl, ivory $5
Plate, 10", Vienna Lace $3
Platter, Swirl, Sunrise......................................$20
Platter, Vienna Lace, oval $8
Platter, Wheat $10
Relish dish, three-part, Turquoise Blue, gold trim.......$12
Snack set, Colonial Lady, ruby and crystal...................$10
Souvenir plate, 10", 1964 World's Fair,
    Golden Shell...$45
Soup bowl, Jane Ray, jadeite $16
Soup bowl, Meadow Green $6
Soup bowl, Swirl, ivory $8
Sugar, Game Bird with decal $10
Sugar, Laurel, Peach Lustre $3
Sugar, Primrose, open $4
Sugar, covered, Shell, Peach Lustre..........................$8
Sugar, covered, Vienna Lace..................................$5
Tumbler, Game Bird with Canada goose decal...........$22
Tumbler, Game Bird with mallard, pheasant or
    grouse decal $12
Vegetable bowl, Lustre Shell $6
Vegetable bowl, Vienna Lace..................................$8

Fire King was made in a variety of kitchenware, ovenware and dinnerware.

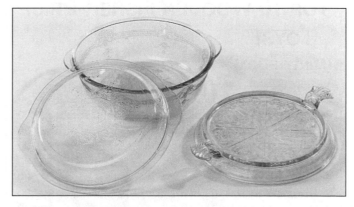

Most collectors of Fire King generally focus on a favorite pattern.

FISHER-PRICE TOYS

The familiar sturdy wood toys with paper lithography made by Fisher-Price are colorful remnants of how toys used to be made. Collectors especially value their quality and nostalgia.

Background and Guidelines: While the rest of the world suffered through the Depression, Fisher-Price set up shop in 1930 in East Aurora, N.Y. Founded by Herman Fisher, Irving Price and Helen Schelle, the company hoped to bring toys of matchless charm and inherent quality to children.

Sixteen toys were introduced in 1931, the first production year, including Granny Doodle and Doctor Doodle, a pair of charming ducks. (See "Value Line" below for their current values.)

Most collectors are familiar with the look of vintage Fisher-Price. Early toys featured a unique, colorful, crisp paper lithography on wood. Such charm today is as rare as some of the early toys.

It didn't take long for Fisher-Price to realize the value of licensing. In 1935, the company issued the Walt Disney Mickey Mouse Band, featuring Mickey and Pluto. That piece alone can command around $2,000 in Mint in Box condition. Other Disney characters and Popeye also became popular Fisher-Price toys.

Musical toys, especially items featuring bells and xylophones, became perennial favorites.

By the late 1950s, plastic was beginning to appear as accents on toys, and by the late 1960s, most of the toys' bodies were made entirely of plastic.

The common Fisher-Price Play Family Little People appeared as early as 1959 in a yellow wooden Safety School Bus. Made of wood, they could be removed from their vehicles. Their body shapes and compositions have changed throughout the years. Today the Little People are about three times the size of the originals and are made of plastic.

Family Play Sets from the 1970s are among the most collected play sets. Three of the most valuable sets include the Play Family Hospital (1976), Play Family Castle (1974), and Play Family A-Frame House (1974). Sesame Street characters are also popular, as is the Little People McDonald's Restaurant.

Today, Fisher-Price is a subsidiary of toy giant Mattel. The company continues to make Little People play sets in a variety of themes, but has expanded its line to include outdoor playground and riding toys, apparel and books.

Trends: Collecting vintage Fisher-Price, especially pre-1950s pieces, can be costly, since it is difficult to find older pieces in premium condition. Many 1930s-40s wooden toys can command $400-$2,000 or more in Mint-in-Box condition.

But collectors shouldn't pass on more modern, plastic Fisher-Price toys. Many toys from the 1960s and later are gaining favor with younger collectors, especially Little People play sets and musical radios, clocks and televisions. The musical toys are still fairly easy to find and can range from $5-$30 in general.

Some of the more common and easy-to-find toys include the Chatter Telephone, Pull-a-Tune Xylophone, Corn Popper and numerous bees and Snoopy dogs. Because of their inherent play value and lengthy history, many were, and still are, used as toys and are often found in less than Mint condition.

Note: Many Fisher-Price toys had several variations, which often means several different values. Also, the date found on the toy may only be a copyright date, which may be earlier than the actual date of manufacture.

Contributor to this section Sean Craig, 9931 18th Ave. W #31, Everett, WA 98204.

Club

•Fisher-Price Collectors Club, 1442 N. Ogden, Mesa, AZ 85205

Recommend Reading from

2000 Toys and Prices, Sharon Korbeck and Elizabeth Stephan
O'Brien's Collecting Toys, Elizabeth Stephan

TOP 10 WOODEN FISHER-PRICE TOYS!

(MINT-IN-BOX)

1. Skipper Sam, 1934, #155	$2,800
2. Popeye the Sailor, 1936, #703	$2,400
3. Popeye, 1935, #700	$2,200
4. Woodsy-Wee Circus, 1931, #201	$2,100
5. Mickey Mouse Band, 1935, #530	$2,100
6. Popeye Cowboy, 1937, #705	$2,100
7. Doughboy Donald, 1942, #744	$2,000
8. Drummer Bear, 1931, #102	$2,000
9. Doctor Doodle, 1931, #100	$2,000
10. Granny Doodle, 1931, #101	$2,000

VALUE LINE

Values shown are for items in Excellent to Mint condition.

The Original Sixteen Fisher-Price Toys

#100 Doctor Doodle	$2,000
#101 Granny Doodle	$2,000
#102 Drummer Bear	$2,000
#103 Barky Puppy	$2,000

The Fisher-Price Donald Duck Drummer toy is worth over $500 in Mint condition.

#104 Lookee Monk $650
#105 Bunny Scoot $2,000
#201 Woodsy-Wee Circus $2,100
#205 Woodsy-Wee Zoo $600
#207 Woodsy-Wee Pets $600
#350 Go 'n' Back Mule $500
#355 Go 'n' Back Bruno $500
#360 Go 'n' Back Jumbo Black Bruno $500
#400 Tailspin Tabby $700
#405 Lofty Lizzy $250
#407 Stoopy Storky $250
#410 Dizzy Dino $800

Other Wooden Fisher Price Toys

Allie Gator, #653, 1960 .... $80-$160
Amusement Park, #932, 1963 .... $100-$200
Baby Chick Tandem Cart, #50, 1953 .... $65-$125
Barky, #462, 1958 .... $75-$125
Barky Buddy, #150, 1934 .... $900-$1,800
Barky Puppy, #103, 1931 .... $1,000-$2,000
Big Bill Pelican, #794, 1961 .... $75-$125
Big Performing Circus, #250, 1932 .... $900-$1,800
Blackie Drummer, #785, 1939 .... $650-$1,000
Bonny Bunny Wagon, #318, 1959 .... $45-$80
Boom Boom Popeye, #491, 1937 .... $800-$1,600
Bossy Bell, #656, 1959 .... $45-$70
Bouncing Bunny Wheelbarrow, #727,
   1939 .... $750-$1,300
Bouncy Racer, #8, 1960 .... $65-$90

Bucky Burrow, #166, 1955 .... $200-$550
Buddy Bronc, #430, 1938 .... $400-$800
Buddy Bullfrog, #728, 1959 .... $65-$125
Bunny Basket Cart, #301, 1957 .... $45-$80
Bunny Basket Cart, #303, 1960 .... $45-$85
Bunny Bell Cart, #520, 1941 .... $250-$550
Bunny Bell Cart, #604, 1954 .... $75-$150
Bunny Cart, #5, 1948 .... $100-$145
Bunny Drummer, #512, 1942 .... $225-$550
Bunny Drummer, #505, 1946 .... $225-$550
Bunny Egg Cart, #28, 1950 .... $70-$125
Bunny Egg Cart, #404, 1949 .... $70-$125
Bunny Engine, #703, 1954 .... $75-$135
Bunny Racer, #474, 1942 .... $225-$550
Busy Bunny Cart, #719, 1936 .... $300-$750
Butch the Pup, #333, 1951 .... $75-$125
Buzzy Bee, #325, 1950 .... $60-$80
Cash Register, #972, 1960 .... $75-$125
Chatter Monk, #798, 1957 .... $65-$145
Chatter Telephone, #747, 1962 .... $45-$65
Choo-Choo Local, #517, 1936 .... $700-$1,500
Chubby Chief, #110, 1932 .... $950-$2,000
Chuggy Pop-Up, #616, 1955 .... $65-$135
Circus Wagon, #156, 1942 .... $300-$650
Concrete Mixer Truck, #926, 1959 .... $300-$625
Corn Popper, #785, 1957 .... $50-$115
Corn Popper, #788, 1963 .... $50-$85
Cotton Tail Cart, #525, 1940 .... $400-$800
Cowboy Chime, #700, 1951 .... $300-$600
Dandy Dobbin, #765, 1941 .... $325-$675
Dashing Dobbin, #742, 1938 .... $400-$850
Ding-Dong Duckey, #724, 1949 .... $225-$575
Dinkey Engine, #642, 1959 .... $50-$95
Dizzy Dino, #407, 1931 .... $400-$800
Doc & Dopey Dwarfs, #770, 1938 .... $1,000-$2,000
Doctor Doodle, #477, 1940 .... $300-$600
Doctor Doodle, #100, 1931 .... $1,000-$2,000
Dog Cart Donald, #149, 1936 .... $1,000-$2,000
Doggy Racer, #7, 1942 .... $300-$600
Donald Cart, #469, 1940 .... $900-$1,800
Donald Duck & Nephews, #479, 1941 .... $700-$1,400
Donald Duck Cart, #544, 1942 .... $350-$750
Donald Duck Cart, #605, 1954 .... $250-$500
Donald Duck Cart, #500, 1937 .... $600-$1,500
Donald Duck Choo-Choo, #450, 1942 .... $450-$900
Donald Duck Choo-Choo, #450, 1940 .... $600-$1,200
Donald Duck Delivery, #715, 1936 .... $750-$1,500
Donald Duck Drum Major, #432, 1948 .... $300-$600
Donald Duck Drum Major, #550, 1940 .... $300-$600
Donald Duck Drummer, #454 .... $225-$500
Donald Duck Pop-Up, #425 .... $650-$1,200
Donald Duck Xylophone, #185, 1938 .... $750-$1,000
Donald Duck Xylophone, #177, 1946 .... $350-$700
Dopey Dwarf, #770, 1939 .... $650-$1,700
Doughboy Donald, #744, 1942 .... $1,000-$2,000

TOP 10 PLASTIC FISHER-PRICE TOYS!

(MINT-IN-BOX)

1. Amusement Park, #932 .... $400
2. Nifty Station Wagon, #234 .... $350
3. Rooms, Sears exclusive, #909 .... $300
4. Castle, #993 .... $120
5. Yellow House with moving van, #952 .... $120
6. Hospital, #931 .... $120
7. Airport with cardboard hangar, #996 .... $100
8. Village, #997 .... $90
9. Musical Shoe, #991 .... $90
10. Dump Truckers, #979 .... $90

Drummer Bear, #102, 1931 .... $1,000-$2,000
Ducky Cart, #51, 1950 .... $85-$145
Ducky Cart, #6, 1948 .... $85-$145
Ducky Daddles, #14, 1941 .... $65-$135
Ducky Daddles, #148, 1942 .... $300-$600
Dumbo Circus Racer, #738, 1941 .... $1,000-$2,000
Easter Bunny, #490, 1936 .... $300-$675
Elsie's Dairy Truck, #745, 1948 .... $700-$1,400
Farm Truck, #845, 1954 .... $300-$600
Farmer in Dell Music Box, #763, 1962 ..... $40-$65
Farmer in the Dell TV Radio, #166, 1963 .... $35-$75
Fido Zilo, #707, 1955 .... $65-$135
Fire Truck, #630, 1959 .... $50-$95
Fuzzy Fido, #444, 1941 .... $200-$550
Gabby Duck, #767, 1952 .... $80-$160
Gabby Goofies, #777, 1963 .... $40-$65
Gabby Goofies, #775, 1956 .... $45-$75
Gabby Goose, #120, 1936 .... $65-$95
Galloping Horse & Wagon, #737, 1948 ..... $350-$750
Go'N Back Jumbo, #360, 1931 .... $900-$1,800
Gold Star Stagecoach, #175, 1954 .... $425-$975
Golden Gulch Express, #191, 1961 .... $95-$165
Granny Doodle, #101, 1931 .... $1,000-$2,000
Granny Doodle & Family, #101, 1933 .... $1,500-$2,000
Happy Helicopter, #498, 1953 .... $225-$425
Happy Hippo, #151, 1962 .... $65-$145
Hot Diggety, #800, 1934 .... $900-$1,800
Howdy Bunny, #757, 1939 .... $650-$1,100
Huckleberry Hound Xylophone, #711,
    1961 .... $225-$475
Huffy Puffy Train, #999, 1958 .... $80-$175
Humpty Dumpty Truck, #145, 1963 .... $65-$125
Humpty Dumpty, #757, 1957 .... $225-$550
Husky Dump Truck, #145, 1961 .... $45-$95
Jack-n-Jill TV Radio, #148, 1959 .... $45-$85
Jingle Giraffe, #472, 1956 .... $175-$375
Jolly Jumper, #793, 1963 .... $50-$85
Jolly Jumper, #450, 1954 .... $75-$165

Juggling Jumbo, #735, 1958 .... $225-$425
Jumbo Jitterbug, #422, 1940 .... $150-$325
Jumbo Rolo, #755, 1951 .... $150-$295
Junior Circus, #902, 1963 .... $200-$395
Katy Kackler, #140, 1954 .... $80-$160
Kicking Donkey, #175, 1937 .... $285-$725
Kitty Bell, #499, 1950 .... $150-$275
Lady Bug, #658, 1961 .... #45-$75
Leo the Drummer, #480, 1952 .... $225-$450
Little Snoopy, 1970s .... $7-$10
Looky Chug-Chug, #161, 1949 .... $175-$325
Looky Fire Truck, #7, 1950 .... $100-$250
Lop-Ear Looie, #415, 1934 .... $300-$600
Lucky Monk, #109, 1932 .... $850-$1,800
Merry Mousewife, #662, 1962 .... $50-$80
Merry Mutt, #473, 1949 .... $75-$145
Mickey Mouse Band, #530, 1935 .... $1,500-$2,100
Mickey Mouse Choo-Choo, #432, 1938 ... $850-$1,800
Mickey Mouse Drummer, #476, 1941 ...... $300-$625
Mickey Mouse Puddle Jumper, #310, 1953 .... $225-$395
Mickey Mouse Safety Patrol, #733, 1956 .... $300-$625
Mickey Mouse Xylophone, #798, 1942 ..... $500-$925
Mickey Mouse Xylophone, #798, 1939 ..... $600-$975
Mickey Mouse Zilo, #714, 1963 .... $325-$575
Molly Moo-Moo, #190, 1956 .... $200-$400
Moo-oo Cow, #155, 1958 .... $80-$160
Mother Goose Cart, #784, 1955 .... $70-$145
Music Box Barn, #764, 1960 .... $45-$90
Music Box Sweeper, #131, 1961 .... $65-$165
Musical Elephant, #145, 1948 .... $325-$700
Musical Push Chime, #722, 1950 .... $50-$95
Musical Sweeper, #225, 1953 .... $65-$170
Musical Sweeper, #100, 1950 .... $135-$275
Musical Tick Tock Clock, #997, 1962 .... $45-$90
Nosey Pup, #445, 1956 .... $75-$155
Patch Pony, #616, 1963 .... $40-$85
Perky the Pot, #686, 1958 .... $65-$135
Peter Bunny Cart, #472, 1939 .... $325-$725
Peter Bunny Engine, #721, 1949 .... $200-$425
Peter Bunny Engine, #715, 1941 .... $225-$475
Peter Pig, #479, 1959 .... $50-$110
Pinky Pig, #695, 1958 .... $65-$145
Pinky Pig, #695, 1956 .... $70-$160
Pinocchio, #494, 1939 .... $400-$975
Pinocchio, #720, 1939 .... $400-$940
Playful Puppy, #625, 1961 .... $60-$120
Playland Express, #192, 1962 .... $80-$165
Pluto Pop-Up, #440, 1936 .... $75-$160
Pony Chime, #137, 1962 .... $65-$135
Pony Express, #733, 1941 .... $200-$445
Poodle Zilo, #739, 1962 .... $65-$145
Pop 'N Ring, #809, 1959 .... $65-$125
Popeye, #700, 1935 .... $1,500-$2,200
Popeye Cowboy, #705, 1937 .... $1,000-$2,100
Popeye Spinach Eater, #488, 1939 .... $650-$1,300

Popeye the Sailor, #703, 1936.....................$1,200-$2,400
Prancing Horses, #766, 1937 ....$400-$900
Pudgy Pig, #478, 1962.....................................$50-$110
Puffy Engine, #444, 1951 ....$75-$145
Pull-A-Tune Xylophone, #870, 1957....................$45-$95
Pushy Doodle, #507, 1933 ....$800-$1,900
Pushy Elephant, #525, 1934.................$1934$600-$1,700
Pushy Piggy, #500, 1932.............................$800-$1,800
Quacko Duck, #300, 1939 ....$250-$600
Quacky Family, #799, 1946 ....$50-$85
Queen Buzzy Bee, #444, 1962............................$50-$80
Rabbit Cart, #52, 1950.....................................$70-$140
Racing Bunny Cart, #723, 1938........................$350-$700
Racing Ponies, #760, 1936...............................$500-$850
Racing Pony, #705, 1933 ....$1,000-$1,475
Racing Rowboat, #730, 1952..........................$225-$475
Raggedy Ann and Andy, #711, 1941 ....$900-$1,975
Rattle Ball, #682, 1959 ....$30-$50
Riding Horse, #254, 1940 ....$900-$1,475
Rock-A-Bye Bunny Cart, #788, 1940................$425-$825
Rock-A-Stack, #627, 1960.................................$25-$40
Roller Chime, #123, 1953.................................$70-$140
Rolling Bunny Basket, #310, 1961 ....$65-$135
Rooster Cart, #469, 1938 ....$225-$575
Safety School Bus, #990, 1962.........................$100-$175
Safety School Bus, #983, 1959 ....$300-$600
Scotty Dog, #710, 1933 ....$850-$1,900

Leo the Drummer is valued at about $450 in Mint condition.

Shaggy Zilo, #738, 1960.....................................$80-$160
Skipper Sam, #155, 1934 ....$1,300-$2,800
Sleepy Sue (Turtle), #495, 1962 ....$45-$90
Smokie Engine, #642, 1960.................................$40-$85
Snoopy Sniffer, #180, 1958 ....$100-$195
Snoopy Sniffer, #180, 1938 ....$200-$475
Snorky Fire Engine, #168, 1960 ....$95-$195
Sonny Duck Cart, #410, 1941 ....$200-$475
Space Blazer, #750, 1953.................................$400-$850
Squeaky the Clown, #777, 1958 ....$225-$550
Stake Truck, #649, 1960....................................$80-$160
Streamline Express, #215, 1935.....................$700-$1,700
Strutter Donald Duck, #510, 1941 ....$300-$700
Struttin' Donald Duck, #900, 1939....................$450-$875
Sunny Fish, #420, 1955 ....$200-$425
Suzie Seal, #460, 1961......................................$40-$85
Tabby Ding Dong, #730, 1939.........................$400-$800
Tailspin Tabby, #400, 1931 ....$350-$700
Tailspin Tabby Pop-Up, #600, 1947 ....$200-$400
Talk-Back Telephone, #747, 1961 ....$70-$140
Talking Donald Duck, #765, 1955 ....$70-$140
Talky Parrot, #698, 1963................................$100-$195
Tawny Tiger, #654, 1962..................................$65-$165
Teddy Bear Parade, #195, 1938 ....$700-$1,700
Teddy Bear Zilo, #777, 1950 ....$50-$165
Teddy Choo-Choo, #465, 1937 ....$400-$825
Teddy Drummer, #775, 1936 ....$600-$1,200
Teddy Station Wagon, #480, 1942 ....$300-$650
Teddy Tooter, #712, 1957 ....$225-$525
Teddy Tooter, #150, 1940 ....$400-$895
Teddy Trucker, #711, 1949 ....$225-$575
Teddy Xylophone, #752, 1948..........................$225-$475
Ten Little Indians TV Radio, #159, 1961 ....$50-$75
This Little Pig, #910, 1963 ....$40-$45
Thumper Bunny, #533, 1942 ....$400-$800
Timber Toter, #810, 1957.................................$100-$175
Timmy Turtle, #150, 1953 ....$80-$160
Tiny Teddy, #634, 1955 ....$75-$145
Tiny Tim, #496, 1957.......................................$70-$135
Tip-Toe Turtle, #773, 1962 ....$45-$95
Toot Toot Engine, #641, 1962............................$45-$90
Tow Truck, #615, 1960 ....$70-$155
Toy Wagon, #131, 1951 ....$250-$500
Trotting Donald Duck, #741, 1937 ....$650-$1,450
Tuggy Turtle, #139, 1959.................................$75-$165
Uncle Timmy Turtle, #125, 1956.......................$100-$195
Waggy Woofy, #437, 1942................................$250-$500
Walt Disney's Carnival, #207, 1936...............$600-$1,200
Walt Disney's Donald Duck, #208, 1936..........$400-$900
Walt Disney's Easter Parade, #475,
    1936..$1,000-$1,900
Walt Disney's Mickey Mouse, #209, 1936 ....$400-$800
Walt Disney's Pluto-the-Pup, #210, 1936..........$450-$800
Whistling Engine, #617, 1957 ....$80-$160
Wiggily Woofer, #640, 1957................................$95-$195

Winky Blinky Fire Truck, #200, 1954 .... $100-$195
Woodsy-Wee Circus, #201, 1931 .... $900-$2,100
Woofy Wagger, #447, 1947 .... $75-$185
Woofy Wowser, #700, 1940 .... $325-$835
Ziggy Zilo, #737, 1958 .... $100-$175

Plastic Fisher-Price Toys

A-Frame, #990, 1973 .... $50-$60
Aero-Marine Search Team, #323, 1979 .... $50-$60
Airlift Copter, #625 .... $17-$25
Airport, #996, 1972 .... $40-$45
Airport crew (carded), #678 .... $12-$15
Airport with cardboard hangar, #996 .... $90-$100
Alpha Probe, #325, 1980 .... $50-$60
Alpha Star, #326, 1983 .... $50-$60
Ambulance, #126 .... $15-$20
Amusement Park, #932, 1963 .... $325-$400
Barnyard Friends, #117 .... $12-$15
Bath and Utility Sets, #725, 1972 .... $35-$40
Beauty Salon, #2453, 1990 .... $30-$35
Boat Hauler, #345 .... $27-$30
Brown House, #952, 1980 .... $25-$30
Bulldozer, #329, 1980 .... $12-$15
Car and Camper, #992, 1979 .... $30-$45
Castle, #993 .... $100-$120
Change-a-Tune Carousel, #170, 1981 .... $35-$40
Choo-Choo, #719, 1963 .... $55-$60
Circus Clowns (carded), #675 .... $12-$15
Circus Train, #991, 1973 .... $22-$35
Construction Workers, #352, 1976 .... $40-$50
Copter, #344 .... $27-$30
Crazy Clown Brigade, #657, 1983 .... $65-$70
Cruise Boat, #2524, 1988 .... $17-$20
Cycle Racing Team, #356, 1977 .... $25-$30
Dare Devil Sport Van, #318, 1978 .... $50-$60
Daredevil Skydiver, #354, 1977 .... $15-$20
Decorator Set, #728, 1970 .... $25-$30
Deep Sea Diver, #358, 1980 .... $30-$40
Dozer, #340 .... $12-$15
Drive-In Movie, #2454, 1980 .... $30-$35
Dump Truckers, #979, 1965 .... $80-$90
Dumptruck, #342 .... $12-$15
Dune Buster, #322, 1979 .... $40-$50
Express Train, #2581, 1987 .... $17-$20
Farm, #2501, 1986 .... $22-$25
Farm Family (carded), #677 .... $12-$15
Farm Fun, #636 .... $8-$10
Farm Set, #331, 1981 .... $20-$30
Ferris Wheel, #969, 1966 .... $45-$75
Ferry, #932, 1979 .... $55-$60
Fire Engine, #2361, 1987 .... $17-$20
Fire Engine, #720, 1969 .... $15-$20
Fire Pumper, #336, 1983 .... $20-$30
Fire Station, #928, 1979 .... $55-$60
Fire Truck, #124 .... $15-$20
Fire Truck Rig, #346 .... $22-$25

Firefighters, #321, 1979 .... $30-$35
Firestar 1, #357, 1980 .... $25-$30
Floating Marina, #2582, 1988 .... $17-$20
Forklift, #343 .... $12-$15
Fun Jet, #182, 1981 .... $25-$30
Fun Jet, #183, 1970 .... $25-$30
Garage, #930, 1970 .... $30-$35
Garage Squad (carded), #679 .... $12-$15
Gas Station, #2455, 1990 .... $30-$35
Goldilocks, #151, 1967 .... $60-$65
Happy Hoppers, #121 .... $30-$40
Highway Dump Truck, #328, 1980 .... $25-$30
Hook & Ladder, #319, 1979 .... $25-$30
Hospital, #931, 1976 .... $100-$120
Houseboat, #985, 1972 .... $40-$50
Humpty Dumpty, #736, 1970s .... $2-$4
Jetliner, #2360, 1986 .... $17-$20
Jetport, #933, 1981 .... $30-$35
Kitchen Set, #729, 1971 .... $25-$30
Lacing Shoe, #146, 1970 .... $70-$75
Lift and Load Depot, #942, 1977 .... $60-$70
Lift and Load Lumber Yard, #944, 1978 .... $45-$50
Lift and Load Railroad, #943, 1978 .... $60-$70
Little Mart, #2580, 1987 .... $17-$20
Little Riders, #656, 1976 .... $6-$7
Little Trucks, #398 .... $22-$25
Load Master Dump, #327, 1984 .... $15-$20
Mail Truck, #127 .... $15-$20
Main Street, #2500, 1986 .... $25-$30
McDonald's, #2552, 1990 .... $60-$75
Merry-go Round, #111, 1972 .... $55-$60
Mini Boat Set, #685, 1969 .... $75-$85
Mini Bus, 1970s .... $3-$5
Mini Camper Set, #686, 1969 .... $75-$85
Mini Snowmobile, #705, 1970 .... $50-$60
Mini Van, #141 .... $7-$10

Fisher-Price toys from the 1960s include the "Chatter Telephone" and "Tip-Toe Turtle," worth about $10 each.

Mini Van, Pampers promotional, #141 ....$7-$10
Motocross Team, #335, 1983 ....$50-$60
Mountain Climbers, #351, 1976 ....$50-$60
Musical Shoe, #991, 1964 ....$80-$90
Neighborhood, #2551, 1988 ....$30-$35
New School, #2550, 1988 ....$25-$30
Nifty Station Wagon, #234, 1960 ....$325-$350
Northwoods Trailblazer, #312, 1977 ....$30-$40
Nursery School, #929, 1978 ....$45-$50
Off-Shore Cargo Base, #945, 1979 ....$75-$85
Patio Set, #726, 1971 ....$35-$40
Play Family Camper, #994, 1972 ....$45-$50
Play Family Circus, #135, 1974 ....$65-$70
Play Family Farm, #915, 1968 ....$25-$35
Play Family Lacing Shoe, #136, 1965 ....$65-$80
Play Family Tow Truck and Car, #718, 1969 ....$75-$85
Play Family Vehicle Assortment, #123 ....$15-$20
Playground, #2525, 1986 ....$12-$15
Police Car, #125 ....$15-$20
Police Patrol Squad, #332, 1981 ....$15-$20
Pool, #2526, 1986 ....$12-$15
Power and Light Service Rig, #339, 1983 ....$25-$35
Power Tow Truck, #338, 1982 ....$20-$30
Race Car Rig, #320, 1979 ....$20-$30
Rescue Copter, #305, 1975 ....$25-$30
Rescue Rig, #337, 1982 ....$15-$20
Rescue Team, #350, 1976 ....$20-$30
Rescue Truck, #303, 1975 ....$30-$40

Rodeo Rig, #330, 1980 ....$15-$20
Rooms, Sears exclusive, #909, 1971 ....$290-$300
Safari, #304, 1975 ....$65-$70
Safety School Bus, #984 ....$325-$350
School, #923, 1971 ....$35-$40
School Bus, #192, 1965 ....$30-$60
Scoop Loader, #341 ....$12-$15
Scuba Divers, #353, 1976 ....$25-$30
Sea Explorer, #310, 1977 ....$50-$60
Sea Shark, #334, 1981 ....$50-$60
Sesame Street Clubhouse, #937, 1977 ....$75-$80
Sesame Street Extras, #940, 1976 ....$25-$30
Sesame Street House, #938, 1975 ....$70-$80
Snorkey Firetruck, #168 ....$300-$350
Snorkey Firetruck, #169 ....$300-$350
Sport Plane, #306, 1975 ....$25-$30
Super Speed Racer, #308, 1976 ....$25-$30
TV Action Team, #309, 1977 ....$70-$80
Village, #997, 1973 ....$80-$90
Western Town, #934, 1982 ....$55-$65
Westerners (carded), #676 ....$12-$15
Wheelie Dragster, #333, 1981 ....$20-$30
White Water Kayak, #355, 1977 ....$25-$30
Wilderness Patrol, #307, 1976 ....$60-$70
Yellow House, #952, 1969 ....$35-$40
Yellow House with moving van, #952 ....$100-$120
Zoo, #916, 1984 ....$20-$25

FISHING COLLECTIBLES

For those of us who, as the bumper sticker says, would rather be fishing, perhaps having a collection of vintage tackle in our dens or a display of old rods and reels on the office wall is the next best thing. Vintage fishing lures and related items are appealing for several reasons—they are colorful, small enough to display, can range in value from $5-$5,000, and perhaps most importantly, they let the fisherman relive those wonderful moments of the big ones that got away. Although they seem to be readily available, it's a challenge to find old lures and other items in top condition. Some old lures can be worth thousands. The norm, though is $5 or $10, up to $200.

Lures—It was probably the native American who first developed the artificial lure on this continent, but the lure as we know it today has its roots in the late eighteenth century. There was little interest in fishing as a sport in early American history but there was much commercial fishing, and probably a little fly fishing by visiting European aristocrats. By then fly fishing as a sport was already well developed in England.

Probably the oldest ancestor of today's modern fishing lure is the "Phantom Minnow." This English lure first made its appearance in America in the early 1800s. The first of these consisted of a metal head and metal fins on either side of a soft body usually made of silk. The "Phantom Minnow" remained essentially the same for the next 75 to 80 years. It underwent a few changes with regard to hooks and leaders, but remained a staple lure into the 1940s.

Known as a bass plug, the first patented lure was the Riley Haskell "Minnow" of 1859. This was followed by a floating model, circa 1876, by the H.C. Brush Co., and the "Flying Hellgrammite," patented by Harry Compstick in 1883, which boasted metal wings and a wood body, the latter becoming the most desirable among collectors worldwide. The first American artificial lure listed in United States patent records (patented in 1876) incorporating a woody body—and confirmed to have been manufactured—was H.C. Brush's "Floating Spinner." There were no further innovations in artificial lures outside of metal spinners and spoons until around 1890. It is at about this time that the first American-made artificial lures appeared, reflecting the look of a natural minnow. The "modern" wood bass plug is attributed to the Heddon Co. late in the 19th century, with the most renowned being their Dowagiac Minnow of 1904.

The use of metal lures preceded wooden plugs, with numerous models produced in both the United States and England in the early 1800s. Using what was close at hand, these were initially just silver dinner spoons with an attached hook. This concept led to what later became known as spinners, which could be either cast or trolled.

Most collectible in this earlier group are the pre-1900 Skinners, the Chicago Spinner and those by J.E. Pepper,

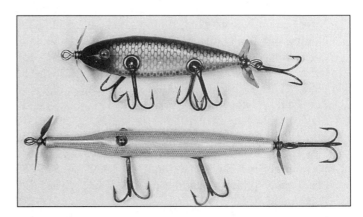

This pair of lures, an Underwater Minnow and a Gar Minnow, both made by the Creek Chub Bair Co., sold for $990 each at a recent auction conducted by Lang Sporting Collectibles of Raymond, Maine.

Chapman and the Hendryx Co. Metal lures from the 1930s and 1940s are also high on collectors' lists. Names to look for are the "Silver Minnow" by Johnson, Arbogast's "Tin Liz," the first "Daredevils" by Eppinger and South Bend's "Tri-Oreno." Also in the metal lure category are torpedo-shaped metal devons, and those made specifically for salmon fishing.

Another lure considered to be one of the most effective is the jig. This type has a single hook, a lead head, and, in its earlier form, a body and tail fashioned of wispy feathers or maribou. Some modern jigs have plastic bodies and curled tails.

General Guidelines: Having the original cardboard or rare jointed wooden boxes add to a vintage lure's value, as do original company catalogs. From 1920 through 1950 many companies produced plugs, most of which are easily found today at reasonable prices. Lately there has been a lot of attention paid to the early plastic lures – some manufacturers were still making wooden lures up into the 1960s. The plastics are still down in the $5 to $15 range for the most part; plenty of hunting grounds still remain as of yet untouched. Many of these early plastics are interesting and make very attractive displays.

There is also a rapidly growing interest in collecting early folk-art-like homemade fishing lures (as well ice-fishing decoys).

Antique fishing lures have increased tremendously in value over the last fifteen years. The wooden lures of the 1920s, '30s and '40s are a must for the sporting collector. Any good wooden lure with good paint is generally worth at least $10, and some bring from $50 to several hundred dollars. The key for the beginning collector is to look at the general condition. Is the paint complete? Be sure that the original paint has age cracks. If it doesn't, it may be a repaint. Consult a long-time collector if you're not sure.

Rods—Rod-making progressed over time, with specific makers preferring different types of wood. In the mid-1800s, the English favored greenheart wood, while Americans used hickory and ash. American rods of the Civil War era looked like the cue sticks used in billiards and sported varnished rattan handles. European varieties had butt sections greenheart wood with bamboo tips, and early examples were mottled. Poachers' rods, made of greenheart and calcutta cane, were fashioned in four sections and hidden in walking sticks or secured in leather cases.

Best known for their resiliency, bamboo fly rods are considered the forte of 19th century American rod makers such as Samuel Phillipe, Charles Murphy and Hiram Leonard. Bamboo rods remain a favorite with many anglers and collectors.

During the 1940s, a Bakelite impregnation process was used to seal the cane fibers and contributed to the rod's durability. Considered "top of the line" among these are rods manufactured by Wright and McGill (Granger series) and the trout rod by Heddon. Gillium, Dickerson and Garrison also produced rods of high quality during the 1950s and 1960s. Heddon models generally had hardwood handles and sported the "leaping bass" decal. American-made rods usually had two tips, whereas many British rods had only one.

General Guidelines: Defects like cracking, rust, bent seats, loose ferrules and replacement parts decrease the value of rods. Short or broken sections also devalue the rod, as do cracked varnish and damaged cork. Steel rods, made during the 1920s-1950s, are generally considered difficult to use but interesting to collectors. On the other hand, most of the fiberglass models, which appeared after World War II, have little collector value with the exception of those by Russ Peak, Winston, the Golden Eagle series by Orvis, and Harry Wilson at Scott-Pow-R-Ply. Custom bamboo bait casting models, by Orvis, Thomas, Leonard and Payne are harder to find, with some commanding values in the thousands of dollars.

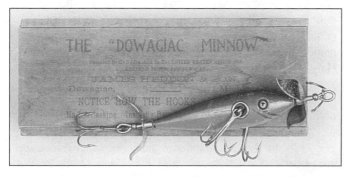

A nice example of a Heddon "Dowagiac Minnow" sold for $1,540 at a Lang Sporting Collectibles auction in Raymond, Maine. The 1902 lure was still in its original wooden, sliding-lid box.

THE ALLURE OF FISHING COLLECTIBLES!

Native Americans created some of the first lures in America. Quite simplistic, yet beautiful, most of them exist in museums today. According to Carl Luckey, author of Old Fishing Lures and Tackle (Krause Publications, 1999), an English-made lure, the "Phantom Minnow," is the oldest manufactured ancestor of today's modern lure. It first appeared in America in the early 1800s and remained essentially the same for nearly 75 years. It featured a metal head and metal fins on either side of a soft body, usually made of silk.

The first commercial spinner baits and spoons appeared in the 1840s-50s, when Julio T. Buel was awarded the first U.S. patent on a spinner bait (1852). The "Floating Spinner," by H.C. Brush, was the first artificial lure to receive a patent (1876). Soon after this wood-bodied lure appeared, real-looking lures of minnows followed.

James T. Heddon, founder of the company which today still bares his name, is considered the first manufacturer of the bass lure, or "plug" as the are called. According to Luckey, here's how it happened:

"It is said that one day Jim Heddon was whiling away some time, waiting for a fishing buddy by the lake, whittling on a chunk of wood. Upon satisfying the whittling urge, he casually tossed the result into the water. What happened next is the legend. To his amazement, a big bass attacked the chunk so violently that it was knocked into the air. Whatever the exact event, that was the moment the idea of making artificial baits out of wood was born in Heddon's mind." So after that, he was making wooden minnows and frogs.

Bud Stewart's hand-carved lures are also quite famous; their folk art status make his handmade lures more desirable and more valuable than many other lures. These lures feature bold colors, swirls, circles and spots; sporting wild paint jobs, they were still neat to look at. Oh, they also caught fish, too.

Companies, such as Heddon, Shakespeare, Pflueger, Creek Chub and South Bend Bair Co. are also known for their unique lures, still popular today among collectors.

A lure's value is based on age, scarcity and condition. Although some vintage lures can sell for hundreds, even thousands, for the most part the lures you will find will be $25 or less. But in general, look for the older lures, because the older it is, the fewer there are, hence the more valuable it will be. And if it has its original box, that adds to the value.

Reels—Originally called "winches," the first 18th century crank reels were made of iron or brass. Of English origin, the first geared reel was hand made around 1780, while the first American multiplying reel is attributed to Kentuckian George Snyder in 1812. Jonathan and Benjamin Meek of Kentucky improved upon this basic design. Reels specifically designed for saltwater fishing followed.

Reels from the Civil War era appeal not only to fishing collectors but to those interested in fine early American nautical pieces.

Centered in the New York area, early saltwater reel manufacturers included Conroy, Bates and Vom Hofe, followed in the early 20th century by Hofe's "big game" reels and drag models by Pflueger. During the early decades of the 20th century, large companies like Shakespeare, Horton, Heddon, Meisselbach, South Bend Tackle, Enterprise (Pflueger) and Hendryx emerged. Later, and noteworthy, are those custom made by Arthur and Oscar Kovalovsky, whose 1940s and 1950s reels are highly regarded in the auction market and among collectors.

Free spoke reels followed World War II. These included the Shakespeare "President," the Pflueger "Supreme," and what is considered by many to be at the apex of this category, the "Ambassadeur" from Abu of Sweden.

General Guidelines: Some of the early German silver fishing reels (typically valued at $150-$400) are good collectible items; however, most poles and reels have not attained this value level, other than the fly rods by some of the famous makers (which can bring $1,000-$3,000). The Meek reel is much in demand by today's collectors.

Fly and Spinning Reels—Called "pirns," the first fly fishing reels were of British 19th century crank design. American fly fishermen of the mid-19th century relied on either British reels or those made by hand; during the 1880s, however, American models made inroads in this market. Again, the names of Orvis, Leonard, Conroy and Vom Hofe came to the fore, Orvis with a simple spool reel, Leonard with his "raised pillar" design, and small, finely-crafted models by Conroy and Vom Hofe that sported rubber side plates and rims of German silver. Also of note were the spool reels by Pflueger and Meisselbach that were distributed between 1895 and 1917.

Offered at a recent auction conducted by Lang Sporting Collectibles of Raymond, Maine, this exceptional musky bait casting reel, made by Meek & Milam of Frankfort, Kentucky, sold for $2,500.

Early models of spinning reels include Scotland's Mallach sidecaster, circa 1884, and the 1905 Illingworth "Mark One." Generally left to European makers, the better reels are from Allcock, Quick, Mitchell, Luxor, Zebco and Alcedo (responsible for the 1960s Orvis models). American makers included Penn, Bache Brown, Pflueger and Fin Nor (circa 1940s-1950s).

General Guidelines: The "Medalist" by Pflueger is the most commonly available to collectors today. Their "Gem" design, circa 1950, is also noted for its reasonable price, with the latter somewhat harder to find and thus of greater value to collectors. Conversely, spring-loaded fly wheels are readily available and have little collectible value.

Flies—From soft to wet there are a plethora of fly types, including streamers, spinners, emergers, soft hackles and nymphs. For those who tie their own, there are fly-tying tools like vices, magnifiers, bobbins, bobbin threaders and specialty pliers. Because provenance is generally unknown, and they can be found in abundance, most collectors search only for those flies tied by specific "names," many of which command several hundred dollars or more. These renowned anglers include Syd Glasso, Preston Jennings, Ruben Cross, Harry Darbee, Carrie Stevens and Roderick Haig-Brown.

On the other hand, gut-eyed flies require no provenance. Wound on blackened hooks and often framed, they are both beautiful and collectible.

General Guidelines: Piquing the interest of serious collectors are flies that remain in their original envelopes or are embedded in the maker's card. L.L. Bean, Orvis and William Mills sold packaged flies, while Hardy, Allcocks and Pflueger provided the popular "spinner-flies," noted for their colorful graphics.

Accessories—In addition to the tools necessary for fly tying, this category includes early hooks (with their contain-

FOR MORE INFORMATION!

Collectors of vintage fishing lures may be interested in the book Old Fishing Lures & Tackle – Identification and Value Guide, Fifth Edition, by Carl Luckey, Krause Publications, 1999. At 672 pages, it's the largest and most comprehensive guide for old fishing lures on the market. It's filled with information and photos on collectible fishing tackle from the 1800s to the 1960s, including historical data and collector values for thousands of lures from hundreds of manufacturers. It also includes information and values for old fishing rods and reels.

ers often generating more interest than the hooks themselves); silk worm gut leaders and lines; colorful bobbers made of cork, quill or wood; casting or practice plugs; lead or "split" shot (along with their containers); landing nets; and creels, as well as rare and desirable Indian fish baskets. Aluminum storage boxes, which can range from simple to fancy, are also collectible, as are leather wallets, which featured wool, paper or imitation felt pages. Hard to find in good condition—and most desirable—are the Victorian handmade styles, which are noteworthy for their parchment pages.

Club
• National Fishing Lure Collectors Club, 22325 B Drive South, Marshall, MI 49068

Recommended Reading
Old Fishing Lures & Tackle—Identification and Value Guide, Carl Luckey

VALUE LINE

Lures
Al Foss, Shimmy Wiggler	$10-$25
Arbogast, Jitterbug	$10-$20
Bass Seeker	$20-$30
Bite-Em Bate Co. Lipped Wiggler lure	$60-$150
Comstock "Flying Hellgrammite" lure	$2,500-$4,000
Crazy Crawler	$25-$75
Creek Chub Bait Co. "Injured Minnow" lure	$10-$25
Creek Chub, Pikie Minnow, wood	$40-$60
Chapman "Allure" #1 and #2 lures	$135-$175
Chapman "Pickerel Spinner" lure	$60-$85

Vintage creels are almost considered works of art by serious collectors. This stunning example, a leather-bound, split-willow basket made by George Lawrence of Portland, Oregon, sold for $2,900 at a Lang Sporting Collectibles auction.

Dalton Special, Shakespeare	$20-$30
Dingbat, wooden	$30-$50
Dingbat, plastic	$5-$10
Wilcox Wiggler	$2,000-$3,000
Florida Fishing Tackle, Dillinger	$5-$10
Florida Shad	$15-$25
Globe	$30-$80
Haskell "Minnow" lure, 1859	$3,000+
Hastings Wilson's Six-in-One Wobbler	$250-$300
Hastings Wilson's Winged Wobbler	$100-$125
Hardy "Devon" lure	$20-$50
Heddon #210 "Surface Minnow" lure, wood	$50-$100
Heddon #210 "Surface Minnow" lure, plastic	$15-$30
Heddon "Crab Wiggler" lure	$50-$100
Heddon "Dummy Double" lure	$600-$1,000
Heddon, Lucky-13, wooden	$30-$70
Heddon "Punkinseed" lure	$50-$250
Hula Popper	$3-$6
Injured Minnow	$6-$25
Keeling "Expert Minnow" lure, 1905-20	$200-$400
Metal devon	$15-$30
Moonlight, 99 percent Weedless	$30-$60
Moonlight Bait	$30-$60
Mustang Minnow	$25-$50
Nip-I-Didee	$40-$60
Paw Paw, Casting Minnow	$15-$35
Pflueger, Pal-O-Mine	$15-$30
Pikie Kazoo	$50-$75
River Pup	$10-$20
River Runt	$20-$60
Shakespeare, Swimming Mouse	$25-$55
South Bend, Bass-Oreno	$20-$50
Surf-Oreno	$50-$150
Tin Liz, 1924	$30-$40
Wiggle Diver, wood	$10-$20
Wotta-Frog	$40-$75

Reels
Abu Ambassadeur #2600, 1958	$30-$50
Abu Limited Edition gold Ambassadeur	$400-$500
Allcock brass fly reel, 1890	$75-$125
Alcedo micron spinning reel	$35-$75
B.C. Milam reel	$375+
Bristol #65 and #66 fly reels	$8-$16
Carlton automatic fly reel, #2925	$50-$90
Chubb bass pirn, 1890	$25-$50
Farlow Saphire fly reel, 1960	$40-$65
Farlow brass pirn crank reel, 1880	$75-$125
Fin-Nor Gold Spinning reel	$150-$250
Fin-Nor fly reel, saltwater, "wedding cake" design	$300-$500
Hardy Jack Scott casting reel	$275-$400
Hardy brass Perfect fly reel, 1900	$400+
Hardy Silex reel	$125-$300
Heddon Chief Dowagiac casting reel	$60-$95
Heddon Model 3-25 casting reel, 1927	$95-$150

Heddon 335 nickel/silver ....$80-$95

Hendryx "raised pillar" brass fly reel...................$15-$30

Hendryx "raised pillar" nickel over brass.............$15-$25

J.F. Meek casting reel, 1835-1840 ....$2,500+

Kovalovsky "big game" reel ....$1,000+

Luxor spinning reel, 1950.....................................$30-$50

Meek and Milam reel, 1851-1878...........................$600+

Montague nickel over brass ....$15-$25

Meisselbach Synploreel #255 casting reel.............$50-$80

Meisselbach saltwater bay reel $35-70

Meisselbach #660 automatic, 1920......................$40-$75

Malloch salmon reel, 1920.................................$100-$195

Montague Imperial 6/0 big game reel.................$95-$150

Orvis trout fly reel, walnut box, 1874 ....$400+

Pennell Tournament Casting nickel silver ....$30-$45

Pflueger Golden West fly reel, 1930 ....$100-$185

Pflueger Superex 3775 automatic fly reel,
     1910..$40-$60

Pflueger Supreme #1573 casting reel....................$25-$40

Pflueger Everlaster bay reel ....$30-$50

Pflueger Adams big game reel ....$125+

Pflueger Summit..$10-$25

Shakespeare Standard Pro.....................................$15-$30

Shakespeare #1847 automatic fly reel...................$10-$25

Shakespeare "Kazoo" fly reel ....$20-$35

Shakespeare Miller-Autocrat big game reel.......$135-$200

Shakespeare President #1970A, 1955....................$15-$30

South Bend #850 surfcasting reel, 1940 ....$10-$20

Talbot (Kansas City, Mo.) casting reel..............$175-$300

Edward Vom Hofe Perfection fly reel, 1900..........$1,500+

Edward Vom Hofe Peerless fly reel; 1883 pat. ....$900+

Edward Vom Hofe Model #521
     saltwater reel ....$165-$300

Edward Vom Hofe Model #721
     "Commander Ross"..$400+

Julius Vom Hofe all metal trout fly reel,
     1889 pat..$200-$300

Julius Vom Hofe 'b-Ocean" big game reel,
     1911 pat..$150-$175

Frederich Vom Hofe brass bay reel,
     pre-Civil War ....$900+

Winchester 4142 casting reel ....$65-$90

Wordens Belt Reel, 1953 ....$45-$65

J.W. Youngs Beaudex fly reel ....$30-$55

Zebco Cardinal spinning reel................................$25-$50

Zebco Zero Hour Bomb spinning reel ....$15-$25

Fly Rods

Abbey & Imbrie Centennial fly rod, 9-1/2', two tips,
     1917...$135-$225

Constable empress fly rod, 8', two tips ....$150-$275

Thomas Chubb Lancewood fly rod, 10',
     1890...$60-$100

Thomas Chubb calcutta bamboo fly rod,
     1900...$100-$200

Devine bamboo fly rod, 9', two tips ....$150-$350

Dickerson fly rod.. $1,000

Edward spinning rods, 6-7', two tips.................$100-$175

Farlow calcutta salmon fly rod, 1900.................$150-$250

Granger Victory fly rod, 7', two tips ....$400-$500

Hardy Phantom fly rod, 9', two tips ....$150-$275

Hardy Marvel fly rod, 7-1/2', two tips...............$300-$500

Heddon #600 bamboo casting fly rod ....$60-$100

Heddon #50 fly rod, 8-1/2' two tips ....$165-$275

Leonard Tournament 8-1/2' trout fly rod,
     two tips...$350-$700

Montague (L.L. Bean label) fly rod, 9-1/2',
     two tips ....$65-$135

Montague Splitswitch casting rod, 5', two tips ......$20-$40

Orvis Battenkill fly rod, 8-1/2', two tips ....$295-$475

Orvis Wes Jordan fly rod, leather case.............$450-$675

Orvis Model #99 fly rod, one tip.......................$175-$300

C.F. Orvis fly rod, one tip, 1900 ....$180-$375

Shakespeare Spring Brook fly rod, 8-1/2',
     two tips, 1950...$40-$85

South Bend #77 bamboo fly rod, 9', two tips.......$65-$125

South Bend #25 Sport Oreno fly rod, 7-1/2',
     two tips...$125-$200

F.E. Thomas salmon fly rod, 10', two tips..........$195-$350

Vom Hofe Big Game bamboo boat rod.............$125-$250

FUTURE TREASURES!

DON'T LET THESE GET AWAY!

Although the most valuable vintage lures are wood, collectors have been paying more attention recently to early plastic lures, according to Carl Luckey, who keeps adding hundreds of listings of early plastic lures to his book's price guide.

For the most part, collectible plastic lures are still very affordable, typically priced in the $5-$15 range.

"Many of these early plastics are interesting and make very attractive displays," he says, adding that this is a segment of the field that still offers lots of collecting opportunities. "There are plenty of hunting grounds yet untouched," he adds.

Many other items are also popular, such as old fishing tackle catalogs. Regardless of the company name, the catalog offers collectors a wealth of interesting and valuable information.

Lure boxes are hot, especially those made by Heddon. Not only do some have terrific pictures on them, they too provide vital information, such as dates and manufacturers' names.

Store displays for lures are also highly desirable. But good luck finding them; they are difficult to find, especially in nice shape. Posters advertising lures, counter displays and window scenes all fall into this category.

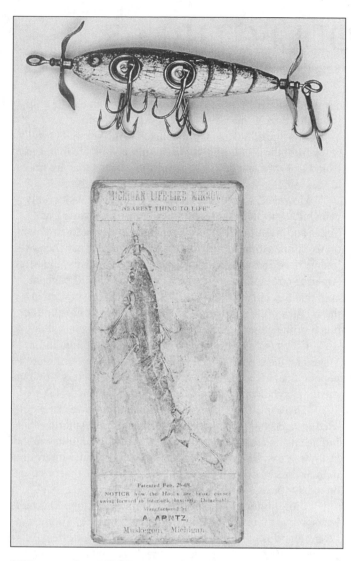

This wooden **Michigan Life-Like Minnow** sold for $415 at a recent Lang Sporting Collectibles auction. An empty box for the same lure, meanwhile, brought a whopping $2,860, demonstrating the scarcity -- and value—of vintage boxes.

Vom Hofe antique wood boat rod ....$100-$195
Winchester Armax fly rod, 9', two tips ....$125-$225
"Cue Stick" hickory rod, ring guides,
    Civil War period ....$295-$425
Winston Lew Stoner, 9', one tip ....$295-$425

Nets
    Hardwood Net, 1950s ....$20-$30
    Hardy Royde landing net ....$150-$200
    Richardson "Harrimac" net, trout size ....$10-$15
    Richardson "Harrimac" net, salmon size ....$30+

Flies
    Hardy Spinner fly, original card............................$10-$15
    Orvis single fly, original wrapper..........................$5-$10
    Gut-eyed fly, blackened hook....................................$15+

Catalogs
    Charles F. Orvis (1900)...$100+
    Meek (reels) ....$100+
    Early Winchester..$100+
    Julius Vom Hofe (1900)..$100+
    Hardy Anglers Guide (pre-1928).............................$100+
    Hardy Anglers Guide (1928-40) ....$50-$100
    Creek Chubb Bait (1930).................................$50-$100
    Folsom Arms (1930).......................................$50-$100
    Pflueger (1920-40)...$25-$50
    South Bend Bait (pre-1940).............................$25-$50
    South Bend Bait (1940-50s)..............................$15-$25
    Heddon Pocket Catalogs ....$15-$25
    L.L. Bean (1950-60s)......................................$15-$25
    Orvis (1950-60)..$15-$25

Miscellaneous
    Fly box, imitation tortoise shell, 1930s......................$50+
    Fly box, blackened aluminum, pre-1910 ....$75+
    Hardy sectioned bag...$100-$150
    Ideal bobber, red/green, 6", 1920s ....$20-$30
    Spooled silk line, good condition ....$8+
    Antique creel, leather closure ....$40-$80
    Indian fish basket, woven twig................................$200+
    Lawrence western creel...$100+

GAMBLING COLLECTIBLES

If you've run out of luck at the blackjack table, maybe it's time to strike it rich with gambling collectibles. Everything associated with gambling and casinos—from playing cards and dice to and casino chips and ash trays—has the potential to be collectible. All of the equipment used in various banking games, such as Chuck-A-Luck, Faro, Hazard, Keno and Roulette, is collectible. So even are illegal devices used by "sharpers"—professional cheaters.

All of the different types of casino "money" are also collected. (In the gaming industry, chips with a stated value are technically called "checks." "Chips" do not have a stated value. Their value is determined at the time of play.)

Other collectibles include playing cards, old books, postcards, prints and photographs.

Background: Gambling has always been a popular pastime in America, as well as a way for "sharpers" to make a quick buck. Today, government agencies and other entities use lotteries to supplement taxes and raise funds for schools, libraries and other civic projects. But many of the efforts in the 18th and 19th century on behalf of states and cities were dishonestly run, making those collectibles even more desirable.

Gambling supply houses located around the country manufactured most of the gambling paraphernalia and equipment, which was generally sold in catalogs. Because most of the equipment offered could be fixed or rigged, the catalog was not meant to be viewed by the general public. These catalogs, which provide excellent information for collectors, are collectibles in their own right. They are, however, quite difficult to find.

Other collectibles include lottery tickets, broadsides, ads and brochures. The ornateness of these items makes them excellent candidates for framing and display.

Chips—Old casino chips, the colorful gambling tokens used at blackjack and craps tables around the world, have emerged as high-stakes collectibles in recent years; many have commanded some surprisingly strong prices during auctions in the late 1990s. Most collectors prefer the $1 and $5

COLLECTOR'S ADVISORY!

In general, chips from defunct casinos are worth more than those from casinos that are still in business. But there are exceptions; chips from some defunct casinos are relatively plentiful because when the casino closed or was sold to another owner, the existing supplies of chips may have been sold by the box full at a sheriff's sale, along with furniture, silverware and other fixtures. Those chips may be on the market in quantities of thousands, so they have little value.

chips because they are generally more affordable. The chip's value depends primarily on supply and demand.

The age of a chip is also a factor in the value. Typically, chips from the 1940s and 1950s are more valuable than those from the 1980s and 1990s. Chips from casinos that are no longer in business are generally also more valuable.

However, some relatively new chips are considerably valuable, especially those with limited issues. Some Las Vegas and Atlantic City hotels regularly offer these commemorative issues to promote events such as boxing matches or lounge headliners, or, as in the case of Atlantic City, the Miss America pageant. In 1997, the Sands issued a $20 pageant chip that has already sold for $100. Collectors who live in these cities often snap up these limited-edition chips before much of the general public has a chance at them.

Chips from some casinos, such as the Flamingo in Las Vegas and the old Playboy Casino in Atlantic City, are more popular than others, There is a crossover of collectors who pursue the Playboy chips to add to their Playboy memorabilia.

There is also an increasing demand for newer chips used in riverboat gambling establishments and American Indian casinos that have proliferated across the country in the last few years. Once again, collectors are especially interested in their limited-edition chips, compared to those that are used on a daily basis.

Punchboards—It seems a certain percentage of Americans just can't resist the chance to take a chance. Today that desire manifests itself in casinos and state-run lotteries. But before the days of electronic slot machines with multicolored flashing lights, simple "punchboards" satisfied the appetite to gamble.

Punchboards consisted of pressed paper with some sort of colorful design on the front. They were usually half an inch to an inch thick. Below the design were rows of small holes—anywhere from 100 to a thousand or more, depending on the board's size.

The player purchased a chance to "punch" one of the holes with a wooden or wire puncher and extract a ticket with a prize on it. Typically, it cost anywhere from five cents to fifty cents to buy a punch; sometimes it was a dollar or more.

Sometimes the prize was cash—usually a quarter, 50 cents, or a dollar. Sometimes the prize was merchandise—candy, cigars, cigarettes, jewelry, radios, clocks, cameras, sporting goods, toys, or beer.

As gambling opponents started to frown on punchboards, the punchboard makers just got more and more clever with the prizes, the graphics, and the types of games offered. Some were printed with trivia questions; others challenged the player to a round of checkers or other simple game before punching out a prize.

By the late 1920s, the jackpots grew larger and the graphics bolder. One punchboard, called "Take It Off," sold its 440 punches for a quarter each. You could win your quarter back, or 50 cents or $1.

Or if you were feeling lucky, you could purchase a shot at the jackpot section, where there was a $20 ticket hidden somewhere.

Today, these old punchboards are popular collectibles that sell for anywhere from $5 to $500, depending on the condition and the graphics depicted on the board. Most sell in the $15-$50 range. Serious collectors seek punchboards that have not been used. Some might show shelf wear, but a premium is paid for those still factory wrapped and unpunched.

Graphics play an important role in value. The "Play Basketball" punchboard, for example, featured basketball players on a red-white-and-blue motif. In the 1930s, a nickel bought a ticket and a chance to win a handmade Havana cigar. An Elvgren pin-up girl, meanwhile, beckoned from a punchboard that advertised Johnson's Chocolates. Another punchboard, "Turkeys, Geese, Ducks, and Chickens," offered players a chance to win a real bird for just a nickel.

Punchboards were found in all kinds of places—drugstores, cafes, cigar stores, grocery stores, taverns, diners and gas stations. Many were sold locally by sports teams and civic organizations as fund-raisers; generally the odds on winning something were usually pretty good, in the 80 to 90 percent bracket.

In order to get around the gambling aspect, some punchboards offered a piece of candy with each purchase. Others offered the purchaser a picture, such as a Mack Sennet bathing beauty.

Similar to punchboards, "pushcards" were another gambling medium of the time. They were made of thin cardboard, and a player simply punched the ticket out with his finger. They usually contained 10 to 200 holes.

Playing cards—There are a wide variety of card deck themes available—literally billions of decks have been printed since the first decks appeared more than 700 years ago in Europe, (1790s in America). Therefore, most collectors focus on one specialized area, a theme such as advertising (hotels, banks, restaurants, alcohol, tobacco), political campaigns, trains, steamboats, airplanes, dogs, horses, beautiful scenes, Art Deco, entertainment, sports or souvenir decks. Most card collectors seek either complete decks, or single cards, usually jokers or the Ace of Spades, which generally carries the manufacturer's name on it and can be used for dating the deck.

You can buy decks of playing cards for as little as 25 cents at second-hand stores or rummage sales, or, if you're interested in a scarce deck from the 1800s, you might pay $1,000 for a deck at auction.

Casino decks are perhaps the cheapest standard decks to pursue. Most are plain Bee or Bicycle brands, but many do display the casino name on the card backs. Used casino decks will have either a small hole punched in them or a small piece clipped from the corner of each card. They can be found in thrift shops for as little as a quarter to $5, but some decks, such as a 1950s Las Vegas deck, may bring as much as $150.

Make sure your deck is complete. If it was printed after 1860, there should be at least one joker in the set, too. Unopened decks bring the most money; lesser-conditioned decks are priced accordingly.

Clubs

• Casino Chips and Gaming Tokens Collectors, P.O. Box 340345, Columbus, OH 43234

• Gaming Times, 4089 Spring Mountain Road, Las Vegas, NV 89102

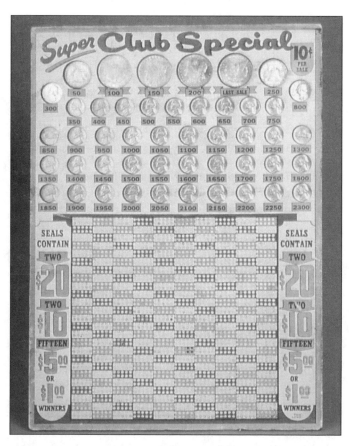

This "Super Club Special" punchboard cost 10 cents a play and offered a change to win up to $20.

VALUE LINE

Casino chips

Atlantis Casino/Resort, $5 chip, Reno ....$7-$10
Circus Circus Casino, Super Bowl Jan. 31, 1999,
    $5 chip, Las Vegas..$5-$7
Dunes Casino, $5 chip, Las Vegas, 1960s ....$200-$250
Eddie's Fabulous 50s, closed casino, $500 chip,
    Reno ....$15-$20

Flamingo, $5 chip, Las Vegas ....$125-$150
Frontier Hotel, $1 chip, Las Vegas, 1967...............$45-$50
Gold Diggers, $5 chip, Cripple Creek, Colo. ....$7-$10
Golden Nugget, $1 chip, Las Vegas........................$4-$5
Hard Rock Casino, Valentine's Day 1998 $5 chip,
    Las Vegas ....$7.50-$10
Hollywood Park Casino, $1 Y2K chip,
    limited edition ....$3-$5
Horseshoe Club, Las Vegas, $5 chip, 1950s ....$45-$50
Hotel Sahara, $3 chip, Las Vegas, 1950s ....$7-$10
Last Frontier, $5 chip, Las Vegas, 1948.................$15-$20
Lucky Slots Casino, closed casino, $1 chip,
    Las Vegas, 1971 ....$15-$20
Playboy Club, $100 chip, Bahamas ....$100-$125
Silver Bird Casino, 50 cent chip, Las Vegas ....$2-$4
Tahoe Plaza, closed casino, $5 chip,
    Lake Tahoe ....$25-$30
Tahoe Village, $25 chip, 1946 ....$10-$15

Playing cards

Alberto Vargas poker cards, deck with box ....$85-$100
"Along the Chicago, Milwaukee & Puget Sound Railway,"
    1910, deck with box ....$75-$85
Art Deco cards, by Einar Nerman, Stockholm,
    1924...$200-$250
Bicycle Wheel Back playing cards, red deck, United States
    Playing Card Co., 1890-1910........................$200-$400
Buster Brown and His Dog Tige, 1906,
    with box...$75-$100
Chicago World's Fair, Columbian Exposition,
    1893, deck ....$50-$75
"Drink Coca-Cola In Bottles," 1956 ....$40-$50
Fifty-Two Art Studies, nudes, 1950s, deck............$25-$35
Girl on Swing, Elvgren, 1950s...............................$45-$60
Goodall's Victorian Playing Cards, England, 1890,
    Queen Victoria ....$75-$100
Maxfield Parrish deck, for Edison Mazda Lamps, "The
    Waterfall," 1930 ....$275-$300
MGM/Sands, Las Vegas, used deck, drilled ....$4-$5
Mickey Mouse Playing Cards, 1930s, Walt Disney
    Enterprises, deck with box ....$50-$60
Mirage Hotel & Casino, Las Vegas, used deck..........$5-$7
Northern Pacific Railroad cards, 1906,
    deck and joker ....$100-$125
Quaker State Motor Oil, new in box.......................$8-$10
Royal Crown Cola, "Best by Taste-Test"...............$20-$25
Silver Slipper, Las Vegas, 1960s-1970s,
    Bee brand deck with box, used ....$4-$6
Smoke & Chew Kids, Plug Cut Tobacco, vintage,
    women posing, ...$525
Southern Pacific Lines, 1940s-1950s,
    deck with box ....$40-$45
Steamboat playing cards, 999, U.S. Playing Card Co.,
    Cincinnati..$15-$20
Tropicana Hotel & Casino, used deck $5
U.S. Army Nurse Corps., by Hoyle ....$10-$15

The Venetian Hotel & Casino, Las Vegas,
    used deck...$5-$7
Wichita Flour Mills Co., Wichita, Kansas, 1930s,
    deck with box ....$25-$30
Yosemite National Park, 1925 Curry Co. deck ......$40-$50

Punchboards

"Barrel of Cigarettes," 10" x 14", 5 cents per punch to
    win packs of cigarettes, 1930s $50
"Basketball," 6-1/2" x 9", 1 cent per punch, 1930s.......$15
"Catch No. 100," 2" x 2-3/4", five cents per
    punch to catch train #100 ....$10
"Dime Stakes," 10" x 13", 10 cents wins cash.......$10-$15
"E-Z Pickin'" 18" x 11", beer barrel design,
    five cents per punch for cash, 1950s ....$20-$25
"Good Punching," 9-1/2" x 9-7/8", cowboy on bronco,
    five cents per punch, 1950s $40
"Home Run Derby," 10" x 12", features a baseball
    diamond...$75
"Huff and Puff", 11" x 9-1/4", wolf and Little Red Riding
    Hood, two cents per punch, 1950s ....$5-$10
"Knockout 100," 2" x 2-3/4", five cents per punch
    to knock out fighter #100 ....$10

CASINO CHIPS HIT THE JACKPOT!

Several records were set during a 1998 auction conducted by The Gaming Emporium, a popular retail store on the famous Atlantic City Boardwalk that specializes in gambling paraphernalia. The auction was something of an oddity because it featured casino chips in denominations of $100 or higher—typically the territory reserved only for advanced collectors.

The top seller was a $100 chip from the Las Vegas Flamingo Hotel. Dating from the Buggsy Siegel era of the 1940s, it sold for a staggering $5,455—the highest price ever paid for a casino chip at auction. Another rare Las Vegas chip, a 1951 $100 chip from Binnion's Horseshoe Club, sold for $4,125.

Among the other highlights: A 1970s $100 Crystal Bay chip from Lake Tahoe went for $880. A $100 chip from Milton Prell's Aladdin in Las Vegas sold for $935. A 1960s Harrah's $100 chip from Reno/Lake Tahoe brought a bid of $798.

An early 1950s $100 chip from the Cal-Neva Biltmore went for $770. A 1985 $100 Las Vegas Bourbon Street chip sold for $825, as did a $100 Las Vegas Freemont Hotel chip. Two Atlantic City Harrah's Marina $5,000 chips (with cancellation notches) realized just under $1,800 for the pair. A dozen other chips brought prices in the $500-$700 range, while the majority of the chips in the 260-lot auction sold for between $200 and $500 each.

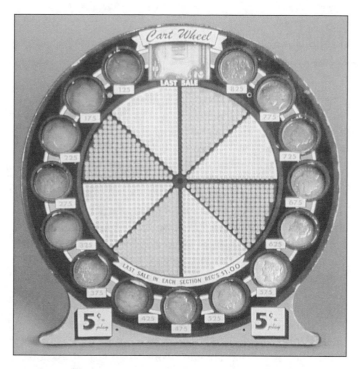

This circular punchboard was just five cents a chance.

"Lulu-Belle," 11" x 12-1/4", five cents
  wins cash, 1930s ....$25-$35
"Nestle's Chocolate" 9" x 8-1/2", two cents
  per punch $45
"Odd Pennies," 6-3/4" x 8-5/8", three cents
  per punch to win cigarettes, 1920s........................... $75
"Professor Charley," 10" x 12", 25 cents per punch
  to win $1, $5 or $10, 1946 .... $20
"Put & Take," a penny to five cents per punch
  for candy bars, 1920s $30
"Release 100," 2" x 2-3/4", five cents per punch
  to release prisoner #100 .... $10
"Ship Ahoy," 9" x 15-1/8", cheesecake graphics,
  10 cents per punch to win $35 .... $135
"Tavern Maid," 9-5/8" x 13-1/2", cheesecake,
  5 cents per punch to win cans of beer, 1938 .... $65

Miscellaneous

Advertising brochure, Mapes Hotel & Casino,
  Reno, defunct ....$5-$7
Ash tray, El Cortez Hotel & Casino,
  Las Vegas, glass ....$10-$15
Ash tray, Hotel Sahara, Las Vegas, 1960s.................$5-$10
Ash tray, Tropicana Hotel & Country Club,
  Las Vegas ....$7-$10
Bingo cage, 9" high, metal, 1941 .... $25
Book, *Gamblers Don't Gamble*, by MacDougall and
  Gumas, 1939 .... $30
Book, *Playing Cards: History & Secrets*, by Benham,
  Spring Books, London $25

Card press, 9-1/2" x 4-1/2" x 3", dovetailed, holds 10
  decks..$150
Catalog, "Bookmaker's Supplies," 19 pages, 1895, illustrated..$35
Catalog, H.C. Evans & Co., "Secret Blue Book," Gam-
  bling Supply, 1936, 72 pages $55
Catalog, 1932 "Blue Book," K.C. Card Co./Mason & Co.,
  gambling supplies, 108 pages $175
Catalog, "Blue Book 40th Anniversary," K.C. Card Co.,
  1958, gambling supplies and ways to cheat......$25-$30
Chip rack, Faro, 18" x 10", blue-green billiard cloth lining
  bottom $75
Chips rack, Roulette, walnut, holds 1,500 chips.........$100
Chips, 160 poker, bone, round, square and rectangular,
  four colors, incised designs, fitted handmade mahogany
  box, 1870s $675
Chips, poker, ivory, scrimshawed florals,
  20 chips $600
Cigarette lighter, Lake Tahoe/Cal Neva, Reno, pictures
  lake on one side..$15-$20
Dealing box, Faro, German silver, unmarked $175
Dice, Meskwaki Casino, Tama, Iowa, five emerald
  green dice ....$5-$10
Dice, celluloid, 5/8", used in chuck-a-luck cage,
  set of three $15
Dice, weighted, black-and-white, always total 12 .... $40
Dice cage, 18-1/2" x 13", nickel-plated brass,
  Mason & Co., Newark, NJ $400
Hopper, Keno, walnut, billiard cloth lining, plated metal
  mouth, acorn finial, carved feet............................$450
Ice bucket, Show Boat Hotel & Casino, Atlantic City, 9"
  high top hat..$15-$20
Instruction card, Gran Casino de la Playa de Marianao,
  Havana, Cuba, Roulette information.................$20-$25
Matchbooks, 25 from Las Vegas casinos, including Gold
  Coast, Showboat, Caesar's Palace, MGM/Grand,
  Tropicana..$10-$15
Postcards, six Las Vegas casinos, including Tropicana,
  Stardust, 1950s.................................$10-$15
Postcard, "Chuck-A-Luck," three woman playing at Wil-
  lows Casino in Reno, real photo, 1931 ....$15-$25
Postcard, "Harold's Club Casino," Reno, 1940 ....$5-$7
Postcard, "Where All Men Are Equal," Detroit Publishing
  Co., 1900s, men at a crap table ....$25-$35
Security patch, Golden Nugget, Las Vegas...................$10
Shot glass, ribbed decoration, porcelain dice
  in bottom $25
Wheel, Roulette, 8" diameter, wood and metal,
  single and double zero decals, 4-prong spinner,
  cloth layout..$40
Wheel, Roulette, wood, double Roulette type,
  14" upper wheel, 20" lower wheel, 1870 ....$1,000
Wheel of Fortune, 60", complete wheel, dice on
  glass face, G. Mason, Chicago $1,100

G.I. JOE

Hasbro took a big gamble in 1964 when it introduced the first G.I. Joe. No right-thinking American boy, after all, would be caught dead playing with dolls. Still, Hasbro wanted to duplicate the success that Mattel was enjoying with its Barbie doll, first issued five years earlier. In effect, Hasbro was looking for a Barbie doll for boys. Advertising the toy as an "action figure" (being careful never to use the word "doll"), the G.I. Joe was everything Hasbro had hoped for—and more. A commercial success for years, G.I. Joe today is one of the most collectible of all toys. In fact, taken together, Barbie and G.I. Joe are the "queen and king" of toy collecting.

Background: The story of G.I. Joe was controversial from the start. Hasbro was not only concerned about the "doll" stigma, there was always the fear that G.I. Joe might be seen as a toy that glorified war. It was, in fact, promoted as "America's Movable Fighting Man." Its introduction at the 1964 New York Toy Fair was lackluster, but when the action figures were released in a New York City test market, shortly after, every test store sold out within a week, and the invasion of America was on. By the end of the first year, G.I. Joe—the Barbie doll for boys—had earned Hasbro a whopping $17 million. (Today, the number is closer to $3 billion and still growing.)

The first G.I. Joes—all 12-inch figures—represented the four main branches of the U.S. military. They included an Army Action Soldier, a Navy Sailor, an Air Force Pilot, and a Marine. Priced at about $4 then, any one of the four original figures would sell for $500 or more today, if found in the original box.

Soon the G.I. Joe line expanded to include African-American figures, talking figures, and one surprise—a female figure. The "G.I. Nurse," decked out in white dress and stockings, was issued in 1967 and was an instant failure. No boy was interested in adding a female doll to his collection of American fighting men. Ironically, the initial failure of the G.I. Nurse doll has made it among the most valuable of all G.I. Joe figures today. Produced in limited quantities, examples have sold for over $3,000 in today's marketplace.

G.I. Joe's military career was threatened in the late 1960s due to the growing real-life conflict in Vietnam. As opposition to the controversial war grew in America, many parents did not want their children playing with "war toys" of any kind. Hasbro, recognizing the controversy, turned G.I. Joe into more of a civilian adventurer rather than a fighting soldier. New sets featured Joe as an astronaut, a frogman, etc.

The overall success of G.I. Joe continued throughout the 1970s with the popular "Adventure Team" series, but by 1976, Hasbro could no longer afford to produce the 12-inch figures because of skyrocketing oil prices that more than tripled the cost of plastics. Instead, in 1977, the company introduced a line of 8-inch figures known as the "Super Joe Adventure Team."

The 1980s saw an even smaller G.I. Joe, one standing just under four inches in height—inspired by the Star Wars action figures that were immensely popular at the time.

But in the 1990s, Hasbro, responding to collector interest, introduced a new wave of 12-inch classic G.I. Joes, along with special figures depicting heroes as diverse as Bob Hope, General Patton and Colin Powell. There have also been G.I. Joe figures issued exclusively for Target, FAO Schwarz, Kay Bee Toys and others. All, of course, are instant collectibles.

General Guidelines: For serious collectors of G.I. Joe, condition is critical. Because they've long been popular playthings for boys, G.I. Joes are hard to find in Mint condition. Finding the boxes is even harder, especially for figures from the 1960s.

It's doubtful a collector will be interested in a figure that saw lots of action on the front lines, but a figure in Mint condition can be worth hundreds or even thousands of dollars. While figures and sets from the 1960s and 1970s tend to bring the highest prices, newer G.I. Joe items from the 1980s and 1990s can also bring prices ranging anywhere from $10 for an easy-to-find item to over $300 for certain sets.

Having the original box can add 50 percent or more to a G.I. Joe's value. For instance, a 1966 Russian Infantry figure in Mint condition without the original package (sometimes called a "loose" figure by collectors) is valued at about $400; but the same figure in Mint condition with its original package could sell for $2,000 or more.

Boxes also aid in identification. Without the box, it is often difficult to identify or date a G.I. Joe figure with certainty. (The date found on a figure's buttocks is a patent date and often not the same as the actual year it was produced.)

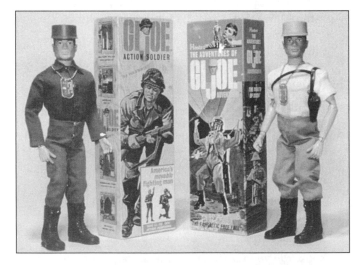

Values for 1960s G.I. Joes increase substantially if you still have the original box.

This GI Joe figure of General Eisenhower, released in the late 1990s, is valued at $75-$100.

Even unclothed G.I Joes of unknown date (in Good or better condition) may have some collector value, especially for parts. Check with a reputable dealer or consult a book to identify the figure and its era.

Rarity also affects prices, and the hard-to-find G.I. Nurse, Action Soldiers of the World, Aquanaut and Talking Astronaut command some of the highest prices today.

Rarity can pertain to an unusual variation as well as a specific figure. For example, while most G.I. Joes contain a trademark scar on faces, scars were rare on the Action Soldiers of the World figures. A scar-faced Action Soldier of the World can bring $1,000 more than the corresponding figure without a scar.

Talking figures and African-American figures are also popular with collectors and may command slightly higher prices. Recent (1990s) editions of classic G.I. Joes are also collectible and have seen prices increase in just a few years for figures still in the box.

Accessories—such as weapons, footlockers and uniforms—are highly collectible, and some can even sell for higher prices than a figure itself. This is because sets are often found with accessories missing, and serious collectors seek individual items to complete the sets.

Accessories increase value. For instance, a Russian Infantry figure dressed only in a basic uniform is worth around $1,600 in Mint-in-Box condition, but the same figure with its additional, original equipment is valued at nearly twice that.

Some G.I. Joe sets featured equipment only, some came with a figure, while still others were vehicle sets. Some 1960s vehicles alone are worth close to $1,000.

Here's the Black version of the 1965 GI Joe Action Soldier. Mint-in-the-Box, it's worth about $2,500. In top condition without the box it's valued at about $800.

Clubs

• G.I. Joe Collectors Club, 12513 Birchfalls Dr., Raleigh, NC 27614

• G.I. Joe Collectors Club, 150 S. Glenoaks Blvd., Burbank, CA 91510

Recommended Reading

GI Joe Identification and Price Guide 1964-1999, Vincent Santelmo

The Complete Encyclopedia to GI Joe, Second Edition, Vincent Santelmo

2000 Toys & Prices, Sharon Korbeck and Elizabeth Stephan

VALUE LINE

With several exceptions (Irwin made some 1960s vehicles), G.I. Joe figures and accessories are manufactured by Hasbro. Prices listed are for figures and accessories in Mint condition without the box. Having the original box generally increases value by two to three times.

G.I. Joe Figure Sets

Action Marine, 1964 .... $150

Action Pilot, 1964 .... $185

Action Sailor, 1964 .... $235

Action Soldier, 1964 .... $185

Action Soldier, Black, 1965 .... $850

Action Soldiers of the World Series, 1966 .... $250-$850

Australian Jungle Fighter, uniform but no
  equipment $275

Australian Jungle Fighter, deluxe set
  (with all equipment) $425

British Commando, standard set, no equipment $275

British Commando, deluxe set
  (with all equipment) $435

Foreign Soldiers of the World, Talking Adventure
  Pack $825

French Resistance Fighter, standard set $275

French Resistance Fighter, deluxe set $350

German Storm Trooper, standard set $300

German Storm Trooper, deluxe set $400

The "Talking GI Joe," dating from 1973-74, is valued at $125-$250 in Mint condition without the box. Having the original box will increase value to $400-$600.

The 1990s Army Helicopter pilot, a female Joe, is currently valued at $75-$100.

Japanese Imperial Soldier, standard set $500
Japanese Imperial Soldier, deluxe set $695
Russian Infantry Man, standard set............................ $335
Russian Infantry Man, deluxe set............................... $425
Adventures of G.I. Joe Series, 1969 .... $250-$750
Aquanaut.. $550
Negro Adventurer (Sears exclusive) $750
Shark's Surprise Set with Frogman............................ $325
Talking Astronaut... $275
Adventure Team, 1970s .... $75-$375
Air Adventurer, 1976 .... $100
Air Adventurer with Kung Fu grip, 1974 .... $135
Black Adventurer, 1970s.................................. $125-$150
Canadian Mountie Set, (Canadian Sears exclusive),
   1967.. $500
G.I. Nurse, 1967... $2,200
Super Joe figures, 1977 .... $40-$75
Talking Action Marine, 1967 .... $250
Talking Action Pilot, 1967 .... $195
Talking Action Sailor, 1967 .... $375
Talking Action Soldier, 1967 .... $160
3-3/4" Series, 1982-1986 .... $5-$100
   Airborne, Series #2, G.I. Joe, 1983 .... $25
   Big Boa, Series #6, Cobra, 1986 .... $7
   Breaker, Series #1, G.I. Joe, 1982 .... $30
   Lady Jaye (female figure), Series #4,
      G.I. Joe, 1984 .... $15
   Scarlett (female figure), Series #1, G.I. Joe, 1982 ...... $75

G.I. Joe Accessories
   Air/Sea Rescue, Action Pilot Series, 1968.................. $500
   Aqua Locker, Adventures of G.I. Joe, 1969 .... $200
   Beachhead Mess Kit, Action Marine Series, 1964 ..... $225
   Dress Parade Adventure Pack, Action Soldier Series,
      1968.. $950
   Landing Signal Officer, Action Sailor Series,
      1966.. $225
   Military Police Uniform, Action Soldier Series,
      1967 $950
   Search for the Abominable Snowman,
      Adventure Team, 1973 .... $225
   Tactical Battle Platform, 3-3/4" Series #4, G.I. Joe,
      1984.. $30
G.I. Joe Vehicle Sets
Amphibious Duck, Action Soldier Series, 1967........ $450
Amphibious Personnel Carrier, 3-3/4" Series #2,
   G.I. Joe, 1983 .... $30
Armored Car, Action Soldier Series, 1967 .... $335
Dreadnok Cycle, 3-3/4" Series #6, Cobra, 1986.......... $12
Fantastic Sea Wolf Submarine, Adventure Team,
   1975.. $125
Spacewalk Mystery Set without Spaceman,
   Adventures of G.I. Joe, 1969 .... $295
Spacewalk Mystery Set with Spaceman,
   Adventure Team, 1970 .... $325
Super Joe Rocket Command Center $115
U.S.S. Flagg (aircraft carrier), 3-3/4" Series #4,
   G.I. Joe, 1984 .... $125

GOLF COLLECTIBLES

Collecting old golf memorabilia—clubs, balls, tees, etc.—is not a new fad. It was first recognized in the late 1970s with reference materials, and since the mid-1980s thousands of new collectors have entered the hobby. An additional tens of thousands putter around the edges of the field, expressing interest in the long-nose woods, feather balls, art and pottery that tells the story of the evolution of golf.

Background: Approximately 500 years ago golf was played along the eastern coast of Scotland, where the land—called links land—was non-arable and mostly sandy; its primary purpose was for grazing sheep.

Early golfers used long, whippy, shafted wooden headed clubs to propel a leather-jacketed ball filled with goose feathers. The delicate wooden headed clubs, usually made by bow makers—Play Club (Driver), Brassie, Long and Short Spoons—were used to sweep the ball from sheep mown grass lies. The Baffie was used to loft the ball over an obstacle or stream from a grass lie.

As a misplayed stroke would damage the delicate feather ball, few iron head clubs were used. Clubs with deep, broad concave faces were forged by the local blacksmith for playing the ball from the sandy lies and were called Bunker or Sand clubs. A small, rounded, cupped-face club was made to extract the ball from the deep hoof and cart tracks and accordingly called a Rut or Track club. A long shallow blade club with very little loft was used to hit the ball from bare hard ground or to hit a low running shot in windy weather. An Approaching Putter and/or Holing Out Putter, usually made from wood, rounded out the set.

General Guidelines: Many collectors enjoy actually using the vintage golf items in their collections. This makes for a whole different type of collector, interested in the usability of the piece in addition to its condition and display potential. Beyond the world of wood-shaft clubs and gutta-percha balls, collectors look for vintage clothes, shoes and tees; also popular are books, instructional aids and advertisements that will help with the identification of old items, and possibly help with the collector's game. Displayable items like prints, pottery and autographed pieces, either modern or vintage, are currently being sought out by lovers of this popular sport.

Wooden-shaft Golf Clubs—Clubs during the feather-ball era were usually made by carpenters, bow makers, barrel makers, wheelwrights and other craftsmen with woodworking backgrounds. The irons were forged by the local armor maker or blacksmith.

A "play club" was used from the tee; a "brassie" was used to strike long, low shots from the fairway; and the "long spoon" and "mid-spoons" were used to hit moderately long-lofted shots. The "short spoon" (sometimes also called a baffie) was used to hit short-lofted shots around the green or over trouble.

DON'T FALL FOR A FAKE "FEATHERIE!"

Many similarly sized balls are easily mistaken for early feather golf balls. Such products, or even balls that are made to fool collectors, are easily identified with a little knowledge. Authentic feather balls are as hard as a modern golf ball, a characteristic which most fakes do not have. They also have the stitching on the inside, as opposed to many old balls that were not made for golf, which will have the stitching showing. Be wary of any ball offered as a featherie, for chances of finding one are slim—much slimmer than the odds that you will detect a less valuable ball posing as a feather ball.

General Guidelines: Value is based on condition, rarity, availability, competition and desirability. Fewer than five percent of all wood shafted clubs are truly valuable. Metal shafted clubs that have been painted or "wood-grained" to look like wood have no collectible value to the "wood shaft collector." Likewise, a club that has been restored or cleaned, is warped or cracked, has heavy rusting and pitting or bad or missing grips will drop substantially in value.

Tens of millions of low grade clubs were made and sold from 1915 to 1935. Spalding, MacGregor, Burke, Kroydon, Hillerich & Bradsby, Wilson, Wright & Ditson and scores of others made clubs with line, dot, hyphen and other face markings. Most of these are common and only have value as conversation pieces, decorations or for their playability.

Vintage Golf Balls—While golf clubs were generally affordable prior to 1850, only the very wealthy could afford the feather balls of the era. A skilled maker could produce no more than three or four balls a day, which resulted in the very high cost. In the late 1840s, gutta-percha—a rubbery compound commonly used to line wooden shipping boxes containing fragile items—was molded into golf balls. The gutta-percha balls were far less expensive and, as a result, golf became more affordable.

As more people took up the game of golf, the courses, clubs and balls were refined. During the late 1800s, many patents were taken out on all forms of golfing artifacts. One of the most significant was the Haskell patent. Working for Goodyear Rubber Company, Coburn Haskell and Bertram Works developed a process of winding thin rubber strips around a central core, then covered these windings with gutta-percha. The "Haskell" ball was the leading factor in the development and refinement of golf clubs and the game as we know it today.

General Guidelines: As with clubs, pre-1800s balls are scarce. Pre-1860 gutta-percha balls are scarcer than "featheries." Named maker balls of both types are even scarcer. Balls with markings on them from this period are among the rarest. There are also a few balls painted for winter play that are highly sought after. While most are red or orange, there have been blue, yellow and black balls noted.

Many collectors cannot afford top-quality examples of odd-pattern balls, gutta-perchas, brambles and wrapped balls. For those who want to collect balls in top quality, signature balls may be the answer. Signature balls are golf balls that were imprinted, at the time of manufacturing, with a professional's name. At present they are plentiful. Most are priced under $50 and can be acquired in top condition.

Common mesh pattern golf balls—circa 1930 from Worthington, Dunlop or Spalding—in above average condition sell for about $75. An identical ball, but with a cover cut or other damage, will bring only $10 to $15.

Faroid or Park Royal balls are so rare and seldom offered, even damaged examples are highly sought after and bring premium prices.

Tees—The earliest tees were not tees at all, but small mounds of sand formed into cones. Shortly before the turn of the century metal cone-shaped molds, mostly made of brass, were in vogue. Many golf courses provided a "Sand Box" with a pail of water at each tee. The player or his caddy used the mold to shape the wet sand for a tee.

During the 1920s, the wooden tee was introduced, along with some wire, plastic, rubber and zinc tees. Tees have been made of aluminum, paper, plastic, steel, wire, zinc, rubber—anything that would raise the ball from the turf. Shapes and forms were stars, triangles, domes, tethers, spinners, molds and just about anything else imaginable.

In the early 1900s, packaging to promote the merchandising of tees became an industry in itself. Tees were packaged in large and small boxes with very ornate designs. Another packaging concept was cloth tee bags, similar to a tobacco pouch, which held 50 or 100 tees. Paper bags were also used to hold 15 to 25 tees. Most bags were white with the printed advertisement of the golf companies.

General Guidelines: Bags or boxes of tees are less valuable if they are only partially full. Tee packets similar to matchbooks are also collectibles and have been produced since the early 1920s. A large variety of brand-name tees were produced, along with tee-holders and advertisements, which are also collectible.

Autographs—The autograph hobby dates back about 1,000 years, and with the first British Open Championship in 1860, golf began to establish itself as a sport. As a result, autographs of golf's greatest players did not escape interest of collectors. Autographed photographs, trading cards, books, golf balls, letters and other items are highly sought after by collectors.

General Guidelines: Modern signatures should be accompanied by a certificate of authenticity, or purchased from a reputable dealer. Many of today's golfers will provide a signature if it is solicited by mail, or can be visited at shows or tournaments, where a signature can be obtained in person.

Books—Golf books cover many categories including instruction, architecture, history, rules, anthologies and fiction. Some reference books generally acquired for information and pricing are highly collectible as well.

In 1457 Scotland's King James II issued a decree outlawing golf because his soldiers were golfing more than practicing their archery skills. This decree became the first printed reference to the game of golf. It wasn't until the golf boom of the 1890s that books on golf were published in great quantities. The most prominent one of this period was *Golf: The Badminton Library* by Horace Hutchinson (1890).

Richard E. Donovan and Joseph S. F. Murdoch collaborated to publish *The Game of Golf and the Printed Word* (1988) which is a bibliography of golf literature in the English language. This is a highly regarded and collectible reference book.

General Guidelines: Prices of books are determined by condition, edition, scarcity and desirability. First printings of first editions command higher prices than later printings.

Books in poor condition (missing pages, broken cover or contents damaged, badly soiled or stained) or library books are generally useful for information only. Underlining, margin notes, repair or rebinding all reduce the value of a book.

This Spalding "diamond-cover" golf ball is typical of the type used in the 1920s and 1930s.

Miscellaneous Golf Collectibles—The wealthy golfer from 1875 to 1930 spared no expense when it came to displaying the game he loved. Collectibles came in the form of trophies, tees, medals, dining utensils, jewelry, smoking paraphernalia, whiskey flasks, music boxes, watches, ink wells and more.

Trophies were made of gold and silver. There were sterling silver toast racks, teapots, knives, forks, and especially spoons with golf motifs, as well as any other dining table items. Whiskey flasks were also made of sterling silver. The businessman had in his den or on his office desk golf-affiliated paperweights, ink wells, pens, clocks, humidors, ashtrays, letter openers and scores of other knickknacks.

Smoking had not yet been demonized and pipe, cigar, and cigarette cases, match safes, humidors, ashtrays and other tobacco related items were made of gold, silver and bronze.

An extensive amount of pottery was made with a golf theme, from some of the most well-known makers—Royal Doulton, Lenox, Copeland, Wedgewood, Kingsware, etc. While earlier pieces were hand-painted, the later pieces contain printed decorations and were produced in larger quantities.

Most glass golf items were produced in England and the United States. A popular glass design involves a sterling silver golfer overlay that was attached to a glass bottle, goblet or pitcher. It is seen in many sizes, as are etched and engraved items.

Contributor to this section: Chuck Furjanic

Clubs
• Golf Collectors Society, P.O. Box 20546, Dayton, OH 45420

• British Golf Collectors Society, Box 13704, North Berwick, West Lothian, EH39 4ZB, Scotland, U.K.

Recommended Reading
Antique Golf Collectibles, 2nd Edition, Chuck Furjanic

VALUE LINE

Prices are for items in Excellent condition.

Clubs
Aluminum head woods, Braddell, Belfast, Ireland, 1890s, leather face insert $650
Beech head, many have leather face inserts $2,250
Diamond back irons, 1910-1915, "Rampant Lion" mark at the toe $70
Gold Medal series putter, 1906-1908, brass blade "Spalding Gold Medal" $65
Gutta-percha face iron, Nicoll, patented 1892, "G. Nicoll, Leven Fife" $2,500
Holing out putter, blacksmith-made, circa 1850, thick long hosel $3,000

Large head brassie, Spalding, 1915, marked "A.G. Spalding Bros." $100
Long-nose putter, 1890s, spliced neck, beech head stamped "D. Anderson" $1,000
Long-nose woods, McEwan, Musselburgh, 1870s, play club or brassie, long head, large lead back weight. "McEwan" mark $2,750
Long-nose woods, Philp, Hugh, St. Andrews, 1850s, "H Philp" in block letters, thorn head ... $10,000
Pretty face woods, various makers, circa 1920s, various pretty face inserts $125
Rake irons, Winton, W & Co., Ltd., circa 1905, The Major, seven pointed tines $6,000
Rut iron, blacksmith-made, 1840-1860, small cupped face, long thick hosel with heavy nicking $3,500
Smooth-face putting cleek, Spalding, circa 1905, "Made in Great Britain" $60
Spalding series putter, 1898-1902, deep smooth-face s teel-blade putter $225
Ted Ray signature irons, circa 1925-1930, each $50
Wry-neck putter, Spalding, circa 1920-25, hyphen-scored, offset hosel, "thistle" marks $65

VINTAGE CLUBS— SEPARATING THE TRASH FROM THE TREASURE!

Not every vintage club is valuable. Here are some tipoffs that a vintage club is common and has little collector value:

No manufacturer's name, or a name like: Biltmore, Hollywood, Thistle, Bonnie, Metropolitan, Columbia, Ace, Majestic

• Metal caps at the end of the grip
• Yardage ranges stamped on the back (for example, "145-155 yds")
• Chromed, chromium or stainless steel heads
• Numbered irons from sets, or "matched set" irons
• Iron faces scored with dots, hyphens or lines
• On the other hand, here some characteristics of an uncommon vintage club that may be valuable:
• Irons with no face markings, or unusual face markings
• Irons or putters with unusual head shapes; wood head putters
• Woods with a thick, curved, oval neck covered with four or five inches of string "whipping"
• Smooth face irons with the following names: Anderson, Park, Army & Navy, Ayres, Carrick, Forgan, Gray and Morris
• Certain Spalding, MacGregor, Condie, Nicoll, Stewart, Gibson and Wright & Ditson clubs with smooth faces

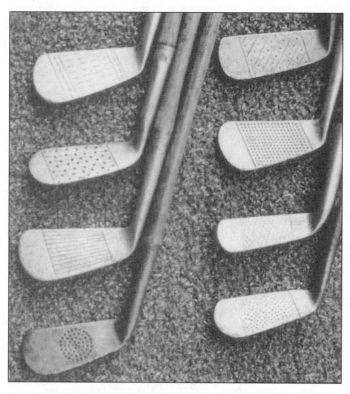

Vintage golf clubs are sometimes identified by the markings on the faces of the irons. Some are less common, like the "ball dot" pattern found on 1915-circa Spalding irons, and the "crisscross" pattern and the "crisscross with dots" pattern typically found on pre-World War I British irons.

Golf Balls

Bramble, rubber core, Goodrich, B F, 1899-1905, "Haskell" and "Pat. Apr. 1, 1899" at poles $325

Bramble, rubber core, Goodrich, B F, 1910, "Haskell Royal" with celluloid cover................................. $800

Bramble, rubber core, Goodyear Rubber Co., 1905, "The Pneumatic" at equator $600

Bramble, rubber core, Goodyear Rubber Co., 1905, "The Pneumatic" at poles........................... $1,250

Bramble, rubber core, various makers, 1905-1920, celluloid or rubber cover $275

Bramble, rubber core, various makers, 1900, gutta-percha cover $325

Bramble, rubber core, Haskell, 1900, "Haskell Bramble" at one pole, "Pat Apr. 11, 99" at other pole............ $500

Diamond cover, Spalding USA, 1920-1930, entire cover with diamonds. "Spalding" at poles $150

Dimple cover, Spalding USA, 1908-1920, Baby Dimple, Domino, Dot, Glory Dimple, and others............... $125

Dimple cover, Spalding USA, 1920-1940, "P.G.A.".... $30

Feather ball, no maker's name, 1840-1860............. $5,000

Feather ball, Gourlay, John Musselburgh, 1840-1860, "J Gourlay" and size number................................. $9,000

Feather ball, Morris, Tom, St. Andrews, 1840-1860, "T Morris" and size number................................. $15,000

Gutta-percha, smooth, no maker's name, 1850-1860, white, brown or black usually with a "test" mark $3,000

Gutta-percha, hand-hammered, no maker's name, 1850-1880 .... $2,000

Gutta-percha, hand-hammered, Forgan, Robert, St. Andrews, 1865-1880, stamped "R Forgan," usually with size number $2,500

Gutta-percha, line cut, remade, no name, 1880-1905 .... $300

Gutta-percha, line cut, various makers, 1880-1905 .... $500

Gutta-percha, bramble, various makers, 1895-1905 .... $450

Gutta-percha, bramble, Spalding, Vardon Flyer, circa 1900, "Vardon Flyer" at both poles....................... $950

Line cut rubber core, Goodrich, B F, Akron, Ohio, 1902, "Haskell" and "Pat. Apr. 1, 1899" in rectangular panels, gutta-percha cover............... $3,500

Mesh cover, various makers, 1910-1940, square markings $75

Warwick, Dunlop, Birmingham, Eng., 1925-1935, alternating rows of square and dimple markings... $175

Tees

Prices shown are for full boxes or bags, unless otherwise noted.

All-My-Tee, various makers, 1930, circular Handi-Pack of nine tees... $75

Bobby Tees, various makers, late 1920s, red wooden goblet-style tees.. $60

Cruickshank steel tees, various makers, 1930, red wire tees with circular top $90

Just Perfect tees, various makers, early 1930s, 18 wooden tees in pale green box $60

K-D sand tee mold, K-D Mfg., Lancaster, PA, 1920s, polished aluminum with spring plunger..................... $475

Keystone sand tee mold, 1920-1930, bakelite plastic with spring plunger $350

No-Looz-Tee, various makers, 1950s-1960s, weighted end, made of rubber $60

Novel-tees, Spurgin Mfg., Chicago, late 1920s, book of 18 paper tees.. $75

Perfect Golf Tee, patented 1927, molded rubber tee secured in the ground by a nail $100

Rex zinc tees, The Rex Co., Chicago, 1930, red box, zinc tees $100

Rite Pencil Tee, WIMO Specialty Co Inc., 1927, long tee with pencil lead at tip, single tee............................. $10

Rubber Manhattan tee, 1920, five-inch-long rubber tee with round weight at one end, tee at other $100

Sand tee mold, 1890-1920, brass with spring plunger $650

Tether tees, various makers, 1900-1930s, "tether" between weith or colorful thistle and the tee.......................... $75

The Reddy Tee, Nieblo Mfg. Co., 1930, wooden tees in green, white and red box $70

The Scot-tee, late 1920s, box of 18 wood tees $100

Tees in bags, various makers, 1930s-40s, draw string bags of fifty and one hundred wooden tees $50

Top Not Tee, various makers, late 1920s, made of both wood and steel, orange and white $60

Autographed Items

Harry Vardon signed photo, 1910-1920...................... $650

Tom Morris signed photo, 1900.............................. $1,500

Ben Hogan signed photo, 1960-1980.......................... $300

Ben Hogan signed photo, 1940-1950.......................... $450

Robert T. Jones, Jr. signed photo, 1955-1970, shaky ballpoint pen signature................................ $650

Robert T. Jones, Jr. signed photo, 1930-1950, black fountain pen signature $2,250

Arnold Palmer signed photo, 1975 .... $40

Byron Nelson signed photo, 1960-1990s...................... $40

Byron Nelson signed photo, 1935-1950, fountain pen, vintage signature $100

Gene Sarazen signed photo, 1960s-1980s $40

Gene Sarazen signed photo, 1925-1950, fountain pen, vintage signature $90

Jack Nicklaus signed photo, 1980................................ $75

Books

Golf Course Mystery by C.K. Steel, 1919 .... $125

History of Golf in Britain by Bernard Darwin, 1952.. $300

Golf; Badminton Library by Horace Hutchinson, 1890.. $325

Scotland's Gift; Golf by C. B. MacDonald, 1928 (reprints $35).. $700

This Game of Golf by Henry Cotton, 1948 .... $60

The Bobby Jones Story by G. Rice and O.B. Keeler, 1953.. $65

Life of Tom Morris by W.W. Tulloch, 1908 .... $1,200

Power Golf by Ben Hogan, 1948 .... $30

Walter Hagen Story by Hagen and M. Heck, 1956.. $125

Encyclopedia of Golf by Steel, Ryde and Wind, 1975.. $35

Golf in the Making by Henderson and Stirk, 1979.. $150

Miscellaneous Collectibles

Ashtray, H. Hoffman, 1920s, glass, intaglio cut $300

Cigarette case, sterling, 1900-1920, golfing scene on cover $575

Golf tees in their original bags or boxes are very popular with collectors.

Creamer, Doulton, early 1900s, Lambeth, England, Uncle Toby series.. $900

Creamer, Royal Doulton, 1930s, Bunnykins $600

Creamer, Wedgewood (England), early 1900s, golfers in white relief.. $650

Crystal decanter, Waterford, 1920, sterling silver hallmarked neck, hand painted golfing scene $2,000

Cuff links, gold golf balls, Dunlop, New York, 1920, nickel size 10k gold mesh $175

Etched glasses, Heissey, circa 1920s, etched golfers $650

Figurine, porcelain, Lladro, 1900s............................. $500

Jardiniere, stoneware, Copeland Spode, 1900, golfers in relief, white on blue or green background $650

Match safe, sterling, Unger, Newark, N.J., 1900-1910, caddy with bag $650

Plate, "The Nineteenth Hole," Royal Doulton, porcelain.. $600

Silver plate ink well, Birmingham, England, 1900, two golf ball inkwells.. $500

Sterling silver spoons, 1900-1920s, golfers on handle $80

Stoneware ewer, Copeland Spode, 1900, golfers in relief, white on green or blue background $1,000

Stoneware pitcher, Copeland Spode, 1900, golfers in relief, white on green or blue background $900

Tankard, silver-rimmed, Lenox, 1905, golfers on green background.. $1,500

Whiskey flask, sterling, Kerr & Co., 1920s, pint size, knickered golfers on front $800

VINTAGE GUITARS

The romance of the guitar is the romance of popular music. Guitars represent a unique, admirable craftsmanship, which at its best approaches Stradivari and the great violin makers of Cremora. The feminine curves and cutaways of classic Gibsons and Fenders, mixed with memories of Elvis, The Beatles, Eric Clapton and Stevie Ray Vaughn with their "axes," has moved the collectibility of these instruments beyond the world of music into that of popular culture.

Background: The vintage electric guitar market began gathering steam in the late 1960s, when musicians realized the instruments of the 1950s and early '60s were superior in playability and tone. Highly sought were Gibson electrics made between 1948 and 1965 (known now as the McCarty-era, a reference to Gibson President Ted McCarty), and Fender instruments made between 1950 and 1965 (known as pre-CBS). In the mid-1960s, McCarty resigned and Fender was bought by the Columbia Broadcasting Co.

It took a while for non-musician collectors to become interested in guitars. When they did, it was a change that increased demand, and value, within this field.

Guidelines: A recognizable maker's name adds value to a guitar. Likewise, age and model are conditions that affect value. Current prices for Gibson McCarty-era and Fender pre-CBS guitars average about $4,500. Mid- to high-end Fenders include the Stratocaster, Telecaster, Esquire, Jazzmaster and Jaguar. Mustangs are less collectible, and bring about $500.

Classic mid- to high-end Gibsons include the Les Paul Standard, Les Paul Junior, Les Paul Custom, SG, Firebird and Flying V.

Other high-end brands include Guild, Gretsch, Martin, Epiphone, National and Rickenbacker. Lower-end brands like Kay, Silvertone, Magnatone, Maybell and Framus sell for $500 or less.

Guitars left in their original condition garner higher prices, taking into consideration the popularity of the brand name. A guitar that has been restored or refinished loses a significant amount of its value—up to 50 percent. Signs that a piece has been restored, repaired or modified are: oversprayed finish; replacement string tuner pegs, volume and tone knobs and switches, pickups, bridge, strap pegs, truss-rod covers and other hardware; and replacement or counterfeit decals.

Any guitar that can be proven to have celebrity ties will be worth a premium, based on the personality's popularity and level of recognition. In 1999, a record was set for the sale of a guitar when Eric Clapton's "Brownie" sold at a Christie's auction in New York. The 1956 sunburst Fender Stratocaster brought the love song "Layla" to life, and was reportedly one of Eric Clapton's favorites. The selling price? $497,500.

Club/Magazine
• Vintage Guitar, PO Box 7301, Bismarck, ND 58507

Celebrity-signed guitars are an increasingly popular collecting category. This group, sold in a recent Christie's auction in New York, includes (from left to right) a Samick guitar signed by members of U2, a Gibson autographed by B.B. King, and a Samick guitar signed by the Eagles. Estimates ranged from $1,000 to $3,000 each.

LEARN THE LINGO!

Here are some of the terms used by guitar players and collectors:

Hollow-body: A guitar body with glued-up back, sides and top, constructed so as to create an acoustic response, or an instrument with such a body. Hollow-body instruments can be electric or acoustic. They are said to be "thin-body" if they are less than three inches deep.

Solid-body: A guitar made of a solid block of wood, or an instrument with such a body. All solid-body instruments are electric.

Natural finish: The grain and color shows through on the top, back and sides of the guitar.

Sunburst finish: Dark around the edges that gradually lightens to a golden-blond in the center. Can be two-color (brown and blond) or three-color (brown, red and blond).

VALUE LINE

Values shown are for guitars in Excellent condition.

Epiphone

Broadway	$850
EM-1	$200
EM-2	$250
Emperor	$350
Emperor Regent	$500
G-310	$150
G-400	$200
Les Paul Custom	$300
Les Paul Standard	$250
S-310	$100
USA Coronet	$350
USA Pro	$300

Fender

Esquire Custom	$3,200
Esquire Custom, 1965-70	$1,500
Jaguar	$650-$800
Jaguar, 1970-75	$500
Jazzmaster	$1,000-$1,500
Jazzmaster, 1970-1980	$500
Stratocaster	$7,000-$10,000
Stratocaster, 1963-64	$6,000
Stratocaster, 1965-66	$4,500
Telecaster, pre-CBS	$3,000-$6,000
Telecaster, CBS	$350-$900

Gibson

Firebird I	$2,500
Firebird III	$3,000
Firebird V	$4,000
Firebird V, reissue	$1,000
Firebird VII	$8,000
Firebird '76	$600
Les Paul Standard, 1868	$1,500
Les Paul Standard, 1969-1971	$1,000
Les Paul Junior, 1954-63	$1,000
Les Paul Custom, 1958-60	$7,000

Gretsch

Astro-Jet	$950
Atkins Axe	$950
Atkins Super Axe	$1,000
Blackhawk	$1,000
Chet Atkins Country Gentleman	$1,000-$3,000
Chet Atkins Hollow Body/Nashville	$1,000-$3,000
Chet Atkins Tennessean, 1962-68	$850-$1,000
Super Chet	$2,000

Martin

D-28E	$1,500
E-18	$300
EM-18	$400
E-28	$600
F-50	$600
F-55	$700
F-65	$500
GT-70	$700
GT-75	$750
GT-75-12	$550

This arch-top guitar, made by the Vega Company of Boston in the 1930s, was offered in a Skinner auction in Boston with a pre-sale estimate of $600-$800.

This 1960 Gibson guitar was sold in a recent Skinner auction in Boston. It carried a $3,000-$5,000 estimate.

HALLMARK ORNAMENTS

Hallmark keepsake ornaments have become a mainstay among collectors, surpassing all other ornament lines in popularity and every-day recognition. Loved for their fun and whimsical nature, Hallmark ornaments speak to their parent company's famous slogan, "When you care enough to send the very best." Today more than 11 million households actively collect them. But due to the wide array of subjects portrayed, even those who don't collect or don't celebrate Christmas usually own a figural Hallmark ornament or two.

Background: Since 1973 Hallmark Cards Inc. has introduced more than 100 series of ornaments that touch every holiday and occasion. The first year 18 pieces were introduced, and they were quite a departure from the colored glass balls that had dominated up until that time. Even with some of its earliest pieces the company beckoned collectors by limiting availability and dating the ornaments.

Hallmark's first collectible series featured designs by Betsey Clark on ball ornaments. The "Betsey Clark" series ran until 1985, when it was retired. In 1976 Hallmark introduced the first "Baby's First Christmas" ornament, which was an instant best-seller and introduced a new tradition to many families.

Hallmark's first collectible series was the Betsey Clark series that ran from 1973 to 1985. The 1976 ornament is valued at about $80

The popular Frosty Friends series debuted in 1980 and continues today. Another big hit, the Rocking Horse series ran from 1981-1996.

Hallmark introduced the Keepsake Ornament Collectors Club in 1987, and wooed collectors by giving members the opportunity to purchase exclusive ornaments.

General Guidelines: Ornaments with their original boxes command the highest prices.

Most Hallmark ornaments have a limited availability of one season, after which time they must be sought out on the secondary market. This, however, is a very loose limit. Many of the more contemporary Hallmark ornaments can be found in abundance on the secondary market, often at or close to retail prices.

Older ornaments and club pieces are more difficult to find and must be obtained at higher prices.

The earliest pieces in Hallmark's most popular collectible series will usually be the most valuable. Some of the most popular series: Here Comes Santa, Carrousel, Frosty Friends, Betsey Clark, Rocking Horse and the Bellringer series.

Some of the most popular pieces today commemorate famous athletes, movie stars and pop culture icons. The earlier Star Wars and Star Trek pieces, produced in the early 1990s, are extremely collectible and command decent prices.

Clubs/Publications

- The Ornament Trader Magazine, PO Box 469, Lavonia, GA 30553-0469

- Collectible Exchange, 6621 Columbiana Rd., New Middletown, OH 44442

- Collectors Mart Magazine, Krause Publications, 700 East State St., Iola, WI 54990

VALUE LINE

Baby's First Christmas
1978	$70
1979 (800QX154-7)	$165
1979 (350QX208-7)	$25

Betsey Clark
1973, first edition	$120
1974, second edition	$70
1975, third edition	$30
1976, fourth edition	$80
1977, fifth edition	$440
1978, sixth edition	$50
1979, seventh edition	$30

1980, eighth edition $30
1981, ninth edition $25
1982, tenth edition $25
1983, eleventh edition $25
1984, twelfth edition $25
1985, thirteenth edition $25

Carrousel Series
1978, first edition $400
1979, second edition $150
1980, third edition $150
1981, fourth edition $75
1982, fifth edition $85
1983, sixth edition $40

Cinnamon Bear
1983, first edition $75
1984, second edition $33
1985, third edition $50
1986, fourth edition $45
1987, fifth edition $25
1988, sixth edition $30
1989, seventh edition $20
1990, eighth edition $20

Collector's Club Pieces
1987, Carrousel Reindeer $60
1987, Wreath of Memories $50
1988, Angelic Minstrel $30
1988, Christmas is Sharing $30
1988, Hold on Tight $75
1988, Holiday Heirloom, 2nd Edition $25
1988, Our Clubhouse $40
1988, Sleighful of Dreams $53
1989, Christmas is Peaceful $30
1989, Collect a Dream $32
1989, Holiday Heirloom, 3rd Edition $25
1989, Noelle $30
1989, Sitting Purrty $45
1989, Visit from Santa $30
1990, Armful of Joy $35
1990, Christmas Limited $92
1990, Club Hollow $30
1990, Crown Prince $40
1990, Sugar Plum Fairy $50
1991, Beary Artistic $35
1991, Five Years Together $40
1991, Galloping Into Christmas $60
1991, Hidden Treasure/Li'l Keeper $35
1991, Secrets for Santa $60
1992, Christmas Treasures $125
1992, Rodney Takes Flight $20
1993, Forty Winks $18
1993, Gentle Tidings $40
1993, Sharing Christmas $30
1994, Holiday Pursuit $19
1994, Jolly Holly Santa $40
1994, On Cloud Nine $15

1994, Sweet Bouquet $15
1995, 1958 Ford Edsel Citation Convertible $50
1995, Barbie: Brunette Debut $35
1995, Collecting Memories $20
1995, Home from the Woods $25
1996, Airmail for Santa $15
1996, Rudolph the Red-Nosed Reindeer $25
1996, Rudolph's Helper $15
1996, Wizard of Ox $50
1992, Chipmunk Parcel Service $22
1992, Santa's Club List $30
1993, It's in the Mail $20
1995, Fishing for Fun $20
1993, Trimmed with Memories $20
1992, Victorian Skater $120
1994, Majestic Deer $30

Frosty Friends
1980, A Cool Yule $650
1981, Eskimo and Husky $400
1982, Icicle $275
1983, Eskimo and Seal on Ice $255
1984, Ice Fishing $70
1985, Arctic Pals/kayak $60
1986, Eskimo and Reindeer $57
1987, Eskimo and Seal $50
1988, Eskimo and Polar Bear $50
1989, Sled $40
1990, Iceberg $30
1991, Ice Hockey $30
1992, Whale $30
1993, Igloo Doghouse $30
1994, Bear and Wreath $25
1995, Eskimo with Polar Bear $20
1996, Seventeenth edition $20
1997, Windsurf Skiing $11

Handcrafted Ornaments
1978, Angel $80
1978, Angels $350
1978, Animal Home $150
1978, Calico Mouse $175
1978, Dove $80

FIRST THINGS FIRST!

Within each series of Hallmark ornaments, the first ornament released most always commands the highest prices, as people start collecting late and seek out the older pieces. Here are some of the most valuable firsts:

Antique Toys, 1978, Carrousel series $400
Santa's Motorcar, 1979, Here Comes Santa series $650
A Cool Yule, 1980, Frosty Friends series $650
Rocking Horse, 1981, Rocking Horse series $600
Cardinals, 1982, Holiday Wildlife series $400
Tin Locomotive, 1982, Tin Locomotive series $650

1978, Joy	$75	1982, Elfin Artist	$50
1978, Holly and Poinsettia Ball	$80	1982, Embroidered Tree	$35
1978, Panorama Ball	$130	1982, Jogging Santa	$45
1978, Red Cardinal	$160	1982, Jolly Christmas Tree	$80
1978, Schneeberg Bell	$180	1982, Peeking Elf	$20
1978, Skating Raccoon	$85	1982, Pinecone Home	$140
1979, A Christmas Treat	$65	1982, Raccoon Surprises	$142
1979, Christmas Eve Surprise	$55	1982, Santa Bell	$50
1979, Christmas Heart	$90	1982, Santa's Workshop	$65
1979, Christmas is For Children	$80	1982, Spirit of Christmas, The	$120
1979, Downhill Run, The	$150	1982, Tin Soldier	$45
1979, Drummer Boy, The	$110	1983, Baroque Angels	$115
1979, Holiday Scrimshaw	$200	1983, Christmas Kitten	$30
1979, Outdoor Fun	$115	1983, Cycling Santa	$120
1979, Ready for Christmas	$130	1983, Embroidered Heart	$20
1979, Santa's Here	$60	1983, Holiday Puppy	$30
1979, Skating Raccoon	$85	1983, Jack Frost	$50
1979, Skating Snowman	$70	1983, Jolly Santa	$27
1980, A Christmas Treat	$65	1983, Madonna and Child	$35
1980, A Christmas Vigil	$100	1983, Mailbox Kitten	$50
1980, A Heavenly Nap	$50	1983, Mouse in Bell	$60
1980, A Spot of Christmas Cheer	$130	1983, Peppermint Penguin	$37
1980, Animal's Christmas, The	$55	1983, Porcelain Doll – Diana	$32
1980, Caroling Bear	$125	1983, Rainbow Angel	$100
1980, Christmas is For Children	$80	1983, Santa's Many Faces	$27
1980, Drummer Boy	$85	1983, Santa's On His Way	$27
1980, Elfin Antics	$190	1983, Santa's Workshop	$80
1980, Heavenly Sounds	$80	1983, Skating Rabbit	$45
1980, Santa	$87	1983, Ski Lift Santa	$60
1980, Santa's Flight	$110	1983, Skiing Fox	$40
1980, Skating Snowman	$70	1983, Unicorn	$60

Holiday Barbie Collection

1980, Snowflake Swing, The	$40	1993, first edition	$125
1981, A Heavenly Nap	$50	1994, second edition	$45
1981, A Well-Stocked Stocking	$75	1995, third edition	$35
1981, Candyville Express	$100	1996, fourth edition	$30
1981, Checking it Twice	$180	1997, fifth edition	$15
1981, Christmas Dreams	$210		
1981, Christmas Fantasy	$75		
1981, Dough Angel	$90		
1981, Drummer Boy	$40		
1981, Friendly Fiddler	$70		
1981, Ice Fairy	$70		
1981, Ice Sculptor	$75		
1981, Love and Joy	$90		
1981, Mr. and Mrs. Claus set	$120		
1981, Sailing Santa	$250		
1981, Space Santa	$100		
1981, St. Nicholas	$45		
1981, Star Swing	$30		
1981, Topsy-Turvy Tunes	$72		
1982, Baroque Angel	$150		
1982, Christmas Fantasy	$75		
1982, Cloisonne Angels	$90		
1982, Cowboy Snowman	$45		
1982, Cycling Santa	$120		

Released in 1991, the "Starship Enterprise" ornament celebrated the 25th anniversary of "Star Trek" and was the first Hallmark Keepsake Ornament that did not have a traditional Christmas theme or image. It has a current value of about $375

The first ornament in the "Here Comes Santa" series is the 1979 "Santa's Motorcar," worth about $650.

The first ornament in the "Rocking Horse" series, introduced in 1981, is valued at about $600.

Mary's Angels

1988, Buttercup	$95
1989, Bluebell	$110
1990, Rosebud	$50
1991, Iris	$35
1992, Lily	$55
1993, Ivy	$20
1994, Jasmine	$15
1995, Camellia	$20
1996, Violet	$7
1997, Daisy	$8

Norman Rockwell

1980, Santa's Visitors	$200
1983, Dress Rehearsal	$30
1984, Caught Napping	$27
1985, Postman & Kids	$21
1986, Checking Up	$18
1987, Christmas Dance	$15
1988, And to All a Good Night	$16
1988, Christmas Scenes	$16
1993, Filling the Stockings	$35
1993, Jolly Postman	$35
1996, Little Spooners	$13

Snoopy & Friends

1979, first edition	$120
1980, second edition	$100
1981, third edition	$80
1982, fourth edition	$105
1983, fifth edition	$75

Star Trek

1991, Starship Enterprise	$375
1994, Klingon Bird of Prey	$31
1995, Captain James T. Kirk	$31
1995, Captain Jean-Luc Picard	$27
1995, Romulan Warbird	$35
1996, Mr. Spock	$15
1996, Star Trek 30 Years	$45
1996, U.S.S. Voyager	$35
1996, U.S.S. Enterprise	$45

Star Wars

1996, Millennium Falcon	$55
1996, Vehicles of Star Wars, set of three	$40
1997, C-3PO & R2-D2	$13
1997, Darth Vader	$25
1997, Luke Skywalker	$20
1998, Star Wars Lunch Box	$13

HALLOWEEN COLLECTIBLES

Here are a few tips to sink your fangs into regarding collectibles from that time of the year when things go bump in the dark of the night.

Halloween is second only to Christmas as the holiday generating the most collectibles. In fact, Americans spend more than $2 billion annually on Halloween decorations. But, unlike Christmas decorations, most vintage Halloween pieces were tossed out after the holiday, making good pieces scarce today.

Collectors seek almost anything associated with the bewitching October 31, the more unusual, the more desirable. Ghosts, skeletons, witches, bats, black cats, owls and jack-o-lanterns are some of the most visible images related to this spooky holiday.

Background and Guidelines: Halloween became popular in the United States in the late 1800s. Postcards, decorations and invitations are among the earliest Halloween collectibles. Postcards, some dating to the early 1900s, are the most popular. Vintage, elaborate postcards can command $50 or more, but nice examples start for as little as $5. You'll find many vintage examples in the $10-$20 range.

Decorations were generally crafted from natural items such as pumpkins and corn stalks, or homemade prior to 1910, when the Dennison Paper Co. set the pace for creating commercial products specifically for this annual celebration. Dennison began producing its annual "Bogie Book" (in itself a collectible) listing its products, Halloween recipes, stories, party ideas and decorating hints.

Dennison and others also began printing Halloween invitations, quite popular in the 1920s and '30s. Vintage pieces, which make nice displays, can bring $10-$20, especially the colorful ones with terrific graphics.

Because of their colorful display potential, 20th-century items generating high interest also include tin noisemakers, jack-o-lanterns, boxed costumes, trick-or-treat bags and intricate crepe paper decorations.

Crêpe paper decorations, dating back to the 1920s, along with those using pressed paperboard, or die-cut and embossed cardboard, are quite scarce. Decorations from the 1930s-50s are highly collectible, too, but don't sell for as much as their earlier counterparts ($25-$50 vs. $50-$75). More recent decorations are even cheaper. Depending on condition and age, vintage party plates, napkins, place cards and table favors will bring between $5-$25.

Trick-or-Treat bags, although they first appeared in the 1930s, were not commonly used until after the war years. These bags, specifically made for toting candy, were made of paper or cloth. Quite often during the 1950s and '60s, bags were given away as promotional tools for stores and businesses. It was only in the 1980s that bags began appearing for sale on store shelves. Vintage bags from the 1940s-60s are what collectors seek today, in part because they are scarce; kids threw the bags out after Halloween. Today, nice examples command $25 or more.

Thus, the general guidelines suggest that anything Halloween related is collectible, with pre-1960s items the most valuable. Victorian paper items from the 1890s sell for $10-$30 each, but some rarer or more elaborate examples command $50-$150.

Boxed costumes were manufactured as early as 1910, by Dennison. Companies such as Halco, Ben Cooper and Collegeville joined the mix in the 1930s-40s with their inexpensive silk-screened fabric costumes. 1960s-70s character costumes by Ben Cooper and Collegeville, such as Batman and Disney characters, are most popular with collectors. But more generic 1940s-60s examples, such as clowns, witches, spacemen, and skeletons, remain popular. Prices vary widely, depending on condition, age and other factors; a vintage costume can range from $10-$100. Masks, and hats, from all eras are also highly collectible.

The jack-o-lantern, which has its origins from a legend about a miserly man name Jack, whose ghost was forced to wander the countryside until judgment day carrying a lantern made from a turnip, remains the most popular symbol and collectible for Halloween. Early jack-o-lanterns from the turn of the century were glass candy containers that could be used as lanterns. The evolution of paper jack-o-lanterns included composition or pressed paper items in the 1910s (worth up to $1,000 if it's an unusual piece in perfect shape) to pressed and formed paperboard by the 1920s.

Some dealers specialize in buying and selling Halloween collectibles. This booth filled with spooky and scary stuff was located at a recent Atlantique City show in Atlantic City, N.J.

Halloween postcards are plentiful and, for the most part, relatively cheap.

Papier-mâché was used beginning in the 1930s; it evolved into lighter and lighter egg carton-like material up until the 1950s (a simple piece can bring $50), when plastic appeared. At this time, a safer light bulb and battery, also more convenient, replaced the customary candle in jack-o-lanterns. The trend today is toward the more unusual pieces, such as those shaped like heads of cats, devils, monkeys, clowns, dogs and elephants. But nice examples featuring traditional faces from the 1930s-40s can sell for $75-$150.

Candy containers, among the most difficult to find of all Halloween collectibles (due in part because candy container collectors were after them first), are highly desirable, especially the earliest character or figural containers. These early glass pieces, in shapes of pumpkins or witches, later included the likes of pumpkin men, cats, vegetable people and other creepy, scary creatures. There are a variety of types, some more detailed than others, some made for more than one year. But the pieces that command premium values are those with mechanical aspects or the addition of glass eyes or noses. Unlike paper collectibles, however, most of these containers were stowed away until the next year.

Containers evolved from the early composition pieces (made by German manufacturers beginning in 1912) to pressed paperboard (formed in a mold, pressed and heated to make rounded surfaces) containers during the 1920s until the 1950s, also mainly made in Germany. These two types, using various production methods, are most actively sought by collectors today. Dennison also created less expensive crêpe-paper-covered containers in the 1910s-20s, when Japan also started making molded cardboard and papier-mâché variations. Recently collectors, thinking the German containers are too expensive, have turned to these versions, modeled after the German style. However, as they evolved, the Japanese styles have surpassed the German containers in quality. Hence, collectors have also turned from these containers to the hard plastic models.

Tin noisemakers, featuring jack-o-lanterns, black cats and witches, can sell for $5-$20 for small generic pieces, up to $100 for older, more elaborate examples of these items, which made a racket when banged, twirled or blown.

Among the Halloween games which exist are those devoted to fortune telling, such as fortune cards, spinners, and punch boards (which all revealed your future) and stunt boards (which commanded you to perform a stunt a before the other partygoers.)

Two of the more popular toys not devoted to fortune telling include "Cat and Witch," similar to pin the tale on the donkey, and the "Plano Magic Stick," a pinwheel-like toy which, if one practices the magic trick, will reverse itself.

Additional Halloween collectibles are dolls and snow domes, which are fairly new to the hobby, along with Halloween-related advertising pieces, jewelry and magazines.

VALUE LINE

Prices listed are for items in Excellent condition

Boxed costumes, generic, with mask,
1940s-50..$40-$70

Candy containers, figural, composition,
1920s ....$150-$400

Candy container, black cat head, pressed cardboard,
cutout eyes and mouth, wire handle, Germany $75

Candy container, pumpkin, glass, painted, scary face,
wire handle...$125

Crepe paper rolls, early 1900s ....$50-$75

Fan foldout, wooden stick, tissue paper, witch riding
broom, 1920s, Germany......................................$30

Figure, black cat, cardboard, flat, movable legs and tail,
Beistle..$20

Ghost, 10", cardboard standup......................................$15

Green Hornet costume, Ben Cooper, 1960s................$150

Howdy Doody costume, Collegeville, 1950s................$85

Horn, 8", paper, orange and black, wood mouthpiece,
Germany..$10

Jack-o-lantern, papier-mache, 1940s $50

Lanterns, figural, paperboard, 1920s..................$150-$500

Lantern, pumpkin, 4", papier-mache, wire handle,
candleholder in base, Germany $75

Lantern, 6", glass and metal, battery operated,
Hong Kong, 1960s...$40

Magazine cover, "The Farmer's Wife," 1925,
costumed boy holding pumpkin on pole $20

Mask, devil, rubber, red, black and white,
rubber ties...$15

Mask, man, wire mesh, painted feature, cloth ties........ $75

Noisemakers, tin, 1920s...$25-$45

Noisemakers, tin, clickers ....$10-$25

Noisemaker, wood with papier-mâché witch,
Germany..$250

Paper decorations, 1920s ....$50-$75

Paper decorations, 1930s-50s...............................$25-$50

Paper decorations, modern...................................$3-$10

Party napkins, package 1930s $35

PEZ dispenser, jack-o-lantern, skull or witch............$1-$3

Postcards, 1908-1914, Tuck, each ....$15-$20

Postcard, "The Magic Halloween," Winsch Schumacker
illustration, pumpkins looking down at woman draped
in sheet ....$100-$125

This "Whirl-O Halloween Fortune and Stunt Game" card is valued at about $35-$50. Party guests had to spin the spinner to find out what embarrassing stunt they had to perform.

Postcard, "A Joyous Halloween," kids looking at black cat
on jack-o-lantern, published by PFB.................$50-$60

Postcard, "An Upsetting Situation," modern Halloween,
1950s, boys pushing over outhouse...................$12-$15

Sheet music, Halloween theme ....$5-$30

Tambourine, lithographed tin, cat face, T. Cohn........... $25

Trick-or-treat bags, paper, 1940s-60s ....$20-$35

Wall decorations, paper, 1930s-40s ....$20-$50

Zorro costume, Ben Cooper, 1950s $75

HAMMERED ALUMINUM

Over the past few years, hammered aluminum has been transformed from one man's hammered trash to another man's hammered treasure.

Background: Although hammered aluminum was produced throughout much of the 20th century, it was from the 1930s to the 1950s that these decorative aluminum trays, candy dishes and similar items enjoyed their heyday.

The very earliest pieces of aluminum were rare, highly prized and highly priced—more valuable even than silver or gold. But that all changed by 1914, when an inexpensive smelting process could be used to turn the expensive metal into a cheap commodity. By the 1930s, Aluminumware had become a common, mass-produced, everyday "handmade" item, affordable to those who were looking for an alternative to silver. It was light, strong and didn't corrode, rust or tarnish.

A variety of items was produced in aluminum, including: ash trays, baskets, bookends, bowls, bun warmers, butter dishes, cake plates, candlesticks, candy dishes, casseroles, chafing dishes, chairs, desk sets, desks, dishes, coasters, cocktail shakers, cups, fruit bowls, ice buckets, jam pots, jewelry, lamps (Everlast and Wendell August Forge), lazy susans, mugs, napkin holders, pitchers, plates, pocketbooks, punch

HOW TO GET HAMMERED!

Here's a tip that will help beginners on a limited budget stretch their collecting dollars to assemble a nice collection of hammered aluminum. When searching for pieces, look for scarce and unique items first and avoid the common. These pieces will be more expensive initially, but you will come out ahead in the long run. That's because the rarer pieces will appreciate in value more quickly than the common items. This means they will cost more later on. By purchasing them now, you can buy more at lower prices. The prices on common pieces, however, will not escalate as quickly. They won't be much more expensive in a few years than they are now. By buying quality pieces now and common pieces later, you should be able to assemble a nice collection and save yourself some money.

The best buys are found in the East and lower Midwest, where aluminum is not yet considered a desirable collectible. Keep your eyes open in rural areas outside of New York City, and in the states of Washington and Oregon. However, aluminum is hot right now in California, so prices are beginning to rise there. The same is true in New York City, where designers are using aluminum pieces.

You can still find lots of bargains in aluminum ware. These cocktail shakers and other pieces of barware were found at flea markets and garage sales for prices ranging from $5 to $30 (Photo courtesy Lynn Wenzel).

sets, salad servers, silent butlers, sugar and creamer sets, syrup servers, tables, trays, tumblers, urns, vases, wastebaskets and more.

There were also a great variety of designs appearing on aluminum ware; animals, flowers, pinecones, and plants are common. The Bamboo pattern, made by Everlast, and the Chrysanthemum pattern, by Continental, are two of the more popular styles from the 1950s. Considering all the different patterns, pieces, embossing, colors and manufacturers, there should be plenty of material to suit the aesthetic interests of any collector.

Some of the better-known companies that produced aluminum ware include: Arthur Armour, Buenilum (Buehner-Wanner Co.), Chadwell, Continental, Cromwell, Everlast, Farber & Shlevin, Hammerkraft, Harmony House, Rodney Kent, Thames, Wendell August Forge, and West Bend. Objects that are marked "patent pending" or have the companies' hallmark on the bottom are especially valuable.

General Guidelines: Hammered aluminum is still an emerging collectible. Prices are not yet firmly established and tend to fluctuate rather dramatically. As aluminum cooking and serving dishes from the 1930s-1950s have become hot collectibles, the prices are rising. But it's not too late to get started. Most pieces are still very affordable.

Many pieces now sell in the $20-$30 range, but a selection is still available for $10-$15, or sometimes even less. Generally, prices over the $100 mark are rare, and only a few pieces—like a large serving cart or a famous designer cocktail set—will top the $200-$300 range. Stunning pieces by Wendell August (a blacksmith), Arthur Armour (designer for August), Kensington (cocktail parties and buffets), Russell Wright and Rodney Kent are popular, but more expensive.

Condition, scarcity and the completeness of the set all contribute to value. You'll find aluminum ware at antique shops and collectibles shows; and, if you're willing to spend the time, you might find some real bargains at flea markets, garage sales, thrift shops or estate auctions.

Club
• Hammered Aluminum Collectors Association, P.O. Box 1346, Weatherford, TX 76086

Recommended Reading
Metalwares Price Guide, Marilyn Dragowick

VALUE LINE

Values shown are for items in Excellent condition.

Ash tray, Kensington, 1930s ....$12-$15
Ash tray, Wendell August, sailboat on water,
    square ....$40-$45
Basket, Continental, Chrysanthemum pattern, square,
    8" x 6" ....$30-$35
Basket, Cromwell, hexagon, flower and fruit design,
    round handle, 10" x 6" ....$15-$20
Basket, Everlast, flowers and leafs pattern, handle,
    9" x 6" ....$15-$20
Bowl, Arthur Armour, square, dogwood and
    butterfly pattern, 8" x 1" ....$45-$50
Bowl, Continental, Chrysanthemum pattern,
    14" ....$40-$50
Bowl, Wendell August, dogwood pattern, 7".........$30-$35
Bread tray, Continental, Chrysthanemum
    pattern..$25-$30
Butter dish, Everlast, Bamboo pattern, 7" ....$20-$25
Candelabra, Wendell August, five lights,
    30" long...$1,000-$1,200
Candy dish, Buenilum, leaf-shaped,
    leaf pattern...$20-$25
Casserole, Arthur Armour, dogwood and
    butterfly pattern ....$75-$100
Casserole, Everlast, flower-and-leaf pattern ....$20-$25
Chafing dish, with tulip finial, includes glass
    container for can of Sterno................................$20-$30
Cigarette box, Continental, Chrysanthemum pattern,
    with glass insert...$50-$65
Coaster set, with matchbook covers, duck pattern,
    1950s ....$35-$50

This sugar-and-creamer set with tray, made by the Buenilum Company, is valued at about $40. It is quite plain but has beautiful handles. (Photo courtesy Lynn Wenzel)

COLLECTOR'S ADVISORY!

There's no need to worry about handling your durable collectibles. Aluminum can be used daily without concern about ruining the finish or lessening its value as a collectible. You can keep your collection in tip-top shape by cleaning it with automobile chrome polish (cream only).

You can also run your things through the dishwasher to keep them nice and bright. But don't do this for things you use every day; dishwashing soap will leave a residue if used too often. So, you can use your aluminum, just like your mom did. But just remember to dry it well! Perhaps the only thing that can hurt aluminum would be to keep liquid in it for any length of time. It will pit and permanently mar the surface.

Coffee pot, Continental, Chrysanthemum
    pattern..$50-$60
Coffee pot, West Bend, colored, electric ....$25-$35
Condiment server, Everlast, 1950s, Bamboo pattern,
    mini Ferris Wheel...$50-$75
Creamer and sugar bowl set, with tray,
    Buenilum Co. ....$40-$50
Crumber and tray, Continental, 1930s ....$30-$40
Dish, Kensington, 1930s ....$50-$100
Gravy boat, Buenilum, 6" x 3"..............................$20-$25
Ice bucket, Everlast, 1930s ....$35-$45
Ice bucket, Everlast, 1950s ....$20-$25
Lazy Susan, Cromwell, fruit and
    flower pattern ....$10-$15
Napkin holder, Wendell August,
    dogwood pattern...$30-$35
Picture frame, signed by Otto Pisoni ....$2,000-$2,100
Pitcher and six tumblers, Everlast,
    Bamboo pattern ....$175-$200

These pieces by Continental are all in the popular Chrysanthemum pattern. They date from the early 1950s (Photo courtesy Lynn Wenzel).

Pitcher, Everlast, Bamboo pattern...........................$40-$50
Pitcher, Kensington, 1930s ....$35-$75
Poinsettias tray, Arthur Armour, 16" diameter ......$50-$60

THE BIRTH OF ALUMINUM

In 1890, American engineer Charles Hall obtained a patent for aluminum. He founded the Pittsburgh Reduction Co. in Niagara Falls, N.Y., and had a research facility in Kensington, Pa. In 1907, it was renamed the Aluminum Company of America (ALCOA). The popular Kensington Ware was first created by ALCOA in 1934.

Sandwich tray, Kensington, cactus pattern ....$35-$40
Serving tray, Farberware, leaf pattern, handles......$30-$35
Serving tray, small, grape pattern ....$12-$15
Serving tray, Westbend, pheasant pattern ....$25-$30
Silent butler, World Hand Forged, 1950s,
    with ash trays ....$30-$40
Silent butler, Everlast, wheat pattern ....$20-$25
Tray, round, Kensington, 1930s ....$50-$75
Tray, bar, Wendell August, geese scene................$50-$55
Tray, bar, Arthur Armour, water lily ....$45-$50
Vase, Russell Wright, round ball vase ....$275-$325
Waste basket, Wendell August Forge,
    "Flying Ducks" ....$125-$150

HANNA-BARBERA COLLECTIBLES

The quick gags of Hanna-Barbera cartoons hit the scene at a time when original animation art for television was scant. Since then America has enjoyed the studio's Saturday morning cartoons, half-hour comedies and other programs for nearly half a century. Scooby-Doo, Huckleberry Hound, The Flintstones, The Jetsons, Yogi Bear, Jonny Quest, The Smurfs; all were the result of a long-ago union between Bill Hanna and Joe Barbera.

Background: Bill Hanna and Joe Barbera met at MGM in the late 1930s, then formed their own studio—Hanna-Barbera—after MGM closed its doors in 1957. Hanna-Barbera's first cartoon was called Ruff & Ready, which was followed by The Huckleberry Hound Show, which received an Emmy. In 1960 The Flintstones became the first half-hour animated situation comedy. Just a few of the other cartoons Hanna-Barbera came out with:

1960s: The Flintstones, The Yogi Bear Show, The Jetsons, Scooby-Doo, Where are You?, Top Cat, QuickDraw McGraw, Magilla Gorilla, Ricochet Rabbit, Space Ghost, Jonny Quest

1980s and on: The Smurfs, The Jetsons Meet The Flintstones, The Snorks

General Guidelines: As today's television pays homage to the older cartoons, the collectibility of the toys and other products that highlight those characters lives on. Items related to the more popular characters usually command higher prices, although the obscure characters are gaining value as the field develops.

Recommended Reading
Saturday Morning TV Collectibles, Dana Cain

VALUE LINE

Prices are for items in Excellent condition.

Atom Ant

Atom Ant coloring book, Whitman #1113	$55
Atom Ant kite, Roalex, 1960s	$75
Atom Ant punch-out set, Whitman, 1966	$100
Atom Ant push puppet, Kohner, 1960s	$50
Atom Ant puzzle, Whitman, 1966	$40
Atom Ant soaky, Purex, 1966	$50
Morocco Mole, Bubble Club soaky, Purex, 1960s	$50
Squiddly Diddly, Bubble Club soaky, Purex, 1960s	$50
Winsome Witch, Bubble Club soaky, Purex, 1960s	$50

Flintstones

Baby Puss vinyl figure, 10", Knickerbocker, 1961	$70
Bamm Bamm bubble pipe, Transogram	$25
Bamm Bamm doll, 15", Ideal, 1962	$100
Bamm Bamm figure, Dakin, 1970, 7"	$35
Bamm Bamm finger puppet, Knickerbocker, 1972	$15
Bamm Bamm soaky, Purex, 1960s	$30
Barney figure, Knickerbocker, 1961, 10", vinyl	$50
Barney finger puppet, Knickerbocker, 1972	$13
Barney night light, Electricord, 1979	$10
Barney Riding Dino toy, Marx, 1960s, 8"	$250
Barney wind-up toy, Marx, 1960s	$175
Barney's car, Flintoys, 1986	$13
Betty figure, Knickerbocker, 1961, 10", vinyl	$95
Betty figure, Flintoys, 1986	$7
Dino bank, china, Dino carrying a golf bag	$90
Dino bank, 1973, hard vinyl, blue with Pebbles on his back	$35
Dino bath puppet sponge mitt, 1973	$18
Dino doll, moveable head and arms	$20
Dino figure, Flintoys, 1986	$7
Dino figure, Dakin, 1970	$50
Dino wind-up, Marx, 1960s	$175
Flintstones, Flintmobile, Flintoys, 1986	$16
Flintstones, Flintstones car, Remco, 1964, battery-operated	$175
Flintstones, set of eight figures, Spoontiques, 1981	$45
Flintstones, set of four figures, Empire, 1976, 3"	$40
Flintstones, set of eight acrylic figures, Imperial, 1976	$35
Fred bubble-blowing pipe, vinyl	$10

Future Treasures? These Hanna-Barbera plastic soap bottles already sell in the $10-$40 range and are sure to increase in value.

This Marx tin wind-up toy of Fred and Dino dates from the early 1960s.

Fred doll, 13", soft vinyl, 1960 .... $90
Fred doll, Perfection Plastic, 1972, 11" $30
Fred figure, Knickerbocker, 1960, 15" $80
Fred figure, Dakin, 1970 .... $45
Fred figure, Flintoys, 1986.. $8
Fred figure, Knickerbocker, vinyl, 1961, 10" $70
Fred finger puppet, Knickerbocker, 1972 .... $13
Fred Flintstone's Bedrock Bank, Alps, 1962,
    9", tin.. $300
Fred Flintstone lithograph wind-up, Marx, 1960s,
    metal, 3-1/2".. $165
Fred Flintstone gumball machine, 1960s, plastic,
    shaped like Fred's head $30
Fred Loves Wilma bank, ceramic $100
Fred night light, 1970, figural $10
Fred policemen figure, Flintoys, 1986 .... $8
Fred push puppet, Kohner, 1960s $25
Fred riding Dino, Marx, 1962, 18",
    battery-operated $300
Fred riding Dino, Marx, 1962, 8", tin, wind-up.......... $300
Great Big Punch Out Book, Whitman, 1961 .... $35
Motorbike, Flintoys, 1986.. $10
Pebbles Bank, 9" $20
Pebbles doll, Ideal, 1963, 15" $110
Pebbles doll, Mighty Star, 1982, vinyl and cloth,
    12" $25
Pebbles figure, Dakin, 1970, 8" $40
Pebbles finger puppet, Knickerbocker, 1972 .... $13
Pebbles Flintstone cradle, Ideal, 1963,
    for a 15" doll $70
Pebbles Soaky, Purex, 1960 .... $30
Police car, Flintoys, 1986.. $13
Wilma figure, Knickerbocker, 1961, 10", vinyl $90
Wilma figure, Flintoys, 1986 .... $7
Wilma Friction Car, Marx, 1962, metal...................... $160

The "Jetsons Out of This World Game" was a 1963 Transogram product. It is worth about $150 today in nice condition

Huckleberry Hound

Hokey Wolf figure, Marx, 1961, TV-Tinykin $25
Hokey Wolf figure, Dakin, 1970................................... $70
Huckleberry Hound bank, Knickerbocker, 1960,
    10", hard plastic... $25
Huckleberry Hound bank, Dakin, 1980, 5" $25
Huckleberry Hound doll, Knickerbocker, 1959,
    18" $35
Huckleberry Hound figure, 1960s, 6",
    glazed china... $30
Huckleberry Hound figure, Marx, 1961,
    TV-Tinykins $25
Huckleberry Hound figure, Dakin, 8" $35
Huckleberry Hound figure, Marx, 1961,
    TV-Tinykins $70
Huckleberry Hound go-cart, Linemar, 1960s,
    6-1/2".. $150
Huckleberry Hound wind-up toy, Linemar,
    1962, 4" $150
Huckleberry Hound wristwatch, Bradley, 1965,
    chrome case, wind-up mechanism $65
Mr. Jinks doll, Knickerbocker, 1959, 13",
    vinyl and plush $45
Mr. Jinks Soaky, Purex, 1960s, 10", Pixie and Dixie
    hard plastic $25
Pixie & Dixie dolls, Knickerbocker, 1960, 12" $40
Pixie & Dixie Magic Slate, 1959 .... $20

Jetsons

Astro doll, Applause, 1990, 10"................................... $20
Elroy toy, Transogram, 1963....................................... $75
Elroy doll, Applause, 1990, 10".................................. $15
George doll, Applause, 1990, 10" $20
Jetsons Birthday Surprise Book, Whitman, 1963,
    Tell-A-Tale book $20
Jetsons Colorform Kit, Colorforms, 1963.................... $70
Judy doll, Applause, 1990, 10"................................... $15
Puzzle, Whitman, 1962, 70 pieces $80
Rosie doll, Applause, 1990, 10" $15

Magilla Gorilla

Droop-A-Long Coyote Soaky, Purex, 1960s, 1
  2" plastic..$45
Droop-A-Long hand puppet, Ideal, vinyl head............$45
Magilla Gorilla book, Golden, 1964,
  Big Golden Book $20
Magilla Gorilla Cannon, Ideal, 1964 ....$70
Magilla Gorilla cereal bowl, MB Inc. $35
Magilla Gorilla doll, 1960s, 11" $50
Magilla Gorilla doll, Ideal, 1966, 18-1/2" $100
Magilla Gorilla plate, 1960s, 8" diameter....................$16
Magilla Gorilla pull toy, Ideal, 1960s,
  with vinyl figure $75
Magilla Gorilla puppet, Ideal....................................$75
Magilla Gorilla push puppet, Kohner, 1960s,
  brown plastic $45
Punkin' Puss Soaky, Purex, 1960s, 11-1/2" $35
Ricochet Rabbit hand puppet, Ideal, 1960s, 11",
  vinyl head $40
Ricochet Rabbit Soaky, Purex, 1960s, 10-1/2",
  plastic $65

Quick Draw McGraw

Auggie Doggie doll, Knickerbocker, 1959, 10",
  plush and vinyl $30
Auggie Doggie Soaky, Purex, 1960s, 10", plastic $40
Baba Looey bank, Knickerbocker, 1960s, 9",
  vinyl, plastic head...$30
Baba Looey doll, Knickerbocker, 1959, 20",
  plush with vinyl...$65

Blabber doll, Knickerbocker, 1959, 15",
  plush and vinyl $50
Blabber Soaky, Purex, 1960s, 10-1/2", plastic............$35
Quick Draw McGraw bank, 1960, 9-1/2", plastic $35
Quick Draw McGraw doll, Knickerbocker, 1959,
  16", plush and vinyl $80
Quick Draw McGraw Moving Target Game,
  Knickerbocker, 1960s..$125
Quick Draw Mold & Model Cast Set, 1960 ....$50
Scooper Doll, Knickerbocker, 1959, 20",
  plush and vinyl $55

Ruff & Reddy

Ruff & Reddy Draw Cartoon Set Color,
  Wonder Art...$80
Ruff & Reddy Go To a Party Tell-A-Tale Book,
  Whitman, 1958..$30
Ruff & Reddy Magic Rub-Off Picture Set,
  Transogram, 1958..$80
Scooby-Doo
Scooby-Doo and the Pirate Treasure Book, Golden,
  1974, Little Golden Book..$10
Scooby-Doo hand puppet, Ideal, 1970s,
  vinyl head $35
Scooby-Doo Paint with Water Book, 1984 ....$10
Scooby-Doo squeak toy, Sanitoy, 1970s, 6" $35

Yogi Bear

Boo Boo doll, Knickerbocker, 1960s, plush,
  9-1/2"..$60
Yogi Bear bubble pipe, Transogram, 1963...................$30
Yogi Bear figure, 1960, 12" $30
Boo Boo figure, 1960, 12" $30
Ranger Smith figure, 1960, 12" $30
Cindy Bear doll, Knickerbocker, 1959, 16".................$65
Yogi and Boo Boo coat rack, Wolverine, 1979,
  48" $65

You can add a plastic Yogi Bear lunch box to your collection for about $30.

Seldom seen complete, the "Jetsons Modeling Clay Set" from Standard ToyKraft is worth at least $100 Mint-in-Box.

Magic Slate, 1963 .... $20
Safety Scissors, Monogram, 1973, on card.................... $7
Snagglepuss figure, Dakin, 1970 .... $50
Snagglepuss Soaky, Purex, 1960s, 9" $25
Snagglepuss Sticker Fun book, Whitman, 1963 .... $20
Yogi Bear and Cindy push puppet set, Kohner,
     1960s, boxed set of two.. $75
Yogi Bear and Pixie & Dixie car game, Whitman $25
Yogi Bear bank, Dakin, 1980, 7" figural...................... $10
Yogi Bear bank, Knickerbocker, 1960s,
     22" figural.. $30
Yogi Bear Cartoonist stamp set, Lido, 1961 .... $50
Yogi Bear doll, Knickerbocker, 1959, 10" $65
Yogi Bear doll, 1962, 6", soft vinyl with
     moveable arms and hands $40
Yogi Bear doll, Knickerbocker, 1960s, 19" plush......... $50
Yogi Bear doll, Knickerbocker, 1959, 16"
     plush with vinyl face $65

Yogi Bear figure, Knickerbocker, 1960s, 9" $45
Yogi Bear figure, Dakin, 1970, 7-3/4" $30
Yogi Bear figure, Marx, 1961, TV-Tinykins $30
Yogi Bear friction toy, 1960s $65
Yogi Bear Ge-Tar, Mattel, 1960s $75
Yogi Bear hand puppet, Knickerbocker $30
Yogi Bear Paint 'em Pals, Craft Master, 1978,
     paint-by-number set $15
Yogi Bear push puppet, Kohner, 1960s......................... $25
Yogi Bear wristwatch, 1963.. $65
Yogi Squeeze doll, Sanitoy, 1979, 12" vinyl................. $16
Yogi Score-A-Matic Ball Toss Game, Transogram,
     1960... $75
Yogi vs. Magilla for President Coloring Book,
     Whitman, 1964... $40
Yogi wristwatch, Bradley, 1967, metal case,
     black vinyl band... $100

HARLEY-DAVIDSON COLLECTIBLES

Collectors are going hog wild for this American icon—Harley-Davidson and its related memorabilia.

According to Harley-Davidson, its motorcycles "began in a shed, went to war, became the symbol of American individualism and ended up king of the road."

Background: Its story begins in 1901, when William Harley, 21, and Arthur Davidson, 20, decided to take the pedal power out of bicycling. Two years later, the legend was born in Milwaukee, Wisconsin. The two men, and Davidson's two brothers, produced their first three motorcycles.

By 1920, the company was the world's largest motorcycle manufacturer, producing more than 28,000 motorcycles, which were sold in 67 countries. It even produced 90,000 motorcycles for the U.S. war efforts in World War II.

"Panhead," "Sportster" and "Fat Boy" models set the standard, as Harley-Davidson led the way while holding onto its "biggest asset—the past."

General Guidelines: Harley-Davidson has a loyal backing of fans—devoted enthusiasts are known as "H.O.G.s," the Harley Owners Group, with more than 300,000 members. They are just as passionate about their memorabilia. And, as the company nears its 100th anniversary, it is producing licensed collectibles to keep fans in hog heaven.

Some of the newer collectibles are of the "limited-edition" variety. Segal Fine Art, in Boulder, Colo., publishes prints by several officially-licensed Harley-Davidson artists, who, in their own styles, each capture the "live to ride, ride to live" sentiments of the H.O.G.s. Popular artists include David Uhl, Scott Jacobs, James Gucwa and Holly Ellsworth.

Christopher Radko, of Elmsford, N.Y., and the Cavanaugh Group of Roswell, Ga., offer many different Christmas ornaments with Harley motifs. Radko has created Free Wheeling Santa and Biker Boot. Cavanaugh offers ornaments that feature exact replicas of real motorcycles. His works include The Leader of the Pack (Santa with a Harley), Santa's Leading Lady (Mrs. Claus on her bike), and Reindeer on Bad Boy (yep, reindeer riding). Cavanaugh also offers snowglobes, such as Up, Up and Away and Santa & Elf with Toy Bag, and limited-edition ceramic steins.

Cavanaugh also offers a wide variety of beanbag animals and plush bears (Babe, Bosco and Cruiser); all have a common interest, a love for Harleys. They even have faux leather biker gear and accessories, too, such as Harley pup tents, saddlebags and sling chairs.

The Franklin Mint has recreated one of the classics –a motorcycle, Billy Bike, from the 1960s film *Easy Rider*. The precision model has functional parts, too. Also available from the Mint is Bobby, a "Biker Baby." Bobby, in a biker vest and red bandana, is a hand-painted porcelain baby who has taken dad's motorcycle keys; he's raring to go.

The ultimate Harley Davidson collectible, of course, is a classic Harley. This example, a museum-quality 1966 Harley Davidson Electra Glide 1200, was offered at a recent Sotheby's auction with a $25,000 estimate. Completely stock and original, the bike has less than 2,000 original miles.

Madame Alexander Dolls of New York created a doll, Cisette, who is decked out from head to toe in leather and wearing fishnet stockings. She too is ready to go her own way. As are the Harley-Davidson Barbie and Ken dolls, produced by Mattel.

Matchbox Collectibles offers replicas of the semi rigs that have carried Harleys from Milwaukee to dealers around the world. Popular models include the 1929, 1937 and 1966 models. There are also two motorcycles to collect.

Vintage Harley collectibles come in all shapes and sizes, from actual motorcycles, to the chains holding the keys used to start them. There's something for everyone who has the Harley-Davidson spirit—photographs; fashions and clothing; police and military items; pins, badges and medals; catalogs, sales literature and brochures; promotional items; dealer collectibles, posters and business cards; motorcycle parts, manuals and accessories; rider tags; keychains and key fobs; postcards; books; calendars; magazines and ads; race programs; Harley-Davidson metal and neon signs; radios; pens and pencils; cigarette lighters, ashtrays and matchbooks; knives; handbags; pocket watches; and toys (pressed steel, die-cast and cast-iron motorcycles).

Club

• Antique Motorcycle Club of America, P.O. Box 300, Sweetser, IN 46987

VALUE LINE

Ad, 1944 *Popular Science* magazine, "These Days Will Come Again," ....$10-$15

Ad, 1947 *Popular Science* magazine, shows new line ....$10-$15

Ad, 1953 *Popular Science* magazine, "Thrilling Power Puts You Miles Ahead in Fun"...........................$5-$10

Ash tray, Deeley H-D Annual Dealer Meeting 1978, red logo in center, ceramic ....$10-$12

Beer can, Daytona 1986, Genuine Beer, aluminum ....$20-$25

Book, *The Complete Harley-Davidson Encyclopedia*, Rafferty, Bramley Books, 1997........................$10-$20

Catalog, 1963, "Widen Your Fun Horizons," 20 pages...$15-$20

Catalog, 1970s, accessory, typical example...........$10-$15

Even Barbie can be a biker babe! Harley Barbie and Ken were issued by Mattel in 1999. Barbie sells for about $200, while Ken is worth about $100.

HARLEY ENTHUSIASTS INCLUDED THE KING!

Since 1916, Harley-Davidson fans have been kept abreast of racing, touring and club news through the pages of The Enthusiast. Today, the magazine, offering a Harley-Davidson viewpoint on life, is published four times annually, making it the longest continually running motorcycle magazine. Pre-1920s magazines are the most highly sought after; some early issues can be worth $200. But perhaps the king of the road is Elvis Presley. The May 1956 issue shows him sitting on a Harley. It can bring as much as $300.

Cigarette lighter, Barlow (B53), with box, shows 1200cc Electra Glide ....$30-$40

Cigarette lighter, Zippo, "95 Years 1903-1998" ....$10-$15

Clock, H-D Motor Oil Co., wall clock, 8" tall, battery-operated ....$20-$25

Coffee mug, black with silver logo ....$5-$10

Dice, with H-D logo in place of #1 on each, black-and-white..$25-$30

Die-cast model, Sportster, Franklin Mint replica of 1957 model, 1:24 scale ....$25-$30

Die-cast model, Panhead, Franklin Mint replica of 1948 model, 1:10 scale ....$25-$35

Handbook, *Rider's Hand Book*, 1926 ....$25-$75

Jersey, black-and-white polyester H-D XR Racing..$30-$40

Lapel pin, "Capitol Drive Plant 50 Years of Producing Powered Trains 1948-1998"...............................10-$15

Magazine, *Harley-Davidson Enthusiast,* typical 1940s-1950s issue ....$10-$20

Magazine, *Saturday Evening Post*, April 7, 1951, shows kids admiring Harley.............................$50-$75

Matchbox, Harley-Davidson motorcycle and sidecar, 1962, 66-B..$45-$75

Matchbox, Harley-Davidson motorcycle, 1980, 50-G ....$3-$7

Match container, Pre-Luxe Premium Deluxe Motor Cycle Oil, 2" tall, 1960s ....$35-$45

Movie poster, *Harley-Davidson and the Marlboro Man*, one-sheet, 1991 ....$30-$40

Neon clock, dealership sign, late 1940s, 18" ....$1,500-$2,000

Oil can, Pre-Luxe Premium Deluxe 1-quart can, 1950s ....$50-$60

Paperweight, H-D Museum, York, Pa., museum medallion in the middle, 1980s ....$20-$25

Pin, bar and shield wrench pin, solid sterling silver vest pin..$30-$35

Pocket watch, Fat Boy, with stand, pouch and chain ....$75-$100

If you can't have the real thing in your garage, how about a nice scale model, like this "Billy Bike" from the Franklin Mint? The bike is a model of the Harley used in the 1969 film "Easy Rider."

Pocket watch, Franklin Mint Heritage, with stand,
 chain and leather sheath ....$75-$100
Postcard, 1964, shows H-D motorcycle, scooter
 and golf cart ....$8-$12
Racing poster, "Harley-Davidson Wins,"
 1940..$100-$300
Rider's cap, leather, 1940s-1950s ....$75-$100
Sales brochure, typical 1950s-60s...........................$6-$12
Sales brochure, typical 1970s ....$3-$5
Service manual, typical 1950s-60s ....$25-$50
Service manual, typical 1970s ....$20-$35
Slot car, Tyco H-D semi truck................................$20-$25
Snow Village sign, "A H-D Holiday,"
 Department 56...$15-$20
Spare parts catalog, 1930s spiral bound................$75-$100
Spark plug, with box, 1950s ....$15-$25

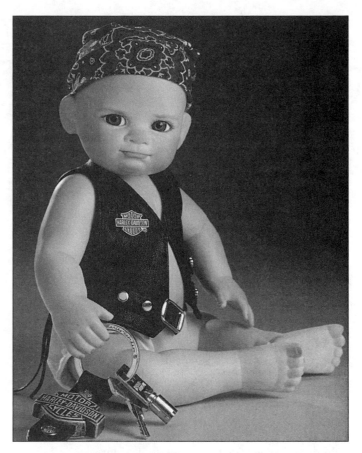

Bobby, the Little Biker Baby, proudly wears his Harley Davidson vest. It was issued by the Franklin Mint with a retail value of $90.

Spray paint, 1970s...$10-$20
Telephone, H-D motorcycle, licensed....................$30-$35
Tie clip, H-D Electra Glide, silver, 1960s............$50-$100

HOLT-HOWARD PIXIEWARE

Among the most fun collectibles to emerge from the 1950s and '60s was Holt-Howard Pixieware, a colorful line of wonderfully whimsical deep-glazed ceramic condiment containers and other kitchen items. A huge commercial success forty years ago, Holt-Howard Pixieware is now enjoying a second life as a hot collectible.

Background: The Holt-Howard Company was started in 1949 by brothers John and Robert Howard and their friend Grant Holt. All three were students at Amherst College in Amherst, Mass. During its early years, the company made primarily Christmas knickknacks, but by the late 1950s was expanding into year-round production of ceramic kitchen and giftware items.

The Holt-Howard Pixieware was a unique concept, just right for the time. America was in the midst of a building boom that included new homes in the suburbs, large kitchens, family rooms and outside barbecues. Americans needed portable containers and jars to transport condiments and other goodies from room to room and from kitchen to patio. Holt-Howard's Pixieware fit the bill perfectly, and looked good doing it. These novelty ceramics were designed with whimsical pixie heads perched atop each container to serve as its cover. The removable heads, which featured wonderfully expressive cartoon-like faces, often also had a built-in serving spoon.

General Guidelines: The cute and colorful Pixieware line was introduced in 1958 with a charming little trio of condiment jars that included a yellow-striped Mustard, a red-striped Ketchup, and a pink-striped Jam 'n' Jelly, all standing just over five inches tall. From the start, it was the adorable facial expressions on the tops of the containers that made them so appealing with consumers then and collectors now. These first three pieces enjoyed the largest production run of any of the Pixiewares, making them still the most commonly found pieces. They have a current value of about $50 each.

A total of some two dozen Pixieware pieces were released by Holt-Howard in 1958, including more condiments, a sugar and creamer set, cherry and onion jars, salt-

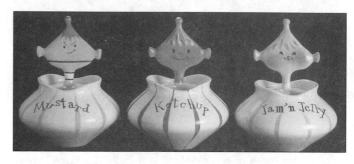

These three guys were the start of the Holt-Howard Pixieware line. They are worth about $50 each today. (Photo courtesy Walter Dworkin, "Price Guide to Holt-Howard Collectibles")

These three whimsical salad dressing jars are worth about $100 each. (Photo courtesy Walter Dworkin, *Price Guide to Holt-Howard Collectibles***)**

and-pepper shakers, liquor decanters, oil-and-vinegar cruets, etc. Today, prices for these original pieces range from $60-$100 each for the smaller pieces to $125-$225 for the larger-size liquor decanters. Also included in the original line was an "Instant Coffee" jar, which is extremely desirable today. Because of her coffee-colored face, the coffee jar is sometimes regarded as a crossover collectible by collectors of Black Americana and has a value of about $150.

After the successful introduction of these first 24 items, Holt-Howard quickly followed up with a new line of 32 more Pixieware gift items that the company called "Cousins by the Dozens." The line included not only more condiment jars, but also bowls, ashtrays, an hors d'oeuvres set, towel hooks, candle holders, vases and more. And that was just the beginning of the Holt-Howard offerings.

The coffee mug—so common today—was actually Holt-Howard's Christmas gift to the world. Among the company's early Christmas items were various Santa Claus mugs and pitchers. The Santa mugs became so popular—mostly because of their larger size—that Holt-Howard started creating coffee mugs for everyday use, not just during the holiday season. As a result of this success, Holt-Howard is generally credited with pioneering the coffee mug as we know it today. Prior to the 1950s, mugs were not in common use.

Over the years, Holt-Howard offered a wonderful assortment of other Santa Claus pieces, including cookie jars, salt-and-pepper shakers, serving trays, candy dishes, ashtrays, planters, and an amazing array of candle holders. Today, all of these Christmas items are very much in demand, with values ranging from $10-$15 for a small salt-and-pepper set to $150 or more for a large Santa cookie jar. A typical Holt-Howard Christmas beverage set, consisting of a pitcher and four mugs is valued at $50-$75.

Among the most successful of all the Holt-Howard creations was its line of "Cozy Kitchen Kitties," condiment jars and other pieces all featuring darling kitty faces. They were tremendously popular. Most of the kittens in this series (though not all) featured plaid or polka-dot scarves around their necks. Dozens of pieces were in the Cozy Kitten line including various salt-and-pepper shakers, ashtray, vases, napkin holders, match holders, spice sets, instant coffee jar, cookie jar, pitcher, cheese board, oil-and-vinegar cruets, sugar-and-creamer set, various condiment jars and more. Today, values vary widely, ranging from $20-$40 each for the common, smaller pieces; $50-$100 for the larger or scarcer pieces; and $100-$200 for the most desirable items.

Playing a sort of cat-and-mouse game, Holt-Howard also released a similar "Merry Mouse" series of pieces about the same time, which featured cute little mouse faces.

Coming along in 1960 was a line of Holt-Howard dinnerware called "Coq Rouge" (French for "Red Rooster"), which featured a rooster design. The line included plates, cereal bowls, and various accessory pieces such as coffee mugs, salt-and-pepper shakers, napkin holders, butter dishes, coffee pots, jam and jelly jars, etc. Today, prices for these pieces begin at $10-$15 for a small plate or cereal bowl to $50-$100 for larger and scarcer pieces, like the coffee pot or cookie jar. The rooster set also included a number of giftware and accessory items, including ashtrays, vases, a wooden recipe box, cigarette box, a 40-inch yardstick caddy with a pocket for scissors, a 24-inch fly swatter, 10-inch pot holder, a set of nesting baskets, etc.

Over the years, in addition to its whimsical pixies, kittens, and roosters, Holt-Howard did exhibit a more serious side, producing numerous other kitchen and household products. Collectors today can find various candle holders, planters, wall pockets, vases, trivets, cutting boards, canisters, mugs, pitchers, liquor decanters and other items displaying the Holt-Howard name. All are collectible, but most desirable are the whimsical treasures from the late 1950s and early '60s.

Among the more interesting—and certainly the most controversial—items produced by Holt-Howard was a coffee mug that pictured President Nixon on a phony three-dollar bill. Sales of the novelty mug were soaring, until federal agents informed Holt-Howard it was illegal to depict U.S. paper money in that fashion, and production was immediately stopped. The Nixon mug, which sold for $1.60 in 1973, is now worth about $75.

Recommended Reading

Price Guide to Holt-Howard Collectibles, Walter Dworkin

VALUE LINE

Values shown are compiled from the "Price Guide to Holt-Howard Collectibles" by Walter Dworkin (Krause Publications) and are for examples in Excellent condition.

1958 Holt-Howard Pixiewares

Mustard, Ketchup or Jam 'n Jelly, each	$50
Instant Coffee	$165
Lil' Sugar and Cream Crock, pair	$90
Olives	$75
Cocktail Olives	$95
Cocktail Cherries	$95
Onions	$75

Included among the many Holt-Howard Christmas items is this pair of "Winking Santa" salt-and-pepper shakers, valued at about $30-$35 for the pair. (Photo courtesy Walter Dworkin, "Price Guide to Holt-Howard Collectibles")

Cocktail Onions $95
Liquor decanter, several varieties................... $175 and up
Bottle bracelets, each $35
"Sam 'n Sally" oil and vinegar cruets, each $125
Spoons with ceramic pixieheads, each......................... $60

1959 Holt-Howard Pixiewares

Relish Jar.. $110
Mayonnaise Jar $110
Honey Jar $300

These charming string holders are part of the Holt-Howard Cozy Kitten series. They are worth about $40-$50 each. (Photo courtesy Walter Dworkin, "Price Guide to Holt-Howard Collectibles")

Chili Sauce.. $185
Salt and Pepper Shakers, pair..................................... $185
"Mustard Max" or "Ketchup Katie," each $110
Sundae Servers ("Nuts" or "Berries"), each $110
Salad Dressing (Russian, French or Italian),
    each ....$100-$115
Hanging Pixie Planter $175

Holt-Howard "Cozy Kitten" Items

Salt & Pepper Shakers, pair (several varieties)......$20-$50
"Memo Minder".. $80
Cottage Cheese Crock... $50
Ashtray/Match Holder $65
Butter Dish, with cover $100
Sugar Shaker $65
Sugar and Creamer Set, pair $60
Ketchup or Mustard, each $165

Holt-Howard Christmas Items

Candle Holders, many varieties, typical pair ....$25-$35
Santa Napkin Holder.. $25
"Winking Santa" Beverage Set
    (pitcher & six mugs) $60
"Winking Santa" Nutmeg Shaker $50
"Winking Santa" Stackable Cream & Sugar, set $35
"Starry Eyed Santa" Pitcher....................................... $35
"Starry Eyed Santa" Mug... $10
Santa "Candy/Cookie" Jar $150
Santa Train Planter.. $45

HOT WHEELS

Although they were introduced in 1968 as simply "The Fastest Metal Cars in the World," Mattel's Hot Wheels soon became the *most popular* metal cars, too, supplanting Matchbox as the toy cars to have.

Background: These 1/64-scale California-style die-cast cars, with large wheels in back and small tires in front, offered a radical departure in styles and colors from their counterparts. And, they were fast on their loop-the-loop tracks.

More than 1,000 different regular-issue models of Hot Wheels have rolled off the lines since 1968; more than 1.7 billion cars in all have been produced. If you count all the variations in paint, interiors, wheels and windshields, you'll find there are thousands of varieties to add to your collection.

These variations are very important. A subtle difference in wheels or color can in some cases mean hundreds of dollars in value. And, because there are so many variations and cars, Hot Wheels pose a challenge to someone who is trying to decide what to collect.

Therefore, many collectors specialize in specific areas, looking for certain types of tires (redlines or blackwalls); models (such as Fords or Chevys); numbered packs; or types of vehicles (such as military or emergency vehicles). The collectors' pins, plastic or metal, are generally $5-$10 each, but some of the more valuable ones are $20.

The number of serious Hot Wheels collectors (considered as those who have more than 100 or 200 cars) has tripled over the past five years, from about 10,000 collectors to more than 30,000. This growth can be attributed, in part, to Hot Wheels' "Treasure Hunt" cars, which became an overnight sensation when they were introduced as limited-edition collectibles in 1995.

General Guidelines: "Redlines" (so called because they have red stripes around their tires), which were produced from 1968-77, are the hardest to find. They are also the most valuable of all Hot Wheels. Corvettes, Mustangs, Camaros and other American muscle cars are popular models among redline collectors. Classic and futuristic concept cars are also good sellers.

Redlines in their original package are extremely scarce, desirable and valuable. The value of these cars is at least two, sometime three, times more than values of cars without the package. Newer Hot Wheels are almost exclusively bought and sold Mint-in-Pack (unless the car was not issued in a pack).

Any car from 1973 is very scarce; Hot Wheels made fewer cars that year and used enamel paint because of the lower cost. Among the redline car colors, white and pink were the least popular, and therefore least produced, so cars with these colors are more valuable than other ones. For example, a scarce pink Hot Wheel can be worth double the value of a car with a more common color.

Blackwalls (1977-late '80s) stretch from the end of the redlines until the beginning of numbered packs, around 1988. During this time, the old-style Hot Wheels were phased out as the cars moved toward a more modern look. The packaging, too, was more colorful. The cars used to be fairly inexpensive, at $7 or less, but now are commanding premium values of $12 or more. It is difficult to find pre-1988 loose cars in Near Mint to Mint condition, let alone in their original package.

Numbered packs (late 1980s to present) were well received by a growing number of Hot Wheels collectors, who were looking for an easy way to collect the cars. Today, this concept has become the most active area in Hot Wheels collecting. It offers collectors many different variations for certain cars, either in paint color, decals or wheels.

The #1 pack is "Old No. 5", a fire engine that is truly tough to find. It commands at least $125 or more. But one of the most popular of the newer cars in numbered packs (#210) is the red Dodge Viper with five-spoke wheels from 1995. It has been sold for $100 or more in some cases.

Many of the "Treasure Hunt" cars have been in demand too. Because they are so valuable and in such demand, many of the new models never even make it to the store shelves. (Many store employees likely have pretty good Treasure Hunt collections.) The first year the cars were issued, 10,000 of each model were made; the next two years, there were 25,000 made of each model.

Hot Wheels has introduced other limited-edition cars over the last five years or so, too. Most of these cars have been created for individuals, businesses and Hot Wheels clubs who have contracted with Mattel to have the cars made for special occasions, such as for conventions or as special giveaways.

These cars, usually made in quantities of a few thousand to 10,000, were sold directly into the hobby by dealers, typically for $10-$15 each. This limited-edition concept started at a

COLLECTING TIP!

Like any collectible, condition plays a key role in value. Hot Wheels collectors are highly sensitive to condition. Problems that might seem like little things to a novice collector—scratched decals, paint nicks and tire wear—all subtract from the value of a car. For instance, a car that is valued at $20 in Mint condition, but has a small paint scratch and tire wear, would sell for around $12. That same $20 car with several major scratches, missing paint and badly worn tires is worth less than $2. If a Hot Wheels car was played with, it will almost always have condition problems that will affect its value.

TIME CAPSULE—1973!

In part because Americans were watching their wallets due to worldwide inflation and an oil crisis, Mattel reduced the number of new models it issued in 1973. And, instead of the shiny spectra-flame finishes used on the earlier models, Mattel used enamel paint for these cars, which were dull compared to the flashier models. Interest in the cars declined, so Mattel released even fewer numbers of cars, making cars from 1973 perhaps the most difficult to find, and some of the most valuable. Mint-in-Package, they can command anywhere from $500 to $1,500, depending on the model (see "Value Line" for specific pricing).

Mattel has issued hundreds of Hot Wheels cars over the years in various styles and variations.

rate of a few each year, but has picked up to several cars each month today. Many collectors are only buying the cars they like, however, instead of buying every car that is issued.

Other limited-edition Hot Wheels cars have been created as mail-in offers from products such as Van de Camp's fish, Little Debbie snacks, Dinty Moore Stew, Tony's Pizza and Malt-O-Meal. McDonald's, Aqua Fresh toothpaste and '76 gas stations have also had Hot Wheels promotions.

Club
• Blues City Hot Wheels Club, 4807 Walden Glen, Memphis, TN 38128

Recommended Reading

Books
2000 Toys & Prices, Sharon Korbeck and Elizabeth Stephan
O'Brien's Collecting Toy Cars and Trucks, Elizabeth Stephan
Die Cast Price Guide, Douglas R. Kelly

Periodicals
Toy Cars & Vehicles
Toy Shop

VALUE LINE

The Top 10 Mattel Classic Hot Wheels
In Mint-in-Package condition.

1. Volkswagen Beach Bomb, surf boards in rear window, 1969 .... $4,500
2. Custom Camero, 1968, white enamel $2,000
3. Snake, 1973, white/yellow $1,500
4. Mongoose, 1973, red/blue.................................. $1,400
5. Mustang Stocker, 1975, white............................. $1,200
6. Carabo, 1974, yellow $1,200
7. Custom Mustang, 1968 .... $1,200
8. Mercedes C-111, 1973 .... $1,200
9. Superfine Turbine, 1973..................................... $1,100
10. Ferrari 312P, 1973... $1,100

The Top 10 Mattel Hot Wheels Numbered Packs

Most Hot Wheels that were produced in numbered packs during the 1980s (#s 1-30) are $30-$65 MIP. Hot Wheels cars produced in numbered packs from 1993-97 are generally $3-$7 MIP. The following values are for examples in Mint-in-Package condition.

1. No. 51, '40s Woodie, 1987, yellow......................... $800
2. No. 49, Rolls-Royce, 1984, blue, whitewalls.......... $300
3. No. 242, '93 Camaro, 1993, blue, Ultra Hots wheels... $200
4. No. 75, Pontiac Banshee, 1990, red, Ultra Hots wheels, gold.. $200
5. No. 355, '67 Camaro, Treasure Hunts, 1995 .... $200
6. No. 98, Nissan 300ZX, 1992, red, Hot Ones wheels, gold $175
7. No. 94, Auburn 852, red, blackwalls, 1991 .... $175
8. No. 88, T-Bird Stock, 1991, black and white, Halvoline decal, blackwalls $175
9. No. 26, '65 Mustang Convertible, 1987, white, whitewalls.. $165
10. No. 89, Mini Truck, 1990, turquoise, Hot Ones wheels, chrome $160

The Top 10 Mattel Hot Wheels Multipacks
In Mint-in-Package condition.

1. Mongoose and Snake Dragster Pak, #5935, 1971... $1,300
2. Go Team, #6428, 1971: Beatnik Bandit, Custom Corvette, Hot Heap, Python................ $1,000+

3. Military Machines, #9504, 1976: AW Shoot,
Gun Bucket, Gun Slinger, Khaki Cooler,
Staff Car, Tough Customer..................................$1,000+
4. Ontario Team 2-Pack, #6429, 1971: Chapparal 2G,
Ford MK IV, Lola GT70, McLaren M6A ....$1,000+
5. Show Team, #6427, 1971: Silhouette,
Splittin' Image, Torero, Turbofire ....$1,000+
6. Indy Team Gift Pack, #6447, 1970: Brabham Repco F1,
Indy Eagle, Lotus Turbine, Shelby Turbine $750
7. H.E.L.P. Machines, #9031, 1975: Chief's Special,
Emergency Squad, Mustang Stocker, Paramedic, Police
Cruiser, Ramblin' Wrecker $600
8. Sizzlin' Six Set, #6431, 1970: Beatnik Bandit, Custom
Cougar, McLaren M6A, Splittin' Image, Turbofire, '31
Ford Woody...$575
9. Fun Machines, #9033, 1975: Backwoods Bomb,
Baja Bruiser, Dune Daddy, Ranger Rig,
Sand Drifter, Super Van $575
10. Streak Machines, #9034, 1975: American Victory,
El Rey Special, Monte Carlo Stocker, Porsche 917,
Torino Stocker, Vega Bomb $575
11. Street Machines, #9032, 1975: Gremlin Grinder,
Mercedes C-111, Mighty Maverick, Porsche 911,
Rodger Dodger, Super Van....................................$575

The Top 10 1973 Hot Wheels
In Mint-in-Package condition.

1. Snake, #6969, white/yellow $1,500
2. Mongoose, #6970, red/blue...................................$1,400
3. Mercedes C-111, #6978, assorted colors $1,200
4. Ferrari 312P, #6973, assorted colors $1,100
5. Superfine Turbine, #6004, assorted colors...........$1,100
6. Prowler, #6965, assorted colors $1,000
7. Porsche 917, #6972, assorted colors $950
8. Ice T, #6980, assorted colors.................................$650
9. Odd Job, #6981, assorted colors $600
10. Police Cruiser, #6963, white $600

Mattel Hot Wheels 1960s-1970s..................... *MNP* *MIP*

	MNP	MIP
Alive '55, #6968, assorted colors, 1973............	$75	$500
Ambulance, #6451, assorted, 1970	$30	$50
Backwoods Bomb, #7670, light blue, 1975.....	$40	$125
Baja Bruiser, #8258, light green, 1976	$300	$1,000
Beatnik Bandit, #6217, assorted, 1968	$15	$45
Buzz Off, #6976, assorted, 1973.....................	$75	$400
Cement Mixer, #6452, assorted, 1970	$20	$45
Classic '36 Ford Coupe, #6253, blue, 1969.....	$10	$25
Classic '57 T-Bird, #6252, assorted, 1969.......	$25	$70
Corvette Stingray, #9241, red, 1976	$30	$80
Custom Camaro, #6208, white enamel, 1968....	$300	$2,000
Custom Cougar, #6205, assorted, 1968	$60	$275
Custom Mustang, #6206, assorted, 1968.........	$65	$425
Custom VW Bug, #6220, assorted, 1968.........	$15	$60
Dune Daddy, #6967, orange, 1975.................	$175	$450
El Rey Special, #8273, light blue, 1974.........	$200	$650
Ferrari 312P, #6417, assorted, 1970................	$20	$30
Formula 5000, #9119, white, 1976	$20	$45
Funny Money, #7621, gray, redline, 1977	$25	$75
Grass Hopper, #7621, light green, 1974	$30	$90
Gremlin Grinder, #9201, chrome, blackwall, 1977..............	$15	$30
Gun Slinger, #7664, olive, 1975	$25	$50
Heavy Chevy, #7619, yellow, 1974..................	$75	$175
Hot Heap, #6219, assorted, 1968.....................	$10	$35
Ice T, #6980, light green, 1974	$30	$75
Indy Eagle, #6263, gold, 1969........................	$50	$200
King Kuda, #6411, assorted, 1970...................	$25	$100
Lotus Turbine, #6262, assorted, 1969.............	$10	$30
Maxi Taxi, #9184, yellow, blackwall, 1977.....	$20	$60
Mercedes C-111, #6978, red, 1974..................	$40	$90
Mighty Maverick, #6414, assorted, 1970	$35	$85
Mongoose, #6970, red/blue, 1973....................	$400	$1,400
Mustang Stocker, #9203, chrome, 1976	$40	$90
Neet Streeter, #9510, chrome, 1976.................	$20	$40
Odd Job, #6981, assorted, 1973	$100	$600
Paddy Wagon, #6966, blue, 1973	$30	$120
Paramedic, #7661, white, 1975........................	$25	$55
Pit Crew Car, #6183, white, 1971	$50	$450
Poison Pinto, #9240, light green, 1976............	$25	$60
Police Cruiser, #6963, white, 1974	$35	$90
Porsche 911, #7648, yellow, 1975	$40	$75
Porsche 917, #6972, orange, 1974...................	$40	$75
Prowler, #6965, light green, 1974...................	$500	$1,000
Ramblin' Wrecker, #7659, white, blackwall, 1977.............	$10	$20
Red Baron, #6964, red, 1973	$30	$200
Rock Buster, #9088, yellow, 1976	$20	$35
Sand Crab, #6403, assorted, 1970....................	$10	$40
Shelby Turbine, #6265, assorted, 1969............	$10	$25
Snake, #6969, white/yellow, 1973	$600	$1,500
Staff Car, #9521, olive, blackwall, 1977........	$500	$750
Steam Roller, #8260, white, 1974....................	$25	$70
Strip Teaser, #6188, assorted, 1971	$65	$200
Sweet "16", #6007, assorted, 1973	$90	$375
Thor, #2880, yellow, 1979	$15	$30

Mint-in-Package, this 1968 Custom Corvette has a value of $250.

This classic 1936 Ford Coupe Hot Wheels car has a value of $25 in Mint-in-Package condition.

Torino Stocker, #7647, red, 1975	$35	$70
Vega Bomb, #7658, green, 1975	$250	$800
Volkswagen Beach Bomb, #6274, surfboards on side, 1969	$50	$275
Whip Creamer, #6457, assorted, 1970	$15	$40
Z Whiz, #9639, blue, 1982	$20	$55

Hot Wheels—Numbered Packs

Mint-in-Pack condition.

1 Old Number 5, 1982, red $125

2 Sol Aire CX4, 1989, black, Ultra Hots wheels, gold $90

6 Blazer 4x4, 1984, black, construction tires, silver $65

7 Troop Convoy, olive $110

10 Baja Breaker, 1989, all-terrain vehicle, white $60

11 '31 Doozie, 1990, maroon, whitewalls $50

12 Roll Patrol, olive, construction tires, black $150

13 Delivery Van—Bob's, 1996, red $20

14 Custom Corvette, 1989 .... $25

18 Mercedes 540K, 1988, black $20

19 Shadow Jet, 1988 .... $65

23 '80s Firebird, 1990, yellow $15

26 '65 Mustang Convertible, 1987, white, whitewalls $165

29 Tail Gunner, 1987, olive, construction tires $90

30 '80s Corvette, 1989, blue $125

31 Cobra, 1995, red, 7-spoke wheels $5

33 Camaro Z-28, 1991, purple $8

34 Bulldozer, 1980 .... $12

36 Baja Bug, 1987, white $35

37 Hot Bird, 1990, white with red interior, Ultra Hots wheels, gold $150

39 Monster Vette, 1987, yellow, construction tires $100

44 '35 Classic Caddy, 1996, blue, 5-spoke wheels $4

45 Rescue Ranger, 1988, red, blackwalls $15

47 '57 Chevy, 1989, turquoise, Ultra Hots wheels $125

51 '40s Woodie, 1987, yellow $800

56 Bronco 4-wheeler, 1990, white, construction tires $45

58 Blown Camaro Z28, 1990, turquoise, Hot Ones wheels $110

59 Sheriff Patrol, 1990, blue $15

65 VW Bug, 1990, red $20

66 Custom Corvette, 1989, red $28

71 Ambulance, 1996, white, sawblade wheels $3

72 School Bus, 1989, yellow $5

75 Pontiac Banshee, 1990, red, Ultra Hots wheels, gold $200

77 Bywayman, 1989, maroon, construction tires, white $125

87 Purple Passion, 1993, purple, whitewalls with flame wheels $8

88 T-Bird Stock, 1991, black and white with Havoline decal, blackwalls $175

89 Mini Truck, 1990, turquoise, Hot Ones wheels, chrome $160

94 Auburn 852, 1991, red, blackwalls $175

95, '55 Chevy, 1991, white $12

106 VW Golf, 1991, white $80

114 Fiero 2M4, 1987, red $85

116 Classic Ferrari, 1991, yellow $15

125 Zender Fact 4, 1991, Silver, Ultra Hots wheels, gold $120

137 Goodyear Blimp, 1992, gray $6

145 Tractor, yellow, construction tires, yellow $10

148 Porsche 930, 1991, purple $50

154 '59 Cadillac, 1991, white, whitewall $4

156 Rodzilla, 1988, purple with red eyes $65

157 '57 Chevy, 1991, yellow, Ultra Hots wheels $11

162 '65 Mustang Convertible, 1995, red, 5-spoke wheels $5

167 '80s Firebird, 1992, orange $7

172 Mazda Miata, 1995, yellow, 7-spoke wheels $55

179 Porsche 959, 1992, purple, Ultra Hots wheels $4

188 Hummer, 1995, brown, plain hood, construction tires $3

192 Corvette Stingray, 1992, green $20

196 3-window '34, 1993, yellow/green $150

200 Custom Corvette, 1995, purple, Ultra Hots wheels $4

204 Oscar Mayer, 1993, yellow and red $5

210 Dodge Viper, 1993, red, 5-spoke wheels $95

213 '57 Chevy, 1993, turquoise, bow tie, Ultra Hots wheels $7

221 Range Rover, 1993, black, construction tires $5

223 Baja Bug, 1992, red $20

233 Toyota MR2 Rally, 1996, white, Ultra Hots wheels $90

242 '93 Camaro, 1993, blue, Ultra Hots wheels $200

253 Mercedes 380, 1994, red, Ultra Hots wheels $4

258 Blazer 4x4, 1994, blue, construction tires, black $6

262 '93 Camaro, 1995, red, 7-spoke wheels $45

266 '59 Caddy, 1995, lavender, 5-spoke wheels $4

271 Dragster, 1996, blue, blackwalls $12

275 Lumina Stocker, 1995, blue with Pontiac front,
   Ultra Hots wheels $125

280 Sharkruiser, 1995, blue, 7-spoke wheels $5

284 Flashfire, 1995, purple, 5-spoke wheels $3

290 '57 Chevy, 1995, blue, 5-spoke wheels $4

293 VW Bug, 1995, pink, 5-spoke wheels $20

303 Street Rodder, 1995, orange,
   construction tires $35

305 Classic Cobra, 1995, lime green, metal base,
   7-spoke wheels $5

315 Ratmobile, 1995, black, 7-spoke wheels $4

320 '59 Caddy, 1995, pink, Real Rider wheels,
   silver $35

321 Corvette Stingray, 1995, green, Real Rider
   wheels, green $40

328 School Bus, 1995, dark windows, blackwalls $20

337 Ramp Truck, 1995, purple, 7-spoke $3

341 '58 Vette Coupe, 1995, pink, 7-spoke wheels $4

342 Mercedes SL, 1996, black with tan interior,
   5-spoke wheels $40

343 Speed Blaster, 1995, blue with black base,
   Ultra Hots wheels $50

344 Camaro Convertible, 1995, red,
   5-spoke wheels $4

347 Power Pistons, 1995, red, Ultra Hots wheels $15

350 Ferrari 355, 1995, yellow, 5-spoke $6

369 Sizzler, 1996, white $4

372 VW Bus, 1996, blue, 5-spoke wheels $65

375 Dog Fighter, 1996, red $4

378 Mustang GT, 1996, red, 3-spoke wheels $20

384 '57 T-Bird, 1996, white with brown flame,
   7-spoke wheels $7

390 Alien, 1996, blue, 5-spoke wheels $3

398 VW Bug, 1996, blue, 7-spoke wheels $5

399 '67 Camaro, 1996, green, 7-spoke wheels $40

405 Custom Corvette, 1996, purple with red interior,
   7-spoke wheels $40

418 Sweet Stocker, 1996, white, 3-spoke wheels $15

423 Wienermobile, 1996, chrome, 5-spoke wheels $4

427 Fire Eater, 1996, red, 5-spoke wheels $3

445 Jaguar 220, 1996, green, 7-spoke wheels $12

449 Camaro Z-28, 1996, orange, 5-spoke wheels $5

450 Corvette Stingray, 1996, white, 7-spoke wheels $4

455 '65 Mustang Convertible, 1996, gold,
   3-spoke wheels $4

463 Pontiac Fiero, 1996, lime green,
   5-spoke wheels $3

474 VW Golf, black, 5-spoke wheels $3

482 Earthmover, 1996, yellow, construction tires,
   silver $3

488 Sting Rod, 1996, gray, construction tires, silver $3

499 Corvette Coupe, 1996, green, 5-spoke wheels $3

509 Firebird Funny Car, 1996, blue, 5-spoke wheels $4

527 Second Wind, 1997, white $5

533 Hummer, 1997, blue, sawblade wheels $3

577 Police Cruiser, 1996, black, 7-spoke wheels $4

591 Porsche 911, 1997, red, 5-dot wheels $3

Hot Wheels Treasure Hunts

   Values are for Mint-in-Package condition (number produced).

353 Olds 442, 1995 (10,000) $60

354 Gold Passion, metallic gold, 1995 (10,000) $80

355 '67 Camaro, 1995 (10,000) $200

356 '57 T-Bird, 1995 (10,000) $50

357 Volkswagen Bug, fluorescent green,
   1995 (10,000) $80

358 '63 Split Window, 1995 (10,000) $70

359 Stutz Blackhawk, 1995 (10,000) $50

360 Rolls-Royce Phantom II, 1995 (10,000) $45

361 Classic Caddy, 1995 (10,000) $45

362 Nomad, 1995 (10,000) $60

363 Classic Cobra, 1995 (10,000) $85

364 '31 Doozie, 1995 (10,000) $45

428 1940s Woodie, yellow-line yellow Real Riders,
   1996 (25,000) $35

428 Woodie, white-line yellow Real Riders,
   1996 (25,000) $75

429 Lamborghini Countach, 1996 (25,000) $22

430 Ferrrari 250, 1996 (25,000) $22

431 Jaguar XJ220, 1996 (25,000) $20

432 '59 Caddy, 1996 (25,000) $28

433 Dodge Viper RT/10, white, 1996 (25,000) $45

433 Viper, red (mispack), 1996 (25,000) $12

434 1957 Chevy, 1996 (25,000) $40

435 Ferrari 355, 1996 (25,000) $18

436 '58 Corvette, 1996 (25,000) $40

437 Auburn 852, 1996 (25,000) $25

438 Dodge Ram 1500, 1996 (25,000) $30

439 1937 Bugatti, 1996 (25,000) $18

578 '56 Flashsider, 1997 (25,000) $30

579 Silhouette II, 1997 (25,000) $15

580 Mercedes 500 SL, 1997 (25,000) $15

THE ULTIMATE TREASURE!

Every collecting area has its Mona Lisa. For example, in the baseball card hobby, it's the famous T-206 tobacco card of Honus Wagner. For Hot Wheels collectors, the ultimate treasure is the 1969 Volkswagen Beach Bomb with the surf boards sticking through the rear window.

This van, likely a reproduction model that never reached store shelves, has been found in five different colors and is valued at $4,000-$5,000. Its more common counterpart (with the surf boards on the side), sells for around $275 (Mint-in-Package) in any of 14 colors.

581 Street Cleaver, 1997 (25,000) $18
582 Lean Machine, 1997 (25,000) $15
583 Hot Rod Wagon, 1997 (25,000) $40
584 Olds Aurora, 1997 (25,000) $15
585 Dog Fighter, 1997 (25,000) $15
586 Buick Wildcat, 1997 (25,000) $15
587 Blimp, 1997 (25,000) $15
588 Avus Quattro, 1997 (25,000) $15
589 Rail Rodder, 1997 (25,000) $24
749 Twang Thang, 1998 (25,000) $15
750 Scorchin' Scooter, 1998 (25,000) $35
751 Kenworth T600A, 1998 (25,000) $18
752 3-Window '34, 1998 (25,000) $22
753 Turbo Flame, 1998 (25,000) $22
754 Saltflat Racer, 1998 (25,000) $14
755 Street Beast, 1998 (25,000) $14
756 Road Rocket, 1998 (25,000) $14
757 Sol-Aire CX-4, 1998 (25,000) $15

A favorite with collectors, the 1971 "Snorkel" is worth $150 in Mint-in-Package condition.

758 '57 Chevy, 1998 (25,000) $20
759 Corvette Stingray II, 1998 (25,000) $16
760 Way-2 Fast, 1998 (25,000) $16

Hot Wheels Accessories

12-Car Rally Case, #5137, 1968 .... $10
24-Car Case, #5138, 1968, vinyl, white and purple
    cars $45
24-Car Super Rally Case, #5142, 1969 .... $6
24-Car Adjustable Case, #5144, 1969,
    yellow with blue and white cars $35
24-Car Collector's Race case, #4976, 1970,
    Custom Mustang, Custom Camaro $35
48-Car Collector's Race Case, #4977, 1970,
    Porsche 917 and Ferrari 312P $40
Automatic Lap Counter, #6270, 1970 .... $15
Construction Co., #5014, 1968 .... $75
Daredevil Loop, #6226, 1968, 360-degree
    drive-in loop-the-loop $15
Dual-Lane Lap Counter, #6476 .... $25
Full Curve Pak, #6225, 1968, banked full
    180-degree curve $15
Half Curve Pak, #6227, 1968 .... $12
Hot Wheels Club Kit, 1970, includes membership card,
    certificate, silver Boss Hoss car, stickers, patches,
    booklet $150
Jump Ramp, #6283, 1969, leap-through-space action,
    two ramps $14
Mongoose and Snake Drag Race Set, #6438,
    1970 .... $500
Service Station, #5013, 1968 .... $65
Speedometer, #6483, 1970 .... $22
Super-Charger, #6294, 1970 .... $45
Talking Service Center, #5159, 1969 .... $80
Trestle 5-Pak, #6284, 1970 .... $15
Tune-Up Tower Performance Center, #6481,
    1970 .... $75
2-Way Super-Charger, #6295 .... $55

HUNTING COLLECTIBLES

North America's first settlers brought with them old country hunting tools—like guns, traps and decoys—to harvest the teeming game of this vast and unsettled wilderness (see also "Fishing Collectibles"). These items were the essentials of early settlers. Antique hunting items have become collectible mainly within the last 25 years. General categories include the following:

Decoys—The origin of bird decoys is sketchy, but records seem to indicate wood decoys were in use as early as the 1770s. Collected primarily as handmade folk art, decoys of geese, shorebirds (plovers, curlews) and ducks command much collector interest.

The carver of a decoy (individual or factory) greatly influences value. Most carvers' markings are found on the bottom of a decoy. Carvers from certain schools of design or regions may bring higher prices than others. Factory-made decoys by Mason are especially valuable.

Condition, of course, is a top consideration. Decoys with much original paint are preferable. Poor repainting, cracks, termites and breaks can detract from a decoy's value. Professional repainting and restoration, however, can improve an otherwise worthless decoy.

Certain species of birds (and in some cases, even the duck's gender) are more valuable than others. Merganser and teal decoys are widely popular, while wood duck decoys are rarer. Drake (male) decoys are more common than hens (females).

Guns—The American settlers brought with them one of their most prized possessions—the black powder musket (or muzzleloader). These early tools also had a companion collectible—black powder. Old muzzleloaders can sell for $150 up to thousands of dollars.

Early waterfowling punt guns are rare and worth more than black powder muskets. They generally command $2,000 to $5,000. Those of unusual length or size may sell for more.

One box of 12 shells for these large guns recently sold for $3,000. The shoulder punt guns in the four-gauge range bring

COLLECTOR'S ALERT!

Calendars and posters have been reproduced. Winchester reproduced its early calendars in the early 1960s. Reproductions also exist for Peters, Remington, and United States Cartridge. Tin signs that are often available at flea markets and shows are sometimes reproductions, too, so be wary of these items. If you know what you are buying and from whom you are buying, you will not get burned.

This advertising sign for "Iver Johnson Champion" sold for just over $2,000 at a Robert Eldred auction in East Dennis, Mass.

from $4,000 to $10,000 depending on the maker. Many large-bore muzzleloaders with twist steel barrels have been sold for between $500 and $2,000. Rust detracts from a gun's value, and to command top dollar, a gun should still be operational.

Powder Cans—Powder cans, often used as decorations, are highly collectible, especially if the graphics are clean and clear. Tin containers with clean graphics can sell for $50 to $300. Containers shaped like wooden barrels are often worth $200 to $400. Cans with paper or printed end labels in Good or better condition command premiums.

Shell Boxes—The first shell boxes were introduced in the late 1800s. The two-piece cardboard boxes were printed with beautiful labels of hunting scenes or color graphics usually on the top and sides of the box. Some had game scenes on the labels and some only had the name of the company. Boxes by U.M.C., Remington, Winchester and Eastern Cartage are especially desirable. Two-piece boxes sell in the $20-$50 range; those with especially clean graphics may command more. After the turn of the century, the one-piece box debuted, but they are not as collectible as two-piece boxes.

Traps—Bear traps are valued at between $150 and $500. Small wooden and wire traps cost from $10 to $150, depending on their condition. Rabbit, fox, mink and beaver traps generally sell for less than $100. Trapper permit buttons, game and fish permits may sell from $30 to $100.

Contributors to this section: Howard Harlan, 4920 Franklin Rd., Nashville, TN 37220, 615-832-0564; Carl Luckey.

Recommended Reading

Books

Krause Publications publishes more than 75 books on collectible guns and weapons, including the following:
Collecting Antique Bird Decoys & Duck Calls, Carl F. Luckey

Flayderman's Guide to Antique American Firearms & Their Values, Norm Flayderman
2000 Standard Catalog of Firearms, 10th Edition, Ned Schwing
Standard Catalog of Winchester, David D. Kowalski
Gun Digest Book of Sporting Clays, Harold Murtz
Gun Digest Book of Trap and Skeet Shooting, Chris Christian
Shotguns for Wingshooting, John Barsness
Complete Guide to Guns & Shooting, John Malloy
Shotgun Digest, 4th Edition, Jack Lewis
Bolt-Action Rifles, Frank de Haas
Remington Firearms, the Golden Age of Collecting, Robert W. D. Ball

Periodicals

Gun List
Military Trader
Gun & Knife Show Calendar

VALUE LINE

Decoys

Values listed are for decoys in Good to Excellent condition by carvers from various regions listed.

Long Island
Thomas Gelston duck decoys	$300-$1,000
Al Ketchum	$1,000-$1,500
Obediah Verity	$1,500-$6,000

Maine
George Huey	$500-$2,500
Gus Wilson Mergansers, black ducks	$1,000-$5,000
Gus Wilson (others)	$750-$3,500
Other Maine carvers	$250-$750

Mason's Decoy Factory
Black Duck	$300-$1,000
Canada Goose	$500-$2,000
Green Wing Teal	$650-$2,000
Mallard	$325-$1,500

Decoys are among the most desirable of all hunting collectibles. This pair, sold at an Eldred's auction in East Dennis, Mass., include a Canada Goose decoy by A.E. Crowell (left) valued at about $1,000; and a Canada Goose decoy from the Mason Decoy factory, restored by A.E. Crowell, that is valued at $2,000-$2,500.

Massachusetts
Elmer Crowell	$650-$6,000
Joe Lincoln	$1,000-$6,000
Benjamin Smith	$525-$2,000

New York State
Sam Denny	$250-$1,000
Frank Lewis	$50-$250
Chauncy Wheeler	$500-$3,000

North Carolina
Lem and Lee Dudley	$2,000-$10,000
Mitchell Fulcher	$2,000-$10,000
Alvira Wright	$4,000-$10,000

Pacific Coast
Horace Crandall	$750-$2,000
Richard Ludwig Jantzen	$750-$3,500

St. Clair Flats
Thomas Chambers	$775-$3,500
Ralph Reghi	$225-$500
George Warin	$750-$1,500

Stratford (Connecticut)
Roswell Bliss	$500-$1,200
Ben Holmes	$500-$2,000
Albert Laing	$1,000-$5,000

Susquehanna Flats
Sam Barnes	$200-$600
Ben Dye	$150-$500
R. Madison Mitchell	$150-$500
R. Madison Mitchell swan decoys	$1,000-$3,000

Wisconsin
August "Gus" Moak	$500-$1,000
Frank Strey	$225-$600

Shot Guns

Values shown are for guns in Good condition.

Browning 12-gauge automatic	$175-$275
Fox shot gun 12-gauge	$375-$425
L.C. Smith 12 gauge	$375-$425
Lefever 12-gauge	$150-$250
Parker shot gun 12-gauge	$375-$700
Remington Model 1900, hammerless shotgun	$275-$800
Springfield Armory Musket	$175-$225
Stevens/Savage 12 gauge	$50-$150
Winchester Lever Action 12 gauge	$75-$150
Winchester double-barrel shotgun	$1,000-$3,500

Shot Shell Boxes

Leader 200 round box	$70-$80
Montgomery Ward two-piece Flying Goose	$45-$60
Montgomery Ward two-piece Mallard	$55-$70
Peters single piece box	$15-$25
Remington Game Load	$55-$80
Remington UMC two-piece	$55-$80
Winchester Ranger (Dog on Point)	$25-$40
Winchester Sunburst	$40-$50
Winchester Super X	$25-$30
Winchester two-piece all brass (empty)	$75-$100

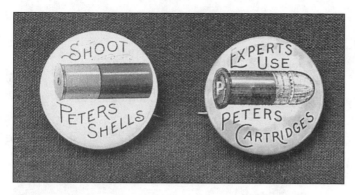

Vintage advertising buttons for shells and cartridges are nice display items. They typically sell in the $20-$40 range.

Traps

Bear traps, Newhouse, Blake and Lamb	$300-$1,000
Beaver traps, Triumph #315	$60
Bird traps, common cage type	$12
Fish traps (Underwood, Evans, Gabriel)	$200-$300
Fly traps	$60
Gibbs Hawl trap	$80
Gibbs mole trap	$40
Leg hold trap, Newhouse, small	$12
Leg hold trap, Newhouse, large	$30
Live wire traps, "Qurouze" type	$25
Minnow Glass Trap	$75
Mole traps, Nash, Kalamazoo, MI	$8
Mouse trap, all metal Victor	$30
Reddick mole traps	$12
Sargent & Co. small	$25
Sargent & Co. large	$40
Triumph small	$5-$6
Triumph large	$25
Wire trap	$10-$15
Wolf traps, Newhouse 4-1/2"	$100
Wolf traps, Hawley and Norton	$150

Paper collectibles

Calendar, DuPont Powder Co., 1908	$325
Calendar, Hercules Powder Co., 1920, "A Surprise Party"	$125
Calendar, Peters Cartridge Co., 1906, "Coming Out Ahead"	$500
Calendar, Remington, 1925, "Let 'Er Rain,"	$500
Calendar, Winchester Arms Co., 1896, "A Finishing Touch"	$650
Catalog, Ambercrombie & Fitch, 1949	$75
Catalog, L.L. Bean, 1932	$50
Catalog, Winchester Arms, 1896	$350
Comic book, *Remington, How to Shoot*	$25
Envelope, Ithaca Gun Co., line drawing of shotgun	$150
Envelope, Remington, hawk chasing fleeing ducks	$275

Vintage calendars often display nice hunting-related artwork. This example is a 1924 Remington calendar.

Hunting license, Illinois, 1908, waterfowl	$175
Hunting license, Connecticut, 1926	$50
Hunting license, New Jersey, 1938	$45
Hunting license, Wisconsin, 1930	$35
Hunting/fishing/trapping license, New York, 1929	$15
Postcard, Remington, factory and shot tower	$25
Postcard, Winchestor, factory	$25
Poster, Hercules Powder Co., 1923, "I'se Lost De Lunch"	$475
Poster, Ithaca Gun Co., 1912, mallard ducks	$550

Poster, Remington, 1907, hunter and
grizzly meet $550
Promotional Flyer, Winchester, model 21 shotgun,
late 1940s $65
Stationery, Ithaca Gun Co., open gun at top $40
Store display, "Winchester Shot Shells Sold Here,"
die-cut, cardboard $1,200

Magazines

The American Rifleman, 1923-30 .... $10-$15
Field and Stream, prior to 1910 .... $25-$30
Field and Stream, 1945-1960 .... $5-$10
Gun Digest, 1946-1949 .... $125-$175
Outdoor Life, 1945-1960 .... $5-$7
Outdoor Life, 1960-present .... $3-$5
Sports Afield, 1960-present .... $3-$5

Miscellaneous

Duck call, Herter's, with box $45

Duck call, red cedar, Charles Perdew,
1930s-1940s $275
Enamel sign, National Wildlife Refuge,
"Unauthorized Entry Prohibited," 1960s............... $225
Metal sign, U.S. Department of the Interior Fish and
Wildlife Service, Bureau of Sport Fisheries and
Wildlife, 1960s $225
Olt "Turkey Hooter Owl Call," with box $50
Oil can, Remington, yellow and blue lithographed $45
Oil can, Winchester, green $50
Powder can, Hazard Powder Co., 1-pound can, green,
red and gold letters $45
Powder can, Hercules Powder Co., 1-pound can,
Infallible Shotgun Smokeless $15
Snipe whistle, Ambercrombie & Fitch, 1900s........... $750
Target ball, glass, 1890s $125
Turkey call, slate box, M.L. Lynch, 1970s................ $225

KITCHEN APPLIANCES

Where would Americans be without our modern kitchen appliances? We take them so much for granted that its hard to imagine there was a time—and really not that long ago—when electrical kitchen appliances seemed like magical contraptions from outer space. The electrification of the home, which began in earnest in the early 1900s, transformed all aspects of life in America, but no room in the home benefited more from this transformation than the kitchen. The development of electrical appliances turned the kitchen from a place of drudgery into a world of comfort and convenience.

Today, these vintage kitchen appliances seem hopelessly archaic next to our modern microwaves and remote-controlled coffee makers, but they have emerged as hugely popular collectibles, desirable both for display and actual use.

While a few hard-core enthusiasts may be looking for old stoves and refrigerators, it is the smaller vintage appliances that are most in demand—everything from old toasters and waffle irons to early popcorn-poppers and malted-milk machines. Many of these early appliances were rather sturdy in their construction, and a surprising number have survived through the decades, much to the delight of today's collectors.

Background: The age of electricity in America began in the 1890s. At the turn of the century, the typical American kitchen was still a rather unenlightened part of the home. All kitchen chores were done by hand, and most families still depended on coal or wood to fuel their kitchen stoves. Even gas stoves were considered a luxury. By around 1910, electrical appliances had started to revolutionize America's kitchens, and the years between 1910 and 1930 saw huge advancements in the field. The 1920s and 1930s, especially, brought an incredible array of appliances into the home.

The very earliest electrical contraptions paid no attention to style or design. Just that they worked was amazing enough, and manufacturers made no attempt to dress them up or hide the workings. Early appliances often had exposed wires, coils, etc. These early pieces are relatively scarce and collected mostly as curious oddities of the past.

As the electricity age exploded, though, more attention was paid to design. The 1930s, especially, brought some wonderful designs, with gleaming chrome, streamlined shapes

COLLECTOR'S ADVISORY!

Be wary of frayed or damaged cords on vintage electrical appliances. If a cord looks damaged or broken, replace it before testing the machine. Removing a bottom plate to replace the cord is generally a fairly easy task, and "old-style" cords are still readily available at many of the better electrical-supply houses.

and Art-Deco-inspired lines. The use of white enameled parts was also popular and gave appliances a crisp, sanitary appearance. Vintage appliances from this era are very much in demand by today's collectors.

The years of World War II affected appliance manufacturing, just as it did all other aspects of American life at the time, and further advances in appliance design and innovation had to wait until the late 1940s and early 1950s. The postwar boom years brought new designs and new appliances, including amazing innovations like the electric frying pan, the toaster oven, and the electric can opener. Appliances sported sleek new designs and even came in colors. New models appeared every year—just like in the automobile market. This era offers a tremendous variety for today's collector.

General Guidelines: Here's a brief look at a few of the more collectible appliance categories.

Toasters—Vintage toasters remain the most collectible of all early electric kitchen appliances. Among the first commercially successful toasters were the Westinghouse "Toaster Stove" and the General Electric D-12, introduced in 1909-1910. The very first electric toasters had simple wire frames to hold the bread against the heating element. Many had decorated porcelain bases and removable overhead warming trays. Today, some of these more desirable early models can sell for hundreds of dollars. Especially rare examples in nice condition can command $1,000 or more.

Also popular with many collectors are the "swing-basket" type toasters dating from the 1920s and first made by Manning Bowman. These models were designed to swing out

Vintage chrome kitchen appliances still look great.

to turn the bread around for toasting on both sides. By 1926, McGraw Electric had developed the first automatic pop-up "Toastmaster," which automatically shut off after reaching the desired amount of toasting. In 1949, Sunbeam offered a bi-metal model operated by "radiant control," which allowed the bread to be lowered automatically and then emerge as toast.

One of the more innovative toaster designs was the 1938 "Toast-O-Lator," which used a novel conveyor-belt approach. You inserted the bread in one end, and it traveled through the machine (much like an automatic car-wash), coming out the other end as toast. A porthole window in the side even allowed viewing of the toasting process as it took place. In actuality, the idea sounded better than it was. Frequent problems with the conveyor belt kept the device from being commercially successful, but the "Toast-O-Lator" remains a favorite with collectors today. Relatively scarce, it typically sells for as much as $200.

Another scarcity that's popular with collectors, selling for $150 or more, is the equally innovative (and even older) "Perc-O-Toaster." Offered by the Armstrong Co. in 1918, this interesting device made coffee and toast at the same time on the breakfast table, using a heating element that radiated heat both up and down. It, too, sounded better than it was.

Waffle Irons—Electric waffle irons starting becoming popular in the teens, when a model introduced by Landers, Frary & Clark was introduced. The market grew quickly throughout the 1920s and '30s. During the 1940s, waffles and pancakes were staples on the menu in most American homes because they could be made with unrationed foodstuffs. As a result, throughout the War years, waffle irons were among the most used of all kitchen appliances.

The late 1940s and 1950s brought the larger, square waffle iron, along with the combination waffle iron-sandwich grill. Later improvements includes waffle irons with removable grids for easier washing and Teflon coating.

Blenders—Blenders came on the scene comparatively late, first appearing on the market in the early 1930s, when the Greene Manufacturing Co. introduced its first model. The Waring "Blendor" arrived in 1937 and dominated this market until 1946, when the first Osterizer appeared. Although advertised as being for the "macerating of fruits and vegetables," early blender companies had a tough time convincing consumers that blenders could be used for anything other than mixing drinks. Collectors like the fact that the shape of the blender lent itself well to Art-Deco-inspired designs.

Mixers—Hamilton Beach offered the first successful electric mixers in the teens and remained one of the dominant names in this area for decades. Mixers for most of the 1920s were dominated by heavy, stationary table-top units made by Hamilton Beach, KitchenAid and others. In 1926 Air-O-Mix introduced its "Whip-All" model, the first combination mixer that could also be used as a portable mixer.

The market was really revolutionized five years later, in 1931, when Sunbeam introduced its first "Mixmaster," the model that became the industry standard for years. Eventu-

ally, mixmasters became lighter and more portable, leading to the first cordless models in the 1960s.

Coffee Makers—The first electric coffee percolator was made by Landers, Frary & Clark in 1908, using their "Universal" trade name. Most modern coffee makers owe their past to the "Coffee Robot," introduced in 1937 by S.W. Farber. It made the coffee, automatically shut off when done brewing and, with a thermostat control, kept the coffee hot indefinitely. At the time, coffee drinkers thought it was nothing short of a miracle.

Fry Pans—The first electric fry pans were an offspring of the old-fashioned chafing dish, a very popular kitchen appliance in the late 1800s. The first mass-produced electric fry pan was introduced by Westinghouse in 1911. The concept did not enjoy the same immediate success as other electrical appliances, mostly because the early models did not have very dependable heat controls, making them a gamble to use (most housewives preferred the reliability of the old-fashioned fry pan.) In fact, electric fry pans did not become popular in America until Sunbeam introduced its "Automatic Frypan" with controlled heat in 1953. The pan had an unusual square configuration, instead of the traditional round shape. By the 1960s, the heat-control units could be removed for easier cleaning.

Irons—Although technically not a kitchen appliance, electric irons fit nicely into this category (because of their size and design), and they are often collected alongside vintage toasters, waffle irons, etc. The iron was among the very first of the electrical appliances. The American Electric Heater Co. was selling electric irons to the laundry trade as early as 1905, and in 1912 the company released its famous "American Beauty" iron for household use.

The "Mysto" iron, released in 1930, was the first electric iron to feature a temperature control, while the "Automatic Heat-Adjusting Speed Iron," produced by Proctor in 1933 was the first to include settings for different fabrics. The "Steam-O-Matic" iron was released in 1938, becoming the first commercially successful over-the-top, good-quality steam iron. Ten years later, Sunbeam advertised its "Ironmaster" as being "hot in 30 seconds," a tremendous improvement over earlier models.

Other Appliances—Collectors also look for vintage electric knives, broilers, hot plates, deep fryers, juicers, egg cookers, coffee grinders, popcorn poppers, etc. Vintage

COLLECTOR'S TIP!

Collectors of vintage kitchen appliances also collect owner's manuals, product brochures, company catalogs, magazine advertisements, and similar items featuring vintage appliances. Early appliances were often sold with an instruction tag containing recipes and other information. These evolved into the more formal owner's manual/recipe books that were common in later years malted-milk machines are especially popular. Often, the more unusual the item the more desirable it is.

Values—For the most part, collectors of vintage electrical appliances want their items to work. Condition is very important. Many a grimy-looking appliance can be carefully cleaned and made presentable, but watch out for dents, dings, broken pieces, etc. Often, electrical cords are frayed, base paint is chipped or worn away, glass and porcelain pieces are chipped or cracked, etc. Also, many pieces are found with burned out motors or heating units. Fortunately, most mechanical and electrical problems can be repaired (professional repair is available but costly!), but external damage can make many pieces undesirable. So it is important to check the overall condition and appearance, as well as testing to see if the machine works.

For many collectors, design is critical. Popular are Art Deco-styled pieces, appliances with unusual designs or features, unusual operating mechanisms, decorations, etc. Chrome-bodied appliances are always more desirable and valuable than painted metal or plastic-bodied appliances. Brass and copper-bodied appliances are also valuable, but scarce.

The values shown below indicate the range of material that is available and the range of prices.

Recommended Reading

300 Years of Housekeepng Collectibles, Linda Campbell Franklin

300 Years of Kitchen Collectibles, Linda Campbell Franklin

Collectibles for the Kitchen, Bath & Beyond, Ellen Bercovici, Bobbie Zucker Bryson

VALUE LINE

Values shown are for appliances that work and are in Very Good to Excellent condition.

Blender, Sears Kenmore, 1950s ....$20-$40
Blender, "Chronmaster Mixall," 1930s chrome
    on black base ....$40-$60
Blender, Polar Cub, A.C. Gilbert, 1929 ....$125-$150
Blender, Hamilton Beach Malt Machine, 1920s,
    Cyclone #1 ....$300-$325
Blender, Silex, 1940s, white cast base ....$35-$45
Blender, Knapp Monarch Whipper, 1930s.............$60-$75
Broiler, Manning Bowman, chrome, 1940............$30-$40
Broiler, Regal, aluminum, 1955 ....$20-$30
Can opener, Udico, 1960, pink and chrome..........$35-$55
Coffee pot (Silex), with burner (GE), 1939 ....$35-$40
Coffee pot, urn shape, chromium on brass,
    Forman ....$15-$30
Coffee pot, "Flavo Matic," West Bend, colored
    aluminum, silo-shaped ....$25-$50
Coffee pot, "Automatic Perculator," General Electric,
    oval shape, unusual ....$25-$35
Coffee pot, "Coffeemaster," Sunbeam, two-tiered,
    very desirable ....$40-$60

Vintage waffle irons, in various sizes and styles, are all popular with collectors.

Coffee pot, "Coffee Robot" set, Farberware, 1937,
    with coffee maker creamer, sugar and tray .....$90-$120
Coffee pot, "Coffeemaker" Presto, completely
    immersible, 1970..$12-$20
Cooker/Roaster, Sunbeam, 1952...........................$35-$50
Cooker/Roaster, Dominion, attached cord ....$30-$50
Deep fryer, "Fri-Well," Dormeyer, 1952................$30-$45
Defroster, anodized aluminum, wood handle,
    Shane Mfg. ....$10-$15
Defroster, aluminum, plastic handle,
    Nu-Rod Inc..$10-$15
Egg cooker, Sunbeam, 4 pieces, 1951 ....$30-$45
Fry pan, "Controlled Heat Automatic Frypan,"
    Sunbeam, 1955...$10-$25
Fry pan, flying saucer shaped, colored aluminum,
    Century Enterprises, scarce..............................$45-$65
Fry pan, "Electric Skillet," GE, turquoise base
    with glass top, unusual ....$60-$75
Hot plate, Edison-Hotpoint, 1910 ....$35-$45
Hot plate, white porcelain enamel,
    Samson United Corp. ....$15-$25
Hot plate, "Signature," Montgomery Ward,
    white with chrome top.......................................$15-$25
Hot plate, "Buffet Queen," Cory Corp., two burners,
    bakelite handles..$20-$25
Hot plate, "Two Heater Electric Stove, Cory Corp.,
    bakelite handle ....$10-$15
Hot plate, "Automatic Heat-Rite Base," Sears,
    1960s ....$10-$15
Iron, "Steam-O-Matic," Waverly Tool Co. ....$20-$30
Iron, "Royal," Brock Snyder Mfg. Co.,
    wood handle ....$15-$30
Knife, "Peel King," with attachments,
    S&H Mfg. Co., 1961 ....$10-$15

Although they are not technically kitchen appliances, vintage irons fit nicely in this general category.

Mixer, "Whip-All," Air-O-Mix, 1920s,
  scarce...$100-$125
Mixer, "Dormey," Dormeyer, hand-held................$10-$20
Mixer, "Mary Dunbar Handymix,"
  Chicago Electric..$25-$40
Mixer, "Mixmaster," Sunbeam, pink,
  desirable...$100-$120
Mixer, "Mixmaster," Sunbeam, white....................$40-$70
Mixer, "Dominion Modern Mode," 1923-33.........$75-$90
Popcorn popper, "Fostoria," McGraw Electric,
  with glass top...$15-$20
Popcorn popper, US Mfg. Co., brick red and tan
  with crank...$20-$25
Popcorn popper, Excel, 1920s................................$25-$30
Popcorn popper, Manning Bowman,
  early 1940s..$15-$20
Popcorn popper, Rapaport, 1920s..........................$25-$35
Popcorn popper, White Cross, 1918,
  National Stamping & Electric...........................$30-$40

Roaster, "Heet-Wel," Welco Inc............................$40-$50
Sandwich grill, "Samson," Samson United Co.,
  plain wood handles..$40-$60
Tea kettle, Sunbeam, made in Canada,
  dome-shaped...$40-$60
Toaster, "Toast-O-Lator," 1930s, scarce.............$125-$200
Toaster, Sunbeam model T-9, desirable classic......$65-$90
Toaster, "Fostoria," automatic pop-up,
  McGraw Electric...$40-$55
Toaster, Edison Appliance Co., 1918, removable
  warming rack, open nickel body.....................$90-$120
Toaster, Heat Master, 1920s-30s, chrome body,
  black bakelite handles, two-slice......................$50-$65
Toaster, Sears Kenmore, early 1940s, chrome,
  black bakelite handles.......................................$25-$30
Toaster, Steel Craft, late 1920s, open, painted
  green wire construction, flip-flop style............$45-$55
Toaster, Sunbeam, early 1920s, chrome body,
  bakelite feet, double wire cages flip over......$125-$150
Toaster, "Toastmaster," 1927 Waters-Genter, chrome
  Art Deco body, pop-up mechanism..............$200-$225
Toaster, Westinghouse "Toaster Stove,"
  1909...$150-$175
Toaster, "Radiant Control," Sunbeam, 1951..........$35-$55
Toaster, "Toastmaster," McGraw Electric,
  1942..$40-$60
Waffle iron/grill, Dominion Electric Co.,
  square with brown bakelite handles..................$40-$60
Waffle iron, Westinghouse, black bakelite
  handles with incised leaf design.......................$40-$55
Waffle iron, "White Cross," National Stampling
  and Electric, unusual...$50-$75
Waffle iron, Manning Bowman Co.,
  chrome with bakelite handles............................$55-$75
Waffle iron, "Twin-O-Matic," Manning Bowman,
  late 1930s, Art Deco design............................$90-$110
Waffle iron, Westinghouse, 1905-21, chrome body,
  removable cabriole legs slip into body............$90-$100
Water pot, Dormeyer, chrome................................$10-$15

LIMITED EDITION COLLECTIBLES

Unlike most collectibles, limited editions are made with collectibility in mind. The most common limited editions are figurines, ornaments, decorative boxes, prints, dolls and plates.

Limited editions are intentionally restricted at the time of production in order to increase their desirability on the primary market, and to increase their value on the secondary market. (The primary market consists of the shops and retail outlets where items are originally offered for sale. The secondary market consists of auction houses, yard sales and Internet arenas in which such products are resold. Prices here can be much higher or lower than the original issue prices seen on the primary market.)

The purest way to limit a product is by number of pieces produced. At the time a piece is issued, the company will announce how many are in existence. The lower the limit—100 or 200 pieces is very low—the more expensive the piece will be on the primary market, and the more likely it will be to increase in value once it hits the secondary market.

Three other ways to limit a product are: by production, meaning pieces will only be produced for a certain number of days; by year, meaning no more pieces will be produced once the year of issue ends; or by the number of orders received, usually meaning the maker will match demand by supplying an unspecified number of pieces. All three of these limits are less desirable than the first, because they do not reveal the specific number of pieces produced.

Manufacturers are now also limiting certain pieces to specific regions of the country, making them available only at collecting events, or making them available only to members of a collecting club. These methods are frustrating for many collectors, but also serve their purpose—secondary market prices for such items often increase immediately, as large groups of people do not have access to the pieces on the primary market.

Having a complete collection is extremely important to collectors of limited editions. Some seek out every piece in a certain series, or all pieces by a certain artist. This makes the first piece in a series, or the earliest pieces by a popular artist, generally more expensive on the secondary market than later pieces.

It is important to note that many similar products are created with no limit, termed open editions. Prices for open edition pieces most often remain at original retail price well after issue date. Some of the most popular figurine, ornament and plate collections—Precious Moments, Hummels, Dreamsicles, Christopher Radko ornaments—consist of open editions, with just a few limited editions thrown into the mix. The limited editions will be more collectible, but an open edition piece can gain desirability if the company decides at some point to retire or close the issue, which would mean the

manufacturer had discontinued production. The piece would then become limited, although the exact number of pieces produced usually remains unknown.

Background: The limited edition market boomed in the United States in the 1970s, but it actually began in the late 1800s with the production of a Christmas plate. Harald Bing of Denmark, director of the Bing & Grondahl porcelain house, commissioned artist Frans August Hallin to design a special plate for the 1895 holiday season. The result was "Behind the Frozen Window," which had an inscription that read "Jule Aften 1895 (Christmas Eve 1895). When enough pieces had been produced to satisfy Bing's needs (the best guess is 500), he had the mold destroyed, creating the first-ever limited-edition plate. The continuing series tradition began the following year when another Christmas plate was created, titled Jule Aften 1896.

The mid-1930s gave rise to what would become one of the most popular figurine collections of modern times. Fashioned after Sister Maria Innocentia Hummel's delightful renderings of young children, the first Hummels appeared on the market in Germany at this time. They have attracted collectors ever since, produced by Goebel of Germany.

During the last 20 years decorative crystal figurines and ornaments, led by Swarovski artists, have grown to become one of the hottest categories among limited editions. Even more recently on the rise is the decorative box, which includes Limoges pieces and also the very popular box figurines of Harmony Kingdom's artisans.

KNOW YOUR LIMITS!

Collectors should be familiar with the terms that manufacturers, dealers and collectors use regarding limited-edition collectibles and their availability. Some of the common descriptions include:

Retired—The piece will no longer be produced by the manufacturer. Often a company will hold a celebration where it "breaks the molds" for newly retired pieces, ensuring that no new pieces will ever be made in that design.

Closed—The number of pieces the company intended to release have been produced.

Suspended—Production of the piece has halted, but could resume again in the future. Often this is done if a problem or error is detected with the design of the piece.

Sold out—Just what it says.

Open—The piece is still being made.

General Guidelines: While the limited edition market began with a plate, the most popular category today is figurines; decorative boxes are also on the rise. Plates have experienced a significant decline in interest since their heyday in the 1970s. The limited edition plates currently being produced should be purchased for their decorative appeal, unless the limit is very restricted or the artist extremely well-known. Older plates can still garner relatively high prices on the secondary market.

Limited editions that are part of a series usually attract more collecting interest than stand-alone pieces. Likewise, those by well-known and respected artists hold value better than those by short-term manufacturers.

Limited edition collectibles are usually, but not always, marked on the base or bottom. Called a backstamp, or bottom stamp, this often incorporates a company logo. It is considered proof of the product's authenticity.

The fewer pieces in circulation and the more difficult they are to find, the more a collector is generally willing to pay. Besides rarity, factors that affect value are condition, backstamp, mold changes, paint and finish changes.

Look to collector's clubs to offer exclusive pieces that are likely to increase in value, depending on the popularity of the artist or line, and the limitations placed on the piece.

Collectibles made of resin, a plastic-like material, are usually less valuable than those made of porcelain or other delicate materials. Resin collectibles are also often produced in open editions, making them less desirable on the secondary market.

Clubs/Associations
•Collector's Information Bureau, 5065 Shoreline Rd., Ste. 200, Barrington, IL 60010, 708-842-2200

Recommended Reading

Books
2000 Price Guide to Limited Edition Collectibles, Fifth Edition, Mary Sieber
Collectors' Information Bureau's Collectibles Price Guide & Directory to Secondary Market Dealers

Periodical
Collectors Mart

VALUE LINE

Values shown are an average of the item's current value on the secondary market and are for examples in Mint condition.

Anna-Perenna Plates
P. Buckley Moss, artist
Christmas at Home, annual Christmas plate, 1995 ..... $125
Christmas Carol, annual Christmas plate, 1989.......... $130
Christmas Eve, annual Christmas plate, 1990 .... $140
Christmas Joy, annual Christmas plate, 1988 .... $100
Christmas Night, annual Christmas plate, 1994.......... $125

Christmas Sleigh, annual Christmas plate, 1987 .... $100
Christmas Warmth, annual Christmas plate, 1992...... $125
Family Outing, American Silhouettes series, 1981 .... $100
Homemakers Quilting, American Silhouettes series, 1984........................ $140
John and Mary, American Silhouettes series, 1982........................ $100
Joy to the World, annual Christmas plate, 1993 .... $125
Leisure Time, American Silhouettes series, 1983........ $90
Night Before Christmas, annual Christmas plate, 1986........................ $100
Noel, Noel, annual Christmas plate, 1984 .... $210
Snowman, The, annual Christmas plate, 1991............ $140
Under the Mistletoe, annual Christmas plate, 1996...... $85

ANRI
J. Ferrandiz Christmas Plates
Christ in the Manger, 1972 .... $250
Christmas, 1973 .... $225
Holy Night, 1974 .... $350
Flight Into Egypt, 1975.. $250
Girl with Flowers, 1976 .... $200
Tree of Life, 1977 .... $100
Leading the Way, 1978.. $180
Drummer, The, 1979.. $200
Rejoice, 1980 .... $200
Spreading the Word, 1981.. $200
Shepherd Family, The, 1982 .... $250
Peace Attend Thee, 1983 .... $200
J. Ferrandiz Woodcarvings
1969 Angel Sugar Heart, closed edition $2,525
1970 Duet, 3", closed edition................................... $175
1970 Duet, 6", closed edition................................... $370
1971 Talking to the Animals, 10", closed edition....... $550
1975 Holy Family, closed edition $670
1976 Cowboy, closed edition $550
1977 Hurdy Gurdy, closed edition $395
1978 Spreading the Word, closed edition $500
1983 Golden Blossom, 20", closed edition.............. $5,160
1983 Welcome, club piece, closed edition................. $400
1984 My Friend, club piece, closed edition.............. $400
1985 Harvest Time, club piece, closed edition $300
1986 Celebration March, club piece, closed edition $250
1987 Will You Be Mine, club piece, closed edition $240
1988 Forever Yours, club piece, closed edition $250
1989 Twenty Years of Love, club piece, closed edition $200
1990 You Are My Sunshine, club piece, closed edition $220
1991 With All My Heart, club piece, closed edition $250

Armani Figurines
Ariel 505C, 1994, Disneyana collection, retired...... $2,500
Beauty and the Beast 543C, 1995, Disneyana collection, retired $1,500

Cinderella 783C, 1992, Disneyana collection,
retired $4,000
Cinderella and the Prince 107C, 1997, Disneyana
collection, retired $825
Daisy 202E, 1994 club event piece, retired $450
Discovery of America—Columbus 867C, 1992,
commemorative $525
Jasmine and Rajah, 1996, Disneyana collection,
retired $1,225
Loving Arms 880E, 1993 club event piece,
retired $500
Pals (boy with dog) 407S, 1990 club event piece,
retired $600
Snow White 199C, 1993, Disneyana collection,
retired $1,900
Springtime 961C, 1992 club event piece, retired $500

Belleek
Christmas plates
Castle Caldwell, 1970 .... $200
Celtic Cross, 1971 .... $85
Flight of the Earls, 1972 .... $70
Tribute to Yeats, 1973 .... $100
Devenish Island, 1974 .... $90
Celtic Cross, The, 1975 .... $90
Dove of Peace, 1976 .... $120
Wren, 1977 .... $80

Bing & Grondahl
Christmas Plates
1895, Behind the Frozen Window $7,000
1896, New Moon $2,400
1897, Sparrows $1,400
1898, Roses and Star $1,000
1899, Crows $2,000
1900, Church Bells.. $1,600
1902, Gothic Church Interior $440
1904, Fredericksberg Hill $180
1905, Christmas Night $180
1906, Sleighing to Church $110
1910, Old Organist, The.. $110
1913, Bringing Home the Tree $50
1914, Amalienborg Castle $25
1915, Dog Outside Window.. $140
1916, Sparrows at Christmas $65
1917, Christmas Boat... $90
1918, Fishing Boat $90
1919, Outside Lighted Window $90
1920, Hare in the Snow.. $80
1921, Pigeons.. $82
1922, Star of Bethlehem $55
1923, Ermitage, The... $80
1924, Lighthouse.. $80
1925, Child's Christmas $80
1926, Churchgoers $80
1927, Skating Couple.. $95
1928, Eskimos.. $70

1929, Fox Outside Farm... $90
1930, Yule Tree $99
1931, Christmas Train $90
1932, Life Boat $95
1933, Korsor-Nyborg Ferry $77
1934, Church Bell in Tower... $77
1935, Lillebelt Bridge $80
1936, Royal Guard $80
1937, Arrival of Christmas Guests.............................. $80
1938, Lighting the Candles $110
1939, Old Lock-Eye, The Sandman............................ $150
1940, Christmas Letters $150
1941, Horses Enjoying Meal....................................... $250
1942, Danish Farm $175
1943, Ribe Cathedral $175
1944, Sorgenfri Castle $100
1945, Old Water Mill, The... $120
1946, Commemorative Cross...................................... $80
1947, Dybbol Mill.. $100
1948, Watchman $65
1949, Landsoldaten $75
1950, Kronborg Castle $110
1951, Jens Bang $100
1954, Royal Boat $89
1955, Kaulundorg Church $123
1956, Christmas in Copenhagen $123
1957, Christmas Candles $139
1958, Santa Claus.. $115
1959, Christmas Eve $129
1960, Village Church... $170
1961, Winter Harmony.. $80
1962, Winter Night $80
1982, Christmas Tree $75

The Enesco Precious Moments Serenity Prayer figurines were released in 1994 with a retail price of $35 each.

The 1958 Bing & Grondahl Santa Claus plate is valued at about $115.

1983, Christmas in Old Town	$70
1984, Christmas Letter, The	$75
1985, Christmas Eve at the Farmhouse	$80
1986, Silent Night, Holy Night	$75
1987, Snowman's Christmas Eve, The	$80
1988, In the King's Garden	$80
1989, Christmas Anchorage	$70
1990, Changing of the Guards	$70
1991, Copenhagen Stock Exchange	$55
1998, Christmas in 1998	$65

Dreamsicles Figurines

1991 Cherub and Child, retired Christmas piece	$45
1991 Forever Yours, retired Christmas piece	$65
1993 A Star is Born, retired club piece	$120
1993 Sweet Dreams, retired Christmas piece	$70
1996 Bundles of Love (Heavenly Classics)	$558

Department 56, Snowbabies Figurines

1986 Climbing on Snowball 7965-0, retired	$100
1986 Hanging Pair 7966-9, retired	$150
1986 Hold on Tight 7956-1, open	$14
1987 Climbing on Tree 7971-5, set of two, retired	$800
1988 Frosty Frolic 7981-2, limited to 4,800	$900
1989 All Fall Down 7984-7, set of four, retired	$55
1991 Fishing For Dreams 6809-8, open	$33

Enesco, Cherished Teddies Figurines

1992 Anna, open	$40
1992 Nathaniel and Nellie, retired	$40
1993 Charity, Easter piece, retired	$100
1993 Daisy, Easter piece, retired	$800
1993 Freda and Tina, open	$65
1993 Teddy Roosevelt, open	$20
1994 Bessie, Easter piece, suspended	$105
1994 Betsey, open	$13
1994 Ingrid, limited to one year	$45
1995 Cub E. Bear, club piece limited to one year	$35
1995 Hilary Hugabear, club piece limited to one year	$40
1995 Mayor Wilson T. Beary, club piece limited to one year	$60

Enesco, Precious Moments Figurines

1976 Prayer Changes Things E1375, suspended	$195
1977 Love is Kind E1379A, suspended	$115

This 1993 Enesco Precious Moments figure, titled "To The Apple of God's Eye," was issued with a $32.50 retail price.

1978 Jesus is Born E2012, suspended $115
1978 Unto Us a Child is Born E2013, suspended....... $115
1979 Christmas is a Time to Share E2802,
    suspended $100
1979 Eggs Over Easy E3118, retired $105
1979 God Loveth a Cheerful Giver E1378,
    retired $900
1980 God Is Love E5213, suspended........................... $75
1980 Thank You For Coming to My Aide E5202,
    suspended $150
1981 Bless This House E7164, suspended $200
1981 There Is Joy in Serving Jesus E7157, retired....... $60
1982 Dropping Over for Christmas E2375,
    retired $100
1982 Taste and See That the Lord is Good E9274,
    retired $160
1983 Praise the Lord Anyhow E9254, retired............. $90
1984 Love is Kind E5377, retired................................ $85
1985 Brotherly Love 100544, suspended $80
1986 Sharing Our Christmas Together 102490,
    suspended $75
1986 Smile Along the Way 101842, retired............... $155
1986 The Spirit Is Willing, But the Flesh Is Weak
    100196, retired $75
1988 Jesus Loves Me 104531, limited to 1,000....... $1,550
1989 I'll Never Stop Loving You 521418, retired $42
1989 I'm So Glad You Fluttered Into My Life
    520640, retired $325

Goebel, Hummel Figurines
Adoration #23/111, 7-1/8", TM 5 .... $375
Angelic Song, #144, TM 6.. $65
Apple Tree Girl, #141/1, TM 5 .... $145
Artist #304, TM 6 .... $90
Barnyard Hero #195/2/0, TM2 .... $115
Boots #143/1, TM 3 .... $175
Cinderella #337, TM 6.. $110
Doll Bath #319, TM 5 .... $75
Eventide, TM 3 .... $135
Feeding Time, #199/1, TM 2 .... $215
Girl With Doll, #239, TM 6 .... $25
Goose Girl, #47/0, TM 2, 4-1/4".............................. $200

Hallmark Ornaments (see separate chapter)
Harmony Kingdom, Box Figurines
    Treasure Jests Collection
Forty Winks, 1992, retired $150
Princely Thoughts, 1992, retired.............................. $150
All Ears, 1993, retired... $60
All Tied Up, 1993, retired.. $70
At Arm's Length, 1993, retired................................. $185
Baby on Board, 1993, retired...................................... $35
Back Scratch, 1993, retired....................................... $950
Day Dreamer, 1993, retired....................................... $200
Hamming it Up, 1993, retired...................................... $50
It's a Fine Day, 1993, retired..................................... $200
Jonah's Hideaway, 1993, retired $185

Reminisce, 1993, retired $165
Side Stepping, 1993, retired...................................... $125
Swamp Song, 1993, retired... $35
Top Banana, 1993, retired... $180
Trunk Show, 1993, retired... $100
Who'd A Thought?, 1993, retired.............................. $950

Lladro Figurines
1969 Beagle puppy lying, retired............................... $250
1969 Beagle puppy pouncing, retired $350
1969 Beagle puppy sitting, retired............................ $275
1971 Dog in Basket, retired $450
1972 Eagles, retired $3,000
1977 Little Red Riding Hood L4965, retired............. $560
1980 Samson and Delilah L5051, retired $1,500
1982 Little Boy Bullfighter L5115, retired................ $400
1984 Swan with Wings Spread L5231, open............. $140
1987 Great Horned Owl L5420, retired..................... $310
1990 Concertina L5695G, retired $350
1990 Mommy, It's Cold L5715G, retired $400

"Good Night" from the Lladro Mother & Child Series, issued in 1987, is now valued at about $375.

1991 Dance of Love L5820G, retired $630
1991 On Her Toes L5818G/M, retired $525
1992 Free Spirit L2220M, retired $235
1992 Just One More L5899G, open $450
1993 Autumn Glow, limited edition of 1,500 .... $900

Miss Martha Originals Figurines

1986 Grandma 1323, retired $3,400
1987 Ben 1504, retired $300
1987 Tat 1801, retired $65
1987 Tiffany 1511, open $32
1988 Maya 1520, retired $380
1989 Bo 1530, retired $70
1990 Jerome 1532, open $32
1990 Thaliyah 778, retired $1,300
1991 Samantha 1542, retired $125
1992 Caitlin 1554, retired $75
1994 Justin 1576, open $37

Swarovski Crystal Pieces

Dolphins, 1990, collectors society piece, retired $1,500
Elephant, 1993, collectors society piece, retired $1,750
Kudu, 1994, collectors society piece, retired $600
Lion, 1995, collectors society piece, retired $600

Love Birds, 1987, collectors society piece,
    retired $5,000
Seals, 1991, collectors society piece, retired $600
Turtledoves, 1989, collectors society piece,
    retired $1,200
Whales, 1992, collectors society piece, retired $650
Woodpeckers, 1988, collectors society piece,
    retired $2,200

Walt Disney Classics Collection Figurines

1992 Bruno from Cinderella, retired $120
1992 Field Mouse, hands not touching, retired $1,400
1992 Field Mouse, hands touching, retired $1,200
1992 Sorcerer Mickey, retired $245
1993 Flight of Fancy, event piece, retired $45
1994 Snow White, flower, retired $200
1996 Donald and Daisy, clef, retired $575
1996 Pinocchio, open $125

Willitts Designs Figurines

Thomas Blackshear's Ebony Visions Collection

Story Teller Premier, The, 1995, sold out $1,100
Dreamer, The, 1996, retired $160
Siblings, The, 1995, retired $150
Guardian, The, 1996, retired $300

VINTAGE LUNCH BOXES

We have television to thank for transforming the once lowly lunch box into the hot collectible that it is today. The metal lunch box has been around since the early 1900s, but it was strictly utilitarian until TV came along in the 1950s and introduced hundreds of popular new characters to American families. Soon those characters were showing up on lunch boxes across the country. It was a tremendous marketing idea, and it created one of the hottest collectibles of the 1980s and 1990s. The once utilitarian lunch boxes that every child carried are now highly-collected remnants of pop culture. Their colorful designs make them popular display pieces.

Background: The first lunch box to feature a popular character was the Hopalong Cassidy box released by Aladdin in 1950. Its immediate success quickly led to the release of other character lunch boxes. Subjects depicted on the boxes mirrored the popular TV personalities of the day—from Western and space heroes to cartoon characters and rock stars. Later, lunch boxes also reflected popular movie themes, like *Mary Poppins* and *Star Wars*.

Aladdin and Thermos were, and still are, the two main manufacturers of lunch boxes. Over the years, collectible lunch boxes have also been made by Ohio Art, Universal, King Seeley Thermos, Adco Liberty and a few other smaller companies. The first generation of collectible lunch boxes were steel. Production of the steel boxes ended in the mid-1980s, and plastic boxes became the norm. Vinyl lunch bags first appeared in the 1960s and continue today.

General Guidelines: Boxes and their corresponding Thermos bottles are often found separately. Both items are collectible. Steel lunch boxes (especially dome or barn-shaped models) are worth more than plastic. But vinyl kits, harder to find in premium condition, run a close second in value. Boxes featuring popular TV, movie, space, Western, Disney, Barbie or cartoon characters are the most collectible.

Condition is important to value. Rust, chipped paint, dents, scratches, and missing latch or handles all contribute to a reduced value for steel lunch boxes. Likewise, plastic boxes and vinyl bags should be free of scratches, punctures, stains,

worn labels or other imperfections to command top value. Be aware that plastic and vinyl boxes and bags are susceptible to heat and exposure to the sun and may exhibit signs of melting.

Recommended Reading

2000 Toys & Prices, Sharon Korbeck and Elizabeth Stephan

VALUE LINE

Steel Lunch Boxes

Values shown are for lunch boxes only (no Thermos bottle) in Near Mint condition (the matching bottle generally increasse value by 30 to 50 percent).

A-Team, King Seeley, 1985	$20
Adam 12, Aladdin, 1973	$65
Addams Family, King Seeley, 1974	$100
Annie Oakley, Aladdin, 1955	$300
Archies, Aladdin, 1969	$75
Astronaut Dome, King Seeley, 1960	$250
Barbie, King Seeley, 1962	$250
Battlestar Galactica, Aladdin, 1978	$50
Beatles, Aladdin, 1966	$400
Bee Gees, King Seeley, 1978	$40
Beverly Hillbillies, Aladdin, 1963	$175
Bonanza, green rim, Aladdin, 1963	$120
Brady Bunch, King Seeley Thermos, 1970	$250
Buck Rogers, Aladdin, 1979	$35

Collectors of vintage lunch boxes can choose from steel, vinyl or plastic. Most are based on popular TV shows.

Bullwinkle & Rocky, Universal, 1962 ....$800
Cabbage Patch Kids, King Seeley, 1984....................$15
Care Bears, Aladdin, 1984 ....$10
Charlie's Angels, Aladdin, 1978 ....$40
Chitty Chitty Bang Bang, King Seeley, 1969 ....$135
Close Encounters, King Seeley, 1978 ....$75
Cracker Jack, Aladdin, 1969......................................$55
Daniel Boone, Aladdin, 1955.....................................$360
Davy Crockett, Kruger, 1955.....................................$360
Davy Crockett/Kit Carson, Adco Liberty, 1955 ....$215
Dick Tracy, Aladdin, 1967 ....$150
Disney School Bus Dome, Aladdin, 1968 ....$60
Disney's Magic Kingdom, Aladdin, 1960 ....$20
Disneyland Monorail, Aladdin, 1968...........................$200
Dr. Seuss, World of, Aladdin, 1970 ....$100
Dukes of Hazzard, Aladdin, 1983................................$50
E.T., Aladdin, 1982 ....$30
Evel Knievel, Aladdin, 1974.......................................$65
Family Affair, King Seeley Thermos, 1969 ....$60
Flintstones, yellow, Aladdin, 1963.............................$160
Get Smart, King Seeley Thermos, 1966 ....$175
G.I. Joe, King Seeley, 1967..$100
Gene Autry, Universal, 1954.......................................$450
Gremlins, Aladdin, 1984 ....$20
Happy Days, American Thermos, 1977........................$40
He-Man & Masters of the Universe, Aladdin, 1984 ....$5
Holly Hobbie, Aladdin, 1979......................................$10
Hopalong Cassidy, Aladdin, 1950 ....$175
Hot Wheels, King Seeley Thermos, 1969.....................$75
Howdy Doody, Adco Liberty, 1954 ....$525
Incredible Hulk, Aladdin, 1978 ....$30
Jetsons Dome, Aladdin, 1963 ....$675
KISS, King Seeley, 1977 ....$100
Knight in Armor, Universal, 1959 ....$850

Land of the Giants, Aladdin, 1968..............................$150
Little House on the Prairie, King Seeley, 1978.............$75
Little Red Riding Hood, Ohio Art, 1982 ....$25
Looney Tunes TV Set, King Seeley, 1959 ....$225
Lost in Space, King Seeley, 1967 ....$600
Mork and Mindy, American Thermos, 1979 ....$25
Munsters, King Seeley Thermos, 1965.........................$370
Muppet Babies, King Seeley Thermos, 1985 ....$10
Peanuts, King Seeley Thermos,
    many variations ....$20-$50
Planet of the Apes, Aladdin, 1974 ....$85
Raggedy Ann & Andy, Aladdin, 1973.........................$25
Rambo, King Seeley Thermos, 1985 ....$10
Roy Rogers Chow Wagon Dome, King Seeley
    Thermos, 1958 ....$245
Sesame Street, Aladdin, 1983 ....$10
Sleeping Beauty, General Steel Ware, 1960 ....$450
Smurfs, King Seeley Thermos, 1983 ....$140
Snow White, Aladdin, 1975..$55
Star Trek Dome, Aladdin, 1968 ....$700
Star Wars, King Seeley Thermos, 1978 ....$40
Strawberry Shortcake, Aladdin, 1980 ....$10
Superman, Universal, 1954 ....$850
240 Robert, Aladdin, 1978..$2,500
Tom Corbett Space Cadet, Aladdin, paper decal,
    1952..$250
Trigger, King Seeley, 1958 ....$235
U.S. Mail Dome, Aladdin, 1969 ....$60
Underdog, Okay Industries, 1974 ....$925
Wagon Train, King Seeley Thermos, 1964 ....$170
Waltons, Aladdin, 1973...$50
Yankee Doodles, King Seeley Thermos, 1975.............$45
Yellow Submarine, King Seeley Thermos, 1968 ....$400
Zorro, Aladdin, 1966...$200

Plastic Lunch Boxes

Values shown are for lunch boxes only (no Thermos bottle) in Near Mint condition (the matching bottle generally increases value by 30 to 50 percent).

Back to the Future, Thermos, 1989..............................$30
Batman, light blue, Thermos, 1989.............................$40
Beauty and the Beast, Aladdin, 1991 ....$20
Big Jim, Thermos, 1976...$85
Care Bears, Aladdin, 1986 ....$10
CHiPs, Thermos, 1977 ....$25
Civil War, Universal, 1961 ....$200
Disney on Parade, Aladdin, 1970.................................$35
Dukes of Hazzard, Aladdin, 1981................................$45
Ewoks, Thermos, 1983 ....$20
Flash Gordon Dome, Aladdin, 1979............................$60
G.I. Joe Live the Adventure, Aladdin, 1986 ....$25
Garfield, food fight scene, Thermos, 1979...................$25
Gumby, Thermos, 1986..$60
Incredible Hulk Dome, Aladdin, 1980.........................$30
Jetsons 3-D, Servo, 1987 ....$75
Jetsons, The Movie, Aladdin, 1990 ....$30

The 1965 Munsters box from King Seeley is a popular item, worth about $275.

Kool-Aid Man, Thermos, 1986......................................$20
Marvel Super Heroes, Thermos, 1990.........................$20
Pee Wee's Playhouse, Thermos, 1987........................$20
Popeye & Son, Servo, 1987.......................................$60
Raggedy Ann & Andy, Aladdin, 1988.........................$45
Rocketeer, Aladdin, 1990...$10
Shirt Tales, Thermos, 1981.......................................$10
Smurfs, Thermos, 1984..$15
Sport Goofy, Aladdin, 1986......................................$30
Teenage Mutant Ninja Turtles, Thermos, 1990............$35
Tom & Jerry, Aladdin, 1989......................................$30
Wayne Gretzky Dome, Aladdin, 1980.........................$125
Where's Waldo?, Thermos, 1990................................$10
Wizard of Oz 50th Anniversary, Aladdin, 1989............$65
Woody Woodpecker, Aladdin, 1972.............................$60
Wuzzles, Aladdin, 1985..$10
Yogi's Treasure Hunt, Servo, 1987............................$30

Vinyl Lunch Boxes

Values shown are for lunch boxes only (no bottle) in Near Mint condition (the matching bottle generally increases value by 15 to 30 percent).

Alice in Wonderland, Aladdin, 1972.........................$215
Alvin & the Chipmunks, King Seeley Thermos,
    1963...$425
Ballerina, Universal, 1960s......................................$800
Barbie, World of, pink box, King Seeley Thermos,
    1971...$75
Barbie and Midge Dome, King Seeley Thermos,
    1964...$525
Beany & Cecil, King Seeley Thermos, 1963...............$550
Beatles Kaboodles Kit, Standard Plastic, 1965..........$625
Bullwinkle, King Seeley, yellow, 1963.......................$450
Captain Kangaroo, King Seeley.................................$500

The Thermos from the 1969 Hot Wheels box is valued at about $25.

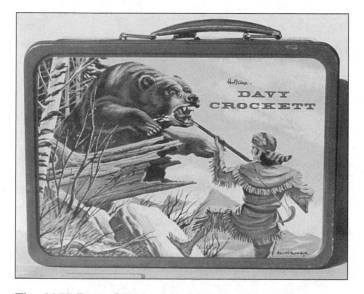

The 1955 Davy Crockett lunch box from Holtemp is valued at about $140.

Casper the Friendly Ghost, King Seeley Thermos,
    1966...$550
Charlie's Angels Brunch Bag, Aladdin, 1978.............$175
Donny & Marie, Aladdin, 1977-78.............................$120
Deputy Dawg, King Seeley Thermos, 1960s...............$550
G.I. Joe, King Seeley Thermos, 1989.........................$185
Gigi, Aladdin, 1962...$300
Highway Signs Snap Pack, Avon, 1988.......................$30
Lassie, Universal, 1960s..$125
Liddle Kiddles, King Seeley Thermos, 1969...............$250
Mary Poppins Brunch Bag, Aladdin, 1966..................$150
Monkees, King Seeley Thermos, 1967........................$400
Pink Panther, Aladdin, 1980......................................$95
Psychedelic, Aladdin, 1969......................................$150
Roy Rogers Saddlebag, brown, King Seeley
    Thermos, 1960..$250
Sleeping Beauty, Aladdin, 1970................................$240
Snoopy Softy, King Seeley Thermos, 1988...................$20
Snow White, Aladdin, 1975.......................................$295

Soupy Sales, King Seeley Thermos, 1966 .... $625
Strawberry Shortcake, Aladdin, 1980 .... $40
Tammy, Aladdin, 1964 .... $250
Tinkerbell, Aladdin, 1969 .... $260
Wonder Woman, yellow box, Aladdin, 1978 .... $200
Yosemite Sam, King Seeley Thermos, 1971 .... $560
Ziggy's Munch Box, Aladdin, 1979 .... $145

Thermos Bottles

Values shown are for bottles in Near Mint condition.

A-Team, steel, King Seeley, 1985 .... $15
Action Jackson, steel, Okay Industries, 1973 .... $200
Addams Family, plastic, King Seeley Thermos,
    1974 .... $25
Archies, plastic, Aladdin, 1969 .... $30
Beatles, steel, Aladdin, 1966 .... $160
Bedknobs & Broomsticks, plastic, Aladdin, 1972 .... $40
Blondie, steel, King Seeley Thermos, 1969 .... $75
Disney Express, plastic, Aladdin, 1979 .... $5
Disneyland Monorail, steel, Aladdin, 1968 .... $115
Fall Guy, plastic, Aladdin, 1981 .... $15
Fonz, The, plastic, King Seeley Thermos, 1978 .... $20
Gentle Ben, plastic, Aladdin, 1968 .... $30
Gomer Pyle, steel, Aladdin, 1966 .... $90
Green Hornet, steel, King Seeley Thermos, 1967 ...... $175

H.R. Pufnstuf, plastic, Aladdin, 1970 .... $50
Hector Heathcote, steel, Aladdin, 1964 .... $90
Holly Hobbie, plastic, Aladdin, 1970s $7
James Bond 007, steel, Aladdin, 1966 .... $135
Land of the Lost, plastic, Aladdin, 1975 .... $35
Little Friends, plastic, Aladdin, 1982 .... $260
Little House on the Prairie, plastic, King Seeley
    Thermos, 1978 .... $35
Lost in Space, steel, King Seeley Thermos, 1967 .... $60
Munsters, steel, King Seeley Thermos, 1965 .... $125
Muppet Babies, plastic, King Seeley Thermos,
    1985 .... $5
Pac-Man, plastic, Aladdin, 1980 .... $5
Planet of the Apes, plastic, Aladdin, 1974 .... $45
Popeye, steel, Universal, 1962 .... $300
Six Million Dollar Man, plastic, Aladdin, 1974 .... $25
Star Wars: Empire Strikes Back, plastic, King
    Seeley Thermos, 1980 .... $10
240 Robert, steel, Aladdin, 1978 .... $325
Twiggy, steel, Aladdin, 1967 .... $80
Underdog, plastic, Okay Industries, 1974 .... $350
Winnie the Pooh, steel, Aladdin $110
Winnie the Pooh, plastic, Aladdin, 1976 .... $70

MAGAZINES—PLAYBOY AND SPORTS ILLUSTRATED

The "Magazines" chapter in the first edition of *Today's Hottest Collectibles*, published two years ago, concentrated on *TV Guide* and *Life* magazine. This time around, we highlight two other highly collectible magazines, *Sports Illustrated* and *Playboy*.

Using centerfolds such as Marilyn Monroe and centerfielders such as Joe DiMaggio, Playboy and Sports Illustrated, have been entertaining male readers for more than 45 years.

People collect these magazines for the beauty of the covers, and the advertisements, historical articles and photos inside. The personality or event featured on the cover, however, is the most important factor in a magazine's value.

General Guidelines: Magazines that feature the likes of DiMaggio, Monroe, Elizabeth Taylor, Michael Jordan and Lucille Ball are some of the most collectible.

Magazines with long track records, such as *Sports Illustrated, Life, Playboy, TV Guide* and *Saturday Evening Post* are popular with collectors. Monster magazines from the 1960s and 1970s are especially hot, along with sci-fi and some music magazines (most notably, early *Rolling Stone*).

Pre-1960 movie magazines have traditionally been popular and are still hot today. And there never seems to be a shortage of collectors for all types of 1950s and 1960s adult magazines, especially those with notable actresses or models in various states of undress.

Pulp magazines—covering themes like crime, detectives, love, horror and romance—from the first half of the 20th century are also popular. Pulp covers were colorful and lurid, making them attractive to buyers. Because these were printed on cheap paper, they are often found in Poor condition today.

People collect magazines in several ways—by celebrity pictured, by event (covers featuring the lunar landing), by cover illustrator. Covers illustrated by Norman Rockwell are especially desirable.

Sports Illustrated—During the 45 years since its debut issue, *Sports Illustrated* has captured some of the sports world's greatest moments on its covers and in its pages.

Although the sport ranks second in terms of appearances on the cover, baseball is the featured granddaddy SI issue of them all. The premiere issue, billed as the nation's first sports weekly, is dated Aug. 16, 1954; the cover price was just a quarter. That issue, which now among collectors has a value of $300 in Near Mint condition, features the Milwaukee Braves' Eddie Mathews swinging at a pitch in Milwaukee's County Stadium.

The issue's value is also driven up by the three pages of 1954 Topps baseball cards inside, featuring Willie Mays, Ted Williams and Jackie Robinson, printed on paper stock.

New York Yankees stars, including Mickey Mantle, are featured on 1954 Topps black-and-white and colored cards included in the magazine's second issue, dated Aug. 23, 1954. This magazine, with a horde of golf bags on the cover, is as rare and as valuable as the first issue.

During its history, more than 2,000 issues of *SI* have been published, with football subjects leading the way with more than 500 appearances. Baseball (more than 400) and basketball (more than 300) are second and third. Hockey has been featured more than 75 times. Boxer Muhammad Ali led all athletes with 32 appearances through 1993, but superstar Michael Jordan caught him early in 1995. Kareem Abdul-Jabbar has 27 appearances to rank third among basketball players.

Leading the way for baseball players, with 10 appearances, is Reggie Jackson. Billy Martin is one of three athletes (the others are Gordie Howe and Willie Mays) to have appeared on a cover in four decades of the magazine's existence—the '50s, '60s, '70s and '80s. Mays also made an appearance on a special fall edition in 1992.

But today, the magazine is perhaps best known for the issue it publishes during the dead of winter, the annual swimsuit edition, featuring beautiful supermodels in swimwear. This magazine is quite popular, to the tune of about four million copies being sold each year. From 1964 on, these magazines are generally the most valuable issues from their corresponding years.

In addition to trying to collect the swimsuit issues, some topics to pursue include favorite players, teams, themes (World Series, All-Stars, Previews), or those named as the magazine's Sportsman of the Year. Some collectors are also

CONDITION IS CRITICAL!

No serious collector wants a magazine with a coffee-cup stain, a major tear or missing pages. The condition of magazines is of paramount importance to values. Newer magazines (from 1960 to the present) have little value in lower grades, since there is a good supply available in prime condition. Older magazines (pre-1960s) are still collectible in lesser conditions since there are relatively few available in top condition. Even an older magazine in Good condition will likely find buyers.

trying to collect an entire run of *SI*s.

The attractive cover photos are what drive the collectibilty of this magazine. Athletes' first cover appearances are especially sought after by those who seek to have them autographed. These issues generally command a higher price than subsequent issues with the same player. Generally, a signed *SI* cover is worth about the value of an unsigned version, plus the value of a signed 8 x 10 photo.

Generally, collectors who seek back issues want them to be in reasonable condition—unripped, uncreased—with the cover attached entirely. But the corners on many issues are often not sharp, especially from the earlier issues. Smudges, rips, tears, missing pages and mailing labels can all lower a magazine's value by 50 percent or more.

Old *SI*s can often be purchased at libraries, flea markets, through hobby publications and mail order houses, and at card shops and shows. On March 26, 1990, *SI* issued a supplemental magazine entitled "35 Years of Covers." This magazine features every cover from 1954 through 1989; it's a worthwhile visual checklist for collectors who are wondering which covers are most appealing.

Playboy—Because *Playboy* has been the authority on fashion, fiction, technology, society and beautiful women since 1953, it's easy to understand who would grace the cover of the first issue—Marilyn Monroe, the silver screen's premier sex symbol.

As an effort to launch a 50-cent magazine, designed as "entertainment for men," the December 1953 premiere edition's cover features a smiling Monroe waving at you. But there's a tantalizing teaser, too—there are full color nudes of the blonde bombshell inside, too!

The rest, as they say, is history—46 years worth, or more than 500 issues, featuring celebrities and Playmates alike, with one thing in common—each in various stages of undress. And

WHAT'S INSIDE COUNTS TOO!

Some people collect Sports Illustrated magazines for the articles inside, too. For example, the Oct. 9, 1961 issue, which features pitcher Joey Jay on the cover, is very popular because it contains a story on Roger Maris' record-breaking 61st home run. This magazine sells for $10-$20. The magazines from the 1998 season, when Mark McGwire and Sammy Sosa were in pursuit of that record, are $7-$12 each and have the potential to rise.

The accomplishments of amateur athletes are also chronicled in the popular "Faces in the Crowd" section. Each athlete is profiled with a small mug shot and brief write-up of what the athlete, perhaps a future star, did. For example, New York Yankees star Don Mattingly appeared in the July 16, 1979 issue (Bjorn Borg cover, $4-$7), while Carl Yastrzemski is in the Aug. 24, 1959 magazine (Yachting cover, $6-$10).

that doesn't include the special newsstand issues or premium issues offered to subscribers. In general, *Playboy* magazines from the 1950s are $50-$100; 1960s are $25-$40; 1970s are $20-$30; 1980s are $15-20; and 1990s are $5-$10.

The values depend on three things—who graces the cover, who the centerfold is, and what female celebrity has also posed in the issue. The annual June issue, devoted to the previous year's Playmate of the Year, also commands a premium value. The issues also feature interviews with celebrities, which is a secondary factor to consider when pricing a magazine. It's also important that the centerfold is intact.

VALUE LINE

Sports Illustrated

The values below are for unsigned magazines in Excellent to Near Mint condition. B = baseball; FB = football; CFB = college football; BB = basketball; CBB = college basketball; H = hockey; FC = first cover; SOY = Sportsman of the Year.

08/16/54 Eddie Mathews (B, FC)	$200-$300
08/23/54 Golf bags	$275-$400
11/22/54 Y. A. Tittle (FB, FC)	$35-$40
04/11/55 Willie Mays, Leo Durocher (BB, FC)	$100-$125
04/18/55 Al Rosen (B)	$75-$100
06/27/55 Duke Snider (B, FC)	$50-$75
07/11/55 Yogi Berra (B, FC)	$25-$50
08/01/55 Ted Williams (B, FC)	$75-$100
09/19/55 Rocky Marciano, boxing	$15-$25
01/02/56 Johnny Podres (B, SOY)	$25-$45
01/09/56 Bob Cousy (BB, FC)	$25-$40
01/23/56 Jean Beliveau (H, FC)	$20-$30
03/05/56 Stan Musial (B, FC)	$30-$50
04/23/56 Billy Martin (B, FC)	$25-$35
05/14/56 Al Kaline, Harvey Kuenn (B, FC)	$25-$40
06/04/56 Floyd Patterson, boxing	$15-$25
06/18/56 Mickey Mantle (B, FC)	$150-$200
06/25/56 Warren Spahn (B, FC)	$25-$35
07/16/56 Reds Musclemen (B)	$35-$60
09/10/56 Whitey Ford (B, FC)	$30-$50
10/01/56 Mickey Mantle, World Series (B)	$75-$100
10/29/56 Paul Hornung (CFB, FC)	$20-$40
03/04/57 Mickey Mantle (B)	$75-$100
03/11/57 Ben Hogan, golf	$20-$40
07/08/57 Ted Williams, Stan Musial (B)	$75-$100
12/23/57 Stan Musial (B, SOY)	$25-$40
06/02/58 Eddie Mathews (B)	$20-$35
07/07/58 Willie Mays, Mickey Mantle (B)	$25-$40
03/02/59 Casey Stengel (B)	$20-$30
04/13/59 Willie Mays (B)	$30-$50
08/10/59 Luis Aparicio, Nellie Fox (B)	$30-$50
10/05/59 Johnny Unitas (FB, FC)	$25-$30
06/13/60 Arnold Palmer, golf	$15-$20
09/12/60 Jack Nicklaus, golf	$20-$30

09/26/60 Jim Brown (FB) ....$20-$35
11/14/60 Bobby Hull (H, FC) ....$15-$25
12/26/60 President, Mrs. Kennedy......................$25-$40
01/09/61 Arnold Palmer, golf ....$15-$25
01/16/61 Bob Cousy (BB) ....$12-$20
03/13/61 Floyd Patterson, boxing ....$10-$15
09/25/61 Bart Starr (FB, FC) ....$20-$30
10/02/61 Roger Maris (B, FC) ....$22-$40
10/30/61 Wilt Chamberlain (BB)........................$20-$30
01/08/62 Jerry Lucas (CBB, SOY) ....$12-$20
03/05/62 Casey Stengel (B) ....$20-$30
04/02/62 Arnold Palmer, golf ....$12-$20
04/30/62 Luis Aparicio (B)................................$15-$25
06/04/62 Willie Mays (B) ....$20-$35
07/02/62 Mickey Mantle (B) ....$75-$125
08/20/62 Don Drysdale (B)................................$20-$30
09/10/62 Jim Taylor (FB, FC)............................$20-$35
10/29/62 Fran Tarkenton (FB, FC) ....$20-$30
11/12/62 Arnold Palmer, Sam Snead, golf............$20-$30
12/17/62 Frank Gifford (FB) ....$20-$35
03/04/63 Sandy Koufax (B, FC) ....$25-$45
04/08/63 Harmon Killebrew (B) ....$20-$30
05/20/63 Paul Hornung (FB) ....$20-$30
06/10/63 Cassius Clay, boxing...........................$25-$40
06/17/63 Jack Nicklaus, golf.............................$12-$20
09/30/63 Whitey Ford (B) ....$15-$25
12/02/63 Roger Staubach (CFB, FC)....................$20-$30
01/20/64 First Swimsuit Issue............................$20-$35
02/03/64 Bobby Hull (H) ....$12-$20
02/24/64 Cassius Clay, boxing...........................$20-$35
03/02/64 Yogi Berra, Casey Stengel (B)...............$20-$30
03/09/64 Cassius Clay, Sonny Liston, boxing ......$20-$30
03/16/64 Gordie Howe (H) ....$15-$25
04/13/64 Sandy Koufax (B) ....$20-$30
05/11/64 Al Kaline (B) ....$15-$25
08/31/64 Brooks Robinson (B) ....$15-$25
09/07/64 Y.A. Tittle (FB) ....$12-$20
10/12/64 Dick Butkus (CFB, FC) ....$20-$30
10/26/64 Tommy Heinsohn (BB).........................$12-$20
11/16/64 Cassius Clay, Sonny Liston, boxing ......$12-$20
12/07/64 Bill Bradley (CBB, FC) ....$12-$20
01/18/65 Swimsuit Issue ....$20-$30
01/25/65 Bobby Hull (H) ....$12-$20
02/08/65 Jerry West (BB) ....$12-$20
04/05/65 Jack Nicklaus, Arnold Palmer, golf........$12-$20
04/12/65 Wilt Chamberlain (BB)........................$15-$25
05/24/65 Cassius Clay, Sonny Liston, boxing ......$15-$25
06/07/65 Cassius Clay, Sonny Liston, boxing ......$15-$25
06/21/65 Mickey Mantle (B) ....$25-$40
07/19/65 Joe Namath (FB)................................$20-$35
08/09/65 Juan Marichal (BB, FC)........................$12-$20
09/06/65 Sugar Ray Robinson, boxing ....$12-$20
10/25/65 Bill Russell (BB, FC)..........................$12-$20
11/22/65 Cassius Clay, Floyd Patterson, boxing....$15-$25
12/20/65 Sandy Koufax (B, SOY) ....$25-$35

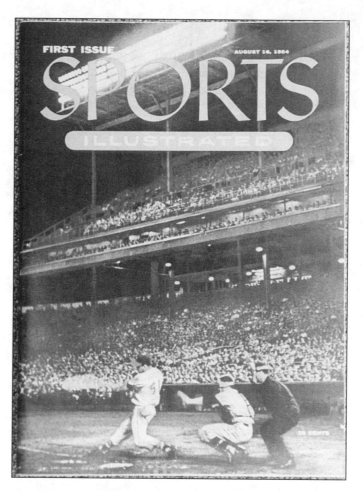

The first issue of "Sports Illustrated" is dated August 16, 1954.

01/10/66 Jim Taylor (FB).................................$12-$20
01/17/66 Swimsuit Issue: Bahamas ....$15-$25
04/04/66 Jack Nicklaus, Arnold Palmer, golf........$12-$20
05/09/66 John Havlicek (BB) ....$12-$20
08/22/66 Paul Hornung, Jim Taylor (FB) ....$12-$20
09/12/66 Gale Sayers (FB)................................$15-$25
10/10/66 Brooks/Frank Robinson (B)....................$15-$25
10/17/66 Joe Namath (FB)................................$15-$25
10/24/66 Elgin Baylor (BB)..............................$12-$20
10/31/66 Bart Starr (FB) ....$12-$20
12/05/66 Lew Alcindor (CBB, FC) ....$25-$35
01/09/67 Bart Starr (FB) ....$12-$20
01/16/67 Swimsuit Issue ....$15-$25
04/03/67 Lew Alcindor (CBB) ....$15-$20
05/08/67 Mickey Mantle (B) ....$25-$35
05/15/67 Koufax/Drysdale/Wills (B) ....$20-$30
07/03/67 Roberto Clemente (B, FC)......................$20-$30
07/10/67 Muhammad Ali, boxing..........................$15-$25
08/21/67 Carl Yastrzemski (B, FC)......................$12-$20
10/16/67 Lou Brock (B, FC)..............................$12-$20
12/11/67 Bobby Orr (H, FC)..............................$15-$20
12/25/67 Carl Yastrzemski (B, SOY)....................$20-$30

03/04/68 Pete Maravich (CBB) ....$30-$40
03/11/68 Johnny Bench (B) ....$12-$25
04/01/68 Lew Alcindor (CBB) ....$12-$20
04/29/68 Jerry West, Elgin Baylor (BB)...........$12-$20
05/27/68 Pete Rose (B, FC) ....$12-$25
06/17/68 Don Drysdale (B)...........................$15-$25
07/08/68 Ted Williams (B) ....$20-$30
07/15/68 Ray Nitschke (FB) ....$12-$20
12/09/68 Joe Namath (FB).............................$12-$25
12/23/68 Bill Russell (BB, SOY)....................$15-$20
01/13/69 Swimsuit Issue..............................$15-$25
01/20/69 Joe Namath (FB).............................$12-$25
01/27/69 Wilt Chamberlain (BB)....................$15-$20
02/03/69 Bobby Orr (H)...............................$15-$20
03/03/69 Vince Lombardi (FB).......................$12-$25
03/17/69 Ted Williams (B) ....$15-$25
03/31/69 Lew Alcindor (CBB) ....$12-$25
04/28/69 Bill Russell (BB) ....$12-$20
05/05/69 Muhammad Ali, boxing....................$12-$25
05/19/69 Walter Alston (B)...........................$12-$20
06/16/69 Joe Namath (FB).............................$12-$25
07/07/69 Reggie Jackson (B, FC) ....$12-$25
07/28/69 S. Jurgenson, Vince Lombardi (FB) ....$15-$20
08/04/69 Bill Russell (BB) ....$15-$20
08/11/69 Joe Namath (FB).............................$12-$25
08/18/69 Hank Aaron (B, FC) ....$15-$25
09/08/69 Ernie Banks, Pete Rose (B) ....$20-$30
10/27/69 Lew Alcindor (BB)..........................$15-$20
12/01/69 Pete Maravich (BB) ....$12-$20
12/22/69 Tom Seaver (B, FC, SOY) ....$20-$30
01/12/70 Swimsuit Issue: Cheryl Tiegs ....$15-$25
01/19/70 Len Dawson (FB) ....$20-$30
02/01/71 Swimsuit Issue...............................$12-$20
02/08/71 Lew Alcindor, Willis Reed (BB) ....$6-$10
03/01/71 Muhammad Ali, Joe Frazier, boxing ......$10-$15
03/15/71 Muhammad Ali, boxing....................$10-$15
05/10/77 Oscar Robertson (BB)........................$6-$10
07/26/71 Muhammad Ali, boxing....................$6-$10
01/17/72 Swimsuit Issue...............................$12-$20
04/10/72 Joe Torre (B) ....$6-$10
05/22/72 Willie Mays (B) ....$6-$10
06/19/72 Bobby Hull (H).............................$6-$10
07/10/72 Johnny Unitas (FB).........................$6-$10

STORE THEM WITH CARE!

Proper care is a must since humidity, heat and light can wreak havoc with magazines. Magazines should be stored in individual plastic sleeves with an acid-free cardboard backing for support. The issues should then be placed in specially designed boxes and stored in a humidity-controlled environment. The sleeves, backing and boxes can be purchased through any number of places, including magazine and comic book dealers.

10/09/72 Joe Namath (FB)...........................$6-$10
01/22/73 Bob Griese (FB)............................$6-$10
01/29/73 Swimsuit Issue..............................$12-$20
04/09/73 Steve Carlton (B) ....$12-$15
04/23/73 Muhammad Ali, boxing....................$7-$12
06/18/73 George Foreman, boxing ....$6-$10
07/30/73 Carlton Fisk (B) ....$10-$15
08/20/73 Bill Russell, Claude Osteen (B)...........$6-$10
10/08/73 Fran Tarkenton (FB) ....$6-$10
11/12/73 Pete Maravich (BB) ....$6-$10
01/14/74 Julius Erving (BB, FC).....................$15-$25
01/28/74 Swimsuit Issue..............................$12-$20
02/04/74 Muhammad Ali, boxing....................$6-$10
03/11/74 Gordie Howe (H)...........................$6-$10
03/18/74 Babe Ruth (B)..............................$6-$10
04/08/74 Pete Rose (B) ....$6-$10
04/15/74 Hank Aaron (B) ....$25-$35
06/17/74 Reggie Jackson (B) ....$6-$10
10/28/74 Muhammad Ali, George Foreman,
    boxing..$6-$10
11/11/74 Muhammad Ali, boxing....................$6-$10
12/23/74 Muhammad Ali, boxing....................$6-$10
01/27/75 Swimsuit Issue: Cheryl Tiegs ....$12-$20
03/03/75 Cincinnati Reds Spring Training (B)........$6-$10
06/16/75 Nolan Ryan (B, FC)........................$25-$35
07/21/75 Tom Seaver, Jim Palmer (B) ....$10-$15
09/15/75 Muhammad Ali, Joe Frazier, boxing ....$6-$10
10/06/75 Reggie Jackson (B) ....$6-$10
10/13/75 Muhammad Ali, Joe Frazier, boxing ......$10-$15
10/20/75 Johnny Bench, Luis Tiant (B)..............$6-$10
12/15/75 George Foreman, Muhammad Ali,
    boxing..$6-$10
12/22/75 Pete Rose (B, SOY) ....$10-$15
01/19/76 Swimsuit Issue..............................$12-$20
06/21/76 George Brett (B) ....$15-$20
08/30/76 Reggie Jackson (B) ....$6-$10
11/01/76 Johnny Bench (B) ....$6-$10
11/22/76 Walter Payton (FB) ....$15-$20
01/24/77 Swimsuit Issue..............................$12-$20
05/02/77 Reggie Jackson (B) ....$6-$10
06/27/77 Tom Seaver (B) ....$6-$10
07/18/77 Rod Carew, Ted Williams (B)..............$6-$10
11/28/77 Larry Bird (CBB, FC).......................$30-$40
01/16/78 Swimsuit Issue..............................$12-$20
08/07/78 Pete Rose (B) ....$6-$10
11/27/78 Magic Johnson (CBB, FC) ....$30-$40
02/05/79 Swimsuit Issue: Christie Brinkley ....$15-$20
03/26/79 Larry Bird (CBB)...........................$6-$10
04/02/79 Earvin Johnson (CBB)......................$6-$10
07/23/79 Nolan Ryan (B)............................$15-$25
08/13/79 Silver Anniversary ....$6-$10
08/27/79 Baseball's Golden Oldies..................$6-$10
12/10/79 Sugar Ray Leonard, boxing ....$6-$10
02/04/80 Swimsuit Issue: Christie Brinkley .... $15-$20
04/14/80 Muhammad Ali, boxing....................$6-$10

08/04/80 Reggie Jackson (B) ....$6-$10
02/09/81 Swimsuit Issue: Christie Brinkley ....$12-$20
04/13/81 George Brett, Mike Schmidt (B).............$10-$15
01/18/82 Dwight Clark (FB)...............................$6-$10
01/25/82 Joe Montana (FB, FC) ....$20-$25
02/08/82 Swimsuit Issue: Carol Alt......................$12-$20
02/15/82 Wayne Gretzky (H).................................$6-$10
10/11/82 Robin Yount (B, FC)..............................$10-$15
11/08/82 John Elway (CFB, FC) ....$10-$15
02/14/83 Swimsuit Issue: Cheryl Tiegs ....$15-$20
03/14/83 Pete Rose, Joe Morgan,
    Tony Perez (B) ....$6-$10
08/15/83 John Elway (FB) ....$6-$10
11/14/83 Dan Marino (FB) ....$6-$10
11/28/83 Michael Jordan (CBB, FC) ....$35-$45
02/13/84 Swimsuit Issue ....$10-$15
07/23/84 Michael Jordan (BB)..............................$20-$30
12/10/84 Michael Jordan (BB)..............................$15-$20
01/14/85 Dan Marino (FB) ....$6-$10
01/21/85 Dan Marino, Joe Montana (FB)..............$10-$15
02/11/85 Swimsuit Issue ....$10-$15
03/25/85 Willie Mays, Mickey Mantle (B)............$10-$15
02/10/86 Swimsuit Issue: Elle MacPherson ....$15-$20
05/12/86 Roger Clemens (B, FC) ....$10-$15
11/17/86 Michael Jordan (BB)..............................$15-$20
02/09/87 Swimsuit Issue: Elle MacPherson ....$15-$20
05/11/87 Reggie Jackson (B) ....$6-$10
07/13/87 Don Mattingly, Daryl Strawberry (B).......$6-$10
12/28/87 Michael Jordan (BB)..............................$15-$20
02/15/88 Swimsuit Issue: Elle MacPherson ....$15-$20
02/22/88 Wilt Chamberlain, Bill Russell (BB)........$6-$10
04/04/88 Mark McGwire, Will Clark (B) ....$6-$10
04/25/88 Muhammad Ali, boxing...........................$6-$10
05/16/88 Michael Jordan (BB)..............................$10-$15
01/30/89 Jerry Rice (FB, FC)...............................$6-$10
Swimsuit Issue: 25th Anniversary ....$15-$20
02/06/89 Mario Lemieux (H, FC)...........................$6-$10
03/13/89 Michael Jordan (BB)..............................$15-$20
04/03/89 Pete Rose (B) ....$6-$10
05/01/89 Nolan Ryan (B) ....$10-$15
05/15/89 Michael Jordan (BB)..............................$15-$20
08/14/89 Michael Jordan (BB)..............................$10-$15
08/21/89 Troy Aikman (FB, FC) ....$6-$10
10/02/89 Joe Montana (FB) ....$6-$10
11/06/89 Joe Dumars, Michael Jordan (BB).........$10-$15
11/13/89 Deion Sanders......................................$6-$10
02/12/90 Swimsuit Issue ....$5-$10
05/07/90 Ken Griffey Jr. (B, FC) ....$8-$15
05/21/90 Michael Jordan (BB)..............................$7-$12
12/17/90 Michael Jordan (BB)..............................$10-$15
01/21/91 Shaquille O'Neal (CBB, FC).................$10-$15
02/18/91 Michael Jordan (BB)..............................$12-$20
04/08/91 Grant Hill (CBB, FC) ....$7-$12
05/27/91 Mickey Mantle, Roger Maris (B) ....$6-$10
06/03/91 Michael Jordan (BB)..............................$15-$20

06/10/91 Michael Jordan, Magic Johnson (BB) ....$10-$15
06/17/91 Michael Jordan (BB)..............................$10-$15
07/29/91 Cal Ripken Jr. (B) ....$10-$15
1991 Special Issue; Red Grange (FB)....................$6-$10
1991 25 Unforgettable Moments ....$7-$12
11/11/91 Jordan/Pippen/Jackson (BB)....................$7-$12
12/23/91 Michael Jordan (BB)..............................$10-$15
03/09/92 Swimsuit Issue: Kathy Ireland.................$6-$10
03/16/92 Ryne Sandberg (B) ....$7-$12
04/13/92 Bobby Hurley (CBB)..............................$6-$10
05/11/92 Michael Jordan, Clyde Drexler (BB)........$7-$12
05/25/92 Michael Jordan (BB)..............................$10-$15
06/15/92 Michael Jordan (BB)..............................$10-$15
06/22/92 Michael Jordan (BB)..............................$10-$15
11/30/92 Shaquille O'Neal (BB) ....$7-$12
02/22/93 Swimsuit Issue ....$6-$10
03/29/93 Jason Kidd (CBB)..................................$6-$10
05/03/93 Joe DiMaggio (B) ....$6-$10
06/07/93 Michael Jordan (BB)..............................$10-$15
06/21/93 Michael Jordan (BB)..............................$10-$15
06/28/93 Michael Jordan (BB)..............................$10-$15
10/18/93 Michael Jordan (BB)..............................$7-$12
02/12/94 Swimsuit Issue: Kathy Ireland,
    Rachel Hunter ....$10-$15
03/14/94 Michael Jordan (B) ....$10-$15
04/18/94 Mickey Mantle (B) ....$6-$10
06/06/94 Ken Griffey Jr. (B) ....$6-$10
02/20/95 Swimsuit Issue ....$6-$10
03/20/95 Michael Jordan (BB)..............................$7-$12
03/27/95 Michael Jordan (BB)..............................$7-$12
05/22/95 Michael Jordan,
    Shaquille O'Neal (BB).................................$7-$12

Collectors prize "Sports Illustrated" magazines for its wonderful cover photos.

08/21/95 Mickey Mantle (B) ....$6-$10
10/23/95 Michael Jordan, Dennis Rodman (BB).....$7-$12
01/29/96 Swimsuit Issue.......................................$6-$10
05/27/96 Michael Jordan, Phil Jackson (BB) ....$7-$12
06/03/96 Michael Jordan (BB)................................$7-$12
06/17/96 Michael Jordan (BB)................................$7-$12
1995-96 Chicago Bulls Championship Edition ....$6-$10
07/08/96 Alex Rodriguez (B, FC)...........................$6-$10
1996 New York Yankees
    Championship Edition.......................................$6-$10
02/21/97 Swimsuit Issue: Tyra Banks....................$6-$10
06/09/97 Michael Jordan (BB)................................$7-$12
06/23/97 Michael Jordan (BB)................................$7-$12
1997-98 Chicago Bulls Championship Edition .....$10-$15
1997 Michael Jordan: 5 NBA Championships ....$7-$12
02/16/98 Michael Jordan (BB)................................$7-$12
06/08/98 Michael Jordan, Scottie Pippen (BB) ....$6-$10
06/15/98 Michael Jordan (BB)................................$7-$12
06/22/98 Michael Jordan (BB)................................$7-$12
08/03/98 Mark McGwire (B)..................................$7-$12
09/07/98 Mark McGwire (B)..................................$7-$12
09/14/98 Mark McGwire (B)..................................$7-$12
09/14/98 Mark McGwire Special Edition................$7-$12
09/21/98 Sammy Sosa (B) ....$6-$10
10/05/98 Mark McGwire (B)..................................$7-$12
10/07/98 Mark McGwire/Sammy Sosa Edition.....$10-$15

Playboy Magazine

Values shown are for examples in Excellent to Near Mint condition (Centerfold is listed first, cover subject is in parentheses).

December 1953, Marilyn Monroe
    (Marilyn Monroe) ....$2,000-$4,000
January 1954, Margie Harrison
    (Merry Christmas)...................................$2,000-$3,000
February 1954, Margaret Scott
    (Hottest Spots in Paris)...........................$1,200-$2,400
March 1954, Dolores Del Monte
    (Model taking off top)..............................$800-$1,600
April 1954, Marilyn Waltz
    (Bunny cartoon) ....$600-$1,200
May 1954, Joanne Arnold
    (Lounging cartoon bunny)........................$600-$1,200
June 1954, Margie Harrison
    (Cartoon bunny popping champagne)...........$450-$900
July 1954, Neva Gilbert
    (Evolution of the bikini)..............................$450-$900
August 1954, Arline Hunter (Sail Boats)...........$400-$800
September 1954, Jackie Rainbow ....$400-$800
October 1954, Madeline Castle
    (Football cheerleader) ....$300-$600
November 1954, Diane Hunter
    (Paris 'Round the World) ....$300-$600
December 1954, Terry Ryan
    (Anniversary issue) ....$300-$600
January 1955, Bettie Page.............................$600-$1,200

CHECK OUT THESE SPECIAL PLAYBOY ISSUES!

Over the years, Playboy has also issued numerous newsstand specials, in addition to their regular monthly issues. Some are tributes to individual women—Vanna White (October 1987, worth about $40), Kimberly Conrad Heffner (December 1989, $25), Dian Parkinson (December 1993, $20), Anna Nicole Smith (January 1995, $30) and Pamela Anderson (May 1996, $55).

Most of the newsstand specials issued during the 1970s are generally worth about $35-$50. Playboy's Book of Lingerie ranges from $15-$20, but two issues, March 1987 and March 1988, are $35 each. Other series include: Bathing Beauties, from the 1990s, generally valued at $15-$20 each; The Best From Playboy, dating from 1964-1980s, generally are worth $20-$40, but 1964 and 1970 are $50 each; College Girls, from the 1990s, generally sell for about $15 each; Girls of Summer, 1980s-90s, are typically $25-$30 each; Nudes, 1990 is $35, 1988 is $15, the rest are in between; Playmate Reviews, 1988 is $35, 1998 is $15, the rest are in between.

February 1955, Jayne Mansfield........................$300-$500
July 1955, Janet Pilgrim...............................$175
October 1955, Marilyn McClintock...........................$100
April 1956, Rusty Fisher (Diana Dors)......................$125
May 1956, Marion Scott (Delores Taylor)..................$125
September 1956, Elsa Sorenson (Diane Harmsen).....$125
February 1957, Jayne Mansfield.........................$75
April 1957, Elain Conte...............................$100
June 1958, Judy Lee Tomerlin......................$65
January 1959, Virginia Gordon.......................$65
April 1959, Nancy Crawford $65
May 1959, Cindy Fuller..............................$30
October 1959, Elaine Reynolds $60
January 1960, Stella Stevens......................$125
February 1960, Susie Scott $65
May 1960, Ginger Young.......................$65
September 1960, Anne Davis (Marlene Renfro) $65
December 1960, Carol Eden (Teddi Smith)..................$85
February 1961, Barbara Ann Lawford.........................$35
June 1961, Heidi Becker $60
February 1962, Kari Knudsen (Cynthia Maddox)........$55
October 1962, Laura Young (Bonnie Jo Halpin) $25
December 1962, June Cochran (Sharleen Conners) $75
February 1962, Toni Ann (Cheryl Lampley) $45
March 1963, Adrienne Moreau (Cynthia Maddox) $25
June 1963, Connie Mason (Jayne Mansfield)...............$60
December 1963, Donna Michelle $85
February 1964, Nancy Joe Hopper
    (Cynthia Maddox)..$45
June 1964, Lori Winston (Mamie Van Doren).............$35

November 1964, Kai Brendlinger (Maria Hoff) $35
February 1965, Jessica St. George (Teddi Smith)......... $35
April 1965, Sue Williams (Lannie Balcom) $35
October 1965, Allison Parks (Penny James)................ $35
April 1966, Karla Conway (Cynthia Maddox) $35
May 1966, Dolly Read (Allison Parks)....................... $35
June 1966, Kelly Burke (Mary Warren)...................... $35
December 1966, Sue Bernard (Nancy Gould) $40
May 1967, Anne Randall (Beth Hyatt) $25
June 1967, Joey Gibson (Sharon Kristie) $25
August 1967, Dede Lind (Lisa Baker) $25
February 1968, Nancy Harwood
    (Paulette Lindberg)..................................... $25
March 1968, Michelle Hamilton (Sharon Kristie)........ $25
May 1968, Elizabeth Jordon (Angela Dorian) $25
February 1969, Lorrie Menconi
    (Nancy Chamberlain) $25
August 1969, Debbie Hooper (Penny James) $25
March 1970, Christine Koren (Barbi Benton) $35
June 1970, Elaine Morton (Claudia Jennings)............. $25
August 1970, Sharon Clark (Linda Donnelly)............. $22
March 1971, Cynthia Hall (Peggy Smith) $25
May 1971, Janice Pennington (Diane Davies)............. $22
August 1971, Cathy Rowland (Christy Miller)............. $22
February 1972, P.J. Lansing (Barbara Carrera)............ $27
May 1972, Deanna Baker (Barbi Benton) $30
October 1972, Sharon Johansen (Lynn Myers)............. $20
February 1973, Cyndi Wood (Jeanette Laxson)............ $20
July 1973, Martha Smith (Karen Christy)..................... $20
October 1973, Valerie Lane (Sheila Ryan) $20
January 1974, Nancy Cameron (Cyndi Wood) $25
March 1974, Pamela Zinszer (Debbie Shelton)............ $20
May 1974, Marilyn Lange (Marsha Kay) $35
April 1975, Victoria Cunningham (Cyndi Wood)........ $20
February 1976, Laura Lyons (Jill De Vries) $20
March 1976, Anne Pennington
    (Vicki Cunningham).................................... $20
January 1978, Debra Jensen (Rita Lee) $25
June 1978, Gail Stanton (Debra Jo Fondren)............... $25
July 1978, Karen Morton (Pamela Sue Martin)............ $20
October 1978, Marcy Hanson (Dolly Parton)............... $25
December 1978, Janet Quist
    (Farrah Fawcett-Majors) $30
January 1979, Candy Loving $45
August 1979, Dorothy Stratten (Candy Loving)........... $40
December 1979, Candice Collins (Raquel Welch) $30
March 1980, Henriette Allais (Bo Derek).................... $20
May 1980, Martha Thomsen (Teri Wells)..................... $20
June 1980, Ola Ray (Dorothy Stratten)........................ $20
January 1981, Karen Price (Barbara Bach)................... $25
June 1981, Cathy Larmouth (Teri Wells) $45
July 1981, Heidi Sorenson (Jayne Kennedy)................ $20
August 1981, Debbie Boostrom (Valerie Perrine) $20
September 1981, Susan Smith (Bo Derek) $20
October 1981, Kelly Tough (Cathy St. George) $20

November 1981, Shannon Tweed (Teri Peterson) $25
December 1981, Patricia Farinelli
    (Bernadette Peters)..................................... $35
March 1982, Karen Witter (Barbara Carrera) $35
April 1982, Linda Rhys Vaughn
    (Mariel Hemingway).................................... $18
June 1982, Lourdes Estores (Shannon Tweed) $25
August 1982, Cathy St. George (Vicki McCarty)......... $25
October 1982, Marianne Gravatte (Tanya Roberts)...... $40
January 1983, Lonny Chin
    (Audrey & Judy Landers).............................. $25
February 1983, Melinda Mays (Kim Basinger)............ $30
May 1983, Susie Scott (Nastassia Kinski)................... $20
June 1983, Jolanda Egger (Marianne Gravatte) $25
August 1983, Carina Persson (Sybil Danning) $18
October 1983, Tracy Vaccaro (Charlotte Kemp) $18
November 1983, Veronica Gamba (Donna Ann).......... $18
December 1983, Terry Nihen (Joan Collins) $20
January 1984, Penny Baker 30th Anniversary
    Bunny $30
April 1984, Lesa Ann Pedriana (Kathy Shower) $35
May 1984, Patty Duffek (Rita Jenrette) $25
July 1984, Liz Stewart (Bo Derek) $18
August 1984 Suzi Schott (Terry Moore Hughes) $17
November 1984, Roberta Vasquez
    (Christie Brinkley) $35
December 1984, Karen Velez (Suzanne Somers) $35
January 1985, Joan Bennett (Goldie Hawn) $25
March 1985, Donna Smith (Shannon Tweed)............... $18
May 1985, Kathy Shower (Karen Velez) $38
June 1985, Devin DeVasquez (Roxanne Pulitzer) $35
July 1985, Marie Carlton (Tracy Vaccaro)................... $30
August 1985, Cher Butler (Kathy Shower)................... $18
September 1985, Venice Kong (Madonna) $25
December 1985, Carol Ficatier (Barbi Benton)............ $25
March 1986, Kim Morris (Sally Field)........................ $17
April 1986, Teri Weigel (Shannon Tweed) $17
May 1986, Christine Ricthers (Kathleen Turner) $17
June 1986, Rebecca Ferratti (Kathy Shower) $20
July 1986, Lynne Austin (Carrie Leigh) $17
November 1986, Donna Edmondson
    (Devin De Vasquez) $25
December 1986, Laurie Carr (Brooke Shields) $30
March 1987, Marina Baker (Janet Jones) $30
May 1987, Kymberly Paige (Vanna White)................... $20
June 1987, Sandy Greenberg (Donna Edmonson)........ $17
August 1987, Sharry Konopski
    (Paulina Porizkova)..................................... $17
November 1987, Pamela Stein (Jessica Hahn) $15
April 1988, Eloise Broady (Vanity) $15
July 1988, Terri Lynn Doss (Cindy Crawford) $35
August 1988, Helle Michaelsen
    (Kimberley Conrad) $18
September 1988, Laura Richmond (Jessica Hahn) $25
March 1989, Laurie Wood (La Toya Jackson)............. $15

The values of "Playboy" magazines depend largely on the cover subject and the Playmate of the Month.

April 1989, Jennifer Jackson (Erika Eleniak) $15
June 1989, Tawnni Cable (Kimberley Conrad)............. $18
July 1989, Erika Eleniak (Shelly Jamison) $35
October 1989, Karen Foster (Pamela Anderson) $35
November 1989, Renee Tenison (Donna Mills) $15
December 1989, Petra Verkaik (Candice Bergen) $25
May 1990, Tina Bockrath (Margaux Hemingway) $15
June 1990, Bonnie Marino (Renee Tenison)................. $35
July 1990, Jacqueline Sheen (Sharon Stone) $45
August 1990, Melissa Evridge (Erika Eleniak) $35
September 1990, Kerri Kendall (Rosanna Arquette) $35
December 1990, Morgan Fox (Sherilyn Fenn) $30
March 1991, Julie Anne Clarke (Stephanie Seymour) . $35
May 1991, Carrie Jean Yazel
　　(Shannon & Tracy Tweed) $15
November 1991, Tonja Christensen
　　(La Toya Jackson) $17
December 1991, Wendy Hamilton
　　(Dian Parkinson) $30
January 1992, Suzi Simpson
　　(Swedish Bikini Team)... $20

May 1992, Vickie Smith (Elizabeth Ward)................... $30
July 1992, Amanda Hope (Pamela Anderson)............. $35
September 1992, Morena Corwin
　　(Sandra Bernhard) $15
December 1992, Barbara Moore (Sharon Stone).......... $18
February 1993, Jennifer Leroy
　　(Stephanie Seymour)... $35
March 1993, Kimberly Donley (Mimi Rogers) $35
May 1993, Elke Jeinsen (Dian Parkinson).................... $15
June 1993, Alesha Oreskovich
　　(Anna Nicole Smith) $18
October 1993, Jenny McCarthy (Jerry Seinfeld) $45
December 1993, Arlene Baxter (Erika Eleniak) $35
March 1994, Neriah Davis (Shannon Doherty) $15
May 1994, Shae Marks (Elle MacPherson) $30
June 1994, Elan Carter (Jenny McCarthy).................... $30
September 1994, Kelly Gallagher (Robin Givens) $15
November 1994, Donna Perry (Pamela Anderson) $30
December 1994, Elisa Bridges (Bo Derek)................... $15
January 1995, Melissa Holiday (Drew Barrymore)...... $45
May 1995, Cynthia Brown (Nancy Sinatra) $12
September 1995, Donna D'Errico
　　(Kimberley Conrad Hefner) $12
December 1995, Samantha Torres
　　(Farrah Fawcett) $25
January 1996, Victoria Fuller (Pamela Anderson)........ $18
May 1996, Shauna Sand (Cindy Crawford)................... $30
July 1996, Angel Lynn Boris (Jenny McCarthy) $20
September 1996, Jennifer Allen (Uma Thurman)......... $15
October 1996, Nadine Chanz (Samantha Fox) $20
November 1996, Ulrika Ericsson (Donna D'errico) $10
December 1996, Victoria Silvstedt
　　(Jenny McCarthy).. $15
January 1997, Jami Ferrell (Marilyn Monroe).............. $15
March 1997, Jennifer Miriam (Faye Resnick) $10
May 1997, Lynn Thomas (Claudia Schiffer) $10
July 1997, Daphnee Lynn Duplaix
　　(Farrah Fawcett) $12
September 1997, Nikki Schieler (Jenny McCarthy,
　　Pamela Anderson) $12
January 1998, Heather Kozar (Shannon Tweed).......... $10
May 1998, Deanna Brooks (Ginger Spice)..................... $8
June 1998, Maria Gil (Pam Anderson, Erika Eleniak,
　　Carmen Electra) $12
October 1998, Laura Lee Cover (Cindy Crawford)...... $12
December 1998, Erica, Nicole and Jaclyn Dahn
　　(Katarina Witt) $25
February 1999, Stacy Marie Fusion
　　(Pamela Anderson)... $10
April 1999, Natalia Sokolova (Sable) $20
May 1999, Yishara Lee Cousino
　　(Charlize Theron) $10

MAGIC MEMORABILIA

Although a magician never reveals his secrets, today there are wannabes who specialize in collecting magic-related items ranging from posters and books that reveal those secrets, to pamphlets issued by the Society of American Magicians, to magic tricks and kits, which pique their attention.

Magic sets have been popular in America and Europe since as early as 1803. Often housed in fine wooden cases, the sets were usually miniature versions of common and popular magicians' tricks.

Background and Guidelines: The earliest magic sets in the United States were Mysto Magic Sets, produced by John Petrie and later by A.C. Gilbert, better known for its Erector sets, as early as 1910. But not every set that says Mysto on it is rare, so it might not necessarily command an exorbitant sum.

The Mysto Magic #5 set, made for 10 years, was often the first set bought by aspiring magicians. It is probably the most common Mysto set, but in Mint-in-Box condition it can still bring $500-$700. The rarest and most desirable Mysto set, however, can bring $2,000 if it is complete. This set, #25, made in 1951, was one of the most elaborate ever made in the United States. It came in a large red suitcase and contained dozens of tricks. Few survive intact today.

Some collectors seek only specific types of magic sets, such as those which feature only coin, handkerchief, rope or card tricks. Others pursue novelty sets, such as "Twenty-One Tricks in a Match Box," which contains a variety of tricks. Sets from other countries, especially those from Spain, Russia and Czechoslovakia, are also pursued, but they are quite rare and scarce.

Celebrity magic sets, those featuring the names, and sometimes the images, of famous magicians, such as Harry Blackstone, Harry Houdini and Mark Wilson, are popular. But character-related sets, though collectible, are not exceptionally valuable because they are not hard to find. These sets include *The Man from U.N.C.L.E.* (made in 1966, by Gilbert, its tricks were named after the show's episodes and promised "only you will know the secret of spy magic!") and James Bond sets.

In 1964, Gilbert produced a set, Martian Magic Tricks, based on the television show *My Favorite Martian.* Many standard tricks, including the "Martian Milky Way" vanishing coin trick, were reworked with an outer space theme, so you could "amaze and mystify your friends."

In the 1960s, Transogram offered a cheaper set, the Magic Kit of Tricks and Puzzles, which, according to the box, offered a "fascinating collection of outstanding magic," and "magic made easy for children." This kit, which included three wire take-it-apart puzzles, a magic wand, and a paddle trick, was a huge seller then. Today it can sell for $50-$75.

A nice three-sheet poster advertising "Thurston the Great Magician" sold for a whopping $13,800 at an auction of magic memorabilia at Swann Galleries in New York.

Also popular with some collectors are a variety of fortune-telling games, the king of which is the Ouija board. The word "Ouija" is actually a combination of foreign two words: the French "Oui" and the German "Ja," which both literally translate to "yes;" the game's mysterious title simply means "Yes…Yes."

The first American Ouija board patent was granted in 1891 to E. Bond, who sold his patent the next year to William Fuld and his Baltimore-based company, Southern Novelty Co. He called his game "Ouija the Oracle Talking Board," and later renamed his company Baltimore Talking Board Co. to better reflect his principal product. In 1966, Parker Brothers bought the rights to the board. One year later, sales hit two million.

But, despite their popularity then, and their continued appearance on toy shelves today, Ouija boards are not particularly valuable as collectibles, primarily because of the superstition and prejudice surrounding them. Prices usually range from $15-$20, although some can sell for more.

However, there are other fortune telling games that do better on the collector market. These include: The Fortune Teller (Milton Bradley, 1908), valued at $100; The Game of Gypsy Fortune Teller (Milton Bradley, 1922) at $10; Black Cat (Parker Brothers, 1897) at $50; The Fortune Telling Game (Parker Brothers, 1890) at $25; The Hand of Fate (Parker Brothers, 1910) at $55; J.R. Singer's Mystic Wanderer (1895) at $75; Funny Fortunes (U.S. Playing Card Co., 1890-1900) at $45; Palmistry (U.S. Playing Card) at $30; and Fortune Telling Game (Whitman Publishing Co., 1934) at $30.

If you are looking for something a bit more expensive, 1870s-1940s posters, lobby cards and billboards promoting famous magicians are scarce and the most valuable. While there are some vintage magic posters that can be had for $20-$200, a classic Harry Houdini poster might set you back thousands. Another famous magician is Chung Ling Soo, who, although an American, passed himself off as the "marvelous Chinese conjurer;" one of his vintage posters might also set you back thousands of dollars.

Other notable magicians from this time period who had beautiful advertising pieces, now highly sought-after, include: Charles Joseph Carter (Carter the Great), Harry Blackstone, Harry Kellar, Howard Thurston, Claude Alexander Conlin (Alexander, the Man Who Knows), Virgil Harris Mulkey (Virgil), Grover George (George) and Milbourne Christopher.

In 1997, Swann Galleries, in New York, held an auction of magic from the collection of Christopher, who devoted a lifetime of scholarly pursuit of the magician's trade. Christopher, an illusionist and spellbinding magician, left behind a massive legacy of vintage books, programs, props, memorabilia, playbills, catalogs and posters that were sold during the 454-lot auction.

As a youngster, Christopher researched every magician who passed through his hometown, Baltimore, and began to build his own library. Soon, he expanded his collection to include other memorabilia, including rare posters and playbills from London, which he visited in 1944 on leave while serving during World War II.

MYSTIFY YOUR FRIENDS WITH MYSTO!

"If you would like to astound and mystify your friends and family with weird exhibitions of sorcery and magic, a Mysto Magic Outfit enables you to duplicate the feats of the world's greatest magicians," say A.C. Gilbert's words in an early 1930s toy catalog promoting his magic set.

The A.C. Gilbert Co. produced one of the greatest toys of its age, the Mysto Magic sets Gilbert designed himself after 1916. The line of approximately 95 Mysto Magic Sets produced after 1916 is one of the greatest contributions to the art of magic anyone has ever made—the nearest competitor created 15 sets. Mysto Magic sets generated youthful interest in aspiring kids and created an avocation in adults.

The last Mysto Magic set was made in 1956. The people who bought these sets at that time are among those who are trying to recapture those times by collecting them today. The sets offered a variety of tricks—about 90 different ones—including tricks with silk handkerchiefs, rings, tubes, balls, cards, coins and bottles.

Virtually every Mysto Magic set came with specially minted Mysto Coins and matching shell, plus instructions or drawings that offered the effect of the illusion and the secret of how to do it. A large two-color poster with a blank space was also included, announcing a magic show, so a budding magician could fill in his name as the star.

In the early 1920s, there were specialty sets focusing on a different area of magic, such as coin tricks, knots, handkerchiefs and card tricks. There were sets in cardboard tubes, wooden boxes with dovetailed corners, and bright red metal suitcases with brass corners or catches.

One set, which came in a large red suitcase, was the Mysto Magic Show Set #25, the most deluxe mass market magic set ever created. The set, produced in 1951, even had legs to turn the suitcase into a table. It included a lift-out upper tray containing Passe Passe bottles, silks, seven Mysto coins, linking rings, five instructional booklets, a poster, mustache and goatee, and a punch-out top hot.

Christopher, who appeared on several television specials when he returned to the United States after the war, also wrote more than 20 books on magic before his death in 1984.

Collecting Tips: Magic sets get a lot of use by aspiring magicians, so pieces are often missing. Serious collectors often check toy catalogs to determine how many pieces were in the original set, then buy incomplete sets to acquire the missing pieces they need. Don't be fooled into thinking that sets that say "100 tricks inside" will contain 100 pieces; quite often the set has fewer pieces and a booklet which details 100 or more tricks which can be used with the same few pieces.

Modern magic sets usually consist of paper and plastic apparatus, which are volatile and harder to keep in prime condition. Sets manufactured for adults are usually sturdier to collect than those made for children. Quite often, the sets created for adults are more valuable—certain Mysto kids sets sell for $100-$200, while professional adult-style models can sell for between $500-$1,000.

Vintage sets often feature metal items, beautifully turned wood, ivory objects and gorgeous silk squares. But when purchasing sets, look for unskilled repairs on the game pieces, such as repainting, which greatly decreases the value of the set.

There are no price guides on magic sets, so values are established by what collectors are willing to pay. At flea markets, many sets sell for $5-$25; toy dealers will list those sets at $10-$50. Rarer sets may command double the value or more, if the set is in pristine condition with all its pieces. In general, individual magic tricks, such as cups and balls, coin tricks, handkerchief tricks, cut and rope tricks, matches to flowers, floating bills and currency, and confetti to flowers, are usually between $5-$15. Good places to look for magic sets and tricks include flea markets, garage sales, thrift stores and antique stores.

Club

• Magic Collector's Association, P.O. Box 511, Glenwood, IL 60425

VALUE LINE

Magic sets

Adams' Abra-Cadabra Magic Set, with 16 tricks, plus wand and booklet......................................$75-$100

Conjuring Tricks game, early 1900s, different magic tricks in wooden box, Bavaria...........................$50-$75

Der Zauberer—The Conjurer, Germany, 1930s, magic set ....$200-$300

The Great Foodini Magic Set, Pressman Toy Corp., 1950s ....$225-$250

Hokus Pokus Magic Set, 1910 ....$400-$600

Mark Wilson's TV Magic Show set, Colonial Enterprise, 1950s..............................$75-$100

Martian Magic Tricks, A.C Gilbert, 1964..........$175-$225

Mysto Magic Set #5, A.C. Gilbert, Mint in Box ....$525-$750

Mysto Magic Exhibition Set, A.C. Gilbert, 1938, smaller version ....$100-$125

Mysto Magic, A.C. Gilbert, 1938, includes makeup and poster...$175-$200

Mysto Magic Set #25, A.C. Gilbert, 1951, Mint in Box ....$1,750-$2,000

Sneaky Pete's Magic Set, Remco, 1958...............$75-$125

Transogram Magic Kit of Tricks and Puzzles, 1960s ....$50-$75

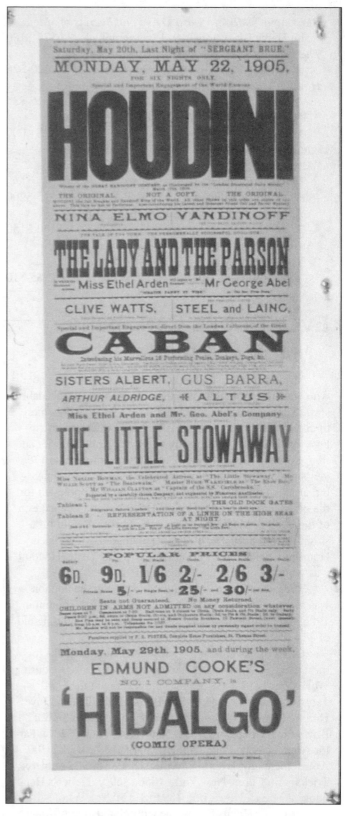

Anything related to Houdini, of course, is considered a treasure. This 1905 theater broadside from an appearance in England sold for $3,220 at a Swann Galleries auction in New York.

Books

Blackstone's Modern Card Tricks and Secrets of Magic,
by Harry Blackstone, 1941, autographed........$75-$100
The Golden Book of Magic, by Clayton Rawson,
the Great Merlini, Golden Press, 1964.............$20-$25
Houdini's Big Little Book of Magic, premium for
American Oil Co., 1927 ....$25-$35
A Magician Among the Spirits, by Harry Houdini,
1924, autographed first edition...........................$1,000

Magic Show Advertising

"Alexander, The Man Who Knows,"
Claude Alexander Conlin, 27" x 41",
red and black lithograph..................................$75-$200
"Ask Alexander," Claude Alexander Conlin,
27" x 41" ....$100-$150
"Australian Tour," or "India Tour," posters for
Virgil Harris Mulkey, 12" x 30", portrait and
illusions, each...$5-$10

A group of four "How To Do" volumes of magic tricks dating from the 1890s sold for $575 at a Swann Galleries auction.

EVEN BOOKS CAN BRING MAGICAL PRICES!

Milbourne Christopher was a magician of some note who was into more than just the hocus-pocus, abracadabra stuff. Though he pulled rabbits out of a hat on stage more than once, his legacy is a wide-ranging collection of vintage magic books, sold during a 1997 Swann Galleries auction. Some of these "how-to" books were more than 175 years old. Many were illustrated. But the highest winning bid attained during the auction was not for a book, but for the original typescript by Harry Houdini for a new edition of the book *A Magician Among the Spirits*. It sold for a stunning $36,800! The 409 pages include corrections in Houdini's hand and by his assistant, Oscar Teale. Houdini was working on it when he died in 1926.

The second highest winning bid during the auction was attained by a book, written and signed by Houdini in 1906. *The Right Way to Do Wrong* brought a winning bid of $14,950.

Other books sold at the auction included: Tricks for the Trenches and Wards, intended for soldiers to use during World War I ($230); Ruse and Subterfuge at the Card Table, Canada, 1902 ($3,450); Book of Riddles and Five Hundred Home Amusements, New York, 1893 ($632); Boy's Own Conjuring Book, New York, 1860 ($201); Parlor Amusements, Philadelphia, 1861 ($138); Dick's 100 Amusements for Evening Parties, 1880 ($69); Gambler's Tricks with Cards, New York, 1850 ($690); Heller's Handbook of Magic, New York, 1891 ($115); The Whole Art of Conjuring, or Hocus Pocus, the Complete Book of Magic, Philadelphia, 1850 ($1,495); and Endless Amusement: A Collection of Nearly 400 Entertaining Experiments, Boston, 1842 ($5,290).

"Australian Tour," or "India Tour," posters for
Virgil Harris Mulkey, 27" x 41", portrait and
illusions, each...$75-$100
"Blackstone, The World's Master Magician,"
18" x 8", Lowe's Theater, 1929.....................$175-$225
"Carter Beats the Devil," window card, 14" x 22",
Otis Litho, 1920 ....$75-$200
"George's Triumphant American Tour," poster for
Grover George, 27" x 41", moonlight scene
with an owl, bats and devils ....$100-$175
"A Gift from the Gods to Mortals on Earth to Amuse
and Mystify," Chung Ling Soo, 20" x 30",
1910..$1,000-$1,300
"The Supreme Master of Magic," poster for Grover
George, 20" x 27"..$200-$700
"The World's Weird Wonderful Wizard," window for
Carter, 14" x 22", Otis Litho, 1920 ....$75-$200

Miscellaneous

Brochure, "Houdini: The Creator of the
Handcuff King Act and Only Legitimate
Jail Breaker," 1912, Victorian Theater, New York,
four pages ....$175-$200
Chiromagica, magnetic magic hand answering board
game, McLoughlin, 1890s?...........................$350-$400
Handcuffs and key, used by Harry Houdini,
with photograph of Houdini ....$2,500-$3,000
The Hand of Fate Fortune Telling Game,
McLoughlin Brothers, 1901 ....$1,750-$2,250
Les Jockos Singes Savants - Jeu Magnetique,
question-answer wheel $850-950
Magic deck of cards based on 1970s television show
"The Magician"...$5-$10
Postcard, Harry Houdini New Year's Greating,
color, 1908..$75-$100

Program, Houdini at the Orpheum Circuit Theater, St. Louis, Mo., 1922, 16 pages........................$75-$100

Wax pack, Blackstone's Magic Tricks, 1963, Philadelphia Chewing Gum Co., features folders explaining 24 different feats of magic by Harry Blackstone, unopened..............................$25-$35

Swann Galleries 1997 Auction Results

Books, *Blackstone's Secret of Magic* and *Blackstone's Modern Card Tricks*, 1929 and 1932, set...............$103

Book, *Handcuff Secrets,* by Harry Houdini, George Routledge & Sons, London, 1910.............$517

Book, *Jap Box Tricks*, by Glenn Gravatt, signed, Los Angeles, 1937...................................$172

Book, *Magic and Mystery Unveiled*, illustrated, New York, 1883 ....$1,265

Book, *Magical Rope Ties and Escapes*, by Harry Houdini, London, 1921...........................$402

Book, *Modern Card Tricks without Apparatus*, by Will Goldston, London, 1915..............................$80

Canes, John Mulholland's, set of three, one ebony and two trick canes................................$1,725

Catalogue, *Illustrated Catalogue of Conjuring Tricks and the Very Latest Creations in Magic*, 160 pages, London, 1877 ....$103

Coin bank, cast magician's coin bank, by Book of Knowledge, with original carton............................$345

"How To Do" volumes, four illustrated pamphlets revealing secrets for sleight of hand, chemical tricks, mechanical tricks and 40 tricks with cards, 1890s...$575

Photographs, 170 photographs of magicians, including better—and lesser-known figures, from early in the century to more recent 1960s portraits, many were promotional shots, some were signed $2,990

Poster, "Alexander, The Man Who Knows," 80" x 109", wearing a white turban, India..........$2,530

Poster, "Christopher's Wonders," 20" x 30", his magical musical revue, 50 fabulous feats.........$201

Poster, "Dante the Famous Magician," shows Beauty, his Arabian Steed, Otis Lithograph Co., Cleveland, 1925...$5,290

Poster, "Karlini, the Great Magician," 35" x 49", shows the magician in his top hat, Vienna..........$1,840

Poster, "Princess Yvonne, The Mystery Girl—Mentalist Supreme," 79" x 82", Triangle Poster Co., Philadelphia..$431

Poster, "Thurston, The Great Magician," 39" x 83", promoting his levitation act, 1910.....................$13,800

This striking three-sheet poster with a clever graphic sold for just under $1,000 at a Swann Galleries auction in New York.

Prop, "Snake in the Basket," two snakes inside, loading rod, two velvet table covers.......................$747

Theater broadside, Harry Houdini appearance in London, England, 1905.......................................$3,220

MILITARIA

Collecting souvenirs of war may be among the oldest pastimes in the world—as old as the first Crusaders who returned with a Saracen sword to hang on the castle wall. Every war has more finely-honed the time-honored soldier's tradition of souvenir hunting.

Some souvenir hunters and collectors have taken a mass-market approach to collecting, helping themselves to anything that was not nailed down—as well as many things that were—providing yet another interpretation of the phrase "the spoils of war." Militaria collecting is not confined to enemy souvenirs; it also represents the perpetuation of a historical record of items used by American, as well as allied forces.

Background: During and after every war, there has been a brisk trade in militaria, not only among the participants, but among civilian collectors as well. For instance, the aftermath of the Revolutionary War found almost every household with a flintlock rifle and powder horn hanging over the mantel.

Following the Civil War, a Scotsman, Francis Bannerman, who had recently emigrated to the U.S., founded a war-surplus empire by purchasing at auction all the Union and captured Confederate war materials he could find. He opened a retail store in New York City, opening the field to many collectors. It's been growing ever since.

General Guidelines: As in most fields of collecting, original condition is of paramount importance, especially in the case of uniforms, headgear and firearms. Those pieces that are in excellent, working condition, with the fewest marks, blemishes or moth holes command the highest prices.

Firearms—In firearms collecting, weapons must bear matching numbers, show little wear or use, and retain all original markings and parts, such as cleaning rods, slings, etc. Beware of rarer pieces that have been repaired or reconstructed by a competent gunsmith. Look for specimens that were made in lesser numbers; these command the highest prices.

Headgear—Make sure all parts, especially straps, helmet plates, liners and trim, are original to the piece. German spike-top helmets are particularly collectible, and, for the more exotic specimens, command outstanding prices. These helmets are difficult to find in original condition, with most lacking one or more of the original components, such as the strap or trim.

Steel helmets, developed during World War I by the warring nations, are highly collectible due to the many different styles and experimental models. The French Adrian helmet of 1915 was used by many countries and individualized by differing helmet plates. German steel helmets from World War I through World War II offer a field of collecting unto themselves, with numerous design variations over the life of the helmet's use. Many helmets have been repainted by dealers or collectors so that they appear to be original.

Collectors can still find headgear from the Revolutionary War, the Napoleanic Wars and earlier campaigns. As always, condition and scarcity determine the selling price. It stands to reason that not many cloth and fabric items have survived 200 to 300 years.

Uniforms—Over the years, uniforms have been personalized with patches, swatches, epaulettes and insignia for reasons of accomplishment and pride. Uniforms from all time periods are collectible.

Uniforms, however, suffer damage from wear, storage and moths. Seams and bindings should be intact for highest value.

Medals and Decorations—Because they are small, often colorful and easy to display, medals and decorations have been collected for hundreds of years. In many cases, these awards are outstanding examples of jeweler's art, designed to exemplify the devotion of soldiers to a higher duty. Campaign medals are usually designed to represent a particular battle, or campaign, covering a particular period in time. Usually such medals will bear a representation that readily identifies the campaign involved.

Orders and decorations for bravery, long service and military merit are usually of a higher quality than campaign medals, with the more rarely awarded medals often surpassing the quality of fine jewelry. Enamels, diamonds, brilliants and other precious gems are to be found in the orders of some countries.

Most collectors prefer to limit their area of collecting to a particular country or group of countries involved in the same conflict; some become so finite as to collect only those medals that were awarded to members of a particular regiment.

It is important to build a reference library covering the subjects of one's interest. An important source of information for the collector is the Orders and Medals Society of America, a group of collectors who have succeeded in maintaining

TRACK DOWN YOUR OLD MILITARY BUDDIES ON THE INTERNET!

"You bonded together at boot camp…Now build a community together." This is the latest phrase to hit cyberspace, courtesy of Planet Alumni's militaryconnections.com.

Planet Alumni, based in Kansas City, designed the site to connect current and former military personnel and their families. The registry-based site is free and lets users create personalized online communities. Members can locate friends and family through a directory, create and post photo albums, post messages, chat in real-time, check an event calendar to plan reunions, and read news of interest.

high standards of professionalism and honesty among dealers and collectors.

Military insignia and badge collectors have proliferated over the last 50 years, with scarcity driving up prices that were quite modest after World War II. The American Society of Military Insignia Collectors (ASMIC) was formed as a focus point for these collectors, and its ranks have steadily grown over the years.

Equipment—This category includes webbed equipment, footgear, survival equipment and load carrying equipment, as well as the personal kit that made life bearable for the fighting man. This equipment differed from country to country, and from war to war. As perishable as this type of equipment tends to be, specimens from the Revolutionary War and every war since can still be found, in relatively good condition.

Collectors who have the room (and the money) also seek original and restored military vehicles, including everything from jeeps and Crossley tenders to deactivated armored fighting vehicles and tanks.

One of the larger organizations devoted to maintaining interest in old fighting vehicles is the Military Vehicle Preservation Association of Independence, Mo. Foreign military vehicles appear on the U.S. market with regular frequency, including German half-tracks, British Ferret and Saracen Armored Cars, as well as general utility vehicles, command cars, ambulances and many others.

Offered at an auction of militaria conducted by Jackson's Auctioneers of Cedar Falls, Iowa, this lot sold for $280. It included two World War I-era dress uniforms and an officer's sword.

Recommended Reading

Books

American Military Collectibles Price Guide, Ron Manion
German Military Collectibles Price Guide, Ron Manion
Japanese & Other Foreign Military Collectibles Price Guide, Ron Manion
Collector's Guide to British Army Campaign Medals, Robert W.D. Ball
World War II Homefront Collectibles, Martin Jacobs
Mauser Military Rifles of the World, Robert W.D. Ball
Military Small Arms of the 20th Century, Ian V. Hogg and John Weeks
Gun Digest Book of Combat Handgunnery, Chuck Taylor
Propaganda Postcards of World War II, Ron Menchene

Periodicals

Military Trader
Gun List
Gun & Knife Show Calendar

VALUE LINE

Firearms

Values are shown for weapons in Excellent condition.

M1795 Type I US Springfield Flintlock Musket, dated 1799	$2,600-$4,500
M1816 French Charleville Flintlock Musket	$1,800-$2,000
British Land Pattern Musket	$1,800-$2,000
British Brunswick P1837 Musket	$900-$1,000
US M1842 Musket	$900-$1,000
French M1853 Musket	$500-$600
US M1855 Rifled Carbine	$2,700-$2,800
British Pattern P1861 Sergeant's Rifle (Confederate)	$1,000-$1,250
US M1870 Rolling Block Standard Navy Rifle	$700-$800
Turkish Peabody-Martini Rifle	$700-$800
German M1871 Mauser Rifle	$400-$500
US M1873 Trapdoor Carbine	$2,200-$2,300
US M1884 Trapdoor Rifle	$500-$600
German M1888 Mauser and Commission Rifle	$150-$200
US M1896 Krag-Jorgensen Rifle	$400-$500
US M1898 Krag-Jorgensen Rifle	$400-$500
US M1898 Krag-Jorgensen Carbine, 26" barrel	$2,200-$2,400
German M1898 Mauser Rifle	$300-$400
British SMLE Mk.III Rifle	$125-$200
US M1903 Springfield Rifle	$400-$500
US M1903 A3 Springfield Rifle	$350-$400
US M1917 Rifle (Enfield)	$175-$250
German K98k Carbine	$350-$400
US MI Garand Rifle, rebuilt, any manufacturer	$400-$450

Headgear

Prices listed are for pieces in Very Good original condition, with original removable parts, such as chinstraps, helmet plates and buttons.

French M1915 Adrian steel helmet,
Russian plate ....$400-$500

French M1915 Adrian steel helmet,
Engineer's plate ....$50-$75

Italian WWI Adrian-style steel helmet,
Bersaglieri ....$75-$100

British WWI steel helmet....................................$25-$50

German leather Uhlan helmet ....$1,500-$1,750

German M1916 steel helmet, plain........................$60-$85

German Prussian EM spike-top helmet ....$275-$325

German M1916 camouflaged steel helmet ....$125-$150

Siamese M1915 Adrian steel helmet ....$75-$100

Mexican M1926 Adrian steel helmet.................$100-$150

Spanish M1926 steel helmet ....$25-$50

M1821 Pattern Bell Crown Shako,
"Massachusetts Militia" ....$1,200-$1,300

Civil War period Infantry Kepi ....$400-$450

Indian Wars Calvary Kepi, c. 1883 ....$500-$600

WWI US Aviator's overseas cap,
French made ....$200-$250

WWI US 90th Div. steel helmet..........................$125-$150

German Waffen SS EM visored hat.............$1,700-$1,800

German M35 steel helmet, Army.......................$300-$400

German Allgemeine SS parade hat ....$1,600-$1,700

German M42 steel helmet, army........................$300-$350

WWII US steel helmet...$20-$30

US Kevlar "Fritz"-style helmet...........................$75-$100

Gas mask, M17A1, complete, with canvas bag,
filters, accessories..$35-$40

Gas mask, M40, complete, with canvas bag ....$75-$100

Camouflage net, for M1 helmets, mesh,
drawstring..$20-$25

Luftwaffe single decal paratrooper helmet,
spanner bolt ....$3,000-$3,500

German ear cut out Cavalry helmet,
Model 1918 ....$2,000-$2,500

Luftwaffe blue canvas pith helmet,
French...$1,250-$1,500

Luftwaffe Herman Goring tropical model 1941 cap,
tan cloth with eagle and bull's eye ....$2,250-$2,500

3rd Reich U-boat rain cap, field gray,
rubberized canvas ....$100-$125

M-1943 goggles, fur lined, in the wrap,
Air Force ....$10-$15

Italian pith helmet, WWII ....$225-$250

Insignia, Metal and Cloth

US Civil War Sergeant's stripes, pair.....................$50-$60

US Civil War Massachusetts Militia Shako Plate ..$40-$50

US Indian Wars Farrier's cloth insignia.................$20-$25

US Spanish American war period Medical
Department collar devices, bronze, pair...................$15

EXTRA! EXTRA! READ ALL ABOUT IT!

World War II, the defining event of the 20th century, was recorded by big-city and small-town papers alike, providing militaria and history buffs an abundance of black-and-white glimpses of those chaotic years. The major headlines attract the most attention, recalling events such as the beginning of the war, the Japanese attack at Pearl Harbor, the Normandy invasion, the death of FDR, V-E Day, the dropping of the first atomic bomb, and V-J Day.

Newspaper headlines that capture the precursor events to the war, such as "Chamberlain Off By Plane to See Hitler; Will Make A Personal Plea To Avert War," are also of interest. Values for papers such as these, in Excellent condition or better, are generally in the $30-$50 range, with some editions, such as the previous example, commanding more. Post-war papers are also pursued by many.

Location papers, published at the site of the event (i.e. Dallas papers for the JFK assassination), always attract greater attention and are therefore more valuable. Honolulu papers covering the Japanese attack on Pearl Harbor lead the way in this category. The most famous and most valuable is an edition of the Honolulu Star-Bulletin of Dec. 7, 1941, whose first extra edition blares: "War! Oahu Bombed By Japanese Planes." In complete, Excellent condition, this paper can be worth more than $1,500. Note, however, that reprints exist, so use caution on this one. Values for other papers providing coverage on Pearl Harbor generally range from $25-$50.

Most D-Day papers are in the range from $15-$40, while those announcing FDR's death may bring $20-$45. V-E Day examples can range from $25-$45, with exceptions approaching $50-$100. V-J papers can usually be purchased for $25-$50, but headlines with outstanding layouts, pictures and color are worth a bit more, as is the case with all other stories.

US WWI Air Service Collar device, officer,
bronze, with silver propeller ....$40-$45

US WWI Tank Corps Collar Device,
1st pattern ....$90-$100

US WWI 32nd Division shoulder patch ....$20-$25

US WWI GHQ shoulder patch ....$30-$40

US WWII AAF pilot's winged badge,
"Sterling" ....$50-$60

US WWII CBI patch, silver bullion,
hand embroidered...$70-$75

Prussia Infantry Lt.'s shoulder insignia,
c. 1890, pair...$60-$75

Prussian WWI machine gunner's sleeve
insignia..$90-$100

Japanese WWII superior private collar insignia ....$15-$20

German WWII "RLB" sleeve insignia...................$50-$60
German WWII Army "Afrika Korps"
  cuff title ....$200-$250

Medals, Insignia, Badges

Prices listed are for items in Fine condition, with original ribbons and no repairs.

US Civil War medal, Army, boxed ....$175-$200
US Indian Wars medal, named..........................$250-$275
US Sampson Medal, named to Marine ....$700-$800
US Cuban Pacification Medal............................$35-$50
US First Haitian Campaign Medal, named..........$90-$100
US WWI Victory Medal, bar "FRANCE" ....$35-$50
US WWII Purple Heart, named to KIA,
  Tarawa ....$700-$750
US WWII European Theater of Operations
  Medal ....$10-$15
US WWII Bronze Star ....$15-$20
US WWII Distinguished Flying Cross ....$20-$25
US Korean War Service Medal............................$10-$15
US Vietnam Service Medal.................................$10-$15
US Gulf War Service Medal ....$15-$20
Imperial German WWI Iron Cross, II Cl ....$25-$30
Imperial Baden War Service Medal ....$25-$30
Imperial Bavarian Order of St. Michael,
  silver and blue, enamel................................$300-$350
Imperial Hesse WWI Bronze Bravery Medal ....$60-$75
Imperial Black Army Wound Badge......................$25-$30
German WWII Iron Cross I Cl, PB........................$60-$75
German WWII "East Front" Medal ....$25-$30
German WWII War Service Cross, II Cl ....$25-$30
Serbian WWI Obolitch Gold Cross
  Bravery Medal..$125-$150
Japanese WWII Red Cross Medal ....$40-$50
Italian WWII Campaign of Liberation Medal,
  1943-45 ....$25-$30
French Legion of Honor, Knight's Grade ....$90-$100
French WWII Croix de Guerre,
  bronze with star ....$35-$45

Military Vehicles

Prices listed are for vehicles in restored, operating condition.

US Renault FT17 Tank $30,000
US WWII Jeep..$5,000
US WWII M3A2 Half-Track $9,000
US M1941 Chevrolet Staff Car............................$6,000
US Stuart "Honey" Light Tank $18,000
German WWII Volkswagen $6,000
German Post-WWII Czech-built SD Kfz 251
  Half-Track $12,000
British 1951 Ferret MkII Armored Car....................$8,000
British Saracen Armored Command Car $8,000

Swords and Knives

Values shown are for items in Excellent original condition.

Civil War Union Presentation Staff and Field
  Officer's Sword, German, inscribed...................$6,000

This lot of assorted French medals, sold at a recent Butterfield & Butterfield auction, includes items from the late 1800s and early 1900s. The entire lot was sold with an estimate of $600-$800.

Civil War Union non-regulation German engraved
  officer's sword...$600-$650
Civil War Bowie Knife, believed
  Confederate ....$500-$550
Civil War Bowie Knife, Union,
  elliptical crossguard ....$600-$650
C.1880 Militia officer's sword, Knight's head
  pommel..$125-$150
US M1902 Army officer's sword......................$200-$250
US M1904 Hospital Corps Knife......................$250-$275
US WWI Trench fighting knife, knuckle bow,
  triangular blade ....$100-$125
US WWI Trench fighting knife, Mk II,
  knuckle duster grip.......................................$175-$200
US WWII Marine Corps fighting knife,
  "K-Bar" ....$175-$200
WWII MI Carbine Bayonet, "Camillus" ....$50-$75
French WWI field-made Trench
  fighting knife ....$75-$100
Imperial German Infantry Hanger, c. 1850........$100-$125
Imperial Saxon Infantry officer's sword,
  engraved and inscribed.................................$750-$800
Imperial M98/05 Sawtooth bayonet....................$75-$100
Hitler youth knife..$60-$75
SA Dagger..$225-$250
Labor Corps Hewer..$250-$275
Engraved dress bayonet ....$200-$225
First Model Luftwaffe dress sword...................$700-$750
Italian WWII Air Force officer's sword.............$200-$225
Japanese WWII Cavalry sword.........................$200-$225

This group of World War II Japanese Army equipment was offered at a Butterfield & Butterfield auction with a $250-$350 pre-sale estimate.

Russian Imperial Shaska ....$600-$650
British c. 1880 socket bayonet ....$75-$85
Austrian M95 bayonet...$35-$50
Spanish M1913 Simpson bayonet.........................$25-$35
Bayonet, M4 Carbine with M8A1 scabbard ....$30-$35
Bayonet, M5 Grand Rifle with M8A1 scabbard ....$30-$35
Machete, GI issue military machete, 12",
　　with injection molded case................................$25-$30
Machete, GI issue military machete, 18",
　　with injection molded case................................$30-$35

Uniforms

Prices listed are for uniforms free of moth holes, repairs and/or replaced insignia.

US Revolutionary War period tail coat,
　　private soldier.. $4,200
US War of 1812 Naval officer's uniform set,
　　complete... $4,200
US Mexican War period officer's
　　undress jacket... $2,500
British officer's mess jacket, Indian Mutiny $1,700
German Hussar officer's dress jacket, c. 1870s $1,000
French Lancer's Tunic, Mexican Expedition,
　　c. 1867 .... $850
US Naval Officer uniform, pre WWI.................$500-$550
US Civil War period artillery officer's mess jacket..... $650

US Spanish-American war Rough Rider's tunic $450
German SW Africa Schutz-Trupp tunic......................$750
WWI French Poilu uniform, complete........................$550
WWI German infantry tunic $325
WWI US officer complete uniform,
　　North Russia Expedition $875
WWII Paratroop uniform, 101st AB,
　　complete field outfit $1,100
WWII US officer's Class A uniform..........................$175
German WWII 1st Sgt. Infantry, field tunic...............$450
Polish WWII Infantry uniform, complete...................$850
Japanese WWII Naval Landing Force field uniform,
　　complete $550
Winter flight suit, WWII Luftwaffe ....$400-$450
Paratrooper jump smock, Third Reich ....$4000-$4,100
Flight Jacket, AAF Type A-2,
　　with Bomb Unit patch ....$1,000-$1,100

Miscellaneous

US and USMC wool blanket.................................$20-$25
GI issue first aid kit, type 8, USMC, complete,
　　with nylon cover...$30-$35
Claymore Mine (M181A anti-personnel mine) bag,
　　with instruction label...$8-$10
WWII emergency communication unit, complete,
　　with waterproof container and parachute......$700-$750
1918 1-quart canteen, U.S. WWI...........................$15-$20
Quarter-pound foot powder, U.S. WWI.................$20-$25
Chow forks, U.S. WWI...$8-$10
Chow set, knife, fork and spoon, U.S. WWI ....$25-$30
Wool mummy sleeping bag, U.S. WWII ....$25-$30
Entrenching shovels, U.S. WWII..........................$15-$20
Mess kit, two-piece, steel, U.S. WWII ....$10-$15
Camo face paint, tube, U.S. WWII ....$3-$5
First Aid field dressing, U.S. WWII ....$2-$3
Winterize kit, for gas mask in cold weather...............$3-$5
Manual, for M17 Mask, how to use ....$3-$5
Health Service hat insignia for a woman, visor,
　　U.S. WWII ....$50-$60
Bronze Swastika paperweight, 5", German ....$75-$85
M001 Civil War brass bugle, reproduction ....$25-$30
Red Cross medal, with ribbon, Japanese,
　　WWII ....$35-$40
Nazi canteen with cup, field-gray
　　wool covered ....$30-$40
Third Reich German army mess tin, used..............$30-$40
Third Reich Adolf Hitler silver sugar
　　cube tongs ....$1,750-$1,900
Parachute, U.S., dated 1943 ....$100-$125
Camouflage clothing bag, USMC........................$25-$30
Signal lamp, WWII, hand held, Japanese ....$300-$400

MODERN DOLLS

In the 1950s America's Baby Boom generation was playing with toys. It was a fertile time, too, for manufacturers to produce a wide variety of dolls, and the resulting pieces are among the most coveted by today's collectors. Some of their favorites, both then and now? Madame Alexander's Cissy, Vogue's Ginny dolls, Ideal's Grow-hair Crissy and Shirley Temple dolls, and Mattel's revolutionary Chatty Cathy. (And, of course, Barbie, who has her own chapter in this book.)

Differing from their predecessors in many ways, these hard plastic and vinyl dolls had extravagant wardrobes, they were often teen-agers, and many had eyes that could blink. Dolls even talked, all firsts that today's collectors played with then—often until their beloved treasures were destroyed—and now seek out in their original condition.

Background: Hard plastic dolls replaced the composition doll—made of a wood pulp mixture—in the 1940s. Hard plastic dolls flourished from the late '40s through the late '50s. At that time doll manufacturers embraced the use of vinyl, which not only withstood the test of time but was also soft and warm to the touch. Eyes, eyelashes and wigs were made of plastic. The "hair" could be washed and combed and, if rooted, would not fall out. These modern dolls mark the beginnings of many dollmaking practices that are still commonly used today.

General Guidelines: Unlike the composition and bisque dolls of decades earlier, dolls made from the late 1940s to the present do not generally suffer from crazing or cracks as they age. The skin surface, however, is susceptible to marks, discoloration and blemishes, all of which deplete the value of a doll. Stains, missing or broken limbs, cracked bodies or cut hair detract severely from a doll's value.

Dolls in original boxes, with any original literature, command premium prices. To command top prices, dolls should be dressed in original clothing and have all original accessories (hats, shoes, etc.). Certain popular outfits may command extra value. Original tags and labels add a premium.

Wigs should be original and not soiled or restyled. A doll with the wig missing is worth very little. Even if the wig is replaced or re-rooted the doll has little value as a collectible.

Original sleep eyes must move freely, and all mechanical parts (including voice boxes) should be operational. Talking dolls with working mechanisms command a premium over dolls that can no longer talk, although mute talking dolls are still collectible.

Be aware of the markings on dolls, often found on the torso, buttocks or back of head. Most composition and modern dolls are marked with the manufacturer's name and date. Sometimes, however, the date may be a copyright date only and not the same as the date the actual doll was manufactured. A doll with a 1966 copyright date may actually have

---

DRESS HER UP!

Certain popular outfits always attract attention within the doll collecting community. Look for the original wardrobes—as opposed to handmade pieces, or generic doll clothes—to be the most collectible. A Littlest Angel dress from the 1956 "Fashion of the Month" club sold in a recent online auction for $25, and a lot of five outfits for Crissy, Ideal's grow-hair doll, sold online for $50.

---

been made in the 1980s.

The Stars: Many, many dolls were produced in the post-war years, but these are among the favorites with today's collectors:

Chatty Cathy—Introduced in 1960, Mattel's Chatty Cathy was the first mass-produced talking doll. She was produced through 1965, with varying eye and skin colors. The first version had blonde hair, a hard-plastic body and a vinyl face. The year a doll was produced does not affect value nearly as much as condition.

Cissy—Introduced in 1955, this popular fashion doll by Beatrice Alexander for the Alexander Doll Co. had many outfits. In 1957 Madame Alexander produced Cissette, a smaller doll that was deemed Cissy's younger sister. Both are very popular among collectors.

Crissy—Ideal's grow-hair doll. The key to value is the condition of her hair, which was often cut or torn out completely. The first edition, produced in 1969, had hair that cascaded to the floor. Dolls from the early 1970s had hair that fell only to the knees. These are the most commonly found today.

Ginny—Produced by Vogue and marketed in the 1950s as the "Fashion Leader in Doll Society." Many dolls in Vogue's line were called Ginny, although a Ginny series was not created until 1952. Vogue tested unusual eye colors, skin colors and wigs when first producing Ginny, and these "transitional" dolls are highly collectible.

Nancy Ann—One of many popular teen dolls produced in the late 1950s (Nancy Ann Storybook Dolls). She had blue sleep eyes, a swivel waist, high-heeled feet and multiple outfits to be purchased separately.

Recommended Reading
Warman's Dolls, R. Lane Herron
200 Years of Dolls, Dawn Herlocher
Modern Doll Rarities, Carla Marie Cross
Crissy Doll and Her Friends, Beth C. Gunther
The World of Dolls, Maryanne Dolan

Mint-in-Box, this "Talking Charmin' Chatty" doll from Mattel is valued at $250.

VALUE LINE

Values shown are for dolls in Near Mint or better condition, unless otherwise indicated.

Alexander Dolls

Alice in Wonderland, 14", hard plastic, blond hair, blue eyes, blue taffeta dress, 1950 .... $700

Amy, 16", cloth doll, dressed mask face, blond hair, painted blue eyes, flowered print dress, replaced shoes and socks, cloth dress tag $80

Baby, 18", hard plastic head, vinyl arms and legs, cloth body, pink organdy dress $85

Binnie Walker, 14", hard plastic, blond hair, black striped dress, yellow pinafore and straw hat, c1950 .... $500

Brenda Starr, 12", vinyl head and arms, hard plastic body and legs, 1964 .... $800

Caroline, 15", vinyl head, blue sleep eyes, rooted hair in orig. set $300

Cissette, 9", hard plastic, jointed knees, blue sleep eyes, orig. outfit $225

Cissette Renoir, 9-1/2", hard plastic, jointed knees $100

Cissy, 20", brown hair, blue sleep eyes, bridal gown and accessories $150

Elise Bridesmaid, 17", vinyl, 1966 .... $250

Fisher Quints, 7" all original clothes, 1964 .... $475

Goldilocks, 14", vinyl head and arms, hard plastic torso and legs, blond synthetic wig, 1978 .... $100

Goya, 21", vinyl $250

Jenny Lind and Cat, 14", vinyl head and arms, hard plastic torso and legs, synthetic wig, sleep eyes, 1969 .... $300

Lissy Ballerina, 12", hard plastic $250

Madame, 21", vinyl $325

Maggie, 14", hard plastic, walker, blond mohair wig, brown sleep eyes $125

Marybel, 16", vinyl head, blond rooted hair, brown sleep eyes, 1959 .... $160

Mary Ellen, 31", hard plastic head, blue sleep eyes, saran wig, hard plastic walker body $215

Melanie, 21", vinyl $275

Nina Ballerina, 14", hard plastic, brown wig, sleep eyes, closed mouth $300

Polly, 17", vinyl, 1965, ball gown $195

Quiz-Kid, 7-1/2", hard plastic head $225

American Character

Baby, 16", composition head, cloth, 1925 .... $125

Betsy McCall, 8", hard plastic, break in seam between legs, orig. outfit with shoes and beret $400

Betsy McCall, 30", 1961, vinyl head and body, blue sleep eyes $250

Bottle Tot, 13", composition head, body mark, orig. tagged clothes $175

Michael Landon, Little Joe, Bonanza, vinyl, fully jointed body, painted brown hair and eyes, molded clothing, c. 1965 .... $65

Sally, 18", composition head, cloth body $200

Sandy McCall, 35", vinyl head and body, blue sleep eyes $530

Sweet Sue Sophisticate, 14", 1953, wedding dress, all orig. accessories and paperwork $500

Sweet Sue Sophisticate, 19", vinyl head $325

Tiny Toodles, 10-1/2", vinyl, molded, painted hair, 1958 .... $25

Tiny Tears, 12", hard-plastic head, vinyl body, curly rooted hair, sunsuit, wood and plastic bathinette, c. 1955 .... $2,500

Tiny Tears, 9", orig. outfit, near mint $175

Toni, 10", collegiate outfit, orig. booklet $70

Toni, 20" $365

Toni, High Society outfit, red shoes and black purse $90

Toodles, 30", 1960 .... $150

Arranbee

Angel Skin, 13", soft vinyl head, magic-skin body and limbs $80

Baby Bunting, 15", vinylite plastic head, stuffed magic-skin body, molded, painted hair $60

Judy, 19", hard plastic, nylon blond wig, braids, metal knob to wind hair back into head, open mouth, 1951 .... $75

Little Dear, 8", stuffed vinyl body, rooted hair, blue sleep eyes, 1956 .... $80

Littlest Angel, 11", vinyl head, hard plastic body, jointed, rooted dark brown hair, 1959 .... $40

Nancy Lee, 14", vinyl, blue sleep eyes, blonde wig, original outfit $250

Nanette, hard plastic, glued-on wig, sleep eyes, 1952 .... $250

Nanette, hard-plastic fully jointed body, saran braided
   wig, blue sleep eyes, closed mouth, 1953 .... $155
Taffy, 23", plastic, socket head, blue eyes, brunette
   saran wig, straight walker legs, 1954 .... $175
Cabbage Patch Kids
Coleco, 1983-89 ....$30-$250
Hasbro, 1989-94, soft body..................................$25-$150
Mattel, 1995-present, soft body ....$25-$150

Effanbee
American Child, Barbara Ann, 16", composition head,
   green sleep eyes, human hair wig $450
Anne Shirley, 18", composition $175
Babette, 11-1/2", composition head and hands,
   stuffed pink cloth body, molded painted brown
   hair, closed eyes and mouth, orig. tags and box,
   1945.. $100
Butterball, 12", all vinyl, molded blond hair,
   original box, 1969 .... $60
Candy Kid twins, 12", vinyl, fully jointed,
   sleep eyes, molded hair, original outfit, 1954 .... $300
Cinderella, 18", 1952 .... $200
Dy-Dee Baby, 10", plastic head, sleep eyes,
   molded hair, orig. clothes, 1950-58........................ $125
Dy-Dee Baby, 14", plastic head, sleep eyes,
   molded hair, orig. clothes, 1950-58........................ $250
Fluffy, 9-1/2", all vinyl, blue sleep eyes, rooted hair,
   1966... $85
Melodie, hard plastic, fully jointed, blue sleep eyes,
   blonde wig, phonograph mechanism inside, 1953,
   with records $650
Miss Chips, all vinyl, jointed, orig. outfit, 1968 .... $85
Patricia Walker, 14", 1952 .... $125
Patsy Baby, 11", composition head........................... $275
Schoolgirl Writing, 18", 1963..................................... $80
Snowsuit Susan, 18", 1967... $85
Sugar Plum, 20", 1980 .... $65

ADVERTISING DOLLS ARE HOT!

Ideal's Little Miss Revlon and American Character's
Toni (Toni home permanents) are two early examples of successful dolls with advertising tie-ins. The tradition continues
today with advertising characters that companies offer as
premiums with the purchase of a product. Like the earlier
advertising tie-ins, many of these characters are highly collectible. Among them are: the 12-inch, hard-plastic Buddy
Lee doll dressed in his traditional outfit (worth about $350);
a 16-inch Jolly Green Giant doll that was a 1969 mail-in premium (about $50); a 12-inch Little Debbie doll that was a
1985 mail-in premium (about $50); a really neat 17-inch Mr.
Peanut doll, complete with monocle on the left eye, that
dates from the 1960s (a bargain at about $20); and a 20-inch
Ronald McDonald doll, issued by Hasbro in 1978 with a
plastic head and a cloth body (about $35).

Sweetie Pie, 21", composition head, blue flirty eyes,
   closed mouth $225
Whistling Jim, composition head, painted eyes,
   molded hair, cloth body, 1950.............................. $275

Horsman
Baby Precious, black, vinyl, voice box, curly wig,
   original dress, bonnet, etc., 1950s $150
Bye-Lo, 14", vinyl head, arms and legs, cloth body,
   molded straight hair $50
Dimples Toddler, 15" $150
Mary Poppins, all vinyl, 1965..................................... $40
Polly, brown vinyl head, painted eyes, painted hair,
   vinyl, voice box, orig. clothes, 1956-58................. $175
Pram Baby, 19", vinyl, jointed head, glass sleep eyes,
   closed mouth, coos.. $65
Ruthie, 12-1/2", all vinyl, rooted black hair $30
Tessie, 18", rooted hair, orig. dress, hard plastic and
   vinyl, pull string for neck $35

Ideal
Baby Snooks, 12", composition head and hands,
   wood torso, wire limbs... $200
Betsy Wetsy, 12", composition head, rubber body,
   jointed at neck, shoulders and hips, drinks,
   wets and cries $50
Betsy McCall, 14", vinyl head, hard-plastic body,
   dark brown curly saran wig, round brown
   sleep eyes, 1953 .... $100
Bonnie Walker, 17", hard plastic, walker,
   blue sleep eyes, open mouth.................................. $85
Bonny Braids, 13", vinyl head, hard plastic body,
   painted eyes, orig. dress, c. 1951, mint in box $375
Crissy, 1969 first version, long grow hair $175
Crissy, 1970s, orig. dress, out of box $35
Crissy, 1972, Moovin Groovin, with box..................... $45
Daddy's girl, smiling mouth, sleep eyes, long
   brunette hair, orig. clothes, early 1960s $800
Little Miss Revlon, 10", vinyl, rooted saran hair,
   sleep eyes, orig. clothes, 1957................................ $95
Lori Martin, all plastic, dark wig, blue sleep eyes,
   orig. clothes $500
Marama, 13", brown composition head, painted brown
   eyes, grass skirt, orange lei $590
Mary Hartline, 16", hard plastic, jointed neck,
   shoulders and hips, nylon wig, sleep eyes.............. $700
Penny Playpal, vinyl head, rooted hair, blue sleep
   eyes, original clothes, 1960................................... $325
Princess Mary, 21", vinyl head, plastic body,
   1952.. $150
Patty Playpal, 36", vinyl head and arms, plastic body,
   rooted brown hair, blue sleep eyes, closed mouth,
   orig. clothes, 1960.. $125
Peter Playpal, all plastic, smiling, blue sleep eyes,
   blonde rooted hair, original outfit, 1960................ $500
Saucy Walker, 22", vinyl head, hard-plastic body,
   1955.. $75

Thumbelina, 20", vinyl head, arms and legs,
    cloth body, rooted dark-blond hair,
    painted blue eyes, music box, 1962 .... $45

Knickerbocker
Holly Hobbie, 12", cloth, 1970s ....$15-$20
Holly Hobbie, 6", cloth, 1970s ....$5-$7
Raggedy Ann and Andy, 12", cloth, 1970s-1990s,
    each ....$15-$30

Mattel
Bozo the Clown, 16", vinyl head, cloth body,
    pullstring, 1962 .... $65
Buffy, 10-1/2", vinyl head, plastic body,
    blond ponytails, painted blue eyes, painted upper
    teeth, pull talk string, holding Mrs. Beasley doll,
    1969 .... $125

There have been numerous Shirley Temple dolls over the years, and all very collectible. This 12-inch doll, made by Ideal in the 1950s, is valued at about $200 in Mint condition.

Cheerful Tearful, 12", vinyl head and body, 1966 .... $35
Chatty Cathy, 19", soft vinyl head, hard plastic body,
    does not talk, 1962 .... $75
Charmin' Cathy, 25", vinyl head and arms,
    plastic body and legs, rooted blond hair,
    blue side-glancing sleep eyes, closed mouth,
    orig. clothes and metal trunk, 1961 .... $100
Donny and Marie Osmond, 10-1/2", vinyl heads,
    plastic bodies, painted eyes, pair, 1977 .... $40
Mrs. Beasley, stuffed body, 22", pull string works,
    1967 .... $250
Truly Scrumptious, 11-1/2", Chitty Chitty Bang Bang,
    vinyl, straight legs, blond hair, pink and white
    gown, matching hat, 1969 .... $90

Nancy Ann Storybook
Autumn, 5" $28
Belgian, 5", #29 .... $300
Bride, #86 .... $50
Bridesmaid Teen, 5-1/2", bisque $30
Christening Baby, 3-1/2", all hard plastic,
    molded painted yellow hair, closed mouth,
    straight baby legs, 1952 .... $25
Daffidown Dilly, 5-1/2", hard plastic $30
Debbie, 11", hard plastic $60
First Communion, 5-1/2", hard plastic $25
French, 5", #25 .... $280
Irish #34, hard plastic, with box $300
Jenny, 5", #161 .... $100
Jeannie, Moonlight and Roses, 6", hard plastic,
    1952 .... $25
Little Bo Peep $100
Little Boy Blue, #115 .... $130
Lori Ann Walker, 10", all hard plastic, head turns,
    glued-on brown wig, 1953 .... $35
Lucy Locket, 5", blue hat $25
Southern Belle, 5-1/2", bisque $28
Valentine, 5-1/2", bisque $20
School Days, 5-1/2", hard plastic $20

Sun Rubber
Betty Bows, 11", rubber, fully jointed, molded hair,
    1953 .... $35
Gerber Baby, 11", all rubber, molded $45
Happy Kappy, 7", rubber body,
    molded painted hair $25
SoWee, 10", bottle, booties, jacket, towel, soap $35
Sunbabe, all rubber, painted eyes,
    molded painted hair, 1950 .... $65
Tod-L-Dee, 10-1/2", rubber body,
    molded painted hair, open nurser mouth,
    molded diaper, shoes and socks $25

Terri Lee Dolls
Baby Linda, 9", all vinyl, molded painted hair,
    black eyes, 1951 .... $90
Ginger Girl Scout, 8" $100

Jerri Lee, 16", hard plastic, jointed at neck,
  shoulders and hips, orig. curly wig, painted eyes,
  orig. clothing and accessories $225
Terri Lee, 16", hard plastic, jointed at neck,
  shoulders and hips, orig. curly wig,
  painted eyes $200
Tiny Jerri Lee, 10", hard plastic, fully jointed,
  blond curly wig, brown sleep eyes,
  closed mouth $175
Tiny Terri Lee, 10", hard plastic, fully jointed,
  blond wig, inset eyes, closed mouth,
  trunk with six tagged outfits $425

Vogue

Baby Dear, 12", all composition, bent baby limbs,
  1961 .... $40
Ginny, 8", 1948-1950, all hard plastic, painted eyes,
  molded hair, mohair wig
  Cinderella $150
  Clown $225
  Coronation Queen $1,100
  Springtime $115
  Valentine $125
Ginny, 8", 1950-1953, moving eyes
  Catholic Nun $165
  Christmas $125
  Mistress Mary $135
  Roller Skating $200
Ginny, 8", 1954, walking mechanism
  Ballerina, poodle cut wig $100
  Rainy Day $75
  School Dress $75
  Springtime $70
Ginny, 8", 1957, bended knees
  Beach outfit $75
  Davy Crockett $80
  Southern Belle $90
  Wee Imp $155
Hansel and Gretel, 7", hard plastic, jointed at neck,
  shoulders and hips, blond mohair wigs $325

Kathe Kruse dolls are popular with collectors. This pair dates from 1978.

Hug-a-Bye Baby, 22", pink pajamas $40
Jeff, 10" $35
Jill, 10", bride's dress $50
Welcome Home Baby, 20" $50

MOVIE MEMORABILIA

Classic movies generate classic collectibles. Autographs, still photos, posters and lobby cards are the most common items. There are also books, films, magazines, sheet music, programs, press kits, and novelties, too. But for those who have outgrown these traditional collectibles, there are also big-ticket items—the actual props and costumes used on the set.

Posters and lobby cards—This area is one of the fastest growing collectible specialties today. But movie posters were originally produced, often quite colorfully and beautifully, with one goal in mind—to promote a particular movie, using remarkable eye-popping, heart-stopping graphics. Ironically, although most of the films from the 1920s-1940s were in black-and-white, many of the posters were in hot, vivid color. They were not mass-produced for public consumption. It has been estimated that in many cases, probably less than 10,000 "one-sheet" posters were produced for movies made during the 1930s.

Generally, the sensational posters were hung outside the theater, then either tossed away or rolled up to be sent to the next theater showing the picture. But, some made it to the walls of star-struck movie buffs, who spirited them away to a safe haven.

Posters were created in several different sizes. One-sheets, 27 by 41 inches, are the most common. Three-sheets, 41 by 81 inches, are comprised of either two or three sections. They are generally worth more than one-sheets. Lobby cards,

11 by 4 inches on heavier stock, were usually printed in sets of eight, each offering a different scene from the movie. Included in the set was a title card, more valuable than the others, because it includes the movie title and stars. A single lobby card is typically worth about 10-25 percent of a corresponding one-sheet poster.

Window cards, 14 by 22 inches, are often found measuring 14 by 18 inches because the four-inch border at the top, which was used to write in dates, was trimmed off. Window cards are generally valued at about 20-40 percent of a corresponding one-sheet. There are also other sizes to consider—larger and smaller—including mini-window cards, jumbo lobby cards, inserts, half-sheets and six-sheets.

Despite some of the high values being attained for movie posters offered for bids in auctions, there are literally thousands of collectible nostalgic posters available for $100 or less. There's even a nice selection available for $25 or less, especially from more recent films.

Posters from the 1950s-70s are quite popular today, as are those featuring Hollywood legends such as Marilyn Monroe and John Wayne, and silent film stars Clara Bow, Charlie Chaplin and Mary Astor (these 1910s posters are scarce and in great demand).

Science fiction and horror films, which usually have terrific graphics, are also favorites, having attained cult followings. Usually they command higher values than early turn-of-the-century posters, which, although older and scarcer, were fairly generic looking. Other factors which influence the value of posters include the graphics and who created the poster's artwork, the condition, the scarcity, the particular movie, and what stars are featured on the poster.

Considered as national treasures, and favorites among serious collectors, are posters from the Library of Congress National Film Registry's 1987 list of 25 top films, including *The Wizard of Oz*, *The Grapes of Wrath*, *Vertigo*, *Gone With the Wind*, *The Maltese Falcon*, *Casablanca* and others.

Autographs—Photographs and index cards are popular items to have autographed. Obtaining a signature in person is not often possible, so many signatures are obtained through the celebrity's agency or studio. In these instances, one can not always be sure that it is an actual signature; someone else may have signed on behalf of the star, or an autopen may have been used. Also, autographs which are personalized to someone are less valuable than those which are not.

Autograph collectors have many options. They can specialize, for example, in signatures of Academy Award winners, autographed first-day covers with commemorative stamps, signatures of famous pairs, such as Ginger Rogers and Fred Astaire, individual stars, or autographs on movie props.

Science fiction films are especially popular with many collectors. This stunning three-sheet poster from the 1951 landmark "The Day the Earth Stood Still" was offered at a Sotheby's auction in New York with a $5,000-$8,000 estimate.

Favorites include: Gene Autry, Lucille Ball, the Beatles, Humphrey Bogart, Clara Bow, James Cagney, Hopalong Cassidy, Lon Chaney Sr., Gary Cooper, Joan Crawford, Bing Crosby, Bette Davis, James Dean, Marlene Dietrich, Douglas Fairbanks, Errol Flynn, Henry Fonda, Clark Gable, Greta Garbo, Judy Garland, Betty Grable, Rita Hayworth, Sonja Heine, Katherine Hepburn, Al Jolson, Boris Karloff, Laurel and Hardy, Vivien Leigh, Bela Lugosi, Madonna, the Marx Brothers, Carmen Miranda, Marilyn Monroe, Paul Newman, Elvis Presley, Ronald Reagan, Roy Rogers, Elizabeth Taylor, Shirley Temple, the Three Stooges, Lana Turner, Rudolph Valentino, John Wayne and Mae West.

Autograph values are derived from several factors, including:

> whether it is on an index card or photograph (more valuable);
>
> whether it is in pencil or pen;
>
> whether it was obtained at the star's height of popularity or after retirement; and
>
> if it is on a letter, and what the letter is about.

IS IT A "RE-ISSUE" OR A "'REPRODUCTION?"

Some movies proved to be so popular that they were re-released—distributed to theaters again, often years after their initial run. Naturally, when a movie was re-released it needed new movie posters to advertise it. Such posters are generally referred to as "re-issue" posters. A re-issue poster can often be identified by an "R" designation in the lower border of the poster; some re-issues contain new wording (such as "Academy Award Winner" or something similar) to indicate the film is a re-release.

Re-issues are every bit as authentic as the original movie posters, but because they were recreated for a re-release, they are usually less valuable than an original poster. Some classic films have seen several re-releases, offering collectors a chance to buy posters that otherwise would be unaffordable. For instance, an original poster for the 1943 Humphrey Bogart classic, Casablanca, is valued at over $5,000; but re-issue posters from when the film was re-released in 1949 and 1956 are typically available for perhaps $300.

Re-issued movie posters should not be confused with "reproduction" posters. Re-issued posters are legitimate posters, issued by their respective studios for display in theaters. Reproduction posters are simply copies of original movie posters reproduced to be mass marketed to the general public. Reproduction posters generally feature only the big box-office classics (Gone With the Wind, The Wizard of Oz, etc.). Most are easily identified. They are typically smaller than the original one-sheet, and they usually display the name of a poster printer not found on the original.

Reproduction posters may have some appeal to a casual movie buff, but they have no collector value to a serious collector.

Still photographs—Still photographs are posed black-and-white or color photos taken on the set of a film, either during, before or after the scene. They usually depict a dramatic or comical moment, but may also be more informal, sometimes showing members of the production staff or cast members rehearsing. Portrait or candid photographs are also taken during special sessions, but these are usually retouched to portray the star in his or her most favorable light. In general, an original still photograph is worth more than a recent copy, no matter how good the copy is. Stills are considered key components of press kits. Generally, still photos can be purchased for less than $20 each, unless they are autographed.

Props and costumes—These artifacts are perhaps the ultimate find for movie memorabilia collectors. Props and costumes do not appear too frequently on the market. If they do, they are usually those being auctioned off by major auction houses, which have obtained the unique treasures from two major studios—M-G-M and 20th Century Fox. These auction houses also frequently sell the possessions of Hollywood personalities, too. The auction catalogs themselves are also considered collectible.

There is one problem (in addition to being able to afford them) to consider when acquiring props and costumes that were supposedly actually used in films. Records are not kept regarding which props were used in which productions. Collectors, therefore, must rely on intuition—make sure you know from whom you are buying. Still photos that document the props from specific scenes can be helpful.

Before buying these collectibles, you can also ask to see a videotape or photograph that shows the item or the star actually using the prop. If possible, obtain letters of authenticity, proof of ownership and other documents which help verify history and provenance. You can also learn how to identify authentic fabric and tailoring techniques from different eras.

Also in this category are the Oscar statues given out at the annual Academy Award ceremonies. They don't come up for sale very often—you have to be pretty desperate to sell your Oscar!—but when they do, they sell for thousands.

Books—Recent film books have not increased in value, and show no signs of doing so; in fact, many have decreased in value. So, the best way to decide which books to collect would be to read them before adding them to your shelves. Movie-related books from the 1930s-1950s, be they autobiographies, biographies or histories, generally sell for between $15-$25. Books before this time are more valuable. Factors which influence the value of a book include: condition, the topics (the more controversial the better), the subject, the photography, and who published it. Books published by smaller, obscure publishers are oftentimes rarer than those published by the larger houses, such as Harper and Row.

If the book is autographed by cast members or the subject discussed in the book, its value, of course, jumps substantially. Screenplays and scripts, difficult to obtain because they are considered property of the film studio, are also pursued. Some screenplays, if they hit the market, sell for $200 or more if they are autographed by cast and crew.

Magazines—Film magazines are either geared toward fans, or to those in the industry, as trade publications, such as *The Hollywood Reporter* and *Daily Variety*. The most highly sought-after vintage fan magazines include *Photoplay, Motion Picture Classic, Shadowland, Motion Picture Magazine, Photo-Play Journal, Feature Movie Magazine, Moving Picture Stories*, and *Movie Weekly*, some of which can be had for less than $10. Generally, a magazine's value is determined by who is on the cover, not what is inside. But, condition also plays a big factor, so it's wise to see if all the pages are intact.

Also, non-film magazines, such as *Life*, sometimes offer worthwhile issues for movie collectors when they have stars on the cover or feature them inside.

Sheet music—Music has always been an integral part of the motion picture. Movie collectors often pursue sheet music, which, from the 1900s to 1950s, was quite popular. The most popular is music featuring a celebrity, such as Elvis Presley, Judy Garland, the Beatles or Al Jolson, on the cover. Most sheet music can be had for $5-$10, and generally less than $20. Exceptions would include rare pieces, which can bring more than $50, or music from blockbusters such as *Gone With the Wind* and *The Wizard of Oz* ($20-$40).

Programs, press books/kits, campaign books—From 1910 to the 1930s, movie theaters produced their own programs to promote current and future films showing at the theater. These pieces often included cast lists and credits for the current productions. The theaters also sold full-color souvenir programs. These programs, usually featuring a color photograph on the cover, included cast and technical credits, a plot synopsis and articles about the production and personalities involved. They can generally be found for between $15-$25 each.

Press books refer to a studio-produced pamphlet intended exclusively for the news media, rather than for exhibitors. Film companies would sometimes produce single sheets—newspaper-sized informational handouts with credit information and promotional stories about the movie.

Press kits are folders that contain a plot summary, biographies, cast and technical credits, production information, and still photographs. It's important to have all the stills included to be considered complete.

Campaign books, today generally 8-1/2 by 14 inches, contain information on the film, plus an illustrated listing about publicity material—lobby cards, posters, banners, bumper stickers, and more.

Novelty items—These include: film-related LPs and sound tracks; paper dolls of favorite personalities; bookplates; coming attraction advertising flyers; cigarette cards featuring film stars; Academy Awards/Oscars programs; posters; tickets; matchbooks; postcards and invitations; notepads featuring silent film stars; dishes; pin buttons; playing cards; spoons; masks; candy and candy tin boxes; cosmetic lines and toiletries; coins; mugs; clothing; paint books; guns; toys; comic books; rings; postcards; and postage stamps. Anything picturing a Hollywood movie star has the potential to be collectible.

COLLECTING TIPS!

In very general terms, the most desirable movie posters are those featuring major stars, blockbuster films and wonderful graphics.

Some film genres are more desirable than others. Always popular are horror films, 1950s and 1960s science fiction movies, classic Westerns, and Disney's animated features, such as Bambi, Pinocchio and Snow White.

Posters from the 1960s and 1970s are attracting much more interest among collectors and are rising rapidly in value. Especially popular are Star Wars, Clint Eastwood's early Westerns, Paul Newman and Robert Redford films, and Audrey Hepburn movies.

Other posters are in demand because they enjoy almost a cult-like following, such as Plan 9 From Outer Space and The Rocky Horror Picture Show.

Collectors should not attempt to repair or restore vintage posters with tape, glue, etc. Always consult a professional restorer. An amateur repair job will almost always detract from a poster's value.

Although one-sheet posters seem to be the most popular item in this field, collectors should also consider other sizes of posters, as well as movie press kits, still photos, animation art, movie star autographs and other items.

VALUE LINE

Movie posters and lobby cards

The following values are actual prices realized at various recent auctions of Hollywood memorabilia.

The African Queen, British three-sheet, 1951........ $13,800
Attack of the 50 Foot Woman, one-sheet, 1958 .... $1,760
Baby Take A Bow, Shirley Temple, one-sheet, 1934... $8,625
Batman, three-sheet, 1966.. $402
The Big Store, Marx Brothers, six-sheet, 1941 .... $8,050
Blonde Venus, 110" x 50", Marlene Dietrich, 1932.. $25,300
Casablanca, French version, one-panel, 1942....... $21,850
The Circus, Charlie Chaplin, one-sheet, 1928 .... $14,375
Cleopatra, one-sheet, 1917.................................. $27,600
Dirty Harry, one-sheet, 1971 .... $375
Dracula, window card, 1931.................................. $25,300
Dracula, one-sheet, 1931 .... $77,000
Flash Gordon, one-sheet, 1936............................. $32,200
Follow the Fleet, Astaire and Rogers, six-sheet, 1936.. $16,100
Frankenstein, one-sheet $180,000
The Ghost of Frankenstein, three-sheet, 1942 .... $2,990
The Graduate, one-sheet, 1968 .... $345

The Grim Game, Harry Houdini, one-sheet,
1919 .... $19,550

Headin' Home, Babe Ruth, set of eight lobby cards,
1920 .... $20,700

Invasion of the Body Snatchers, one-sheet,
1956 .... $2,750

The Jazz Singer, Al Jolson, one-sheet, 1927 .... $17,250

King Kong, one-sheet, 1933 .... $52,250

The Klondike Kid, one-sheet, 1932 .... $57,500

Lawless Nineties, John Wayne, six-sheet, 1936 .... $7,475

The Maltese Falcon, one-sheet, 1941 .... $6,325

The Phantom of the Opera, six-sheet, 1925 .... $57,500

Saved by the Belle, Three Stooges, one-sheet,
1939 .... $26,450

Snow White and the Seven Dwarfs, one-sheet,
1937 .... $14,950

Some Like It Hot, one-sheet, 1959 .... $1,600

The Sound of Music, one-sheet, 1965 .... $460

Viva Las Vegas, Elvis Presley, one-sheet, 1964 .... $862

You Can't Cheat an Honest Man, W.C. Fields,
one-sheet, 1939 .... $6,900

Other Movie posters and lobby cards

Price ranges taken from dealer lists, show sales, etc.

All About Eve, one-sheet, VG .... $250-$275

All The King's Men, one-sheet, VG .... $100-$125

Animal House, one-sheet .... $75-$100

Annie Hall, one-sheet, VG .... $50-$75

Ben-Hur, one-sheet, VG .... $2,500-$2,600

Breakfast at Tiffany's, lobby card .... $75-$150

The Bridge on the River Kwai, one-sheet, VG ..... $75-$100

Citizen Kane, one-sheet, one-sheet .... $11,000-$13,000

The Deer Hunter, one-sheet, VG .... $15-$25

E.T. The Extra-Terrestrial, one-sheet .... $35-$45

Field of Dreams, one-sheet .... $25-$30

Forrest Gump, one-sheet .... $30-$50

From Here to Eternity, one-sheet, VG .... $125-$150

The Godfather, one-sheet, VG .... $50-$75

Godzilla, one-sheet, 1956 .... $1,500-$2,000

Goldfinger, one-sheet .... $250-$300

Hamlet, one sheet, VG .... $300-$350

Her Love Story, one-sheet .... $2,000-$3,000

The Hunchback of Notre Dame, Disney,
one-sheet .... $30-$40

It's A Wonderful Life, one-sheet .... $4,500-$5,500

Jaws, lobby card .... $15-$30

King Kong, lobby card .... $500-$1,000

The Mask, one-sheet .... $15-$25

Monty Python Live at the Hollywood Bowl,
one-sheet .... $15-$20

North by Northwest, one-sheet .... $300-$400

One Flew Over the Cuckoo's Nest, one-sheet,
VG .... $75-$100

On the Waterfront, one-sheet, VG .... $200-$250

Ordinary People, one-sheet, VG .... $5-$10

Patton, one-sheet, VG .... $40-$60

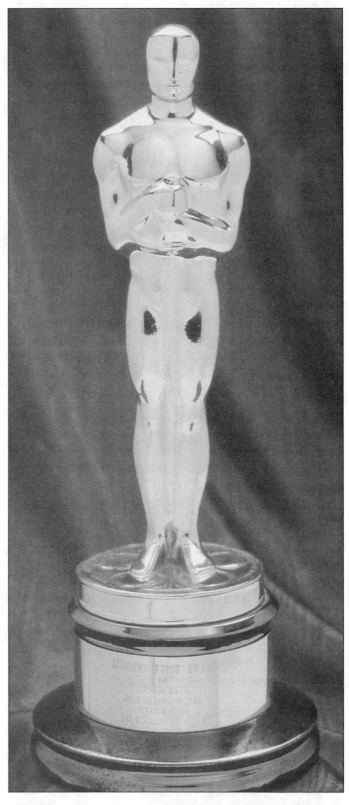

Oscars rarely come up for sale, but when they do, they sell for thousands. This 1943 Oscar, the Academy Award presented to Hal Wallis for Best Picture, sold for a record $145,000 at a Christie's auction in New York.

A one-sheet poster from everyone's favorite movie, "It's A Wonderful Life," sold for over $6,000 at a Butterfield & Butterfield auction.

Platoon, one-sheet, VG ....$7-$15
Psycho, house card ....$350-$500
Pulp Fiction, one-sheet ....$40-$60
Rain Man, one-sheet, VG ....$15-$20
Rocky, one-sheet, VG ....$30-$50
Rocky Horror Picture Show, lobby card ....$30-$50
Schindler's List, one-sheet, VG ....$5-$10
Seven Year Itch, one-sheet ....$1,200-$1,500
The Silence of the Lambs, one-sheet, VG ....$15-$25
Snow White, Disney, one-sheet ....$7,500-$12,000
The Sound of Music, one-sheet, VG ....$50-$75
This Gun For Hire, one-sheet, 1942 ....$3,000-$4,000
Tom Jones, one-sheet, VG ....$30-$50
Toy Story, one-sheet ....$20-$30
True Grit, one-sheet ....$125-$150
Uncle Buck, one-sheet ....$10-$15
The Virginian, one-sheet ....$4,000-$6,000
West Side Story, one-sheet ....$200-$275

Yellow Submarine, the Beatles, one-sheet..........$200-$400
You Can't Cheat An Honest Man,
    one-sheet ....$800-$1,500

Movie props and costumes

The following values are actual prices realized at various recent auctions of Hollywood memorabilia.

Academy Award Oscar, *Casablanca*, "Best Picture"
    1942...$145,500
Academy Award Oscar, *The Philadelphia Story*,
    "Best Screen Play" $14,950
Baseball jersey, worn by Richard Pryor in *The Bingo
    Long All-Stars & the Travelling Motor Kings*........$230
Batmobile, from the 1989 movie $189,500
Bicycle, red and white, from *Pee-Wee's Big
    Adventure* $9,200
Bra, worn by Marilyn Monroe in *Some Like
    It Hot* $14,000
Buick Phaeton convertible, 1940, used in
    Casablanca..$211,500
Cape, worn by Bette Davis in *The Virginia
    Queen* $3,450
Captain's suit, worn by W.C. Fields in
    Mississippi...$4,887
Carriage, horse-drawn, used by Dorothy and Toto
    and the gang in *The Wizard of Oz* $40,250
Charlie McCarthy dummy, Edgar Bergen's
    original $112,500
Chimpanzee costume, worn by Roddy McDowell in
    Planet of the Apes $5,460
Coat, brown silk velvet, worn by Errol Flynn in
    Captain Blood $31,050
Cocktail dress, worn by Goldie Hawn in
    Overboard $201
Dress, worn by Julie Andrews in
    The Sound of Music..$29,900
Dress, worn by Marilyn Monroe in
    There's No Business Like Show Business..........$46,000

A TRULY MAGICAL HOLLYWOOD MOMENT!

As the audience hooted and hollered encouragement, magician David Copperfield interrupted his show in Raleigh, N.C., one February night in 1996 to successfully bid on and win the Batmobile used in the 1989 Batman movie. His winning bid—$189,500! He also purchased ventriloquist Edgar Bergen's original Charlie McCarthy dummy during a 1995 auction. This time, he "only" paid $112,500. His intentions were to display the doll at his Copperfield Museum in Nevada. He also paid small change, $9,775, for the dancer Fred Astaire's tuxedo and tails and black sweater worn by him in the movie Funny Face.

Evening gown, full-length silk, worn by
Raquel Welch in *Myra Breckenridge* $316
Fred and Barney costumes, worn in *The Flintstones*,
pair $5,175
Gloves, black vinyl, 15-inch elbow length, worn by
Michelle Pfeiffer as Catwoman in
Batman Forever $4,830
Gown, full-length, worn by Faye Dunaway in
Little Big Man $4,600
Gown, worn by Vivien Leigh in
Gone With the Wind $33,350
Leisure suit, polyester, worn by John Travolta in *Saturday
Night Fever* $145,500
Military sweatsuit, worn by Tom Hanks in
Forrest Gump $4,600
Munchkin costume, *The Wizard of Oz* $10,925
Outfit, skirt, blouse, jacket, scarf, hat, purse, boots,
worn by Katherine Hepburn in
Rooster Cogburn $6,900
Outfit, worn by Dolly Parton in *Best Little
Whorehouse in Texas* $4,600
Outfit, brown flannel Arabian vest, worn by
Rudolph Valentino in *Son of the Sheik* $5,750
Overcoat, twill, worn by Bing Crosby in *Dixie* $402
Prison outfits, red-and-beige striped, worn by
Steve McQueen and Dustin Hoffman in
Papillon $13,800
Riding jacket, herringbone, worn by Clark Gable in
Gone With the Wind $19,550
Shoes, leopard-skin, worn by Jayne Mansfield in
Will Success Spoil Rock Hunter? $4,600
Space uniform, three-piece, worn by
Charlton Heston in *Planet of the Apes* $10,350
Sperm suit, used in Woody Allen's *Everything You
Always Wanted to Know About Sex* $1,150
Suit, herringbone, three-piece, worn by Robert Redford
in *Butch Cassidy & The Sundance Kid* $9,200
Ten Commandments, fiberglass tablets, from
The Ten Commandments $81,700
Tunic and tights, worn by Leslie Howard in
Romeo and Juliet $4,600
Tunic, floor-length, worn by Marlon Brando in
Julius Caesar $374
Tuxedo, worn by Warren Beatty in *Bugsy* $4,312
Western outfit, jacket, shirt, pants and vest,
worn by John Wayne in *The Cowboys* $10,350
Wheelchair, used by Freddie Krueger in
A Nightmare on Elm Street 3 .... $6,900

Other Movie Props and Costumes
Price ranges taken from dealer lists, show sales, etc.
Bolero jacket, worn by Bob Hope in
Road to Morocco $1,100
Gown, worn by Elizabeth Taylor in *Rhapsody* $950
Jacket, worn by Marlon Brando in
The Missouri Breaks $1,595

Pants, worn by Yul Brynner in *The King and I* $1,300
Shoes, white canvas, worn by James Caan in
Honeymoon in Vegas $85
Trenchcoat, worn by Humphrey Bogart in
Casablanca $85,000
Tunic, worn by Errol Flynn in *The Prince and
the Pauper* $1,995
Tuxedo, worn by James Dean in *Giant* $60,000

Movie Star Autographed Items
Rosco "Fatty" Arbuckle, 8" x 10" sepia-tone
photo .... $1,000-$2,000
Fred Astaire, black-and-white photo .... $500-$700
Lauren Bacall, color photo .... $150-$200
Humphrey Bogart, black-and-white photo .... $700-$800
Sean Connery, color photo .... $200-$300
Joan Crawford, signed letter, 1936 .... $350-$550
Bette Davis, black-and-white photo .... $300-$400
James Dean, signed Life magazine,
1955 .... $3,000-$4,000

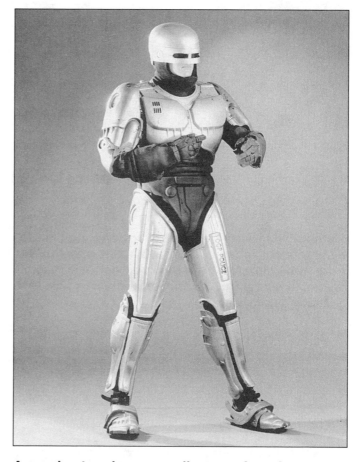

A growing trend among collectors of movie memorabilia is owning the actual props and costumes from their favorite films. Most of these one-of-a-kind collectibles are expensive. This costume from "Robocop 2" sold for $9,200 at a recent Butterfield & Butterfield auction.

Memorabilia from Academy-Award-winning films is a favorite collecting category. This one-sheet poster from "One Flew Over the Cuckoo Nest" is already valued at nearly $1,000. This example was sold at a Sotheby's auction.

Olivia de Havilland, clipped signature .... $100-$150
W.C. Fields, black-and-white from
    Never Give A Sucker An Even Break .... $600-$900
Clark Gable, parchment paper .... $350-$450
Judy Garland, signed photo for
    A Star Is Born .... $400-$500
Lillian Gish, 7" x 9" black-and-white photo ...... $400-$600
Tom Hanks, signed army helmet prop from
    Forrest Gump .... $700-$900
Daryl Hannah, color photo for *Attack of the
    50 Foot Woman* .... $100-$200
Tippi Hedren, autographed *The Birds*
    videocassette .... $100-$200
Sonja Heinie, black-and-white photo .... $200-$300
Audrey Hepburn, handwritten note on
    postcard .... $250-$350
Pee Wee Herman, signed *Life* magazine with
    Pee Wee cover .... $200-$300
Alfred Hitchcock, black-and-white photo .... $500-$700
Al Jolson, signed federal tax document,
    1950 .... $300-$400
Boris Karloff, signed typed letter, 1961 .... $300-$450
Buster Keaton, signed contract, 1933 .... $500-$700
Grace Kelly, handwritten letter .... $600-$800
Carol Lombard, black-and-white photo .... $500-$700
Carol Lombard, color photo .... $800-$1,000
Marilyn Monroe, sepia-tone photo .... $8,000-$10,000
Jayne Mansfield, 5" x 7" black-and-white .... $300-$400
Arnold Schwarzenegger, rubber prop knife .... $400-$500
Jimmy Stewart, 6" x 4" marker drawing of Harvey,
    signed .... $400-$600
Oliver Stone, autographed director's chair .... $300-$400
Sharon Stone, 11" x 14" color photo from
    Basic Instinct .... $350-$450
Elizabeth Taylor, black-and-white photo .... $100-$150
John Travolta, 3-1/2" x 5-1/8" black-and-white
    publicity photo .... $100-$150
Lana Turner, black-and-white photo .... $100-$150
John Wayne, signed letter .... $300-$400
Orson Welles signed check .... $250-$350
Mae West, signed check, 1979 .... $200-$300

MOVIE MONSTERS

Some things are hard to explain. Take monsters, for instance. Years ago, they chased us. Now, we're chasing them. Instead of running from the likes of Wolf Man, Dracula and Frankenstein, we are, in fact, pursuing them, through monster-related collectibles.

Background: The monsters first became popular in the movies—mostly from Universal Studios—in the 1930s and 1940s. When these cinema ghouls rose from the dead during "Shock Theater" telecasts years later, store shelves began filling up with merchandise to meet the demand for an area that had been untapped 20 years earlier.

Among the first to pay tribute to these monsters was Marx, which created a six-inch wind-up Frankenstein toy in 1960, and then a series of six-inch plastic figures. Aurora issued its first model kit in 1961, a Frankenstein kit, followed by what many consider to be the "holy grail" of monster models—a gigantic Frankenstein model, a 1/5 scale model kit of "Big Frankie." The 1960s also saw Pez dispensers, Soaky bottles, Halloween costumes and other items with monster themes.

During the 1970s, many licensed products were paper-related—puzzles, trading cards and "Famous Monsters" magazine. Remco and Milton Bradley joined the fold during the '80s, with their product lines of games and action figures.

General Guidelines: Lurking within the category of monster collectibles are toys, action figures, games, movie posters and lobby cards, comics, magazines and books, models, costumes and masks, and trading cards.

Toys—Complete, unopened, in-the-package items carry premium values. Puzzles and games should have all of the original parts, and a game board in nice condition. If you have the original box, in Mint shape, with a particularly stunning piece of artwork or graphic design, you'll get top dollar.

Action figures—Figures that are missing accessories, such as a weapon, or that have been discolored by sunlight or age, are worth less.

Movie posters—The most valuable posters are those advertising the first releases of the movie. Prior to 1980, most posters were folded; if your poster is folded, but is in perfect condition otherwise, it can still command a top dollar. Lobby cards, however, are never folded. These 11 by 14 cards, featuring actual scenes, are printed on durable paper and are suitable for framing.

Comics, magazines and books—It's difficult to find comics in Mint condition, with no wrinkles, tears, stains or water spots. Therefore, most of the ones you'll see will be in Good shape, or worse—perhaps missing a page, having a loose or torn cover, or having writing on it. Look for bargains on these comics, as something to read, enjoy and cherish as a collectible, not an as investment. These tips apply to magazines and books, too, although they are not as common as comic books.

RAY HARRYHAUSEN'S MONSTERS

Ray Harryhausen's rise to stardom began with his box office hit The Beast from 20,000 Fathoms in 1953, but this brilliant filmmaker's career spanned more than three decades, spawning such other classics as 20 Million Miles to Earth (1957); Clash of the Titans (1981); Earth vs. The Flying Saucers (1956); First Men in the Moon (1964); It Came from Beneath the Sea (1955); Jason and the Argonauts (1963); Mysterious Island (1961); One Million Years B.C. (1966) and many more.

In addition to the vast variety of model kits released for these movie's, Harryhausen merchandise includes action figures, masks, books, comic books, magazines, records, movie posters and lobby cards, and Super 8 films. As a general rule, most of these items are priced below $100 and fall into the price ranges for similar Universal Monsters categories.

High-end examples include 1980s resin model kits by Billiken for 20 Million Miles to Earth (Ymir, more expensive than the Beast, is worth $400-$700) and movie poster one-sheets for the Beast ($350-$550). Other movie poster sheets generally fall between $200-$400, with the less popular Three Worlds of Gulliver and The Wonderful World of the Brothers Grimm at the low end ($35-$70).

Models—For vintage plastic kits, the highest prices are reserved for models still in the box that have never been assembled. During the last decade, vinyl and resin kits have become quite popular throughout the country, dominating the old classics. Collectors are putting less emphasis on packaging for these kits; prices are determined more by regional supply and demand. Often these newer, costly kits, professionally crafted and painted, make beautiful display pieces.

Costumes and masks—Factors to consider when pricing items such as classic Ben Cooper masks and Collegeville costumes include whether the item is loose or with its box, or complete. Condition and tagging are important considerations for full-head latex masks, such as those made by Don Post in the 1960s, depicting the likes of the Wolf Man, Dracula and Frankenstein.

(Note: Japanese movies had their own monsters, led, of course, by Godzilla, Rodan and others. They will be covered in a future edition of this book.)

Recommended Reading

Collecting Monsters of Film and TV, Dana Cain

VALUE LINE

Universal Monsters

The Bride of Frankenstein

Famous Monsters magazine cover, February 1963,
    issue #21 $60-$225

Halloween costume, 1980, Collegeville.................$50-$75

Model kit, Aurora, 1965....................................$350-$900

Movie poster, 1935, one-sheet ....$40,000-$50,000

Movie poster, 1953 re-release, one-sheet........$750-$1,000

The Creature from the Black Lagoon

Aquarium toy, moves and connects to an air pump,
    Penn-Plax, 5", 1971....................................$250-$350

Bubblegum charm, 1960s ....$20-$25

Creature from the Black Lagoon Mystery Game,
    Hasbro, 1963 ....$250-$300

Famous Monsters magazine cover, issue #103 ......$15-$20

Flicker ring, silver base, 1960s ....$40-$65

Glass, Universal Monsters series, 1960s..............$75-$100

Halloween costume, Ben Cooper, 1973.................$50-$75

Key chain, 4", soft plastic, China, 1991.................$10-$15

Life-size Creature, 7', foam latex standee, limited
    edition, Michael Burnett, 1993 ....$3,000-$4,000

Lobby card, 3-D version, 1954 ....$175-$300

Mask, Don Post, 1967.......................................$200-$300

Model kit, Aurora, 1963....................................$150-$400

Model kit, Billiken, 1991 ....$50-$100

Movie poster, one-sheet, 3-D version,
    1954..$4,000-$6,000

Movie poster, one-sheet, 3-D re-issue, 1972......$150-$200

Movie poster, one-sheet, *Revenge of the Creature,*
    1955..$600-$900

**The Universal Studios monsters were featured in a
line of Aurora model kits in the 1960s.**

Movie poster, one-sheet, *Creature Walks Among Us,*
    1956..$450-$700

Nodder, bobbing head doll, Japanese,
    1960s..$100-$150

PEZ dispenser, pearl green, 1965......................$150-$200

Pinball machine, Bally, 1992 ....$1,750-$2,000

Soaky bubble bath bottle, 10", Colgate-Palmolive,
    1960s..$100-$150

Dracula

Autographed Bela Lugosi photo ....$125-$185

Famous Monsters cover, issue #30 ....$75-$100

Figure, Dreadful Dracula, Mad Monster series,
    8", Mego, 1972...$100-$200

Figure, with patch and ring, Remco, 8", 1980 ....$50-$75

Flicker ring, silver base......................................$35-$50

Game, Dracula Mystery Game, Hasbro,
    1963..$175-$225

Halloween costume, Ben Cooper, 1963 ....$50-$100

Inflatable Dracula, Doritos/Pepsi promo, 32",
    1990s..$25-$40

Mask, Don Post, 1967..$200-$250

Model kit, Aurora, 1962.....................................$250-$300

Model kit, glow version, Aurora, 1969 ....$50-150

Model kit, Monogram, 1983 ....$20-$30

Movie Poster, Dracula, one-sheet,
    1931..$45,000-$65,000

Movie poster, Dracula, one-sheet, re-release,
    1947..$3,000-$5,000

Paint-by-Number set, Hasbro, 1963..................$175-$300

Puzzle, 200 pieces with canister, APC, 1974.........$20-$30

Wallet, Hasbro, 1963..$100-$150

Bram Stoker's Dracula, ceramic mug,
    (Coppola film), 1992 ....$5-$10

Bram Stoker's Dracula, model kit, vinyl,
    Horizon, 1990s..$35-$65

Bram Stoker's Dracula, pewter figure,
    Spirit of the Wolf, 1992...................................$15-$20

Frankenstein

Bendee, AHI, 4", 1974...$30-$40

Bendee, JustToys, 1991...$5-$10

Blushing Frankenstein, 13", plastic, tin base,
    battery-op, Rosko, 1960s.............................$200-$350

Electronic talking Frankenstein, neon, 16",
    Playskool, 1992...$20-$35

Figure #1, AHI, 8", 1973 ....$100-$200

Figure, glows with removable clothes, 8",
    Remco, 1978 ....$30-$60

Figure, 3", plastic, Palmer Plastics, 1963 ....$25-$35

Figure, Monster Frankenstein, Mad Monster series,
    8", Mego, 1972...$25-$100

Flicker ring, silver or blue base, 1960s ....$40-$50

Frankenstein Mystery Game, Hasbro, 1963 ......$150-$225

Glass, Universal Monster series, 6-1/2",
    1960s ....$75-$100

Halloween costume, Ben Cooper, 1963...............$75-$125

Life magazine, Karloff/Frankenstein cover,
    March 15, 1968 ....$20-$30
Life-size Frankenstein, foam latex standee,
    7' ....$2,500-$3,500
Lobby card, Frankenstein, 1931 ....$2,000-$4,000
"MAD" magazine cover, issue #89,
    September 1964 ....$15-$30
Mask, Don Post, 1967 ....$225-$275
Model kit, Aurora, 1961 ....$75-$250
Model kit, Gigantic Frankenstein, "Big Frankie,"
    Aurora, 1964 ....$750-$1,200
Model kit, glow version, Aurora, 1969 ....$50-$150
Model kit, Monsters of the Movies, Aurora,
    1974 ....$150-$250
Model kit, Billiken, 1991 ....$75-$125
Monster head speaker, Actwell Plastics,
    1964 ....$450-$650

COLLECTING TIPS AND TRIVIA!

Universal Monsters rule the collecting world, with the Creature of the Black Lagoon considered the king; he reigns as the favorite, and is 100 times more in demand than others. Frankenstein and Dracula (most imitated and most copied) finish two and three.

Universal could not copyright its classic films (because they were based on famous works of literature), but wary collectors need only look for the Universal Studios name, which is stamped on most officially licensed toys. The company also copyrighted its monster makeup. Therefore, other studios, such as the British film company Hammer Films, which has released dozens of its own Dracula and Frankenstein movies during the 1950s and '60s, can be distinguished from the classics.

1960s magazine ads from Famous Monsters of Filmland were the source for some kids to purchase monster toys, which weren't available to them in local drug stores.

Remco's Creature from the Black Lagoon and Phantom of the Opera action figures, later added to its original line of four released in 1980 (Dracula, Frankenstein, the Mummy and the Wolf Man), are scarce. These figures glow and grab things when you press a button on their backs.

In 1997, the U.S. Postal Service issued a set of five commemorative postage stamps honoring Dracula, Frankenstein, the Mummy, the Phantom of the Opera and the Wolf Man.

A continuing trend in collecting, high-end model and resin kits, began during the 1980 with offerings from Billiken, Horizon and Tskuda.

The Mummy (1932, Boris Karloff) original movie poster sold at auction for a record-breaking $453,000 in 1997.

The Mole People items are scarce; prices for existing items reflect their high demand.

Movie poster, Frankenstein, one-sheet,
    1931 ....$60,000-$90,000
Movie poster, Frankenstein, re-release, one-sheet,
    1961 ....$150-$225
Necklace, "Wear a Weirdo," Frankenstein's head
    as a pendant, 1960s ....$20-$35
Nodder, composition, name on base,
    early 1960s ....$100-$175
Paint-by-Number set, Hasbro, 1963 ....$175-$300
PEZ dispenser, 1960s ....$150-$250
Puzzle, 200 pieces in canister, APC, 1974 ....$20-$35
Puzzle, Frankenstein vs. Wolf Man, Jaymar,
    1963, small box, 7x10 ....$75-$100
Soaky bubble bath bottle, 1960s ....$75-$150
Tin, Walking Frankenstein, battery-op, 12-1/2",
    Marx, 1963 ....$1,000-$1,750
Tin, wind-up, 6", Marx, 1960 ....$175-$350
Wallet, Hasbro, 1963 ....$100-$150

The Hunchback of Notre Dame
"Famous Monsters" magazine cover,
    issue #33 ....$15-$25
Flicker ring, round, 1960s ....$20-$30
Mask, Don Post, 1965 ....$250-$350
Model kit, Aurora, 1964 ....$100-$300
Model kit, glow version, Aurora, 1969 ....$50-$150
Movie poster, Lon Chaney silent film,
    1923 ....$20,000-$30,000

Invisible Man
Movie poster, *The Invisible Man*, one-sheet,
    1933 ....$30,000-$40,000
Movie poster, *The Invisible Man Returns*,
    one-sheet, 1940 ....$750-$1,000
Movie poster, *The Invisible Man's Revenge*,
    one-sheet, 1944 ....$200-$300

The Mole People
Mask, Don Post, 1965 ....$350-$400
Hands to accompany rubber mask, Don Post,
    1965 ....$75-$100
Model kit, Billiken, 1980s $85-135
Movie poster, one-sheet, 1956 ....$500-$750

The Mummy
Bendees, Vic's 1979 ....$10-$15
Board game, Curse of the Mummy's Tomb,
    Games Workshop, 1988 ....$10-$15
Board game, Voice of the Mummy, Milton Bradley,
    1971 ....$15-$20
Figure, Lincoln International, 8", removable clothes,
    1975 ....$75-150
Figure, glows, with patch and ring, Remco, 8",
    1980 ....$25-$50
Figure, Mini-Monster, non-glow version, Remco,
    3-3/4", 1983 ....$75-125
Figure, plastic, 2-1/2", MPC, mid-1960s ....$15-$25
Figure, Horrible Mummy, Mad Monster series,
    8", Mego, 1972 ....$50-$100

Movie posters from the Universal Studios monster films are extremely desirable and generally expensive. This one sold for $6,900 at a Butterfield & Butterfield auction.

Flicker ring, round, 1960s ....$20-$30
Halloween costume, Ben Cooper, 1973 ....$20-$35
Life-size Mummy, foam latex standee,
    Illusive Concepts, early 1990s ....$1,000-$1,500
Lobby card, *The Mummy*, 1932....................$2,500-$5,000
Lobby card, *The Mummy's Tomb*, 1948.................$30-$75
Mask, Don Post, 1967..$200-$250
Model kit, Aurora, 1963......................................$75-$300
Model kit, Luminators, Revell/Monogram,
    1991...$15-$20
Model kit, Monogram, 1983 ....$20-$35
Model kit, Billiken, 1990 ....$100-$150
Movie poster, *The Mummy*, one-sheet,
    1932..$60,000-$100,000
Movie poster, *The Mummy's Curse*, one-sheet,
    1944...$800-$1,200
Mummy Mystery Game, Hasbro, 1963 ....$150-$225
Paint-by-Number set, Crafthouse, 1975................$15-$30
Puzzle, jigsaw, Jaymar, 1963, small box,
    7x10..$75-$125
Soaky bubble bath bottle, 1963...........................$75-$100
Tin wind-up, 9" Robot House, 1992 ....$85-$125
Wallet, Hasbro, 1963...$100-$150

The Phantom of the Opera
Famous Monsters magazine cover, issue #3 ......$250-$400
Famous Monsters magazine cover, issue #10 ......$60-$150
Famous Monsters magazine cover,
    issue #171 or #208 ....$5-$8

Figure, glow-in-the-dark, 6", Marx reproduction,
    Uncle Milton, 1990 ....$10-$15
Figure, glows, with patch and ring, Remco, 8",
    1980..$175-$325
Figure, Mini-Monster, non-glow version, Remco,
    3-3/4", 1983...$25-$40
Figure, Mini-Monster, glow version, Remco,
    3-3/4", 1980s ....$15-$25
Flicker ring, round, 1960s....................................$20-$30
Game, Phantom of the Opera Mystery Game,
    Hasbro ....1963$175-$225
Halloween costume, Ben Cooper, 1963 ....$80-$160
Mask, Don Post, 1967.......................................$200-$250
Model kit, Aurora, 19643....................................$75-$300
Model kit, Aurora, Frightening Lightning,
    1969..$250-$350
Model kit, Aurora, glow version, 1969...............$50-$150
Model kit, Billiken, 1980s ....$200-$250
Model kit, Horizon, 1988.....................................$40-$60
Monster Times magazine cover, issue #40,
    1970s ....$4-$8
Movie poster, 1925 silent, one-sheet,
    Lon Chaney Sr...................................$25,000-$35,000
Movie poster, 1929 re-release,
    one-sheet ....$11,000-$15,000

You could add a Jaymar "Mummy" puzzle to your collection for about $15.

Movie poster, one-sheet, Claude Rains,
 1943 ....$1,200-$1,600
Nodder, wind-up, Japanese, 1963 ....$75-$100
Wallet, Hasbro, 1963..$100-$150

The Wolf Man

Bendee, Vic's 1979 ....$10-$15
Button, 7/8", b&w photo on colored background,
 1960s ....$15-$20
Famous Monsters magazine cover, issue #99 ....$12-$15
Figure #1, AHI, 8", 1973 ....$100-$225
Figure, Lincoln International, 8", removable clothes,
 1975..$75-$150
Figure, limited edition, 60th Anniversary, Placo,
 10"..$15-$20
Figure, Human Wolfman, Mad Monster series,
 8", Mego, 1972..$75-$200
Figure, glows, with patch and ring, Remco,
 8", 1980 ....$75-$125
Figure, Mini-Monster, glow version, Remco, 3-3/4",
 1980s, ...$25-$45
Figure, Mini-Monster, non-glow version, Remco,
 3-3/4", 1983..$50-$75
Flicker ring, silver or blue base, 1960s ....$35-$50
Game, Wolf Man Mystery Game, Hasbro,
 1963..$250-$325
Lobby card, The Wolf Man, 1941 ....$600-$2,000
Mask, Don Post, 1967..$225-$300
Mask, Don Post, rubber, 1976..............................$60-$85
Model kit, Aurora, 1962..$75-$300
Model kit, glow version, Aurora, 1969................$25-$150
Model kit, Wolfman's Wagon, Aurora,
 1965..$300-$400
Model kit, Monsters of the Movies, Aurora,
 1974..$175-$250
Model kit, Monogram, 1983 ....$20-$35
Movie poster, The Wolf Man, one-sheet,
 1941..$12,000-$16,000
Movie poster, The Wolf Man, one-sheet,
 1951 re-release ....$750-$1,000
Nodder, model kit, Uncle Gilberts ....$40-$60
Paint-by-Number set, Hasbro, 1963..................$175-$300
PEZ dispenser, 1960s..$175-$250
Puzzle, 200 pieces in canister, APC, 1974.............$20-$30
Puzzle, jigsaw, Jaymar, 1963,
 small 7" x 10" box..$75-$125
Soaky bubble bath bottle, 1963............................$85-$150
Tin wind-up, 9" Robot House, 1992 ....$85-$125
View-Master reel set, GAF, 1978..........................$10-$15

Miscellaneous Universal Monsters

Abbott & Costello Meet Frankenstein lobby card,
 1948..$75-$125
Abbott & Costello Meet Frankenstein movie poster,
 1948..$800-$1,200
Abbott & Costello Meet the Mummy movie poster,
 1955 ....$150-$250

Book, *Movie Monsters*, make-up tips,
 Scholastic paperback...$3-$5
Book, *Movie's Greatest Monsters*, paperback,
 Willow Wisp Press, 1983 ....$5-$10
Book, *Monster Hall of Fame,* Dynamite,
 Scholastic, 1978 ....$8-$12
Boris Karloff's Monster Game, Gems, 1965 .....$125-$200
Coloring book, *Universal Monsters*, Golden
 (Western Publishing), 1991 ....$5-$10
Creature Features game, Athol, 1975 ....$50-$75
House of Frankenstein, Super 8mm film,
 Castle Films...$25-$50

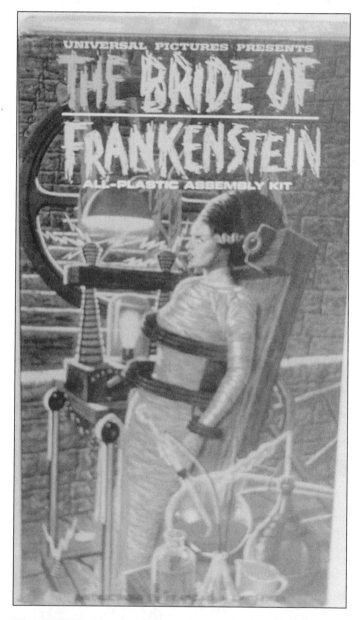

**The 1965 "Bride of Frankenstein" model kit by Aurora
is a valuable one, worth about $850 Mint-in-Box.**

Lunch box and thermos, "Universal's Movie
Monsters," Aladdin, 1979 ....$85-$125
Mad Monster Castle, Mego, vinyl, 1974 ....$300-$600
Monster Old Maid card game, Milton Bradley,
1963...$40-$60
Movie poster, *House of Frankenstein*, one-sheet,
1944..$2,000-$3,000
Movie poster, *American Werewolf in London*,
Universal, 1981 ....$15-$25
Movie poster, *I Was a Teenage Werewolf*,
Michael Landon, 1957 ....$125-$200
Movie poster, *Teen Wolf*, Michael J. Fox,
1980s ....$15-$25
Movie poster, *Werewolf of London,* one-sheet,
Universal, 1935 ....$11,000-$15,000
Record LP, *Themes from Classic SF,*
Fantasy and Horror Films................................$15-$25
Universal Monster Mansion Game, Milton Bradley,
1981..$40-$65
Wrapping paper roll, Universal Monsters, Unique,
1991...$5-$10

Miscellaneous Movie Monster Items

Attack of the 50-Foot Woman movie poster,
one-sheet, Allied Artists, 1958...............$1,200-$2,000
Blob model kit, 5", resin, Blob on diner,
Lunar Models ....$75-$100
Blob movie poster, one-sheet, Paramount,
1958...$150-$250
Curse of the Demon movie poster, one-sheet,
Columbia...$100-$150
Dr. Jekyll as Mr. Hyde model kit, Aurora,
1964..$200-$300
The Fly movie poster, one-sheet,
20th Century Fox, 1958..................................$75-$150
Planet of the Vampires movie poster, one-sheet,
American Intl., 1965 ....$500-$600
Reptilicus model kit, resin, Monster Fun..............$65-$85
Them! movie poster, one-sheet, Warner Brothers,
1954..$350-$500
The Thing model kit, Billiken, 1980s.................$150-$300
War of the Colossal Beast movie poster,
American Intl., 1958 ....$125-$200

NATIVE AMERICAN ARTIFACTS

An area of collecting that was once confined to the Southwest, Native Americana has caught the interest of the entire nation. The intricately patterned baskets and beadwork, the chipped arrowheads, tools and weapons, and the vibrantly dyed rugs and fabrics make for a diverse field. Add to that the fact that each tribe used different raw materials, and the result is a myriad of cultures and traditions reflected in the artifacts that were left behind.

Background: Since there is little native-written history from which to glean information, artifacts play a key role in revealing America's history from an aboriginal perspective. The weaponry, textiles, body adornments, tools, utensils, pottery and baskets used by various tribes during their fight to retain their land and heritage are aggressively sought by today's collectors.

The oldest documented Native American culture is the Sandia, which dates from 15,000 B.C. It is estimated that there were 10 million Native Americans scattered throughout the country when the explorers arrived. The ensuing treatment of the American Indian tribes by the U.S. government—the latter of which was intent on bringing these "savages" around to its way of thinking—is grim.

By the late 1800s the Indian wars were over and tribes were relegated to reservations. The beadwork, baskets, pots and jewelry made during this early reservation period are beautiful and highly collectible.

Today's Native American craftspeople have been forced to organize in an attempt to curb the importation of cheap, non-Indian made goods. Modern goods should either come directly from the crafter to ensure authenticity, or otherwise be guaranteed to be authentic by way of a reputable dealer or certificate of authenticity.

General Guidelines: Items connected with famous Indian chiefs, as well as other historical items, are extremely popular in today's collecting market. Also items associated with a battle or other notable event, mid-19th century artwork, early schoolbooks from reservations, and vintage garments are taking the forefront in this field.

With older chipped and flaked stone tools, look for signs of the maker's work on all sides of the piece; newer pieces, which are still valuable but not as much so, may be worked on just one side.

Newly made arrowheads and other chipped artifacts sell for $10-$50. Many prehistoric artifacts can be had for between $25 and $200. Even if an old artifact is accompanied by a certificate of authenticity, be sure to check with the authenticator to ensure the certificate is not a fake.

Artifacts will often command higher prices in the region in which the tribe is located. Navajo rugs, Hopi kachina dolls, Zuni fetish necklaces, Mimbres pottery, intricate Plains Indian

This 50-by-80-inch Navajo German town blanket sold for $9,200 at an auction conducted by Jackson's in Cedar Falls, Iowa.

beadwork and finely woven baskets from the Northwest tribes are much in demand among today's collectors. Beadwork, especially, has become expensive; fine old examples of beaded gauntlets and moccasins bring high prices.

Club
•Genuine Indian Relic Society, 195 Barringon Dr. E., Roswell, GA 30076

Recommended Reading

Warman's Native American Collectibles, John A. Shuman III
North American Indian Artifacts, Sixth Edition, Lar Horthem

VALUE LINE

Arapaho beaded moccasins, 19th century	$1,500
Blackfoot gauntlets, beaded, with history	$300
Blackfoot jacket, buckskin, beaded, with history	$500
Chilcotin moccasins, ca. 1870	$1,500
Chilcotin burden basket, 15-1/2"	$800
Chilcotin basket, coiled, lidded, 6-1/2"	$200
Chippewa deerskin pipe bag	$175
Cree beaded belt, ca. 1925, 36"	$300
Cree beaded saddle, diamond design, 1920, 18"	$3,000
Cree moccasins, beaded	$400
Deerskin gauntlets, beaded with floral design	$400
Eastern Algonquin birch bark hat	$275
Fetish necklace, shell	$100
Fetish necklace, carved bone	$100
Hopi Kachina doll, polychrome wood	$1,000
Hopi vase	$250
Inuit cooking bowl, stone, 11"	$300
Inuit ivory and fossil bone artifacts	$700
Inuit grease bowl, lidded, wood, 6"	$300
Inuit hunter's necklace, carved bone	$200
Inuit soapstone carving, bear, man and seal	$300
Iroquois tomahawk, trade iron head	$700
Iroquois wall mask	$100
Kalamath basket, 7"	$350
Klikitat basket, 14"	$750
Lillooet carry basket	$150
Lillooet tray, circular, double-handled, 18-1/2"	$350
Lillooet basket, oval, handled, ca. 1920	$300
Little Big Man photograph	$150

Lytton basket, flared, 9-1/2"	$300
Lytton basket, heart-shaped, 11"	$350
Makah basket, square, lidded, geometric design, 3-3/4"	$400
Makah basket, lidded, 3/4"	$200
Micmac lidded basket	$150
Moccasins, fully beaded, ca. 1920	$800
Mukluks, beaded	$100
Navajo bracelet, silver and turquoise	$200
Navajo earrings, silver inlaid	$100
Navajo fetish necklace, carved, seven strand, multi-stone	$400
Navajo fetish necklace, turquoise inlaid	$150
Navajo fetish necklace, carved bone, dolphin	$150
Navajo "lazy lines" rug, c. 1930, 8' x 5'	$500
Navajo rug, dyed homespun wool, geometric patterns	$600
Navajo rug, dyed homespun wool, animals with brown background	$500
Navajo wide ruins rug, woven wool	$350
Navajo wool blanket, woven, 18" x 37"	$100
Nayarit sitting figure, 7-1/2"	$1,500
Nayarit painted dish, 1-1/4"	$200
Northern Plains bow, ca. 1890	$400

A Butterfield & Butterfield auction of Native American art included this Apache pictorial olla (left) that was offered with an estimate of $7,000-$9,000; and a Zia polychrome pottery jar (right) that had an $8,000-$12,000 pre-sale estimate.

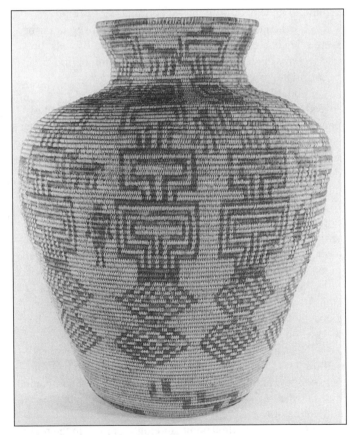

This Apache basket sold for $9,200 at a Dunning's auction in Elgin, Ill.

Northwest coast dagger, copper with carved
    bone handle, 30"... $2,000
Northwest coast totem pole....................................... $150
Oil painting, "Wild Horse Roundup",
    Chicago 1928 .... $5,000
Osage medicine bag, 16" $400
Plains beaded and quilled bridle, Sioux.................. $1,500
Plains buffalo lance, hand-wrought............................ $700
Plains pouch, beaded, 7" $500
Plains pipe tomahawk, iron, 20" $700
Puget Sound basket, zigzag pattern, 12"................. $1,000
Scrapper, flint... $100
Sioux beaded doll, 12" $600
Sioux beaded doll, 12" $650
Sioux pottery bowl, 10" $100
Sioux knife case, fully beaded, 11"............................ $700
Sioux beaded pipe bag, 30"...................................... $1,500
Sioux beaded knife sheath, 8-1/2" $350
Southwestern polychrome pottery Olla, Acoma,
    white clay with geometric decorations................ $4,000
Southwest basketry bowl $350
Southwest kachina doll, 12".. $500
Tlingit basket, 7-1/2" $1,250
Tlingit basket, ca. 1870, 10" $1,100
Tlingit horn spoon, four figures, abalone inlaid, ca.
    1880, 8" $1,300
Trade beads, early Dutch $200

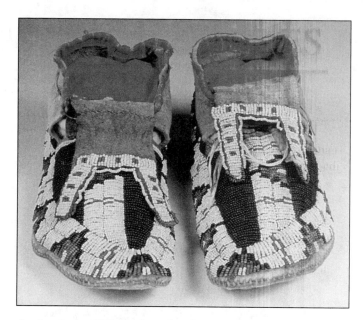

A nice pair of Sioux beaded hide moccasins brought a top bid of $1,035 at a Jackson's auction in Cedar Falls, Iowa.

Woodlands purse, beaded, 7"...................................... $450
Zuni fetish necklace, carved stone $150
Zuni squash blossom necklace.................................... $750

PAPERWEIGHTS

The word "paperweight" is actually something of a misnomer. Introduced in mid-19th century France, these delicate glass treasures may have been called "paperweights," but even back then they were considered far too beautiful just to hold down paper. This should come as no surprise, of course, to the thousands of people who collect paperweights today. For them, vintage paperweights are precious works of art, like classic paintings or sculpture—and, and as it turns out, they are also rock-solid investments. In fact, over the past three decades, through good economic times and bad, antique paperweights are one of the few collectibles that have continued to increase in value.

Some sell for astounding prices. In 1990, a rare, highly desirable French paperweight sold for a record $258,000; and, although the better paperweights often do command prices in the thousands, this is still a hobby where knowledgeable collectors can get started for under $100 and find a nice selection of pieces in the $300-$600 range.

Background: Most in demand by today's collectors are antique paperweights made between 1845 and 1860 by Baccarat, Clichy and Saint Louis, the three most prominent glass factories in France at the time. The skilled artists at these factories created exquisite paperweights depicting delicate flowers, exotic birds, dazzling butterflies, and other fragile designs—all encased in clear crystal. It was the most demanding of all the glassmaking skills.

Some of the paperweights were comprised of "millefiori," which literally means "a thousand flowers"— tiny glass canes whose cross sections reveal microscopic patterns as delicate as snowflakes.

But the fine art of the paperweight was not exclusive to France. Also becoming increasingly collectible are antique paperweights from American glassworks, primarily the New England Glass Company, the primary producer of paperweights in the United States.

And in recent years, the art of making paperweights has enjoyed something of a renaissance—both in France and America—as contemporary glassmakers carry on the tradition, combining the classic French designs with modern technology to create a whole new generation of beautiful paperweight treasures.

General Guidelines: The true treasures of the paperweight hobby sell for thousands, but you don't have to a millionaire to collect paperweights. Collectors will find a nice selection in the $100-$500 range and many more beauties for less than $1,000. As with most collectibles, it is probably best to specialize—either by theme (birds, flowers, fish, etc.), or by a specific artist or company. Some collectors specialize in American-made paperweights, modern paperweights or miniature paperweights (those under two inches in diameter, which are generally more modest in price).

But no matter what you choose, quality is critical. The value of a paperweight depends on design, maker, craftsmanship, condition and rarity. In a *Today's Collector* article, a spokesman for L.H. Selman Ldt., of Santa Cruz, Calif., the nation's largest paperweight dealer, offered the following criteria for evaluating a paperweight:

Clarity of the glass—Is it clear, or does it have a yellow tinge?

Imperfections—Are there any cracks, bruises or scratches?

Color—Are the colors bright and vibrant, or do they appear washed out or dull?

Execution—Study the complexity of the design; also is it well-centered?

Artist and factory—Was it produced by a reputable maker? When it comes to antique paperweights, those made by Baccarat, Clichy, and Saint Louis are the most desirable and offer the best investment potential.

Creativity—Is the design attractive and original?

These antique paperweights sold at a recent L.H. Selman auction for prices ranging from $1,100 for the Clichy weight at bottom center to $6,600 for the rare Baccarat "snake" weight at top center. (Photo courtesy L.H. Selman, Santa Cruz, Calif.)

Trends: Traditionally, the paperweight market, which has a tremendous record as an investment collectible, has been dominated by paperweights from 19th-century France. These classic French pieces still command the highest prices, but in recent years, prices have also been rising dramatically for two other categories of collectible paperweights: American-made paperweights and modern paperweights.

Until a few years ago, it was uncommon for an antique American-made paperweight to sell for over $1,000; but now, American-made examples—especially those made by the New England Glass Company and the Mount Washington Glass Company—can sell for thousands and starting to rival their French counterparts.

Also attracting more interest are investment-grade contemporary paperweights, which can also sell in the thousands. Modern paperweight artists whose work commands the highest prices include Paul Stankard, Rick Ayotte, Chris Buzzine, Randall Grubb and a handful of others. While most antique paperweights are not signed in any way, almost all modern weights are signed and dated in some fashion.

Clubs

• International Paperweight Society, 761 Chestnut St., Santa Cruz, CA 95060

• Paperweight Collectors Assoc. Inc., P.O. Box 1059, Easthampton, MA 01027

VALUE LINE

Values below reflect actual prices realized from recent paperweight auctions conducted by paperweight specialist L.H. Selman, Ltd., Santa Cruz, Calif. The descriptions are condensed and not complete.

Antique Paperweights

Clichy, close concentric piedouche weight, pink and green rose surrounded by concentric complex canes, footed pedestal formed with green and white staves, extremely rare $23,000

Clichy, outstanding color ground circular garlands millefiori weight with a large central pink and green rose, set in a rich turquoise color ground surrounded by complex canes of various colors and designs $18,700

Baccarat, dated magnum scattered millefiori weight with the Gridel silhouettes of a moth, roosters, elephant, pheasant, dog, horse, monkey and goats, extremely rare $14,300

A rare and unusual "triple" weight sold for $45,000 at a Selman auction. (Photo courtesy L.H. Selman, Santa Cruz, Calif.)

Clichy, C-scroll garland millefiori weight with a large central pink and green rose $11,000

Clichy, double clematis bouquet weight with three blossoms in pink, blue and auburn on stems with buds and leaves; flowers are tied with a pink ribbon, extremely rare $8,800

Baccarat bouquet weight consisting of a formal arrangement with a pansy, a red double clematis, three white blossoms with ruby centers and a yellow bud on a star-cut ground, very rare $8,250

Baccarat, paneled honeycomb carpet ground weight with a flower-shaped design with petals shaped from cobalt blue and ruby arrow/six-pointed star canes and other complex canes, very rare $8,250

Clichy, close concentric millefiori mushroom weight with a chain of twelve pink and green roses amidst circlets of complex canes in various colors......... $7,700

Saint Louis, carpet ground weight with the central silhouette of Punchinello...................................... $7,700

Clichy, cinquefoil garland on lace weight with a five-looped ruby garland of pastry mold canes around a complex concentric arrangement $7,150

Clichy, very nice close concentric millefiori weight with a chain of twenty-four pink and green roses and a circlet of twelve green and white roses alternating with cherry pastry mold canes $4,100

New England Glass Co., crown, red, white, blue and green twists interspersed with white latticinio emanating from a central pink, white and green complex floret/cog cane, minor bubbles in glass.................... $2,200

Clichy, close packed millefiori piedouche weight with quatrefoil, pastry mold, cog, stardust and bulls-eye canes in various colors, set on a blue and white-striped pedestal.................................... $2,200

Clichy, chequer weight with a central pink and green rose and a purple and white rose amidst complex canes of various colors $2,000

Modern paperweights are beginning to rival their antique cousins in price. These four contemporary weights, all 1970s and 1980s examples from the Saint Louis factory of France, sold at a Selman auction for prices ranging from $450 to $2,000. (Photo courtesy L.H. Selman, Santa Cruz, Calif.)

Clichy, close concentric millefiori weight with circlets of complex cog and stardust/bulls-eye canes in various colors, arranged in a green and white stave basket.. $1,650

Clichy, emerald color ground star-pattern millefiori garland weight with three concentric star-shaped garlands of bulls-eye, cog and star-shaped canes in various colors $1,550

Clichy, miniature nosegay weight with three cane flowers and leaves $1,100

Sandwich Glass Company, double poinsettia, red flower with double tier of petals, green and white Lutz rose, green stem and leaves, bubbles between petals $1,100

Clichy, spaced millefiori weight with a central pink and green rose surrounded by an edelweiss cane, moss cane, cog canes, pastry mold canes and bulls-eye canes in various colors............................ $990

Val St. Lambert, patterned millefiori, four red, white, blue, pistachio and turquoise complex canes circlets spaced around central pink, turquoise and cadmium green canes circlet, canes set on strips of lace encircled by spiraling red and blue torsade, minor blocking crease $825

Clichy, concentric millefiori drawer pull with four pink and white roses amidst canes of various colors... $650

Saint Louis, scrambled millefiori weight the silhouette of a dancing man and a cross amidst whole and broken complex canes $650

Clichy, miniature spaced millefiori weight with cog, edelweiss, six-pointed star, moss and pastry mold canes in various colors $525

Baccarat rock weight, also called mountains of the moon and sand dunes, features a sandy ground flecked with green glass and mica........................... $475

New England Glass Company, scrambled millefiori weight with whole and broken complex cog canes twisted ribbon and filigree in various colors $330

Sandwich Glass Company, spotted fantasy flower weight, flower has six yellow-spotted blue petals around a copper aventurine center on a stalk with green leaves, pontil scar on base $275

Contemporary Paperweights

Paul Stankard, bouquet, yellow meadowreath, blue forget-me-nots, red St. Anthony's fire, white bellflowers, and white chokeberry blossoms and buds, 1977 .... $2,200

Paul Stankard, 1975 spiderwort plant from the American Floral Series...................................... $1,975

Saint Louis, basket of fruit, six pears, three plums and three red cherries, bed of green leaves, swirling latticinio basket, handle with encased lace twist, limited edition of 250, date/signature cane, 1985... $1,430

Delmo Tarsitano, wasp with translucent yellow wings and striped brown and yellow abdomen, beige and amber millefiori field made to resemble wasp's nest, six and one faceting, DT signature cane $1,320

Chris Buzzini, 1994 artist's proof scarlet columbine weight, ruby blossom with yellow center and stamens... $1,100

Delmo Tarsitano, blackberry weight, rare................... $990

Charles Kaziun, concentric millefiori, heart, turtle silhouette, shamrocks, six pointed stars and floret canes encircled by purple and white torsade, turquoise ground flecked with goldstone, K signature cane $990

Paul Stankard, stylized flower weight containing a pale pink blossom with yellow and orange stamens, on a stalk with yellow-green leaves, powder-blue ground, pre-1976 .... $935

Perthshire, crown, central complex cane with projecting red and blue twisted ribbons alternating with latticinio ribbons, date/signature cane, limited edition of 268, 1969 .... $770

Rick Ayotte, yellow finch with yellow breast and head, black and white wings, perched on branch, faceted, signed and dated, limited edition of 25, 1979.. $550

Debbie Tarsitano, bouquet weight containing two turquoise blossoms, an amethyst blossom, opening white buds and five pink bellflowers on gathered stems... $475

Paul Ysart, pink fish with translucent red fins, sandy ground encircled by ring of spaced bubbles........... $440

Leonard DiNardo, Hopi Indian, burgundy over white double overlay, traditional Indian pattern cutting, signed and dated, 1984.............................. $330

Some paperweights can bring truly astounding prices. This rare weight, known as "Bird in the Nest," made the French glass factory, Pantin, sold for an incredible $182,600 at a Selman auction. (Photo courtesy L.H. Selman, Santa Cruz, Calif.)

William Manson, compound triple butterfly, three pink, white, powder blue, green and gold aventurine, and yellow millefiori butterflies, approaching pink double clematis on bed of green leaves, encircled by garland of pink and white complex canes, date/signature cane, 1981... $330

Baccarat, yellow carpet, twelve zodiac silhouette canes, tiny yellow florets ground, date/signature cane, limited edition of 300, 1972......................... $300

PETROLIANA

From the very earliest days of the automobile, cars ran on gasoline, so companies that sold gasoline competed for motorists' dollars by establishing and heavily promoting strong brand identities.

Gas stations usually had a distinctive look to identify them as part of a chain, and everything from advertising signs to oil cans carried the company's easy-to-spot color scheme and corporate logo. From the red star labels on Texaco lubricants to blue-and-yellow Sunoco gas pumps and the red Mobil Pegasus horse, the oil industry's products and equipment were colorful symbols of life on wheels.

Gas station artifacts are known as "petroliana." Some examples include antique gasoline pumps and the ornate globes that sat atop them, porcelain signs from vintage gas stations, oil cans and other packaging, advertising and promotional items created by oil companies and even obsolete service station equipment.

Many old-car hobbyists enjoy collecting and displaying petroliana.

General Guidelines: Petroliana is hot in today's old-car hobby. Along with the increased interest, prices are escalating, although there may be some degree of overkill and market saturation setting in. Watch for reproduction items which are plentiful and extremely authentic looking.

Items in most demand today include products of service station suppliers that did not stay in business long; porcelain signs from the 1930s to 1950s; glass oil containers; metal quart oil cans; marine and racing petroliana; oil can banks given away as service station premiums; gas pump globes with aircraft graphics; vintage road maps; air machines with globes; and globes with ethyl or premium incorporated into their graphics.

Petroliana collectibles can be found at flea markets, antique shows and shops—and don't forget automobile swap meets. Another good source might be to inquire at your local service stations or find someone who worked for one of the many oil companies.

Clubs/Associations

• International Petroliana Collectors Association, P.O. Box 937, Powell, OH 43065-0937

• Iowa Gas Swap Meet, 2417 Linda Drive, Des Moines, IA 50322

Recommended Reading

Petroliana Identification and Price Guide, Mark Anderton

Old Cars Weekly (newspaper)

PETROLIANA COLLECTIBLES TIMELINE

1900s—Gas pumps, some of the most expensive petroliana items, were first used at filling stations in the early 1900s. The most desirable are those from the 1930s and 1940s.

1900s-1950s—This time frame offers some of the most valuable, coveted advertising signs, those promoting specific brands and parts. Condition and graphics drive the values of signs, which can be in the more common forms of tin and metal, or paper, cloth or porcelain.

1900s-1940s—License plate attachments from this period are rare; they were attached to the car, and license plates were hung from their hooks.

1910—Glass globes were first designed in 1910.

1910s—Tin oil cans were created, in various shapes and sizes, during this time. In the 1960s, however, plastic bottles began being used for oil bottles. Today, collectors look for the older tin cans, especially those with terrific graphics, which are the most desirable.

1930s – Gas-station-attendant's badges from this time can bring $750 to $1,500 each.

1940s-1970s—Many service stations gave away plastic figural gas-pump salt-and-pepper-shakers, molded in Missouri. Corporate colors were used on most pumps at company-owned stations, but independent owners could order pumps with their own colors; these variations are rarer, and more valuable.

1950s—Tin toy gas stations made during this time are hot items now, with prices tripling over the last 10 years or so.

VALUE LINE

Values shown are for items in Very Good to Excellent condition.

Service Station Premiums

Amalie Motor Oil light-up clock,
  15" diameter ....$250-$300
Amoco radio, looks like a pump, with box,
  4-1/2" x 2-1/2" ....$50-$100
Atlantic salt and pepper shakers, plastic, set........$50-$150
Cities Service pocket knife ....$25-$75
Cities Service rubber ball.....................................$25-$50
Cities Service thermometer...............................$150-$250

Conoco salt and pepper shakers, plastic, set .... $30-$60
Esso cooler .... $20-$50
Esso Flit Sprayer can .... $5-$30
Esso knife .... $90-$200
Esso plate .... $100-$400
Esso rubber tiger .... $20-$50
Esso salt and pepper shakers, plastic, set .... $30-$60
Esso sewing kit .... $35-$75
Marathon key chain .... $35-$50
Marathon metal map rack .... $100-$225
Marathon thermometer .... $50-$125
Mobil bowl .... $40-$100
Mobil glass set of 6 .... $40-$80
Mobilgas lighter .... $50-$150
Mobilgas phone .... $50-$150
Mobilgas pocket mirror .... $125-$225
Mobiloil porcelain thermometer,
   32-1/2" x 4-1/4" .... $300-$600
Oilzum light-up clock, Choice of Champions,
   round .... $500-$800
Phillips 66 Farm Service cooler .... $50-$150
Phillips 66 plastic slide puzzle .... $5-$20
Phillips 66 salt and pepper shakers, plastic, set ..... $25-$50
Quaker Alcohol Anti-Freeze thermometer,
   metal .... $150-$300
Quaker State metal tray .... $150-$250
Quaker State neon light-up clock .... $500-$700
Red Crown Gasoline porcelain thermometer
   .... $1,500-$2,500
Shell inkwell .... $200-$400
Shell map book .... $75-$150
Shell metal bottle opener .... $50-$100
Shell pocketknife .... $40-$80
Shell tin bank .... $300-$500
Shell wooden clock .... $2,000-$3,500
Sinclair plastic Dino bank .... $20-$50
Sinclair radio, looks like a pump, with box .... $50-$125
Socony Gasoline and Polarine brush .... $10-$30
Standard Oil checker game .... $50-$150
Standard Oil salt and pepper shakers, plastic,
   set .... $50-$150
Sunoco cuff links, with box .... $100-$200
Sunoco Zippo lighter, with box .... $45-$90
Texaco metal lighter .... $150-$250

Gasoline Pump Globes

Aladdin Gas, metal body .... $275-$350
American Gas, metal body .... $300-$350
Amoco, glass body, blue and white .... $250-$300
Ashland Plus, plastic body .... $100-$150
Ashland Kerosene, plastic body .... $150-$200
Atlantic Capitol Gasoline, metal body .... $350-$425
Atlantic Hi-Arc, glass body .... $350-$450
Atlantic Imperial, glass body .... $250-$325
Atlantic Premium, glass body .... $700-$1,000
Bay Gas, plastic body .... $250-$350

Bolivar Gas, glass body .... $500-$700
Boron Supreme, glass body .... $100-$250
Browder Special Gasoline, glass body .... $250-$350
Calso Gasoline, glass body .... $400-$600
Champlin Presto Gasoline, glass body .... $300-$450
Cities Service Oils, metal body .... $500-$800
Conoco, plastic body .... $150-$225
Deep Rock, plastic body .... $250-$400
Derby Gasoline, glass body .... $400-$600
Dixie Oils Gasoline, plastic body .... $400-$650
Duro Gasoline, glass body .... $250-$500
Elreco Regular, glass body .... $250-$400
Esso, glass body .... $250-$400
Esso Extra, glass body .... $300-$500
Falcon Ethyl, plastic body .... $400-$800
Filtered Gasoline, glass body .... $200-$500
Foster Supertane Oil Co., glass body .... $400-$800
Frontier Gas, glass body .... $500-$1,500
General Motor Fuel, metal body .... $750-$1,200
Hornet Gasoline, plastic body .... $150-$400
Imperial, metal body .... $250-$500
Imperial Premier Gasoline, metal body .... $300-$500
Kanotex, glass body .... $750-$1,500
Marathon, glass body .... $400-$800
Metro, glass body .... $300-$600
Mobilgas, glass body .... $300-$600
Mobil Kerosene, metal body .... $600-$1,100
Musgo, glass body .... $4,000-$7,000
Phillips 66, plastic body .... $350-$500
Power Esso, glass body .... $250-$400
Power G, glass body .... $100-$300
Purol-Pep, metal body .... $300-$600
Red Aro Gasoline, glass body .... $350-$700
Richfield Premium, plastic body .... $300-$500

Values may vary from region to region. These old Gulf tins would be more desirable in the Pittsburgh area than on the West Coast. They range in value from $15 to $75.

Old gas pumps and globes are popular with serious collectors, who look for treasures at old car shows and swap meets. These old pumps were offered at the annual Iola Old Cars Show, in Iola, Wisconsin, the largest event of its kind in the Midwest.

Royal Gasoline, metal body ....$200-$600
Shamrock, plastic body ....$200-$500
Sinclair Dino Supreme, plastic body ....$150-$325
Skelly Premium, plastic body ....$100-$200
Socony, metal body ....$250-$500
Spunkey's Ethyl, glass body ....$300-$450
Blue Sunoco, metal body ....$300-$450
Super Flash Ethyl, glass body ....$800-$1,500
Texaco, glass body ....$400-$900
Tidex, metal body ....$250-$425
Tydol Flying A Kerosene, glass body ....$500-$1,000
White Rose, Canadian, glass body..................$750-$1,500
Zephyr, glass body ....$300-$500

Gasoline Pumps

Atlantic White Flash Erie pump, restored..........$400-$800
Mobil Special gas pump, restored...................$900-$2,000
Phillips 66 gas pump, restored ....$1,000-$2,500
Richfield gas pump, restored............................$400-$600
Shell gas pump, restored ....$1,000-$2,000
Sinclair gas pump, restored..........................$1,500-$3,000
Texaco Fire Chief gas pump, restored ....$1,000-$2,000

Visible Gasoline Pumps

American, 360-V, 10-gal., circa 1923 ....$1,270-$2,130
Butler, Model 61, 10-gal., square,
    circa 1924 ....$2,185-$3,220
Correct Measure, lighthouse, 10-gal.,
    circa 1928 ....$1,340-$1,975
Fry, Model 87, 10-gal., circa 1926...............$1,850-$2,875
Wayne, 519-C, 10-gal., circa 1919...............$2,080-$3,150

Miscellaneous Petroliana

Attendant's hat, Amoco ....$180-$230
Attendant's hat, Esso...$150-$225
Attendant's hat, Sunoco ....$150-$250
Bottle rack, Pennzoil..$200-$500
Chalkboard ad, Pennzoil "Ask For It,"
    masonite ....$10-$80
Crate, Hippo Oil Products...................................$100-$300
Curb sign, Kendall "Sold Here In
    Sealed Cans" ....$500-$750
Curb sign, Mobiloil..$200-$450
Curb sign, Oilzum...$3,500-$9,000
Curb sign, Pennzoil...$300-$500
Electric lamp, Amoco, 18 " ....$100-$150
Oil rack, Mobiloil...$150-$500
Shirt, Esso ....$20-$50
Shirt, Phillips 66 ....$10-$50
Shirt, Texaco, cloth ....$100-$200
Sign, "Charge Accounts of American Oil Co.
    Honored Here," porcelain...................$50-$80
Sign, "Amoco Courtesy Cards Honored Here,"
    metal...$100-$150
Sign, "Atlantic Credit Cards Honored Here,"
    porcelain...$100-$150
Sign, "Conoco Free Travel Information,"
    metal...$1,000-$1,500
Sign, "Mobil Travel Information Center,"
    metal...$50-$150
Sign, Sunoco, light up...$200-$400
Suggestion box, Mobiloil.....................................$100-$300
Tire display sign, Montgomery Ward retail auto
    center, to check worn tires...............$75-$140
Windshield wash cabinet, Film-Fyter, for use at
    service station, unused ....$50-$75

Car Care Products/Parts/Tools

Archer Lubricants, tin quart..................................$25-$50
Atlantic White Flash tin license plate
    attachment ....$45-$90
Cadillac Chromium Cleaner, quart tin can, full .....$20-$30
Capitol Lubricant one pound tin grease.................$10-$30
Champion commercial spark plug, part J-10,
    with box...$10-$15
Firestone tire tube repair kit, tin can, complete .....$15-$25
Freedom license plate attachment, bulldog..........$50-$125
Many Miles Transmission Oil, tin, gallon ....$275-$500
Mobil Freezone, tin...$30-$75
Mobil Hydrotone, eight ounce ....$5-$25

Mobilgas license plate attachment ....$100-$300
Peak Anti-Freeze, one gallon, tin........................$15-$25
Pennzoil Motor Grease, tin, 25 pound ....$40-$80
Phillips 66 antifreeze tester.................................$20-$50
Pure as Gold pound grease.................................$50-$125
Quaker State greases ....$10-$50
Red Hat Motor Oil rear view mirror ....$5-$25
Richfield Anti-Freeze, tin, gallon.......................$40-$100
Richfield Brake Fluid, tin, gallon.........................$5-$25
Sinclair bulk oil dispenser................................$195-$250
Sun Light Axle Grease, tin.................................$15-$50
Tydol Flying A Battery Service kit ....$200-$400

Motor Oil, Quart Cans

Ace High ....$40-$80
Aero Eastern..$190-$250
Conoco Super...$5-$25
Dixie Supreme ....$25-$75
Falcon...$30-$100
Golden Leaf ....$20-$75
Grand Champion...$300-$600
Marathon ....$125-$250
Mother Penn...$40-$100
Norwalk Premium Motor Oil...............................$20-$80
Phillips 66 ....$25-$75
Power-lube ....$1,000-$2,000
Quaker State...$15-$35
Rajah...$325-$500
Richlube ....$30-$80
Sterling ....$30-$100

Motor Oil, One-Gallon Tin Cans

Agalion..$150-$200
All Pen ....$20-$50
Amoco...$5-$25
Deep Rock...$100-$250
Hippo Oil ....$100-$300
Oilzum..$400-$600
Pennzoil...$25-$150
Sinclair Opaline ....$1,100-$1,800
Wolf's Head ....$40-$80

Motor Oil, Two-Gallon Tin Cans

Aero..$20-$50
Air Chief ....$50-$100
Amoco...$50-$100
A-penn...$5-$20
Around the World ....$50-$100
Atlantic Capital ....$5-$50
Blue Eagle ....$50-$100
Bull's Head..$50-$100
Capitol...$35-$50
Cross Country ....$15-$50
Economy ....$50-$100
Empire State..$20-$100
Oneida ....$50-$150
Pennsey ....$25-$75
Pep Boys ....$200-$500
Wake Up Viz ....$80-$200

Vintage signs advertising gas and oil products have been popular with collectors for years and are increasing dramatically in value.

Motor Oil, Other Sizes

Ace High Motor Oils, tin, five-gallon
   easy pour ....$80-$100
Admiral Penn, tin, five quart...............................$150-$200
Amoco, tin, half gallon ....$50-$70
Atlas, tin, five gallon ....$25-$75
Booster, tin, five gallon ....$120-$200
Cross Country, tin, five gallon ....$2-$50
Freedom, tin, five quart ....$50-$125
Kendall, tin, five gallon......................................$50-$150
Penn Drake Premium, tin, five quart....................$10-$40
Texaco, tin, five gallon ....$100-$175

Advertising Signs

Amalie Motor Oil porcelain sign ....$300-$400
Atlantic Refining Co. porcelain sign....................$350-$450
Atlantic Premium porcelain sign ....$50-$100
Barnsdall Super-Gas Ethyl porcelain sign ....$40-$120
Esso Elephant Kerosene porcelain sign ....$400-$650
Husky Hi Power porcelain sign ....$350-$425
Marathon Motor Oils tin sign ....$150-$300
Mobil Regular porcelain sign.............................$25-$100
Penn Drake metal sign ....$100-$200
Quaker State metal sign ....$25-$150
Shell Premium Gasoline porcelain sign..........$800-$1,200
Signal Diesel Fuel porcelain sign ....$500-$1,000
Sinclair Pennsylvania Motor Oil,
   porcelain sign ....$200-$400
Texaco porcelain sign.......................................$400-$650
Valvoline Motor Oil metal sign...........................$80-$200
Veedol skater tin sign ....$1,000-$1,500

Paper/Cardboard/Cloth Memorabilia

Amoco Lubricants paper banner, "put Spring in
   your Car!" ....$20-$50
Atlantic Maximum Mileage blotter ....$50-$100
Atlantic Refining Co. cloth flag ....$50-$100
Conoco lubrication book....................................$300-$500

This advertising bank, a promotional item from Amoco, would probably sell for about $5.

Deep Rock, paper poster, "makes engine sing" .... $5-$10
Esso 1935 lubrication guide .... $50-$100
Esso 1953 calendar .... $20-$90
Esso Lubrication cardboard ad .... $100-$300
Esso Mobil silk cloth advertisement,
    framed .... $100-$300
Kendall Motor Oil, nylon banner .... $10-$40
Pure road map of Michigan, 1956 .... $5-$10
Quaker Brand Anti-Freeze cloth banner .... $20-$50
Red Indian Pathfinder road map .... $50-$150
Richlube cloth banner .... $100-$150
Shell poster, "cars love Shell," paper .... $40-$80
Sinclair 50th year book .... $20-$50
Skelly cardboard fan .... $100-$200
Sunoco Passenger Car Chart .... $10-$50
Texaco cloth salt bag .... $50-$100
Texaco nylon flag .... $50-$125
Texaco paper mask .... $25-$75

Harley-Davidson Motorcycle Petroliana
Genuine Harley-Davidson Motor Oil can,
    one gallon, 1938 .... $445-$700
Genuine Harley-Davidson Motor Oil can,
    five gallon, with pour spout, 1925 .... $650-$1,000
H-D Gunk Motorcycle Cleaner, full, 1955 .... $85-$100
H-D Silver Heat Resistant Finish, full pint,
    1940 .... $20-$50
Touch-up paint, glass jar, full, 1958 .... $20-$50

PEZ DISPENSERS

In 1952, Americans saw the inauspicious introduction of an Austrian mint in a handy little dispenser. Long popular in the homeland, the pocket candy lost something in the translation. The marketing cure for this was successful beyond all expectations.

Background: PEZ was created in 1927 in Vienna, Austria, as a peppermint candy and breath mint sold in a clever package which dispensed the candies one at a time. Highly successful in Europe, it became the fashionable adult candy of its time. But its launch in America found a disinterested public.

Soon PEZ would be reinvented for the American market as a children's candy with fruit-flavored candies replacing the staid pfefferminz of old (PEZ derives its name from the first, middle and last letters in this word). The dispensers, which didn't exist until 1948, looked somewhat like a disposable cigarette lighter, without the now-familiar character heads. But after their introduction to the United States, soon they were redesigned and given colorful heads in the shapes of popular cartoon characters (some of the first licensed characters are thought to be Popeye, Donald Duck and Mickey Mouse). American children quickly claimed the new candy as their own.

Today PEZ, one of the most recognizable commercial names, is available everywhere, from the local Kmart to the corner convenience store, and few Americans can see a dispenser without it evoking a few childhood memories. This ability to reconnect us, either with our own childhoods or with our national past, is central to collectibility in any field, and a PEZ dispenser holds a rich postwar legacy in its tiny plastic container.

PEZ collectors nationwide have formed clubs, published newsletters and held national conventions. Long ago, kids threw away the dispensers, but these once lowly candy holders have grown in popularity and respect to the point that rare dispensers are now highly-prized collectibles and have even been sold by internationally-known auction houses like Christie's.

General Guidelines: The PEZ market has developed some noteworthy variations on standard collecting procedures. In many fields, a toy still in the original package commands a premium over the same toy with no package. This is not usually the case in PEZ collecting. Before blister cards, PEZ dispensers were packaged in boxes or cellophane bags, which did not allow for either display or handling of the toys themselves.

Since dispenser stems are easily interchangeable, PEZ authorities hold that only variations in head configuration or coloring affect value. There is generally no difference in value between dispensers with different colored stems but the same head. PEZ color variations only count when they are in the heads.

Finally, there is the matter of "feet and no feet." This refers to the presence or absence of a flattened rounded base on the stem resembling flat shoes. PEZ dispensers released in America before 1987 were all of the "no-feet" variety, so a dispenser with feet was made after 1987. But, unfortunately, it's not that easy. Certain older molds continued to be produced with no feet even after 1987, but these are generally common dispensers with little variance in value between feet and no-feet varieties. The major difference in value here applies to older, no-feet dispensers that were discontinued and perhaps reissued after 1987 with feet.

There are many avenues for finding PEZ dispensers (more than 300 character mold-variation heads exist), including ads in toy collecting publications, toy shows, antique stores, flea markets, rummage sales, chain stores and drug stores. National conventions are scheduled annually now, too, allowing Pezheads to meet and trade.

One recommendation for beginning collectors is to buy the new pieces (usually at less than $3 each today) and gradually add to their collections. However, beginners should be aware of doctored dispensers, those which others are trying to pass off as originals. Some may have been redesigned or repainted to look like PEZ characters which were never distributed; others may have had the "feet" carefully amputated.

Trends: PEZ dispensers have seen mixed performance at shows, but values are on the rise, with the most sought-after dispensers being the Bridge; Mueslix, a European comic character; Pineapple; Vucko (1984 Olympic Wolf) and Make-A-Face, a dispenser packaged with attachable plastic facial features, much like Mr. Potato Head. Few of these dispensers are ever found complete or packaged.

Another PEZ category fast on the rise in popularity are "advertising regulars." These look like regular non-headed dispensers, but with a company's name or logo on the side.

THE TOP 10 PEZ DISPENSERS
(IN MINT CONDITION)

1. Make-A-Face, American card $3,400
2. Elephant $3,200
3. Witch "regular" $3,200
4. Make-A-Face, German Super Spiel card $3,000
5. Lion's Club Lion $3,000
6. Mueslix $2,950
7. Pineapple $2,850
8. Space Trooper $2,000
9. Make-A-Face, no card $2,000
10. Bride $2,000

Quite limited, due to small production runs for each company, these are highly sought after today. The Witch regular ("regular" in PEZ jargon refers to dispensers without feet) is a favorite among collectors. These orange dispensers, which experts conclude have only a handful in existence, have a black witch painted on the side

Low-end common dispensers have been selling in large quantities, but many new collectors are hedging at the price points of dispensers in the $75 and up range, indicating this is still strongly a collector-based market. The top of the market appears healthy, with reports of dispensers achieving two and three times prior estimates at auction. Universal Monsters are among the most popular dispensers, including the various variations that were created.

Die-cuts are also popular with collectors. Each dispenser has an image cut out on the side which corresponds to the character portrayed by the dispenser. There are only five of these types: Easter Bunny, the rarest; Casper the Ghost; Mickey Mouse, which features Minnie Mouse on it; Donald Duck; and Bozo the Clown.

Rubber-headed dispensers from the 1970s, featuring the likes of superheroes such as Batman, Batgirl, Wonder Woman, the Joker and Penguin are also popular, as is the series called "Eerie Spectres." This line has six creatures in it: Air Spirit, Diabolic, Vamp, Zombie, Spook and Scarewolf; figures range in value from $150-$300 in Excellent to Mint condition.

In 1995, PEZ Candy released its "regulars" as a return to an adult dispenser with peppermint candy. These dispensers, available in several colors and designs, but without heads, are designed for those who don't like the fruit flavors or for frumps who don't want to be seen carrying a cartoon-character dispenser in their three-piece suit.

Some collectors also pursue PEZ advertisements, premiums and other memorabilia. These include balloons, clickers ($10-$15 each), masks (Ghoul Mask is $200-$300; Hobo is $45-$65; Spiderman or Hulk, $25-$35; Cave Man or Old Man, $200-$300 each), paper inserts (included with the dispenser, ranging in value from $50-$200), yo-yos and ash trays. They are all generally harder to find than dispensers. PEZ Candy has also licensed its name for use on watches, Hallmark ornaments and clothing.

Counter display boxes, featuring the likes of football players, Universal Monsters, Disney characters, and Super Heroes are also collectible, with values often ranging from $250-$500, depending on condition and what is portrayed on the box. For example, a 1960s Popeye box can be worth $500-$750. Vending boxes from the 1960s will fetch $50-$225, while those from the 1970s can bring $20-$50.

Contributors to this section: John Devlin, 5541 Oakville Center, Suite 119, St. Louis, MO 63129-3554; Richard Belyski, PEZ Collector's News, P.O. Box 124, Sea Cliff, NY 11579

Club
•Fliptop Preservation Society, 1368 Dearing Downs Circle, Birmingham, AL 35080

VALUE LINE

Values shown are for Excellent to Mint condition.

Advertising regular, no feet, no head, advertising
    on side must be complete ....$650-$1,200
Air Spirit, no feet, reddish triangular
    fish face ....$175-$250
Alpine, 1972 Munich Olympics, no feet, green
    hat with beige plume, black mustache ....$700-$900
Arlene, with feet, pink head, Garfield's
    girlfriend..$2-$5
Asterix, no feet, blue hat with wings, yellow
    mustache, European ....$800-$1,400
Asterix (1998 foreign issue), head different
    than old..$3-$5
Astronaut A, no feet, helmet, yellow visor,
    small head ....$400-$575
Astronaut B, no feet, green stem, white helmet,
    yellow visor, large head..................................$115-$175
Baloo, with feet, Jungle Book..............................$12-$25
Baloo, no feet, Jungle Book....................................$20-$40
Barney Bear, with feet, brown head,
    white cheeks and snout, black nose $15-30
Barney Bear, no feet, brown head, white cheeks
    and snout, black nose ....$30-$45
Barney Rubble, Flintstones.......................................$1-$2
Baseball dispenser set, no feet, baseball glove
    with ball, bat, white home plate,
    marked "PEZ"...$500-$750
Baseball glove, no feet, brown baseball glove
    with white ball...$165-$220
Batman, with feet, blue ....$3-$6
Batman, no feet, blue cape, mask and hat............$75-$120

Most of the major "Star Wars" characters were featured on PEZ dispensers.

Batman, Soft Head Superhero, no feet,
blue mask ....$125-$175
Betsy Ross, no feet, dark hair and white hat,
Bicentennial issue ....$130-$175
Boba Fett...$1-$3
Bouncer Beagle...$5-$6
Bozo the Clown, die-cut Bozo and Butch on stem,
no feet, white face, red hair and nose...........$140-$200
Bride, no feet, white veil, light brown,
blond or red hair.......................................$950-$2,000
Brutus, no feet, black beard and hair ....$145-$250
Bugs Bunny, no feet, gray head with
white cheeks...$5-$10
Bugs Bunny...$1-$3
Bugs Bunny, with feet, gray head with
white cheeks...$2-$4
Bullwinkle, no feet, brown head,
yellow antlers ....$200-$250
Bunny 1990, with feet, long ears, white face.............$1-$3
Bunny 1999 ....$1-$3
Bunny Original A, no feet, narrow head and
tall ears ....$275-$375
Bunny Original B, no feet, tall ears and full face,
smiling buck teeth ....$275-$375
Bunny with fat ears, no feet, wide ear version,
yellow..$20-$35
C-3PO ....$1-$3
Camel, with feet, brown face with red fez hat ....$35-$50
Candy Shooter, black gun with PEZ monogram
on stock ....$85-$150
Candy Shooter, red body, white grip, with
German license and double PEZ candy ....$50-$75
Candy Shooter on card....................................$350-$550
Captain (Paul Revere), no feet, blue hat,
Bicentennial issue ....$130-$175
Captain America, blue mask...............................$75-$100
Captain America, no feet, blue cowl, black
mask with white letter A ....$95-$150
Casper the Friendly Ghost, no feet, white face..$100-$200
Casper the Friendly Ghost, die-cut ....$165-$225
Charlie Brown, with feet, blue cap, smile with
red tongue at corner..$10-$15
Charlie Brown, with feet, blue cap,
eyes closed ....$45-$75
Charlie Brown, with feet, crooked smile,
blue cap ....$1-$2
Chewbacca ....$1-$3
Chip, no feet, black top hat, tan head with white
sideburns, brown nose, foreign issue ....$80-$125
Clown, with feet, green hat, foreign issue
(Merry Music Makers) ....$3-$6
Clown with chin, no feet, long chin,
hat and hair..$50-$80
Clown with collar, no feet, yellow collar, red hair,
green hat ....$45-$80

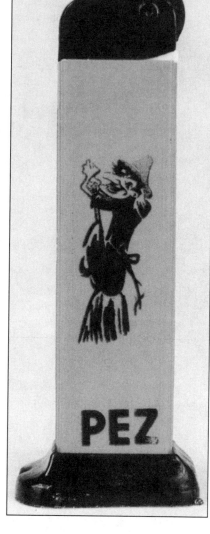

Among the most valuable PEZ dispensers is this one, known as the "Witch regular" by advanced collectors. Very scarce, it is worth over $3,000.

Cool Cat, with feet, orange head, blue snout,
black ears...$35-$60
Cow A, no feet, cow head, separate nose..............$60-$95
Cow B, no feet, blue head, separate snout, horns,
ears and eyes ....$50-$100
Cowboy, no feet, human head, brown hat..........$225-$300
Creature from Black Lagoon, no feet, green head
and matching stem, with copyright ....$225-$275
Daffy Duck..$1-$3
Daffy Duck A, no feet, black head, yellow beak,
removable white eyes ....$10-$15
Daffy Duck B, with feet, black head,
yellow beak ....$3-$5
Dalmatian pup, with feet, white head with left ear
cocked, foreign issue.....................................$35-$55
Daniel Boone, no feet, light brown hair under
dark brown hat, Bicentennial issue ....$150-$215
Darth Vader ....$1-$3
Dino the Dinosaur ....$1-$2

Dinosaurs, PEZ-A-SAURS line, four different
   dinosaurs, each ....$1-$3
Donald Duck, die-cut...........................$135-$185
Donald Duck A, no feet, blue hat, one-piece head
   and bill, open mouth..........................$12-$25
Donald Duck B, with feet, blue hat, white head
   and hair with large eyes, removable beak ....$1-$3
Donkey Kong Jr., no feet, blonde monkey face, dark
   hair, white cap with "J" on in, with box........$350-$650
Dopey, no feet, flesh colored die-cut face with
   wide ears, orange cap ....$175-$225
Dr. Skull B, no feet, black collar............................$10-$15
Droopy Dog A, with feet, white face, flesh snout,
   black movable ears and red hair.........................$5-$25
Droopy Dog B, with feet...$5-$6
Dumbo, with feet, blue head with large ears,
   yellow hat..$30-$50
Dumbo, no feet, gray head with large ears,
   red hat...$50-$85
Easter Bunny die-cut, no feet, die-cut...............$450-$575
Elephant, gold or black ....$2,600-$3,200
Fireman, no feet, black mustache, red hat with
   gray #1 insignia ....$75-$95
Foghorn Leghorn, with feet, brown head, yellow beak,
   red wattle ....$60-$85
Foghorn Leghorn, no feet, brown head, yellow beak,
   red wattle ....$75-$95
Football player, no feet, white stem, red helmet
   with white stripe..$100-$150
Frankenstein, no feet, black hair, gray head ......$180-$300
Fred Flintstone, Flintstones..$1-$2
Garfield, with feet, orange head ....$1-$2
Garfield with teeth, with feet, orange head,
   wide painted toothy grin......................................$1-$2
Garfield with visor, with feet, orange face,
   green visor..$1-$2
Gorilla, no feet, black head with red eyes and
   white teeth ....$50-$80
Green Hornet, no feet, green mask and hat,
   two hat styles exist ....$175-$255
Groom, no feet, black top hat, white bow tie.....$250-$425
Gyro Gearloose ....$5-$6
Henry Hawk, with feet...$55-$80
Henry Hawk, no feet, light brown head,
   yellow beak ....$60-$95
Hippo, no feet, green stem with "Hippo"
   printed on side, foreign issue ....$700-$925
Huey, Dewey or Louie Duck, with feet, red,
   blue or green stem and matching cap,
   white head and orange beak ....$5-$10
Hulk A, no feet, dark green head, black hair ....$30-$60
Hulk B, no feet, light green head, dark
   green hair...$25-$30
Hulk B, with feet, light green head, tall dark
   green hair..$3-$6

Indian brave, no feet, small human head,
   Indian headband with one feather,
   Bicentennial issue ....$100-$200
Indian chief, no feet, war bonnet,
   Bicentennial issue ....$100-$110
Indian woman, no feet, black hair in braids with
   headband ....$95-$175
Jerry (Tom & Jerry), with feet, brown face,
   multiple piece head ....$8-$10
Jerry (Tom & Jerry), no feet, brown face,
   pink lining in ears...$100-$200
Jiminy Cricket, no feet, green hatband and collar,
   flesh face, black top hat.................................$180-$260
Joker, Soft Head Superhero, no feet, green
   painted hair...$125-$175
Kermit the Frog, with feet, green head ....$1-$2
Lion with crown, no feet, black mane, green head
   with yellow cheeks and red crown ....$45-$100
Lion's Club lion, no feet, stem imprinted "1962
   Lion's Club Inter'l Convention".............$2,000-$3,000
Little Orphan Annie, no feet, light brown hair,
   fresh face with black painted features...........$100-$160
Maharajah, no feet, green turban with
   red inset ....$35-$50
Make-A-Face, no card, feet, oversized head
   with 18 facial parts.................................$1,700-$2,000
Make-A-Face, American card......................$2,400-$3,400
Mary Poppins, no feet, flesh face, reddish hair,
   lavender hat ....$900-$1,100
Mickey Mouse A, no feet, black head and ears,
   pink face, mask with cut out eyes and mouth,
   nose pokes through mask ....$60-$85

SHOULD I KEEP THEM IN THE ORIGINAL PACKAGE?

If you are collecting PEZ dispensers because you love them, take them out of their cellophane bags, put them on display and enjoy them. However, if the dispenser is on a blistercard, it is wise to keep it intact, mint in package. It will show some increase in value because the card itself is unusual, especially if it has an unusual shape, contest or gimmick on it.

There are only a few dispensers that one should really keep in the package. The Stand By Me dispenser is a packaged set; its authenticity is dependent upon it being intact as originally given out by Columbia Pictures in 1986. The set includes one package of candy, a miniature poster from the movie Stand By Me, and a Boy PEZ Pal. It comes in a small plastic bag that is stapled at the top.

The other dispensers in this category are the 1970s Candy Shooter and the 1980s Space Gun. These both include cards that are very displayable and add to the dispensers' value.

Mickey Mouse B, no feet, painted face, non-painted black eyes and mouth ....$85-$140

Mickey Mouse C, no feet, flesh face, removable nose, painted eyes ....$10-$15

Mickey Mouse D, no feet, flesh face, mask embossed white and black eyes ....$5-$10

Mickey Mouse die-cut, no feet, die-cut stem with Minnie, die-cut face mask ....$120-$175

Mickey Mouse die-cut, no feet, die-cut stem with Minnie, painted face ....$125-$225

Mickey Mouse E, with feet, flesh face, bulging black and white eyes, oval nose ....$1-$3

Monkey, with feet, tan monkey face in brown head, foreign issue ....$10-$25

Monkey sailor, no feet, cream face, brown hair, white sailor cap, whistlehead ....$40-$50

Mowgli, no feet, black hair over brown head, Jungle Book ....$20-$35

Mowgli, with feet, black hair over brown head, Jungle Book ....$5-$20

Mueslix, no feet, white beard, mustache and eyebrows, European ....$2,800-$2,950

Obelix, no feet, red mustache and hair, blue hat, European ....$800-$1,400

Obelix (1998 foreign issue), head different than old ....$3-$5

Octopus, no feet, black, orange or black head ....$35-$75

Octopus, no feet, red head......................................$70-$90

Olive Oyl, no feet, black hair and flesh painted face ....$125-$225

Panther, no feet, blue head with pink nose.........$100-$200

Papa Smurf, with feet, red hat, white beard, blue face ....$2-$3

Pear, no feet, yellow pear face, green visor......................................$800-$1,000

Pebbles Flintstone, Flintstones ....$1-$2

Penguin, with feet, penguin head with yellow beak and red hat, foreign issue ....$5-$6

Penguin (Batman villain), Soft Head Superhero, no feet, yellow top hat, black painted monocle, whistlehead......................................$130-$175

Personalized regular, no feet, no head, paper label for monogramming......................................$175-$200

Petunia Pig, with or without feet, black hair in pigtails......................................$25-$40

Pineapple, no feet, pineapple head with greenery and sunglasses ....$2,350-$2,850

Pinocchio A, no feet, red or yellow cap, pink face, black painted hair ....$145-$180

Pinocchio B, no feet, black hair, red hat ....$110-$140

Pirate, no feet, red cap, patch over right eye ....$45-$75

Policeman, no feet, blue hat with gray badge ....$45-$70

Princess Leia ....$1-$3

Psychedelic eye, no feet, decal design on stem, beige or black hands, many color variations..........$200-$450

Psychedelic eye, 1998 limited-edition, has 1967 copyright date......................................$10-$20

Psychedelic flower, no feet, stem with decal on side, many color variations ....$225-$500

Raven, no feet, black head, beak and glasses.........$35-$60

Regular, no feet, no head, stem with top only, assorted colors, 1990s issues......................................$2-$3

Regular, no feet, no head, stem with top only, 1950s ....$80-$160

Ringmaster, no feet, white bow tie, white hat with red hatband, black handlebar mustache ....$200-$325

Road Runner A, no feet, purple head, yellow beak ....$25-$40

Road Runner B, with feet, purple head, yellow beak ....$15-$20

Rudolph, no feet, brown deer head, red nose.........$35-$60

Sailor, no feet, blue hat, white beard..................$110-$160

Santa, full body stem with painted Santa suit and hat ....$135-$190

Santa Claus A, no feet, ivory head with painted hat ....$80-$125

Santa Claus B, no feet, small head with flesh painted face, black eyes, red hat ....$85-$150

Santa Claus C, no feet, large head with white beard, flesh face, red open mouth and hat......................$5-$10

Santa Claus C, with feet, removable red hat, white beard ....$1-$2

Sheriff, no feet, brown hat with badge..............$110-$165

Smurf, no feet, blue face, white hat ....$3-$6

Snoopy, with feet, with white head and black ears......................................$1-$2

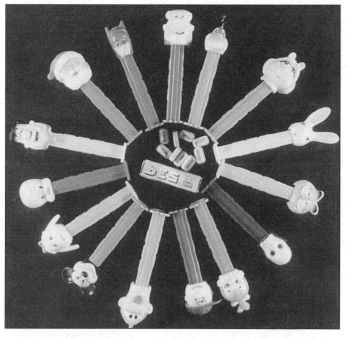

Newer PEZ dispensers are only worth about $2 each, but are great additions to a growing collection.

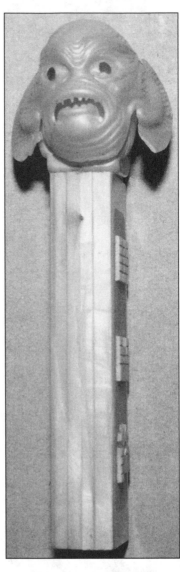

In Mint condition, the "Creature from the Black Lagoon" PEZ dispenser is a $275 item.

Snow White, no feet, flesh face, black hair with
   ribbon and matching collar ....$170-$220
Snowman, no feet, black hat, white face.................$5-$10
Space gun, 1950s, various colors.......................$275-$425
Space gun, 1980s, silver or red, loose...................$55-$85
Space gun, 1980s, silver or red,
   on blister pack ....$150-$200
Spaceman, no feet, clear helmet over
   flesh-color head ....$90-$150
Spider-Man A, no feet, red head with
   black eyes...$10-$15
Spider Man B, with feet, bigger head ....$1-$2

Stand By Me, dispenser packed with mini film
   poster and candy..$140-$185
Stewardess, no feet, light blue cap,
   blonde hair...$130-$175
Sylvester, with feet, black head, white whiskers,
   red nose ....$1-$3
Sylvester, no feet, black head, white whiskers,
   red nose ....$10-$15
Taz..$1-$3
Teenage Mutant Ninja Turtles, four different
   characters ....$1-$3
Thor, no feet, yellow hair, gray winged
   helmet..$225-$325
Thumper, with feet, no Disney logo......................$30-$50
Thumper, no feet, orange face, with logo ....$200-$300
Tinkerbelle, no feet, pale pink stem, white hair,
   flesh face with blue and white eyes...............$180-$230
Tweety 1999...$1-$3
Tweety Bird, with feet, yellow head ....$1-$3
Tweety Bird, no feet, yellow head ....$10-$17
Tyke, with feet, brown head.................................$10-$25
Uncle Sam, no feet, stars and stripes on hat band,
   white hair and beard, Bicentennial issue.......$150-$225
Vucko Wolf, 1984 Sarajevo Olympics issue,
   with feet..$650-$775
Winnie the Pooh, with feet, yellow head ....$60-$70
Winter Olympics Snowman, 1976 Innsbruck,
   red nose and hat, white head with arms extended,
   black eyes, blue smile ....$375-$425
Witch 1 piece, no feet, black stem with witch embossed
   on stem, orange one-piece head ....$225-$300
Witch 3 piece A, with feet, red head and hair,
   green mask, black hat...$3-$7
Witch 3 piece B, no feet, chartreuse face,
   black hair, orange hat ....$70-$120
Witch regular, orange stem with black witch
   graphics, no head....................................$1,700-$3,200
Wolf Man, no feet, black stem, gray head ....$200-$275
Wonder Woman, Soft Head Superhero, no feet,
   black hair and yellow band, with star...........$100-$165
Wonder Woman, with feet, red stem.........................$1-$3
Wonder Woman, no feet, black hair and yellow
   band with red star...$5-$10
Yoda ....$1-$3
Zombie, no feet, burgundy and black
   soft head ....$175-$250
Zorro, no feet, black mask and hat.........................$55-$65

POLITICAL MEMORABILIA

Political memorabilia is often associated with the election of candidates for public office, but non-campaign items—such as mourning ribbons worn for Abraham Lincoln's death, inaugural materials, and buttons protesting Prohibition—are collectible as well.

Background: Each campaign throughout history has tempted the public with yet another gimmick, usually with considerable success. This has created a collector's bonanza, including a range of items like the ever-popular buttons and pins, paper memorabilia (including prints and cartoon depictions of the candidates) and a plethora of novelty items. An increase in the scope of campaign items occurred around the time of the 1840 William Henry Harrison campaign and escalated thereafter. By the beginning of the 20th century, the influx of immigrants even necessitated that some of the written materials be offered in native languages.

Items generally have greater value if they relate to figures who played dominant roles during significant periods of U.S. history, or if they relate to those who were merely notable for their colorful speech or behavior.

Pins, Buttons, Lapel Devices and Medals

Pins and buttons are commonly associated with political campaigns. Although rare buttons command high prices, campaign buttons are the most popular collectible due to their availability, ease of display and general low cost. The period between 1896 and 1920 is considered the "golden age" of campaign buttons, with hundreds of companies contributing to their manufacture. They are noteworthy for innovative designs and unusual graphics.

Buttons and pins offer the collector a multitude of choices, from early clothing styles commemorating the inauguration of George Washington to colorful rhinestone pins bolstering the candidacy of General Dwight Eisenhower.

"Jugate" buttons pictured the two candidates (president and vice president). "Coattail" buttons featured the presidential candidate and a Senate or similar candidate, although in some cases even two or more candidates rode the coattails of the presidential contender on the campaign "button" trail.

The graphics and mechanical devices found on many early pins and buttons make them particularly collectible. Mechanical pins were especially ingenious; when opened, they revealed the candidate's picture.

There were also beautiful porcelain studs, as well as celluloid buttons. Although invented in 1839, celluloid did not reach general usage until the mid-19th century and was not used in the political arena until the 1880s. Celluloid advanced in popularity during the 1896 campaign of William McKinley, which also ushered in the mass production of pin-back buttons.

Campaign buttons and ribbons are favorites of collectors of political memorabilia.

Popular during the mid-19th century were two-piece buttons, lapel studs and brooches, all of which are included in a wide variety of lapel items. Small lapel studs for the buttonhole were produced in large quantities in the late 19th century. Some of the most interesting were in eye-catching shapes like drums, flags and hats. Over 500 types were produced during this period, making it a fertile field for collectors. Brass lapel pins from more recent campaigns, like those in the outline of various states with the candidate's name inside the "boundaries," are particularly colorful and appealing.

General Guidelines: For avid button collectors design generally takes precedence, as do unusual themes, such as those calling attention to Teddy Roosevelt's association with the Rough Riders. Picture buttons that show both the Presidential and Vice Presidential contenders are also more desirable than single candidate buttons.

Condition is important, although minor defects can be overlooked in rare items. Scarcity, of course, adds to the collectibility and value of any button. Dents, rust, scratches and tears detract from value. Campaign budget restrictions and buttons for local and state campaigns translate into less distribution and fewer buttons.

Buttons used to promote a "non-running" candidate during the party nominating convention are generally of little value.

Buttons from the 1920 Cox-Roosevelt campaign are rare. Although not exciting in design, few exist in the varying styles produced, making these among the rarest. Also scarce are pins from the campaigns of James Davis in 1924.

Third party items are also worthy of consideration in rounding out any serious collection. Silk screen designs on cloth from modern campaigns are rare and desirable. Beginning around 1972, psychedelic designs also contributed to colorful presentations.

Ribbons, Ribbon Badges, Silks

Campaign ribbon badges from early campaigns (1800-1864) are less limited for the collector than other items in the textile category, like banners and early silks. Although many fall into the rarer category, some campaigns, like William Henry Harrison's, inundated the voters with over 150 designs, making this series a coup for the specialized collector.

Ribbon badges had a medal or celluloid button or sheet on the fabric or suspended from it. Some overly-large ribbons, referred to as fringes and tassels, sported fringes of metallic threads featuring elaborate symbols and inscriptions.

The majority of ribbons from this period were lithographed in black. Rarely in dark colors, background shades were generally white, cream or other pale hues. Most emphasized symbols or issues pertinent to the voter, such as ribbons for the "Know Nothing" party covering a variety of subjects in about 25 different designs. Many of these were imprinted with the names of cities, towns and villages, even specific wards.

Bar clasps on other ribbons featured items exclusively associated with a given candidate. Until 1932, select individuals traveled to the home of the presidential candidate and formally notified him of his victory, making ribbons worn by the 50 to 100 members of these now defunct notification committees of historical and political interest.

General Guidelines: Silks are more rare. Card-mounted portrait silks made by the Thomas Stevens Company of Coventry, England, are extremely limited, with only five concerning American subjects—Washington, Harrison, Grant and Mr. and Mrs. Cleveland—plus two variants, now known to exist. The one picturing President and Mrs. Cleveland has a cigarette advertisement on the card mount. There were also silks for the Confederacy, although only a few styles are known. These include the Stars and Bars with the names of President Jefferson Davis and his Vice President Alexander Stephens, and possibly one other designed for the inauguration. Embroidered ribbons manufactured by the aforementioned Stevens Company remain the most desirable in this category. Called Stevengraphs, they appeared as bookmarks and portrait silks.

Multi-color ribbon designs for candidate Henry Clay; ribbons for Martin Van Buren; Franklin Pierce; Andrew Jackson; Winfield Scott; John Quincy Adams; Lewis Cass; and the majority of those produced for the "Know Nothing" party are rare.

Ferrotypes

Unlike voters today who view their candidates almost daily on television, during the mid- to late 19th century ferrotypes, or tintypes, were one of the few ways for the public to see a likeness of the candidate. Framed in brass of varying shapes and, more rarely, made of plush cloth, the candidate's face usually appeared on one side with his running mate on the reverse. Less often, both candidates were shown together, with a pin on the back.

By placing a hole at the top, ferrotypes could then be displayed by hanging them from the lapel. This style first appeared during the campaigns of 1860, with over 300 different types known to have existed.

In 1864, a variation of the earlier ferrotype was offered, with the pictures framed in thin sheets of metal that were stamped in elaborate designs in raised relief. Called shell badges, they were usually of copper or brass.

This time period also introduced the albumin print. Simply a paper photograph, it was understandably popular because of its lower production cost and eventually replaced its predecessors. Although shell models continued until about 1904, by the 1880s ferrotypes were rarely seen on the campaign circuit, replaced instead by cardboard photo badges.

General Guidelines: The scarce survival of ferrotypes from the 1860-1864 period makes them more valuable, as does the interest of Lincoln collectors for these campaign lapel items. For example, a Lincoln/Johnson ferrotype in elaborate brass frame can command upwards of $20,000.

Textiles/Fabric/Banners

Information on political textiles is limited, making this an oft-overlooked category for collectors. Parade banners and campaign ribbons, for instance, were common to early campaigns, but they remain more obscure and less understood than other political collectibles.

Some of these textiles are referred to as campaign chintzes, but, for the most part, they were simply swatches of fabric in varying sizes that featured the candidate and/or his campaign. They ranged from simple depictions to elaborate illustrations appropriate to the period or the candidate. Campaign chintzes were introduced for George Washington's inauguration in 1789 and continued through the Civil War. With the exception of the 1872 and 1880 campaigns, few were seen after that time. Also of interest are the small quilts called "crazy quilts" that were a product of the 1840 and 1880 campaigns.

Early campaign and parade banners, and those that hung in the candidate's headquarters, also fall into the textile category. These were often of expensive fabrics and hand-painted, not only with simple slogans but also in unique designs and pictures. Many are now considered fine examples of early American folk art. Although some command attention for their skillful graphics, by the end of the 19th century banners were produced commercially and lost much of their individuality. Nonetheless, these later styles remain of interest to collectors who focus on particular campaigns. By the 1930s and 1940s, however, headquarter banners had become a thing of the past.

General Guidelines: Rarely found today are the large canvas banners from 1876-1928 that were often suspended across streets. Smaller versions were intended for hanging in the windows of homes; printed on both sides, these same rare miniatures might well have been used as salesmen's samples.

Paper and Art

Cartoons and drawings have been an ongoing source of amusement to the public. Many were found in newspapers and periodicals, some appeared on postcards and sheet music, and still others were displayed on trade cards. Many advertisements can also be found depicting candidates touting everything from beer to sewing machines.

Political cartoons are exaggerations of figures and topics and are intended more to ridicule than to evoke laughter. An offshoot of cartoons is found in the caricature-exaggerated but less direct and more irreverent depictions of candidates.

Paintings of political figures by renowned artists of the day were frequently converted to prints. Purchased primarily by wealthy individuals, engravings were also prevalent during this country's early history, and all now fall into the political collectible category.

Stone lithographs, which were introduced in 1820, brought prints into the realm of the general public. Along with cartoons and broadsides, they filled a need, providing information about the candidates, however questionable their accuracy. Patriotic and overblown, they became an entirely separate art form.

Certain series present a challenge to collectors, like those by Currier and Ives from 1851 to 1868 portraying all the presidents from Washington to Lincoln in front of a draped background of either red or green. Here the goal is to find the entire series in the same background color.

Lithographs were also made for presidential birthplaces, deathbed scenes, inaugurations, etc. In addition to Currier and Ives, the chief publishers of these lithographs were Buford, Prang, Kellog, Endicott, Baille, Sarony and Robinson. Today, even small book prints of political figures from later periods comprise part of this collecting genre.

More formal entries in the paper category are items like invitations to inaugural balls and personal papers and letters. Not to be overlooked were postcards touting individual candidates. The early 1900s brought many postcard designs that are particularly creative, including mechanicals, and thus desirable to collectors.

Here too are paper posters and banners, campaign and anti-campaign biographies and brochures, paper ballots and electoral tickets. Prior to the advent of machines, voting was accomplished by ballots or electoral tickets, and during the 1920s and 1930s these were often as large as newspaper sheets. While some simply listed the candidates, others were complete with pictures. The smaller electoral tickets first appeared around 1824 and were used as voter reminders, listing candidates for a particular party and sometimes featuring portraits and patriotic symbols. Tickets showing the candidates, or those for third party candidates, are generally most desirable.

General Guidelines: Although the genre began in the mid-1700s, collectibles from that period are rare and costly. The presidency of Andrew Jackson, however, occurred at the beginning of the stone lithography period, making cartoons about the Jackson presidency more widespread. During the 1860s, dual colors came into prominence, with cartoon lithographs from this period being particularly noteworthy. Soon, weekly publications were brimming with cartoons, and by the time of the Civil War most daily newspapers carried them. Even foreign publications featured cartoons about American political figures.

Several early American cartoonists dominated the field, including David Claypool Johnson, Doolittle, Charles, Tinsdale, Clay, and Thomas Nast.

Surprisingly, cartoons before the 1870s are often easier to obtain. Not only did later ones from newspapers and magazines require only one master copy, but when wood pulp replaced rag in newspapers their deterioration was much more rapid.

Tobacco Products

Snuff boxes made of pewter or tin are popular collectibles; early models were made of papier-mâché, enameled, lacquered and decorated with political pictures.

Although he was disgraced in office, Richard Nixon memorabilia is very much in demand.

While most snuff boxes enjoyed popularity from the 1820s until around 1880, some are known to feature George Washington. One of these is made of tortoiseshell, with Washington's picture encased in its glass top.

Cigar cases also appeared, but their popularity lasted from 1840-1850. Dating from 1904, some candidates' pictures decorated cigar bands.

Replete with ingenious designs, political pipes are very popular in today's market. The bowls of some are carved into busts in the likeness of favored candidates. Others feature items like eagles and shields and are often inscribed with political slogans. Most were made of white clay or briar.

Match boxes also feature political candidates. Some were made of cast iron.

Lighters and cigarette packages first appeared in the 1930s. The campaign of 1956 sported particularly attractive designs featuring styles for running mates Dwight D. Eisenhower and Richard Nixon, and others for their opponents Adlai Stevenson and Estes Kefauver. In 1964, presidential opponents Barry Goldwater and Lyndon Johnson both offered small lighters with their pictures on brass medalets. Other lighters sported campaign slogans and, of course, the elephant or donkey. Cigarette boxes were also used to promote the opposing candidacies of Richard Nixon and George McGovern.

General Guidelines: Rare tobacco-related collectibles include McKinley and Bryan meerschaum pipes, French-made briar pipe with bust of FDR, 1880 Winfield Hancock rebus puzzle pipe and a double-covered cigar box with framed lithographic portraits of Blaine and Logan.

Hats

As seen on the floor of every political convention, hats have always promoted a favorite candidate. Fragile, they are hard to find, since most were unwearable by the time convention week had ended.

In earlier days, however, the hat assumed a place of honor and was treated accordingly, making those prime collectibles today. In some instances, the adornments attached to the hat garner more attention than the hat itself. One example is the early tricorner with colorful cockades that were worn for the Thomas Jefferson/John Adams political duel. The lines were clearly drawn, with Jefferson supporters attaching red, white and blue rosettes and Adams supporters favoring brown and black.

There were also parade hats, beach hats, cowboy hats, beanies, baseball caps, straw skimmers, yarmulkes, coonskin varieties, ski caps, even painters' caps. One 1896 model was fashioned from a Boston newspaper, which folded one way to promote the candidacy of William Jennings Bryan and another to favor William McKinley. After 1948, some campaigns made assembling even easier, providing cardboard models with instructions.

Toys and Banks

Often manufactured in limited quantities, political toys are hard to find; however, due to a general lack of interest, their cost to the collector remains fairly low. Mechanical and still banks are the main items in this category, but everything from dolls and marbles to battery-operated figures and board games depicted politics.

Political Causes; Splinter Parties

Apart from the usual political campaigns involving but a few parties, items for particular causes also fall into the venue of political memorabilia. These would include such diverse groups as the National Women's Party, the Native American Party, the Know Nothings, and early labor movements like the Wobblies (Industrial Workers of the World). Prior to 1900, materials pertaining to such groups were most often of paper, with the category later dominated by buttons. With movements like those involving civil rights, abortion, nuclear power, and the Black Panthers, this category has become especially active since 1960.

Founded in 1869, the Prohibition Party has participated in every campaign since, as well as promoting its cause in the interim. The movement spawned a host of other groups, like the Women's Christian Temperance Union, the Anti Saloon League, the Washington Temperance Society (Washingtonians) and the Cold Water Army (a children's temperance group).

Suffragette materials ran the gamut from parade sashes, tote bags and broadsides to china and tin window hangers.

Anti-prohibition and anti-suffrage items were equally popular. These included decals, bar items, beer schooners, and canes with beer barrel tops from the 1933 Chicago World's Fair.

An early advocate for women's rights and outspoken nonconformist was Victoria Claflin Woodhull, who ran for president in 1872 and was a prime target for cartoonists like Thomas Nast. Also prominent in the movement was Belva Ann Lockwood, nominated for president by the National Equal Rights Party in 1884. Materials relating to both Woodhull and Lockwood are rare.

In addition to a 1872 campaign poster, only three items are known for the latter—the paper, "Equal Rights," a campaign rebus puzzle ribbon and a card featuring Lockwood with a movable paper skirt.

General Guidelines: Especially rare are all items for Victoria C. Woodhill, Prohibition Party lapel pins/buttons from the campaigns of 1872, 1876 and 1880, as well as Wobblie literature.

Clocks and Watches

The earliest political timepiece is from the Harrison 1840 campaign. Watch fobs also conveyed political themes. Although most were of brass, there were also celluloid models, some with fiberboard or leather backings. One of the earliest wristwatches is from the Woodrow Wilson campaign, with others following in more contemporary campaigns, many in caricature stylings.

General Guidelines: All 19th century clocks and pocket watches are rare. Especially noteworthy are the 1888 pocket watch with a Harrison/Morton jugate and the 1896 one featuring a McKinley portrait. Considered quite rare is a 1920 pocket watch with Cox/Roosevelt on the dial.

Contributor to this section: Robert Ball

Clubs

• American Locals Political Items, 1111 W. Whiteside, Springfield, MO 65807

• The American Political Items Collectors, P.O. Box 340339, San Antonio, TX 78234

• The Political Bandwagon, P.O. Box 348, Leola, PA 17540

• The Political Collector, P.O. Box 5171, York, PA 17405

• The Thomas Nast Society, Morristown/Morris Township Library, Miller Road, Morristown, NJ 07960

Recommended Reading

Hake's Guide to Presidential Collectibles, Ted Hake

VALUE LINE

Pins, Buttons, Lapel

Bryan/Sewell jugate, "Victory 1896" ....$200+
Cox/Roosevelt jugate (Americanize America), 1920 ....$40,000+
Davis/Bryan jugate, 1924 ....$950-$1,200
Harding/Coolidge jugate, sepia/cream, 1920 ....$1,800-$2,200
Parker/Davis jugate, "Shure Mike," 1904 ....$675-$775
Roosevelt/Johnson jugate, 1912 ....$1,000+
Taft and Wilhelm II jugate, "Sixth Annual German Day, Aug. 8, 1910" ....$200-$250
Warren Harding/Calvin Coolidge jugate, 1920........1,000+
Kennedy brass inaugural medal, 1961 ....$45-$65
Washington inaugural button, inscribed "March the Fourth 1789 Memorable Era," brass ....$1,500+
Inauguration badge, brass hanger/pink ribbon, 1949 ....$45-$60
Pre-1872 large medalets...$175+
Hoover and wife clothing buttons, celluloid cover, brass rims, 1932 .... $100-$125/pr
Van Buren clothing button, brass, 1840 ....$200-$250
Cleveland/Hendricks button, brass, 1884...............$25-$45
T. Roosevelt "Welcome" button, 1904.........$1,900-$2,250
"Be Safe with Hoover," 1932................................$40-$50
"Come Clean Geraldine" (Reagan campaign) 1984..$5-$10

"Every 'Buddy' for Wilkie," 1940 ....$325-$375
"For Vice President Franklin D. Roosevelt," 1920...$1,900-$2,250
"Landon on the New Deal," 1936 ....$2,250-$2,800
"Make the White House the Dwight House," 1952...$10-$15
"Me for Al" (Smith campaign), 1928 ....$50-$70
"On the Right Track with Jack," 1960 ....$30-$40
"Teddy's Terrors" (L.A. Rough Riders convention), early 1900s ....$450-$500
"Truman Fights for Human Rights," 1948........$200-$225
"U.S. for Ike,"1952 ....$75-$100
"Veterans for Ike," blue and white, 1952 ....$15-$20
"Win with Wilson," 1916......................................$35-$50
"Youth for Kennedy,"1960.................................$250-$275
Al Smith Day (button and ribbons), 1928..........$275-$325
Blaine stickpin, plumed knight, 1884 ....$200-$250
Landon/Knox, felt sunflower with elephant, 1936..$20-$30
Lincoln/Hamlin ferrotype, lapel device, 1860..$450-$500
McKinley/Atlanta Peace Jubilee, 1898..............$125-$175
Taft "The Gunnison Tunnel Opening," Montrose, CO, elliptical design, 1910...........................$275-$325
Truman Minnesota Club, brown and gold, 1948..$175-$200

Coattail Buttons

Carter/Mondale/Moynihan, 1976...........................$5-$10
Hoover/Allen/Young, 1928 ....$55-$75
"Roosevelt-Lehman American Labor Party," 1936...$10-$15
"Vote Harriman/Roosevelt/CIO," litho, 1944 ....$15-$20
"Work and Wages/Roosevelt/Curley," 1932 ......$300-$350
"Wilkie/Vanderbilt," red, white and blue, 1940..$125-$150

Ribbons, Ribbon Badges, Silks

Ribbon, Blaine/Logan pictures, red and gold, 1884..$50-$75
Ribbon, Cleveland, red, white, blue and gold, paper photo, 1888...$85-$125
Ribbon, "I Am for Bryan and American Manhood," 1908..$40-$50
Ribbon, Garfield/Arthur, colorful design, dual photos, 1880 ....$200-$250
Ribbon, Wm. Jennings Bryan, "The Commoner," 1908..$60-$75
Ribbon badge, "Grant and Colfax," 1872 ....$500-$550
Ribbon badge, Harrison, celluloid sheet w/portrait, 1892..$100-$125
Ribbon badge, "Henry Clay Pride of America," 1844..$175-$225
Ribbon badge, "McKinley and Hobart," celluloid jugate, 1896 ....$175-$200
Ribbon badge, Wm. Jennings Bryan, tin frame, cardboard photo, metal bell, 1908...................$60-$75

Ribbon-shaped bookmark, Harrison/Reid,
 celluloid, paper photos, 1892 ....$125-$150

Ferrotypes

"Abraham Lincoln" ferrotype, velvet-covered rim,
 Hamlin on reverse, 1860 ....$425-$525

Grant ferrotype, fabric rim, stickpin, 1868 ....$225-$300

"John C. Breckenridge" ferrotype, brass rim;
 Lane on reverse, 1860 ....$375-$450

Lincoln ferrotype, brass shell frame,
 reverse paper label, 1864..............................$600-$700

Lincoln ferrotype, brass rim with stickpin,
 1864..$375-$450

McClelland/Pendleton jugate ferrotype, 1864 ....$9,000+

Stephen A. Douglas ferrotype, doughnut-style,
 silvered brass, Hershel Johnson on reverse,
 1860...$2,400-$2,600

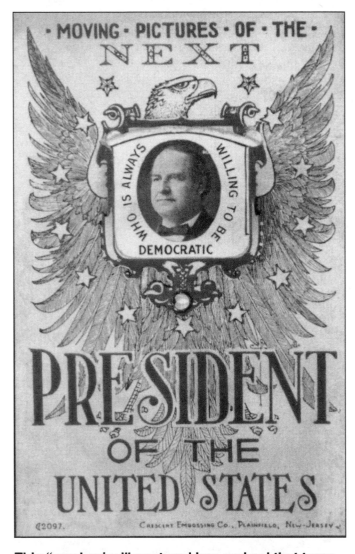

This "mechanical" postcard has a wheel that turns to show pictures of all of the candidates. For a postcard, it is very expensive, valued at $500 or more.

"Grant/Colfax" jugate, pictures on front, brass
 shell frame, pin back, 1868 ....$450-$550

"Grant/Wilson" jugate ferrotype, brass shell frame,
 pin on reverse, 1872 ....$1,000-$1,200

Greeley/Brown jugate front, shell frame, reverse
 pin/Greeley portrait on back, 1872..........$1,700-$1,900

Hayes/Wheeler jugate ferrotype, stickpin
 reverse, 1876 ....$500-$700

Textiles/Fabric/Banners

Campaign flags..$150+

Canvas banner, Smith, 1928.............................$375-$425

Fabric banner, Hoover, blue and orange,
 1932..$250-$300

Fabric banner, Roosevelt, yellow fringe, 940 ....$50-$75

Bandana, Cleveland/Thurman, black and white,
 1888..$200-$250

Bandana, Harrison, elaborate black, white and
 red design, 1888 ....$350-$400

Bandana "I Like Ike," 1952...............................$25-$50

Bandana "McGovern for President," 1972 ....$40-$60

Bandana, Parker/Davis, 1904............................$350-$400

Bandana, Teddy Roosevelt, red, white and
 brown, 1912...$150-$200

Bandana, "Tippicanoe and Morton Too," Harrison/
 Morton, red, white and blue, 1888 ....$175-$225

Bandana, "Win with Ike," red, white and blue,
 1952...$50-$75

Bandana, "Win With Ike for President," 1956 ....$50-$75

Bandana, Wm. Henry Harrison, 1888................$350-$400

Handkerchief, "G.O.P. Republican Party,"
 elephant, red, white and blue, 1964 ....$15-$20

Kerchief, Harrison/Morton, black and white,
 wide dotted border, 1888..............................$150-$200

Kerchief, "We Want Wilkie," red, white and blue,
 1940..$50-$75

Kerchief, William Howard Taft, 1908................$250-$300

Paper and Art

Ballot, 1920 Presidential ballot, with party
 electors ....$75-$100

Book, The Goldwater Cartoon Book, 1964 ....$10-$15

Book, The Heroic Life of William McKinley,
 48 pages, campaign biography, 1902 ....$15-$25

Booklet, Republican party platform booklet,
 24 pages, jugate cover, 1932 ....$25-$30

Cartoons, Pre-1872 cartoons and black and
 white prints...$200-$800

Paper, "Who is James Buchanan?" black-and-white
 portrait, 1856.. $350-$400

Photo, Roosevelt framed inauguration jugate photo,
 1933..$75-$100

Political almanacs ....$100-$600

Postcard, "Dewey-Warren The Way Ahead,"
 1948..$10-$20

Postcard, "For President, Woodrow Wilson,"
 1916..$10-$20

Postcard, "Give us Roosevelt or Give us Taft," 1908...$20-$35

Postcard, "Pull my Tail and See the Next President," elephant with Taft photo..................................$50-$75

Postcard, "Taft," caricature, fabric clothing with brass buttons, 1908..$50-$75

Postcard, "TR, Coming Home, Glad Tidings," Taft with elephant and Uncle Sam dancing, 1910 ....$35-$50

Postcard, "Vote for John P. Kennedy," 1960 ....$10-$20

Poster, "Calvin Coolidge," sepia, 1924..................$35-$50

Poster, "Elect Congressman Nixon U.S. Senator," Nixon portrait, cardboard, 1950 ....$30-$40

Poster, "For Vice President Spiro T. Agnew," paper, 1968..$35-$45

Poster, "Forward with Roosevelt," black-and-white, cardboard, 1936...$75-$100

Poster, "Goldwater and Miller," red, white and blue, cardboard, 1964...$25-$40

Poster, "James M. Cox," black-and-white, paper, 1920...$175-$225

Poster, "Johnson/Humphrey for the USA," paper, 1964..$10-$15

Poster, "Roosevelt and Johnson," black-and-white, paper, 1912...$125-$150

Poster, "Warren G. Harding," brown and white, paper, 1920...$75-$100

Print, Currier and Ives, "Abraham Lincoln/Andrew Johnson," 1864 ....$1,000-$1,300

Program, Official Program 43rd Inauguration 1957, 48 pages, Rockwell cover ....$35-$50

Program, Wilson inauguration, 1917 ....$75-$100

Program, 1948 Republican National Convention ....$25-$50

Sheet music, Colorful pre-1880 ....$175-$800

Ticket, Democratic National Convention Guest ticket; 1940...$5-$10

Ticket, Greeley Liberal Republican ticket, 1872..$65-$85

Ticket, Levering/Hale National Prohibition ticket, 1896..$65-$85

Ticket, Truman inauguration ticket; 1949...............$20-$25

Trade card, Cleveland/Stevenson, 1892, "Ale & Beef Co."...$25-$45

Window poster, "Keep Pennsylvania Liberal, Forward with Roosevelt," black and white, 1936............$75-$85

Tobacco Products

Ashtray, Ford photo, black-and-white, China, 1974..$10-$15

Ashtray, McKinley, silver, silver bug with brass nail, 1896..$225-$275

Cigar, Al Smith on colorful label, jumbo, 1928..$35-$50

Cigars, boxed bubble gum cigars, "I Like Adlai" on inside lid, 1952..$25-$45

Cigar box, "Bryan and Sewall-16-1" cigar box; wooden; 1896$65-$100

Cigar box, "Presidents-Roosevelt and Garner," white, wooden, jugate paper label, 1932.........$75-$100

Cigar box, "Square Deal," Roosevelt, wooden, 1904..$75-$100

Cigar/card cases, hand-painted ....$350-$650

Clay pipe, Bryan, no stem, 1908......................$75-$100

Clay pipe, Henry Clay, without stem, 1844.......$200-$250

Match holder, Greeley, cast iron, 1872 ....$225-$275

Match pack, Johnson/Humphrey, jugate photos, 1964..$3-$5

Matchsafe, Bryan, silvered brass, 1896 ....$125-$175

Pipe, Al Smith, carved portrait, celluloid stem, 1928..$175-$225

Snuffboxes, papier mache ....$150+

Hats

Beaver hat, felt, paper label of Cleveland/Harrison, with running mates inside, 1892 ....$225-$375

Inscribed miniature china/glass hats ....$125-$250

Inscribed miniature terra cotta hats....................$75-$175

Harrison campaign hat, beige, Harrison/Morton on inside label, 1888 ....$225-$300

Kennedy plastic hat, red, white and blue, paper band, 1960..$40-$50

Styrofoam hat, "Goldwater in '64," white with black and gold band with Goldwater pictures, 1964..$25-$35

Unmarked miniature styles (dependent on materials).................................$75-$175

Western hat,"L.B.J. for the U.S.A.", orange felt, 1964..$20-$25

Toys and Banks

Bank, Al Smith celluloid, red, white and blue, 1928..$150-$175

Bank, FDR, metal with bronze finish, 1940..........$35-$50

Bank, Goldwater, 1964 ....$25-$35

Bank, Tammany, cast iron, movable politician, 1872..$400-$450

Bust, Teddy Roosevelt, marble, sulphide bust..$135-$175

Cap bomb, McKinley cast-iron, with signature, 1896..$300-$350

Card game, "Roosevelt at San Juan," 1899........$150-$175

Dart board, Anti-Agnew dart board, "Et tu Spiro," 1972..$25-$35

Football, "Win One More for the Gipper Reagan-Bush" (N.Y. Republicans), miniature plastic, 1984 .....$15-$20

Game, "Anti-Kennedy New Frontier/The Game Nobody Can Win," 1962 ....$45-$60

Game, "Bluff," board, Kennedy and Khrushchev, 1963..$50-$75

Puppet, Johnson donkey, hand puppet, 1964 ....$10-$15

Puzzle, "Playing Possum with Taft," jigsaw, with box, 1909..$125-$150

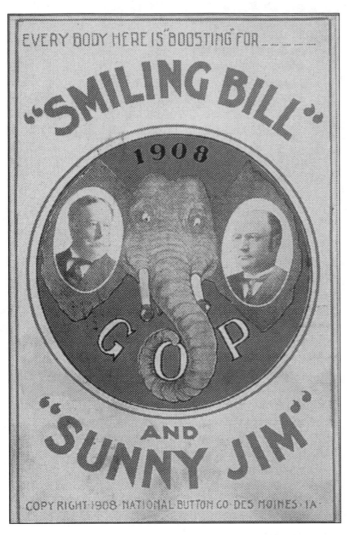

This rare postcard shows the two members of the 1908 Republican ticket. It is valued at $1,500.

Puzzle, Roosevelt/Garner inaugural jigsaw puzzle;
jugate pictures/Capitol; 1932 ....$30-$45
Scales, Harrison/Cleveland, bisque figures,
1888 ....$1,150-$1,350
Wind-up, Jimmy the Walking Peanut toy,
1980 ....$25-$35
Political Causes and Splinter Parties
Bar set, Mr. Dry, coffin-shaped ....$100-$150
Button, "Vote for My Sake" (child),
Prohibition ....$15-$20
Clock, mantel, cast iron, cocktail party figures,
moveable arms ....$150-$200
Decal, Anti-Prohibition, donkey, elephant and
beer keg ....$75-$100
Hatchet pin, Carry Nation brass, mother of pearl,
with rhinestone ....$100-$125
Hatchet pin, Carry Nation iron ....$25-$75
Jugate, "Socialist Candidates
1912/Debs-Seidel" ....$175-$225

Periodicals, women's suffrage ....$75-$250
Postcard, Anti-Saloon League ....$10-$15
Ribbon, WCTU button, white, 1928, inscribed
"WCTU/Vote for Hoover" ....$60-$75
Washingtonian ribbons ....$30-$75

Clocks and Watches
Clock, Rough Rider, brass, 1904 ....$250-$300
Clock, F.D.R. The Man of the Hour, metal,
1936 ....$150-$200
Clock, pictures all presidents from Washington
through LBJ, electric, 1964 ....$40-$50
Clock, red, white and blue figure of Agnew, plastic,
electric, 1973 ....$50-$75
Pocket watch, Cox/Roosevelt on dial, 1920 ....$25,000
Pocket watch, Carter/Mondale in '76,
with silver case ....$45-$60
Watch fob, Roosevelt and Fairbanks, brass;
1904 ....$25-$35
Watch fob, Roosevelt, high relief portrait,
copper, 1904 ....$25-$40
Watch fob, Taft, celluloid with fiberboard,
1908 ....$125-$175
Watch fob, William J. Bryan, celuloid and leather,
1908 ....$50-$75
Watch fob, Woodrow Wilson, celluloid,
1912 ....$75-$100
Wristwatch, Nixon-Agnew, "Watch them Doing
Time for You," 1974 ....$85-$125

Miscellaneous Items
Ashtray, I Like Ike! ceramic, elephant, 1952 ....$30-$40
Bottles, Figural busts ....$150+
Bow tie, "I'm for Kennedy," white with embroidery,
1960 ....$75-$100
Box, Jackson inauguration, wood with litho portrait,
1829 .... $3,000
Bust, NRA bust of FDR, metal with gold finish, red,
white and blue eagle ....$85-$125
Fan, "The Roosevelt Creed," pictures Teddy Roosevelt,
ad on back, 1916 ....$30-$50
Fan, FDR, Garner, and Cabinet, 1933 ....$50-$60
Fan, "Goldwater Fan Club," cardboard, 1964 ....$30-$40
Horn, McKinley, "Patriotism/Protection/Prosperity,"
tin, 1896 ....$75-$100
Noisemaker, "Roosevelt/Fairbanks," wood slats with
gear wheel, 1904 ....$125-$175
Pitcher, Garfield, white ceramic, raised portrait and
banner, 1880 ....$400-$450
Pitcher, shaped like bust of Eisenhower in military
uniform, 1952 ....$75-$100
Plate, bust of Garfield, pressed clear glass mourning plate,
"We Mourn our Nation's Loss," 1881 ....$30-$40
Platter, W.H. Taft/J.S. Sherman, oval, portraits,
1908 ....$40-$50
Pocket mirror, Taylor campaign, pewter, French,
1848 ....$500-$525

Pocket mirror, "It's an Elephant's Job No Time for Donkey Business," 1936 ....$125-$175

Salt and pepper shakers, President John F. Kennedy and Mrs. Kennedy; 1961 ....$30-$40

Sheet music, "Hail, Brave Garfield," 1880 ....$35-$45

Sheet music, "March on with Adlai and John," 1952...$40-$55

Sheet music, "Never Swap Horses When You're Crossing a Stream," 1916..................................$25-$35

Sheet music, "That Grand Old Party," 1948 ....$15-$20

Sunglasses, "I Like Ike," plastic with blue ribbons, 1952...$30-$40

Tie, Eisenhower, Ike with yellow lightning and Capitol...$45-$55

Tile, McKinley profile, ceramic, light blue, 1896...$35-$50

Tray, Bryan/Stevenson ....$650-$700

Tray, Teddy Roosevelt..$500-$550

Umbrella, McKinley handle, 1896....................$450-$500

Vest; "Vote Nixon Lodge Experience Counts," red, white and blue stripes, 1960.............................$35-$45

POSTCARDS

Postcards have been popular in America ever since U.S. postal regulations first allowed them in 1872. Prior to this, early souvenir cards were produced, depicting tourist attractions and special events around the world. These early postcards were called "pioneer" cards. Most of these were illustrations on government-printed postal cards or privately printed souvenir cards. Writing was allowed on one side of these cards, with only the address on the other side.

From 1898 to 1918, European publishers, especially English and German, printed many cards. In 1898, private printers were granted permission by the U.S. Congress to sell cards inscribed "Private Mailing Card" (PMC). In 1901, Congress granted permission to use the word "postcard." At this time, the message was still only allowed on one side of the card and the address on the other.

In 1907, divided backs were allowed, permitting the sender to write a note on the left side of the card and place the address on the right. Linen postcards became popular in the 1940s and chrome cards in the 1950s.

General Guidelines: The two general collecting categories of postcards are known as "views" and "topics."

Views are pictures or photographs of places like cities, states and monuments. Views of small towns are usually more rare than those of large cities. Some of these postcards are made from actual photographs and are called "real-photo" postcards. Real-photo postcards are highly sought after.

Topics are postcards centering on a particular theme, such as holidays, advertising or Black Americana. It's easy to find many vintage topic postcards. Some of the major publishers were Tuck, Paul Finkenrath, Detroit, Whitney and Winsch. Many postcard publishers used a different logo or style for printing the words "Post Card," so by checking the back of the card, you may be able to determine the publisher.

Among the most collectible postcards are those that feature advertising, artist signatures, Black Americana, characters, hold-to-light, holidays, paper toys, political themes, sets and installments, and souvenir postcards.

Advertising postcards promoted products. Some popular advertising postcards are Bull Durham, Campbell's Soup, Coca-Cola and Cracker Jack. Political postcards promoted a particular candidate or political party. And souvenir postcards depict tourist attractions or special events. Black Americana cards portray African-Americans, often in early racist stereotypes.

Artist-signed postcards are cards in which the artist signed the *original* artwork used to print the postcard. Sometimes, the signature gets cropped or completely lost from the printed postcard. A missing or cropped signature does not necessarily render the card uncollectible, especially if the artist has an identifiable style. Some popular postcard artists include Frances Brundage, Ellen Clapsaddle, H.B.G. (Griggs) and Rose O'Neill.

Characters were frequently depicted on postcards, from favorite TV show personalities to comic characters. Some popular postcard characters are Felix the Cat, Mickey Mouse and Kewpie.

When held to light, hold-to-light postcards result in a changed image. There are two categories of hold-to-light cards. The first, and more common, are transparencies. Transparencies have a hidden inner layer that contains an image only seen when the card is held to light. The second type are die-cut cards. The top layer has small die-cut shapes that shine with illuminated color when they are held against the

Holiday postcards are among the most popular categories. This patriotic example would appeal to collectors of postcards, Thanksgiving memorabilia, and Uncle Sam collectibles.

KEEP THEM SAFE!

Because postcards are made of paper, proper preservation is essential to maintaining their value and visual appeal. Cards should be kept in a cool, dry and dark place. Sunlight and humidity can damage cards. Plastic storage sleeves should be free of PVC, which damages paper with extended exposure. If storing postcards in albums, use ones with acid-free paper.

light. All hold-to-light cards require a significant amount of light to enjoy their full effect. These hold-to-light cards can have values into the hundreds of dollars.

Paper toy postcards are often paper dolls to cut out that have changes of outfits on other postcards. Books of paper doll postcards were also produced. Another popular postcard toy is the mechanical paper doll. The body is separate from the arms and legs of the doll; when cut out, they can be assembled with paper fasteners or strings, resulting in a mechanical doll. Unused cards carry a premium.

Some collectors look for sets, or a group of postcards, that center on one theme, for instance days of the week or the zodiac. Installments are sets that consist of three or more cards that, when pieced together, form the entire picture. These are sometimes called puzzle cards.

Condition is essential when grading a postcard. Collectors look for those in Near Mint to Mint condition. Rounded corners, tears, creasing, dirt and fading decrease a card's value.

Contributor to this section: Susan Brown Nicholson, P.O. Box 595, Lisle, IL 60532.

Clubs

• Bay State Post Card Club, P.O. Box 334, Lexington, MA 02173

• Borderland Post Card Club, 1024 Oneida, El Paso, TX 79912

• Cape Cod Post Card Club, Short Neck Road, South Dennis, MA 02173

• Hawaii Postcard Club, P.O. Box 15273, Honolulu, HI 96830

• Illinois State Post Card Club, Corn Belt Philatelic Society Postcard Division, Box 625, Bloomington, IL 61702-0625

• Orange County Post Card Club, 10601 Ketch Ave., Garden Grove, CA 92643

• Tucson Post Card Exchange Club, 820 Via Lucitas, Tucson, AZ 85718

• Webfooters Post Card Club, 4838 N. Lombard St., Portland, OR 97236-1072

Recommended Reading
Postcard Collector (monthly publication)

VALUE LINE

Note: The values of the higher priced postcards on this list are compiled from various specialty postcard auctions and represent the high end of pricing in this hobby. The vast majority of postcards sell for under $20.

American Airlines System Map, sepia $8
April's Fool Day, Bernhardt Wall, Ullman #156,
    owl and skull $16
Circus Training Animals, Ringling Bros., Sarasota $8
Elves, New Year's Greeting, embossed, gilded $5
Glass car from General Motors Exhibit, N.Y.
    World's Fair $15
Halloween, E. Weaver #2399 .... $8
Hawaii, "Royal Hula-Hula Dancers" $7
Joan Crawford, MGM logo $12
Nude Woman, sitting on porch railing $6
President Franklin Roosevelt in auto at Little White
    House, Warm Springs, Ga. $25
Rudolph Valentino playing chess $20
Uncle Sam says to Kaiser, "My Hat's in the Ring" $10
Valentine's Day, Cupid, "A Token of Love" $4
James Jeffries vs. Jack Johnson, ad for heavyweight
    championship of the world, July 4, 1910,
    shows fighters, plus an inset view of a
    baseball game .... $300-$400
O'Brien's Farm Sausage, wagon advertising, 1950,
    by Dexter Press $30
Josephine Baker, real photo of her, with a
    German Shepherd .... $150-$175
Olympia Beer, "It's the Water," Olympia, Wash.,
    by E.C. Kropp Co. $50

"Real photo" postcards of train stations, like this one in East Alton, Ill., are very collectibles.

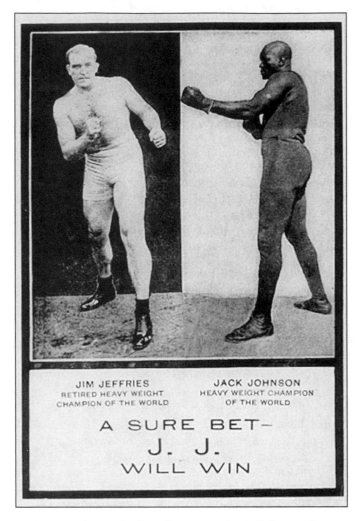

Although the majority of postcards sell for under $25, some, like this one promoting a heavyweight boxing match between Jack Johnson and Jim Jeffries, can be worth hundreds. It was offered in an auction conducted by Postcards International of Hamden, Conn.

Postcards by renowned artists, like this example by Art Nouveau artist Alphonse Mucha, can be worth hundreds. This example was offered in an auction by Postcards International of Hamden, Conn.

"Golly!! Don't I Like Chicken," black boy, rare
American woven silk, published by Lybold &
Huettner, Brooklyn...$375-$425
Hoover Vacuum, real photo, ad for the Hoover
Electric Suction Sweeper, 1909, New Berlin,
Ohio.. $65
1908 Presidential Campaign, Taft vs. Bryan, portraits,
plus text, The Patriotic Publishing Co.,
Little Rock, Ark. ....$200-$225
Charles Lindbergh, "Our Hero," real photo $75
"Keep Coolidge," 1924 presidential campaign,
black and white ....$175-$200
Easter Greetings, signed Louis Wain, published by
J. Salmon, England.. $40
Balloon Race, 1907, St. Louis, balloon is titled
"Anjou," real photo.......................................$100-$125

A Happy New Year, mountain is face of old man,
child on sled $40
Woman With Cattails, artwork by Raphael Kirchner,
scarce American issue ....$200-$225
Army soldier, WWI ad for Chesterfield cigarettes,
by Lyendecker $35
Peace Dove, by Pablo Picasso, anti-war/anti-atomic
bomb text on back, French ....$75-$100
Cow-Drawn Sleigh, North Dakota bachelor on his
way to see his girl, 1911, by Fred Olson................. $35
Cynthia, by Harrison Fisher, published in
Cosmopolitan ....$75-$100
The Cunard Liner Lusitania, real British photo,
by Davidson Bros.. $35
Saint Paul Sports Carnival, 1917, with skier, skater,
fireworks, also advertises the National Ski
Tournament ....$100-$125

Motorcycle ad, "Ride the Great New 1946 Indian Chief," linen $125

Panning Gold, 1913, gold-seeker with pan and shovel, near Dahlonega, Ga. .... $125-$150

Happy Hallowe'en, "May the witches of Hallowe'en brew for you a very happy future," by the Gibson Art Co. $30

Ambulance, Canadian Women's Motor Ambulance, four medical attendants in front, real photo .... $75-$100

Coney Island, "The Beach," by Edw. Lowey, N.Y., 1900s $35

Our Gang, the kids with pilot Dal Speer promoting General Alloys Monoplanes, 1929, Boston .... $150-$175

1933 World's Fair, futuristic-style illustration of Sky Ride, advertising Valdura paints .... $100-$125

Cincinnati Stadium, "Ball Park, National League, Cincinnati, O", 1910 .... $75-$100

Titanic, "The Largest Ship in the World. Wrecked on her maiden voyage," real photo of launch, published by Tom Harvey, Rudruth, England .... $600-$700

7th National Automobile Show, Madison Square Garden, New York, 1907, Harburg Tire Company .... $350-$400

Two Hours Catch, Kankakee River, Wheatfield, Ind., real photo .... $50-$75

Santa Advertising, for Huyler's Bonbons and Chocolates, children writing to Santa are asking for him to send some Huyler's .... $250-$300

Joe DiMaggio's Restaurant, San Francisco, with Joe, Vince and Dom DiMaggio, linen, by Curt Teich $175

Bantam 60, linen advertisement for "America's Only Economy Car," published by the American Bantam Car Co., Butler, Pa. .... $250-$300

"Washington Crisps," patriotic illustrated box of corn cereal between two dogs, real photo ..... $250-$300

Shylock, sketches from Shakespeare, the Merchant of Venice, signed Sydney Carter, published by Hildesheimer & Co., London $35

Electrical Exposition, Boston, 1909 .... $300-$350

Harley-Davidson with sidecar, U.S. flag on front handlebars .... $125-$150

Cowgirl, "Typical Scene on South Dakota Prairies," by Fish, 1908 .... $75

Ladies Orchestra, at the House of David religious colony and amusement park, Benton Harbor, Mich. .... 125-$150

Golfer, female, ad for Falstaff Bottle Beer, real photo $125

Dance Marathon, Bobby and George doing the Cuzi-Q, 864 hours .... $100-$125

Empire State Building, cross section of the world's tallest building, real photo $60

1965 New York World's Fair, plastic 3-D for the Florida Pavilion, woman water skier .... $500-$600

Settlers, "Sunday Visitors on the Claim," real photo by Leland Art Co., 1909 .... $45

Chicago Cubs 1907, real photo of the team, published by F.P. Burke .... $750-$850

RAILROAD MEMORABILIA

Railroads have been operating in the United States since the 1830s, and to collectors that translates to nearly 170 years worth of collectibles. Beginning collectors may collect all kinds of railroad items, but most choose to specialize, concentrating either on a particular type of collectible (like lanterns) or on a specific railroad (like the Milwaukee Road).

General Guidelines: The most important factors in determining the value of an item are the railroad name, condition of the item and type of item. Items from short line railroads, especially those that are defunct, are highly desirable. Nevertheless, items used by the larger railroads in their early years can also be valuable.

Another factor that affects value is the historical significance of the railroad, which was evidenced by its popularity with the artists, photographers and journalists of the time.

Condition is critical. Check closely for cracks, especially on china items. Holloware pieces should be dent-free and free of blemishes on silver plating. Both china and holloware serving pieces must have lids.

Lanterns are highly collectible and can be bent slightly, but corrosion pitting would be acceptable only on rare examples. Lanterns with cracked globes have no value. Paper items, such as passes and schedules, should be free of creases, water stains, glue, tape and other marks to command top prices.

Unlike like many other collecting categories, when it come to railroad collectibles, original packaging is rarely important. The significance of railroad artifacts is that they were actually used by railroads and represent much of our history.

The most expensive categories of railroad collectibles are locks, lanterns, china and holloware.

China & Silver Holloware

Railroad china and silver holloware have long enjoyed a premier position among railroad collectibles. The price of a piece of china depends on many factors, including the railroad, the pattern, the condition and the particular setting piece. China with chips or cracks has little value. Certain setting pieces—such as butter pats, egg cups, gravy boats and demitasse sets—are particularly desirable.

Beware of counterfeits, however. Some are crude with "over glaze" decals, but higher-quality counterfeits may be difficult to detect. Expertly-restored pieces, fraudulently sold as undamaged, can fool even experienced collectors.

Train Hardware & Fixtures

Hardware and fixtures include items used on the engine, cars and caboose. Items such as builder's plates or bells have a secondary interest for most collectors; however, almost any collector would like to have a big brass bell or an embossed step stool. Embossed markings are highly desir-able, but many train items were not marked. Beware of fake cuspidors, especially those embossed with the Union Pacific Railroad initials, full name or logo.

Station Items

Baggage tags, telegraph items and other station items are popular, but scarce. Brass baggage tags can be a challenge to collect. Many stations had their own shape. Original tags consisted of the station tag with strap and the claim tag carried by the passenger. Tags and straps are rarely found together, so collectors often seek just the brass station tags.

Station signs can be painted wood, painted steel or porcelain enameled steel. Values depend mostly on the railroad and the condition.

Lanterns

There were many manufacturers of lanterns from the 1850s to the 1960s. Lanterns made before 1880, however, are extremely rare. The glass globes and thin steel and wire tie frames were fragile, so few premium examples of old lanterns exist.

The least valuable lanterns have short globes (3-1/2 to 4-1/2 inches tall) and come from a large railroad. These were made after 1910. The most valuable lanterns have tall globes (5-3/8-to 6 inches) and come from the defunct short lines, with the railroad name embossed on both the frame and the globe.

Colored globes are more valuable than clear globes. Red is the most common color. Cast globes (with the railroad name embossed in raised letters) are considerably more valuable than etched ones. A lantern with an unmarked globe is considered a "frame," and the globe has no value except for the display.

Avoid fakes by learning about the markings on authentic globes.

Assuming the same railroad marking, the "bell bottom" and the brass top lanterns are more valuable than those with the wire bottom or the steel top. The value of a lantern is based on the railroad, the condition, type of frame, type and color of the globe and its marking, and the lantern manufacturer.

Locks

The most desirable locks are embossed examples from defunct short lines. The most favored types are the large brass lever switch or car locks, the round lever push key type, or the E. C. Simmons Hardware locks embossed "KeenKutter" on the front with the railroad name on the back. Stamped brass locks have greater value than steel locks, but the criteria for value is about the same. The name of a manufacturer who went out of business in the mid-1800s can add appreciable value to a lock.

Nearly fifty lock manufacturers have been identified on the old railroad locks. One of the favorite locks, the KeenKutter, is identified only with the jobber's name and logo. Many railroad locks were sold to the railroads through jobbers, but the jobber's name was not usually marked on the lock. E. C. Simmons was the most common. The name "E.H. Linley" (a St. Louis jobber for Wilson Bohannan locks) also appeared on locks.

Paper Items

Annual passes and timetables are the most popular and valuable. The most desirable paper items have attractive color artwork, such as scenic views. The most valuable annual passes, however, are not made of paper, but rather sterling silver and leather. Railroad playing cards must be complete decks and in their original box; frayed or creased corners reduce the value.

Contributor to this section: Frank Arnall, P.O. Box 253, Claremont, CA 91711.

Clubs

• Railroadiana Collectors Association Inc. (RCAI), 795 Aspen, Buffalo Grove, IL 60089

• Key, Lock & Lantern, P.O. Box 65, Demarest, NJ 07627

VALUE LINE

Dining Car China

Abbreviations used: TM: Top mark or logo; BS: Bottom stamp or logo; NBS: No bottom stamp or logo.

Bouillon cup and saucer, Kansas City Southern, Foxbury pattern, NBS ....$22-$25
Bread plate, Florida East Coast, seahorse pattern, NBS ....$6-$10
Cereal bowl, CM St P & P, "Traveler," BS ....$30-$35
Cereal bowl, CB & Q, "Violets and Daisies," NBS ....$20-$25
Cereal bowl, Union Pacific, "Harriman Blue," ES ....$20-$25
Cup and saucer, C&O, "Chessie," NBS.............$150-$175
Cup and saucer, Southern Pacific, "Prairie Mountain Wildflowers," BS..$70-$75
Cup, Santa Fe, "California Poppy," sometimes BS..$10-$15
Demitasse cup and saucer, D&RGW, "Prospector," NBS ....$250-$275
Demitasse cup and saucer, CM St P & P, "Traveler," BS..$140-$150
Demitasse cup and saucer, Union Pacific, "Winged Streamliner," BS..$45-$50
Demitasse cup and saucer, Missouri Pacific, "The Eagle" ....$125-$150

Dinner plate, Union Pacific, "Challenger," sometimes BS ....$30-$35
Dinner plate, Santa Fe, "Adobe" ....$70-$80
Dinner plate, Southern Pacific, "Prairie Mountain Wildflowers," BS..$60-$75
Dinner plate, Denver & Rio Grande, "Blue Adam," NBS ....$25-$30
Gravy boat, Santa Fe, "California Poppy," sometimes BS ....$150-$175
Oval platter, 8", B&O, "Centenary" ....$90-$100
State Capitals plate, Missouri Pacific, "Diesel Service" ....$275-$300

This old railroad lamp stands about 18 inches high, including the handle. It has four different colored lights (red, blue, yellow, and clear) for signaling. It is worth about $125-$150.

Railroad collectors would love this old advertising mirror for The Travelers Insurance Company of Hartford. It would probably sell in the $65-$75 range.

Dining Car Silver Holloware
Butter pat, Southern Pacific ....$25-$30
Celery plate, Rio Grande Western, BS..............$110-$125
Cereal bowl, top marked "FEC" ....$25-$30
Coffee pot, individual, CB&Q ....$65-$75
Coffee pot, individual, Illinois Central ....$200-$225
Coffee pot, individual, C&NWRY.........................$45-$50
Creamer, individual, NYNH&H RR,
   "New Haven" ....$45-$50
Creamer, Baltimore & Ohio, BS............................$45-$50
Sugar bowl, covered, D&RG RR,
   "Curecanti"...$350-$375
Sugar bowl, Missouri Pacific, top marked
   "The Eagle" ....$35-$40
Syrup pitcher, D&RG RR, "Curecanti"
   logo..$250-$275
Teapot, individual, Florida East Coast,
   "Royal Poinciana" BS FEC H Co. ....$18-$20

Dining Car Silver-Plated Flatware
Fork, "FEC" in circle ....$9-$10
Fork, Santa Fe ....$12-$15
Knife, marked "NYC" ....$10-$15
Serving spoon, marked "D&RG" ....$75-$85
Spoon, Southern Pacific ....$10-$12
Sugar tongs, marked "UPRR"................................$45-$50

Miscellaneous Dining Car Items
Napkin, C.R.I. & P..$8-$10
Napkin, Denver & Rio Grande, "Curecanti"
   logo..$125-$140
Table cloth, white, Burlington Route.....................$15-$20
Table cloth, white, Baltimore & Ohio....................$12-$15
Table cloth, white, Pullman ....$12-$15
Water glass, NYC, "20th Century Limited"...........$10-$15
Water glass, Union Pacific ....$8-$10

Railroad China Items
Ashtray/pencil holder, Missouri Pacific, 6" tall $65
Baked potato dish, Delta Line, pre-1950 ....$30
Bread plate, UP Desert Flower, 5-1/2", Syracuse,
   1962, MT...$35
Bouillon cup, SP Prairie Mountain Wildflower,
   Syracuse, NM...$50
Butter pat, ATSF, California Poppy, no marker mark,
   NM $15
Butter pat, CB&Q, Violets and Daisies, 3-3/8",
   Buffalo, NM $100
Butter pat, FEC Carolina, Sterling, 1949,
   "Florida East Coast Railway," VG $30
Candlestick holder, Wabash Meridale, 9-1/2",
   Syracuse, 1934, MT $45
Celery dish, Erie Akron, 10" long, Shenango, MT.......$35
Celery dish, NYC Vanderbilt, 10-1/2", Ohio Pottery,
   NM $50
Cereal bowl, CN Queen Elizabeth, Royal Doulton,
   7-1/2", MT..$25
Coffee cup, Mimbreno, 2-3/4", Syracuse, 1963..........$100
Compartment plate, C&O Car Ferry, 9-1/2",
   Syracuse, 1958, MT $175
Covered sugar, KCS Roxbury, 2-3/4" high,
   Syracuse, 1952, MT $20
Cup and saucer, demitasse, KCS Roxbury, Syracuse,
   1938, MT...$25
Cup and saucer, demitasse, CN Queen Elizabeth,
   Royal Doulton, MT $50
Cup and saucer, Missouri Pacific Eagle, NM $175
Cup and saucer, N&W Dogwood, Syracuse, 1956,
   NM $15
Cup and saucer, SP Prairie Mountain Wildflower,
   1945, NM $75
Dessert plate, ATSF, California Poppy, 1970s,
   MT..$15
Dessert plate, SP Prairie Mountain Wildflower,
   7-1/4", Syracuse, NM..$30
Dessert plate, UP Desert Flower, 6-1/2", Syracuse,
   1954, NM $15
Dinner plate, Adobe Econorim, 1954, Syracuse China
   9-1/2", EX $125
Dinner plate, Centenary, Harper's Ferry in food well,
   Lamberton, 1927, NM..$175
Dinner plate, SP Prairie Mountain Wildflower, 9-1/2",
   Syracuse, EX $60
Dinner plate, Wabash Meridale, 9-1/2", Syracuse,
   1954, EX $25
Double egg cup, UP Desert Flower, Syracuse, 1958,
   MT..$75
Gravy boat, D&RGW Blue Adam, 3-1/4" high............$50
Oatmeal bowl, UP Desert Flower, 6-1/4", Syracuse,
   1955, MT...$35
Plate, UP Circus Series, 8-1/4", Syracuse, 952, MT.....$90

Platter, oval, SP Sunset, 12-1/2" by 8-1/2", Syracuse, 1924, VG $225

Sauce dish, SP Prairie Mountain Wildflower, Syracuse, NM $15

Service plate, IC Pirate, VG $125

Service plate, KCS Roxbury, Syracuse, 10-1/2", 1968, NM $15

Soup plate, CN Queen Elizabeth, Royal Doulton, 9-1/2", MT $30

Railroad menus

Baltimore & Ohio Railroad George Washington Bicentennial menu, 1932, 7" x 10", VG $35

Chicago and North Western System Railroad, dining car menu, 1948, A Century of North Western Service! ....$10-$15

CP Canadian luncheon menu, A La Carte and Table 'D Hotel selections, 1961, 8-1/2" x 11", G $7

GN Empire Builder Indian lunch menu, Aug. 28, 1939, 6-1/2" x 10", NM $35

Great Lakes Transit Corporation dinner menu, 1928, 5-1/2" x 8-3/4", EX $15

Harvey House in Chicago Union Station lunch menu, 1962, 5-3/4"x11-3/4", tri-fold, EX $15

NP Breakfast menu, June 1962, 8-1/2"x11", EX $10

NP North Coast Limited Traveler's Rest, 7-1/2" x 11-1/2", 1962, VG $10

Santa Fe Dining Car Service menu, pictures Ranchos de Taos, by E.L. Blumenschein from the Santa Fe collection of famous paintings of the Southwest, 7" x 9-1/2", 1972, mint $15

Silver Meteor Railroad, dining car menu, 1948, Seaboard Railroad Air Line through the Heart of the South, Feb. 20, 1948 ....$25-$35

Train Hardware and Fixtures

Berth ladder, Pullman ....$55-$75

Box car seal, O.S.L. RR ....$2-$5

Brass locomotive bell, 18" diameter ....$600-$650

Builders plate, American Locomotive Co., 1912 ....$165-$175

Builders plate, Baldwin Locomotive Works, 1923 ....$175-$200

Builders plate, General Electric, oval shape ....$35-$50

Caboose coal stove ....$275-$300

Coal shovel, wood handle, M.P. RR ....$5-$7

Cuspidor, Pullman, nickel plated ....$85-$100

Door knobs, pair, emblem L&N ....$100-$125

Light fixture, caboose, iron ....$30-$35

Locomotive pressure gauge, 6" diameter ....$20-$25

Locomotive whistle, 16" tall, heavy brass ....$250-$275

Luggage rack, Pullman, 36" ....$80-$100

Oiler can, long spout, NYC System ....$35-$50

Smoking stand, D & RGW, brass ....$250-$275

Step stool, B&O emblem on side ....$175-$200

Ticket punch, P RR ....$15-$20

Station Items

Cast iron stove ....$250-$275

Door lock, brass, inscribed UP ....$20-$25

Fire extinguisher, RY EX AGY, wall mount ....$40-$50

Porcelain enameled sign, Railway Express Agency, 12" x 72" ....$175-$200

Steel sign, painted white on black, Western Pacific, Feather River Route, 23" x 26" ....$150-$175

Steel sign, painted steel, Naegale (Colorado), 9" x 50" ....$140-$150

Telegraph key ....$15-$20

Wall clock, Santa Fe ....$275-$300

Locks

Abbreviations: Emb: Railroad name or initials cast in raised letters; FB: Railroad name or initials embossed in large letters across the back; E: Railroad name or initials embossed in vertical panel on back; BL: Brass lever type; PT: Pin tumbler type; LPK: Lever push key type, 2-1/4" diameter.

VGN RY, FB, BL $400

N&W RY, FB, BL, Fraim $50

A&IP, E, BL $475

P RR, FB, BL $175

D&IG RR, FB, BL $1,000

Tex & Pac RY, E, BL $950

So Pacific Co., CS-44, Switch, E, BL $75

USY&T Co., E, BL $85

Union Pacific, Switch, E, BL $65

L&N RR, E, BL $110

St.J &G.I. Ry., E. BL $950

ERIE R.R., E, BL $175

Frisco, stamped, steel, Adlake $25

A.T.&S.F. Ry., stamped, steel, Adlake $7

CS&CC RR, stamped, steel, Adlake $150

NYOS RR, stamped, iron, J.A. Goeway $250

AL&S, PT, Best $25

C&A RR, stamped, BL, Union Brass $65

U.P. RR, stamped, BL, Adlake $15

CR RR, stamped, BL, H.C. Jones $275

MO. PAC. Ry., Men's Toilet Lock, LPK, emb $825

IC RR, LPK, emb $85

N&W Ry, LPK, emb $165

A.T. & S.F., stamped, RACO $7

S.P. Co., stamped, steel, Fraim $12

New Jersey Central, stamped, PT, Corbin $35

C&O, emb, PT, Yale $25

Paper items

Annual pass, Denver & Rio Grande, 1892 ....$200

Annual pass, Denver & Rio Grande Western, 1932 ....$30

Annual pass, Southern Pacific, 1947 ....$8

Annual pass, Baltimore & Ohio, 1952 ....$5

Annual pass, New York Central, 1938 ....$14

Annual pass, Illinois Central, 1928 ....$12

Annual pass, A.T.&S.F., 1894 ....$75

Annual pass, Pennsylvania Railroad, 1949 ....$3-$5

Annual pass, Atlanta & West Point Railroad,
1931 ....$8-$10
Folding picture book, Santa Fe, California, 1931 ....$25
Map of system, large, Missouri Pacific.....................$40
Map of system, large, Southern Pacific......................$45
Matchbooks, most railroads $3
Playing cards, Amtrak...$5
Playing cards, Western Pacific $12
Playing cards, Rio Grande with logo $27
Playing cards, D&RG, multiple scenes.....................$40
Playing cards, Southern Pacific, Sunset logo,
    multiple scenes $25
Playing cards, Florida East Coast, multiple scenes.......$30
Rules book, O.R. & N. Co., 1912 ....$20
Stock certificate, Erie Railroad, 1955 ....$15
Stock certificate, Chicago, Rock Island & Pacific,
    recent $3
Timetable, Northern Pacific, 1883, ornate $250
Timetable, St. Louis & San Francisco, Frisco $3
Timetable, Rio Grande, 1961, Moffat Tunnel Route $4
Timetable, D&RG, 1887, Curecanti logo $100
Timetable, B&O, 1957..$4
Timetable, Burlington Route, 1956...............................$3
Timetable, Washington Sunset Route, 1915 ....$30
Timetable, NYC, 1935 ....$15
Wells Fargo receipt, 1890 ....$40

Miscellaneous

Adjustable wrench, 18", SP Co.................................$25
Badge, SP RR Railroad Police...................................$200
Badge, UP RR Police $250
Badge, Patrolman, Reading Railway Co.....................$150
Baggage sticker, Santa Fe logo $5
Brakeman's hat and badge,
    New York Central System......................................$150
Brakeman's hat and badge, NYC RR $100
Brass baggage tag, P RR Co, one part $20
Brass baggage tags, A.T.&S.F. RR, two parts,
    station and claim $100
Brass baggage tag, Sierra Ry. Co. of Cal,
    one part...$175
Cap badge, PORTER $25
Cap badge, TRAINMAN, Erie (RR) $100
Cigar box, Burlington Route......................................$50
Cigarette lighter, Great Northern, 1950s......................$45
Cold chisel, 8" B&O RR..$5
Conductor badge, Conrail $75
First aid box, CN RR $17
Gold keystone pin, P RR...$25
Label pin, ACL logo $15
Man's tie, D&RG $30
Paperweight, PC RR, white metal................................$7
Paperweight, U.P. RR shield design, brass $25
Pencil, Railway Express Agency $2
Smoking stand, D.& R.G.W., brass,
    bottom marked $350

Ticket punch, 1930s $22
Tie bar, A.T.&S.F. $5
Watch fob, Iowa Route-Burlington $150
Wool blanket, Union Pacific logo $250

Badges

AMTRAK attendant silver hat badge $20
AMTRAK trainman gold hat badge $22
Australian Station assistant hat badge with number $30
BCE Railway Co., motorman badge, red with white
    letters, #1725, missing back pin $35
British Columbia police, set of two hat badges $115
Canadian Northern breast badge..................................$15
Canadian Northern conductor hat badge,
    gold with black lettering $60
Canadian Northern lapel pin, silver with
    black lettering..$10
Canadian Northern police hat badge, gold trim
    with cobalt blue inlay $50
Canadian Pacific police hat badge, old, copper shield
    with beaver on top $100
Canadian Pacific brass shoulder badge,
    worn by CPR police $20
Canadian Pacific hat badge $15
Canadian Pacific Hotels waiter breast badge,
    silver and blue, with number $30
LIRR trainman hat badge...$30
NYNH & NRR trainman hat badge $55
Sleeping car porter badge, silver with
    black lettering..$20

Railroad Books

*The American Heritage History of Railroads
    in America*, Oliver Jensen, 1975, VG.....................$30
The American West, Lucius Beebe and Charles Clegg,
    Bonanza Books, 1955, dust jacket, MT $20
*A Century of Reading Company Motive Power,
    Reading Lines 1852-1941*, softcover,
    by the Reading Railroad Co. ....$15-$20
*The Crookedest Railroad in the World: A History
    of the Mt. Tamalpais and Muir Woods Railroad
    of California*, Wurm and Graves, Howell-North,
    1960 2nd ed., 123 pages, hardcover,
    dust jacket, EX $25
The Electric Railway in Theory and Practice,
    Oscar T. Crosby and Louis Bell, W.J. Johnson Co.,
    1893, 2nd ed., 416 pages, hardcover, VG $25
Elements of Railroad Engineering—1923, by
    William G. Raymond, published by John Wiley &
    Sons, N.Y., 453 pages..................................$20-$25
*General Motors Engine Maintenance Manual Model
    567B Locomotive Engine*, 3rd ed., 1,211 pages,
    softcover ed., EX $30
High Iron: A Book of Trains, Lucius Beebe,
    Bonanza Books, 1938, 225 pages, hardcover,
    dust jacket, EX $20

Mansions on Rails, Lucius Beebe, 1959, hardcover,
382 pages, dust jacket, VG...................................... $85

*Pacific Slope Railroads—Steam on Rails, Mexico to
Canada,* George B. Abdill, Bonanza Books, 1959,
182 pages, hardcover, dust jacket, EX $20

Rails West, George B. Abdill, 1960, hardcover,
191 pages, VG... $35

*Redwood Railways: A History of the Northwestern
Pacific Railroad and Predecessor Lines,*
Gilbert H. Kneiss, 1956, Howell-North, fourth
printing, 1960, 165 pages, hardcover, dust jacket,
EX $25

Trains in Transition, Lucius Beebe, Bonanza Books,
1941, 210 pages, hardcover, dust jacket, EX $20

The Twilight of Steam Locomotives, Ron Ziel, 1963,
hardcover, dust jacket, 208 pages, dust jacket,
VG $35

Railroad Ephemera

Ad, Santa Fe Railroad, original, 1955 issue of
Holiday Magazine ....$5-$7.50

Booklet, B&O Century of Progress, Chicago World's
Fair, 24 pages, 1934, NM.. $25

Booklet, Grand Trunk Railway System, Oct. 13, 1904,
59 pages, VG $50

Brochure, Pullman 1939, World's Fair Exhibit,
Art Deco, 19 pages, 1939, VG $20

Brochure, SP/CRI&P Golden State Limited,
12 pages, 1931, VG... $10

Calendar, 1937 Pennsylvania Railroad, EX, framed,
28" x 28" ....$250-$275

Check, Michigan, Indiana & Illinois Line RR,
Aug. 21, 1909... $5

Check, National Car Line Co., Aug. 8, 1912................. $4

Check, National Transportation & Terminal Co.,
March 10, 1913 .... $4

Check, Minneapolis & St. Louis Railroad Co.,
Feb. 10, 1913 .... $5

Investigation report, The Bussey Bridge
Train Disaster, March 14, 1887................................ $40

Rule book, New York Central System,
Instructions for Operators (Signalmen),
April 28, 1957, 32 pages ....$2-$4

Rule book, Erie Railroad Rules of the Operating
Department, Nov. 30, 1952, 140 pages,
hardcover...$10-$15

Schedule, The Chicago and NorthWestern Railway,
The Short Line to Chicago and all points East,
fold-out, 52 panels, Oct. 1, 1885, VG $60

Time schedule, LTR&T Tahoe Tavern, Lake Tahoe CA,
ca. 1900-10, eight pages, VG $8

Tourist brochure, ATSF Santa Fe Off the
Beaten Path in New Mexico and Arizona,
31 pages, 1925, 8" x 9", VG..................................... $20

Tourist brochure, CB&Q Burlington Escorted Tours,
44 pages, 1926, 6" x 9", EX $15

*Through the American Rockies
on the Northern Pacific*

NORTHERN PACIFIC

28 Ranges of Mountains
Seen from Northern
Pacific Main Line Trains

This 8-by-11-inch, four-part foldout was an advertising brochure from the Northern Pacific Railroad. It is valued at $15-$25.

Tourist brochure, CB&Q From Wagon Wheel to
Stainless Steel, 20 pages, 1947, 8" x 9", VG $8

Tourist brochure, C&NW Summer Tours under
Escort, Dept. of Tours, 56 pages, 1931, EX $20

Tourist brochure, CRI&P Rock Island: Colorado
under the Turquoise Sky, 32 pages, 1924, EX $15

Tourist brochure, DL&W Lackawanna Railroad:
Mountain and Lake Resorts, 111 pages, 1909,
6-1/2" x 9-1/4", EX $85

Tourist brochure, MILW Yellowstone via Gallatin
Gateway, MT, 26 pages, 1953, 8" x 9", VG $14

Tourist brochure, NP Burlington Escourted Tours,
11 pages, 1941, 8" x 9", MT $7

Tourist brochure, UP/C&NW The Challenger, tri-fold,
24" x 9", ca. late 1930s/early 1940s, MT $15

Railroad Lanterns

Adams & Westlake, S.P.CO lantern, wire ring bottom,
single guard around globe, Adlake Kero
4-43 ....$45-$60

B&O Railroad lantern, red, Adams & Westlake Co.,
Adlake Kero # 4-32.......................................$150-$175

Canadian Northern H.L. Piper, bamboo wood handle,
minor rust, short red globe, dated 1/44 .... $50

Canadian Northern H.L. Piper, small dent on dome,
short clear globe, dated 1/56 .... $40

Canadian Northern H.L. Piper, small dent on dome,
etched CNR, clear globe, dated 4/51 .... $45

Canadian Northern caboose marker lamp, H.L. Piper,
complete, G $175

CPRY E.T. Wright, tall globe lantern, cast CPR clear
globe, chromed $150

Canadian Northern wall lamp, CNR embossed on pot,
two-piece wall mount $175

D&H Railroad lantern, Handlan, red, acid etched
D&H on clear glass globe .... $50-$75

Indiana Harbour Belt RR lantern, Adlake Kero type,
clean globe, pot and burner .... $45-$55

GNRY Armspear, 1925, short red globe $60

L&N RR lantern, orange amber globe, 1925,
missing entire burner assembly .... $150-$200

NYCS railroad lantern, Dressel marked NYCS,
cobalt blue globe .... $175-$225

Penn System RR Tail Tall globe lantern, red cast
globe, PS in logo, Adlake Reliable type,
pot and burner .... $50-$75

Pennsylvania Lines railroad lantern, Adlake Reliable,
1908-13 .... $100-$125

Soo Line RR lantern, yellow globe .... $7-$100

Union Pacific RR switch lamp, Adlake,
two green/two lenses, MT $200

Cobalt blue Adlake railroad signal lantern,
VG condition .... $45-$60

Railroad Lapel Pins

Amalgamated Transit Union $8

B of RT, 10 or 20 years, each $15

B of RT, 25 or 30 years, each $20

British Columbia, CROR Training $7

British Columbia Ski Team $10

British Columbia Telecommunications $10

B&O Railroad 10-year service pin,
Service/Welfare .... $45-$50

Canadian Association of Train Dispatchers,
5, 10, 15 or 20 years, each $10

Canadian Northern, Expo 86 IMAX logo $10

Canadian Northern, Super Train $10

Canadian Pacific, Alberta Division $7

Canadian Pacific, award pin $8

Canadian Pacific, 100 years $8

Canadian Pacific, Rogers Pass Project $10

Canadian Pacific, Vancouver Division, 1994 .... $7

Canadian Pacific, 3/4" tall pin, CPR beaver and
shield logo .... $3-$4

Quebec North Shore, safety award $15

Southern British Columbia, CROR, 1990 .... $10

Southern British Columbia, 1-Year No Injury $12

UTU, 40 years $12

Railroad Miscellaneous

Ashtray, Wilmington and Western Railroad,
enamel .... $7-$10

Clock, Canadian Northern, black metal casing,
battery-operated, CN logo on face $65

Coat hanger, Canadian Northern $10

Conductor's step stool, New York Central Railroad,
metal .... $100-$125

Conductor's uniform, pants, suspenders, vest, jacket,
hat, B&O emblems .... $125-$175

First aid kit, Pennsylvania Railroad,
PRR marked contents, tin .... $35-$50

First aid kit, Canadian Northern, metal, new $30

Lunch box, Canadian Pacific Railroad, 1970,
Ohio Arts .... $45-$55

Matches, British Columbia, pack of four $5

Matches, Frisco, 25 packages in a box car $15

Matches, Rock Island, pack of six $4

Matches, Union Pacific, pack of six $4

Membership pin, Brotherhood of Railroad Trainmen,
10-year pin, 1/2" diameter, 10K gold-filled,
EX $10

Mug, decorative, steam engine, stamped Bavaria
Schumann Arzberg, Germany .... $10-$12

Playing cards, L & N Railroad Centennial 1850-1950,
complete, includes 2 jokers, from Mobile .... $35-$50

Portable telephone for caboose, gray metal case,
7" x 5" x 9-1/2" $50

Railroad crossing lights, four lights on the set,
two posted in opposite directions from the
others .... $200-$250

Step stool, Canadian Pacific, aluminum, G $200

Telegraph insulator, white ceramic, "CPR" on dome,
minor chips $5

Telegraph insulator, beehive shape, "Canadian Pacific
Rly. Co." embossed on bottom $5

Torch, B&O, 9-1/2" fabricated from sheet metal,
marked "B&O RR" on bottom $65

Torch, PRR, 9" cast iron, marked "PRR Dayton
Malleable Iron Co. 189" on side $65

Uniform buttons, each $3

Watering can, marked PRR, 12" x 10" $50

Railroad Postcards

Alford Station, train leaving for Montrose, PA,
Herald Post, used, #739, VG $5

Baltimore and Ohio Building, Baltimore #657, MT $5

B&O Depot, Youngstown, Ohio, 1910,
SH Knox & Co., A2910 .... $6-$8

Broad Street Station, Pennsylvania RR, Philadelphia,
used, #736, EX $3

Buffalo, Rochester and Pittsburgh Depot, Rochester,
NY, GB&S, used, #T971, EX $10

CPR Depot and Mount Rundle, real photo,
hand-colored, #33, MT $5

CPR Station, Durham, Ontario, used, #549, VG $4

CRI&P Passenger Station, Davenport, IA,
Rock Island Post Card Co., #618, NM $7

Dickinson House and NYC Station, Corning, NY,
Curetich, #432, EX $6

Donner Pass Railroad Snowsheds on U.S. Highway 40,
Norden CA, Frashers Photos, NM $2

East 26th Street Car overturned at 18th and Frank,
Aug. 3rd, 1915, Erie, PA, used, #400, NM $15

Electric Engine and Power House of Detroit River
Tunnel, Detroit, #743, MT $10

Electric Locomotive in Underground Tunnel, Chicago,
VO Hammon, #494, NM $5

Electric Train Arriving at Venice, CA,
Ed. H. Mitchell, used, #259 .... $7

Erie Depot, Elmira, NY, Rubin Bros., #427, NM $7

General View of the Bridge at Nicholson, PA,
A. Campbell, real photo, used, #742, NM $10

High Bridge, Georgetown Loop, mountains,
trains and trestle, embossed, #717, NM $6

Illinois Central Depot, Chicago, VO Hammon,
#131, EX $4

Lackawanna's new passenger station, Hallstead, PA,
used, #740, G $3

New Lackawanna Station, Scranton, PA,
used, #735, VG $5

New Santa Fe Depot, Colorado Springs, CO, HHT,
unused, #612, VG $6

New York Central Station, Utica, NY, Curteich,
#443, EX $6

Olympian descending eastern slope of the Rockies,
Curteich, #313, MT $8

Oriental Limited, Great Northern RR,
Scenic Hot Springs, WA, used, #710, NM $8

O.S.L. R.R. Depot, Pocatello, Idaho .... $8-$10

Railroad Station, NYNH&HRR Co., Brockton, MA,
printed in Germany, used, #315, NM $4

Rock Island Depot, Topeka, KS, #196, MT $5

Santa Fe Roundhouse, Albuquerque, NM, #570,
EX $4

Scene on Youngstown/Southern Electric Line,
Youngstown, OH, AC Besselman, used, #661,
EX $3

Southern Pacific Company Compound Malet Engine,
Souvenir Publishing, #704, MT $10

Sunset Express at Yuma, AZ, Souvenir Publishing,
#621, NM $7

Tarrucca Viaduct at Susquehanna, PA, Baker Bros.,
#741, EX $5

Tunnel in Cow Creek Canyon, Shasta Route,
Southern Pacific RR, HHT, unused, #25, EX............ $3

Union Depot, Grand Junction, Colo., used, #545,
VG $4

Union Depot, 3rd and Douglas, Sioux City, IA,
Hornick Hess & More, #452, EX........................... $5

Union Station, Pennsylvania RR, Baltimore, #725,
EX $3

Union Station, Salt Lake City, #448, EX $6

U.S. Naval Academy, Washington, Baltimore and Annap-
olis Electric Railroad Co., #701, EX...................... $4

Railroad Stocks

Beech Creek RR, steam engine................................. $10

B&O Railroad cancelled stock certificate, mid to late
1950s, very early train pulling a freight car,
two open air passenger carriages........................ $6-$10

Boston and Albany Railroad Co., Indian between
city pictures, 1950s $12

Bush Terminal Co., seated allegorical female.............. $10

Canada Southern, smoking funnel train
leaving station $12

Central of Georgia, man with hammer $10

Chesapeake & Ohio, C&O logo with two men $12

Chesapeake & Ohio Railway Co., oncoming
steam engine, 1905, vertical............................... $45

Chesapeake & Ohio Railway Co., man on horseback
watching train, 1906, vertical............................. $35

City Railway, Dayton, electric trolley with
19th century passengers $35

Erie-Lackawanna RR, man, woman and
company logo $7

Hudson and Manhattan Railroad Co., train going
through tunnel $12

Lionel, orange/blue, small boy playing
with two toy trains... $80

Missouri Pacific two men flanking train, oil well $7

Missouri, Kansas, and Texas Railroad Company,
vignette of a steam locomotive coming out of a roundhouse .... $9-$10

Mohawk and Malone Railway Co., green horizontal format bond, buck with antlers, 1960s....................... $15

New York Central bond, vignette of engine 3404
pulling passenger train $22

New York, Chicago and St. Louis Railroad Co.,
male and female flanking famous logo, 1950s........... $8

Norfolk & Western, no vignette, fancy green border,
beige background, 1880s.................................... $35

Pennsylvania RR, state seal with two horses,
orange/green.. $6

Pennsylvania RR, picture of train in famous
horseshoe curve.. $8

Philadelphia Traction Co., horse drawn carriage and
streetcars... $12

Pittsburgh & Lake Erie Railroad Co., train, ship
and city scene, 1950s $7

Pittsburgh, Youngstown and Ashtabula Railway Co.,
man on horseback watching train, 1970s $12

Reading Co., Monopoly stock, train with two
allegorical females $8

Seatrain Lines, man with navigational instruments and
globe.. $7

Southern Railway, two men flanking an industrial
    scene $10
St. Louis-San Francisco Railway, man in front of
    city scene, vertical $15
Union Pacific Corp., vignette of three men $7
Ware River RR, oval picture of a man $25
West Shore RR, river scene, ships, train $20
Western Maryland Railway, Mercury in front of
    diesel loco $7
Western Maryland Railway, uncommon issue,
    steam train in station $40

Railroad switch keys

Atchison, Topeka, Santa Fe, brass railroad key ..... $15-$20
Baltimore & Ohio RR Co., pocket wear,
    F.S. Hardware $15
Belt RR of Chicago Route, light pocket wear $16
British Columbia Railway, Adlake $14
Burlington Northern, pocket wear, Adlake $11
Burlington Route, pocket wear, Adlake $16
Canadian National, embossed marks, R.M. Co. $12
Canadian National brass railroad key .... $10-$13
Canadian National, steel key .... $10-$12
Canadian Pacific, embossed marks, R.M. Co. $12
Canadian Pacific switch keys, CPR .... $12-$15
Chesapeake & Ohio, pocket wear $13
Chicago & NorthWestern, light pocket wear,
    Adlake $16
Chicago Rock Island & Pacific, pocket wear,
    Adlake $16

Dining car china is very popular with railroad collectors. This berry dish from the Union Pacific is worth about $15-$30.

Cleveland, Cincinnati & St. Louis, pocket wear $18
Denver & Rio Grande, light pocket wear, Adlake $19
Duluth Missabee & Iron Range, light pocket wear,
    Adlake $18
Grand Trunk Railroad brass key .... $20-$25
Grand Trunk Western, pocket wear $18
Gulf Mobile & Ohio, near new $16
Illinois Central Gulf, crinkle, Adlake $13
Indiana Harbor Belt, pocket wear $16
International Great Northern, pocket wear $22
Kansas City Southern, Adlake, near new $16
Louisville & Nashville, small key, pocket wear $14
Missouri Pacific, near new $12
New York Central, pocket wear $14
Pacific Great Eastern, pocket wear, Adlake $36
Penn Central, pocket wear, Adlake $16
Southern Pacific, pocket wear, Adlake $16
St. Louis & San Francisco, pocket wear, Adlake $14
Western Pacific, pocket wear, Adlake $22

Railroad Timetables

Atlantic Coast Line, 1960 .... $7
ATSF Santa Fe Railway, Aug. 5, 1945, 64 pages,
    VG $8
ATSF Santa Fe Railway, Feb. 29, 1948, six pages,
    wallet-size, NM $6
Burlington Route, 1964 .... $8
C&O Passenger Train, Michigan Lines, April 26,
    1964, six pages, NM $7
Colorado and Southern Railroad, Feb. 20, 1938,
    12 pages, MT $18
CRI&P Rock Island, July 27, 1930, 20 pages, EX $20
Delaware and Hudson, Dec. 7, 1947, 10 pages,
    NM $14
DRG Rio Grande, April 16, 1961, 6-page double
    fold-out, NM $5
Erie Railroad System, May 20, 1943, 20 pages,
    NM $12
Grand Funk Railway System, May 1, 1906,
    24 pages, F $17
Gulf Mobile and Ohio Railroad, Jan. 2, 1941,
    28 pages .... $50-$75
Illinois Central, October-December 1942, 36 pages,
    EX $12
Illinois Central, 1964 .... $7
Illinois Terminal, April 26, 1953, 6-page fold-out,
    EX $10
Milwaukee Road, June 6, 1948, 44 pages, NM $8
New York Central, Jan. 16, 1921, F $7
New York Central, Sept. 24, 1944, accordion fold,
    EX $5
New York Central West Shore, Sept. 21, 1909,
    folds to 9-1/4" x 31", G $20
Northern Pacific Railway Company, June 1, 1967,
    eight pages, EX $4
Pennsylvania Railroad, Nov. 5, 1944, 16 pages, EX $6

PRR No. 13, Eastern Region Philadelphia Terminal Division, April 27, 1947, employees only .... $5-$7

Reading Railway System, 1947, 12 pages, NM............. $6

Rock Island, 1962 .... $10

SCL, 1969 .... $8

Seaboard Air Line Railroad, June 15, 1950, 24 pages, EX $12

Seaboard, 1955.. $10

SL&SF Frisco Lines, October 1944, 28 pages, G........ $10

Southern Pacific, March-April 1941, 56 pages, EX...... $12

Southern Pacific, 1955 .... $14

Southern Railway, 1964 .... $7

Southern Railway System, the Crescent line, 1952, in Good condition.. $25-$30

Union Pacific, 1966.. $8

Western Pacific, California Zephyr, Sept. 27, 1953, eight pages, EX $7

Western Pacific, California Zephyr, 1962 .... $12

Railroad Watches

American Waltham Watch Co., 18S, 15J, ca. 1917 .... $125-$150

American Watch Co., 18S, ca. 1867 .... $250-$275

Ball Hamilton, 16S, 21J, Model 333, ca. .... $450-$475

Ball Hamilton, 16S, 21J, ca. 1929 .... $475-$500

Elgin, 16S, 15J Hunter Case, 1904 .... $225-$250

Elgin, 16S, 17J Hunter Case, ca. 1916............... $325-$350

Hamilton, 16S, 23J, model 950, ca. 1940s......... $750-$775

Hamilton, 16S, 21J, model 992, ca. 1907 .... $225-$250

Hamilton, 16S, 21J, model, 992B, ca. 1950s... $425-$450

Hampden, 18S, 17J, Special Railway, ca. 1897 .... $200-$225

Illinois, 16S, 21J, Bunn Special Model 14, 1916.. $375-$400

Illinois, 16S, 21J, Bunn Special, 1924 .... $350-$375

Illinois, 16S, 23J, Bunn Special 163, ca. 1930 .... $1,200-$1,300

Illinois, 16S, 21J, Bunn Special 161A Ytype IIB, 1,700 made, ca. 1932 .... $900-$950

Illinois, 16S, 21J, Elvinar Type IIE, 4,234 made, ca. 1932 .... $1,100-$1,200

Illinois, 16S, 21J, Burlington, 1920 .... $300-$325

Illinois, 16S, 21J, Burlington, 1923 .... $300-$325

Illinois, 16S, 19J, Roosevelt, ca. 1923 .... $175-$200

Illinois, 16S, 23J, Sangamo, ca. 1902 .... $550-$575

Illinois, 16S, 21J, Sangamo Getty Model 5, 1901.. $625-$650

Illinois, 16S, 23J, Sangamo, 1910..................... $800-$825

Illinois, 16S, 23J, Sangamo Special Model 10, 3,400 made, ca. 1920 .... $800-$825

Illinois, 18S, 15J, C. Wheaton Keywind, ca. 1882 .... $250-$275

South Bend, 16S, 19J, Model 219, 1916 .... $350-$375

South Bend, 16S, 17S, Model 223, 1910........ $950-$1,000

South Bend, 16S, 21J Model 227, ca. 1927 .... $250-$275

Waltham Keywind, 18S, 11J, Wm. Ellery Model, ca. 1883 .... $250-$275

RECORDS

The total dominance of cassette tapes and compact discs in recent years has made phonograph records virtually obsolete. But many old records are still very collectible, and some have significant value. If you know what to look for, there are plenty of collectible 45s and albums just waiting to be discovered at neighborhood garage sales and local flea markets.

Background: The earliest records, known as 78s, were either 10 inches or 12 inches in diameter. In the late 1940s, the 33-1/3 rpm and 45 rpm records were introduced.

The success and popularity of Elvis Presley and The Beatles spawned a great interest in record collecting. With the advent of the compact disc (CD) in 1983, the record's days as the pre-eminent format for music were numbered. A few new titles are still issued on vinyl, and many of these could become hot collectibles because they are manufactured in very small quantities.

General Guidelines: Condition is everything! The better a record plays and looks, the more it is worth. A nearly perfect record, with no visible signs of wear, will typically sell for five to ten times the price of an average record.

To command top value, record albums should include any inserts that came with them. Singles (45s and 78s) should be protected by a sleeve.

No record is completely worthless unless it can no longer be played. Many collectors will accept less-than-perfect copies of records—especially rare or scarce records—but such examples will not bring top dollar.

FUTURE TREASURES?

Colorful album covers (along with 45 rpm picture sleeves) are seeing a surge in popularity—primarily for display purposes—with people seeking covers in the best possible condition. In fact, some collectors are now seeking vintage album covers as objects of art—similar to old movie posters—to decorate their offices or game rooms. For these collectors, who don't intend to ever actually play the records, the condition of the vinyl record (or even the presence of the record) is secondary. The condition of the cover, of course, is critical. Expecting this trend to continue, some savvy collectors are already searching flea markets and yard sales for nice record album covers (if they are cheap enough), regardless of the condition of the record inside, or even if there is a record inside. The best albums for this purpose are colorful covers displaying nice photos of popular artists, albums displaying colorful psychedelic graphics, and soundtracks of popular movies. The better the graphics, the more desirable the cover.

Surprisingly, as a general rule, the less popular a record was, the more valuable it will be. Although this seems contrary to conventional logic it makes sense in terms of supply and demand. Big hits—like Buddy' Holly's "Peggy Sue"—sold in the millions and many have survived; but a lesser-known record, like Holly's "Blue Days, Black Nights" was produced in far fewer numbers. Today, a serious Buddy Holly fan might pay as much as $200 or $300 for a nice example of "Blue Days, Black Nights," while a copy of "Peggy Sue" might bring $25 or $30. When scouring record bins at yard sales and flea markets, it might be better to snap up unfamiliar songs and artists rather then grab the monster hits.

This is especially true when it comes to rhythm and blues artists and doo-wop groups from the 1950s and early 1960s. The following groups—The Hornets, The Prisonaires, The Larks, the Nu-Tones, The Windsors, The Hide-A-Ways, The Celtics, The Mello-Moods, the Belltones and others—all have records worth $3,000 or more, but most people have never heard of them. There are countless examples of other little-known artists whose records are also incredibly valuable to serious collectors. If you spot an unfamiliar record from the Fifties or early Sixties that, by the title, label or artist, appears to be an early R&B or doo-wop record, you might want to take a chance on it, assuming it's not too pricey.

Here are some other general guidelines in various categories of record collecting:

78 rpm records: Although they are the oldest form of commercial records, the majority of 78s are not in great demand and are less valuable than most people might think. Some categories of 78s are collectible, though, including early Country and Western, blues, jazz and early rock and roll. The most collectible artists are blues stars of the 1920s and 1930s; early Gene Autry and Hank Williams; Louis Armstrong and other pre-swing band leaders; Charlie Parker, Miles Davis and other post-World War II jazz greats; Elvis Presley; and almost any rock-and-roll 78 made after 1957. In the late 1950s, it was standard procedure for major rock artists, like Elvis, Chuck Berry, Rick Nelson, etc. to issue the same records on both 78 and 45 rpm versions. Virtually every early rock record in the 78 rpm format is collectible, even though very few are ever played. The vast majority of 78s, however, bring only a few dollars or less.

45 rpm records: The 7-inch 45 rpm single—the small record with the big hole—was introduced in 1949. Many are very collectible today, but condition is critical. Condition is especially important when it comes to very popular records. Elvis Presley's "Hound Dog," for example, sold millions of copies, and most were played to death. Well-worn copies of "Hound Dog" are relatively common today, but an original Mint copy would be a true rarity.

Picture sleeves, featuring a photo of the artist, at least double the value of the record, and often will increase it many times. Picture sleeves even without the record are collectible and are often more valuable than the vinyl. This is because picture sleeves were often discarded or damaged and comparatively few survived.

Promotional 45s, given to radio stations, are always worth at least as much as their regular counterparts and are usually worth more.

Many early RCA Victor records featuring colored wax are especially collectible.

In general, the most valuable 45s fall into the following categories:

Near Mint and Mint examples of hit singles, especially from the 1950s and 1960s.

Original small-label recordings of songs that later became hits on major national labels. For example, the Beach Boys' first record, "Surfin," was originally issued on the tiny California "X" label. After it started selling, the record was reissued on the Capitol label, where it became a national hit. A Near Mint copy of "Surfin" on the "X" label is one of the true treasures of the record collecting hobby today and would bring as much as $1,000. A copy of "Surfin" on the Capitol label, meanwhile, is worth $5-$15, depending on condition. (Similar scenarios took place for dozens of other hit songs during the 1950s-60s rock era.)

Hit songs by obscure artists or one-hit wonders in top condition.

Obscure recordings and lesser-known songs by major artists.

Classical records: Look for classical recordings on the RCA Red Seal Living Stereo and Mercury Living Presence labels, both made from about 1958-62. Condition is even more important with classical records than with most other forms of music.

Country & Western: For two years in the early 1990s, both BMG Music and Columbia House, the two major record clubs, made *vinyl records* of albums that were otherwise available to the general public on just compact discs and cassettes. Most of these records were done in pressings of 5,000 or fewer—extremely limited numbers in a hobby this large—and most of these were country titles. As these become better known to collectors, their value should increase. Among those artists otherwise unavailable on LP records are Billy Ray Cyrus, Wynonna Judd (as a solo artist) and Trisha Yearwood.

Doo-Wop: Many doo-wop records (vocal groups of the 1950s) are nearly impossible to find in general circulation. The lesser-known the record, the more valuable it is.

Jazz: Small label 78 rpms from the 1920s and 1930s are particularly desirable, especially artists such as King Oliver, and the New Orleans Rhythm Kings. Original pressings of per-formances by the acknowledged legends—Charlie Parker, Miles Davis, Glenn Miller, John Coltrane—are highly sought-after. Also in demand are 1950s multi-record collections.

Novelty/Comedy: The most important records in this category are "break-in" records, a simulated interview in which the answers are excerpts from current hit songs. Examples by Buchanan and Goodman, who invented break-in records in 1956, are the most sought-after, along with Dickie Goodman as a solo act. Other collectible novelty records are those relating to fads, TV shows, politics, or particular artists (such as Elvis and The Beatles). Also collectible are albums by stand-up comedians. Among the most collectible in this field are Bob Newhart, Bill Cosby, George Carlin and Redd Foxx. Novelty songs, like the Chipmunks, Monster Mash, etc. also have a following.

Children's records: Most generic children's albums not considered collectible, unless they have a celebrity tie-in, such as Disney, Howdy Doody, etc. Collectors of Disney memorabilia, for example, highly value Disney records (and their colorful picture sleeves).

The Beatles and Elvis: Anything by the Beatles as a band is collectible; but values vary greatly. Especially collect-ible are mono copies of *Sgt. Pepper's Lonely Hearts Club Band* and *Magical Mystery Tour*; 45 rpm picture sleeves; and late-1960s pressings of Capitol albums with a lime-green label. In general, for the Beatles as solo artists, the less popu-lar something was, the more valuable it is.

Any record by Elvis Presley is collectible. Tribute records that came out after Presley's death are collected as well. While anything by Elvis is collectible, it is not necessarily valuable. The more unusual an item is, the more valuable it is. The most sought-after Elvis items are his first five records, released on the Sun label. Common Elvis 45s and albums are inexpensive and not likely to increase much in value, unless they are in Near Mint condition. Most of Presley's records, however, saw lots of use and are nearly impossible to find in prime condition, especially those from the 1950s.

Elvis collectibles with enduring value include 45 rpm picture sleeves; photos that were enclosed with original 1960s albums; any promotional items; and mono versions of Pres-ley's late 1960s albums, which were produced in fewer quan-tities than their stereo counterparts.

(Note: Elvis and The Beatles each have their own chapters.)

Rock and Pop: Aside from The Beatles and Elvis, the most collectible rock is by performers from the 1960s British Invasion, such as The Rolling Stones, the Animals, the Who, the Yardbirds, etc. Among American performers with collect-ing potential are Bob Dylan, The Lovin' Spoonful, and The Mamas and the Papas.

Other commonly-collected rock is the pop/garage mate-rial of the period, such as Paul Revere and the Raiders; late 1960s album rock, such as Jimi Hendrix, The Doors, Love, Cream and Buffalo Springfield; 1970s classic rock, such as Jethro Tull, Pink Floyd and David Bowie; and heavy metal, including Black Sabbath, KISS, Motley Crue and Metallica.

Also eagerly sought are early singles by seminal rockers like Chuck Berry, the Everly Brothers, Little Richard, Buddy Holly, Ricky Nelson, etc; girl groups, such as the Shirelles, the Crystals and the Ronettes; teen idols such as Paul Anka, Frankie Avalon and Fabian; surf music including The Beach Boys; and other popular early 1960s performers such as Chubby Checker, Roy Orbison, Dion, The Four Seasons, etc. Virtually every artist enshrined in the Rock and Roll Hall of Fame would be considered collectible.

Any record with the involvement of Phil Spector or Brian Wilson—as performer, writer or producer—is highly sought after.

Since popular music was primarily a singles medium until the late 1960s, albums by rock artists released during their heyday are among the most collectible of all records. This is especially true of records in true stereo.

Alternative Rock: Early records on local labels by "alternative" artists who later became famous—such as R.E.M., Nirvana and Soundgarden—have the most potential as collectibles.

Soul and Rhythm & Blues: Blues 78s are among the rarest and most sought after. Robert Johnson 78s routinely sell for hundreds of dollars, and into four figures for discs in better shape. Early 1950s 45s by blues and R&B artists also are hard to find in any condition. Easily, the most collectible soul records are those recorded by Motown Records, including artists like The Supremes, Temptations, Miracles, Marvin Gaye and Stevie Wonder.

In many cases, soul records are more sought-after overseas than in the United States. Albums by soul artists are hard to find, and even albums that topped the charts are increasing in value. Early Motown 45s are difficult to find in Near Mint condition, and picture sleeves from the 1960s are extremely scarce.

Soundtracks: Soundtrack albums of everything from Broadway plays to TV shows and movies are a very popular collecting category. While albums are the most collected, there is also some interest in multi-record 45 rpm sets from the early to mid 1950s and in 45s of TV theme songs. The 45 sets must have their original box or sleeves to be of significant value.

Original pressings of soundtracks from the 1950s are worth more than their counterparts from the 1960s, which, in turn, are worth more than those from the 1970s and 1980s. Any soundtrack with music by Elvis Presley or The Beatles commands a premium.

Check the fine print if you encounter local cast recordings; someone famous might be lurking in the credits, and those can be worth hundreds once they become known to the collecting community.

Clubs

• Keystone Record Collectors, P.O. Box 1516, Lancaster, PA 17608

• International Association of Jazz Record Collectors, P.O. Box 75155, Tampa, FL 33675

Recommended Reading

Books

The Beatles Memorabilia Price Guide, Third Edition, Jeff Augsburger, Marty Eck and Rick Rann
Goldmine Price Guide to Rock 'n' Roll Memorabilia, Mark Allen Baker
Standard Catalog of American Records, Tim Neely
Goldmine Record Album Price Guide, Tim Neely
Goldmine Price Guide to 45 RPM Records, Tim Neely
Goldmine 45 RPM Picture Sleeve Price Guide, Charles Szabla
Goldmine British Invasion Record Price Guide, Tim Neely and Dave Thompson
Goldmine Jazz Album Price Guide, Tim Neely
Goldmine Heavy Metal Record Price Guide, Martin Popoff
The Complete Book of Doo-Wop, Dr. Anthony J. Gribin & Dr. Andrew M. Schiff
Forever Lounge, John Wooley, Thomas Conner & Mark Brown
Goldmine Promo Record & CD Price Guide, Fred Heggeness and Tim Neely
Goldmine Comedy Record Price Guide, Ronald L. Smith

Goldmine Country Western Record & CD Price Guide, Fred
 Heggeness
Goldmine Christmas Record Price Guide, Tim Neely

Periodicals

Goldmine
Discoveries

VALUE LINE

*Values shown are taken from the Goldmine Standard
Catalog of American Records and are for records in Excellent
condition, a grade also known by many record collectors as
Very Good Plus (VG+). Records in Near Mint condition will be
worth approximately twice the value shown. Records in Very
Good condition will be worth approximately half the value
shown. Records in Good condition will be worth approximately
10 to 15 percent of the value shown.*

45 rpm Records

Values shown are for records only, with no picture sleeve.

Johnny Ace, most titles on Duke label	$20
Allman Brothers Band, typical example	$2
Ames Brothers, typical title on Coral or RCA	$7
Bill Anderson, typical example	$2-$5
Andrews Sisters, typical Capitol or Decca	$6-$8
Animals, typical MGM label	$6
Paul Anka, ABC-Paramount label	$6-$10
Paul Anka, RCA Victor	$4-$7
Annette, Buena Vista label	$5-$8
Eddy Arnold, most 1950s RCA Victor titles	$10-$15
Eddy Arnold, 1960s RCA Victor	$3-$5
Chet Atkins, 1950s RCA Victor	$10-$12
Chet Atkins, 1960s RCA Victor	$4-$7
Frankie Avalon, typical Chancellor	$5-$10
Bachman-Turner Overdrive, Mercury	$2
Joan Baez, typical example	$2-$3
Lavern Baker, 1950s Atlantic	$10-$20
Hank Ballard, 1959-1964 King	$8-$12
Les Baxter, 1950s	$5-$7
Beach Boys, Surfin on "X" label	$500
Beach Boys, most 1960s Capitol examples	$3-$6
Harry Belafonte, 1950s RCA Victor	$5-$7
Tony Bennett, 1950s Columbia	$5-$8
Chuck Berry, 1950s Chess	$12-$20
Chuck Berry 1960s Mercury	$3-$5
Big Bopper, "Chantilly Lace" on "D" label	$100
Big Bopper, Mercury label	$7-$10
Big Maybelle, 1950s Okeh label	$15-$20
Blood, Sweat and Tears, Columbia	$2-$3
Bobbettes, 1950s Atlantic	$10-$15
Pat Boone, most 1950s Dot	$8-$15
Pat Boone, most 1960s	$3-$6
Brothers Four, 1960s Columbia	$4-$6
James Brown, 1950s Federal	$10-$15

**Very popular with a growing number of collectors
(and increasing in value) are "Extended Play" 45
rpms. They measure seven inches, just like a regular 45, but they came in heavy cardboard jackets
(like a 12-inch album) and typically contained four
songs (two on each side). Produced for a relatively
short time in the late 1950s and early 1960s,
Extended Plays are not as common as either singles
or albums. Many are very desirable. This late 1950s
EP of Buddy Holly and the Crickets sold for nearly
$900 at a record auction.**

James Brown, 1960s King	$6-$8
Dave Brubeck, 1950s-60s	$5-$8
Sonny Burgess, "Red Headed Woman" on Sun label	$75
Jerry Butler, 1959-60 Abner label	$15
Jerry Butler, 1960s Mercury	$4-$5
The Cadillacs, "Gloria" on Josie label, 1954	$250
The Cadillacs, 1960s reissue of above	$12
The Cadillacs, most other Josie examples	$15-$25
Freddie Cannon, 1959-1964 Swan	$6-$10
Carpenters, typical example	$2-$3
Chad and Jeremy, typical example	$4-$5
Challengers, typical example	$5-$10
Bobby Charles, 1950s Chess	$20-$25
Bobby Charles, 1950s Imperial	$10
Ray Charles, most 1950s Atlantic	$10-$15
Ray Charles, most ABC	$5
Chubby Checker, most 1960s Parkway	$6-$8
The Checkers, early 1950s King	$100-$500
Chicago, typical example	$2-$3
Chipmunks, typical Liberty	$6-$8

Chordettes, typical 1950s example ....$5-$8
Chords, 1950s Cat label ....$25-$50
Jimmy Clanton, typical Ace example ....$5-$10
Eric Clapton, typical example ....$2-$3
Dave Clark Five, 1960s Epic ....$5-$7
Dee Clark, typical 1950s-early 60s ....$6-$12
Patsy Cline, 1950s Coral example $15
Patsy Cline, typical Decca example ....$5-$10
Eddie Cochran, "Skinny Jim" on Crest.......................$150
Eddie Cochran, 1950s Liberty ....$15-$20
Nat King Cole, most Capitol examples....................$4-$7
Perry Como, most 1950s RCA Victor.......................$5-$7
Sam Cooke, 1950s Keen ....$12-$14
Sam Cooke, 1960s RCA Victor ....$5-$10
Crests, typical Coed example...................................$12-$15
Crew Cuts, 1950s Mercury or RCA..........................$6-$8
Crickets, 1950s Brunswick or Coral ....$15-$30
Crickets, 1960s Liberty ....$12-$15
Jim Croce, most examples $2
Crystals, early 1950s Deluxe ....$100-$150
Crystals, 1960s Philles..$8-$12
Danny and the Juniors, "At the Hop"
 on Singular label $500
Danny and the Juniors, 1950s ABC-Paramount ....$12-$20
Bobby Darin, 1950s Atco ....$10-$15
Bobby Darin, 1960s Atco ....$5-$10
Bobby Darin, 1960s Atlantic $4
Sammy Davis Jr., typical example ....$3-$6

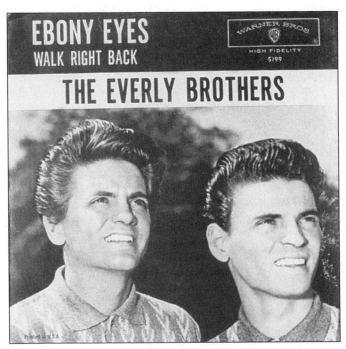

Picture sleeves from 45p rpm records are generally scarcer and more valuable than the records themselves. This Everly Brothers picture sleeve from 1961 is worth about $20 in nice condition.

Doris Day, 1949-1950 Columbia ....$10-$20
Doris Day, 1951-1960 Columbia ....$4-$8
Diamonds, early 1950s Atlantic.........................$250-$300
Diamonds, later 1950s Mercury.............................$8-$10
Bo Diddley, 1950s Checker ....$12-$20
Bo Diddley, 1960s Checker ....$6-$10
Dion, most 1960s Columbia examples ....$6-$8
Doobie Brothers, typical example................................$2
Eagles, most examples $2
Duane Eddy, most Jamie examples........................$8-$12
Duke Ellington, most examples ....$5-$7
Everly Brothers, most Cadence.............................$10-$12
Everly Brothers, most Warner Bros. ....$5-$8
Everly Brothers, most Barnaby..............................$2-$3
Fabian, 1950s Chancellor.....................................$12-$25
Eddie Fisher, most examples.................................$3-$7
Five Keys, early 1950s Aladdin ....$200-$400
Five Keys, later 1950s Capitol ....$15-$25
Flamingos, early 1950s Chance ....$500-$1,000
Flamingos, most later 1950s Checker...................$25-$40
Flamingos, most examples on "End" label ....$10-$15
Four Aces, most 1950s Decca...............................$5-$10
Four Freshmen, most 1950s Capitol ....$4-$6
Four Lads, most 1950s Columbia ....$5-$7
Four Preps, most 1950s Capitol ....$6-$10
Four Seasons, typical example,
 Vee Jay or Philips...$6-$8
Four Tops, most 1960s Motown..............................$4-$5
Connie Francis, most 1950s MGM ....$10-$15
Connie Francis, most 1960s MGM ....$5-$10
Bobby Fuller Four, "I Fought the Law"
 on Exeter label...$175
Bobby Fuller Four, "I Fought the Law" on Mustang......$8
Lesley Gore, most 1960s Mercury.........................$5-$7
Grand Funk Railroad, most examples......................$2-$3
Grateful Dead, "Stealin" on Scorpio label.................$300
Grateful Dead, most examples ....$2-$5
Bill Haley and His Comets, early 1950s Essex......$25-$50
Bill Haley and His Comets, later 1950s Decca......$12-$20
Hawks, 1950s Imperial ....$30-$60
Jimi Hendrix, most Reprise examples ....$5-$8
Buddy Holly, "Words of Love" on Coral...................$250
Buddy Holly, most other Coral examples ....$20-$25
Buddy Holly, most Decca examples ....$100-$150
Tab Hunter, most examples...................................$7-$10
Bill Joel, most examples $2
KISS, most examples ....$3-$6
Brenda Lee, most 1950s Decca.............................$7-$12
Brenda Lee, most 1960s Decca..............................$4-$7
Lettermen, most examples ....$2-$4
Jerry Lee Lewis, most 1950s-1965 Sun ....$10-$15
Jerry Lee Lewis, most other examples....................$2-$10
Little Richard, most 1950s Specialty ....$12-$20
Little Richard, early 1950s RCA Victor ....$150-$250
Bob Marley and the Wailers, most examples.............$2-$4

Marshall Tucker Band, most examples ....$2-$3
Dean Martin, most 1950s Capitol ....$5-$8
Dean Martin, most 1960s Reprise...........................$2-$5
Johnny Mathis, most examples ....$2-$4
McGuire Sisters, most examples..............................$3-$6
Mello-Tones, early 1950s Columbia or
    Decca..$150-$200
Mitch Miller, most examples ....$3-$5
Mills Brothers, most examples ....$4-$7
Moby Grape, most examples ....$2-$4
Monkees, most examples ....$5-$8
Marilyn Monroe, most examples ....$15-$25
Moonglows, early 1950s on Chance..............$300-$1,000
Moonglows, later 1950s on Chess ....$15-$30
Ricky Nelson, most 1950s Imperial......................$10-$15
Ricky Nelson, most 1960s Imperial.........................$7-$10
Ricky Nelson, most Decca ....$3-$7
Roy Orbison, most Monument examples.................$7-$10
Roy Orbison, most MGM examples ....$5-$7
Patti Page, early 1950s Mercury ....$5-$10
Patti Page, most 1960 and later ....$2-$5
Partridge Family, most examples ....$2-$3
Les Paul, early 1950s Decca ....$20-$50
Peter and Gordon, most examples ....$5-$6
Bobby Boris Pickett, Garpax label.......................$12-$20
Wilson Pickett, most examples ....$3-$5
Queen, most examples ....$2-$4
Johnny Ray, most examples ....$4-$7
Ronettes, most Philles examples...........................$10-$12
Royal Teens, most examples..................................$10-$15
Bobby Rydell, most 1960s Cameo ....$5-$8
Neil Sedaka, most RCA Victor ....$5-$10
Shangri-Las, most 1960s Red Bird $10
Bobby Sherman, most examples ....$2-$5
Shirley and Lee, most early 1950s Aladdin ....$15-$40
Frank Sinatra, most 1950s Capitol..........................$5-$10
Frank Sinatra, most early 1950s Columbia............$10-$25
Frank Sinatra, most RCA Victor ....$5-$8
Frank Sinatra, most 1960s Reprise ....$4-$10
Percy Sledge, most Atlantic.....................................$3-$5
Sonny and Cher, most 1960s Atco $5
Bruce Springsteen, most examples ....$2-$3
Rod Stewart, most examples ....$2-$4
Supremes, "I Want a Guy" on Motown $750
Supremes, most Motown hits...................................$4-$8
Temptations, most examples ....$2-$4
Three Suns, most examples......................................$4-$6
Joe Turner, 1951-53 Atlantic ....$50-$100
Joe Turner, later 1950s Atlantic ....$10-$15
Ventures, 1960s Dolton ....$6-$10
Gene Vincent, most 1950s Capitol.........................$12-$25
Andy Williams, most examples ....$2-$6
Hank Williams, most 1950s MGM ....$12-$25
Wrens, 1950s Rama ....$75-$200
Yardbirds, most examples ....$7-$20

Record Albums
Angels, Smash label...$25
Angels, Caprice label..$60-$100
Annette, most Buena Vista.....................................$25-$50
Association, most albums ....$5-$10
Frankie Avalon, most Chancellor..........................$15-$25
Joan Baez, most Vanguard ....$6-$12
Beau Brummels, Autumn label.............................$20-$25
Harry Belafonte, most RCA Victor.......................$6-$12
Brook Benton, most Mercury ....$10-$15
Blood, Sweat and Tears, most Columbia ....$4-$7
Bob B. Soxx and the Blue Jeans, Phillies label $250
Gary U.S. Bonds, Legrand label ....$35-$50
Pat Boone, most Dot ....$6-$12
Box Tops, Bell label... $10
Brothers Four, typical album....................................$6-$8
Johnny Burnette, most Liberty..............................$20-$25
Cadillacs, most Jubilee.......................................$100-$150
Glen Campbell, most Capitol....................................$5-$7
Ace Cannon, typical album......................................$6-$12
Freddie Cannon, Swan label $100
Freddie Cannon, Warner Bros.............................$15-$20
Carpenters, typical album ....$4-$8
Vikki Carr, most albums ....$5-$9
Champs, Challenge label ....$50-$100
Chubby Checker, most Parkway ....$15-$20
Chicago, most Columbia...$5-$10
Chiffons, most 1960s Laurie..............................$50-$100
Chordettes, most Cadence and Columbia ....$20-$25
Jimmy Clanton, most Ace......................................$40-$50
Dee Clark, Abner label ....$75-$100

COLLECTOR'S ADVISORY!

Although the listings below offer an idea of the general range of collectible records, a comprehensive price guide is essential for anyone entering this hobby on a serious basis. The various "Goldmine" price guides from Krause Publications are highly recommended.

A detailed price guide is especially critical for artists such as the Beatles, Elvis Presley, Rolling Stones, Beach Boys, etc., whose records have been issued and re-issued many times over the years, resulting in many, many variations of the same record—each with a different value. In some cases, one version of a record may be worth just a few dollars, while another, scarcer version of the same title might be worth hundreds or even thousands. Sometimes the color of the label can affect a record's value, or a subtle change on the album cover. Frequently, stereo and mono versions of the same record have different values. Sometime the stereo version is worth more; sometimes the mono version is. These are the kinds of details that only a comprehensive record price can provide.

DJ and promotional copies of records are often more desirable than the corresponding regular version. This DJ copy of a 1968 Otis Redding album is worth about $50 in Near Mint condition.

Dee Clark, Vee Jay	$25-$40
Patsy Cline, most Decca	$15-$25
Patsy Cline, MCA, Hilltop or Everest	$5-$10
Eddie Cochran, 1957 Liberty	$150-$300
Eddie Cochran, 1960s Liberty	$50-$100
Eddie Cochran, Sunset, United Artists, or 1980s Liberty	$4-$12
Joe Cocker, typical album	$4-$7
Perry Como, typical album	$4-$10
Contours, Gordy label	$250
Contours, Motown	$3-$5
Sam Cooke, Keen label	$100
Sam Cooke, 1960s RCA Victor or Famous labels	$15-$20
Dave Baby Cortez, most albums	$10-$20
Cowsills, typical album	$6-$8
Floyd Cramer, typical album	$6-$10
Johnny Crawford, Del-Fi label	$10-$20
Creedence Clearwater Revival, most Fantasy	$4-$10
Crests, Coed label	$200-$400
Crew Cuts, 1950s Mercury	$25
Crickets, 1960 Coral	$100-$200
Crickets, 1960s Liberty	$50-$75
Crickets, 1950s Brunswick	$300-$400
Jim Croce, typical album	$5-$10
Crystals, Philles label	$100-$200
Spencer Davis Group, 1960s United Artists	$10-$20
Bobby Day, 1959 Class label	$300

Del Vikings, 1950s Luniverse label	$500
Del Vikings, 1960s Dot label	$100
Bo Diddley, most 1960s Checker	$15-$30
Dino, Desi and Billy, typical album	$10
Donovan, typical 1960s album	$5-$10
Patty Duke, most United Artists	$10-$15
Duprees, 1960s Coed label	$150-$200
Duane Eddy, most Jamie	$15-$40
Electric Prunes, Reprise	$15-$20
Embers, JCP label	$75-$100
Emerson, Lake and Palmer, typical album	$4-$6
Fabian, Chancellor	$25-$40
Fendermen, Soma label	$500-$2,000
Five Satins, 1950s Ember	$150-$250
Roberta Flack, typical album	$3-$5
Fleetwood Mac, typical 1970s album	$4-$10
Fleetwoods, most 1960s Dolton	$10-$20
Four Aces, 1950s Decca	$15-$25
Four Freshmen, 1950s-early 1960s Capitol	$10-$25
Four Lads, most 1950s-60s Columbia	$10-$20
Four Seasons, most 1960s Philips	$8-$15
Four Tops, most Motown	$8-$12
Four Tunes, Jubilee label	$125
Peter Frampton, typical album	$4-$5
Connie Francis, most 1960s MGM	$10-$15
Aretha Franklin, typical album	$5-$10
Freddie and the Dreamers, typical 1960s	$10-$12
Bobby Fuller Four, 1960s Mustang	$40-$75
Gaylords, 1950s-60s Mercury	$10-$12
Bobby Goldsboro, typical 1960s-70s album	$8-$10
Leslie Gore, most 1960s Mercury	$15-$20
Grassroots, most Dunhill	$10-$15
Grateful Dead, typical album	$6-$10
Hall and Oates, typical album	$4-$6
Herman's Hermits, most 1960s MGM	$5-$7
Buddy Holly, 1950s Coral	$75-$200
Buddy Holly, most 1960s Coral	$25-$75
Buddy Holly, 1961 Decca	$150
Hollywood Argyles, Lute label	$400
Hondells, Mercury	$25-$40
Honeys, Warner Bros.	$300
Hullaballoos, Roulette	$25-$35
Tab Hunter, typical album	$10-$20
Impalas, Cub label	$200-$300
Michael Jackson, typical album	$4-$6
Bill Joel, typical album	$4-$6
Elton John, typical album	$4-$6
Johnny and the Hurricanes, 1950s-1960 Attila, Big Top or Warwick	$100-$200
Jack Jones, typical album	$4-$7
Tom Jones, typical album	$5-$7
Andy Kim, typical album	$6-$7
Kingston Trio, typical 1950s-60s album	$8-$15
Knickerbockers, 1960s Challenge label	$50-$100
Al Kooper, typical album	$5-$7

Major Lance, Okeh label..$15-$20
Brenda Lee, most 1960s Decca..........................$10-$20
Brenda Lee, most MCA ....$4-$6
Lettermen, typical album ....$4-$7
Bobby Lewis, 1961 Beltone, label...................... $100
Bobby Lewis 1960s United Artists $10
Gary Lewis and the Playboys, 1960s Liberty ....$7-$10
Liberace, 1950s Columbia ....$20-$40
Liberace, most others ....$4-$7
Gordon Lightfoot, typical album ....$4-$7
Little Eva, Dimension label ....$75-$100
Loggins and Messina, typical album ....$4-$6
Julie London, most 1950s-60s Liberty.................$10-$15
Barry Manilow, typical album.............................$2-$5
Manfred Mann, 1960s Ascot or United Artists......$15-$25
Al Martino, typical 1960s Capitol ....$5-$7
Johnny Mathis, typical album ....$4-$10
The McCoys, 1960s Bang or Mercury.................$12-$15
Mello-Kings, Herald label ....$150-$300
Bette Midler, typical album ....$4-$6
Midnighters, 1950s Federal ....$1,500-$3,000
Midnighters, 1960s King ....$100-$300
Roger Miller, typical album ....$5-$10
Steve Miller Band, typical album.........................$4-$7
Mindbenders, 1960s Fontana ....$10-$15
Guy Mitchell, King label $150
Guy Mitchell, most Columbia ....$15-$20
Chad Mitchell Trio, typical album.......................$7-$10
Mott the Hoople, typical album ....$4-$8
Anne Murray, typical album ....$4-$5
Ricky Nelson, most 1960s Decca or Imperial ....$12-$20
Ricky Nelson, 1957 Verve $125
Sandy Nelson, most 1960s Imperial ....$8-$12
Leonard Nimoy, 1960s Dot label ....$$25-$40
Olympics, early 1960s Arvee label......................... $100
Dolly Parton, typical album ....$4-$8
Paul and Paula, 1960s Philips ....$15-$20
Penguins, Dooto label ....$100-$400
Peter, Paul and Mary, typical 1960s album............$5-$12
Gene Pitney, most 1960s albums ....$10-$15
Lloyd Price, late 1950s-early 1960s
    ABC-Paramount................................$20-$25
Johnny Ray, most 1950s Columbia......................$20-$25
Helen Reddy, typical album ....$4-$5
Paul Revere and the Raiders,
    most 1960s-70s albums ....$7-$15
Righteous Brothers, most 1960s Moonglow,
    Philles or Verve ....$10-$20
Linda Ronstadt, typical album ....$4-$6
Sam the Sham and the Pharaohs, 1960s MGM......$12-$20
Tommy Sands, 1950s Capitol ....$15-$25
Boz Scaggs, typical album ....$4-$6
Jack Scott, 1960s Top Rank ....$75-$100
Jack Scott, 1950s Carlton................................$75-$150
Sha Na Na, typical album ....$5-$7

Bobby Sherman, typical album...................................... $7
Simon and Garfunkel, typical album ....$5-$7
Percy Sledge, 1960s Atlantic............................$12-$25
Smothers Brothers, typical album..........................$7-$12
Rick Springfield, typical album ....$4-$5
Springfields, 1960s Philips ....$15-$20
Cat Stevens, typical album................................$5-$10
Dodie Stevens, 1960s Dot................................$15-$20
Gale Storm, 1950s Dot....................................$15-$25
Strawberry Alarm Clock, 1960s Uni ....$20-$25
Barbra Streisand, typical album ....$4-$8
Donna Summer, typical album.............................$4-$6
James Taylor, typical album................................$4-$8
Three Suns, 1950s-early 1960s RCA ....$10-$25
Trashmen, 1964 Garrett label........................$100-$150
Troggs, 1960s Fontana or Atco ....$15-$25
Turtles, 1960s White Whale................................$10-$20
Uriah Heep, typical album ....$4-$5
Vanilla Fudge, 1960s Atco ....$6-$10
Bobby Vee, most 1960s Liberty.........................$12-$25
Gene Vincent, most 1950s-early 60s Capitol.....$200-$500
Bobby Vinton, typical album ....$5-$10
Warren Zevon, typical album $5
Zombies, 1960s Parrot ....$20-$30

45 RPM Picture Sleeves

Values shown are for picture sleeves in Excellent condition; values are for the sleeve only, with no record.

Paul Anka, typical example ....$12-$15
Animals, typical example....................................$12-$14
Frankie Avalon, typical example..........................$10-$15
Archies, typical example.. $8
Beach Boys, "Barbara Ann" ....$60-$80
Beach Boys, "Ten Little Indians" $100
Beach Boys, typical example, 1960s ....$10-$20
Chuck Berry, typical example...........................$15-$25
Eddie Cochran, "Mean When I'm Mad" $1,000
Sam Cooke, typical example...............................$12-$15
Bobby Darin, typical example ....$10-$20
The Diamonds..$40-$50
Dion, typical example ....$10-$20
Everly Brothers, "Wake Up Little Susie" $100
Everly Brothers, typical example, 1950s-60s ....$15-$25
Fabian, typical example ....$15-$20
Four Seasons, typical example, 1960s ....$10-$15
Four Tops, typical example ....$10-$20
Peter Frampton, typical example ....$2-$3
Connie Francis, typical example............................$6-$15
Lesley Gore, typical example..............................$8-$12
Grassroots, typical example ....$5-$8
Herman's Hermits, typical example.......................$7-$10
Tommy James and the Shondells,
    typical example ....$5-$8
Jan and Dean, typical example............................$10-$15
Jay and the Americans, typical example...................$4-$7
Billy Joel, typical example.. $2

Records from the original British Invasion in the mid-1960s are a popular collecting category. This Searchers album was released in several variations and is valued at between $30 and $50 in Near Mint condition, depending on the version.

Davy Jones, typical example..................................$15-$20
Kingston Trio, typical example................................$8-$15
Led Zeppelin, "Stairway to Heaven" $60
Brenda Lee, typical example 1960s........................$8-$15
Gary Lewis and the Playboys, typical example ....$6-$8
Lovin Spoonful, typical example..............................$6-$8
Marcels, typical example ....$25-$40
Clyde McPhatter, typical example ....$10-$15
Monkees, typical example ....$10-$15
Ricky Nelson, typical example ....$10-$15
Oliva Newton-John, typical example ....$3-$5
Roy Orbison, typical example................................$10-$15
Buck Owens, typical example....................................$4-$6
Peter and Gordon, typical example ....$5-$10
Bobby Boris Pickett, typical example....................$20-$25
Gene Pitney, typical example...................................$8-$14
Rolling Stones, "We Love You" $200
Rolling Stones, "Street Fighting Man" $6,000
Rolling Stones, 'Not Fade Away"...............................$125
Rolling Stones, "Satisfaction" $100
Rolling Stones, "Heart of Stone"...............................$250
Rolling Stones, "Beast of Burden" $900
Rolling Stones, typical 1960s London..................$10-$20
Ronettes, typical example ....$40-$50
Linda Ronstadt, typical example................................$2-$3
Searchers, typical example...................................$15-$25
Jack Scott, typical example...................................$20-$25
Supremes, typical example ....$10-$15
Turtles, typical example...$5-$10
Gene Vincent, "The Night Is So Lonely" $1,000

RUBY RED GLASS

In the earliest of times only the wealthy could afford glass, a material that was treasured much like gold and silver. As the production process became automated and cost-effective, glass became available to nearly everyone. In today's society glass is taken for granted for its many everyday uses, but the process that yields ruby red glass has never become common. Neither has its output, for collectors of ruby red glass cherish their scarlet pieces, from tableware to oil lamps and perfume bottles.

Background: The ancient Egyptians were known to create red glass by adding copper during the production process. The key to making ruby red glass, however, was lost for centuries, and although Venetian glassmakers grasped for it over and over, it remained out of reach. The process was not rediscovered until 1670, in Bohemia. Through the 1900s the ruby red color was achieved with the use of gold chloride as a coloring agent.

In the late 1930s, selenium replaced gold as the preferred coloring agent for molded or pressed glass, but gold was still commonly used in blown glass. With machine-made glass, copper is usually used to achieve the rich ruby color, although a few glassmakers still use the expensive gold process.

In the 1940s there was a resurgence of interest in ruby red glass, and it became a popular look for tableware. It was at this time that the Anchor Hocking Co. introduced its patented Royal Ruby line of red glass, which was made using copper to achieve the rich color. The glass had a deep, even hue, and was more cost-effective to produce than other ruby red glass. Royal Ruby was amply produced, and was used in many Depression patterns.

A great number of companies have produced ruby red glass using many different processes, and it is still being produced today. Many ruby red glass items are coated with clear crystal in order to minimize the use of the expensive gold ruby glass.

General Guidelines: Ruby red glass is made in a variety of hues, from the deep colors of the gold ruby pieces to the lighter cranberry glass, which contains less gold chloride. There are even more companies that make the glass than there are hues. Among them: Fenton, Duncan & Miller, Imperial, Blenko, Westmoreland and Viking. It is important to know the markings of each company when collecting its ruby red patterns.

Anchor Hocking's Royal Ruby was produced in large numbers. It is plentiful, and is one of the most commonly collected types of red glass. Its production ceased in 1943 when WWII impacted the availability of copper. Production of Royal Ruby resumed in 1977, and all of these newer pieces are embossed with the company's trademark.

Older glass will show signs of wear and roughness around the base.

This Royal Ruby punch set would probably sell in the $75-$125 range.

Ruby red and other colored glass is often termed either flashed or stained. These are two processes used to add color to clear glass, commonly used with ruby red glass because its production process is expensive. Ruby-stained pieces are in general worth twice as much as their clear-glass counterparts.

With flashed pieces, either clear glass was dipped in colored glass, or colored glass was dipped in molten clear glass, creating a thin layer of colored glass, either over or under clear glass.

Stained pieces have a layer of color painted on clear glass, then are refired for permanency. This was an inexpensive way to create colored glass, but is still very collectible. The color can be easily scratched, and older pieces of stained-ruby glass should have small signs of wear in the color; otherwise they may be newer reproductions. Another way to distinguish original ruby stain is by its deep, rich color; reproductions approach iridescence and are much paler.

Often stained or flashed glass is etched with a pattern, making a clear-glass design on the colored glass. Names and dates were often etched into stained pieces to commemorate certain events. These small pieces are called souvenir glass.

Recommended Reading

Warman's Glass, Ellen T. Schroy
Fifty Years of Collectible Glass 1920-1970, Tom and Neila Bredehoft
Warman's Pattern Glass, Ellen T. Schroy
American & European Decorative Art Glass & Price Guide, Kyle Hustfloen

VALUE LINE

Ashtray, Fostoria, coin glass with four frosted coins, 7-1/2" $20
Basket, Fenton, Hobnail pattern, 1985, 7" $30
Berry bowl, Royal Ruby, 8", Burple $25

These Ruby Red pieces, consisting of a sugar, creamer and cup-and-saucer, are worth about $10-$12 each.

Bowl, Blenko, ruffled edge, 15"..................................... $25
Bowl, Fenton, pineapple, 11", crimped, three feet...... $180
Bowl, Fenton, cupped, 8", 1929.................................... $90
Bowl, Fostoria, 9" oval, coin glass with frosted coins.. $50
Bowl, Imperial, reeded design, 1930s............................ $25
Bowl, Viking, Hobnail pattern, fluted........................... $20
Candleholders, 6-1/2" $33
Candy dish, Fenton, 7", 1996, covered......................... $40
Candy dish, Imperial, 6", 1970s, covered,
    IG on bottom $50
Candy dish, Viking, with lid $30
Creamer, flashed, 8" $25
Compote, flashed.. $20
Decanter, Bavarian cut-glass, 10",
    with four 3" glasses $150

Decanter, Blenko, crackle glass, fluted, 11", 1930s...... $25
Glass, carnival, 8 oz., 1997 .... $15
Heart, Westmoreland, 8" x 7" $30
Ice Bucket, Fenton, Plymouth pattern, 1933............... $130
Juice glasses, Royal Ruby, set of four.......................... $25
Oil lamp, flashed, 15" x 15".. $30
Pickle dish, New Martinsville, 7", diamond design,
    1930s $30
Pitcher, Avon... $30
Pitcher, crackle-glass, 7-1/4" $20
Pitcher, Depression glass, tilted, 6" $55
Pitcher, Imperial, reeded design, 1930s $130
Pitcher, Fenton, cranberry, 7"...................................... $60
Pitcher, slant, Royal Ruby, 6" x 5-1/2" $45
Pitcher, Royal Ruby, 9" $30
Plate, Fenton, 10", Sheffield pattern, 1936 .... $80
Plate, unmarked, 11" $35
Plate, Imperial, 7", Cape Cod pattern $30
Plate, Imperial, 8" square, Mt. Vernon design $30
Plate, Westmoreland, heart-shaped,
    M. Gregory design, 1983 .... $70
Plate, Westmoreland, 12-1/2", Doric pattern,
    1981.. $150
Platter, New Martinsville, 12", 1980s, handled $50
Punch set, Royal Ruby, 10 cups................................... $100
Relish dish, Royal Ruby, leaf shaped, 2" x 5" $5
Salt and pepper shakers, Fenton, Georgian pattern,
    1930s, chrome lids $120
Toothpick holder, 1904, flashed, two small chips $30
Tumbler, Avon, 5-1/2", Cape Cod................................ $10
Tumblers, Royal Ruby, set of eight.............................. $40
Vase, Blenko, 10-1/2", ruffled top, 1980..................... $10
Vase, Duncan & Miller, 14", 1940s,
    cornucopia style $175
Vase, Fenton, 12", 1931, floral engraved design......... $200
Vase, Fenton, 7", Sheffield pattern, 1936..................... $55
Wine glass, Blenko, 1930s... $10

SALT AND PEPPER SHAKERS

Vintage salt-and-pepper shakers are a bit like old cocktail shakers: you can enjoy using them everyday—except you won't need a designated driver afterward.

Prior to 1900, salt was set on the table in tiny glass bowls called salt cellars or open salts. The Victorian era saw the advent of the elaborate glass and fine china salt and pepper shakers.

The first novelty shaker was patented near the turn of the century, and by 1920, novelty shakers were the popular choice for holding spices for the table. The advent of the fam-

ily road trip during the mid-to late 1940s caused a boom in sales of salt and pepper shakers as small, inexpensive souvenirs (much like snow globes of later years). Interest in novelty shakers manufactured today is just as strong as those made prior to 1960.

Novelty shakers made between 1940 and today are extremely popular collectibles. Made in interesting shapes of ceramic, metal, glass, plastic or wood, they are quite affordable, typically $10 to $50 per pair.

Finding shakers with manufacturers' marks is the exception rather than the rule. The base of the shakers was often quite small and, after the plug had been added, there was little space for a mark. Occasionally, a paper sticker bearing the manufacturer's name is found intact. More often, the shakers bear no mark at all. For more accurate identification, a price guide with photographs may be helpful.

General Guidelines: Sets command higher prices than individual pieces. Shakers featuring Disney characters, advertising characters or Black figures are especially popular. Collect only sets in Very Good or better condition. Make sure the set has the proper two pieces and base, if applicable. China shakers should show no signs of cracking. Original paint and decoration should be intact on all china and metal figurals. All parts should be present, including the closure.

Collectors compete with those in other areas, such as advertising, animal groups, Blacks and holiday collectors. Many shakers were stock items which had souvenir labels later affixed to them. The form, not the label, is the important element.

LEARN THE LINGO!

Collectors of salt-and-pepper shakers seem to speak their own language. Here are some of the terms you may run across:

Advertising sets: Used to advertise a specific product.

Art glass: Shakers made by famous glass companies, usually in patterns to match stemware. These are not considered novelty shakers and can have surprisingly high prices.

Bench-sitters: Two shakers perched on a small wooden bench, often kissing.

Carriers: A three-piece set consisting of a holder and two shakers.

Condiment sets: A third container (a mustard) sits with the shakers on a tray.

Go-withs: The shakers represent two different objects with the same theme.

Hangers: A three-piece set consisting of a holder and two shakers hanging from the holder.

Holders: A third piece holds the shakers.

Huggers: Patented in 1949 by Ruth van Tellingen, this type of shaker has arms (or necks) which entwine, making the figures appear to be hugging.

Mechanical sets: The shakers move in some way.

Miniatures: Tiny, not full-sized, shakers.

Nesters: A set in which the holder itself may be one of the shakers.

Nodders: Shakers with small, bobbing heads.

One-piece sets: The salt and pepper are both contained in one divided shaker.

Sitters: A set where one shaker sits on top of the other.

Souvenir or Landmark: Shakers made in a shape of a state, building or monument, such as the Statue of Liberty or the Empire State Building. Usually sold on site or at a nearby roadside shop.

Two-sided: These shakers have faces on the front and back of both shakers.

This pair of shakers in a caramel slag cactus pattern sold for $275 at an auction conducted by Jackson's in Cedar Falls, Iowa.

The colored sets, in both transparent and opaque glass, command the highest prices; crystal and white sets the lowest. Although some shakers, such as the tomato or fig, have a special patented top and need it to retain their value, it generally is not detrimental to replace the top of a shaker.

Garage sales and flea markets are great places to look for shakers. With a lot of luck, you might be able to assemble an impressive collection for under $100 in a short amount of time.

Serious collectors will find their specific shakers and sets at antique shows and shops, but at higher prices.

Beginners would be wise to concentrate on a certain category, especially if space is a problem. For example, a collector might look for animals, vegetables, transportation, Black Americana, sports themes or states of the Union.

But if space is no object, you can buy anything that appeals to you. You will find lots of variety and an endless assortment to choose from.

Collectors of salt and pepper shakers have thousands to choose from. They are a wonderful collectible: small, colorful, great to display and, for the most part, very affordable.

Trends: Serious, traditional collectors often look down on figural and souvenir types, but if these are your favorites, don't worry about it. Sentiment and whimsy are prime collecting motivations. The large variety and current low prices indicate a potential for long-term price growth.

The following are among the hottest categories of salt-and-pepper shakers:

Advertising—Shakers depicting advertising characters were often offered as premiums for buying certain products. Characters may include Borden's Elsie the Cow, Big Boy and RCA Victor's Nipper the Dog.

Art Deco—Early plastics and ceramics in a variety of bold colors and the geometric shapes of the 1930s and 1940s.

Black Americana—Shakers featuring Mammy, Aunt Jemima and other stereotypical African-American characters are highly collectible and often hard to find today.

Character—Cartoon characters, in any shape or form, are always collectible, especially characters from Walt Disney, Warner Bros., DC Comics or others.

Lustreware—Painted ceramic shakers from the 1930s and 1940s characterized by a glistening peach colored glaze. Most often made in Japan, featured hand-painted scenes with cottages, florals and fruits.

Native American—Often depict stereotyped images of Native Americans.

Club

•Salt & Pepper Novelty Shakers Club, P.O. Box 3617, Lantana, FL 33465

SIZING UP SHAKERS!

Salt and pepper shakers come in three general sizes. The largest, those designed to sit on a kitchen stove for use during cooking, are referred to as a "range" set and usually average 5 to 8 inches tall. "Table sets," the most common size used for dining, average 2 to 5 inches, while "miniature" sets, mainly decorative and rarely functional, are usually no more than 1 to 1-1/2 inches tall.

Materials used to make the shakes is very important to collectors. Clay is the most popular. How the clay is fired determines whether the final product is earthenware, stoneware, bone china or hard paste porcelain. But generally every shaker made of clay is usually referred to as ceramic.

Besides ceramic shakers, you'll also find sets made of plastic, metal, wood, wood composition (sawdust and glue), glass, chalkware (plaster of paris), cardboard, and a few more exotic materials, like bone or ivory.

VALUE LINE

Advertising

Big Boy Restaurants, sets from the 1970s ....$175-$225
Borden's Elsie holding twins ....$60-$85
Budweiser beer bottles, plastic and metal.............$20-$30
Coca-Cola, ceramic bottles ....$60-$75
Colonel Sanders ....$75-$85
Fifi and Fido, Ken-L-Ration dog and cat food.......$25-$30
Firestone, U.S. Rubber, tires ....$50-$65
Greyhound buses...$75-$100
Heinz Ketchup bottles...$5-$15
Keebler, Elf and Tee, in basket ....$50-$60
Mr. Peanut, ceramic set...$40-$50
Sealtest, milk bottles, 3-1/4" ....$20-$25

Animals

Bears, yellow snuggle type, van Tellingen.............$40-$50
Cats, white..$40-$50
Chicks, yellow, hatching from white eggs,
    Japan..$20-$30
Ducks, yellow snuggle type, van Tellingen ....$50-$60
Fawns, laying down ....$70-$80
Fish, gray..$45-$55
Fish, orange...$40-$50
Pheasants, tall, Rosemeade ....$40-$50
Poodles..$40-$50
Quail..$40-$50
Rabbits, yellow snuggle type, van Tellingen ....$40-$50
Scotties, orange dogs playing instruments.............$75-$85

"WHEN IT RAINS IT POURS!"

Salt today is nothing like the salt our forefathers had to contend with.

Prior to about 1911, even though sodium was not yet linked to high blood pressure, salt had an even bigger problem: It would cake unmercilessly when hit with humidity. Caked salt did not shake, so salt shakers were not generally used. The accepted method of serving salt on the table was in "open salts," where diners merely reached over and pinched the amount they wanted out of the open salt dish.

We have Joy Morton, owner of the Morton Salt Co., to thank for putting an end to lumpy salt. In 1911, Morton added moisture-absorbing fillers to its salt, with such impressive results that the company confidently adopted the now-famous "When It Rains, It Pours" slogan.

With that development, salt could actually be shaken from a shaker, a convenience that eventually led to the demise of the open salt dish. And with the prosperity of the industrial age, Americans were able to indulge themselves with frivolous items, like figural salt and pepper shakers.

Advertising and novelty shakers are a very popular category. These El Paso gas pump shakers stand about 2-1/2 inches tall.

Art Glass

Peachblow, Wheeling..$325-$350
Pigeon Blood, Periwinkle variant ....$110-$125
Rubena, enamel, pewter top...............................$200-$225

Black Americana

Black maid and butler, 4-1/4" ....$150-$175
Luzianne Mammy Coffee mammy in green skirt,
    plastic, 5"..$275-$300
Luzianne Mammy Coffee mammy, in red skirt, reproduction ....$75-$100
Boy sitting with whole watermelon, girl with legs outstretched and watermelon slice on her leg
    ....$50-$60
Wooden black chef and mammy heads, Japan,
    3-1/4"...$30-$40

Depression-Era Glass

Block Optic, green ....$40-$50
Cameo, green ....$75-$85
Cloverleaf, green..$35-$45
Colonial knife and fork, green ....$145-$160
Doric, pink ....$40-$50
English Hobnail, green, round base ....$85-$100

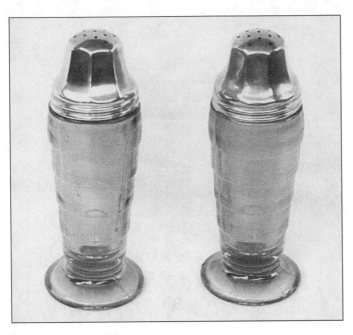

There are many salt and pepper shakers available to collectors of Depression glass. Most sell in the $35-$75 range. These are in the Moderntone pattern.

Floral, pink, large..$55-$65
Florentine #2, green ....$45-$55
Madrid, footed, amber...$100-$115
Manhattan, pink ....$50-$60
Mayfair, flat, pink..$70-$80
Miss America, clear ....$325-$350
Newport, amethyst ....$45-$55
Normandie, amber...$55-$65
Patrician, amber ....$65-$75
Princess, topaz...$80-$90
Sharon, amber ....$45-$55
Tea Room, pink ....$60-$70

Disney
Donald Duck and Daisy, Japan, 1960s, 4"............$40-$50
Donald Duck and Ludwig von Drake, Japan,
    paper label ....$150-$165
Dumbo, redware, Japan, 3-1/8" ....$15-$20
Flower ....$165-$175
Mickey Mouse, in chair, Good Co. (Applause Inc.),
    1989, Korea ....$20-$25
Lady and The Tramp, Japan, 1960s, 3-1/2" ....$65-$80
Mickey and Minnie Mouse, Germany, 1930s,
    2-1/2"...$500-$600
Mickey and Minnie Mouse, Japan, 1940s ....$200-$250
Mickey and Minnie Christmas elfs, Enesco,
    1990s ....$20-$25
Mowgli, Calico Imports, Japan ....$200-$225
Pinocchio, Japan, 1960s, 5" ....$150-$175
Pluto, WDP Incised, gold trim, 1950s ....$70-$80

Figural shakers, which take the form of people, animals and other things, are probably the most popular category.

Skunk "Flower" from Bambi, 1940, full bee,
    Goebel ....$125-$150
Snow White, Dopey, 1990s, 4" ....$25-$30
Winnie the Pooh and Rabbit, on tray, Enesco,
    1960s ....$250-$300

Miniatures, Arcadia Ceramics, 1950-60s
Candlesticks ....$15-$20
Eggs and sausage ....$10-$15
Fish and creel ....$10-$15
Mailbox and packages..$15-$20
Marriage license and ring.......................................$20-$25
Outhouses...$15-$20
Toaster and toast ....$15-$20
Washtub and scrub board ....$25-$30

Miscellaneous
Bugs Bunny, 1970s ....$150-$175
Casper the Friendly Ghost, USA, 1990s, 6" ......$100-$150
Corn, standing...$55-$65
Dennis the Menace, Japan, 1960s, 4" ....$45-$60
Egg in frying pan, Japan ....$10-$15
Felix the Cat, Japan, 1950s, 3" ....$400-$450
Golfer, ball, on tray, Goebel...............................$185-$200
Marvin the Martian, Applause Inc., 1994 ....$25-$30
Munich priests...$65-$75

Popeye, Japan, 1950s, 4" ....$125-$150

Porky Pig, in wheelbarrow, Japan, 1950s,
4" ....$125-$150

Shmoos, Japan, 1950s, 4" ....$125-$175

Tomatoes, ceramic, Japan, 1950s..........................$10-$15

Personalities

Charlie Chaplin, USA, 1950s.................................$75-$100

Emmett Kelly, Japan, 1960, 5-3/4" ....$75-$100

President Kennedy, in rocker ....$50-$60

Laurel and Hardy, Japan, 1950s, 4-1/2" ....$450-$500

Dean Martin and Jerry Lewis, unmarked..........$275-$325

Marilyn Monroe, Clay Art, 1980s........................$25-$30

Richard Nixon and Spiro Agnew, K. Wolf Studios,
1990s ....$15-$20

Santa Claus...$65-$75

Opalescent

Argonaut Shell, blue ....$60-$70

Fluted Scrolls, canary...$65-$75

Reverse Swirl, white ....$45-$55

Windows Swirl, cranberry ....$100-$125

Opaque

Bird, blue, handle ....$100-$110

Bulging petal, green pair.......................................$45-$55

Forget-Me-Not, pink variegated slag ....$20-$30

Guttate, green...$30-$40

Inverted fan and feather, pink slag ....$800-$850

Melonette, blue, pair ....$45-$55

Rib & Swirl, blue ....$45-$55

Square Scroll, pink..$25-$35

Sold by Glasses, Mugs & Steins of Sun Prairie, Wis., this group of beer-related shakers includes two pairs of Budweiser shakers that sold for $200-$250 a pair; and two pairs of beer-bottle shakers that went for $50-$75 a pair.

Pattern Glass

Acorn, pink ....$45-$55

Feather...$20-$30

Fish, blue..$65-$75

Fish, blue and white ....$100-$115

Klondike, amberette, pair....................................$225-$250

Nestor, amethyst..$55-$65

Nevada ....$30-$40

Red Block..$60-$70

Wheat and barley, blue..$35-$45

Souvenirs

The Alamo, Texas, Japan, 1940s, pair ....$15-$20

Disneyland Castle, 1960s, metal, pair....................$20-$25

Golden Gate Bridge, Japan, pair ....$30-$35

Mount Rushmore, Japan, 1950s, pair.....................$15-$20

SCIENCE FICTION & SPACE TOYS

The powerful draw of characters that range from Buck Rogers and Flash Gordon to Captain Kirk, Dr. Who and beyond has made space and science fiction collecting one of the fastest growing areas in all of collecting. Collectors have nearly a century of collectibles and dozens of characters to search for.

Background: Coming to the public first through 1920s newspaper strips and then radio shows, Buck Rogers did more than explore worlds in his 25th century—he paved the way for all kinds of sci-fi toy merchandising. Flash Gordon soon followed, and the rivalry for fans was intense between the two early science fiction heroes. While Buck Rogers was the first to arrive in print, Flash Gordon made it to theaters first with his 1936 film debut. When Rogers hit the big screen three years later, moviegoers may have wondered whether they were seeing double, and with good reason—actor Buster Crabbe portrayed both heroes!

As radio succumbed television during the 1950s, more space heroes, like Captain Video (1949) and Tom Corbett (1950) took their adventures into American homes with stunning results. But none of these early forays could equal the singular trajectory taken by Gene Roddenberry's *Star Trek*, which originally aired from 1966-1969 and subsequently gained a phenomenal following in syndication and beyond. No other sci-fi TV series has spawned so many films and spin-off series, not to mention the astonishing array of toys and collectibles ranging from action figures to starships.

When it comes to space adventure, however, George Lucas' epic *Star Wars* (1977) remains unparalleled for its sheer all-around success. The top-grossing film of all time during its first theatrical release, Star Wars sparked a merchandising frenzy unlike any other before it; more than 500 licensees issued related products, in the process setting new standards for licensing. Star Wars sequels *The Empire Strikes Back* (1980) and *Return of the Jedi* (1983) only strengthened its domination of the science fiction genre and collectible market. Toys in this category range from ray guns and board games to robots, action figures and play sets. Virtually every manufacturer has capitalized on these valuable licenses.

General Guidelines: As essential as six-shooters are to cowboy westerns, ray guns are perhaps the epitome of science fiction toys. Louis Marx produced a significant number of space guns both generic and character-related. Disney, Hubley and Wyandotte made memorable space gun contributions as well.

Ray guns have since given way to action figures, which seem to be the most popular science fiction toys on today's collectible market. Figures in original boxes and on original cards are the most valuable.

Star Wars toys (which, in this book, have a separate chapter) lead the pack. The first *Star Wars* action figures were marketed in 1977 by Kenner. Truly the Holy Grail for collectors, they may sell for $100 or more each in original packaging. Toys featuring science fiction sensations Land of the Giants and Lost in Space are highly collectible, particularly robots, premiums and model kits.

Robots from many eras, especially Japanese examples from the 1960s and earlier, are highly collectible.

Flash Gordon and Buck Rogers are among the most collectible early (pre-World War II) science fiction characters. Vintage Buck Rogers toys top collectors' lists, even in less than Excellent condition.

The fastest growing areas are *Star Wars* and *Star Trek*; some figures and play sets from 1977 and later are selling for hundreds of dollars.

Any space or science fiction toy is collectible, but not necessarily valuable. Don't pass on nondescript spaceships and figures, although those associated with a hit TV show or movie are often worth more.

Collecting Tips: When traveling into the world of science fiction and space toys, keep the following in mind:

Female figures, villainous aliens and variation figures are what drive the action figures market, one of the predominant areas of collectibles in the 1990s. Heroes tend to be produced in great abundance, because most people like them. So that makes aliens, villains, rouges and disreputable char-

---

THE TOP 10 SPACE AND SCIENCE FICTION TOYS

(IN MINT IN PACKAGE CONDITION)

1. Lost in Space doll set, Marusan/Japanese $7,000
2. Buck Rogers Solar Scouts Patch, Cream of Wheat, 1936 ....$7,000
3. Buck Rogers Cut-Out Adventure Book, 1933 .....$6,000
4. Space Patrol Monorail Set, Toys of Tomorrow, 1950s $4,200
5. Buck Rogers roller skates, Marx, 1935 ....$3,600
6. Buck Rogers pocket watch, E. Ingraham, 1935 ....$3,500
7. Buck Rogers costume, Sackman Bros., 1934 ......$2,500
8. Big Loo, Marx, 1960s $2,500
9. Lost In Space Switch-and-Go Set, Mattel, 1966 ....$2,300
10. Buck Rogers 25th Century Scientific Laboratory, Porter Chemical, 1934..$2,200

---

acters, plus females, relatively scarce. Variations in figures are sought-after too, but it takes training to find them before the scarce variations are published in collectors' magazines. They usually draw highest prices when they are first discovered, but sometimes allegedly scarce figures actually turn out to be easy to find, so you might do better to wait and look.

In order to be worth collecting, any hardcover book must be in Near Mint condition, with the dust jacket in similar shape. The only defect in a dust jacket that does not significantly reduce value is "price-clipping," where a small portion of the inside front flap of the dust jacket is cut to remove the original price. This was commonly done to books given as gifts and by some used book dealers who wanted to charge more than the original price. It is a pointless practice today, because the price is also printed on the bar code box in back. Ex-library copies, not necessarily scarce or valuable, can be a useful source for missing dust jackets.

First-edition hardcovers of the first book by an author who later becomes famous have seen the greatest collector interest and are the most valuable. First-edition paperbacks of the author's first books are a lot more valuable than reprint paperbacks, but still do not generally become incredibly valuable. In addition, paperback print runs are about 10 times as large as hardcover books, so they are rarely very scarce.

Pulp magazines, the dominant form of science fiction publishing from 1926 until the late 1940s, are generally found in Very Good condition or less. Stories written by certain authors—Isaac Asimov, Ray Bradbury, Edgar Rice Burroughs, H.P. Lovecraft and Robert A. Heinlein—are more valuable than most, as are those featuring Buck Rogers.

The original legendary model kit company was Aurora. Its models are the highest priced in the field. Aurora

made famous models for *The Invaders, Land of the Giants, Lost in Space* and *Star Trek*. When it went out of business, some of its former employees formed Addar and made a number of famous models for *Planet of the Apes*. Today, much of the action in new model kits is in expensive vinyl kits.

Buck Rogers was the first of the great space heroes. Many of his accessories, such as his Rocket Gun and Space Helmet, have become part of the familiar background of all space adventures. As a 1930s radio character, Buck had a club, the Solar Scouts, which you could join. There were plenty of premiums for a young fan to acquire. These are all quite valuable today.

Every movie produces posters, sometimes many different ones. Posters for really good movies become valuable, as do posters for really bad movies such as *Plan 9 From Outer Space*. Science fiction and horror movies are popular with poster collectors, so prices are a little higher than for mundane movies, but posters for recent movies can often be had for $10-$15.

Clubs

• Lost in Space Fan Club, 550 Trinity A Club, Westfield, NJ 07090

• Star Trek: The Official Fan Club, P.O. Box 111000, Aurora, CO 80011

Recommended Reading

Vintage Toys, Volume I: Robots and Space Toys, Jim Bunte, Dave Hallman and Henry Mueller
2000 Toys & Prices, Sharon Korbeck and Elizabeth Stephan
Science Fiction Collectibles Identification & Price Guide, Stuart W. Wells III
UFO and Alien Collectibles Price Guide, Dana Cain

Considered a true classic by serious collectors, the 1960s "Lost in Space" Robot by Remco is worth at least $500 in mint condition.

VALUE LINE

Action Figures

Values shown are figures in Mint-in-Package condition.

Battlestar Galactica (Mattel 1978-79)
Baltar	$75
Boray	$75
Commander Adama	$40
Cylon Centurian	$40
Cylon Commander	$110
Daggit, brown or tan	$30
Imperious Leader	$30
Lucifer	$110
Ovion	$35
Starbuck	$40

Buck Rogers (3-3/4") (Mego 1979)
Ardella	$15
Buck Rogers	$40
Doctor Huer	$20

Draco	$20	Alien figure, Kenner, 18", 1979	$200
Draconian Guard	$20	Alien model kit, Tsukuda, 1980s	$225
Killer Kane	$15	Alien Warrior model kit, Halcyon	$30
Tiger Man	$15	Aliens Colorforms set, Colorforms	$20
Twiki	$30	Aliens Computer Game, Commodore, 1985	$15
Wilma Deering	$25	Glow Putty, Laramie	$15

Lost in Space (Trendmasters 1998)

Battle Armor Don West	$8
Cryo Chamber Judy or Will Robinson	$8
Cyclops	$15
Dr. Smith	$15
Judy Robinson	$15
Proteus Armor Dr. Smith or John Robinson	$8
Tybo the Carrot Man	$15
Will Robinson	$15

Planet of the Apes (Mego 1973-75)

Astronaut Burke, boxed	$130
Astronaut Burke, carded	$100
Astronaut Verdon, boxed	$140
Astronaut Verdon, carded	$125
Astronaut, boxed	$150
Astronaut, carded	$100
Cornelius, boxed	$140
Cornelius, carded	$100
Dr. Zaius, boxed	$150
Dr. Zaius, carded	$100
Galen, boxed	$140
Galen, carded	$100
General Urko, boxed	$130
General Urko, carded	$100
General Ursus, boxed	$120
General Ursus, carded	$100
Soldier Ape, boxed	$140
Soldier Ape, carded	$100
Zira, boxed	$150
Zira, carded	$100

Star Trek (3-3/4") (Mego 1974-80)

Arcturian	$150
Betelgeusian	$150
Captain Kirk	$35
Decker	$35
Dr. McCoy	$35
Ilia	$20
Klingon	$150
Megarite	$150
Mr. Spock	$35
Rigellian	$150
Scotty	$35
Zatanite	$150

Other Space and Science Fiction Toys

Values shown are for items in Excellent condition.

Alien/Aliens

Alien Blaster Target Set, HG Toys	$170
Alien Chase Target Set, HG Toys	$165
Alien costume, Ben Cooper	$65

Movie viewer, Kenner, "Alien Terror" clip	$75

Battlestar Galactica

Battlestar Galactica model kit, Monogram, 1979	$25
Battlestar Galactica steel lunch box, 1978 Aladdin	$45
bottle	$15
Colonial Viper model kit, Monogram, 1979	$25
Colorforms Adventure Set, Colorforms, 1978	$20
Cylon Base Star model kit, Monogram, 1979	$30
Cylon Helmet Radio, 1979	$15
Cylon Raider model kit, Monogram, 1979	$25
Cylon Warrior costume, 1978	$15

COLLECTING IN SEPARATE WORLDS!

Science fiction literature, largely a 20th century phenomena, is generally divided into two categories—the book world and the media world. Readers reside in the book world; they collect books, magazines, cover art and attend conventions to meet their favorite authors and artist.

Those favoring the media world collect movie memorabilia, action figures and toys, comic books and trading cards. They seek autographs from major and minor movie stars and cast members from their favorite television shows.

But there is crossover among these two worlds. Readers will go see Star Trek and watch TV shows, while some media fans will read science fiction books. Although they often times know little or nothing about the collectibles in each other's worlds, members in both worlds are collectors, pursuing space-theme items in six general categories—action figures; books and magazines; comic books; models and statues; toys; and trading cards.

Examples of values for hardcover first-edition books include: The Martian Chronicles, (Ray Bradbury, 1950, Doubleday, $850); I, Robot (Isaac Asimov, 1950, Gnome Press, $1,250); Fantastic Voyage (Asimov, 1966, Houghton Mifflin, $200); The Puppet Masters (Robert Heinlein, 1951, Doubleday, $500); Reach for Tomorrow (Arthur C. Clarke, 1956, Ballantine, $500); Earthlight (Clarke, Ballantine, 1955, $1,000); Planet of the Apes (Pierre Boulle, 1963, Vanguard, $125); Dune (Frank Herbert, 1955, Chilton, $1,500); Brave New World (Aldous Huxley, 1932, Doubleday, signed, $1,500); A Princess of Mars (Edgar Rice Burroughs, 1917, McClurg, with dust jacket, $10,000); Nineteen Eighty-four (George Orwell, 1949, Harcourt, red dust jacket, $500); The War of the Worlds (H.G. Wells, 1898, Harper, $300).

Galactic Cruiser, Larami, 1978 .... $8
Game of Starfighter Combat, FASA, 1978 .... $15
L.E.M. Lander, Larami, 1978 .... $8
Lasermatic Pistol, Mattel, 1978 .... $30
Lasermatic Rifle, Mattel, 1978 .... $40
Poster Art Set, Craft Master, 1978 .... $10
Puzzles, Parker Brothers, 1978 .... $10
Space Alert Game, Mattel, 1978 .... $12

Buck Rogers

Buck Rogers in the 25th Century Pistol Set, Daisy,
    1930s $300
25th Century Police Patrol Rocket, Marx, 1935,
    tin wind-up $800
25th Century Scientific Laboratory, Porter Chemical,
    1934 .... $1,300
Atomic pistol, Daisy, 1946 .... $250
Battle Cruiser Rocket, Tootsietoy, 1937 .... $190
Buck Rogers 25th Century Rocket, Marx, 1939 .... $550
Buck Rogers badge, enameled, premium $125
Buck Rogers and the Doom Comet Book, Whitman,
    1935, Big Little Book $90
Buck Rogers figure, Tootsietoy, 1937 .... $150
Buck Rogers knife, premium $125
Buck Rogers, steel lunch box, 1979 Aladdin $35
    bottle $20
Buck Rogers movie projector, premium $200
Buck Rogers telescope, premium $105
Buck Rogers wristwatch, Huckleberry Time,
    1970s $100
Buck Rogers wristwatch, E. Ingraham, 1935 .... $650
Chemistry set, Grooper, 1937, advanced $700
Chief Explorer badge, 1936, gold $350
Colorforms set, Colorforms, 1979 .... $15
Cut-Out Adventure Book, 1933,
    Cocomalt premium $3,000
Flash Blast Attack Ship Rocket, Tootsietoy, 1937 ..... $150
Flying saucer, 1940s, paper $112
Helmet and Rocket Pistol set, Einson-Freeman,
    1933 .... $250
Lite-Blaster Flashlight, 1936 .... $260
Official Utility Belt, Remco, 1970s $35
Pencil box, American Pencil, 1930s $125
Pendant watch, Huckleberry Time, 1970s $185
Pocket knife, Adolph Kastor, 1934 .... $900
Pocket watch, E. Ingraham, 1935 .... $1,500
Punching bag, Morton Salt, 1942 .... $75
Puzzle, Milton Bradley, 1950 .... $35
Rocket ship, Marx, 1934 .... $425
Roller skates, Marx, 1935 .... $2,350
Rubber band gun, 1940 .... $75
Saturn ring, Post Corn Toasties, 1946 .... $500
Solar Scouts patch, Cream of Wheat, 1936 .... $5,000
Sonic Ray Gun, Norton-Honer, 1955 .... $115
Space Ranger kit, Sylvania, 1952 .... $100
Strato-Kite, Aero-Kite, 1946 .... $35

A recent Auctions Unlimited auction included (from top to bottom) a "Buck Rogers 25th Century Pistol" by Daisy that sold for $137, a "Buck Rogers Atomic Pistol" by Daisy that went for $275, and a "Numatic Space Gun" that brought $40.

Super Foto Camera, Norton-Honer, 1955 .... $70
Two-Way Transceiver, DA Myco, 1948 .... $130
View-Master set, View-Master, 1979 .... $8
Walkie Talkies, Remco, 1950s $125
XZ-35 space gun, 7", Daisy, 1934 .... $180

Captain Midnight

Air Heroes Stamp Album, 1930s $75
Captain Midnight medal, 1930s $125
Captain Midnight Flight Patrol Wings badge, 1941, pre-
    mium $72
Captain Midnight Flight Commander Signet ring,
    1957, premium $1,000
Captain Midnight Spy Scope, 1947, premium $80
Cup, Ovaltine $50
Membership manual, 1930s $55
Secret Society Decoder with key, 1949 .... $175

Captain Video

Captain Video Game, Milton Bradley, 1952 .... $125
Captain Video Secret Seal Ring, 1950s, premium $300
Comic book, Captain Video No. 1, Fawcett,
    1951 .... $375
Flying saucer ring, 1950s $1,000
Galaxy Spaceship riding toy, 1950s $425
Interplantary Space Men figures, 1950s $90
Mysto-Coder, with photo, 1950s $175
Rite-O-Lite Flashlight Gun, Power House Candy,
    1950s $80
Rocket Tank, Lido, 1952 .... $95
Secret Seal ring, 1950s $400
Space Port Play Set, Superior, 1950s $425
Troop Transport Ship, Lido, 1950s $95

Defenders of the Earth

Defenders Claw Copter, Galoob, 1985 .... $16
Garax battle action figure, Galoob, 1985 .... $16

This "Planet of the Apes" General Ursus figure, a 1975 Mego product, is worth about $100 Mint-on-Card.

Garax Swordship, Galoob, 1985 .... $16
Gripjaw vehicle, Galoob, 1985 .... $16
Lothar battle action figure, Galoob, 1985 .... $11
Mandrake the Magician battle action figure, Galoob, 1985 .... $10
Ming the Merciless battle action figure, Galoob, 1985 .... $11
Mongor figure, Galoob, 1985 .... $23
Phantom battle action figure, Galoob, 1985 .... $10
Phantom Skull Copter, Galoob, 1985 .... $10
Puzzle $13

Defenders of the Universe
Battling Black Lion Voltron Vehicle, LJN, 1986 .... $13
Coffin of Darkness Voltron Vehicle, LJN, 1986 .... $10
Doom Blaster Voltron Vehicle, LJN, 1986 .... $13
Doom Commander figure, Matchbox, 1985 .... $7
Green Lion Voltron Vehicle, LJN, 1986 .... $13
Hagar figure, Matchbox, 1985 .... $7
Hunk figure, Matchbox, 1985 .... $7
Keith figure, Matchbox, 1985 .... $7
King Zarkon figure, Matchbox, 1985 .... $7
Lance figure, Matchbox, 1985 .... $7
Motorized Lion Force Voltron Vehicle Set, LJN, 1985 .... $13
Pidge figure, Matchbox, 1985 .... $7
Prince Lothar figure, Matchbox, 1985 .... $7
Princess Allura figure, Matchbox, 1985 .... $7
Robeast Mutilor figure, Matchbox, 1985 .... $7
Robeast Scorpious figure, Matchbox, 1985 .... $7

Skull Tank Voltron Vehicle, LJN, 1986 13
Vehicle Team Assembler, LJN, 1986 .... $13
Voltron Motorized Giant Commander, LJN, 1984 .... $25
Zarkon Zapper Voltron Vehicle, LJN, 1986 .... $16

Doctor Who
Ace figure, Dapol, 1986 .... $16
Anniversary Set, Dapol, 1986 .... $390
Cyberman Robot Doll, Denys Fisher, 1970s $350
Dalek Army Gift Set, Denys Fisher, 1976 .... $60
Dalek Bagatelle, Denys Fisher, 1976 .... $100
Dalek Shooting Game, Marx, 1965 .... $325
Doctor Who card set, Denys Fisher, 1976 .... $26
Doctor Who doll, Denys Fisher, 1976 .... $130
Ice Warrior, Dapol, 1986 .... $13
Mel figure, Denys Fisher, 1976 .... $13
Tardis figure, Denys Fisher, 1976 .... $325

Flash Gordon
Automatic Disintegrator, Hubley $300
Book bag, 1950s $30
Captain Action outfit, Ideal, 1966 .... $275
Flash figure, Mattel, 1979 .... $16
Flash figure, Galoob, 1986 .... $10
Flash Gordon Air Ray Gun, Budson, 1950s $350
Flash Gordon and Alien model kit, Revell, 1965 .... $100
Flash Gordon and the Perils of Mongo book, Whitman, 1940, Big Little Book $60
Flash Gordon Arresting Ray Gun, Marx, 1939 .... $295
Flash Gordon costume, Esquire Novelty, 1951 .... $145
Flash Gordon game, House of Games, 1970s $25
Flash Gordon hand puppet, 1950s, rubber head $145
Flash Gordon kite, 1950s, paper $90
Flash Gordon Dome plastic lunch box, 1979 Aladdin .... $60, bottle $20
Flash Gordon Radio Repeater Clicker Pistol, Marx, 1930s $350
Flash Gordon signal pistol, Marx, 1930s $325
Flash Gordon water pistol, Marx, 1940s $130
Flash Gordon wristwatch, Bradley, 1979 .... $115
Pencil box, 1951 .... $120
Puzzles, Milton Bradley, 1951, set of three $180
Rocket fighter, Marx, 1939, wind-up $295
Rocket ship, Mattel, 1979 .... $35
Sunglasses, Ja-Ru, 1981 .... $5
Three-Color Ray Gun, Nasta, 1976 .... $13
Two-Way Telephone, Marx, 1940s $100
View-Master set, View-Master, 1963 .... $35
View-Master set, View-Master, 1976 .... $10
Wallet, 1949 .... $115
Water pistol, Marx, 1950s $260

Land of the Giants
Colored pencil set, Hasbro, 1969 .... $100
Colorforms set, Colorforms, 1968 .... $50
Costumes, Steve Burton, Giant Witch or Scientist, Ben Cooper, 1968, each $60
Double Action Bagatelle Game, Hasbro, 1969 .... $65

Flying saucer, Remco, 1968......................................$100
Land of the Giants coloring book, Whitman, 1968 ......$35
Land of the Giants comic book, #1, Gold Key,
    1968...$15
Land of the Giants steel lunch box, 1968 Aladdin......$150
    bottle...$50
Land of the Giants Diorama, Aurora, 1968 ....$365
Motorized Flying Rocket, Remco, 1968....................$130
Movie viewer, Acme, 1968..$45
Painting set, Hasbro, 1969 ....$65
Puzzle, Whitman, 1968 ....$55
Rub-Ons, Hasbro, 1969..$50
Shoot & Stick Target Rifle Set, Remco, 1968............$145
Signal Ray Space Gun, Remco, 1968 ....$115
Space sled, Remco, 1968 ....$325
Spaceship Control Panel, Remco, 1968....................$325
Spindrift model kit, Aurora, 1968............................$450
Target set, Hasbro, 1969 ....$100
Trading cards, Topps, 1968, set of 55 ....$450
View-Master set, GAF, 1968......................................$35
Walkie Talkies, Remco, 1968 ....$130
Wrist flashlight, Bantam Lite, 1968..........................$50

Lost in Space

3-D Fun set, Remco, 1968 ....$775
Chariot model kit, Lunar Models, 1987.....................$50
Costume, Ben Cooper, 1965 ....$130
Diorama model kit, Aurora, 1966.............................$650
Helmet and gun set, Remco, 1967 ....$525
Laser water pistol $50
Lost in Space Dome, 1967 King Seeley Thermos,
    steel lunch box $600
    bottle...$60
Lost in Space, large model kit with chariot, Aurora,
    1966...$1,485
Lost in Space, small model kit, Aurora, 1966.........$1,020
Lost in Space model kit, The Robot, Aurora,
    1968...$880
Note pad, June Lockhart on front $40
Puzzles, Milton Bradley, 1966 ....$65
Robot, Remco, 1960s...$310
Robot, Aurora, 1966 ....$650
Robot, AHI, 1977..$35
Robot, Remco, 1966 ....$450
Roto-Jet gun set, 1966..$1,300
Saucer gun, AHI, 1977..$50
Switch-and-Go set, Mattel, 1966 ....$1,500

IN THE BEGINNING!

The name science fiction was actually invented in the late 1920s, by the acknowledged father of sci-fi, Hugo Gernsbach, editor of Amazing Stories. His magazine, and the others that sprang up in the 1930s, were the primary places that science fiction was published for almost 25 years.

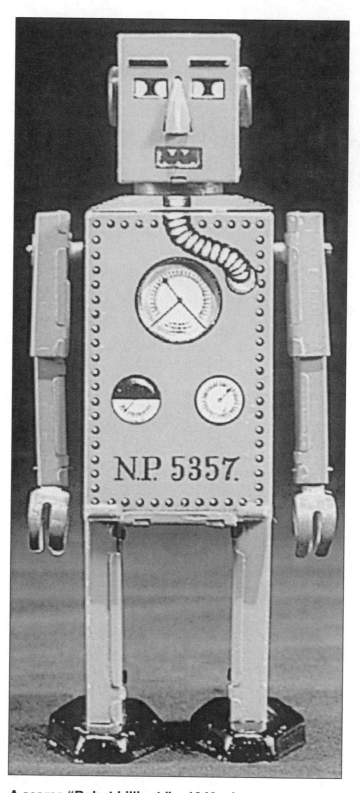

A scarce "Robot Lilliput," a 1940s Japanese robot, sold for over $8,000 at a Sotheby's auction in New York.

View-Master set, GAF, 1967..............................$40
Walkie Talkies, AHI, 1977.................................$50

Planet of the Apes

Color-Vue set, Hasbro, 1970s $45
Dr. Zaius bank, Play Pal, 1967 ....$25
Fun-Doh Modeling Molds, Chemtoy, 1974.................$30
Galen bank, Play Pal, 1960s $35
Planet of the Apes Activity Book, Saalfield, 1974 ....$30
Planet of the Apes Coloring Book, Saalfield, 1974 ......$30
Planet of the Apes steel lunch box, 1974 Aladdin .$85 bot-
    tle..$45
Puzzles, H.G. Toys..$10
View-Master set, GAF, 1967.............................$25
Wastebasket, Chein, 1967 ....$35

Space: 1999

Adventure Play set, Amsco/Milton Bradley, 1976 ....$50
Astro Popper Gun, 1976 ....$10
Colorforms Adventure Set, Colorforms, 1975.............$16
Commander Koenig figure, Mattel, 1976 ....$30
Cut and Color Book, Saalfield, 1975 ....$10
Dr. Russel figure, Mattel, 1976 ....$30
Eagle Freighter, Dinky, 1975 ....$50
Eagle One model kit, MPC, 1976 ....$80
Eagle One Spaceship, Mattel, 1976 ....$300
Eagle Transport, Dinky, 1975 ....$50
Film Viewer TV Set, 1976 ....$20
Galaxy Time Meter, 1976 ....$10
Moon Base Alpha model kit, MPC, 1976.................$30
Moonbase Alpha play set, Mattel, 1976 ....$50
Puzzle, HG Toys, 1976 ....$10
Space Expedition dart set, 1976.........................$10
Space: 1999, coloring book, Saalfield....................$20
Space: 1999 steel lunch box,
    1976 King Seeley Thermos $55
        bottle..$25
Talking View-Master set, View-Master, 1975.............$20
Utility belt set, Remco, 1976 ....$40
Walking Spaceman, 1975.................................$150

Star Trek

Action Toy Book, Random House, 1976 ....$10
Clock, 1986..$20
Colorforms set, Colorforms, 1975 ....$20
Comb and brush set, 1977...............................$20
Communicators walkie talkies, Mego, 1976.............$100
Controlled Space Flight, Remco, 1976,
    Enterprise $115
Enterprise model kit, AMT, 1966 ....$350
Enterprise wristwatch, Rarities Mint, 1989 ....$80
Enterprise inflatable, Sterling, 1986....................$30
Figurine paint set, Milton Bradley, 1979 ....$20
Flashlight, 1976, phaser shape $8
Helmet, Remco, 1976 ....$80
Kirk bank, Play Pal, 1975 ....$35
Kirk costume, Ben Cooper, 1975.........................$13
Kirk or Spock costumes, Ben Cooper, 1967..............$16

Kite, Hi-Flyer, 1975, Spock or Enterprise $20
Klingon costume, Ben Cooper, 1975 ....$13
Klingon Cruiser model kit, AMT, 1968......................$155
Klingon Cruiser model kit, Aurora 1972 ....$68
Metal detector, Jetco, 1976 ....$145
Needlepoint kit, Arista, 1980 ....$23
Paint-by-Numbers set, Hasbro, 1972, large $50
Pennant, Image Products, 1982, "Spock Lives" $8
Phaser, Remco, 1975......................................$50
Phaser gun, Remco, 1967.................................$115
Puzzle, H.G. Toys, 1976, Kirk, Spock, McCoy $6
Spock bank, Play Pal, 1975................................$35
Spock Bop Bag, 1975 ....$80
Spock costume, Ben Cooper, 1973 ....$16
Spock model kit, AMT, 1973..............................$130
Star Trek Color and Activity Book, Whitman,
    1979...$5
Star Trek Dome, steel lunch box, 1968 Aladdin,........$700
    bottle...$375
Tracer gun, Rayline, 1966.................................$65
U.S.S. Enterprise Action Play Set, Mego, 1975 ....$180
U.S.S. Enterprise model kit, Aurora, 1972 ....$89
Utility belt, Remco, 1975.................................$65
View-Master set, GAF, 1974..............................$16
Vulcan Shuttle Model, Ertl, 1984 ....$25
Wastebasket, Chein, 1977 ....$50
Water pistol, Azrak-Hamway, 1976 ....$30

Water pistol, Aviva, 1979 ....$20
Writing tablet, 1967 ....$16
Yo-Yo, Aviva, 1979 ....$10

Tom Corbett

Binoculars $100
Flash X-1 Space Gun $95
Model Craft Molding Super Set, Kay Standley,
   1950s $165
Official Space Pistol, Marx, 1950s $80
Official Sparking Space Gun, Marx $130
Polaris wind-up spaceship, Marx, 1952 ....$325
Push-Outs book, Saalfield, 1952 ....$50
Puzzles, Saalfield, 1950s $30
Rocket Scout ring, 1950s $16
Signal Siren Flashlight, Usalite, 1950s $115
Space Academy Play Set, Marx, 1950s $310
Space Cadet 2 Spaceship, Marx, 1930s,
   tin wind-up $375
Space Cadet Atomic Rifle, 1950s $165
Space cadet belt, 1950s $105
Space gun, 1950s $120
Space suit ring, 1950s $16
Tom Corbett Coloring Book, Saalfield, 1950s $40
Tom Corbett decoder, 1950s, cardboard, premium $52
Tom Corbett portrait ring, 1950s $35
Tom Corbett Space Cadet badge, 1950s, premium $75
Tom Corbett wristwatch, Ingraham, 1950s $425
View-Master set, Sawyer's, 1950s $50

Robots

Answer Game Machine, battery-operated robot
   performs math tricks $650
Attacking Martian, S.H., 1960s $100
B.O. Robot, 1950s $450
Big Loo, Marx, 1960s $1,250
Chief Robotman, KO, 1965 ....$850
Cragstan's Mr. Robot, Cragstan, 1960s $400
Electric Robot, Japan, 1960s $250
Forbidden Planet Robby, Masudaya, 16" $115
Forbidden Planet Robby, Masudaya, 5" $23
Frankenstein, Marx, 1960s $250
Laughing Robot, Marx $70
Launching Robot, S.H., 1975 ....$35
Mechanized Robot, 1960s $600
Moon Creature, Marx, 1960s $170
Mr. Atom, Advance Toys, 1960s $300
Mr. Machine, Ideal, 1961 ....$195
Mr. Mercury, Marx, 1960s $500
Piston Robot, Japan, 1970s $100
Radio control robot, Bilko, 1970s $35
Robot the Wonder Toy, Ideal, 1960 ....$130
Robot Commando, Ideal, 1960s $300
Sky Robot, S.H., 1970s $30
Sparky Robot, KO, 1960 ....$65
Television Space Man, Alps, 1950s $450

Spaceships

Eagle Lunar Module, 1960s $115
Friendship 7 ....$50
Inter-Planet Toy Rocketank Patrol, Macrey, 1950 ....$45
Jupiter Space Station, TN/Japan, 1960s $125
Moon-Rider Spaceship, Marx, 1930s, tin wind-up $200
Mystery Spaceship, Marx, 1960s $75
Rocket Fighter, Marx, 1950s $375
Rocket Fighter Spaceship, Marx, 1930s $200
Satellite X-107, Cragstan, 1965 ....$130
Sky Patrol Jet, TN/Japan, 1960s $425
Solar-X Space Rocket, TN/Japan $65
Space Bus $500
Space Pacer, 1978 ....$29
Space Survey X-09 ....$350
Space Train, 1950s $26
Spaceship, Marx $60
Super Space Capsule, 1960s $100
X-3 Rocket Gyro, 1950s $35

This "Planet of the Apes" model kit by Addar is worth about $60-$75 in Mint-in-Box condition.

View-Master Reels

Values shown are examples in Mint-in-package condition.

Buck Rogers, L15 .... $8
Close Encounters of the Third Kind, J47 .... $15
Dr. Who, BD187 or BD216 .... $75
E.T. The Extra-Terrestrial, N7 .... $18
Flash Gordon in the Planet Mongo $25
Mork and Mindy, K67 .... $8
Planet of the Apes, BB507 or B507 .... $35
Space: 1999, BD150 or BB451 .... $25
Star Trek—The Motion Picture K57 .... $12

Games

Buck Rogers in the 25th Century, card,
   1936 All-Fair ....$160-$350
Buck Rogers and His Cosmic Rocket Wars,
   board, 1934....................................$200-$350
Battlestar Galactica, board,
   1978 Parker Brothers.........................$15-$25
Doctor Who, board, 1980s Denys Fisher.............$75-$100
Fantastic Voyage, board, 1968 Milton Bradley......$25-$40
Flash Gordon, board, 1977 Waddington/House
   of Games ....$2-$35
Land of the Giants, board, 1968 Ideal................$100-$160

Lost in Space, board, 1965 Parker Brothers.........$75-$120
Mork and Mindy, board, 1978 Milton Bradley......$15-$25
Space: 1999, board, 1975 Milton Bradley ....$15-$25
Star Trek, board, 1979 Milton Bradley ....$40-$60
Star Trek, board, 1960s Ideal ....$100-$135
Planet of the Apes, board,
   1974 Milton Bradley ....$45-$65

Other

Astro Base, Ideal, 1960..$325
Astronaut costume, Collegeville, 1960 ....$25
Astronaut costume, Ben Cooper, 1962 ....$25
Atomic Ray Gun, Hiller, 1949 ....$225
Cherilea space gun, Marx $40
Dan Dare & the Aliens Ray Gun, 1950s....................$155
Martian bobbing head, 1960s.......................................$35
Men Into Space space helmet, Ideal, 1960s.................$50
My Favorite Martian coloring book, Whitman............$20
Rocket gun, Jak-Pak, 1958...$13
Space water pistol, Nasta, 1976 ....$10
Space Ghost coloring book, Whitman $30
Voyage to the Bottom of the Sea Scout Play Set,
   Remco, 1964 ....$600
Voyage to the Bottom of the Sea Seaview Play Set,
   Remco, 1964 ....$650

VINTAGE SEWING COLLECTIBLES

People often try to glean the history of fashion from Hollywood movies, and the garments preserved by society's upper echelon. Sewing items, however, offer a wonderful glimpse at what it took to make the real woman's wardrobe—and that of her family. Although the clothing was often worn until threadbare and then thrown out, the sewing patterns, advertisements and tools used by the everyday tailor show the story behind the outfits. The daily work of our grandmothers and great-grandmothers is commemorated in this collecting category.

Background: Sewing was considered an essential skill of the 19th century woman, as evinced by a wealth of early American samplers. Regardless of her economic and social status, most every woman was skilled in sewing and dressmaking. In fact, as recently as 50 years ago sewing items were still found in almost every home in America.

Many of the earliest sewing tools were made of wood. During the Victorian era a vast assortment of practical, as well as whimsical, sewing devices appeared on the market. Among them were tape measures, pincushions, stilettos for punchwork and crochet hooks. Sewing birds—attached to table tops to hold fabric—were a standard fixture in the parlor. Sized paper patterns were introduced in the mid-1800s and quickly caught on. By the 1870s several companies were competing to produce the best paper patterns, which evolved into the tissue-paper variety seen today.

In the late 1910s the treadle-foot sewing machine gave way to electric power. Paired with the sized patterns, sewing became a breeze compared to the earlier efforts. Soon Hollywood's influence would hit the sewing world, with patterns and fabrics that brought a little bit of the glamour of the big screen within reach for the average family.

General Guidelines: Collectors tend to favor sterling silver items, from thimbles to darning eggs, stilettos and thread holders. Advertising and souvenir items also attract a lot of attention – needle cases and sewing kits were important advertising giveaways in the 20th century. Although many plastic items are available, they do not attract a significant amount of collecting interest. Figural items—tape measures, sewing birds, etc.—are always popular because of their display potential.

Many old sewing machines are still going for relatively low prices, as are tissue paper patterns which can be found for a few dollars. Many of the patterns are purchased for the purpose of making and wearing the clothes. Those for clothing styles that are back in vogue, therefore, often attract more interest than pieces that are older or more historically significant.

Clubs

• International Sewing Machine Collectors Society, 1000 E. Charleston Blvd., Las Vegas, NV 89104

• Thimble Collectors International, 6411 Montego Bay, Louisville, KY 40228

COLLECTING TIP!

The best way to date tissue paper patterns is with the accompanying catalogs and magazines that were produced. Such materials make both a useful and an interesting addition to any collection of sewing materials. Check local fabric stores to see if they are looking to get rid of any old materials. Also consider using sewing machine advertisements and catalogs, along with other reference materials, both to complement and to authenticate your collection.

VALUE LINE

Advertisement, 1957 Singer sewing machine	$8
Bobbin, ivory, Chinese, Victorian carved flowers	$60
Bobbins, treadle-style machine, 1-1/8"	$10
Button hook, bone handle, 2-1/2"	$20
Button hook, mother-of-pearl handle, 6"	$45
Catalog, "Button Sampler," Albert/Adams, Grammercy, 1951, 140 pages	$20
Catalog, "Davis Sewing Machine," New York, N.Y., 1895, 18 pages	$25
Catalog, "Domestic Sewing Machine," New York, N.Y., 1883, 26 pages	$35
Catalog, "New Home Sewing Machine," 1900, 12 pages	$12
Catalog, "Singer Manufacturing Co.," N.J., 1900, eight pages	$25
Catalog, Wilson Sewing Machine Co., Chicago, IL, 26 pages	$40
Chatelaine, silver, three love tokens, 1880s	$110
Crochet hooks, whale bone, carved, 3-piece set	$250
Darner, glass, cobalt blue	$135
Patterns, 1920s-1940s	$10
Embroidery hoop, Shaker, 6", walnut and cherry, table clamp, handmade	$150
Embroidery scissors, steel, Germany	$45
Magazine, *The Tailors*, E. Butterick & Co, 1880s	$30
Mending kit, Bakelite, with thimble cap	$30
Needle case, Bakelite, shaped like a doll	$35
Needle case, silver, ribbed	$25

Vintage thimbles are easy to display and still very affordable. This pair, a floral Pickard china thimble and a West German floral thimble, would sell in the $12-$20 range.

Advertising thimbles are a popular collecting category. These Coca-Cola and Campbell's thimbles are recent examples that are available for only about $2 each.

Oil can, "Singer"	$10
Pattern, Butterick, 1898, #1103, skirt	$75
Pattern, Butterick, 1930s, princess slip	$20
Pattern, McCalls, #2901, 1908, girl's size 14 dress	$65
Pattern, McCalls, Ginny doll outfits, 1957	$25
Pattern, McCalls, blouse size 16, 1931	$40
Pattern, McCalls, #1855, 1954, girl's size 8	$2
Pattern, Vogue, size 16, Paris original, Paquin suit, 1956	$65
Patterns, 1940s, Butterick, Vogue, McCalls, four patterns	$7
Pin cushion, black girl, print fabric	$40
Pin cushion, stuffed dog with tape measure as tongue, Japan, corduroy	$25
Pin cushion, slipper, beaded leather, 5", 1950s	$65
Pin cushion, doll, arms at head	$20
Sewing basket, pink wicker, 1950s, gray felt poodle, oval	$35
Sewing basket, weaved, brass hinges	$35
Sewing bird, 1853, two blue pin cushions, good condition	$130
Sewing bird, iron, brass heart-shaped thumbscrew	$125
Sewing box, Victorian, ivory implements, crimson velvet, brass trim, includes scissors, needle cases	$250
Sewing box, antique, dovetailed, holds parts and accessories, patented 1899	$20
Sewing box, brass St. Bernard decoration, wooden, blue fabric inside	$75

Sewing kit, occupied Japan, metal, blue velvet pin cushion lid, with thimble and thread	$10
Sewing set, bone and ivory, shuttle, button, crochet hooks, etc.	$60
Singer children's toy sewing machine, 1910-14, model 20	$150
Singer sewing book, 1950, 244 pages	$20
Sewing bird clamp, Victorian, brass	$75
Tape measure, thimble on top with spools of thread	$25
Tape measure, metal, turtle-shaped	$50
Tape measure, Colgate Fab Soap, celluloid	$15
Tape measure, black boy and alligator, 1920s, made in Japan, celluloid	$200
Tape measure, red apple, green leaf reveals tape, "United Device Corp."	$15
Tape measure, John Deere, 1919, celluloid, "Parisian Novelty Co."	$60
Tape measure, Eiffel Tower, 3", metal	$300
Tape measure, celluloid fruit basket, 2" long	$50
Tape measure, Maxfield Parrish art, celluloid	$250
Tape measure, 1904 St. Louis World's Fair, celluloid	$50
Tape measure, silver metal pig, corkscrew tail to release tape	$100
Thimble, Victorian, 10K gold	$100
Trade card, Singer Sewing Machine, 1899	$20
Trade card, Domestic Sewing Machine Co.	$10
Trade cards, JP Coats, Merrick, Clarks	$6

SPACE MEMORABILIA

Man has always been fascinated by outer space.

So, too, have collectors. Science fiction and space toys have been popular since the early days of Buck Rogers and Flash Gordon.

Now you can add actual space memorabilia to the list. Not toys or games, but the real thing: historic artifacts from actual space flights—everything from authentic space suits worn by real astronauts to items that have gone to the moon and back. For those can afford it, these are new space "toys." They're not really antiques—there's nothing more than 40 years old—but memorabilia from the U.S. and Soviet space programs is fast becoming one of today's hottest collectibles. And it's a collecting area that's just starting to take off.

Background: The U.S.-Russian space race began during the Cold War years of post-World War II. The Soviets took the early lead with their launch of "Sputnik," the world's first satellite, on October 4, 1957. "Explorer," the first U.S. satellite, came some four months later. Both countries launched their first men into space in 1961, the Soviets sending Yuri Gagarin on April 12; and America sending Alan Shepard on May 5. The space race continued at a furious pace throughout the 1960s, culminating with the historic Apollo 11 flight, which saw the first Americans land on the moon in July of 1969, fulfilling President Kennedy's bold prediction of landing a man on the moon before the end of the decade.

The sixth and final moon mission came in 1972. For the past three decades, America's space program has concentrated mainly on shuttle missions and unmanned exploratory flights to Mars and beyond.

One especially significant mission in the space race was a joint mission conducted by the U.S. and Soviets in July of 1975, when a U.S. Apollo crew linked up with a Russian Soyuz crew in space—sort of a brief truce in both the space race and the Cold War. Because of its historical significance, memorabilia related to this flight is especially desirable.

General Guidelines: Authentic space memorabilia is not common, but it is more plentiful than most people might think. Thousands of people have been involved in both the U.S. and Soviet space programs over the past five decades, and many souvenirs and other items have found their way into private hands and collections. In the disarray following the break-up of the Soviet Union, especially, many items from the Russian space program were spirited away and found new homes in the United States and elsewhere.

Still, authentic space memorabilia is not something you're likely to find at the local flea market or yard sale—unless, of course you live in John Glenn's or Buzz Aldrin's neighborhood. Most of the better material in this hobby lies in the domain of the major auction houses. Sotheby's and Superior Stamp & Coin are two of the auction firms that have held major sales of space memorabilia in the past few years. As this collecting area grows—and more and more items find their way into private collections—space memorabilia will start showing up in the more traditional collecting arenas, like collector shows and on-line auctions.

As you might expect, the true treasures of this hobby—everything from actual space suits to tiny vials of moon dust—are very expensive, selling for many thousands of dollars, and beyond the reach of the average collector. But there are plenty of more affordable space-related artifacts to look for, including autographs or astronauts and cosmonauts, books, newspapers and magazines, uniform patches, commemorative buttons and ribbons, photographs, contractor's models, training manuals, other technical documents, and so on.

For serious collectors, the most desirable pieces are what the hard-core enthusiasts call "flown" items—material

For collectors who can afford it, these are the real space toys. Actual space suits, like this one offered in a recent Sotheby's auction, are worth thousands.

that was actually taken into space and brought back. Items that went to the moon and back are especially coveted. Less valuable are prototype pieces or items that were used in training and not for actual missions.

Some of the items that have been sold in past auctions have been truly amazing. In one Sotheby's sale, a collector stunned the gallery when he paid $400,000—about ten times the pre-sale estimate—for a group of moon rocks, really just three small specks, brought back by an unmanned Soviet lunar mission. Selling for even more was an authentic "flown" Russian space capsule, used on a real space flight, which went for $500,000. In another auction, another "flown" Soviet capsule—this one launched by the Russians on March 23, 1961 with a mannequin on board—failed to sell with an estimate of one million dollars. The capsule was used for a test mission twenty days before Cosmonaut Yuri Gagarin made his first manned flight. Gagarin's handwritten logbook from that historic flight sold for $320,000, while a congratulatory telegram he received from Nikita Krushchev upon his return went for $60,000. (Other Soviet space capsules have sold for as much as $1.5 million.)

The values shown in the "Value Line" are taken from various recent auctions and should serve as a good indicator of the range of prices and material that is available. Also included are a few toys, games, puzzles and other commercial space-related items.

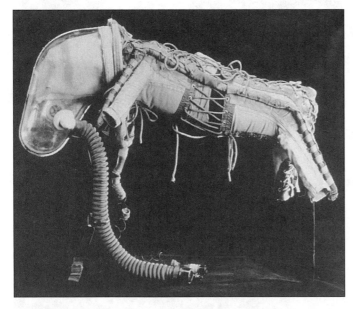

Among the more unusual items in a recent Sotheby's auction of space memorabilia was this doggie space suit from the Soviet program.

VALUE LINE

U.S. Space Program Memorabilia

Autographed photo of seven original
    Mercury astronauts $3,200
Autographed photo of Grissom, White and Chaffee
    (the three astronauts died in a 1967 launch-pad
    fire) $3,850
Autographed photo, Gus Grissom $250
Autographed photo, Alan Shepard $185
Autographed postal cover (flown), taken to the moon
    and back by Buzz Aldrin on Apollo 11, autographed
    by Aldrin, Armstrong, and Collins $25,000
Autographed postal cover, Christa McAuliffe $1,500
Board Game, "Countdown," 1967 .... $75
Board Game, "Shuttle Command," Universe Games,
    1985 .... $40
Cape Kennedy souvenir felt pennant, mid-1960s $50
Commemorative button and ribbon from 1962
    John Glenn flight $70
Contractor's plastic model of original
    Mercury capsule $850
Contractor's model of Saturn rocket, 10" long $450
Contractor's model of early Gemini capsule, 8" $1,250
Contractor's model of Apollo spacecraft, 21" $1,500
Crew patch, flown on Apollo 11 by
    Buzz Aldrin $1,850
Flag, small, silk American flag carried into space by
    Ed White and flown outside during America's
    first space walk $3,000
Flag, small American flag carried to moon and
    back by Buzz Aldrin $2,500
Heat shield fragments from John Glenn's historic
    space capsule $1,100
Heat shield fragment from Apollo 13 spacecraft,
    1/2" piece in glass display case $450
Helmet, early high-altitude test-pilot helmet,
    1956 .... $550

STRANGE COLLECTIBLES!

Generally, when you buy something at auction, you expect to take possession of it immediately. That's not always the case, however, at an auction of space memorabilia. In one of the more bizarre auction highlights, a buyer once paid $60,000 for a lunar rover used by the Soviets during one of their unmanned moon missions. The only problem is that the rover is still there, marooned on the moon's surface, some 240,000 miles away, with no chance it will ever be brought back to earth. The buyer, in effect, paid $60,000 for a bill of sale—and the assurance that if he ever gets to the moon, at least he won't have to rent a car.

Historic newspapers and magazines,
typical example ....$5-$35
Jigsaw puzzle, "Astronauts of Apollo 11" 1969 .... $60
Lunar rover novelty license plate, flown to moon and
back by Apollo 15 crew $6,900
Manual, countdown manual for John Glenn's
first flight, 1962, used by Guenter Wendt $1,750
Model kit, "Tranquillity Base" lunar model kit,
1969, Revell $60
Moon dust, small vial from Apollo 12 mission,
removed from Charles Conrad's space suit....... $37,000
Orange flying suit, used by Jim Irwin during survival train-
ing in the Panama jungle (and for painting his house in
retirement) $675
Phonograph record, "To the Moon," 1969,
with book, Time/Life............................ $40
Space food, freeze-dried potato soup, returned
unopened from space flight $3,850
Space helmet, complete, used by Ed White............. $8,250
Space suit, early full-pressure suit designed by
B.F. Goodrich in 1957 .... $7,500
Space suit, training suit used by Gus Grissom......... $6,000
Space suit, back-up suit used by Wally Schirra $4,500
Space suit glove, believed used by ill-fated Apollo
1 crew $2,850

Soviet Space Memorabilia

Bank, "Sputnik," lithographed tin, with space dog
"Laika," 1958 .... $150
Chess set, first chess set used in space.................. $30,000
Letter, delivered to Cosmonaut Vladimir Shatalov on
board Soyuz 4 during a daring capsule-to-capsule ren-
dezvous, first letter delivered to space............. $110,000
Slide rule, used by chief engineer of Soviet space
program $190,000
Space capsule, "Kosmos," unmanned photo-reconnais-
sance spy satellite, flown in space
Oct.-Nov. 1978.............................. $112,000
Space suit, high-altitude canine pressure suit
designed for Soviet space dogs $25,000
Space suit, complete from 1973 Soyuz-Salyut
program $31,000
Space suit, worn by Cosmonaut Alexei Leonev on
historic 1975 Apollo/Soyuz joint mission....... $140,000
Training suit, used by Cosmonaut Alexei Leonev,
first man to walk in space............................... $230,000
Yuri Gagarin, handwritten flight record from
first manned flight $320,000
Yuri Gagarin, handwritten and autographed
manuscript of speech....................................... $110,000

This is the book in which THE ASTRONAUTS tell their first-hand story of the first Americans in space.

Alan B. Shepard, Jr.   Walter M. Schirra, Jr.

Donald K. Slayton   M. Scott Carpenter   John R. Glenn, Jr.

Virgil I. Grissom   L. Gordon Cooper, Jr.

PUBLISHED BY POCKET BOOKS, INC.   PRINTED IN U.S.A.

A more conventional collectible is this book auto-graphed by the seven original U.S. astronauts. It was offered at a Superior Galleries auction with a $1,500 estimate.

Yuri Gagarin, flight instructions from chief
flight engineer $65,000
Yuri Gagarin, medal awarded by
Soviet government...$55,000
Yuri Gagarin, wrist watch, personally owned........$32,500
Yuri Gagarin, autographed photo............................$6,500

SPORTS MEMORABILIA

"Programs, here! Get your programs here!"

Chances are, if you have been to a major league sporting event, you've heard the vendors hawking their wares, those collectible reminders of the day you spent in a big league stadium or park.

Maybe, just maybe, if you were really lucky that day, you caught a foul ball, which now sits on your mantelpiece. And, if you were lucky enough to bat a thousand, after the game you were able to meet the player who hit the ball into the stands. And he signed the ball for you. It's the dream of every little leaguer.

But one does not have to limit himself to the elusive foul ball, or even autographs. Over the past century, when you consider that there are four major professional sports, you'll realize thousands and thousands of different eclectic sports collectibles have been produced.

Do you want to buy Pete Rose's 1978 Silver Wraith Rolls Royce? ($44,000) The boyhood home of Mickey Mantle? ($60,500). How about a 1950s Zamboni machine used by the New York Rangers in Madison Square Garden? ($500-$700).

Those items were on the market during sports auctions, a good place to find the unusual items. But for the average collector, there are lots of things to collect. This chapter will cover the mainstream items. If, however, you are looking for the oddball items, there are dealers who specialize in these.

For more information on sports-related autographs, bobbing head dolls, cereal boxes and *Sports Illustrated*, see the corresponding chapters in this book.

Equipment—Whether it's a Hall of Famer's game-used uniform or one of the exact replica jerseys made by Mitchell and Ness Co. of Philadelphia, memorabilia comes in all different shapes, styles and price ranges.

Whereas owing a souvenir such as a program from a game is a nostalgic reminder of a certain event, owning an item such as a hockey stick that was handled at one time by Gordie Howe puts a collector a little bit closer to a legendary sporting figure.

Some collectors specialize in a favorite player or team, while others collect on a much broader scale—such as an entire sport.

Equipment collecting spans the gamut of uniforms, gloves, bats, helmets, sticks, skates and game apparel. Your best chance of obtaining game used items—if you don't get them directly from the player—is to build a base of experience, trusted collectors.

There are also books available from Krause Publications that will give you great tips and pointers on these collectibles. So, that might be a wise purchase before heading off to buy that Michael Jordan game-used Chicago Bulls jersey.

Team publications—Although some exist from the 1950s, it wasn't until the late 1950s that what we now consider as yearbooks and media guides were produced by professional teams on a regular basis. Most yearbooks from the 1960s offer collectors an affordable alternative for less than $100. Those from the 1940s and 1950s can bring top dollar, depending on scarcity and age.

To be classified as a yearbook, generally a publication must have photographs of every player on the 25-man roster, plus biographies and statistics. Media guides, which debuted in the 1940s, were given to radio, television and newspaper beat reporters who covered professional teams during the season. They are designed to provide almost every imaginable kind of biographical and statistical tidbits to the reporters; the reporters quite often were the only source from which collectors could obtain a media guide, but in recent years teams have made copies available to fans.

Programs—Many fans purchase a souvenir program to keep score in when they attend a professional game, as reading material, or to have autographed (which increases its value). Unscored programs are preferred, but if the scoring is done neatly the program does have intrinsic value; it provides a history of what happened and can trigger fond memories.

Condition is a key factor in determining a program's value. The nicer it is, the more valuable it will be. In general, football programs from the 1930s are worth $85-$100; those

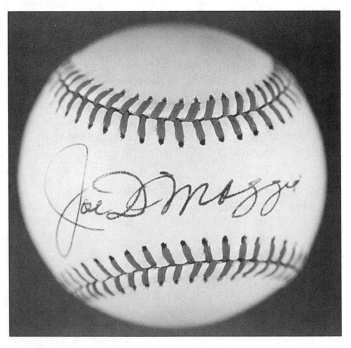

Collectors generally prefer "single-signed" autographed baseballs containing just one signature. A Joe DiMaggio autographed ball is worth about $350.

from 1940-45 are worth $45-$60; those from 1946-50 are worth $25-$50; those from the 1950s are worth $20-$30; those from the 1960s are worth $15-$35; those from the 1970s are worth $6-$8; those from the 1980s are worth $5-$6; and those from the 1990s are worth $5 or less.

In general, NBA programs from the 1960s are $20-$25, while those from the 1970s are $10-$20. Special events bring more. Hockey programs from the 1930s can bring $50-$75, while those from the 1940s can bring $40-$50. Programs from the 1960s can bring $25-$35, while those from the 1970s are worth $15-$25. Programs from the 1980s are up to $15

Baseball regular season programs from before 1900 might set you back $500-$750; 1900s-1910 will be in the $200-$500 range; 1910-19, $75-$200; 1920-29, $35-$75; 1930-39, $20-$35; 1940-49, $15-$25; 1950-59, $10-$25; 1960-69, $5-$25. Everything after 1970 is usually less than $15.

The most valuable programs are generally World Series programs, which have been produced since 1903, and Stanley Cup, NBA Finals and Super Bowl programs. World Series programs, especially from championship teams, are in more demand than those from All-Star games and regular season games. Since 1974, only one program has been produced for the World Series for both teams participating. This holds true for Super Bowl programs. The first two are in great demand.

Books—Four main factors determine the value of a book: scarcity, desirability, condition and edition. Condition greatly affects the value—torn pages, coffee stains and general wear and tear all reduce the value. A lack of a dust jacket also drops the book's value. To be worth top dollar, a book should also be a first printing of a first edition. Books which have little or no value to collectors would be those which are discards from libraries.

Autographs add to the book's value. It can be signed by the author or the subject, or both. But a biography of a superstar does not automatically mean that book is valuable. For example, there is no scarce Mickey Mantle biography. But there is a hard-to-find biography of Rocky Colavito; since it is scarcer, it is more valuable.

There is no guarantee that a book will appreciate dramatically, so the average collector is advised to collect books he enjoys for his own sake. You might consider specializing – team, player, genre, topic. You can find books all over – garage sales, card shows, library sales, antiquarian books sales, hobby publications, used book stores and used book dealers.

Games—Generally, player or team-related games are in greater demand than more generic games. Board games are more valuable than card games. Other factors which can influence a value include the games age (older is more valuable); company (Milton Bradley and Parker Brothers are two of the top); graphics and illustrations (higher quality and more colorful are more valueable); box and board style (wood and metal are more valuable than cardboard); theme; and completeness (no missing parts).

Commemoratives—Commemorative covers and postcards is a category that is ideally suited for sports collecting.

Famous athletic events and individual player accomplishments can be celebrated and remembered long after they occur.

Commemorative covers or cachets usually depict an achievement and often contain a postmark from the nearest U.S. Post Office. Autograph(s) can add extra value and importance to the items. Notable cachet producers include Gateway Stamp Co., Historic Limited Editions Z Silk Cachets and Wild Horse Cachets.

Also included in this category are Hall of Fame art postcards. Perez-Steele Galleries has issued series of postcards since 1980; generally, these cards range from $5-$15 unsigned, with a few exceptions. Autographed postcards are also more valuable. Goal Line Hall of Fame postcards, which honor pro football's best, are generally $2-$3, with a few exceptions.

Chicagoland Processing Enviromint offers commemorative limited-edition medallions, paying tribute to athletes who have set milestones or broken records. Team efforts have also been recognized on the company's one troy ounce silver medallions, which are officially licensed by their respective leagues. In general, the medallions will bring $35-$60 each, but sets will bring $125-$150.

Highland Mint offers medallions and cards honoring players from each of the four major sports. The company creates replicas of superstar players' trading cards in bronze, silver and gold varieties.

Pins—Press pins, which have been issued since 1911, are distributed to members of the media by the host team for World Series and baseball All-Star games. The lapel pin provides the reporters legitimate access to cover the game.

Generally, the better looking the pin is, and the better condition it is in, the more valuable it will be. Also, because fewer reporters cover the All-Star game, there are fewer of these pins available when compared to World Series pins.

In general, here's a price range for World Series pins for each decade: 1910s ($2,500-$18,000); 1920s ($375-$4,000); 1930s ($225-$5,000); 1940s ($250-$2,400); 1950s ($125-$500); 1960s ($50-$300); 1970s ($50-$375); 1980s ($25-$175); and 1990s ($50-$150).

Super Bowl pins generally range from $1,540 for Super Bowl I, to $125 for Super Bowl XXXIII in 1999.

Ticket stubs and schedules—Ticket stubs do not command high prices unless they are from All-Star, playoff, World Series, NBA Finals or Super Bowl games. Tickets from a game where a significant achievement or record occurred are also worth more than a ticket from a regular season game. Special commemorative tickets and unused tickets often are worth a bit more, too.

The most valuable ticket stubs have seat numbers, which are generally printed in a different color ink in a separate press run. Those without, generally from the 1940s and 1950s, and sold in large blocks, are usually of little or no value because they are artist's proofs.

Baseball team schedules offer collectors an inexpensive alternative to the big-ticket items that may anchor a fan's col-

A game-worn (and autographed) jersey from basket-ball Hall of Famer Larry Bird is worth at least $3,500.

on. Also, schedules for defunct teams carry a slight premium as well, as do those which are scarce localized versions and those featuring team or player photos.

In general, here are values: 1901-1909 ($150); 1910-19 ($100); 1920-29 ($75); 1930-39 ($35); 1940-49 ($30); 1950-59 ($25); 1960-69 ($15); 1970-79 ($10); 1980-89 ($2).

Pennants—Since almost every kid who had a felt pennant tacked it up on his bedroom wall, it's unusual to find a vintage pennant in well-preserved, investment grade condition. Most, measuring 12" x 30", have pinholes in them and can be purchased for less than $50.

Today's versions, often available at stadiums and arenas, are made in large quantities, so look for 1950s and before models, and concentrate on pennants for popular teams, championship teams, teams which no longer exist, or those which commemorate a specific event.

Although it probably isn't going to offer big returns as an investment piece, a pennant can still add a nice decorative touch to any memorabilia display.

Note: This is a huge and varied collecting area. The "Value Line" below includes representative items to demonstrate the range of prices and material available.

Recommended Reading

Books

2000 Standard Catalog of Sports Memorabilia, Tom Mortenson
2000 Baseball Card Price Guide, Sports Collectors Digest
2000 Sports Collectors Almanac, Sports Collectors Digest
2000 Standard Catalog of Baseball Cards, Bob Lemke
2000 Standard Catalog of Football Cards, Sports Collectors Digest
2000 Standard Catalog of Basketball Cards, Sports Collectors Digest
Baseball Memorabilia Price Guide, Tuff Stuff Magazine
Getting Started in Card Collecting, Sports Collectors Digest
Mickey Mantle Memorabilia, Mark K. Larson, Rick Hines and Dave Platta
Platinum Inserts Sports Cards, Sports Collectors Digest
Collecting Michael Jordan, Oscar Garcia
Malloy's Sports Collectibles Value Guide, Roderick Malloy
All Sport Autograph Guide, Mark Allen Baker
Baseball Autograph Handbook, Mark Allen Baker
The Complete Guide to Baseball Memorabilia, Mark K. Larson
The Complete Guide to Football, Basketball & Hockey Memorabilia, Mark K. Larson
Sports Equipment Price Guide, David Bushing

Periodicals

Sports Collectors Digest
Tuff Stuff
Sportscards Magazine & Price Guide
Certified Card Price Guide

lection. The limits are endless. The easiest way to add to your collection is to contact the professional teams for season ticket information.

Because they are used for advertising purposes, the schedules for each team can have a variety of different sponsors each year. Thus, in addition to being available from the team, they can be found in all sorts of places, too—restaurants, banks, sporting goods stores, liquor stores, radio stations, motels and hotels, ticket outlets, convenience stores, and kiosks along interstate highways.

Condition plays a factor in a schedule's value. It is more valuable if it isn't damaged, ripped or torn, or marked

VALUE LINE

Baseball Equipment

Hank Aaron, 1967 Atlanta Braves home jersey,
game-used $16,995

Dick Allen, 1973-75 Hillerich & Bradsby
game-used bat $495

Roberto Alomar, Toronto Blue Jays game-used
batting helmet $795

Wade Boggs, 1982 Louisville Slugger
game-used bat $1,295

Bobby Bonilla, 1992-93 New York Mets
game-used cap $95

George Brett, 1984 Kansas City Royals road jersey,
used $3,000

Ellis Burks, Franklin game-used batting gloves $65

Roberto Clemente, 1960s Pittsburgh Pirates
game-used batting helmet $3,000

Rick Dempsey, 1974 New York Yankees
road jersey $425

Doug DeCinces, 1987 Adirondack game-used bat $70

Bill Dickey, store model glove .... $50-$150

Steve Garvey, 1981 Los Angeles Dodgers
home jersey, signed, used $1,195

Cito Gaston, 1970s Adirondack game-used bat $110

Juan Gonzalez, 1990 Texas Rangers game-used cap,
signed $145

Kent Hrbek, 1992 Minnesota Twins home jersey,
used $695

Von Hayes, 1986-89 Louisville Slugger
game-used bat $40

Chuck Knoblauch, Franklin game-used
batting glove $35

Whitey Kurowski, store model glove .... $50-$175

Paul Molitor, 1988 Milwaukee Brewers road jersey,
used $1,095

Mickey Mantle, 1965-68 Louisville Slugger
game-used bat, signed $10,995

Amos Otis, store model glove .... $30-$60

Jim Palmer, 1970s Baltimore Orioles
game-used cap $350

Bip Roberts, 1991 San Diego Padres road jersey,
used $350

Brooks Robinson, store model glove .... $30-$85

Gary Sheffield, 1990 Milwaukee Brewers
game-used batting helmet $175

Ozzie Smith, 1977-79 Hillerich & Bradsby
game-used bat, signed $695

Rennie Stennett, 1978 Pittsburgh Pirates home jersey,
used $350

Darryl Strawberry, Eaton game-used batting glove $50

Danny Tartabull, 1992 Worth game-used bat,
cracked $80

Frank Thomas, 1995 Chicago White Sox
home jersey, used $2,500

Luis Tiant, store model glove .... $35-$75

Otto Velez, 1993 Louisville Slugger game-used bat,
cracked $90

Mo Vaughn, 1997 Boston Red Sox home jersey,
used $895

Robin Ventura, 1993 Louisville Slugger
game-used bat $175

Honus Wagner, store model glove .... $750-$1,500

Walt Weiss, 1990s Oakland A's game-used cap,
signed $65

Basketball Equipment

Mark Aguirre, 1992-93 Los Angeles Clippers
home jersey, used $395

Rick Barry, 1970s Golden State Warriors
warm-up jacket, signed $2,950

Larry Bird, 1980s Converse game-used shoes,
signed $995

Randy Breuer, 1991-92 Minnesota Timberwolves
road jersey, used $350

Clyde Drexler, Avias, game-used shoes, signed $225

Joe Dumars, 1990-91 Detroit Pistons home jersey,
used $525

Patrick Ewing, 1992 Eclipses, Olympic
game-used shoes, signed $895

Rick Fox, 1993-94 Boston Celtics home warm-ups, complete $425

Walt Frazier, 1970s New York Knicks home jersey
and pants, used $3,500

Anfernee Hardaway, 1994-95 Orlando Magic
road jersey, used $1,495

Michael Jordan, 1992-93 Chicago Bulls white,
used $8,250

John Koncak, Reeboks, game-used shoes,
autographed $185

Chris Mullin, 1992 Olympic uniform with shorts,
used, signed $3,500

Dikembe Mutombo, Black Adidas, game-used shoes,
signed $395

Gary Payton, 1991-92 Seattle SuperSonics
warm-up $450

Rony Seikaly, 1990-91 Miami Heat road jersey,
used $495

John Stockton, 1997-97 Utah Jazz road jersey,
used $1,250

Jack Sikma, Converse, game-used shoes, signed $100

Reggie Theus, 1987 Sacramento Kings warm-up $195

James Worthy, 1993-94 Los Angeles Lakers
home jersey, used $895

Football Equipment

Marcus Allen, 1994 Kansas City Chiefs game-used football shoes $495

Ken Anderson, Cincinnati Bengals home jersey,
used $795

Edgar Bennett, 1998 Chicago Bears game-used cleats,
signed $100
Dick Butkus, Chicago Bears home jersey, used $3,250
Lynn Dickey, 1980s Green Bay Packers white jersey,
used $500
Mel Gray, 1970s St. Louis Cardinals road jersey,
used $350
Sonny Jurgensen, 1970s Washington Redskins home jer-
sey, used $3,700
Joe Morris, late 1980s New York Giants white jersey,
used $695
Joe Namath, 1972 New York Jets home jersey,
used $7,000
Jerry Rice, 1994 Pro Bowl jersey, blue, used........... $1,495
Art Still, Nike cleats, red and white, used, signed $195
Vinny Testaverde, 1990s Tampa Bay Buccaneers
home jersey, used $450
Rod Woodson, early 1990s Pittsburgh Steelers
black jersey, used $750

Hockey Equipment

Tony Amonte, Easton aluminum game-used stick,
signed $135
Tom Barrasso, 1990-91 Pittsburgh Penguins
home jersey, used $950
Ed Belfour, Cooper goalie stick, used, signed $255
Paul Coffey, 1993 All-Star game jersey, used,
signed $1,995
Kevin Dineen, game-used gloves, Philadelphia Flyers
black-and-white... $95
Marcel Dionne, 1984 Sher-wood game used stick $350
Dirk Graham, 1991-92 Chicago Blackhawks
road jersey, Captain's C patch, used...................... $800
Wayne Gretzky, 1988-89 Los Angeles Kings white,
used, signed... $6,500
Bobby Holik, Christian game-used stick $60
Gordie Howe, 1947-48 Detroit Red Wings jersey,
used $30,000
Brett Hull, 1989-90 St. Louis Blues white knit jersey,
used $2,700
Jari Kurri, Edmonton Oilers game-used Bauer Custom
Supreme 2000 skates, signed $550
Reed Larson, Koho game-used stick, signed $75
Eric Lindros, Bauer Supreme skates, used.............. $1,200
Mark Messier, 1991-92 New York Rangers home,
used $2,500
Petr Nedved, Sher-wood game-used stick, signed...... $125
Joel Otto, 1990 Calgary Flames playoff jersey,
used $495
Joe Sakic, 1980s Quebec Nordiques home jersey, Cap-
tain's C patch, used $1,750
Kevin Stevens, Pittsburgh Penguins game-used
hockey gloves... $500
Bryan Trottier, Victoriaville game-used stick,
signed ....$225-$250
Darcy Wakaluk, 1993-94 Dallas Stars black knit,
used $750

Team Publications

Anaheim Mighty Ducks 1993-94 media guide............. $12
Atlanta Braves 1974 yearbook.................................... $20
Atlanta Falcons 1973 media guide.............................. $16
Baltimore Orioles 1967 yearbook............................... $50
Boston Bruins 1972-73 media guide........................... $40
Boston Celtics 1961-62 media guide ....$40-$60
Brooklyn Dodgers 1955 yearbook............................ $300
Buffalo Bills 1971 yearbook $40
California Angels 1983 yearbook ....$8-$12
Chicago Blackhawks 1971-72 media guide................. $30
Chicago Cubs 1953 yearbook $50
Cincinnati Bengals 1969 media guide $27
Cleveland Browns 1987 yearbook $8
Cleveland Cavaliers 1993-94 media guide.................... $8
Dallas Cowboys 1965 yearbook $27
Detroit Red Wings 1966-67 media guide $75
Detroit Tigers 1980 yearbook ....$8-$15
Edmonton Oilers 1981-82 media guide $35
Green Bay Packers 1965 yearbook ....$100-$125
Houston Astros 1966 yearbook................................... $75
Houston Rockets 1971-72 media guide $20
Indiana Pacers 1968-69 media guide $30
Indianapolis Colts 1984 media guide............................ $6
Jacksonville Jaguars 1995 media guide $6
Kansas City Royals 1991 media guide $12
Los Angeles Dodgers 1976 yearbook....................$12-$18
Miami Dolphins 1985 yearbook $20
Milwaukee Brewers 1981 media guide....................$6-$8
Milwaukee Bucks 1971-72 media guide...................... $25
Minnesota Twins 1978 yearbook $12
Montreal Expos 1984 media guide $6
New England Patriots 1972 media guide $13
New Jersey Devils 1993-94 media guide $10
New York Islanders 1978-79 media guide $25
New York Jets 1966 yearbook $60
New York Mets 1969 yearbook ....$100-$125
New York Rangers 1947-48 media guide $200
New York Yankees 1951 yearbook ....$175-$200
Oakland A's 1969 media guide $20
Oakland Raiders 1966 media guide $27
Philadelphia Athletics 1949 yearbook ....$60-$125
Philadelphia Eagles 1974 yearbook............................ $20
Philadelphia Flyers 1967-68 media guide.................... $35
Philadelphia 76ers 1968-69 media guide..................... $45
Phoenix Suns, 1976-77 media guide........................... $10
Pittsburgh Pirates 1973 media guide........................... $35
Pittsburgh Steelers 1958 media guide $40
Quebec Nordiques 1974-75 media guide...................... $30
Sacramento Kings 1996-97 media guide $7
San Antonio Spurs 1982-83 media guide $8
San Diego Padres 1984 media guide............................ $10
San Francisco 49ers 1979 media guide........................ $20
Seattle Seahawks 1976 yearbook................................ $25
St. Louis Blues 1990-91 media guide $9

St. Louis Cardinals 1990 media guide, baseball $8
Tennessee Titans 1998 yearbook $8
Texas Rangers 1996 yearbook $10
Toronto Maple Leafs 1965-66 media guide $75
Vancouver Canucks 1970-71 media guide $60
Washington Senators 1946 media guide $60

Programs

1903 World Series, Pittsburgh .... $15,000-$30,000
1915 World Series, Philadelphia A's .... $2,500-$3,000
1921 World Series, New York Yankees .... $1,500-$3,000
1929-30 Stanley Cup Finals, Montreal/Boston $1,500
1935 World Series, Chicago Cubs .... $350-$550
1939 MLB All-Star Game,
    New York Yankees .... $800-$1,000
1949 World Series, Brooklyn .... $200-$250
1952-53 Stanley Cup Finals, Montreal/Boston $400
1953 NBA All-Star Game, Fort Wayne $600
1957 World Series, Milwaukee .... $100-$175
1960-61 NHL All-Star Game, Montreal $100
1963 World Series, Los Angeles .... $60-$75
1964-65 NBA Finals, Boston at Los Angeles $195
1964 NBA All-Star Game, Boston $175
1965 MLB All-Star Game, Minnesota .... $75-$125
1967 Super Bowl I, Green Bay/Kansas City ..... $275-$395
1971-72 NBA Finals, Los Angeles at New York $125
1973-74 NHL All-Star Game, Chicago $35
1975 World Series, Cincinnati/Boston .... $25-$50
1976 Super Bowl X, Dallas/Pittsburgh .... $125-$195
1979 NBA All-Star Game, Detroit $50
1979-80 Stanley Cup Finals, New York Islanders/Philadel-
    phia $75
1982 World Series, Milwaukee/St. Louis $15
1983-84 NBA Finals, Boston at Los Angeles $75
1986 MLB All-Star Game, Houston .... $5-$15
1987 Super Bowl XX, Chicago/New England .... $20-$30
1989 NBA All-Star Game, Houston $25
1992 Super Bowl XXVI, Washington/Buffalo ...... $15-$25
1992-93 Stanley Cup Finals,
    Los Angeles/Pittsburgh $25
1996-97 NHL All-Star Game, San Jose $8
1997 World Series, Cleveland/Florida $10

Books, hardcover

Babe: The Legend Comes to Life,
    by Robert W. Creamer, 1974 .... $50
Ball Four, by Jim Bouton with Leonard Schecter,
    1970 .... $50
Bobby Orr: My Game, by Bobby Orr and
    Mark Mulvoy, 1974 .... $20
Ditka, An Autobiography, by Mike Ditka with
    Don Pierson, 1986 .... $15
Drive, the Story of My Life, Larry Bird with
    Bob Ryan, 1989 .... $25
The Game, by Ken Dryden, 1983 .... $12.50
Gretzky, An Autobiography, by Wayne Gretzky with
    Rick Reilly, 1990 .... $25

Guidry, by Ron Guidry and Peter Golenbock,
    1980 .... $15
Hang Time, Days & Dreams with Michael Jordan,
    by Bob Greene, 1992 .... $30
Instant Replay: The Green Bay Diary of Jerry Kramer,
    by Dick Schaap, 1968 .... $25
It's Good to Be Alive, by Roy Campanella, 1959 .... $45
Joe Jackson, by Donald Gropman, 1979 .... $50-$60
Life on the Run, by Bill Bradley, 1976 .... $25
Looking Deep, by Terry Bradshaw with
    Buddy Martin, 1989 .... $35
Loose Balls, by Terry Pluto, 1990 .... $25
Me and the Spitter, by Gaylord Perry with
    Bob Sudyk, 1974 .... $50
The Mickey Mantle Story, by Mickey Mantle and
    Ben Epstein, 1953 .... $150
My Turn at Bat, by Ted Williams with
    John Underwood, 1969 .... $45
Rocket Man, by Roger Clemens with
    Peter Gammons, 1987 .... $30
Sandy Koufax, Strikeout King, by Arnold Hano,
    1964 .... $40
Tarkenton, by Jim Klobuchar with Fran Tarkenton,
    1976 .... $15
They Call Me Gump, by Lorne "Gump" Worsley with
    Tim Moriarity, 1975 .... $20
Willie Stargell—An Autobiography, by
    Willie Stargell and Tom Bird, 1984 .... $25
Winfield, A Player's Life, by Dave Winfield with
    Tom Parker, 1988 .... $35

Games

ABC Monday Night Football, Aurora, 1972 .... $8-$40
All-Star Baseball, Cadaco-Ellis, 1962 .... $15-$40
Baseball, Milton Bradley, 1940s .... $35-$50

This game-worn Ken Griffey Junior jersey sold for $2,500, a price that will seem an incredible bargain once Griffey is retired and in the Baseball Hall of Fame. Griffey has the best chance of any current player of breaking Hank Aaron's career home run record.

Big League Baseball Game, 3M Corp., 1971 ....$14-$30

Blue Line, 3M, 1968 ....$25-$60

Classic Major League Baseball Game, Classic,
1990...$7.50-$15

Football, Parker Bros., 1898 ....$295-$495

Hank Aaron Baseball Game, Ideal, 1973.............$50-$125

Harlem Globetrotters Game, Milton Bradley,
1971...$30-$75

Ice Hockey, Milton Bradley, 1942 ....$25-$40

Jackie Robinson Baseball Game, Gotham Pressed
Steel Corp. 1948..$425-$725

The Johnny Unitas Football Game, Play-Rite,
1960...$125-$150

Mickey Mantle's Big League Baseball, Gardner & Co.,
1962...$125-$325

Official Baseball Game, Milton Bradley,
1970...$55-$125

Oscar Robertson's Pro Basketball Strategy,
Research Games, 1964 ....$70-$175

Pro Draft, Parker Bros., 1974...............................$15-$40

Pursue the Pennant, Pursue the Pennant, 1984 ......$25-$60

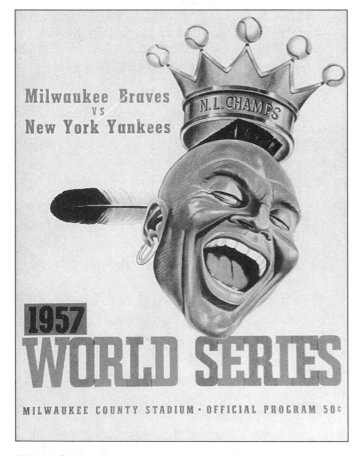

World Series programs, especially those from the 1970s and earlier, are very desirable. This 1957 Series program from the Milwaukee Braves is worth $150 in nice condition.

Slapshot, Avalon Hill, 1982 ....$5-$12

Statis Pro Baseball, Avalon Hill, 1979..................$17-$40

Strat-O-Matic Baseball, Strat-O-Matic, 1961 ....$100-$250

Touchdown, Milton Bradley, 1930s ....$150-$250

Willie Mays "Say Hey" Baseball, Centennial Games,
1958...$190-$450

Commemoratives

Goal Line Hall of Fame postcard, Terry Bradshaw,
unsigned $10

Goal Line Hall of Fame postcard, Art Donovan,
unsigned $3

Goal Line Hall of Fame postcard, Bob Griese,
unsigned $4

Goal Line Hall of Fame postcard, Ray Nitschke,
unsigned $3

Goal Line Hall of Fame postcard, Roger Staubach,
unsigned $12

Goal Line Hall of Fame postcard, Paul Warfield,
unsigned $3

Perez-Steele Celebration postcard, Jocko Colon,
signed ....$150-$500

Perez-Steele Celebration postcard, Mickey Mantle,
signed ....$125-$250

Perez-Steele Celebration postcard, Ted Williams,
signed ....$80-$175

Perez-Steele Great Moments postcard, Ty Cobb,
unsigned $20

Perez-Steele Great Moments postcard, Juan Marichal,
signed ....$10-$20

Perez-Steele Great Moments postcard, Frank Robinson,
signed $25

Perez-Steele Hall of Fame postcard, Ernie Banks,
unsigned $15

Perez-Steele Hall of Fame postcard, Rod Carew,
unsigned $5

Perez-Steele Hall of Fame postcard, Don Drysdale,
unsigned $10

Perez-Steele Hall of Fame postcard, Bob Lemon,
unsigned $10

Perez-Steele Hall of Fame postcard, Gaylord Perry,
unsigned $5

Perez-Steele Hall of Fame postcard, Robin Yount,
unsigned $5

Press pins

MLB All-Star Game, 1958, Baltimore ....$400-$650

MLB All-Star Game, 1977,
New York Yankees ....$100-$125

MLB All-Star Game, 1996, Philadelphia ....$50-$100

World Series, 1928, St. Louis Cardinals ....$875-$1,200

World Series, 1935, Detroit Tigers ....$600-$800

World Series, 1947, Brooklyn Dodgers ....$400-$800

World Series, 1969, New York Mets.................$200-$300

World Series, 1976, Cincinnati Reds ....$125-$175

World Series, 1991, Atlanta Braves ....$60-$100

Super Bowl I, Green Bay/Kansas City $1,540

Super Bowl III, New York Jets/Baltimore $850
Super Bowl X, Pittsburgh/Dallas ....$325-$350
Super Bowl XIX, Miami/San Francisco ....$130-$175
Super Bowl XXIII, Cincinnati/San Francisco ...$124-$135
Super Bowl XXIV, San Francisco/Denver $125

Pennants

Atlanta Falcons, 1970s.. $10
Boston Red Sox, 1940s, baseball over stadium,
    gray and red.. $100
Buffalo Bills, 1980s, white, with updated logo............. $35
Cincinnati Reds, 1969, picture pennant $95
Dallas Cowboys, 1970s... $25
Detroit Red Wings, 1969, white on red $45
Green Bay Packers, 1950s, player running on state of Wis-
    consin $95
Houston Rockets, 1994-95 NBA Champions $5
Kansas City Kings, 1970s, red, white and blue $25
Los Angeles Rams, 1960s, ram's head in circle,
    white on gold.. $45
Milwaukee Brewers, 1970, barrel man swinging bat,
    gold on blue.. $55
Montreal Canadiens, 1993-94, team autographed $95
New York Giants, late 1970s, quarterback throwing $35
New York Islanders, 1980s $5
New York Knicks, 1960s, large basketball,
    blue on orange $55
Pittsburgh Pirates, 1960, N.L. Champions, pirate holding
    sword $135
San Francisco 49ers, 1960s, helmet, red,
    white and gold.. $40
Washington Redskins, 1970s,
    Indian head on helmet $30

Miscellaneous

Ash tray, Alan Ameche's Restaurant in Baltimore $75
Bank, Indiana Pacers, ABA, ceramic............................ $75
Beer can, 1977 Iron City Pittsburgh Steelers 1976
    Super Bowl Champions, pictures team ....$5-$8
Bottle cap, 1967-68 Coca-Cola Hank Aaron NL All-Star,
    N19.. $35
Bottle cap, 1967-68 Coca-Cola Bob Uecker, Philadelphia
    Phillies, P10 ....$8.50
Bottle cap, 1964 Coke NFL All-Stars Mike Ditka $10
Bottle cap, 1964 Coke NFL-All-Stars Merlin Olsen $6
Bottle cap, 1964-65 Coca-Cola Hockey
    Jean Beliveau.. $25
Bumper sticker, 1972 Boston Bruins,
    "Get the Cup Back"... $20
Coca-Cola bottle, NBA All-Star Weekend,
    Salt Lake City Utah, 1993.. $20
Coca-Cola bottle, Cal Ripken Jr. Record-Breaking Year,
    1995.. $3
Cup, 7-Eleven Pete Maravich $35
Cup, 1972 7-Eleven Jim Plunkett $6.50
Cup, 1972 7-Eleven Pete Rose....................................... $25
Cup, 1972 7-Eleven Carl Yastrzemski $25

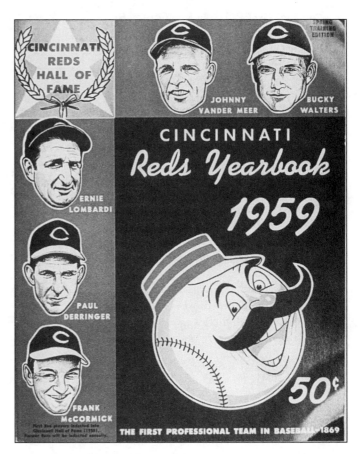

Yearbooks are popular with fans of specific teams. This 1959 Cincinnati Reds Yearbook is a relative bargain at about $50.

Cup, 1973 7-Eleven Luis Tiant $4
Exercise set, Mickey Mantle's Isometric Minute a Day
    Home Gym.. $95
Hockey boot wax, Phil Esposito can, 1960s $40
Ice scraper, Cincinnati Reds, on cardboard display $30
Jersey patch, 1973-74 Boston Bruins
    50th Anniversary $35
Magnet, Larry Bird Night, Feb. 4, 1993 .... $20
Mask, Michael Jordan, sponsored by Chicago area Chev-
    rolet-Geo Dealers and Jordan's Restaurant.............. $12
Megaphone, New York Giants, 1960s, "Go With The
    Giants" $135
Menu, Joe DiMaggio's Fisherman's Wharf
    Restaurant... $50
Mirror, Seagrams Roberto Clemente, 1980s............... $100
Mirror, Seagrams Jim Plunkett, 1980 .... $40
Movie poster, A League of Their Own, 1992 .... $35
Movie poster, Hoop Dreams, 1994 .... $15
Mug, Pittsburgh Pirates World Champions, glass......... $35
Pencil set, Mickey Mantle... $25
Pillow cases, Wayne Gretzky, 1980s............................ $15
Pop can, 1976-77 RC Cola Terry Bradshaw ....$10-$12
Pop can, 1976-77 RC Cola Mick Tingelhoff ....$5-$7

Pop can, 1977 RC Cola Ken Griffey Sr. ....$2-$3.50
Pop can, 1978 RC Cola Lyman Bostock......................... $1
Postage stamp, Roberto Clemente, 1984,
    20-cent stamp, unused.. $3
Postage stamp, Lou Gehrig, 1988, 25-cent stamp,
    unused .... 85 cents
Postage stamp, Vince Lombardi, 1997,
    32-cent stamp, unused...................................... 40 cents
Poster, 1968 Sports Illustrated Tony Oliva ....$12-$18
Poster, 1968-71 Sports Illustrated
    Larry Csonka..$20-$25
Poster, 1968-71 Sports Illustrated Bobby Hull ......$40-$50
Poster, 1969 Sports Illustrated John Hadl..............$15-$18
Poster, 1969 Sports Illustrated
    Reggie Jackson..$90-$120
Record, 1964 Auravision Al Kaline............................. $35
Record, Mickey Mantle "My Favorite Hits"
    album..$150-$175
Record, 1967 Green Bay Packers Reviews
    Season Highlights $45

Record, "Havlicek Stole The Ball," 1966,
    Celtics highlights.. $65
Ruler, Minnesota Twins all-time team $25
Serving tray, Minnesota Vikings, 14".........................$11
Sheet music, "Babe Ruth! Babe Ruth! We Know
    What He Can Do," by J. W. Spencer..................... $650
Sheet music, "Hail to the Redskins" $65
Sheet music, "I Love Mickey," by Teresa Brewer,
    Ruth Roberts and Bill Katz ....$75-$100
Sheet music, "Take Me Out to The Ball Game,"
    by Jack Norworth and Albert Von Tilzer $600
Stadium seat, Chicago Stadium $200
Stadium seat, Yankee Stadium.................................... $800
Store display, Joe Namath, 1970s, for Dingo Boots,
    with box.. $125
Tennis shoes, Pete Maravich shoe box and shoes......... $95
Tobacco tin, Chicago Cubs ....$70-$90
Wallet, Boston Braves, leather, World Series $185
Writing tablet, Ty Cobb, 6" x 9" lined notepad,
    Cobb on cover $175

STAMPS

For more than 150 years, stamp collecting, touted as the world's most popular hobby, has been attracting thousands of collectors. It's a very personal hobby—you can pick and choose what you want to collect.

Just about everything imaginable has been portrayed on a stamp at some point in time, so the hobby suits everyone.

General Guidelines: The value of a stamp depends largely on its "grade" and "condition," along with such factors as age, quantity issued, and scarcity and demand. In stamp collecting, "Grade" is a rough measurement of the relationship between the printed design and its edges or margins, a characteristic that also is often referred to as a stamp's centering. Generally speaking, the more nearly equal width all margins of a stamp are and the farther those equal margins are from the printed design, the more desirable the stamp will be to collectors. "Condition," meanwhile, refers to the overall appearance and quality of the stamp, which, of course, can enhance or detract from the value of the stamp.

Values shown in the "Value Line" below reflect the prices that you may expect to pay for a stamp in fault-free condition, free of any detectable defects. Defects of condition include: tears, scrapes, thins (places where some of the paper is missing from the back of the stamp, often due to inept removal), stains, brown spots, absence of the original gum, disfiguring cancellations or postal markings, torn or clipped perforations, creases, pinholes, fading, oxidized pigments, and pieces missing. The more these conditions exist, the less valuable the stamp.

Clubs/Associations

• The American Philatelic Society, P.O. Box 8000, State College, PA 16803

• The American Stamp Dealers Association, 3 School Street, Glen Cover, NY 11542-2548

Recommended Reading

Books

2000 Brookman Stamp Price Guide, David S. Macdonald

2000 Krause-Minkus Standard Catalog of U.S. Stamps, Third Edition, Maurice Wozniak

2000 Catalogue of Errors on U.S. Postage Stamps, Ninth Edition, Stephen R. Datz

Krause-Minkus Standard Catalog of Canadian & United Nations Stamps, George Cuhaj

Periodical

Stamp Collector (bi-weekly)

COLLECTOR'S ADVISORY!

It is considered fraudulent to knowingly represent and sell regummed stamps as original-gum copies, which is often attempted to obtain the considerably higher price that such original-gum stamps typically command. Similarly, it is fraudulent to chemically or otherwise remove a light cancellation from a stamp and offer it as unused. Both regumming and removal of cancellations have some skilled practitioners, which is why the consultation of an expert is recommended for valuable, mint stamps.

VALUE LINE

Values shown are for unused, fine-very fine stamps (UnFVF) and used, fine-very fine stamps (UseFVF) for issues prior to 1940. Post-1940 releases use grades for mint, unused stamps and cancelled very fine stamps (UseVF). Used stamps refer to those that have been canceled correctly in the course of performing their intended function.

Regular Postal Issues

1847 Benjamin Franklin, 5 cent, red brown .... $4,500/$500

1847 George Washington, 10 cent, black .... $17,500/$1,250

1851 Benjamin Franklin, 1 cent, blue, Type I .... $175,000/$15,000

1851 George Washington, 5 cent, blue, Type III .... $7,500/$1,600

1856 Thomas Jefferson, 5 cent, red brown, Type I .... $8,500/$900

1860 Benjamin Franklin, 30 cent, orange .... $850/$300

1861 Thomas Jefferson, 5 cent, buff .... $9,000/$425

1862 George Washington, 24 cent, lilac .... $400/$55

1866 Abraham Lincoln, 15 cent, black .... $650/$72

1869 Pony Express, 2 cent, brown .... $225/$28

1869 Early Locomotive, 3 cent, ultramarine .... $175/$8

1869 Shield and Eagle, 10 cent, yellow .... $1,000/$90

1869 Signing of Declaration of Independence, 24 cent, green and violet .... $3,100-$550

1870 Daniel Webster portrait, 15 cent, orange .... $2,600/$750

1870 Oliver Perry, 90 cent, carmine .... $4,250/$550

1871 Edwin Stanton, 7 cent, vermilion .... $1,325/$275

1872 Henry Clay, 12 cent, pale violet .... $14,000/$1,750

1873 Benjamin Franklin, 1 cent, ultramarine ..... $70/$1.25

1875 Zachary Taylor, 5 cent, Prussian blue ...... $145/$5.50

1882 Alexander Hamilton, 30 cent, black ...... $300/$22.50

1882 James Garfield, 5 cent, olive brown .... $80/$3

1883 George Washington, 2 cent, r
ed brown ....$20/20 cents

1890 Ulysses Grant, 5 cent, chocolate .... $47.50/$2

1890 Daniel Webster, 10 cent, deep bluish
green ....$95/$2.25

1894 James Garfield, 6 cent, red brown.......... $115/$17.50

1894 William T. Sherman, 8 cent,
purple brown ....$95/$12.50

1894 James Madison, $2, dark blue............... $1,900/$650

1902-03 Andrew Jackson, 3 cent,
dark red violet ....$52.50/$2.25

1902-03 Martha Washington, 8 cent,
violet black..............................$42.50/$1.60

1902-03 Benjamin Harrison, 13 cent,
black brown ....$42.50/$6.50

1911 George Washington, 4 cent,
brown..$22.50/75 cents

1917 James Madison, $2, dark blue....................$325/$45

1922 Theodore Roosevelt, 5 cent,
Prussian blue ....$17.50/20 cents

The first U.S. postage stamp, picturing Ben Franklin, dates from the 1840s. It can sell for as much as $4,500.

1922 Rutherford B. Hayes, 11 cent,
turquoise blue..............................$1.50/50 cents

1922 Niagara Falls, 25 cent, green............$17.50/75 cents

1923 Benjamin Franklin, 1 cent, green.......$1.45/20 cents

1923 William McKinley, 7 cent, black ....$8/75 cents

1923 American Indian, 14 cent, blue...........$4.75/80 cents

1923 Bison, 30 cent, olive brown...............$32.50/50 cents

1923 Golden Gate, 20 cent,
carmine red....................................$22.50/20 cents

1923 Lincoln Memorial, $1,
purple brown ....$45/50 cents

1925 Warren Harding, 1-1/2 cent,
yellow brown.........................$2.75/25 cents

1930-32 William H. Taft, 4 cent,
yellow brown.....................90 cents/20 cents

1938 John Adams, 2 cent, rose ....25 cents/20 cents

1938 White House, 4-1/2 cent, gray ....25 cents/20 cents

1938 Martin Van Buren, 8 cent,
olive green.........................45 cents/20 cents

1938 James Knox Polk, 11 cent,
cobalt......................................75 cents/15 cents

1938 Millard Fillmore, 13 cent,
blue green...............................$2.25/20 cents

1938 James Buchanan, 15 cent, slate.......65 cents/20 cents

1938 Chester A. Arthur, 21 cent,
slate blue ....$2.25/20 cents

1938 William Howard Taft, 50 cent,
light red violet ....$8.50/20 cents

1938 Calvin Coolidge, $5, carmine and
black .... $115/$4.50

1954 Statue of Liberty, 3 cent, violet.......25 cents/20 cents

1955 Susan B. Anthony, 50 cent, red violet......$2/20 cents

1955 Patrick Henry, $1, dark lilac ....$7/20 cents

1956 Mount Vernon, 1-1/2 cent,
brown carmine....................................25 cents/20 cents

1956 The Alamo, 9 cent, rose lilac ....25 cents/20 cents

1956 Independence Hall, 10 cent,
brown purple ....25 cents/20 cents

1956 Monticello, 20 cent, bright blue......50 cents/20 cents

1958 Statue of Liberty, 8 cent,
deep blue and carmine.........................25 cents/20 cents

1958 Paul Revere, 25 cent,
deep blue green ....$1.50/20 cents

1959 Bunker Hill Monument, 2-1/2 cent,
slate blue ....25 cents/20 cents

1959 Hermitage Issue, 4-1/2 cent,
blue green...........................25 cents/20 cents

1961 John H. Pershing, 8 cent,
brown.....................................25 cents/20 cents

1962 Evergreen Wreath and Burning Candles,
4 cent, green and red ....25 cents/20 cents

1963 U.S. Flag and White House, 5 cent,
blue and red.......................25 cents/20 cents

1963 Christmas Tree and White House, 5 cent,
dark blue, indigo and red......................25 cents/20 cents
1965 Angel Gabriel, 5 cent, red,
green and yellow ....25 cents/20 cents
1966 Franklin D. Roosevelt, 6 cent,
black brown ....25 cents/20 cents
1966 Albert Einstein, 8 cent, violet ....25 cents/20 cents
1966 John Bassett Moore, $5, dark gray.................$10/$3
1966 Traditional Christmas, 5 cent,
multicolored ....25 cents/20 cents
1967 Albert Gallatin, 1-1/4 cent,
light green ....25 cents/20 cents
1967 John F. Kennedy, 13 cent,
brown.. 25 cent/20 cents
1967 Frederick Douglass, 25 cent,
maroon ....50 cents/20 cents
1967 Eugene O'Neill, $1, dark purple ....$2.25/50 cents
1968 Henry Ford, 12 cent, black...............25 cents/20 cents
1968 John Dewey, 30 cent, purple ....55 cents/25 cents
1968 Thomas Paine, 40 cent,
dark blue..75 cents/25 cents
1968 Lucy Stone, 50 cent, maroon ....$1/25 cents
1968 Flag over White House, 6 cent, dark blue,
green and red.......................................25 cents/20 cents
1968 Flying Eagle Serviceman's Airlift, $1,
multicolored .... $3/$2
1970 Dwight D. Eisenhower, 6 cent,
blue..25 cents/20 cents
1971 Ernie Pyle, 16 cent, brown..............30 cents/25 cents
1971 U.S. Postal Service, 8 cent,
multicolored ....25 cents/20 cents

STAMPS GRADING

Stamp graders use a scale a bit different than most collectors. The two primary grades are: fine—visibly off-center on two sides, with margins or perforations either just touching or barely clear of the printed design on one side; or very fine—barely off-center on one side, with all margins or perforations almost equally distant and well clear of the printed stamp design.

An intermediate grade, the predominant grade for stamps that have been collected for more than a century, is referred to as fine-to-very fine, or f-vf. These stamps are perceptibly off-center to one side, or very slightly off-center on two sides, with the stamp design printed clear of all sides and untouched by any of the margins.

Stamps of grades lower than fine-to-very-fine (such as very good and fine) usually sell for less than the f-vf copies. Stamps of higher grade than fine-to-very-fine (including very fine and the elusive extremely fine or superb) sell for more than the stamps priced here.

1973 Crossed Flags, 10 cent,
red and blue...25 cents/20 cents
1973 Jefferson Memorial, 10 cent,
blue..25 cents/20 cents
1974 Zip Code, 10 cent, multicolored .....25 cents/20 cents
1974 Elizabeth Blackwell, 18 cent,
purple ....30 cents/25 cents
1974 Swinging Bell, 6.3 cent,
brick red ....25 cents/20 cents
1974 Dove of Peace, 10 cent,
multicolored ....25 cents/20 cents
1975 Capitol Dome, 9 cent,
green on gray paper.............................25 cents/20 cents
1975 Colonial Printing Press,
orange on gray paper...........................25 cents/20 cents
1975 Old North Church, 24 cent,
red on blue paper.................................50 cents/25 cents
1976 American Eagle and Drum, 7.9 cent,
red on canary paper.............................25 cents/20 cents
1976 Saxhorns, 7.7 cent,
brown on canary paper ....25 cents/20 cents
1977 Contemplation of Justice, 10 cent,
purple on gray paper ....25 cents/20 cents
1977 Quill Pen and Inkwell, 1 cent,
blue on green paper ....25 cents/20 cents
1977 Reading and Learning, 4 cent,
maroon on green paper........................25 cents/20 cents
1978 Sandy Hook Lighthouse, 29 cent,
blue on blue paper ....50 cents/25 cents
1978 Steinway Grand Piano, 8.4 cent,
blue on canary paper ....25 cents/20 cents
1978 Kerosene Table Lamp, $2, multicolored......$3.50/$1
1979 Railroad Conductor's Lantern, $5,
multicolored .... $8.50/$2.25
1979 Country Schoolhouse, 30 cent,
green on blue paper.....................................$1/30 cents
1979 Santa Claus Christmas Tree Ornament,
15 cent, multicolored...........................45 cents/20 cents
1980 Weaver Manufactured Violins, 3.5 cents,
purple on yellow paper........................25 cents/20 cents
1980 Sequoyah, 19 cent, brown ....30 cents/20 cents
1981 George Mason, 18 cent, blue ....30 cents/20 cents
1981 Rachel Carson, 17 cent, green........30 cents/20 cents
1981 Electric Auto, 17 cent, blue............35 cents/25 cents
1981 Fire Pumper, 20 cent,
fire engine red.....................................40 cents/30 cents
1981 Mail Wagon, 9.3 cent, dark red.......25 cents/20 cents
1982 Bighorn Sheep, 20 cent, blue ....45 cents/20 cents
1982 Crazy Horse, 13 cent,
light maroon ....35 cents/20 cents
1982 Robert Millikan, 37 cent, blue ....60 cents/20 cents
1982 Hansom Cab, 10.9 cent, purple.......25 cents/20 cents
1982 Locomotive, 2 cent, black ....25 cents/20 cents
1982 Stagecoach, 4 cent, brown...............25 cents/20 cents

The first U.S. commemorative stamps were an 1893 series depicting the Landing of Columbus. This example is valued at $15-$20.

1982 Kitten and Puppy, 13 cent,
multicolored ....35 cents/20 cents
1982 Igor Stravinsky, 2 cent, brown ....25 cents/20 cents
1983 Sleigh, 5.2 cent, red........................25 cents/20 cents
1983 Handcar, 3 cent, green.....................25 cents/20 cents
1983 Thomas H. Gallaudet, 20 cent,
green..25 cents/20 cents
1983 Pearl Buck, 5 cent,
red brown ....25 cents/20 cents
1984 Railroad Caboose, 11 cent, red ....25 cents/20 cents
1984 Baby Buggy, 7.4 cent, brown..........25 cents/20 cents
1985 Sinclair Lewis, 14 cent, gray...........25 cents/20 cents
1985 Oil Wagon, 10.1 cent, blue..............25 cents/20 cents
1985 John J. Audubon, 22 cent, blue.......40 cents/20 cents
1985 Tricycle, 6 cent, brown....................25 cents/20 cents
1985 School Bus, 3.4 cent, green.............25 cents/20 cents
1985 Stutz Bearcat, 11 cent, green...........25 cents/20 cents
1986 William Jennings Bryan, $2,
purple ....$3.25/75 cents
1986 Father Flanagan, 4 cent, purple.......25 cents/20 cents
1986 Dog Sled, 17 cent, blue ....30 cents/20 cents
1986 Bernard Revel, $1, blue............................$2/25 cents
1986 Bread Wagon, 25 cent,
orange brown......................................40 cents/20 cents
1987 Tow Truck, 8.5 cent, dark gray ....50 cents/20 cents
1987 Mary Lyon, 2 cent, blue ....25 cents/20 cents
1987 Locomotive, 2 cent, black ....25 cents/20 cents
1987 Canal Boat, 10 cent, sky blue..........25 cents/20 cents
1987 Red Cloud, 10 cent, carmine red.....25 cents/20 cents
1987 Racing Car, 17.5 cent,
blue violet...30 cents/20 cents
1988 Flags with Clouds, 25 cent,
multicolored ....35 cents/20 cents

1988 Owl and Grosbeak, 25 cent,
multicolored ....40 cents/20 cents
1988 Popcorn Wagon, 16.7 cent,
dark rose...35 cents/20 cents
1988 Tugboat, 15 cent.............................30 cents/20 cents
1988 Railroad Mail Car, 21 cent,
green..35 cents/20 cents
1988 Elevator, 5.3 cent, black ....25 cents/20 cents
1988 Tandem Bicycle, 24.1 cent,
deep blue violet ....40 cents/20 cents
1989 Johns Hopkins, $1, blackish blue........$1.75/20 cents
1989 Beach Umbrella, 15 cent,
multicolored ....30 cents/20 cents
1990 Seaplane, $1, dark blue and red ....$2/50 cents

1990 Bobcat, $2, multicolored..............................$4/$1.25

1990 Circus Wagon, 5 cent,
    carmine red............................25 cents/20 cents

1991 Fawn issue, 19 cent,
    multicolored ....40 cents/20 cents

1991 Lunch Wagon, 23 cent, blue ....50 cents/20 cents

1991 Hot Air Balloon, 19 cent,
    multicolored ....30 cents/20 cents

1991 Flags on Parade, 29 cent,
    multicolored ....50 cents/20 cents

1991 Cardinal, 30 cent, multicolored.......45 cents/20 cents

1991 Santa Descending a Chimney, 29 cent,
    multicolored ....45 cents/20 cents

1991 Wendell L. Wilkie, 75 cent,
    maroon ....$1.25/50 cents

1992 Circus Wagon, 5 cent, red ....25 cents/20 cents

1993 Futuristic Space Shuttle, $2.90,
    multicolored ....$6.50/$2.50

1993 Rose, 29 cent, multicolored ....50 cents/20 cents

1993 Pine Cone, 29 cent,
    multicolored ....50 cents/20 cents

1994 Tractor Trailer, 10 cent, green.........25 cents/20 cents

1994 Fishing Boat, 19 cent,
    multicolored ....50 cents/20 cents

1994 Moon Landing, $9.95, multicolored ....$25/$10

1994 Cardinal in Snow, 29 cent,
    multicolored ....50 cents/20 cents

1995 Circus Wagon, 5 cent, red ....25 cents/20 cents

1995 Pink Rose, 32 cent, pink,
    green and black ....80 cents/30 cents

1995 Ferryboat, 32 cent, deep blue..........75 cents/20 cents

1995 Space Shuttle Challenger,
    $3 multicolored ....$6/$3

1995 Space Shuttle Endeavor, 10.75 cent,
    multicolored ....$21/$8

1995 Milton S. Hershey, 32 cent,
    chocolate brown ....65 cents/20 cents

1996 Red-Headed Woodpecker, 2 cent,
    multicolored ....25 cents/20 cents

1996 Jacqueline Cochran, 50 cent,
    multicolored ....$1.20/40 cents

1996 Cal Farley, 32 cent, green................65 cents/20 cents

1996 Yellow Rose, 32 cent,
    yellow and multicolored......................75 cents/25 cents

1997 Statue of Liberty, 32 cent,
    multicolored ....75 cents/20 cents

1997 Flag Over Porch, 32 cent,
    multicolored ....60 cents/20 cents

1998 Uncle Sam, 33 cent,
    multicolored ....50 cents/20 cents

1998 Shuttle Landing, $3.20, multicolored ....$4/$2.75

1998 Shuttle Piggyback Transport, $11.75,
    multicolored ....$14/$8

The "Inverted Jenny," so-named because the airplane is upside-down, is America's most famous error stamp. The 24-cent stamp is very rare, selling for over $100,000.

Commemorative Issues

1904 Map of Louisiana Purchase, 10 cent,
    red brown ....$125/$25

1907 Pocahontas, 5 cent, indigo ....$85/$22.50

1913 Panama Canal, 2 cent, rose red ....$15/50 cents

1925 Battle of Lexington, 2 cent, carmine red......$5/$3.50

1925 Viking Ship (Norse-American Centennial),
    5 cent, indigo and black ....$15/$12.50

1928 Wright Airplane (Aeronautics Conference),
    2 cent, carmine red ....$1.25/$1

1931 Red Cross Nurse and Globe, 2 cent,
    black and scarlet................................25 cents/20 cents

1932 Ski Jumper (Olympic Winter Games), 2 cent, carmine red................................40 cents/25 cents

1934 Whistler's Mother (Mother's Day), 3 cent,
    reddish violet................................25 cents/20 cents

1934 Grand Canyon, 2 cent, red ....25 cents/20 cents

1935 Michigan Centennial, 3 cent,
    dark lilac................................25 cents/20 cents

1936 Susan B. Anthony, 3 cent,
    reddish purple................................25 cents/20 cents

1939 Tower of the Sun (Golden Gate Exposition),
    3 cent, light reddish violet...................25 cents/20 cents

1939 Sandlot Baseball Game (Baseball Centennial),
    3 cent, violet...$2.25/20 cents

1940 Louisa May Alcott, 5 cent,
    gray blue................................40 cents/20 cents

1940 Samuel Langhorne Clemens, 10 cent,
    sepia ....$2.25/$1.75

1940 Horace Mann, 1 cent, emerald ....25 cents/20 cents
1940 Booker T. Washington, 10 cent,
    sepia ....$2.50/$1.75
1940 Jane Addams, 10 cent, sepia ....$1.50/$1
1940 Eli Whitney, 1 cent, emerald...........25 cents/20 cents
1940 Alexander Graham Bell, 5 cent,
    gray black...$1.25/50 cents
1940 Pony Express Rider, 3 cent,
    chestnut ....35 cents/20 cents
1940 90mm Anti-Aircraft Gun (Army and Navy),
    2 cent, rose ....25 cents/20 cents
1942 Victory Eagle (Win the War), 3 cent,
    violet...25 cents/20 cents
1944 Telegraph Wires and Posts (Telegraph Centennial),
    3 cent, bright purple ....25 cents/20 cents
1945 U.S. Sailors (Navy), 3 cent, blue ....25 cents/20 cents
1946 Smithsonian Institution, 3 cent,
    brown purple ....25 cents/20 cents
1948 George Washington Carver, 3 cent,
    bright purple ....25 cents/20 cents
1948 Sutter's Mill, Calif., 3 cent,
    violet...25 cents/20 cents
1948 Francis Scott Key, 3 cent,
    carmine..25 cents/20 cents
1948 Clara Barton and Red Cross, 3 cent,
    carmine..25 cents/20 cents
1949 Pioneer and Ox Cart, 3 cent,
    blue green.......................................25 cents/20 cents
1949 Edgar Allen Poe, 3 cent,
    bright purple ....25 cents/20 cents
1950 Supreme Court Building, 3 cent,
    bluish violet....................................25 cents/20 cents
1952 American Farm, 4-H Emblem, 3 cent,
    blue green.......................................25 cents/20 cents
1952 Mount Rushmore, 3 cent,
    blue green.......................................25 cents/20 cents
1953 National Guard, 3 cent,
    light blue ....25 cents/20 cents
1953 Truck, Farm and City (Trucking Industry),
    3 cent, violet...................................25 cents/20 cents
1955 Great Lakes and Freighter (Soo Lock Centennial),
    3 cent, blue ....25 cents/20 cents
1957 Teacher and Students, 3 cent,
    brown purple ....25 cents/20 cents
1958 Minnesota Lakes (Statehood), 3 cent,
    emerald green ....25 cents/20 cents
1959 NATO Emblem, 4 cent, blue...........25 cents/20 cents
1960 Boy Scouts of America, 4 cent, red,
    deep blue and deep ocher ....25 cents/20 cents
1960 Pony Express Rider, 4 cent,
    sepia ....25 cents/20 cents
1960 Campfire Girls Insignia, 4 cent,
    blue and red....................................25 cents/20 cents
1960 Andrew Carnegie, 4 cent, claret......25 cents/20 cents

FIVE TIPS TO PROTECT YOUR COLLECTION!

Paper stamps are fragile, so handle them with care. You can purchase a pair of stamp tongs, designed with special tips that do not damage the stamp; don't just use a pair of cosmetic tweezers.

Anything that will be holding the stamps should be archival-quality acid-free paper—files, albums, envelopes, plastic sheets.

Use mounting corners (transparent little envelopes used to hold each corner of the stamp in place) or hinges (small rectangles of special gummed paper). Do not use tape—not even magic tape! It will damage your stamps.

There are also self-mounting pages with strips of plastic attached to them; you slip your stamp into the strip. But make sure it is archival-quality plastic.

Before you soak stamps off old letters, it would be wise to get some professional advice; some collectors want the whole envelope, too.

1961 Nurse Lighting Candle, 4 cent, blue,
    black, orange and flesh........................25 cents/20 cents
1962 Girl Scouts of America, 4 cent,
    red...25 cents/20 cents
1963 Emancipation Proclamation, 5 cent,
    bright blue, scarlet and indigo.............25 cents/20 cents
1964 Artillery in Action (The Wilderness), 5 cent,
    brown, purple and black ....25 cents/20 cents
1964 Sam Houston, 5 cent, black.............25 cents/20 cents
1964 John F. Kennedy and Eternal Flame,
    5 cent, gray blue ....25 cents/20 cents
1964 Amateur Radio, 5 cent, purple ....25 cents/20 cents
1965 Winston Churchill, 5 cent, black.....25 cents/20 cents
1965 Stop traffic accidents, 5 cent, green,
    black and red ....25 cents/20 cents
1966 Circus Clown, 5 cent, red, blue,
    pink and black ....25 cents/20 cents
1966 Great River Road, 5 cent, salmon, blue,
    olive yellow and yellow.......................25 cents/20 cents
1967 Davy Crockett, 5 cent, green,
    black and yellow ....25 cents/20 cents
1968 Walt Disney, 6 cent,
    multicolored ....25 cents/20 cents
1969 Professional Baseball, 6 cent, yellow,
    red, black and green ....$1.25/20 cents
1969 Football, 6 cent, red and green........45 cents/20 cents
1970 Stone Mountain Memorial, 6 cent,
    gray black..25 cents/20 cents
1971 Douglas MacArthur, 6 cent, red,
    blue and black ....25 cents/20 cents
1971 Prevent Drug Abuse, 8 cent, blue,
    deep blue and black............................25 cents/20 cents

1972 PTA, 8 cent, yellow and black ....25 cents/20 cents

1972 Tom Sawyer, 8 cent, multicolored ..25 cents/20 cents

1973 Lyndon B. Johnson, 8 cent,
multicolored ....25 cents/20 cents

1974 VFW Emblem, 10 cent,
red and blue ....25 cents/20 cents

1974 Energy Conservation, 10 cent,
multicolored ....25 cents/20 cents

1975 Collective Bargaining, 10 cent,
multicolored ....25 cents/20 cents

1975 Bunker Hill, 10 cent,
multicolored ....25 cents/20 cents

1976 Diving (Olympic Games) 13 cent,
multicolored ....25 cents/20 cents

1977 Peace Bridge, 13 cent, blue.............25 cents/20 cents

1978 Carl Sandburg, 13 cent,
brown and black ....25 cents/20 cents

1979 Robert F. Kennedy, 15 cent,
blue...30 cents/20 cents

1979 John Steinbeck, 15 cent,
dark blue..30 cents/20 cents

1979 Albert Einstein, 15 cent, brown ......30 cents/20 cents

1979 W.C. Fields, 15 cent,
multicolored ....30 cents/20 cents

1980 Helen Keller and Anne Sullivan, 15 cent, multicolored..30 cents/20 cents

1981 American Red Cross, 18 cent,
multicolored ....30 cents/20 cents

1981 Beat Alcoholism, 18 cent,
blue and black ....65 cents/20 cents

1981 Space Achievement issue, 8 different,
18 cent, multicolored..........................30 cents/20 cents

1982 George Washington, 20 cent,
multicolored ....35 cents/20 cents

1982 Jackie Robinson, 20 cent,
multicolored ....$2.50/20 cents

1982 Ponce de Leon, 20 cent,
multicolored ....35 cents/20 cents

1983 Babe Ruth, 20 cent, blue.................35 cents/20 cents

1984 National Archives, 20 cent,
multicolored ....35 cents/20 cents

1984 Jim Thorpe, 20 cent,
dark brown ....75 cents/20 cents

1984 Smokey Bear, 20 cent,
multicolored ....35 cents/20 cents

1984 McGruff, the Crime Dog, 20 cent,
multicolored ....35 cents/20 cents

1984 Roberto Clemente, 20 cent,
multicolored ....$3.50/20 cents

1985 Social Security Act, 22 cent,
dark blue and light blue......................35 cents/20 cents

1985 Duck Decoys issue, 4 different, 22 cent, multicolored, each ....40 cents/20 cents

1985 International Youth Year issue,
4 different, 22 cent, multicolored.................$1/20 cents

1986 Fish Booklet issue, 5 different, 22 cent,
multicolored ....$1.75/20 cents

1987 Enrico Caruso, 22 cent,
multicolored ....35 cents/20 cents

1987 Steam Locomotive issue, five different,
22 cents, multicolored ....75 cents/25 cents

1988 Cats issue, 4 different, 22 cents,
multicolored ....$1/20 cents

1988 Roses (Love), 45 cents,
multicolored ....$1.35/20 cents

1988 Classic Cars issue, 5 different, 25 cents,
multicolored ....$2/50 cents

1988 Antarctic Explorers issue, 4 different,
25 cents ....$1/20 cents

1989 Mount Rainier (Washington), 25 cent,
multicolored ....75 cents/20 cents

1989 Steamboats issue, 5 different, 25 cent,
multicolored ....75 cents/20 cents

1989 Moon Landing Anniversary, $2.40,
multicolored ....$6/$2.25

1989 Dinosaurs issue, 4 different, 25 cent,
multicolored ....$1.25/20 cents

1990 Classic Films issue, 4 different, 25 cent, multicolored..$2/20 cents

1990 Sea Mammals issue, 4 different, 25 cent, multicolored..75 cents/20 cents

1991 Numismatics, 29 cent,
multicolored ....45 cents/20 cents

1991 Basketball Centennial, 29 cent,
multicolored ....45 cents/20 cents

1991 American Comedians issue, 5 different,
29 cent, multicolored..........................45 cents/20 cents

Duck stamps are popular collecting category. The first one, issued in 1934 with artwork by "Ding" Darling, is valued at $500-$600/

This error stamp, known in the stamp hobby as the "C.I.A. Invert," is valued at about $18,000. Dating from 1979, it has the circled flame in the wrong place. The error was discovered by employees of the Central Intelligence Agency.

1992 Olympic Baseball, 29 cent,
  multicolored ....$1/20 cents
1992 Voyage of Columbus issue, 4 different,
  29 cent, multicolored.................................$1/20 cents
1993 Elvis Presley, 29 cent,
  multicolored ....45 cents/20 cents
1993 Grace Kelley, 29 cent, blue ....45 cents/20 cents
1993 Circus issue, 4 different, 29 cent,
  multicolored ....45 cents/20 cents
1993 Rock 'n Roll, 7 different, 29 cent,
  multicolored ....45 cents/20 cents
1993 Aids Awareness, 29 cent,
  red and black ....45 cents/20 cents
1994 Love, 52 cent, multicolored ....$1.50/35 cents
1994 Norman Rockwell, 29 cent,
  multicolored ....50 cents/20 cents
1994 Popular Singers issue, 5 different,
  multicolored ....75 cents/50 cents
1994 Blues and Jazz Singers, 8 different,
  multicolored .... 50 cent/25 cents
1995 Richard M. Nixon, 32 cent,
  multicolored ....50 cents/20 cents

1995 Recreational Sports issue, 5 different,
  32 cent, multicolored..........................50 cents/20 cents
1995 Marilyn Monroe, 32 cent,
  multicolored ....75 cents/20 cents
1995 Louis Armstrong, 32 cent,
  multicolored ....50 cents/20 cents
1996 Marathon, 32 cent, multicolored.....50 cents/20 cents
1996 Breast Cancer Awareness, 32 cent,
  multicolored ....50 cents/20 cents
1996 James Dean, 32 cent,
  multicolored ....50 cents/20 cents
1996 Riverboats issue, 5 different, 32 cent,
  multicolored ....75 cents/50 cents
1996 Hanukkah, 32 cent,
  multicolored ....75 cents/20 cents
1996 Cycling, 50 cent, multicolored...................$2.50/$1
1997 Love, 55 cent, multicolored ....$1/30 cents
1997 Legendary Coaches, 4 different,
  multicolored ....50 cents/20 cents
1997 Humphrey Bogart, 32 cent,
  multicolored ....50 cents/20 cents
1997 Classic Movie Monsters issue, 5 different,
  32 cent, multicolored..........................50 cents/20 cents
1998 Sylvester and Tweetie, 32 cent,
  multicolored ....50 cent/25 cent

**Commemorative issues with more than 10 stamps
in the series**

1968 Historic Flags issue, 10 different, 6 cent, multicolored...40 cents/30 cents
1976 50 State Flag issue, 13 cent,
  multicolored ....55 cents/40 cents
1982 50 State Birds, 20 cent, multicolored.......$1/50 cents
1986 Presidents Souvenir Sheets of 9, 22 cents,
  sheet is...$5.25/$4.50
  single stamps are ....50 cents/40 cents
1987 American Wildlife issues, 50 different,
  22 cents, multicolored............................$1.50/55 cents
1991 Space Exploration issue, 10 different,
  29 cent, multicolored..........................45 cents/20 cents
1991 1941: A World at War issue, 10 different,
  29 cent, multicolored..........................80 cents/45 cents
1992 Wildflowers issue, 50 different, 29 cent,
  multicolored ....95 cents/60 cents
1992 1942: Into the Battle issue, 10 different,
  29 cent, multicolored..........................75 cents/45 cents
1993 World War II 1943 issue, 10 different,
  29 cent, multicolored..........................75 cents/45 cents
1994 Silent Screen stars issue, 10 different,
  29 cent, multicolored..........................45 cents/20 cents
1994 1944: Road to Victory issue, 10 different,
  29 cent, multicolored, sheet of 10 is ....$8.75/$7
  singles are..75 cents/70 cents
1994 Revised Legends of the West, 20 different,
  29 cent, multicolored..........................45 cents/20 cents

1995 Civil War issue, 20 different, 32 cent, multicolored ....75 cents/50 cents

1995 1945: Victory at Last Pane issue, 10 different, 32 cent, multicolored sheet is.................................$9/$8 singles are...80 cents/40 cents

1995 Jazz Musicians, 10 different, 32 cent, multicolored ....50 cents/20 cents

1995 Comic Strip Classic issue, 20 different, 32 cent, multicolored...........................75 cents/50 cents

1996 Atlanta 1996 Centennial Olympic Games issue, 32 cent, multicolored...........................75 cents/50 cents

1996 Endangered Species issue, 15 different, 32 cent, multicolored...........................50 cents/20 cents

1997 The World of the Dinosaurs issue, 15 different, 32 cent, multicolored......75 cents/50 cents

1997 Classic American Aircraft issue, 20 different, 32 cent, multicolored...........................75 cents/50 cents

1997 Classic American Dolls issue, 15 different, 32 cent, multicolored..........................75 cents/50 cents

1998 Celebrate the Century 1900s issue, 15 different, 32 cent, multicolored, sheet is.................. $12.50/$9.50 singles are..50 cents

1998 Celebrate the Century 1910s issue, 15 different, 32 cent, multicolored sheets are...............$12.50/$9.50 singles are..50 cents

1998 Celebrate the Century 1920s issue, 15 different, 32 cent, multicolored, sheet is..........................$15/9.50 singles are...75 cents/50 cents

1998 American Art issue, 20 different, 32 cent, multicolored...50 cents/20 cents

1998 Celebrate the Century 1930s issue, 15 different, 32 cent, multicolored...........................75 cents/50 cents

STAR WARS COLLECTIBLES

The *Star Wars* trilogy—among the top-grossing films of all time—spawned a line of toys that changed the face of the industry.

Background and General Guidelines: Before *Star Wars*, large-sized action figures were produced of superheroes or perhaps television characters—anywhere from six to 12 inches tall. But Lucasfilm along with Kenner (the major licensee of *Star Wars* toys) decided that smaller was better. The 3-3/4-inch size became the industry standard, making larger action figures seem bulky in comparison. Even the mighty G.I. Joe surrendered to the smaller size.

Why this change in size was made is open to speculation, but here's something to consider—how big would your Millennium Falcon have to be to fit a 12-inch Han Solo action figure into the cockpit? (And how many kids would it take to lift it?) While Kenner's plastic Millennium Falcon was not produced to true scale, it still allowed a figure to sit in the cockpit with room for more in the main hold.

Star Wars also set the stage for what has become the staple of the toy industry: Movie tie-ins. Licensing is now the name of the game for most toy companies, so if a movie is expected to do well at the box office, then there will assuredly be a line of toys and collectibles associated with it. The next time you wander through the aisles of your favorite toy store and delight over the number of toys dedicated to that latest blockbuster movie, you can give thanks to *Star Wars*.

While there was a period between 1984 and 1995 when *Star Wars* toys seemed to cool and few if any new items appeared on the market, that all changed with the news that George Lucas was updating the old movies and releasing a series of three new *Star Wars* "prequels." Buoyed by renewed interest, new lines of *Star Wars* action figures were released by Kenner in July 1995, and Galoob began issuing *Star Wars* Micro Machines in 1996. While neither line of toys has reached the level of the original toys of the late 1970s and early 1980s, they still helped bring *Star Wars* toys to a new generation of fans.

Hasbro, the licensee for *Episode I* toys, is betting that *Star Wars* will be in our minds for years to come, boosting toy sales to unprecedented heights. Since *Star Wars* toys, games, soundtracks and books have resulted in $4 billion in sales since the first movie debuted in 1977, this is probably a safe bet. According to *USA Today*, analysts predict spin-off sales could exceed $1 billion during 1999 alone.

But how collectible are these new toys? Well, remember that the main reason the original toys are so collectible is because they were taken out of the package -- kids back then weren't going to leave their Luke Skywalker with telescoping lightsaber sitting in the blisterpack. As is the case with most hobbies, items are collectible because they are rare. While

children might still play with their Darth Maul and Jar Jar Binks action figures, their parents will stash Mint, unopened toys in the attic. And since 90 percent of all toy collectors will be doing the same thing, don't expect your Obi-Wan action figure to put your kids through college, although they will, of course, all be collectible.

While the new *Star Wars* toys may not have great value, the market may show an increase in the value of certain original toys. Obi-Wan Kenobi, often thought to be a supporting character, will become a major player with the release of the prequels, thereby making his action figures from the original three movies even more desirable. New villain Darth Maul has the potential to become the new cult figure, eclipsing Boba Fett as the current favorite of true fans, so watch for his figures to rise in value at a faster pace than other characters. But don't expect the value of R2-D2 with sensorscope to fluctuate much with the release of the new movie since figures of this popular droid will again flood the market.

Contributors to this section: Chris Fawcett, cfawcett@ix.netcom.com; Gus Lopez, 4756 University Place NE #124, Seattle WA 98105, lopez@halcyon.com

Recommended Reading

Star Wars Collectors Pocket Companion, Stuart Wells
2000 Toys & Prices, Sharon Korbeck and Elizabeth Stephan
The Galaxy's Greatest Star Wars Collectibles Price Guide, Stuart W. Wells III

VALUE LINE

Top 10 Star Wars Action Figures
(in Mint in Package condition)
1. Luke with Telescoping Saber, Original 12, 3", 1977 .... $4,410
2. Jawa, Vinyl Cape, Original 12, 3", 1977 .... $3,200
3. Anakin Skywalker, Power of the Force, 3", 1985 .... $2,150
4. Yak Face with coin, Power of the Force, 3", 1985 .... $1,710
5. Boba Fett, 3", 1978 .... $920
6. Droids, Boba Fett, 3", 1985 .... $790
7. AT-AT Driver with coin, Power of the Force, 3" $660
8. IG-88, 12", 1980 .... $640
9. Han Solo, Large Head, Original 12, Action Figures, 3", 1977 .... $620
10. Early Bird Figures—Luke, Leia, R2-D2, Chewbacca, 3", 1977 .... $610

Top 10 Star Wars Toys
(in Mint in Package condition)
1. TIE Bomber, die-cast, 1979 .... $830
2. Tatooine Skiff, Power of the Force $670
3. Cantina Adventure Set, Sears Exclusive, 1977 ...... $640
4. Jawa Sand Crawler, battery-operated, 1977 .... $610
5. Sonic Land Speeder, JC Penney exclusive, 1977 .... $580
6. A-Wing Fighter, Droids box, 1983 .... $580
7. 63rd Coin, lightsaber, Kenner, 1985 .... $500
8. Death Star Space Station, 1977 .... $480
9. Millennium Falcon, 1982 .... $390
10. Cloud City Play Set, Sears exclusive, Empire Strikes Back, 1981 .... $350

STAR WARS TRADING CARDS!

Although there have been several high-end card sets issued during the 1990s, featuring high-tech innovations, the rise in popularity of Star Wars trading cards can be traced to humble beginnings offered by Topps, then king of the hill in the trading card industry. Topps hit the jackpot by securing a Star Wars license and revolutionized the entertainment card business by negotiating for permission to summarize plots. In addition to several issues by Topps during the 1990s, other companies to tap the market during this time include Metallic Images and Metallic Impressions. Here is a roundup of Star Wars trading cards (with values for cards in Mint condition).

Star Wars Series I, blue (Topps 1977, 66 cards, 11 stickers): set is $125, single card is $1.25, unopened pack is $10-$15; stickers are $4, complete set is $40.

Star Wars Series II, red (Topps 1977, 66 cards, 11 stickers): set is $75, single card is 50 cents, unopened pack is $7.50-$12; stickers are $4, complete set is $40.

Star Wars Series III, yellow (Topps 1977, 66 cards, 16 stickers): set is $40, single card is 50 cents, unopened pack is $7.50-$12; stickers are $4, complete set is $40.

Star Wars Series IV, green (Topps 1978, card #s 199-264, sticker #s 34-44): set is $40, single card is 40 cents, unopened pack is $4-$8; stickers are $1, set is $30.

Star Wars Series V, orange (Topps 1978, card #s 265-330, sticker #s 45-55): set is $40, single card is $1.25, unopened pack is $4-$5; stickers are $3, complete set is $30.

Empire Strikes Back Series I, red (Topps 1980, 132 cards, 33 stickers): set is $42, single card is 50 cents, unopened pack is $5-$7.50; stickers are $2, set from all three series is $60.

Empire Strikes Back Series II, blue (Topps 1980, 132 cards, 33 stickers): set is $30, single card is 55 cents, unopened pack is $3-$5; sticker is $1.50.

Empire Strikes Back Series III, yellow (Topps 1980, 88 cards, 22 stickers): set is $35, single card is 50 cents, unopened pack is $1-$3; sticker is $1.50.

Return of the Jedi Series I, red (Topps 1983, 132 cards, 33 stickers): set is $30, single card is 35 cents, unopened pack is $2-$3; stickers are $1.

Return of the Jedi Series II (Topps 1983, 88 cards, 22 stickers): set is $30, single card is 50 cents, unopened pack is $2-$3; stickers are 75 cents.

Star Wars Collectibles

The first value shown is for a "loose" Mint figure/the second value is for a figure Mint-in-Package.

12-inch Action Figures
A New Hope
Cantina Band Aliens .... $15/$20
Grand Moff Tarkin, 1998 .... $15/$20
Greedo, 1998 .... $15/$20
Luke in ceremonial garb, 1998 .... $15/$20
Sandtrooper, 1998 .... $15/$20

Collector's Series
Admiral Akbar, 1997 .... $15/$20
Boba Fett, 1997 .... $15/$20
C-3PO, 1997 .... $15/$20
Chewbacca, 1997 .... $15/$20
Darth Vader, 1996 .... $15/$20
Han Solo, 1996 .... $15/$20
Lando Calrissian, 1997 .... $15/$20
Luke as X-Wing Pilot, 1997 .... $15/$20
Luke in Bespin outfit, 1997 .... $15/$20
Luke Skywalker, 1996 .... $15/$20
Obi-Wan Kenobi, 1996 .... $15/$20
Princess Leia, 1997 .... $15/$20
Stormtrooper, 1997 .... $15/$20
TIE Fighter Pilot, 1997 .... $15/$20
Tusken Raider .... 1997$15$20

Empire Strikes Back
AT-AT Driver, 1998 .... $15/$20
Boba Fett, 1979 .... $150/$400
Han in Carbonite .... $15/$20
Han in Hoth gear, 1998 .... $15/$20
IG-88, 1980 .... $210/$640
Leia in Hoth gear .... $15/$20
Luke in Hoth gear, 1998 .... $15/$20
Snowtrooper, 1998 .... $15/$20

Return of the Jedi
Banquin D'an, 1998 .... $15/$20
Chewbacca (chained), 1998 .... $15/$20
Emperor Palpatine, 1998 .... $15/$20
Luke as Jedi Knight, 1998 .... $15/$20

Special 2-Packs
Grand Moff Tarkin and Imperial Gunner .... $30/$40
Han and Luke in Stormtrooper disguise .... $30/$40
Han in Hoth gear with Tauntaun .... $25/$50
Leia as Jabba's prisoner and R2-D2 .... $30/$40
Luke as Jedi Knight and Bib Fortuna .... $30/$40
Luke in Hot gear with Wampa .... $30/$40
Wedge Antilles and Biggs Darklighter .... $30/$40

Star Wars

Boba Fett, 1979 .... $160/$410
C-3PO, 1979 .... $75/$195
Chewbacca .... $60/$145
Darth Vader, 1978 .... $70/$165
Han Solo, 1979 .... $150/$310
Jawa, 1979 .... $110/$270
Luke Skywalker .... $105/$290
Obi-Wan Kenobi, 1979 .... $125/$250
Princess Leia, 1977 .... $100/$250
R2-D2, 1979 .... $60/$155
Stormtrooper, 1979 .... $80/$175

Trilogy 3-Packs

Luke with poncho (Tatooine), Han with flight jacket,
   Leia in Boushh disguise .... $20/$80
R2-D2 with scope, R5-D4, Ewok .... $20/$80

Trilogy assortment

Jawa, 1998 .... $15/$20
R2-D2, 1998 .... $15/$20
Yoda, 1998 .... $15/$20

3-inch Action Figures

Cinema Scene 3-Packs

Cantina Aliens—Labria, Nabrun Leids, Takeel .... $3/$10
Cantina Showdown—Obi-Wan Kenobi, Ponda Baba,
   Dr. Evazan .... $3/$10
Death Star Escape—Luke and Han in Stormtrooper dis-
   guise, Chewbacca .... $3/$10
Final Jedi Duel—Darth Vader, Luke,
   Emperor Palpatine .... $3/$10
Jaba the Hut's Dancers—Rystall, Greeata,
   Lyn Me .... $3/$10
Jedi Spirits—Anakin Skywalker, Yoda,
   Obi-Wan Kenobi .... $3/$10
Mynock Hunt—Han, Leia, Chewbacca .... $3/$10
Purchase of the Droids—Luke, C-3PO,
   Uncle Owen .... $3/$10
Rebel Pilots—Wedge Antilles, B-Wing Pilot
   (Ten Nunb), Y-Wing Pilot .... $3/$10

Dark Empire

Clone Emperor, 1998 .... $3/$6
Imperial Sentinel, 1998 .... $3/$6
Kyle Katarn, 1998 .... $3/$6
Luke Skywalker, 1998 .... $3/$6
Princess Leia Organa Solo, 1998 .... $3/$6

Dark Forces

Darktrooper, 1998 .... $3/$6

Deluxe 2-Packs

Boba Fett vs. IG-88 .... $6/$10
Droopy McCool and Barquin D'an .... $6/$10
Leia and Han .... $6/$10
Leia and Luke .... $6/$10
Leia and R2-D2 .... $6/$10
Leia and Wicket the Ewok .... $6/$10
Max Rebo and Doda Bodonawieedo .... $6/$10
Prince Xizor vs. Darth Vader .... $6/$10
Sy Snooties and Joh Yowza .... $6/$10

Droids

A-Wing Pilot, 1985 .... $45/$175
Boba Fett, 1985 .... $25/$790
C-3PO, 1985 .... $25/$110
Jann Tosh, 1985 .... $8/$25
Jord Dusat, 1985 .... $8/$20
Kea Moll, 1985 .... $8/$35
Kez-Iban, 1985 .... $8/$20
R2-D2, 1985 .... $25/$85
Sise Fromm, 1985 .... $20/$85
Thall Joben, 1985 .... $8/$25
Tig Fromm, 1985 .... $18/$80
Uncle Gundy, 1985 .... $8/$20

Empire Strikes Back

2-1B, 1980 .... $10/$105
4-LOM .... $12/$165
AT-AT Commander, 1980 .... $8/$50
AT-AT Driver, 1981 .... $9/$65
Bespin security guard, black, 1980 .... $10/$65
Bespin security guard, white, 1980 .... $10/$65
Bossk, 1980 .... $10/$105
C-3PO, with removable limbs, 1982 .... $8/$70
Cloud Car Pilot, 1982 .... $18/$65
Dengar, 1980 .... $8/$55
FX-7, 1980 .... $8/$55
Han in Bespin outfit, 1981 .... $12/$130
Han in Hoth gear, 1980 .... $10/$95
Han Rebel Soldier, 1980 .... $7/$70
IG-88, 1980 .... $11/$90
Imperial Commander, 1981 .... $9/$50
Imperial TIE Fighter Pilot, 1982 .... $11/$105
Lando Calrissian .... $12/$65
Leia in Bespin gown, 1980 .... $20/$105
Leia in Hoth gear, 1981 .... $20/$110
Lobot, 1981 .... $8/$40
Luke in Bespin outfit, 1980 .... $20/$175
Luke in Hoth gear, 1982 .... $13/$70
R2-D2 with Sensorscope .... $11/$70
Rebel Commander, 1980 .... $8/$40
Snowtrooper, 1980 .... $12/$100
Tautaun, solid belly, 1980 .... $20/$60
Tautaun, split belly, 1982 .... $19/$60
Ugnaught, 1981 .... $10/$55
Wampa, 1982 .... $15/$55
Yoda, 1981 .... $25/$115
Zuckuss, 1982 .... $12/$90

Ewoks

Dulok Scout, 1985 .... $8/$16
Dulok Shaman, 1985 .... $8/$20
King Gomesh, 1985 .... $8/$16
Logray, 1985 .... $8/$20
Urgah, 1985 .... $8/$18
Wicket, 1985 .... $9/$20

Heir to the Empire

Grand Admiral Thrawn, 1998 .... $3/$6

Mara Jade, 1998 ....$3-$6
Spacetrooper, 1998 ....$3-$6

Mail-Away Figures

Admiral Ackbar ....$9/$19
Anakin Skywalker ....$30/$40
AT-AT Commander ....$8/$15
AT-ST Driver ....$10/$15
C-3PO with removable limbs ....$8/$15
Emperor Palpatine ....$11/$17
Han in Hoth gear ....$12/$20
Han in Trenchcoat ....$14/$20
Luke in Hoth gear ....$14/$20
Nien Nunb ....$8/$20
Pruneface ....$9/$15
R2-D2 with Sensorscope ....$10/$15

Power of the Force

2-1B Medic Droid, 1997 ....$3/$10
4-LOM, 1997 ....$3/$10
8D8 Droid, 1998 ....$3/$6
A-Wing Pilot with coin, 1985 ....$50/$95
Admiral Ackbar, 1997 ....$3/$10
Amanaman with coin, 1985 ....$95/$210
Anakin Skywalker, 1999 ....$3/$6
Anakin Skywalker with coin, 1985 ....$30/$2,150
ASP-7 Droid, 1997 ....$3/$10
AT-AT Driver, 1998 ....$3/$6
AT-AT Driver with coin ....$9/$660
AT-ST Driver, 1997 ....$3/$10
AT-ST Driver with coin ....$10/$55
Aunt Beru, 1999 ....$3/$6
B-Wing Pilot with coin, 1985 ....$9/$30
Barada with coin, 1985 ....$45/$85
Bib Fortuna, 1997 ....$3/$10
Biggs Darklighter, 1998 ....$3/$6
Biker Scout with coin, 1985 ....$12/$85
Boba Fett, 1996 ....$3/$10
Bossk, 1997 ....$3/$10
C-3PO, 1995 ....$3/$10
C-3PO with removable limbs and backpack,
    1998 ....$3/$6
C-3PO with removable limbs and coin ....$8/$70
C-3PO, Shop Worn, 1999 ....$3/$6
C-3PO with Millennium minted coin ....$5/$10
Captain Piett, 1998 ....$3/$6
Chewbacca, 1995 ....$3/$10
Chewbacca (Hoth), 1998 ....$3/$6
Chewbacca as Boushh's Bounty, 1998 ....$3/$6
Chewbacca in Bounty Hunter disguise, 1996 ....$3/$6
Chewbacca with coin ....$9/$95
Chewbacca with Millennium minted coin ....$5/$10
Darth Vader, 1995 ....$3/$10
Darth Vader, 1998 ....$3/$6
Darth Vader with removable helmet, 1998 ....$3/$6
Darth Vader with coin ....$15/$95
Dash Rendar, 1996 ....$3/$6

Death Star Droid with Mouse Droid, 1998 ....$3/$6
Death Star Gunner, 1996 ....$3/$10
Death Star Trooper, 1998 ....$3/$6
Dengar, 1997 ....$3/$10
Emperor Palpatine, 1998 ....$3/$6
Emperor Palpatine, 1997 ....$3/$10
Emperor Palpatine with coin, 1985 ....$10/$85
Emperor Palpatine with Millennium
    minted coin ....$5/$10
Emperor's Royal Guard, 1997 ....$3/$6
Endor Rebel Soldier, 1998 ....$3/$6
EV-9D9, 1997 ....$3/$6
EV-9D9 with coin, 1985 ....$85/$145
Gamorrean Guard, 1985 ....$3/$6
Gamorrean Guard with coin ....$9/$310
Garindan (Long Snoot), 1997 ....$3/$10
Grand Moff Tarkin, 1997 ....$3/$10
Greedo, 1996 ....$3/$10
Han in Bespin outfit, 1997 ....$3/$6
Han in Bespin outfit, with Millennium
    minted coin ....$5/$10
Han in Carbonite, 1996 ....$4/$6

Star Wars **fans have plenty of characters to choose from.**

Han in Carbonite with coin, 1985 .... $100/$230
Han in Endor Gear, 1997 .... $3/$10
Han in Hoth Gear, 1996 .... $4/$10
Han in trenchcoat with coin .... $15/$430
Han Solo, 1995 .... $4/$10
Hoth Rebel Soldier, 1997 .... $3/$10
Imperial Dignitary with coin, 1985 .... $45/$75
Imperial Gunner with coin, 1985 .... $65/$120
Ishi Tib, 1998 .... $3/$6
Jawa, 1996 .... $3/$10
Jawa with coin, 1985 .... $14/$80
Lak Sirvak, 1998 .... $3/$6
Lando as General, 1998 .... $3/$6
Lando as General Pilot with coin, 1985 .... $60/$115
Lando as Skiff Guard, 1997 .... $3/$10
Lando Calrissian, 1996 .... $3/$10
Leia as Jabba's prisoner, 1997 .... $3/$6
Leia in Boushh disguise, 1996 .... $3/$6
Leia in Endor gear with Millennium
     minted coin .... $5/$10
Leia in Ewok celebration outfit, 1998 .... $3/$6
Leia in Hoth gear, 1998 .... $3/$6
Leia with all-new likeness, 1998 .... $3/$6
Lobot, 1998 .... $4/$6
Luke as Jedi Knight, 1996 .... $3/$6
Luke as Jedi Knight with green saber with coin,
     1985 .... $30/$210
Luke as X-Wing pilot, 1996 .... $3/$10
Luke as X-Wing pilot, with coin, 1985 .... $10/$90
Luke in battle poncho, with coin .... $65/$115
Luke in battle poncho, with Millennium
     minted coin .... $5/$10
Luke in Bespin outfit, 1998 .... $3/$6
Luke in ceremonial garb, 1997 .... $3/$6
Luke in Dagobah fatigues, 1996 .... $3/$10
Luke in Hoth gear, 1997 .... $3/$6
Luke in Imperial Guard disguise, 1996 .... $3/$6
Luke in Stormtrooper disguise, 1996 .... $3/$10
Luke in Stormtrooper disguise, with coin,
     1985 .... $140/$400
Luke Skywalker, 1998 .... $3/$6
Luke Skywalker, 1995 .... $3/$10
Luke with blast shield helmet, 1998 .... $3/$6
Lumat, with coin, 1985 .... $15/$55
Malakili (Rancor Keeper), 1997 .... $3/$6
Momaw Nadon (Hammerhead), 1996 .... $3/$10
Mon Mothma, 1998 .... $3/$6
Nien Nunb, 1997 .... $3/$6
Nikto, with coin .... $14/$590
Obi-Wan Kenobi, 1998 .... $3/$6
Obi-Wan Kenobi, 1995 .... $3/$10
Obi-Wan Kenobi, with coin, 1985 .... $15/$90
Orrimaarkpo (Prune Face), 1998 .... $3/$6
Paploo, with coin, 1985 .... $14/$45
Ponda Baba, 1997 .... $3/$10

KENNER COMES UP EMPTY!

Despite trying to rush to market after Star Wars became a smash hit, Kenner was able only to muster some boxed puzzles, a board game and paint sets before Christmas 1977. But it did market an empty box; the Early Bird Certificate Kit, that came with a coupon good for the first four action figures by mail early in 1978. The kits sold for around $10. Today, in sealed condition along with the white cardboard mailer containing the first figures, the cost would be 30 to 50 times that.

Pote Snitkin, 1998 .... $3/$6
Prince Xizor, 1996 .... $3/$6
Princess Leia, 1995 .... $3/$10
Princess Leia, 1998 .... $3/$6
R2-D2, 1995 .... $3/$10
R2-D2, 1998 .... $3/$6
R2-D2 with Datalink and Sensorscope, 1998 .... $3/$6
R2-D2 with pop-up Lightsaber, with coin,
     1985 .... $95/$150
R5-D4, 1996 .... $3/$10
Rebel Fleet Trooper, 1997 .... $3/$10
Ree-Yees, 1998 .... $3/$6
Romba, with coin, 1985 .... $35/$55
Saelt-Marae (Yak Face), 1997 .... $3/$6
Sandtrooper, 1996 .... $3/$10
Snowtrooper, 1997 .... $3/$6
Snowtrooper, with Millennium minted coin .... $5/$10
Stormtrooper, 1995 .... $3/$10
Stormtrooper, with coin .... $12/$180
Teebo, with coin .... $12/$135
TIE Fighter Pilot, 1996 .... $3/$10
Tusken Raider, 1996 .... $3/$10
Ugnaught, 1998 .... $3/$6
Warok, with coin, 1985 .... $35/$60
Weequay Skiff Guard, 1997 .... $3/$10
Wicket and Logray, 1998 .... $3/$6
Wicket, with coin, 1985 .... $20/$165
Yak Face, with coin, 1985 .... $165/$1,710
Yoda, 1998 .... $3/$6
Yoda, 1996 .... $3/$10
Yoda, with coin .... $25/$510
Zuckuss, 1998 .... $3/$6

Promotional 3-inch figures

B'omarr Monk .... $0/$10
Figrin D'an (Cantina Band Member) .... $0/$15
Han in Stormtrooper disguise .... $0/$15
Mace Windu .... $5/$10
Muftak and Kabe .... $10/$20
Obi-Wan Kenobi Spirit .... $0/$15
Oola and Salacious Crumb .... $10/$15
STAP and Battle Droid .... $10/$15

Return of the Jedi

8D8, 1983...$9/$35
Admiral Ackbar, 1983...$9/$30
AT-AT Commander ....$9/$25
AT-ST Driver...$10/$30
B-Wing Pilot ....$9/$20
Bib Fortuna ....$14/$35
Biker scout, 1983 ....$12/$40
Chief Chirpa, 1983...$10/$30
Emperor Palpatine, 1983....................................$10/$45
Emperor's Royal Guard ....$12/$55
Gamorrean Guard, 1983......................................$9/$30
General Madine, 1983...$10/$40
Han in Trenchcoat, 1984...................................$15/$40
Klaatu, 1983...$10/$20
Klaatu in Skiff guard outfit, 1983 ....$13/$35
Lando Calrissian, 1983 ....$13/$35
Leia in battle poncho, 1984...............................$25/$45
Leia in Boushh disguise, 1983 ....$16/$45
Logray, 1983 ....$11/$30
Luke as Jedi Knight, blue saber, 1983 ....$45/$165
Luke as Jedi Knight, green saber, 1983 ....$30/$85
Lumat, 1983 ....$25/$40
Nien Nunb, 1983...$8/$30
Nikto, 1984 ....$14/$25
Paploo ....$25/$45
Pruneface, 1984..$9/$25
Rancor Keeper, 1984...$10/$20
Rancor Monster, 1983...$10/$20
Rebel Commander, 1983......................................$8/$25
Rebel Commando, 1983..$9/$25
Ree-Yees, 1983 ....$8/$25
Squid Head, 1983..$13/$30
Sy Snooties and the Rebo Band, 1984 ....$30/$180
Teebo, 1984 ....$12/$30
Weequay..$8/$20
Wicket, 1984 ....$20/$40

Star Wars

Boba Fett, 1978..$20/$920
C-3PO, Original 12, 1977 ....$12/$125
Chewbacca, Original 12, 1977...........................$9/$220
Darth Vader, Original 12, 1977..........................$15/$230
Death Squad Commander, Original 12, 1977 ......$10/$175
Death Star Droid, 1978 ....$12/$155
Early Bird Figures, Luke, Leia, R2-D2,
    Chewbacca, 1977 ....$220/$610
Greedo, 1978..$10/$115
Hammerhead, 1978..$9/$150
Han Solo, large head, Original 12, 1977.............$18/$620
Han Solo, small head, Original 12, 1977.............$25/$580
Jawa, cloth cape, Original 12, 1977 ....$14/$220
Jawa, vinyl cape, Original 12, 1977...............$250/$3,200
Luke as X-Wing Pilot, 1978, ...$10/$130
Luke Skywalker, Original 12, 1977 ....$30/$320

Luke with Telescoping Saber, Original 12,
    1977..$220/$4,410
Obi-Wan Kenobi, Original 12, 1977 ....$15/$185
Power Droid, 1978 ....$8/$125
Princess Leia, Original 12, 1977........................$35/$250
R2-D2, Original 12, 1977 ....$12/$175
R5-D4, 1978...$12/$130
Snaggletooth, blue body, Sears exclusive,
    1978..$200/$0
Snaggletooth, red body, 1978.............................$10/$160
Stormtrooper, Original 12, 1977 ....$12/$230
Tusken Raider, Original 12, 1977 ....$15/$230
Walrus Man, 1978..$11/$135

Banks

C-3PO, ceramic, Roman, 1977 ....$25/$50
Chewbacca, Sigma, 1983 ....$25/$35
Darth Vader, Adam Joseph, 1983........................$9/$13
Darth Vader, ceramic, Roman, 1977 ....$50/$75
Darth Vader, silver plated, Leonard Silver,
    1981..$45/$65
Emperor's Royal Guard, Adam Joseph, 1983.........$9/$13
Gamorrean Guard, Adam Joseph, 1983.................$30/$50
Jabba the Hut, Sigma, 1983 ....$25/$35
Kneesaa Bank, Adam Joseph, 1983.......................$7/$10
R2-D2, Adam Joseph, 1983.................................$7/$10
R2-D2, ceramic, Roman, 1977 ....$25/$35
Wicket, Adam Joseph, 1983 ....$7/$10
Yoda, Sigma, 1983 ....$25/$35
Yoda, lithographed tin with combination dials ......$11/$16

Bisque Figures

Boba Fett, bisque, Towle/Sigma, 1983 ....$30/$45
Darth Vader, bisque, Towle/Sigma, 1983..............$30/$45
Galactic Emperor, bisque, Towle/Sigma, 1983......$20/$30
Gamorrean Guard, bisque, Towle/Sigma, 1983 .....$20/$30
Han Solo, bisque, Towle/Sigma, 1983 ....$25/$35
Lando Calrissian, bisque, Towle/Sigma, 1983.......$30/$45
Luke Skywalker, bisque, Towle/Sigma, 1983 ....$30/$45

Board Games

Star Wars Adventures of R2-D2 Game,
    Kenner, 1977 ....$20/$30
Star Wars Battle at Sarlacc's Pit,
    Parker Brothers, 1983...................................$15/$25
Star Wars Escape from Death Star, Kenner,
    1977..$15/$25
Star Wars Monopoly, Parker Brothers, 1997 ....$20/$35
Star Wars ROTJ Ewoks Save the Trees,
    Parker Brothers, 1984...................................$15/$25
Star Wars Wicket the Ewok, Parker Brothers,
    1983..$12/$20
Star Wars X-Wing Aces Target Game, 1978 ....$30/$50

Books

Burger Chef Fun Book, 1978.................................$6/$8
Chewbacca and C-3PO Coloring Book, Kenner........$2/$4
Chewbacca and Leia Coloring Book, Kenner...........$2/$4
Chewbacca's Activity Book, Random House ....$3/$5

Chewbacca, Han, Leia and Lando Coloring Book,
 Kenner .... $2/$4
Darth Vader and Stormtroppers Coloring Book,
 Kenner .... $2/$4
Empire Strikes Back Coloring Book, 1980 .... $5/$7
Empire Strikes Back Panorama Book,
 Random House .... $15/$20
Empire Strikes Back Pop-Up Book,
 Random House,1980 .... $10/$15
Empire Strikes Back Sketchbook, Ballantine,
 1980 .... $14/$20
Escape from the Monster Ship Book,
 Random House, 1985 .... $6/$8
Ewoks Coloring Book, Kenner, 1983 .... $7/$10
Fuzzy as an Ewok, Random House, 1985 .... $6/$8
How the Ewoks Saved the Trees, Random House,
 1985 .... $6/$8
Jedi Master's Quiz, Random House, 1985 .... $6/$8
Lando Fighting Skiff Guard Coloring Book,
 Kenner, 1983 .... $2/$4
Lando in Falcon Cockpit Coloring Book, 1983 .... $2/$4
Learn-to-Read Activity Book, Random House,
 1983 .... $6/$8
Luke Skywalker Coloring Book, Kenner, 1983 .... $2/$4
Max Rebo Coloring Book, Kenner, 1983 .... $7/$10
My Jedi Journal, Ballantine .... $7/$10
R2-D2 Coloring Book, Kenner .... $2/$4
Return of the Jedi Activity Book, Happy House,
 1983 .... $5/$7
Return of the Jedi Coloring Book, 1984 .... $2/$4
Return of the Jedi Maze Book, 1983 .... $2/$4
Return of the Jedi Monster Activity Book,
 Happy House, 1983 .... $2/$4
Return of the Jedi Picture Puzzle Book,
 Happy House, 1983 .... $2/$4
Return of the Jedi Pop-Up Book,
 Random House, 1983 .... $10/$12
Return of the Jedi Punch-Out Book,
 Random House .... $10/$12
Return of the Jedi Sketchbook, Ballantine,
 1983 .... $11/$16
Return of the Jedi Word Puzzle Book,
 Happy House, 1983 .... $5/$7
Star Wars Pop-Up Book, Random House,
 1978 .... $10/$16
Star Wars Poster Art Coloring Set, Craft Master,
 1978 .... $9/$13
Star Wars Questions and Answers About Space Book,
 Random House, 1979 .... $5/$7
Star Wars Sketchbook, Ballantine, 1977 .... $14/$15
Sticker Book, 256 stickers, Panini, 1977 .... $23/$35
Yoda Coloring Book, Kenner .... $2/$4

Star Wars Cereal boxes
Apple Jacks, with Droids comic, Kellogg's, 1995 .... $15
Apple Jacks, with Star Wars comic,
 Kellogg's, 1995 .... $10
Boo Berry, with card offer, General Mills, 1978 .... $150

Boo Berry, with sticker offer, General Mills,
 1978 .... $150
C-3PO's, with C-3PO mask, Kellogg's, 1984 .... $30
C-3PO's, with Chewbacca mask. Kellogg's, 1984 .... $30
C-3PO's, with Darth Vader mask, Kellogg's, 1984 ...... $30
Cheerios, with poster offer, General Mills, 1978 .... $50
Cheerios, with tumbler offer, General Mills, 1979 .... $50
Chocolate Crazy Cow, with card offer,
 General Mills, 1978 .... $150
Cocoa Puffs, with card offer, General Mills,
 1978 .... $75
Cocoa Puffs, with sticker offer, General Mills,
 1978 .... $75
Corn Pops, with Making of Star Wars, Kellogg's,
 1995 .... $10
Count Chocula, with card offer, General Mills,
 1978 .... $150
Count Chocula, with sticker offer, General Mills,
 1978 .... $150
Franken Berry, with card offer, General Mills,
 1978 .... $150
Franken Berry, with sticker offer, General Mills,
 1978 .... $150
Froot Loops, with Han Stormtrooper offer,
 Kellogg's, 1995 .... $10
Lucky Charms, with hang glider offer,
 General Mills, 1978 .... $75
Raisin Bran, with Star Wars video ad, Kellogg's,
 1995 .... $10
Strawberry Crazy Cow, with card offer,
 General Mills, 1978 .... $150
Trix, with hang glider offer, General Mills,
 1978 .... $75

Star Wars Cereal Premiums
Card, set of 18, General Mills, 1978 .... $3
Han Stormtrooper, Kellogg's, 1995 .... $10
Hang glider, set of four, General Mills, 1978 .... $8
Kite, General Mills, 1978 .... $30
Making of Star Wars video, Kellogg's, 1995 .... $5
Micro Collection figures, Kellogg's, 1984 .... $10
Poster, set of four, General Mills, 1978 .... $2
Rebel Rocket, set of four, Kellogg's, 1984 .... $10
Star Wars comic, Kellogg's, 1995 .... $5
Stick-R-Card, set of 10, Kellogg's, 1984 .... $2
Stickers, set of 16, General Mills, 1978 .... $15
Tumbler, General Mills, 1978 .... $15

Clocks
3-D, electric, quartz, Bradley, 1982 .... $16/$23
C-3PO and R2-D2 alarm clock, Bradley, 1980 ...... $15/$25
Droid, wall clock, Bradley .... $20/$30
Empire Strikes Back, wall clock, Bradley .... $20/$30
Portable clock/radio, Bradley, 1984 .... $11/$16

Clothing
Chewbacca bandolier strap, 1983 .... NA/$15
Darth Vader belt buckle, Leather Shop, 1977 .... $14/$20

R2-D2 and C-3PO belt buckles, Leather Shop,
1977 .... $14/$20
Return of the Jedi belt, Leather Shop, 1977 .... $5/$7
Yoda backpack, Sigma .... $14/$20

Star Wars Coins
2-1B, Kenner, 1985 .... $120
63rd Coin, lightsaber, Kenner, 1985 .... $500
A-Wing Pilot, Kenner, 1985 .... $5
Anakin Skywalker, Kenner, 1985 .... $75
AT-AT, Kenner, 1985 .... $75
AT-ST driver, Kenner, 1985 .... $10
B-Wing Pilot, Kenner, 1985 .... $10
Barada, Kenner, 1985 .... $5
Bib Fortuna, Kenner, 1985 .... $75
Biker Scout, Kenner, 1985 .... $10
Boba Fett, Kenner, 1985 .... $75
C-3PO, Kenner, 1985 .... $10
Chewbacca, Kenner, 1985 .... $10
Creatures, Kenner, 1985 .... $75
Darth Vader, Kenner, 1985 .... $10
Droids, Kenner, 1985 .... $75
Emperor, Kenner, 1985 .... $10
Emperor's Royal Guard, Kenner, 1985 .... $50
EV-9D9, Kenner, 1985 .... $5
FX-7, Kenner, 1985 .... $120

Gamorrean Guard, Kenner, 1985 .... $10
Greedo, Kenner, 1985 .... $75
Han Carbonite, Kenner, 1985 .... $10
Han Hoth, Kenner, 1985 .... $5
Han original, Kenner, 1985 .... $120
Han Solo Rebel (trenchcoat), Kenner, 1985 .... $10
Hoth Stormtrooper, Kenner, 1985 .... $120
Jawas, Kenner, 1985 .... $10
Lando General, Kenner, 1985 .... $5
Lando with Cloud City, Kenner, 1985 .... $75
Luke Jedi, Kenner, 1985 .... $10
Luke, original, Kenner, 1985 .... $50
Luke Poncho, Kenner, 1985 .... $5
Luke Stormtrooper, Kenner, 1985 .... $5
Luke with Tauntaun, Kenner, 1985 .... $75
Luke X-Wing, Kenner, 1985 .... $10
Luke X-Wing, small, Kenner, 1985 .... $30
Lumat, Kenner, 1985 .... $10
Millennium Falcon, Bend Ems, 1994 .... $5
Obi-Wan Kenobi, Kenner, 1985 .... $10
Princess Leia, Boushh, Kenner, 1985 .... $120
Princess Leia, original, Kenner, 1985 .... $120
R2-D2 pop-up lightsaber, Kenner, 1985 .... $5
Stormtrooper, Kenner, 1985 .... $10
Tusken Raider, Kenner, 1985 .... $120
Warok, Kenner, 1985 .... $5
Wicket, Kenner, 1985 .... $10
X-Wing, Bend Ems, 1994 .... $5
Yak Face, Kenner, 1985 .... $75
Yoda, Kenner, 1985 .... $10
Zuckuss, Kenner, 1985 .... $120

Cookie Jars
C-3PO cookie jar, ceramic, Roman, 1977 .... $150/$250
Darth Vader, R2-D2 and C-3PO cookie jar,
hexagon, Sigma .... $55/$80
R2-D2 cookie jar, ceramic, Roman, 1977 .... $90/$150

Electronics
Darth Vader speaker phone, ATC, 1983 .... $40/$60
Duel Racing Set, Lionel, 1978 .... $40/$75
Give-A-Show Projector, with filmstrips, Kenner,
1979 .... $25/$35
Luke Skywalker AM headset radio .... $95/$150
Movie viewer, Kenner, 1978 .... $15/$20

Fast Food
Boba Fett toy, Taco Bell, 1997 .... $3/$5
Cloud City toy, Taco Bell, 1997 .... $3/$5
Death Star spinner toy, Taco Bell, 1997 .... $3/$5
Empire Strikes Back glasses, Burger King, 1980 ...... $4/$8
Empire Strikes back sticker album, Burger King,
1980 .... $4/$20
Glasses, Burger King, 1977 .... $5/$10
Millennium Falcon toy, Taco Bell, 1997 .... $1/$2
Mirror Cube toy, Taco Bell, 1997 .... $1/$2
Puzzle cube, Taco Bell, 1997 .... $1/$2
R2-D2 toy, Taco Bell, 1997 .... $1/$2

┌───┐

READ ALL ABOUT IT!

Whatever the format, comic books have been one of the best bets for Star Wars fans wanting to keep the adventure going between films since 1977. Comic book stores are the best place to find new and old Star Wars comics from Dark Horse, which, in it's Dark Empire I and II sequels, built on the legend George Lucas laid down in the first three movies. Dark Horse's comics have played a key role in helping maintain the conceptual presence of Star Wars in the years until the theatrical re-releases and the first prequel.

Most comics issued by Dark Horse can be found for between $3-$10 in Mint condition, unless it is the first issue of a new series. Notable examples include issues #1 (Dec. 1991) and #2 (Feb. 1992) of Star Wars: Dark Empire, at $22 each.

Collectors looking for excitement between the release of Star Wars: The Phantom Menace and the two prequel films, set for release in 2002 and 2005, can turn to Marvel Comics. From 1977 to 1986, it supplied regular doses of original Star Wars comics adventures to fans—and published more than 100 issues during the challenging periods between film releases of that era. Marvel's 107 issues of Star Wars are generally $20-$30, except for the last issue, #107, from September 1986, at $65. The first issue, July 1977, is $70, but a rare 35-cent test-market version can bring $425.

└───┘

Return of the Jedi glasses, Burger King, 1983...........$3/$5

Star Wars Episode I, cup toppers, Taco Bell, 1999...............$2/$3

Star Wars Episode I, cup toppers, Kentucky Fried Chicken, 1999 ....$2/$3

Star Wars Episode I, cup toppers, Pizza Hut, 1999, $2/$3

Star Wars Episode I, Flying Bucket toppers, Kentucky Fried Chicken, 1999...............$2/$3

Star Wars Episode I, KFC Buckets, Kentucky Fried Chicken, 1999 ....$4/$6

Star Wars Episode I, Planet Coruscant, Pizza Hut, 1999...............$3/$5

Star Wars Episode I, Planet Naboo, Kentucky Fried Chicken, 1999 ....$3/$5

Star Wars Episode I, Planet Tatooine, Taco Bell, 1978...............$3/$5

Star Wars Funmeal boxes, Burger King, 1978.......$25/$40

Star Wars poster, Pizza Hut, 1998...............$1/$3

Yoda toy, Taco Bell, 1997 ....$1/$2

Halloween costumes

Admiral Ackbar, Ben Cooper, 1983 ....$5/$10

Boba Fett, Ben Cooper, 1979...............$5/$10

C-3PO, Ben Cooper, 1977 ....$5/$10

Chewbacca, Ben Cooper, 1977 ....$5/$10

Darth Vader, Ben Cooper, 1977 ....$5/$10

Gamorrean Guard, Ben Cooper, 1983 ....$5/$10

Klaatu, Ben Cooper, 1983...............$5/$10

Leia, Ben Cooper, 1977 ....$5/$10

Luke, Ben Cooper, 1977 ....$5/$10

Luke X-Wing pilot, Ben Cooper, 1977 ....$5/$10

R2-D2, Ben Cooper, 1977...............$5/$10

Stormtrooper, Ben Cooper, 1977 ....$5/$10

Wicket, Ben Cooper, 1983 ....$5/$10

Yoda, Ben Cooper, 1980 ....$5/$10

Kits

Flying R2-D2 rocket kit, Estes, 1978...............$9/$13

TIE Fighter rocket kit, Estes, 1978 ....$11/$16

X-Wing Fighter rocket kit, Estes, 1978 ....$11/$16

X-Wing with Maxi-Brutel rocket kit, Estes, 1978...............$18/$25

Medals

Chewbacca, W. Berrie, 1980...............$6/$8

X-Wing, W. Berrie, 1980 ....$6/$8

Micro Series

Bespin Control Room, 1982 ....$12/$35

Bespin Freeze Chamber, 1982 ....$25/$65

Bespin Gantry, 1982...............$12/$30

Death Star Compactor, 1982...............$30/$70

Death Star Escape, 1982 ....$15/$40

Death Star World, 1982...............$50/$155

Hoth Generator Attack, 1982...............$15/$35

Hoth Ion Cannon, 1982...............$20/$45

Hoth Turret Defense, 1982...............$20/$40

Hoth Wampa Cave, 1982 ....$15/$35

Hoth World, 1982...............$50/$155

Imperial TIE Fighter, 1982 ....$30/$60

Millennium Falcon, 1982...............$175/$390

Snowspeeder, 1982 ....$50/$155

X-Wing Fighter, 1982 ....$25/$60

Miscellaneous

Chewbacca/Darth Vader bookends, Sigma ....$25/$35

Darth Vader duty roster...............$5/$7

Darth Vader SSP Van, Kenner, 1978...............$20/$25

Empire Strikes Back dinnerware set...............$15/$25

Inflatable lightsaber, Kenner, 1977 ....$45/$60

Intergalactic passport and stickers, Ballanine, 1983...............$7/$10

Original Fan Club Kit, 1977 ....$10/$15

Original Press Kit, 1977...............$25/$45

Return of the Jedi candy containers, figural, set of 18, Topps, 1983 ....$20/$30

Star Wars dinnerware set...............$20/$30

Sticker set and album, Burger King ....$7/$10

Yoda hand puppet...............$14/$20

Yoda Jedi Master Fortune Teller Ball ....$20/$30

Mugs

C-3PO, ceramic, Sigma...............$16/$23

Chewbacca, ceramic, Sigma ....$18/$25

Darth Vader, ceramic, Sigma ....$16/$23

Gamorrean Guard, ceramic, Sigma...............$10/$20

Han Solo, ceramic, Sigma...............$23/$35

Lando Calrissian, ceramic, Sigma ....$16/$23

Leia, ceramic, Sigma...............$20/$30

Luke Skywalker, ceramic, Sigma...............$20/$30

Play sets

Cloud City play set, Sears exclusive, 1981 ....$100/$350

Dagobah, 1982...............$25/$85

Darth Vader's Star Destroyer ....$50/$170

Hoth Ice Planet, 1980...............$40/$95

Imperial Attack Base, 1980...............$20/$65

Rebel Command Center, 1980...............$75/$210

Turret and Probot, 1980 ....$30/$90

Play-Doh

Ewoks Play-Doh set...............$11/$16

Ice Planet Hoth Play-Doh set...............$16/$23

Jabba the Hutt Play-Doh set...............$11/$16

Star Wars Action Play-Doh set ....$20/$30

Posters

Ben Kenobi/Darth Vader, Proctor & Gamble, 1978...............$9/$13

Chewbacca, Burger King, 1978 ....$5/$7

Dagobah, Burger King, 1980 ....$5/$7

Darth Vader, Nestea, 1980 ....$5/$7

Darth Vader, Proctor & Gamble, 1980...............$5/$8

Darth Vader, Burger King, 1978 ....$5/$7

Death Star, Proctor & Gamble, 1978 ....$5/$8

Empire Strikes Back 1981 re-release...............$12/$35

Empire Strikes Back 1982 re-release...............$12/$35

Empire Strikes Back advance ....$45/$100

Empire Strikes Back Poster Album Vol. 1 .... $10/$15
Empire Strikes Back Radio Program poster .... $15/$20
Empire Strikes Back Special Edition .... $9/$20
Hoth poster, Burger King, 1980 .... $5/$7
Luke Skywalker, Nestea, 1980 .... $5/$7
Luke Skywalker, Proctor & Gamble .... $5/$8
Luke Skywalker, Burger King, 1978 .... $5/$7
R2-D2 and C-3PO poster, Proctor & Gamble,
   1980 .... $5/$8
R2-D2 poster, Burger King, 1978 .... $5/$7
Return of the Jedi 1985 re-release .... $12/$30
Return of the Jedi Special Edition .... $9/$20
Revenge of the Jedi, with date .... $60/$150
Revenge of the Jedi, without date .... $100/$200
Star Destroyer, General Mills, 1978 .... $5/$10
Star Wars 1982 re-release .... $20/$50
Star Wars Birthday, 1st anniversary .... $250/$600
Star Wars Mylar advance .... $70/$175
Star Wars Radio Program, Golden .... $23/$35
Star Wars second advance .... $70/$175
Star Wars Second Edition .... $9/$20
Star Wars Episode I, The Phantom Menace .... $9/$20
TIE Fighter and X-Wing poster, General Mills,
   1978 .... $30/$40

Punching Bags
Chewbacca, Kenner, 1977 .... $20/$40
Darth Vader, Kenner, 1977 .... $15/$30
Jawa, Kenner, 1977 .... $45/$65
R2-D2, Kenner, 1977 .... $15/$30

Puzzles
Attack of the Sand People, 140 pieces, Kenner .... $5/$7
Cantina Band, 500 pieces, Kenner .... $6/$8
Han Solo and Chewbacca, 140 pieces, Kenner .... $6/$8
Jabba the Hutt, Craft Master, 1983 .... $4/$7
Jawas Capture R2-D2, 140 pieces, Kenner .... $4/$6
Luke and Leia Leap for Their Lives, 500 pieces,
   Kenner .... $6/$8
Luke Skywalker, 500 pieces, Kenner .... $6/$10
Space Battle, 500 pieces, Kenner .... $7/$10
Stormtroopers Stop the Landspeeder, 140 pieces,
   Kenner .... $5/$7
Trapped in the Trash Compactor, 140 pieces,
   Kenner .... $5/$7
Victory Celebration, 500 pieces, Kenner .... $6/$8
X-Wing Fighters Prepare to Attack, 500 pieces,
   Kenner .... $6/$8

School supplies
C-3PO pencil tray, Sigma .... $24/$35
C-3PO tape dispenser, Sigma .... $23/$35
R2-D2 string dispenser with scissors, Sigma .... $20/$30
Yoda tumbler/pencil cup, Sigma .... $20/$30

Star Wars Buddies
C-3PO, Hasbro, 1998 .... $3/$6
Cantina band member, Hasbro, 1998 .... $3/$6
Chewbacca, first version, Hasbro, 1998 .... $5/$10

Chewbacca, second version, Hasbro, 1998 .... $3/$6
Darth Vader pillow, 1983 .... $9/$13
Jabba the Hutt, Hasbro, 1998 .... $3/$6
Jawa, Hasbro, 1998 .... $3/$6
Max Rebo, Hasbro, 1998 .... $3/$6
R2-D2, Hasbro, 1998 .... $3/$6
Salacious Crumb, Hasbro, 1998 .... $3/$6
Wampa, Hasbro, 1998 .... $3/$6
Wicket, Hasbro, 1998 .... $3/$6
Yoda, Hasbro, 1998 .... $3/$6
Yoda sleeping bag, Hasbro, 1998 .... $16/$23

Toothbrushes
Electric toothbrush, Kenner, 1978 .... $16/$23
Snow Speeder toothbrush holder, Sigma .... $25/$35
Wicket toothbrush, battery-operated, 1984 .... $9/$13

Die-Cast Vehicles
Darth Vader's TIE Fighter, 1979 .... $20/$55
Land Speeder, 1979 .... $30/$70
Millennium Falcon, 1979 .... $35/$155
Slave I, 1979 .... $25/$85
Snowspeeder, 1979 .... $25/$90

Action Figures account for the majority of *Star Wars* collectibles. This 12-inch Chewbacca figure from Kenner is valued at about $150 in Mint-in-Package condition.

Star Destroyer, 1979 .... $50/$175
TIE Bomber, 1979.. $300/$830
TIE Fighter, 1979... $50/$60
Twin-Pod Cloud Car, 1979 .... $50/$80
X-Wing Fighter, 1979 .... $25/$75
Y-Wing Fighter, 1984.. $25/$160

Droids Vehicles

A-Wing Fighter, Droids Box, 1983.................... $250/$580
ATL Interceptor, 1985.. $20/$60
Imperial Side Gunner, 1985 .... $20/$55

Empire Strikes Back Vehicles

AT-AT, 1980 .... $100/$240
Rebel Transport, 1980... $40/$100
Scout Walker, 1982 .... $20/$60
Slave I, 1980 .... $50/$200
Snowspeeder .... $40/$85
Twin-Pod Cloud Car, 1980 .... $40/$85

Ewoks Vehicles

Ewoks Fire Cart, 1985 .... $10/$25
Ewoks Woodland Wagon, 1985 .... $20/$60

Power of the Force

Ewok Battle Wagon, 1985 .... $45/$135
Imperial Sniper Vehicle, 1985............................ $50/$85
One-Man Sand Skimmer, 1985............................ $40/$80
Security Scout Vehicle, 1985 .... $55/$120
Tatooine Skiff.. $300/$670

Return of the Jedi Vehicles

B-Wing Fighter, 1984 .... $60/$125
Ewok Combat Glider, 1984 .... $10/$25
Imperial Shuttle, 1984... $150/$300
Speeder Bike, 1983 .... $15/$30
TIE Interceptor, 1984 .... $50/$110
Y-Wing Fighter, 1983.. $50/$125

Star Wars Vehicles

Darth Vader's TIE Fighter, 1977........................ $50/$130
Imperial TIE Fighter, 1977 .... $40/$150
Jawa Sand Crawler, battery operated, 1977 .... $200/$610
Land Speeder, battery operated, 1977.................. $25/$75

Millennium Falcon, 1977................................... $90/$300
Sonic Land Speeder, JC Penney exclusive,
    1977.. $180/$580
X-Wing Fighter, 1977 .... $25/$120

Watches

C-3PO and R2-D2, digital, Bradley, 1970s........... $55/$80
C-3PO and R2-D2, digital, rectangular, Bradley,
    1970s .... $30/$45
C-3PO and R2-D2, digital, round face, Bradley,
    1970s .... $45/$65
C-3PO and R2-D2, digital, round, musical, Bradley,
    1970s .... $70/$100
C-3PO and R2-D2, vinyl band, Bradley,
    1970s .... $45/$60
C-3PO and R2-D2, vinyl band, photo, Bradley,
    1970s .... $30/$45
C-3PO and R2-D2, white border, photo, Bradley,
    1970s .... $45/$65
Darth Vader, digital, Bradley, 1970s .... $30/$45
Darth Vader, star and planet on face, Bradley,
    1970s .... $45/$65
Darth Vader, vinyl band, Bradley, 1970s .... $30/$45
Droids, digital, Bradley, 1970s .... $30/$45
Ewoks, vinyl band, Bradley, 1970s....................... $30/$45
Jabba the Hutt, digital, Bradley, 1970s .... $30/$45
Wicket the Ewok wristwatch, Bradley, 1970s........ $30/$45
Yoda, Bradley, 1970s .... $30/$45

Weapons

Droids lightsaber, 1985 .... $50/$200
Laser pistol, 1980.. $20/$85
Lightsaber, 1980.. $15/$70
Lightsaber, 1980.. $20/$55
Three-position laser rifle, 1980.......................... $50/$200
Biker Scout's laser pistol, 1984 .... $25/$70
Lightsaber .... $20/$50
Han Solo's laser pistol .... $20/$115
Inflatable lightsaber, 1977.................................. $35/$150

SUPERMAN AND BATMAN COLLECTIBLES

Fighting for truth and justice for more than sixty years, Superman and Batman are the original superheroes and among the most collectible characters of all time.

Background: Superman was the creation of Joe Shuster and Jerry Siegel, the artist and writer team who met while they were teenagers working on their high school newspaper in Cleveland. They dreamed up the Superman character in the late 1930s, and sold the idea to National Periodical Publications, an emerging comic book company that would later become the giant DC Comics. The very first "Superman" story appeared in the June 1938 issue of *Action Comics* and was so popular that within a year of his initial appearance, Superman not only had his own quarterly comic book, but was also a daily comic strip in hundreds of newspapers across the country.

Within a few years, Superman had his own radio show, with Bud Collyer (better known for hosting early TV game shows like *Beat the Clock*) playing the lead, and was also the subject of a series of Paramount cartoons and a pair of 15-chapter film serials starring an actor named Kirk Alyn.

In 1951, Lippert Pictures released the first full-length Superman movie, *Superman and the Mole Men*, starring character actor George Reeves, the man who would literally become Superman for millions of babyboomers. The success of the film led to the classic *Superman* TV series, also starring Reeves, that ran from 1953 to 1957—and for many years beyond that in syndication. (The show is still popular today.) Later years, of course, saw another TV series, *Lois and Clark, the New Adventures of Superman*, and four new *Superman* feature films, with Christopher Reeve playing the Man of Steel.

Batman trailed Superman, but not by much—about a year, as a matter of fact. The creation of artist Bob Kane, Batman, the Caped Crusader, made his initial appearance in the May 1939 issue of *Detective Comics*. Within a year he had his own title and a loyal sidekick, Robin, the Boy Wonder. Together they became known as the Dynamic Duo. Much of Batman's success stemmed from the villains he was up against, a series of menacing characters that included Catwoman, the Joker, Riddler, Penguin and others.

As the 1940s progressed, Batman became a newspaper comic strip and the subject of a pair of movie serials. Throughout the 1950s and early 1960s, Batman remained a popular comic-book hero, and then, in 1966, his popularity soared to new levels with the debut of the *Batman* TV show, starring Adam West and Burt Ward, with various celebrities playing the villain roles. Although canceled during its third season, the campy TV show had a huge following of dedicated fans and remains popular to this day. Batman was also

featured in animated cartoon shows in the 1960s and 1970s, and then enjoyed renewed popularity with several Batman feature films, the first of which was released in 1989, starring Michael Keaton.

General Guidelines: Collectibles exist from every period of Superman's long career. In general, the older the material the more valuable it will be. Items from the 1940s, especially, are scarce, typically selling for hundreds, or even thousands, of dollars. Superman collectibles from the 1950s—the era of the George Reeves TV show—are very much in demand and increasing in value. Most have a copyright line on

"Action Comics" No. 1, dating from June 1938, is among the most valuable of all comic books, worth $75,000 or more in Mint condition. This example was sold at a Sotheby's auction.

them indicating either "National Publications, Inc." or "National Comics Publications." The majority of Batman collectibles date from the era of the 1960s TV show and later.

Condition for both Superman and Batman collectibles is, of course, critical; and items still in their original package or box will at least double the value of most vintage items. Having the original box for more recent items will typically increase value by 25 to 50 percent. The graphics of the box or package will also affect value. Since the majority of collectors seek these items for display purposes, the more attractive the graphics, the more desirable the item will be.

The values shown in the "Value Line" below demonstrate the range of material that is available.

Trends: Superman and Batman, as characters, have both already stood the test of time. They have succeeded in comic books, in newspaper strips, on radio, on television and in the movies. And, more importantly, they have remained popular from generation to generation for more than six decades—one of the true tests of a legitimate collectible. Some of their collectibles have sold for astounding prices—another indicator of a solid investment area. Superman and Batman items will continue to be made, and the vintage items should continue to increase in value.

In recent years, some advanced collectors, not satisfied with the "traditional" mass-produced commercial and premium items, have been seeking out the unique, one-of-a-kind collectibles, such as props and costumes from the Batman and Superman TV shows and movies. In one recent auction, for instance, the actual Batman and Robin costumes worn by Adam West and Burt Ward in the ABC television series sold for a whopping $23,000.

Recommended Reading

2000 Toys & Prices, Sharon Korbeck and Elizabeth Stephan

Among the several Superman lunch boxes issued over the years is this 1967 box from King Seeley, valued at about $150.

VALUE LINE

Values shown are items in Excellent condition without the original box (unless indicated).

Superman Collectibles

Bicycle siren, Empire, 1970s $25
Badge, Fo-Lee Gum, 1948, shield-shape, brass....... $3,500
Cigarette Lighter, Dunhill, 1940s, battery-operated,
    table-top, chrome $1,000
Children's Dish Set, Boontonware, 1966, plate,
    bowl & cup $115
Cinematic Picture Pistol, Daisy, 1940, metal gun with
    28-scene film $775
Coloring Book, Whitman, 1966.................................... $30
Coloring Book, Saalfield, 1940s $350
Comic Book, *Action Comics* #1, 1938.................. $75,000
Comic Book, *3-D Adventures of Superman,*
    with 3-D glasses, 1950s $120
Comic Book, Mini Comic, Kellogg's,
    1955..$125-$200
Crayon-By-Numbers Set, Transogram, 1954 .... $225
Cup, Burger King, 1984, one of four $7
Doll, Ideal, 1940, 13", wood & composition $1,000
Doll, Toy Works, 1977, 25", cloth $25
Energized Superman figure, Remco, 1979, 12",
    battery-operated $70
Fan Card, National Comics, 1950s $150
Film Viewer, Acme, 1947, with two films $225
Flying Superman, Transogram, 1955,
    12" plastic figure propelled by rubber band $115
Hand Puppet, Ideal, 1966, 11", cloth & vinyl.............. $45
Hair Brush, Monarch, 1940 .... $160
Hair Brush, Avon, 1976 .... $25
Kite, Pressman, 1966 .... $75
Kite, Hiflyer, 1982 .... $10
Lunch Box, 1954, Adco Liberty $1,000
Lunch Box, 1967, King-Seeley.................................. $150
Moccasins, Penobscot Shoe, 1940s $500
Official Magic Kit, Bar-Zim, 1956,
    complete in box... $750
Official Superman Costume, Ben Cooper, 1954,
    complete in box... $275
Official Superman Playsuit, Ben Cooper, 1970,
    in box.. $40
Official Superman Playsuit, Funtime Playwear,
    1954... $400
Official Superman Two-Piece Kiddie Swim Set,
    1950s, swim fins and goggles $150
Paint-by-Numbers Watercolor Set, Transogram,
    1954... $225
Patch, 1940s, several available....................... $500-$2,000
Patch, 1970s .... $10-$35
Pen, Jaffe, 1947.. $400

Pencil Box, Mattel, 1966 .... $60
Pennant, 1940s $750
Pennant, 1973, 35th anniversary $25
Pillow, 1960s $65
Pin, 1940s, Kellogg's $25
Pogo Stick, 1977 .... $50
Puzzle, Saalfield, 1940 .... $350
Puzzle, 1960s-70s, various .... $15-$25
Ring, Superman Gum, Gum, Inc., 1940 .... $15,000
Ring, Nestle's, 1978 .... $50
Roller Skates, Larami, 1975 .... $55
School Bag, Acme, 1950s, vinyl $150
Scrap Book, Saalfield, 1940 .... $150
Soaky, Avon, 1978 .... $40
Statue, Syracuse Ornament, 1942, 6",
    composition $2,750
Superman Action Game, American Toy Works,
    1940s $1,500
Superman and Supergirl Push Puppets, Kohner,
    1968, pair $400
Superman Beanie, 1940s $700
Superman Belt, Pioneer, 1940s $500
Superman Belt Buckle, 1940s $150
Superman Book and Record Set, Peter Pan, 1970s,
    two stories & record $10
Superman Candy Ring, Leader Novelty, 1940,
    gold finish, hidden compartment, decal $7,500
Superman Christmas Card, 1940s $150
Superman City Game, Remco, 1966,
    complete in box $300
Superman Crazy Foam, American Aerosol, 1970s $50
Superman Crusader Ring, 1940s $165
Superman Cut-Outs, Saalfield, 1940 .... $1,500
Superman Electronic Question and Answer Quiz Machine,
    1966, Lisbeth Whiting Co., battery-operated $125
Superman Figure, 1980s, various .... $35-$50
Superman Golden Muscle Building Set,
    Peter Puppets Playthings, 1954, in box $1,000

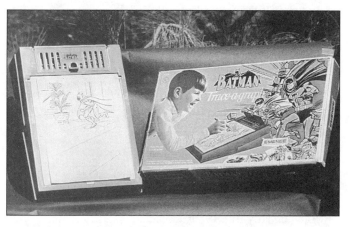

The "Batman Trace-a-Graph" toy by Emenee is valued at about $150 Mint-in-Box.

The Batman character was introduced in "Detective Comics" No. 27, which dates from May 1939 and is a treasure among both Batman and comic book collectors. This example sold for $68,500 at a Sotheby's auction.

Superman Trading Cards, 1980s,
    complete set of 88 .... $15-$25
Superman Junior Defense League Pin, 1940s $150
Superman Junior Horseshoe Set, Super Swim $100
Superman Junior Swim Goggles, Super Swim,
    1950s $85
Superman Krypton Rocket, Park Plastics, 1956 .... $300
Superman Paint Set, American Toy Works,
    1940s $750
Superman Phone Booth Radio, Vanity Fair, 1978 .... $65
Superman Pinball Game, Bally, 1978,
    full-size arcade game $550
Superman Pop-Up Book, Random House, 1979 .... $25
Superman Radio, 1973, depicts Superman from
    waist up $75
Superman Supertime Wristwatch, National Comics,
    1950s $525
Superman-Tim Magazine, 1940s, typical issue ...... $50-$60
Suspenders, Pioneer, 1948 .... $500

The Aurora Batman model kit from the 1960s is popular with collectors and valued at about $300 Mintin-Box.

Telephone, AT&E, 1979, plastic $750
Trading Cards, Gum Inc., 1940,
    set of 72 .... $5,000-$7,000
    Individual card .... $50-$100
TV Guide, September 1953,
    George Reeves cover .... $150-$250
Wristwatch, New Haven Clock, 1939 .... $1,200
Wristwatch, Una-Donna, 1986 .... $20

Batman Collectibles

Bat Cycle, Toy Biz, 1989 .... $12
Bat-Troll Doll, Wish-Nik, 1966 .... $150
Batboat, Duncan, 1987 .... $20
Batcave Play Set, Mego, 1974, vinyl $250
Batman "Punch-O" Drink Mix, 1966,
    one paper packet $35
Comic Book, 3-D Comic, DC, 1966,
    with 3-D glasses $150
Hand Puppets, Batman & Robin, Ideal, 1966,
    12" plastic and vinyl, each $150
Batman Annual, 1965-66 hardcover book,
    reprints of 1950s comics $30

Batman Bank, 1989, figural, from Batman Cereal $7
Batman Arcade Game, Bluebox, 1989, electronic $125
Batman Batarang Toss, Pressman, 1966 .... $250
Batman Bendy Figure, Diener, 1960s, on card $70
Batman Cartton Kit, Colorforms, 1966 .... $55
Batman Cereal Box, Kellogg's, 1966,
    with Yogi Bear $750
Batman Cereal Box, Ralston, 1989 .... $50
Batman Crazy Foam, 1974 .... $45
Batman Dinner Set, 1966, ceramic, three-piece $75
Batman Figure, Ideal, 1966, 3" $25
Batman Figure, Applause, 1988, 15" $25
Batman Figure and Parachute, CDC, 1966 .... $50
Batman Flying Copter, Remco, 1966 .... $85
Batman Fork, Imperial, 1966, 6" stainless steel $25
Batman Halloween Costume, Ben Cooper, 1965,
    mask and cape $40
Batman Helmet and Cape Set, Ideal, 1966 .... $250
Batman Kite, Hiflyer, 1982 .... $15
Batman Lamp, Vanity Fair, Taiwan $75
Batman Movie Lobby Display, 1989,
    Michael Keaton cardboard stand-up $135
Batman Meets Blockbuster Coloring Book,
    Whitman, 1966 .... $45
Batman on a String Figure, Fun Things, 1966 .... $30
Batman Paint-by-Number Set, Hasbro, 1965 .... $85
Batman Pencil Box, Empire, 1966,
    gun-shaped box with Batman pencils $55
Batman Pillow, 1966, 10" x 12", with 1940s logo $35
Batman Pinball Game, Marx, 1960s,
    tin litho with plastic casing $85
Batman Play Set, Ideal, 1966, eleven pieces with charac-
    ters and vehicles $1,000
Batman Record, SPC, 1966, 45 rpm record,
    sleeve shaped like Batman's head $35
Batman Road Race Set, 1960s, slot car set $250
Batman String Puppet, Madison, 1977 .... $20
Batman Superhero Stamp Set, 1970s $25
Batman Target Game, Hasbro, 1966 .... $85
Batman Utility Belt, Ideal, 1960s $3,000
Batman Wastepaper Basket, 1966, 10", tin litho $65
Batman Wristwatch, Quintel, 1991, digital $15
Batman Yo-Yo, Spectra-Star, 1989 .... $7
Batman/Robin Flasher Ring, Vari-Vue, 1966 .... $25
Batmobile, Simms, 1960s, plastic car on card $50
Batmobile, AHI, 1972, battery-operated, tin litho,
    11" $150
Batmobile, Bandai, 1980s $60
Batmobile, Toy Biz, remote control, 1989 .... $30
Batmobile Radio, Bandai, 1970s $95
Batphone, Marx, 1966 .... $125
Batscope Dart Launcher, Tarco, 1966 .... $45
Batwing, Toy Biz, 1980s $20
Beach Towel, 1966, Batman hitting crook $100
Bread Wrapper, New Century Bread, 1966 .... $40

The 1950s "TV Guide" with Superman and George Reeves on the cover is one of the more valuable "TV Guides", worth about $200 in nice condition.

Cake Decoration, 1960s, Batman or Robin,
   2" plastic...$20
Catwoman Watch, Consort, 1991 ....$15
Cave Tun-L, New York Toy, 1966 26" tunnel..........$1,000
Charm Bracelet, 1966, on card $60
Christmas Ornament, Presents, 1989 ....$10
Coins, Transogram, 1966, plastic coin set $50
Dinner Plate, child's, 1966, Boontonware,
   7" plastic...$30
Dot-to-Dot and Coloring Book,
   Vasquez Brothers, 1967.......................................$45
Milk Carton, Reiter and Hart, 1966 ....$300
Pajama's, child's Wormser, 1966 ....$475
Puzzle, Whitman, 1966, frame tray $30
Gotham City Stunt Set, Tonka, 1989 ....$50
Inflatable TV Chair, 1982 ....$20

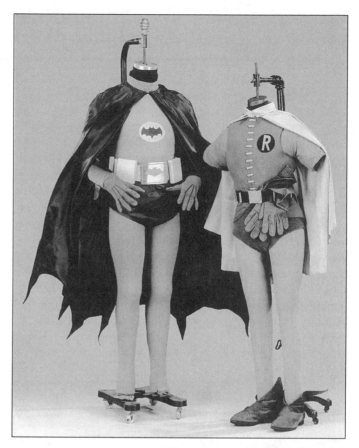

For the really serious collector, here are the actual costumes worn by Adam West and Burt Ward in the 1960s "Batman" TV show. Sold at a Butterfield & Butterfield auction, the pair of costumes sold for $23,000.

Joker Bank, Mego, 1974 ....$60
Joker Figure, Presents, 15" vinyl $20
Joker Figure, Applause, 1988, vinyl $20
Joker Van, Ertl, 1989, die-cast vehicle on card...............$8
Life Magazine, March 1968, Adam West as
   Batman on cover $45
Official Bat-Signal Sticker, Alan-Whitney, 1966..........$20
Pain-by-Number Book, Whitman, 1966 ....$45
Paper Mask, 1943, newspaper premium to
   promote first comic strip $1,500
Party Hat, 1972, Amscan cardboard hat depicts
   Batman & Robin $15
Penguin Returns Model Kit, Horizon $20
Ray Gun, 1960s, 7"..$225
Robin Figure, Ideal, 1966, 3" plastic $20
Robin Figure, Presents, cloth and vinyl.......................$20
Robin Figure, Applause, 1988 ....$20
Shooting Arcade, AHI, 1970s..$80
Sticker Fan with Batman Book, Watkins-Strathmore,
   1966..$45
Talking Alarm Clock, Janex, 1975................................$85
TV Guide, March 1966, Adam West cover.................$150

Superman and Batman Collectibles   417

TEDDY BEARS

The story of the first teddy bear has been told, revised and exaggerated so many times over the years that the real truth has probably been lost forever. But, regardless of how it actually happened, the introduction of that first cuddly teddy bear began a relationship between bears and their owners that has lasted a hundred years and shows no signs of diminishing.

Background: The origin of the teddy bear dates back to 1902, when President Theodore Roosevelt went to the border of Mississippi and Louisiana to settle a boundary dispute between the two states. The president was called on to help draw a new line between the two states. During a break in the tense negotiations, Roosevelt was invited to go hunting on the Mississippi Delta. Several variations of that day have been reported. Some say a malnourished bear was driven from the woods for the president to shoot. Some say a small, sickly bear was tied to a tree for him to shoot. Others say it was not a bear, but a cub that the president was instructed to shoot.

Combining America's favorite pastimes, baseball and collecting, is this early (circa 1905) Steiff teddy bear in a homemade baseball uniform. The teddy bear, which was purchased new in a Chicago department store, was sold by the original owner's family at a Theriault's auction for $2,600—twice its pre-sale estimate. Theriault's, which has been specializing in doll and teddy bear auctions for more than 25 years, is located in Annapolis, Maryland.

The only certainty is that Roosevelt refused to shoot the bear because, whatever the particular circumstances, he considered it unsportsmanlike. A popular political cartoonist of the day, Clifford K. Berryman, of *The Washington Post,* heard of the incident and immortalized it in a cartoon. The cartoon, which was reprinted in newspapers around the country, pictured a small bear with a rope around its neck being held by a man in Rough Rider clothing. Roosevelt had his back to the bear with his arm outstretched, indicating he was not going to shoot. The caption, "Drawing the line in Mississippi," gave the cartoon a double meaning.

Among those captivated by the cartoon was Brooklyn shopkeeper Morris Michtom, who displayed the cartoon in his store window, alongside a toy bear his wife had made. A sign identified the stuffed animal as "Teddy's Bear," and a legend was born. By 1907, the Michtoms had moved to a new building and opened the Ideal Novelty and Toy Company.

Michtom, according to family history, wrote President Roosevelt for permission to call the new toy a "Teddy" bear. Reportedly, although no letter has ever been found to verify this fact, the President responded: "I do not know what use my name is to a stuffed animal business, but you are welcome to use it."

Although a war hero and a man who achieved greatness as President of the United States, Theodore Roosevelt's greatest contribution to America might have been his role in developing a lovable and enduring children's toy. Roosevelt probably never dreamed, on that cold day in November of 1902, that a simple act of good sportsmanship would lead to a lasting treasure called the "teddy bear."

Today, Germany, along with the United States and Great Britain, remain the leading countries to produce teddy bears, one of the few toys which has stayed in its same basic form over the years.

General Guidelines: Teddy bears were intended to be loved, hugged and played with by children, so some of the most-loved teddies did not survive. Those that did often bore the marks of their owners' affections forever.

This wear and tear contributes to the decreased supply of early bears on the market today. The availability of bears manufactured before World War II is limited, and examples found, even in poor condition, can be extremely pricey.

Condition is the most significant factor in determining the value of a teddy bear. To command top prices, fur covering should be in Excellent or better condition. Foot pads, however, can be tolerated in a worn or slightly worn condition.

Bears with the manufacturer's original identification mark (be it a button, label or tag) command higher prices. Early Steiff bears are the most coveted of all bears because of their rarity and value. Identifying a bear's manufacturer can

COLLECTING IN MINIATURE!

Like their bigger cousins, miniature teddies were produced by the major manufacturers, like Steiff, Schuco, Ideal, Chad Valley and Bing.

Smaller Steiff bears are nearly as hard to find as their large counterparts, but the prices are less. Smaller Schuco bears are easier to find. These bears have one major identifying characteristic—a metal torso. If you carefully squeeze the bear body and it feels extremely hard, chances are it is a Schuco metal body.

Schuco also produced teddy bears that had perfume bottles inside, accessed by removing the teddy bear's head. Nice examples can sell for $300-$500. Schuco also produced a teddy bear "compact," whose jointed body contained an oval mirror on one side and a powder puff and tray on the other. These bears can bring $1,000-$1,500.

Schuco's "Yes-No" bears, in a variety of sizes, are also popular. The smaller size, less than six inches, creates the illusion that he is following your every move. This is done when the operator moves the tail mechanism that changes the position of the head from up and down to back and forth. They generally sell in the $300-$500 range. Larger sizes can range from $1,500-$5,000, depending on factors such as size, condition and year of issue.

Here are representative values of a few of the more desirable miniature teddy bears:

Star Gazer, 5-1/2", mohair, glass stickpin eyes,
  Steiff, pre-1920s... $600
6", beige mohair, head swivels, jointed limbs,
  brown floss nose and mouth, Steiff, 1960s $250
3-1/2" perfume bottle bear, green mohair,
  Schuco, 1920s-30s $1,000
5" perfume bottle bear, brown mohair, Schuco,
  1920s-30s $700
2-1/2" gold compact bear, with lipstick, powder
  and puff, Schuco, 1930s.. $600
3-1/2" dark gold mohair, black glass bead eyes,
  black floss nose, Steiff, 1910 .... $800
3-1/2" gold Original Teddy, with tag,
  Steiff, 1950s $300
5-1/4" pink mohair, brown floss nose and mouth,
  rattle Teddy, Steiff.. $1,750
2-3/4" bright gold mohair, metal eyes, floss nose,
  Schuco, 1970s $175
2-3/4" cinnamon mohair, metal eyes, Schuco,
  1960s-70s $200

Provenance can be a very important factor in determining the value of a teddy bear. This early Steiff bear came to America with its original owner in 1905. It remained in a woven and leather bag for 90 years, until it was sold at a Theriault's auction a few years ago for $6,000 -- twice its pre-sale estimate.

Distinguishing features of early Ideal bears are short mohair, a wide and triangularly-shaped head, an elongated slim body, wide-apart eyes and ears, and pointed pads on the feet. Ideal bears from the 1950s and '60s are commonly found with the features painted onto a molded vinyl face, and with large sleep eyes. They were often unjointed with bodies of rayon plush.

In some cases, repair or restoration can increase the value of a bear. Normally a bear obviously repaired and dressed in inappropriate clothing would be of lesser value. If it could be documented, however, that a child did the repair in a long-ago decade, the value could actually increase.

Miniature bears take up less space, but are not proportionally cheaper than large bears. In fact, a miniature bear in Good condition can be more expensive than its full-size counterpart! With all bears, facial appeal and rare color variations can increase value.

Bears manufactured in the late 1960s and 1970s are still abundant and can be found at very reasonable prices—even at yard sales and second-hand stores. But the legion of fans is growing and the market has exploded over the last decade. Teddy bears that only recently would have sold in the hundreds of dollars are now selling in the thousands and sometimes tens of thousands at auctions.

The Best Advice: The most important part of a bear's value may be its emotional appeal, which, unfortunately, is totally subjective. People can be as much in love with a $5 bear as a $5,000 bear. No solid advice can be given about the

be difficult with older bears since many were not marked or lost the original manufacturer's identification marks over time. Just looking at the bear, however, can give one clues to its origin. Distinguishing features of an old Steiff bear are an elongated muzzle, arms, feet and hump.

This pair of Steiff teddy bears sold a recent Theriault's auction for around $2,500 each.

emotional appeal of a teddy bear, except this: If you think a bear is adorable and it calls to you, it will probably have the same effect on another teddy bear collector down the line.

Basically, teddy bears are simply just too subjective a collectible to be anchored by any traditional method of defining value. In the final analysis, the best advice may be not to collect teddy bears with the hope of ever reselling them, because by the time you go to it, you probably won't be able to bring yourself to. That is both the essential lure and the eternal burden of the teddy bear collector.

Collecting Tips: Here are some general things to look for when attempting to evaluate a vintage teddy bear:

Manufacturer—Popular manufacturers to look for include Steiff, Ideal, Knickerbocker, Schuco, Chad Valley, Gund and Dakin.

Fabric—Wool mohair was commonly used before WWI, artificial silk plush around 1930, cotton plush after WWII and synthetic plush after the early 1950s.

Label—Is there a fabric label? Original cardboard hang tags are usually missing, but fabric labels sewn into a seam may still be present.

Condition—Some wear and tear is typical and many signs of distress can be repaired, but thin, rotting plush or fabric is difficult to salvage.

Body proportions—Long, thin arms and muzzle or a hump on the back generally indicate the bear was made before WWII, but variations between manufacturers make it important to consult a good reference book.

Articulation—Many old bears are jointed, but during the 1960s production costs made it popular to produce unjointed bears.

Ears—Original ear positions are important in manufacturer identification and dating. Check around the seam of the bear's head for any holes to indicate the ears may have been replaced.

Eyes—Plastic eyes generally indicate the bear was made after 1950, while glass eyes indicate the bear was manufactured after 1920. Boot-button eyes were used before WWI.

Paws—Felt was commonly used for paw pads in early bears; velvet was popular in the 1930s, while trimmed plush or leather (real or synthetic) was used later. Ultrasuede paw pads were made after the 1970s.

Clubs

• Good Bears of the World Club, P.O. Box 13097, Toledo, OH 43613-0097

• Teddy Bear Boosters Club, 19750 S.W. Peavine Mountain Rd., McMinnville, OR 97128

• B.E.A.R., Bear Enthusiasts All-Round, 313 Glenoaks Blvd., Glendale, CA 91207

• Steiff Clubs USA, 225 Fifth Ave., Suite 1022, New York, NY 10010

• National Doll & Teddy Bear Collector, P.O. Box 4032, Portland, OR 97208-4032

VALUE LINE

3-1/2" high, golden mohair, metal frame, tummy opens to reveal oval mirror and powder puff tray, Schuco $350

3-3/4" high, compact bear, gold mohair, lipstick under the head, powder/puff inside body, Steiff, 1920 .... $1,000

5" high, Teddy Threesome, mohair, swivel head, stationary legs, collar with bell, felt paws, Steiff $75

5" high, white mohair, plastic brads, Schuco................ $75

5" high, perfume bear, gold mohair, metal bead eyes and glasses, Schuco, 1925 .... $950-$1,100

6" high, Bedtime Bear, brown mohair, straw stuffed, glass eyes, sewn nose and mouth, jointed, Steiff, 1900s $175

6" high, Pouting Bear, brown plush, foam stuffing, molded face, sitting, Knickerbocker, 1950s $25

6-1/2" high, Berg Bear, gold plush, straw stuffed, Austria $100

7" high, Bear-at-Brunch, gold mohair, straw stuffed, stick-pin eyes, sewn nose and mouth, jointed, swivel head, Germany $175

7" high, Scooter Bear, plush, windup, on wheels $175

10" high, Cocoa Bear, white felt, stuffed, button eyes, 1940s $50

11" high, Classic Pooh, Winnie the Pooh, limited edition, 1990s, Steiff $250

11" high, Riding Bear, stuffed, blue and white checked, metal tricycle, red wood wheels $150

11" high, brown mohair, swivel head, gold muzzle, glass eyes, Zotty $150

11" gold mohair, glass eyes, Knickerbocker $275

11" high Playmate Bear, gold mohair, stuffed, sewn nose and mouth, jointed, 1950s $75

12" high, Smokey the Bear, Ideal, 1953 .... $50

12" high, white mohair, glass eyes, flannel pads, Steiff, 1912 ....$1,750-$1,850

12" high, short gold mohair, glass eyes, head swivels, arms/legs jointed, excelsior stuffing, Ideal, 1907 .... $1,500

13" high, gold mohair, swivel head, glass eyes, Hermann $125

13" high, cinnamon mohair, shoe button eyes, Steiff, 1910 ....$2,450-$2,550

14" high, light brown mohair, glass eyes, felt pads, shaved muzzle and eye area, Steiff, 1960s $475

16" high, Gentle Ben, black plush, plastic eyes, pink mouth, red felt tongue, pull string, Mattel, 1967 .... $50

16" high, brown and white mohair, glass eyes, Bing, 1920s ....$3,500-$3,700

16" high, The Original Ideal Teddy Bear, 75th anniversary commemorative, brown plush, label, special-edition box, Ideal, 1978 .... $75

16" high, Yogi Bear, brown plush, stuffed, molded face, yellow paws, green felt tie, Knicker-bocker, 1959 .... $100

16" high, tan mohair, button eyes, original lease and muzzle, Steiff, 1910 ....$6,000-$6,500

20" high, off-white mohair, shoe button eyes, Steiff, 1920 ....$3,500-$3,600

26" high, Beaver Valley Polar Bear, white plush, hinged jaw with teeth, hand-made eyes, limited edition of 25, signed on foot .... $1,000-$1,200

Light brown mohair bear, fully jointed, stuffed with excelsior and cotton, 22" tall, has a growler but no eyes, possibly English, circa 1930 .... $250

1920s Schuco yes-no bear $275

Steiff white miniature bear, 1950s $275

THERMOMETERS

When Galileo created the world's first thermometer in 1593, he could not have envisioned that four centuries later, his modest little invention would lead to a huge field of collectibles. Many types of thermometers have been invented since Galileo's first tinkerings, and as long as the weather continues to change, more sophisticated thermometers will continue to enhance our lives. For collectors, however, thermometers go way beyond our simple need to know the temperature.

Background: The modern age of thermometers can be traced to the work of Gabriel D. Fahrenheit, the German physicist and inventor who not only made the first mercury thermometer in 1714, but also came up with the Fahrenheit temperature scale, which is still in general use throughout the United States today. (Much of the rest of the world, interestingly, prefers the Celsius scale, while the scientific community records its temperatures on the Kelvin scale.)

The mass-production of thermometers in America dates back to 1851, when the Taylor Company of Rochester, N.Y., began making inexpensive thermometers to be sold in the nation's hardware stores. Shortly after, thermometers were starting to be used as advertising vehicles to promote various

This is an example of what collectors call a "bi-metal thermometer. It dates from the mid-1880s. (Photo courtesy Dick Porter, Onset, Mass.)

COLLECTOR'S ADVISORY!

Collectors should be aware that reproductions of some of the classic advertising thermometers have invaded the market. Many of these counterfeits use a paper label, while the original was painted and has the maker's name stamped on the back in ink. Modern metal thermometers often just look too new, lacking the natural aging that results from long exposure to the weather.

products. By the early 1900s, thermometers were being used to promote everything from soft drinks to gasoline. Today, these advertising thermometers are the most popular with collectors.

Over the years, major U.S. manufacturers of thermometers have included Cooper, Kessler, Hartley Gove & Sons, Maximum, PSG Industries, Taylor, Wahl and Weksler.

Collecting Trends: Collectible thermometers fall into six broad categories, according to Richard Porter, who owns what is probably the world's largest collection of thermometers and displays them at his Thermometer Museum in Onset, Mass. Porter's categories include the following:

Advertising Thermometers—The most popular category, as far as collectors are concerned, advertising thermometers feature the designs, slogans and logos of various products or businesses. Over the years, thermometers have advertised everything from gas stations and funeral homes to cigarettes and root beer. Most tend to be rather large; they were originally designed for display outside a gas station or country store. But some advertising thermometers were small enough to be given away as premiums. The value of advertising thermometers depends largely on what product is being advertised and age. In general, the older an advertising thermometer is, the more valuable it will be. And, of course, the more popular and desirable product names will also increase value. Collectors also look for clever graphics, bright colors, nice designs and classic slogans.

Antique Thermometers—Generally, this category includes thermometers dating from prior to 1900. Early thermometers, from the mid-1800s, are sought mostly by serious collectors of scientific instruments and tend to be pricey. Some sell in the hundreds, but according to Porter, two examples, both from the mid-1800s in Excellent condition with carved wood inlays, have sold for over $5,000.

Souvenir Thermometers—Growing rapidly in popularity with collectors are souvenir thermometers, the small, inexpensive thermometers sold at gift shops across America. Similar to snow globes, they promote cities, zoos, beaches, fairs and other attractions.

Cute Thermometers—These could also be described as "novelty" thermometers and are fun to collect.

Ordinary Thermometers—This category is a broad one that includes general, everday thermometers that lack advertising. Thermometers used daily by chefs, doctors and others also fit into this category.

Unusual Thermometers—This category consists of thermometers that are…well, unusual. They generally present great difficulty when trying to determine their age or value, but they can make a nice addition to a collection.

General Guidelines: In addition to being attractive, collectors also want their thermometers to work. In most cases, a thermometer cannot be adjusted, except by moving the tube, most of which are held in place by adhesive or brackets. However, broken thermometers can sometimes have their tubes successfully replaced, rendering them workable and, therefore, more valuable.

The size and shape of the glass tube, its bore and the bulb, also affect a thermometer's value. In general, the larger the glass tube and its bore, the more valuable it will be. Typically, larger thermometers, in general, are more valuable than smaller ones.

"Filling-station" type thermometers are among the most in demand by collectors. They generally offer nice, colorful graphics and are great to display. Most advertise gas and oil products, soft drinks, tobacco products, liquor, etc.

"Chandelier" thermometers, originally used in mansions and on railroad parlor cars, are rare and considered true treasures among serious collectors.

Mercury-filled thermometers are more valuable than those filled with alcohol. Among alcohol thermometers, those filled with green or blue-tinted alcohol are more desirable than thermometers exhibiting the more common red alcohol. Thermometers with faded alcohol are less valuable than those displaying nice bright color.

The type of material used for the backing plate of the thermometer will also affect its value. Materials such as glass, porcelain and red clay, which stand up to weather better than metal, plastic or wood, are also more collectible. Porcelain and glass thermometers in particular (without chips, of course) command the highest prices, especially those of older vintage. Thermometers featuring exotics woods (mahogany, rosewood, oak, ebony) and/or carvings always command a premium. Flaws, such as scratches, dents, chips, fading and rust, will significantly reduce the value of a thermometer.

VALUE LINE

Values shown are for working thermometers in Excellent condition.

Antique Thermometers

Wet/Dry Bulb, Taylor Co., 1880s .... $185 and up

"Chandelier" style thermometer, Taylor Co., 1887 .... $200 and up

This rare chandelier-style thermometer, designed for use in a train car, is valued at over $200. (Photo courtesy Dick porter, Onset, Mass.)

Tin case, late 1800s $150

Wood bath floaters, 1900 .... $50-$60

Enameled Metal Case, 1880s .... $50 and up

Vertical V-grooved backing plate, 1850-1900 .... $85 and up

Wood backing plate.. $45 and up

Physician's pocket bi-metal thermometer, 1900.. $100 and up

German-made silver pocket thermometer......... $95 and up

Champagne bowl floater .... $65 and up

Bi-metal thermometers, 1880s ....$90-$100

A.J. Dodge, wall model, wood frame, 8", 1900.......... $650

B.T. Co., wood with green enamel, 8" $150

C.P. Scott, cottage barometer, wood frame $250

C.M. Mfg. Co., wall model, cast-iron frame 13", 1890.. $400

L.C. Tower, "Weather Prognosticator," wood frame, brass, 9"... $450

Motometer, desk model, brass frame, round dial, 1910... $350

Tycos, chandelier model, brass frame, three-sided, 8-1/2", rare $1,700

Advertising Thermometers

Ex-Lax, gas-station type, 39".....................................$200
Pepsi-Cola, gas-station type, 1940s, 26"...................$175
Chesterfield, tin litho cigarette pack, 18", 1950s $185
Coca-Cola, gas-station type, bottle-shape,
   18-30"..$90-$125
Prestone, gas-station type, 36".................................$75
Mail Pouch Chewing Tobacco, gas-station type,
   39"...$75
Purolator Filters, gas-station type, 28"......................$65
Orange Crush, gas-station type, 28" $65
Orange Crush, bottle-cap style, 16", 1950s $95
Hires Root Beer, gas-station type $70
Hire Root Beer, bottle-shape, 29" $100
Royal Crown Cola, gas-station type, 29", 1940s $100

Mail Pouch Tobacco, gas-station type, 72",
   1930s $450
Ed Pinaud's Hair Tonic, 27", 1915........................$3,500
Winston, 9", round, 1960s...$65

Souvenir Thermometers

Florida ceramic animals, glass tube or bi-metal,
   1950s-1970s $15
Keys to cities or attractions, 1930s ....$20-$30
Sailing vessels, ship's wheels, horses, horseshoes,
   1930S ....$15-$20
Wall hanger or electric outlet cover $25
National monuments and battlefields,
   1930s to present $30
Wind mills or Dutch shoes, 1940s ....$10-$20
Pine slab, 1930s $25
Towers or obelisks, 1890s to present ....$20 and up
Animals on pedestals and pine slabs,
   1920s to present $20

Advertising thermometers, like this one for Hires Root Beer, were commonly seen on the walls of gas stations or country stores. They are the most popular category for collectors today. (Photo courtesy Dick Porter, Onset, Mass.)

This inexpensive advertising thermometer is on a piece of cardboard. Examples like this are generally valued at $10 or less. (Photo courtesy Dick Porter, Onset, Mass.)

Ordinary Thermometers

Chef's $10
Microwave $15
Medical $5
Oven $6
Lab, bright red alcohol or mercury $8
Refrigerator $6
Dairy floaters $10
Photo lab $8
Swimming pool floater $15
Auto dashboard $6
Boiler, bi-metal $25
Antifreeze tester, glass tube $5
Incubating, glass tube with narrow range $12
Hot/cold alarm $15
Double and triple scale .... $20 and up
Beehive (uncommon) $35
Brewers .... $50 and up
Grain silo $25
Aquarium or reptile $8

Turkey breast $20
Stove pipe safety $10

Cute Thermometers

Canary on a perch, bi-metal $20
Swiss Weather House, 1913 to present $15
Miniature frying pan, bi-metal, 1950 .... $25
Tie-clasp, 1970s $15
Cracker Jack prizes, 1920s-30s $50
Shells $20
Fountain pen or ball-point pen $25
Pocket watch or wristwatch, 1970s-present $25

Unusual Thermometers

St. Labre's Fish Skeleton, 1960s-1980s $12
French soldier's hat paperweight, 1900s $45
Muffler or windshield shape, 1930s-1950s $50
Recording thermometers, drum or disk,
    1930s-present $100
Postcard, heat-sensitive or liquid crystal, 1980s-90s $5
Plum bob, 1940s $45

Classic Tin Toys

Today's toys may be durable, but most are made of plastic, which just doesn't hold the charm and nostalgia of yesterday's tin creations. Those tin toys, made in large numbers mainly before World War II, are among the priciest collectible toys today.

Background and General Guidelines: Metal toys produced before World War I can be considered true works of art, especially since tin toys were often painstakingly hand painted. But the advent of chromolithography changed the way most toys were produced. Chromolithography was actually developed late in the 19th century. The technique allowed multicolored illustrations to be printed on flat tin plates, which were molded into toys. Starting in the 1920s, lithographed tin toys began to dramatically change toy production. American manufacturers could produce these colorful toys more inexpensively than the classic European toys that had dominated the toy market until this time.

With mass production came mass appeal. New tin mechanical toys were based on the characters and celebrities that were popular at the time. Newspaper comic strips and Walt Disney characters provided already popular subject matter for toy marketers.

Among the most well-known makers of mechanical tin toys were Marx, Chein, Lehmann and Strauss. Others included Courtland, Girard, Ohio Art, Schuco, Unique Art and Wolverine. Many of these manufacturers had business relationships with each other. Over the years, some would be found working together, producing toys for others, distributing others' toys or being absorbed by other companies. There even appeared to be some pilfering and reproducing others' ideas.

One of the advantages of lithography was that it allowed old toys to be recycled in many ways. When a character's public appeal began to wane, a new image could be printed on the same body to produce a new toy. Or, when a toy company was absorbed by another, older models could be dusted off and dressed up with new lithography. Many of the mechanical tin wind-up toys show up in surprisingly similar versions with another manufacturer's name on them.

Of the companies listed here, Marx was no doubt the most prolific. The company's founder, Louis Marx, at one time was employed by another leading toy maker, Ferdinand Strauss. He left Strauss in 1918 to start his own company.

Many of the popular Marx tin wind-ups were based on popular characters. One of the most sought-after is the Merrymakers Band, a group of mouse musicians. Some of the other highly valued character toys are the Amos 'n Andy Walkers, the Donald Duck Duet, Popeye the Champ, Li'l Abner and his Dogpatch Band and the Superman Rollover Airplane.

While Marx went on to produce many different kinds of toys, other companies, such as Chein, specialized in inexpensive lithographed tin. And like Marx, Chein also capitalized on popular cartoon characters, producing several Popeye toys, among others. J. Chein and Company, which was founded in 1903, was best known for its carnival-themed mechanical toys. Its Ferris Wheel is fairly well known among toy collectors and was made in several lithographed versions, including one with a Disneyland theme. Chein also produced a number of affordable tin banks.

Girard was founded shortly after Chein, but didn't start producing toys until 1918. It subcontracted toys for Marx and Strauss in the 1920s. In fact, several Girard and Marx toys are identical, having been produced in the same plant with different names on them. Marx later took over the company in the 1930s.

New Jersey-based Unique Art isn't known for an extensive line of toys, but it produced some that are favorites among tin toy collectors.

There are many other companies that produced lithographed tin toys not included in this section, particularly German and Japanese companies. Lehmann and Schuco, both German firms, are the only non-American toy makers listed in this guide. More lithographed tin toys can be found in the vehicles section of this book.

Trends: Older tin litho toy values are holding their own. However, due to the scarcity that has been created by collectors building and maintaining their collections, the values will continue to rise.

Remember, the better the condition, the better the value, especially with tin. Any character toys in Excellent condition or better are certain winners. Those with the original box are true treasures.

Tin robots have virtually become and endangered species. Whether wind-up or battery-operated, they are now

---

THE TOP 10 TIN TOYS!
(IN MINT CONDITION)

1. Popeye the Heavy Hitter, Chein	$6,500
2. Popeye Acrobat, Marx	$5,500
3. Popeye the Champ, Marx	$4,600
4. Mikado Family, Lehmann	$3,900
5. Red the Iceman, Marx	$3,500
6. Mortimer Snerd Hometown Band, Marx	$2,500
7. Popeye the Punching Bag, Chein	$2,500
8. Lehmann's Autobus, Lehmann	$2,500
9. Popeye Express, Marx	$2,400
10. Hott and Trott, Unique Art	$2,300

quite difficult to find. Those that are on the market generally command premium prices.

Contributor to this section: Leo Rishty, 2563 Jardin Lane, Weston, FL 33327.

Recommended Reading

Books
O'Brien's Collecting Toys, Elizabeth Stephen
2000 Toys & Prices, Sharon Korbeck and Elizabeth Stephen
O'Brien's Collecting Toy Cars and Trucks, Elizabeth Stephen

Periodicals
Toy Shop
Toy Cars & Vehicles

VALUE LINE

Values shown are for toys in Excellent to Mint condition.

Chein miscellaneous

Army Drummer, 1930s	$115-$175
Disneyland Tea Set, 15-piece set	$175-$500
Dolly's Washer, washing machine	$100-$300
Easter Basket, nursery rhyme figures	$55-$100
Melody Organ Player	$125-$175
Player Piano, eight rolls	$325-$500
Scuba Diver, 10" long	$120-$185
Space Ride	$230-$350

Chein Wind-ups

Army Cargo Truck, 1920s	$390-$600
Army Plane	$230-$350
Barnacle Bill, 1930s, waddles	$550-$850
Cat, with wood wheels	$65-$100
Clown Boxing, 8" tall	$390-$600
Disneyland Ferris Wheel, 1940s	$650-$1,200
Disneyland Roller Coaster	$620-$1,200
Duck, 1930, 4" high, waddles	$75-$100
Handstand Clown	$125-$200
Jumping Rabbit, 1925	$165-$200
Mechanical Fish, 1940s, 11" long	$50-$75
Merry-Go-Round, with swan chairs	$775-$1,200
Pelican	$165-$250
Pig	$60-$95
Playland Merry-Go-Round, 1930s	$850-$1,200
Roller Coaster, 1938, with two cars	$425-$650
Santa's Elf, 1925	$390-$600
Speedboat, 14" long	$145-$225
Yellow Cab, 7" long	$300-$400

Lehmann

Ajax Acrobat, does somersaults	$1,425-$2,200
Crocodile, walks, mouth opens	$475-$725
Dancing Sailor	$975-$1,500
Flying Bird	$475-$750
Li-La Car, women passengers	$1,200-$1,850

This 9-inch wind-up drummer toy by Chein is a good buy at about $150.

Ostrich Cart	$650-$975
Paddy Riding Pig	$1,175-$1,800
Sea Lion	$250-$375
Skier, 1920s	$850-$1,300
Taxi, 1920s	$750-$1,150
Zig-Zag, handcar vehicle	$1,300-$2,000

Marx Buildings and Rooms

Airport, 1930s	$195-$300
Automatic Car Wash	$225-$350
Automatic Garage, family car	$245-$375
Brightlite Filling Station, 1930s	$425-$650
Bus Terminal, 1937	$295-$450
City Airport, two metal planes, 1938	$195-$300
Dick Tracy Automatic Police Station, station and car	$625-$950
Greyhound Bus Terminal, 1938	$195-$300
Home Town Drug Store, 1930s	$295-$450
Home Town Meat Market, 1930s	$300-$465
Metal Service Station, 1949-50	$275-$425
Model School House, 1960s	$80-$125
New York World's Fair Speedway, two red cars, 1939	$495-$750
Newlyweds' Bedroom, 1920s	$165-$500
Newlyweds' Kitchen, 1920s	$165-$500
Roadside Rest Service Station, Laurel and Hardy, stools, 1935	$1,050-$1,600

Service Station, two pumps, two friction vehicles, 1929...$495-$750
Sky Hawk Flyer, wind-up, two planes, tower..$210-$325
Sunnyside Garage, 1935 ....$425-$650
TV and Radio Station...$225-$350
Used Car Market, 1939 ....$425-$650
Whee-Whiz Auto Racer, 1925 ....$495-$750

Marx Miscellaneous Toys

Army Code Sender, pressed steel ....$35-$50
Baby Grand Piano...$100-$250
Cat Pushing Ball, 1938 ....$100-$150
Jumping Frog ....$65-$100
King Kong...$60-$95
Mysterious Woodpecker ....$80-$125
Rooster ....$100-$150
Toto the Acrobat ....$165-$250

Marx Trains

Crazy Express Train, 1960s ....$195-$300
Disneyland Express, 1950s ....$425-$650
Disneyland Train, with Goofy, 1950.................$225-$350
Engine Train, 1960s ....$110-$170
Flintstones Choo Choo Train, "Bedrock Express," 1950s ....$390-$600
Mickey Mouse Express Train, 1952 ....$390-$900
New York Central Engine Train.........................$325-$500
Subway Express, 1954 ....$310-$475

Wagons and Carts

Busy Delivery, 1939..$475-$750
Farm Wagon, 1940s ....$100-$150
Horse and Cart, 1934 ....$130-$200
Horse and Cart, with Clown Driver, 1923 ....$225-$350

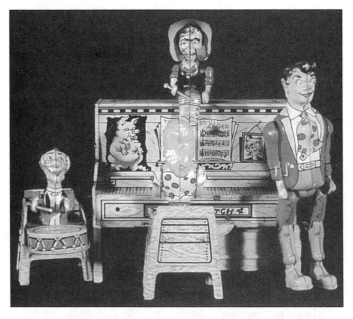

Li'l Abner and his Dogpatch Band by Unique Art is a very desirable tin toy, worth about $1,000 Mint-in-Box.

Popeye Horse and Cart, wind-up ....$550-$850
Two Donkeys Pulling Cart, 1940s ....$180-$275
Wagon with Two-Horse Team, 1940s ....$145-$225

Marx Wind-up Toys

Amos 'n Andy Walkers, 1930, each ....$1,075-$1,800
Ballerina..$145-$225
Bear Cyclist, 1934...$115-$175
Big Parade, 1928...$685-$1,050
Butter and Egg Man......................................$1,175-$1,800
Carter Climbing Monkey, 1921 ....$190-$290
Charlie McCarthy Bass Drummer, 1939.........$750-$1,150
Cowboy on Horse, 1925.....................................$115-$175
Dapper Dan Coon Jigger, 1922.....................$900-$1,300
Donald Duck Duet, Donald and Goofy, 1946...$780-$1,200
Drummer Boy, 1939..$475-$725
Ferdinand the Bull and Matador, 1938 ....$500-$800
Flipping Monkey..$130-$200
Gobbling Goose, 1940s.......................................$210-$325
Hey Hey the Chicken, 1926 ....$1,450-$2,220
Honeymoon Express, 1940s, circular train and plane ....$360-$550
Howdy Doody, with Clarabell, 1950 ....$875-$1,350
Jazzbo Jim, 1920s...$625-$1,200
Knockout Champs Boxing Toy, 1930s ....$295-$450
Little Orphan Annie and Sandy, 1930s.............$475-$725
Mickey Mouse ....$400-$600
Moon Creature ....$225-$350
Mortimer Snerd Bass Drummer, 1939.........$1,450-$2,200
Mother Goose, 1920s ....$250-$500
Mystery Cat, 1931...$165-$250
Pecos Bill, 1950s...$130-$200
Pinocchio, 1950s...$425-$650
Poor Fish, 1936 ....$115-$175
Popeye and Olive Oyl Jiggers, 1936............$1,175-$1,800
Porky Pig with Rotating Umbrella, 1939..........$525-$800
Ring-A-Ling Circus, 1925 ....$775-$1,200
Snappy the Miracle Dog, 1931 ....$130-$200
Subway Express, 1950s ....$110-$170
Tom Tom Jungle Boy..$150-$200
Walking Popeye, 1932 ....$700-$1,000
Wise Pluto ....$165-$250
WWI Soldier ....$80-$125
Zippo Monkey, 1938 ....$150-$200

Mattel Jacks in the Box

Flipper...$75-$125
Mother Goose..$15-$25
Porky Pig..$75-$150
Super Chief ....$200-$300
Tom & Jerry ....$45-$100
Woody Woodpecker...$75-$150

Mattel Musical Toys

Hickory Dickory Dock Clock ....$25-$40
Man on the Flying Trapeze ....$100-$145
Sing a Song of Sixpence ....$35-$65

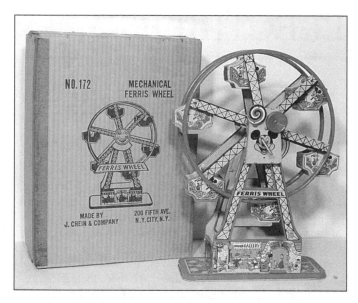

The Chein Mechanical Ferris Wheel is considered a classic by collectors of tin toys. It is worth about $800 in top condition.

Ohio Art

Automatic Airport ....$325-$500
Circus Shooting Gallery, 1960s ....$100-$200
Coast Guard Plane..$75-$100
Coney Island Roller Coaster, 1950s...................$200-$300
Doll Stroller ....$60-$80
Donald Duck Carpet Sweeper...........................$100-$250
Jungle Eyes Shooting Gallery, 1960s..................$75-$150
Little Red Riding Hood Tea Set,
   seven-piece set..$200-$350
Mexican Boy Tea Set, nine-piece set ....$100-$200
Mickey Mouse Tray ....$100-$200
Mother Goose Tea Set, seven-piece set.............$150-$250
Ten Little Indians Spinning Top...........................$25-$35
Three Little Pigs Spinning Top ....$25-$35
Watering Can ....$30-$40

Schuco

1917 Ford..$80-$125
Airplane and pilot, 1930s..................................$225-$350
Clown Playing Violin, 1950s ....$225-$350
Combinato Convertible, 1950s ....$165-$250
Dancing Mice, 1950s ....$225-$350
Dancing Monkey with Mouse, 1950s ....$210-$325
Drummer, 1930s...$210-$325
Fox and Goose, 1950s..$250-$375
Juggling Clown ....$225-$350
Mickey and Minnie Dancing ....$1,150-$1,750
Monkey Drummer, 1950s ....$195-$300
Monkey on Scooter, 1930s................................$195-$300
Tumbling Boy, 1950s...$165-$250

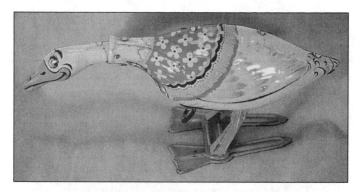

"Gertie the Galloping Goose" by Unique Art is a $300 item in Mint condition.

Unique Art

Miscellaneous toys

Artie the Clown in his Crazy Car......................$390-$595
Butter and Egg Man ....$825-$1,250
Casey the Cop ....$575-$895
Dandy Jim...$750-$1,000
Flying Circus..$825-$1,000
G.I. Joe and his K-9 Pups..................................$225-$300
Hee Haw..$225-$300
Howdy Doody & Buffalo Bob at Piano ....$1,300-$2,000
Krazy Kar ....$335-$515
Motorcycle Cop ....$400-$500
Rodeo Joe Crazy Car ....$250-$400
Sky Rangers ....$400-$625

Wolverine

Arithmetic Quiz Toy, 1950s ....$50-$75
Battleship, 1930s...$120-$185
Crane ....$65-$100
Drum Major ....$150-$300
Drum Major, round base, 13" ....$165-$250
Express Bus...$210-$325
Jet Roller Coaster..$200-$300
Merry-Go-Round ....$390-$595
Mystery Car ....$165-$250
Sandy Andy Fullback..$295-$450
Snow White Stove...$35-$50
Submarine ....$165-$250
Sunny and Tank...$130-$200
Sunny Suzy Deluxe Washing Machine ....$95-$200
Yellow Taxi, 1940s..$225-$350
Zilotone, 1920s ....$750-$1,150

Wyandotte

Airplane Carousel, 1930s...................................$200-$375
Carnival Set, 1930s ....$500-$1,000
Hoky Poky, 1930s..$250-$350
Model Shooting Gallery, 1930s ....$200-$300
Mother Duck with Baby Ducks ....$90-$125
Trapeze Artist, 1930s ....$200-$325

TOBACCO COLLECTIBLES

If current legislative trends continue, tobacco may someday be as hard to find as a good drink was during Prohibition. When that day happens, the thousands of different cigar, cigarette and pipe accessories produced over the years will become even more in demand by collectors, but increasingly hard to find.

The list of smoking collectibles includes cigar cutters, cigar bands, match safes, pipes, ashtrays, lighters, cigarette cases, humidors, advertising materials, cigarette boxes, cigarette holders, match covers, cigar boxes, pocket lighters, cigarette dispensers, pipe racks, pipe rests, cigarette packs and more. Many of these collectibles are still in uncharted waters, making them good opportunities for early-bird collectors, who may find them at easy-on-the-pocket prices.

The broad field of tobacco-related collectibles includes the following general categories:

Advertising—Tobacco-related advertising items have been hot collectibles for years. Many of the smaller items are popular, due in part because their size allows them to be stored or displayed in space-tight apartments and small homes. There are more than 50,000 forms of tobacco advertising dating from 1900 to the 1940s, with an expansive price range, too. For example, a 1920s small die-cut figure of a man selling "Four Roses Tobacco" can sell for $100 to $15,000. Relatively inexpensive items are available, too, however. Ads from national magazines will set you back $5-$10. They make an attractive display piece when framed.

Trade cards that advertise cigar brands are highly collectible, too. They can be rare and expensive; a Currier & Ives piece may sell for $75-$100. Tobacco-related post cards, those depicting cigar making, advertising, or retailing, are also collectibles. Generally, they range from $10-$15 each, unless they have a real photo, which can increase the value to $20-$25.

Humidors—Humidors, containers for storing tobacco popular from the mid-1800s to the turn of the century, are finding a niche, especially those made of Majolica or terra cotta. Particularly appealing are figurals, featuring a sponge receptacle for keeping the tobacco moist, that depict people, cats, dogs, frogs, pigs and animals. Rare examples of an early humidor in good condition can sell for $3,500; others, in good condition, with minor restorations, may be as low as $50.

Cigar bands and labels—Cigar bands and cigar box labels are popular with collectors because their exuberant colors, exotic designs and handy size make them ideal for display. It's estimated that more than 100,000 cigar factories were active in the United States at the turn of the century, using compelling illustrations and attention-demanding brand logos; today, they provide collectors a myriad of brands to pursue. Most of the labels sell for $5-$10, but early examples of Cuban lithographs can be as high as $40-$50.

Cigar cutters—Nineteenth-century cigar cutters, often highly imaginable and usually made of brass, are gaining prominence in two ways—as collectibles, and for practical use today, as smoking cigars has again become fashionable. Three styles of cigar cutters were made—for desktops, for cigar store counters and those made to be tucked into a pocket ($150-$500).

Countertop cutters, starting at $125 and up, generally advertise cigar brands. Many desktop cutters, ranging from $200 to as much as $1,200, portray masculine interests, such as horses and dogs.

Tobacco cutters—Before pre-packaging, tobacco was delivered to merchants in bulk form. Tobacco cutters were used to cut the tobacco into desired sizes. Examples include: Arrow-Cupples Co. (worth about $45); Pennsylvania Hardware Co., 1900 ($50); Star Brand Tobacco, 1885 ($50); RJ Reynolds Co., original black japanned finish ($95); Griswold, No. 3 ($110); Master Workman, original label ($115); Keen Cutter, EC Simmons ($150); Battle Ax ($175); Spear Head, ornate ($225); and Paraflint, brass dog, engraved sides ($225).

Cigarette Cases—As more and more women began smoking cigarettes after World War I, the manufacture of feminine cigarette cases began to surge, especially in the 1930s. In addition to their practical use, the cases were also fashion statements, so multiple variations were created to satisfy a clamoring market. Popular through the 1930s were cases with pearl-encrusted designs, stylized enamel motifs, gold mesh sparked by rhinestones, raised signets where an initial or name was engraved, touches of either real gems or faux jewels, and more.

The basic shapes (columnar, round, rectangular, envelope, flat and full) were fashioned of everything from gold metal, gold mesh and silver to cloisonné and wood.

Vintage cigar box labels featuring Native American themes are especially popular and generally sell for prices in the hundreds.

Some cigarette cases were paired with matching lighters, others with compacts. Some were offered as a smart one-piece unit that combined the cigarette case with a lighter or a design incorporating a case, lighter and compact. Brand names such as Volupte, known for its elegant cases with silver or gold finish, and Evans, which made a variety of attractive cases, are quite popular today. Also considered favorites are Art Deco cases, silver and gold-wash cases, and "Plain Jane" cases from the 1940 and 1950s, which are plentiful and can be purchased for $5-$10.

Men's cases were also plentiful through the 1930s. Because they were kept in jacket and shirt pockets, most men's cases were typically flat rectangles or squares. Some included the owner's name or initials.

The materials used for men's cases included rich silver, baked enamel in varied colors and design motifs, chrome, leather and the then-new hard plastic called Bakelite. Some cases were designed to hold a single row of cigarettes; others accommodated two rows.

Lighters—Cigarette lighters were also made in various shapes and sizes, including patterned china, leather, gold and enameled surfaces. They were available everywhere, from

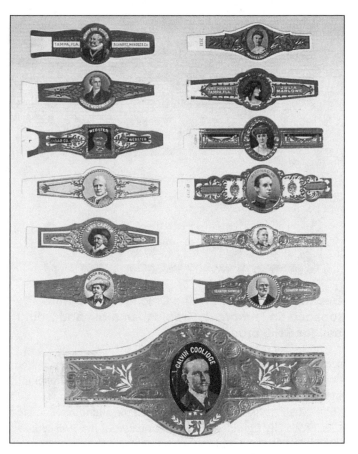

Cigar box labels can sell for a few dollars each to over a hundred. They have depicted various subjects over the years, including U.S. presidents.

fine jewelry stores to dime stores. The Ronson lighter, featuring a flowing silver design, was so appealing that it was a popular gift selection for special occasions. Windproof Zippo lighters were also popular; today they are selling for $20. A round, solid chrome "fireball" lighter from the early 1940s can bring $75.

Ashtrays—Ashtrays were also made in different sizes—large, small or purse-size; and for different places—table, desk or floorstanding. Oversize ashtrays—round, square or rectangular—were also created from ceramic and metal and catered to the needs of cigar and pipe smokers. Collectors are most interested in ashtrays that have advertising, such as those for local eating establishments or tourist attractions.

Large chrome ashtrays from the 1930s with glass inserts can sell for $50 today, as can 1950s wrought iron and ceramic ashtrays designed to hold a drink and cigarettes. Floor-standing ashtrays with a fiberglass lighted base and ceramic top will be one area in great demand in the near future.

Match safes—Ornamented match safes are readily available today in a wide range of prices. These were marketed from the mid-19th century until the early 1900s, when lighters replaced matches. Many have richly embossed metal, are embellished with carvings of floral borders, and feature

THESE PIPES ARE SO HOT THEY'RE SMOKIN'!

The workmanship, delicate carvings, and varied subjects of the carvings have always attracted collectors to Meerschaum pipes. The Meerschaum pipe received its name from the fine, compact, clay-like material from which it is fashioned. When exposed to extreme heat and tobacco this material takes on a dark, rich patina. Pipes have been made from the clay-like material since the 18th century, and they have always been highly prized among pipe smokers for their color as well as for their often ornately carved designs.

These designs range from simple forms to complex and intricate configurations, including portrait pipes, a woman ice skater, a lion's head, and an elaborate carving of cherubs playing musical instruments.

Today, and for years past, Meershcaums have been valued by collectors who are willing to pay good money for an outstanding example. A winning bid of $1,610 was obtained during a 1998 auction for a Meerschaum pipe in a gold plated ferrule case. The pipe, completed with an amber bit, is a carved bust of Franz Joseph and a pyramid of elephants holding a human figure.

A large cased Meershaum pipe (with an amber bit) dated 1892, in the form of a bearded buccaneer, sold for $1,265 in the same auction. A bid of $488 bought a cased Meerschaum cheroot holder, carved in the form of a Victorian woman wearing a muff and ice skates.

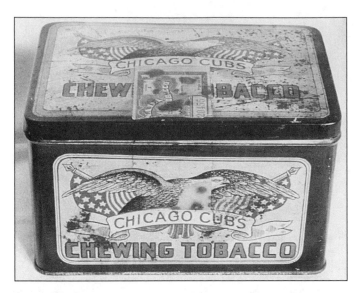

Because of its tie-in to the Chicago Cubs, this tobacco tin is more desirable than most and would sell for $150 or more.

scenes of houses, animals, flowers and portraits. They can be broken down into categories such as silver, celluloid, enamel, figurals, advertising and Art Nouveau.

Match strikers have also attracted the attention of collectors, especially figurals from the last quarter of the 19th century that include a match holder and a roughened area for striking. Nice figural match strikers can range from $200-$600.

Trends: Interest is increasing in pocket tobacco tins and any advertising of a metal, paper or cardboard material that is die-cut, such as Joe Camel, a counter ad of the Marlboro Man, or the perky little Philip Morris bellhop figure.

Cigar boxes are another area where interest has increased, in part because collectors, who are seeing tins become more valuable, are realizing they can get the same image on a cigar box for less. Cigar boxes, generally $5-$10, are more valuable if they are made in unusual shapes, such as books, mailboxes and treasure chests; the unusual shapes appear on the market about one every 20 boxes.

Most boxes are collectible because they have beautiful images on the inside; these boxes are also more valuable than those which have just a statement or name of the cigar inside the cover. Cigar boxes that are tied to the tobacco industry's history are also collected, such as those that, for example, are historically significant because a president may have smoked those cigars.

Envelopes, letterheads, billheads and receipts associated with cigar companies or the stores which sold the products are also gaining interest among collectors. These paper products, often containing nice lithography and engraving, are not as expensive as cigar labels.

Club

• Society of Tobacco Jar Collectors, 6370 Kirby Ridge Cove, Memphis, TN 38119.

Cigarette Packs

Benson & Hedges, Menthol 100's, 4-pack,
1965 ....$2-$5
Camel Turkish & Domestic Blend Cigarettes,
4-pack, R.J. Reynolds Co., 1960s ....$5-$10
Chesterfield, 9-pack, Liggett & Myers, 1920s.......$20-$35
Chesterfield, 20-pack, Liggett & Myers, 1935 ....$5-$10
Chesterfield, 20-pack, Liggett & Myers, 1960s.........$2-$5
Kool Mild Menthol King-Size, 20-pack, 1950s.......$5-$10
Kool Mild Menthol Tipped, 20-pack, Buy
War Bonds and Stamps, 1943 ....$20-$35
Lucky Strike, 20-pack, American Tobacco Co.,
1935..$20-$40
Marlboro, 4 Class A Cigarettes, Philip Morris,
1975 ....$2-$5
Mecca Cigarettes, 20-pack, American Tobacco Co.,
1930s ....$20-$40
Pall Mall Famous Cigarettes, 20-pack, England,
1975..$2-$5
Pall Mall Famous Cigarettes, 5-pack,
American Tobacco Co., 1965 ....$2-$5
Philip Morris King Size, 4-pack, Philip Morris,
1960s ....$5-$10
Piedmont Cigarettes, 20-pack, Liggett Group,
1970s ....$5-$10
Salem, 4-pack, Menthol Fresh, Filter, R.J. Reynolds,
1965 ....$2-$5
Viceroy, 4-pack, complimentary package,
B&W Tobacco Corp., 1960s ....$2-$5
Viceroy Filter Tip, King-Size, 20-pack,
B&W Tobacco Corp., 1955...............................$5-$10
Virginia Slims, Menthol-Filter, 5-pack,
Benson & Hedges, 1980s ....$2-$5
Winston, King Size filter, 4-pack, R.J. Reynolds,
1965...$5-$10

Miscellaneous Collectibles

Ashtray, porcelain steel, for 7-20-4 Cigars ....$35-$45
Ashtray, with match holder, Austria ....$75-$100
Cigar box, Benson & Hedges, holds 25,
wood and paper, 1930s.....................................$20-$30
Cigar box, Harvard Cigars, wooden, 1917.............$40-$50
Cigar box, Tennyson, 5 cents, tin,
lithographed ....$75-$100
Cigar box, King Edward Invincible Mild Tobaccos,
1950s ....$30-$40
Cigar box, copper plated,
2-1/2" x 8-1/2" x 5-1/2" ....$100-$125
Cigar box, figural, bear pulling a
Bock Havana sled...$725-$800
Cigarette case, leather, tortoise shell and
brass interior, hinged, 3-1/2" x 4-1/4"..........$200-$225

Cigar clipper, 14k gold, scissors, Europe,
  1890s-1920s ....$75-$175
Cigar cutter, counter type, cast iron,
  Empire Tobacco Co., Quebec.........................$50-$60
Cigar cutter, pocket or desk type, bronze,
  owl or eagle shape, Austria, 1880-1910.......$350-$700
Cigar cutter, with brass matchbox,
  2-1/4" x 1-3/4"..$200-$250
Cigar cutter, steel on wood base,
  5" x 8-1/2" x 3-1/4" ....$75-$100
Cigar dispenser, tin and glass, 10-cent coin-operated,
  9-1/2" x 6" x 16" ....$1,000-$1,250
Cigar holder, carved Meerschaum, 3-1/4" ....$75-$100
Cigar holder, Bakelite, transparent, with lined,
  labeled case, 4"..$50-$75
Cigar holder, Windsor, amber ....$100-$150
Cigar jar, molded glass......................................$75-$100
Cigar machine, countertop, Cigaromat Corp.
  of America, New York ....$375-$425
Humidor, Lighter, Ronson, table model,
  Crown model, 1930s-1960s ....$10-$20
Humidor, Benson & Hedges, large, mahogany,
  brass inlays, sits on a table ....$2,250-$3,250
Humidor, Benson & Hedges, mahogany,
  1920s ....$1,250-$1,500
Humidor, Buck Cigars
  "King of the Range".................................$750-$1,000
Humidor, counter display, Garcia Grande Cigars,
  Brunhoff ....$275-$325
Lighter, Ronson, table model, Spartan model,
  1950s ....$20-$40
Lighter, Ronson, lighter/cigarette case combination,
  Pal model, 1940s-1960s ....$30-$50
Matchholder, frog sitting on a stump, cast metal,
  2" x 6-1/2" x 4" ....$275-$325
Pipe, Meerschaum, mid-19th century ....$100-$175
Smoking stand with ashtray and matchbox holder,
  Bradley & Hubbard ....$150-$200
Tobacco cutter, Cremo Cigars,
  5-1/4" x 5-1/2"..$100-$150

Tobacco Advertising Items
Bloodhound 10-Cent Cuts, cardboard box.................. $100
Brown's Mule, diecut display,
  cardboard box with 15 plugs $150
Camel, ad, "Read the truth: when they learn to smoke,
  they flock to Camel," 1928....................................$45
Cannon Ball Chewing Tobacco,
  memo booklet giveaway...$10
Chesterfield, magazine ad, 1930s-1950s........................$5
Chesterfield Plant, postcard, 1950s................................$5
Day's Work, diecut display cardboard box
  with 12 plugs $75
Duke's Cameo Cigarette Tobacco, wood chair, litho-
  graphed back has a nicely dressed
  young woman $50

Egyptienne Luxury, cardboard cigarette box,
  1909...$25
J.K. McKee & Co. Confectionery and
  Cigar letterhead $13
King Clay 5-cent Cigars, advertising fan, baseball score-
  card on back, cardboard ....$50-$75
L&M, magazine ad, James Arness, 1959 ....$5
L&M, postcard...$4
London Life, cardboard cigarette box, 1910.................$20
Model Tobacco Co. Plant, postcard, 1957 ....$5
Old English Curve Cut, cardboard box,
  4-3/4" x 3-3/4", EX $25
Our Advertiser, 2-1/4 oz. cloth pouch,
  unopened, NM..$25
Our Advertiser, 7 oz. cloth pouch, unopened, NM $70
Prince Albert, magazine ad $3
Red Fox Chewing Tobacco, memo
  booklet giveaway...$10
RJR, postcard, Winston cigarette plant, 1940s $7
RJR, stock certificate, 1948 ....$30

Vintage tobacco tins are among the most popular of all advertising tins, which collectors love for their display potential.

Tobacco signs

Camel Cigarettes and Prince Albert,
cardboard sign with Santa, 1940s $200
Camel Cigarettes, Christmas cardboard sign with
Santa, 1930s $375
Camel Cigarettes, "So Mild, So Good, Sold Here,"
tin sign... $175
Granger Rough Cut, heavy cardboard sign,
man and woman, 1930s.. $50
L&M, round diecut tin sign $85
Prince Albert, tin sign, "The National Joy
Smoke Sold Here".. $125

Tobacco Tags

American Navy $10
B.F. Hanes, Our Senator $20
Bird in Hand, NM $18
D.H. Spencer & Son, Calhoun, NM............................ $18
F.G. Flynt, Pride of Winston $18
Harvey's National Leaf $7
Irwin & Poston, Sweet Mash $25
J.G. Flynt, Pride of Winston $20
Lash's Select $7
P.H. Hanes, Early Bird $10
P.H. Hanes, Just Out $12
Piedmont #11 .... $12
RJR, Mickey $8
RJR, Strawberry... $9
Stater Bros., Day's Work $8
Sun Cured, Ram's Horn $7
Taylor Bros., Ram's Horn $10

Mark Twain was featured on several cigar box labels. This example sold for $300 in a recent auction conducted by Cerebro of East Prospect, Pa.

Tobacco Tins

Allen & Ginter Dixie Chop Cut Plug, barrel tin $250
Arcadia Tobacco, horizontal flat box tin..................... $12
Auto Tobacco, horizontal flat box tin $17
Bagdad Tobacco, pocket tin... $65
Belfast Cigars, vertical box tin.................................... $30
Benton Tobacco, vertical box tin $20
Black and White Tweenies, small flat cigar tin............ $75
Blue Boar, cylindrical tobacco tin............................... $17
Bond Street Tobacco, pocket tin $20
Briggs Tobacco, pocket tin... $15
Bridley's Mixture, cylindrical tobacco tin $8
Camel, horizontal flat cigarette tin.............................. $30
Cameron's, horizontal box tobacco tin $40
Carolina Gem Long Cut, square corners.................... $125
Chesterfield Cigarette, small round tin $15
Christan Peper, vertical box tobacco tin $12
Dill's Best, cylindrical tobacco tin $25
Dixie Queen, lunch pail tobacco tin............................ $85
Dutch Masters, cylindrical cigar tin............................ $30
Eight Brothers, cylindrical tobacco tin $15
Eight Brothers, cylindrical pail tobacco tin $85
George Washington, key top canister............................ $35
Half and Half Tobacco, collapsible pocket tin $20
Half and Half Tobacco, pocket tin $20
Half and Half, cylindrical tobacco tin.......................... $12
Handsome Dan, horizontal tobacco tin......................... $50
Hiawatha, horizontal box tobacco tin $60
La Pallina, horizontal box cigar tin.............................. $12
Lady Churchill, horizontal box cigar tin...................... $20
Lucky Strike, horizontal box tobacco tin $17
Mayo's, lunch box tobacco tin $80
My Pal, horizontal box tobacco tin $20
Old Chum, vertical tobacco tin $30
Old English, flat square tobacco tin $12
Omar Cigarettes, horizontal box tobacco tin $15
Patterson's Seal, lunch pail tobacco tin........................ $75
Penn's, square box tobacco tin $20
Piper Heidsieck Chewing, square flat tobacco tin........ $10
Player's Cigarettes, horizontal box tin $15
Prince Albert, pocket tobacco tin................................. $25
Prince Albert, round canister top $35
Repeater, horizontal box tobacco tin............................ $50
Sail, cylindrical tobacco tin.. $15
Sir Walter Raleigh, pocket tobacco tin......................... $25
Stag, pocket tobacco tin $50
Sweet Burley Light, round tobacco tin $50
Sweet Caporal $15
Sweet Cuba, lunch pail tobacco tin $25
Tiger, horizontal tobacco tin $45
Tuxedo, cylindrical tobacco tin.................................... $15
Twin Oaks, pocket tobacco tin..................................... $60
Union Leader, pocket tobacco tin $15
Velvet, pocket tobacco tin $35
Yale, horizontal box tobacco tin $15

VINTAGE TOOLS

Probably more than any other antique or collectible, antique hand tools are a reflection of life as it once was. What could be more nostalgic than the very items used to create the past?

Background and General Guidelines: Although they are just as useful today as when they were first made, many vintage tools are strictly display pieces. But collectors also face competition from those who are interested in buying the old tools because they actually want to use them, rather than buying expensive new tools. Nevertheless, vintage tools are, fortunately, for the most part, still plentiful. You can generally find them in antique malls and shops, at auctions and garage sales. Flea markets are where you can often find the best deals.

There's a wide range of tools to be collected, too, including: axes, planes, tool chests, wagons, tobacco carriers, ox yokes, ice tongs, mallets, cross-cut saws, barrels, tubs, anvils, spuds, augers, tobacco cutters, stitching horses, shoe lasts, grindstones, cradle scythes, hay forks, wooden rakes and more.

Because there are so many different variations on individual tools, it's difficult to use price ranges for values. However, there are several good price guides available that give values for specific tools. The vast majority of tools can be found for less than $50, with many others under $25—wooden mauls at $5, adzes at $10 and planes at $15-$20.

Planes—Wood and metal planes, used to smooth wood and cut designs can be traced to ancient Rome. Records indicate that the wood plane industry started to develop toward the end of the 18th century, peaking about 1860. By 1945, only a few makers remained. The metal plane industry, on the other hand, began around 1830; however, by 1940 electrical-powered equipment had dominated the industry.

Carpenters' planes are of special importance, commanding attention for their beauty, versatility of design and size variations. Wooden planes have been used for over 2,000 years. Those seen by collectors today most likely date from the first 75 years of the 19th century. Appearing in England just prior to the 19th century, the work of professional plane-makers was authenticated by the stamping of their names near the top of the front face of their products. From that point on, the majority of British and American wooden planes carried their maker's name.

Stanley Tools provide the broadest area for collecting metal planes. Stanley began producing metal planes in 1869, which increased in popularity during the last quarter of the 19th century, almost totally replacing the earlier wooden varieties. Almost all Stanley tools carry a model number and are easily identified.

The maker's imprint is a major factor in determining the value of a wooden plane. The imprint is a stamped impression embossed near the top of the front face of the tool. A common imprint increases the value slightly, but the stamp of several early 18th century New England makers (Nicholson, Chelor, for example) can increase the value by $1,000 or more.

Measuring and Layout Tools—Early carpenters used a folding rule for measurements. Before the advent of the "zig-zag" folding six-foot rule, the two-foot "four-fold" rule was most often used, although there were also two-fold and six-fold models. The four-fold type consisted of four six-inch strips, usually of boxwood (ivory in premium grades), held together by brass or nickel silver hinges. Because graduations on the outside of these strips suffered from pocket wear, they are often unreadable, making those with clear markings highly prized. Makers' names can increase values, with the rarest Stanley ivory rules commanding hundreds of dollars.

Plumb bobs were suspended from a string to make certain that work was truly vertical. Made in a variety of shapes, they were usually of brass, although lead, steel, ivory and even wood were also used. Of particular interest to collectors are those by Stanley with an integral reel to hold the sting. Older styles with ornate shapes can command hundreds of dollars, while those of museum quality are often valued at well over a thousand.

Wood levels are made of cherry, mahogany, rosewood, ebony or boxwood. The smaller sizes are rarer, especially the Stanley 6" and Stratton 6-1/2". Premium levels had all edges protected by inlaid brass strips, while cast-iron levels, with elaborate filigree designs between top and bottom surfaces, are generally brittle. Inclinometer levels, which are used to measure the slope of a surface by means of a dial indicator, are valuable with original, unbroken glass level vials.

Axes and Hatchets—These "edge tools" were second in importance only to rifles among early settlers on the American frontier. Chief among carpenters' tools from this period was the axe. Hand-forged with wooden handles, they were often decorated with distinctive patterns, the designs having been passed down from generation to generation. The axe, or hatchet, was also a necessary tool for latheing, shingling and barrel-making.

DISPLAY THEM!

Although many tools just don't display very well, buck saws and cross-cut saws look great hanging on a wall—if it is big enough—as do smaller tools hung together, such as wrenches. Planes display well on shelves.

Tools can also be displayed in areas that one would not normally consider as showcases for antiques, such as garages, storage sheds and basements. They can add a nostalgic touch compared to otherwise modern, drab spaces used today by other collectors.

Although vintage tools are rarely fragile, they are susceptible to rust. So keep them away from moisture, tools' greatest enemy, by storing them in a dry location.

The single-edge felling axe took a variety of shapes. Except for those with a desirable maker's name stamped into the head, they are quite inexpensive. The broad axe was used for hewing tree trunks into squared timbers and had a longer cutting edge, a one-sided bevel and a canted handle.

Contributors to this section: John Whelan, 38 Colony Court, Murray Hill, NJ 07974; Bill Rigler, Route 2, Box 152, Wartrace, TN 37183.

Clubs

- Midwest Tool Collectors Association, Rt. 2, Box 152, Wartrace, TN 37183

- Early Trades & Craft Society, 11 Blythe Place East, Northport, NY 11731

- L.I. Antique Tool Collector's Association, 31 Wildwood Drive, Smithtown, NY 11787

- Early American Industries Association, 167 Bakersville Road South, Dartmouth, MA 02748

- Collectors of Rare and Familiar Tools Society (CRAFTS), 38 Colony Court, Murray Hill, NJ 07974

VALUE LINE

Miscellaneous Tools

Beader, Stanley No. 66, with replacement
blades ....$100-$125
Bit gauge, Stanley No. 49, with box ....$20-$25
Butt gauge, Stanley No. 95G ....$20-$25
Calipers, Goodell Pratt, No. 505...........................$25-$30
Carving tools, Miller Falls, No. 1, set of 6 ....$100-$125
Clapboard marker, Stanley 88, adjustable..............$40-$50
Dowel jig, Stanley No. 59, 6 drill guides, box.......$40-$50
Dowel machine, Stanley No. 77, 3/8" cutter,
box..$375-$425
Drill, Miller Falls type ....$100-$125
Gouge, Ibbotson Peace & Co.,
graduated set of 9, cast steel..........................$200-$250
Grooving router, Preston, adjustable,
three cutters, three fences................................$75-$100
Hammer, Adz head, Cheney No. 777 ....$50-$75
Hammer, Snowball, wrapped handle,
brass clip ....$40-$50
Level, Goodell Pratt, 18", cast iron,
double pump...$15-$20
Level, Stratton Brothers No. 10, bound 12",
rosewood ....$175-$200
Oat and wheat grinder, cast iron, wooden box,
Superior Drill Co...$400-$450
Parallel ruler, Carrington's patent, wood,
paper label..$50-$75
Ratchet brace, Consolidated Tool Works Inc., No. 808,
knob controlled, hardwood handles ....$50-$65
Rachet brace, Keystone, WA Ives Mfg. Co., lever controlled, hardwood handles ....$65-$75

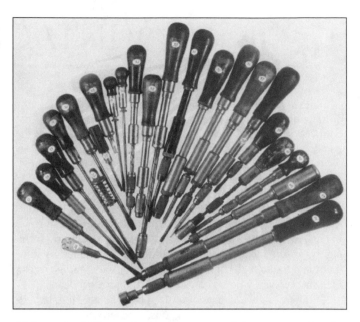

Old push drills and vintage screwdrivers are plentiful. This group was part of lot of some 70 pieces of this type that sold at an Eldred's auction in East Dennis, Mass., with an estimate of $700-$1,000 for the entire lot

Screwdriver, 18-1/2" Cowles Hardware Co., cabinetmaker's type ....$45-$50
Sharpening stone, 13-3/4" mounted on block, carved
designs, "James N. Roser, 1826" ....$350-$400
Socket set, PS & W Co., set of 12 in original
wood box, applewood handles ....$375-$450
Wrench, W & C Wynn & Co., patent,
combination wrench, pliers, buggy wrench,
hammer, screwdriver ....$75-$100

Wood Planes

Common makers or unmarked beech
bench planes...$15-$30
Applewood planes...$25-$50
Exotic woods..$50-$75
Compass planes..$45-$75
T. Napier planes ....$100-$125
Coachmaker's boxwood planes..........................$20-$125

Axes

Common felling ....$10-$20
Rare names like Fordham & Hedges ....$100-$125
Broad axes...$50-$85
Cooper's axes, W. Greaves...............................$100-$125
Continental...$200-$375
Goosewing axes ....$175-$200
Goosewing axes, Pennsylvania ....$250-$275
Goosewing axes, Beatty....................................$600-$625
Continental Goosewing.....................................$650-$700
Continental Goosewing decorated ....$1,000-$1,100
Continental decorated bearded side axe.......$1,650-$1,750
Marbles Safety Axe...$100-$175

Boring Tools

Erlandsen Bow drill ....$275-$325
Bow drill, brass & ebony ....$50-$75
Bow drill, boxwood & ebony..........................$150-$175
Bow drill, ivory handle ....$525-$550
Bow drill, blackwood handle ....$450-$500
Bear "eggbeater" drills.............................$5-$50
Iron Braces ....$15-$75
Primitive wooden braces ....$85-$800
Sheffield unplated braces ....$60-$200
Sheffield plated braces ....$100-$700
Ultimatum braces....................................$300-$600
Ultimatum beech filled long form ....$1,400-$1,500
French 16th century decorated iron
    brace ....$2,300-$2,500
English shipwright's brace, 17th century.....$5,400-$5,500
Cherry or mahogany levels, common makers,
    20" or longer...............................$10-$50
Rosewood, brass bound levels, common makers
    20" or longer...............................$50-$200

Chisels and Gouges

Paring chisels ....$5-$20
Mortise chisels ....$10-$30
Lock Mortise ....$10-$30
Carving chisel sets, per piece......................$15-$25

Saws

Common examples.....................................$5-$20
Brass backed saws...................................$45-$65
Early Shaw & Marshall, 18" ....$175-$225
Disston D15 ....$125-$150
Disston D23 ....$175-$200
Disston 240, stair saw ....$50-$60
Fret saws, rosewood Shaker pattern..................$275-$300

Wrenches

Common wrenches.....................................$1-$5
Bemis & Call Monkey wrench ....$75-$100
Coes (early 4") ....$45-$55
Coes Key wrench, 32"................................$125-$140
Eifel Plierwrench ....$30-$40
John Deere wrench...................................$100-$125
Planet Jr. wrench ....$15-$20
Winchester S wrench ....$20-$30
Unusual adjustable Alligator wrench.................$225-$275

Tool boxes

Common carpenter's boxes ....$5-$25
Cabinetmakers chests................................$400-$1,250

Special Purpose Planes

#9 Cabinet Maker's Black Plane......................$850-$2,500
#10 Cabinet Maker's Rabbet..........................$100-$200
#10-1/2 Cabinet Maker's Rabbet ....$350-$1,850
#11 Beltmaker's ....$75-$275
#12 Veneer Scraper ....$50-$125
#13 Circular ....$45-$125
#20-1/2 Circular ....$85-$115
#39 Dado..$60-$150
#40 Scrub ....$55-$65
#41 Miller's Patent Plow ....$450-$1,100

#43 Miller's Patent Plow ....$125-$325
#45 Combination Plow ....$50-$250
#46 Skew..$75-$275
#48 Tongue & Groove.................................$25-$100
#50 Combination.....................................$100-$200
#52 Chute Board and Plane...........................$1,300-$1,500
#55 Combination Plow ....$125-$650
#56 Corebox...$750-$850
#60 Block...$200-$250
#62 Low Angle ....$250-$550
#65 Block...$50-$75
#66 Hand Beader.....................................$65-$150
#70 Box Scraper.....................................$45-$60
#75 Bull Nose Rabbet ....$20-$65
#78 Duplex ....$20-$60
#79 Side Rabbet ....$25-$60
#80 Steel Case Rabbet ....$225-$275
#81 Cabinet Scraper ....$15-$50
#85 Cabinet Scraper Plane ....$500-$575
#90 Steel Cased Rabbet ....$150-$200
#92 Cabinet Maker's Rabbet..........................$100-$125
#95 Edge Trim ....$125-$175
#96 Chisel Gauge ....$100-$125
#97 Edge Plane ....$225-$450
#98 Side Rabbet ....$50-$65
#112 Cabinet Scraper................................$75-$150
#113 Circular Plane ....$75-$175
#141 Bullnose Plow ....$300-$350
#146 Tongue & Groove Match ....$125-$150
#148 Tongue & Groove Match ....$100-$125
#164 Low Angle (low knob) ....$50-$65
#171 Door Trim ....$375-$425
#180 through #192 Rabbets, each.....................$10-$60
#193 Fibre Board Plane ....$35-$115
#194 Fibre Board Beveler ....$25-$100
#196 Curve Rabbet Plane.............................$625-$1,300
#278 Rabbet & Filletster ....$125-$300
#289 Filletster & Rabbet ....$125-$225
#340 Furring Plane..................................$850-$950
#444 Dovetail ....$525-$875
#602 Bedrock Smooth.................................$450-$500
#604 Bedrock Smooth.................................$60-$100
#605 Bedrock Jack ....$40-$100
#606 Bedrock Fore ....$50-$125
#607 Bedrock Jointer ....$115-$225

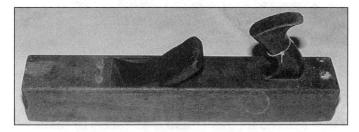

Common vintage wood planes look great and generally sell in the $10-$25 range.

TRANSISTOR RADIOS

The mid- to late-fifties was a great time in America. James Dean was king, cars had fins, and rebellious teenagers were enjoying a raucous new music known as rock and roll. Coming along at just the right moment was another new invention: the transistor radio.

Today these old pocket gems are popular collectibles—and, surprisingly, they don't even have to work. Although some collectors buy old transistor sets to actually listen to, most buy them for display purposes. Serious collectors are more interested in style than sound, and in most cases, the value of a transistor radio depends more on appearance and rarity than on fidelity. If a radio plays, it is certainly a plus; but even if it doesn't, it could still have considerable value.

General Guidelines: Sorting out the good from the bad is easier with transistor radios than with many other types of collectibles. Here are some general guidelines:

Most collectible transistor radios were made between 1954 and 1963. Radios from this era are easy to spot because they all have the old Civil Defense markings on their dials. Look for triangles, dots, arrows or similar symbols between the "6" and "7" positions on the low end of the dial and just before the "16" position at the top end. These "Conelrad" markings were required on all American-made radios during the Cold War era, and today they serve as the single best way to identify a collectible transistor radio. If a radio does not display the CD marking, it is not old enough to be considered collectible.

Collectible transistor radios are AM only. A very few collectible sets may also have a short wave or a marine band with it, but never FM. (The FM band did not become popular until well after the transistor's golden age.) This actually works to the benefit of savvy collectors. Because radios without FM are no longer popular with the general public, you may find some old transistor sets at bargain prices at yard sales or flea markets because the owner has no practical use for them and is not aware of their collectible value.

Generally, collectors prefer smaller transistor radios to large ones. If it doesn't fit in your shirt pocket—or perhaps your coat pocket—it is probably not valuable. (Two exceptions to this rule are the Sylvania Thunderbird and the Raytheon STP-1, both of which are larger but very much in demand.)

Early transistor radios made in either the United States or Japan are the most collectible. Some sets from Germany and England are also collectible, but there is little interest in sets from Hong Kong, Taiwan or Korea. Collectors prefer the rare and the unusual. So far, there is little demand for the common "mass market" sets produced by G.E., Westinghouse, Admiral, Sylvania, Silvertone, etc. The majority of sets by these manufacturers typically sell for under $50 (many are under $25), but there are some exceptions. The very first General Electric models (released in 1955), for example, can sell for as much as $150.

Condition and appearance are critical to a radio's value. As with many other collectibles of this type, transistor radios still in their original box (complete with instructions, leather case, etc.) always command a substantial premium, but most collectors look for nice, clean radios that display well. Any chip or crack in the case will instantly cut a radio's value in half. A large missing chunk could render the piece almost worthless. Scratches, dents in the grill, battery acid corrosion and other defects will also lower the value. Radios don't have to be in perfect condition to be valuable, but, as with baseball cards, comic books, or virtually any other collectible, do not expect to get a Mint or a Near-Mint price for a radio that is flawed. But even radios missing a knob, carrying handle or other part, may have value as a parts radio for a serious collector, especially if it's a rare model.

Colored radios are always better than their corresponding black or white example. Popular colors of early transistor sets include red, green, tan, pink, orange and blue.

Collectors generally do not prefer leather transistor sets (with the exception of the scarce Bulova 250 and the Raytheon 8TP). Plastic radios that can be removed from a leather carrying case are a nice find, but most sets permanently encased in leather are not in great demand (they tend to be larger than pocketsize anyway).

Also, most collectors are not interested in sets that are advertised as "Solid State" or that have more than eight transistors. Both of these types are later models and considered too new to be classics.

Specific sets to look for include the Regency TR1. Introduced just in time for the 1954 Christmas season, this

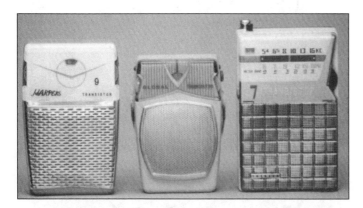

These three early 1960s Japanese models all exhibit a "reverse plastic" design, where the underside of the clear plastic is painted. Shown are a Harper GK900, a Global GR711 and a Toshiba 7TP-352M. In nice condition, they are worth about $80-$100 each. (Photo courtesy Bruce Phillips, Stratham, N.H.)

model is considered the first of the American-made transistor radios. Its success prompted other manufacturers, such as Raytheon, Zenith and others, to rush their first transistor radios onto the market. Demand for any of these early American-made sets is tremendous.

The Japanese invasion began in 1957, when Sony introduced its model TR-63. In order to compete successfully in the U.S. market, Japanese manufacturers offered transistor radios with slick designs and bright colors. Many of these early Japanese models (dating from 1957 to 1963) featured unusual shapes, interesting tuning windows, chrome or gold-colored speaker grilles, and other design elements that make them favorites with today's collectors. Especially interesting and popular are radios featuring "reverse plastic," a technique where the underside of clear plastic was painted, resulting in a unique and stunning appearance. Collectors consider many of these first-generation Japanese models to be hand-held art. They are to transistor collectors what Catalin radios are to their tube-radio collecting cousins.

Unfortunately, pressure to lower prices drove the nice styling out of the Japanese sets, and by the mid-1960s, the Japanese models were as dull and boxy as most of the American sets of the day.

Many collectors of early transistor radios are also interested in the following related sets:

Boys Radios—Sold as toys to escape a higher import tax, these Japanese radios had only two transistors and did not usually display the Civil Defense markings mentioned above. They are generally marked on the back "2 Transistor," "2TR," or "Boys Radio." Most were cheaply made, but there were some nicer ones. Today, they are generally valued in the $25-$50 range, although an especially desirable one could bring as much as $100.

Crystal Radios—Made without transistors, crystal radios typically used a single diode. They had no batteries and did not have a speaker (you listened through an earphone). Tuning was often done with a tuning rod, rather than a dial. Crystal radios are of interest to today's collectors because they were made in a variety of different shapes, such as rockets, satellites, pens and watches. They generally are valued in the $20-$100 range.

Solar Radios—These innovative models were powered by solar cells attached to either the top of the radio or the carrying handle. The largest manufacturer of solar radios was Hoffman, but models were also produced by Admiral, Zenith and others. Today, American-made models typically sell for up to $100, with Japanese versions bringing less.

Watch sets—Early pocket transistor radios with watches in them are collectible (typically selling for $40 and up), but fold-up travel clock radios are, so far, not very desirable.

Micro Transistors—Japan's attempts to miniaturize radios were taken to the extreme with these micro-sets that can measure as small as an inch square. The first models were the "Micronic Ruby" series by Standard, which were strictly transistors. Sony improved the idea in 1966 using integrated circuits for its micro radios. Today, the Standard micros sell for $50 and up, while a Sony micro may bring twice that.

Contributor to this chapter: Bruce Phillips, 127 Bunker Hill Ave., Stratham, NH 03885.

Club
•Transistor Network, 32 West Main Street, Bradford, NH 03221

Recommended Reading
Transistor Radios A Collector's Encyclopedia & Price Guide, David and Robert Lane

Among the most valuable of all American-made transistor radios is the Bulova 250 (far left), a 1955 model valued at nearly $500 in nice condition. The Regency TR1 (center) dates from 1954 and is considered the first transistor radio. It is worth about $250-$300. The first Japanese transistor that was exported to the United States was the 1955 Sony TR63 (far right), now worth over $400. (Photo courtesy Bruce Phillips, Stratham, N.H.)

┌─ **WHAT TO LOOK FOR!** ─────────

Here, in alphabetical order, are ten brands of early transistor radios that are especially desirable:
• Bulova
• Crown
• Global
• Hoffman
• Mitchell
• Raytheon
• Regency
• Sony
• Toshiba
• Zephyr

This model, known by collectors as the Toshiba "Lace," because of its lace grill, is a collecting classic, valued at about $400-$450. (Photo courtesy Bruce Phillips, Stratham, N.H.)

VALUE LINE

The following values are for radios in nice condition with no cracks, chips, scratches, missing parts, etc.

Admiral YG 161 "Clipper," with short wave, 1962 ...... $40
Admiral Y2063, 1961 "Super 7" $25
Admiral 7M12, 1957, 7 transistor $50
Admiral Y2231GPS, 1962, 6 transistor $15
Admiral 751, 1958, 8 transistor $25
Admiral 802, 1957, 8 transistor $40
Admiral 537, 1956, 8 transistor $35
Admiral 7L12, Solar Powered, 1956, radio only $150
Arvin 60R403, 1957, 4 transistor $20
Arvin 62R48, 1962, 8 transistor $20
Arvin 8576, 1957, 5 transistor $135
Bulova 250, 1955 .... $500
Bulova 290, late 1950s, 4 transistor $75
Bulova 620, late 1950s, 4 transistor $100
Bulova 672, 1961, 6 transistor $100
Bulova 1012, 1964 .... $15
Candle PTR-83, 1963 .... $50
Champion Boys Radio, 1962, 2 transistor $75
Channel Master 6501, 1959 .... $90
Channel Master 6516, 1961, 7 transistor $60
Channel Master 6505, 1963 .... $30

Channel Master 6479, 1965 .... $5-$10
Commodore "Super DeLuxe" $50
Continental TR-100, 1960 .... $50
Continental TR-300, 1960, 8 transistor $35
Continental TR-680, 1964 .... $5-$10
Coronet BL-206P Boy's Radio, 1960, 2 transistor $50
Crown TR-670 "Six Transistor," 1959 .... $50
DeWald K-544, 1957, leather $200
DeWald K-702-B, 1955, 6 transistor, leather $75
DeWald L-414, 1959, leather $50
Elgin, most mid-'60s models .... $5-$10
Emerson 555, 1960 .... $60
Emerson 707, 1961, 7 transistor $45
Emerson 844 "Miracle Wand," 1957 .... $60
Emerson 856, hybrid (tubes & transistors), 1956 .... $100
Emerson 888 "Atlas," 1958, 8 transistor $100
Emerson 888 "Explorer," 1958, 8 transistor $150
Emerson 888 "Satellite," 1958, 8 transistor $150
Emerson 888 "Vangard," 1959, 8 transistor $125
Emerson 888 "Pioneer," 1958, 8 transistor $100
Emerson 888 "Transtimer," (clock radio),
    leather case, 1959 .... $100
Emerson 988 "Rambler," 1959, 8 transistor $85
Firestone, most models .... $40-$60
Fleetwood "Transistor Six," early 1960s $40
General Electric 675, 676, 677, or 678,
    1955 .... $100-$150
General Electric, most 1956-1959 models .... $20-$40
General Electric, most 1960-1965 models .... $5-$20
Global GR-711, 1962 .... $100
Global GR-900, 1963 .... $125
Harpers GK 900, 9 transistor $100
Hi-Delity, early 1960s, most models .... $10-$20
Hitachi TH-666, 1958, 6 transistor $100
Hitachi TH-667, 1960, 6 transistor $75
Hitachi WH-761M, 1961, with marine band $25
Hitachi WH-822, 1960, with short wave $45
Hoffman BP-411 or TP-411, solar radio $650
Hoffman KP-706, 1959, solar radio $300
Hoffman KP-709 "Solar," 1963 .... $150
Lafayette FS-91, 1961, 9 transistor $200
Lafayette FS-112, 1959 6 transistor $40
Lafayette FS-200, 1960 6 transistor $40
Lafayette FS-280, 1965, 10 transistor,
    with short wave $15

Lafayette TR-1660, 1964, 6 transistor ....$5-$10
Lloyd's, most models ....$5-$15
Magnavox AM-2, 1956......................................$75-$100
Magnavox AM-5, 1957..$50-$75
Magnavox, most 1960-65 models ....$10-$20
Midland, most 1964-65 models ....$5-$10
Mitchell 1101, 1102, or 1103, 1955-56,
    4 transistor...$400
Motorola 7X23E "Power 10," 1958 ....$250
Motorola 56T1, 1955, 5 transistor $225
Motorola 66T1, 1957, 6 transistor $150
Motorola 6X39A "Weatherama," 1958,
    6 transistor, two bands......................................$125
Motorola 7X25P, 1959, 7 transistor $40
Motorola X14E, 1960, 6 transistor $60
Motorola, most models 1961-1964 ....$10-$25
NEC NT-61, 1960, 6 transistor $110
Norelco, most 1960-64 models ....$15-$30
Olympic 447, 1956, 4 transistor................................$125
Olympic 666 or 766, 1959 ....$50
Olympic, most 1960-1963 models ....$15-$30
Panasonic, most 1962-66 models...........................$5-$20
Peerless, most 1963-65 models ....$5-$20
Philco T-7, 1956, 7 transistor $90
Philco most models 1957-59.................................$25-$45
Philco, most models 1960-65 ....$10-$25
Raytheon 8TP, 1955 ....$250
Raytheon, 1955-56, most models......................$150-$225
RCA 7-BT-9J, 1955, 6 transistor $175
RCA, most 1956-1959 models...............................$50-$80
RCA, most early '60s models ....$10-$20
Realistic, most 1961-62 models ....$20-$35
Realtone TR-1088 "Comet", 1959............................$150
Realtone TR-801 "Electra," 1960 6 transistor $65
Realtone TR-1623 "Transistor Clock Radio,"
    1962...$85
Realtone, most 1963-64 models............................$10-$20
Regency TR-1, 1954, red, gray, black,
    or white ....$300-$500
Regency TR-1, 1954, green or mahogany ....$500-$700
Regency TR-1G, 1956 ....$200
Regency TR-4, 1957 ....$150
Regency TR-5, 1957 ....$80
Rocket A1 crystal set, early 1960s............................$50
Ross, most 1964-65 models ....$5-$15
Sears 6204, 1965, 7 transistor ....$5-$10
Sharp TR-182, 1959..$50
Sharp, most 1963-64 models..................................$5-$15
Silvertone 206, 1959, 4 transistor $25
Silvertone, 1213 "All Transistor 500," 1959 ....$20
Silvertone 1201, 1960, 4 transistor $15
Silvertone 1203, 1961, 6 transistor $20
Silvertone 4205, 1963, 6 transistor $15
Silvertone 5202, 1963, 7 transistor ....$5-$10
Silvertone, most 1963-65 models ....$5-$15
Sony TR-63, 1957..$500
Sony ICR-120, Micro radio, Integrated Circuit,
    1970..$200

Collectors love early Japanese transistors for their great designs. This group includes a 1961 Six Transistor Fleetwood, worth about $50; a rare 1962 Toshiba 8TP-90 with a concentric ring grill, worth about $700; and a 1962 Realtone TR-1088, valued at about $125. (Photo courtesy Bruce Phillips, Stratham, N.H.)

Sony TFM-121, 1961 early AM-FM $60
Sony TR-510, 1961 ....$100
Sony, most models 1963-65 ....$10-$20
Standard "Micronic" models.................................$85-$150
Star-Lite, most 1964-65 models..............................$5-$10
Sylvania 3102 "Thunderbird," 1957 ....$350
Sylvania, most 1958-1960 models........................$30-$40
Sylvania, most 1961-65 models ....$5-$15
Toshiba 5TR-193 (lace grille), 1959 ....$400
Toshiba 7TP-352M $100
Toshiba 8TP-90, 1962 ....$700
Toshiba, many late '50s-early '60s models............$20-$50
Trancel TR-60 ....$125
Trancel, most 1960-63 models...............................$15-$30
Trans-ette, most 1962-64 models.........................$10-$25
Trav-ler, TR-250-A or TR-251-A, 1958 ....$75
Trav-ler, TR-282, 1958 ....$40
Trav-ler, most early '60s models..........................$15-$25
Truetone D-3614A, 1956, 4 transistor $100
Truetone D-3715A, 1957, 4 transistor $90
Truetone, most 1960-63 models.............................$10-$25
Truetone, most 1964-65 models..............................$5-$10
Westinghouse "Escort" (with watch, lighter,
    flashlight), 1968 ....$100
Westinghouse, most 1957 models.........................$50-$75
Westinghouse, most 1958-59 models ....$20-$45
Westinghouse, 1960-63 models.............................$10-$25
Viscount 6TP-102, 1962, 6 transistor $125
York, most models ....$5-$10
Zenith Royal 500, 1955-56, 7 transistor,
    pink or tan ....$150-$200
Zenith Royal 500, 1955-56, 7 transistor, white...........$100
Zenith Royal 200, 300 or 400, 1958-1961,
    7 transistor...$40-$75
Zephyr AR-600, 1962 ....$200

TV Toys

When television became wildly popular in the early 1950s, marketers figured out they could sell toys and other items based on popular TV characters. (This was nothing new; they had done the very same thing with radio characters in the 1930s and '40s.) Now with television in its sixth decade, we have some sixty years worth of TV collectibles to look for. It's one of the most fascinating and fastest growing categories in all of collecting. With about 4,000 different TV shows on the air since the age of television began, there are literally tens of thousands of items to collect. The price ranges for these items can be less than $10 (especially for items from newer shows) to hundreds of dollars for items from the 1950s, 1960s and 1970s.

General Guidelines: Collectors often collect by show, by genre (Western, comedy, etc.) or by type of collectible, like board games or dolls. Look for items in the best condition possible. On newer items—post-1970—look for collectibles in Near Mint condition or better. Items that are still in their original packaging are highly desirable. In fact, on post-1980 items, the market is very much geared toward items that are Mint-in-Box.

Each era had its favorite shows and characters. These are often the most collectible today. Items to look for from the 1950s and earlier are those related to the early TV cowboys—Gene Autry, Hopalong Cassidy, Roy Rogers and The Lone Ranger. Items from later Westerns, such as *Bonanza* and *Maverick*, are also popular.

The 1960s might have seen the finest television shows ever made, as far as many are concerned. Among those with the most collectible toys are *Batman, Lost In Space, The Green Hornet, Man from U.N.C.L.E., Hogan's Heroes, The Addams Family, The Munsters, The Beverly Hillbillies, Gilligan's Island, The Flintstones, I Spy* and *The Monkees*. Cool shows. Cool toys. These are also classic shows that have a cult following, which contributes greatly to how in-demand the toys will be.

While the 1970s was a time of excessive bad taste and even worse television, there were actually some shows that spawned neat toys, including *Charlie's Angels, The Six Mil-*

lion Dollar Man, The Bionic Woman, The Brady Bunch, The Partridge Family, Chips, M*A*S*H*, Happy Days and *Welcome Back, Kotter.*

Items from the 1980s and 1990s shows have proven less collectible, but *The X-Files, The Simpsons* and *Beverly Hills 90210* are a few current shows with toys and other memorabilia that may prove collectible in the future.

Recommended Reading

Saturday Morning TV Collectibles, Dana Cain
Collecting Monsters of Film and TV, Dana Cain
Hake's Guide to Cowboy Character Collectibles, Ted Hake
Television's Cowboys, Gunfighters & Cap Pistols, Rudy A. D'Angelo
TV Toys and The Shows That Inspired Them, Cynthia Boris Liljeblad
The Monkees Collectibles Price Guide, Marty Eck

VALUE LINE

Values shown are for examples in Excellent condition.

A-Team
Board game, Parker Bros. $15
Card game, The Adventures with B.A., Parker Bros., 1983...$15
Colorforms, Lazer Blazers 3-DHolographic Stickers, MIP, 1983 ....$8
Comic books, Marvel, 1984...$5
Doll, Mr. T, 12" Galoob, 1983 ....$85
Grenade toss..$50
Halloween bag, "Loot Bag," plastic, Unique Industries, Mr. T $3
Kite, Mr. T. Hi-Flyer, MIP $20
Lunch box, thermos, steel, 1985 ....$40
Off-Road Attack Cycle $45
Party hats, four cones, nice graphics, 1983, MIP...........$8
Puzzle, Mr. T., 18" x 24" MIP.......................................$10

Addams Family
Coloring book, family portrait on the cover, Saalfield, 1965..$20
Dolls, Lurch, Morticia, Fester, Remco, 1964, each $575
Fester's Mystery Light Bulb, lights up in your mouth, 1964-66 ....$50
Game board, The Addams Family Game, Ideal, 1964..$35
Model house, complete with ghosts, Aurora, 1964..$500
Puppets, Ideal, 1964...$65

I'LL SWAP YA!

Here's a tip: Trade. Easy, huh? You were into Batman three years ago; now you're into the Addams Family (the release of major movies will do that to you). Suggest a trade—your Corgi Batmobile for a set of Addams Family puppets. You swap and everybody goes home with something fresh. You just never know what a dealer will trade for until you ask.

Thing bank, generic hand in box bank, 1964-66 .... $70
View-Master, three-wheel with story booklet,
    #B486 .... $115

ALF
Board game, The ALF Board Game, Coleco Games,
    1987 .... $10
Coloring book, ALF Helps Out, Alien Prod.,
    unusued, 1988 .... $10
Doll, plush, 18", Alien Prod., 1986 .... $20
Doll, plush clip-on, 4" $5
Doll, plush, with suction cups, 7", Applause, 1989 ...... $10
Halloween costume, 1986, MIP $20
Lunch box, plastic $25

All in the Family
Game, Archie Bunker's Card Game, 1971 .... $20
Goblet, Archie Bunker for President, 1972 .... $20
Pinback button, Archie Bunker for President,
    1970s $15
Record, 1971 .... $15

Batman
Art Kit, Paint-by-Number, Hasbro, 1966 .... $50
Coins, plastic, feature characters, Transogram,
    1966 .... $30
Coloring book, Whitman, 1966 .... $20
Flying Copter, Remco, 1966 .... $65
Game board, Batman and Robin Game, Hasbro,
    1965 .... $35
Game, target, plastic revolver and darts, Hasbro,
    1966 .... $85
Model, Batman, Aurora, 1964 .... $250
Model, Batmobile, Aurora, 1966 .... $200
Model, Robin, Aurora, 1966 .... $125
Pajamas, child's two-piece, Wormser, 1966 .... $800
Phone, Batman Hot Line, Marx, 1966 .... $125
Play set, Ideal, 1966 .... $550
Puppets, hand puppets, vinyl, glove-style, Ideal,
    1966 .... $65
Record set, Golden Records, 1966 .... $65
Soaky, Batman or Robin, Colgate-Palmolive, 1966 ..... $50
Stamp set, rubber, Kellogg's, 1960s $200
Trace-A-Graph, light table, drawings, Emenee,
    1966 .... $85
Utility belt, include Batarang, handcuffs, flashlight,
    more for crime fighting, Ideal, 1966 .... $600

Ben Casey
Book, paperback, *A Biography of Vince Edwards*, Televi-
    sion's Ben Casey, Belmont, 1962 .... $17
Coloring book, Saalfield $20
Game, Ben Casey "The Drama of Life in a Big Metropoli-
    tan Hospital," Transogram, 1961 .... $25
Hospital cart, wheeled, plasma stand and bottle, accesso-
    ries, Transogram, 1962 .... $185
Play set, Play Hospital Set, Transogram, 1962 .... $35
Play Suit, child's scrubs, "Ben Casey" embroidered
    over pocket $50

You could add this nice Mattel "Flipper" jack-in-the-box to your collection for about $40-$50.

Beverly Hillbillies
Car, Clampett's truck replica, plastic, Ideal, 1963 ...... $350
Card game, The Beverly Hillbillies, Milton Bradley,
    1963 .... $30
Coloring book, Watkins, 1964 .... $35
Coloring set, sketches, crayons and paints, Standard
    Toykraft, 1963 .... $30
Costume, Jed Clampett, Ben Cooper, 1963 .... $150
Lunch box, family in the truck, family in Bugtussle, Alad-
    din, 1963 .... $50
Punch-out book, figures, car, mansion, Whitman,
    1964 .... $20
Puzzle, jigsaw, family photo, Jaymar $30
Puzzle tray, three puzzle trays, Milton Bradley,
    1963 .... $30
View-Master, three reels, booklet, #B570, GAF $35

Beverly Hills 90210
Booklets, 3" x 5", paperbacks, each $5
Bookmarks, Book Bites, photo-shaped, set of four,
    1991 .... $15
Cologne spray $15
Doll, Brenda, Mattel, 1991, 12" MIB $75
Doll, Dylan, Mattel, 1991, 12" MIB $75

Frisbee, Wham-O, 1991, MIP......................................$17
Game, Entangle, Cardinal..$30
Gift bag, cast photos, Cleo, 1991..................................$15
Lipstick and nail polish set...$15
Pencils, set of three, Fasco, 1991.................................$10

Bewitched
Broom, 36" long, Samantha head on top, Amsco,
    1965..$30
Doll, Samantha, red gown with witch hat, Ideal,
    1965..$250
Card game, Stymie, Milton Bradley, 1965...................$35
Coloring book, Treasure, 1965......................................$35
Costume, Samantha, Ben Cooper, 1965......................$150
Game board, T. Cohn, 1965..$25

Bionic Woman
Board game, The Bionic Woman, Parker Brothers,
    1976..$20
Coloring fun book, Treasure Books, 1976....................$15
Cup or tumbler, plastic, Dawn, 1976, each.................$12

This "Mod Squad" puzzle from Milton Bradley is valued at about $40.

Cut out doll, Bionic Woman Doll Dressing Book,
    Stafford Pemberton, 1978.......................................$30
Doll, Jamie Sommers, Kenner, 1976............................$50
Eyeglass case, Bionic Eyewear, Hudson, 1977...........$20
Paint-by-Number set, 9" x 12" picture and paints,
    Craft Master, 1976..$25
Play-Doh, action play set, Kenner, 1977......................$30
Puzzle, jigsaw, different versions, APC, each..............$12

Bonanza
Coloring book, two versions, Saalfield, 1965, each......$15
Comics, 37 different issue, Dell/Gold Key,
    1960-70, each..$15
Game, Bonanza Rummy, Parker Bros., 1964..............$35
Gun and holster, Bonanza logo, Halpern Co.,
    1965..$75
Lunch box, thermos, four Cartwrights riding
    the range, Aladdin, 1963..$75
Model, three snap-together figures, Revell, 1966.......$125
Puzzle, Joe firing at bad guy, 125 pieces,
    Milton Bradley, 1964..$25
Record album, Lorne Greene's Welcome to the
    Ponderosa, RCA Victor, 1964.................................$25
View-Master, three reels, booklet, GAF, 1964.............$25
Wagon, accessories to make four-in-one, American Char-
    acter, 1965...$100

Brady Bunch
Activity book, Whitman, 1975.......................................$30
Board game, The Brady Bunch Game, Whitman,
    1973..$150
Brain twisters, five tricky metal puzzles, Larami,
    1973..$35
Coloring book, Whitman, 1974......................................$30
Lunch box, metal, thermos, King Seeley, 1969..........$200
Paper dolls, Greg and Marcia, Whitman, 1974............$50
Sticker fun book, Whitman, 1973.................................$65
View-Master, three reels, booklet, Grand Canyon Adven-
    ture, #B568, GAF, 1971..$40

Captain Kangaroo
Presto Slate on board, 1960s.......................................$35
Record, 45 rpm, 1957..$25
Record, 45 rpm, 1962..$20

Charlie's Angels
Beauty sets, Sabrina, Kelly, Kris or Jill, comb and
    mirror, Fleetwood, 1977, each................................$20
Board game, Charlie's Angels game, Milton Bradley,
    1977..$25
Dolls, Kelly, Sabrina, Kris, Jill, Hasbro, 1977, each....$45
Farrah Fawcett Creme Rinse/Conditioner, Faberge,
    8-ounce, 1970s..$20
Farrah doll, 12", Mego, 1980.......................................$55
Hair dryer, comb, curlers, Fleetwood, 1977................$35
Jewels and case, Fleetwood, 1977..............................$25
Lunch box, metal, thermos, Aladdin, 1978..................$45
Paper dolls, Sabrina, Kelly, Jill, Toy Factory,
    1977, each..$35

Sunglasses, with case, Fleetwood, 1977 .... $25
Target set, two guns, six darts, target, Placo Toys, 1977

ChiPs
Board game, ChiPs Game, Ideal, 1981 .... $30
Dolls, Jon, Ponch or Sarge, Mego, 1980, each $45
Model, ChiPs helicopter, Revell, 1980 .... $25
Motorcycle, with logo, die-cast, Imperial, 1980 .... $25
Puzzles, jigsaw, HG toys $12
Wallet, Imperial, 1981 .... $20

Daniel Boone
Coloring book, The Fess Parker Coloring Book, Saalfield, 1964 .... $25
Figure, Daniel Boone, Remco, 1964 .... $100
Game board, Fess Parker Trail Blazers, Milton Bradley, 1964 .... $25
Lunch box, Fess Parker Daniel Boone, thermos, King Seeley, 1965 .... $50
Paint set, Paint-by-Number, Standard Toykraft, 1964 .... $50
Play set, cowboys and Indians, Marx $125
View-Master, three reels, booklet, #B479, GAF, 1964 .... $15

Dark Shadows
Comic books, 35 issues, Gold Key, 1969-76, each $20
Game, Barnabas Collins Dark Shadows Game, Milton Bradley, 1969 .... $40
Game, Dark Shadows Game, Whitman, 1968 .... $50
Model, Barnabas Vampire Van, MPC, 1969 .... $90
Pillows, Horror Head, Centsable, 1969 .... $65
View-Master, three reels, folio, #B503, GAF $75

Donny & Marie
Colorforms dress-up kit, Colorforms, 1977 .... $30
Coloring book, Donny & Marie, Whitman, 1977 .... $20
Costume, Donny, Collegeville, 1977 .... $25
Diary, Donny on cover, Continental Plastics, 1977 ..... $15
Dolls, Donny or Marie, Mattel 1976 .... $35
Guitar, Donny & Marie, Lapin, 1977 .... $50
Marie's Make Up Set, Gordy, 1976 .... $15
Necklace, 16" chain, Osbro, 1977 .... $15

Dr. Kildare
Comics, nine issues, Dell, 1962-65 .... $20
Game, Dr. Kildare Perilous Night Game, Ideal, 1963 .... $50
Game board, Dr. Kildare Medical Game For The Young, Ideal, 1962 .... $25
Punch-Out book, Junior Doctor Kit, Golden, 1962 ...... $25
Puzzle, jigsaw, 100 pieces, show sketches, Milton Bradley, 1962 .... $25
Stethoscope, Dr. Kildare Thumpy-The HeartBeat, Amson, 1962 .... $35

Dukes of Hazzard
Coloring book, 1981 .... $15
Finger racers, Knickerbocker, 1981 .... $20
Model kit, General Lee, original issue, MIB $65
Puzzle, MIB $25

Record, 45 rpm, photo sleve, sealed $15
View-Master, three reels, booklet $15

Emergency
Board game, Milton Bradley, 1973 .... $25
Fireman's helmet, plastic, 1970s $75
Lunch box, thermos, steel, 1973 .... $85
Record, Great Adventures $30
Halloween costume, Collegeville, 1975 .... $50

Family Affair
Coloring book, Buffy and Mrs. Beasley cover, Whitman, 1968 .... $10
Doll, 6" poseable Buffy with Mrs. Beasley, Mattel, 1967 .... $65
Doll, Mrs. Beasley, life-size replica, with talk box, Mattel, 1968 .... $125
Game board, The Family Affair game, Whitman, 1971 .... $20
Lunch box, Buffy and Cissy, thermos, King Seeley, 1969 .... $30
Paper dolls, Buffy and Jody set, boxed, Whitman, 1970 .... $20
View-Master, three reels, little book, #B571, GAF $25

Flintstones
Comic book, Gold Key, 1970s $10
Doll, Pebbles, 15", Ideal, 1963 .... $125
Figure, Barney, Dakin, 1970 .... $65
Figure, Dino, Dakin, 1970 .... $85
Figure, Fred, Dakin, 1970 .... $65
Figure, Pebbles, Dakin, 1970 .... $65
Flip book, It's About Time, 1977 .... $12
Horn, 1960s $75
Jell-O mold, 1988 .... $10
Paddy Wagon motorized kit, Remco, 1961 .... $325
Push puppet, Dino, 1960s $80
Wind-up, Barney, tin, 3-1/2", Marx, 1960s $200
Wind-up, Fred riding Dino, 18", Marx, 1963 .... $700

Relatively scarce in complete condition, this 1958 "Zorro" Play Set from Marx is valued at $750-$800 in Excellent condition.

Flying Nun

Chalk board, activity board, Screen Gems, 1967........ $100
Coloring book, Saalfield, 1968 .... $40
Doll, Sister Bertrille, 4", Hasbro, 1960s $100
Paper dolls, Saalfield, 1969.................................. $50
View-Master, three reels, booklet, #B495,
    GAF, 1967 .... $45

Get Smart

Card game, Get Smart, mini-board, Ideal, 1966 .... $25
Coloring book, Get Smart!, Saalfield, 1965 .... $20
Game board, The Get Smart Exploding Time Board
    Game, Ideal, 1965 .... $35
Lunch box, cartoon drawings of Max, thermos,
    King Seeley, 1966 .... $65
Model, Get Smart car, AMT, 1967 .... $50
Radio/lipstick tube, MPC, 1966.............................. $50
Radio/pen, fountain pen radio, MPC, 1966 .... $35

Gomer Pyle, U.S.M.C.

Board game $65
Lunch box, thermos, steel, 1966 .... $250
Record, Shazam! Gomer Pyle U.S.M.C.,
    Columbia, 1965 .... $30

Green Hornet

Bubble gum ring, rubber, in cello pack, Frito Lay........ $55
Car, Black Beauty replica, Corgi, 1966 .... $175
Charm bracelet, chain with five charms,
    Greenway, 1966....................................... $110
Colorforms, vinyl stick-on people,
    Colorforms, 1966 .... $50
Coloring book, Whitman, 1966 .... $20
Comics, three issues, Gold Key, 1967, each $45
Costume, jumpsuit and mask, Ben Cooper, 1966 .... $125
Drawing set, light table, illustrations, Lakeside,
    1966.. $125
Figure, bendable, Lakeside, 1966 .... $25
Flasher pin, Hornet's face to mad hornet,
    GPI, 1967 .... $25
Flasher rings, eight different, Chemtoy,
    1960s, each... $75
Game board, Green Hornet Quick Switch game,
    Milton Bradley, 1966 .... $50
Lunch box, Black Beauty shot, thermos,
    King Seeley, 1967 .... $175
Model, Black Beauty, Aurora, 1966 .... $250
Paint set, two sets, Hasbro, 1966 .... $125
Playing cards, educational cards, Ed-U-Cards,
    1966.. $35
View-Master, #B488, three reels, booklet, GAF.......... $75
Whistle, plastic, Hornet and Kato, Bantam Lite,
    1966.. $25
Wrist radio, 4" with straps, Remco, 1966 .... $125

Gunsmoke

Comics, 27 issues, Dell/Gold Key, 1956-70, each........ $25
Figure, Heroes of the West series, Hartland Plastics,
    1960s $50

Game board, Gunsmoke Game, features Matt Dillon,
    Lowell, 1950s.. $65
Game, target shoot, dart pistols, cardboard villains,
    Park Plastic, 1958 .... $50
Holster set, double holster set with copper clad grips,
    Leslie-Henry.. $375
Lunch box, metal, Matt Dillon in action, thermos, Alad-
    din, 1959... $100
Pistol, cap, Marshall Matt Dillon cap pistol,
    Leslie-Henry, 1950s $90
Play set, Official Gunsmoke Dodge City, Marx,
    1960.. $1,275
Puzzle, 100 pieces, Marshall Dillon holds mob in jail,
    Whitman, 1960 .... $25
View-Master, three reels, booklet, #B589, GAF.......... $25

Happy Days

Board game, Happy Days, Parker Brothers, 1976 .... $20
Colorforms, The Fonz, Colorforms, 1976 .... $25
Glasses, six different, Libbey Glass Co.,
    1976, each $20
Kite Fun Book, with the Fonz, Western Publishing,
    1978.. $15
Paper doll, 14" Fonzie, Toy Factory, 1976.................. $30
Scrapbook, The Official Fonzie Scrapbook,
    Grosset & Dunlap, 1976.............................. $10
Soda can, 35 different cans, R.C. Cola, 1978 .... $10
View-Master, three reels, booklet, GAF, 1974............ $25

Hardy Boys

Disco Amplifier, Shaun Cassidy, portable,
    Vanity Fair, 1977 .... $45
Costume, Joe Hardy, Ben Cooper, 1970s................... $40
Guitar, Shawn Cassidy as Joe Hardy, Carnival Toys,
    1978.. $65
Model, Hardy Boys' van, Revell, 1978...................... $40
Poster Put-Ons, adhesives, Joe Hardy,
    or Joe and Frank Hardy, Bi-Rite, 1977 .... $10

Hogan's Heroes

Comics, nine issues, Dell, 1966-69, each $15
Game board, Hogan's Heroes Bluff Out game, Tran-
    sogram, 1966.. $35
Lunch box, metal, domed, Hogan and Schultz,
    thermos, Aladdin, 1966.............................. $85
Model, Hogan's Heroes WWII Jeep, MPC, 1968........ $35
Record, Hogan's Heroes Sing the Best of
    World War II, Liberty Records, 1967...................... $25

Howdy Doody

Belt buckle, figural head, metal, 1960s...................... $40
Game, Electric Doodler, 1950s $150
Lunch box, steel, Adco Liberty, 1954.......................$475

Kung Fu

Halloween costume, Caine, Ben Cooper, 1973............ $35
Lunch box, metal, action scene, King Seeley,
    1974.. $100
Target set, Multiple Toymakers, 1975....................... $30
View-Master, three reels, booklet, #B598,
    GAF, 1974 .... $25

Laugh-In

Brunch bag, vinyl, 1968 ....$75
Coloring book, unused, 1960s $15
Lunch box, thermos, steel, 1969 ....$175
Paper doll booklet, Saalfield, 1969 ....$50
View-Master, three reels, booklet, #B497,
    GAF, 1968 ....$30

Laverne & Shirley

Board game, Laverne and Shirley,
    Parker Brothers, 1977..............................$30
Costume, Laverne or Shirley, Collegeville, 1977 ....$35
Dolls, Laverne and Shirley two-pack, Mego,
    1977 ....$125
Pocketbook Mad Money Purse, Harmony, 1977 ....$20
Puzzles, jigsaw, three different, HG Toys,
    1976, each $15
Secretary set, Harmony, 1977 ....$20
View-Master, three reels, booklet, #J20,
    GAF, 1978 ....$20

M*A*S*H

Dog tags, stainless steel $20
Fan photo, cast $15
Figure, B.J., 3-3/4", MIP...............................$25
Figure, Colonel Potter, 3-3/4", MIP $25
Figure, Father Mulcahy, 3-3/4", MIP $25
Figure, Hawkeye, 3-3/4", MIP $25
Figure, Hot Lips, 3-3/4", MIP $25
Figure, Winchester, 3-3/4", MIP $25
Model kit, helicopter $20
Model kit, The Swamp..................................$20
Vodka bottle, MIB.......................................$40

Man from U.N.C.L.E.

Cap firing cane, aluminum, plastic bullets,
    Marx, 1966 ....$65
Car, Gun Firing Thrush-Buster, Corgi, 1966 ....$85
Car, die-cast, Playart, 1968 ....$200
Coloring book, Solo and Kuryakin,
    Whitman, 1967 ....$45
Dolls, Solo and Kuryakin, AC Gilbert, 1965 ....$100
Game board, The Man From U.N.C.L.E. game,
    Ideal, 1965..$25
Gun/cigarette lighter, hard plastic, Ideal, 1966............$85
Gun set, Napoleon Solo, Ideal, 1965 ....$350
Lunch box, metal, action graphics, thermos,
    King Seeley, 1966 ....$125
Model, sporty car, AMT, 1967......................$85
Model figures, Illya or Napolean, Aurora, 1966........$300
Puppets, six, for fingers, Dean, 1966 ....$325
Puzzle, "Illya's Battle Below," Milton Bradley,
    1966 ....$50
Secret Message Pen, double-tipped,
    American Character, 1966........................$200
Spy Magic Tricks, mystery gun, playing cards,
    Gilbert, 1965 ....$325
View-Master, three reels, booklet,
    Sawyers/View-Master, #B484 ....$30
Watch, Secret Agent Watch, Bradley, 1966 ....$300

Monkees

Car, Monkeemobile, die-cast, Corgi, 1967 ....$235
Flip books, 16 styles, flipped photos create story,
    Topps, 1967 ....$55
Game board, Hey! Hey! The Monkees game,
    Transogram, 1967..................................$50
Guitar, plastic, Mattel, 1966........................$65
Lunch box, vinyl, four heads on box, thermos,
    King Seeley, 1967 ....$125
Model, Monkeemobile, plastic, MPC, 1967 ....$65
Puppet, one Monkee head for each finger,
    talking toy, Mattel, 1966 ....$85
Puzzle, jigaw, 11" x 17" $30
View-Master, three reels, booklet, #B493, GAF...........$30

Mork & Mindy

Activity book, Wonder Books, 1979...............$15
Card game, Mork & Mindy, Milton Bradley, 1978 ......$20
Costume, Mork, Ben Cooper, 1978 ....$30
Dolls, Mork or Mindy, Mattel, 1979 ....$35
Mittens, "Nano, Nano," PPC, 1979................$20
Radio, Mork from Ork Eggship,
    Concept 2000, 1979 ....$50
Scrapbook, The Official Mork & Mindy Scrapbook, Wall-
    aby, 1979 ....$10
Talking doll, Mork, rag, Mattel, 1979..............$30

The Munsters

Comic books, 16 different issues, Gold Key,
    1965-68 ....$25
Doll, Herman, soft cloth body and plastic head,
    Mattel, 1964 ....$125
Dolls, Grandpa, Lily and Herman, rubber,
    oversized heads, Remco, 1964 ....$50
Game board, The Munsters' Picnic, Hasbro, 1965.......$75
Game board, Munster's Masquerade Party game,
    Hasbro, 1965 ....$75
Model, Munster Koach Toy, no assembly required,
    AMT, 1964 ....$150

**Board games (along with lunch boxes) are among
the most popular category of TV collectibles. This
1960s Ideal game is valued at $100-$125 in Excellent
condition.**

Model, diorama, Munsters at Home, Aurora, 1964..$500

Puppet, Herman, talking doll, Mattel, 1964.................$90

Puzzle, family sing-along, Whitman, 1965..................$25

View-Master, three discs and booklet, #B481 ....$115

The Outer Limits

Comic books, Dell, 18 different, 1964-69, each $10

Costume, polyester jumpsuit with monsters, monster mask, Collegeville, 1964......................................$150

Game board, The Outer Limits game, Milton Bradley, 1964 ....$150

Model kit, The Sixth Finger, Golden Era Models $75

Puzzles, jigsaw, six different, 8" x 13", Milton Bradley, 1964, each $100

The Partridge Family

Board game, The Partridge Family game, Milton Bradley, 1971 ....$35

Bus, Partridge Family bus, plastic, with 8 figures, Remco, 1973 ....$500

Coloring book, family on bus, Saalfield, 1971 ....$30

Colorforms, David Cassidy Dress-Up Kit, Colorforms, 1972 ....$40

Comic books, Charlton, 1970s, each $15

Guitar, David Cassidy, Carnival Toys, 1970s.............$100

Paint and Color Album, David Cassidy, Artcraft, 1971 ....$35

In the 1960s kids could make their own "Land of the Giants" spaceship out of toothpicks. Today, the Remco kit is worth about $50 in Excellent condition.

Paper dolls, Saalfield, 1972.......................................$50

Puzzle, David Cassidy, life-size, 84 pieces, APC, 1973 ....$75

Sheet music, "I Think I Love You," Columbia $20

Pee-Wee Herman

Coloring book, Scholastic, 1979.................................$15

Doll, talking, with pull string, MIB $150

Figure, 6", Pee-Wee with scooter, MIP.......................$40

Lunch box and thermos, plastic, 1987 ....$30

View-Master, three discs and booklet, #4074, GAF...$15

The Rat Patrol

Coloring book, eight pages, Saalfield, 1966 ....$25

Comic books, six, 1967, each $20

Costume, leader of the pack, Ben Cooper, 1967...........$65

Doll, Jack Moffit, Marx, 1967 ....$80

Game board, Rat Patrol Desert Combat game, Transogram, 1967 ....$50

Jeep, Midget Motors Jeep, Remco, 1967.....................$50

Lunch box, metal, action scenes, thermos, Aladdin, 1967,...$50

Model, diorama, battle scene, Aurora, 1967.................$80

Play set, dolls, accessories, Marx, 1967.....................$700

The Rifleman

Comics, Dell/Gold Key, 1959-64................................$35

Figure, cowboy and horse, Hartland, 1960 ....$65

Game board, The Rifleman Game, Milton Bradley, 1959 ....$50

Gun, plastic replica of Lucas's Winchester, Hubley, 1959 ....$75

Lunch box, Lucas and bank robbers, metal, thermos, Aladdin, 1961 ....$125

Paint set, Paint-by-Number, cutouts, Standard Toykraft, 1960...$75

Play set, tin houses, figures, fences, horses, wagon, accessories, Marx, 1959...$425

Playsuit, cowboy outfit, logo and Lucas McCain, Pla-Master, 1959 ....$175

S.W.A.T.

Cap gun, .45, 1975 ....$30

Model, police helicopter, 1977 ....$20

Puzzle, 1975 ....$20

Rifle, 1975..$25

Scooby-Doo

Coloring book, 1982 ....$15

Lunch box, thermos, steel, King Seeley, 1973............$100

Radio, Scooby-Doo, 1970s $75

View-Master, "That's Snow Ghost," GAF 1972 ....$15

Six Million Dollar Man

Activity book, Rand McNally, 1977 ....$15

Board game, The Six Million Dollar Man, Parker Brothers, 1975..$20

Costume, Steve Austin, Ben Cooper, 1974...................$20

Doll, Steve Austin, with bionic grip, Kenner, 1975......$55

Play-Doh set, Kenner, 1977 ....$20

Poster Put-Ons, Steve Austin adhesives, Bi-Rite, 1978... $10

Raincoat, yellow, with logo, Steve Austin on back, Universal, 1976 .... $50

Tattoos and stickers, Kenner, 1976 .... $15

Trash can, Steve Austin in action, Cheinco, 1976 .... $35

View-Master, three reels, booklet, #B559, GAF.......... $20

Wristwatch, The Six Million Dollar Man, Universal, 1976 .... $85

Voyage to the Bottom of the Sea

Coloring book, book and crayons, Whitman, 1964 .... $25

Comics, 16 different, Dell/Gold Key, 1961-70, each $15

Four-Way sub gun, makes four different guns, Remco, 1965 .... $575

Game board, Voyage to the Bottom of the Sea, Milton Bradley, 1964 .... $50

Lunch box, Seaview and characters, thermos, Aladdin, 1967 .... $75

Model, Flying Sub, Aurora, 1968 .... $300

Model, Seaview, Aurora, 1966.................................... $300

Play set, Submarine Scout set, Remco, 1965.............. $100

View-Master, #B483, GAF $15

Welcome Back, Kotter

Card game, Welcome Back, Kotter, Milton Bradley, 1976 .... $20

Chalkboard, Kotter and the Sweathogs, Board King, 1976.. $60

Colorforms, Welcome Back, Kotter, Colorforms, 1976 .... $20

Costume, Kotter, Collegeville, 1976 .... $25

Educational calculating wheel, multiplying wheel, Pamco, 1976 .... $15

Folders, whole group or individual Sweathogs, Mead, 1977... $7

Magic slates, two styles, Whitman, 1977 .... $20

Paint-by-Number, Sweathogs, Craft Master, 1976 .... $35

Puzzles, jigsaw, several different, HG Toys, 1976, each $15

View-Master, three reels, booklet, #J19, GAF, 1977 .... $20

Zorro

Action set, hat, mask, whip, knife, Marx, 1958 .... $250

Bean Bag Game, Gardner Toys, 1960........................... $70

Comics, Dell, 1959-61, each.. $65

Costume, Zorro, mask, Ben Cooper, 1958.................. $125

Game board, Whitman, 1965 .... $25

Game board, Walt Disney's Zorro Game, Whitman, Parker Bros. 1966... $35

Game, target, with dart gun, Knickerbocker, 1950s $45

Lunch box, Aladdin, Zorro posing, thermos, 1966....... $75

Model, Aurora, Zorro kit, 1965 .... $200

Paint set, four canvases, oil paints, Hassenfeld, 1960.. $50

Play set, town with trees, fences and figures, Marx, 1958 .... $700

Puzzle, jigsaw, Jaymar, 1958 .... $25

View-Master, three reels, booklet, #B469, GAF.......... $40

Miscellaneous TV Shows

Adam-12, comic books, Whitman, 1974, each............. $20

Bugaloos, lunch box, metal, thermos, Aladdin, 1971 .... $65

Davy Crockett, child's vest, 1950s.............................. $55

Dragnet, Jack Webb official badge, Knickerbocker, 1955.. $150

Eight is Enough, puzzle, jigsaw, APC, 1978 .... $15

Family, Kristy McNichol doll, Mego, 1978.................. $40

Fantasy Island, Tattoo costume, Ben Cooper, 1978...... $35

Flipper, coloring book, Whitman, 1966 .... $25

Gidget, Fortune Teller game, Milton Bradley, 1966... $35

Gilligan's Island, board game, The New Adventures of Gilligan, Milton Bradley, 1974 .... $35

Good Times, doll, J.J. Shindana Toys, 1975................. $50

Green Acres, paper doll book, two dolls, Whitman, 1967.. $60

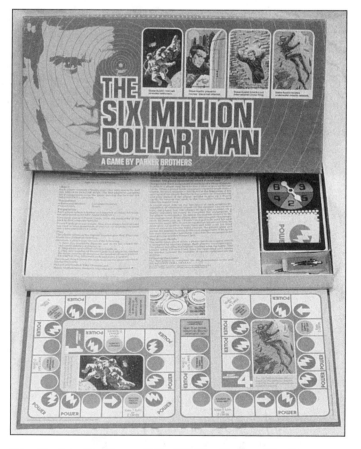

The Parker Brothers "Six Million Dollar Man" game is a good buy at $10-$15, but make sure it's complete.

H.R. Pufnstuf, vinyl puppets, eight different,
Remco, 1970, each $65

I Dream of Jeannie, decorative bottle, Jim Beam,
1964 .... $75

Julia, paper dolls, four, Saalfield, 1969, each $50

Kojak, toy gun on keychain, MIP $25

Lassie, plush doll, 13" long, with original tags,
rubber face, 1950s $75

Leave It To Beaver, Little Golden Book,
Whitman, 1959 .... $25

Life and Times of Grizzly Adams, trash can,
Cheinco, 1977 .... $30

Little House on the Prairie, costume, Laura,
Ben Cooper, 1970s $25

Little House on the Prairie, dolls, Laura or Carrie, Knickerbocker, 1978 .... $50

The Love Boat, World Cruise game,
Ungame, 1980 .... $25

The Love Boat Playset, Multi-Toys, 1983 .... $100

Mod Squad, puzzle, jigsaw, Milton Bradley,
1969, shows cast... $45

My Favorite Martian, Martian Magic Tricks,
boxed set, 1964... $250

The Patty Duke Show, coloring book,
Whitman, 1966... $30

Punky Brewster, coloring book, Golden, 1986 .... $5

Petticoat Junction, paper doll booklet, 1964 .... $50

Ren & Stimpy, card game, 1992 .... $20

Ren & Stimpy, cereal premium, target toss, 1994 .... $25

Sigmund and the Sea Monsters Game, board,
Milton Bradley, 1975 .... $30

Starsky and Hutch, handcuffs and wallet set,
Fleetwood, 1976... $35

That Girl, coloring book, Saalfield, 1970 .... $30

That Girl, paper doll booklet, Saalfield, 1967.............. $45

Three's Company, jigsaw puzzle, Chrissy,
APC, 1978 .... $20

Three's Company, doll, Chrissy, Mego, 1978.............. $50

T.J. Hooker, wallet, cuffs and badge, 1982, MIP $10

Vega$, binoculars, 1978, MIP...................................... $25

The Waltons, Farmhouse playset, Mego, 1974........... $100

The Waltons, paper dolls, 27 pieces and two dolls, Whit-
man, 1974.. $30

Wonder Woman, doll, Mego, 1978 .... $75

VEHICLE TOYS

Modern man has always been fascinated with machines that move. Partial evidence of this is the amazing number of toy vehicles that have been produced in the 20th century. In fact, it could be reasonably argued that toy vehicles are collected more than any other type of toy.

With the dawn of the modern industrial age, the mass production of full-sized automobiles and their toy counterparts seemed to go hand-in-hand. As cars rolled off the assembly lines, their miniature replicas were not far behind.

Cars and trucks weren't the only toy vehicles, however. Any sort of vehicle—including boats, planes and horse-drawn wagons—was a natural for miniaturization. The types and manufacturers of toy vehicles were as varied as the real things, too. Toy makers crafted them with everything from cast iron and tin to wood and plastic.

The earliest toy automobiles came along soon after their big daddy originals in the late 19th century; they were produced in cast iron. But it wasn't until after World War I that toy automobile production really began to hit its stride.

Today, vehicle toys—from airplanes to buses to cars to trucks—come in every shape, size, scale and medium. Collectors never run out of choices, and that's why toy vehicle collecting never slows down.

Background and General Guidelines:
Arcade, A.C. Williams and Hubley were major makers of cast-iron vehicles in the late 1800s. These sturdy vehicles, among the best known and sought-after, have been known to sell for $10,000 or more for prime examples.

Although it began producing toys in the late 1800s, Arcade Manufacturing, of Freeport, Ill., didn't issue its first toy vehicle—a replica of a Chicago Yellow Cab—until around 1920. After that, several realistic models of actual cars, trucks and busses followed. The company's slogan was "They Look Real."

During this time, a Pennsylvania company, Hubley, was also producing fine quality cast-iron vehicles, mainly horse-drawn wagons, trains and guns. By the 1930s, the company was producing its most well-known products, many patterned after actual automobiles of that time.

A.C. Williams, beginning in the late 1800s, was also making cast-iron vehicles, but on a smaller scale. The Ohio-based company's toys, designed for the five-and-dime stores of that time, are difficult to identify because the toys bear no markings.

Although heavy cast-iron toys ruled the market at the turn of the century, lithographed tin toys found a niche during the 1920s, led by Louis Marx. This leader produced an extensive line of tin toy cars, trucks, airplanes and farm equipment, but also began offering steel, and later, plastic versions.

Beginning in the mid-1900s, large toy trucks were now being made of pressed steel and cast metal by companies like Buddy L., Structo, Tonka and Smith-Miller. Buddy L, one of the most famous producers of heavy-duty trucks, created toys meant for kids to play with, not for sitting on a dresser or bookshelf.

Heavy-duty constructed Buddy L toys from the 1920s and 1930s, produced by the Moline Pressed Steel Co. of Moline, Ill., are among that company's most valuable collectible vehicles. Starting in the 1930s, the company began using lighter-weight materials. These issues, and those thereafter, do not command the high collector prices as those issued during the company's heyday.

Smith-Miller trucks, produced by a company that specialized in "famous trucks in miniature," also offered large trucks, using cast-metal and aluminum. The company, founded by Bob Smith and Matt Miller, was later known as Miller-Ironson Corp., but is more commonly known as Smitty Toys. The Smith-Miller name continues today, through limited-edition trucks, but the company has made its mark with its Mack trucks, due to their outstanding quality.

Additional toy vehicle producers during this time included Marx, Wyandotte and, after World War II, numerous Japanese companies, such as Bandai, which used tin. Bandai produced wind-up, friction and battery-operated cars. Auburn Rubber Co., of Auburn, Ind., specialized in rubber toys.

Smaller die-cast vehicles, generally three to six inches long, came on the scene in the 1920s with Tootsietoys leading the way. The trade name, which began appearing regularly during the Roaring Twenties, originates from Tootsie, the name of the daughter of the company's founder, Samuel Dowst. By the 1930s, Tootsietoys was producing some of what have become the company's most highly prized toys.

THE TOP 10 VEHICLE TOYS!
(IN MINT CONDITION)

1. Packard Straight 8, Hubley $15,000
2. Checker Cab, No. 175, Arcade............................ $12,000
3. Elgin Street Sweeper, Hubley $11,500
4. World's Greatest Circus Truck, Keystone $10,000
5. Ingersoll-Rand Compressor, Hubley.................. $10,000
6. Motorized Sidecar Motorcycle, Hubley $10,000
7. Ahrens-Fox Fire Engine, Hubley $8,000
8. Seven-Man Fire Patrol, Hubley........................... $7,500
9. Tractor Dredge (on Treads), Buddy L.................. $7,500
10. White Bus, No. 319, Arcade $7,400

But its Federal vans from the 1920s are among the most sought-after vehicles, especially those with company logos.

Being mass produced and economically priced, Tootsietoys were widely available in the five-and-dime arena. The success of these products no doubt led to several competitors.

One of those competitors, Barclay, produced vehicles of a lesser quality, but offered a few innovations, such as replacing metal tires with white rubber ones during the 1930s, and switching from wood to metal for axles. After World War II, black tires replaced the white versions.

Meanwhile, in Europe, Dinky toys were being produced from 1933 though the 1970s in England and France. Generally of high quality, these toys were generally 1:43 in scale.

Other highly collectible small die-cast vehicles are Corgi (beginning in the late 1950s, by England's Mettoy Co.), Mattel's Hot Wheels, and Matchbox, one of the best known series of toy cars. Although the Matchbox company, Lesney, is better known for its three-inch vehicles, it also produced several larger vehicles before it began the Matchbox line. Some of these early Lesney vehicles are valued at up to $2,000 each.

The England-based company, which began after World War II, is derived from a combination of the founders' two names, LESlie and RodNEY Smith. After tinkering with several products, the company hit paydirt with its "Matchbox" line, issuing its 1-75 Series of 75 models each year.

Due to the popularity of this series, a United States company, Mattel, began producing its line of colorful hot rods that appealed to youngsters—Hot Wheels, with their California-type appeal. Lesney, which had been producing as many as 5.5 million cars a week, soon lost the battle with the California-based Mattel and went into receivership. Matchbox was later restructured, sold twice and eventually landed with Tyco Toys, which, in 1996, was purchased by Mattel. Thus, Mattel now offers the Matchbox line of cars. Today, these small-scale, die-cast vehicles enjoy a high level of interest among collectors for their size, detail and relative affordability.

General Guidelines: Rarity is a key factor with cast-iron and steel vehicles from the 1930s and earlier—therefore Near Mint or better examples can cost almost as much as an actual automobile. Vintage cast iron is almost never found in Mint condition, so imperfections may be more acceptable than those found on a small die-cast car.

Defects in die-cast vehicles may lessen their value 25 percent or more. Boxes are hard to come by for earlier vehicles, but almost all modern vehicle collectors desire original packages.

Numerous body style and color variations can greatly affect vehicle pricing. Vehicles in rarer colors will be worth more. Sure-fire winners among vehicle toys are those bearing advertising logos or character images, such as a Buddy L Coca-Cola truck, a Corgi Batmobile or James Bond car, Marx's Charlie Chaplin car or Tootsietoy's Buck Rogers destroyer.

Anything from the 1940s or earlier is worth picking up if the price is right. But beware of the many current reproductions in cast iron and other metals.

Trends: Values remain strong for vehicle toys of all kinds. Demand for die-cast examples, including Hot Wheels, Johnny Lightning and Matchbox, has been on the rise as many children who grew up with these toys are reaching their late 20s and early 30s.

Attempting to meet this nostalgic collector demand, some replicas and reissues are reaching the retail and secondary marketplaces at reasonable prices. By contrast, while values for cast-iron toys haven't experienced drastic declines, they will bear close watching as their main collecting audience ages.

Contributor to this section: Arcade, Conrad Schwager, 10321 N. Trails Edge Dr., Peoria, IL 61615.

Clubs

- American International Matchbox, 532 Chestnut St., Lynn, MA 01904

- Aviation Toys, P.O. Box 845, Greenwich, CT 06836

- Dinky Toy Club of America, P.O. Box 11, Highland, MD 20777

- Toy Car Collectors Club, 33290 W. 14 Mile Road, #454, West Bloomfield, MI 48322

Recommended Reading

Books

O'Brien's Collecting Toy Cars & Trucks, Elizabeth Stephan
O'Brien's Collecting Toys, Ninth Edition, Elizabeth Stephan
2000 Toys & Prices, Sharon Korbeck and Elizabeth Stephan
Die Cast Price Guide, Douglas R. Kelly

Periodicals

Toy Cars & Vehicles
Toy Shop

VALUE LINE

Values shown are for items in Excellent to Mint condition. Certain variations (such as color or accessories) may increase value. Cars in original boxes or packaging command a premium. Hot Wheels are listed in a separate chapter.

Arcade (cast iron, 1920s-1930s)

A.C.F Bus, 1927	$2,200-$3,500
Allis-Chalmers Tractor Trailer, 1937, #2650, 13" long, with trailer	$375-$500
Ambulance, 1932, #187	$700-$1,200
Anthony Dump Truck, 1927	$1,500-$2,400
Austin Racer, 1932, #175X	$90-$135
Austin Wrecker, 1932, #177X	$150-$225
Borden's Milk Bottle Truck, 1936, #2640X	$1,200-$2,500
Buick Opera Coupe, 1927	$2,900-$4,900
Buick Sedan, 1927	$2,500-$4,000

Caterpillar Tractor, 1931, #266X ....$75-$100
Caterpillar Tractor, 1930, #271 ....$800-$1,300
Checker Cab, 1932, #157...........................$8,000-$12,000
Chevrolet Coupe, 1934, rumble seat..................$250-$350
Chevrolet Sedan, 1934 ....$110-$180
Chief Fire Chief Coupe, 1934, #1230..........$2,500-$3,400
Corn Harvester, 1939, #4180 ....$175-$250
Double Decker Bus, 1939, #3180 ....$450-$750
Dump Truck, 1936, #2320 ....$130-$200
Express Truck, 1929, #214X............................$250-$400
Fire Engine, 1941, #6990................................$950-$1,525
Fire Ladder Truck, 1936, #1820 ....$250-$400
Ford Model A Coupe, 1928, #113X ....$300-$400
Ford Model T Coupe, 1923.............................$300-$450
Ford Model T Stake Truck, 1927....................$925-$1,250
Fordson Tractor, 1928, #273 ....$150-$200
Greyhound Lines Bus, 1937, #3850 SP ....$275-$400
Ice Truck, 1941, #1933 ....$355-$540
International Dump Truck, 1936, #3030......$1,600-$2,200
International Stake Truck, 1936, #3090.......$1,100-$2,000
Mack Cement Mixer, 1931 ....$900-$1,200
Mack High Dump Truck, 1931, #244X ....$1,600-$2,300
Mack Tank Truck, 1925 ....$1,600-$2,800
Nash Coupe, 1943...$400-$650
National Trailways Bus, 1937, #3870..........$1,200-$1,700
New York World's Fair Bus, 1939, #3750 ....$200-$300
Oliver Tractor, 1941, #3560 ....$500-$700
Pontiac Sedan, 1935, #1350............................$250-$375
Racer, 1932, #137 ....$180-$240
Red Baby Dump Truck, 1923, #1 ....$1,500-$2,500
Stake Truck, 1929, #213 ....$200-$325
Tank, Army, 1941, #3960.................................$200-$300
Tractor, 1941, #7200.......................................$270-$360
Trailer, Farm, 1929, #288................................$150-$250
White Bus, 1928, #319....................................$5,500-$7,400
Wrecker, 1937, #1503 ....$150-$200
Yellow Cab, 1936, #1580Y ....$2,800-$4,000
Yellow Couch Double-Decker Bus,
    1925...$2,500-$4,000

Auburn (rubber, 1930s-1940s)

1947 Buick Coupe, #100 on license ....$115-$150
Airport Limousine...$40-$50
Allis-Chalmers Tractor, 1950...........................$40-$50
Army Jeep ....$7-$10
Army Recon Half Truck ....$15-$20
Battleship, 1941 ....$25-$30
Clipper Plane, 1941...$20-$25
Dive Bomber, 1937 ....$20-$25
Earthmover..$25-$30
Fire Engine...$25-$30
Fire Truck...$10-$15
Ford, 1930s ....$20-$25
John Deere Tractor..$40-$50
Motorcycle ....$30-$40
Police Cycle, 1950s..$75-$100

Classic vintage vehicle toys in nice condition can sell for thousands. This group, sold at a recent Christie's auction in New York, includes (top row) a 1930s Chien Hercules tinplate Motor Express Truck that went for $750, a 1927 Sturditoy pressed steel Wells Fargo Truck that sold for $2,300; (middle row) a 1928 Buddy-L pressed steel Baggage Line Truck that brought $2,185, a 1925 Buddy-L steelplate Oil Tanker Truck that went for $1,725; and (bottom) a 1929 Buddy-L pressed steel Passenger Bus that sold for $3,680.

Race Car, red, rubber ....$65-$85
Racer, rubber..$30-$40
Rescue Truck..$25-$30
Sedan, green ....$25-$30
Stake Truck ....$25-$30
Submarine, 1941 ....$20-$27
Telephone Truck ....$55-$75

Bandai (tin, 1950s-1960s, friction unless noted)

1956 Buick, green ....$60-$85
1956 Chevrolet Convertible, cream ....$315-$450
1958 Chrysler Imperial Convertible, maroon ....$245-$350
1958 Ford Station Wagon, two-tone green ....$85-$125
1958 Ford Ranchero Pickup Truck ....$175-$225
1961 Plymouth Valiant, blue.............................$105-$150
1964 Ford Fairlane, red.....................................$50-$85
1965 Ford Mustang, cream/black ....$90-$125
1967 Chevrolet Camaro, battery ....$100-$140
Cadillac, 1959, white ....$175-$225
Chevrolet Corvette, 1963, red ....$125-$175
Cougar, white, battery..$150-$200
Ferrari, 1958, silver, battery..............................$550-$850
Ferrari and speed boat set, 1958 ....$650-$900
Fiat 600, 1950s, blue..$70-$100
Ford Convertible, 1955, green ....$650-$900
Ford F.B.I. Mustang, 1965, black and white......$100-$140

Ford GT, 1960, red, battery ....$150-$200
Ford Mustang, 1967, red, battery ....$125-$175
Ford Ranchero, 1955...$250-$350
Ford Thunderbird, 1965, red and black ....$175-$225
Ford Wagon, 1957, blue and white ....$150-$200
Jaguar 3.4 Sedan, 1960s, light green.................$125-$175
Land Rover, 1960, red..$100-$150
Lincoln Continental, 1958,
    turquoise and white ....$250-$375
Lincoln Continental and Cabin Cruiser,
    1958...$550-$800
Lotus Elite, 1950s, red and black......................$100-$150
Mercedes-Benz 219 Convertible, blue..............$125-$175
Old Timer Police Car, battery operated ....$95-$125
Plymouth Ambulance, 1961, white.....................$50-$75
Plymouth Valiant, blue wind-up ....$75-$100
Porsche 911, 1960s, white, battery operated......$150-$200
Rolls-Royce Convertible, 1950s ....$300-$450
Taxi, 1950s ....$115-$150
Volkswagen, 1960, red, battery...........................$75-$100
Volkswagen Bus, 1960s, red and white,
    battery...$150-$275
Volkswagen Truck, 1960s, blue, battery ....$150-$200

Barclay (die-cast, 1930s-1940s)
Armoured Car, 1937 ....$25-$35
Beer Truck..$25-$35
Coupe, 1930s...$40-$55
Dirigible Plane, 1930s...$10-$15
Double-Decker Bus..$30-$40
Fordson Tractor #203...$20-$25
Howitzer Cannon ....$25-$35
Milk Truck #377..$40-$55
Monoplane ....$30-$40
Mortar Cannon...$30-$40
Race Car...$40-$55
U.S. Army Single Engine Transport Plane,
    1940...$15-$20

Buddy L (pressed steel, 1920s-1960s)
Aerial Ladder and Emergency Truck, 1952.......$300-$400
Aerial Ladder Fire Engine, 1961 ....$185-$250
Air Mail Truck, 1930 ....$1,000-$1,400
Allied Moving Van, 1941................................$900-$1,200
Army Combination Set, 1956 ....$400-$500
Army Staff Car, 1964...$150-$200
Army Supply Truck, 1956 ....$150-$175
ArmyTruck, 1940...$200-$250
Auto Hauler, 1970..$95-$130
Baggage Truck, 1930-32..................................$5,000-$7,000
Big Brute Mixer Truck, 1971...............................$50-$70
Big Brute 3-piece Road Set, 1971.......................$150-$200
Big Mack Dumper, 1967.......................................$100-$140
Borden's Milk Delivery Van, 1965 ....$200-$275
Brute Cement Mixer Truck, 1968 ....$55-$75
Brute Farm Tractor-n-Cart, 1969 ....$40-$55
Brute Fire Department Set, 1970 ....$115-$150

Brute Fire Pumper, 1969..$50-$75
Brute Hook-N-Ladder, 1969.................................$40-$55
Brute Road Grader, 1970 ....$75-$100
Buddy L Milk Farms Truck, 1945 ....$300-$450
Buddywagon, 1966 ....$150-$200
Camper, 1965 ....$75-$100
Catapult Airplane and Hangar, 1930............$1,200-$1,500
Cattle Transport Truck, 1956 ....$115-$150
Cement Mixer on Treads, 1929-31 ....$3,500-$4,500
Cement Mixer Truck, 1964..................................$95-$125
City Baggage Dray, 1939.....................................$250-$300
Coal Truck, 1927..$1,000-$2,000
Coca-Cola Delivery Truck, 1964 ....$95-$125
Colt Sportsliner, 1968 ....$45-$65
Concrete Mixer, 1949...$150-$200
Country Squire Wagon, 1965...............................$115-$150
Dandy Digger, 1953..$115-$150
Deluxe Convertible Coupe, 1949 ....$450-$600
Deluxe Rider Delivery Truck, 1945....................$200-$270
Deluxe Rider Dump Truck, 1945.........................$115-$150
Desert Rats Command Car, 1967.........................$75-$100
Dr. Pepper Delivery Truck Van, 1966.................$130-$175
Dump Truck, 1941 ....$130-$175
Dump Truck, 1935 ....$485-$650
Dump-n-Dozer, 1962 ....$115-$150
Dumper with Shovel, 1963 ....$115-$150
Express Truck, 1930-32 ....$4,500-$6,000
Extension Ladder Fire Truck, 1945 ....$300-$400
Family Camping Set, 1964 ....$75-$100
Fast Delivery Pickup, 1949 ....$150-$200
Fire and Chemical Truck, 1949............................$185-$250
Fire Department Set, 1960 ....$375-$500
Fire Engine, 1925-29 ....$800-$1,600
Fire Pumper, 1968..$150-$200
Fire Truck, 1928..$800-$1,200
Fire Truck, 1930..$1,000-$1,600
Fire Truck, 1939...$700-$1,000
Fire Truck, 1948...$200-$250
Fisherman, 1962..$120-$160
Flivver Dump Truck, 1926.................................$1,000-$1,500
Flivver Scoop Dump Truck, 1926-27 ....$2,500-$3,500
Four-Engine Transport, 1949 ....$300-$400
Giant Digger, 1933...$395-$525
Giant Hydraulic Dumper, 1961............................$200-$275
GMC Airway Express Van, 1957.........................$350-$450
GMC Brinks Bank Set, 1959 ....$350-$450
GMC Coca-Cola Route Truck, 1957 ....$300-$400
GMC Livestock Set, 1958....................................$400-$500
GMC Self-Loading Auto Carrier, 1959 ....$300-$400
Hertz Auto Hauler, 1965......................................$150-$200
Highway Construction Set, 1962 ....$300-$400
Highway Hawk Trailer Van, 1985 ....$75-$100
Hook & Ladder Fire Truck, 1923 ....$1,800-$2,400
Hose Truck, 1933..$750-$1,000
Husky Dumper, 1961 ....$125-$140

Husky Tractor, 1966...$75-$100
Hydraulic Dump Truck, 1926 ....$800-$1,000
Hydraulic Hi-Lift Dumper, 1953 ....$115-$150
Hydraulic Sturdy Dumper, 1969 ....$75-$100
Hydraulic Water Tower Truck, 1933............$1,000-$1,700
Ice Truck, 1926 ....$900-$1,600
Insurance Patrol, 1925 ....$1,000-$1,300
International Dump Truck, 1935.......................$485-$650
Jolly Joe Popsicle Truck, 1948 ....$425-$550
Jr. Animal Farm Set, 1968 ....$185-$250
Jr. Animal Ark, 1970..$60-$80
Jr. Beach Buggy, 1971 ....$50-$70
Jr. Canada Dry Delivery Truck, 1968 ....$150-$200
Jr. Dump Truck, 1967 ....$75-$100
Jr. Fire Emergency Truck, 1969 ....$75-$100
Jr. Fire Snorkel Truck, 1968...........................$150-$200
Jr. Kitty Kennel, 1968 ....$85-$115
Jr. Sanitation Truck, 1968 ....$115-$150
Jr. Sportster, 1968...$55-$75
Kennel Truck, 1966...$145-$190
Ladder Truck, 1939..$200-$300
Lumber Truck, 1926 ....$1,300-$2,700
Mechanical Crane, 1952 ....$225-$300
Milkman Truck, 1961 ....$175-$225
Mister Buddy Ice Cream Truck, 1966 ....$75-$100
Mobile Construction Derrick, 1953 ....$250-$350
Model T Flivver Truck, 1924....................$1,500-$2,000
Moving Van, 1924.....................................$2,000-$3,000
Overhead Crane, 1924 ....$2,000-$3,000
Overhead Trailer Truck, 1939.........................$550-$700
Pepsi Delivery Truck, 1970..............................$95-$125
Police Colt, 1968...$75-$100
Polysteel Dumper, 1959 ....$150-$200
Polysteel Hydraulic Dumper, 1962....................$100-$130
Polysteel Milkman Truck, 1960.......................$100-$130
Pumping Fire Engine, 1929 ....$3,500-$4,000
Railway Express Truck, 1930 ....$1,000-$2,000
REA Express Truck, 1964 ....$300-$400
Red Cross Ambulance, 1958.............................$95-$125
Rider Dump Truck, 1945 ....$245-$325
Ruff-n-Tuff Cement Mixer Truck, 1971 ....$55-$75
Road Builder Set, 1963 ....$300-$400
Ryder Van Lines Trailer, 1949 ....$525-$700
Sand and Gravel Truck, 1926.....................$1,000-$1,200
Sand Loader, 1931 ....$250-$350
Sanitation Service Truck, 1967 ....$150-$200
Scoop-n-Load Conveyor ....1956 $85-$115
Sears Roebuck Delivery Truck Van, 1967 ....$200-$275
Self-Loading Car Carrier, 1964 ....$95-$125
Shell Pickup and Delivery, 1952......................$185-$250
Ski Bus, 1967...$115-$150
Sprinkler Truck, 1929 ....$1,500-$2,000
Stake Body Truck, 1921................................$1,500-$2,000
Standard Oil Tank Truck, 1936-37..................$500-$1,000
Station Wagon, 1963.......................................$115-$150

Steam Shovel, 1921-22 ....$250-$500
Street Sprinkler Truck, 1930-32..................$1,000-$1,900
Suburban Wagon, 1964 ....$100-$140
Super Market Delivery, 1956 ....$115-$150
Tank and Sprinkler Truck, 1924.....................$900-$1,700
Texaco Tank Truck, 1959................................$250-$400
Transport Airplane, 1946 ....$300-$400
Trailer Van Truck, 1956.................................$225-$300
Traveling Crane, 1928................................$1,900-$2,500
Traveling Zoo, 1967.......................................$115-$150
Trench Digger, 1928-31 ....$3,500-$5,000
United Parcel Delivery Van, 1941....................$450-$650
U.S. Mail Delivery Truck, 1956.......................$300-$500
Utility Dump Truck, 1941...............................$130-$175
Warehouse Set, 1959......................................$225-$300
Water Tower Truck, 1929..........................$4,500-$6,000
Wild Animal Circus, 1966 ....$225-$300
Wrecker Truck, 1930 ....$1,000-$2,500
Yellow Taxi with Skyview, 1948......................$400-$600
Zoo-A-Rama, 1968 ....$150-$200

Corgi (die-cast, 1950s-1960s)
Adams Probe 16...$25-$40
AMC Pacer..$20-$35
Army Equipment Transporter ....$105-$175
Austin A60 Driving School ....$65-$110
Austin London Taxi, yellow interior....................$55-$90
Austin Mini Van..$60-$100
Austin Police Mini Van...................................$75-$175
Batbike ....$60-$125

Over the years, Matchbox produced several lines of toy vehicles, including a series of "Models of Yesteryear." Having vehicles in their original boxes can increase the value substantially.

Batboat, red seats	$90-$175
Batcopter	$35-$95
Batmobile, no tow hook	$300-$500
Beach Buggy & Sailboat	$30-$50
Beatles' Yellow Submarine	$270-$450
Bedford Army Tanker	$210-$350
Bedford Daily Express Van	$90-$150
Bedford Fire Tender	$90-$150
Bedford Milk Tanker, rubber tires	$150-$250
Bedford Tanker	$20-$35
Beep Beep London Bus	$40-$65
Bell Army Helicopter	$35-$60
Bentley Continental	$65-$110
Berliet Dolphinarium Truck	$85-$175
Bertone Shake Buggy	$18-$30
Bloodhound Loading Trolley	$60-$100
Bloodhound Missile	$105-$175
BMC Mini-Cooper S Rally	$60-$100
Breakdown Truck	$18-$30
BRM Racing Car	$75-$125
Buick & Cabin Cruiser	$120-$200
Buick Police Car	$27-$45
Buick Riviera	$45-$75
Campbell Bluebird	$85-$175
Captain America Jetmobile	$36-$60
Caterpillar Tractor	$105-$175
Chevrolet Camaro SS	$45-$95
Chevrolet Caprice Classic	$36-$60
Chevrolet Charlie's Angels Van	$15-$40
Chevrolet Coca-Cola Van	$20-$35
Chevrolet Impala	$75-$125
Chevrolet Impala Taxi	$75-$125
Chevrolet State Patrol Car	$75-$125
Chitty Chitty Bang Bang	$270-$425
Chopper Squad Helicopter	$30-$50
Circus Cage Wagon	$84-$140
Circus Crane Truck	$120-$200
Circus Human Cannonball Truck	$45-$75
Citroen DS 19 Rally	$105-$175
Citroen Le Dandy Coupe	$105-$175
Citroen Winter Olympics Car	$105-$200
Coast Guard Jaguar XJ12C	$27-$45
Commer Ton Ambulance	$55-$90
Commer Ton Pickup	$45-$75
Commer Holiday Mini Bus	$45-$75
Commer Military Police Van	$80-$130
Concorde-First Issues, Japan Airlines	$420-$700
Corporal Missile Launcher, 1960-61	$55-$90
Corvette Sting Ray	$60-$100
Daily Planet Helicopter	$36-$60
Datsun 240Z	$20-$35
Decca Airfield Radar Van	$180-$350
Dodge Livestock Truck	$50-$85
Dropside Trailer	$15-$25
ERF 44G Moorhouse Van	$150-$250
ERG 64G Earth Dumper	$45-$75
Euclid TC-12 Bulldozer	$120-$200
Ferrari 308GTS	$20-$35
Ferrari Berlinetta 250LM	$45-$75
Ferrari Daytona	$20-$35
Fiat 1800	$36-$60
Fiat 2100	$33-$55
Fire Bug	$30-$50
Fire Engine	$24-$40
Ford Capri	$20-$35
Ford Car Transporter	$30-$50
Ford Consul	$65-$110
Ford Cortina Estate Car	$55-$90
Ford Escort 13 GL	$12-$20
Ford Esso Tank Truck	$25-$40
Ford Exxon Tank Truck	$25-$40
Ford Gulf Tank Truck	$25-$40
Ford Mustang Fastback	$45-$95
Ford Sierra	$15-$20
Ford Thunderbird 1957	$15-$25
Ford Torino Road Hog	$20-$35
Ford Transit Milk Float	$25-$40
Ford Transit Wrecker	$35-$60
Fordson Power Major Tractor	$75-$125
Futuristic Space Vehicle	$18-$30
Ghia-Fiat 600 Jolly	$90-$150
Golden Eagle Jeep	$15-$20
GP Beach Buggy	$20-$35
Green Hornet's Black Beauty	$275-$500
Hardy Boys' Rolls-Royce	$105-$200
Hillman Hunter	$65-$125
Hillman Imp	$45-$75
Honda Prelude	$15-$20
Hughes Police Helicopter	$30-$50
Jaguar 2.4 Litre	$80-$130
Jaguar E Type	$65-$110
Jaguar XJS	$15-$25
James Bond Aston Marton, 4"	$150-$275
James Bond Moon Buggy	$275-$525
James Bond Space Shuttle	$45-$75
Jeep & Horse Box	$25-$40
Jeep CJ-5	$15-$20
Jeep FC-150 Pickup	$55-$90
JPS Lotus Racing Car	$45-$75
Karrier Butcher Shop	$100-$165
Karrier Dairy Van	$75-$125
Karrier Mobile Grocery	$110-$185
Kojak's Blue Regal	$40-$85
Lamborghini Miura	$45-$75
Land Rover 109WB	$18-$30
Land Rover Breakdown Truck	$35-$60
Land Rover Circus Vehicle	$90-$150
Lincoln Continental	$90-$150
Lotus Eleven	$95-$160
Lotus Racing Car	$35-$60

Lunar Bug ....$40-$85
Mack Esso Tank Truck...................................$30-$50
Mack Exxon Tank Truck..................................$25-$40
Marcos Matis ....$35-$55
Massey Ferguson 165 Tractor..........................$55-$90
Massey Ferguson Combine................................$90-$150
Massey Ferguson Tractor with Fork ....$90-$150
Mazda 4x4 Open Truck....................................$20-$35
Mazda Camper Pickup......................................$25-$40
Mercedes-Benz 220SE Coupe ....$60-$100
Mercedes-Benz 240D Taxi................................$18-$30
Mercedes-Benz 300SL Coupe ....$65-$110
Mercedes-Benz Ambulance...............................$20-$35
Mercedes-Benz Police Car................................$18-$30
Mercedes-Benz Tanker ....$18-$30
Metropolis Police Car ....$30-$50
MGC GT ....$75-$125
Milk Truck & Trailer ....$90-$150
Monkeemobile ....$225-$375
Morris Marina ....$25-$40
Motorway Ambulance.......................................$15-$25
NASA Space Shuttle...$45-$75
National Express Bus..$15-$20
Olds Toronado & Speedboat.............................$90-$150
Oldsmobile Super 88..$60-$100
Oldsmobile Toronado.......................................$55-$90
Penguinmobile ....$30-$65
Peugeot 505 Taxi..$15-$20
Playground ....$450-$750
Plymouth Sports Suburban ....$60-$100
Police Land Rover..$25-$40
Pontiac Firebird..$75-$125
Popeye's Paddle Wagon ....$300-$525
Porsche 917..$20-$35
Porsche 924 ....$15-$25
Porsche Carrera 6 ....$45-$75
Priestman Cub Crane ....$75-$125
Priestman Shovel & Carrier..............................$135-$225
Quartermaster Dragster....................................$45-$75
Radio Roadshow Van.......................................$35-$60
RAF Land Rover & Bloodhound.......................$240-$400
Range Rover Ambulance ....$30-$50
Renault 11 GTL ....$25-$40
Renault 5 Turbo ....$18-$30
Renault Floride...$55-$95
Renegade Jeep..$15-$20
Riley Pathfinder..$65-$110
Riley Pathfinder Police Car..............................$75-$125
Road Repair Unit ....$25-$40
Rolls-Royce Silver Ghost ....$25-$40
Rolls-Royce Silver Shadow ....$40-$65
Rover 2000...$45-$75
Rover 2000 Rally ....$75-$125
Rover 2000TC..$45-$75
Rover 90...$75-$125

Tonka is among the best-known names among toy vehicles. This Tonka "Sportsman" pickup, complete with cap and boat is valued at about $300 in Mint condition with its original box.

Saint's Jaguar XJS...$45-$75
Saint's Volvo P-1800...$85-$175
Scammell Circus Crane Truck ....$275-$450
Scania Bulk Carrier...$9-$15
Scania Container Truck......................................$9-$15
Scania Dump Truck ....$9-$15
Shadow-Ford Racing Car...................................$15-$25
Silver Jubilee Landau..$25-$40
Silverstone Racing Layout.................................$600-$1,200
Simon Snorkel Fire Engine................................$55-$90
Spider-Bike ....$60-$100
Spider-Buggy ....$75-$125
Spider-Copter...$45-$85
Starsky & Hutch Ford Torino.............................$55-$100
Studebaker Golden Hawk ....$85-$140
Stunt Motorcycle...$105-$175
Sunbeam Imp Rally...$35-$55
Superman Set ....$120-$225
Supermobile ....$45-$75
Tarzan Set...$150-$275
Thunderbird Missile & Trolley ....$85-$165
Tipping Farm Trailer..$15-$25
Touring Caravan..$25-$40
Toyota 2000 GT ....$25-$40
Tractor with Shovel & Trailer.............................$100-$165
Triumph Acclaim Driving School........................$25-$40
Triumph TR2...$100-$175
Tyrrell P34 Racing Car ....$30-$55
U.S. Racing Buggy ....$25-$45
Unimog Dump Truck...$30-$50

Vanwall Racing Car ....$55-$90
Volkswagen 1200, red interior ....$90-$150
Volkswagen Breakdown Van...........................$75-$125
Volkswagen Driving School...............................$40-$70
Volkswagen Pickup ....$65-$110
Volvo Concrete Mixer.....................................$45-$75
Volvo P-1800..$60-$100
VW Polo Police Car......................................$25-$40
VW Racing Tender & Cooper.........................$75-$125
White Wheelie Motorcycle ....$20-$35
Wild Honey Dragster ....$40-$65

Dinky (die-cast, 1930s-1970s)

A.W. Ensign, #68a, 1940 ....$300-$450
Airspeed Envoy, #62m, 1945-49.....................$125-$200
Ambulance, #30F..$160-$275
AMX Tank, #F80C/817....................................$75-$100
Atco Delivery Van, type 2, #28N, 1935-40........$375-$850
Atalanta, #66a, 194 ....0$450-$650
Austin/London Taxi, #284, 1972-79 ....$35-$75
Bedford Military Truck, #25WM/60 ....$125-$250
Beechcraft Baron, #715, 1968-76 ....$60-$90
B.E.V. Truck, #14A/400, 1954-60 ....$30-$70
Blaw Knox Bulldozer, #561.............................$75-$115
Boeing 737, #717, 1970-75 ....$45-$90
Boeing Flying Fortress, #62g, 1945-48 ....$125-$225
Bristol Blenheim, #62B, 1945-48 ....$95-$120
Cadillac Eldorado, #131, 1956-62 ....$95-$135
Caravan, postwar, #30G..................................$60-$85
Centurian Tank, #651......................................$50-$75
Chevrolet El Camino, #449, 1961-68 ....$65-$100
Citroen Milk Truck, #F586, 1961-65................$275-$600
Commer Fire Engine, #955, 1955-69 ....$85-$135
Continental Touring Coach, #953, 1963-66.......$200-$350
DeSoto Diplomat, orange, #F545, 1960-63 ....$85-$125
D.H. Albatross, #62w, 1939-41 ....$275-$400
D.H. Sea Vixen, #738, 1960-65 ....$65-$110
Dodge Royal, #191, 1959-64 ....$115-$150
Empire Flying Boat, #60x, 1938-40 ....$600-$1,000
Euclid Dump Truck...$75-$115
Foden Mobilgas Tanker, #941, 1954-57 ....$350-$750
Ford Thunderbird, South African issue,
     #F565 ....$250-$600
Ford Police Car, #F551, 1960s.........................$100-$150
Ford Transit Van, #417, 1978-80 ....$20-$30
General Monospar, #66e, 1940 ....$300-$350
Gloster Meteor, #70e/732, 1946-62 ....$25-$35
GMC Tanker, #F823 ....$250-$500
Guy Van, Lyons, #514.................................#550-$1,600
Hawker Hurricane, #62h, 1939-41....................$70-$115
Hayrake, #324, 1954-71..................................$40-$60
Jaguar XK 120, white, #157, 1954-62 ....$200-$400
Jeep, #F816 ....$75-$115
Junkers JU89, #62Y, 1945-49 ....$160-$225
Klingon Battle Cruiser, #357, 1976-79 ....$45-$70
Leland Tanker, Corn Products.....................$1,200-$3,000

Leopard Moth, 66b, 1940.................................$225-$300
Mercury Seaplane, #63b, 1939-41 ....$100-$175
Military Ambulance, #626................................$45-$75
Motor Truck, red/blue, #22C ....$350-$650
Mustang Fastback, #161, 1965-73 ....$55-$75
Nord Noratlas, #804, 1960-64 ....$250-$400
Percival Gull, #66c, 1945-48 ....$125-$150
Pickford's Delivery Van, type 1, 28B,
     1934-35 ....$500-$1,000
Plymouth Fury Sports, #115, 1965-69 ....$55-$80
Plymouth Plaza Taxi, #266, 1960-67 ....$95-$150
Police Motorcycle Patrol, #37B, 1938-40 ....$75-$125
Police Motorcyclist, #37B, 1946-48 ....$45-$70
Potez 63, #64c, 1939-48..................................$250-$400
Prisoner Mini-Moke.......................................$200-$340
Range Rover Ambulance, #268, 1974-78 ....$35-$50
Road Grader, #963, 1973-75 ....$45-$70
Rolls-Royce, #30B, 1946-50 ....$100-$125
Royal Mail Van, #260, 1955-61 ....$115-$150
Sea King Helicopter, #724/736, 1971-79.............$35-$85
Searchlight, prewar, #161A..............................$250-$500
Short Shetland Flying Boat, #701, 1947-49 ......$550-$750
Silver Jubilee Bus, #297, 1977 ....$35-$70
Spitfire, #62A, 1945-49...................................$75-$125
Spitfire II, #741, 1978-80 ....$80-$135
Streamlined Fire Engine, #25H/25,
     1946-53 ....$100-$175
10 Ton Army Truck, #622, 1954-63 ....$50-$75
Thames Flat Truck, #422/30R, 1951-60 ....$75-$110
Town Sedan, #24C, 1934-40 ....$130-$200
Twin Engined Fighter, #70d/731, 1946-55 ....$25-$35
U.S.S. Enterprise, #371/803, 1980.....................$45-$70
Vickers Viscount, #706, 1956-65 ....$125-$200
Volkswagen 1300 Sedan, #129, 1965-76 ....$35-$75
Vulcan Bomber, #749/707/99, 1955-56.......$1,500-$4,000
Whitley Bomber, #62t, 1937-41........................$300-$350
Willeme Semi Trailer Truck, F36B/896,
     1959-71 ....$130-$225

Hubley (cast iron, late 1800s-1960s)

Ahrens-Fox Fire Engine, 1932....................$6,500-$8,000
America Plane..$5,000-$7,000
Auto Fire Engine, 1912................................$5,550-$7,000
Auto Truck, 1920, 17-1/2" ....$1,650-$2,250
B-17 Bomber...$185-$250
Bell Telephone Truck, 1930, 10" ....$1,000-$1,500
Buick Convertible ....$60-$80
Coupe, 1928, 8-1/2" ....$1,100-$1,500
Delta Wing Jet...$95-$125
Dump Truck, 7-1/2" ....$335-$450
Elgin Street Sweeper, 1930.......................$8,000-$11,500
Fire Engine, 1920s, 10-3/4" ....$5,750-$7,500
Flying Circus...$70-$90
Ford 961 Powermaster, 1961 ....$250-$400
Ford Sedan, 1930s...$100-$185
Harley-Davidson Motorcycle, 1932..................$450-$800

Hook and Ladder Truck, 1912, 23" ....$3,000-$4,500
Huber Road Roller, 1927 ....$2,250-$3,750
Indian Air Mail, 1929 ....$2,650-$3,500
Indian Armoured Car, 1928 ....$3,500-$6,000
Ingersoll-Road Compressor, 1933 ....$6,500-$10,000
Limousine, 1918 ....$325-$400
Lindy Plane, 13-1/4" ....$1,750-$2,000
Milk Truck, 1930 ....$200-$295
Motorcycle ....$600-$800
Packard Roadster, 1930...................................$145-$250
Police Patrol, 1919.......................................$1,450-$2,500
Railway Express Truck ....$225-$275
Piper Cub Plane..$75-$115
Racer, 1931, 10-3/4" ....$150-$250
Roadster, 1920 ....$150-$225
School Bus ....$85-$125
Sea Plane..$55-$75
Service Coach ....$900-$1,500
Seven Man Fire Patrol, 1912.....................$5,700-$7,500
Stake Truck, 12"...$150-$200
Station Wagon...$75-$100
Steam Shovel...$115-$150
Studebaker...$600-$800
Tow Truck, 9"...$225-$275
Tractor Shovel, 1933 ....$1,650-$2,000
Traffic Car, 1930 ....$950-$1,500
U.S. Air Force ....$45-$75
Wrecker, 5" ....$95-$125
Yellow Cab, 1940...$500-$700

Johnny Lightning/Topper (1960s-1970s)
'32 Roadster ....$25-$60
A.J. Foyt Indy Special..$40-$60
Al Unser Indy Special.....................................$100-$200
Baja ....$45-$125
Big Rig ....$65-$150
Bubble ....$45-$75
Bug Bomb ....$40-$90
Condor...$150-$200
Custom Camaro, prototype $1,000
Custom Charger, prototype $1,000
Custom Continental, prototype $2,000
Custom Dragster, without canopy.....................$35-$75
Custom Dragster, mirror finish ....$150-$225
Custom Dragster, with plastic canopy ....$60-$100
Custom El Camino, with opening doors ....$100-$250
Custom El Camino, mirror finish.....................$200-$350
Custom El Camino, with sealed doors...............$100-$300
Custom Eldorado ....$125-$275
Custom Ferrari, mirror finish ....$300-$450
Custom Ferrari ....$150-$275
Custom Ferrari, with sealed doors ....$35-$80
Custom GTO, mirror finish.............................$200-$350
Custom GTO, with sealed doors......................$125-$350
Custom GTO, with opening doors ....$100-$300
Custom Mako Shark, mirror finish ....$200-$500

Custom Mako Shark, sealed doors........................$40-$75
Custom Mako Shark, opening doors.................$125-$300
Custom Mustang, prototype................................. $1,000
Custom Spoiler ....$35-$65
Custom T-Bird, opening doors..........................$75-$225
Custom T-Bird, mirror finish ....$200-$400
Custom T-Bird, sealed doors.............................$80-$250
Custom Toronado, mirror finish......................$450-$600
Custom Toronado, sealed doors ....$300-$500
Custom Toronado, opening doors ....$225-$400
Custom Turbine, unpainted interior ....$25-$45
Custom Turbine, painted interior ....$25-$100
Custom Turbine, mirror finish ....$150-$225
Custom XKE, opening doors ....$150-$275
Custom XKE, mirror finish.................................$300-$450
Custom XKE sealed doors ....$35-$80
Double Trouble ....$75-$100
Flame Out ....$60-$100
Flying Needle...$45-$100
Frantic Ferrari ....$35-$45
Glasser..$40-$75
Hairy Hauler...$65-$150
Jumpin' Jag ....$35-$80
Leapin' Limo ....$50-$125
Mad Maverick ....$75-$150
Monster ....$40-$75
Movin' Van ....$35-$65
Nucleon ....$35-$80
Parnelli Jones Indy Special ....$40-$60
Pipe Dream...$65-$150
Sand Stormer...$20-$35
Sand Stormer, black roof ....$50-$100
Screamer ....$45-$75
Sling Shot..$50-$95
Smuggler ....$35-$75
Stiletto ....$60-$85
TNT..$40-$75

Fire trucks were especially popular with boys in the 1940s and 1950s. This Tonka Pumper Truck is valued at about $400 in Mint-in-Box condition.

Triple Threat ....$40-$90
Twin Blaster ....$65-$150
Vicious Vette ....$35-$80
Vulture...$75-$130
Wasp...$80-$100
Wedge ....$45-$75
Whistler..$75-$125
Wild Winner..$60-$125

Keytsone (large scale steel, early 1900s)
Air Mail Plane...$2,400-$2,800
Ambulance ....$1,500-$2,000
Coast to Coast Bus ....$1,700-$2,500
Dump Truck ....$500-$720
Fire Truck...$1,000-$1,600
Moving Van...$1,500-$2,000
Rapid Fire Air Mail Plane.........................$3,000-$4,200
Steam Roller...$300-$600
Steam Shovel..$175-$225
Tank Truck ....$1,800-$2,200
Truck Loader...$375-$500
U.S. Army Truck......................................$900-$1,300
World's Greatest Circus Truck.................$5,000-$10,000
Wrecker..$1,000-$1,500

Marx (tin, 1930s-1960s)
727 Riding Jet ....$225-$300
Air Force Truck......................................$125-$300
Airplane, 1926..$225-$300
Ambulance, 11".....................................$175-$375
American Tractor, 1926, wind-up.......................$225-$300
American Van Lines Bus, wind-up.....................$100-$130
Army Airplane, 1938 ....$190-$250
Army Bomber, 1935 ....$450-$600
Army Tank, 1940s, wind-up ....$225-$375
Army Truck, 20......................................$75-$125
Auto Transport Truck, 1931......................$375-$525
Blondie's Jalopy, 1941 ....$500-$850
Cadillac Coupe, 1931, 11"....................$300-$525
Caribbean Luxury Liner, 15" ....$75-$225
Carpenter's Truck, 1940s ....$250-$350
Cement Mixer Truck, 1930s ....$350-$525
Climbing Tractor, 1930, wind-up.....................$150-$325
Coca-Cola Truck, 1940s, 17".....................$200-$250
Cross Country Flyer ....$550-$725
Daredevil Flyer, 1929, 19" ....$170-$325
Delivery Truck, 1940 ....$175-$225
Dick Tracy Police Car, 9" ....$225-$350
Donald Duck Go-Kart, 1960s, friction ....$130-$325
Doughboy Tank, 1942, 10", wind-up.................$225-$450
Driver Training Car, 1930s, wind-up ....$120-$225
Dump Truck, 1950s, friction........................$75-$100
Falcon..$75-$175
Fire Chief Car, 1936, 8" ....$250-$425
Flying Zeppelin, 1930, 17", wind-up.................$525-$750
Gravel Truck, 1930 ....$150-$250
Greyhound Bus, 1930s, wind-up ....$150-$200

Hill Climbing Dump Truck, 1932, wind-up ......$210-$375
Hook and Ladder Fire Truck, 1950, 24"............$135-$225
Hot Rod #23, 1967, friction ....$75-$90
Jalopy, 1950s, friction ....$200-$250
Jeep, 1946-50 ....$130-$200
Jet Plane, 1950s, friction....................................$90-$195
King Racer, 1925, wind-up ....$575-$750
Luxury Liner Boat, friction................................$150-$250
Mack Army Truck, 1929, 13-1/2"....................$350-$600
Mack Dump Truck, 1930, 19" ....$450-$650
Mickey Mouse Disney Dipsy Car, 1953,
    wind-up ....$665-$875
Midget Tractor, 1940, wind-up, copper color ......$60-$125
Milk Truck, 1940 ....$90-$120
Motorcycle Delivery Toy, 1932, wind-up ....$275-$500
Motorcycle Policeman, 1920s, wind-up ....$150-$325
Mystery Car, 1936...$250-$375
Navy Jeep, wind-up ....$75-$100
Overseas Biplane, 1928, wind-up ....$275-$395
Pan American, 1940..$150-$525
Peter Rabbit Eccentric Car, 1950s, wind-up ......$375-$500
Pet Shop Truck, 11" ....$200-$250
Police Motorcycle with Sidecar, 1930s,
    3-1/2" wind-up ....$650-$850
Popeye Flyer, 1936, Wimpy, Swee'Pea ....$900-$1,600
Power Grader, 17-1/2" ....$100-$125
Racer #4, 5", wind-up ....$125-$195
Range Rider, 1930s, wind-up.............................$375-$500
Refrew Tank, wind-up..$125-$200
Rollover Airplane, 1947, wind-up ....$300-$575
Rolls-Royce, 1955, friction...................................$60-$80
Rookie Cop, 1940, wind-up ....$275-$425
Royal Van Co. Mack Truck, 1927.....................$375-$600
Sanitation Truck, 1940s ....$200-$270
School Bus, 11-1/2", pull toy ....$200-$325
Sky Flyer, 1927 ....$340-$450
Snoopy Gus Wild Fireman, 1926....................$750-$1,150
Sparkling Army Tank, 1942, wind-up ....$150-$300
Sparkling Tractor, 1939, wind-up ....$75-$235
Sparkling Warship, 14", wind-up.......................$75-$195
Stake Bed Truck, 14" ....$150-$200
Station Wagon, 1950, 7", wind-up ....$200-$325
Stutz Roadster, 1928, wind-up ....$500-$750
Tow Truck, 1935, 10"...$200-$250
Tractor, 1941, wind-up.......................................$175-$300
Tractor with Earth Grader, 1950s, wind-up ....$60-$190
Tricky Motorcycle, 1930s, wind-up...................$150-$250
Tricky Taxi, 1940s, wind-up ....$275-$375
Truck Train, 1933, 41", five trailers ....$400-$525
Tugboat, 1966, battery ....$75-$195
Turnover Army Tank, 1938, wind-up ....$225-$375
U.S. Mail Truck, 1950s, 14" ....$350-$450
V.F.D. Fire Engine, 1940s, 14" ....$180-$295
Whoopee Car, 1930s, wind-up..........................$580-$775
Wrecker Truck, 1930s.......................................$225-$290

Yellow and Green Tractor, 1930, wind-up ....$135-$335
Yellow Taxi, 1927, wind-up ....$425-$575
Yogi Bear Car, 1962, friction ....$85-$195
Zeppelin, 1929, 28", pull toy ....$600-$800

Matchbox (die-cast, 1960s-1970s)

1957 Chevy, #4-H, 1979 ....$8-$12
1957 Ford T-Bird, #42-G, 1982 ....$5-$6
Armored Truck, #69-E, 1978...........................$5-$8
Aston Martin Racing Car, #19-C, 1961 ....$30-$45
Austin Taxi Cab, #17-B, 1960 ....$50-$70
Bedford Ambulance, #14-C, 1962 ....$60-$80
Bedford Low Loader, #27-A, 1956....................$350-$450
Big Bull, #12-F, 1975....................................$6-$8
Blue Shark, #61-C, 1971................................$4-$6
BP Petrol Tanker, #25-C, 1964 ....$15-$20
Cadillac Sedan, #27-C, 1960 ....$30-$40
Camper, #38-G, 1980....................................$5-$7
Caterpillar Tractor, #8-B, 1959 ....$35-$45
Cement Mixer, #3-A, 1953 ....$35-$45
Chevy Van, #68-E, 1979 ....$5-$7
Cobra Mustang, #11-H, 1982...........................$3-$5
Coca-Cola Lorry, #37-B, 1957........................$75-$140
Corvette, #62-G, 1979....................................$4-$6
D-Type Jaguar, #41-B, 1960 ....$100-$150
Dodge Challenger, #1-H, 1976 ....$5-$8
Dodge Charger, #52-C, 1970 ....$6-$8
Dodge Wreck Truck, #13-D, 1965....................$500-$700
Dumper Truck, #48-C, 1966 ....$20-$25
Ferrari Berlinetta, #75-B, 1965 ....$20-$25
Field Car, #18-E, 1969................................$145-$200
Foden Ready Mix Concrete Truck,
   #26-B, 1961...................................$130-$180
Ford Fairlane Police Car, #55-B, 1963 ....$55-$100
Ford Fairlane Station Wagon, #31-B, 1960 ....$30-$35
Ford GT, #41-D, 1970....................................$7-$20
Ford Mustang, #8-F, 1970................................$25-$50
Ford Pickup, #6-E, 1970................................$7-$15
Ford Thunderbird, #75-A, 1960.........................$35-$45
Formula Racing Car, #28-H, 1982.....................$3-$5
Greyhound Bus, #66-C, 1967 ....$35-$45
Hot Chocolate, #46-G, 1972 ....$4-$5
Hovercraft, #72-D, 1972................................$7-$10
Jaguar Mark 10, #28-C, 1964 ....$65-$90
Jeep CJ5, #72-C, 1970................................$7-$10
John Deer Tractor, #50-B, 1964......................$20-$30
Lamborghini Miura, #33-D, 1970.....................$40-$50
Land Rover, #12-B, 1959................................$55-$75
Lincoln Continental, #31-C, 1964 ....$15-$20
London Bus, #5-A, 1954................................$45-$65
Mack Dump Truck, #28-E, 1970 ....$5-$15
Maxi Taxi, #72-F, 1973................................$3-$4
Mercedes-Benz 300 SE, #46-D.........................$10-$20
Mercedes-Benz Taxi, #56-F, 1980 ....$4-$5
Mercury Cougar, #62-C, 1968 ....$10-$15
Mercury Station Wagon, #73-E, 1972 ....$5-$7

MG Midget, #19-A, 1956 ....$60-$75
Model A Ford, #73-G, 1979 ....$3-$5
Pantera, #8-H, 1975 ....$45-$60
Peterbilt Tanker, #56-G, 1982 ....$25-$40
Plymouth Grand Fury Police Car, #10-G, 1979........$4-$5
Pontiac Firebird, #4-G, 1975 ....$7-$12
Pontiac Trans Am, #16-G, 1982 ....$3-$4
Quarry Truck, #6-A, 1954................................$30-$50
Road Dragster, #19-F, 1970 ....$4-$6
Road Roller, #1-B, 1953................................$45-$65
Road Tanker, #11-A, 1955.........................$265-$360
Rolls-Royce Phantom V, #44-B, 1964 ....$20-$30
Safari Land Rover, #12-C, 1965 ....$10-$20
Shunter, #24-F, 1978................................$5-$7
Slingshot Dragster, #64-D, 1971.....................$10-$15
Snorkel Fire Engine, #13-G, 1977 ....$5-$7
Stake Truck, #20-A, 1956.........................$75-$100
Sugar Container Truck, #10-C, 1961 ....$55-$75
Swamp Rat, #30-F, 1976................................$4-$6
Television Service Van, #62-B, 1963....................$40-$50
U.S. Mail Jeep, #5-G, 1978.........................$10-$15
Volks Dragon, #31-E, 1971 ....$4-$5
Volkswagen Camper Car, #34-D, 1968.................$20-$25
Weasel, #73-F, 1974................................$4-$6
Woosh-n-Push, #58-E, 1972 ....$4-$5
Zoo Truck, #35-E, 1981................................$7-$10

Smith-Miller (cast-metal and aluminum, 1940s-1950s)

"B" Mack Lumber Truck, 1954 ....$650-$1,000
"L" Mack Army Materials Truck, 1952...........$500-$750
"L" Mack Merchandise Van, 1951.................$695-$1,000
Chevrolet Bekins Van, 1945 ....$350-$750
Chevrolet Coca-Cola Truck, 1945 ....$600-$850
Chevrolet Lumber, 1946 ....$195-$275
Ford Coca-Cola Truck, 1944 ....$650-$900
GMC Coca-Cola Truck, 1954.........................$450-$750
GMC Dump Truck, 1950................................$200-$285
GMC Kraft Foods, 1948 ....$300-$450
GMC Material Truck, 1949 ....$175-$265
GMC Oil Truck, 1947................................$185-$265
GMC Rexall Drug Truck, 1948 ....$750-$1,000
GMC Timber Giant, 1948 ....$285-$495
GMC U.S. Treasury Truck, 1952.....................$325-$475

Structo (pressed steel, early 1900s)

Ambulance Truck, 1928................................$800-$1,350
Auto Builder Auto, 1918................................$1,100-$1,500
Auto Builder Racing Auto, 1919 ....$900-$1,200
Bearcat Auto, 1919 ....$1,400-$2,000
Caterpillar Tractor, 1921.........................$500-$850
Climbing Military Tank, 1929 ....$700-$1,100
Climbing Tractor, 1929................................$600-$1,100
Contractor Truck, 1924.........................$850-$1,000
Dump Truck, 1924-32................................$300-$450
Excavator, 1931................................$600-$950
Fire Insurance Patrol, 1928 ....$500-$700
Giant Truck Builder Dump Truck, 1919......$1,300-$1,850

Future treasures? These cars from the 1990s Johnny Lightning Racing Dreams Series may be tomorrow's treasures.

High Wheel Tractor/Trailer, 1919	$1,000-$1,500
Hook and Ladder Truck, 1930	$450-$690
Lift Crane, 1924	$150-$225
Lone Eagle Airplane, 1928	$800-$1,100
Motor Dispatch, 1929	$1,000-$1,400
Moving Van, 1928	$650-$950
Pile Driver, 1924	$200-$300
Police Patrol, 1928	$650-$950
Pumping Fire Engine, 1928	$1,000-$1,400
Red Rider Truck, 1931	$450-$750
Road Grader, 1922	$350-$650
Roadster, 1924	$1,500-$2,000
Screen Side Truck, 1928	$650-$1,000
Sky King Airplane, 1929	$1,000-$1,500
U.S. Mail Truck, 1928	$700-$1,100
Whippet Military Tank, 1920	$650-$1,000
Yuba Tractor, 1919	$1,000-$1,475

Tonka (pressed steel, 1950s-1960s)

Ace Hardware Semi Truck, 1955	$425-$850
Airport Service Truck, 1962	$225-$300
Allied Van Lines, 1953	$200-$350
Army Troup Carrier, 1964	$150-$250
Back Hoe, 1963	$145-$250
Big Mike with V-Plow, 1957	$500-$850
Bulldozer, 1960	$75-$125
Car Hauler, 1961	$250-$400
Cargo King, 1956	$150-$250
Carnation Milk Van, 1955	$225-$400
Cement Truck, 1960	$200-$300
Coast to Coast Stores Truck	$170-$295
Crane and Clam, 1949	$145-$245
Crane and Clam, 1947	$145-$245
Cross Country Freight Semi Truck, 1955	$225-$475
Deluxe Fisherman, 1960, with boat	$200-$400
Deluxe Fisherman, 1960 with houseboat	$225-$425
Deluxe Sportsman, 1958	$225-$375
Dump Truck	$135-$200
Dump Truck, 1955-57	$125-$250

Dump Truck and Sandloader, 1961	$200-$300
Eibert Coffee Van, 1954	$340-$575
Fire Department Rescue Van	$150-$275
Fire Jeep, 1963-64	$200-$325
Gambles Pickup Truck, 1955-63	$200-$300
Gambles Semi Truck, 1956	$270-$450
Gasoline Tanker, 1957	$400-$850
Gasoline Tanker, 1958	$450-$900
Giant Bulldozer, 1961	$175-$240
Grain Hauler, 1952-53	$175-$250
Green Giant Transport Truck, 1953	$200-$400
Green Giant Utility Truck, 1953	$160-$300
Hi-Way Dump Truck, 1956	$150-$300
Hi-Way Mobile Clam, 1961	$225-$340
Hi-Way Mobile Dragline, 1960	$225-$345
Hydraulic Aerial Ladder, 1957	$200-$400
Hydraulic Dump Truck, 1957	$175-$250
Hydraulic Land Rover, 1959	$500-$1,000
Ladder Truck, 1959	$325-$600
Ladder Truck, 1954	$225-$450
Livestock Van, 1952-53	$150-$275
Log Hauler	$150-$250
Minute Maid Box Van, 1955	$400-$675
Parcel Delivery Van, 1954	$200-$400
Pickup Truck, 1955	$250-$350
Pickup Truck, with camper, 1963	$195-$300
Pickup Truck, Stake Trailer, 1957	$225-$400
Power Lift Truck and Trailer, 1948	$260-$500
Ramp Hoist, 1963	$250-$550
Rescue Squad Van, 1960-61	$250-$500
Road Grader, 1953	$75-$125
Sanitary Service Truck, 1959	$350-$750
Shovel, 1964	$90-$150
Sportsman Pickup Truck, 1959	$225-$300
Standard Tanker, 1961	$450-$700
Star-Kist Tuna Box Van, 1954	$500-$700
Steam Shovel, 1953	$125-$245
Steam Shovel, 1949	$130-$210
Steam Shovel, 1947	$120-$240
Steel Carrier, 1950-53	$180-$265
Suburban Pumper, 1959	$250-$425
Suburban Pumper, 1957	$200-$375
T.F.D. Tanker, 1958	$425-$800
Thunderbird Express Semi Truck, 1959	$200-$400
Tonka Air Express, 1959	$265-$400
Tonka Express, 1950	$300-$500
Tonka Farms Stock Rack Truck, 1957	$225-$400
Tonka Marine Service, 1961	$350-$500
Tonka Toy Transport Truck, 1949	$225-$325
Tractor and Carry-All, 1949-50	$200-$300
Trencher, 1963	$100-$200
U.S.A.F. Ambulance	$160-$250
Utility Truck, 1950-53	$175-$200
Wrecker Truck, 1949-53	$175-$225

Tootsietoy (small die-cast, 1920s-1950s)

Atlantic Clipper..$10-$20
Army Half Truck, 1941......................................$55-$75
Army Jeep, 1950s..$25-$40
Army Tank, 1939-41...$50-$100
Armored Car, 1938-41 ....$35-$65
Baggage Car...$15-$30
Battleship, 1939 ....$20-$35
Beechcraft Bonanza ....$10-$35
Boat Trailer ....$15-$20
Borden's Milk Tank Car.....................................$20-$35
Box Car ....$20-$35
Buck Rogers Battlecruiser, 1937 ....$110-$165
Buick Coupe, 1924...$42-$65
Buick Delivery Van...$35-$50
Buick LeSabre, 1951..$45-$70
Buick Sedan ....$35-$55
Caboose..$15-$25
Cadillac Coupe ....$60-$85
Carrier ....$25-$40
Caterpillar Bulldozer...$45-$55
Chevrolet Ambulance, 1950 ....$25-$50
Chevrolet Bel Air, 1955 ....$30-$50
Chevrolet El Camino..$25-$40
Chevrolet Fastback, 1950..................................$20-$35
Chrysler New Yorker, 1953...............................$35-$55
Chrysler Windsor Convertible, 1950 ....$90-$120
Civilian Jeep, 1950...$20-$35
Coal Car ....$15-$25
Corvair, 1960s...$55-$75
Cross Country Bus ....$45-$65
Cruiser, 1939 ....$15-$25
Crusader ....$50-$75
Destroyer, 1939 ....$20-$40
Dodge Pickup..$30-$40
F-94 Starfire, 1970s..$15-$35
Farm Tractor ....$100-$145
Federal Bakery Van, 1924..................................$85-$110
Ferrari Racer, 1956 ....$40-$65
Fire Hook and Ladder ....$40-$50
Ford Coupe, 1934..$50-$75
Ford F1 Pickup, 1949...$20-$35
Ford Falcon, 1960 ....$15-$30
Ford Roadster...$40-$60
Ford Shell Oil Truck ....$60-$85
Ford Station Wagon, 1962 ....$40-$55
Freighter, 1940...$20-$45
GMC Greyhound Bus, 1948 ....$35-$55
Graham Sedan, 1933-35....................................$115-$150
Greyhound Bus, 1937-41 ....$60-$80
Hook and Ladder..$75-$90
Horse Trailer ....$15-$20
Hose Wagon, postwar ....$25-$40
International Standard Oil Truck ....$75-$100
Jaguar Type D, 1957 ....$15-$25

LaSalle Convertible..$200-$300
Limousine ....$40-$65
Lincoln ....$400-$500
Lincoln Wrecker...$425-$600
Log Car ....$15-$25
Low Wing Plane ....$30-$50
Mack Coal Truck, 1925 ....$100-$250
Mack Milk Truck ....$110-$175
Mack Transport, 1941 ....$500-$750
Mercury, 1952...$20-$40
Model T Pickup, 1914...$40-$50
Navy Jet, 1970s...$10-$30
Oil Tanker, postwar ....$25-$40
Oldsmobile 98, 1955 ....$25-$40
Pennsylvania Engine ....$30-$50
Piper Cub ....$15-$30
Plymouth, 1957 ....$15-$20
Pontiac Sedan, 1950...$25-$45
Refrigerator Car ....$15-$30
Roadster ....$100-$140
Santa Fe Engine ....$20-$35
Shell Oil Truck ....$85-$120
Smitty, 1932 ....$250-$500
Steamroller, 1931-34...$150-$200
Stratocruiser ....$50-$110
Submarine, 1939 ....$15-$30
Texaco Oil Truck...$85-$120
Thunderbird Coupe, 1955 ....$30-$40
Transport Plane, 1941 ....$75-$110
TWA Electra..$20-$45
U-Haul Trailer ....$15-$30
Uncle Walt, 1932 ....$300-$450
Uncle Willie, 1932 ....$300-$450
U.S. Army Plane, 1936 ....$25-$50
V.W. Bug, 1960 ....$25-$30
Waco Bomber..$80-$150
Yacht, 1940 ....$15-$30

A.C. Williams (small cast iron, 1900s-1930s)

1930s Chrysler Convertible...............................$400-$500
1930s Coupe...$250-$350
1930s Sedan, 5"..$250-$350
Ford Roadster, 1936..$550-$650
Mack Bulldog Gasoline Tank Truck, 7" ....$450-$600
Moving Van, 1930..$225-$300
Pickup Truck, 1926..$150-$200
Racer, 1932 ....$450-$600
Taxi, 1920 ....$350-$500

Winross

Alpo...$45-$50
Amana ....$45-$50
Anderson Windows ....$60-$65
Avis Truck Rental ....$35-$45
Borden Milk Tanker ....$90-$110
Bubble Yum ....$65-$75
Bud Light ....$100-$125

California Raisins...$70-$80
Campbell's Soup...$80-$90
Coca-Cola, Ford Aeromax cab ....$200-$300
Coors, Ford cab...$200-$250
Cracker Jack..$250-$300
Domino's..$50-$60
Eastman Kodak, Mack cab................................$400-$500
Emergency Fire, 3000 cab ....$325-$350
Georgia Pacific..$300-$350
Girl Scout Cookies...$65-$75
Goodwrench...$125-$150
Hardee's ....$70-$80
Hawaiian Punch ....$125-$150
Hostess Cakes ....$70-$80
Johnson Wax ....$30-$40
Kraft ....$70-$80
Lancaster Farm Toy Show ....$175-$200
Leinenkugel Brewery..$45-$55
Lysol...$30-$40
McDonald's...$50-$60
Morton Salt ....$80-$90
Mountain Dew ....$45-$55
Nabisco ....$95-$110
Nestle's Quik..$80-$90
Pepsi...$175-$200
Quaker State..$150-$200
Red Hawk Racing ....$100-$120
Schmidt's Beer...$125-$150
Seven Up ....$100-$125
Shasta...$35-$45
Sony ....$65-$75

Sunoco, Ford Aeromax cab................................$250-$300
SuperAmerica ....$35-$45
Totinos..$40-$50
U.S. Mail ....$65-$75
United Way ....$40-$50
Westman's 32" Transport Tanker, 3000 cab.......$200-$250
Wonder Bread ....$75-$80
Yoplait Yogurt ....$40-$50

Wyandotte (pressed steel, 1930s)
Ambulance, 11-1/4" ....$150-$185
Army Bombing Plane ....$65-$85
Battleship ....$55-$70
China Clipper Plane ....$200-$300
Circus Truck and Wagon....................................$950-$1,400
Contractor's Truck ....$125-$175
Coupe...$75-$90
Defense Bomber Airplane..................................$150-$225
Engineer Corps Truck ....$130-$190
Gasoline Truck..$200-$300
Hook 'n Ladder Truck..$130-$160
Ice Truck ....$190-$250
Medical Corps Truck ....$175-$250
Milk Truck ....$190-$250
Rocket Racer..$75-$100
S.S. America Boat...$75-$100
Semi-Trailer Dump Truck....................................$90-$150
Soap Box Derby Racer..$100-$150
Stake Truck ....$65-$80
Station Wagon..$300-$450
Zephyr Roadster...$600-$750

VINTAGE CLOTHING

In this category, Victorian clothes, and those from the 1920s-30s, have taken the back seat of late to trendy items from the 1960s and '70s. As today's fashion designers reintroduce the pieces of yesteryear to the catwalk, enthusiasts search thrift shops and rummage sales for vintage fashions to call their own. Some of the hottest items today? Levi's jeans, Hawaiian shirts, early tennis shoes and neckties—all of which can occasionally be found in clearance bins for mere pennies. The key is to know what you're looking for and what makes it truly vintage. It couldn't hurt to also know what's desirable in Japan, a country in which America's vintage fashions are as hot as it gets.

Background: Originally popular in the 1960s as a means of self-expression, hippie chic became a clever way to dress despite the '70s economic crunch. It also brought ethnic costume into the mainstream in America, influenced by the '70s craft revival that showcased knitwear, embroidery and tie-dyeing. Like collectors today, hippies shopped second-hand stores for one-of-a-kind originals. Such clothes are still popular today as a tie to one of America's most colorful decades.

Another strong influence on the world of vintage fashions is the clothes' lasting appeal overseas, in Japan. With the strong U.S. presence in that country following World War II came a strong appreciation of American fashions. Among the items that made their mark in Japan—and continue to attract the teenagers of that country—are Levi's jeans, tennis shoes, military flight jackets and Hawaiian and bowling shirts.

General Guidelines: Obtaining old catalogs is a good way to identify and authenticate vintage clothing. The catalogs are rather inexpensive online and in thrift shops, and can also sometimes be obtained from department stores, etc., at no charge. If nothing else, old catalogs will familiarize a collector with the common style touches—collar style and shape, leg flare, button choice—that dominated each decade. Knowing a rough estimate of the age of a piece of clothing is essential.

Products popular in Japan—Levis, tennis shoes, military flight jackets—generally garner higher prices, especially online. Also becoming desirable in Japan are crazy daisy patterns and other typically 1970s American items.

In general, brand name and designer items from the 1940s through the 1970s are more valuable than their no-name counterparts. Collectors are interested in representative design trends of each era—the first mini-skirts, American flag motifs or distinctive platform shoes, for example.

Levis—Levis is the most popular brand of denim with collectors today. The serge material originally used to make Levis was imported from Nimes, France. It was referred to as "serge de Nimes," and in English the "de Nimes" was melded into the word denim. In the early years Levis were considered strictly work clothes for farmers, ranchers and miners. Over time they developed into acceptable casual wear, and today they are very aggressively collected by the Japanese, as well as people in the United States.

LOOK FOR THE RED THREAD!

The most popular collectible Levis are called red lines, identifiable by the red thread used on the inside seams. Among red lines, single-stitch is more valuable than double-stitch. In Japan, where vintage Levis are very desirable, red lines are known as "akamimis."

In 1971 Levis switched from using the traditional indigo dyes to the more modern chemical dyes. Jeans produced before this change are the most valuable. Serious collectors can recognize vintage jeans by looking at the fabric, but the tab tag can also give away the jeans' age. The small red tab tag on vintage jeans (those produced before 1971) is called a Big "E" tab, because the word "Levis" appears in all capital letters.

Holes, stains and faded color all diminish value. Check the inside of the pockets to discover how much a pair of jeans has faded from its original color. Levi blue jeans—as opposed to stone-washed, or colored denim—are usually the most valuable, as long as condition is acceptable. Colored jeans, however, are gaining popularity.

The button on an authentic pair of Levis should say "Levi Strauss", and any rivets will carry the letters "L.S. & Co.—S.F."

Hawaiian shirts -- Hawaiian shirts, also called Aloha shirts, were printed on cotton and silk until rayon was invented in the mid-1920s. From the 1920s through the 1950s the shirts were hand silk-screened, a process which resulted in more artistic shirts than the latter, which were roller-printed with more repetitive designs.

Vintage shirts—those made before 1955—command very high prices, and can be spotted by a few characteristics: two lines of stitching at the shoulders, with no stitching visible on the collar; strong bleed-through of colors to the inside of the shirt; a loop closure for the top button, not a hole; buttons shaped like coconut or bamboo were common in the earlier years; and a worn tag with a brand name like Kahala, Wong's, Paradise Sportswear, Kamehameha, Hale, Iolani and Shaheen's. If a shirt has any pockets they should be matched to the fabric pattern behind the pocket, making them nearly invisible. This indicates that a shirt is of high quality.

Bowling shirts—With bowling shirts, the older shirts are more detailed—often with elaborately embroidered designs—and have bright color combinations. The collars, as with Hawaiian shirts, do not have top-stitching in vintage items. Look for vintage tags from popular companies like Hilton, King Louie and Nat Nast. Vintage rayon shirts are most valuable, followed by embroidered cotton shirts. Knit shirts are the least valuable.

"The Wallstreet of Collecting"

MANION'S INTERNATIONAL AUCTION HOUSE, INC.

Vintage Denim & Classic Clothing

AUCTION #193E

Vintage tennis shoes, Levis and other denim have become so popular that some auction houses hold specialty auctions devoted exclusively to this material. This catalog from a recent Manion's auction in Kansas, City, Kansas, shows the range of material available.

Neckties—Never have ties been as flashy as they were in the 1940s, specifically from 1946-48. As the rest of a man's outfit became drab during the World War II era, the tie was used to liven things up. Hand-painted ties of the era are highly collectible, as are Hawaiian ties, which can sell for hundreds, even thousands, of dollars. Many ties, however, can be had for as little as one dollar, with a more common price being between $5 and $20. They are often sold in groupings, and so the price for a single tie can average out to mere pennies.

Tennis shoes—The tennis shoe has come a long way since its inception. Even Michael Jordan's Air Jordan, first introduced in 1985, has evolved to become a much more complex shoe. It is the simplicity of yesteryear's sneakers that collectors crave with this item. Any holes, cracks or other signs of serious wear greatly detract from the shoe's value. Highly collectible brands are Nike, Air Jordans, Adidas, Converse and Puma. This is one more category that is very popular overseas.

IS BIGGER BETTER?

WHEN TO SUPER-SIZE!

Size does matter when it comes to vintage clothes, but the same rules don't apply in all categories. Avoid outgrowing your collection by keeping these guidelines in mind when shopping vintage:

Within the world of Hawaiian shirts, yesterday's size large is today's size medium; the clothes simply were not made to be as roomy as they are today. Since many collectors of vintage clothing wear their finds, vintage size large can command higher prices simply because more people will "fit in".

The opposite is true when buying and selling Levis, which are popular in small sizes. When not shopping for your own wardrobe—in which case your size, obviously, is best—Levis command the highest prices when they have 28 to 32-inch waists, and comparable lengths. Still, as styles change and people begin wearing their pants bigger, the ideal size may change. Acceptable waist size ranges from 27-42 inches.

With tennis shoes, it's best to take the middle road in terms of size. A men's size 9 is ideal, with sizes 8-10 being the most acceptable and commanding the highest prices.

"Hale" 1940s, rayon..$150
"Hale", 1950s...$300
"Hukilau", pocket pattern doesn't line up.....................$40
JC Penney's, 1950s, rayon $100
JC Penney's, 1940s, rayon $225
"Made in California", 1940s, black, boys size,
    hibiscus pattern, boys size.....................................$200
"Made in California", 1950s $150
"Mahinanani", 1950s, hand-print, rayon,
    wood buttons, matching print pockets........................$50
"National", 1940s, rayon, loop closure $100
"Pali Hawaiian Style", hand print, size large $650
"Pali Hawaiian Style", 1950s, matching pockets,
    bamboo buttons $15
"Paradise Found", 1960s, rayon, Honolulu,
    wooden buttons $40
"Polynesian Sportswear", 1940s, rayon.....................$100
"Richard Douglas", made in Hawaii, rayon,
    X-Large size $110
"Royal Hawaiian", 1940s, made in Honolulu,
    coconut buttons $225
"Royal Hawaiian", 1960s, rayon, metal buttons $45
Vintage Levis Jeans
Black stitching at back pockets, 517s, 32 x 32,
    zipper fly $40
Indigo denim, big E, Talon 42 zipper, 28 x 27.............$35
Jacket, brushed denim, big E, snap front, size large $20
Red line, blue denim, button-fly 501s, 28 x 32,
    small E..$40
Red line, blue denim, button-fly 501s, 29 x 32,
    small E..$30
Red line, double stitch, small E, button-fly 501s,
    34 x 32..$80
Red line, double stitch, small E, button-fly 501s,
    36 x 30..$70
Red line, indigo denim, Talon 42 zipper, 28 x 26........$25
Red line, indigo denim, big E, button fly,
    36 x 29..$300
Red line, indigo denim, big E, Talon zipper,
    27 x 32..$420
Red line, indigo denim, button-fly 501s, 36 x 34..........$80
Red line, indigo denim big E, button-fly 501s,
    33 x 30..$400
Red line, indigo denim, big E, zipper fly, 33 x 30 ......$500
Red line, indigo denim, button-fly 501s, big E,
    28 x 30..$165
Red line, indigo denim, button-fly 501s, big E,
    33 x 33..$500
Red line, indigo denim, button-fly 501s, small E,
    36 x 32..$280
Red line, indigo denim, button-fly 501s, small E,
    31 x 36...$71
Red line, indigo denim, button-fly 501s, small E $100
Red line, indigo denim, button-fly 501s, small E $75
Red line, single stitch, indigo denim, button fly,
    small E, 35 x 30..$250
Red line, single stitch, small E, button-fly 501s,
    35 x 32..$250

Red line, single stitch, small E, button-fly 501s,
    33 x 30..$150
White denim, big E, Scovill zipper, 36 x 27 ....$20

Vintage Neckties
Bebop era look $10
Palm tree and grass in shades of brown,
    4-3/8" wide..$45
Hawaiian tie, "Kanaka Tie", made in Hawaii,
    1960s $10
"Raxon" tie in "Art of India" pattern, 1940s................$45
Novelty tie with box, 1950s, rayon, pattern on
    tie reads "bullsh*t"..$30
Emilio Pucci necktie, 1960s, silk, bold colors $40
"Carpaccio's the Dream of Ursula", 1940s,
    silk-screened, 3" wide..$30

Vintage Tennis Shoes
Adidas Campus $150
Adidas Runner $150
Adidas Stan Smiths $150
Adidas Superstar $250
Air Jordan, first edition $450
Air Jordan, second edition $400
Air Jordan, third edition...$325
Air Jordan, fourth edition...$325
Air Jordan, high top, 1992 ....$170
Converse Chuck Taylor...$250
Converse One Star...$150
Nike Air Street Defender, 1995 ....$60
Nike Bruin...$125
Nike Dunk..$275
Nike Orange Swoosh, high top, 1980 ....$75
Nike Orange Swoosh, women's, 1980...........................$50
Nike Rainbow $125
Nike Road Runner...$125
Nike Taylor $80
Nike Terminator $350

This vintage Hawaiian shirt, with a "Kahala" label was in a group of four similar shirts that sold as one lot for $800 at a recent Christie's auction in New York.

WARNER BROS.

"What's up, doc?" Along with "sufferin' succotash!" and "I tawt I taw a puddy tat," Bugs Bunny's trademark phrase has become part of the pop-culture lexicon. Unlike many cartoon characters, the cast of the Looney Tunes and Merrie Melodies shorts grows more popular with each generation that tunes in. Today's Warner Bros. characters are young, hip, and mass-produced—they line store shelves as everything from beanbag plush to crazy straws. Much of the new product has yet to gain any collecting value, but hundreds of products have been made to commemorate the characters from the 1930s through today. The depth of the Warner Bros. characters' field, both in availability and price, is as great as the depth of their fan base. Most everyone has heard Porky Pig stammering out his heartfelt farewell at the end of a cartoon, one of the most recognizable goodbyes around: "That's all, folks." But for this field there's no end in sight as the older collectibles remain in demand, and the new are only just beginning to develop a collector base.

Background: The story behind Looney Tunes and Merrie Melodies began when Leon Schlesinger formed an alliance with the Warner brothers, along with animators Hugh Harman and Rudolph Ising, in 1930. The first Looney Tunes cartoon, *Sinkin' in the Bathtub*, premiered that year—just two years after Disney introduced Mickey Mouse in *Steamboat Willie*. The Merrie Melodies cartoon series debuted in 1931.

Looney Tunes' first breakout character, Porky Pig, hit the small screen in the 1935 film short *I Haven't Got a Hat*. Daffy Duck debuted in 1937, and the character that would launch Looney Tunes' popularity, Bugs Bunny, was introduced in 1940.

Bugs opened the door for an expanding cast of characters, including Foghorn Leghorn, Wile E. Coyote and Road Runner, Pepe Le Pew, Tweety, Sylvester, Elmer Fudd and Yosemite Sam.

Vintage Looney Tunes collectibles include a cute 1930s tin wind-up Porky Pig toy.

The Bugs Bunny Game by Ideal is worth about $40-$45.

STUTTERIN' SUCCOTASH!

What do Daffy Duck and Sylvester have in common? They both have speech problems, as do most of the Looney Tunes characters. It's a large part of their charm, but what was the inspiration behind the impediment? It's been said that Leon Schlesinger himself, producer of the Looney Tunes cartoons during their earliest years, was affected by a rather pronounced lisp. The animators borrowed their boss's speech patterns to give voice to Daffy Duck, and were surprised to find it met with his approval. The voice was later modified and given to another character, that lovable "puddy tat" named Sylvester. He's best remembered as the kitty that was always trying to eat Tweety Bird—yet another Looney Tune that struggles with pronunciation.

Warner Bros. continues to attract children today with its Tiny Toons cartoon, released in 1990, and the WB television network, launched in 1995 with Michigan J. Frog as its mascot. A broad base of new cartoon characters, from the Animaniacs crew to Pinky and the Brain, fill hours of television programming.

Soon to follow would be *Space Jam*, a full-length film starring Michael Jordan opposite Bugs Bunny and the rest of the Looney Tunes gang. Bringing the older characters to the big screen in a live-action and animated film cast even more attention on the Looney Tunes.

For those fans who are in love with the merchandise that commemorates these characters, Warner Bros.'s nationwide chain of Studio Stores consistently showcase the newest and most popular product.

General Guidelines: As the new characters and merchandise becomes more popular, vintage Warner Bros. and Looney Tunes material is gaining popularity, and value. Various products were produced during the 1970s, many of which are still relatively affordable today. In the mid-1970s, Welch's produced jelly jars featuring the Looney Tunes characters, which sell today for around $15 each. Figural bubble-bath bottles ($12-$45), toys and figures by Dakin ($20-$75) and vinyl figural banks ($75-$200) by the N.V. Vinyl Products Corp. all were created during the 1970s.

Toys from the 1940s and '50s are some of the most high-priced collectors' pieces. They include: valuable items produced by Richie Prem; Bugs Bunny button premiums worth up to $75; and a Colorforms set, the Bugs Bunny Cartoon Kit, that is worth $125 in mint-in-box condition.

VALUE LINE

Values shown are for items in Excellent condition.

Bugs Bunny, bank, Dakin, 1971 .... $30
Bugs Bunny, bank, Dakin, 1940s $80
Bugs Bunny, Bendy, Applause, 1980s, 4" $10

Bugs Bunny, charm bracelet, 1950s (Bugs, Tweety, Sniffles, Fudd etc.) $40
Bugs Bunny, Chatter Chum, Mattel, 1982 .... $20
Bugs Bunny, clock, Litech, 1972, 12" x 14" $75
Bugs Bunny, Colorforms set, Colorforms, 1958 .... $65
Bugs Bunny, costume, with mask, Collegeville, 1960s $16
Bugs Bunny, figure, Dakin, 1971, 10" $25
Bugs Bunny, figure, Dakin, 1976, yellow globes in "Cartoon Theater" box $20
Bugs Bunny, figure, Warner Bros., 1975, 5-1/2", ceramic $35
Bugs Bunny, figure, Warner Bros., 1975, 3", ceramic $20
Bugs Bunny, hand puppet, Zany, rubber head, 1940s $70
Bugs Bunny, snow dome, miniature, Applause, 1980s $10
Bugs Bunny, night light, Applause, 1980s $10
Bugs Bunny, soaky, soft rubber $16
Bugs Bunny, talking alarm clock, Janex, 1974, battery-operated $75
Bugs Bunny, talking doll, Mattel, 197150
Bugs Bunny, wristwatch, Lafayette, 1978 .... $40
Daffy Duck, bank, Applause, 1980s $15
Daffy Duck, figure, Applause, 1980s, 4" bendy $15
Daffy Duck, figure, Dakin, 1968, 8-1/2" $25
Daffy Duck, figure, Dakin, 1970s $30
Elmer Fudd, hand puppet, Zany, 1940s, rubber head $65
Foghorn Leghorn, figure, Dakin, 1970, 6-1/4" $40
Foghorn Leghorn, figure, Applause, 1980s, PVC $50

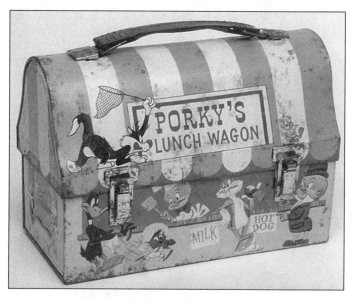

It would cost you about $375 to add this "Porky's Lunch Wagon" lunch box from King Seeley to your collection. It dates from 1959.

New cookie jars featuring Looney Tunes characters are available for $40-$100.

Foghorn Leghorn, hand puppet, 1940s, Zany,
  rubber head.. $55
Foghorn Leghorn, hand puppet, 1960s, 9",
  fabric with vinyl head................................ $60
Pepe Le Pew, figure, Dakin, 1971, 8" $50
Pepe Le Pew, Goofy Gram, Dakin, 1971 .... $50
Porky and Petunia, figures, Warner Bros., 1975,
  4-1/2"... $16
Porky Pig, bank, 1930s, bisque (orange,
  blue and yellow)... $100
Porky Pig, doll, Mattel, 1960s, 17", cloth with
  vinyl head.. $30
Porky Pig, doll, Gund, 1950, 14" $80
Porky Pig, doll, Dakin, 1968, 7-3/4",
  black velvet jacket...................................... $20
Porky Pig, soaky $30
Porky Pig, umbrella, 1940s, 3" figure on end $75
Road Runner and Wile E. Coyote, lamp, 1977,
  12-1/2"... $35
Road Runner, bank, standing on base $10
Road Runner, costume, Collegeville, 1960s $30
Road Runner, doll, Mighty Star, 1971, 13"..... $16
Road Runner, figure, Dakin, plastic,
  Cartoon Theater... $16
Road Runner, figure, Dakin, 1971, Goofy Gram $25

Road Runner, figure, Dakin, 1968, 8-3/4" $25
Road Runner, hand puppet, Japanese, 1970s, 10",
  vinyl head.. $7
Speedy Gonzales, figure, Dakin, 1970, 7-1/2"..... $25
Speedy Gonzales, figure, Dakin, 5" vinyl $20
Sylvester and Tweety, bank, 1972, vinyl......... $25
Sylvester and Tweety, figures, Warner Bros.,
  1975, 6" $16
Sylvester, figure, Dakin, 1976, Cartoon Theater........... $16
Sylvester, figure, Dakin, 1971, Sylvester on
  fish crate $25
Sylvester, figure, Dakin, 1969...................... $20
Sylvester, figure, Oak Rubber, 1950, 6"......... $30
Sylvester, hand puppet, Zany, 1940s, rubber head........ $65
Sylvester, soaky, Colgate $16
Tasmanian Devil, bank, Applause 1980s $10
Tasmanian Devil, doll, Mighty Star, 1971, 13"............. $16
Tasmanian Devil, figure, Superior, 1989, 7" $5
Tweety, doll, Dakin, 1969, 6", moveable
  head and feet $16
Tweety, figure, Dakin, Cartoon Theater, 1976 .... $16
Tweety, figure, Dakin, on bird cage, 1971 ..... $25
Tweety, figure, Dakin, 1971, Goofy Gram,
  holding red heart $25
Tweety, hand puppet, Zany, 1940s, rubber head $65
Tweety, soaky, Colgate, 1960s, 8-1/2", plastic.............. $16
Wile E. Coyote and Road Runner, figures,
  Royal Crown, 1979, 7"............................... $20
Wile E. Coyote, doll, Mighty Star, 1971, 18" plush $16
Wile E. Coyote, doll, Dakin, 1970, on explosive
  box.. $30
Wile E. Coyote, figure, Dakin, 1976,
  Cartoon Theater.. $16
Wile E. Coyote, figure, Dakin, 1971, Goofy Gram $25
Wile E. Coyote, figure, Dakin, 1968, 10" $23
Wile E. Coyote, hand puppet, Japanese, 1970s,
  10", vinyl head $7
Wile E. Coyote, night light, Applause, 1980s............... $23
Yosemite Sam, mini snow dome, Applause, 1980s $16
Yosemite Sam, musical snow dome, Applause,
  1980s $30
Yosemite Sam, figure, Dakin, 1978, Fun Farm............. $20
Yosemite Sam, figure, Dakin, 1968, 7"......... $23
Yosemite Sam, figure, Dakin, 1971,
  on treasure chest.. $25
Yosemite Sam, nodder, 1960s, 6-1/4".......... $100

WESTERN AMERICANA

Western Americana is a collecting area that has exploded over the past decade. Once limited primarily to the American Southwest, cowboy collectibles are now popular throughout the United States—and around the world. Collectors everywhere, it seems, have developed a renewed passion for the Old West. The realm of Western Americana is diverse Virtually everything associated with life on the old frontier is desirable, but most popular is the traditional cowboy gear: Boots, hats, chaps, saddles, spurs and gunleather.

Background: There are several different approaches to collecting cowboy antiques. Some collectors look for the worn and battered equipment used by the actual working cowboys of the Old West—the gear used by the brave buckaroos on their long cattle drives of the 1870s and 1880s. Other collectors enjoy the more romantic Western gear used by rodeo stars or Wild West show performers. These items featured fancier, high-quality decoration and include the flashy wide-brimmed Stetson hats, multi-colored "wooly" chaps and similar accessories. Still another group of collectors likes the glitzy gear used by the Hollywood cowboys—the silver-decorated parade saddles, wildly embroidered boots, fancy cowboy shirts, etc.

General Guidelines: Value depends on condition, rarity and maker. In general, items displaying well-known maker's marks are more desirable and more valuable than unmarked, "generic" pieces that could be ordered from general-merchandise catalogs like Sears & Roebuck or Montgomery Ward. Cowboy gear that is decorated with silver or elaborate designs has more value than plain examples. Also, items associated with people (clothing, spurs, hats, holsters) are generally in stronger demand than horse-related items, such as bridles and bits.

Here are some guidelines for the most popular categories of Western Americana:

Holsters and Gun Belts—Nothing symbolizes the Wild West as much as a cowboy's leather gunbelt and holster. The two together are called a "rig" by collectors. Traditionally gun belts and holsters held little value for gun collectors,

Fancy spurs, sometimes known as "cowboy jewelry," can get very expensive. This pair, made by G.S. Garcia, sold for over $17,000 at the Mesa show (Photo courtesy Bill Manns).

but now the leather rigs are often more valuable than the guns they once carried. Very popular with cowboy collectors, they frequently command some of the highest prices of all Western collectibles. Values range from perhaps $200 for a simple generic model originally sold by catalog, to thousands of dollars for fancier models. Among the more desirable makers are Meanea, Heiser and Myres. Nice examples typically bring $500 to $2,000 and more. Fancy models decorated with silver bring the higher prices. Especially desirable rigs have sold at auction for over $10,000.

Saddles—Made by the major manufacturers of the day—Meanea, Gallatin and Collins of Cheyenne, Wyo., or Frazier and Gallup of Pueblo, Colo.—saddles from 1870-1900 are typically known as "slick fork" models. Prices for nice, authentic examples start at about $500 and go into the thousands. Nice 1880s trail saddles, made by frontier saddleries, typically sell in the $1,000-$5,000 range. Saddles of generic manufacture, originally sold through catalogs like Sears and Montgomery Ward are not as desirable and bring less than half the value of a marked saddle.

Commanding top dollar are saddles made by Heiser, Main & Winchester and Edward Bohlin, a Swedish immigrant who became known as the "saddle maker to the stars." Stunning examples of Bohlin saddles have sold at auction for over $30,000.

Spurs—With antique cowboy gear now being elevated to "decorative art" status, vintage spurs have become especially popular because they are easy to display and have a rugged beauty that truly symbolizes the Old West.

There are two main schools of Western spur design: Texas and California. The "Texas-style" spurs, worn by the actual cattle-driving cowboys, were relatively heavy and sim-

COLLECTING TRENDS!

All types of cowboy collectibles have been increasing in value in recent years, but according to expert William Manns (who provided much of the information for this chapter), among the hottest trends right now are cowgirl antiques—items associated with the women of the Old West. Especially desirable are cowgirl boots, scarves, riding skirts, belts, beaded gloves, and photographs and Wild West Show posters depicting cowgirls.

ple in design. Generic iron spurs of this type from the late 1800s generally sell in the $150 to $600 range. More popular with today's collectors are Texas-style spurs made by manufacturers such as Kelly, Crockett, McChesney, and Garcia, which typically sell in the $350-$1,500 range. Especially nice to display are spurs adorned with silver steer heads, arrows, snakes, stars, playing-card suits and other traditional Western decorations. Among the more interesting spurs sought by collectors today are "gal leg" spurs, a style of spur by made by McChesney in the shape of a woman's leg—a scandalous thing in Victorian times. They typically sell for $500-$1,000.

The most elaborate spurs are the fancy "California-style" spurs, which were heavily influenced by Mexican artists in old California. Sometimes called "cowboy jewelry," they are typically lighter in weight and design than Texas spurs, with fine, elegant engraved silver inlays. They typically sell for $1,000 to $5,000 a pair—and up. California-style

You never know where a treasure might be hiding. This rare Main & Winchester saddle, dating from the 1890s, was found in a Pennsylvania antique shop for $300. Offered later at the Cody Old West Auction, it sold for a record $46,750 (Photo courtesy Bill Manns).

spurs by major makers demand the higher prices. They include G.S. Garcia, Mike Morales, L.D. Stone, Rafael Gutierrez, Jose Figueroa, Schnitker and Buermann, among others. Outstanding examples can command Western-size prices. A record was set several years ago when a pair of presentation spurs made by G.S. Garcia sold at auction for $46,000.

Chaps—Chaps range in price from $300 to $2,000 and higher. The straight-leg "shotgun" variety chaps were the most popular with the working cowboy of the late 1800s. Rather plain in design, they typically have fringe running the length of the leg and large patch pockets. These are usually priced in the $700 to $1,500 range. Chaps with fancy studding and designs, and those from respected makers, bring the higher prices, but even well-worn, unmarked chaps typically sell in the $500-$700 range.

A more elaborate style of chaps, known as "batwings" because of their shape, were popular with cowboys from the 1890s through the 1920s, as were the distinctive "woolies," those hairy-looking chaps often worn by movie and TV cowboys. Both are very popular with collectors today. Ornately decorated batwing chaps can bring from $1,500 to $5,000, while fancy woolies in nice condition with a maker's mark can sell for $2,500 and higher.

Boots—You can't be a cowboy without boots. Vintage boots are sought by today's collectors, both to wear and for display. Again, the price range is wide—from under $100 to over $1,000. Collectible boots date from the 1870s to the 1940s or even the 1950s. Many collectors, in fact, consider the late 1940s and early 1950s to be the golden age of cowboy boots. "Boot art" from this era featured colorful designs of bright butterflies, eagles, cactus and other Western symbols. These elaborate, fancy boots were often the type worn by the popular movie and TV cowboys of the era, and they typical command the higher prices.

Cowboy Hats—Available in many different styles, authentic cowboy hats from the 1870s to the 1930s are generally valued in the $75-$500 range. Stetson cowboy hats always bring top prices. The classic Stetsons with a five-inch brim, high crown and "pencil-rolled" edge sell in the $500 to $1,000 range. Vintage sombreros are also popular. An elaborately embroidered Stetson sombrero once sold at a Scottsdale show for a record $4,400.

Hat accessories, like leather or horsehair hat bands, are also popular with collectors. A penitentiary-made horsehair hat band will typically sell for several hundred dollars. (It was customary for prisoners in the Old West to fashion horsehair hat bands, bridles, and other items to help pass the time. Prison-made horsehair bridles can sell for prices ranging from $500 to over $2,000.)

Miscellaneous Cowboy Gear—Other popular cowboy collectibles include studded cowboy cuffs (most sell in the $100-$500 range); fancy bits ($300-$1,500); rodeo scarves ($25-$200); rawhide riata, the cowboy's rope ($75-$300); steer-horn chairs ($1,200-$3000); leather saddlebags ($250-$700); authentic lawmen's badges ($100-$200); vintage branding irons ($25-$200); and paper items such as vintage photos and letters, old Western maps, Wild West Show posters and programs, "Wanted" posters, mining certificates, and other historical documents ($25-$2,000). Material related to Buffalo Bill is especially desirable. Nice posters from Buffalo Bill's Wild West Shows have sold for prices in the $2,000-$5,000 range.

The list of miscellaneous collectible Western Americana actually includes anything and everything associated with life on the frontier: clothing furniture, paintings, glassware, bottles, saloon items, blankets, canvas canteens, gambling items, surveying and scientific instruments, advertising signs and tins, mining tools, ranching and farming implements, etc.

Contributor to this chapter: Bill Manns, P.O. Box 6459, Santa Fe, NM 87502.

Recommended Reading
Collecting the Old West, Jim and Nancy Schaut

These dazzling heavily studded batwing chaps, made by the Fred Mueller Saddlery in Denver, sold for over $4,500 at the Cody Old West Auction. (Photo courtesy Bill Manns)

VALUE LINE

The list below includes general ranges for certain categories of cowboy collectibles, along with specific values for some of the better items sold at recent auctions and shows. Average and common pieces are generally worth less than the values shown here.

Bits, fancy silver inlay ....$300-$1,500

Boots, 1940s-1950s, color inlays ....$150-$500

Boots, 1930s, inlaid leather decorated with
    bronc-buster design $750

Bridle, horsehair, prison-made, circa 1900,
    two colors ....$500-$1,200

Bridle, horsehair, as above, five or
    more colors..$1,000-$3,500

Chaps, straight-leg, shotgun-style, fringed .....$500-$1,200

Chaps, batwing, 1890s-1920s, studded...........$400-$1,000

Chaps, batwings, 1890s-1920s,
    ornately decorated ....$1,500-$5,000

Chaps, woolies, $700-$2,000

Chaps, woolies, fancy with maker's
    mark ....$2,000-$4,000

You can't be a cowboy without cowboy boots. This fancy pair of inlaid leather boots decorated with a bronc buster went for $740 at the Cody Old West Auction. (Photo courtesy Bill Manns)

Chaps, Bohlin, batwing style, brown, tooled billet (belt), engraved SS buckle, mounted with eight 1878 silver dollars $1,980

Chaps, Hamley, wide, over 1,000 metal studs, circa 1919 .... $4,510

Cowgirl's outfit, authentic skirt and vest from Buffalo Bill's Wild West Show $7,000

Cuffs, studded, 1900-1930 ....$100-$400

Gloves, women's beaded riding ....$150-$1,500

Gun belt and holster, prices vary greatly ....$200-$3,500

Gun belt and holster, Bohlin, two-tone floral carved, large engraved SS buckle $1,260

Hats, classic Stetson, five-inch brim, pencil-rolled edge ....$500-$1,000

Holster and gun, fast draw, Colt SA 38-40 revolver, used by stunt man Mark Swain $2,200

Holster and gun, Visalia, .38-caliber Smith & Wesson revolver, made for Alamedo County Sheriff's Posse, 1930s $3,850

Poster, "Pawnee Bill" Wild West show, 1888, rare $12,000

Poster, "Buffalo Bill" Wild West show, exceptional example $13,000

Saddle, 1870-1900, prices vary greatly ....$500-$3,000

Saddle, cowgirl astride-style, vintage ....$500-$1,200

Saddle, Licthenberger and Ferguson, silver-mounted parade $7,500

Saddle, F.A. Meanea, full-carved, loop-seat style $22,000

Saddle, fancy silver parade saddle made for Hollywood star Harry Carey $14,500

Saddle, Main & Winchester, 1890s, full seat, hooded stirrups, original horsehair girth, tooled floral border pattern $46,750

Saddle, Main & Winchester, 1870s, half-seat design with tapaderos, raised floral carving, Mint condition (world record price) $55,000

Saddlebags, vintage, leather...............................$200-$700

Scarves, rodeo ....$25-$200

Spurs, iron, generic, 1870-1900 ....$100-$500

Spurs, Texas-style, silver inlay maker's mark ....$300-$1,200

Spurs, California-style, fancy silver inlay ....$1,000-$5,000

Spurs, Edward Bohlin, gold and silver engraved, parade spurs, 1940.. $29,500

Spurs, silver mounted, Bohlin, Hollywood, McChesney, #125-2, tooled leather Bohlin straps $3,400

Spurs, silver mounted, Cox, John, Canon City, prisoner #4307, 4" shanks, fancy nickel-spotted leather straps by R.T. Frazier Saddlery, Colorado... $13,200

Spurs, silver mounted, Garcia, G.S., #44, early mark, 14-point rowels $7,150

Spurs, silver mounted, Eddie Hulbert, Montana, Cheyenne-style heel band, engraved button design, 2-1/4" 18-point rowels..................................... $11,600

Spurs, silver mounted, Mike Morales, California-style, engraved shield, snowshoes and eagle motif....... $5,500

Spurs, silver mounted, Phillips & Gutierrez, eagle bit.. $5,610

Spurs, silver mounted, Qualey Bros., fully engraved, card-suit design, raised silver buttons, tooled leather straps $12,100

Spurs, silver mounted, L.D. Stone, marked "1900," silver-mounted drop shank, engraved button heel band, silver inlaid rowels, orange 2-1/4" domed-button beaded conchos, basketweave leather straps....... $6,050

Spurs, silver mounted, Jesus Tapia, circa 1916...... $23,650

Spurs, silver mounted, Wauley Bros. $12,100

Spurs, "gal leg" by Tom Johnson, 1915.................... $900

Steerhorn chairs ....$1,000-$2,500

WOMEN'S COMPACTS, HANDBAGS & ACCESSORIES

Ladies bedroom accessories from the late 1800s and early 1900s can generally be found for less than $100 at antique shops and flea markets. But don't forget to look for boudoir items at garage sales and on-line auction sites, where there are bargains to be had. You can find items such as combs, compacts, hatpins and holders, and antique beaded bags.

Antique beaded bags—Beaded bags from the late 18th century to the early 20th century are needlework masterpieces of artistry, the jewels among collectible purses. The variety is infinite among these miniature works of art. Usually each bag had its own story; most bags were homemade and passed down among family members from generation to generation. Therefore, they are relatively plentiful.

Bags, often with fringe on the bottom, have been created in all sorts of sizes and in many ways, including knitted and crocheted styles. Beading has been done on all kinds of canvas, on loose fabrics, such as lace net or flour sacking, on soft leathers, on commercial ring meshes and on other fabrics. Early bags emphasized this beautiful artwork, using glass beads that maintained their brilliant colors; this made them more decorative than practical. They were often considered status symbols; the more beads and more elaborate the design, the wealthier the owner was.

Although most bags, often smaller, were made by women at home, some of the finest were made by skilled professional bead workers; these larger bags, made by European artists and those who came to the United States to work in the garment industry, had intricate designs featuring scenes and landscapes, floral designs and figurals. Their craftsmanship and beauty were unsurpassed. Restoration, in itself an art, is an accepted practice among collectors, as long as it is done correctly.

MARKET TRENDS!

Most antique beaded bags were hand made at home, and there were dozens of patterns used to create them. According to author Evelyn Haertig, an expert on antique purses, French and Italian figurals and scenics with lacy and intricate fringe are most desirable. Other popular patterns include: abstracts; animals; bead and tambour; bead with tapestries; children; dated and signed; early science; Egyptology (scarce); fable/mythological; figurals; florals; funeral; multi-colored solids; Oriental themes; scenics; solids with swags; Turkish rug patterns; and Venetian scenics (rare).

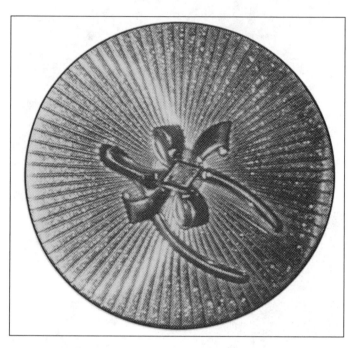

This white metal loose-powder compact with wishbone and jewel in the center is valued at $25 to $50. It dates from about 1940. (Photo courtesy Beth Wheeler)

During the early 20th century, purse patterns and supplies were sold in stores and through ladies magazines. Patterns back then ranged from 10 to 25 cents, while frames were 25 to 50 cents. Beads cost about 10 cents per thousand. An 8-by-9-inch purse could take several months to complete and would require more than 120,000 beads—it would cost $25 to make this purse, a pricey sum back then. But compare that cost to the values today of top-of-the-line antique purses, those displaying flawless scenes or figural designs, and you'll see why collectors get excited. Today, those purses can bring $700 to $5,000!

But by the 1940s, the beading process had simplified, on its way to being a lost art. No longer were little glass beads were being used; instead, plastic beads and frames were being mass-produced for sale in department stores.

Antique beaded bags can be found at estate sales, shows, major auctions, antique shops and flea markets. Values will depend on age, condition, pattern, desirability and other factors. Beginners can get started for $50 or less, while advanced collectors may pay $5,000 for a rare and particularly desirable bag.

This nickel-silver Sesquicentennial Commemorative vanity bag on a pendant chain depicts the Liberty Bell. Made by Evans, circa 1926, it is valued at about $75. (Photo courtesy Beth Wheeler)

Author Evelyn Haertig, an expert on antique purses, says collectors should consider certain characteristics before buying a bag. These include the intricacy and rarity of the pattern; the size of the beads (smaller and finer were used to make the more attractive, intricate patterns); the skill displayed; the size of the purse and whether it had a lining; the colors used; the fringing on the bag (patterned is more valuable than solid); the overall condition and appeal of the purse; and the condition and type of frame used.

Ladies' compacts—As women became "liberated" during the early 1900s and began entering the business world, no longer was the use of makeup frowned upon. Women rou-

tinely began using cosmetics as a daily grooming ritual, so portable cosmetic containers became a necessity during the height of their popularity (1920-1950).

Reflecting the mood of the time, compacts were made in all types of shapes, colors, combinations, motifs and styles—Art Deco and Art Nouveau figures, detailed floral designs, rhinestone motifs. They used natural and man-made materials such as Lucite, Plexiglas, plastic, celluloid, wood, ebonite, leathers, alligator, snakeskin, bi-metal, gold-tone metal, nickel silver, sterling silver, tortoiseshell, ivorene.

The variety of compacts included commemoratives, premiums, souvenirs (for fairs, states, ocean liners, landmarks and tourist attractions), enamels, patriotic, figurals and Art Deco. Famous movie actresses and cartoon and fictional characters, such as Betty Boop and Minnie Mouse, often graced the lids. Combinations included compacts with cigarette cases, hatpins, canes, music boxes, watches and lighters.

Compacts were sold in gift shops, dime and jewelry and department stores across the country. But by the late 1950s, women were opting for the "Au Naturel" look. The term "vintage" describes compacts from the first half of the 20th century, not contemporary examples. You might find them at secondhand stores, flea markets, antique shops, rummage sales and collectibles shows.

Original cosmetics do not enhance the value of the compact. Compacts should be in good repair, with no missing or broken parts. Minor flaws may be repaired, but have it done professionally so the value is not affected. Do not remove an original mirror. A professionally resilvered or repaired mirror is more desirable than a mirror replaced with a new one.

It's wise to keep information about the piece and an inventory of your collection. Videotaping or photographing a collection is a good idea for those who have an extensive or quite valuable collection. Remember to make copies of your records and tapes, however. You may also want to have a certified appraisal done on your collection; for insurance purposes, keep this information with your records.

Combs—Hair ornaments, among the first accessories developed by primitive man, generally had a single pair of teeth which were used to untangle hair and keep it out of one's face. Quite often, remnants of early ornaments and combs, those having many teeth, can be found during archeological excavations.

Ornaments, many featuring gold, silver and gemstones, were prominent during the late 1800s and early 1900s. Combs, made from horns, were first produced in America during the Revolutionary War, when imports from England were restricted. But the most plentiful combs to collect are the beautiful celluloid (moldable plastic) combs from the Victorian era of the 1830s-1900, which replaced the likes of horn, bone, wood, ivory and tortoiseshell combs from earlier times. Although quite functional, combs from this period were often used as decorations.

Prevalent in the late 1700s, horn combs were hand-carved from animal horns, which were cheap and readily available for those crafting them. Today, these combs are readily available at reasonable prices. In addition to the previously mentioned materials, silver, gold, brass and aluminum were also later used to make combs. These combs were often quite fancy and quite expensive; many had real gems embedded into the design.

While many of the fancy combs are in museums, there are still carved and sculpted tortoiseshell combs to be had. But they continue to increase in value.

Hatpins and hatpin holders—Around 1850, when oversize hats were fashionable, hatpins became quite popular for women who wanted to keep their hats on their heads. Different materials were used to decorate the pin ends – gem stones, precious metals, china, enamel, crystal and shells. Decorative subjects were plentiful, from commemoratives to insects. Art Nouveau pins (1895-1910s) are highly desirable.

Containers were also created to keep hatpins in place on dresser tops. The holders, made of gold, glass, porcelain, china, crystal, silver and copper, were produced by major manufacturers such as Wedgwood, Meissen, R.S. Prussia, R.S. Germany and Nippon.

Club

• Antique Comb Collectors Club International, 4901 Grandview, Ypsilanti, MI 48197

VALUE LINE

Beaded bags

Art Deco-era purse with silver-plated frame; black and yellow beads with center blue and lavender design; three levels of beads make up fringe design; 6" x 10" ....$250-$325

A romantic scene, shows man, playing a stringed instrument, and woman sitting alongside a creek; French jeweled frame; 8" x 11" ....$600-$700

A majestic bird with sweeping tail; French frame of brown stones and enameled flowers; 6" x 10" ....$500-$600

Victorian beaded floral purse; shows cabbage roses on a divided cream and blue background; frame is marked "Made in CzechoSlovakia," 5-1/2" x 10" ....$475-$575

Victorian glass bead purse; decorated with a castle scene; silver-plated frame; Art Nouveau; 6" x 11" ....$350-$425

1960s purse, made of shiny faceted beads, 7" x 9" with button closure, lined with black fabric and metal zippers, with handle ....$5-$10

One hank (12 loops) of vintage metal seed beads, made in France, size 9, with original paper bag, for purse repairs, 1920s-1930s ....$10-$15

The Pilcher gold-plate square compact (upper left) with etched filigree pattern dates from the mid-1940s. It is valued today at $50-$75. The "Nail Care 'n Such" (center) is worth $35-$55, while the unmarked rectangular compact (right) with gold-tone-and-white metal stripes is worth about $35.

THE ULTIMATE COLLECTIBLE COMPACT!

In 1951, Elgin American offered the exquisite "Bird-In-Hand" compact hand-signed by artist Salvador Dali. The bird-shaped white-metal case was highlighted with gold-tone details and tucked inside a turquoise fabric drawstring pouch that was nestled into a turquoise suede presentation case.

Inside were spaces for lipstick, pills and powder. Each featured a framed mirror in the lid. Originally, the case was available in three different finishes. The satin bronze case sold for $15, the case in silver finish was $25, and the sterling silver case with 14-karat gold retailed for $100. Extremely popular with today's collectors, the current value is $1,500-$1,700.

New Bead Book, by Emma Post Barbour, by National Trading Co., Chicago, Ill., 1924, 28 pages........$10-$15

Combs/Hair Ornaments

Back comb, celluloid, bright teal blue pearlescent, embedded rhinestones, 1920s ....$40-$50

Back comb, hearts and flowers filigree design, row of five long teeth, imitation ivory, 1910 ....$30-$40

Back comb, decorative wirework, prongset rhinestone, wide row of multiple teeth, imitation tortoiseshell, c. 1880 ....$85-$100

Barrette, rhinestone, 2-1/2", c. 1950 ....$20-$25

This unmarked opaque glass dresser box, measuring about 7 inches long, sold for just over $500 at an auction conducted by Jackson's of Cedar Falls, Iowa.

Celluloid comb, Victorian, peacock motif,
1840-1880 ....$75-$85
Celluloid comb, with rhinestones,
c. 1915-1920...................................$100-$125
Hair clip, rhinestone, c. 1930, price for pair ....$20-$25
Hairpin, Art Deco, amber, c. 1925 ....$45-$50
Hairpin, tortoiseshell, SS filigree, English,
Victorian, c. 1890 ....$75-$100
Horn comb, with lead crown, 1830s ....$75-$85
Ornament, plastic, black, with box-shaped
decoration on top, seven past rhinestones on
box sides, c. 1960 ....$25-$30
Ornament, elongated star shape, rhinestone,
large paste diamond center, long, silver-colored
clip, c. 1960 ....$15-$20
Set of English Blue Steel Graining Combs, 1900s,
three combs with four different widths, metal case,
Ridgely Trade Mark ....$10-$15
Side comb, celluloid, imitation amber, pearlescent-colored
overlay, embedded rhinestones, c. 1926............$25-$30
Tiara, encircles gathered hair, hand-set rhinestones,
c. 1940 ....$75-$100
Tortoiseshell comb, with garnets,
early 19th century..$300-$325
Vintage hair combs with rhinestones, for side of
bun or unswept hairdo.......................$10-$12
Walnut showcase, for Maximum Combs, 15 " x 8", "
select your favorite style," with glass front, by United
Drug Company Rubber Department,
Boston, Mass. ....$50-$75
Wood comb, Ashanti Tribe, Ghana, 1800s ....$125-$150

Compacts/Accessories
Brush set, sterling silver, with mirror, 1940s ....$65-$75
Clothes brush, sterling silver, late 1800s ....$25-$30

Compact, American Beauty, gold-tone or white
metal, with rhinestone on cover ....$35-$50
Compact, Amita, damascene, gold and silver
floral motif, black matte lid, Japan................$100-$125
Compact, Art Deco, blue enamel geometric pattern,
rose-cut diamond closure and front motifs,
14K yellow gold.......................................$2,500-$3,000
Compact, Champleve, red and goldtone, hand-mirror
shape, lipstick concealed in handle, red cabochon lipstick thumbpiece, Italy ....$350-$375
Compact, Coro, vanity case and watch, horseshoe shape,
black enamel, snap closing, powder and rouge compart-
ments ....$150-$175
Compact, Coty, gold-tone, with plastic log on
lid inset...$25-$35
Compact, Coty, gold-tone, with teal plastic inset,
1935...$40-$50
Compact, Coty, air spun gold-tone, with floral
design on lid ....$35-$40
Compact, Coty, hand-mirror shape, plastic,
lipstick in handle ....$50-$65
Compact, Croco, round blue, blue zipper, decorative multicolored court inset on lid, Israel.....................$50-$60
Compact, Elgin American, sterling silver,
with etched flowers on cover........................$125-$150
Compact, Elgin American, gold-tone case,
with engine-turned motif on lid ....$40-$50
Compact, Elgin American, gold-tone, colorful
enamel swirls, G.E. color logo on top...........$150-$160
Compact, Elgin American, compact/music box,
silvered, three gilt deer on lid, Anniversary Waltz,
black carrying case.......................................$125-$150
Compact, Elizabeth Arden, light blue
harlequin-shaped ....$125-$150
Compact, Elizabeth Arden, round, gold-tone case, with
blue enamel and "N" monogram on lid ....$30-$45
Compact, Evans, pink and yellow gold-tone,
basket weave ....$200-$215
Compact, Illinois Watch Case Co., compact/watch combination, round, gold-tone, engraved design
on lid ....$200-$215

HERE'S WHAT TO LOOK FOR!

Vintage compacts were made by the following manufacturers: Charles of the Ritz; Colleen Moore; Coty; Dorothy Gray; Elizabeth Arden; Evans; Evening in Paris; Helena Rubinstein; Jonteel; Lady Esther; Princess Pat; Richard Hudnut; Ritz; Tangee; Tre-Jur; Woodbury; and Yardley.

Today's collectors also seek compacts made by the following manufacturers: Elgin American; Evans; Illinois Watch Co.; Stratton of London; Volupte; Wadsworth; and Whiting & Davis.

Compact, Lampl, light blue enamel, five colorful 3-D scenes from Alice in Wonderland encased in plastic domes on lid ....$200-$225

Compact, Lampl, compact/cigarette case, gold-tone, rhinestones and green faux gemstones on lid, center compact flanked by cigarette compartment...$140-$150

Compact, Lancome, square, black ....$30-$45

Compact, Lin-Bren, leather, green, envelope motif coin holder on lid...................................$85-$100

Compact, Luzier's, oblong, black and gold ....$25-$45

Compact, Napier, SS, clamshell shape ....$65-$75

Compact, Petit Point, vanity case, scalloped half-moon shape, gold-tone...........................$150-$175

Compact, Pilcher gold-plate square, with etched filigree pattern, 1945 ....$55-$75

Compact, Rex Fifth Avenue, gold-tone, loose-powder with flower basket on lid ....$60-$75

Compact, Rex Fifth Avenue, painted, enameled, two pink flamingos, turquoise background .....$90-$100

Compact, Rosenfield, zippered gold-tone, multicolor confetti sparkles and thread, Israel ....$40-$45

Compact, SF Co., Fifth Avenue, small round compact with snakeskin on cover ....$25-$40

Compact, Volupte, hand shape, gold-tone, lace gloved ....$225-$240

Compact, Volupte, vanity pouch, light blue collapsible leather ....$85-$100

Compact, Wadsworth, fan-shaped, gold-tone, with fan on lid ....$45-$55

Compact, round, with hand-painted portrait in center, unmarked ....$75-$90

Compact, unmarked, rectangular gold-tone, with black enamel top, embellished with rhinestones, 1930s...$60-$75

Compact, sterling silver fan-shaped, unmarked, circa 1970 ....$95-$115

Compact, square, gold-tone, hand-painted roses, 1920s ....$50-$60

Compact, gold-tone, marked "Switzerland" ....$35-$50

Compact, "Nail Care 'n Such"..............................$35-$55

Compact, small, round nickel-silver, on a finger ring, unmarked, 1930s ....$35-$45

Compact, unmarked, gold-tone, with papercut silhouette inset, 1920s ....$55-$65

Compact, white loose-powder, with wishbone and jewel in the center, 1940s...................................$25-$50

Compact, beetle shape, novelty, plastic, red ......$100-$125

Compact, nickel-and-silver rouge on pendant chain ....$75-$100

Compact, black enamel, painted poodle on white enamel disk on lid ....$40-$50

Compact, gold-tone, heart-shaped, purple inlaid in black plastic lid ....$75-$85

Manicure set, celluloid..$12-$15

Ladies' beaded hand bags have been increasing steadily in value in recent years.

Vanity bag, gold plated, with shield on pendant chain ....$125-$150

Vanity bag, nickel-silver sesquicentennial commemorative on pendant chain, by Evans, circa 1926............$75-$85

Hatpins and hatpin holders

Art Deco, Bakelite, 1920s....................................$35-$40

Art Deco, scallop shell, celluloid, imitation ivory..$35-$40

Art Deco, Egyptian motif, brass and celluloid..$125-$135

Art Nouveau, French ivory, marbelized inset ....$65-$75

Brass, lacy opeNWOrk, large rhinestones on
dome top..$35-$40

Brass, owl, figural ....$40-$50

Carnival glass, flying black bat, figural,
silver luster..$35-$40

Celluloid, phoenix bird design, imitation amber,
oval disc, applied brass.....................................$65-$75

Celluloid, fan shape, coral-color beads,
imitation ivory ....$25-$30

Celluloid, hollow conical shape, imitation
tortoiseshell ....$20-$25

Celluloid, black and ivory palmette, 1920 ....$65-$75

Crystal, teardrop shape inside, handcut, attached to
10-1/2" brass pin ....$125-$150

Cloisonné, foil back, script mark, Japan................$75-$85

Jet glass, cut and faceted, 3-1/4"..........................$90-$100

Peacock eye glass, three-sided motif,
gilded brass ....$75-$85

Sterling silver, Art Noveau design, 12" ....$75-$85

Sterling silver, six sided, floral decorations ....$60-$75

Hatpin holder, china...$50-$100

Hatpin holder, Egyptian motif, pink and white,
bisque, 5-1/4", 1909 ....$125-$150

Hatpin holder, Art Nouveau, bronzed metal, woman,
bust, flowering leaves, 1900s ....$900-$100

Hatpin holder, butterfly and berry pattern,
carnival glass, blue, Fenton ....$700-$750

Hatpin holder, cobalt, blue, with six 9" hatpins,
2-1/4" x 7-1/4"..$25-$30

Hatpin holder, Nippon, 2-1/2" x 2" x 2-1/2",
hand painted with flowers and trees in yellow,
green, blue and orange, with vintage pins.........$15-$20

WORLD'S FAIRS COLLECTIBLES

Much of what we see in the modern world was marked at conception by a world's fair. Visitors to these celebrations of society's advancements could pick up any number of souvenirs as they browsed, from key rings and ashtrays to posters and toys. The number of products made to commemorate each fair is vast. For this reason collectors usually focus on one fair, or one type of item.

Background: Fairs date back to the Middle Ages, when people would travel great distances to view the tools, spices, silks and crafts offered by street vendors.

It was not until 1851 that the World's Fair and Exposition movement began with The Great Exhibition of 1851 in London. It was the brainchild of Prince Albert, husband of Queen Victoria, who wanted to gather all the civilized nations of the world under one roof. He did so in a gigantic building called the Crystal Palace. The event attracted 14,000 exhibitors from all over the world displaying fine arts, expensive furniture, delicate porcelain, cut glass, machinery, Colt guns and printing presses.

The first World's Fair in America was held in 1853 in New York City, and was also called the Crystal Palace. Unlike its namesake, this world's fair was not very successful, even though P.T. Barnum was one of its large investors and Otis displayed his new Safety Elevator.

To date there have been over 100 recognized fairs and expositions, of which about 50 are considered to have been major events. The airplane, telephone and Ferris wheel—as well as the ice cream cone and hot dog—are among the many advancements that were introduced at world's fairs. Other significant events and inventions that are linked to world's fairs:

1876 (Centennial Exposition, Philadelphia) the telephone was first displayed

1889 (Int. Universal Exposition, Paris) Gustav Eiffel built his miraculous tower

1893 (World Columbian Exposition, Chicago) that all-important snack, Cracker Jack, was introduced

1901 (Pan-American Exposition, Buffalo) President McKinley was assassinated

1904 (Louisiana Purchase Exposition, St. Louis) First gave us iced tea, ice cream cones and hot dogs on a bun

1925 (Exposition of Decorative Arts and Modern Industries, Paris) best remembered for its dramatic display of Art Deco

1933-34 (Century of Progress, Chicago) introduced the world to Sally Rand and her risqué "Fan Dance"

1939-40 (World's Fair of Tomorrow, New York City) introduced television

Many of the items from the 1939 New York World's Fair featured the distinctive shapes of the Trylon and Perisphere, the event's most famous buildings.

General Guidelines: As America's baby boomers come of age, items from the later world's fairs are becoming more collectible. Especially popular are items from the 1964-65 New York World's Fair, which are still relatively inexpensive.

Items from the first few World's Fairs are still the most valuable, as they scarcely turn up for sale. Items from the more historically significant world's fairs have become highly collectible, but even souvenirs from these events can be purchased inexpensively.

Among the most collectible items to look for are paper ephemera (tickets, fair guidebooks, posters, postcards), ruby red glass (and other glassware) and spoons. Condition determines value.

Prices are almost always higher in the city or area where an exposition was held. Items from local and state fairs have little value, except to collectors of local (city or state) memorabilia.

Contributor to this section: Mike Pender, World's Fair Collector's Society, P.O. Box 20806, Sarasota, FL 34276-3806.

Clubs

• World's Fair Collector's Society Inc., P.O. Box 20806, Sarasota, FL 34276

• 1904 World's Fair Society, 12934 Windy Hill Drive, St. Louis, MO 63128

• Trans-Mississippi Exposition Historical Association Inc., P.O. Box 55063, Omaha, NE 68155

- World of Century 21 Club Inc., P.O. Box 80445, Seattle, WA 98108

- Pan-American Expo Collectors Society, One Fir Top Drive, Orchard Park, NY 14127

VALUE LINE

1851, London Crystal Palace (the Great Exposition)
Binoculars, ivory and brass, "Exposition De Wondres 1851" $50
Book, *The Great Exposition*, by Tally $100
Cup, porcelain, white ground, blue picture of Crystal Palace $125
Pipe, white clay, picture of Crystal Palace on bowl $175

1853, New York Crystal Palace
Coin, so-called dollar, 1-7/8", obverse is Liberty seated, reverse is Crystal palace $300
Print, "The Burning of the Crystal Palace," Currier & Ives $300

1876, Philadelphia (Centennial Exposition)
Book, *History of the Centennial*, 6" x 9" 874 pages $75

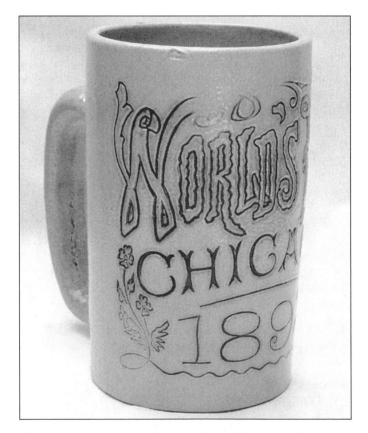

This mug is a souvenir from the 1893 fair in Chicago.

Booklet, *Centennial Book*, 2-1/2" x 3", 16 pages., issued by Orange Judd Co. $15
Brooch, black glass, Victorian $25
Fan, 5" handheld, looks like a firecracker when in its case $220
Inkwell, glass, Memorial Hall $100
Shoe, frosted glass, Gillinder $40
Souvenir cards, set of eight $25
Stevengraph, 1-1/2" x 9-3/4", Lincoln $125
Stevengraph, 1-1/2" x 9-3/4", Washington $125
Textile, Memorial Hall, eagle on top, star border 18-1/2" x 24-1/2" $75
Ticket, unused $40
Trade card, Traveler's Insurance Co., color $22

1889, Paris (International Universal Exposition)
Clock, Eiffel Tower shape, 19", cast-iron, alarm $400
Guide book $40
Sheet music, 11" x 14", "World's Fair Gallop" by William May $10
Textile, 22" x 22" bird's eye view of Fair $65
Trade card, Gold Coin Stoves and Ranges, shows Machinery Hall, corner creases $6

1893, Chicago (World's Columbian Exposition)
Advertising trade card, Traveler's Insurance Co., color $22
Barber bottle, 10-1/2" high, bulbous, gold-imprinted Columbus medal $150
Bell, art glass, etched with frosted handle $110
Brochure, Penn. RR $60
Cane, pull-out map of World's Columbian Exposition $350
Change tray $30
Children's fold-out book, "Little Folks History of the US," $50
Cup, German, 3" $60
Darning egg, Peachblow art glass, gold writing, 5-1/2" $750
Doll furniture, chairs, sofas, soft lead, price for each piece $35
Fan, hand, large $50
Handkerchief, Columbus landing in the New World $25
Imprinted handkerchief, small $20
Large wooden cane $100
Matchsafe, Columbus head $125
Medal, brass, two piece, "Wisconsin—Columbian Exposition 1893" $20
Medallion, 1-3/4"d, Ferris wheel, aluminum $35
Mini jug $60
Periodical, *The Youth's Companion* $30
Plate, ABC theme, Staffordshire, shows buildings from fair, 7-1/4" $200
Pop-Up, 12-1/8" x 10-1/4", Electrical Building, Hall of Mines, Wisconsin State Building $150
Postcards, set of eight, Goldsmith $70

Puzzle, egg shape, silvered brass, Christopher
    Columbus portrait, "1492-1892"............................$50
Ribbon, silk, souvenir $75
Sterling silver demitasse spoon..........................$20
Straight razor, with box, Joseph Allen & Sons $25
Sugar spoon...$25
Ticket, admission, Manhattan Day, NY, Oct. 21,
    1893...$38
Token, Ferris wheel, aluminum............................$18
Token, Jackson's Napa Soda, aluminum.....................$37
Toothpick Holder, ruby glass, thumbprint $85
Woven silk bookmark $100

1898, Omaha (Trans-Mississippi Exposition)
Cordial cup, ruby-stained, etched souvenir...................$36
Cup, ruby-stained, 3" $27
Handkerchief, embroidered...................................$7
Souvenir cup, ruby flashed....................................$58
View book $25

1901, Buffalo (Pan-American Exposition)
Booklet, 20 pages, "Streets of Mexico".....................$30
Bowl, marked C.P. Co. Chittenango China, 3" $18
Fork and knife, made from iron nails............................$6
Letter opener, buffalo..$30
Mug, stoneware, beer $225
Plate, milk glass, gold trim, shows Electric Tower $15
Postcard, unused $3
Poster, 25" x 48", Maid of the Mist $1,200
Souvenir book $25
Spoon, Agricultural building. $5
Stickpin, embossed copper-colored tin $12
Stickpin, frying pan shape, embossed buffalo head......$36
Vase, 6" high, Indian Congress $175
Whiskey glass, etched, "Pan-American Exposition
    1901"..$60

1904, St. Louis (Louisiana Purchase Exposition)
Bust, Napoleon, green base, 14" $100
Clock, 10" high, shaped like Festival Hall..............$1,800
Corset, in original box...$30
Handkerchief, 10" x 10", various prints
    embroidered on one corner $35
Key ring, brass $15
Matchsafe, Jefferson and Napoleon......................$85
Matchsafe, plated, relief scenes $55
Official guide book $25
Plate, clear, lattice design......................................$25
Playing cards, deck $100
Pocket knife, Cascade Gardens.............................$125
Print, Swedish pavilion, 18" x 14" print $40
Salt and pepper shakers, 3"...................................$45
Spoon, Palace of Electricity, nickel plate.....................$15
Tobacco canister, black aluminum $50
Token, "Compliments of Huyler's" $10
Toothpick holder, milk glass.................................$30
Tray, 3-1/4" x 5", litho, tin, issued by American
    Can Co...$50

Tumbler, 5" high, milk glass $30
**1915, San Francisco (Panama-Pacific International
    Exposition)**
Book, Art of the Exposition, 6" x 9".........................$25
Fountain pen, Mint in Box $75
Medals, 1-3/4" diameter, opening day and closing
    day, ribbons, colorful, pair $125
"Novagem" souvenir, large gem, box labeled
    Tower of Jewel $340
Program, Exposition horse racing track...................$130
Trade card $10
Watch fob, brown with rhinestones,
    18K gold inlay..$25
1926, Philadelphia (Sesquicentennial Exposition)
Book, *Sesqui-Centennial*, 6-1/2" x 9-1/4",
    500-plus pages...$35
Compact, 2-1/2" diameter, Liberty Bell in center........$50
Lamp, 8" high, glass Liberty Bell shade.....................$60
Pin, blue Liberty Bell, "Crane's Ice Cream Served Every-
    where—Keep Cool During The Fair" $15
1933, Chicago (Century of Progress)
Bracelet, engraved slip-on...$10
Change tray, 4-1/2" diameter, round, bronzed,
    12 relief buildings and fountain, box $22

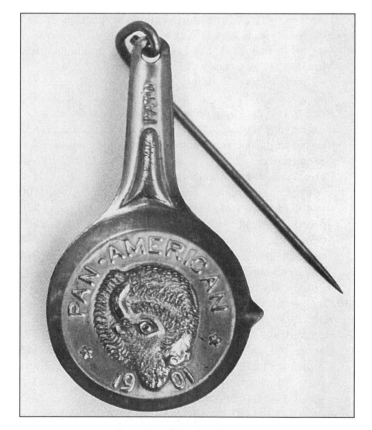

**This stick pin dates from the 1901 Pan American
Exposition.**

You could add "The Official New York World's Fair Game" by Milton Bradley to your collection for about $50. It is from the 1964 fair.

Cigarette case, Art Deco, Stewart's Private Blend, "Made in Bavaria"....................................$75
Cookbook, *The Wonder Book of Good Meals*..............$20
Crumb set, engraved with World's Fair pavilions, white metal..$25
Guide book, *1933 Century of Progress*, Art Deco cover $24
Handkerchief, nice graphic, in cellophane package......$15
Key, 8-1/2" long, metal, "Key to Chicago World's Fair 1933" $20
Mirror, oval, "A Century of Progress, 1933", Towers Federal Building $16
Photograph, 10" x 60", panoramic view $75
Plate, 8-1/4" diameter, pictures Carillon Tower, marked "Pickard" $35
Playing cards, each card has different view, sealed deck $40
Purse, beaded, green and white, marked "Century of Progress 1934" $100
Ring, comet, marked "World's Fair" $20
Spoons, set of six, with book and original box $65
Stamps, world's fair scenes....................................$6
Teaspoon, gold $10
Toy, Greyhound bus, 11-1/2" long, tandem, blue and white, Arcade....................................$400

1939, New York (World's Fair of Tomorrow)
Ashtray, Firestone tire....................................$75
Bag, suitcase shape, contains pictures to color..........$175
Banner, felt, 26" x 8", "World of Tomorrow 1939"......$15
Certificate of attendance $65
Charm bracelet, brass, seven scenic charms $15
Cigarette case, in original box $95
Coaster, cardboard, punch-out of Trylon and Perishpere..$25
Compact $50
Flipbook, hula girl..$15

Guide book, British Pavilion, 122 pages.....................$15
Letter opener $15
Magazine, *Popular Science*, parachute jump on cover $30
Map, 11" sq., multicolored, Tony Sarg $50
Perfume bottle..$25
Pinback button, "I Have Seen the Future" $20
Plate, Tiffany & Co., shows Trylon and Perishpere..$200
Playing cards, Tiffany, deck....................................$85
Sheet music, Dawn for a New Day, George and Ira Gershwin $35
Sheet music, *Yours for a Song* $45
Snow dome, Trylon and Perishpere inside.................$100
Souvenir book, Official Souvenir Book, spiral bound, Trylon and Perishpere illustration..........................$50
Teapot, Hall China Co., cobalt blue $300

1962, Seattle (Century 21 Exposition)
Candy Dish, 7" diameter, Space Needle, silver overlay $50
Cigarette Lighter, space $12
Creamer and Sugar, miniature $20
Decanter, whiskey..$15
Salt and Pepper Shakers, Space needle shape, plastic $20
Shoe horn, metal, gilt, crown design on handle..........$18
Tray, 11" diameter, litho, tin, Space Needle $18

1965, New York
Book, pop-up..$17
Booklet, Progressland, Disney exhibit......................$18
Bottle, Jim Beam..$20
Bumper sticker..$15
Butter dish..$20
Drinking glasses, embossed, set of six......................$20
Fan, hand-held with box $20
Felt pennant..$20
Game, World's Fair Game, Milton Bradley, original box $25
Glass, Shaefer Beer..$25
Groundbreaking brochures (ea.) $4
Hard hat, white plastic, crown front with full color sticker, Arlington Hat Maker..........................$30
License plate $35
Magazine, *Life*, May 1, 1964, opening day.................$20
Official guide book $15
Official titanium medal (small)..................................$10
Paint Set, complete in box $150
Poster, Progressland, Disney exhibit..........................$40
Rain bonnets, various, in small case ....$10-$15
Souvenir Book, *Official Souvenir Book*, 7" x 10", 24 pages..$20
Souvenir Map..$20
Tray, round, Unisphere..$25
Trivet, 4-3/4" square, tile with wooden frame, picture of Unisphere, original box $20
Wastebasket, metal, approximately 12" tall.................$95

WRESTLING COLLECTIBLES

Pro wrestling back in the 1960s and '70s was known as the "grunt and groan" sport, consisting of large men applying headlocks and twisting arms for minutes at a time while the referee shouted, "Do you give up?"

But those days of grunts and groans are long gone.

Background: In the 1980s, Hulkamania began running wild, and the World Wrestling Federation was dominating the wrestling market. People were actually willing to view matches on pay-per view—in 1987, more than 93,000 people witnessed WrestleMania III at the Pontiac Silverdome.

Although no one could have predicted the popularity professional wrestling has recently attained, welcome to the age of "sports entertainment," where every match is a soap opera. During the 1990s, it was through cable television that these stories were being resolved, pushing wrestling to new heights.

Soon, the WWF had competition from the World Championship Wrestling, which began competing for the same fans, as well as wrestlers. Wrestling's popularity was fueled even more.

Of course, wrestling is about more than the action in the ring and the spectacle surrounding it. There has been a boon of licensed memorabilia that has been produced for wrestling fans, from $150 replica championship belts to trading cards.

General Guidelines: Like the sport, the history of wrestling collectibles has taken a similar path. The majority of collectibles from the 1960s and 1970s are autographed photos and programs and wrestling magazines (generally $5-$20 each). But in 1985 and 1987, Topps released sets of WWF trading cards and stickers. A few more card sets were released by other companies before the 1980s ended. That would be the end of the wrestling card market, until recently.

Topps released sets of WCW trading cards in 1998 and 1999. DuoCards released a set of WWF cards in 1998 and WrestleMania Live cards in 1999.

BEAUTY AND THE BEASTS!

Kimberly, the original Nitro Girl, is often considered the leader of that group. The Nitro Girls have helped WCW's Nitro show become one of the highest rated programs on cable television. The group as a whole is popular with wrestling fans, but Kimberly's autographs are still holding steady at $25. Miss Elizabeth, Randy "Macho Man" Savage's #1 fan, and the WWF's first female star from the late 1980s, is also at $25, while her LJN action figure is worth $75. But Sable, the WWF's blonde bombshell, has surpassed her predecessors in the fans' eye, in part through the pages of Playboy magazine and as a guest star on several television shows. Sable's autograph is bringing $40.

Wrestling's increase in popularity has also led to an increase in the value of older card sets. Just 10 years ago, the 1985 Topps WWF was priced at $7; now it is at $30, with the Jesse "the Body" Ventura cards the top ones to get.

Wrestling figures have had a steadier market, with figures being released every year in some form since the mid-1980s. Wrestling figures have become a hot commodity lately, with new figures being released all the time.

Some of the early figures are commanding big bucks these days. If these figures are in their original packaging, you can expect to get top dollar.

The wrestling collectibles market has not lagged behind other collectible markets. If there is a hot trend in the collectibles industry, such as beanie babies, you can expect wrestling to get a piece of the action.

With no letdown in sight for professional wrestling, its collectibles should continue to be in demand for a long time. Keep in mind, however, that this market is rapidly changing, especially for current wrestlers, whose in-ring performances during the course of the year can greatly affect the value of their items—both upward and downward. Regional interest and other factors may also cause the value of an item to vary from one part of the country to another; these prices are only a guide.

Recommended Reading

Professional Wrestling Collectibles, Kristian Pope

VALUE LINE

Autographs

Values shown are for autographed 8"x10" photos

Captain Lou Albano	$15
Andre the Giant	$125
"Stone Cold" Steve Austin	$40
Bob Backlund	$20
Buff Bagwell	$20
Paul Bearer	$10
Brutus Beefcake	$20
Chris Beniot	$20
Bam Bam Bigelow	$15
Eric Bischoff	$20
Steve Blackman	$10
Tully Blanchard	$15
The Blue Meanie	$10
Nick Bockwinkel	$15
Booker T	$20
Boss Man	$15
D 'Lo Brown	$15

King Kong Bundy	$15
Christian	$10
Chyna	$20
The Crusher	$25
Debra	$25
Disco Inferno	$15
Droz	$10
Edge	$15
Miss Elizabeth	$25
Ric Flair	$35
Terry Funk	$15
Vern Gagne	$15
Gangrel	$10
The Godfather	$15
Bill Goldberg	$35
Goldust	$15
Gorgeous George	$60
Eddy Guerrero	$20
Bart Gunn	$10
B.A. Billy Gunn	$10
Scott Hall	$30
Hardcore Holly	$10
Bret Hart	$25
Jimmy Hart	$15
Owen Hart	$25
Bobby Heenan	$20
Hunter Hearst Hemsley	$25
Curt Hennig	$25
Larry Hennig	$15
Mark Henry	$15
Honky Tonk Man	$15
Hulk Hogan	$40
Iron Sheik	$15
"Road Dog" Jesse James	$20
Jeff Jarrett	$20
Chris Jericho	$20
Kane	$25
Kimberly	$25
Konnan	$15
Killer Kowalski	$15
Kurrgan	$10
Jerry "The King" Lawler	$25
Lex Luger	$25
Rocky Maivia	$30
Dean Malenko	$20
Mankind	$25
Vince McMahon	$20
Shawn Michaels	$30
Midian	$10
Rey Mysterio Jr.	$15
Kevin Nash	$40
Diamond Dallas Page	$30
"Rowdy Roddy" Piper	$25
Harley Race	$15
Raven	$20

Stevie Ray	$20
Dusty Rhodes	$20
Jake "The Snake" Roberts	$20
Jim Ross	$10
Terri Runnels	$15
Sable	$40
Bruno Sammartino	$25
Saturn	$10
Randy Savage	$30
Ken Shamrock	$20
Tiger Ali Singh	$15
Sergeant Slaughter	$25
Al Snow	$15
Jimmy "Superfly" Snuka	$20
Rick Steiner	$20
Scott Steiner	$20
Sting	$30
Big John Studd	$50
Sunny	$20
Test	$15
Ultimate Warrior	$25
The Undertaker	$25
Val Venis	$25
Jesse Ventura	$40
Viscera	$10
Baron Von Raschke	$15
Paul Wright	$20
X-Pac	$20
Yokozuna	$15
Larry Zbyzsko	$20

Action Figures
World Wrestling Federation (Hasbro, 1990-94)
Values shown are examples in Mint-in-Package condition.

1-2-3 Kid	$75
Adam Bomb	$35
Akeem	$75
Andre the Giant	$150
Ax	$30
Bam Bam Bigelow	$20
Bart Gunn	$35
Berzerker	$15
Big Bossman (1990)	$16
Big Bossman (1992)	$15
Billy Gunn	$35
Bret Hart (1992)	$25
Bret Hart (1993 mail-in)	$75
Bret Hart (1994)	$15
British Bulldog	$15
Brutus the Barber (1990)	$25
Brutus the Barber (1992)	$25
Bushwackers (two-pack)	$20
Butch Miller	$15
Crush (1993)	$25
Crush (1994)	$15

Demolition (two-pack) $45
Doink the Clown $15
Dusty Rhodes $300
Earthquake $30
El Matador $15
Fatu $15
Giant Gonzales $15
Greg the Hammer $30
Hacksaw Jim Duggan (1991) $15
Hacksaw Jim Duggan (1994) $15
Honky Tonk Man $50
Hulk Hogan (1990) $25
Hulk Hogan (1991) $20
Hulk Hogan (1992) $20
Hulk Hogan (1993 mail-in) $100
Hulk Hogan (1993, no shirt) $20
I.R.S. $15
Jake "The Snake" Roberts $20
Jim Neidhart $15
Jimmy "Superfly" Snuka $25
Kamala $25
Koko B. Ware $60
Legion of Doom (two-pack) $40
Lex Luger $30
Ludwig Borga $35
Luke Williams $15
Macho Man (1990) $25
Macho Man (1991) $35
Macho Man (1992) $35
Macho Man (1993) $15
Marty Jannetty $15
Mountie $15
Mr. Perfect (1992) $35
Mr. Perfect (1994) $25
Nailz $25
Nasty Boys (two-pack) $80
Owen Hart $35
Papa Shango $15
Razor Ramon (1993) $30
Razor Ramon (1994) $18
Repo Man $15
Ric Flair $15
Rick Martel $15
Rick Rude $30
Rick Steiner $18
Ricky "The Dragon" Steamboat $15
Rockers (two-pack) $20
"Rowdy Roddy" Piper $30
Samu $15
Scott Steiner $15
Sgt. Slaughter $30
Shawn Michaels (1993) $25
Shawn Michaels (1994) $15
Sid Justice $15
Skinner $15

Smash $25
Tatanka (1993) $15
Tatanka (1994) $15
Ted Dibiase (1990) $20
Ted Dibiase (1991) $15
Ted Dibiase (1994) $15
Texas Tornado $50
Typhoon $30
Ultimate Warrior (1990) $25
Ultimate Warrior (1991) $20
Ultimate Warrior (1992) $40
Undertaker (1992) $18
Undertaker (1993 mail-in) $50
Undertaker (1994) $25
Virgil $15
Warlord $15
Yokozuna $30

American Wrestling Association (Remco, 1985)

Values shown are examples in Mint-in-Package condition.

Baron Von Raschke/Rick Martel 2-pack $50
Greg Gagne/Jim Brunzell 2-pack $70
Curt Hennig/Greg Gagne 2-pack $60
Nick Bockwinkel/Larry Zbyszko 2-pack $80
Jerry Blackwell/Stan Hansen 2-pack $90
Referee, grey or brown hair $100
Sheik Adnan $130
Marty Jannetty $100
Nord the Barbarian $120
Shawn Michaels $120
Buddy Rose $100
Doug Sommers $100
Boris Zukoff $130

World Wrestling Federation (LJN, 1985-89)

Values shown are examples in Mint-in-Package condition.

Adrian Adonis $50
Andre the Giant $60
Bam Bam Bigelow $100
Big John Studd $30
Bobby "The Brain" Heenan $30
Brutus Beefcake $50
Elizabeth $75
George "The Animal" Steele $30
"Hacksaw" Jim Duggan $50
Honky Tonk Man $60
Hulk Hogan white shirt $250
Hulk Hogan red shirt $300
Jesse Ventura $40
Jimmy Hart $30
Ken Patera $50
King Harley Race $200
King Kong Bundy $50
Paul Orndorff $30
Randy Savage $60

"Ravishing Rick" Rude $110
Rick Martel $125
Ted Dibiase $50
Tito Santana $50
Ultimate Warrior $150
Vince McMahon $40
British Bulldogs 2-pack $200
Hart Foundation 2-pack $600
Killer Bees 2-pack $200
Strike Force 2-pack $400

World Championship Wrestling (Galoob, 1990)
Values shown are examples in Mint-in-Package condition.

Arn Anderson, white $20
Barry Windham, black $20
Brian Pillman, orange $20
Butch Reed $30
Lex Luger, blue $20
Ric Flair, blue $20
Rick Steiner, purple $20
Ron Simmons $30
Scott Steiner, yellow $20
Sid Vicious, black $20
Sting, blue $20
Sting, black $20
Sting, orange $20
Tom Zenk $20

World Championship Wrestling (Justoys, 1990), Bendies
Values shown are examples in Mint-in-Package condition.

Arn Anderson $15
Barry Windham $15
Brian Pillman $15
Butch Reed $20
Lex Luger $15
Ric Flair $15
Rick Steiner $20
Ron Simmons $20
Scott Steiner $20
Sid Vicious $15
Sting $15
Tom Zenk $15

World Wrestling Federation (Justoys, 1994-present), Bendies
Values shown are examples in Mint-in-Package condition.

Bret Hart, pink $20
Diesel $10
Doink the Clown $15
Lex Luger $15
Razor Ramon $10
British Bulldog $4
Undertaker $4
Goldust $4

Yokozuna $4
Sunny $4
Mankind $4
Steve Austin $4
The Rock $6
Hunter Hearst Hemsley $4
Owen Hart $4
Crush $4
Chyna $4
Sable $4
Cactus Jack $4
Billy Gunn $4
Road Dog $4

World Wrestling Federation (Playmates, 1997)
Values shown are examples in Mint-in-Package condition.

Undertaker 14" $40
Undertaker 9" $10
Sid 9" $10

Ringmasters
Values shown are examples in Mint-in-Package condition.

Bret Hart $8
Goldust $5
Shawn Michaels $5
Sid $5
Undertaker $5
Yokozuna $8
Steve Austin/Bret Hart 2-pack $15
Yokozuna/Ahmed Johnson 2-pack $15
Owen Hart/Shawn Michaels 2-pack $15
Sid/Vader 2-pack $15
Mankind/Undertaker $15
Savio Vega/Goldust $15

Strech'ums
Bret Hart $10
Sid $10
Undertaker $10
Shawn Michaels $10

World Championship Wrestling (Toybiz, 1999)
Values shown are examples in Mint-in-Package condition.

Bill Goldberg $6
Diamond Dallas Page $6
Hollywood Hogan $6
Kevin Nash $6
Lex Luger $6
Macho Man $6
Scott Hall $6
Sting $6
The Giant $6
Kevin Nash/Giant 2-pack $20
Sting/Hollywood Hogan $25
Macho Man/Miss Elizabeth $20

Ring Fighters

WWF Series I Attitude Bears

WWF Series II Attitude Bears

WWF Mini Attitude Bears

WCW Series I Nitro Bears and Wolves

WCW Beanie Wrestlers

Miscellaneous

This action figure of Diesel by Jakks is worth about $45.

Die-cast cars, WCW/NWO, Racing Champions 1998, featuring Curt Hennig, Buff Bagwell, Bret Hart, Disco Inferno, Hollywood Hogan, Randy Savage, 1:64 scale, each ....$8-$10

Die-cast cars, WCW/NWO, Racing Champions 1998, featuring Konnan, Raven, Scott Hall, Bret Hart, Lex Luger, Elizabeth, 1:24 scale, each..............$25-$30

Die-cast cars, WCW/NWO, Racing Champions 1998, Street Rods: Goldberg, 12 different models, 1:64 scale, 24K Nitro, each $20

Die-cast cars, WCW/NWO, Racing Champions 1999, Street Rods: Bret Hart, Macho Man, Sting, Goldberg, Lex Luger, Diamond Dallas Page, 1:64 scale, hoods open, each......................................$8

Die-cast cars, WCW/NWO, Racing Champions 1999, Street Rods: Goldberg, Bret Hart, Hollywood Hogan, Sting, Raven, 1:64 scale, hoods closed, each.............$8

Die-cast cars, WCW/NWO, Racing Champions 1999, Street Rods: Bam Bam Bigelow, Rick Flair, Lex Luger, Bret Hart, 1:24 scale, hoods open, each...................$30

Die-cast cars, WCW/NWO, Racing Champions 1999, Street Rods "Main Event:" DDP, Konnan, Giant, Goldberg, Disco Inferno, Brian Adams, 1:64 scale, each $8

Doll, WWF Bone Crunchin' Buddies, stuffed, The Rock, Steve Austin or the Undertaker $35

Doll, WWF super-size stuffed Hulk Hogan dolls, Ace Novelty, 1991, 2' $25

Doll, WWF super-size stuffed Hulk Hogan dolls, Ace Novelty, 1991, 3' $50

Foam finger, Sting, 22" long $10

Foam figure, Hulk Hogan, 22" long............................$10

Foam hat, Green, Randy "Macho Man" Savage, says "OOOOoooh Yeah"..$10

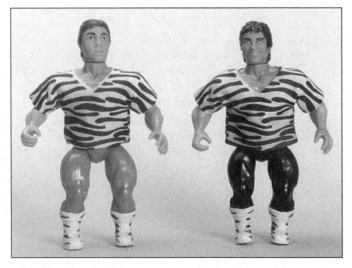

These 1985 figures of The Rockers are worth about $100 each.

Game, Superstar Pro Wrestling Game, board, 1984, Super Star Game ....$13-$20

Game, Verne Gagne World Champion Wrestling, board, 1950, Gardner ....$115-$175

Game, World Champion Wrestling Official Slam O' Rama, board, 1990, International Games............$8-$12

Game, Wrestling Superstars, board, 1985, Milton Bradley ....$13-$20

Game, WWF Wrestling Game, board, 1991, Colorforms ....$8-$12

Growth chart, WCW full-size chart, 3' 7', Goldberg or Kevin Nash, each $25

Halloween costumes, printed jumpsuits, foam muscle chest, vinyl mask, Steve Austin, Kane, the Undertaker, each..$40

Lunch box, WWF, plastic, 1986, Thermos $10
bottle...$5

Kite, Ultimate Warrior, 4' x 2', Spectra, 1990, Mint in Bag $5

Magazine, *Big Time Wrestling*, May 1964, "The Big O" cover $20

Magazine, *Inside Wrestling*, September 1974, Killer Kowalski cover...$10

Magazine, *Pro Wrestling Illustrated*, July 1988, Hulk Hogan/Andre the Giant cover $10

Magazine, *WWF Magazine*, August 1987, Ken Patera cover $5

Magazine, *Wrestling Monthly*, January 1972, Bruno Sammartino cover $10

Magazine, *Wrestling Revue*, October 1970, Dick "The Bruiser" cover...$10

Magazine, *Wrestling Revue*, Winter 1960, Lou Thesz cover...$15

Masks, full-head, soft vinyl, "Stone Cold" Steve Austin ($25), Shawn Michaels, Goldust, The Undertaker, Sable, each $35

Pennants, WCW, Sting, Hollywood Hogan, Diamond Dallas Page, Bret Hart or Randy Savage, each................$8

Megaphone, Jimmy Hart megaphone $5

Microphone, Official WWF Vince McMahon ringside microphone, MIP $15

Pen set, WWF superstars, set of three, Bret Hart, Shawn Michaels and The Undertaker $10

Pillow, WWF, Hulk Hogan, Big Boss Man, Jake "The Snake" Roberts or Ultimate Warrior, stuffed, Ace Novelty, 1991, each...$8

Poster, Lincoln Park, Mass., matches, April 12, featuring tag teams Ivan Putski and Dom DeNucci vs. Louis Cyr and Ivan Koloff, plus other star bouts $25

Poster book, 12x18, eight WWF wrestlers in each, set of two...$10

Program, Nov. 29, 1951, matches in Amarillo, Texas, Gorgeous George cover...............................$10

Program, WWF program, Jan. 14, 1985, Long Island, NY, Mike Rotundo and Barry Windham cover $5

Standup, life-size, WWF, Shawn Michaels, The Under-
taker, Rocky Maivia or Steve Austin,
Advance Graphics, 1998, each...................................$30
Sticker album, *Hulk Hogan's Rock 'n' Wrestling Sticker
Album*, Diamond Publishing, 1986, 32 pages $10
Straw, WWF drinking straw, Steve Austin or The Under-
taker, each...$5
Suspenders, WWK, kids, WWF War Zone,
Steve Austin or WWF Superstars, each $15
Ticket, WCW commemorative, July 6, 1998,
Nitro, features Goldberg...$20
Ticket, WCW Starcade '98, features Kevin Nash........$20
Valentine's Day cards, WCW/NWO, box of 30,
1999...$5
Video, The Glory Days of Wrestling: The Way It
Was '50s and '60s, two-tape boxed set,
90 minutes, black-and-white and color $2

Trading Cards (Mint)

1982 Wrestling All-Stars A, set (36) $40
1 Andre the Giant $10
2 Hulk Hogan $8
13 Bruno Sammartino $2
20 Bruiser Brody $2
27 Ric Flair $7
All others ....50 cents-$1.50
1982 Wrestling All-Stars B, set (36)..........................$30
7 Kerry Von Erich..$3.50
20 Jesse Ventura $15
All others ....50 cents-$2
1983 Wrestling All-Stars, set (36) $30
7 Jimmy Snuka $4
9 Lou Thesz $5
27 Antonio Inoki $3
All others ....50 cents-$2
1985 Topps WWF, set (66) $30
11 Jesse Ventura $4
38 Jesse Ventura $4
39 Ventura/Putski $4
61 Jesse Ventura $4
62 Jesse Ventura $4
All others ....10 cents-$2
1985 Topps WWF Stickers, set (22) $20
4 Jesse Ventura $5
9 Hulk Hogan $2.50
11 Hulk Hogan $2.50
16 Hulk Hogan $2.50
21 Andre the Giant $5
22 Hulk Hogan $2.50
All others ....30 cents-$1
1986 Monte Gum Wrestling Stars, set (100) $50
Hulk Hogan and Ric Flair cards, each.....................$2-$3
All others ....30 cents-$1.75
1987 Topps WWF, set (75) $20
2 Andre the Giant $2
54 The Giant is Slammed $2

58 The Challenge $2
All others ....10 cents-$1.50
1987 Topps WWF Stickers, set (22) $10
1 Bret Hart..$1
2 Hulk Hogan $2.50
4 Randy Savage $1.50
17 Andre the Giant $5
All others .... 30 cents-50 cents
1988 Wonderama NWA, set (343) $125
1 Ric Flair $5
48 Ric Flair/Sting $5
68 Ric Flair $5
89 Nikita Koloff/Ric Flair $5
107 Michael Hayes/Ric Flair $5
162 Ric Flair/Michael Hayes $5
175 Four Horsemen..$2.25
197 Michael Hayes/Ric Flair $5
219 Dusty Rhodes/Ric Flair $5
227 Ric Flair/Robert Gibson $5
252 Ron Garvin/Ric Flair $5
270 Ric Flair/Ron Garvin $5
339 Four Horsemen..$2.25
All others ....20 cents-$1
1994 Action Packed WWF, set (42)............................$35
1 Bam Bam Bigelow $1.75
4 Diesel..$5
5 Razor Ramon $4
7 Shawn Michaels $3.50
12 The Undertaker $2
13 "Macho Man" Randy Savage $1.50
15 Bret Hart...$2
17 1-2-3 Kid $2.50
26 Andre the Giant $7
31 Diesel..$5
37 Razor Ramon $4
38 Shawn Michaels $3.50
40 Bret Hart...$2
42 Undertaker/Paul Bearer $2
All others ....20 cents-$1
1995 Action Packed WWF, set (42)............................$30
3 Razor Ramon $3
4 Diesel..$3.50
21 Diesel...$3.50
25 Shawn Michaels $3
38 Shawn Michaels $3
All others ....75 cents-$1.75
1995 Cardz WCW, set of 100 ....$25
Common cards .... 10 cents
1998 DuoCards WWF, set (72)..................................$15
6 Steve Austin $1.50
8 The Rock $1
11 Steve Austin $1.50
15 The Rock $1
22 Sable $1
All others .... 10 cents-75 cents

Mankind has become one of the most popular current wrestlers. This Jakks figure is currently worth about $15 but may climb.

1998 DuoCards WWF autographs, set (13)	$300
1 Steve Blackman	$15
2 Chyna	$30
3 Billy Gunn	$30
4 Owen Hart	$60
5 Hawk	$20
6 Jacqueline	$15
7 Road Dog	$30
8 Mankind	$30
9 Paul Bearer	$15
10 Redemption card	$40
11 Sable promo	$60
12 Sable, unsigned	$20
13 The Rock	$45
1998 Topps WCW/NWO, set (72)	$15
1 Hollywood Hogan	$1.50
3 Kevin Nash	$1
9 Goldberg	$1
65 Hollywood Hogan	$1.50
68 Goldberg	$1
All others	10 cents-75 cents

1998 Topps WCW/NWO signatures, set (37)	$900
Arn Anderson	$40
Giant	$40
Hollywood Hogan	$80
Chris Jericho	$45
Kevin Nash	$100
Diamond Dallas Page	$60
Raven	$40
All others	$20-$35
1998 Topps WCW/NWO chrome, set (10)	$40
C5 Hollywood Hogan	$10
C6 Kevin Nash	$10
All others	$3-$7
1998 Topps WCW/NWO stickers, set (10)	$8
S1 Goldberg	$1.50
S5 Hollywood Hogan	$2
S6 Kevin Nash	$2
1999 Artbox WWF, set (40)	$20
2 Stone Cold Stunner	$1.50
7 Stone Cold Stunner	$1.50
33 Whoop-Ass 101	$1.50
34 Austin vs. Mankind	$1.50
36 Austin vs. Kane	$1.50
38 The Rattlesnake	$1.50
All others	40 cents-$1
1999 DuoCards WWF, WrestleMania Live, set (54)	$16
5 Wrestlemania III	$1.25
7 Wrestlemania IV	$1.25
8 Wrestlemania V	$1
28 The Rock	$1
35 "Stone Cold" Steve Austin	$1.50
All others	10 cents-75 cents
1999 Topps WCW/NWO, set (72)	$15
4 Goldberg	$1
33 Hollywood Hogan	$1.50
43 Kevin Nash	$1
65 Goldberg Triumphant!	$1
67 Hogan for President	$1.50
68 Big Sexy	$1
All others	10 cents-75 cents
1999 Topps WCW/NWO, set (37)	$1,000
Bam Bam Bigelow	$40
Ms. Elizabeth	$40
Goldberg	$100
Scott Hall	$75
Bret Hart	$80
Kimberly	$50
Randy Savage	$60
Sting	$100
All others	$20-$35

YO-YOS

Yo-yos are currently enjoying a resurgence in popularity, and enough vintage yo-yos are found in old toy chests to keep prices low. The tricks that can be learned on the yo-yo make it one of those simple toys—along with the hula hoop, Slinky and jump rope—that seemingly never changes and yet endures.

But the yo-yo has indeed changed. It became flying saucer-shaped during the space race of the 1960s. It has held the mark of dozens of Hollywood stars and advertising characters, and it was made of plastic starting in the 1960s. In the 1970s, manufacturers began weighting the rim for longer spin, and today Yomega markets a yo-yo with a "brain."

While the earliest of yo-yoers would "walk the dog" and go "around the world" at local tournaments, today's yo-yoers delight in tricks like "splitting the atom" and the "brain twister." They participate in worldwide events and are always looking for unique yo-yos that will perform today's tricks. As a result, the modern toys in this field can exceed the older versions in price and collectibility.

Background: This simple toy has been played with around the world for centuries, but it became widely recognized as the yo-yo in the 1920s, at the hands of Pedro Flores.

Flores came to America from the Philippines, where the yo-yo had been played with for hundreds of years. It was also rumored to have been used as a weapon, a tidbit that is contested by some experts.

Originally called a "flat-top," Duncan has produced butterfly yo-yos since 1958.

Flores started his own company, named the product a "yo-yo," and held spinning contests to promote and popularize its use. Flores's yo-yos were the first to have the string looped around the axle rather than tied to it. This allowed the yo-yo to spin, or "sleep", at the end of the string.

Donald F. Duncan took note of Flores's yo-yo and the popularity of the spinning contests. Duncan purchased the right to market the yo-yo in 1928 and used a fleet of yo-yo professionals to teach tricks via traveling demonstrations and contests. Flores kept ties with the company by continuing to demonstrate the tricks that could be done with a yo-yo.

Throughout the 1930s and '40s America went crazy for yo-yos, playing with the spinning return top and learning tricks like "walking the dog" and "rocking the baby." In the 1950s and '60s the yo-yo's popularity continued.

Although Duncan had trademarked the word "yo-yo" in 1932, the name was determined to be a generic term in 1965 and Duncan lost his exclusive right to its use. The court ruling was a big break for competitors—among them Cheerio, Hi-Ker and Goody—who had earlier been forced to call their products whirl-a-gigs, come-backs, returning tops, etc.

Also in 1965 Duncan was forced into bankruptcy, in part because of excessive legal fees. Flambeau Plastics Co. purchased the name, and this company still manufactures and sells Duncan yo-yos today.

General Guidelines: Original Flores yo-yos are aggressively sought out by yo-yo collectors. One sold online

LEARN THE LINGO!

Yo-yos often have one of these words written on them, or just be known as this type of product:

Butterfly: A variant shape in which yo-yos were produced. Also called thunderbirds, they have wider axles than other yo-yos.

Executive: In addition to being a toy, yo-yos have been recognized for their ability to relieve stress. This prompted many companies to come out with an "executive" model, geared toward the professional.

Jeweled: A wooden yo-yo that is adorned with rhinestones. They were popular in the '50s and most sell for relatively low prices ($10 and up).

Junior: A yo-yo that is smaller than the tournament yo-yo and made for beginners.

Premiums: Yo-yos that were given away by fast food chains, soft drink companies, banks, etc., as a form of advertisement for the product.

Tournament: Yo-yos that were deemed to have been made for experts.

recently for more than $750, and some go for more than $1,000. Other companies that produced yo-yos during the earlier years are Bandalore, Cheerio, Hi-Ker, Chico, Dell, Fli-Back, Festival, Goody, Imperial and Royal. Earlier yo-yos were made of wood and tin.

Modern producers include the Hummingbird Toy Co., Tom Kuhn Custom Yo-Yos and Yomega.

Many yo-yos can be bought and sold for between $5 and $25. Yo-yo collectors like to play with their finds, so keeping it in the original packaging isn't quite as important as it is with other collecting fields. Still, yo-yos produced after 1959 command higher prices if found in the original plastic packaging.

Earlier pieces are identified by the seal—either embossed or in sticker form—found on the side of the yo-yo. This is very important to collectors, allowing them to identify the maker of each yo-yo. The condition and shape of the seal also affects pricing, and its absence would significantly diminish the price of any yo-yo.

Strings, tournament patches and other yo-yo memorabilia is also highly collectible.

Clubs

• Yo-yo Times, P.O. Box 1519-CLM, Herndon, VA 22070

• American Yo-yo Association, 14534 Wallingford, Seattle, WA 98133

Tin lithographed yo-yos feature bright colorful designs. Some also have holes punched in the outer edge which produce a whistling sound when the yo-yo spins.

THE WHO'S WHO OF YO-YOS!

In 1974, President Richard Nixon garnered a little positive attention when he played with a yo-yo on stage at the Grand Ole Opry. That yo-yo, signed by Nixon, sold at auction for more than $16,000.

A yo-yo that was sent into space by NASA in 1985 later sold for nearly $5,000. The space shuttle Discovery carried the toy up to see what effect microgravity would have on it. The yo-yo refused to sleep, and it had to be thrown down rather than dropped.

VALUE LINE

Alfani, executive, aluminum with cedar stand	$36
Black Mag, Cyko Precision, modern	$35
Cheerio, Beginner, wood, black and red, 1940s	$20
Cold Fusion GT yo-yo	$90
Dell Plastics, Sleeper King Big D, on plastic card	$15
Duncan, 1930s, tin-litho, whistling, lots of wear and dings	$55
Duncan, 1930s, wooden, bicolor	$85
Duncan, 1930s, tin whistling yo-yo	$240
Duncan, 1950s, junior, red/yellow	$10
Duncan, 1950s, O-Boy, wood, red/black	$35
Duncan, 1960s, pink Mardi Gras yo-yo	$100
Duncan, 1960s, butterfly, no string	$10
Duncan, 1970s, beginner, no string	$10
Duncan, 1972, velvet	$60
Duncan, 1980s, Black Jewel, on card	$30
Duncan, Big "T", blue tournament	$125
Duncan, butterfly, wooden, green, gold leaf stamped "small butterfly" seal, glitter enamel	$100
Duncan, Gold Seal, tournament, 1930s	$20
Duncan, Hyper Imperial, mint in package, blue	$5
Duncan, Imperial, orange	$5
Duncan, Oh-Boy, tournament	$15
Duncan, Shrieking Sonic Satellite	$75
Duncan, tournament, black glitter	$25
Duncan Turn Top	$30
Duncan, World Class, mint on card, red	$10
Festival, Dragonfly, white wood	$20
Fli-Back, beginner, blue, 1960s	$15
Fli-Back, tournament	$130
Flores, mint, red, "Flores original yo-yo official tournament top"	$760
Flying Disc, wooden, bicolor	$20
Goldeneye 24K-gold plated yo-yo	$55
Hi-Ker, butterfly (flat top), red/white stripe, 1950s	$150
Hi-Ker, professional top, wooden	$35
Hummingbird, Master Award, given at contests	$50
Lumar, #33, beginner, made in Great Britain, tin	$85

Lumar, Championship, made in Great Britain $60
National Convention Mark McGwire yo-yo $30
New SB2 Tom Kuhn silver yo-yo $60
No Jive, mint, 1979, with box and string $20
Royal, jewelled tournament, wooden, gold leaf
    stamped seal $300
Royal, thunderbird (butterfly), 1960s, wood,
    triangular decal seal $400
Tom Kuhn, Pocket Rocket, mini, polished
    aluminum $17
Tom Kuhn, Sleep Machine $30
Twin Twirler, yellow, plastic $30
Whirl-King, standard, wooden $15
Yomega, Metallic Missile yo-yo $40
Premiums, Promotionals and Character Yo-Yos
Alka-Seltzer, Speedy $5
American Tobacco Co., "American Achievers,"
    wood, given to employees $12
Batman, 1970s $8
Bozo the Clown, tin, marked "Bozo the Clown—Larry
    Harmon Pictures 1976" $15
Burger Chef, copyright 1972 .... $6
Charlie Brown, green plastic $10
Coca-Cola, c. 1980, Russell Super,
    "Enjoy Coca-Cola" $11
Coca-Cola, modern, shaped like a bottle cap $6.50
Cracker Jack, 1950s, plastic $15
Curious George, metal, modern $7
Disney, Donald Duck, Walt Disney Productions,
    c. 1950s-60s $15
Freddy Krueger $5
G.I. Joe, 1988 .... $5
Grateful Dead, wooden $15

Jerry Garcia, maple, "Gimme four, I'm still on tour,"
    in velvet bag $35
John Deere, from historic site in Grand Detour, Ill. $20
KISS, 1998-99 Psycho Circus tour, silver coins
    on sides $35
Kitty Clover Potato Chips, wooden,
    Duncan beginner $25
McDonald's, plain red $13
Montgomery Wards, Duncan beginner $3
Mountain Dew $6
New Era Potato Chips, Duncan beginner $10.50
New York World's Fair, 1939, wooden $85
Paul Bunyan's Forest Camp, wooden $10
Pee Wee Herman, 1988, on card $15
Pepsi $6
Pez, tin, mid-'50s $350
Pez, plastic, 1970s $8
Plastic yo-yo, marked "Richard Nixon Library and Birth-
    place," plastic with metal axle $10
Rice Krispies, Duncan Glow-Imperial,
    glows in the dark $8
Rosie O'Donnell Show, Yomega, plastic $25
Roy Rogers and Trigger, 1940s, bright yellow on
    card, with extra string, marked All Western Plastics $15
Scooby-Doo, lights up and talks $10
Smothers Brothers, wooden yo-yo with Yo-Yo
    Man video $10
Snoopy as the Red Baron $10
Spider-Man, Duncan $15
Super Sugar Crisp, Duncan, YoYolympics $15
Thomas the Tank Engine, tin litho, modern $3
TRON, Duncan, vari-vue flicker, sides glow,
    1980s $40

This plastic glow in the dark yo-yo was a tie-in to the 1993 movie "A Nightmare Before Christmas."

Wooden yo-yos make interesting tourist souvenirs, such as this example from the Corn Palace in Mitchell, South Dakota.

FIND OUT WHAT'S HOT IN TODAYS MARKET

Antique Trader's™ Antiques & Collectibles Price Guide 2001
edited by Kyle Husfloen
The leading pricing guide provides the best source possible for in-depth and detailed coverage of hundreds of collecting fields. Covers the major categories of ceramics, furniture and glass, plus a diverse range of others. New areas of collecting are also presented so readers can keep abreast of current market trends. Some 600 photographs highlight over 20,000 entries.

Softcover • 6 x 9 • 912 pages
3,000 b&w photos
Item# AT2001 • $16.95

New Edition

100 Greatest Baby Boomer Toys
by Mark Rich
Relive your childhood with this nostalgic picture book of toys from your past. The 100 greatest toys are ranked in popularity and value listings are included for many more. And, if you're not already a collector, you may become one after seeing the values of some of those deep-in-the-closet keepsakes.

Softcover • 8-1/4 x 10-7/8 • 208 pages
250 color photos
Item# BOOM • $24.95

NEW

Warman's™ Advertising
by Don & Elizabeth Johnson
More than 10,000 listings, 16 pages of color and 650 black-and-white photos of hundreds of different advertisers including Betty Crocker, Campbell's, Coca-Cola, Domino's Pizza, General Motors, Harley-Davidson, Kellogg's, Levi's, McDonald's, Pepsi-Cola, and Zero. Also includes collecting hints, history, references, collections, collector's clubs, websites and reproduction alerts.

Softcover • 8-1/2 x 11 • 304 pages
650 b&w photos • 70 color photos
Item# WADV • $24.95

2001 Toys & Prices
8th Edition
edited by Sharon Korbeck & Elizabeth Stephan
Space toys fans will now have an easier-to-use section, including a spotlight on ultra-hot robots. Both the casual collector and veteran enthusiast will find over 58,000 values on more than 20,000 toys including cast-iron banks, lunch boxes, board games, Barbie, PEZ, space toys, Fisher-Price, Hot Wheels, restaurant toys and more. More than 20 chapters make this compact guide indispensable as a reference guide.

Softcover • 6 x 9 • 936 pages
700 b&w photos • 8-page color section
Item# TE08 • $18.95

NEW

Kiddie Meal Collectibles
by Alex G. Malloy and Robert J. Sodaro
This new book, compiled by two leading experts in contemporary collectibles features 208 pages filled with facts, photos, descriptions, and current marketplace prices. Premiums offered by more than thirty restaurant franchises are covered in detail, complete with current values for mint-in-package items, mint-out-of-package items, individual objects, and complete sets.

Softcover • 8-1/2 x 11 • 208 pages
400+ b&w photos • 32-page color section, 100 color photos
Item# AT5161 • $24.95

New Edition

Saturday Morning TV Collectibles '60s '70s '80s
by Dana Cain
This encyclopedia is filled with information on 1960s to 1980s kids' show collectibles. If you're already a veteran collector, this guide is great, as it features in-depth listings, prices and photos of your favorite Saturday morning program collectibles. If you're a novice or beginning hobbyist, you'll find your favorite character collectibles and how much you should pay. More than 3,500 items priced and nearly 1,000 photos.

Softcover • 8-1/2 x 11 • 288 pages
750 b&w photos • 16-page color section, 200 color photos
Item# TOON • $24.95
